The Handbook of
Fixed Income Securities

The Handbook of
Fixed Income Securities

FRANK J. FABOZZI
and
IRVING M. POLLACK

Editors

1983

DOW JONES-IRWIN
Homewood, Illinois 60430

This publication is designed to provide accurate and
authoritative information in regard to the subject matter
covered. It is sold with the understanding that the
publisher is not engaged in rendering legal, accounting, or
other professional service. If legal advice or other expert
assistance is required, the services of a competent
professional person should be sought.

*From a Declaration of Principles jointly adopted by a Committee
of the American Bar Association and a Committee of Publishers.*

ISBN 0-87094-306-5
Library of Congress Catalog Card No. 82–71874

Printed in the United States of America

3 4 5 6 7 8 9 0 M P 0 9 8 7 6 5 4

FJF's corner
   To the memory of my grandparents,
   Lucia and Francesco Fabozzi
   Maria and Biagio Falzone

IMP's corner
   To my family,
   Shirley, Janet,
   and Joan

Foreword

Although buy-and-hold is a realistic option for investors who buy equities, it is an act of wanton imprudence for investors in debt securities. Ultimately, of course, a debt security reverts to cash, and thereafter earns nothing for its owner. Well before the maturity date, however, its entire pattern of market behavior changes with the passage of time. This means that active management of fixed-income securities is an inescapable responsibility.

Lenders of money have two other factors to worry about. First, will the borrower meet all payments of interest and principal when due? Second, how much will those payments buy in terms of goods, services, and financial assets as the repayments come in?

From these three painfully obvious considerations—the impact of time, the credit-worthiness of the borrower, and the relation of predetermined dollar payments to a changing price level—stems an extraordinarily complex collection of tools, techniques, risk and return calculations, and forecasting models for the active manager to worry about. In a world in which the variety of issuers and issues seems to proliferate continuously, this is no job for people who are seeking soft berths.

It is, indeed, an area where constant study is essential. What happens in any given market, in any given moment, or in any given economic environment is relevant for all the other markets, moments, and environments. Our learning requirements give us no surcease.

This volume is essential for those who recognize the importance of meeting those requirements. It leaves no stone unturned, and has about the most skilled stone-turners one would want to put to this particular task. Whether we turn to it for a guide to action, for a grasp of the facts, or for an understanding of fundamental theory, the answers we seek are here.

Peter L. Bernstein
President of Peter L. Bernstein Inc.,
and Editor of
The Journal of Portfolio Management

Preface

Dynamic changes in the financial markets in recent years have intensified the interest of investors in fixed income securities. In the late 1960s interest rates began to rise, making fixed income securities more competitive with other investment vehicles such as common stock. As rates continued to rise throughout the 1970s and early 1980s and as erratic monetary policy caused interest rates to fluctuate substantially, borrowers began issuing fixed income contracts that offered more attractive investment characteristics to an investing public that had become concerned with committing funds in a volatile interest rate environment. Moreover, improved techniques for managing fixed income portfolios in such an investment climate were developed.

This book is designed to provide extensive coverage of not only the wide range of fixed income securities but also investment strategies and the interest rate environment. It is intended for both the novice investor and the professional money manager. Each chapter is written by an authority on the subject. Many of these authorities have written books, monographs, and/or articles in leading journals on their topic.

The *Handbook* is divided into four parts. Part 1 provides general investment information with which an investor must be familiar in order to understand the risks and rewards associated with fixed income securities. The securities—money market instruments, U.S. Treasury and agency obligations, corporate bonds, preferred stock, tax-exempt obligations, mortgages, pass-through securities, and international fixed income instruments—are explained in Part 2. Fixed income financial contracts that allow the holder to purchase additional bonds (contingent takedown options), redeem bonds before maturity (put bonds), and convert securities into common stock are also explained in Part 2. Investment management strategies are discussed in Part 3, followed by a comprehensive discussion of the determinants of the level of interest rates, the term structure of interest rates, and interest-rate forecasting in Part 4.

We extend our deep personal appreciation to the contributing authors, the editorial advisory board (Peter E. Christensen, Sylvan G. Feldstein, H. Gifford Fong, Michael D. Joehnk, Marcia Stigum, Richard R. West, and Arthur Williams III) and the following individuals who provided us with assistance in this project: Arthur Blutter (Blutter Associates), Patrick Casabona (St. John's University), Mark Castelino (Powers-Vogel Research), Michael Dohan (Queens College, CUNY), Jack Clark Francis (Bernard Baruch College, CUNY), Gary L. Gastineau (Kidder, Peabody & Co., Inc.) Richard V. Howe (The First National Bank of Chicago), David S. Kidwell (University of Tennessee), Robert W. Kopprasch (Salomon Brothers Inc), Thomas A. Shively (The First National Bank of Chicago), Melvyn Stein (Stein, Rubine & Stein), Richard S. Wilson (Merrill Lynch Pierce Fenner & Smith), and Frank G. Zarb (Lazard Freres & Co.).

An editorial footnote is needed to explain the use of the pronoun *he* in some parts of the *Handbook*. In most instances, when referring to a person the contributors used the term *investor*. It became necessary, however, to use a pronoun at certain times. The pronoun *he* was selected by contributors for convention. They felt that alternatives such as *he/she* or *he or she* or *s(he)* are awkward. The use of the generic *he* throughout this *Handbook*, then, is meant to include both sexes.

Frank J. Fabozzi
Irving M. Pollack

Contributors

Francesco Andina Vice President, Julius Baer Securities Inc.

Steven P. Baum, Ph.D. Vice President, Salomon Brothers Inc

Peter E. Christensen Vice President, The First Boston Corporation

Noreen M. Conwell Pension Fund Administrator, Merrill Lynch, Pierce, Fenner & Smith, Inc.

Frank J. Fabozzi, Ph.D., C.F.A., C.P.A. Professor of Economics, Fordham University

Sylvan G. Feldstein, Ph.D. Vice President and Bond Analyst, Moody's Investors Service, Inc.

Michael G. Ferri, Ph.D. Associate Professor of Finance, University of South Carolina

H. Gifford Fong President, Gifford Fong Associates

Gary L. Gastineau Manager of the Options Portfolio Service, Kidder, Peabody & Co., Inc.

Margaret Darasz Hadzima, C.F.A. Vice President, Bonds, Scudder, Stevens & Clark

Jane Tripp Howe The First National Bank of Chicago

James W. Jenkins, Ph.D., C.F.A. President, Sterling Wentworth Corporation, and Associate Professor, Brigham Young University

Michael D. Joehnk, Ph.D., C.F.A. Professor and Chairman, Department of Finance, Arizona State University

Frank J. Jones, Ph.D. Executive Vice President, New York Futures Exchange

Ira A. Kawaller, Ph.D. Director, New York Office, International Monetary Market

Robert W. Kopprasch, Ph.D., C.F.A. Vice President, Salomon Brothers Inc

Martin L. Leibowitz, Ph.D. Managing Director, Bond Portfolio Analysis Group, Salomon Brothers Inc

Nicholas J. Letizia, J.D., C.P.A. Donaldson, Lufkin & Jenrette

Steven C. Leuthold Managing Director, The Leuthold Group

A. Michael Lipper, C.F.A.   President, Lipper Analytical Services, Inc.

Allan M. Loosigian   President, A. M. Loosigian & Co.

Richard C. McEnally   Professor of Finance, University of North Carolina

William C. Melton, Ph.D.   Vice President—Senior Economist, Investors Diversified Services, Inc.

Laura Nowak, Ph.D.   Assistant Professor of Economics, Fordham University

Morris W. Offit   Chief Executive Officer, Julius Baer Securities Inc.

Frank K. Reilly, Ph.D., C.F.A.   Dean and Bernard J. Hank, Professor of Business Administration, University of Notre Dame

John C. Ritchie, Jr., Ph.D.   Professor of Finance, Temple University

Christopher J. Ryan, J.D.   Attorney, Ruskin, Schlissel, Moscou & Evans

Harry C. Sauvain, D.S.C.   Professor Emeritus of Finance, Indiana University

Christina Seix, C.F.A.   Director of Bond Management, MacKay-Shields Financial Corporation

Dexter Senft   Vice President, Fixed Income Research, The First Boston Corporation

Rupinder S. Sidhu   Associate, Strategic Services Group, Merrill Lynch White Weld, Capital Markets Group

Cornelia M. Small   Vice President, Economics, Scudder, Stevens & Clark

Marcia Stigum, Ph.D.   President, Stigum & Associates

Michael Waldman   Vice President, Salomon Brothers Inc

Anthony J. Taranto   Thomas J. Lipton, Inc.

Arthur Williams III, C.F.A.   Vice President—Pension Fund Investments, Merrill Lynch, Pierce, Fenner & Smith, Inc.

Benjamin Wolkowitz   Vice President, Citicorp Futures Corporation

W. David Woolford   Vice President, The First National Bank of Chicago

Contents

Discount. Bond Purchased at a Discount when the Discount Is
Not an Original-Issue Discount. Dividends. Capital Gain and Loss
Treatment: *Capital Gain and Loss Treatment for Individuals.*
Capital Gain and Loss Treatment for Corporations. Deductibility
of Interest Expense Incurred to Acquire or Carry Securities.

Compound Interest: *Computing Future Value. Illustration 1.*
Illustration 2. Computing Future Value of an Ordinary Annuity.
Illustration 3. Present value: *Computing Present Value.*
Illustration 4. Computing Present Value of an Ordinary Annuity.
Illustration 5. Illustration 6. Yield Measures: *Current Yield.*
Yield-to-Maturity. Yield-to-Call. Realized Compound Yield. Bond
Price Volatility: *Bond Price Volatility and Coupon Rate. Bond*
Price Volatility and Maturity. Bond Price Volatility and the Initial
Yield Level. Bond Price Volatility and Duration.

The Cash Market for Government Securities: *Primary Market.*
Secondary Market. Interest-Rate Determination: *Rationale for*
Interest-Rate Determination. The Structures of Interest Rates.
Overview of Interest-Rate Determination.

Long-Term Interest Rates—The First Cut. Short-Term Interest
Rates—The First Cut. Long-Term Interest Rates—A Second Cut.
Short-Term Interest Rates—A Second Cut. "Real" Rates of
Interest: It Ain't Necessarily So. "Real" Interest Only in Periods of
Inflation. Observations. "Real" Interest and Short-Term Rates.

Introduction. Types of Indices. Measuring Risk of Indices.

PART 2

Overview of the Money Market. Treasury Bills: *Determining the*
Yield on Bills. Bill Quotes. Buying Bills. Selling Bills. Bills Held to
Maturity. Commercial Paper: *Issuers of Paper. Issuing*
Techniques. Paper Maturities. Paper Yields. Risk and Ratings.
Buying Dealer Paper. Buying Direct Paper. Buying Bank Paper.
Bankers' Acceptances. Negotiable Certificates of Deposit:
Computing the Yield of a CD, Given Its Price. Computing Price,
Given Yield. Breaking Out Accrued Interest. Holding Period
Yield. A Secondary CD. Sensitivity of Return to Sale Rate and
Length of Holding Period. Compounding.

Financial Analysis: *Traditional Ratio Analysis. Analysis of the
Components of Return on Equity. Nonfinancial Factors.*
Indenture Provisions: *Utility Indentures. Industrial Indentures.
Financial Indentures.* Utilities: *Segments within the Utility
Industry. Financial Analysis. Nonfinancial Factors.* Finance
Companies: *Segments within the Finance Industry. Financial
Analysis.* The Rating Agencies and Brokerage Houses: *Rating
Agencies. Brokerage-House Services.*

The Taxation of Municipal Bonds. Equivalent Taxable Yield.
Description of the Instruments: *Bonds. Hybrid and Special Bond
Securities. Notes. Newer Market Sensitive Debt Instruments.* The
Buyers of Municipal Bonds: *Commercial Banks. Insurance
Companies. Households (Individual Investors).* The Credit-Rating
Agencies: *Moody's Investors Service. Standard & Poor's. How
the Rating Agencies Differ.* Municipal Bond Insurance: *The
Insurers. Underwriting Criteria Used by Insurers. Credit-Rating
Agencies View of Municipal Bond Insurance. Market Pricing of
Insured Municipal Bonds.* Yield Relationships within the
Municipal Bond Market: *Differences within an Assigned Credit
Rating. Differences between Credit Ratings. Differences between
In-State, General Market, and Territorial Issues. Differences
between Maturities.* Forecasting Municipal Bond Yields by
Monitoring Trends in Other Markets. The Primary and Secondary
Markets: *The Primary Market. The Secondary Market.* Regulation
of the Municipal Securities Markets.

Introduction: *The First Influence: Defaults and Bankruptcies. The
Second Influence: Strong Investor Demand for Tax Exemption.*
The Legal Opinion: *General Obligation Bonds. Revenue Bonds.
Legally Untested Security Structures and New Financing
Techniques. The Need for Reliable Legal Opinions.* The Need to
Know Who *Really* Is the Issuer: *For General Obligation Bonds.
For Revenue Bonds.* On the Financial Advisor and Underwriter:
*The Need for Complete, Not Just Adequate, Investment Risk
Disclosures. The Importance of Firm Reputation for
Thoroughness and Integrity.* General Credit Indicators and
Economic Factors in the Credit Analysis: *For General Obligation
Bonds. For Revenue Bonds.* Red Flags for the Investor: *For
General Obligation Bonds. For Revenue Bonds.*

What is a Mortgage? Qualifying for a Mortgage. Mortgage
Insurance. Servicing. Where Does Mortgage Money Come from?
What Types of Properties Are Mortgaged? Nontraditional Mort-
gages: *Graduated-Payment Mortgages (GPMs). Pledged-Account*

Warrants and Stock Rights Distinguished. Warrants and Call Options Distinguished. Leverage and Minimum Values. Warrant Premiums. Summary of Warrants.

Hypothetical CTO Example. The Intrinsic Value of an Option. The Option's Profit. The Break-Even Price and Yield. Probability Models. The Black-Scholes Option Valuation Approach. Applying Option Models to "Fixed Income" Options. Profit Analysis. Aggressive Strategy: The CTO Unit "Double-Up." Defensive Strategy: CTO plus CDs. Average Yield. CTO Variations.

Early Put Issues. Basic of a Put. An Example. The Value of the Put. In-the-Money Puts. Altering the Example for an Issue at Par. The Importance of the Yield Curve. The Yield Curve and Multimaturity Bonds (Multiple Exercise Dates). Multimaturity Bonds as Investor Call Options. The Strike Yield. Put Ratio.

Introduction. U.S.–Pay International Bond Investing: *Eurodollar Bonds. Yankee Bonds.* Foreign-Pay International Bond Investing: *The Markets. Components of Return.* The Rationale for International Bond Investing: *Superior Rates of Return. Diversification.* The Impact of Foreign Bonds on a U.S. Bond Portfolio.

Introduction. Domestic Instruments: *United Kingdom. Germany. Netherlands. Switzerland. Canada. Japan. Foreign Instruments: Bonds. Floating-Rate Notes. Convertible Bonds and Bonds with Warrants.* Money Market Instruments: *Certificates of Deposit. Floating-Rate CDs (FRCDs). Asian-Dollar CDs.* Bankers' *Acceptances. Promissory Notes. Treasury Bills.*

Nature of Bond Portfolio Analysis.

Tax-Free Portfolios: *Realized Compound Yield for the Tax-Free Portfolio. A New Concept: The Effective Par Rate. Realized*

PART 1

General Investment Information

An Introduction to Fixed Income Securities

1

MICHAEL D. JOEHNK, Ph.D., C.F.A.*
Professor and Chairman of the
Department of Finance
Arizona State University

Ever since interest rates began to climb in the late 1960s, the appeal of various types of fixed income securities has increased in a similar fashion. Today such securities as bonds, preferred stock, and convertible issues are found in an increasing number of investment portfolios and are being actively used to fulfill a variety of investor objectives. Basically two things have occurred to alter the investment appeal of fixed income securities: (1) interest rates moved to levels that were highly competitive with other securities and (2) at the same time, these market rates began to fluctuate widely and provided investors with attractive capital gains opportunities. Such behavior was, of course, predictable, since the yields and price performance of good- to high-grade fixed income securities are sensitive to changes in market interest rates. This book is devoted exclusively to fixed income securities—to the substantial return opportunities inherent in this investment vehicle, to the various investment strategies that can be employed, and to the different kinds of fixed income securities that are available to portfolio managers. The present chapter provides an introduction to and an overview of fixed income securities; in it, we'll

---

* Parts of this chapter were adopted from the author's book, *Fundamentals of Investing*, coauthored with Lawrence J. Gitman (New York: Harper & Row, 1981).

look at reasons for investing in fixed income securities, the market for these securities, sources of risk exposure, and the type of risk-return relationship to expect with such investment vehicles.

WHY INVEST IN FIXED INCOME SECURITIES?

Like any other type of investment vehicle, bonds and other forms of fixed income securities provide investors with two kinds of income: (1) They provide current income, and (2) they can often be used to generate varying amounts of capital gains. The current income, of course, is derived from the periodic receipt of dividend and/or interest payments. Capital gains, in contrast, are earned whenever market interest rates fall. A basic trading rule in the market for fixed income securities is that interest rates and security prices move in opposite directions.[1] When interest rates rise, prices fall; and when rates drop, prices move up. So it is possible to buy fixed income securities at one price and, if market interest-rate conditions are right, to sell them some time later at a higher price. Of course, it is also possible to incur a capital loss should market rates move against the investor. Taken together, the current income and capital gains earned from bonds and other types of fixed income securities can lead to *attractive and highly competitive investor yields*.

In addition to their yields, fixed income securities are a versatile investment outlet. They can be used conservatively by those who primarily (or exclusively) seek high current income as a way to supplement their income sources. Or they can be used aggressively for trading purposes by those who actively go after capital gains. Fixed income securities have long been regarded as excellent vehicles for those seeking current income, but it has only been since the advent of high and volatile interest rates that they have also become recognized as excellent trading vehicles. This is so because investors have found that the number of profitable trading opportunities has increased substantially as wider and more frequent swings in interest rates began to occur. Finally, because of the generally high quality of many fixed income securities, they can also be *used for the preservation and long-term accumulation of capital*. Many investors regularly and over the long haul commit all or a major portion of their investment funds to fixed income securities because of this investment attribute. Some investors, in fact, may never use any other type of investment vehicle.

Advantages and Disadvantages of Ownership

One of the advantages of investing in fixed income securities is the highly competitive rates of return that are available, even with nomi-

---

[1] The reason for this relationship is explained in Chapter 4.

nal amounts of trading and minimal risk exposure. Another advantage is the occasional opportunity to realize substantial capital gains. Also attractive to some investors are the tax shields that can be obtained with certain types of issues; municipal obligations are perhaps the best known in this regard, but there are also some unusual tax advantages to Treasury and agency issues.[2]

On the other side, there are disadvantages to investing in fixed income securities. For the individual investor, one of the biggest disadvantages is the relatively large denomination of many of these issues. Another is that the coupons or dividend rates are fixed for the life of the issue[3] and therefore cannot move up over time in response to the ravages of inflation: 5 percent coupons purchased by investors in the early 1960s may have been attractive at the time of acquisition, but they are not very competitive today. In fact, inflation is probably the biggest worry for fixed income investors today. Not only does inflation erode the purchasing power of the principal portion of the investment, but it also has a strong influence upon the behavior of interest rates. That is, inflation can lead to violent swings in interest rates and, in so doing, produce violent swings in the market behavior of fixed income securities, all of which can cause substantial capital losses. A final disadvantage is the often inactive secondary markets for these securities, which tends to limit the amount of aggressive trading and speculation that can take place.

What Are the Choices?

Fixed income securities derive their name from the fact that their level of current income, as defined by the issue's coupon or dividend rate, is fixed for a stipulated period of time, usually the life of the issue. In essence, the security's claim on the income of the issuer is set at a fixed amount. A 12 percent coupon on a $1,000 bond means that the issuer has to pay the bondholder $120 per year for the use of the money—nothing more, nothing less. Likewise, a $5 dividend rate on a preferred stock means the same thing: that the issuer is required to pay "rent" of precisely $5 per year for each share of preferred stock outstanding.

Investors and portfolio managers can select from a number of different types of fixed income securities; these include:

- Money market instruments
    Short-term debt securities, such as Treasury bills, commercial paper, CDs, money market certificates

---

[2] See Chapters 9, 10 and 15.
[3] There are exceptions, such as variable rate instruments and extendable notes.

- Bonds
  - Treasury issues
  - Agency issues
  - Municipal bonds
  - Corporates
  - Institutional obligations
- Preferred stock
- Convertible issues
  - Convertible bonds
  - Convertible preferreds
- Investment company shares (mutual funds)
  - Open- and closed-end funds
  - Investment trusts
- Financial futures
- Put and call options on fixed income securities
  - Not yet a reality but a definite possibility in the near future

Although each of the listed types will be reviewed in detail in later chapters, a perusal of the above list reveals that investors/portfolio managers can find fixed income securities with short-term maturities (money market instruments), or they can choose to go long term (with bonds, preferreds, and convertibles). In addition, they can acquire a position in a managed portfolio of fixed income securities via a mutual fund, or they can deal in financial assets that are linked to the price behavior of certain kinds of fixed income securities by trading financial futures or, possibly in the future, put and call options.

Briefly, money market instruments are low-risk, highly liquid, short-term, unsecured IOUs that are issued by banks, nonfinancial corporations, the U.S. Treasury, various agencies of the U.S. government, and state and local governments. The minimum denominations of these securities are relatively large (seldom are they less than $10,000), and trading lots can be substantial (usually $100,000–$250,000 or more). Major money market instruments include U.S. Treasury bills, federal funds, Eurodollars, negotiable certificates of deposit, commercial paper, bankers acceptances, repurchase agreements, and notes and bills issued by federal agencies and municipal governments. Like the money market, the bond market is an immense institution: by year-end 1980, the volume of bonds outstanding was approaching the $1.5 trillion mark. It is made up of five segments, the largest of which deals in issues of the U.S. Treasury. The fastest growing segment of the U.S. bond market is that for agency issues: These are the obligations of the various political subdivisions of the U.S. government (i.e., either government-sponsored corporations or federal agencies). The issuers include such organizations as the Tennessee Valley Authority, U.S. Postal Service, Government National Mortgage Association (GNMA), and the Federal Home Loan Bank.

The municipal sector is another part of the bond market; this is the "tax-exempt" segment wherein state and local government bonds are traded.[4] The major nongovernmental sector of the market is the corporate segment. The market for corporates is customarily subdivided into several segments, which include industrials (the most diverse of the groups); public utilities (the dominant group in terms of volume of new issues); rail and transportation bonds; and financial issues (bonds issued by banks and other financial institutions). Not only is there a full range of bond quality available in the corporate market, but it also has the widest range of different types of issues—from first mortgage bonds and convertible issues to serial bonds and variable rate notes. By far the smallest segment of the market, institutional bonds are marketed by a variety of private, nonprofit institutions, such as schools, hospitals, and churches. Many of the issuers are affiliated with religious orders, and hospitals make up the primary source of issues.[5]

Although preferred stocks are actually a form of equity, they are considered fixed income securities because their level of current income is fixed (i.e., they carry a fixed dividend, which is paid quarterly). By the end of the 1970s, there were approximately 800 preferred stocks listed on the major exchanges, and their estimated market value was some $25 billion. Most of these stocks were utility issues, although there is a growing number of industrial preferreds. One attraction of preferreds as a form of fixed income security is the fact that 85 percent of preferred dividends received by corporations are tax exempt (leading to yields on preferred stocks that are normally slightly *less* than comparable corporate bonds). Convertible securities, initially issued as bonds or preferreds, are subsequently convertible into shares of the issuing firm's common stock. So long as the convertible is outstanding, it has the same underlying attributes of any

---

[4] Municipal issuers include states, counties, cities, and other political subdivisions, such as school districts and industrial development authorities. These issues are considered tax exempt, since the interest they pay is free from federal income taxation and normally from taxation by the state and local authorities in the state in which they were issued.

[5] Institutional bonds are not discussed in this book, primarily because the market is so small and there is a definite paucity of interest in the market on the part of institutional investors. Such obligations are issued, in serial form, by a variety of private nonprofit (often religious-affiliated) institutions. Even though these obligations have a virtually spotless default record, they regularly provide returns that are 1 to 1½ percentage points above comparable corporates. They do so because the secondary market for these issues is almost nonexistent. For more information on institutional bonds, see: John T. Emery and Robert J. Halonen, "Determinants of Bond Yields: The Case of Non-Profit Institutions," *Mississippi Valley Journal of Business & Economics*, Spring 1974, pp. 49–58; and Thomas J. Kenny, "Institutional Bond Market Expansion Predicted for Coming Decade," *Mid-Continent Banker*, March 1971, pp. 22–32.

other fixed income security (bond or preferred), except that under
certain conditions its price behavior is linked to movements in the
underlying common stock.

In addition to investing directly into various types of fixed income
securities, investors can also invest indirectly into these securities via
investment company shares (such as mutual funds) and financial futures. Without a doubt, the hottest property today in the mutual fund
industry is the money fund, which is nothing more than a mutual fund
that invests in a portfolio of money market instruments. There are also
fully managed bond funds available, or if that's not to their liking,
investors can buy units in an investment trust, which represents little
more than an interest in an *unmanaged* (limited life) portfolio of corporate or municipal bonds. For investors interested only in capital
gains, financial futures may be the answer; in essence, they provide a
vehicle for speculating on the behavior of interest rates. A financial
future (or interest rate future as it is also known) is nothing more than
a commodities futures contract. A relatively new form of financial
asset (these instruments did not exist before October 1975) is the
financial future. Financial futures trading is carried out in Treasury
bills, commercial paper, domestic CDs, GNMA pass-through certificates, Treasury notes, and Treasury bonds.

Equity versus Fixed-Income Investments

As the above review suggests, fixed income investors and portfolio
managers have a vast array of investment vehicles to choose from.
This is in sharp contrast to equity investors, who basically have four
alternatives: common stocks; options, such as warrants and puts and
calls; mutual funds; and when the conditions are right, convertible
securities. Including all the exchanges and the complete over-the-
counter market, there are tens of thousands of different common
stocks available to investors. Admittedly some of these are quite
small, and because they are only regionally traded, they have very
limited markets. Even so, although fixed income investors have a
greater diversity as far as types of issues are concerned, equity investors
probably hold the upper hand with respect to a larger number of
different issuers.

Although the investment objectives may be the same in either case,
investing in equity securities is not at all like investing in fixed income securities. To begin with, the analytical and selection process
for equity securities is far more complex and less certain. That is, the
dividend and price performance of common stock is subject to not
only economic and market forces, but also corporate and financial
variables; the net result is considerable uncertainty in formulating
future expectations. High-grade fixed income securities, in contrast,

are heavily influenced by a single variable—the behavior of interest rates—which simplifies the credit analysis and selection process. (This is not to suggest, however, that the task is an easy one! Rather, because there is less variability between returns of individual securities, the actual selection process with fixed income securities is a bit less uncertain.) Unfortunately, forecasting interest rates is not an easy task in itself, and the task is made even more difficult by the presence of a *complex structure of yield spreads* (which is constantly changing with movements in interest rates).

Equity investors seek high levels of return from capital gains and current income, and the same can certainly be said of investors/ portfolio managers who deal in fixed income securities. Clearly, on a risk-return continuum, fixed income investors have just as many options to choose from as equity investors—they can select the bluest of blue chips or, if they are so inclined, decide to go with very high risk, speculative vehicles.[6] Moreover, the introduction of aggressive management strategies to fixed income securities (such as the use of margin, bond swaps, interest-rate speculation, and financial futures) has enhanced the investment appeal of fixed income securities and improved the return potential of such portfolios. Although equities have historically been viewed as superior investment vehicles relative to fixed income securities, the comparative advantage seems to have shifted dramatically in the past decade or so. For example, the widely quoted study by Lawrence Fisher and James Lorie reveals that, over the 40-year period from 1926 to 1965, the average rate of return from common stocks was a hefty 9.3 percent.[7] When these rates of return are contrasted with those available from bonds, the latter appear meager indeed. The Hickman[8] study of bond returns over the 44-year period ending in 1943 shows an annual rate of return of 5.6 percent,

---

[6] A special type of speculative bond vehicle is the "junk bond." Highly popular in some circles of Wall Street, the junk bond is simply a low-rated, speculative-grade (BB or Ba) obligation that lacks the bond merits and characteristics of investment-grade issues. They offer high yields but also possess high exposure to risk, reflecting doubt by bond analysts about an issuer's ability to keep up interest payments and eventually pay back the face value of the bond. Unlike investment-grade fixed income securities, the fortunes of junk bonds are closely tied to the future outlook of the issuing firm or municipality (the movements of interest rates often have little, if any, affects on the price behavior of junk bonds). Because they lack many of the usual characteristics of fixed income securities, junk bonds are not covered in this handbook. Those who want more information about these securities are directed to Jerry Edgerton, "Junk Bonds: Wall Street Lays a Golden Egg," *Money*, May 1978, pp. 79–83.

[7] Lawrence Fisher and James H. Lorie, "Rates of Return on Investments in Common Stock: The Year-by-Year Record, 1926–65," *Journal of Business*, July, 1968, pp. 291–316.

[8] W. Braddock Hickman, *Corporate Bond Quality and Investor Experience*, a study by the National Bureau of Economic Research (Princeton, N.J.: Princeton University Press, 1958).

whereas Lawrence Fisher and Roman Weil[9] suggest that only about 3.5 percent was earned on bonds over the period 1926 to 1968.

The situation began to change, however, as the decade of the 1960s came to a close. To wit, in a more recent study, Roger Ibbotson and Rex Sinquefield showed that although stocks have dominated the investment universe over the long run, the comparative annual returns from 1969 through 1980 favored fixed income securities about half of the time.[10] Apparently, the lofty and violent yields that prevailed during this period have created a whole new investment environment in which fixed income obligations are now more competitive with equities for the investor's dollar. Further, aggressive bond management tactics are becoming more widely adopted, and as a result the returns on fully managed portfolios are improving accordingly. In fact, this more aggressive approach to bond portfolio management was reviewed in an article by Daniel Ahearn, who showed that in the first half of the 1970s fully managed bond portfolios far outperformed the Standard & Poor's 500 Stock Average.[11] Thus, bonds and other forms of fixed income securities have come into their own and are today viewed as highly competitive with the equity side of the market.

AN OVERVIEW OF THE MONEY AND CAPITAL MARKETS

Fixed income securities are found in both the money and capital markets. Essentially, short-term debt instruments with maturities of one year or less are traded in the money market, whereas the capital markets deal in financial claims with maturities greater than one year. Such instruments not only include long-term debt obligations but equity securities as well. Looking only at the fixed income securities element, the capital market dominates the money market in terms of size (the former is perhaps two to three times the size of the latter), though the money market holds the upper hand with respect to overall quality of the obligations traded and the liquidity/marketability of the instruments.

The money market is the economic area in which short-term credit instruments are bought and sold; it is a vital part of our nation's financial system. It is the market in which commercial banks and other

---

[9] Lawrence Fisher and Roman L. Weil, "Coping with the Risk of Interest-Risk Fluctuations: Returns to Bondholders from Naive and Optimal Strategies," *Journal of Business,* October 1971, pp. 408–31.

[10] Roger G. Ibbotson and Rex A. Sinquefield, *Stocks, Bonds, Bills and Inflation: The Past and The Future (1981 Edition),* (Charlottesville, Va.: Financial Analysts Research Foundation, 1981).

[11] Daniel S. Ahearn, "The Strategic Role of Fixed Income Securities," *Journal of Portfolio Management,* Spring 1975, pp. 12–16.

businesses adjust their liquidity positions, the federal reserve conducts its monetary policy, and the federal government sells its debt to finance day-to-day operations. In the money market, businesses, governments, and sometimes individuals borrow or lend funds for short periods—usually 1 day to 120 days. Actually, the money market consists of a collection of markets, each trading distinctly different financial instruments. There is no formal organization, such as the New York Stock Exchange. Central to the activity of the money market are the dealers and brokers who specialize in one or more money market instruments; such dealers buy securities for their own position and sell from their security inventories when a trade takes place. Generally speaking, money market instruments are financial claims that have low default risk, short maturities, and high marketability.

The most important function of the money market is to provide a vehicle that enables economic units to adjust their liquidity positions. Almost every economic unit—financial institution, business corporation, or governmental body—has a recurring problem of liquidity management. Money market instruments allow these units to bridge the gap between cash receipts and cash expenditures, thereby solving their liquidity needs. More than anything else, an efficiently functioning money market provides liquidity to the economy, which ultimately fosters the flow of funds to the most important use throughout the nation.

In contrast to the money markets, capital markets involve financial claims with relatively high degrees of price risk. They include common and preferred stocks, and debt securities with maturities greater than one year, mutual funds, stock options, warrants, and financial futures contracts. Capital markets facilitate the transfer of funds from savers to borrowers, and in so doing, they enhance the economic development and vitality of the country. Because of the lengthy maturities that exist with the securities, the existence of a secondary market is especially important because it allows investors and financial institutions to alter the liquidity, composition, and risk of their portfolios in response to new information and/or to changes in general market conditions. Such secondary markets provide the needed liquidity to the capital markets. After all, conditions change, and individual and institutional investors need ways to alter their investment positions.

RISK EXPOSURE IN FIXED INCOME SECURITIES

Investors in fixed income securities are exposed to a variety of potential risks. Depending upon the investment particulars and market climate, some types of risks are going to be more important than others, and some may be of insignificant importance. The major sources of risk include the following:

Interest-rate risk
Purchasing power risk
Market risk
Liquidity (or marketability) risk
Business risk (or risk of default)
Issue-specific risks
   Reinvestment risk
   Call risk
   Price risk

The most important of these is interest-rate risk, which measures the variability of bond returns/prices as caused by changes in the level of interest rates. Because of the relationship between bond prices and interest rates, no segment of the market (except perhaps for the highly speculative issues) is free of this important and powerful force. The price stability of investment-grade securities is mainly a function of interest-rate stability and, therefore, interest-rate risk. Purchasing power and market risk are closely related to interest-rate risk. Purchasing power risk is linked to inflation and the loss of purchasing power over time; market risk, in contrast, is the effect of the market (in general) upon the price behavior of securities. In the latter case, since virtually all segments of the market for fixed income securities are responsive to interest rates, it follows that market risk is directly related to interest-rate risk. Also, though purchasing power may decline over time with a given level of inflation, what is more important to bond investors is the impact of inflation on yields and prices. For although the level of inflation affects the promised yield, *changes* in the rate of inflation (or inflation expectations) lead to changes in the level of interest rates and therefore changes in the prices of seasoned issues.

Marketability risk has to do with the liquidity of an obligation and the ease with which the issue can be sold at or near prevailing market prices. Smaller issues and those with thin secondary markets will often experience marketability difficulties and are therefore subject to such risk. Marketability is important in defining the yield performance of an obligation—the greater the assumed marketability risk, the greater the required yield. Finally, business risk is the risk of default as reflected by the financial and operating risks of the issuer. Business risk is relevant to corporate fixed income securities (bonds, preferred stocks, and convertibles) as well as municipal and institutional obligations. Fortunately, agency ratings are available to help in measuring the amount of business risk exposure. They are not perfect, but they do provide an excellent starting point for the assessment of such risk exposure. The quality of an obligation as reflected in agency ratings has an influence on the promised yield of a security—the lower the default risk, the higher the agency rating and the lower the prevailing yield to maturity. Business risk, along with marketability risk, has an *insignificant* impact on price behavior because it only affects prevailing levels of yields. In contrast, interest-rate risk and purchasing power risk can have *dramatic* effects on the price behavior of an obligation over time and therefore are extremely important to investors in fixed income securities.

The final source of risk is, like default risk, issue specific and has more of an impact on the prevailing level of yields than changes in yield (and therefore price behavior). One of these is reinvestment risk, which has to do with the ability of an investor to reinvest principal and/or coupon/dividend receipts at an attractive rate. It is a particularly important risk for those investors holding short-term securities as well as obligations that derive a major portion of their return from coupon, for example, high-coupon, high-yielding premium bonds. For such investors, the rate of return that can be obtained on reinvested proceeds over the life or investment horizon of a security can have a substantial effect on the level of yield actually realized from an investment. In fact, depending upon the coupon and maturity of an obligation, reinvestment results can represent as much as half (or more) of the total return on an investment and therefore have a dramatic effect on determining whether or not realized yield will live up to promised yield.[12]

Call risk is another form of risk to which some fixed income investors are exposed. Whenever a security, such as a bond, carries a call feature that gives the issuer the right to prematurely retire the obligation, investors face the risk that the issue will be called out from under them, in which case, they will be left with no alternative but to reinvest the funds in less attractive (lower yielding) investment vehicles. This is an especially important feature for investors holding current coupon or premium bonds during periods when interest rates are falling, and the likelihood of a call (for refunding purposes) are increasing. Finally, there is price risk—a type of exposure that is obviously linked to movements in interest rates, but that can have a greater or lesser impact on price behavior depending upon the maturity of the obligation held. Other things being equal, price risk increases as the term to maturity of an obligation increases. Thus, short-term money market instruments have much less exposure to price risk than long issues and therefore are considered attractive when interest rates are rising. In contrast, the prices of long maturities will fluctuate over wide ranges with movements in interest rates and, as a result, are used by investors who are going after capital gains during periods of declining interest rates.

---

[12] See Chapter 4.

As we noted above, some risks have a primary impact on price behavior, and others effect differential yields at a given time. Certainly, both catagories of risk will effect holding-period returns. Interest rate, purchasing power, and market risk are reflected in comparative price behavior over time. Other things being equal, the greater the change in interest rates, the greater the impact on the market value/price of an obligation. Liquidity, business risk, and issue-specific risk, in contrast, are reflected in differential promised yields. For example, the higher the default risk, the greater the comparative promised yield of an obligation at any time. The same can be said of an issue that lacks marketability, or one that has substantial call or reinvestment risk.

Risk-Return Relationships

Modern capital market theory maintains that when the universe of financial assets is evaluated in terms of risk-return characteristics, an upward-sloping market line will occur—greater return will be accompanied by greater risk. Financial assets that characteristically exhibit high levels of return logically should possess higher levels of risk. Compared with other market vehicles, fixed income securities have traditionally been viewed as low risk, and therefore the rates of return demanded by investors have been correspondingly modest. A brief review of historical bond yields will quickly confirm this. In the absence of abnormal inflation (in the 1950s and early 1960s), the returns for fixed income securities were low. Since the late 1960s, however, when the inflation rate increased, the level of yields on fixed income securities increased accordingly. In periods of high economic uncertainty, such as the recession of 1974, yields on low-rated obligations (Baa and below) tend to move to levels that greatly exceed those on comparable higher rated issues—the risk premiums on the securities increases substantially. This is rather common in periods of economic stress and points out the effect of perceived risk of default on investor returns. Because the risk of default for low-rated obligations is naturally believed to increase during economic recessions, the yield on such obligations responds quite predictably by moving up.

Clearly the risk-return behavior of fixed income securities is compatible with traditional capital market theory. Capital market theory, however, also relates the risk-return behavior of fixed income securities to other types of financial assets. Because fixed income securities are considered to be relatively conservative investments, we would expect long-term obligations, such as bonds, to be on the lower end of the capital market line. Numerous tests have been conducted on capital market behavior, and one of the earlier studies examined the comparative risk-return characteristics of 14 classes of long-term securities. Government bonds, various grades of corporate bonds, preferred stock, and common stock were all compared in terms of their risk premium behavior; the results confirmed a priori expectations to the extent that bonds and preferred stocks provided both lower risk and return than their common stock counterpart.[13] Other studies have also provided evidence that supports expected risk-return behavior in the context of a capital market line.[14]

The inverse relationship between risk and return is depicted in Exhibit 1. The point labeled R_f in the figure reflects the fact that it is

Exhibit 1
Capital Market Line

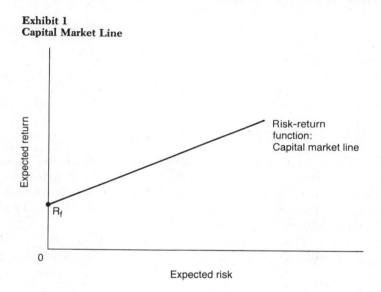

possible to receive a positive return for zero risk; the return associated with such an investment is commonly referred to as the risk-free rate of interest, R_f. In practice, the risk-free rate is about equal to the return on a short-term U.S. government security and represents the return to investors for giving up current period consumption in order to invest. A wide variety of risk-return combinations are associated with each type of investment vehicle. Some common stocks offer low returns and low risk; others exhibit high returns and high risk. In general, the risk-return characteristics of each of the major investment vehicles can be depicted on a capital market line as shown in Exhibit 2. Although the locations of the risk-return axes are only approximate, it should be clear that an investor can select from a wide variety of vehicles, each

---

[13] Robert M. Soldofsky and Roger L. Miller, "Risk Premium Curves for Different Classes of Long-Term Securities," *Journal of Finance*, June 1969, pp. 429–46.

[14] Ibbotson and Sinquefield, *Stocks, Bonds, Bills and Inflation*.

Exhibit 2
Risk-Return Trade-offs

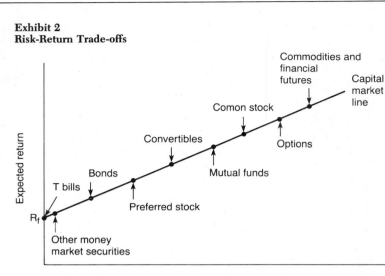

having certain characteristic risk-return behavior. Of course, such behavior is the reason for the diversification benefits of fixed income
securities. That is, because bonds have risk-return profiles that are
different from those of equity securities, they provide viable diversification opportunities for portfolio managers.

AN OVERVIEW OF THE BOOK

This book is organized into four parts. The first part provides a
review of the basic features of fixed income securities as well as their
tax treatment. Also addressed are yield measures, price volatility, interest-rate properties, and fixed income indices.

The second part deals with fixed income instruments. Starting with
money market securities, the vehicles examined include Treasury obligations, agency issues, corporate bonds, preferred stock, tax-exempt
securities, mortgages and pass-through securities, fixed income mutual funds, convertible issues and bonds with warrants attached, securities with contingent takedown and early redemption options, and
international fixed income securities. Throughout this part of the
book, consideration is given not only to issue characteristics and risk-
return performance, but also to the credit analysis of such securities.

Having looked at the alternative investment vehicles, part three
addresses the very important issue of bond investment management.
Important bond portfolio concepts and investment strategies are examined here, including measures of performance, horizon analysis,
bond swaps, yield spreads and yield curves, margin trading, dedicated

pension strategy, and the use of financial futures and options for hedging purposes. Any discussion of bond portfolio management would be incomplete without saying something about duration; we provide extensive coverage of this important concept in two full chapters devoted exclusively to the properties of duration and bond portfolio immunization.

Part four then deals with interest rates and interest-rate forecasting, including the role of the Federal Reserve in impacting interest rates, the term structure of interest rates, and techniques for forecasting interest rates. The two appendixes to this book provide a discussion of the tax implications of exchange offers and general information about retirement plans for individuals.

Features of Fixed Income Securities

2 **MICHAEL G. FERRI, Ph.D.**
Associate Professor of Finance
University of South Carolina

The purpose of this chapter is to explore some of the most important features of bonds and preferred stock and to provide the reader with a taxonomy of terms and concepts that will be of assistance in the reading of the specialized chapters to follow. We will first offer a discussion of the attributes of bonds and proceed later to an account of analogous aspects of preferred stock.

BONDS

Type of Issuer

One of the most important characteristics of a bond is the nature of its issuer. Though foreign governments and firms do raise capital in the American financial markets, the three largest issuers of debt are domestic corporations, municipal governments, and the federal government. Within each of these classes of issuer, however, one can find additional and significant differences. Domestic corporations, for example, include regulated utilities as well as unregulated manufacturers. Further, each firm may sell differing kinds of bonds: Some debt may be publicly placed, other bonds may be sold directly to one or only a few buyers; some debt is collateralized by specific assets of the company, and other debt may be unsecured. Municipal debt is also varied: "general obligation" bonds (or GOs in the jargon of the bond market) are backed by the full faith, credit, and taxing power of the governmental unit issuing them; "revenue bonds," on the other hand, have a safety or creditworthiness that depends upon the vitality and success of particular units (such as schools or hospitals or water systems) within the municipal government. Within the federal government, many departments and agencies have the authority to sell bonds. The U.S. Treasury has the most voracious appetite for debt, but the bond market often receives calls from such units as the Export-Import Bank, the Federal Home Loan Bank, and other agencies of the federal government.

It is important for the investor to realize that, by law or practice or both, these different borrowers have developed different ways of raising debt capital over the years. As a result, the distinctions among the various types of issuers correspond closely to differences among bonds in yield, denomination, safety, maturity, tax status, and such important provisions as the call privilege and sinking fund. As we discuss the key features of fixed income securities, we will point out how the characteristics of the bonds vary with the obligor or issuing authority.

Maturity

A key feature of any bond is its *term to maturity*, the number of years during which the borrower has promised to meet the conditions of the debt (which are contained in the bond's *indenture*). A bond's maturity is the date on which the debt will cease to exist and the firm will redeem the issue by paying the face value or principal. One indication of the importance of the maturity is that the code word or name for every bond contains its maturity (and coupon). Thus, the title of the Exxon bond due or maturing in 1998 is given as "Exxon 6.5 percent '98." In practice, the words *maturity, term,* and *term to maturity* are used interchangeably to refer to the number of years remaining in the life of a bond. Technically, however, maturity denotes the date the bond will be redeemed, and term or term to maturity denotes the number of years until that date.

A bond's maturity is crucial for several reasons. First, maturity indicates the expected life of the instrument or the number of periods during which the holder of the bond can expect to receive the coupon payments and the number of years before the principal will be paid. Second, the yield on a bond—its yearly rate of return—depends substantially on its maturity. (See Chapter 4 for a fuller account of the relationship between maturity and yield.) Third, the volatility of a bond's price is closely associated with maturity: Changes in the market level of rates will wrest much larger changes in price from bonds of long maturity than from otherwise similar debt of shorter life. (Chapter 4 discusses this point in detail.) Finally, bonds with long terms may be safer than debt with shorter maturities: The issuers of longer term bonds have a higher likelihood of finding favorable conditions for retirement, which usually occurs through a refinancing, than the obligors whose bonds have a short life.

When considering a bond's maturity, the investor should be aware of any provisions that modify, or permit the issuer to modify, the maturity of a bond. Though corporate bonds are typically *term bonds* (issues that have a single maturity), they contain arrangements by which the firm either can or must retire the debt early, in full or in part. Many corporates, for example, give the issuer a *call privilege*, which permits the firm to redeem the bond before the scheduled maturity under certain conditions (these conditions are discussed below). Some U.S. government bonds have the same provision. Many industrials and some utilities have *sinking-fund provisions*, which mandate that the firm must retire a goodly portion of the debt, in a prearranged schedule, during its life and before the stated maturity. Typically, municipal bonds are *serial bonds* or, in essence, bundles of bonds with differing maturities. (Some corporates are of this type, too.)

Usually, the maturity of a corporate bond is between 10 and 30 years; the shorter maturities are more characteristic of banking or financial issues, and utilities are more likely to employ the longer maturities. Government bonds range in life from 1 to 20 or more years (though, technically, Treasury issues of 1 to 10 years are called notes), but the number of bonds with maturities exceeding 10 years is relatively small. The "term component" of municipal debt—the longest lived part of the serial issue—tends to have a maturity between 15 and 20 years.

Coupon and Principal

A bond's *coupon* is the periodic interest payment made to owners during the life of the bond. The coupon is always cited, along with maturity, in any quotation of a bond's price. Thus, one might hear about the "Duke Power 14.375 due in 1987" or the "Sears 8 due in 2006" in discussions of current bond trading. In these examples, the coupon cited is in fact the *coupon rate* or rate of interest that, when multiplied by the *principal* or face value of the bond, provides the value of the coupon payment. Typically, but not universally, half of the coupon payment is made in semiannual installments. Most bonds are "bearer bonds" whose investors clip coupons and send them to the obligor for payment. Some bonds are "registered issues," and their owners receive the payment automatically at the appropriate time. A small class of industrial bonds, called income bonds, contain a provision that permits the firm to omit or delay the payment of coupons if the firm's earnings are too low. Because it combines the riskiness of equity with the limited return of debt, this kind of bond is not popular with many investors. Recently, some corporations and municipalities have begun to issue a "zero-coupon" debt (see Chapter 12).

One reason that debt financing is popular with corporations is that the coupon payments are tax-deductible expenses. As a result, the true aftertax cost of debt to a profitable firm is usually much less than the stated coupon rate. The level of the coupon on any bond is typically close to the level of yields for issues of its class at the time the bond is first sold to the public. Although some original-issue, deep-discount bonds have recently been offered to the market, firms usually try to set the coupon at a level that will make the market price close to par value. This goal can be accomplished by placing coupon rate near the prevailing market rate.

To many investors, the coupon is simply the amount of interest they will receive each year. However, the coupon has another major impact on an investor's experience with a bond. The coupon's size influences the volatility of the bond's price: The larger the coupon, the less the price will change in response to a shift in market interest rates. Thus, the coupon and the maturity have opposite effects on the variability of a bond's price. (See Chapter 4 for more analysis of this point.)

The form of payment of the coupon depends upon whether the bond is a bearer bond or a registered issue. If a bond is registered, the issuer knows the identity of the owners of the debt and automatically submits the coupon payments to them at the appropriate time. The bearer bond is more common. The interest on this type of debt is paid when the holder presents a coupon to the company's agent. Recently, the U.S. government began to issue new bonds in book-entry form. Under this arrangement, the bond consists of a computerized record, rather than a physical document. Generally, the change from prior practice has received a good welcome.

The *principal* or *face value* of a bond is the amount to be repaid to the investor either at maturity or at those times when the bond is called or retired according to sinking-fund provisions. But the principal plays another role, too. It is the basis on which the coupon rests; the coupon is the product of the principal and the coupon rate. For most corporate issues, the face value is $1,000; many government bonds have larger principals, up to $10,000 or $25,000; and many municipal bonds come in denominations of $5,000.

Yields

Participants in the bond market use two calculations to describe the expected or present return on a bond. The first, and simpler, calculation is the *current yield*, which is the ratio of the coupon to the current price. For example, a bond with a price of 91 (which is 91 percent of par, or $910 for a corporate bond with a face value of $1,000) and a coupon of 9.5 (or 9.5 percent of par) has a current yield of 10.44 percent. *The Wall Street Journal*'s tables for trading in the bond market report this yield.

Despite its wide use and simplicity, the current yield is deficient because it neglects the principal to be paid at maturity. To account for this rather large cash flow, investors utilize the conceptually and computationally more complex measure of *yield-to-maturity*. The yield-to-maturity, often referred to as yield, is the rate of interest an investor would have to earn if an investment equal to the price of the bond were capable of generating the semiannual coupon payments and the principal of the bond in exactly the yearly pattern promised by the issuer. For example, suppose a bond is selling at $961.60 and has a coupon of $80 per year for the next 20 years. The holder of such a bond would expect to receive $40 every six months for 20 years and $1,000 at the end of the 20th year. What rate of interest on an investment of $961.60 would be able to produce those cash flows and leave nothing after the payment of the $1,000? The answer is a yearly compounding rate of 8.4 percent, which is the yield-to-maturity of this bond.

The yield-to-maturity is an application of the discounting technique known as internal rate of return (or IRR). The IRR of any series of payments is that discount rate that makes the present value of the payments just equal to the price or cost of the asset that generates the flows. The yield and the price of any bond are negatively related: As the price of the bond rises, the yield falls, and vice versa. For example, had the price of the bond in the preceding example been $1,010.00, the yield would have been 7.90 percent; and if the price had been $847.80, the yield would have been 9.40 percent. Yield must rise if price falls because any given future cash flows can be generated with a lower investment *if* the yearly, compounded rate of interest increases. Similarly, yield would fall as price rose because it would take a smaller rate of interest to generate set future cash flows if the initial investment were to increase. (Further discussion of this matter may be found in Chapter 4.)

Price Quotes

As we mentioned above, the prices of most bonds are quoted as percentages of par value or face value. (The exception to this rule is generally the municipal issue, which is quoted on a yield basis. This point will receive some more attention in Chapter 15.) To convert the price quote into a dollar figure, one simply multiplies the price by the par value. The following table will illustrate the matter. Thus a bond with a par of $1,000 and a price of "91¾" has a market value or price of $917.50.

Par Value	Price Quote	Price as a Percentage of Par	Price in Dollars
$ 1,000	91¾	91.75%	$ 917.50
5,000	102½	102.5	5,125.00
10,000	87¼	87.25	8,725.00
25,000	100⅞	100.875	25,218.75

Call and Refunding Provisions

If a bond's indenture contains a *call feature* or *call provision*, the issuing firm or governmental entity retains the right to retire the debt, fully or partially, before the scheduled maturity. The chief benefit of such a feature is that it permits the borrower, should market rates fall, to replace an old, expensive bond with a new, low-yielding issue. The call feature has added value for corporations and municipalities, which may in the future wish to escape the restrictions that frequently characterize their bonds (about the disposition of assets or collateral). The call feature provides an additional benefit to corporations, which might want to use unexpectedly high levels of cash to retire outstanding bonds or might wish to restructure their balance sheets.

The call provision is detrimental to investors, who run the risk of losing a high-coupon bond when rates begin to decline. When the borrower calls the issue, the investor must find other outlets, which presumably would have lower yields than the bond just withdrawn through the call privilege. Another problem for the investor is that the prospect of call limits the appreciation in a bond's price that could be expected when interest rates start to slip.

Because the call feature benefits the issuer and potentially disadvantages the lender, callable bonds carry higher yields than bonds that cannot be retired before maturity. This difference in yields is likely to grow when investors believe that market rates are about to fall and that the borrower may be tempted to replace a high-coupon debt with a new, low-coupon bond. (Such a transaction is called refunding.) However, the higher yield alone, is not sufficient compensation to the investor for the call privilege. Thus the price at which the bond may be called, termed the call price, is normally higher than the principal or face value of the issue. The difference between call price and principal is the *call premium*, whose value is usually one year's interest in the first few years of a bond's life and declines systematically toward zero thereafter.

An important limitation on the borrower's right to call is the *period of call protection* or *deferment period*, which is a specified number of years in the early life of the bond during which the issuer may not call the debt. Such protection is another concession to the investor and comes in two forms. Some bonds are *noncallable* (often abbreviated NC) for any reason during the deferment period; other bonds are nonrefundable (NR) for that time. The distinction lies in the fact that nonrefundable debt may be called for reasons of merger or reorganization if the firm uses unborrowed or internally generated funds for the transaction. The market attaches a higher value to the protection from refunding, even though it is less extensive than the provision of noncallability.

Variations in call protection mirror the type of issuer of the bond. Industrial debt is usually nonrefundable for 10 years but immediately callable for other reasons. Public utility bonds tend to be noncallable for five years. Treasury bonds with 20 years to maturity are noncallable for at least the first 15 years, and debt of federal agencies has protection against call for 10 years. Municipal bonds tend to offer 10 years of protection against call. It is important to note that debt from federal sources is seldom called or refunded for purposes of saving interest payments; rather, government debt managers attempt to refund debt in a way that is consistent with stability in the capital markets.

Some years ago, *Barron's* carried an article on refunding entitled "The Unwelcome Call." A firm's exercise of its call privilege is unwelcome because of its impact on an investor's return. The following example will illustrate the point. Suppose an investor is holding a bond with an 11 percent coupon and 13 years of remaining maturity. The expected return, seven years ago when the bond was purchased at par ($1,000) was 11 percent. The deferment period, now passed, was set at five years. Suppose further that the company can now float a new 20-year bond for a rate of 9 percent and that the call premium on the old debt is $85 (and initially was $110, or one year's interest).

In the investor's view, the existence of the call has two unpleasant consequences. First, the market value of the bond cannot exceed par plus call premium, or $1,085. If the firm did not have the option to buy at that price, the value of the bond would have risen to more than $1,150, which is the present value of the remaining interest payments and principal, discounted at the current market rate of 9 percent. But no investor will pay more than $1,085, the price at which the firm can force a bondholder to sell. The second consequence is that the realized return is lower than the originally expected 11 percent. The yearly return from initial purchase to call, seven years later, is approximately 9.5 percent, which is the discount rate equating the purchase price of $1,000 to the present value of seven years of $110 in coupons and a call price of $1,085. Further, an investor who reinvests the proceeds in a bond of like maturity and risk can expect a return of only 9 percent per year over the remaining 13 years of the original planning period. Hence the investor's likely return from the original investment and the forced second one is rather substantially below the 11 percent originally expected when the investor bought a bond with only limited protection from call.

The example has raised the question of when the firm might find it profitable to refund an issue. It is important for investors to understand the process by which a firm decides whether it ought to retire an old bond and issue a new one. A simple and brief example will illustrate that process and introduce the reader to the kinds of calculations to make when trying to predict whether a bond will be refunded.

Suppose a firm's outstanding debt consists of $30 million in a bond with a coupon of 10 percent, a maturity of 15 years, and a lapsed deferment period. The firm can now issue a bond, with a similar maturity, for an interest rate of 7.8 percent. Assume that the issuing expenses and legal fees amount to $200,000. The call price on the old bond is $1,050.

The firm must pay, adjusted for taxes, the sum of call premium and expenses. This sum is $850,000, given that the tax rate is 50 percent and the call premium is $1.5 million.[1] Such a transaction would save the firm a yearly sum of $330,000 in interest (which equals the interest of $3 million on the old bond less the $2.34 million on the new, adjusted for taxes) for the next 15 years.[2] The rate of return on a payment of $850,000 now in exchange for a yearly savings of $330,000 per year for 15 years is about 38 percent. This rate exceeds the firm's aftertax cost of debt (now at 7.8 percent times .5 or 3.9 percent) and makes the refunding a profitable transaction.[3]

Sinking-Fund Provision

The *sinking-fund provision*, which is typical for publicly and privately issued industrial bonds and not uncommon among certain classes of utility debt, requires the obligor to retire a certain amount of the outstanding debt each year. Generally, the retirement occurs in one of two ways. The firm may purchase the amount of bonds to be

---

[1] Both expenses are tax-deductible expenses for the firm. The total expense is the call premium of $1.5 million plus the issuing expenses and legal fees of $200,000. The aftertax cost is equal to the before-tax cost times (1 − tax rate). Hence the aftertax cost is $1.7 million times (1 − .5), or $850,000.

[2] The new interest expense would be $30 million times .078. The aftertax cost of the interest expense is $660,000 times (1 − .5).

[3] Most analysts believe that the "hurdle rate" for refunding must be the aftertax cost of debt, which equals the product of the yield-to-maturity and (1 − marginal tax rate of the firm).

retired in the open market if their price is below par, or the company may make payments to the trustee empowered to monitor the indenture and the trustee will call a certain number of bonds chosen by lottery. In the latter case, the investor would receive the prearranged call price, which is usually very close to par value. The schedule of retirements varies considerably from bond to bond. Some issuers, particularly in the private-placement market, retire most if not all of their debt before maturity. In the public market, some companies may retire as little as 20 percent or 30 percent of the outstanding par value before maturity. Further, many companies write a deferment period into the indenture, permitting them to wait five years or more before beginning the process of sinking-fund retirements. Government debt is generally free of this provision.

It is generally conceded that sinking-fund provisions redound, on balance, to the benefit of the investor. The sinking-fund requirement assures an orderly retirement of the debt so that the final payment, at maturity, will not be too large. Second, the provision enhances the liquidity of some debt, especially the smaller issues and Eurobonds, which have thin secondary markets. Third, the prices of bonds with this requirement are presumably more stable because the issuer may become an active participant on the buy side when prices fall. For these reasons, the yields on bonds with sinking-fund provisions tend to be less than those on bonds without them, all else being the same.

Sometimes, however, the sinking fund can work to the disadvantage of an investor. Suppose that an investor is holding one of the early bonds to be called for a sinking fund. All of the time and effort put into analyzing the bond would now have become wasted, and the investor would have to choose new instruments for purchase. Also, an investor holding a bond with a high coupon at the time rates begin to fall is still forced to relinquish the issue. For this reason, in times of high interest rates one might find investors demanding higher yields from bonds with sinking funds than from other debt.

The sinking-fund provision may also harm the investor's position through the *doubling option*, which is part of many corporate bond indentures. With this option, the corporation is free to retire twice the amount of debt the sinking fund requires and to do it at the call price set for sinking-fund matters. Of course, the firm will exercise this doubling option only if the price of the bond exceeds the sinking-fund price (usually near par), and this happens when rates are relatively low. If, as is typically the case, the sinking-fund provision becomes operative before the lapse of the call-deferment period, the firm can retire much of its debt with the doubling option and can do so at a price far below that of the call price it would have to pay in the event of refunding. The impact of such activity on the investor's position is obvious: The firm can redeem at or near par many of the bonds that appear to be protected from call and that have a market value above the face value of the debt.

Convertible Debt

A *convertible bond* is one that can, after a lapse of a deferment period, be exchanged for specified amounts of common stock in the issuing firm. The conversion cannot be reversed, and the terms of the conversion are set by the company in the bond's indenture. The most important term is *conversion price* or *conversion ratio*, which dictates the number of shares of common to which the holder of the convertible has a claim. For example, Dana Corporation recently issued an A-rated debenture with a 5.875 percent coupon and a maturity of 25 years; the bond has a conversion ratio of 13.22 shares for one bond, or a conversion price of $75.64 per share. Typically, the conversion ratio falls through time, in a schedule contained in the indenture.

The *conversion value* is the market value of the shares into which the bond can be converted. At issuance, that value is less than the face value of the bond, and the difference between them is the *conversion premium*. If the value of the stock grows over time, then the difference begins to favor conversion from fixed income to common stock.

Should investors delay conversion despite a rising price of common, the firm can exert a certain amount of pressure on the bondholders by exercising the call privilege, which is a part of almost all convertible debt. The specified call price is usually equal to or less than par plus one year's interest and can accordingly be much less than the market value of the common stock, which may have appreciated since the convertible was first issued. Another form of pressure on the investor to convert has already been mentioned—the conversion ratio falls through time as the conversion price rises. Investors thus have an incentive not to keep the fixed income security too long in the face of a rising common stock price.

Companies issue convertible bonds for several reasons. The conversion feature produces a yield on the bond that is below that of otherwise similar "straight" or nonconvertible issues. Also, the interest on a convertible may appeal to many investors who want the cash flow and safety of a bond while still enjoying the prospects of capital gains should the company's stock begin to perform well. Third, convertibles offer a firm a chance to avoid dilution in earnings per share, which a new equity issue might bring about. Such a consideration would be important to a firm about to embark on a project whose earnings will not materialize for some time. By using convertible debt instead of new common, the firm can expect that its number of shares will not increase until investors see improved earnings and higher prices for common stock. Fourth, convertible bonds are also tempting to management that believes the market is underestimating its firm's potential. Though small and aggressive firms have been ready to use this financing tool, some large concerns have also employed convertible debt as a funding mechanism.

Convertibles offer investors the relatively safe income of a bond as well as the opportunity for capital gains should the price of the stock do well. Thus a convertible bond is like a straight bond with a very long call option. As a result, convertibles often have higher prices than nonconvertible debt of similar characteristics. Convertibles are especially attractive to those institutions forbidden by regulatory agencies from holding common stock. By buying convertibles these institutions can participate in the stock market even though they are holding bonds.

Anyone interested in convertibles should take notice of two potential problems. First, the yields on convertibles, as mentioned above, are substantially below that of straight debt. Second, convertibles tend to be *subordinated debentures*, a form of debt that has a somewhat residual claim on the firm's income and assets in the case of liquidation. In fact subordinated debt usually has a lower credit rating than otherwise similar bonds. Thus, even though the convertible bond promises the relatively safe income of a fixed income security, the investor should realize that it is often a junior debt and inferior to other forms of debt in important respects. Techniques for analyzing convertible bonds are discussed in Chapter 22.

Warrants

A *warrant* is an option a firm issues that permits the owner to buy, from the firm, a certain number of shares of common stock at a specified price. It is not uncommon for publicly held corporations to issue warrants with new bonds. Firms issue bonds sweetened by warrants in order to decrease the cost of debt and, eventually, to increase the amount of equity in the firm when investors exercise their warrants. Though many small and marginal firms issue bonds with warrants, it is not uncommon for large firms to employ this technique in raising new debt capital.

One of the most valuable aspects of a warrant is that it has a rather long life: Most warrants are in effect for at least two years from issuance, and some are perpetual.[4] Another key feature of the warrant is the *exercise price*, the value for which the warrant holder can buy stock from the corporation. This price is normally set at 15 percent or so above market price of common at the time the bond is issued.

---

[4] This long life contrasts sharply with the three to nine months during which call options, similar to warrants, are exercisable.

Frequently, the exercise price will rise through time, according to the schedule in the bond's indenture. Another important characteristic of the warrant is its *detachability*. Detachable warrants can be sold to third parties who can exercise them with the firm. These warrants are often actively traded on the American Stock Exchange. Other warrants can be exercised only by the bondholder, and these are called nondetachable warrants.

The chief benefit to the investor is the financial leverage the warrant provides. The following example illustrates the point. Suppose that a company's warrant that allows the holder to buy one share of common has an exercise price of $55, that its market value is $3, and that it is detachable. Suppose further that the price of the stock is now $50. If the price of the allied common were to rise to $60, or an increase of 20 percent, the price of the warrant would grow to at least $5 (the difference between the market value of the stock and the price at which the warrant holder can get shares from the company). The warrant's value would then have risen by more than 66 percent. The prospect of such large gains explains why bonds with warrants are more attractive to investors than is similar debt without warrants. Hence the price of a bond with a warrant is higher (and its yield is lower) than that of an otherwise similar bond without a warrant. (A further discussion of warrants appears in Chapter 22.)

PREFERRED STOCK

Preferred stock is a form of equity or ownership in a publicly held corporation. As the term implies, the claims of the holders of preferred stock are superior in some important ways to those of the owners of the other form of equity, common shares. The firm must pay dividends on preferreds before it is free to distribute earnings to holders of common stock. Also, in the event of liquidation, the owners of preferreds have a prior claim on any assets that may remain after the creditors have been satisfied. One difference between preferred and common is that holders of preferred are not normally permitted a voting power in the management of the firm.

The dividend on a preferred stock is, like the coupon on a bond, a fixed payment. A preferred with a dividend of 8 percent and a par value of $100 (which is a typical value) would receive $80 per year. However, the dividend is unlike the coupon on a bond in that the firm is not legally bound to pay the dividend. The company may decide to omit or delay the dividend without suffering the consequences it would meet if it omitted a coupon payment. Some dividends are cumulative, which means that the firm must eventually pay arrearages on any previously omitted dividend payments. Other dividends are noncumulative, and the firm may skip them without the liability of having to pay them later. A very small number of preferreds called participating entitle the investor to receive extra dividends in the case when common dividends exceed the level of dividends on preferred issues.

Public utilities are the prime issuers of preferred stock. Their aim in using this hybrid security is to increase the equity portion of their balance sheet or to prepare the way for a later flotation of new debt. Industrial concerns use preferred primarily in the special cases of merger or acquisition. The type of preferred used then is *convertible preferred*, which will be discussed later. Industrial firms find preferred an unsuitable form of financing because the dividend payments are not tax deductible, as are interest payments on bonds. If the tax rate of a firm is near 50 percent, then the true aftertax cost of debt capital is nearly half as large as the rate on preferred equity. Utilities, by contrast, have an easier time passing costs along to customers and consequently are not reluctant to employ preferred stock in their capital structure.

The expected rate of return on preferred stock is easy to calculate. Because it is a form of equity and a perpetuity, preferred stock has no maturity or principal to be redeemed (with the exceptions of some cases to be analyzed later). Thus the price of preferred is simply the discounted value of an unlimited series of fixed dividend payments. It can be shown that the return on preferred is approximately equal to the ratio of the dividend to the price. (This calculation resembles the current yield on bonds discussed above.) For example, if the Duke Power preferred with a dividend of $8.70 has a price of $61, then its yield is 14.26 percent. This figure is the one reported in *The Wall Street Journal* table of trades from the preceeding day on the market. As is the case with bonds, the price and yield of preferred stock vary inversely: A rise in yield brings about a fall in price, and vice versa. Further, the yields on preferreds tend to correspond closely to and move in concert with the yields on other long-term fixed income securities. Any utility may have more than one preferred stock outstanding at any time, and the different instruments are designated by their dividend level. For example, Duke Power currently has at least four preferreds outstanding—one with a dividend of 8.7 percent, another with a dividend of 8.2 percent, a third with a dividend of 2.69 percent, and so on.

Preferreds have a number of characteristics that are analogous to those discussed above in connection with corporate bonds. The first is the call provision. By such a provision the issuer has the right to redeem, under certain circumstances and at a price near par plus one year's dividend, the outstanding preferred stock. Normally the issuer will be motivated to call the stock when rates fall below the level in effect when the stock was first issued. Again, as in the case of bonds, saved payments are the goal of early retirement. Also the issuer has usually granted the investor a deferment period during which the stock cannot be called. As in the case of bonds, the actual call provisions can vary considerably from stock to stock, company to company, and time to time.

Preferred stock also often contains a sinking-fund provision, which mandates that the issuer retire a given percentage of the issue at scheduled periods after issuance. Investors holding a stock with this provision tend to calculate its yield in a manner similar to the yield-to-maturity on bonds. Obviously, a preferred stock with a sinking fund bears a strong resemblance to a typical corporate bond: Both have fixed, periodic payments, both have maturities, and both have large par value payments at the time of maturity.

Finally, as mentioned above, some preferred stock is convertible into shares of common of the issuing company. This instrument has been popular in the arrangement of mergers and acquisitions. If an acquiring company offers convertible preferreds in exchange for common stock in the acquired firm, the owners of that stock have no immediate tax liability. By accepting the convertible preferred, the owners of the acquired firm can receive a steady stream of high dividends and decide when, and to what extent, they might want to convert into common shares of the acquiring firm.

One more interesting facet of preferred stock requires mention here. The dividends from preferred stock are not fully taxable if the owner of the stock is a corporation. As a result of this rule, corporations tend to be active buyers of the preferreds of other companies, particularly the utilities. This point will be treated in greater detail in Chapters 3 and 13.

CONCLUSION

This chapter has provided an introduction to some of the fundamental attributes of bonds and preferred stock. The chapter has explored, in a preliminary way, such matters as the yields and pricing of these instruments, the motivation behind the issuance of the securities, and the key features of the assets. We have examined to some extent the impact on the investor's experience of such characteristics as call features, sinking-fund provisions, and convertibility. It is our hope that this chapter will supply the reader with a general knowledge of the instruments and provide a conceptual and terminological background for the later chapters that will investigate, in some detail, each of the features discussed above.

The bond market has become a very exciting investment arena. A decade of high and volatile interest rates has had two important effects: (1) It has created a variability in bond prices and returns that have offered both large gains and large risks to its investors; (2) the recent past has encouraged issuers and investors alike to experiment with unusual types of debt and fixed income securities. The zero-coupon debt of several years to maturity, the money market mutual fund, and variable rate instruments are only some of the exciting developments of our time. In fact, this present time is a specially interesting one to investors and analysts of the bond markets, and later chapters will discuss some of the changes and innovations that make this period a particularly important one in financial history.

Federal Income Tax Treatment of Fixed Income Securities

3

FRANK J. FABOZZI, Ph.D., C.F.A., C.P.A.
Professor of Economics
Fordham University

The purpose of this chapter is to explain the provisions of the Internal Revenue Code that the investor should be cognizant of in order to make intelligent investment decisions.

SOME DEFINITIONS

Gross Income, Adjusted Gross Income, and Taxable Income

Investors often use the term *income* in a very casual way. The Internal Revenue Code (IRC), however, provides a more precise definition of income. The IRC distinguishes between gross income, adjusted gross income and taxable income. *Gross income* is all income that is subject to income tax. For example, interest income and dividends are subject to taxation. However, there is a statutory exemption for interest from certain types of debt obligations, as explained later in this chapter. For such obligations, interest income is not included in gross income. Gross income for an individual and a corporation is determined in the same manner.

Adjusted gross income is gross income minus certain business and other deductions. For example, for investors an important deduction from gross income to arrive at adjusted gross income is the long-term capital gain deduction. This deduction will be discussed later in this chapter.

Taxable income is the amount on which the tax liability is determined. It is found by subtracting the personal exemption allowance and other permissible deductions (other than those deductible in arriving at adjusted gross income) from adjusted gross income. For a corporation, all permissible deductions are treated as business deductions. Therefore, adjusted gross income is meaningless for a corporation.

Tax Basis of a Capital Asset, Capital Gain, and Capital Loss

The IRC provides for a special tax treatment on the sale or exchange of a capital asset. The instruments described in this book—debt obligations, preferred stock, and shares of investment companies specializing in fixed income securities—would qualify as capital assets in the hands of a qualified owner. In order to understand the tax treatment of a capital asset, the tax *basis* of a capital asset must first be defined. In most instances the *original basis* of a capital asset is the price paid by a taxpayer on the date it is acquired.[1] The *adjusted basis* of a capital asset is its original basis increased by capital additions and decreased by capital recoveries.

The proceeds received from the sale or exchange of a capital asset are compared to the adjusted basis to determine if the transaction produced a capital gain or capital loss. If the proceeds exceed the adjusted basis, the taxpayer realizes a *capital gain*; on the other hand, a *capital loss* is realized when the adjusted basis exceeds the proceeds received by the taxpayer.

Classification of Taxpayers: Dealers, Traders, Investors

For tax purposes, taxpayers are classified as either dealers, traders, or investors. The classification is important because it determines whether capital gain or loss provisions are applicable and the treatment of transaction costs.[2]

---

[1] When securities are purchased in a package, it is necessary to unbundle the package in order to determine the basis for each security. The general rule for determining the basis of each security is to allocate the cost of the package based upon the total fair market value of the unit immediately after the acquisition. For example, suppose that a unit package containing one bond and one share of preferred stock is purchased for $950. Immediately after the acquisition, the bond sells for $900 and the preferred stock for $85. The total value of the unit is therefore $985. The original basis of the bond is then 91.4 percent ($900 divided by $985) of the acquisition cost, or $868.30 (.914 times $950). The original basis of the preferred stock is $81.70 (.086 times $950).

[2] The classification is also important because it determines whether "wash sales" provisions are applicable. (A wash sale is defined in footnote 29.)

Traders and investors are entitled to realize capital gains and losses. Dealers, on the other hand, are not. In the case of dealers the securities held are considered inventory, and any gains or losses are treated as ordinary gains or losses rather than capital gains or losses.[3] A dealer in securities is a merchant of securities who is regularly engaged in the acquisition of securities and subsequent resale to customers with a view to the gains and profits that may be derived as a result of such transactions. A dealer may be an individual, partnership, or corporation.

A trader is a person who buys and sells for his or her own account rather than the account of a customer, and the frequency of such transacting is such that the person may be said to be engaged in such activities as a trade or business. Investors, like traders, transact for their own accounts. However, transactions are occasional and much less than required in a trade or business.

Regardless of the classification of the taxpayer, expenses incurred to acquire a security are treated as part of the acquisition cost. Selling expenses, however, are handled differently for traders and investors compared with dealers. Traders and investors must deduct the selling expenses from the sale price when determining whether a capital gain or loss is realized. For dealers, selling expenses are deducted as a business expense.

INTEREST INCOME

Interest received by a taxpayer is included in gross income, unless there is a specific statutory exemption indicating otherwise. Therefore, if a taxpayer purchases $10,000 in face value of a corporate bond that has a coupon rate of 12 percent, the taxpayer expects to receive $1,200 per year. If that amount is actually received by the taxpayer in the tax year, it is included in gross income.

Interest received on debt issued by any state or political subdivision thereof,[4] the District of Columbia, any possession of the United States, and certain local and urban agencies operating under the auspices of the Department of Housing and Urban Development is not included in gross income. As explained later, there is also a maximum lifetime exclusion on interest paid on certain savings certificates.

---

[3] There is an exception. If a dealer (1) clearly designates that certain securities are being held for investment purposes when the securities are acquired and (2) does not hold the securities primarily for sale to customers in the ordinary course of business after the designation, then gains or losses on the designated securities qualify for capital gain and loss treatment.

[4] Because of financing practices by some state and local governments that Congress viewed as abusive, Congress imposed limitations on the issuance of tax-exempt obligations in various amendments to the Internal Revenue Code of 1954. The limitations involved industrial development bonds and arbitrage bonds. See Chapter 15.

The statutory exemption of the interest received from debtors who are state and local governments (both referred to as municipalities in this chapter) is supposedly based upon the reciprocal immunity doctrine of the United States Constitution. This doctrine holds that states cannot interfere in the operations of the federal government, and the latter cannot interfere in the operations of the former. By taxing interest income on municipal obligations, it is argued that the ability of the state to finance its operations would be impaired. Although the exemption is still part of the Internal Revenue Code, many political analysts believe that since the passage of the 16th Amendment to the Constitution, the exemption has been based upon political reasons rather than on constitutional grounds.

Likewise, interest paid on debt issued by the U.S. government and its agencies are exempt from income taxation by state and local governments but not from federal income taxes. Interest income by U.S. territories, the District of Columbia and certain local urban agencies operating under HUD are also exempt from all state and local income taxes.[5] Usually, a state exempts the interest income from its own debt obligations, its agencies, and its political subdivisions from its state and local income taxes. However, a state usually taxes the interest income from obligations of other states and political subdivisions.

The Economic Recovery Tax Act (ERTA) of 1981 included a provision that granted individuals a lifetime exclusion from gross income of $1,000 for a single return and $2,000 for a joint return of interest income earned on qualified tax-exempt savings certificates issued by qualified savings institutions. To qualify, the savings certificates must have been issued during the period from October 1, 1981, to January 1, 1983.

Beginning January 1, 1985, the ERTA of 1981 grants individual taxpayers a 15 percent interest exclusion of "qualified interest income" over "qualified interest expense." The maximum exclusion is $450 for a single taxpayer and $900 for a joint return. Qualified interest income includes (1) interest on deposits in banks, savings and loan associations, credit unions, and other savings or thrift institutions regulated under state or federal law (e.g., real estate investment trusts and regulated investment companies), and (2) interest from corporate, federal, state, or local bonds subject to tax. Qualified interest expense is all deductible interest expense except for that incurred with property used primarily as a dwelling unit or incurred on trade or business loans. If a taxpayer does not itemize deductions, that taxpayer does not have to reduce qualified interest income by qualified interest expense.

---

[5] The Economic Recovery Tax Act of 1981 extended tax-exempt status to interest paid on state or local government obligations issued before January 1, 1985, where the proceeds are used to purchase mass-transit vehicles leased to a government-owned transit system, and to obligations issued by qualified volunteer fire departments.

As explained in Chapter 4, a portion of the income realized from holding a debt obligation may be in the form of a capital gain rather than coupon interest. The IRC (as explained later in this chapter) provides for favorable tax treatment for certain capital gains. The tax treatment of the income from holding a debt instrument will therefore have a major impact on the aftertax return realized by an investor.

For example, suppose $10,000 of a 15-year corporate bond is purchased at par and the issuer promises to pay 12 percent of par annually, that is, the coupon rate is 12 percent. The yield to maturity would be 12 percent.[6] Assuming the bonds are held to maturity and the company makes the promised interest payments on schedule, then $1,200 is reported in the taxpayer's gross income each year. When the bonds mature and are redeemed by the issuer for $10,000, the amount received represents the return of the taxpayer's investment and is therefore not subject to taxation.[7] Suppose instead that $10,000 of face value of 15-year corporate bonds with a coupon rate of 9.5 percent had been purchased for $8,279. The yield to maturity for this bond would be 12 percent, the same yield as the bonds purchased at par value; however, in this case a portion of the income is in coupon interest received of $950 (.095 times $10,000), and the remainder is provided in the form of a capital gain of $1,721 ($10,000 redemption value minus $8,279). Investors may prefer the bonds selling at a discount[8] because the capital gains would be taxed at a preferential rate.[9]

Unlike debt instruments whose interest payments are taxable, the capital gain portion of a tax-exempt bond is unattractive for an investor who seeks tax-free income. This is because although the coupon interest received is exempt from federal income taxation, the capital gain portion is subject to taxation, albeit at a lower rate than coupon interest received from a taxable obligation. This point should be kept in mind when considering the acquisition of a tax-exempt obligation.[10] To repeat, subject to the exceptions noted later, *the portion of income that is exempt from federal taxation for a tax-exempt obligation is the coupon interest received, not the capital gain portion.*

---

[6] The yield to maturity is explained in Chapter 4.

[7] Recall that the tax basis for the bonds would be their cost of $10,000. Since the proceeds received are $10,000 at redemption, there is neither a capital gain nor a capital loss.

[8] This is not true for original-issue, deep-discount bonds discussed later in this chapter.

[9] Notice that a definitive statement about the preference for the bonds selling at a discount is not made. Although there is a tax advantage if the bonds are held to maturity, you will see there are other factors—expected movement of interest rates and need for current income, for example—that affect the investor's preference.

[10] As explained in Chapter 15, there is a formula suggested for determining the equivalent taxable yield for a tax-exempt obligation. This formula is only an approximation because it assumes that all of the income is tax free; that is, it assumes the obligation is acquired at approximately par value.

Because of the importance of distinguishing between income in the form of a capital gain (or loss) and interest income, the investor must be familiar with certain rules set forth in the IRC. These rules are summarized below.

Accrued Interest

Usually, interest is paid semiannually. The interest earned by the seller from holding the bond until the disposal date is called accrued interest. For example, if a corporate bond whose issuer promises to pay $60 on June 1 and December 1 for a specified number of years is sold on October 1, the seller is usually entitled to accrued interest of $40 ($60 times ⅔) for the four months that the seller held the bond.

Let us look at the tax position of the seller and the buyer, assuming that our hypothetical bond is selling for $900 in the market and that the seller's adjusted basis for this bond is $870. The buyer must pay the seller $940, $900 for the market price plus $40 of accrued interest. The seller must treat the accrued interest of $40 as interest income. The $900 is compared to the seller's adjusted basis of $870 to determine whether the seller has realized a capital gain or capital loss. Obviously, the seller has realized a capital gain of $30. When the buyer receives the December 1 interest payment of $60, only $20 is included in gross income as interest income. The basis of the bond for the buyer is $900, not $940.

Not all transactions involving bonds require the payment of accrued interest by the buyer. This occurs when the issuer of the bond is in default of principal or interest or the interest on the bonds are contingent on sufficient earnings of the issuer.[11] Such bonds are said to be quoted flat. The acquisition price entitles the buyer to receive the principal and unpaid interest for both past scheduled payments due and accrued interest. Generally, for bonds quoted flat, all payments made by the issuer to the buyer are first considered as payments to satisfy defaulted payments or unpaid contingent interest payments and accrued interest before acquisition. Such payments are treated as a return of capital. As such, the proceeds reduce the cost basis of the bond. On the other hand, accrued interest after the acquisition date is considered interest income when received.

For example, suppose the issuer of a corporate bond is in default of two scheduled interest payments of $60 each. The interest payments are scheduled on April 1 and October 1. The bond is sold for $500 on August 1. Assume that on October 1 of the year of acquisition the issuer pays the bondholder $120. The buyer would treat the payment

---

[11]A bond whose interest is contingent upon sufficient earnings by the issuer is called an income bond and is discussed in Chapter 12.

as a return of capital of $120, since it represents the two defaulted interest payments. Hence the adjusted basis of the bond is $380 ($500 minus $120) and is not considered interest income. Suppose that two weeks later the issuer pays an additional $60 to the bondholder. This payment must then be apportioned between accrued interest before the acquisition date of August 1 and accrued interest after the acquisition date. The latter is $20, since the bond was held by the buyer for two months. Thus $40 of the $60 payment reduces the adjusted basis of $380 prior to the second payment to $340 and is not treated as interest income. The $20 of accrued interest since the acquisition date is treated as interest income.

Bond Purchased at a Premium

When a bond is purchased at a price greater than its redemption value at maturity, the bond is said to be purchased at a premium.[12] For a taxable bond purchased by a nondealer taxpayer, the taxpayer may elect to amortize the premium ratably over the remaining life of the security. In the case of a convertible bond selling at a premium, however, the amount attributable to the conversion feature may not be amortized. The amount amortized reduces the amount of the interest income that will be taxed. In turn, the basis is reduced by the amount of the amortization.

For a tax-exempt bond, the premium *must* be amortized. Although the amount amortized is not a tax-deductible expense since the interest is exempt from taxation, the amortization reduces the original basis.

For example, suppose on January 1, 1981, a calendar-year taxpayer purchased *taxable* bonds for $10,500. The bonds have a remaining life of 10 years and a $10,000 redemption value at maturity. The coupon rate is 7 percent. The premium is $500. The taxpayer can amortize this premium over the 10-year remaining life. If so, the amount amortized would be $50 per year ($500 divided by 10).[13] The coupon interest received of $700 ($10,000 times 0.07) would then be effectively reduced by $50. At the end of 1981, the first year, the original basis of $10,500 is reduced by $50 to $10,450. By the end of 1985 the bond would be held for five years. The adjusted basis would be $10,250 ($10,500 minus $250). If the bond is held until retired by the issuer at

---

[12] A bond will sell at a premium so that the effective interest rate of the bond is adjusted to reflect the prevailing interest rate on securities of comparable risk and remaining maturity. For a further discussion, see Chapter 4.

[13] There is a method that provides the precise value of the amount that should be amortized each year. This is known as the scientific, or effective-interest-rate, method. However, this method provides lower amortization in the earlier years than the straight-line method of amortization used in the example. Consequently, the straight-line method is preferred for taxable bonds if the taxpayer elects to amortize the premium.

maturity, the adjusted basis would be $10,000, and consequently there would be no capital gain or loss realized. If the taxpayer does not elect to amortize the premium, the original basis is not changed. Consequently, at maturity the taxpayer would realize a capital loss of $500.

Had our hypothetical bond been a tax-exempt bond, the premium would have had to be amortized. The coupon interest of $700 would be tax exempt, and the amortization of $50 would not be a tax-deductible expense.[14] Instead, the basis would be adjusted each year.

As an illustration of the amortization for a bond purchased some time during the tax year rather than at the beginning of the tax year, let's take an actual case. In April 1981 Albany County South Mall 10s maturing 4/1/85 sold for approximately $270,285. The redemption value at maturity per bond is $250,000. Suppose that a calendar-year taxpayer purchased the bond on April 1, 1981. The premium is $20,285 ($270,285 minus $250,000).

The number of months remaining to maturity is 48 (four years times 12 months). Consequently, the monthly amortization is $422.60. At the end of 1981 the original basis of $270,285 is reduced by the amortization corresponding to the number of months the bond was held for in 1981. Since the bond was held for nine months (April 1 to December 31), the original basis is reduced by $3,803.40 ($422.60 times nine months). Hence, the adjusted basis is $266,481.60 ($270,285 minus $3,803.40) at the end of 1981.

Suppose the bond is sold on October 31, 1982, and the taxpayer receives $260,000. To determine whether there is a capital gain or loss, the adjusted basis must be ascertained. Since the bond was held for 19 months, amortization is $8,029.40 ($422.60 times 19 months) and the adjusted basis is $262,255.60 ($270,285 minus $8,029.40). Hence the taxpayer would realize a capital loss of $2,255.60, the difference between the adjusted basis of $262,255.60 and the proceeds received of $260,000.

So far in our illustration we have used the original basis and the remaining number of years to maturity to determine the amount to be amortized. In the case of a callable bond, the taxpayer may elect to compute the amortization based upon the earlier call date *if a smaller deduction results compared to using the number of years remaining to maturity.* For example, suppose an investor purchased a bond that has 10 years remaining to maturity for $1,300. The redemption value at maturity is $1,000; however, the bond may be called in six years for

---

[14] In the case of tax-exempt bonds, the scientific method of amortization would be preferred, since the adjusted basis would be higher than if the straight-line method were used. Consequently there would be a greater capital loss or smaller capital gain if the bonds were sold before maturity.

$1,150. If the bond is a taxable bond, then the first election the investor must make is whether or not to amortize the premium. If the investor elects to amortize the premium, then the investor may elect to base the amount of the amortization upon the call price and date rather than upon the redemption value at maturity if the deduction is less. If the amount amortized is based upon the redemption value at maturity, then the annual amount deducted would be $30, since the premium is $300 and there are 10 years remaining to maturity. If the earlier call date is used, the amount of the premium is $150. The annual deduction is $25 per year, since there are six years to the call date.

Should a bond be called before its maturity date, any unamortized portion of the premium is treated as an ordinary loss in the year the bond is called. For example, consider our hypothetical 10-year bond that is callable in 6 years. If the bond were actually called in the sixth year, an investor who did not elect to amortize the premium would realize an ordinary loss of $150 (original basis of $1,300 minus call price of $1,150). Notice what happens if the premium is amortized. Amortization based upon the maturity date would result in a capital gain of $30.[15] Of course, amortization based upon the call date would have generated neither a capital gain nor loss.

As noted earlier, no portion of the premium attributable to the conversion feature of a convertible bond may be amortized. For example, suppose a 15-year convertible bond with a 9.5 percent coupon rate is selling for $1,400. The investor must determine what portion of the premium is due to the conversion value. Suppose the investor determines that nonconvertible bonds with the same quality rating and years remaining to maturity are selling to yield 8.1 percent. A 15-year bond priced to yield 8.1 percent would sell for $1,120.30 per $1,000 of redemption value at maturity.[16] Consequently, the premium that the investor may elect to amortize is based upon $1,120.30, *not* $1,400.

Bond Purchased at a Discount

A bond purchased at a price less than its redemption value at maturity is said to be bought at a *discount*. The tax treatment of the discount depends upon whether the discount represents *original-issue discount* or a bond that was not sold at an original-issue discount but is purchased in the secondary market at a discount.

---

[15] The adjusted basis would be the original basis of $1,300 minus the amount amortized over the six years of $180 ($30 times six).The capital gain is therefore the call price of $1,150 minus the adjusted basis of $1,120.

[16] See Chapter 4 for the pricing of bonds.

Original-Issue Discount

When bonds are initially sold, they may be sold at a price less than their redemption value at maturity. There are three reasons a debt obligation may be sold at a discount. First, an increase in interest rates between the time the coupon rate is set by the issuer and the bonds are actually sold will force the issuer to sell the bonds at a discount. Second, bonds offering an original-issue discount are attractive to some institutional investors, as explained in Chapter 12. Consequently, the bonds can be sold at a lower cost to the issuer than bonds sold at par value. Finally, some short-term debt obligations, such as Treasury bills and commercial paper, are sold on a discounted or noninterest-bearing basis.[17]

The tax treatment of an original-issue discount depends on the issuance date. For obligations issued prior to July 2, 1982, the ratable monthly portion of the original-issue discount must be amortized and included in gross income. For obligations issued after July 2, 1982, the amount of the amortization is determined by the scientific or effective interest method. This means that amortization is lower in the earlier years, gradually increasing over the life of the obligation on a compounding basis. Regardless of the date of issuance, the amount amortized is added to the adjusted basis. The post-July 2, 1982 rules, however, do not apply to tax-exempt obligations.

There are three exceptions to this general rule. First, since the interest on tax-exempt bonds is not included in gross income, the amortized discount is not included in gross because it constitutes interest income. Second, the holder of Series EE and E savings bonds may elect to have the original-issue discount on these bonds taxed when the bonds are redeemed rather than having the accrued interest income taxed annually.[18] Third, for noninterest-bearing municipal and federal obligations maturing in one year or less from the date of issue, the discount is not accrued. Instead, the interest is recognized as earned only when the obligation is redeemed or sold.

To illustrate the rule for a bond issued prior to July 2, 1982, let us use an actual case. On March 15, 1981, Martin Marietta Corporation issued debentures carrying a 7 percent coupon rate and due 30 years later. This issue was a pioneering offering of original-issue *deep*-discount bonds. The offering price was $538.35 per $1,000 of redemption value at maturity. The original-issue discount was therefore $461.65. The number of remaining months to maturity was 360 (30 years times 12 months) at the time of the offering. Hence, the ratable monthly amortization is $1.28 per $1,000 par value. In 1981 the bond would be

---

[17] Treasury bills and commercial paper are discussed in Chapter 8.

[18] For a further discussion, see Chapter 10.

held for 9½ months. Hence, interest income of $12.16 must be included in the 1981 gross income of a calendar-year taxpayer in addition to the coupon interest paid by the issuer. The adjusted basis of the bond at the end of 1981 would be $550.51.

There are three more points the investor should be familiar with when dealing with original-issue discount bonds. First, original-issue discount is treated as zero if the discount is less than one fourth of 1 percent of the redemption value at maturity multiplied by the number of complete years to maturity. For example, suppose a bond maturing in 20 years is initially sold for $990 for each $1,000 of redemption value at maturity. The original-issue discount is $10. The redemption value multiplied by the number of years to maturity is $20,000. The original-issue discount is .0005 of $20,000. Since it is less than one fourth of 1 percent (.0025), the original-issue discount is treated as zero; that is, the investor does not have to amortize the discount and report it as gross income. Instead, the rule discussed in the next section is applicable.

Second, if an original-issue discount bond is sold before maturity, subsequent holders must continue to amortize the original-issue discount. However, if the price paid by the subsequent holder is greater than the adjusted basis of the previous holder, then a deduction of the monthly amortization is allowed by the new holder. The amount that the new holder is entitled to reduce the monthly amortization is determined by dividing the excess of the price paid over the adjusted basis of the previous holder by the number of remaining months to maturity. For example, suppose the original purchaser of the Martin Marietta Corporation bonds discussed above sold the bonds on June 15, 1982, for $557.55. Since the adjusted basis to the original bondholder is $557.55,[19] the new bondholder must continue to report $1.28 per month as interest income in his or her gross income. If less than $557.55 is paid, the same amount is still reported. However if $730.05 is paid for the bond, the new bondholder can reduce the monthly amortization of the original-issue discount by $.50. This is determined as follows. The excess of the price paid over the adjusted basis of the previous holder, the original purchaser in this case, is $172.50 ($730.05 minus $557.55). Since there are 345 months remaining to maturity, the reduction is found by dividing $172.50 by 345. Consequently, the monthly amortization of the new holder is $.78 ($1.28 minus $.5).

The third point to keep in mind is that an investor may have to pay taxes on interest included in gross income but not received in cash. Consequently, original issue discount obligations are unattractive for portfolios of individual investors and institutions subject to taxation.

---

[19] The adjusted basis is the original basis of $538.35 plus amortization for 15 months of $19.20.

Bond Purchased at a Discount when the Discount Is Not an Original-Issue Discount

The rule for the tax treatment of a bond acquired at a discount when the discount does not represent an original-issue discount is simple. The discount is *not* amortized. The original basis is therefore unchanged. The difference between the original basis and the proceeds received when the bond is disposed of determines whether there is a capital gain or loss.

The buyer of a tax-exempt obligation should realize that the statutory exemption of interest income applies only to the coupon interest and the amortization of the original-issue discount. For example, the Boston Massachusetts' 6.3s due 4/1/88 sold in April 1981 at $11,474 per bond. Since the redemption value at maturity is $15,000, the discount is $3,526 ($15,000 minus $11,474). Furthermore, the discount is *not* original-issue discount. Although annual interest income of $945 ($15,000 times .063) is exempt from federal taxation, the capital gain of $3,526 that would be realized if the bond were held until maturity would be treated as a capital gain. Disposal of the bond prior to maturity would result in a capital gain or loss depending upon whether the proceeds are greater than or less than $11,474, respectively.

DIVIDENDS

Preferred stock and investment companies specializing in fixed income securities are discussed later in this book.[20] Both investment vehicles pay dividends rather than interest. The general rules applicable to these investment vehicles are discussed in this section.

Corporations make cash distributions to shareholders.[21] Not all cash distributions, however, are taxed. For individual taxpayers, only that portion of the distribution representing dividends is included in gross income, subject to a $100 dividend exclusion for a single return and $200 for a joint return beginning January 1, 1982.[22] A *dividend* is defined as a payment made by a corporation out of earnings and profits of each taxable year. Dividend income is taxed as ordinary income. Any portion of a distribution that does not represent a dividend is treated as a return of capital. No tax is paid on that portion; instead, the basis of the stock is reduced by that amount.[23]

---

[20] Preferred stock is discussed in Chapter 13. Chapters 20 and 21 are devoted to investment companies specializing in fixed income securities.

[21] A corporation may make distributions in a form other than cash to holders of its common stock.

[22] Beginning 1982, holders of qualified *common stock* who participate in a dividend reinvestment plan of public utilities will be able to exclude $750 for a single return and $1,500 for a joint return.

[23] If the distribution that is not a dividend exceeds the adjusted basis, it is treated as a capital gain.

Corporate recipients of dividend payments must include the entire amount in gross income. However, there is a special deduction that a corporation can take against dividend payments.[24] A corporate tax-payer is entitled to a deduction equal to (1) 85 percent of a dividend received from a domestic corporation[25] and (2) 100 percent of the dividend received from a corporation that is a member of a controlled group with the recipient corporation. For this reason, the treasurer of a corporation contemplating a fixed income investment would prefer a high-quality preferred stock issue to a high-quality, long-term debt instrument.

Dividends are also paid by regulated investment companies, such as a mutual fund.[26] Investment companies sell their own securities to the public and reinvest the proceeds in a large number of securities. The shareholder of an investment company participates in the return generated from holding and transactions involving these securities. The return earned by the investment company can therefore be in the form of interest, dividends, or capital gains. However, the dividend from an investment company to its shareholders is designated by the investment company in a written notice to its shareholders not later than 45 days after the close of the taxable year as either ordinary dividends or capital gains. Ordinary dividends are treated in the same way as preferred stock dividends. However, any portion of the dividend that represents tax-exempt income realized by the investment company is under certain conditions tax-exempt to the shareholder.[27] The amount classified as a capital gain is considered a long-term capital gain and treated accordingly as explained later in this chapter.

Not all of the long-term capital gain realized by the investment company is actually paid in cash to the shareholders. In that case, the investment company will pay the income tax on that portion retained. The shareholder, however, is deemed to have paid the tax on the undistributed capital gain, which can be refunded or credited to the shareholder. Moreover, the shareholder increases the basis of the share of the investment company by an amount equal to the excess of the long-term capital gains over the capital gains tax included in the shareholder's total long-term capital gains.[28]

CAPITAL GAIN AND LOSS TREATMENT

Once a capital gain or capital loss is determined for a capital asset, there are special rules for determining the impact on adjusted gross

[24] Section 243(a) of the IRC.

[25] There is a limitation based upon the taxable income of the corporation.

[26] Section 852(a) of the IRC sets forth specific requirements for a regulated investment company to be granted special tax treatment.

[27] Section 852(b)(5) of the IRC specifies the conditions for the tax-exempt portion of interest income to be tax free to the shareholder.

[28] Section 852(b)(3)(D) of the IRC.

income. The tax treatment for individuals and nondealer corporations is explained in this section.

Capital Gain and Loss Treatment for Individuals

To determine the impact of transactions involving capital assets on adjusted gross income, it is first necessary to ascertain whether the sale or exchange has resulted in a capital gain or loss that is long term or short term. The classification depends upon the length of time the capital asset is held by the taxpayer. The general rule is that if a capital asset is held for one year or less, the gain or loss is a short-term capital gain or loss.[29] A long-term capital gain or loss results when the capital asset is held for one day more than one year, or longer. Usually, the day of acquisition is not counted in determining the holding period, but the day of sale is counted.

Second, all short-term capital gains and losses are combined to produce either a *net short-term capital gain* or a *net short-term capital loss*. The same procedure is followed for long-term capital gains and losses. Either a *net long-term capital gain* or a *net long-term capital loss* will result.

Third, an overall *net capital gain* or *net capital loss* is determined by combining the amounts in the previous step. If the result is a net capital gain, the entire amount is added to gross income. However, net long-term capital gains are given preferential tax treatment. A deduction is allowed from gross income in determining adjusted gross income. The permissible deduction is 60 percent of the excess of net long-term capital gains over net short-term capital losses.[30] Exhibit 1 provides six illustrations of the treatment of a net capital gain.

If there is a net capital loss, it is deductible from gross income. The amount that may be deducted, however, is limited to the lesser of (1) $3,000 (but $1,500 for married taxpayers filing separate returns), (2) taxable income without the personal exemption and without capital gains and losses minus the zero bracket amount, and (3) the total of net short-term capital loss plus half the net long-term capital loss. The third limitation is the so-called $1 for $2 rule and is the basic difference between the tax treatment of net short-term capital losses and net

---

[29] An exception to this general rule applies to wash sales. A wash sale occurs when "substantially identical securities" are acquired within 30 days before or after a sale of the securities *at a loss*. In such cases, the loss is not recognized as a capital loss. Instead, the loss is added to the basis of the securities that caused the loss. The holding period for the new securities in connection with a wash sale then includes the period for which the original securities were held. The rule is not applicable to an individual who is a trader, nor to an individual or corporate dealer.

[30] A capital gain deduction taken by an individual could result in a minimum tax liability.

Exhibit 1
Tax Treatment of a Net Capital Gain

	Illustration Number					
	(1)	*(2)*	*(3)*	*(4)*	*(5)*	*(6)*
1. Net long-term capital gain (loss)............	$35,000	$35,000	$35,000	$ 0	($3,000)	($8,000)
2. Net short-term capital gain (loss)...........	(15,000)	15,000	0	15,000	15,000	15,000
3. Net capital gain: increase in gross income	20,000	50,000	35,000	15,000	12,000	7,000
4. Excess of net long-term capital gain over net short-term capital loss...............	20,000	35,000	35,000	0	0	0
5. Capital gains deduction (60 percent of line 4).............	(12,000)	(21,000)	(21,000)	0	0	0
6. Increase in adjusted gross income (line 3 minus line 5)........	8,000	29,000	14,000	15,000	12,000	7,000

long-term capital losses. The former is deductible dollar for dollar, but the latter requires $2 of long-term capital loss to obtain a $1 deduction.

Because of the difference in the tax treatment of net long-term capital losses and net short-term capital losses, the order in which these losses are deductible in a tax year are specified by the Treasury. First, net short-term capital losses are used to satisfy the limitation. Any balance to satisfy the limitation is then applied from net long-term capital losses using the $1 for $2 rule. Any unused net short-term or net long-term capital losses are carried over on a dollar-for-dollar basis.[31] When they are carried over, they do not lose their identity but remain either short term or long term. These losses can be carried over indefinitely until they are all utilized in subsequent tax years.

Exhibit 2 provides 10 illustrations of the net capital loss deduction rule. In the illustrations it is assumed that taxable income as defined in (2) above is greater than $3,000, and the taxpayer, if married, is not filing a separate return.

Capital Gain and Loss Treatment for Corporations

The procedure for determining a net capital gain or loss is the same as that for individuals. The tax treatment of any net capital gain or loss differs from that of individuals in the following two ways.

First, a corporation is not entitled to a net capital gain deduction for the excess of net long-term capital gains over net short-term capital losses. Instead the excess is subject to an alternative tax computation that limits the tax to 28 percent of the gain. The tax attributable to the excess of net long-term capital gains over net short-term capital losses is the lesser of (1) the tax liability on the taxable income when the excess is included in taxable income (i.e., regular tax computation) and (2) the tax liability on taxable income that is reduced by the excess, plus a 28 percent tax on the excess. The latter tax computation is the alternative tax computation.

Second, no deduction is allowed for a net capital loss. However, net capital losses can be carried back to three preceding taxable years and carried forward five taxable years to offset any net capital gains in those years.[32] Although there are exceptions, the general rule is that any unused net capital loss after the fifth subsequent year can never be used by a corporate taxpayer. Net capital losses are not carried over in character. Instead, they are carried over as a short-term capital loss.

---

[31] However, in determining the amount of the net capital loss deduction in a future tax year, the $1 for $2 rule applies.

[32] There is a limitation on the amount that can be carried back. The amount cannot cause or increase a net operating loss in the taxable year it is carried back to. Net capital losses are applied to the earliest year as a carry-back or carry-over.

Exhibit 2
Tax Treatment of a Net Capital Loss

					Illustration Number					
	(1)	(2)	(3)	(4)	(5)	(6)	(7)	(8)	(9)	(10)
1. Net long-term capital gain (loss)...	$ 0	($7,000)	($7,000)	($7,000)	($3,000)	($4,000)	$6,000	($4,000)	($12,000)	$ 4,000
2. Net short-term capital gain (loss)..	(5,000)	0	(5,000)	(2,000)	(1,000)	0	(7,000)	1,000	2,000	(14,000)
3. Net capital loss	5,000	7,000	12,000	9,000	4,000	4,000	1,000	3,000	10,000	10,000
4. Capital loss deduction*..........	3,000	3,000	3,000	3,000	2,500	2,000	1,000	1,500	3,000	3,000
5. Long-term capital loss carryover...	0	1,000	7,000	5,000	0	0	0	0	4,000	0
6. Short-term capital loss carryover ..	2,000	0	2,000	0	0	0	0	0	0	7,000

* Assumes that the taxpayer (1) is not married or if married is not filing a separate return and (2) has taxable income without the personal exemption and without capital gains and losses minus the zero bracket amount greater than $3,000.

DEDUCTIBILITY OF INTEREST EXPENSE INCURRED
TO ACQUIRE OR CARRY SECURITIES

An investment strategy discussed in Chapter 34 involves the borrowing of funds to purchase or carry securities. Although interest expense on borrowed funds is a tax-deductible expense, the investor should be aware of the following two rules relating to the deductibility of interest expense to acquire or carry securities.

First, there are limitations applicable to individual taxpayers when funds are borrowed to acquire or carry securities.[33] The amount of interest that can be deducted is $10,000 plus the amount of any net investment income. For example, if an individual taxpayer receives net investment income of $50,000 but incurred interest expense of $80,000, only $60,000 may be deducted in the current tax year. The balance of $20,000 will be carried over to the next tax year.

Second, the IRC specifies that interest paid or accrued on "indebtedness incurred or continued to purchase or carry obligations, the interest on which is wholly exempt from taxes," is not tax deductible.[34] It does not make any difference if any tax-exempt interest is actually received by the taxpayer in the taxable year. Courts have found that the rule applies where the taxpayer (1) holds defaulted obligations,[35] (2) holds a tax-exempt obligation before interest begins to accrue,[36] and (3) seeks to produce a taxable profit rather than tax-exempt interest.[37] The nondeductibility of interest expenses also applies to debt incurred or continued in order to purchase or carry shares of a regulated investment company (e.g., mutual fund) that distributes exempt interest dividends.[38]

To understand why interest related to debt incurred to purchase or carry tax-exempt obligations is disallowed as a deduction, consider the following example. Suppose a taxpayer in the 50 percent marginal tax bracket borrows $100,000 at an annual interest cost of 12 percent, or $12,000. The proceeds are then used to acquire $100,000 of municipal bonds at par with a coupon rate of 8 percent, or $8,000 interest per year. If the $12,000 interest expense were allowed as a tax-deductible expense, the aftertax cost of the interest expense would be $6,000. Since the interest received from holding the municipal bonds is $8,000, the taxpayer would benefit by $2,000 after taxes.

---

[33] Section 163(d) of the IRC. For corporate taxpayers and taxpayers who incur interest expense for business purposes, the limitation does not apply.

[34] Section 265(2) of the IRC.

[35] *Clyde C. Pierce Corp.* v. *Commissioner*, 120 F.2d 206 (1941).

[36] *Illinois Terminal Railroad Co.* v. *United States*, 375 F.2d 1016,1022 (1967).

[37] *Denman* v. *Slayton*, 282 U.S. 514 (1931).

[38] Section 265(4) of the IRC.

In the absence of direct evidence that the purpose of the indebtedness was to purchase or carry tax-exempt obligations, the rule is generally *not* applicable where a taxpayer's investment is "insubstantial." For individual taxpayers, the IRS will presume an investment is insubstantial if in the tax year under consideration the average amount of the tax-exempt obligations does not exceed 2 percent of the average value of the portfolio of investments and any assets held in the active conduct of the taxpayer's trade or business.[39] For the purposes of applying this rule, the investments in the portfolio are valued according to their adjusted basis. For a nondealer corporation, an insubstantial investment will be presumed to exist if in the taxable year the average amount of the tax-exempt obligations is not in excess of 2 percent of the average total assets held in the active conduct of the corporate taxpayer's trade or business.[40]

In the absence of direct evidence that the purpose of the indebtedness was to purchase or carry tax-exempt obligations, there is another circumstance in which the rule does not apply to individual taxpayers. The circumstances occurs when the individual taxpayer incurs personal indebtedness to purchase goods and services for *personal consumption*, or to purchase a residence, or to improve a residence or other real property that is held for *personal* use.[41]

An acceptable argument to overcome the IRS's presumption that indebtedness was incurred by an individual taxpayer to purchase or carry tax-exempt obligations is that there was no market for the obligation. Such a situation, however, is unlikely to exist for the preponderance of tax-exempt obligations. The IRS's presumption is not rebutted, however, by demonstrating that the obligations would have to be sold at a loss or that the amount of cash that would have been generated from the liquidation of the obligation would have been less than the amount of indebtedness incurred.[42]

When there is no direct evidence linking the debt incurred to the tax-exempt obligations purchased or carried by a nondealer corporation, the IRS will generally not presume an indirect link unless there is evidence that the amount borrowed is in excess of the amount the corporation needs to carry on its business. One indication of excess borrowing is when "the taxpayer invests a disproportionally large portion of its liquid assets in tax-exempt obligations and there are no facts indicating that such investment is related to the reasonable needs of

---

[39] Revenue Procedure 72–18. Portfolio investments include "transactions entered into for profit (including investment in real estate) which are not connected with the active conduct of a trade or business."

[40] Revenue Procedure 72–18.

[41] Revenue Procedure 72–18.

[42] Revenue Procedure 72–18.

the taxpayer's business. . . ."[43] The acquisition of short-term, tax-exempt obligations that are frequently liquidated in order to provide funds for the use in a taxpayer's operations would generally not be inferred by the IRS to be indirectly linked to indebtedness incurred by the taxpayer. However, the IRS may make an inference of an indirect link "with respect to indebtedness which is itself short term and is incurred other than in the normal course of the taxpayer's trade or business."[44]

The question of the purpose of incurring indebtedness when there is no direct link depends upon the underlying fact. For example, in one case a nondealer corporate taxpayer used municipal bonds as collateral for a short-term loan. The proceeds of the short-term loan were used to satisfy the taxpayer's current operating expenses. The interest deduction on the short-term loan was denied by the court because it was thought that, at the time the municipal bonds were acquired, the taxpayer should have anticipated the need for additional financing to meet current operating expenses.[45] Yet the interest on indebtedness incurred by the same corporate taxpayer in order to finance the construction of a new plant was allowed by the court. The court justified the deduction on the grounds that the corporate taxpayer's liquidity would be threatened if it were required to dispose of the municipal bonds.[46]

Other cases have established that even though a taxpayer continues to carry tax-exempt securities after borrowing funds, the interest deduction would be allowed if there is a good business reason for doing so rather than disposing of the securities.[47] However, even though there may be a good business reason, the deduction would be denied if the dominant reason for borrowing funds is to hold the securities.[48]

---

[43] Revenue Procedure 72–18.

[44] Revenue Procedure 72–18.

[45] *Wisconsin Cheeseman v. United States*, 388 F.2d 420 (1968).

[46] *Wisconsin Cheeseman v. United States*.

[47] For example, in *R.B. George Machinery Co.*, 26 B.T.A. 594 (1932) (Acquiesced C.B. XI–2,4), the nondealer corporate taxpayer acquired nonnegotiable obligations in the course of business operations as payment for its services to the tax-exempt entity. In yet another case, a nondealer taxpayer was required to hold such obligations as a condition to providing a service or product to a state or local government. *Commissioner v. Bagley & Sewall Co.*, 221 F.2d 944 (1955).

[48] *Illinois Terminal Railroad Co.* v. *United States*.

Bond Yield Measures and Price Volatility Properties

4 **FRANK J. FABOZZI, Ph.D., C.F.A., C.P.A.**
Professor of Economics
Fordham University

To make investment decisions, the investor must be capable of determining the yield on an investment. A bond may provide three sources of income to an investor over the time it is held: (1) the contracted periodic interest payments, (2) interest from the reinvestment of the periodic interest payments, and (3) capital gain (or loss) resulting from the disposal of the security. Several measures of the yield on a bond are discussed in this chapter. Since a measure may not take into account all three sources of income offered by a bond, the investor should understand the drawback of each measure. In Chapter 28, a more thorough treatment of bond yield measures is presented. Special yield measures are computed for money market instruments, and they are discussed in Chapter 8.

A fundamental relationship illustrated in this chapter is that the price of a fixed income security moves in the opposite direction of the change in the yield that investors require. Consequently, as market participants require a higher (lower) yield, the price of a bond falls (rises). However, not all bonds change by the same magnitude for a given change in yield. The response of bond prices to a change in yield depends upon certain characteristics of the bond. The characteristics that influence bond price volatility are discussed in this chapter.

To appreciate the bond yield measures and price volatility properties, the investor should understand the concepts of compound interest and present value. The following two sections discuss these concepts.

COMPOUND INTEREST

One of history's wealthiest bankers, Baron Rothschild, was once asked if he could name the Seven Wonders of the World. Although he responded he could not, he did tell his questioner what he thought was the Eighth Wonder of the World. "The Eighth Wonder should be utilized by all of us to accomplish what we want," he stated. "It is compound interest."[1]

The concept of compound interest is very simple. When a principal is invested, interest is earned on the principal in the first period. In subsequent periods interest is earned on not only the original principal invested but also on the interest earned in previous periods. Thus interest is being earned on an amount that is increasing over time.

For example, suppose that $1,000 is invested today earning 8 percent interest compounded annually. The amount at the end of one year will be $1,080 ($1,000 times 1.08). The $80 represents the interest earned for one year. If the principal and interest are reinvested for another year, the amount at the end of the second year will be $1,166.40 ($1,080 times 1.08). The amount at the end of two years can be broken down as follows:

Original principal...	$1,000.00
First year's interest	80.00
Second year's interest on original principal..................	80.00
Second year's interest on interest ($80 times .08)............	6.40
	$1,166.40

Reinvestment of $1,166.40 for a third year would produce $1,259.71 ($1,166.40 times 1.08). The third-year interest of $93.31 ($1,166.40 times .08) is comprised of $80 interest on the original principal of $1,000 plus $13.31 interest on the $166.40 interest earned in the first two years.

It is the interest on interest that explains the snowballing effect of money to multiply itself under compound interest. To highlight this point, suppose the $1,000 is invested for 50 years earning 8 percent interest compounded annually. The amount at the end of 49 years would be $43,427.42. Just how this amount is determined will be

---

[1] Loraine L. Blaire, *Your Financial Guide for Living* (Englewood Cliffs, N.J.: Prentice-Hall, 1963), p. 62.

explained later. At the end of 50 years, the amount will be $46,901.61 ($43,437.42 times 1.08). The interest in the 50th year is $80 interest on the original principal plus $3,394.19 interest on the $42,427.42 interest earned in the first 49 years.

Had interest been based on simple interest, the investment would not have grown as much compared to compound interest. With simple interest, only interest on the original principal is realized. Interest is not earned on the interest earned in previous years. For example, if $1,000 is invested earning 8 percent simple interest for two years, the amount at the end of the second year will be $1,160. The amount is composed of the original principal of $1,000 plus two years of simple interest of $80 per year. Recall that if interest is compounded, the amount at the end of the second year is $1,166.40. The difference between simple interest and compound interest is only $6.40 in this example. However, as the time increases over which the principal is invested, the difference between the amount resulting from simple and compound interest is no longer trivial. For example, at the end of 50 years, simple interest would produce an amount equal to $5,000 ($1,000 plus 50 times $80), but the amount assuming compound interest would be $46,901.61!

Computing Future Value

To determine the future value of a principal invested today, the following formula is used:

$$FV = P(1 + r)^n$$

where

FV = future value
P = original principal invested
r = the nominal or simple interest rate (as a decimal)
n = number of periods

The expression $(1 + r)^n$ means multiply $(1 + r)$ by itself n times. For example, if n is 4, then the expression $(1 + r)^4$ is

$$(1 + r) \text{ times } (1 + r) \text{ times } (1 + r) \text{ times } (1 + r)$$

Illustration 1

What is the future value of $80 invested today earning 10 percent compounded annually for six years?

In terms of the formula for future value, P is $80, n is 6, and r is 10 percent. The expression $(1 + .10)^6$ is then:

$$(1.10) \times (1.10) \times (1.10) \times (1.10) \times (1.10) \times (1.10) = 1.7716$$

Hence

$$FV = \$80 \ (1.7716) = \$141.73$$

(End of Illustration 1.)

It can become quite tedious to compute the value for the expression $(1 + r)^n$. Most preprogrammed calculators have an option that computes this value. Alternatively, there are tables available that provide the value of $(1 + r)^n$. Exhibit 1 is an abridged future value table that provides the value of $(1 + r)^n$. Notice that at the intersection of the 10 percent column and 6 period row, the value is 1.7716. This is the same value computed for $(1.10)^6$ in Illustration 1.

Thus far it has been assumed that interest is compounded annually. When interest is compounded more than one time per year, the formula provided above can still be used. It is only necessary to adjust the interest rate and the number of compounding periods. The interest rate per compounding period is calculated by dividing the annual interest rate by the number of times interest is compounded per year. Multiplying the number of times interest is compounded per period by the number of years gives the number of periods that should be used. Thus the formula given above becomes:

$$FV = P \left(1 + \frac{r}{m}\right)^{Nm}$$

where

m = number of times interest is compounded each year
N = number of years

For example, suppose interest is assumed to be compounded quarterly for five years. The adjusted interest rate to be used in the formula and the table is the annual interest rate (r) divided by four (m). The number of compounding periods is five years (N) times four (m) or 20.

Illustration 2

Instead of assuming annual compounding in Illustration 1, suppose interest is compounded semiannually (i.e., twice per year). The adjusted interest rate is 5 percent (10 percent divided by 2). The number of compounding periods is 12 (2 times 6). From Exhibit 1, the future value of $1 assuming 5 percent interest compounded per period for 12 periods is 1.7959. Hence, the future value of $80 is

$$FV = \$80 \ (1.7959)$$
$$= \$143.67$$

Exhibit 1
Future Value of $1 at the End of n Periods

Period	1%	2%	3%	4%	5%	6%	7%	8%	9%	10%	11%	12%	13%	14%	15%
1	1.0100	1.0200	1.0300	1.0400	1.0500	1.0600	1.0700	1.0800	1.0900	1.1000	1.1100	1.1200	1.1300	1.1400	1.1500
2	1.0201	1.0404	1.0609	1.0816	1.1025	1.1236	1.1449	1.1664	1.1881	1.2100	1.2321	1.2544	1.2769	1.2996	1.3225
3	1.0303	1.0612	1.0927	1.1249	1.1576	1.1910	1.2250	1.2597	1.2950	1.3310	1.3676	1.4049	1.4429	1.4815	1.5209
4	1.0406	1.0824	1.1255	1.1699	1.2155	1.2625	1.3108	1.3605	1.4116	1.4641	1.5181	1.5735	1.6305	1.6890	1.7490
5	1.0510	1.1041	1.1593	1.2167	1.2763	1.3382	1.4026	1.4693	1.5386	1.6105	1.6851	1.7623	1.8424	1.9254	2.0114
6	1.0615	1.1262	1.1941	1.2653	1.3401	1.4185	1.5007	1.5869	1.6771	1.7716	1.8704	1.9738	2.0820	2.1950	2.3131
7	1.0721	1.1487	1.2299	1.3159	1.4071	1.5036	1.6058	1.7138	1.8280	1.9487	2.0762	2.2107	2.3526	2.5023	2.6600
8	1.0829	1.1717	1.2668	1.3686	1.4775	1.5938	1.7182	1.8509	1.9926	2.1436	2.3045	2.4760	2.6584	2.8526	3.0590
9	1.0937	1.1951	1.3048	1.4233	1.5513	1.6895	1.8385	1.9990	2.1719	2.3579	2.5580	2.7731	3.0040	3.2519	3.5179
10	1.1046	1.2190	1.3439	1.4802	1.6289	1.7908	1.9672	2.1589	2.3674	2.5937	2.8394	3.1058	3.3946	3.7072	4.0456
11	1.1157	1.2434	1.3842	1.5395	1.7103	1.8983	2.1049	2.3316	2.5804	2.8531	3.1518	3.4785	3.8359	4.2262	4.6524
12	1.1268	1.2682	1.4258	1.6010	1.7959	2.0122	2.2522	2.5182	2.8127	3.1384	3.4984	3.8960	4.3345	4.8179	5.3502
13	1.1381	1.2936	1.4685	1.6651	1.8856	2.1329	2.4098	2.7196	3.0658	3.4523	3.8833	4.3635	4.8980	5.4924	6.1528
14	1.1495	1.3195	1.5126	1.7317	1.9799	2.2609	2.5785	2.9372	3.3417	3.7975	4.3104	4.8871	5.5347	6.2613	7.0757
15	1.1610	1.3459	1.5580	1.8009	2.0789	2.3966	2.7590	3.1722	3.6425	4.1772	4.7846	5.4736	6.2543	7.1379	8.1371
16	1.1726	1.3728	1.6047	1.8730	2.1829	2.5404	2.9522	3.4259	3.9703	4.5950	5.3109	6.1304	7.0673	8.1372	9.3576
17	1.1843	1.4002	1.6528	1.9479	2.2920	2.6928	3.1588	3.7000	4.3276	5.0545	5.8951	6.8660	7.9861	9.2765	10.761
18	1.1961	1.4282	1.7024	2.0258	2.4066	2.8543	3.3799	3.9960	4.7171	5.5599	6.5435	7.6900	9.0243	10.575	12.375
19	1.2081	1.4568	1.7535	2.1068	2.5270	3.0256	3.6165	4.3157	5.1417	6.1159	7.2633	8.6128	10.197	12.055	14.231
20	1.2202	1.4859	1.8061	2.1911	2.6533	3.2071	3.8697	4.6610	5.6044	6.7275	8.0623	9.6463	11.523	13.743	16.366
21	1.2324	1.5157	1.8603	2.2788	2.7860	3.3996	4.1406	5.0338	6.1088	7.4002	8.9491	10.803	13.021	15.667	18.821
22	1.2447	1.5460	1.9161	2.3699	2.9253	3.6035	4.4304	5.4365	6.6586	8.1403	9.9335	12.100	14.714	17.861	21.644
23	1.2572	1.5769	1.9736	2.4647	3.0715	3.8197	4.7405	5.8715	7.2579	8.9543	11.026	13.552	16.627	20.361	24.891
24	1.2697	1.6084	2.0328	2.5633	3.2251	4.0489	5.0724	6.3412	7.9111	9.8497	12.239	15.178	18.788	23.212	28.625
25	1.2824	1.6406	2.0938	2.6658	3.3864	4.2919	5.4274	6.8485	8.6231	10.834	13.585	17.000	21.230	26.461	32.918
26	1.2953	1.6734	2.1566	2.7725	3.5557	4.5494	5.8074	7.3964	9.3992	11.918	15.080	19.040	23.990	30.166	37.856
27	1.3082	1.7069	2.2213	2.8834	3.7335	4.8223	6.2139	7.9881	10.245	13.110	16.739	21.324	27.109	34.389	43.535
28	1.3213	1.7410	2.2879	2.9987	3.9201	5.1117	6.6488	8.6271	11.167	14.421	18.580	23.883	30.633	39.204	50.065
29	1.3345	1.7758	2.3566	3.1187	4.1161	5.4184	7.1143	9.3173	12.172	15.863	20.624	26.749	34.616	44.693	57.575
30	1.3478	1.8114	2.4273	3.2434	4.3219	5.7435	7.6123	10.062	13.267	17.449	22.892	29.959	39.116	50.950	66.211

Source: Frank J. Fabozzi, *Equipment Leasing: A Comprehensive Guide for Executives* (Homewood, Ill.: Dow Jones-Irwin 1981), p. 88.

When interest was assumed to be compounded annually, the future value was $141.73. Compounding more times within a year results in more interest on interest and therefore a greater future value. (End of Illustration 2.)

Computing Future Value of an Ordinary Annuity

An annuity is a series of equal dollar payments for a specified number of periods. An annuity for which payment occurs at the end of the period is referred to as an ordinary annuity.[2] In this chapter, when we refer to an annuity we mean an ordinary annuity.

When realized compound yield is discussed later in this chapter, it will be helpful to have a means of quickly computing the future value of an ordinary annuity. Therefore the computation of the future value of an ordinary annuity will be illustrated.

Illustration 3

Suppose that today (time period 0) you expect to receive $40 every six months for the next seven years. Each payment will be made at the end of the period. That is, you will receive the first payment at the end of period 1, the second payment at the end of period 2, and so on. Exhibit 2 illustrates the timing of the 14 payments of $40. Suppose that each time a $40 payment is received it can be invested for the remainder of the 14 periods and that the interest rate earned each six months is 5 percent. What is the future value of this ordinary annuity?

For each payment of $40 the number of periods that it can be invested must be determined. Then the future value of each $40 investment must be computed. The total future value is the sum of the future value of the 14 investments of $40. As shown in Exhibit 2, the future value of this ordinary annuity is $783.93. (End of Illustration 3.)

Rather than go through the lengthy computations shown in Exhibit 2, a shortcut procedure is available. Tables are available that provide the future value of an ordinary annuity of $1 per period. Exhibit 3 is an abridged version. The value from the table should then be multiplied by the annuity payment, $40 in Illustration 3, to obtain the future value of the annuity. For example, from Exhibit 3 the future value of ·an ordinary annuity of $1 per period for 14 periods assuming a 5 percent interest rate per period is 19.598. Hence the future value of an ordinary annuity of $40 is $40 times 19.598, or $783.92.

---

[2] An annuity in which the payment occurs at the beginning of the period is called an annuity due.

Exhibit 2
Future Value of an Ordinary Annuity of $40 Per Period for 14 Periods

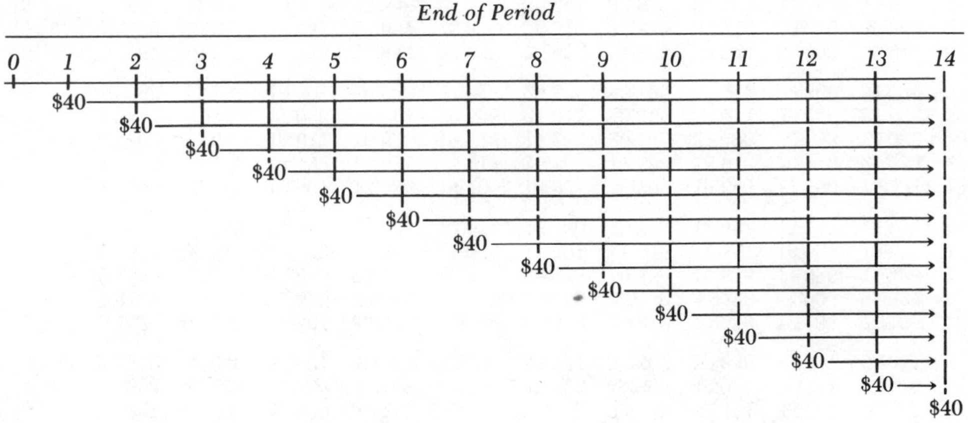

End of Period

	Future Value at the End of Period 14		
	Number of Periods Invested	FV of $1 at 5 Percent from Exhibit 1	FV of $40
	13	1.8856	$ 75.42
	12	1.7959	71.84
	11	1.7103	68.41
	10	1.6289	65.16
	9	1.5513	62.05
	8	1.4775	59.10
	7	1.4071	56.28
	6	1.3401	53.60
	5	1.2763	51.05
	4	1.2155	48.62
	3	1.1576	46.30
	2	1.1025	44.10
	1	1.0500	42.00
	0	1.0000	40.00
	Total future value		$783.93

Exhibit 3
Future Value of an Ordinary Annuity of $1 per Period for N Period

Number of Periods							Interest Rate								
	1%	2%	3%	4%	5%	6%	7%	8%	9%	10%	11%	12%	13%	14%	15%
1	1.0000	1.0000	1.0000	1.0000	1.0000	1.0000	1.0000	1.0000	1.0000	1.0000	1.0000	1.0000	1.0000	1.0000	1.0000
2	2.0100	2.0200	2.0300	2.0400	2.0500	2.0600	2.0700	2.0800	2.0900	2.1000	2.1100	2.1200	2.1300	2.1400	2.1500
3	3.0301	3.0604	3.0909	3.1216	3.1525	3.1836	3.2149	3.2464	3.2781	3.3100	3.3421	3.3744	3.4069	3.4396	3.4725
4	4.0604	4.1216	4.1836	4.2465	4.3101	4.3746	4.4399	4.5061	4.5731	4.6410	4.7097	4.7793	4.8498	4.9211	4.9934
5	5.1010	5.2040	5.3091	5.4163	5.5256	5.6371	5.7507	5.8666	5.9847	6.1051	6.2278	6.3528	6.4803	6.6101	6.7424
6	6.1520	6.3081	6.4684	6.6330	6.8019	6.9753	7.1533	7.3359	7.5233	7.7156	7.9129	8.1152	8.3227	8.5355	8.7537
7	7.2135	7.4343	7.6625	7.8983	8.1420	8.3938	8.6540	8.9228	9.2004	9.4872	9.7833	10.089	10.405	10.730	11.066
8	8.2857	8.5830	8.8923	9.2142	9.5491	9.8975	10.259	10.636	11.028	11.435	11.859	12.299	12.757	13.232	13.726
9	9.3685	9.7546	10.159	10.582	11.026	11.491	11.978	12.487	13.021	13.579	14.164	14.775	15.416	16.085	16.785
10	10.462	10.949	11.463	12.006	12.577	13.180	13.816	14.486	15.192	15.937	16.722	17.548	18.420	19.337	20.303
11	11.566	12.168	12.807	13.486	14.206	14.971	15.783	16.645	17.560	18.531	19.561	20.654	21.814	23.044	24.349
12	12.682	13.412	14.192	15.025	15.917	16.869	17.888	18.977	20.140	21.384	22.713	24.133	25.650	27.270	29.001
13	13.809	14.680	15.617	16.626	17.713	18.882	20.140	21.495	22.953	24.522	26.212	28.029	29.985	32.088	34.351
14	14.947	15.973	17.086	18.291	19.598	21.015	22.550	24.214	26.019	27.975	30.095	32.392	34.883	37.581	40.504
15	16.096	17.293	18.598	20.023	21.578	23.276	25.129	27.152	29.360	31.772	34.405	37.279	40.418	43.842	47.580
16	17.257	18.639	20.156	21.824	23.657	25.672	27.888	30.324	33.003	35.949	39.190	42.753	46.672	50.980	55.717
17	18.430	20.012	21.761	23.697	25.840	28.212	30.840	33.750	36.973	40.544	44.501	48.883	53.739	59.117	65.075
18	19.614	21.412	23.414	25.645	28.132	30.905	33.999	37.450	41.301	45.599	50.396	55.749	61.725	68.394	75.836
19	20.810	22.840	25.116	27.671	30.539	33.760	37.379	41.446	46.018	51.159	56.940	63.439	70.749	78.969	88.211
20	22.019	24.297	26.870	29.778	33.066	36.785	40.995	45.762	51.160	57.275	64.203	72.052	80.947	91.024	102.44
21	23.239	25.783	28.676	31.969	35.719	39.992	44.865	50.422	56.764	64.002	72.265	81.698	92.470	104.76	118.81
22	24.471	27.299	30.536	34.248	38.505	43.392	49.005	55.456	62.873	71.402	81.214	92.502	105.49	120.43	137.63
23	25.716	28.845	32.452	36.617	41.430	46.995	53.436	60.893	69.531	79.543	91.148	104.60	120.20	138.29	159.27
24	26.973	30.421	34.426	39.082	44.502	50.815	58.176	66.764	76.789	88.497	102.17	118.15	136.83	158.65	184.16
25	28.243	32.030	36.459	41.645	47.727	54.864	63.249	73.105	84.700	98.347	114.41	133.33	155.62	181.87	212.79
26	29.525	33.670	38.553	44.311	51.113	59.156	68.676	79.954	93.323	109.18	128.00	150.33	176.85	208.33	245.71
27	30.820	35.344	40.709	47.084	54.669	63.705	74.483	87.350	102.72	121.09	143.08	169.37	200.84	238.49	283.56
28	32.129	37.051	42.930	49.967	58.402	68.528	80.697	95.338	112.96	134.20	159.82	190.69	227.95	272.88	327.10
29	33.450	38.792	45.218	52.966	62.322	73.639	87.346	103.96	124.13	148.63	178.40	214.58	258.58	312.09	377.16
30	34.784	40.568	47.575	56.084	66.438	79.058	94.460	113.28	136.30	164.49	199.02	241.33	293.20	356.78	434.74

If a table is not available or if a table does not include the interest rate needed, the following formula can be used to obtain the future value of an ordinary annuity of $1 per period:

$$\text{FV of an ordinary annuity of } \$1 = \frac{(1 + r)^n - 1}{r}$$

where

n = number of payments
r = simple interest rate per period

For example, if r is 5 percent and n is 14, the future value of an ordinary annuity of $1 per period is

$$\frac{(1 + .05)^{14} - 1}{.05} = 19.5986$$

PRESENT VALUE

The notion that money has time value is one of the basic concepts in investment management. Money has time value because of the opportunity to invest money received at some earlier date at some interest rate. As a result, money to be received in the future is less valuable than money that could be received at an earlier date.

Computing Present Value

The process of determining the amount that must be set aside today in order to have a specified future value is called discounting. The amount that must be set aside today in order to have a specified future value is called the present or discounted value. The formula for the present value of $1 in the future is:

$$PV = \frac{FV}{(1 + r)^n}$$

where

PV = present value
FV = future value
 r = interest rate or discount rate
 n = number of periods

Note that the formula for the present value is derived by solving the formula for the future value of $1 for the original principal, P, and demonstrates that the present value procedure is the reverse of the future value calculations demonstrated above.

Illustration 4

Suppose an investor expects to receive $1,000 seven years from now. Assuming the investor can earn 12 percent compounded annually on any sum invested today, what is the present value of this future sum?

Using the formula for present value, we have FV = $1,000, r = 12 percent, and n = 7. The expression $(1 + .12)^7$, found in Exhibit 1, is 2.2107. Hence the present value is

$$PV = \frac{\$1,000}{2.2107}$$

$$= \$452.35$$

By placing $452.35 today into an investment that earns 12 percent compounded annually, the investor will have $1,000 at the end of seven years. (End of Illustration 4.)

Present value tables are also available. Exhibit 4 shows the present value of $1, which is found by dividing one by $(1 + r)^n$, as mentioned above. The columns show the interest or discount rate. The rows show the number of discounting periods. The present value of $1 obtained from Exhibit 4 is then *multiplied* by the future value to determine the present value. For example, the present value of $1,000 seven years from now assuming 12 percent interest compounded annually is

PV = $1,000 (PV of $1 from Exhibit 4)
 = $1,000 (.4523)
 = $452.30

There are two facts you should note about present value. Look again at Exhibit 4. Select any interest rate and look down the column. Notice that the present value decreases. That is, the greater the number of periods over which interest could be earned, the less must be set aside today for a given dollar amount to be received in the future. Next select any period and look across the row. As you look across, the interest rate increases and the present value decreases. The reason is the higher the interest rate that can be earned on any amount invested today, the less must be set aside to obtain a specified future value.

So far, the present value of a single future sum has been illustrated. The principle is the same if there is a series of future sums at different times. Each future sum must be discounted individually to obtain its present value. Then the present values are added to obtain the present value for the series of future sums.

Computing Present Value of an Ordinary Annuity

In the case of an annuity, it is a simple task to compute the present value of the series. Exhibit 5 provides the present value of an ordinary

Exhibit 4
Present Value of $1

	Discount rate																		
Period	1%	2%	3%	4%	5%	6%	7%	8%	9%	10%	11%	12%	13%	14%	15%	16%	18%	20%
1	.9901	.9804	.9709	.9615	.9524	.9434	.9346	.9259	.9174	.9091	.9009	.8929	.8850	.8772	.8696	.8621	.8475	.8333
2	.9803	.9612	.9426	.9246	.9070	.8900	.8734	.8573	.8417	.8264	.8116	.7972	.7831	.7695	.7561	.7432	.7182	.6944
3	.9706	.9423	.9151	.8890	.8638	.8396	.8163	.7938	.7722	.7513	.7312	.7118	.6931	.6750	.6575	.6407	.6086	.5787
4	.9610	.9238	.8885	.8548	.8227	.7921	.7629	.7350	.7084	.6830	.6587	.6355	.6133	.5921	.5718	.5523	.5158	.4823
5	.9515	.9057	.8626	.8219	.7835	.7473	.7130	.6806	.6499	.6209	.5935	.5674	.5428	.5194	.4972	.4761	.4371	.4019
6	.9420	.8880	.8375	.7903	.7462	.7050	.6663	.6302	.5963	.5645	.5346	.5066	.4803	.4556	.4323	.4104	.3704	.3349
7	.9327	.8706	.8131	.7599	.7107	.6651	.6227	.5835	.5470	.5132	.4817	.4523	.4251	.3996	.3759	.3538	.3139	.2791
8	.9235	.8535	.7894	.7307	.6768	.6274	.5820	.5403	.5019	.4665	.4339	.4039	.3762	.3506	.3269	.3050	.2660	.2326
9	.9143	.8368	.7664	.7026	.6446	.5919	.5439	.5002	.4604	.4241	.3909	.3606	.3329	.3075	.2843	.2630	.2255	.1938
10	.9053	.8203	.7441	.6756	.6139	.5584	.5083	.4632	.4224	.3855	.3522	.3220	.2946	.2697	.2472	.2267	.1911	.1615
11	.8963	.8043	.7224	.6496	.5847	.5268	.4751	.4289	.3875	.3505	.3173	.2875	.2607	.2366	.2149	.1954	.1619	.1346
12	.8874	.7885	.7014	.6246	.5568	.4970	.4440	.3971	.3555	.3186	.2858	.2567	.2307	.2076	.1869	.1685	.1372	.1122
13	.8787	.7730	.6810	.6006	.5303	.4688	.4150	.3677	.3262	.2897	.2575	.2292	.2042	.1821	.1625	.1452	.1163	.0935
14	.8700	.7579	.6611	.5775	.5051	.4423	.3878	.3405	.2992	.2633	.2320	.2046	.1807	.1597	.1413	.1252	.0985	.0779
15	.8613	.7430	.6419	.5553	.4810	.4173	.3624	.3152	.2745	.2394	.2090	.1827	.1599	.1401	.1229	.1079	.0835	.0649
16	.8528	.7284	.6232	.5339	.4581	.3936	.3387	.2919	.2519	.2176	.1883	.1631	.1415	.1229	.1069	.0930	.0708	.0541
17	.8444	.7142	.6050	.5134	.4363	.3714	.3166	.2703	.2311	.1978	.1696	.1456	.1252	.1078	.0929	.0802	.0600	.0451
18	.8360	.7002	.5874	.4936	.4155	.3503	.2959	.2502	.2120	.1799	.1528	.1300	.1108	.0946	.0808	.0691	.0508	.0376
19	.8277	.6864	.5703	.4746	.3957	.3305	.2765	.2317	.1945	.1635	.1377	.1161	.0981	.0829	.0703	.0596	.0431	.0313
20	.8195	.6730	.5537	.4564	.3769	.3118	.2584	.2145	.1784	.1486	.1240	.1037	.0868	.0728	.0611	.0514	.0365	.0261
21	.8114	.6598	.5375	.4388	.3589	.2942	.2415	.1987	.1637	.1351	.1117	.0926	.0768	.0638	.0531	.0443	.0309	.0217
22	.8034	.6468	.5219	.4220	.3418	.2775	.2257	.1839	.1502	.1228	.1007	.0826	.0680	.0560	.0462	.0382	.0262	.0181
23	.7954	.6342	.5067	.4057	.3256	.2618	.2109	.1703	.1378	.1117	.0907	.0738	.0601	.0491	.0402	.0329	.0222	.0151
24	.7876	.6217	.4919	.3901	.3101	.2470	.1971	.1577	.1264	.1015	.0817	.0659	.0532	.0431	.0349	.0284	.0188	.0126
25	.7798	.6095	.4776	.3751	.2953	.2330	.1842	.1460	.1160	.0923	.0736	.0588	.0471	.0378	.0304	.0245	.0160	.0105
26	.7720	.5976	.4637	.3607	.2812	.2198	.1722	.1352	.1064	.0839	.0663	.0525	.0417	.0331	.0264	.0211	.0135	.0087
27	.7644	.5859	.4502	.3468	.2678	.2074	.1609	.1252	.0976	.0763	.0597	.0469	.0369	.0291	.0230	.0182	.0115	.0073
28	.7568	.5744	.4371	.3335	.2551	.1956	.1504	.1159	.0895	.0693	.0538	.0419	.0326	.0255	.0200	.0157	.0097	.0061
29	.7493	.5631	.4243	.3207	.2429	.1846	.1406	.1073	.0822	.0630	.0485	.0374	.0289	.0224	.0174	.0135	.0082	.0051
30	.7419	.5521	.4120	.3083	.2314	.1741	.1314	.0994	.0754	.0573	.0437	.0334	.0256	.0196	.0151	.0116	.0070	.0042

Source: Frank J. Fabozzi, *Equipment Leasing: A Comprehensive Guide for Executives* (Homewood, Ill.: Dow Jones-Irwin 1981), p. 91.

Exhibit 5
Present Value of an Ordinary Annuity of $1 per Period for n Periods

Discount rate

Number of Periods	1%	2%	3%	4%	5%	6%	7%	8%	9%	10%	11%	12%	13%	14%	15%
1	0.9901	0.9804	0.9709	0.9615	0.9524	0.9434	0.9346	0.9259	0.9174	0.9091	0.9009	0.8929	0.8850	0.8772	0.8696
2	1.9704	1.9416	1.9135	1.8861	1.8594	1.8334	1.8080	1.7833	1.7591	1.7355	1.7125	1.6901	1.6681	1.6467	1.6257
3	2.9410	2.8839	2.8286	2.7751	2.7232	2.6730	2.6243	2.5771	2.5313	2.4869	2.4437	2.4018	2.3612	2.3216	2.2832
4	3.9020	3.8077	3.7171	3.6299	3.5460	3.4651	3.3872	3.3121	3.2397	3.1699	3.1024	3.0373	2.9745	2.9137	2.8550
5	4.8534	4.7135	4.5797	4.4518	4.3295	4.2124	4.1002	3.9927	3.8897	3.7908	3.6959	3.6048	3.5172	3.4331	3.3522
6	5.7955	5.6014	5.4172	5.2421	5.0757	4.9173	4.7665	4.6229	4.4859	4.3553	4.2305	4.1114	3.9976	3.8887	3.7845
7	6.7282	6.4720	6.2303	6.0021	5.7864	5.5824	5.3893	5.2064	5.0330	4.8684	4.7122	4.5638	4.4226	4.2883	4.1604
8	7.6517	7.3255	7.0197	6.7327	6.4632	6.2098	5.9713	5.7466	5.5348	5.3349	5.1461	4.9676	4.7988	4.6389	4.4873
9	8.5660	8.1622	7.7861	7.4353	7.1078	6.8017	6.5152	6.2469	5.9952	5.7590	5.5371	5.3282	5.1317	4.9464	4.7716
10	9.4713	8.9826	8.5302	8.1109	7.7217	7.3601	7.0236	6.7101	6.4177	6.1446	5.8892	5.6502	5.4263	5.2161	5.0188
11	10.3676	9.7868	9.2526	8.7605	8.3064	7.8869	7.4987	7.1390	6.8052	6.4951	6.2065	5.9377	5.6870	5.4527	5.2337
12	11.2551	10.5753	9.9540	9.3851	8.8633	8.3838	7.9427	7.5361	7.1607	6.8137	6.4924	6.1944	5.9177	5.6603	5.4206
13	12.1337	11.3484	10.6350	9.9856	9.3936	8.8527	8.3577	7.9038	7.4869	7.1034	6.7499	6.4235	6.1218	5.8424	5.5831
14	13.0037	12.1062	11.2961	10.5631	9.8986	9.2950	8.7455	8.2442	7.7862	7.3667	6.9819	6.6282	6.3025	6.0021	5.7245
15	13.8651	12.8493	11.9379	11.1184	10.3797	9.7122	9.1079	8.5595	8.0607	7.6061	7.1909	6.8109	6.4624	6.1422	5.8474
16	14.7179	13.5777	12.5611	11.6523	10.8378	10.1059	9.4466	8.8514	8.3126	7.8237	7.3792	6.9740	6.6039	6.2651	5.9542
17	15.5623	14.2919	13.1661	12.1657	11.2741	10.4773	9.7632	9.1216	8.5436	8.0216	7.5488	7.1196	6.7291	6.3729	6.0472
18	16.3983	14.9920	13.7535	12.6593	11.6896	10.8276	10.0591	9.3719	8.7556	8.2014	7.7016	7.2497	6.8399	6.4674	6.1280
19	17.2260	15.6785	14.3238	13.1339	12.0853	11.1581	10.3356	9.6036	8.9501	8.3649	7.8393	7.3658	6.9380	6.5504	6.1982
20	18.0456	16.3514	14.8775	13.5903	12.4622	11.4699	10.5940	9.8181	9.1285	8.5136	7.9633	7.4694	7.0248	6.6231	6.2593
21	18.8570	17.0112	15.4150	14.0292	12.8212	11.7641	10.8355	10.0168	9.2922	8.6487	8.0751	7.5620	7.1016	6.6870	6.3125
22	19.6604	17.6580	15.9369	14.4511	13.1630	12.0416	11.0612	10.2007	9.4424	8.7715	8.1757	7.6446	7.1695	6.7429	6.3587
23	20.4558	18.2922	16.4436	14.8568	13.4886	12.3034	11.2722	10.3711	9.5802	8.8832	8.2664	7.7184	7.2297	6.7921	6.3988
24	21.2434	18.9139	16.9355	15.2470	13.7986	12.5504	11.4693	10.5288	9.7066	8.9847	8.3481	7.7843	7.2829	6.8351	6.4338
25	22.0232	19.5235	17.4131	15.6221	14.0939	12.7834	11.6536	10.6748	9.8226	9.0770	8.4218	7.8431	7.3300	6.8729	6.4642
26	22.7952	20.1210	17.8768	15.9828	14.3752	13.0032	11.8258	10.8100	9.9290	9.1609	8.4881	7.8957	7.3717	6.9061	6.4906
27	23.5596	20.7069	18.3270	16.3296	14.6430	13.2105	11.9867	10.9352	10.0266	9.2372	8.5478	7.9426	7.4086	6.9352	6.5135
28	24.3164	21.2813	18.7641	16.6631	14.8981	13.4062	12.1371	11.0511	10.1161	9.3066	8.6016	7.9844	7.4412	6.9607	6.5335
29	25.0658	21.8444	19.1885	16.9837	15.1411	13.5907	12.2777	11.1584	10.1983	9.3696	8.6501	8.0218	7.4701	6.9830	6.5509
30	25.8077	22.3965	19.6004	17.2920	15.3725	13.7648	12.4090	11.2578	10.2737	9.4269	8.6938	8.0552	7.4957	7.0027	6.5660

Source: Frank J. Fabozzi, *Equipment Leasing: A Comprehensive Guide for Executives* (Homewood, Ill.: Dow Jones-Irwin 1981), p. 94.

annuity of $1 for n periods for selected interest rates. As noted earlier in this chapter, the payments occur at the end of each period in the case of an ordinary annuity.[3] The present value of an ordinary annuity is computed by multiplying the value from Exhibit 5 by the annuity payment.

Illustration 5

Suppose an investor makes an investment that is expected to engender $80 at the end of each year for the next seven years and an additional $1,000 at the end of the seventh year. What is the present value of this investment if the investor seeks a 12 percent return?

The present value of this investment can be computed in two steps. First, the present value of $80 per year is computed using the present value ordinary annuity table, Exhibit 5. The present value is $365.10, as shown below:

PV of $80 per year for seven years

  = $80 (PV of $1 per year at 12 percent from Exhibit 5)

  = $80 (4.5638)

  = $365.10

Next, the present value of $1,000 seven years from now is determined using a 12 percent discount rate. The present value is $452.30 as shown earlier. Therefore the present value of the investment is $817.40 ($365.10 plus $452.30). The investor who pays more than $817.40, will expect to realize a return on the investment that is less than 12 percent; however, a rate of return on the investment greater than 12 percent will be expected if the investor can acquire the investment at cost of less than $817.40. (End of Illustration 5.)

Illustration 6

Suppose that the investment in the previous illustration will still produce $80 each year; however, the interest will be received in two equal installments every six months. The investor seeks a 6 percent semiannual rate of return from this investment. The present value is then $814.10, as shown below:

PV of $40 for 14 six-month periods

  = $40 (PV of $1 each six months at 6 percent from Exhibit 5)

  = $40 (9.2950)

  = $371.80

---

[3] The present value of an annuity due of $1 per period can be obtained from Exhibit 5 as follows: (1) find the present value for n minus one payments in Exhibit 5, and (2) add $1 to the value found in (1). For example, the present value of an annuity due of $1 for five years at 6 percent interest is the present value of an ordinary annuity of $1 for four years from Exhibit 5 ($3.5460) plus $1, or $4.5460.

PV of \$1,000 at the end of 14 six-month periods

$$= \$1,000 \text{ (PV of \$1 at 6 percent from Exhibit 4)}$$
$$= \$1,000 \text{ (.4423)}$$
$$= \$442.30$$

Present value of investment $= \$371.80 + \$442.30$
$$= \$814.10$$

(End of Illustration 6.)

There is also a general formula that can be used to compute the present value of an ordinary annuity of \$1. The formula is[4]

$$\text{Present value of an ordinary annuity of \$1} = \frac{1 - \dfrac{1}{(1 + r)^n}}{r}$$

To illustrate the use of this formula, let us compute the present value of an ordinary annuity of \$1 for seven years assuming 12 percent interest compounded annually ($r = .12$ and $n = 7$).

$$\frac{1 - \dfrac{1}{(1.12)^7}}{.12} = \frac{1 - .4523492}{.12} = 4.5638$$

YIELD MEASURES

As stated at the outset of this chapter, there are three potential sources of income to an investor who holds a bond: (1) the contracted interest payments, (2) income from the reinvestment of the periodic interest payments, and (3) capital gain (or loss) from disposal of the security. The four yield measures discussed below—current yield, yield-to-maturity, yield-to-call, and realized compound yield—take one or more of these sources into consideration when determining the investor's return on investment.

The following hypothetical bond will be used to illustrate the yield measures:

$$\text{Years to maturity} = 7$$
$$\text{Coupon rate} = 8 \text{ percent}$$
$$\text{Market price} = \$814.10$$
$$\text{Redemption value at maturity} = \$1,000$$
$$\text{Frequency of interest payments} = \text{semiannual}$$

Since this bond is selling below its redemption value at maturity (or par value), the bond is said to be selling at a discount.

---

[4] For an annuity due, the corresponding formula is

$$\left[\frac{1 - \dfrac{1}{(1 + r)^{n-1}}}{r} \right] + 1$$

Current Yield

The current yield relates the annual dollar coupon interest to the market price. It can be expressed mathematically as follows:

$$\text{Current yield} = \frac{\text{Annual dollar coupon interest}}{\text{Market price}}$$

For our hypothetical bond, the current yield is

$$\frac{\$80}{\$814.10} = 0.098 = 9.8 \text{ percent}$$

The current yield exceeds the coupon rate when a bond is selling at a discount. The opposite is true when a bond is selling at a premium. For example, if the market price of our hypothetical bond is $1,089 rather than $814.10, the current yield is 7.3 percent ($80 divided by $1,089).

The drawback of the current yield is that it does not take into consideration the two other sources of income—reinvestment of interest and capital gain (or loss). To illustrate the latter source, suppose the bond is held to maturity. At that time, the issuer will redeem the bond for $1,000. The investor who purchased the bond for $814.10 will realize a capital gain of $185.90 ($1,000 minus $814.10). Had the bond been purchased for $1,089, there would be a capital loss of $89.

Yield-to-Maturity

Unlike the current yield, the yield-to-maturity does take into account any capital gain or loss. The yield-to-maturity does consider the reinvestment of the contracted periodic payments; *however, it implicitly assumes that these payments are reinvested at the yield-to-maturity.*

The yield-to-maturity is the discount rate that equates the present value of the promised cash flow (coupon payments plus redemption value at maturity) to the market price.[5] Thus the yield-to-maturity takes the time value of money into consideration. When a yield-to-

---

[5] The general formula for the yield-to-maturity for a bond paying interest semiannually is:

$$P = \sum_{t=1}^{2n} \frac{C/2}{\left(1 + \frac{r}{2}\right)^t} + \frac{R}{\left(1 + \frac{r}{2}\right)^{2n}}$$

where

P = price of bond
n = number of years to maturity
C = annual dollar coupon interest
r = yield-to-maturity
R = redemption value of bond at maturity

Exhibit 6
Worksheet for the Computation of the Yield-to-Maturity of an 8 Percent Coupon Bond—Maturing in Exactly 7 Years, and Priced at $814.10

Discount Rate (percent)	PV of an Annuity of $1 for 14 Periods*	PV of an Annuity of $40 for 14 Periods†	PV of $1 14 Periods Hence‡	PV of $1,000 14 Periods Hence§	Total PV of Cash Flow
4%	$10.5631	$422.52	$.5775	$577.50	$1,000.02
5	9.8986	395.94	.5051	505.10	901.04
6	9.2950	371.80	.4423	442.30	814.10
7	8.7455	349.82	.3878	387.80	737.62
8	8.2442	329.77	.3405	340.50	669.82

* From Exhibit 5.
† $40 times PV of an annuity of $1 for 14 periods.
‡ From Exhibit 4.
§ $1,000 times PV of $1 14 periods hence.

maturity is quoted, the market price used to make the computation is the offer price and does not include accrued interest and commissions.

Let us go through the computation of the yield-to-maturity once. Later it will be explained how this yield can be determined without the necessary trial-and-error computations given below. The worksheet for determining the yield-to-maturity for our hypothetical bond is shown as Exhibit 6. Now remember what our objective is—to determine the discount rate that equates the present value of the 14 payments of $40 every six months (beginning six months from now) plus the present value of the redemption value of $1,000 at maturity to the market price of the bond ($814.10).

An arbitrary starting point of 5 percent was selected. The present value of the promised cash flow is $901.04. This discount rate produces a present value that is greater than the bond's market price of $814.10. Since a higher discount rate lowers the present value, a higher discount rate must be tried. Skipping 6 percent for the moment, we see that a 7 percent discount rate produces a present value for the promised cash flow that is less than the market price. Consequently, the discount rate we are searching for must be less than 7 percent, but greater than 5 percent. When a 6 percent rate is used, the present value of the promised cash flow is equal to the market price. But 6 percent is *not* the yield-to-maturity because the time period in the discounting process is six months. To annualize the yield, the *convention* is to double the discount rate. The yield-to-maturity of our hypothetical bond is therefore 12 percent.[6]

---

[6] Technically, the yield should be annualized using the following formula:

$$(1 + \text{Discount rate})^2 - 1$$

In our example, we would find the annualized yield to be

$$(1.06)^2 - 1 = 1.1236 - 1 = .1236, \text{ or } 12.36 \text{ percent}$$

The discrepancy between the yield-to-maturity as conventionally computed (i.e., doubling of the semiannual discount rate) and the correct procedure for annualizing explains why bonds carrying a coupon rate equal to the prevailing market interest rate may be selling slightly below par.

This convention also presents problems when comparing bonds that do not have the same number of coupon payments per year. This can be corrected by adjusting the conventional yield-to-maturity as follows:

$$\text{Adjusted yield-to-maturity} = \left(1 + \frac{\text{Conventional yield-to-maturity}}{m}\right)^m - 1$$

where

m is the number coupon interest payments per annum

For example, if the conventional yield-to-maturity for three hypothetical bonds that pay interest annually, semiannually, and monthly is 12 percent, the adjusted yield-to-maturity would be as follows:

Fortunately, it is unnecessary to go through time-consuming computation to determine the yield-to-maturity because tables are available. The tables are part of a book usually referred to as a yield book, basis book, or bond value tables. Sample pages from a yield book are shown in Exhibit 7.

The yield book is organized as follows. Each page corresponds to a coupon rate. A yield book may increment the coupon rate by one eighth or one fourth of 1 percent. Exhibits 7(a), 7(b), and 7(c) are three sample pages from a yield book for an 8 percent coupon rate. The top row of each page indicates the time remaining to maturity. The time increments can be given in terms of months, quarters, six months, or years. In the yield book from which the pages were abstracted, monthly periods are used up to 5 years, quarterly to 10 years, and semiannually to 40 years. (The bold number on the pages in Exhibit 7 refers to the number of years, and the number after the hyphen refers to the number of months.) In the first column, the yield-to-maturity ("yield") is given.

The values appearing within the table are the bond values expressed as a percentage of par value. For example, at the intersection of 7–0 and 10.00 is 90.10. This value is interpreted as follows: A bond with a coupon rate of 8 percent, seven years remaining to maturity, and priced to yield 10 percent will sell for 90.10 percent of its par value. For a bond with a par value of $1,000, this means that the bond will sell for $901.00. Notice the agreement of this value with the present value found in Exhibit 6. When the 8 percent coupon bond with seven years remaining to maturity is discounted at 5 percent, which corresponds to a 10 percent yield-to-maturity, the present value of the bond is found to be $901.02.

Let us return to our original task of using the yield book to find the yield-to-maturity given the coupon rate, remaining time to maturity, and market price of the bond. First, locate the page in the yield book that corresponds to the coupon rate and time remaining to maturity for the bond whose yield is sought. Second, look down the column corresponding to the time remaining to maturity until the market price of

---

If annual, m = 1

$$\text{Adjusted yield-to-maturity} = \left(1 + \frac{.12}{1}\right)^1 - 1 = .12$$

If semiannual, m = 2

$$\text{Adjusted yield-to-maturity} = \left(1 + \frac{.12}{2}\right)^2 - 1 = .1236$$

If monthly, m = 12

$$\text{Adjusted yield-to-maturity} = \left(1 + \frac{.12}{12}\right)^{12} - 1 = .1268$$

Exhibit 7
Sample Pages from a Yield Book

8% — YEARS and MONTHS

Yield	3-5	3-6	3-7	3-8	3-9	3-10	3-11	4-0
4.00	112.65	112.94	113.23	113.51	113.79	114.08	114.36	114.65
4.20	111.97	112.25	112.51	112.78	113.05	113.32	113.59	113.86
4.40	111.30	111.56	111.81	112.06	112.31	112.56	112.82	113.07
4.60	110.63	110.88	111.11	111.34	111.58	111.81	112.05	112.29
4.80	109.97	110.20	110.41	110.63	110.85	111.07	111.30	111.52
5.00	109.31	109.52	109.72	109.93	110.13	110.34	110.55	110.76
5.20	108.66	108.86	109.04	109.23	109.42	109.61	109.80	110.00
5.40	108.01	108.19	108.36	108.53	108.71	108.88	109.06	109.24
5.60	107.36	107.53	107.69	107.84	108.00	108.17	108.33	108.50
5.80	106.72	106.88	107.02	107.16	107.31	107.45	107.60	107.75
6.00	106.09	106.23	106.36	106.48	106.61	106.75	106.88	107.02
6.10	105.77	105.91	106.03	106.15	106.27	106.39	106.52	106.65
6.20	105.46	105.59	105.70	105.81	105.93	106.05	106.17	106.29
6.30	105.14	105.27	105.37	105.48	105.58	105.70	105.81	105.93
6.40	104.83	104.95	105.04	105.14	105.24	105.35	105.46	105.57
6.50	104.52	104.63	104.72	104.81	104.91	105.00	105.11	105.21
6.60	104.21	104.31	104.39	104.48	104.57	104.66	104.75	104.85
6.70	103.90	104.00	104.07	104.15	104.23	104.32	104.40	104.50
6.80	103.60	103.68	103.75	103.82	103.90	103.98	104.06	104.14
6.90	103.29	103.37	103.43	103.50	103.56	103.64	103.71	103.79
7.00	102.98	103.06	103.11	103.17	103.23	103.30	103.37	103.44
7.10	102.68	102.75	102.79	102.85	102.90	102.96	103.02	103.09
7.20	102.38	102.44	102.48	102.52	102.57	102.62	102.68	102.74
7.30	102.07	102.13	102.16	102.20	102.24	102.29	102.34	102.39
7.40	101.77	101.82	101.85	101.88	101.92	101.96	102.00	102.05
7.50	101.47	101.51	101.54	101.56	101.59	101.62	101.66	101.70
7.60	101.17	101.21	101.22	101.24	101.27	101.29	101.32	101.36
7.70	100.88	100.91	100.91	100.93	100.94	100.96	100.99	101.02
7.80	100.58	100.60	100.60	100.61	100.62	100.63	100.65	100.68
7.90	100.28	100.30	100.30	100.30	100.30	100.31	100.32	100.34
8.00	99.99	100.00	99.99	99.98	99.98	99.98	99.99	100.00
8.10	99.70	99.70	99.68	99.67	99.66	99.66	99.66	99.66
8.20	99.40	99.40	99.38	99.36	99.35	99.34	99.33	99.33
8.30	99.11	99.10	99.07	99.05	99.03	99.01	99.00	99.00
8.40	98.82	98.81	98.77	98.74	98.72	98.69	98.68	98.66
8.50	98.53	98.51	98.47	98.43	98.40	98.37	98.35	98.33
8.60	98.24	98.22	98.17	98.13	98.09	98.06	98.03	98.00
8.70	97.96	97.93	97.87	97.82	97.78	97.74	97.71	97.68
8.80	97.67	97.63	97.57	97.52	97.47	97.42	97.39	97.35
8.90	97.39	97.34	97.28	97.22	97.16	97.11	97.07	97.03
9.00	97.10	97.05	96.98	96.92	96.85	96.80	96.75	96.70
9.10	96.82	96.76	96.69	96.61	96.55	96.49	96.43	96.38
9.20	96.54	96.48	96.39	96.32	96.24	96.18	96.11	96.06
9.30	96.26	96.19	96.10	96.02	95.94	95.87	95.80	95.74
9.40	95.98	95.91	95.81	95.72	95.64	95.56	95.49	95.42
9.50	95.70	95.62	95.52	95.42	95.34	95.25	95.17	95.10
9.60	95.42	95.34	95.23	95.13	95.04	94.95	94.86	94.79
9.70	95.14	95.05	94.94	94.84	94.74	94.64	94.55	94.47
9.80	94.87	94.77	94.66	94.54	94.44	94.34	94.25	94.16
9.90	94.59	94.49	94.37	94.25	94.14	94.04	93.94	93.85
10.00	94.32	94.21	94.08	93.96	93.85	93.74	93.63	93.54
10.20	93.77	93.66	93.52	93.39	93.26	93.14	93.03	92.92
10.40	93.23	93.11	92.96	92.81	92.68	92.55	92.42	92.31
10.60	92.69	92.56	92.40	92.24	92.10	91.96	91.82	91.70
10.80	92.16	92.02	91.84	91.68	91.52	91.37	91.23	91.10
11.00	91.63	91.48	91.29	91.12	90.95	90.79	90.64	90.50
11.20	91.10	90.94	90.75	90.56	90.39	90.22	90.06	89.91
11.40	90.58	90.41	90.21	90.01	89.83	89.65	89.48	89.32
11.60	90.06	89.88	89.67	89.47	89.27	89.08	88.90	88.73
11.80	89.55	89.36	89.13	88.92	88.72	88.52	88.33	88.15
12.00	89.04	88.84	88.60	88.38	88.17	87.96	87.77	87.58

(a)

8% — YEARS and MONTHS

Yield	6-3	6-6	6-9	7-0	7-3	7-6	7-9	8-0
4.00	121.92	122.70	123.45	124.21	124.95	125.70	126.42	127.16
4.20	120.69	121.42	122.12	122.84	123.53	124.23	124.91	125.59
4.40	119.47	120.16	120.82	121.49	122.13	122.79	123.41	124.06
4.60	118.28	118.92	119.53	120.15	120.75	121.36	121.94	122.54
4.80	117.09	117.69	118.25	118.84	119.39	119.96	120.50	121.05
5.00	115.92	116.47	117.00	117.54	118.05	118.57	119.07	119.58
5.20	114.77	115.28	115.76	116.25	116.72	117.21	117.66	118.14
5.40	113.62	114.09	114.53	114.99	115.42	115.86	116.28	116.71
5.60	112.50	112.93	113.32	113.74	114.13	114.53	114.91	115.31
5.80	111.38	111.77	112.13	112.51	112.86	113.23	113.56	113.92
6.00	110.28	110.63	110.95	111.30	111.60	111.94	112.24	112.56
6.10	109.74	110.07	110.37	110.69	110.98	111.30	111.58	111.89
6.20	109.19	109.51	109.79	110.10	110.37	110.67	110.93	111.22
6.30	108.66	108.95	109.22	109.50	109.76	110.04	110.28	110.56
6.40	108.12	108.40	108.64	108.91	109.15	109.41	109.64	109.90
6.50	107.59	107.85	108.08	108.33	108.55	108.79	109.00	109.24
6.60	107.06	107.30	107.51	107.75	107.95	108.18	108.37	108.59
6.70	106.53	106.76	106.95	107.17	107.35	107.57	107.74	107.95
6.80	106.01	106.22	106.39	106.60	106.76	106.96	107.12	107.31
6.90	105.49	105.68	105.84	106.03	106.18	106.36	106.50	106.68
7.00	104.98	105.15	105.29	105.46	105.59	105.76	105.89	106.05
7.10	104.46	104.62	104.74	104.90	105.01	105.16	105.28	105.42
7.20	103.95	104.10	104.20	104.34	104.44	104.57	104.67	104.80
7.30	103.45	103.57	103.66	103.78	103.87	103.99	104.07	104.19
7.40	102.94	103.05	103.13	103.23	103.30	103.41	103.47	103.57
7.50	102.44	102.54	102.59	102.68	102.74	102.83	102.88	102.97
7.60	101.94	102.02	102.06	102.14	102.18	102.26	102.29	102.37
7.70	101.45	101.51	101.54	101.60	101.62	101.69	101.71	101.77
7.80	100.96	101.00	101.02	101.06	101.07	101.12	101.13	101.17
7.90	100.47	100.50	100.50	100.53	100.52	100.56	100.55	100.58
8.00	99.98	100.00	99.98	100.00	99.98	100.00	99.98	100.00
8.10	99.50	99.50	99.47	99.47	99.44	99.45	99.41	99.42
8.20	99.02	99.01	98.96	98.95	98.90	98.90	98.85	98.84
8.30	98.54	98.52	98.45	98.43	98.37	98.35	98.29	98.27
8.40	98.06	98.03	97.95	97.91	97.84	97.81	97.73	97.70
8.50	97.59	97.54	97.45	97.40	97.31	97.27	97.18	97.14
8.60	97.12	97.06	96.95	96.89	96.79	96.73	96.64	96.58
8.70	96.66	96.58	96.46	96.39	96.27	96.20	96.09	96.03
8.80	96.19	96.10	95.97	95.88	95.76	95.67	95.55	95.47
8.90	95.73	95.63	95.48	95.38	95.24	95.15	95.02	94.93
9.00	95.28	95.16	95.00	94.89	94.74	94.63	94.48	94.38
9.10	94.82	94.69	94.52	94.40	94.23	94.11	93.95	93.84
9.20	94.37	94.23	94.04	93.91	93.73	93.60	93.43	93.31
9.30	93.92	93.76	93.57	93.42	93.23	93.09	92.91	92.78
9.40	93.47	93.30	93.10	92.94	92.74	92.58	92.39	92.25
9.50	93.03	92.85	92.63	92.46	92.24	92.08	91.88	91.73
9.60	92.59	92.39	92.16	91.98	91.76	91.58	91.37	91.21
9.70	92.15	91.94	91.70	91.50	91.27	91.09	90.86	90.69
9.80	91.71	91.49	91.24	91.03	90.79	90.59	90.36	90.18
9.90	91.28	91.05	90.78	90.57	90.31	90.11	89.86	89.67
10.00	90.84	90.61	90.33	90.10	89.83	89.62	89.36	89.16
10.20	89.99	89.73	89.43	89.18	88.89	88.66	88.38	88.16
10.40	89.14	88.86	88.54	88.27	87.96	87.71	87.42	87.18
10.60	88.31	88.01	87.66	87.38	87.05	86.78	86.46	86.21
10.80	87.48	87.16	86.79	86.49	86.14	85.85	85.52	85.25
11.00	86.67	86.32	85.94	85.62	85.25	84.94	84.59	84.31
11.20	85.86	85.50	85.09	84.75	84.37	84.05	83.68	83.38
11.40	85.06	84.68	84.26	83.90	83.50	83.16	82.78	82.46
11.60	84.28	83.88	83.43	83.06	82.64	82.29	81.89	81.56
11.80	83.50	83.08	82.62	82.23	81.79	81.43	81.01	80.67
12.00	82.73	82.29	81.82	81.41	80.96	80.58	80.15	79.79

(b)

8% — YEARS and MONTHS

Yield	30-6	31-0	31-6	32-0	32-6	33-0	33-6	34-0
4.00	170.12	170.71	171.28	171.84	172.39	172.94	173.47	173.99
4.20	165.01	165.53	166.05	166.55	167.04	167.52	168.00	168.46
4.40	160.12	160.59	161.05	161.49	161.93	162.36	162.78	163.19
4.60	155.45	155.86	156.27	156.67	157.06	157.43	157.80	158.17
4.80	150.98	151.34	151.70	152.05	152.40	152.73	153.06	153.38
5.00	146.70	147.02	147.34	147.65	147.95	148.24	148.53	148.81
5.20	142.60	142.88	143.16	143.43	143.69	143.95	144.20	144.45
5.40	138.67	138.92	139.16	139.40	139.63	139.85	140.07	140.28
5.60	134.91	135.12	135.33	135.54	135.74	135.93	136.12	136.30
5.80	131.30	131.49	131.67	131.84	132.02	132.18	132.34	132.50
6.00	127.84	128.00	128.16	128.31	128.45	128.60	128.73	128.87
6.10	126.16	126.31	126.46	126.59	126.73	126.86	126.99	127.11
6.20	124.52	124.66	124.79	124.92	125.04	125.16	125.28	125.39
6.30	122.92	123.04	123.16	123.28	123.39	123.50	123.61	123.71
6.40	121.34	121.45	121.56	121.67	121.77	121.87	121.97	122.06
6.50	119.80	119.90	120.00	120.10	120.19	120.28	120.37	120.45
6.60	118.28	118.38	118.47	118.56	118.64	118.72	118.80	118.88
6.70	116.80	116.89	116.97	117.05	117.12	117.20	117.27	117.34
6.80	115.35	115.43	115.50	115.57	115.64	115.70	115.77	115.83
6.90	113.93	114.00	114.06	114.12	114.18	114.24	114.30	114.35
7.00	112.53	112.59	112.65	112.71	112.76	112.81	112.86	112.91
7.10	111.17	111.22	111.27	111.32	111.36	111.41	111.45	111.49
7.20	109.83	109.87	109.91	109.96	110.00	110.03	110.07	110.11
7.30	108.51	108.55	108.59	108.62	108.66	108.69	108.72	108.75
7.40	107.22	107.26	107.29	107.32	107.34	107.37	107.40	107.42
7.50	105.96	105.99	106.01	106.03	106.06	106.08	106.10	106.12
7.60	104.72	104.74	104.76	104.78	104.80	104.81	104.83	104.85
7.70	103.51	103.52	103.54	103.55	103.56	103.57	103.59	103.60
7.80	102.32	102.32	102.33	102.34	102.35	102.36	102.37	102.37
7.90	101.15	101.15	101.16	101.16	101.16	101.17	101.17	101.17
8.00	100.00	100.00	100.00	100.00	100.00	100.00	100.00	100.00
8.10	98.88	98.87	98.87	98.86	98.86	98.86	98.85	98.85
8.20	97.77	97.76	97.75	97.75	97.74	97.73	97.73	97.72
8.30	96.69	96.68	96.66	96.65	96.64	96.63	96.62	96.61
8.40	95.63	95.61	95.59	95.58	95.57	95.55	95.54	95.53
8.50	94.58	94.56	94.54	94.53	94.51	94.49	94.48	94.46
8.60	93.56	93.54	93.52	93.49	93.48	93.46	93.44	93.42
8.70	92.55	92.53	92.50	92.48	92.46	92.44	92.42	92.40
8.80	91.57	91.54	91.51	91.49	91.46	91.44	91.42	91.40
8.90	90.60	90.57	90.54	90.51	90.48	90.46	90.43	90.41
9.00	89.65	89.61	89.58	89.55	89.52	89.50	89.47	89.45
9.10	88.71	88.68	88.64	88.61	88.58	88.55	88.53	88.50
9.20	87.80	87.76	87.72	87.69	87.66	87.63	87.60	87.57
9.30	86.90	86.86	86.82	86.78	86.75	86.72	86.69	86.66
9.40	86.01	85.97	85.93	85.89	85.86	85.83	85.79	85.76
9.50	85.14	85.10	85.06	85.02	84.98	84.95	84.92	84.88
9.60	84.29	84.24	84.20	84.16	84.12	84.09	84.05	84.02
9.70	83.45	83.40	83.36	83.32	83.28	83.24	83.21	83.17
9.80	82.63	82.58	82.53	82.49	82.45	82.41	82.38	82.34
9.90	81.82	81.77	81.72	81.68	81.64	81.60	81.56	81.53
10.00	81.02	80.97	80.92	80.88	80.84	80.80	80.76	80.72
10.20	79.47	79.42	79.37	79.33	79.28	79.24	79.20	79.16
10.40	77.97	77.92	77.87	77.82	77.78	77.74	77.70	77.66
10.60	76.52	76.47	76.42	76.37	76.33	76.28	76.24	76.20
10.80	75.12	75.07	75.02	74.97	74.92	74.88	74.84	74.80
11.00	73.77	73.71	73.66	73.61	73.57	73.52	73.48	73.44
11.20	72.46	72.40	72.35	72.30	72.26	72.21	72.17	72.13
11.40	71.19	71.13	71.08	71.03	70.99	70.94	70.90	70.86
11.60	69.96	69.91	69.86	69.81	69.76	69.72	69.68	69.64
11.80	68.77	68.72	68.67	68.62	68.57	68.53	68.49	68.45
12.00	67.62	67.57	67.52	67.47	67.42	67.38	67.34	67.30

(c)

Source: Reproduced from Publication #63, *Expanded Bond Values Table*, copyright 1970, pages 873, 876, and 883, Financial Publishing Company, Boston, Mass.

the bond (expressed as a percentage of par value) is found. Finally, look across the row to obtain the yield.

The procedure can be illustrated using our hypothetical bond. Exhibit 7(b) represents the appropriate page of the yield book, since it contains bond values for a bond with a coupon rate of 8 percent and seven years remaining to maturity. The market price of our hypothetical bond is $814.10, or 81.41 percent of par. Looking down column 7–0 we find the value of 81.41 in the row corresponding to a yield of 12 percent. This, of course, agrees with our previous computation that indicated the yield-to-maturity for our hypothetical bond to be 12 percent.

Everything went smoothly in our illustration. The exact time remaining to maturity was on the table, and so was the exact market price. Suppose instead that our hypothetical bond had seven years and one month remaining to maturity and a market price of $904. Neither input needed to determine the yield-to-maturity is included on the sample page. What can be done in such cases? The yield-to-maturity can be approximated by interpolating the values presented in the yield book. Such an approach may be satisfactory for a investor with a small sum to invest. However, for a portfolio manager with substantial funds to invest, such an approach would be inadequate. In such instances, portfolio managers usually have on-line access to a precanned computer program that provides the yield-to-maturity given the three input values. For a cost of less than $25, an investor can purchase a pocket calculator that includes a feature to compute the yield-to-maturity.

The investor should be cognizant of the following relationships of the coupon rate, current yield, and yield-to-maturity:

Price of the Bond	Relationship
Selling at par	Coupon rate = Current yield = Yield-to-maturity
Selling at a discount	Coupon rate < Current yield < Yield-to-maturity
Selling at a premium	Coupon rate > Current yield > Yield-to-maturity

Yield-to-Call

As explained in Chapter 2, a bond may be called by the issuer before maturity. Consequently, a conservative investor will compute the yield on a bond in two ways: (1) assuming the bond is held to maturity, and (2) assuming the bond is called by the issuer. The latter yield is referred to as the yield-to-call. A conservative investor uses the lower of the two yields in determining the promised "yield" on the bond because it represents a minimum yield that may be realized.

At the outset, it must be noted that the yield-to-call, like the yield-to-maturity, is a traditional measure that is *not* a good measure to employ in order to evaluate the investment merits of alternative bonds available to the investor. This is so for two reasons. First, it assumes the coupon interest payments before the issue is called will be reinvested at a rate equal to the yield-to-call. Hence it suffers from the same problem as the yield-to-maturity. Second, it does not recognize what will happen to the proceeds after the bond is called. Consequently, since the yield-to-maturity assumes a time commitment of funds greater than the yield-to-call, a direct comparison of these two yields is inappropriate. These drawbacks of the yield-to-call are discussed in the next section. In this section, the yield-to-call is explained. Moreover, an important related concept, the "crossover yield," which will be useful in the discussion in the next section, will also be explained.

The yield-to-call is defined as the discount rate that equates the present value of the promised cash flow if the bond is called (coupon payments plus call price) to the market price. To illustrate the computation of the yield-to-call, suppose our hypothetical bond is selling for $1,089.37 instead of $814.10. Further, assume the bond is callable three years from now at 104.2 (i.e., $1,042). A trial-and-error approach can be used to determine the yield-to-call for this bond. If a 3 percent discount rate is used, the present value is the market price of $1,089.37, as shown below:

PV of an annuity of $1 for six periods at 3 percent	× Semiannual coupon rate	
5.4172	× $40	= $ 216.69

plus

PV of $1 six periods hence at 3 percent	× Call price	
.8375	× $1,042	872.68
Present value of bond if called		= $1,089.37

Doubling the discount rate gives the yield-to-call. Hence the yield-to-call is 6 percent.

The yield-to-maturity for the bond can be found using the yield book. From Exhibit 7, we find that an 8 percent coupon bond with seven years remaining to maturity and a price of 108.91 offers a yield-to-maturity of 6.4 percent. Since our hypothetical bond has a market price of 108.94, its yield-to-maturity is approximately 6.4 percent. Therefore a conservative investor may use the yield-to-call as the "yield," since it is less than the yield-to-maturity.

When the call price is greater than the redemption value, which it usually is when a bond can be called, there are methods for approximating the yield-to-call.[7] Since there are specialized yield-to-call books published and pocket calculators with preprogrammed features to compute the yield on an investment, the approximation methods are not discussed in this chapter. It may not be necessary, however, to compute the yield-to-call. Remember that if the yield-to-call is greater than the yield-to-maturity, then the latter is the minimum "yield."

There is a simple procedure to quickly determine if the yield-to-maturity is less than the yield-to-call. The procedure requires determining the yield at which the yield-to-maturity and yield-to-call are equal. This is called the crossover yield.[8] If the yield-to-maturity is greater than the crossover yield, then it is less than the yield-to-call. On the other hand, if the yield-to-maturity is less than the crossover yield, then the minimum yield is the yield-to-call. Furthermore, once the crossover yield is computed at the time of acquisition, it continues to serve as the benchmark at every time up to the call date for determining the minimum yield.

The crossover yield is computed by finding the yield-to-maturity of a bond created as follows. The remaining life of the bond created is the difference between the remaining life of the callable bond and the remaining time before the bond can be called. The price of the new bond is the call price of the callable bond, and the coupon rate is the same as the callable bond. For example, for our hypothetical callable bond the difference between the remaining life of the bond (seven years) and the remaining life before the bond can be called (three years) is four years. The price of the created bond is 104.2, which is the price of the callable bond. The coupon rate for the created bond is 8 percent, the same as for the callable bond. The crossover yield is then the yield-to-maturity of a bond with a coupon rate of 8 percent, four years remaining to maturity, and a market price of 104.2. The yield-to-maturity for this bond can be found by using the yield book. Exhibit 7(a) is the relevant page from the yield book. As can be seen, the yield-to-maturity is approximately 6.8 percent.

Since the yield-to-maturity of the callable bond (6.4 percent) is less than the crossover yield (6.8 percent), the yield-to-call is the lower yield. Moreover, as the market price of the callable bond changes between now and the call date, the crossover yield of 6.8 percent will still apply.

The foregoing discussion helps to understand why it is not necessary for the investor to be concerned about the yield-to-call if a bond is selling at or below par. In such cases the created bond will have a yield-to-maturity less than the coupon rate if the call price of the callable bond is above par. Hence the crossover yield is less than the

---

[7] See Sidney Homer and Martin L. Leibowitz, *Inside the Yield Book* (Published jointly: Englewood Cliffs, N.J.: Prentice-Hall, and New York: New York Institute of Finance, 1972), pp. 164–67.

[8] Ibid., pp. 60–63.

coupon rate of the callable bond. The yield-to-maturity of the callable bond, on the other hand, will be greater than the coupon rate if the bond is selling below par and equal to the coupon rate if the bond is selling at par. Therefore, the yield-to-maturity of the callable bond is greater than crossover yield. Since the yield-to-maturity of the callable bond is greater than the crossover yield, the yield-to-maturity is less than the yield-to-call. Furthermore, this relationship holds at all times until the call date.

In addition to its use in determining whether the yield-to-call is less than the yield-to-maturity, the crossover yield has an important interpretation that will be discussed in the next section.

Realized Compound Yield

When using the yield-to-maturity as a measure of investment return, it is assumed that the coupon interest can be reinvested at a rate equal to the yield-to-maturity. That is, if the yield-to-maturity is 12 percent, it is assumed that the coupon interest payments can be reinvested to yield 12 percent.

To see the importance of the interest-on-interest component of total return, consider a bond selling at par with seven years remaining to maturity and carrying a 12 percent coupon rate. The total return for this bond consists of two sources: (1) coupon interest of $60 every six months for seven years and (2) interest from the reinvestment of the coupon interest. Since the bond is assumed to be selling at par, there is no capital gain or loss.

The future value generated from the reinvestment of coupon interest at 12 percent annually can be found by multiplying the future value of an annuity of $1 by the semiannual coupon interest. Thus for the bond under examination we have:

$$\begin{matrix} \text{FV of \$60 for 14} \\ \text{six-month periods} \end{matrix} = \$60 \times \begin{matrix} \text{FV of \$1 each six months} \\ \text{at 6 percent interest from Exhibit 5} \end{matrix}$$

$$= \$60 \times 21.015$$

$$= \$1,261$$

The coupon interest is $840 ($60 times 14). Hence the balance, $421 ($1,261 minus $840), represents the interest-on-interest component of the total return. For this bond, interest-on-interest accounts for 33 percent ($421 divided by $1,261) of the total return.

The importance of the interest-on-interest component becomes greater the longer the maturity. For example, if the 12 percent coupon bonds selling at par had a remaining life of 30 years instead of 7 years, the total return would be $31,987. Since coupon interest payments are $3,600 ($60 times 60 semiannual coupon payments), interest-on-interest is $28,387 ($31,987 minus $3,600) or 89 percent of the total return.

For a bond selling at a discount from par, interest-on-interest makes up less of the total return for bonds of equal time remaining to maturity and the same yield-to-maturity. This can be illustrated with the hypothetical bond used to illustrate the computation of the yield-to-maturity. Recall that the bond carries an 8 percent coupon rate, has seven years remaining to maturity, and has a market price of $814 (rounded to the nearest dollar). The yield-to-maturity for this bond is 12 percent. The total return consists of (1) coupon interest payments of $560, (2) interest-on-interest of $281, and (3) a capital gain of $186 ($1,000 minus $814). The interest-on-interest component accounts for 27 percent of the total return ($281 divided by $1,027). For the 12 percent, seven-year par bonds, the interest-on-interest component makes up 33 percent of the total return.

The interest-on-interest component of a long-term bond selling at a discount would be a substantial portion of the bond's total return, just as in the case of a bond selling at par. In fact the longer the term of the bond, the less important is the capital gain component compared with the other two components. For example, a bond with 30 years remaining to maturity, carrying a coupon rate of 8 percent, and selling at $677 will have a yield-to-maturity of 12 percent. The total return for this bond is $21,648, consisting of: (1) coupon interest payments of $2,400, (2) interest-on-interest of $18,925, and (3) a capital gain of $323. The capital gain component is only 1.5 percent of the total return. For the seven-year bond selling at a discount, the capital gain component represented 18 percent of the total return. The interest-on-interest component for the 30-year bond selling at a discount is about 87 percent, which is approximately the same as in the case of the 30-year bond selling at par.

As would be expected, bonds selling at a premium are more dependent upon the interest-on-interest component of the total return.

Because of the importance of the rate that the coupon interest is assumed to be reinvested, a measure of return that can be used for investment decisions must take into account interest-on-interest. Homer and Leibowitz suggest a comprehensive measure that takes into consideration all three sources of a bond's return.[9] The measure they suggest reveals the fully compounded growth rate of an investment under varying reinvestment rates. They call this measure the realized compound yield.

The steps to compute the realized compound yield are as follows:

1.   Compute the total future dollars that will be received from the investment. This is equal to the sum of the coupon payments, the interest-on-interest from reinvesting the coupon payments at an assumed reinvestment rate, and the redemption value.

---

[9] Homer and Leibowitz, *Inside the Yield Book.*

2.   Divide the amount found in the previous step by the invest-ment. The resulting amount is the future value per dollar invested.

3.   Find the interest rate that produces the future value per dollar invested. This can be done by using a future value of $1 table such as Exhibit 1 or by solving the following equation:

$$\text{(Future value per dollar invested)}^{\frac{1}{\text{no. of periods}}} - 1$$

4.   Since interest is assumed to be paid semiannually, double the interest rate found in the previous step. The resulting interest rate is the realized compound yield.

The 12 percent, seven-year bond selling at par will be used to demonstrate the computation of the realized compound yield. The reinvestment rate assumed is 10 percent. The steps are as follows:

1.   The total future dollars to be received consists of the coupon interest and interest-on-interest of $1,176[10] and the redemption value of $1,000. Hence the total future dollars to be received is $2,176.

2.   Since the investment is $1,000, the future value per $1 invested is $2.176 ($2,176 divided by $1,000).

3.   From Exhibit 1 it can be seen that the interest rate that will produce a future value of $2.176 for a $1 investment made for 14 periods is between 5 and 6 percent. Using the formula, or consulting a more detailed table, the interest rate of 5.7 percent would produce a future value of $2.17.

4.   Doubling 5.7 percent we get a realized compound yield of 11.4 percent.

A property of the realized compound yield is that it will be between the yield-to-maturity and the reinvestment rate. Therefore when the reinvestment rate is the same as the yield-to-maturity, the realized compound yield is the same as the yield-to-maturity. When the rein-vestment rate is greater than the yield-to-maturity, the realized com-pound yield will be greater than the yield-to-maturity. The realized compound yield will be less than the yield-to-maturity when the rein-vestment rate is less than the latter.

The difference in basis points between the realized compound yield and the yield-to-maturity depends not only on the reinvestment rate but also on the remaining life of the bond and the coupon rate. The longer the term-to-maturity, the more important will be the inter-

---

[10] FV of $60 for 14   = $60 × FV of $1 each six months
        six-month periods   at 5 percent interest from Exhibit 5
                             = $60 × 19.598
                             = $1,176

Note that since the annual reinvestment rate is assumed to be 10 percent, a 5 percent semiannual interest rate is used in the future value computation.

est-on-interest component for a given coupon rate and yield-to-maturity. Consequently, the longer the term of a bond, the closer its realized compound yield will be to the reinvestment rate. On the other hand, the shorter the maturity, the closer the realized compound yield will be to the yield-to-maturity.

For a given term-to-maturity and yield-to-maturity, the lower the coupon rate, the less of a bond's total return depends on the interest-on-interest component. Therefore, holding all other factors constant, the realized compound yield will deviate from the yield-to-maturity by more basis points for a given reinvestment rate the lower the coupon rate.

Exhibit 8 shows the realized compound yield under different assumptions for the reinvestment rate for the four bonds discussed in this section. The reader can verify the properties of the realized compound yield stated in the preceding discussion.

Exhibit 8
Realized Compound Yields for 7-Year and 30-Year Bonds with a 12 Percent Yield-to-Maturity: Coupon Rates 12 Percent and 8 Percent

	Realized Compound Yield* 7-Year Bonds		30-Year Bonds	
Reinvestment Rate	12 Percent Coupon, Price = 100	8 Percent Coupon, Price = 81.41	12 Percent Coupon, Price = 100	8 Percent Coupon, Price = 677
8%	10.8%	11.1%	9.3%	9.4%
10	11.4	11.6	10.6	10.8
12	12.0	12.0	12.0	12.0
14	12.6	12.5	13.3	13.3
16	13.2	13.0	15.0	14.9

* The yield-to-maturity for each bond is 12 percent.

Realized compound yield should also be used to measure the minimum yield for a callable bond selling at a premium. As discussed in the previous section, the selection of a minimum yield based upon the lesser of the yield-to-maturity and yield-to-call is deficient because it does not consider the reinvestment opportunities available to the investor. A proper analysis would consider the realized compound yield assuming the bond is not called and assuming the bond is called. Using the callable bond discussed in the previous section, the realized compound yield approach will be illustrated. Information about the callable bond is summarized below:

Coupon rate = 8 percent
Time remaining to maturity = seven years
Market price = $1089.40

Time to first call = three years
Call price = $1,042
Yield-to-maturity = 6.4 percent
Yield-to-call = 6 percent
Crossover yield = 6.8 percent

To compute the realized compound yield, the reinvestment rate must be specified. It is assumed in this illustration that the coupon interest and principal, if the bond is called, can be reinvested earning 5 percent per annum (2.5 percent semiannually).

The realized compound yield if the bond is *not* called and held to maturity is 6 percent as shown below:

1. The total future dollars to be received consists of the coupon interest and interest-on-interest of $661 and the redemption value at maturity of $1,000. The total future dollars to be received is therefore $1,661.

2. The future value per $1 invested is $1.52 ($1,661 divided by $1,089.4).

3. From Exhibit 1 it can be seen that the interest rate that will produce a future value of $1.52 if $1 is invested for 14 periods is 3 percent.

4. Doubling 3 percent we obtain the realized compound yield of 6 percent.

The realized compound yield if the bond is called is 5.4 percent as shown below:

1. Determination of the total future dollars to be received if the bond is called requires several computations, each of which is explained below.

a. *Coupon interest and interest-on-interest up to the call date:* There are six coupon payments of $40 per period between the contemplated acquisition date and the call date. The future value of the coupon interest and interest-on-interest assuming the $40 coupon interest payments are reinvested at 2.5 percent per period is $256.

b. *Future value at maturity of coupon interest and interest-on-interest expected up to the call date:* The $256 computed in the previous step can be reinvested for the remaining number of periods until maturity earning 2.5 percent per period. Since there are eight periods (four years) between the call date and maturity, $256 will grow to $312.[11]

c. *Coupon interest and interest-on-interest to maturity for the funds reinvested after the bond is called:* The call price is $1,042. This amount can be reinvested earning 5 percent per annum. The

---

[11] The future value of $1 invested for eight periods at 2.5 percent is 1.2184.

annual coupon interest from the reinvestment of the funds would be $52.10 ($1,042 times .05) or $26.05 semiannually. Reinvesting $26.05 for eight periods earning 2.5 percent per period would give $228 at the end of eight periods.

The total future dollars to be received is b plus c plus the redemption value of $1,042. Hence the total future dollars to be received is $1,582 ($312 + $228 + $1,042).

2. The future value per dollar invested is $1.45 ($1,582 divided by $1,089.40).

3. From Exhibit 1 it can be seen that the interest rate that will produce a future value of $1.45 for a $1 investment made for 14 periods is between 2 and 3 percent. The approximate rate is 2.7 percent.[12]

4. Doubling 2.7 percent we get a realized compound yield if the bond is called of 5.4 percent.

The minimum yield is therefore 5.4 percent, the realized compound yield if the bond is called.

The crossover yield is helpful to know since it also tells which realized compound yield will be the minimum yield. The crossover yield can be interpreted as the average reinvestment rate that must be earned by the investor to fare better by having the bond called.[13] If the reinvestment rate is greater than the crossover yield, the realized compound yield if the bond is called will exceed the realized compound yield if the bond is held to maturity. Therefore the minimum yield is the realized compound yield assuming the bond is held to maturity. The more likely case is that the reinvestment rate will be less than the crossover yield. In that case the realized compound yield if the bond is held to maturity will exceed the realized compound yield if the bond is called. The latter will then be the minimum yield. In our illustration the 5 percent reinvestment rate assumed is less than the crossover yield of 6.8 percent. Hence the realized compound yield if the bond is called is the minimum yield.

BOND PRICE VOLATILITY

From our discussion of the time value of money, it should be clear that the price of a bond changes in the opposite direction from the change in the yield required by investors. For example, if a 9 percent coupon bond with 20 years remaining to maturity is selling at 100 (par) to yield 9 percent, the price of the bond will decrease to 91.42 if market yields increase by 100 basis points to 10 percent. The increase in market yields decreases the price of the bond by 8.58 percent. If, on the other hand, market yields decline by 100 basis points

---

[12] $1.027^8 = 1.4521$

[13] Homer and Leibowitz, *Inside the Yield Book*, pp. 62–63.

to 8 percent, the price of the bond will increase by 9.9 percent to 109.90. In addition the change in the price of the bond will be greater the greater the change in the yield required by investors. For example, for the 9 percent coupon, 20-year bond, an increase in market yields from 9 percent to 11 percent (a 200-basis-point increase) will result in a decrease in the price of the bond from 100 to 83.95. Hence, for a 200-basis-point increase in yield, the price of the bond will fall by 16.05 percent compared with 8.58 percent for a 100-basis-point increase in yield.

For a given initial market yield and a given change in basis points, the percentage change in the price of the bond will depend upon certain characteristics of the bond. The relationship between bond price volatility and these characteristics of a bond are illustrated in the remainder of this chapter.

Before proceeding, it is important to understand that the volatility we will be discussing is the change that will result from an *instantaneous* change in market yields. Even if market yields do not change, the price of a bond selling at a premium or discount will change due to the passage of time. For example, consider a bond with a 7 percent coupon rate, 20 years remaining to maturity, and selling at 81.60 to yield 9 percent. If the bond is held for one year and market yields remained at 9 percent, the price of the bond would increase to 81.95, since it would have 19 years remaining to maturity. The increase in price from 81.60 to 81.95 results from an accretion process that will eventually increase the price of the bond to its par value at maturity. For a bond selling at a premium, the price of a bond decreases as it approaches maturity if market yields remain constant. Consider, for example, a bond with a coupon rate of 12 percent, 20 years remaining to maturity, and selling for 127.60 to yield 9 percent. The price of the bond after one year has passed will be 127.07 if market yields do not change. This results from the amortization of the premium. The relationship between the price of a bond and the remaining time to maturity assuming that market yields are unchanged is shown in Exhibits 9 and 10.

Bond Price Volatility and Coupon Rate

For a given maturity and initial market yield, the volatility of a bond's price increases as the coupon rate decreases. This is illustrated in Exhibit 11. The term to maturity is 20 years, and the initial yield is 9 percent. The price of the bond for coupon rates between 5 percent and 12 percent at 1 percent increments for eight hypothetical changes in the market yield are shown in the top panel of the exhibit. In the second panel, the percentage change in the price of the bond is shown.

Exhibit 9
**Time Path of the Value of a 7 Percent Coupon, 20-Year Bond If the Required Yield
Begins and Remains at 9 Percent**

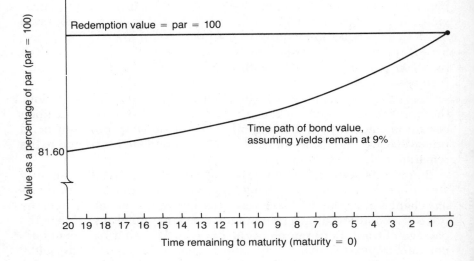

Exhibit 10
**Time Path of the Value of a 12 Percent Coupon, 20-Year Bond if the Required Yield
Begins and Remains at 9 Percent**

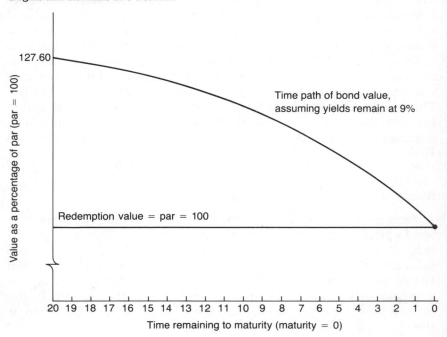

Coupon Rate

	5 Percent	6 Percent	7 Percent	8 Percent	9 Percent	10 Percent	11 Percent	12 Percent
Initial Price	$63.20	$72.40	$81.60	$90.80	$100.00	$109.20	$118.40	$127.60
Price If Yield Changes by:								
−200 bp	$78.64	$89.32	$100.00	$110.68	$121.36	$132.03	$142.71	$153.39
−100	70.31	80.21	90.10	100.00	109.90	119.79	129.69	139.59
−50	66.61	76.15	85.69	95.23	104.77	114.31	123.85	133.39
−10	63.86	73.13	82.39	91.66	100.93	110.19	119.46	128.73
+10	62.54	71.68	80.82	89.95	99.09	108.22	117.36	126.49
+50	60.03	68.91	77.80	86.68	95.56	104.44	113.32	122.20
+100	57.10	65.68	74.26	82.84	91.42	100.00	108.58	117.16
+200	51.86	59.88	67.91	75.93	83.95	91.98	100.00	108.02
Percentage Change in Price If Yield Changes by:								
−200 bp	+24.43%	+23.37%	+22.55%	+21.89%	+21.36%	+20.91%	+20.53%	+20.21%
−100	+11.25	+10.79	+10.42	+10.13	+9.90	+9.70	+9.54	+9.40
−50	+5.40	+5.18	+5.01	+4.88	+4.77	+4.68	+4.60	+4.54
−10	+1.04	+1.01	+0.97	+0.95	+0.93	+0.91	+0.90	+0.89
+10	−1.04	−0.99	−0.96	−0.94	−0.91	−0.90	−0.88	−0.87
+50	−5.02	−4.82	−4.66	−4.54	−4.44	−4.36	−4.29	−4.23
+100	−9.65	−9.28	−9.00	−8.77	−8.58	−8.42	−8.29	−8.18
+200	−17.94	−17.29	−16.78	−16.38	−16.05	−15.77	−15.54	−15.34
Ratio of Percentage Price Change to Yield Movement in Basis Points If Yield Changes by:								
−200 bp	−.1222%	−.1169%	−.1128%	−.1095%	−.1068%	−.1046%	−.1027%	−.1011%
−100	−.1125	−.1079	−.1042	−.1013	−.0990	−.0970	−.0954	−.0940
−50	−.1080	−.1036	−.1002	−.0976	−.0954	−.0936	−.0920	−.0908
−10	−.1040	−.1010	−.0970	−.0950	−.0930	−.0910	−.0900	−.0890
+10	−.1040	−.0990	−.0960	−.0940	−.0910	−.0900	−.0880	−.0870
+50	−.1004	−.0964	−.0932	−.0908	−.0888	−.0872	−.0858	−.0846
+100	−.0965	−.0928	−.0900	−.0877	−.0858	−.0842	−.0829	−.0818
+200	−.0897	−.0865	−.0839	−.0819	−.0803	−.0789	−.0777	−.0767

An implication of this property of price volatility is that bonds selling at a discount are more responsive to changes in market yield, all other factors equal, compared with bonds selling at or above par. Moreover, the deeper the discount resulting from the divergence between the coupon rate and market yield, the greater the responsiveness of the bond's price to changes in market yield. The greatest price response is offered by zero-coupon debt obligations. From a purely capital gain or loss perspective, therefore, investors would avoid bonds selling at a discount if interest rates are expected to rise; however, bonds selling at a discount rate are attractive if interest rates are anticipated to decline.

Notice in Exhibit 11 that the percentage change in the price of a bond is not the same for both an increase and decrease of the same number of basis points. The difference between the percentage change in price increases as the amount of the change in basis points increases. For small changes in basis points, such as 10 basis points, the percentage price change is almost symmetrical. As the coupon rate increases, the difference between the percentage change in price for a given change in basis points decreases.

For analysis purposes, it would be helpful to be able to express the percentage change in price in terms of some fixed volatility factor times the change in yield. Unfortunately, this is not possible because the relationship between the percentage change in the price of a bond is not linear and not symmetrical with respect to yield changes. This can be seen in the third panel in Exhibit 11, which shows that the ratio of the percentage price change to the change in yield is not constant.

The change in the price of the bond, however, is only one consideration in evaluating the investment merits of a particular bond issue. Recall that even though interest rates may decline so that the price of the bond increases, the interest-on-interest component of the bond's total return will decrease due to the lower reinvestment rate. It seems that we are missing an important element in assessing the relative attractiveness of a bond issue. That element is the period of time the investor plans to hold the bond. This period is commonly referred to as the investor's investment horizon. In Chapter 29 a framework for evaluating the attractiveness of a bond for a given investment horizon is explained.

Bond Price Volatility and Maturity

The volatility of the price of a bond increases the longer the remaining term to maturity, all other factors constant. For bond's yielding 9 percent and with a coupon rate of 9 percent, this property is illustrated in Exhibit 12.[14]

---

[14] Once again it can be seen that the percentage change in price is not symmetrical for a given change in basis points and a given maturity, except for very small changes. The difference in the percentage change in price decreases as the maturity increases.

Exhibit 12
Bond Price Volatility for 9 Percent Coupon Bonds Selling at Par

			Years to Maturity				
	1	5	10	15	20	25	30
Initial Price	$100.00	$100.00	$100.00	$100.00	$100.00	$100.00	$100.00
Price If Yield Changes by:							
−200 bp	$101.90	$108.32	$114.21	$118.39	$121.36	$123.46	$124.94
−100	100.94	104.06	106.80	108.65	109.90	110.74	111.31
−50	100.47	102.00	103.32	104.19	104.77	105.15	105.40
−10	100.09	100.40	100.65	100.82	100.93	101.00	101.04
+10	99.91	99.61	99.35	99.19	99.09	99.02	98.98
+50	99.53	98.05	96.82	96.04	95.56	95.25	95.06
+100	99.07	96.14	93.77	92.31	91.42	90.87	90.54
+200	98.15	92.46	88.05	85.47	83.95	83.07	82.55
Percentage Change If Yield Changes by:							
−200 bp	+1.90%	+8.32%	+14.21%	+18.39%	+21.36%	+23.46%	+24.94%
−100	+0.94	+4.06	+6.80	+8.65	+9.90	+10.74	+11.31
−50	+0.47	+2.00	+3.32	+4.19	+4.77	+5.15	+5.40
−10	+0.09	+0.40	+0.65	+0.82	+0.93	+1.00	+1.04
+10	−0.09	−0.39	−0.65	−0.81	−0.91	−0.98	−1.02
+50	−0.47	−1.95	−3.18	−3.96	−4.44	−4.75	−4.94
+100	−0.93	−3.86	−6.23	−7.69	−8.58	−9.13	−9.46
+200	−1.85	−7.54	−11.95	−14.53	−16.05	−16.93	−17.45
Ratio of Percentage Price Change to Yield Movement in Basis Points If Yield Changes by:							
−200 bp	−.0095%	−.0416%	−.0711%	−.0920%	−.1068%	−.1173%	−.1247%
−100	−.0094	−.0406	−.0680	−.0865	−.0990	−.1074	−.1131
−50	−.0094	−.0400	−.0664	−.0838	−.0954	−.1030	−.1080
−10	−.0090	−.0400	−.0650	−.0820	−.0930	−.1000	−.1040
+10	−.0090	−.0390	−.0650	−.0810	−.0910	−.0980	−.1020
+50	−.0094	−.0390	−.0636	−.0792	−.0888	−.0950	−.0988
+100	−.0093	−.0386	−.0623	−.0769	−.0858	−.0913	−.0946
+200	−.0093	−.0377	−.0598	−.0727	−.0803	−.0847	−.0873

An implication of this property of price volatility is that if interest rates are expected to increase, bond prices will decrease by a greater percentage for long-term bonds compared to short-term bonds, all other factors constant. Therefore, from a purely capital loss perspective, an investor will avoid long-term bonds (holding everything else constant) if interest rates are expected to rise. Conversely, since the percentage change in prices of long-term bonds will increase by a greater percentage than short-term bonds, investors will prefer long-term bonds from a purely capital gain perspective when interest rates are projected to fall.

Once again, remember that the capital gain or loss resulting from a change in market yield is only one component of the total return from holding a bond. The technique discussed in Chapter 29 can be employed to evaluate the relative investment merit of holding a bond over the investor's investment horizon given the investor's projection about the future movement of interest rates.

Bond Price Volatility and the Initial Yield Level

The two properties of bond price volatility just demonstrated measured the change in yield in terms of basis points. For example, if yields change from 9 percent to 10 percent, the change in yield was measured as 100 basis points. Alternatively, the change in yield can be measured as a percentage change from the initial yield. Using our previous example, the percentage change in yield is 11.11 percent if yields increase to 10 percent from a 9 percent initial yield.

Regardless of whether the movement in yields is measured by the change in basis point or as a percentage of the initial yield, the two properties of bond price volatility discussed above hold. An additional property of bond price volatility when the movement is based upon the expected percentage change from an initial yield level is that for a given percentage change in yield, bond price volatility increases the higher the initial yield level, all other factors constant. This property is illustrated in Exhibit 13.

Exhibit 13
Bond Price Volatility for a 9 Percent Coupon, 20 Year Bond for 25 Percent Increase in Market Yield

Initial Yield	New Yield after 25 Percent Increase	Change in Basis Points	Initial Price	New Price	Percentage Change in Price
4.00%	5.00%	100 bp	168.39	150.21	−10.80%
6.00	7.50	150	134.67	115.41	−14.30
8.00	10.00	200	109.90	91.42	−16.82
10.00	12.50	250	91.42	74.48	−18.53
14.00	17.50	350	66.67	53.12	−20.32

It is not difficult to understand why this occurs. The higher the initial yield, the greater the change in the number of basis points for a given percentage change in yield. Therefore, since bond price volatility depends upon the magnitude of the change in basis points, the higher the initial yield level, the greater the bond's price volatility for a given percentage change in yield. An implication of this property is that as yields rise, bond price volatility increases.

Bond Price Volatility and Duration

A pitfall with using the maturity of a bond as a measure of the timing of its cash flow is that it only takes into consideration the final payment. To overcome this shortcoming, Professor Frederick R. Macaulay in 1938 suggested using a measure that would account for all cash flows expected.[15] The measure he suggested, known as duration, is a weighted average term-to-maturity where the cash flows are in terms of their present value. Mathematically, duration is measured as follows:

$$\text{Duration} = \frac{\text{PVCF}_1 \, (1)}{\text{PVTCF}} + \frac{\text{PVCF}_2 \, (2)}{\text{PVTCF}} + \frac{\text{PVCF}_3 \, (3)}{\text{PVTCF}} + \cdots + \frac{\text{PVCF}_n \, (n)}{\text{PVTCF}}$$

where

PVCF_t = the present value of the cash flow in period t discounted at the prevailing yield-to-maturity

t = the period when the cash flow is received

n = remaining number of periods until maturity

PVTCF = total present value of the cash flow from the bond where the present value is determined using the prevailing yield-to-maturity

For a bond in which there are no sinking-fund or call effects and in which interest is paid semiannually, the cash flow for periods 1 to $n - 1$ is just one half of the annual coupon interest.[16] The cash flow in period n is the semiannual coupon interest plus the redemption value. The discount rate is one half the prevailing yield-to-maturity. The resulting value is in half years when semiannual interest payments are used in the computation. To obtain duration in terms of years, dura-

---

[15] Frederick R. Macaulay, *Some Theoretical Problems Suggested by the Movement of Interest Rates, Bond Yields, and Stock Prices in the United States Since 1865* (New York: National Bureau of Economic Research, 1938).

[16] The cash flow when the effects of a sinking fund or call must be considered is explained in Chapter 35.

tion in half years is divided by two.[17] Since the price of a bond is equal
to its cash flow discounted at the prevailing yield-to-maturity, PVTCF
is nothing more than the current market price including accrued interest.

Exhibit 14 shows how the duration of a 7 percent coupon bond with
eight years to maturity and selling for $887.70 to yield 9 percent is
computed assuming coupon interest is paid semiannually. The duration for this bond is 6.1335 years.

Exhibit 14
Worksheet for Computation of the Duration of a 7 Percent
Coupon Bond with Eight Years to Maturity Selling at
$887.70 to Yield 9 Percent (semiannual interest payments
assumed)

Period	Cash Flow	PV at 4.5 Percent	PVCF	PVCF × Period
1	$ 35	.9569	$ 33.4915	33.4915
2	35	.9157	32.0495	64.0990
3	35	.8763	30.6705	92.0115
4	35	.8386	29.3510	117.4040
5	35	.8025	28.0875	140.4375
6	35	.7679	26.8765	161.2590
7	35	.7348	25.7180	180.0260
8	35	.7032	24.6120	196.8960
9	35	.6729	23.5515	211.9635
10	35	.6439	22.5365	225.3650
11	35	.6162	21.5670	237.2370
12	35	.5897	20.6395	247.6740
13	35	.5643	19.7505	256.7565
14	35	.5400	18.9000	264.6000
15	35	.5167	ʼ18.0845	271.2675
16	1035	.4945	511.8075	8,188.9200
			887.6935	10,889.4080

$$\text{Duration in half years} = \frac{10,889.4080}{887.6935}$$
$$= 12.2671$$

$$\text{Duration in years} = \frac{12.2671}{2}$$
$$= 6.1335$$

Three properties of a bond's duration should be noted. First, except
for zero coupon bonds, the duration of a bond is less than its maturity.
Second, the duration of a bond decreases the greater the coupon rate.
Finally, as market yields increase, the duration of a bond decreases.
These properties are demonstrated in Chapter 35.

---

[17] In general, if there are m coupon payments per year, then duration in years is
computed by dividing the duration based upon m payments per year by m.

The specific link between a bond's duration and its bond price volatility for small changes in interest rates was demonstrated by Professors Michael Hopewell and George Kaufman.[18] They show that

Percentage change in bond's price

$$= -(\text{Modified duration}) \times \left(\frac{\begin{array}{c}\text{Change in market yield} \\ \text{in basis points}\end{array}}{100} \right)$$

where modified duration is duration divided by (1 + market yield/the number of coupon payments per year).

For example, the duration of the 7 percent coupon bond with eight years to maturity and selling to yield 9 percent is 6.1335. Hence modified duration is 6.1335/(1 + .09/2), or 5.8694. The percentage decline in the bond's price if market yields rise by 50 basis points is 2.93 percent as shown below:

$$= -(5.8694) \times \left(\frac{50}{100} \right)$$
$$= -2.93 \text{ percent}$$

The use of duration as a measure of the responsiveness of a bond's price to a change in market yields is only one application of how this concept can be used in bond portfolio management. Another important application deals with the trade-off that arises as interest rates change over the investor's investment horizon. As noted several times earlier, as interest rates increase, the price of the bond declines, but the portion of the total return from interest-on-interest increases. When interest rates decrease over the investor's investment horizon, the opposite is true. The portion of the total return resulting from interest-on-interest decreases, but the price of the bond increases. To immunize a bond portfolio from this interest rate risk so as to achieve a targeted return over an investment horizon, it has been demonstrated that the duration of the portfolio should be set equal to the investment horizon. This application of duration is discussed in Chapter 36.

SUMMARY

This chapter explained the basic elements of bond yield mathematics. In addition to illustrating how each yield measure is computed, the drawback of the conventional yield-to-maturity measure is explained and a better measure, the realized compound yield, is introduced. The investor should now understand why the yield-to-matu-

[18] Michael H. Hopewell and George C. Kaufman, "Bond Price Volatility and Term to Maturity: A Generalized Respecification," *American Economic Review*, September 1973, pp. 749–53.

rity only provides a *promised yield* and that yield will not necessarily be equal to the return realized by the investor at the end of the investor's investment horizon. A further discussion of a bond's total return is provided in Chapter 28, and a framework for evaluating the investment merit of a bond over the investor's investment horizon is discussed in Chapter 29.

The factors that influence the volatility of a bond's price are also explained in this chapter. The duration of a bond is a concept with important implications for bond portfolio management. Although this concept is introduced in this chapter, a more detailed treatment is provided in Chapter 35.

The Determinants of Interest Rates on Fixed Income Securities

5

Frank J. Jones, Ph.D.
Executive Vice President
New York Futures Exchange

Benjamin Wolkowitz, Ph.D.
Vice President
Citicorp Futures Corporation

This chapter discusses the determination of interest rates on fixed income securities. In discussing the determination of interest rates, first the determination of the general level of interest rates at a specific time, and then the factors that cause differences in interest rates at a specific time are considered. The interest rates on securities issued by the U.S. Department of the Treasury (hereafter Treasury) are commonly accepted as the benchmark interest rates in the U.S. economy and, typically, in the world. Thus a topic related to interest-rate determination, the market for Treasury securities, is also discussed in this chapter.

The interest rates on Treasury securities are commonly accepted as being reflective of the general level of interest rates because there are more of Treasury securities outstanding than of any other securities in the world, the Treasury issues securities of every maturity spectrum on a regular basis, and Treasury securities have virtually no credit risk. The next section in this chapter discusses the primary and secondary markets for Treasury securities.

Following the Treasury security markets section is the discussion of interest-rate determination. This discussion is structured so that the conceptual analysis is followed by applications of the conceptual conclusions. Most of these applications use Treasury securities as the basis for comparison. The first part of this discussion considers the determination of the general level of interest rates, which can be considered "the" interest rate. The three major rationales or theories for interest-rate determination—liquidity preference, loanable funds, and inflation and the real rate of interest—are discussed. A synthesis of these approaches is also provided. A fourth rationale, the "tone of the market," is also reviewed and shown to have an impact on interest rates in the short term.

The second part of the discussion on interest-rate determination discusses the factors that cause differences among interest rates at a specific time, that is, why not all interest rates are equal to the general level of interest rates. There are three such factors or reasons for differences among interest rates.

The first factor is maturity. The impact of maturity on a security's interest rate is considered in the context of three hypotheses, the liquidity hypothesis, the expectations hypothesis and the segmentation hypothesis.

Differences among interest rates on securities at a time also occur due to differences in credit risk. Investors respond to a risk-return trade-off in that the greater the risk associated with a particular security, that is, the less creditworthy the issuer, the greater the required return. This concept of credit risk is explained and illustrated with a number of actual market examples.

A third important reason for differences among interest rates on securities is taxability, with regard to the tax exemption on coupons for municipal securities, the difference in tax treatment between coupon return and capital appreciation, and flower bonds. The subject of taxability and its impact on interest rates is also discussed.

The chapter concludes with an overview of interest-rate determination, which combines all the concepts introduced and demonstrates how they interact to determine market interest rates. This synthesis of theory and actual experience, relying on Treasury issues as a basis for comparison, provides a comprehensive overview of interest-rate determination.

THE CASH MARKET FOR GOVERNMENT SECURITIES

The liabilities of the U.S. Treasury outstanding are greater in magnitude than the liabilities of any other institution in the world. The Treasury has, over time, issued liabilities to raise funds to finance its budget deficits. During recent years there has been a substantial increase in the amount of Treasury liabilities outstanding, as indicated in Exhibit 1.

Exhibit 1
Outstanding Treasury Securities ($ millions)

End of Fiscal Year of Month	Amount Outstanding			Securities Held by					
				Government Accounts			The Public†		
	Total	Public Debt Securities	Agency Securities	Total	Public Debt Securities	Agency Securities	Total	Public Debt Securities	Agency Securities
1973	468,426*	457,317*	11,109	125,381	123,385	1,996	343,045	333,932	9,113
1974	486,247	474,235	12,012	140,194	138,206	1,988	346,053	336,029	10,024
1975	544,131	533,188	10,943	147,225	145,283	1,942	396,906	387,905	9,001
1976	631,866	620,432	11,433	151,566	149,611	1,955	480,300	470,821	9,478
T.O.	646,379	634,701	11,678	148,052	146,105	1,947	498,327	488,327	9,730
1977	709,138	698,840	10,298	157,295	155,490	1,805	551,843	543,350	8,493
1978	780,425	771,544	8,881	169,477	167,973	1,504	610,948	603,571	7,377
1979	833,751	826,519	7,232	189,162	187,683	1,478	644,589	638,836	5,754
1980	914,317	907,701	6,616	199,212	197,743	1,469	715,105	709,958	5,147
1981	1,003,941	997,855	6,086	209,507	208,056	1,450	794,434	789,799	4,636
1980–Nov.	920,316	913,752	6,564	191,223	189,753	1,470	729,094	723,999	5,094
Dec.	936,686	930,210	6,476	193,925	192,464	1,461	742,761	737,746	5,015
1981–Jan.	940,528	934,073	6,455	190,995	189,520	1,475	749,533	744,553	4,980
Feb.	956,898	950,498	6,399	193,449	191,974	1,474	763,449	758,524	4,925
Mar.	970,901	964,531	6,370	192,314	190,855	1,459	778,587	773,676	4,911
Apr.	970,326	964,026	6,300	195,463	194,004	1,460	774,863	770,022	4,840
May	974,758	968,497	6,261	199,356	197,897	1,458	775,402	770,600	4,803
June	977,350	971,174	6,176	201,377	199,919	1,457	775,973	771,255	4,719
July	979,388	973,250	6,139	200,032	198,578	1,455	779,356	774,672	4,683
Aug.	986,312	980,193	6,119	200,455	199,001	1,454	785,857	781,192	4,665
Sept	1,003,941	997,855	6,086	209,507	208,056	1,450	794,434	789,799	4,636
Oct.	1,011,111	1,005,042	6,069	206,303	204,853	1,449	804,808	800,189	4,620
Nov.	1,019,324	1,013,303	6,021	203,544	202,103	1,441	815,780	811,200	4,580

* Excludes issues to IMF and other international lending institutions to conform with the budget presentation and the source for this table.
† Includes holdings of Federal Reserve Banks.
Source: Monthly Treasury Statement of Receipts and Outlays of the United States Government and *Treasury Bulletin*, February 1981.

As of January 31, 1981, the Treasury had total liabilities outstanding of $934.1 billion. Of this total, $628.5 billion was in marketable securities, and the remainder was in a nonmarketable type. This section focuses on marketable Treasury securities.

Because Treasury securities are liabilities of the U.S. Department of the Treasury, and in effect of the U.S. government, they are perceived to have virtually no credit risk. On the basis of credit risk, the yields on Treasury securities are thus lower than those of any private security.

Due to their large volume outstanding, the broad range of maturities available, the low credit risk, and the liquidity of their secondary market, Treasury securities are widely held. Holders of substantial amounts include foreign governments and government agencies, commercial banks, nonbank financial institutions, nonfinancial institutions, and individuals. Because of their unique characteristics and because they are widely held, Treasury debt securities make up a fundamental component of the securities markets and the basis for analyses of these markets.

It is important to distinguish between the two different types of marketable Treasury securities—discount and coupon securities. The fundamental difference between these two types of securities is the form in which the holder receives interest and, as a result, the prices at which they are issued.

On coupon securities explicit interest payments are periodically (typically every six months) made by the Treasury while the securities are outstanding. On the other hand, on discount securities there is no payment of interest by the Treasury to the holders from the time of issue until the maturity day when the principal is repaid. This difference in the way in which interest is paid causes a difference in issue prices between these two types of securities, as discussed below.

According to current Treasury practices, all Treasury securities with maturities of one year or less are issued as discount securities, and all securities with maturities of more than one year are issued as coupon securities. Treasury discount securities are called bills. Treasury coupon securities with maturities between 1 and 10 years are called notes, and with maturities of greater than 10 years are called bonds.

On coupon securities, the annual coupon is specified before the issue, and an amount equal to half the annual coupon is paid to the holder every six months, beginning six months after the issue date through the maturity date. For example, if a Treasury security is issued with an 8 percent coupon, a $40 payment is made every six months for a maturity value of $1,000.

Consider the issue prices of discount and coupon securities. Both issue prices are related to the maturity value or par value of the security, which is the amount paid by the Treasury to the holder of the security on the maturity day of the security. Since the coupon payment of coupon securities represents the payment of interest during the time the security is outstanding, the initial issue price of a Treasury coupon security is approximately the same as its maturity value. Thus Treasury coupon securities are issued at about par, the maturity value. If interest rates subsequently increase, the coupons of newly issued bonds will be higher, and thus the price of the bonds previously issued at lower coupons will sell at a price below its maturity value, that is "at a discount" to par. Contrarily, if interest rates subsequently decrease, the coupons of newly issued bonds will be lower than the coupon of the previously issued bonds, and thus the price of the bonds previously issued at higher coupons will sell at a price above its maturity value, that is "at a premium" to par. Note that interest rates and prices move in opposite directions.

On the other hand, because no explicit interest is paid on a discount security, the security must be issued at a price that is at a discount to its maturity value such that the difference between the initial discount price and the final maturity price represents the return to the holder of the security.

Exhibit 2 shows the relationship between issue prices and maturity values for Treasury discount and coupon securities.

There are two major components of the Treasury security market: (1) the primary market, that is, the market on which the securities are originally issued, and (2) the secondary market, that is, the market for the postissue trading of these securities.

Primary Market

Marketable securities are typically issued on an auction basis by the Treasury with the assistance of the Federal Reserve System.

The Treasury has found that it can reduce the rate at which it issues its debt, and thus its interest cost, particularly when issuing substantial amounts to fund large budget deficits, by issuing Treasury securities on a regular basis (i.e., having a stable schedule for auctioning securities with specific maturities). Such regularity provides the purchasers of Treasury debt with firm expectations regarding the timing of issuances of the various types of Treasury securities. The regularization of the Treasury funding process has developed such that there are now several regular cycles on which the Treasury auctions and issues specific maturities of debt. Exhibits 3 and 4 provide data on the recent issues according to these various cycles for discount securities and for coupon securities, respectively. A description of these cycles is provided in Exhibit 5. Exhibits 6 and 7 provide examples of Treasury announcements for the auctions and issues of Treasury discount and coupon securities, respectively.

Exhibit 2
Price Behavior of Treasury Discount and Coupon Securities

A. Treasury discount securities

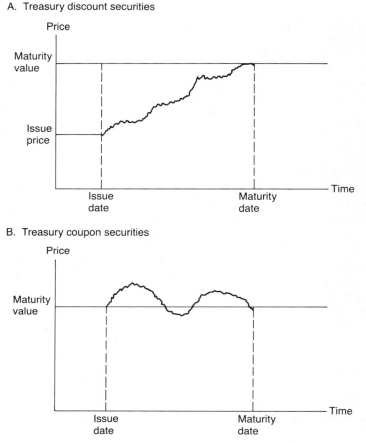

B. Treasury coupon securities

As indicated in Exhibits 3 and 5, there are three discount security (Treasury bill) cycles. Every Monday the Treasury auctions 91-day Treasury bills. These bills are issued on the following Thursday and mature on the Thursday 13-weeks (91 days) later. On the same cycle, every Monday the Treasury also auctions 182-day bills, which are issued on the following Thursday and mature on the Thursday 26 weeks, or 182 days, after their issue date. The third Treasury bill cycle is the "year bill" cycle. On this cycle, every fourth Thursday the Treasury auctions a 52-week Treasury bill, which is issued on the following Thursday and matures on the Thursday 52 weeks, or 364 days, later.

Note that initial 91-day and 182-day Treasury bills mature every Thursday, and initial 364-day Treasury bills mature every fourth Thursday. Note also that during the last 91 days of its maturity, an initial 182-day Treasury bill is indistinguishable from an initial 91-day Treasury bill issued 91 days after it. Likewise during the last 182 days of its maturity a 364-day Treasury bill is indistinguishable from an initial 182-day Treasury bill issued 182 days after it.

As indicated in Exhibits 4 and 5, there are several auction cycles for Treasury coupon issues. Although none of these cycles is immutable, the auction cycles for the two-year and four-year Treasury notes and the refunding cycle have been fairly stable during recent years. In addition, there have been 5-year and 20-year auction cycles.

Since it contains the Treasury long bond, typically 30 years in maturity, the refunding cycle is most important. The Treasury refunding cycle involves the issue of three coupon securities, typically a short note, a long note, and a long bond, during the February, May, August, and November quarterly cycle months. The securities to be auctioned and issued on the Treasury refunding cycle during the February, May, August and November quarterly cycle months are usually announced late in the month prior to auction, as illustrated in Exhibit 7. The three securities are auctioned on different days early in the refunding month and issued on the 15th day of the month. Typically the three issues include, with slight deviations, a 3½-year Treasury note (the short note), a 10-year Treasury note (the long note), and a long bond, which has usually had 30 years to maturity and 25 years to call.[1]

The fact that these Treasury cycles are not immutable is illustrated by two recent deviations. During 1979 the Treasury twice included only two securities in its refunding cycle, both times omitting the short-term note. During February 1979, the Treasury issued only an 8-year note and the 29-year, 9-month bill, and in May 1979 it issued only a 10-year and a 30-year bond. More recently, during January 1981, the Treasury began issuing a 20-year bond, actually a 20-year, 1-month bond, and discontinued the issue of the previously issued 15-year bond. The reason for the latter change appears to be that the 15-year bond had been generally considered to be unpopular, as indicated by the fact that its yield has been substantially above the Treasury yield curve. The immediate reaction to the 20-year cycle has been much more favorable; its yield has been closer to the yield curve than the

---

[1] By statute, the Treasury cannot issue bonds with coupons greater than 4.25 percent, which limits its ability to issue long-term debt. Originally, with respect to this statute, a bond was defined as any security over 5 years in maturity; as of 1976 a bond is now defined as any security over 10 years. Congress has granted exemptions to the ceiling on an annual basis. On October 1, 1980, the Treasury was authorized to have $70 billion of debt outstanding above the 4.25 percent ceiling. As of April 2, 1981, $58.6 billion of that authority had been used.

Exhibit 3
Treasury Bill Auctions

Issue Date	91 Day			182 Day			364 Day		
	Maturity	Amount ($ billions)	Rate	Maturity	Amount ($ billions)	Rate	Maturity	Amount ($ billions)	Rate
5/08/80	8/7	$3.5	9.728%	11/6	$3.5	9.495%	—	—	—
5/15/80	8/14	3.5	8.604	11/13	3.5	8.782			
5/22/80	8/21	3.5	8.953	11/20	3.5	8.923			
5/27/80							5/21/81#	$4.00	8.341%
5/29/80	8/28	3.5	7.675	11/28	3.5	7.753*			
6/05/80	9/4	3.9	8.036	12/4	3.8	8.165			
6/05/80	6/6	2.0		(2-day cash management bill)					
6/12/80	9/11	2.8	6.500	12/11	2.8	6.935			
6/19/80	9/18	3.9	6.369	12/18	3.9	6.662			
6/24/80							6/18/81#	4.00	7.491
6/26/80	9/25	3.5	7.077	12/26	3.5	7.108			
7/03/80	10/2	4.0	8.149	1/2/81	4.0	8.097†			
7/10/80	10/9	4.0	8.209	1/1/81	4.0	8.114			
7/17/80	10/16	4.0	8.169	1/15/81	4.0	8.110			
7/22/80							7/16/81#	4.00	7.669
7/24/80	10/23	4.0	7.881	1/22/81	4.0	7.906			
7/31/80	10/30	4.0	8.221	1/29/81	4.0	8.276			
8/07/80	11/6	4.0	8.877	2/5/81	4.0	8.867			
8/14/80	11/13	3.8	8.723	2/12/81	3.8	8.8915			
8/19/80							8/13/81#	4.00	8.963
8/04/80	9/16	3.0	8.498	(43-day cash management bill)					
8/21/80	11/20	3.8	9.411	2/19/81	3.8	9.765			
8/28/80	11/28	3.9	10.025‡	2/26/81	3.9	10.250			
9/04/80	12/4	3.8	10.124	3/5/81	3.8	10.250			
9/11/80	12/11	3.8	10.060	3/12/81	3.8	10.234			
9/16/80							9/10/81#	4.00	9.967
9/18/80	12/18	3.8	10.638	3/19/81	3.8	10.875			
9/25/80	12/26	3.8	10.460§	3/26/81	3.8	10.824			
10/02/80	1/2/81	3.9	11.524‖	4/2/81	4.0	11.718			
10/09/80	1/8/81	3.9	11.295	4/9/81	3.9	11.140			

Date	Rate	Price	Date	Rate	Price	Date	Rate	Value
10/14/80			4/16/81	3.9	11.281			
10/16/80	3.9	11.338	4/23/81	3.9	11.407	10/8/81*	4.00	11.136
10/23/80	3.9	11.413	4/30/81	3.9	12.284			
10/30/80	3.9	12.331	5/7/81	4.0	13.269			
11/06/80	4.0	13.344	5/14/81	4.0	13.231			
11/13/80	4.0	13.514	(44 day cash management bill)			11/5/81**	4.00	12.219
12/31/80	4.0	13.885	5/21/81	4.0	13.917			
11/20/80	4.0	14.309	5/28/81	4.2	14.030‡‡			
11/28/80	4.0	14.384††	6/4/81	4.3	14.544			
12/04/80	4.5	14.649	(141-day cash management bill)					
12/03/80	3.0	15.25	6/11/81	4.0	15.069	12/3/81	4.00	13.261
12/11/80	4.0	16.335	6/18/81	4.1	15.423			
12/18/80	4.2	16.667	6/25/81	4.0	14.032			
12/26/80	4.0	14.992	(120-day cash management bill)					
12/31/80	4.0	14.775	7/02/81	4.2	13.411			
1/02/81	4.3	13.908	(16-day cash management bill;			12/31/81	4.5	12.074
1/06/81	2.5	17.033	reopening)					
1/08/81	4.2	13.601	7/09/81	4.2	13.182			
1/15/81	4.3	15.317	7/16/81	4.3	14.228			
1/22/81	4.3	15.595	7/23/81	4.3	14.471	1/28/82	4.5	13.033
1/29/81	4.3	15.199	7/30/81	4.3	14.121			
2/05/81	4.3	14.657	8/06/81	4.3	13.735			
2/12/81	4.5	15.397	8/13/81	4.5	14.430			
2/19/81	4.3	15.464	8/20/81	4.3	14.760			
2/26/81	4.3	14.103	8/27/81	4.3	13.611	2/25/82	4.5	12.801
3/05/81	4.3	14.463	9/03/81	4.3	14.133			
3/12/81	4.3	13.996	9/10/81	4.3	13.427			
3/19/81	4.3	12.758	9/17/81	4.3	12.096			
3/26/81	4.3	12.695	9/24/81	4.3	12.274	3/25/82	4.5	11.481
4/01/81	6.0	13.672	(22-day cash management bill; reopening 4/29/80 issue)					
4/02/81	4.3	12.501	10/01/81	4.3	12.078			
4/09/81	4.3	14.147	10/08/81	4.3	13.783			
4/16/81	4.0	13.783	10/15/81	4.0	13.646	4/22/82	4.5	12.991
4/23/81	4.0	13.553	10/22/81	4.0	13.621			

Exhibit 3 (*concluded*)

Issue Date	91 Day			182 Day			364 Day		
	Maturity	Amount ($ billions)	Rate	Maturity	Amount ($ billions)	Rate	Maturity	Amount ($ billions)	Rate
4/30/81	7/30/81	4.0	14.190	10/29/81	4.0	14.042			
5/07/81	8/06/81	4.0	15.963	11/05/81	4.0	15.104			
5/14/81	8/13/81	4.0	16.433	11/12/81	4.0	15.531	5/20/82	4.0	14.623
5/21/81	8/20/81	4.0	16.034	11/19/81	4.0	15.025			
5/28/81	8/27/81	4.0	16.750	11/27/81	4.0	15.675			
6/05/81	6/25/81	6.0	17.946	(20-day cash management bill)					
6/03/81	6/18/81	3.0	18.480	(15-day cash management bill)					
6/04/81	9/03/81	4.0	15.456	12/03/81	4.0	14.491			
6/11/81	9/10/81	4.0	14.982	12/10/81	4.0	14.000			
6/18/81	9/17/81	4.0	13.451	12/17/81	4.0	13.356	6/17/82	4.0	13.146
6/25/81	9/24/81	4.0	14.337	12/24/81	4.0	13.939			
7/02/81	10/01/81	4.0	13.909	12/31/81	4.0	13.621			
7/09/81	10/08/81	4.0	14.400	1/07/82	4.0	14.050			
7/16/81	10/15/81	4.0	14.558	1/14/82	4.0	14.230	7/15/82	4.0	13.735
7/23/81	10/22/81	4.0	15.563	1/21/82	4.0	15.318			
7/30/81	10/29/81	4.3	15.065	1/28/82	4.3	14.790			
8/04/81	8/27/81	3.0	16.200	(23-day cash management bill)					
8/06/81	11/05/81	4.3	15.674	2/04/82	4.3	15.571			
8/13/81	11/12/81	4.3	15.235	2/11/82	4.3	15.122	8/12/82	4.5	14.542
8/20/81	11/19/81	4.5	15.705	2/18/82	4.5	15.644			
8/27/81	11/26/81	4.5	15.832	2/25/82	4.5	15.854			
9/01/81	9/17/81	4.5	16.313	(16-day cash management bill)					
9/03/81	12/03/81	4.5	15.583	3/04/82	4.5	15.646			
9/10/81	12/10/81	4.5	15.611	3/11/82	4.5	15.795	9/09/82	4.75	15.056
9/10/81	9/17/81	2.0	17.280	(9-day cash management bill)					
9/17/81	12/17/81	4.5	14.412	3/18/82	4.5	14.657			
9/24/81	12/24/81	4.5	14.198	3/25/82	4.5	14.129			
10/01/81	12/31/81	4.5	14.669	4/01/82	4.5	14.932			
10/08/81	1/07/82	4.5	14.206	4/08/82	4.5	14.218	10/07/83	5.0	14.580

Date	Rate	Yield	364-day Mat. Date	Rate	Yield
10/15/81	4.5	13.526			
10/22/81	4.5	13.613			
10/29/81	4.7	13.352			
11/05/81	4.7	12.695	11/04/82	5.0	13.159
11/12/81	4.7	11.128			
11/19/81	4.7	10.693			
11/27/81	4.7	10.560			
12/03/81	4.7	10.400	12/02/82	5.0	10.506
12/07/81	3.0	10.656			
12/07/81	2.0	11.186			
12/10/81	4.7	10.404			
12/17/81	4.7	11.101			
12/24/81	4.7	11.037			
12/31/81	4.9	11.690	12/30/82	5.25	12.501
1/05/82	3.0	12.326			
1/07/82	4.9	11.658			
1/14/82	4.9	12.121			
1/21/82	4.9	12.505			
1/28/82	5.0	13.364	11/27/83	5.25	13.143
2/04/82	5.0	13.85			
2/11/82	5.0	14.099			
2/18/82	5.0	14.74			
2/25/82	4.9	12.430	2/24/83	5.25	13.180

Date	Rate	Yield
4/15/82	4.5	13.500
4/22/82	4.5	13.795
4/29/82	4.7	13.619
5/06/82	4.7	12.721
5/13/82	4.7	11.510
5/20/82	4.7	10.972
5/27/82	4.7	10.915
6/03/82	4.7	10.701
(45-day cash management bill)		
(163-day cash management bill)		
6/10/82	4.7	10.772
6/17/82	4.7	11.595
6/24/82	4.7	11.838
7/01/82	4.9	12.448
(163-day cash management bill)		
7/08/82	4.9	12.282
7/15/82	4.9	12.806
7/22/82	4.9	13.102
7/29/82	5.0	13.530
8/05/82	5.0	13.846
8/12/82	5.0	13.933
8/19/82	5.0	14.36
8/26/82	4.9	12.695

* 183 day—matures on Thanksgiving.
† 183 day—matures on New Year's Day.
‡ 92 day—matures on Thanksgiving.
§ 92 day—matures on Christmas Day.
‖ 92 day—matures on New Year's Day.
* 359 day—Tuesday issue—Thursday maturity.
** 364 day—First-Thursday issue—Thursday maturity cycle.
†† 90 day—Issued on Friday.
‡‡ 181 day—Issued on Friday.

Exhibit 4
Treasury Coupon Security Auctions

Cycle	*Issue Date*	*Maturity*	*Coupon*	*Maturity Date*	*Amount ($ billions)*	*Rate*
(R)	05/15/80	3¼ years	9¼%	08/15/83	$3.5	9.32%
(R)	05/15/80	9½ years	10¾	11/15/89	2.0	9.88
(R)	05/15/80	30 years	10	05/15/10	2.0	10.12
(5/15)	06/05/80*	5 years, 2½ months	9⅝	08/15/85	3.0	9.66
(2)	06/04/80*	2 years	9⅜	05/31/82	4.0	9.37
(2)	06/30/80	2 years	8⅝	06/30/82	4.26	8.63
(4)	06/30/80	4 years	8⅞	06/30/84	3.2†	8.99
(5/15)	07/09/80	14 years, 10 months	10⅜	05/15/95	1.5	10.42
(2)	07/31/80	2 years	8⅞	07/31/82	4.5	8.97
(R)	08/15/80	29¼ years	10⅜	11/15/09	1.5	10.71
(R)	08/15/80	10 years	10¾	08/15/90	2.75	10.81
(R)	08/15/80	3¼ years	9⅞	11/15/83	4.51	9.88
(2)	09/02/80	2 years	11⅛	08/31/82	4.5	11.24
(5/15)	09/03/80	5 years, 2½ months	11¾	11/15/85	3.0	11.76
(2)	09/30/80	2 years	11⅞	09/30/82	4.5	11.93
(4)	09/30/80	4 years	12⅛	09/30/84	3.0	12.13
(5/15)	10/14/80	15 years, 1 month	11½	11/15/95	1.5	11.61
(2)	10/31/80	2 years	12⅛	10/31/82	4.3	12.24
(R)	11/17/80	3 years, 6 months	13¼	05/15/84	3.75	13.31
(R)	11/17/80	10 years	13	11/15/90	2.25	13.07
(R)	11/17/80	30 years	12¾	11/15/10	2.0	12.81
(2)	12/01/80	2 years	13⅞	11/30/82	4.5	13.99
(5/15)	12/08/80	5 years, 2½ months	13½	02/15/86	3.0	13.52
(2)	12/31/80	2 years	15⅛	12/31/82	4.5	15.15
(4)	12/31/80	4 years	14	12/31/84	3.3	14.03
—	01/05/81	7 years	12⅜	01/15/88	2.5	12.49
(20)	01/12/81	20 years, 1 month	11¾	02/15/01	1.5	11.82
(2)	02/02/81	2 years	13⅝	01/31/83	4.5	13.69
(R)	02/17/81	3½ years	13¼	08/15/84	3.85	13.37
(R)	02/17/81	9 years, 9 months‡	13	11/15/90	2.5	12.89
(R)	02/17/81	29¾ years	12¾	11/15/10	2.25	12.68
(2)	03/02/81	2 years	13⅞	02/28/83	5.4	13.97
—	03/04/81	5 years, 2 months	13¾	05/15/86	3.3	13.79
(2)	03/31/81	2 years	12⅝	03/31/83	4.75	12.65
(4)	03/31/81	4 years	13⅜	03/31/85	3.5	13.49
(20)	04/02/81	20 years, 1 month	13⅛	05/15/01	1.75	13.21
—	04/06/81	7 years	13¼	04/15/88	2.75	13.34

(2)	04/30/81	2 years	14½	04/30/83	4.25	14.58
(R)	05/15/81	3 years	15¾	05/15/84	3.0	15.81
(R)	05/15/81	10 years	14½	05/15/91	1.75	14.56
(R)	05/15/81	30 years	13⅞	05/15/11	2.0	13.99
(2)	06/01/81	2 years	15⅝	05/31/83	4.25	15.72
(5/15)	06/03/81	5 years, 5 months	13⅞	11/15/86	3.0	13.95
(2)	06/30/81	2 years	14⅝	06/30/83	4.25	14.72
(4)	06/30/81	4 years	14	06/30/85	3.25	14.04
(20)	07/02/81	20 years, 1 month	13⅜	08/15/01	1.75	13.45
(5/15)	07/15/81	7 years	14	07/15/88	3.00	14.07
(2)	07/31/81	2 years	15⅞	07/31/83	4.5	15.92
(R)	08/17/81	3¼ years	16	11/15/84	4.25	15.96
(R)	08/17/81	10 years	14⅞	08/15/91	2.25	14.98
(R)	08/17/81	29¾ years‖	13⅞	05/15/11	2.0	14.06
(2)	08/31/81	2 years	16¼	08/31/83	4.75	16.26
(5/15)	09/08/81	5 years, 2 months	16⅛	11/15/86	3.25	16.14
(2)	09/30/81	2 years	16	09/30/83	4.75	16.12
(4)	09/30/81	4 years	15⅞	09/30/85	3.25	15.91
(20)	10/07/81	20 years, 1 month	15¾	11/15/01	1.75	15.78
(5/15)	10/14/81	7 years	15⅜	10/15/88	3.0	15.40
(2)	11/02/81	2 years	15½	10/31/83	4.75	15.56
(R)	11/16/81	3 years	14⅜	11/15/84	4.5	14.43
(R)	11/16/81	10 years	14¼	11/15/91	2.25	14.33
(R)	11/16/81	30 years	14	11/15/11	2.0	14.10
(2)	11/30/81	2 years	12⅛	11/30/83	4.8	—
(5/15)	12/02/81	5 years, 2 months	12¾	02/15/87	3.25	12.83
(2)	12/31/81	2 years	13	12/31/83	4.75	13.06
(4)	12/31/81	4 years	14⅛	12/31/85	3.25	14.16
(20)	01/06/82	20 years, 1 month	14¼	02/15/02	1.75	14.25
(7)	01/13/82	7 years	14⅝	01/15/89	3.25	14.74
(2)	02/01/82	2 years	15	01/31/84	5.25	15.08
(R)	02/16/82	3 years	14⅝	02/15/85	5.01	14.63
(R)	02/16/82	10 years	14⅝	02/15/92	2.5	14.68
(R)	02/16/82	29 years, 9 months#	14	11/15/11	2.5	14.56
(2)	03/01/82	2 years	15⅛	02/29/84	5.25	15.21

* Postponed due to uncertainty over changing of the national debt ceiling.
† Reduced $50,000 because of debt ceiling.
‡ Reopening of 13 percent of 11/15/90 issued during November 1980.
§ Reopening of 12¾ percent of 11/15/10 issued during November 1980.
‖ Reopening of 13⅞ percent of 5/15/11 issued during May 1981.
\# Reopening of 14 percent of 11/15/11 issued during November 1981.

15-year bond yield has been. Thus the Treasury has every quarter since January 1981 issued a 20-year, 1-month bond on the January, April, July, and October quarterly cycle, which thus mature on the refunding cycle months.

Both Treasury bills and Treasury coupon issues are sold on an

Exhibit 5
Treasury Auction Cycles

Discount securities:

Three-month (91-day) Treasury bills	Auctioned every Monday; issued on the following Thursday.
Six-month (182-day) Treasury bills	Same auction and issue cycle as for three-month Treasury bills. Thus, 182-day Treasury bills eventually trade in consonance with 91-day Treasury bills.
Fifty-two week (364-day) Treasury bills	Auctioned every fourth Thursday; issued the following Thursday. Thus 364-day Treasury bills eventually trade in consonance with 182-day and then 91-day Treasury bills.

Coupon securities:

(2)	*Two-year Treasury notes:* Every month, normally near the end of the month (although often substantially before or after the end of the month), a two-year note is auctioned and issued that matures at the end of the month 24 months hence.
(4)	*Four-year Treasury notes:* Four-year Treasury notes are auctioned and issued during the last weeks of the March/June/September/December quarterly cycle months for maturity on the last day of these months four years hence. These notes eventually become two-year notes and thereafter trade in consonance with newly issued two-year notes.
(5/15) *5-year/15-year*	Typically, on the January, April, July, October quarterly cycle, the Treasury auctions and issues, during alternate quarters, 5-year notes and 15-year bonds. These bonds are dated to mature on the 15th day of the February/May/August/November quarterly cycle months (and thus the long-term notes and bonds issued on the refunding cycle eventually trade in consonance with these issues—see below). This cycle, however, has not followed this pattern without exception. For example, a 15-year bond was substituted for a 5-year note as issued on 10/10/78 (to mature on 2/15/93) and on 4/18/79 (to mature on 2/15/94). And an extra 5-year note was issued on 9/3/80 (to mature on 11/15/85).

Exhibit 5 (*concluded*)

(R) *Refunding cycle*	The refunding cycle is based on the quarterly February/May/August/November cycle months. Refunding cycle notes and bonds are issued on the 15th day of the February/May/August/November months and are auctioned on different days during the two weeks prior to the issue. Each refunding issue has typically contained three issues: (1) an anchor issue note in the 3- to 3½-year range, (2) a longer term note, typically between 7 and 10 years, and (3) a long-term bond, typically between 20 and 30 years. The issues in the refunding cycle are subject to some variations, however. For example, during two recent auctions (May 1979 and February 1979, for example) there were only two auctioned.

auction basis. Treasury bills are auctioned on a price basis wherein the bids are made on the basis of the price, to not more than three decimal places (e.g., 98.237). Bids are taken by the Treasury and securities allocated from the high price to the low price until the Treasury has allocated the total amount of the announced issue. The successful bids are awarded at their actual bid price. Those who have bid at the lower prices are not allocated bills. Bids may also be made on a non-competitive basis. Such bids include no price, only a quantity. These bids are completely allocated at the average price of the successful bids. Noncompetitive bids are usually made by small, noninstitutional savers and tend to increase during periods of high interest rates, when Treasury yields surpass the return on savings accounts and similar instruments.

Different auction methods have been used by the Treasury for auctioning coupon issues. The most common auction method is to require the bids to be made on a *yield* basis, to two decimal points, for example 11.27 percent. The Treasury then allocates the securities, beginning with the lowest yield bid to the highest yield until the announced amount is fully subscribed. The average yield of those receiving an allocation is used to determine the coupon of the newly issued bonds. The coupon is usually set slightly less than the average yield so that the new bonds are issued at a slight discount to par. The price paid by each successful bidder is determined from the coupon on the issue established by the Treasury and the yield bid by the particular bidder.

If the current yield on an outstanding bond of approximately the same maturity as that which the Treasury plans to auction is approximately the same as the coupon on the outstanding issue (that is, the issue is trading at about par), the Treasury may announce the reissue of this outstanding security (i.e., an additional amount of this outstanding security is auctioned). In this case, since the coupon is predetermined, the auction is done on a price basis rather than on a yield basis.

Exhibit 6

FEDERAL RESERVE BANK OF NEW YORK
Fiscal Agent of the United States

[Circular No. 9049]
[April 8, 1981]

OFFERING OF TWO SERIES OF TREASURY BILLS

$4,000,000,000 of 91-Day Bills, To Be Issued April 16, 1981, Due July 16, 1981

$4,000,000,000 of 182-Day Bills, To Be Issued April 16, 1981, Due October 15, 1981

To All Incorporated Banks and Trust Companies, and Others Concerned, in the Second Federal Reserve District:

Following is the text of a notice issued by the Treasury Department:

The Department of the Treasury, by this public notice, invites tenders for two series of Treasury bills totaling approximately $8,000 million, to be issued April 16, 1981. This offering will result in a paydown for the Treasury of about $275 million, as the regular 13-week and 26-week bill maturities were issued in the amount of $8,279 million. The $3,000 million of additional issue 38-day cash management bills issued March 9 and maturing April 16, 1981, will be redeemed at maturity.

The $8,279 million of regular maturities includes $2,284 million currently held by Federal Reserve Banks as agents for foreign and international monetary authorities and $1,772 million currently held by Federal Reserve Banks for their own account. The two series offered are as follows:

91-day bills (to maturity date) for approximately $4,000 million, representing an additional amount of bills dated July 22, 1980, and to mature July 16, 1981 (CUSIP No. 912793 6W1), currently outstanding in the amount of $8,339 million, the additional and original bills to be freely interchangeable.

182-day bills for approximately $4,000 million, to be dated April 16, 1981, and to mature October 15, 1981 (CUSIP No. 912793 7W0).

Both series of bills will be issued for cash and in exchange for Treasury bills maturing April 16, 1981. Tenders from Federal Reserve Banks for themselves and as agents for foreign and international monetary authorities will be accepted at the weighted average prices of accepted competitive tenders. Additional amounts of the bills may be issued to Federal Reserve Banks, as agents for foreign and international monetary authorities, to the extent that the aggregate amount of tenders for such accounts exceeds the aggregate amount of maturing bills held by them.

The bills will be issued on a discount basis under competitive and noncompetitive bidding, and at maturity their par amount will be payable without interest. Both series of bills will be issued entirely in book-entry form in a minimum amount of $10,000 and in any higher $5,000 multiple, on the records either of the Federal Reserve Banks and Branches, or of the Department of the Treasury.

Tenders will be received at Federal Reserve Banks and Branches and at the Bureau of the Public Debt, Washington, D.C. 20226, up to 1:30 p.m., Eastern Standard time, Monday, April 13, 1981. Form PD 4632-2 (for 26-week series) or Form PD 4632-3 (for 13-week series) should be used to submit tenders for bills to be maintained on the book-entry records of the Department of the Treasury.

Each tender must be for a minimum of $10,000. Tenders over $10,000 must be in multiples of $5,000. In the case of competitive tenders the price offered must be expressed on the basis of 100, with not more than three decimals, e.g., 99.925. Fractions may not be used.

Banking institutions and dealers who make primary markets in Government securities and report daily to the Federal Reserve Bank of New York their positions in and borrowings on such securities may submit tenders for account of customers, if the names of the customers and the amount for each customer are furnished. Others are only permitted to submit tenders for their

own account. Each tender must state the amount of any net long position in the bills being offered if such position is in excess of $200 million. This information should reflect positions held as of 12:30 p.m., Eastern time, on the day of the auction. Such positions would include bills acquired through "when issued" trading, and futures and forward transactions as well as holdings of outstanding bills with the same maturity date as the new offering, e.g., bills with three months to maturity previously offered as six month bills. Dealers, who make primary markets in Government securities and report daily to the Federal Reserve Bank of New York their positions in and borrowings on such securities, when submitting tenders for customers, must submit a separate tender for each customer whose net long position in the bill being offered exceeds $200 million.

Payment for the full par amount of the bills applied for must accompany all tenders submitted for bills to be maintained on the book-entry records of the Department of the Treasury. A cash adjustment will be made on all accepted tenders for the difference between the par payment submitted and the actual issue price as determined in the auction.

No deposit need accompany tenders from incorporated banks and trust companies and from responsible and recognized dealers in investment securities for bills to be maintained on the book-entry records of Federal Reserve Banks and Branches.

Public announcement will be made by the Department of the Treasury of the amount and price range of accepted bids. Competitive bidders will be advised of the acceptance or rejection of their tenders. The Secretary of the Treasury expressly reserves the right to accept or reject any or all tenders, in whole or in part, and the Secretary's action shall be final. Subject to these reservations, noncompetitive tenders for each issue for $500,000 or less without stated price from any one bidder will be accepted in full at the weighted average price (in three decimals) of accepted competitive bids for the respective issues.

Settlement for accepted tenders for bills to be maintained on the book-entry records of Federal Reserve Banks and Branches must be made or completed at the Federal Reserve Bank or Branch on April 16, 1981, in cash or other immediately available funds or in Treasury bills maturing April 16, 1981. Cash adjustments will be made for differences between the par value of the maturing bills accepted in exchange and the issue price of the new bills.

Under Sections 454(b) and 1221(5) of the Internal Revenue Code of 1954 the amount of discount at which these bills are sold is considered to accrue when the bills are sold, redeemed or otherwise disposed of, and the bills are excluded from consideration as capital assets. Accordingly, the owner of these bills (other than life insurance companies) must include in his or her Federal income tax return, as ordinary gain or loss, the difference between the price paid for the bills, whether on original issue or on subsequent purchase, and the amount actually received either upon sale or redemption at maturity during the taxable year for which the return is made.

Department of the Treasury Circulars, Public Debt Series—Nos. 26-76 and 27-76, and this notice, prescribe the terms of these Treasury bills and govern the conditions of their issue. Copies of the circulars and tender forms may be obtained from any Federal Reserve Bank or Branch, or from the Bureau of the Public Debt.

This Bank will receive tenders for both series up to 1:30 p.m., Eastern Standard time, Monday, April 13, 1981, at the Securities Department of its Head Office and at its Buffalo Branch. Tender forms for both series are enclosed. Please use the appropriate forms to submit tenders and return them in the enclosed envelope marked "Tender for Treasury Bills." Forms for submitting tenders directly to the Treasury are available from the Government Bond Division of this Bank. Tenders not requiring a deposit may be submitted by telegraph, subject to written confirmation; no tenders may be submitted by telephone. *Payment for Treasury bills cannot be made by credit through the Treasury Tax and Loan Account. Settlement must be made in cash or other immediately available funds or in Treasury securities maturing on or before the issue date.*

Results of the last weekly offering of Treasury bills are shown on the reverse side of this circular.

ANTHONY M. SOLOMON,
President.

Exhibit 6 (*concluded*)

RESULTS OF LAST WEEKLY OFFERING OF TREASURY BILLS
(TWO SERIES TO BE ISSUED APRIL 9, 1981)

Range of Accepted Competitive Bids

	91-Day Treasury Bills *Maturing July 9, 1981*			*182-Day Treasury Bills* *Maturing October 8, 1981*		
	Price	Discount Rate	Investment Rate[1]	Price	Discount Rate	Investment Rate[1]
High	96.486[a]	13.902%	14.61%	93.180[b]	13.490%	14.68%
Low	96.400	14.242%	14.98%	92.972	13.902%	15.16%
Average	96.424	14.147%	14.88%	93.032	13.783%	15.02%

[1] Equivalent coupon-issue yield.   [b] Excepting one tender of $680,000.
[a] Excepting two tenders totaling $20,000.

(30 percent of the amount of 91-day bills   (62 percent of the amount of 182-day bills
bid for at the low price was accepted.)   bid for at the low price was accepted.)

Total Tenders Received and Accepted

	91-Day Treasury Bills *Maturing July 9, 1981*		*182-Day Treasury Bills* *Maturing October 8, 1981*	
By F.R. District (and U.S. Treasury)	Received	Accepted	Received	Accepted
Boston	$ 71,470,000	$ 48,970,000	$ 67,560,000	$ 47,560,000
New York	6,263,410,000	3,059,410,000	5,081,445,000	3,263,445,000
Philadelphia	34,675,000	34,675,000	19,955,000	19,955,000
Cleveland	56,095,000	51,095,000	131,310,000	101,310,000
Richmond	55,055,000	55,055,000	44,035,000	44,035,000
Atlanta	58,480,000	58,480,000	58,210,000	58,210,000
Chicago	881,035,000	501,035,000	443,895,000	208,895,000
St. Louis	28,625,000	26,625,000	24,440,000	24,440,000
Minneapolis	13,860,000	13,860,000	10,740,000	10,140,000
Kansas City	51,810,000	51,810,000	38,155,000	38,155,000
Dallas	25,040,000	25,040,000	15,315,000	15,315,000
San Francisco	439,250,000	187,250,000	441,580,000	227,580,000
U.S. Treasury	187,535,000	187,535,000	241,855,000	241,855,000
TOTALS	$8,166,340,000	$4,300,840,000	$6,618,495,000	$4,300,895,000
By class of bidder Public				
Competitive	$5,969,120,000	$2,103,620,000	$4,103,905,000	$1,786,305,000
Noncompetitive	922,420,000	922,420,000	783,730,000	783,730,000
SUBTOTALS	$6,891,540,000	$3,026,040,000	$4,887,635,000	$2,570,035,000
Federal Reserve	900,000,000	900,000,000	737,460,000	737,460,000
Foreign Official Institutions	374,800,000	374,800,000	993,400,000	993,400,000
TOTALS	$8,166,340,000	$4,300,840,000	$6,618,495,000	$4,300,895,000

Secondary Market

The secondary market for Treasury securities is the most liquid financial market in the world. This market is "made" by a group of U.S. government securities dealers who continually provide bids and offers on outstanding Treasuries. A current list of primary reporting dealers as specified by the Federal Reserve Bank of New York (FRBNY) is provided in Exhibit 8.

Dealers continuously provide bids and offers on specific outstanding government securities, buying for and selling from their inventories. Dealers' earnings are derived from three sources. First, dealers profit from their market making through the difference in their bid/ask quotes, the spread. The bid/ask spread is a measure of the liquidity of the market for the issue, as discussed below. Second, to the extent that dealers hold inventories, they also profit from price appreciation of their inventories (or price depreciation of securities they have shorted) but experience a loss from their inventory positions if prices decline. Finally, dealers may profit on the basis of "carry," the difference between the interest return on the securities they hold and the

Exhibit 7

**FEDERAL RESERVE BANK
OF NEW YORK**
Fiscal Agent of the United States

Circular No. **8944**
October 30, 1980

TREASURY ANNOUNCES NOVEMBER QUARTERLY FINANCING

*To All Banking Institutions, and Others Concerned,
in the Second Federal Reserve District:*

The following statement was issued yesterday by the Treasury Department:

The Treasury will raise about $3,100 million of new cash and refund $4,922 million of securities maturing November 15, 1980, by issuing $3,750 million of 3½-year notes, $2,250 million of 10-year notes and $2,000 million of 30-year bonds.

The $4,922 million of maturing securities are those held by the public, including $752 million held, as of today, by Federal Reserve Banks as agents for foreign and international monetary authorities. In addition to the public holdings, Government accounts and Federal Reserve Banks, for their own accounts, hold $1,401 million of the maturing securities that may be refunded by issuing additional amounts of new securities. Additional amounts of the new securities may also be issued to Federal Reserve Banks, as agents for foreign and international monetary authorities, to the extent that the aggregate amount of tenders for such accounts exceeds the aggregate amount of maturing securities held by them.

Printed on the reverse side is a table summarizing the highlights of the offerings. Copies of the official offering circulars will be furnished upon request directed to our Government Bond Division (Tel. No. 212-791-6619). In addition, enclosed are copies of the forms to be used in submitting tenders.

This Bank will receive tenders at the Securities Department of its Head Office and at its Buffalo Branch up to 1:30 p.m., Eastern Standard time, on the dates specified on the reverse side of this circular as the deadlines for receipt of tenders. *All competitive tenders,* whether transmitted by mail or by other means, must reach this Bank or its Branch by that time on the specified dates. However, for investors who wish to submit noncompetitive tenders and who find it more convenient to mail their tenders than to present them in person, the official offering circular for each offering provides that *noncompetitive* tenders will be considered timely received if they are mailed to this Bank or its Branch under a postmark no later than the date preceding the date specified for receipt of tenders.

Bidders submitting noncompetitive tenders should realize that it is possible that the average price may be above par, in which case they would have to pay more than the face value for the securities.

Payment with a tender may be in the form of a personal check, which need not be certified, an official bank check, or a Federal funds check (a check drawn by a depository institution on its Federal Reserve account). Please note that the Treasury Department has now authorized us to accept checks or drafts drawn on money market or mutual funds. All checks must be drawn payable to the Federal Reserve Bank of New York; *checks endorsed to this Bank will not be accepted.* Payment may also be made in cash or in Treasury securities maturing on or before the issue date of the securities being purchased.

Recorded messages provide information about Treasury offerings and about auction results: at the Head Office — Tel. No. 212-791-7773 (offerings) and Tel. No. 212-791-5823 (results); at the Buffalo Branch — Tel. No. 716-849-5046. Additional inquiries regarding these offerings may be made by calling, at the Head Office, Tel. No. 212-791-6619, or, at the Buffalo Branch, Tel. No. 716-849-5016.

ANTHONY M. SOLOMON,
President.

Exhibit 7 (*concluded*)

HIGHLIGHTS OF TREASURY
OFFERINGS TO THE PUBLIC
IN NOVEMBER 1980 FINANCING

SECURITIES TO BE ISSUED NOVEMBER 17, 1980

	3½-Year Notes	10-Year Notes	30-Year Bonds
Amount Offered:			
To the public	$3,750 million	$2,250 million	$2,000 million
Description of Security:			
Term and type of security	3½-year notes	10-year notes	30-year bonds
Series and CUSIP designation	Series G-1984 (CUSIP No. 912827 LE0)	Series B-1990 (CUSIP No. 912827 LF7)	Bonds of 2005-2010 (CUSIP No. 912810 CS5)
Maturity date	May 15, 1984	November 15, 1990	November 15, 2010
Call date	No provision	No provision	November 15, 2005
Interest coupon rate	To be determined, based on the average of accepted bids	To be determined, based on the average of accepted bids	To be determined, based on the average of accepted bids
Investment yield	To be determined at auction	To be determined at auction	To be determined at auction
Premium or discount	To be determined after auction	To be determined after auction	To be determined after auction
Interest payment dates	May 15 and November 15	May 15 and November 15	May 15 and November 15
Minimum denomination available	$5,000	$1,000	$1,000
Terms of Sale:			
Method of sale	Yield auction	Yield auction	Yield auction
Accrued interest payable by investor	None	None	None
Preferred allotment	Noncompetitive bid for $1,000,000 or less	Noncompetitive bid for $1,000,000 or less	Noncompetitive bid for $1,000,000 or less
Payment by non-institutional investors	**Full payment to be submitted with tender**	**Full payment to be submitted with tender**	**Full payment to be submitted with tender**
Deposit guarantee by designated institutions	Acceptable	Acceptable	Acceptable
Key Dates:			
Deadline for receipt of tenders	**Wednesday, November 5, 1980, by 1:30 p.m., EST**	**Thursday, November 6, 1980, by 1:30 p.m., EST**	**Friday, November 7, 1980, by 1:30 p.m., EST**
Settlement date (final payment due from institutions)			
a) cash or Federal funds	Monday, November 17, 1980	Monday, November 17, 1980	Monday, November 17, 1980
b) readily collectible check	Thursday, November 13, 1980	Thursday, November 13, 1980	Thursday, November 13, 1980
Delivery date for coupon securities	**Monday, November 24, 1980**	**Monday, November 24, 1980**	**Friday, November 28, 1980**

financing costs of these securities. Dealers, typically, do not have sufficient capital to own outright the securities they hold in their inventory, so their inventories are financed. When the interest return on the securities they hold is greater than the financing cost, a "positive carry" exists, and thus a profit results from this differential. In the opposite case of "negative carry," dealers experience a loss from carrying their inventory.

Since dealer financing is of a very short maturity and the securities held in inventory are almost always of a longer maturity, the carry is positive when long-term interest rates are higher than short-term in-

Exhibit 8
List of the Government Securities Dealers Reporting to the
Domestic Reports Division of the Federal Reserve Bank of
New York

ACLI Government Securities, Inc.
Bache Halsey Stuart Shields Inc.
Bank of America NT & SA
Bankers Trust Company
A. G. Becker Incorporated
Briggs, Schaedle & Co., Inc.
Carroll McEntee & McGinley Incorporated
The Chase Manhattan Bank, N. A.
Chemical Bank
Citibank, N. A.
Continental Illinois National Bank & Trust Company of Chicago
Crocker National Bank
Discount Corporation of New York
Donaldson Lufkin & Jenrette Securities Corporation
The First Boston Corporation
First National Bank of Chicago
Goldman, Sachs & Co.
Harris Trust and Savings Bank
E. F. Hutton & Company, Inc.
Kidder, Peabody & Co., Incorporated
Aubrey G. Lanston & Co., Inc.
Lehman Government Securities Incorporated
Merrill Lynch Government Securities Inc.
Morgan Guaranty Trust Company of New York
Morgan Stanley & Co., Inc.
The Northern Trust Company
Paine, Webber, Jackson & Curtis Incorporated
Wm. E. Pollock & Co., Inc.
Chas. E. Quincey & Co.
Salomon Brothers
Smith Barney, Harris Upham & Co., Incorporated
Stuart Brothers N.Y. Hanseatic Division
United California Bank
Dean Witter Reynolds Incorporated

Note: This list has been compiled and made available for statistical purposes only and has no significance with respect to other relationships between dealers and the Federal Reserve Bank of New York. Qualification for
the reporting list is based on the achievement and maintenance of reasonable
standards of activity.
Source: Domestic Reports Division, Federal Reserve Bank of New York,
August 28, 1980.

terest rates and negative when short-term interest rates are higher
than long-term interest rates.[2] Obviously, when carry is negative, the
dealers generate a loss on carrying their inventories and attempt to
minimize the size of their inventory for this reason.

The typical mechanism for financing Treasury securities is the repurchase agreement, or "repo," which is basically a collaterized loan

---

[2] This relationship between short-term and long-term interest rates is the basis for
the yield curve, as discussed in the next section.

wherein the Treasury securities owned by the dealer are used as collateral to the lender on the loan to the dealer. Repurchase agreements are typically of very short maturity, commonly one day. Longer repurchase agreements are called term repos. The market for term repos becomes quite thin as the maturity lengthens.

The secondary market for Treasury securities also includes brokers who intermediate between dealers. However, brokers, unlike dealers, do not buy and sell for their own inventories but simply arrange trades between dealers for a commission. The dealers pay the brokers a commission for arranging trades between themselves and others. Currently there are four Treasury securities brokers.

Bids and offers in the dealer market for Treasury bills are made on a discount basis, not a price basis, in basis points. (A basis point is 1/100th of 1 percent in discount return; for example, the difference between 10.00 percent and 10.01 percent is one basis point.) Thus a bid/offer quote may be 11.63 percent/11.61 percent. This discount is converted into a price for delivery, as discussed below.

On the other hand, bids and offers for coupon instruments are made on the basis of price to 1/32 of 1 percent of par, which is taken to be $100. For example a quote of 97−19 refers to a price of 97 and 19/32. Thus, on the basis of $100,000 par value, a change in a price of 1 percent is consistent with $1,000 and 1/32 with $31.25. Exhibit 9 provides an example of dealer quotes for the most actively traded Treasury securities, and a selection of other securities.

The government securities dealers work closely with the Federal Reserve System and the Treasury in several ways. First and most importantly, the FRBNY, on behalf of the Board of Governors of the Federal Reserve System (hereafter Fed), conducts its open-market operations and its repo and reverse repo transactions through auctions with the primary dealers. Such activities are conducted by the FRBNY among the dealers on an auction basis in a matter of minutes. Second, as a basis of its conduct of monetary policy, the FRBNY gets information on a frequent basis from the primary dealers about the condition of the financial markets. Finally, although primary dealers do not underwrite Treasury issues in the same way corporate bonds are underwritten by investment banks, the dealers to a large extent provide the same function. To provide this function dealers frequently bid actively at the auctions and subsequently redistribute the bonds they are allocated to their customers. Of course, if the prices decline before they are redistributed, the dealers experience underwriting losses.

There are two other components of secondary markets, in addition to the market for the spot buying and selling of Treasury securities and the repo market, that are closely associated with the Treasury spot market. The first of these is the market for shorting specific government securities. In this market a dealer or other institution sells a

Exhibit 9
Dealer Quote for Treasury Securities*

```
:FEDERAL   FUNDS    10.41  :        U S MONEY MARKETS
:SOURCE GARVIN GUYBUTLER   :   TREAS BILLS 10.41        EURODEPOSITS   10.33: GY RP 10.16:
: BID 8 7/8   OPM 9        :   3M  8.26-21  +.25  :        3M  10 1/4 -3/8 :O/N    8.00-12:
: ASK 9       HGH 9        :   6M  9.48-43  +.15  :        6M  11 3/16-5/16:1WK    8.50-37:
:LAST 9       LOW 9        :   YR  9.84-79  +.20  :        YR  12 1/16-3/16:2WK    8.62-50:
                           :                           OTHER MATS SEE P12/1MO    8.75-50:
```

GOVT COUPONS		10.41		CDS–BID					:BAS–BID				
					EARLY		LATE	10.07		:EARLY		LATE	10.07
13.125	7/84	102.02–07	–08:	SEP	9.15 –25	9.25	–15		:	8.90 –20	:	8.90	–20
13.125	8/85	102.12–17	–15:	OCT	9.35 –15	9.45	–15		:	9.00 –20	:	9.10	–20
14.875	6/86	106.24–29	–20:	NOV	9.60 UNC	9.65	–05		:	9.40 UNC	:	9.50	+10
13.750	8/87	104.16–21	–19:	DEC	10.25 +35	10.30	+20		:	9.80 +10	:	9.95	+25
14.500	8/89	108.09–14	–11:	JAN	10.55 +05	10.55	+05		:	10.20 UNC	:	10.20	UNC
13.750	5/92	106.10–15	–25:	FEB	10.50 –05	10.50	–10		:	10.15 +05	:	10.10	+05
14.250	2/02	113.21–26	–05:	DLR COMMERCIAL PAPER	8/19/82				: BANK RATE				
13.875	5/11	112.06–11	–03:	30	8.75 90	9.25	180		9.625:PRIME		14.00–15.00:		
14.000	11/11	112.22–27	–36:	60	9.00 120	9.375	240		9.875/BRKER		11.00–12.50:		

* Source: Telerate Screen, p. 5.

security it does not own, that is, "shorts" the security with an agreement that the security will be returned at some future date. The short accomplishes this by borrowing a security from another dealer or institution. Of course the interest forgone by the lender must be paid by the borrower. There is a fairly active short market for actively traded government securities, but it is confined mainly to government security dealers.[3]

The second component is the "when-issued market," or "W/I market," wherein Treasury securities are traded prior to the time they are issued by the Treasury. The when-issued trading for both Treasury bills and Treasury coupon issues extends from the day the auction is announced until the issue day. All deliveries on when-issued trades occur on the issue day of the Treasury security traded.

The institutional arrangements of the Treasury securities markets are described in this section. Interest rates on Treasury securities are the benchmark interest rates in the U.S. financial system. The next section contains a discussion of the factors affecting interest-rate determination.

INTEREST-RATE DETERMINATION

In this section we shall discuss how interest rates are determined. The first part of this section focuses on the determination of "the" interest rate or, alternatively, the general level of interest rates, for which a Treasury security interest rate (either a 91-day Treasury bill rate or a long-term Treasury bond rate) is the benchmark. The second part then considers why, at any time, a variety of levels of interest rates coexist. This discussion relates to the rationales for structures of interest rates. The concluding part of this section provides an overview of interest-rate determination.[4]

---

[3] In many ways the repo transaction is similar to the shorting transaction. However, in the repo transaction the borrower of funds who puts up a Treasury security as collateral is subject to market risk, whereas in the short transaction the borrower of the security is subject to market risk.

[4] This chapter discusses interest rates as though the interest rates on securities were directly comparable. Interest rates on all securities, however, are not, without adjustment, directly comparable. Typically, market makers refer to the value of securities in terms of their prices, not their interest rates. The interest rates on the securities are then calculated from their prices. Interest rates are important because they provide a common basis for comparing the returns on securities of different maturities and of different principal values. For these reasons, interest rates are always calculated on an annual basis, typically for $100 of maturity value. However, in calculating interest rates from prices, different assumptions are used for different securities. Thus within the general term *interest rate* are included the returns on several types of securities that are calculated according to different assumptions and are called, alternatively, discount return, yield, bond equivalent yield, repo equivalent yield, and other measures of return. Thus in comparing interest rates on different securities, adjustments must often be made so

Rationale for Interest-Rate Determination

In a broad sense the economy can be conceived of as being composed of two sectors—the real sector and the financial sector. The real sector is involved with the production of goods and services with physical resources—labor and capital. Important examples of components of the real sector include automobile production, steel production, and housing construction. The financial sector is concerned with the transfer of funds from lenders to borrowers. Important examples of components of the financial sector include commercial banks, insurance companies, and securities dealers.

In the financial sector equilibrium is attained when the demand for borrowed funds equals the supply of loanable funds, as discussed below. The interest rate is the variable that causes this equality or equilibrium.

To an individual deciding whether to currently consume an amount of funds or abstain from consumption and supply the funds to the financial sector (that is, save) the interest rate can be viewed as compensation for abstaining from current consumption. For example, an individual with $100 of disposable income when the interest rate is 10 percent must decide between consuming the $100 today or saving it for one year, after which the individual would have $110 to consume. The $10 of added consumption is in effect a reward for abstaining from current consumption. The greater the reward, that is, the higher the interest rate, the more a saver should be willing to supply loanable funds. In the aggregate, the supply of loanable funds is directly related to the interest rates, which are reflected in the upward sloping supply curve of Exhibit 10.

The steepness of this curve depends on the saver's preference for future consumption relative to present consumption. The greater this preference for savings, the flatter the supply curve—the more willing a saver is to save. In this case there is a greater increase in savings for a given increase in interest rates.

To a borrower of funds, the interest rate represents a cost. In the context of the preceding example, at an interest rate of 10 percent borrowing $100 for one year will cost the borrower $10 in interest. To a business borrower, this $10 interest expense is the cost of borrowing to improve capital plant and equipment. If a business borrower can make operations sufficiently more efficient and consequently more profitable as a result of becoming more capital intensive, then borrowing should occur. The higher the interest rate, however, the

---

that the interest rates compared are calculated on the basis of the same assumptions. However, the magnitudes of the differences among interest rates calculated on the basis of different assumptions are in most cases small. This chapter ignores the effect of different assumptions used in calculating interest rates and uses the term *interest rate* as though the returns on all securities were comparable.

Exhibit 10
The Supply and Demand of Loanable Funds

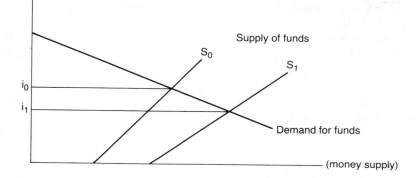

greater must be the profitability associated with an investment for it to pay off. Since more investments will pay off at low interest rates than at high interest rates, the demand for funds by borrowers will decline as interest rates rise. For this reason, the demand for funds curve in Exhibit 10 is downward sloping.

The catalyst for achieving equality between the aggregate supply of funds and the aggregate demand for funds in the financial system is the interest rate. The financial sector is not, however, one uniform, homogenous market. Rather the financial sector is composed of a number of financial institutions and markets that, although distinct, are interrelated. Each of these specific components of the financial sector is specialized, attracting funds from specific types of savers and making funds available to specific types of borrowers.

There is, however, some substitution in which savers and/or borrowers who usually borrow or lend in one part of the financial sector may switch to a different part because of a change in relative interest rates. For example, small savers that had typically deposited their funds in thrift institutions have in the recent high-rate environment responded to relative interest rates and shifted to money market funds.

Interest rates bring the supply and demand for funds into equality in each part of the financial system and operate in the same way to bring the total or aggregate supply and demand for funds in the financial system into equality.

Interest rates are not constant, rather they vary over time. Understanding what affects interest rates and why they are variable is key to understanding the operations of the financial sector. The determination of the general level and variability of interest rates is explainable by several different theories or frameworks. The three major theories, liquidity preference, loanable funds, and inflation and the real rate of interest, are described below. In addition to a general conceptual discussion of the theories, a discussion of how these theories can be used in practice is provided. The focus in this section is on the general level of interest rates, not on any particular interest rate.

Liquidity Preference. "Liquidity preference" is synonomous with the "demand for money." And, as is the case with the demand for other financial assets and liabilities, the demand for money is dependent on the level of interest rates.

The relationship between the demand for money and interest rates can be explained in two ways. The first relies on a Keynesian construction called the speculative demand for money. In this approach, it is assumed that the investor has as investment alternatives either holding cash, which has a zero return and no risk, or holding a bond that has two forms of return, a coupon return and a potential capital gain or loss. If the capital loss on bonds is large enough to exceed the coupon return, the total return on bonds will be negative, and holding money, even at a zero return, would be preferable.

Since the prices of and interest rates on fixed income securities move inversely, bonds incur a capital loss when interest rates rise and a capital gain when interest rates fall. Thus, when interest rates are low, there will typically be an expectation that they will rise, thus resulting in a capital loss on bonds. In anticipation of such a capital loss, holding cash is preferable. Conversely, if interest rates are presently high, they will typically be expected to decline, so that a capital gain on bonds is anticipated and holding bonds is preferable.

Interest rates affect the relative demand for money and bonds as illustrated by a downward sloping demand curve shown in Exhibit 11. The demand for money increases as the current interest rate decreases because the lower the present interest rate is, the more it is expected to rise, and thus the greater the expected capital loss is and the more investors are inclined to hold money. With respect to Exhibit 11, as the interest rate rises from i_2 to i_1, the quantity of money demanded decreases from Q_2 to Q_1.

A second way to explain the relationship between interest rates and the demand for money is to conceive of the interest rate as the foregone return for holding money instead of an interest-bearing asset. Consequently, the higher the rate of interest, the greater is the return foregone by holding money, and the less money is held. In other words, according to Exhibit 11 as interest rates rise, the cost of holding money rather than an interest-earning asset rises. Consequently, as interest rates rise a smaller amount of money is held.

According to either explanation, the liquidity preference theory of interest rates explains the level of the interest rate in terms of the

Exhibit 11
The Supply and Demand of Money

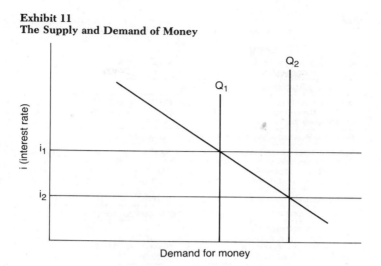

Demand for money

supply and demand for money. Thus if the Fed increases(decreases) the supply of money and there is no change in the demand relationship, the interest rate will decrease(increase). Again referring to Exhibit 11, increasing the supply of money from Q_1 to Q_2 while leaving the demand relationship unchanged results in a lower equilibrium interest rate. In general, an increase in the supply or a decrease in the demand for money will cause interest rates to decline, whereas a decrease in supply or an increase in demand will cause interest rates to rise.

The liquidity preference theory of interest-rate determination can be used for determining both short-term and long-term changes in interest rates.

A partial, short-term analysis of interest-rate determination is based solely on tracking and analyzing short-term movements in the money supply. Since the Fed has the primary responsibility for determining the money supply, there has developed a school of interest-rate analysts commonly known as Fed watchers who continually monitor and interpret the Fed's activities to infer from these activities the Fed's intentions regarding future activities that will affect the money supply and, consequently, interest rates.[5] The weekly money supply statistics announced by the Fed on Friday afternoons and widely disseminated by the financial press are carefully examined for indications of changes in Fed policy that could affect interest rates. Exhibit 12 provides a weekly table of Federal Reserve money supply statistics. An additional discussion of how the Fed's money supply data are interpreted is provided below.

---

[5] Fed watching is the subject of Chapter 45.

Exhibit 12
Weekly Federal Reserve Money Supply Statistics

Federal Reserve

Wednesday, July 28, 1982 All data in millions of dollars	Latest Week	Previous Week	Year Ago
Monetary Aggregates Daily averages			
M-1 (One-Week Lag) *	$450,800	R $451,600	$428,500
Adj. Monetary Base (Fed. Res. Board) *	172,713	R172,686	n.a.
Adj. Monetary Base (St. Louis Fed) */	178,100	178,600	n.a.
Reserve Position, All Member Banks Daily averages			
Required Reserves	40,056	40,359	40,884
Total Reserves Held, Including Vault Cash	40,327	R 40,665	41,285
Excess (Deficit) Reserves	271	R 306	401
Less: Non-seasonal, Non-extended Borrowing at Federal Reserve Banks	336	323	1,720
Equals: Free (Net Borrowed) Reserves	(65)	R (17)	(1,319)
Reserve Position, Eight Major New York Banks Daily averages			
Excess (Deficit) Reserves	0	64	n.a.
Borrowings at Federal Reserve	57	39	n.a.
Net Federal Funds Purchases	10,269	R11,238	n.a.
Basic Reserve Surplus (Deficit)	(10,326)	R(11,213)	n.a.
Federal Reserve Credit Outstanding Daily averages			
Gov'ts. and Agencies Held Outright	141,220	142,215	130,298
Gov'ts. and Agencies Under Repurchase	0	1,252	1,389
Float	1,708	R 2,011	3,094
Other Assets	9,057	8,916	10,261
Other Factors Affecting Reserves Daily averages			
Gold Stock	11,149	11,149	11,154
Special Drawing Rights	4,018	3,875	3,068
Currency in Circulation	147,103	147,899	137,732
Treasury Deposits	3,358	3,181	3,063
International			
Gov't. Securities Held for Foreign Central Banks and Int'l. Fin. Institutions	95,851	96,479	n.a.
Ten New York Banks, Balance Sheet Items Wednesday, July 21			
Total Loans, Adjusted	113,491	115,301	n.a.
United States Treasury Securities	6,062	5,834	n.a.
Tax-Exempt Securities	11,376	11,725	n.a.
Demand Deposits, Adjusted	24,959	25,764	n.a.
Total Time and Savings Deposits Excluding Large† C.D.'s	34,941	34,807	n.a.
Large Negotiable Certificates of Deposit	35,329	34,846	n.a.
Total Loans, Credit Demand Wednesday, July 21			
Business Loans, All Large Banks	210,426	212,092	181,014
All Other Commercial, Industrial Loans* *	206,508	207,769	176,844
Business Loans, New York Banks* *	59,467	60,779	n.a.
Business Loans, Chicago Banks* *	n.a.	24,022	19.599
Commercial Paper	182,877	181,285	n.a.

R Revised.   * Seasonally adjusted.   † Over $100,000.   * * Excluding acceptances.
n.a. Not available.

Source: *The New York Times.*

In addition to watching and interpreting the market money supply data, the Fed's open-market operations and their affect on the federal funds rate are continuously monitored. As an example, the following discussion recently appeared in *The Wall Street Journal* (January 20, 1982):

Some specialists said the recent rise in the funds rate reflected an apparently tougher stance adopted by the Fed late last month in supplying reserves to the banking system. And many contend the recent surge in the money supply will force the Fed to get even tougher.

A longer-term application of the liquidity preference theory is based on the relationship between the money supply and the level of Gross National Product (GNP). This relationship is formally expressed by the equation: $M \times V = P \times Y$ (called the quantity theory of money), where V is the velocity of money, P is the price level, and Y is real gross national product. The product of P and Y, $P \times Y$, is nominal GNP, referred to simply as GNP.

According to this theory, if the level of the money supply over some future time period is less(greater) than the actual amount needed to support the expected level of GNP, then the level of interest rates is likely to rise(fall). It is due to this relationship that economic forecasters go through the complex exercise of predicting GNP and the money supply and their interrelationship in order to provide forecasts of interest rates.[6]

Predicting GNP and money supply relationships is usually conducted in the context of large econometric models of the U.S. economy. These multiequation models attempt to capture the complex interactions in the economy that result in the determination of interest rates, GNP, and money supply. The results of such models are frequently the basis for long-range financial planning by corporations and others.

Loanable Funds.   The loanable funds theory of interest-rate determination is based on the reasoning related to the supply and demand for loanable funds provided at the beginning of this section. This theory of interest-rate determination depends on the supply of funds available for lending by savers and the demand for such loanable funds by borrowers. As indicated above, as the return to lending rises (as interest rates rise), the supply of loanable funds increases. Conversely, when interest rates decline, the return to lenders declines; thus so does the supply of such funds.

Since interest rates represent a cost to borrowers, the opposite relationship applies to borrowers: As interest rates rise, borrowers' demand for funds decreases, and as interest rates decline, borrowers' demand for funds increases. These relationships are illustrated by Exhibit 13.

In Exhibit 13 the equilibrium level of interest rates is r_0, and the quantity of funds lent and borrowed at that rate is E_{LF}. if the interest rate were initially higher than r_0, for example r_1, then the supply of funds, S_{LF}, would exceed the demand, D_{LF}, at that rate. This excess supply of funds would exert downward pressure on interest rates,

---

[6] See Chapter 47 for a thorough discussion of interest-rate forecasting.

Exhibit 13
The Supply and Demand of Loanable Funds

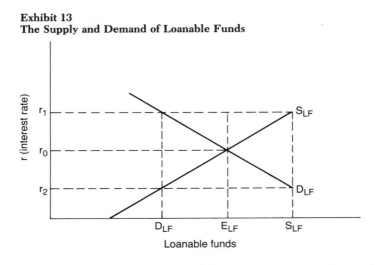

Loanable funds

causing them to decrease to r_0, the point at which supply and demand would be in equilibrium. Alternately, if rates were below the equilibrium level, for example at r_2, then the demand would exceed the supply. The effect of market pressures in this case would be to cause interest rates to increase again to the equilibrium level, r_0.

The loanable funds theory of interest-rate determination applies to aggregate borrowing and lending in the economy. If, at a given interest rate, intended aggregate borrowing is greater than intended aggregate lending, then interest rates will rise. Then the actual measured levels of borrowing and lending at the higher level of interest rates will be equal. If intended aggregate borrowing is less than intended aggregate lending, interest rates will decline until the actual measured levels of borrowing and lending will be equal at the lower level of interest rates.

To apply the loanable funds theory, aggregate borrowing and lending is typically divided into its components or sectors, as illustrated in Exhibit 14. Even though some borrowers and lenders can shift among types and maturities of sources and uses of funds and some cannot, a structure or taxonomy such as shown in Exhibit 14 can be used in either case for determining aggregate borrowing and lending. This structure is useful for summarizing actual, measured aggregate borrowing and lending for past years, as done for 1976–1981 in Exhibit 14; as indicated above, borrowing and lending must be equal.

The structure is also useful for forecasting interest rates.[7] For this purpose, an estimate is developed of the expected or intended levels of borrowing and lending of each type shown in Exhibit 14 over a

---

[7] See Chapter 47.

Exhibit 14
Summary of Supply and Demand for Credit ($ billions)

1. Summary of Supply and Demand for Credit ($ Billions)

	1976	1977	1978	1979	1980	1981e	1982p	Amt. Out. 31Dec81e	Table Refer.
			Annual Net Increases in Amounts Outstanding						
Net Demand									
Privately Held Mortgages	70.5	108.0	116.0	105.0	70.9	72.2	71.7	1,230.3	2
Corporate & Foreign Bonds	39.1	39.1	31.8	36.1	37.9	27.4	28.8	536.9	3
Subtotal Long-Term Private	109.6	147.1	147.8	141.1	108.8	99.6	100.5	1,767.2	
Short-Term Business Borrowing	14.1	49.0	76.0	91.4	55.0	127.1	142.1	742.7	8
Short-Term Other Borrowing	40.7	50.7	65.5	52.8	20.7	47.0	59.7	555.9	8
Subtotal Short-Term Private	54.8	99.7	141.5	144.2	75.7	174.1	201.8	1,298.6	
Privately Held Federal Debt	73.0	74.5	81.7	77.4	118.0	113.5	135.4	1,003.6	6
Tax-Exempt Notes and Bonds	17.6	28.9	32.5	27.7	33.0	31.0	30.7	397.5	4
Subtotal Government Debt	90.6	103.4	114.2	105.1	151.0	144.5	166.1	1,401.1	
Total Net Demand for Credit	**255.0**	**350.2**	**403.5**	**390.4**	**335.5**	**418.2**	**468.4**	**4,466.9**	▼
Net Supply[1]									
Thrift Institutions	70.5	82.0	73.5	55.9	57.9	-39.7	41.1	832.8	9
Insurance, Pensions, Endowments	49.0	68.1	73.2	63.6	75.4	70.8	76.7	808.8	9
Investment Companies	2.9	7.0	6.4	25.5	22.5	69.4	64.0	149.9	9
Other Nonbank Finance	12.9	13.4	18.9	26.4	16.6	33.3	41.4	240.4	9
Subtotal Nonbank Finance	135.3	170.6	172.0	171.3	172.3	213.2	223.1	2,031.8	9
Commercial Banks[2]	60.8	84.1	105.9	103.9	83.3	115.0	126.8	1,289.9	10
Business Corporations	9.0	-2.3	-0.9	8.3	3.7	6.8	7.7	98.9	11
State & Local Government	4.0	13.3	11.1	9.5	7.3	11.0	8.2	87.1	11
Foreign[3]	19.6	47.2	58.8	8.9	37.9	17.9	16.0	296.1	11
Subtotal	228.7	312.9	346.9	301.9	304.5	363.9	381.8	3,803.8	
Residual (mostly household direct)	26.3	37.3	56.6	88.5	31.0	54.3	86.6	663.1	12
Total Net Supply of Credit	**255.0**	**350.2**	**403.5**	**390.4**	**335.5**	**418.2**	**468.4**	**4,466.9**	▲
Percentage Growth in Outstandings									
Total Credit	11.0	13.6	13.8	11.7	9.0	10.3	10.5		
Government	13.1	13.2	12.9	10.5	13.7	11.5	11.9		
Household	11.5	14.7	14.7	11.1	5.8	7.2	7.4		
Corporate	8.1	12.4	13.5	14.1	9.0	13.7	13.4		
Long-Term	10.3	12.9	11.7	9.8	7.5	6.4	6.1		
Short-Term	11.9	14.5	16.2	13.9	10.6	14.3	14.6		
Held by Nonbank Finance	13.6	15.1	13.2	11.6	10.5	11.7	11.0		
Commercial Banks	8.3	10.5	12.0	10.5	7.6	9.8	9.8		
Foreign	18.5	37.6	34.1	3.8	15.8	6.4	5.4		
Household Direct	7.1	9.4	13.1	18.1	5.4	8.9	13.1		

[1] Excludes funds for equities, cash and miscellaneous demands not tabulated above.
[2] Domestically chartered banks and their domestic affiliates.
[3] Includes U.S. branches of foreign banks.

Note: Figures in tables may not add to totals due to rounding.

Source: "1982 Prospects for Financial Markets", Salomon Brothers, January 4, 1982, p. 20.

period of time. Then the sum of all types of borrowing (aggregate borrowing) is compared with the sum of all types of lending (aggregate lending). If the former is greater than the latter, interest rates are forecast to increase. And due to the increase in interest rates, actual borrowing would be less than expected borrowing and actual lending would be greater than expected lending. Then, *ex post*, actual measured borrowing and lending would be equal. For example, the data in Exhibit 14 provide estimates of the actual measured sources and uses of funds in 1982 after interest rates changed to their equilibrium levels.

Often, instead of developing as complete a taxonomy of borrowing and lending as described above, analysts focus on only the major types of borrowing and lending, such as federal government borrowing, business borrowing, and mortgage borrowing. Then by forecasting increases or decreases in these types of borrowing, the analysts assess whether there will be upward or downward pressures on the interest rate.

A popularization of the application of the loanable funds theory on a sectoral basis is referred to as crowding out. Large federal deficits require the U.S. Department of the Treasury to increase the amount of debt it has outstanding; and the issue of Treasury debt is alleged to compete with private-sector borrowing, assuming a fixed supply of available credit. Thus an increase in the demand for funds by the Treasury causes interest rates to increase and forces out the private-sector issues. An example of the crowding out application of the loanable funds theory appeared recently in *The Wall Street Journal* (1981):

> Many dealers said they continue to be concerned about the size of the Treasury's financing needs. Traders also expressed nervousness over recent increases in short-term interest rates. But many said they remain confident that bond prices will rebound early next year, mainly because they anticipate further evidence of erosion in the economy.

And another example appeared in a *New York Times* story (1981):

> Unusually heavy year-end Government borrowings continued to weigh on the money market last week, raising short-term rates a point on average and reducing prices of longer-term coupon securities as much as two points, or $20 for each $1,000 of face value.

Thus the crowding-out concept derives from the loanable funds theory but focuses only on Treasury borrowing. Most applications of loanable funds use an intermediate approach between a complete taxonomy of sources and uses of funds and only a single use of funds; they consider a few major uses of funds and perhaps changes in the aggregate supply of funds.

Inflation and the Real Rate of Interest   Interest rates represent a rate of return for lenders and a cost to borrowers. To be a meaningful representation of cost or return, however, interest rates should be related to the rate of change of prices. The significance of this relationship can be considered by the following example. Consider a saver who has placed $5,000 in a money market fund earning a return of 12 percent per year. At the end of a year the saver has $5,600, a 12 percent increase in purchasing power. If, however, the price level had increased by 10 percent per year, then the net increase in purchasing power of the savings would be only 2 percent.

The 12 percent return on the savings is referred to as the nominal rate of interest, since it measures the percent increase in the nominal number of dollars earned or paid over a period of time. The measure of change in purchasing power of 2 percent is referred to as the real rate of interest since it measures the real change in purchasing power. The difference between these two rates is the rate of inflation. Thus the real rate of interest (IR) equals the nominal rate of interest, (IN) minus the rate of inflation (DP): $IR = IN - DP$.

From the lender's perspective, the real rate of interest represents the increase in real purchasing power resulting from foregone consumption—savings. From the borrower's perspective, the real rate of interest represents the real cost of borrowing. The inflation component of the nominal rate of interest the borrower pays on the borrowed funds represents a deterioration of the principal of the loan (often described as paying back in cheap dollars), not a real cost of borrowed funds. A business should as a decision rule continue to borrow and invest until the real rate of return on investments equals the real rate of interest paid on borrowing.

Thus there are two major determinants of the real rate of interest. The first is the return on investment—the return to capital. If a business can improve its efficiency of operations and earn a higher rate of return from investment, it will be inclined to pay a higher real rate of return on borrowed funds. The other influence is the preference of consumers. The more consumers want to consume currently rather than forego consumption, the higher the real rate of return will have to be to induce them to alter their plans and save.

Then the real rate of interest and the rate of inflation jointly determine the nominal rate of interest. The effect of the rate of inflation on the nominal rate of interest is to cause the nominal rate to change so that the real rate is unaffected by the rate of inflation. Lenders, unless subject to a "dollar illusion," are concerned with the return of the real purchasing power on their savings rather than the nominal return. Such concern causes consumers to negotiate for nominal rates that keep their real rate of return at least constant. Thus, to the extent their savings are sensitive to the real rate of interest, an increase in inflation without a corresponding increase in the real rate of interest will cause a decrease in savings. Consequently, there is upward pressure on the nominal rate of interest during periods of inflation, which prevents the real rate of interest from decreasing below its original level. To prevent savings from decreasing requires an increase in the nominal rate equal to the increase in the rate of inflation.

Inflation has a somewhat similar effect on the willingness of borrowers to pay a higher nominal rate of interest for funds. Inflation affects the return on investment by affecting the prices of goods and services produced. An investment earning a given amount net of the interest on borrowings will earn a higher nominal amount after inflation because the value of the goods and services produced by the investment have been inflated. If the interest payments on the borrowings do not increase as well, then the real rate of return on investment will also increase. Presumably, under such circumstances borrowers will continue to increase their demand for funds until the nominal cost of borrowing has increased such that the real cost is at its preinflation level.

Over time, however, the real rate of interest may change for two reasons. First, the real rate of interest, since it is the real return on capital, may decrease during recessions because of a substantial amount of unused capital and a low return to the used capital. Similarly, it may increase during periods of economic growth because all capital is productively employed.

The second reason for changes in the real rate relates to *unexpected* changes in the rate of inflation. The nominal interest rate on a security at any time should reflect the *expected* average rate of inflation over the maturity of the security. If the financial markets *expect* a higher rate of inflation in the future, nominal interest rates should increase to reflect these expectations. However, if inflation changes unexpectedly, the initial nominal rate of interest will not correctly reflect the change, and the actual real rate of interest over the period will be different from the normal level of the real rate in the opposite direction of the unexpected change in the rate of inflation.

Consider the following example. Between times T_0 and T_1 the nominal rate of interest is 8 percent, the rate of inflation is 5 percent, and the real rate of interest is 3 percent. Assume these are the normal levels.

Assume that at T_1 the rate of inflation *unexpectedly* increases to 6 percent. Since the change is unexpected, the nominal rate does not change, and thus the real rate of interest decreases to 2 percent. Assume that by T_2 the financial markets recognize the change in the rate of inflation and the nominal rate of interest increases to 9 percent, restoring the real rate of interest to 3 percent.

At T_3 the rate of inflation *unexpectedly* decreases to its original level of 5 percent. Because the change is unexpected, the nominal rate remains at 9 percent, so the real rate increases to 4 percent. By T_4 the financial market recognizes the change in the rate of inflation, the nominal rate of interest decreases to 8 percent, and the real rate of interest decreases to its original normal level of 3 percent. Thus, although expected changes in the rate of inflation should have no effect on the real rate of interest, unexpected changes in inflation will cause the real rate of interest to change in the opposite direction.

Typically, interest rates are referred to in nominal terms. Similarly, interest rate determination models relate to the nominal rate of interest. As discussed above, the nominal rate of interest and the rate of inflation are directly related. Since the nominal rate of interest is, by definition, equal to the real rate of interest plus the rate of inflation, the rate of inflation is a major component of the level of the nominal rates of interest. In fact, given the levels of inflation and interest rates that have been observed during the last decade, changes in the nominal rate of interest have been due in greater measure to changes in inflation than to changes in the real rate of interest.

Exhibit 15 provides a plot of the real rate of interest from 1965 until recently. Calculations of the real rate of interest can be made from

Exhibit 15
The Real Rate of Interest

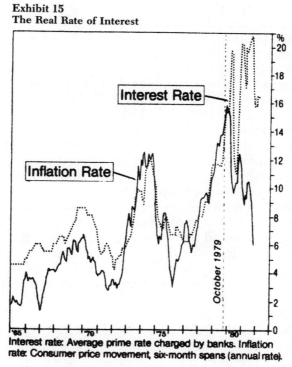

Interest rate: Average prime rate charged by banks. Inflation rate: Consumer price movement, six-month spans (annual rate).

Sources: U.S. Commerce Department.

different measures of the rate of inflation and different interest rates, although in concept the measure of the inflation rate used should be the expected inflation rate over the maturity of the security whose interest rate is used. The interest rate can be either a short-term or a long-term interest rate. Very often the inflation rate used is based on an average over several previous periods or a projection of the trend of the past inflation rate into the future. The real rate of interest in the plot in Exhibit 15 equals the 91-day Treasury bill interest rate minus the contemporanious quarterly change in the Consumer Price Index (CPI). Alternatively, the real rate plotted could have been the long-term Treasury bond rate minus an expected long-term rate of inflation.

Exhibit 15 shows that there has been considerable variation in the real rate of interest, the difference between the interest rate and the inflation rate, since 1981. These changes in the real rate have been due both to changes in the strength of the economy and errors in inflationary expectations.[8] Although the correlation is less than perfect, the real rate of interest tends to be low during recessions and high during periods of economic strength. Recently, the real rate of interest has been at historic highs.

To summarize, in models of the determination of the nominal rate of interest, the factors that affect the rate of inflation and the real rate of interest should be considered separately. Since there has been even greater volatility in the rate of inflation than in the real rate of interest, an accurate determination of the rate of inflation is an important part of an accurate determination of the nominal rate of interest.

Synthesis. The three different theories or rationales of the level of interest rates that were described in this section are not exclusive but, rather, are compatible and complementary ways of considering interest-rate determination. The liquidity preference theory, which considers the supply and demand for money, and the loanable funds theory, which considers the supply of and demand for loanable funds, are equivalent ways of considering interest-rate determination. A model that included both money and loanable funds would show that these two theories would determine the same interest rate. The impact of the inflation and the real rate of interest theory on the level of interest rates is complementary to the other two explanations by introducing the effect of inflation to either. Thus the three theories described in this section should be viewed as a unified approach to interest-rate determination.

Tone of the Market. The factors discussed above that affect interest rates—the supply and demand for money, the supply and demand for funds, and the inflation rate—are objective in nature. These fundamental factors undoubtedly determine the level of interest rates after some lag. But there is another type of influence on interest rates that responds very quickly—within hours, or even minutes, and at times

---

[8] Some observers claim that the real rate of interest has been high recently because the real rate contains a risk premium to account for the increased volatility of interest rates since October 1979, when the Fed announced that it would devote more attention to controlling the money supply and less to controlling the interest rate.

includes subjective as well as objective factors—this type of influence is called the tone of the market.

The tone of the market determines the very short-run direction and volatility of interest rates and is due to actions by professionals in the interest-rate markets, mainly dealers in government securities, corporate bonds, and municipal bonds, and also large institutional investors in these securities. The professionals continually monitor the nation's and the world's economic, political, and social condition and quickly assess their likely impacts on interest rates. In particular, they watch for changes in the condition of the nation's economic goals, inflation, unemployment, economic growth, and balance of payments and watch for changes in economic policies, monetary policy, and fiscal policy. Even more specifically, they monitor the volume of new issues of Treasury, corporate, and municipal debt that will be brought to the market in the next few days and weeks and Fed open-market operations and monetary policy.

By monitoring and quickly assessing the likely impact of these factors on interest rates, the professionals are able to rapidly alter their portfolio strategies in view of new information. If dealers and portfolio managers expect interest rates to increase, they reduce the size of their portfolio to avoid losses, thus lowering the demand for securities and increasing interest rates. In response to the same expectations, they may reduce their holdings of long-term securities but increase their holdings of short-term securities, thus increasing long-term rates relative to short-term rates, a normal phenomenon during times of rising interest rates. Through these portfolio activities, the expectation that interest rates will rise actually causes interest rates to rise, at least for a short period of time. If interest rates are expected to decrease, the opposite will occur.

At times professionals may respond not only to recent information but to expectations or anticipations of future information. Operating on the basis of future information is more subjective than operating after the release of new information. And at times the psychology of the market may be counter to the fundamental factors: Professionals may expect future information that will reverse interest-rate trends based on recently available data.

The tone of the market, whether determined by objective (fundamental) or subjective (psychological) factors, affects interest rates very quickly. And activities by professionals that set the tone of the market by quickly translating new information or expectations of future information into present interest-rate changes add to the efficiency of the financial markets.

The following quote from *The Wall Street Journal* indicates the nature and importance of the tone of the market:

Bond prices swung widely as speculators stepped up their involvement in the credit markets.

The Treasury recently offered 8⅜% bonds of 2008, for example opened at 99²²⁄₃₂ bid, 99²⁴⁄₃₂ asked, traded as high as 100 bid, 100⁴⁄₃₂ asked only to finish the session at their opening levels.

The earlier firming came as dealers purchased inventory for possible markups in any subsequent resumption of the strong price rally of the past two weeks.

The Structures of Interest Rates

It is often asked what determines or affects "the" interest rate as if there were a single interest rate. However, from the financial markets it is obvious that there is not one but several interest rates. And although these interest rates may move, in general, in the same direction at the same time, the amounts of their movements and at times even the direction of their movements may differ substantially. Thus the spreads, or differences, between interest rates vary. These observations are illustrated by Exhibit 16.

This section discusses the factors that tend to make interest rates differ among themselves. These factors are often the basis for the "structures" of interest rates. There are three different structures of interest rates, and even if securities are identical in every other respect, their interest rates may differ because of maturity, credit risk, and taxability. These three structures of interest rates are discussed below.

Maturity Structure (Term Structure) of Interest Rates.[9] This section considers the relationship between a security's interest rate and its term to maturity. This relationship is usually referred to as the maturity structure or term structure of interest rates. A common analytical construct in this context is the yield curve (or term structure curve), which is a curve illustrating the relationship between the interest rate and the maturity of securities that are identical in every way other than maturity.

There are three distinct explanations of the relationship between the maturities of securities and their interest rates.

Liquidity Hypothesis. Although there are several aspects to a security's liquidity, the major aspect is the security's potential for capital gain or loss, often called market risk. The major determinant of a security's market risk is its maturity, since the longer the security's maturity, the greater the price change for a given change in its interest rate. For example, the prices of Treasury bonds are more volatile than the prices of Treasury bills.

---

[9] For a more detailed discussion of this subject, see Chapter 46.

Exhibit 16
Plot of Interest Rates

MONEY MARKET RATES

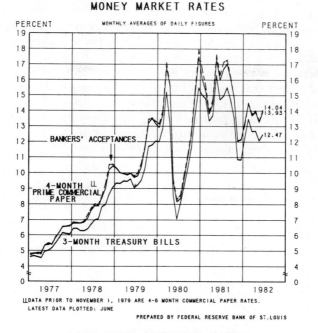

LLDATA PRIOR TO NOVEMBER 1, 1979 ARE 4-6 MONTH COMMERCIAL PAPER RATES.
LATEST DATA PLOTTED: JUNE

PREPARED BY FEDERAL RESERVE BANK OF ST. LOUIS

LONG-TERM INTEREST RATES

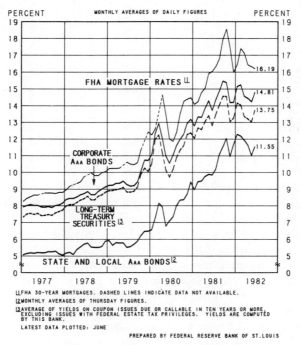

LLFHA 30-YEAR MORTGAGES. DASHED LINES INDICATE DATA NOT AVAILABLE.
L2MONTHLY AVERAGES OF THURSDAY FIGURES.
L3AVERAGE OF YIELDS ON COUPON ISSUES DUE OR CALLABLE IN TEN YEARS OR MORE, EXCLUDING ISSUES WITH FEDERAL ESTATE TAX PRIVILEGES. YIELDS ARE COMPUTED BY THIS BANK.
LATEST DATA PLOTTED: JUNE

PREPARED BY FEDERAL RESERVE BANK OF ST. LOUIS

Source: Monetary Trends, *Federal Reserve Bank of St. Louis*, December 23, 1981.

Since there is a trade-off between the risk and the return on a security, investors typically require a higher return to invest in a security with higher risk. Because a security with a longer maturity has greater market risk and, for this reason, less liquidity, interest rates should increase with maturity as a compensation to investors. This relationship between the level of interest rates and the maturity of a security is called the liquidity preference hypothesis and is illustrated in Exhibit 17. This hypothesis does not purport to be a complete explanation of the term structure of interest rates, but only a complement to the other explanations described below.

Exhibit 17
Liquidity Preference: The Relationship between the Level of Interest Rates and Maturity

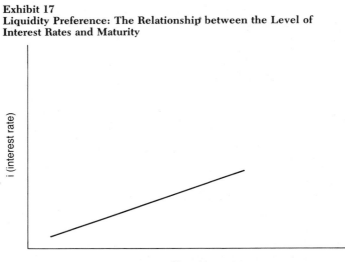

Expectations Hypothesis. The expectations hypothesis begins with a premise considered in a preceding section, that lenders desire to maximize their return from providing funds and borrowers desire to minimize their cost of borrowing funds. However, unlike the preceding discussion, the expectations hypothesis explicitly considers how lenders and borrowers attain their objectives over a period of time rather than just at any moment in time.

To consider the temporal aspect of maximizing investment return and minimizing borrowing cost and how these decisions affect the relationship between interest rates and maturities, consider a two-period planning horizon. Consider each period to be one year, although it could be any other discrete period of time. A lender considering strategy over this two-period planning horizon has two alternatives—either to purchase a security with a maturity equal to the two periods or purchase a security with a one-period maturity with the intention of reinvesting for an additional period at the end of the first period. The lender's decision will depend on a comparison of the currently available two-period interest rate with the average of the currently available one-period rate and the expected one-period rate, one period hence. Obviously, the lender will select the strategy with the higher anticipated return.

The borrower who is planning over the same two-period horizon is also faced with two alternatives—either to issue a security with a two-period maturity or to issue a one-period security with the intention of issuing another one-period security, one period hence. The borrower's decision will be based on the total cost of funds over the two periods. If the two-period interest rate is less than the average of the current one-period rate and the one-period rate expected one period hence, then the borrower will issue a two-period security. Otherwise, the borrower will sequentially issue two, one-period securities.

The decisions made separately by lenders and borrowers will affect the relative interest rates over the two-period horizon. For example, if the two-period interest rate exceeds the average of the one-period rate and the expected one-period rate one period hence, then all lenders would choose to invest for two periods and all borrowers would sequentially issue two, one-period securities. As a consequence, there would be an excess supply of funds in the two-period market, causing the two-period interest rate to decrease, and an excess demand for funds in the one-period market, causing the one-period interest rate to increase. According to the expectations hypothesis, the interest rates will continue to change until the current two-period rate equals the effective rate for two sequential one-period securities. Under this circumstance, both borrowers and lenders will be indifferent between a single two-period transaction and two sequential one-period transactions, and thus interest rates will be in equilibrium.

The expectations hypothesis is also applicable to a larger number of periods. However, the basic conclusion that the current long-term rate should equal the average of the current and expected future short-term rates remains the same. As a result, borrowers and lenders will be indifferent between relying on a long-term security or a series of short-term securities.

The expectations hypothesis does not imply that all interest rates will be equal, only that the average of the observed and anticipated short-term rates will equal the long-term rate. If interest rates are expected to remain stable, however, so that future short-term rates are expected to equal the currently observed short-term rate, then current interest rates across all maturities will be equal, as illustrated by the yield curve shown in Exhibit 18. This is a "flat" yield curve.

Exhibit 18
Flat Yield Curve

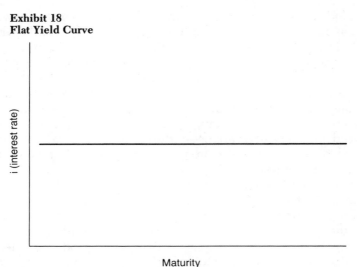

Maturity

If rates are expected to increase, the shape of the yield curve will be different. With an anticipated increase in interest rates, lenders will purchase short-term securities so that they can earn the higher anticipated rate after their initial short-term-maturity security matures and they subsequently reinvest in another short-term security at a higher rate, and also so that they avoid the capital losses that longer term securities would incur when interest rates rise. Borrowers, on the other hand, would be induced to issue long-term securities in order to lock in the currently low rates for a long period of time, thereby eliminating the need for issuing new securities at the higher rates. These actions of lenders and borrowers would result in an excess supply of short-term funds, causing short-term rates to decrease, and an excess demand for long-term funds, causing short-term rates to increase. These pressures on short- and long-term interest rates would produce an upward-sloping yield curve as illustrated in Exhibit 19.

According to the expectations hypothesis, these pressures on interest rates will continue until, again, the current long-term interest rate equals the average of the current and expected short-term rates. For example, if the current one-year rate is 12 percent, the expected one-year rate one year hence is 13 percent, and the expected one-year rate two years hence is 14 percent, then the current two-year rate would be 12.5 percent, and the current three-year rate should be the average of these three one-year rates, 13 percent.[10] Thus the yield curve based on the current one-year, two-year, and three-year rates would be upward sloping.

---

[10] This example ignores the effect of compound interest.

Exhibit 19
Upward-Sloping Yield Curve

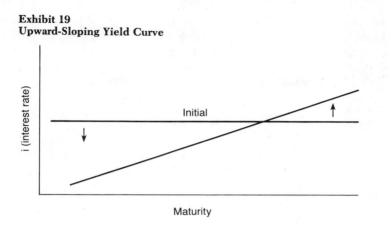

The explanation is similar if interest rates are expected to decrease in the future. In this case, lenders would purchase only long-term securities in an attempt to lock in currently high interest rates before rates decrease and to reap the capital gain that would result from the decrease in interest rates. Borrowers, on the other hand, would issue only short-term securities, thereby paying currently high rates for a short period of time with the expectation of subsequently issuing longer term securities when rates decrease. Consequently, there would be an excess supply of funds in the long-term market and an excess demand for funds in the short-term market, which would cause long-term interest rates to decrease and short-term interest rates to increase. These pressures on interest rates would result in a downward-sloping, or inverted, yield curve as illustrated in Exhibit 20.

Exhibit 20
Downward-Sloping Yield Curve

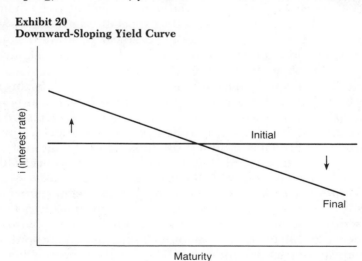

As indicated above, the liquidity hypothesis is not intended to be a complete explanation of the term structure of interest rates. Rather it is intended to supplement the expectations hypothesis. The combined effects of the liquidity hypothesis and the expectations hypothesis are shown in Exhibit 21.

Exhibit 21
Expectations Hypothesis plus Liquidity Hypothesis

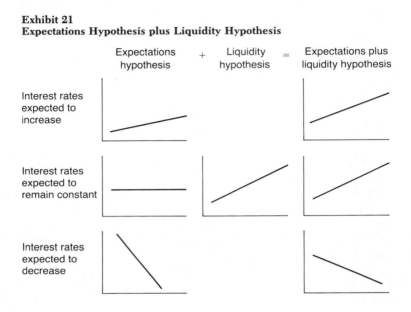

The expectations hypothesis produces a horizontal yield curve when interest rates are normal, an upward-sloping yield curve when interest rates are low, and a downward-sloping yield curve when interest rates are high. Supplementing the expectations hypothesis with the liquidity hypothesis, which always predicts an upward-sloping yield curve, provides an upward bias to a yield curve based only on the expectations hypothesis. Indeed upward-sloping yield curves have historically been the most frequently observed, and for this reason upward-sloping yield curves are frequently referred to as normal yield curves. During recessionary periods, when interest rates are low and are expected to increase, the yield curve has a steep upward slope. When the economy is strong, credit is tight, and interest rates are high, however, downward-sloping yield curves are observed. Both observations are consistent with the expectations hypothesis.

Segmentation Hypothesis. The basis for the segmentation hypothesis is the antithesis of the basis for the expectations hypothesis. Whereas the expectations hypothesis assumes that both borrowers and lenders are able to alter the maturity structure of their portfolios, each group shifting among the maturities of their respective borrowings or investments, the segmentation hypothesis assumes that both borrowers and lenders are constrained to particular segments of the maturity spectrum for institutional and legal reasons. For such market participants, shifting among maturities is not feasible, and therefore various maturity securities are not considered to be substitutes for one another, independent of the levels of the various interest rates.

In practice, there are numerous financial market participants whose borrowings or investments are, for a variety of reasons, constrained to only one portion of the maturity spectrum. For example, pension fund managers and insurance companies have a relatively small amount of their investments in short-maturity securities, whereas commercial banks and thrifts have a relatively small amount of their investments in long-term bonds.

If indeed the market is segmented so that borrowers and lenders active in the market for one maturity are unlikely to be active in the market for any other maturity, then the interest rate associated with a particular maturity would have to be the result of the supply and demand pressures for only that maturity. Consequently, a change in supply and demand factors in one maturity will affect the interest rate for only that maturity and have no impact on the interest rate for any other maturity.

The segmentation hypothesis and the expectations hypothesis are competing, incompatible explanations of the relationship between interest rates and maturities on securities. For technical reasons, resolving which is the more correct explanation of the relationship is an intractable problem. In reality there are probably some elements of both theories that are correct while neither one is completely correct in explaining the relationship. In particular, it is unlikely that all borrowers and lenders are locked into one portion of the available maturity structure and unable to switch to another when interest rates dictate. Alternatively, there are undoubtedly some market participants who are restricted to particular segments of the maturity structure.

Either hypothesis could provide correct conclusions without the hypothesis holding in its extreme version. For example, for the expectations hypothesis to apply, not all borrowers and lenders have to be able to shift among maturities on the basis of relative interest rates, only enough to affect the relative interest rates. Similarly, for the segmentation hypothesis to apply, not all borrowers and lenders have to be restricted to particular segments of the maturity range, only enough so that the interest rates associated with each maturity segment are influenced by different supply-and-demand considerations. Observers of debt markets have noted characteristics supportive of both hypotheses in their less-than-extreme versions. However, most observers tend to support the expectations hypothesis complemented by the liquidity hypothesis as the dominant explanation for the observed relationship between interest rates and maturity.

The combined expectations hypothesis/liquidity hypothesis description of the maturity structure of interest rates can be applied to the actual behavior of the financial markets. The conclusions that can be drawn from a combination of the expectations hypothesis and the liquidity preference hypothesis are that when the level of interest rates is normal the yield curve will have a slight upward slope—the long-term rates will be slightly greater than short-term rates. When the general level of interest rates is low, the term structure will have a steeper upward slope. Finally, when the level of interest rates is high, the term structure will have a downward slope. Pragmatically, the segmentation hypothesis adds nothing that either contradicts or supports this observation.

Empirical observations support conclusions derived from the expectations and the liquidity hypotheses. Exhibits 22, 23, and 24 show

Exhibit 22
Yield Curve—November 12, 1981

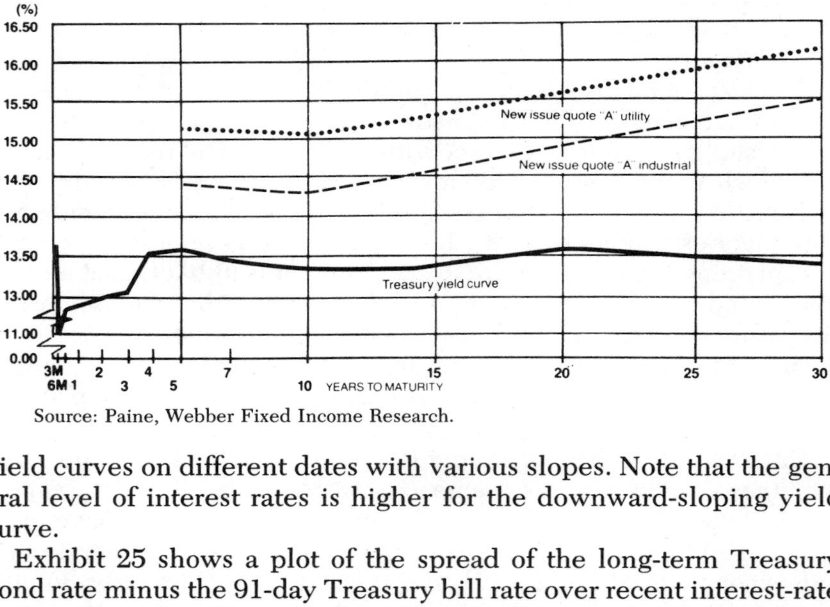

Source: Paine, Webber Fixed Income Research.

yield curves on different dates with various slopes. Note that the general level of interest rates is higher for the downward-sloping yield curve.

Exhibit 25 shows a plot of the spread of the long-term Treasury bond rate minus the 91-day Treasury bill rate over recent interest-rate cycles. Note that the spread tends to be large and positive at low levels of interest rates and negative at high levels of interest rates. These results are consistent with the conclusions of the combined expectation hypothesis and the liquidity hypothesis.

Credit Risk.   The two major characteristics of a security are return and risk. In turn, there are two major types of risk, market risk and credit risk. Market risk refers to the volatility of the price of a security due to changes in the general level of interest rates. The market risk of

Exhibit 23
Yield Curve—September 3, 1981

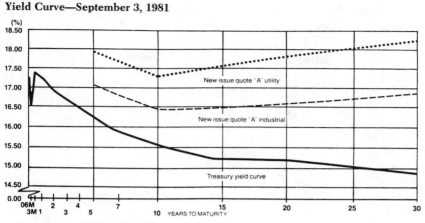

Source: Paine, Webber Fixed Income Research.

Exhibit 24
Yield Curve—August 5, 1982

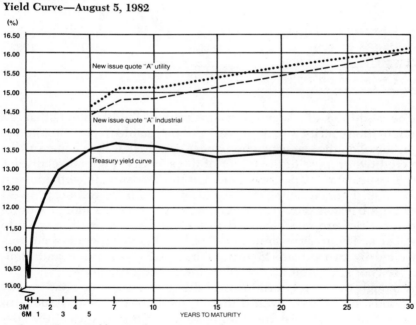

Source: Paine, Webber Fixed Income Research.

a security is thus determined primarily by its maturity, since the
longer the maturity, the greater the price change of the security for a
given magnitude of interest-rate change in the opposite direction.
Thus the term structure of interest rates relates to the market risk of a
security. This section considers the other type of risk, credit risk.

Exhibit 25
30-Year Treasury Bond minus 91-Day Treasury Bill Yield Spread

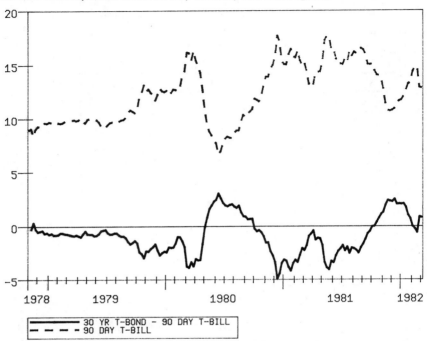

The credit risk of a security is a measure of the likelihood that the issuer of the security, the borrower, will be unable to pay the interest or principal on the security when due. Credit risk is thus a measure of the creditworthiness of the issuer of the security. Federal securities, that is issues of the U.S. Department of the Treasury, have the lowest credit risk. Federal agencies are perceived to have the next lowest credit risk because they are backed by the federal government. Corporate securities are rated lower than federal agencies with respect to credit risk. The relative credit risks of long-term corporate securities are rated by two private financial corporations—Moody's and Standard & Poor's. Exhibit 26 describes their rating categories.

Although the creditworthiness of different issuers of bonds affect the bonds' credit risk, even different bonds of the same issuer can have different credit risk depending on the characteristics of the specific bond. For example, a debenture, an unsecured bond, may have a higher credit risk than a bond that is collateralized by real or financial assets or a sinking-fund bond of the same issuer.

Some money market instruments are also rated by private financial corporations.[11] Both Standard & Poor's and Moody's rate commercial

---

[11] Money market instruments are described in Chapter 8.

Exhibit 26
Corporate Bond Rating Categories*

Standard & Poor's Rating Categories†	Description
AAA (Aaa)	Bonds rated AAA have the highest rating assigned by Standard & Poor's to a debt obligation. Capacity to pay interest and repay principal is extremely strong.
AA (Aa)	Bonds rated AA have a very strong capacity to pay interest and repay principal and differ from the highest rated issues only in small degree.
A (A)	Bonds rated A have a strong capacity to pay interest and repay principal, although they are somewhat more susceptible to the adverse effects of changes in circumstances and economic conditions than bonds in higher rated categories.
BBB (Baa)	Bonds rated BBB are regarded as having an adequate capacity to pay interest and repay principal. Whereas they normally exhibit adequate protection parameters, adverse economic conditions or changing circumstances are more likely to lead to a weakened capacity to pay interest and repay principal for bonds in this category than for bonds in higher rated categories.
BB (Ba) B (B) CCC (CCa) CC (Ca)	Bonds rated BB, B, CCC and CC are regarded, on balance, as predominantly speculative with respect to capacity to pay interest and repay principal in accordance with the terms of the obligation. BB indicates the lowest degree of speculation and CC the highest degree of speculation. While such bonds will likely have some quality and protective characteristics, these are outweighed by large uncertainties or major risk exposures to adverse conditions.
C	The rating C is reserved for income bonds on which no interest is being paid.
D	Bonds rated D are in default, and payment of interest and/or repayment of principal is in arrears.
Plus(+) or Minus (−):	The ratings from "AA" to "B" may be modified by the addition of a plus or minus sign to show relative standing within the major rating categories.

* These Standard & Poor's corporate bond rating categories also apply to municipal bonds.
† The ratings in parentheses refer to the corresponding ratings of Moody's Investors Service, Inc.
Source: Standard & Poor's Corporation.

paper issues. For example, the grades usually acceptable to commercial paper investors are Standard & Poor's A–1, A–2, and A–3 and Moody's Prime–1, Prime–2, and Prime–3. Exhibit 27 provides descriptions of the Standard & Poor's commercial paper rating categories. However, other money market instruments, such as domestic bank negotiable certificates of deposit (CDs), are not rated by these agencies.

Interest rates are higher for securities with greater credit risk, since investors have to be compensated for the additional risk. Conse-

Exhibit 27
Standard & Poor's Commercial Paper Rating Definitions

Rating Category	Description
A	Issues assigned this highest rating are regarded as having the greatest capacity for timely payment. Issues in this category are delineated with the numbers 1, 2, and 3 to indicate the relative degree of safety.
A–1	This designation indicates that the degree of safety regarding timely payment is either overwhelming or very strong. Those issues determined to possess overwhelming safety characteristics will be denoted with a plus (+) sign designation.
A–2	Capacity for timely payment on issues with this designation is strong. However, the relative degree of safety is not as high as for issues designated "A–1."
A–3	Issues carrying this designation have a satisfactory capacity for timely payment. They are, however, somewhat more vulnerable to the adverse effects of changes in circumstances than obligations carrying the higher designations.
B	Issues rated "B" are regarded as having only an adequate capacity for timely payment. However, such capacity may be damaged by changing conditions or short-term adversities.
C	This rating is assigned to short-term debt obligations with a doubtful capacity for payment.
D	This rating indicates that the issue is either in default or is expected to be in default upon maturity.

quently, the interest rate on a Treasury security is less than that on a AAA corporate security, which is in turn less than that on an A corporate security, all with the same maturity. Exhibit 28 shows the spread between 30-year Treasury bonds and 30-year AAA corporate bonds and the spread between 30-year corporate AAA bonds and 30-year A corporate bonds against the level of the 30-year Treasury bond interest rate. Note that these spreads tend to widen when interest rates are high and to narrow when interest rates are low. This is consistent with a "flight to quality," an increased preference by investors for low credit risk instruments when interest rates are high and investors perceive low credit risk borrowers as vulnerable. Exhibit 29 shows the interest rates by credit rating at a specific time.

Exhibit 30 shows a plot of the spread between 90-day Treasury bills and 90-day industrial commercial paper against the Treasury bill interest-rate level. This money market spread similarly shows a widening when interest rates are high and a narrowing when interest rates are low, that is a flight to quality at high interest rates.

The credit-risk structure of interest rates explains variations in the interest rates on various securities of the same maturity due to differences in the credit risk of the issuers and issues. In addition, the size

Exhibit 28
30-Year AAA Corporate Bond minus 30-Year Treasury Bond Yield Spread and
30-Year A Corporate Bond minus 30-Year AAA Corporate Bond Yield Spread

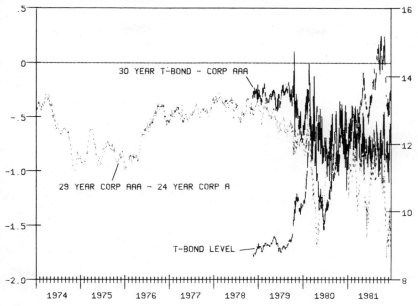

Exhibit 29
Bond Interest Rates by Credit Rating

	Industrials	Treasuries	Utilities
Baa.	17.25%		18.70%
A.	16.25		17.75
Aa.	15.55		17.50
Aaa.	15.15		—
Bell System Debentures			17.00
30-Year Treasuries		14.40%	

Source: *Bondweek*, February 8, 1982, p. 9.

of the spreads between securities with high credit risk and low credit risk varies with the level of interest rates.

Taxability Structure. There are three aspects of taxability that cause interest rates on different securities to differ at a specific time.

Tax-Exempt Municipals. The coupon payments on Treasury and corporate bonds are subject to the federal personal income tax. Consequently, the aftertax yield on Treasury and corporate bonds is less than the coupon yield by an amount determined by the bondholder's tax bracket. It is not legal, however, for the federal government to tax

Exhibit 30
90-Day Commercial Paper minus 90-Day Treasury Bill Yield Spread

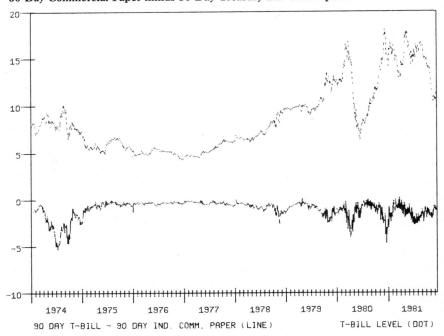

90 DAY T-BILL - 90 DAY IND. COMM. PAPER (LINE)   T-BILL LEVEL (DOT)

the coupon payment on state and local securities.[12] Since municipal securities are tax exempt, their aftertax yield is the same as their pretax yield. Because investors are concerned with aftertax rather than pretax yields, municipal securities can be issued with lower coupons than the coupons on similar Treasury or corporate securities. For example, to an investor in the 50 percent tax bracket, a 6 percent municipal security selling at par has the same aftertax yield as a 12 percent Treasury or corporate security.

Thus municipal bond interest rates differ from the interest rates on Treasury and corporate bonds because of the difference in taxability. Exhibit 31 shows the spread in the yields between a 30-year Treasury bond and a 30-year AAA municipal security. Notice that the yield spread is always positive, that is, the yield on Treasury bonds is higher than the yield on municipal bonds.

The magnitude of the spread changes over the interest-rate cycle for two reasons. First, municipal bonds have a higher credit risk than

---

[12] Neither can state and local governments tax the coupon payments of federal securities, but this exemption is not as important as the federal exemption on state and local government securities because the income tax rates of state and local government are lower than federal income tax rates.

Exhibit 31
30-Year Treasury Bond minus 30-Year Municipal Bond Yield Spread

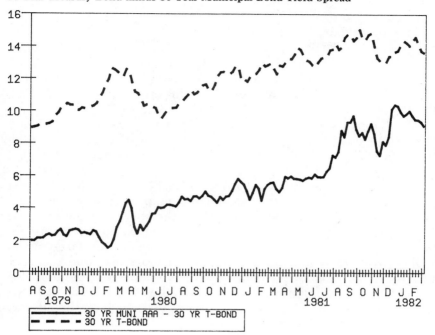

Treasury bonds, and the phenomenon related to the flight to quality discussed in the last section is applicable. Here the flight to quality is from municipals to Treasuries when interest rates are high. In this case, however, since the rate on Treasury bonds is higher than the rate on municipal bonds, the flight to Treasury bonds during times of high interest rates tends to narrow the spread.

In addition, the spread between Treasury and municipal bond yields changes over the interest-rate cycle for reasons of taxability. The spread is the absolute difference between the Treasury and the municipal bond interest rates. However, the tax rate as it is applied to the coupon on Treasury securities has a relative or proportional effect. Thus, for example, to an investor in the 50 percent tax bracket a 4 percent municipal security has the same aftertax yield as an 8 percent Treasury security, for a spread of 4 percent. However, a 6 percent municipal security has the same aftertax yield as a 12 percent Treasury security, for a spread of 6 percent. Similarly, an 8 percent municipal security has the same aftertax yield as a 16 percent Treasury security, for a spread of 8 percent. Thus, because of the proportional nature of the federal personal income tax, the absolute spread between Treasury and municipal bonds varies over the interest-rate cycle, being larger when interest rates are high and smaller when interest rates are low.

Overall, due to the flight to quality the spread between Treasury and municipal bonds narrows when interest rates are high, and due to the proportional nature of the income tax, the spread widens when interest rates are high. Thus the two effects are countervailing. Based on the Treasury bond/municipal bond interest-rate spread shown in Exhibit 31, the latter effect of interest rates on the spread dominates the former effect.

The spread between municipal and Treasury bonds may also vary structurally due to changes in tax legislation that affect the level of the personal income tax and the attractiveness of other tax shelters that compete with municipal securities as tax-reducing investments.

Level of Coupon.   A second aspect of taxability also causes interest rates among different securities, even of the same issuer and maturity, to differ. This aspect is the magnitude of the coupon of the security. Although coupon payments on Treasury and corporate bonds are taxed at the personal income tax rate, capital gains are taxed at the capital gains tax rate. If a bond is held for more than one year, the long-term capital gains tax rate, which is 40 percent of the personal income tax rate, will apply. Consequently, the aftertax value of 1 percent of pretax coupon return is less to an investor than the aftertax value of 1 percent of pretax capital gains.

The yield-to-maturity of a bond, as it is commonly calculated, includes both the coupon return and the return due to capital gain or loss (the difference between the current market price and the par value of the bond) on an annual basis as if the security were held to maturity. If, for example, a 30-year security with an $80 coupon is selling for $1,000, its 8 percent yield-to-maturity is entirely due to the coupon return. If another 30-year security with a $60 coupon is initially selling for $773.77 for an 8 percent yield-to-maturity, its yield-to-maturity consists of a 7.75 percent coupon return, and the remainder is due to the capital gain over the 30-year life. Since this low-coupon "discount security" (a security selling for less than its maturity value of $1,000) has a portion of its return due to capital gains, which is taxed at a lower rate, the aftertax return on the low-coupon discount bond is greater than that of the high-coupon bond selling at "par" (its maturity value of $1,000). Therefore the price of the discount bond will be bid up, and thus the yield-to-maturity at its new actual trading price will be somewhat less than the 8 percent yield on the par bond. The lower yield on the discount bond will compensate for its more favorable tax treatment.

Thus low-coupon discount bonds normally sell at a yield somewhat lower than high-coupon bonds selling at par or at a premium (at a price greater than its maturity value) or even at a smaller discount

Exhibit 32
11¾ Percent Treasury Bond minus 7⅝ Percent Treasury Bond Yield Spread

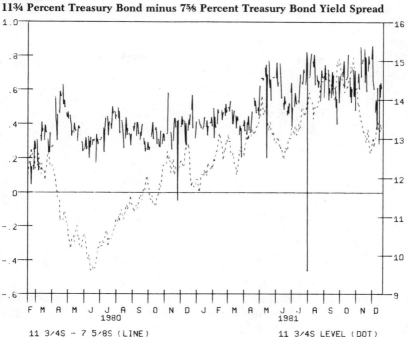

11 3/4S − 7 5/8S (LINE)   11 3/4S LEVEL (DOT)

because of this tax advantage. Exhibit 32 shows the yield spread between high-coupon, 11¾ percent, and low-coupon, 7⅝ percent, Treasury securities over the past two years. Notice that the yield spread, almost without exception, is positive (the yield on the high-coupon bond is greater than the yield on the low-coupon bond).

Exhibit 33 illustrates that although the pretax yield of the highest coupon Treasury bonds shown is highest, the aftertax yield of these bonds is not. Due to taxability alone, the yields on all these bonds would be equal if they were identical in every way other than coupon. However, they also have different maturities and different times since issuance.

Flower Bonds. Several Treasury bonds issued during the 1950s and early 1960s exhibit another type of taxability. These bonds, known as flower bonds, are acceptable *at par* in payment of federal estate taxes when owned by the decedent at death. These bonds, identified in Exhibit 34, were issued with low coupons. On January 1, 1977, the capital gain realized at the holder's death was made taxable, thus, to some extent, reducing the tax advantage of flower bonds.[13]

---

[13] See Chapter 9 for the conditions imposed by the Treasury to use flower bonds to pay federal estate taxes.

Exhibit 33
Before-Tax and Aftertax Yields on U.S. Treasury Bonds (12/4/81)

Coupon	Pre-tax Yield-To- Maturity	Aftertax Yield	Issue Date	Maturity Date
7⅝%...........	12.12†	7.11	2/15/77	2/15/07/02
7⅞	12.14	7.08	11/15/77	11/15/07/02
8¼	12.45	7.23*	5/15/75	5/15/05/00
8⅜	12.37	7.15	8/15/78	8/15/08/03
8¾	12.45	7.14	11/15/78	11/15/08/03
9⅛	12.51	7.11	5/15/79	5/15/09/04
10	12.59	7.01	5/15/80	5/15/10/05
10⅜	12.66	6.99	11/15/79	11/15/09/04
11¾	12.79	6.84	2/15/80	2/15/10/05
12¾	12.77	6.65†	11/17/80	11/15/10/05
13⅞	12.85*	6.68	5/15/81	5/15/11/06
14	12.85*	6.68	11/16/81	11/15/11/06

* Highest.
† Lowest.
Source: "Government Securities Quotations," Continental Bank, Chicago, Ill.

Due to their tax advantages, the (pretax) yields on these bonds is lower than on other Treasury bonds without the estate-tax eligibility provision, as shown in Exhibit 34.

Interest Rate Structure: A Summary.   Factors that affect interest rates tend to affect all interest rates in generally the same way. For this reason, discussions of the determinants of interest rates often seem as if there were a single interest rate. This section provides the transition

Exhibit 34

Issue Date	Coupon	Maturity Date	Size of Issue ($ billions)	Yield*
Flower Bonds				
5/01/53	3¼%	Jan. 15, 1978–83	$1.1	12.73%
4/05/60	4¼	May 15, 1975–85	0.9	9.86
6/03/58	3¼	May 15, 1985	0.6	8.98
2/14/58	3½	Feb. 15, 1990	2.0	5.87
8/15/62	4¼	Aug. 15, 1987–92	2.3	6.21
1/17/63	4	Feb. 15, 1988–93	0.13	5.93
4/18/63	4⅛	May 15, 1989–94	0.9	5.87
2/15/55	3	Feb. 15, 1995	0.39	4.55
10/03/60	3½	Nov. 15, 1998	1.5	4.78
Recently Issued Nonflower Bonds				
(10 year)	14⅝%	Feb. , 1992		14.70%
(20 year)	14¼	Feb. , 2002		14.76
(30 year)	14	Nov. , 2006–11		14.50

* *The Wall Street Journal*, February 12, 1982, p. 44.

from the consideration of a single interest rate to the actual multiplicity of interest rates observed in the financial world.

There are three major structures of interest rates that contribute to the multiplicity of interest rates observed: the maturity structure, the credit-risk structure, and the taxability structure. There are, in addition, other factors that cause differences in interest rates. One such factor is the liquidity of the security, often measured by the size of the bid/ask spread (the smaller the spread, the more liquid the security). The liquidity of a security may depend on the size of the original issue or the time since the original issue. Securities tend to be less liquid if the original-issue size was small and as the time since original issue increases. These aspects of liquidity supplement the market-risk aspect discussed above.

The fundamental factors that affect these three structures, and changes in the relationships among interest rates on the basis of these structures over the interest-rate cycle, are discussed in this section.

Overview of Interest-Rate Determination

Four potentially exclusive rationales for determining the level of "the" interest rate: liquidity preference, loanable funds, inflation and the real rate of interest, and the tone of the market have been discussed. The perspective was on the factors that affect the general level of interest rates at a specific time, not on the differences among various interest rates at a specific time. We then discussed the structures of interest rates, the factors that tend to, given the general level of interest rates, affect the differences among specific interest rates at a specific time. As discussed, the three major factors are the maturity, the credit risk, and the taxability of the specific security. Now we shall integrate these various perspectives on interest-rate determination.

Most models of interest-rate behavior, whether used for explaining past interest-rate behavior or forecasting future interest-rate behavior, and whether they are judgmental or econometric models, incorporate elements of the liquidity preference, loanable funds, and inflation and the real rate of interest rationales. Thus these three rationales are viewed as complimentary rather than competitive as explanations for interest-rate behavior. There are, however, some differences in the applicability of these three rationales and also the tone of the market rationale depending on whether the short-run or long-run responses of interest rates are being considered and whether short-term or long-term interest rates are being considered.

Liquidity preference is a very important explanation of very short run changes in interest rates, particularly changes in short-term interest rates in response to changes in the money supply. Money supply announcements made by the Federal Reserve Bank of New York every Friday afternoon (for the week ending on Wednesday nine days before) are closely watched, and the financial markets respond very quickly to them.

The nature of the response of interest rates, particularly short-term interest rates, to money-supply announcements has changed significantly during the last decade. If it was announced a decade ago that money supply had increased significantly, interest rates declined and vice versa, as expected by the liquidity preference rationale. However, today when an announcement is made that money supply has increased significantly, interest rates usually increase rather than decrease, and vice versa. There are two reasons for this change in response.

First, since the mid-1970s the Federal Reserve System has, as an important part of its implementation of monetary policy, set ranges for future money-supply growth. It then conducts monetary policy so that the actual money-supply growth fits within these ranges. Thus an announcement of a large increase in the money supply is now interpreted by the markets as requiring the Federal Reserve System to subsequently tighten money-supply growth to keep the money-supply growth within the announced ranges. The markets, thus anticipating a subsequent decline in money-supply growth, respond by making interest rates increase in response to the expected tightening. Here again the liquidity preference rationale is operable, but now the market responds to expectations of subsequent money-supply growth rather than to the announcement of the past money-supply growth.

The second reason for the change in response is that inflation has become a more important force in determining interest rates. In view of the quantity theory of money, there is an important relationship between money supply and inflation. Thus an announcement of a high growth in the money supply often causes market participants to conclude that inflation will accelerate, at least if this money-supply growth rate continues, thus causing interest rates to increase due to the inflation and real rate of interest rationale. For both of these reasons, interest rates now often increase rather than decrease when there is an announcement of an increase in the money supply.

Essentially, all explanations of the level of interest rates include some measure of the money supply as a determinant, particularly for short-term interest rates, and particularly for short-run changes. The liquidity preference rationale, however, is also used for determining the level of interest rates on a longer term basis. This use is implemented, as discussed above, in the context of the quantity theory of money: $M \times V = P \times Y$. By forecasting a likely growth in the money supply, M, and a likely range of increases in real GNP, Y, an assumption about the likely range of inflation, P, can be made from the quantity theory. From this rate of inflation and an assumption about the real rate of interest, the nominal rate of interest can be determined. This conceptual construction obviously relies jointly on the liquidity preference and the inflation and real rate of interest rationales of interest-rate determination.

The loanable funds rationale is typically used to explain and forecast interest rates on a long-term basis and applies, in general, to both long- and short-term interest rates. By developing a taxonomy of the likely sources and uses of funds over a period of time, as provided above, and including an assumption about changes in the money supply, a forecast of potential imbalances between the supply and demand for funds can be made. Projected imbalances of supply over demand are then used as the basis for forecasting a decrease in interest rates and of demand over supply for forecasting an increase in interest rates.

It is in this context that crowding out (borrowing by the federal government sector, which makes borrowing by the private sector more expensive or impossible) is considered. In addition, increased borrowing by the business or consumer sectors put upward pressures on interest rates, and vice versa. In the loanable funds context, short- and long-term sources and uses of funds are typically aggregated, thus implicitly assuming substitutability among securities of various maturities.

With the recent higher levels of inflation, the inflation and real rate of interest rationale has become very important in explaining the nominal level of interest rates. As discussed, although they are attributable both to variations in inflation and variations in the real rate of interest, variations in the nominal rate of interest are more attributable to the former than the latter. Thus the real rate of interest might vary over a range of from −1 percent to 4 percent, and inflation might vary over a range of 5 percent to 15 percent. Therefore including a measure of inflation in an explanation for the general level of interest rates is essential.

However, it is more difficult to include an accurate measure of the determinants of the real rate of interest. In general, the real rate of interest tends to vary over the business cycle, being high during periods of prosperity and low during periods of recession. Most explanations of the general level of interest rates include inflation explicitly but do not consider the real rate of interest explicitly.

Thus most explanations of the general level of interest rates include elements of the liquidity preference, loanable funds, and the inflation and real rate of interest rationales, although there are some differences in emphasis depending on whether short-term or long-term interest rates and whether short-term changes or long-term changes in the rates are being considered. The "tone of the market" rationale should also be considered in determining interest rates, although typically only for very short run changes and mainly in the short-term interest rates. Therefore models that forecast quarterly interest rates often do not include the tone of the market.

Having determined the general level of interest rates, or "the" interest rate, by the methods summarized above, consideration can be given to determining specific interest rates on specific securities. To make this determination, given the general level of interest rates, the maturity, the identity of the issuer, and the taxability of the specific security must be considered—that is, the interest rate on the specific security must be considered with respect to the three structures of interest rates discussed above. In relating a specific interest rate to the general level of interest rates, two issues must be considered: (1) the normal spread between the specific interest rate and an interest rate reflective of the general level of interest rates, such as the 90-day Treasury bill rate or the long-term Treasury bond rate, and (2) variations in the magnitude in this spread over the interest-rate cycle.

The conclusions of the three maturity structures of interest rates are as follows. When the level of interest rates is low, interest rates increase with maturity (the term structure-of-interest-rate curve has a positive slope. And when the level of interest rates is high, interest rates decrease with maturity (the term structure-of-interest-rate curve has a negative slope. Thus short-term interest rates vary through a much wider range than the long-term interest rates, as illustrated in Exhibit 35. And thus the spread between short-term and long-term interest rates (long term minus short term) varies considerably over the interest-rate cycle and becomes less positive (or more negative) as interest rates increase.

Exhibit 35
Interest-Rate Variability by Maturity

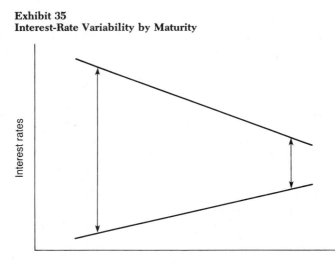

Maturity

With respect to the identity of the issuer, the greater the credit risk of the issuer, the higher the interest rate on the security. It is in this regard that Treasury securities are the benchmark for interest rates. The Treasury has the lowest credit risk of any issuer, and thus Treasury securities have the lowest adjustment for credit risk. Different issues of the same issuer may also have different credit risks due to the nature of the securities. The spread between high credit-risk interest rates and low credit-risk interest rates (high credit risk minus low credit risk) increases with the level of interest rates, due to a "flight to quality" when interest rates are high.

Finally, the taxability of the issue must be considered. The most important aspect of taxability relates to municipal securities whose coupons are exempt from the federal income tax. Due to this tax exemption, actual pretax interest rates on municipals are lower than on Treasury and corporate securities. Because taxes are on a relative or proportionate basis, the spread between Treasury and municipal securities (Treasury rate minus municipal rate) widens (narrows) as the level of interest rates increases (decreases).

Another aspect of taxability relates to the magnitude of the coupon, which determines the degree of the discount or the premium of a security, since coupon income is taxed as personal income and capital appreciation as capital gains. Thus the higher the coupon on a security, the higher will be its interest rate to compensate for the greater tax liability. Finally, flower bonds have lower yields due to their estate-tax advantages.

Overall, the determination of interest rates occurs in two steps. First, the general level of interest rates is determined by the eclectic combination of the methods described above. Second, the appropriate spread between the interest rate on the specific security being considered and the general level of interest rates is determined by considering the factors that affect the structures of interest rates. The benchmark interest rate used in such spread analysis is typically the interest rate on a U.S. Treasury debt security.

Interest Rates and Inflation*

6

STEVEN C. LEUTHOLD
Managing Director
The Leuthold Group
An Associate of Lynch Jones and Ryan

Everyone knows inflation brings high interest rates . . . government officials, economists, fixed income managers, stockbrokers, corporate executives, the man on the street. We are all aware of this truism. And the higher the inflation, the higher the interest rates. Who would argue with that?

Investment people also know there is actually a measurable direct relationship between prevailing long-term rates and the rate of inflation, the real rate of interest. We also know that accelerating inflation means higher interest rates and decelerating inflation strongly implies lower interest rates. Who would argue with that, at least until recently?

The impact of inflation on interest rates varies as one progresses up the yield curve to longer maturities and, of course, we also know that short-term interest rates are typically lower than long-term rates.

Today, the preceding axioms are still broadly accepted. They had come to be viewed as truisms, unchallenged, undisputed common knowledge. Most of us, because this thinking was universally accepted, assume that historic financial data convincingly confirm these beliefs. We don't view these axioms as theory, we view them as fact. Billions of dollars are committed every year on these assumptions.

* This chapter is abstracted from the author's book and reprinted with permission from *The Myths of Inflation and Investing* by Steven C. Leuthold, published by Crain Books Division of Crain Communications, Inc. Copyright 1980 by Steven C. Leuthold.

Surprisingly, long-term economic history does not strongly support these accepted truisms, and in some cases history appears to contradict what most of the investment business has come to believe as indisputable fact.

Obviously, what occurred in the past is not a rubber stamp for the future. Conditions change and what worked yesterday does not always work tomorrow. Relationships that existed then may not exist now. Our purpose is not to disprove these broadly accepted investment axioms, but we do want to make the reader aware that these truisms have not always been true. *They are not natural laws.* This does not mean one should become an atheist on the subject, only a skeptical agnostic. If we can shake your faith, open your eyes, you may avoid some unpleasant future investment traps. Blind faith may be comforting today, but if unwarranted, it can get you in a mess of trouble down the road.

The statistics, tables, and charts that follow are derived from a series of historic financial data covering almost 200 years of short- and long-term interest rates and consumer prices in the United States and England. The sources and the annual data employed can be found in *The Myths of Inflation and Investing.* It is believed that basic data are as accurate and reliable as any available.

LONG-TERM INTEREST RATES—THE FIRST CUT

High inflation means high interest rates, while price stability and deflation are accompanied by lower interest rates. Right? Wrong!

The first simple test of this truism was classifying 188 years of average annual yields for quality long-term U.S. bonds back to 1792. The annual yields were then separated into the three following environments (based on annual changes in the CPI).

1. Inflation years: years in which the CPI was up 1.6 percent or more.
2. Stable years: years in which the CPI was up or down 1.5 percent or less.
3. Deflationary years: years in which the CPI declined 1.6 percent or more.

The results of this classification are below:

		High-Quality Long-Term Bonds	
		Average Yield	*Median Yield*
89 Inflation years	(47%)	4.94	4.87
42 Stable years	(22)	4.19	4.25
57 Deflation years	(31)	5.07	5.01
188 Years	100	4.81	4.83

As can be seen from the table above, long-term interest rates have typically between 10 to 15 basis points higher in deflationary years than in inflationary years. In the 57 deflationary years shown above, the average yield was 5.07 percent; and in the inflationary years, it was only 4.94 percent. Stable years had the lowest average yields, 4.19 percent.

SHORT-TERM INTEREST RATES—THE FIRST CUT

The first test here involved classifying 149 years of average annual returns on prime commercial paper, four- to six-month paper or a reasonable proxy, back to 1831. These yields were then separated and averaged in the same three environments, again based on annual changes in the CPI.

Again, we defined inflation years as those in which the CPI was up 1.6 percent or more. Stable years were those in which the CPI was up or down 1.5 percent or less, and deflation years were those in which the CPI was down 1.6 percent or more.

The results are tabulated below:

		High-Quality Short-Term Paper	
		Average Yield	Median Yield
71 Inflation years	(48%)	5.49	5.40
39 Stability years	(26)	4.83	4.69
38 Deflation years	(26)	6.30	5.45
148 Years	100	5.50	5.28

Again, this approach showed that short-term rates have been higher in deflationary years than in inflationary years. Indeed, the difference in average returns was almost 80 basis points in favor of the deflationary years. Once again, the stable years showed the lowest interest rates, as expected. But the surprise is the relationship between the inflationary and deflationary years.

There is a third surprise for many readers. Short-term rates historically have been higher than long-term rates on both an average and a median basis. If we look at the period from 1831 through 1979, where both long and short rates are available, we find that the average short-term rate was 5.50 percent and the median short-term rate was 5.28 percent. The average long-term rate for the same period was 4.54 percent, 96 basis points lower, and the median long-term rate was 4.37 percent, 91 basis points lower.

	Short Rates	Long Rates	Difference
Average	5.50%	4.54%	−.96
Median	5.28	4.37	−.91

So what really is the normal shape of the yield curve? Today, what is viewed as the abnormal or inverted yield curve has historically been the most prevalent—short rates higher than low rates. Only in the 30 years or so during which Federal Reserve actions could control the money markets have long rates consistently been higher than short rates. These days may be past. In the last decade or so, long rates have been higher than short rates only about 60 percent of the time. Perhaps free-market forces are once again becoming the controlling factor.

This meat-axe division of the historic yield data is admittedly crude. Simple annual rates of inflation or deflation can and have fluctuated widely from year to year, and some kind of smoothing of inflation data is appropriate. However, in this simple form the data seem to contradict today's accepted interest-rate/inflation-rate theory that implies inflation means higher interest rates than does deflation.

Second, the average yields and median yields for the three environments are likely all much lower than most readers would have thought. The average prevailing long-term yield of 4.81 percent for the entire 188-year period seems absurdly low when compared to current levels. Also the average yield of 5.50 percent for short-term rates might seem a bit on the low side.

Yield statistics for 1980 and 1981 are not incorporated in the tables and calculations herein. Although inclusion of this data does alter certain of the averages cited, the differences are not material to the overall observations and conclusions.

That first cut was disturbing, but don't completely throw out the inflation/interest-rate dogma yet. A more careful analysis of the historic data, while not supporting much of the inflation/interest-rate theory which is currently in vogue, does reveal it is not all wrong.

LONG-TERM INTEREST RATES—A SECOND CUT

The analysis that follows covers the same 188 years of U.S. inflation and deflation as measured by the CPI. This time the CPI data are smoothed via a three-year centered average of annual rates. The same 188 years of average annual interest rates for high-quality, long-term, fixed income securities are employed.

This more careful analysis indicates—to some extent at least—that inflation environments of 4 percent and above historically have been accompanied by higher-than-average long-term interest rates. However, the relationship is a far cry from what most economists and fixed income investment professionals currently believe. The analysis also indicates that higher deflation levels also are accompanied by higher-than-average levels of long-term rates.

Exhibits 1, 2, and 3 detail the findings. Notice that Exhibit 3 and the last two columns in Exhibit 1 exclude the very low long-term interest

Exhibit 1
Long-Term Interest Rates, 1791–1979

Inflation/Deflation Environment	All Years			Excluding 1939–1950 As Artificial Years		
	Years	Average	Median	Years	Average	Median
Inflation 9%+	14	6.09%	5.50%	13	6.36%	5.52%
Inflation 6–8%	14	5.05	5.07	10	6.02	5.39
Inflation 4–5%	17	5.25	6.01	15	5.61	6.02
Inflation 2–3%	29	4.08	3.93	26	4.25	3.98
Inflation 1%............	28	4.22	4.28	27	4.28	4.32
0	19	4.68	4.52	19	4.68	4.52
Deflation 1%...........	18	4.61	4.62	17	4.72	4.77
Deflation 2–3%	22	5.09	5.24	22	5.09	5.24
Deflation 4–5%	15	4.96	4.81	15	4.96	4.81
Deflation 6%+	11	5.70	5.75	11	5.70	5.75
	187	4.81%	4.82%	175	4.95%	4.93%

Exhibit 2
Average Long-Term Interest Rates by Inflation/Deflation Environments

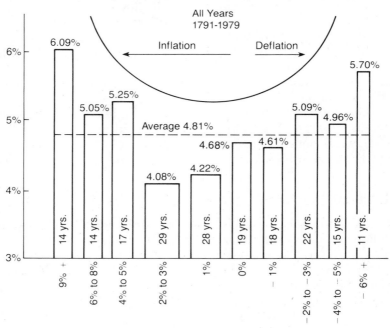

rates of 1939 to 1950 from calculations. In this period it can be argued that nonmarket circumstances unnaturally restrained interest rates. First, World War II held down interest rates, and an excess profits tax put a ceiling on dividends. Then the Treasury and the Federal Reserve Bank Board cooperatively kept interest rates pegged. During

Exhibit 3
Average Long-Term Interest Rates by Inflation/Deflation Environments

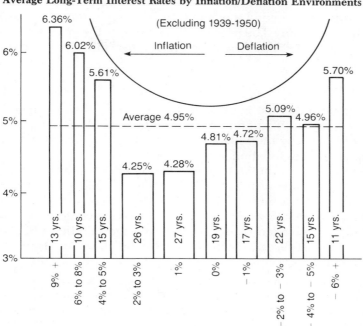

this time the entire government market was supported by the federal reserve banks, fixing long government bonds at 2.5 percent and three-month Treasury bills at 0.38 percent. This pegging agreement lasted until the spring of 1951. During this period of artificial rates there were significant bursts of inflation.

Some might argue that U.S. long-term rates prevailing in that period, averaging below 2.9 percent in our data base, are unrealistic, artificially depressed by the U.S. government. The other side of the argument is that there have been other circumstances of "artificially" depressed interest rates in this country's history, as well as England's and Europe's. And, no matter what the reason, no matter what extraneous forces were present, that's the way it was. All the data should, therefore, be included. While personally favoring this latter position, we will present the data both ways, but the same conclusions can be drawn no matter which way the cake is sliced.

Looking now at Exhibits 1 and 2, and 3, we can see that whether we include or exclude the 1939 to 1950 "artificial" years, the average interest rate when inflation exceeded 4 percent was above 5 percent, and in years of relative price stability it did not top 4.75 percent. However, in years of price deflation the interest rate on long-term bonds again increased, peaking at a 5.7 percent rate in years of more than 6 percent deflation. The charts reveal this symmetry clearly.

It is also clear from Exhibit 1 that the average interest rate has trailed the inflation rate significantly. For example, in the 14 years when inflation exceeded 9 percent, the average interest rate on long-term bonds was only 6.09 percent. If we exclude the years which some regard as artificial, then this average interest rate rises only to 6.36 percent.

Now on to some observations:

- Long-term interest rates typically rise above their average levels in the higher inflation-rate environments of 4 percent and above, but historically the inflationary impact is less than close to keeping pace with inflation acceleration.
- Counter to current thought, in inflation environments of 6 percent and above, long-term rates do not typically reflect the rate of inflation plus "real interest" of 2 percent to 3 percent. Our research reveals in the 28 years where the three-year centered average of inflation exceeded 6 percent, the average nominal interest rate was, in most cases, actually below the inflation rate itself, a negative real rate of interest.
- In deflationary environments, long-term interest rates also appear to typically rise above their average levels. This is especially pronounced in environments of steeper deflation, 6 percent and above.
- The best environment for relatively low long-term yields appears to be a stable to modestly inflationary environment. As was demonstrated earlier, this same conclusion also holds true for the stock market.

Why do rates seem to rise at both ends of the spectrum—at higher inflation levels and higher deflation levels—while remaining relatively low in the middle? One explanation might be that these extremes represent periods of severe economic problems. Investments during these periods, even in top-quality corporate bonds, appear to involve a higher level of risk. Thus they must provide higher potential returns to be attractive. In higher deflation periods, the risk is usually depression; and in higher inflation periods the risk is twofold, loss of purchasing power and the possibility of economic collapse. Periods of relative price stability, on the other hand, also are typically periods of economic stability and prosperity.

SHORT-TERM INTEREST RATES—A SECOND CUT

Let's take a look now at the short-term interest-rate history. This analysis covers the years between 1831 and 1979, examining historic short-term rates in eight separate inflationary and deflationary environments. We used the consumer price index to define the periods, but unlike the preceding treatment of long-term rates these annual inflation data are not averaged or smoothed. We feel that four- to six-month short rates are most validly analyzed against shorter term inflationary or deflationary conditions.

Again we present the data in two ways. The first includes all years; the second excludes the 1939 to 1950 period to eliminate possible distortions from this "artificial" period.

Once again, you can see that interest rates are lowest in periods of relative price stability and then generally rise as the inflation rate or deflation rate increases (see Exhibit 4). However, with short-term

Exhibit 4
Short-Term Interest Rates, 1831–1979

Inflation/Deflation Environment	All Years			Excluding 1939–1950 As Artificial Years		
	Years	Average	Median	Years	Average	Median
Inflation 10%+	12	6.27%	5.84%	10	7.35%	6.69%
Inflation 6–9%.....................	17	5.61	5.36	14	6.61	5.86
Inflation 3–5%.....................	21	5.32	5.55	20	5.56	5.64
Inflation 2%	20	5.23	5.00	18	5.47	5.24
Stability (1% inflation—1% deflation).	40	4.79	4.52	36	5.21	4.80
Deflation 2–3%.....................	21	6.57	5.62	21	6.57	5.62
Deflation 4–5%.....................	8	6.60	5.89	8	6.60	5.89
Deflation 6%+.....................	10	4.94	4.81	10	4.94	4.81

rates the symmetry is not as smooth as in the case of long-term rates. The short-term interest rate trails the inflation rate. The average rate in periods of very high inflation (10 percent or more) was only 6.27 percent including all years, and 7.35 percent excluding the "artificial" years. Again some observations:

- Short-term rates typically rise somewhat above their average levels in higher inflation environments, but far less than one might expect. This work again indicates that interest rates, this time short-term rates, do not keep pace with accelerating inflation.

- Counter to current theory, history does not substantiate the hypothesis that interest rates reflect the rate of inflation plus "real interest" of even 1 percent to 2 percent. In the 29 years tabulated, where inflation was 6 percent and above, the average short-term interest rate, even in nominal terms, was below the inflation rate, again a negative real rate of interest.

- As with long-term rates, deflation, except at levels of 6 percent or more, also seems to be accompanied by higher short-term interest rates. However, unlike the long-term rate correlation, short rates fell significantly in the higher deflationary years. This may be a function of slackening short-term demand for funds. These 10 high deflation years also tended to be recession or business contraction years. In this environment, the demand for short-term funds is at a low ebb

• As with longer term rates, there seems to be some evidence that periods of relative price stability are a favorable environment for short-term rates.

All things considered, inflation does not necessarily have controlling impact on short-term rates. It appears that business-cycle pressures, with expanding and contracting demand for credit, have a significantly greater impact on short-term rates than do inflation/deflation or price stability. Also, it seems that the perceived economic credit risk factor does not play the important role it does with longer term rates. Short-term credit instruments, because of the very limited time horizons, do not seem to have much variation in risk premiums.

In summary then, regardless of the 1981 experience, it appears that typically neither long-term nor short-term interest rates keep pace with inflation, though both tend to move in the same direction as inflation. However, both long and short rates initially increase with deflation except that short-term rates begin to decline again when the deflation rate reaches 6 percent or more.

"REAL" RATES OF INTEREST: IT AIN'T NECESSARILY SO

Professional investors, economists, politicians, businesspeople and bankers, with few exceptions, still accept the theory of a "real" rate of interest. The "real" rate of interest is arrived at by subtracting the inflation rate from the quoted (nominal) interest rate. Thus, if nominal interest rates are 9 percent and the current inflation rate is 6 percent, then the real interest rate would be 3 percent. The rationale behind this theory of "real" interest is that inflation erodes the value of a dollar, so a lender who lends money for five years at 6 percent is a real loser if inflation over that five years runs at 7 percent, or even only 6.5 percent. In effect, the lender actually has lost money at a rate of 1 percent or 0.5 percent per year. Obviously, this is not good business.

Therefore, a lender who expects inflation to run at 7 percent during the next five years should charge interest of 10 percent. This would give a "real" rate of interest (that is, a real return) of 3 percent per year.

This all seems to make sense from the lender's standpoint. The theory of "real" interest rates has been around for a long time, at least in academic circles. Professional fixed income investors, underwriters, and bond issuers began focusing on the concept in the last decade or so.

One of the primary reasons for this awareness was a chart that regularly appeared in *Monetary Trends,* a monthly publication of the Federal Reserve Bank of St. Louis. This bank was and is a leader in espousing monetary theory, and its weekly and monthly publications are among the most widely read reports in the investment world.

The chart shown as Exhibit 5 first appeared on the back cover of *Monetary Trends* where it was immediately apparent to a reader, and

Exhibit 5
Yields on Highest Grade Seasoned Corporate Bonds

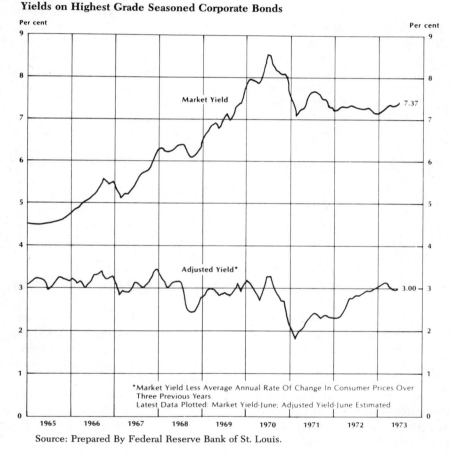

Source: Prepared By Federal Reserve Bank of St. Louis.

it "proved" to many professionals that the theory of "real" interest rates was fact. Perhaps it was some kind of natural law. The chart shows market interest rates climbing steadily from about 4.5 percent at the beginning of 1965 to a peak of about 8.5 percent in 1970, with a few fluctuations along the way, and then settling at about 7.4 percent through 1972 and 1973. Through all of this, the adjusted yield (the market yield less the annual rate of change in consumer prices over the three previous years) hovered fairly consistently around 3 percent, with one plunge as low as 2 percent at the beginning of 1971. This apparent historic documentation, combined with the appealing rational underlying theory, led to an almost universal acceptance.

Admittedly, the chart is impressive. The adjusted yield or "real" rate of interest has remained remarkably stable in the period covered. The approach very neatly rationalized and perhaps justified the high rates of the late 1960s and 1970s, rates that were unprecedented for most living investors.

This writer was introduced to the world of investments in 1960. Back then no professionals, except perhaps a few on the lunatic fringe, believed long-term high-grade bonds could ever, in their lifetime, yield more than 6 percent. But the 6 percent barrier was broken in 1968. It was a new world and there just had to be an explanation, a rationale. Rates kept going up, moving through 7 percent in the next two years, then 8 percent. But "real" interest rate theory could explain it all. Lenders, of course, were very pleased with this thesis because it provided an excellent defense against consumer and political charges of usury and excessive profits. After all, when the inflation erosion of the dollar was subtracted, their "real" return was only a skimpy 2 percent to 3 percent.

But one of the problems encountered in applying the theory of "real" interest rates to a current situation is determining what the inflation adjustment factor should be. The key is really the future inflation rate, and that may not be the same as past experience. The St. Louis Fed, in its chart calculation, used the average annual rate of inflation, as measured by the CPI, over the previous three years as a proxy for expected future rates. But this did not fit very well in 1974 and 1975, so the statistics were rejuggled.

Theorists maintain the proper inflation rate adjustment is the expected rate of future inflation. Few, however, are willing to stick their necks out and actually predict future inflation, and as we have seen, economists also have a very poor record for predicting inflation, even one year in advance. Thus, the past typically continues to serve as a proxy for the future. Factoring in 1974 and 1975, it was found the past inflation-rate/interest-rate correlation fits better if a five-year average of past inflation is used instead of a three-year average as a proxy for expected inflation. But more on that later.

First, let's take a look at the long-term history of "real" interest volatility year to year. In Exhibit 6 the deflation rate has been added to the nominal interest rate during periods of deflation because the dollar becomes worth more in such periods. In periods of inflation, the inflation rate has been subtracted from the nominal interest rate to determine the "real" rate.

As can clearly be seen, the "real" rate of interest is far more volatile

Exhibit 6
"Real" Interest 1791–1909—Long-Term Interest Rates Adjusted for Inflation/Deflation

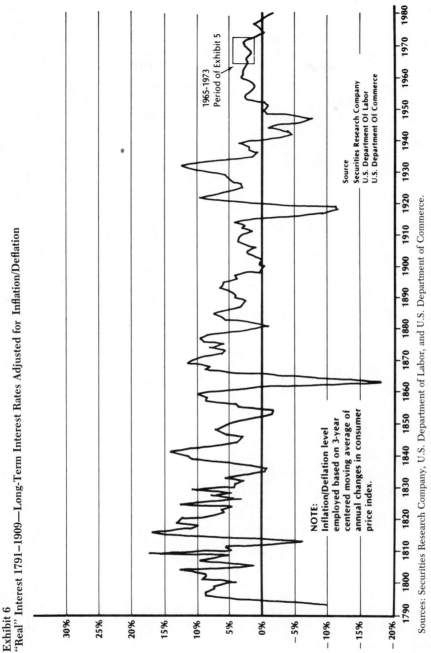

Sources: Securities Research Company, U.S. Department of Labor, and U.S. Department of Commerce.

than perceived. Even when inflation and deflation have been
smoothed with a three-year average, the swings have run from a positive 17 percent to a negative 18 percent. During the Civil War inflation, for example, the "real" rate of interest plunged to a minus 18
percent. Similarly, it plunged to minus 12 percent in the World War I
inflation and then climbed to more than 12 percent in the 1930s. On
two other occasions, early in the history of the nation, the "real" interest rate rose to more than 15 percent. In late 1981 (not shown in
Exhibit 6) it spurted up to 6 to 7 percent, the highest levels since the
1930s.

There have been 10 periods of negative "real" interest, ranging
from 1 year to 10 years in duration. But the relative stability of "real"
interest from the mid-1950s through 1969 is unique. And this is the
statistical base of evidence most commonly used to support the concept of "real" interest. No similar extended period of stability can be
found in the almost 200 years covered by the chart.

If we look at Exhibit 7, we can see that at first glance the "real" rate
of interest appears to be just what the experts say—about 3 percent.
Between 1792 and 1979 the median long-term bond rate was 4.84
percent, and the average annual inflation rate was 1.5 percent. Subtracting the latter from the former we get a "real" rate of interest of
3.34 percent.

Exhibit 7
Variable "Real" Rates

1792–1979	Median annual long-term bond rate	4.84%
	Less: average annual inflation rate	(1.50)
	"Real" rate of interest	3.34%
1792–1979	Inflation years only, where three-year centered moving aver-age is 2.5 percent or more.	
	Median annual long-term bond rate	4.84%
	Less: median annual inflation rate	(5.20)
	"Real" rate of interest	−0.36%
1792–1979	High inflation years only, where three-year centered moving average is 5.5 percent or more.	
	Median annual long-term bond rate	5.06%
	Less: median annual inflation rate	(8.50)
	"Real" rate of interest	−3.44%

However, if we take the academician's first approach and assume a
three-year moving average of inflation as the appropriate inflation-
adjustment factor, and if we include only inflation years (years where
the inflation rate is 2.5 percent or more), then we get a different picture. Now the "real" interest rate is minus 0.36 percent.

If we look at high inflation years only (years when the inflation rate
is 5.5 percent or more), then the picture is even gloomier because the

"real" rate of interest declines to minus 3.44 percent. This is not very helpful to those who maintain there is a constant "real" rate of interest and that it hovers between 2 percent and 3 percent, basing their investment actions on this axiom.

If we look at the history in 30-year periods (see Exhibit 8), the picture becomes even more confusing because the "real" interest rate was highest in the earliest periods (in the 1792–1821 and 1822–1851 periods). It then declined continuously, except that in the most recent 30-year period, 1950–1979, it edged up again to 1.66 percent.

Exhibit 8
Annual Bond, Inflation and "Real" Interest Rates, 1792–1979

Years	Average Long-Term Bonds	Compounded Annual Inflation Rate	Real Rate of Return
By 30-year periods:			
1792–1821	6.24%	0.65%	5.59%
1822–1851	5.06	−0.36	5.42
1852–1881	5.07	1.02	4.05
1882–1911	3.62	0.36	3.26
1912–1941	4.06	1.39	2.67
1942–1971	3.81	3.43	0.38
Most recent 30 years:			
1950–1979	5.48%	3.82%	1.66%
By 15-year periods:			
1792–1806	6.36%	2.90%	3.46%
1807–1821	6.13	−1.56	7.69
1822–1836	4.80	0.71	4.09
1837–1851	5.32	−1.42	6.74
1852–1866	5.24	4.26	0.98
1867–1881	4.90	−2.12	7.02
1882–1896	3.68	−1.15	4.83
1897–1911	3.56	1.90	1.66
1912–1926	4.49	4.11	0.38
1927–1941	3.64	−1.26	4.90
1942–1956	2.80	4.18	−1.38
1957–1971	5.11	2.69	2.42
Most recent 15 years:			
1965–1979	7.15%	5.66%	1.49%

Breaking history into 15-year periods gives more erratic results, with the "real" rate reaching a high of 7.69 percent in the 1807–1821 period and a low of minus 1.38 percent in the 1942–1956 period.

How then, do the experts conclude that the "real" interest rate is stable over time? It depends on when you look at it.

It is almost as though economic history started in 1954, the year most of the monetary experts' "long term" charts begin. The question is, is this a result of laziness or inadequate data? Perhaps it is that the earlier data failed to support their "theory" with any degree of consistency.

The concept of a "real" rate of interest is widely held, but it does not appear to be a natural law. It is not a truism that has prevailed forever. Like many investment concepts and theories, sometimes it works and sometimes it doesn't.

"REAL" INTEREST ONLY IN PERIODS OF INFLATION

Exhibit 9 groups years into inflationary periods. For example, there have been 28 years since 1790 when inflation ranged between 0.5 percent and 1.4 percent. In these 28 years, the "real" interest rate averaged 3.27 percent. In the 17 years when inflation ranged between 1.5 percent and 2.4 percent, the nominal interest rate averaged 4.15 percent, and the "real" rate declined to an average of 2.14 percent. As the inflation rate increases, the "real" interest rate declines steadily, until at an inflation rate of more than 7.5 percent (17 years) the nominal interest rate averages 5.72 percent, but the "real" interest rate is minus 6.69 percent! The inclusion of 1980 and 1981 would modify this slightly. Using this method, 1980 provided a positive return of less than 1 percent, and the "real rate" for 1981 averaged 6 percent. This brings the average negative rate of return down about 100 basis points from that in Exhibit 9.

Exhibit 9
"Real" Interest Rates on Long-Term Bonds (three-year centered average inflation)

Inflation Environment	Years	Nominal Rate Average	Nominal Rate Median	Real Rate Average	Real Rate Median
7.5%+.................	17	5.72	5.48	−6.69	−5.88
5.5–7.4%	13	5.30	5.13	−1.14	−0.84
3.5–5.4%	15	5.27	6.01	0.81	1.28
2.5–3.4%	15	3.98	3.55	1.03	0.62
1.5–2.4%	17	4.15	4.37	2.14	2.43
0.5–1.4%	28	4.25	4.28	3.27	3.07

Exhibit 10 presents annual "real" interest rates for those years in which the three-year average of inflation was 2.5 percent or higher. This eliminates deflation distortion as well as periods of relative price stability. All qualifying inflation years, 1793 through 1980, are included (61 years in all). An additional 45 years of mild inflation ranging from 0.5 percent to 2.4 percent, have been tabulated. But it was believed that these data were actually more representative of an economic condition of relative price stability. These 45 years are also examined in *The Myths of Inflation and Investing*.

Exhibit 10
"Real" Long-Term Interest Rates in 2.5 Percent plus Inflation Years (using 3-year centered average of CPI as inflation proxy)

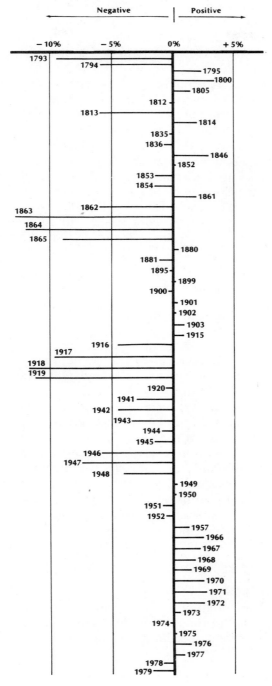

Exhibit 10 shows that the volatility of "real" interest rates in periods of inflation is similar to the volatility shown in Exhibit 9. There have been 28 years of positive "real" interest inflation environments and 33 years of negative "real" interest. In only 8 out of the 61 years the "real" interest rate exceeded 2 percent less than 14 percent of the time. Again in Exhibit 10, the only period of reasonable consistency appears to be the more recent period through 1977. Exhibit 10 also supports another earlier conclusion: If the theory espousing a continuing, relatively stable level of "real" interest rates is some form of natural law, Moses must have brought it down from the mountain on a stone tablet sometime in the early 1950s.

Taking a closer look, Exhibit 11 recasts the annual "real" interest-rate data into specific inflation environments. Four environments were selected with approximately the same number of years falling in each environment. Environment I includes years in which the three-year average of inflation was 7.5 percent or higher; environment II was the 5.5 percent to 7.4 percent range; environment III was 3.5 percent to 5.4 percent; and environment IV was 2.5 percent to 3.4 percent.

OBSERVATIONS

The conclusions are immediately obvious: The higher the inflation rate, the less likely a positive "real" rate of interest is to be achieved. Further, the 2 percent to 3 percent "real" rate of interest rule of thumb never prevailed with inflation above 5.5 percent until 1981, although it did come close in 1976. If investors strongly believed that long-term quality bonds are priced in terms of nominal rates, which would return a "real" rate of 2 percent to 3 percent plus compensation for anticipated erosion of the dollar through inflation, they had better think again because "it ain't necessarily so," not if a three-year average of past inflation is used as a proxy for future inflation. Even in periods of relatively mild inflation—2.5 percent to 3.4 percent—the "real" interest rate was only 1 percent or less in 10 of 15 years.

We have also run the same test applying the now more popular five-year average of past inflation as the proxy for anticipated inflation. This works a little better, but not much.

"REAL" INTEREST AND SHORT-TERM RATES

The concept of "real" interest rates usually is applied to long-term interest rates. Data relating to short-term rates (average annual rates for four- to six-month prime commercial paper or equivalent) dating back to 1831 have been accumulated but are not presented in this chapter.

Exhibit 11
"Real" Long-Term Interest Rate in Inflation Years (three-year centered average)

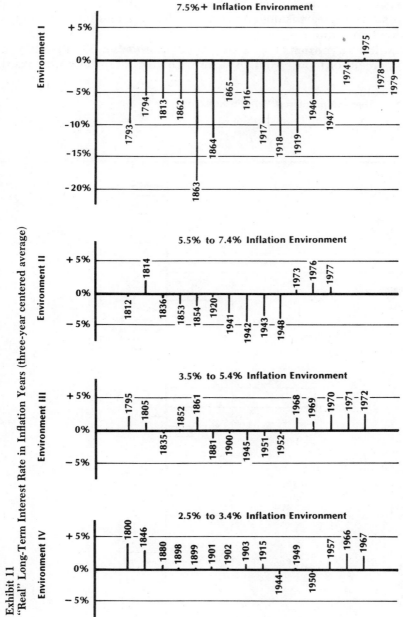

Comparing apples with apples, the annual average short-term rate was run against the annual inflation rate. Smoothing the inflation rate across several years is not appropriate when the credit instrument has a life of six months or less.

Exhibit 12 presents the "real" rate of interest for 53 inflation years (2.5 percent or more) from 1831 through 1979. Exhibit 13 breaks the

Exhibit 12
"Real" Short-Term Interest Rates in Inflation Years

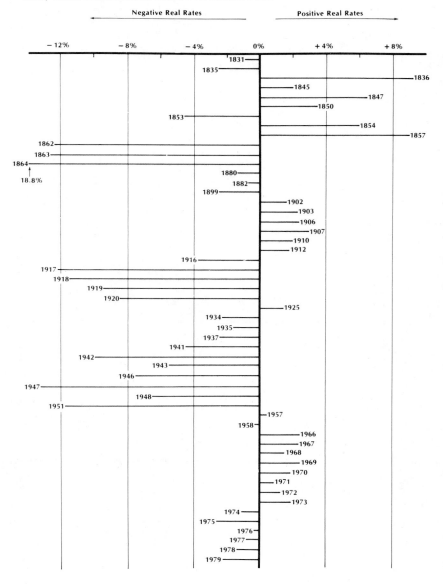

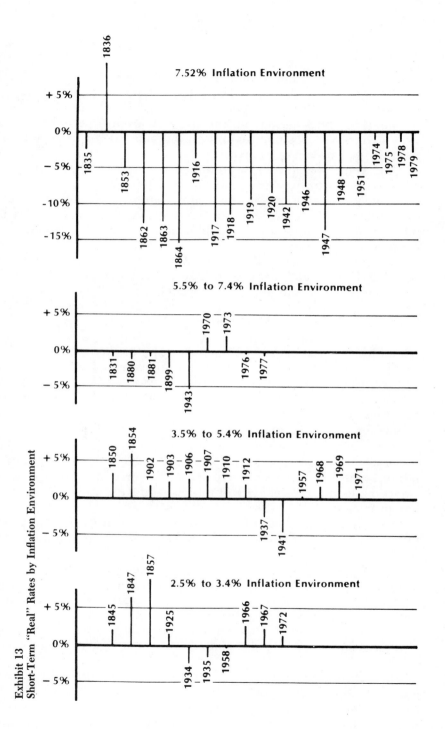

Exhibit 13
Short-Term "Real" Rates by Inflation Environment

same data down in the same four inflation environments used earlier, but this time it is based on existing annual rates of inflation.

As can be seen from Exhibit 12, 22 of the inflation years (42 percent) recorded positive "real" short-term interest rates, but in only 13 years did the rate exceed 2 percent.

The 1966–1973 period and the early 1900s are the only periods with a consistent positive real return, but since 1973 the real short-term rate has become negative.

Thus trying to analyze short-term rates using the concept of "real" return appears to be a frustrating proposition. Inflation appears to have even less influence on short rates than on long rates. Business-cycle considerations are far more important, and the concept of "real" interest rates has little obvious application in short-term money market investing.

The breakdown of "real" short-term rates by inflation environment (see Exhibits 12 and 13) demonstrates that short rates very rarely match inflation rates in inflation environments of 5.5 percent or more. This occurred in only 3 of 29 years recorded. In only one year did the "real" rate of interest rise to more than 2 percent.

In years when inflation was more than 5.5 percent, the average real rate of interest was minus 5.37 percent. The median rate was minus 4.26 percent. In years when inflation was between 2.5 percent and 5.4 percent, the average "real" interest rate was 1.76 percent, and the median "real" rate was 2.01 percent. For all years when inflation was in excess of 2.5 percent, the average "real" rate of interest was minus 2.14 percent, and the median rate was minus 0.89 percent.

In summary, there seems to be little longer term evidence supporting or even suggesting the conclusion that market or nominal rates of interest (long or short term) are historically intrinsically composed of two components: the real rate of interest and a quantifiable expected rate of inflation.

Further, the relative stability of "real" interest from the mid-1950s through 1969 appears to be a rarity and should not be relied upon in future years.

Many of today's authorities on interest rates can be validly criticized for their dogmatic attitudes, their failure to engage in historic supportive research, and their propensity to juggle the facts and time frames to support their conclusions.

In periods of higher inflation, the currently popular quantitative formulas used to justify and explain existing nominal rates have rarely worked at all.

The entire concept of an intrinsic "real" rate of interest has been almost blindly accepted by most investors, economists, and now politicians as economic fact. Few have bothered to critically examine or even question the validity of this concept. The experts are being taken at face value, just as was the case with the "stocks are an inflation hedge" doctrine.

Even though the concept of an intrinsic "real" rate appears to be theory and not fact, it will continue to be an important consideration in the long-term fixed income markets for years to come. If enough people, especially those who control the investment of massive amounts of capital, believe this is an economic truism, they will act accordingly. When sailors thought the world was flat, they sailed as if it was.

This work is not intended to be a definitive, landmark rebuttal of the "real" rate theory. Rather, we hope the discussion may stimulate further sophisticated critical analysis of the concept. While bits and pieces of the study may be validly attacked, it is still clear that no undisputable evidence exists to substantiate the existence of an intrinsic "real" rate of interest. And for literally billions of dollars to be invested annually based on the supposed existence of such a rate, based on the shaky evidence that does exist, borders on the incredible.

It is equally amazing that the academicians in this nation continue to teach this concept in the economics departments and business schools, without so much as a qualification. It's the gospel, to be accepted without question. John Maynard Keynes was once quoted as saying "history is for undergraduates." Maybe that's the problem.

To investors, pension officers, corporations, and professional portfolio managers, we close with this warning combining two well-worn quotes: "Ignorance may well be bliss," but keep in mind, "it ain't necessarily so." In future years the "real" rate of interest may go the way of other once mighty investment myths.

Fixed Income Indices

7

ARTHUR WILLIAMS III, C.F.A.
Vice President—Pension Fund Investments
Merrill Lynch, Pierce, Fenner & Smith, Inc. ·

NOREEN M. CONWELL
Pension Fund Administrator
Merrill Lynch, Pierce, Fenner & Smith, Inc.

INTRODUCTION

As investors become increasingly interested in analyzing their fixed income investments, the need for appropriate benchmarks against which to measure portfolios also grows. This trend has created the need for more accurate and more specific fixed income indices to measure fixed income investments. Fortunately, the marketplace has recognized this need and has developed a large number of indices for use by fixed income investors and analysts. Most of these indices are listed in Exhibits 1 through 7, together with their most important characteristics.[1]

---

[1] Further information regarding some of the indices may be obtained from the following representatives:

Howard B. Harmon, Jr., VP—senior fixed income specialist, Merrill Lynch, Pierce, Fenner & Smith, Inc., (212) 637–8373.

Andrea R. Priest, Lipper Analytical Distributors, Inc., (212) 269–4080.

Ronald J. Ryan, director of fixed income research and strategy, Lehman Brothers Kuhn Loeb, Inc., (212) 558–2602.

Elliot Shurgin, assistant manager, Statistical Research Department, Standard & Poor's Corporation, (212) 248–3460.

Earl Stephens, Moody's Investors Service, Inc., (212) 553–0495.

Statistical Section, *Barron's National Business and Financial Weekly*, (413) 592–7761.

The development of an index to measure a phenomenon requires deciding what is to be measured, how each component is to be weighted (equally or by some other method), and the statistical technique to be applied to the weighted data. For fixed income investments, this simple sounding process is extremely complex. The problems in establishing bond indices are the following:

1. It is difficult to find accurate and consistent information as to the prices of bonds at a point in time. Whereas most of the stocks in which institutional investors invest are traded on stock exchanges, bonds are traded over-the-counter, and hence it is difficult to establish the timing and price of transactions.
2. Bonds change characteristics as time passes. For instance, a 20-year bond today is a 19-year bond a year from today, and 19-year bonds behave somewhat differently from 20-year bonds.
3. The transition of bonds from one category to another creates the need to add and subtract bonds from categories.
4. Newly issued bonds being added to an index have different yield levels from existing bonds and thus perform slightly differently.

TYPES OF INDICES

There are at least three types of indices that might be of interest to investors: those relating to price, yield, and total return. Price indices measure only the prices of bonds; yield indices measure yield to maturity (although they could also measure current return); and total-return indices show the return an investor would have achieved in a certain type bond over a given period through a combination of price change, coupon interest, and interest on interest. The total-return index, which is more comprehensive than the others, breaks out the return attributable to the three major factors impacting bonds and totals them to provide a true rate of return based on the assumption as to reinvestment rate.

MEASURING RISK OF INDICES

Increasingly, investors are concerned not only with return but also with the risk taken in achieving that return. This has created the need to measure the riskiness of portfolios and indices. A number of methods have been established for this purpose. Chapter 44 discusses how the risk in fixed income portfolios can be measured. Since bond indices are really just specific portfolios, these techniques can be applied to indices as well.

Exhibit 1
Corporate Bond Indices

Index Name	Number of Securities	Total MV, PV* ($ billions)	Securities Included	Type (yield, total return, etc.)†	Weighting	Calculation	Period and Base Amount	YTM or Coupon and Period	Number of Years to Maturity	Beginning Date of Index	Source of Bond Prices	Historical Information and Frequency
Salomon Brothers High-Grade LT AAA–AA............	845	PV = $82.58	AAA–AA	Total return	Par value	Arithmetic	1978 = 100	y = 15.45% 11/1/81	23 years	1/1/69	Salomon Trading Desks	1969 monthly
Salomon Brothers LT A..............		PV = 58.00	A	Total return	Par value	Arithmetic	1978 = 100	c = 8.92 11/1/81	22 years	1/1/78	Salomon Trading Desks	1969 monthly
Salomon Brothers High-Grade LT AAA–AA–A..........		PV = 140.00	AAA–AA–A	Total return	Par value	Arithmetic	1978 = 100	c = 8.648 11/1/81	23 years	1/1/78	Salomon Trading Desks	1969 monthly
Barron's Best Grade Bonds............	10	N/A	Aaa	YTM	Equally	Bond value tables	N/A	y = 13% 11/12/81 c = 5¼% 11/12/81	15 years 11/12/81	1/32	The Wall Street Journal	No
Barron's Intermediates Grade Bonds............	10	N/A	Baa	YTM	Equally	Bond value tables	N/A	y = 14½% 11/12/81 c = 7⅜% 11/12/81	20 years 11/12/81	7/76	The Wall Street Journal	No
Dow Jones 20 Bonds Average..........	20	N/A	Aaa	YTM	Equally	Bond value tables	N/A	y = 14⅛% 11/12/81 c = 7½% 11/12/81	20 years 11/12/81	7/76	The Wall Street Journal	No
Dow Jones 10 Industrial Bonds Average...........	10	N/A	Aaa	YTM	Equally	Bond value tables	N/A	y = 13¾% 11/12/81 c = 6¾% 11/12/81	12 years 11/12/81	4/15	The Wall Street Journal	No

											The Wall Street Journal		No
Dow Jones 10 Public Utility Bond Average.....	10	N/A	Aaa	YTM	Equally	Bond Value tables	N/A	y = 14½% 11/12/81 c = 8⅜% 11/12/81	20 years 11/12/81	4/15	Salomon Brothers	1971— weekly; 1900— monthly	
Standard & Poor's Corp. Composite Bond Yield Average–AAA..........	8–AAA Ind. 8–AAA Util. 16	N/A	AAA	YTM	Equally	Arithmetic	N/A	y = 15.36% 10/21/81	20–25 years 10/21/81	4/37	Salomon Brothers	1971— weekly; 1937— monthly	
Standard & Poor's Corp. Composite Bond Yield Average–AA..........	8–AA Ind. 8–AA Util. 16	N/A	AA	YTM	Equally	Arithmetic	N/A	y = 15.75% 10/21/81	20–25 years 10/21/81	1/37	Salomon Brothers	1971— weekly; 1937— monthly	
Standard & Poor's Corp. Composite Bond Yield Average–A..........	7–A Ind. 8–A Util. 15	N/A	A	YTM	Equally	Arithmetic	N/A	y = 15.97% 10/21/81	20–25 years 10/21/81	1/37	Salomon Brothers	1971— weekly; 1937— monthly	
Standard & Poor's Corp. Composite Bond Yield Average–BBB..........	7–BBB Ind. 8–BBB Util. 15	N/A	BBB	YTM	Equally	Arithmetic	N/A	y = 16.94% 10/21/81	20–25 years 10/21/81	1/37	Salomon Brothers	1971— weekly; 1937— monthly	
Standard & Poor's Corp. Composite Bond Price Index–AAA ..	8–Inds AAA 8–Util AAA 16	N/A	AAA	Price	Equally	Converted into a price assuming 4 percent coupon and 20 years maturity	N/A	c = 4% 10/21/81 p = 29.84% 10/21/81	20 years 10/21/81	1/37	Salomon Brothers	1971— weekly; 1900— monthly	

N/A = not available.
* MV = market value; PV = par value. Unless otherwise indicated, amount represents MV.
† YTM = yield-to-maturity.

Exhibit 1 (*continued*)

Index Name	Number of Securities	Total MV, PV* ($ billions)	Securities Included	Type (yield, total return, etc.)†	Weighting	Calculation	Period and Base Amount	YTM or Coupon and Period	Number of Years to Maturity	Beginning Date of Index	Source of Bond Prices	Historical Information and Frequency
Standard & Poor's Industrial Bond Yield Average–AAA	8–Inds AAA 8–Util AAA 16	N/A	AAA	YTM	Equally	Arithmetic	N/A	y = 15.22% 10/21/81	15–25 years 10/21/81	1/37	Salomon Brothers	1971—weekly; 1937—monthly
Standard & Poor's Industrial Bond Yield Average–AA	8–Inds AA 8–Util AA 16	N/A	AA	YTM	Equally	Arithmetic	N/A	y = 15.46% 10/21/81	15–25 years 10/21/81	1/37	Salomon Brothers	1971—weekly; 1937—monthly
Standard & Poor's Industrial Bond Yield Average–A	7–Ind A 8–Util A 15	N/A	A	YTM	Equally	Arithmetic	N/A	y = 15.63% 10/21/81	15–25 years 10/21/81	1/37	Salomon Brothers	1971—weekly; 1937—monthly
Standard & Poor's Industrial Bond Yield Average–BBB	7–Ind BBB 8–Util BBB 15	N/A	BBB	YTM	Equally	Arithmetic	N/A	y = 16.68% 10/21/81	15–25 years 10/21/81	1/37	Salomon Brothers	1971—weekly; 1937—monthly
Lehman Brothers Kuhn Loeb Corp. Bond Index	4,270	181.308	AA–	Total return	Market value	Arithmetic	N/A	y = 14.30% 11/81	1 year+	12/72	Lehman Brothers Kuhn Loeb	12/72—monthly
Lehman Brothers Kuhn Loeb Intermediate Corp. Bond Index	1,484.5	62.144	AA–	Total return	Market value	Arithmetic	N/A	y = 14.11% 11/81	1 year+	12/72	Lehman Brothers Kuhn Loeb	12/72—monthly
Lehman Brothers Kuhn Loeb Long-Term Corp. Bond Index	2,785.5	119.164	AA–	Total return	Market value	Arithmetic	N/A	y = 14.40% 11/81	1 year+	12/72	Lehman Brothers Kuhn Loeb	12/72—monthly

Lehman Brothers Kuhn Loeb Industrial Bond Index............	876.5	52.673	AA−	Total return	Market value	Arithmetic	N/A	y = 13.92% 11/81	1 year+	12/72	Lehman Brothers Kuhn Loeb	12/72—monthly
Lehman Brothers Kuhn Loeb Utility Bond Index............	2,829.5	94.246	AA−	Total return	Market value	Arithmetic	N/A	y = 14.35% 11/81	1 year+	12/72	Lehman Brothers Kuhn Loeb	12/72—monthly
Lehman Brothers Kuhn Loeb Finance Bond Index............	564.0	34.388	AA	Total return	Market value	Arithmetic	N/A	y = 14.73% 11/81	1 year+	12/72	Lehman Brothers Kuhn Loeb	12/72—monthly
Lehman Brothers Kuhn Loeb Aaa Bond Index.....	1,048.5	440.593	AAA	Total return	Market value	Arithmetic	N/A	y = 12.81% 11/81	1 year+	12/72	Lehman Brothers Kuhn Loeb	12/72—monthly
Lehman Brothers Kuhn Loeb Aa Bond Index.....	985.5	43.207	AA	Total return	Market value	Arithmetic	N/A	y = 14.0% 11/81	1 year+	12/72	Lehman Brothers Kuhn Loeb	12/72—monthly
Lehman Brothers Kuhn Loeb A Bond Index......	1,819.5	66.924	A+	Total return	Market value	Arithmetic	N/A	y = 14.53% 11/81	1 year+	12/72	Lehman Brothers Kuhn Loeb	12/72—monthly
Lehman Brothers Kuhn Loeb Baa Bond Index....	929.5	25.874	BBB+	Total return	Market value	Arithmetic	N/A	y = 15.43% 11/81	1 year+	12/72	Lehman Brothers Kuhn Loeb	12/72—monthly
Moody's Aaa Industrial Bond Average	10	N/A	Aaa	YTM	N/A	Arithmetic	N/A	c = 10½%	25 years	1918	Newspaper	1918—monthly
Moody's Aa Industrial Bond Average	10	N/A	Aa	YTM	N/A	Arithmetic	N/A	c = 10¼%	23⅜ years	1918	Newspaper	1918—monthly
Moody's A Industrial Bond Average	10	N/A	A	YTM	N/A	Arithmetic	N/A	c = 13¼%	26⅞ years	1918	Newspaper	1918—monthly

N/A = not available.
* MV = market value; PV = par value. Unless otherwise indicated, amount represents MV.
† YTM = yield-to-maturity.

Exhibit 1 (*continued*)

Index Name	Number of Securities	Total MV, PV* ($ billions)	Securities Included	Type (yield, total return, etc.)†	Weighting	Calculation	Period and Base Amount	YTM or Coupon and Period	Number of Years to Maturity	Beginning Date of Index	Source of Bond Prices	Historical Information and Frequency
Moody's Baa Industrial Bond Average	10	N/A	Baa	YTM	N/A	Arithmetic	N/A	c = 10⅛%	18¼ years	1918	Newspaper	1918—monthly
Moody's Industrial Average	40	N/A	Aaa,Aa,A Baa	YTM	N/A	Arithmetic	N/A			1918	Newspaper	1918—monthly
Moody's Aaa Public Utility Average	10	N/A	Aaa	YTM	N/A	Arithmetic	N/A	c = 12⅛%	36½ years	1918	Newspaper	1918—monthly
Moody's Aa Public Utility Average	10	N/A	Aa	YTM	N/A	Arithmetic	N/A	c = 13¾%	29 years	1918	Newspaper	1918—monthly
Moody's A Public Utility Average	10	N/A	A	YTM	N/A	Arithmetic	N/A	c = 15%	28¾ years	1918	Newspaper	1918—monthly
Moody's Baa Public Utility Average	10	N/A	Baa	YTM	N/A	Arithmetic	N/A	c = 15½%	28¾ years	1918	Newspaper	1918—monthly
Moody's Public Utility Average	40	N/A	Aaa,Aa,A Baa	YTM	N/A	Arithmetic	N/A			1918	Newspaper	1918—monthly
Moody's Aa Railroad Bond Average	8	N/A	Aa	YTM	N/A	Arithmetic	N/A	c = 6⅜%	21 years	1918	Newspaper	1918—monthly
Moody's A Railroad Bond Average	10	N/A	A	YTM	N/A	Arithmetic	N/A	c = 6%	18⅝ years	1918	Newspaper	1918—monthly
Moody's Baa Railroad Bond Average	5	N/A	Baa	YTM	N/A	Arithmetic	N/A	c = 5⅝%	23 years	1918	Newspaper	1918—monthly
Moody's Railroad Bond Average	23	N/A	Aa,A,Baa	YTM	N/A	Arithmetic	N/A			1918	Newspaper	1918—monthly

Index	Number	MV/PV	Quality	Return	Weighting	Average	Base	Coupon/Yield	Maturity	Start	Source	Period
Moody's Aaa Corp. Composite	20	N/A	Aaa utilities and industrials	YTM	N/A	Arithmetic	N/A		15 years+	1918	Newspaper	1918—monthly
Moody's Aa Corp. Composite	20	N/A	Aa utilities and industrials	YTM	N/A	Arithmetic	N/A		15 years+	1918	Newspaper	1918—monthly
Moody's A Corp. Composite	20	N/A	A utilities and industrials	YTM	N/A	Arithmetic	N/A		15 years+	1918	Newspaper	1918—monthly
Moody's Baa Corp. Composite	20	N/A	Baa utilities and industrials	YTM	N/A	Arithmetic	N/A		15 years+	1918	Newspaper	1918—monthly
Moody's Corp. Average Composite	80	N/A	High-quality utilities and industrials	YTM	N/A	Arithmetic	N/A		15 years+	1918	Newspaper	1918—monthly
Merrill Lynch	3983	MV = 184.0 PV = 286.8	A/AA	Total return	Market value	Arithmetic	12/31/72 = 100	c = 8.930% y = 15.796% 10/81	17.72 10/81	12/31/72	Merrill Lynch Bond Pricing	1973
Merrill Lynch Long Term (15 years+)	2106	MV = 105.0 PV = 177.3	A/AA	Total return	Market value	Arithmetic	12/31/72 = 100	c = 9.091% y = 15.831% 10/81	24.07 10/81	12/31/72	Merrill Lynch Bond Pricing	1973
Merrill Lynch Long Term (15 years+), High Quality	784	MV = 51.5 PV = 87.3	AA/AAA	Total return	Market value	Arithmetic	12/31/72 = 100	c = 9.043% y = 15.648% 10/81	25.44 10/81	12/31/72	Merrill Lynch Bond Pricing	1973
Merrill Lynch Long-Term (15 years+), High-Quality Utilities	519	MV = 27.0 PV = 47.0	AA/AAA	Total return	Market value	Arithmetic	12/31/72 = 100	c = 8.855% y = 15.677% 10/81	27.91 10/81	12/31/72	Merrill Lynch Bond Pricing	1973

N/A = not available.
* MV = market value; PV = par value. Unless otherwise indicated, amount represents MV.
† YTM = yield-to-maturity.

Exhibit 1 (*continued*)

Index Name	Number of Securities	Total MV, PV* ($ billions)	Securities Included	Type (yield, total return, etc.)†	Weighting	Calculation	Period and Base Amount	YTM or Coupon and Period	Number of Years to Maturity	Beginning Date of Index	Source of Bond Prices	Historical Information and Frequency
Merrill Lynch Long-Term (15 years+), High-Quality Utilities—Coupons 4–5.99 Percent.........	64	MV = 1.6 PV = 4.2	AAA/AAA	Total return	Market value	Arithmetic	12/31/72 = 100	c = 4.961% y = 15.057% 10/81	19.43 10/81	12/31/72	Merrill Lynch Bond Pricing	1973
Merrill Lynch Long-Term (15 years+), High-Quality Utilities—Coupons 6–7.99 Percent.........	154	MV = 5.7 PV = 11.8	AA/AAA	Total return	Market value	Arithmetic	12/31/72 = 100	c = 7.242% y = 15.408% 10/81	24.64 10/81	12/31/72	Merrill Lynch Bond Pricing	1973
Merrill Lynch Long-Term (15 years+), High-Quality Utilities—Coupons 8–9.99 Percent.........	240	MV = 12.4 PV = 22.0	AA/AAA	Total return	Market value	Arithmetic	12/31/72 = 100	c = 8.708% y = 15.637% 10/81	28.47 10/81	12/31/72	Merrill Lynch Bond Pricing	1973
Merrill Lynch Long-Term (15 years+), High-Quality Utilities—Coupons 10–11.99 Percent.........	23	MV = 2.1 PV = 3.0	AA/AAA	Total return	Market value	Arithmetic	9/30/74 = 100	c = 11.136% y = 15.963% 10/81	34.84 10/81	9/30/74	Merrill Lynch Bond Pricing	1973
Merrill Lynch Long-Term (15 years+), High-Quality Industrials.........	108	MV = 11.4 PV = 18.8	AA/AAA	Total return	Market value	Arithmetic	12/31/72 = 100	c = 8.951% y = 15.195% 10/81	22.57 10/81	12/31/72	Merrill Lynch Bond Pricing	1973

Merrill Lynch Long-Term (15 years+), High-Quality Industrials— Coupons 6–7.99 Percent 32	MV = 2.2 PV = 4.1	AA/AAA	Total return	Market value	Arithmetic	12/31/72 = 100	c = 7.303% y = 14.778% 10/81	21.11 10/81	12/31/72	Merrill Lynch Bond Pricing	1973
Merrill Lynch Long-Term (15 years+), High-Quality Industrials— Coupons 8–9.99 Percent 59	MV = 6.7 PV = 11.4	AA/AAA	Total return	Market value	Arithmetic	12/31/72 = 100	c = 8.696% y = 15.215% 10/81	21.82 10/81	12/31/72	Merrill Lynch Bond Pricing	1973
Merrill Lynch Long-Term (15 years+), High-Quality Industrials— Coupons 10–11.99 Percent 9	MV = 1.1 PV = 1.5	AA/AAA	Total return	Market value	Arithmetic	12/31/72 = 100	c = 10.990% y = 15.513% 10/81	27.65 10/81	12/31/72	Merrill Lynch Bond Pricing	1973
Merrill Lynch Long-Term (15 years+), High-Quality Finance 38	MV = 3.4 PV = 5.7	AA/AAA	Total return	Market value	Arithmetic	12/31/72 = 100	c = 9.181% y = 15.979% 10/81	22.60 10/81	12/31/72	Merrill Lynch Bond Pricing	1973
Merrill Lynch Long-Term (15 years+), High-Quality Finance— Coupons 6–7.99 Percent 8	MV = .5 PV = 1.0	AA/AAA	Total return	Market value	Arithmetic	12/31/72 = 100	c = 6.987% y = 15.628% 10/81	22.41 10/81	12/31/72	Merrill Lynch Bond Pricing	1973

N/A = not available.
* MV = market value; PV = par value. Unless otherwise indicated, amount represents MV.
† YTM = yield-to-maturity.

Exhibit 1 (*continued*)

Index Name	Number of Securities	Total MV, PV* ($ billions)	Securities Included	Type (yield, total return, etc.)†	Weighting	Calculation	Period and Base Amount	YTM or Coupon and Period	Number of Years to Maturity	Beginning Date of Index	Source of Bond Prices	Historical Information and Frequency
Merrill Lynch Long-Term (15 years+), High-Quality Finance—Coupons 8–9.99 Percent	22	MV = 1.9 PV = 3.4	AA/AAA	Total return	Market value	Arithmetic	12/31/72 = 100	c = 8.739% y = 15.894% 10/81	22.45 10/81	12/31/72	Merrill Lynch Bond Pricing	1973
Merrill Lynch Long-Term (15 years+), High-Quality Finance—Coupons 10–11.99 Percent	4	MV = .6 PV = .8	AA/AAA	Total return	Market value	Arithmetic	9/30/74 = 100	c = 11.447% y = 16.423% 10/81	21.80 10/81	9/30/74	Merrill Lynch Bond Pricing	1973
Merrill Lynch Long-Term (15 years+), Medium-Quality	132	MV = 53.5 PV = 90.0	A/A	Total return	Market value	Arithmetic	12/31/72 = 100	c = 9.138% y = 16.010% 10/81	22.74 10/81	12/31/72	Merrill Lynch Bond Pricing	1973
Merrill Lynch Long-Term (15 years+), Medium Quality Utilities	962	MV = 29.8 PV = 52.3	A/BBB	Total return	Market value	Arithmetic	12/31/72 = 100	c = 9.279% y = 16.675% 10/81	23.20 10/81	12/31/72	Merrill Lynch Bond Pricing	1973
Merrill Lynch Long-Term (15 years+), Medium-Quality Utilities—Coupons 4–5.99 Percent	34	MV = .5 PV = 1.3	A/A	Total return	Market value	Arithmetic	12/31/72 = 100	c = 5.297% y = 16.085% 10/81	16.58 10/81	12/31/72	Merrill Lynch Bond Pricing	1973

Merrill Lynch Long-Term (15 years+), Medium-Quality Utilities—Coupons 6–7.99 Percent	306	MV = 6.2 PV = 13.1	A/BBB	Total return	Market value	Arithmetic	12/31/72 = 100	c = 7.317% = y = 16.510% 10/81	19.26 10/81	12/31/72	Merrill Lynch Bond Pricing	1973
Merrill Lynch Long-Term (15 years+), Medium-Quality Utilities—Coupons 8–9.99 Percent	444	MV = 14.2 PV = 25.8	A/BBB	Total return	Market value	Arithmetic	12/31/72 = 100	c = 8.896% = y = 16.595% 10/81	23.91 10/81	12/31/72	Merrill Lynch Bond Pricing	1973
Merrill Lynch Long-Term (15 years+), Medium-Quality Utilities—Coupons 10–11.99 Percent	92	MV = 3.5 PV = 5.4	A/BBB	Total return	Market value	Arithmetic	12/31/72 = 100	c = 10.690% = y = 16.831% 10/81	24.77 10/81	12/31/72	Merrill Lynch Bond Pricing	1973
Merrill Lynch Long-Term (15 years+), Medium-Quality Industrials............	256	MV = 19.2 PV = 29.9	A/A	Total return	Market value	Arithmetic	12/31/72 = 100	c = 8.891% = y = 14.700% 10/81	22.55 10/81	12/31/72	Merrill Lynch Bond Pricing	1973
Merrill Lynch Long-Term (15 years+), Medium-Quality Industrials—Coupons 6–7.99 Percent	64	MV = 7.6 PV = 11.2	A/A	Total return	Market value	Arithmetic	12/31/72 = 100	c = 7.504% = y = 12.410% 10/81	22.91 10/81	12/31/72	Merrill Lynch Bond Pricing	1973

N/A = not available.
* MV = market value; PV = par value. Unless otherwise indicated, amount represents MV.
† YTM = yield-to-maturity.

Exhibit 1 (*continued*)

Index Name	Number of Securities	Total MV, PV* ($ billions)	Securities Included	Type (yield, total return, etc.)†	Weighting	Calculation	Period and Base Amount	YTM or Coupon and Period	Number of Years to Maturity	Beginning Date of Index	Source of Bond Prices	Historical Information and Frequency
Merrill Lynch Long-Term (15 years+), Medium-Quality Industrials—Coupons 8–9.99 Percent	142	MV = 7.8 PV = 13.4	A/A	Total return	Market value	Arithmetic	12/31/72 = 100	c = 8.981% y = 15.991% 10/81	21.14 10/81	12/31/72	Merrill Lynch Bond Pricing	1973
Merrill Lynch Long-Term (15 years+), Medium-Quality Industrials—Coupons 10–11.99 Percent	27	MV = 2.0 PV = 3.0	A/A	Total return	Market value	Arithmetic	12/31/72 = 100	c = 11.194% y = 16.353% 10/81	25.10 10/81	12/31/72	Merrill Lynch Bond Pricing	1973
Merrill Lynch Long-Term (15 years+), Medium-Quality Finance	52	MV = 2.5 PV = 4.5	A/A	Total return	Market value	Arithmetic	12/31/72 = 100	c = 8.770% y = 16.712% 10/81	20.42 10/81	12/31/72	Merrill Lynch Bond Pricing	1973
Merrill Lynch Long-Term (15 years+), Medium-Quality Finance—Coupons 6–7.99 Percent	11	MV = .5 PV = 1.1	A/A	Total return	Market value	Arithmetic	12/31/72 = 100	c = 6.792% y = 16.064% 10/81	22.19 10/81	12/31/72	Merrill Lynch Bond Pricing	1973

				Total return	Market value	Arithmetic	12/31/72 = 100			12/31/72	Merrill Lynch Bond Pricing	1973
Merrill Lynch Corp. Long-Term (15 years+), Medium-Quality Finance—Coupons 8–9.99 Percent	34	MV = 1.6 PV = 2.9	A/A				12/31/72 = 100	c = 8.954% y = 16.912% 10/81	20.12 10/81	12/31/72	Merrill Lynch Bond Pricing	1973
Merrill Lynch Long-Term (15 years+), Medium-Quality Finance—Coupons 10–11.99 Percent	4	MV = .2 PV = .3	A/A				12/31/72 = 100	c = 11.168% y = 16.895% 10/81	18.26 10/81	12/31/72	Merrill Lynch Bond Pricing	1973
Merrill Lynch Intermediate Term (5–9.99 years)	714	MV = 32.4 PV = 43.5	A/AA				12/31/72 = 100	c = 9.920% y = 15.882% 10/81	7.68 10/81	12/31/72	Merrill Lynch Bond Pricing	1973
Merrill Lynch Intermediate Term, (5–9.99 years) High-Quality	213	MV = 14.5 PV = 19.4	AA/AAA				12/31/72 = 100	c = 9.709% y = 15.483% 10/81	7.73 10/81	12/31/72	Merrill Lynch Bond Pricing	1973
Merrill Lynch Intermediate-Term (5–9.99 years) High-Quality Utilities	95	MV = 3.7 PV = 5.3	AA/AAA				12/31/72 = 100	c = 8.360% y = 15.208% 10/81	8.10 10/81	12/31/72	Merrill Lynch Bond Pricing	1973

N/A = not available.
* MV = market value; PV = par value. Unless otherwise indicated, amount represents MV.
† YTM = yield-to-maturity.

Exhibit 1 (*continued*)

Index Name	Number of Securities	Total MV, PV* ($ billions)	Securities Included	Type (yield, total return, etc.)†	Weighting	Calculation	Period and Base Amount	YTM or Coupon and Period	Number of Years to Maturity	Beginning Date of Index	Source of Bond Prices	Historical Information and Frequency
Merrill Lynch Intermediate-Term (5–9.99 years), High-Quality Utilities— Coupons 4–5.99 Percent	56	MV = .9 PV = 1.6	AA/AA	Total return	Market value	Arithmetic	12/31/72 = 100	c = 4.609% y = 15.176% 10/81	7.48 10/81	12/31/72	Merrill Lynch Bond Pricing	1973
Merrill Lynch Intermediate-Term (5–9.99 years), High-Quality Utilities— Coupons 6–7.99 Percent	2	MV = .05 PV = .09	AA/AA	Total return	Market value	Arithmetic	12/31/72 = 100	c = 6.106% y = 15.489% 10/81	9.78 10/81	12/31/72	Merrill Lynch Bond Pricing	1973
Merrill Lynch Intermediate-Term (5–9.99 years), High-Quality Utilities— Coupons 8–9.99 Percent	2	MV = .03 PV = .04	AA/AA	Total return	Market value	Arithmetic	9/30/74 = 100	c = 8.859% y = 14.794% 10/81	8.39 10/81	9/30/74	Merrill Lynch Bond Pricing	1973
Merrill Lynch Intermediate-Term (5–9.99 years), High-Quality Utilities— Coupons 10–11.99 Percent	4	MV = .6 PV = .8	AAA/AA	Total return	Market value	Arithmetic	12/31/72 = 100	c = 10.552% y = 15.423% 10/81	8.30 10/81	12/31/72	Merrill Lynch Bond Pricing	1973

Merrill Lynch Intermediate-Term (5–9.99 years), High-Quality Industrials.. 37	MV = 3.2 PV = 4.0	AA/AAA	Total return	Market value	Arithmetic	12/31/72 = 100	c = 10.957% y = 15.177% 10/81	7.84 10/81	12/31/72	Merrill Lynch Bond Pricing	1973
Merrill Lynch Intermediate-Term (5–9.99 years), High-Quality Industrials—Coupons 6–7.99 Percent 3	MV = .2 PV = .3	AA/AAA	Total return	Market value	Arithmetic	12/31/72 = 100	c = 7.205% y = 14.936% 10/81	6.86 10/81	12/31/72	Merrill Lynch Bond Pricing	1973
Merrill Lynch Intermediate-Term (5–9.99 years), High-Quality Industrials—Coupons 8–9.99 Percent 5	MV = .3 PV = .5	AA/AAA	Total return	Market value	Arithmetic	12/31/74 = 100	c = 9.255% y = 15.188% 10/81	7.35 10/81	12/31/74	Merrill Lynch Bond Pricing	1973
Merrill Lynch Intermediate-Term (5–9.99 years), High-Quality Industrials—Coupons 10–11.99 Percent 9	MV = 1.0 PV = 1.3	AA/AAA	Total return	Market value	Arithmetic	12/31/72 = 100	c = 10.446% y = 15.365% 10/81	7.15 10/81	12/31/72	Merrill Lynch Bond Pricing	1973
Merrill Lynch Intermediate-Term (5–9.99 years), High-Quality Finance 37	MV = 3.7 PV = 5.3	AA/AAA	Total return	Market value	Arithmetic	12/31/72 = 100	c = 8.668% y = 15.255% 10/81	7.83 10/81	12/31/72	Merrill Lynch Bond Pricing	1973

N/A = not available.
* MV = market value; PV = par value. Unless otherwise indicated, amount represents MV.
† YTM = yield-to-maturity.

189

Exhibit 1 (*continued*)

Index Name	Number of Securities	Total MV, PV* ($ billions)	Securities Included	Type (yield, total return, etc.)†	Weighting	Calculation	Period and Base Amount	YTM or Coupon and Period	Number of Years to Maturity	Beginning Date of Index	Source of Bond Prices	Historical Information and Frequency
Merrill Lynch Intermediate-Term (5–9.99 years), High-Quality Finance—Coupons 6–7.99 Percent	7	MV = .5, PV = .8	AA/AAA	Total return	Market value	Arithmetic	12/31/72 = 100	$c = 7.048\%$, $y = 15.379\%$ 10/81	6.63 10/81	12/31/72	Merrill Lynch Bond Pricing	1973
Merrill Lynch Intermediate-Term (5–9.99 years), High-Quality Utilities—Coupons 8–9.99 Percent	5	MV = .6, PV = .8	AA/AAA	Total return	Market value	Arithmetic	6/30/74 = 100	$c = 9.069\%$, $y = 15.591\%$ 10/81	6.62 10/81	6/30/74	Merrill Lynch Bond Pricing	1973
Merrill Lynch Intermediate-Term (5–9.99 years), High-Quality Finance—Coupons 10–11.99 Percent	7	MV = .6, PV = .7	AA/AAA	Total return	Market value	Arithmetic	12/31/72 = 100	$c = 11.207\%$, $y = 15.791\%$ 10/81	7.19 10/81	12/31/72	Merrill Lynch Bond Pricing	1973
Merrill Lynch Intermediate-Term (5–9.99 years), Medium Quality	501	MV = 17.9, PV = 24.0	A/BBB	Total return	Market value	Arithmetic	12/31/72 = 100	$c = 10.091\%$, $y = 16.205\%$ 10/81	7.63 10/81	12/31/72	Merrill Lynch Bond Pricing	1973

Merrill Lynch Intermediate-Term (5–9.99 years), Medium-Quality Utilities 315	MV = 9.0 PV = 12.2	A/BBB	Total return Market value Arithmetic	12/31/72 = 100	c = 10.012% y = 16.217% 10/81	7.68 10/81	12/31/72	Merrill Lynch Bond Pricing	1973
Merrill Lynch Intermediate-Term (5–9.99 years), Medium-Quality Utilities—Coupons 4–5.99 Percent 142	MV = 1.8 PV = 3.4	A/BBB	Total return Market value Arithmetic	12/31/72 = 100	c = 4.674% y = 15.864% 10/81	7.34 10/81	12/31/72	Merrill Lynch Bond Pricing	1973
Merrill Lynch Intermediate-Term (5–9.99 years), Medium-Quality Utilities—Coupons 6–7.99 Percent 30	MV = .5 PV = .8	A/A	Total return Market value Arithmetic	7/31/76 = 100	c = 6.931% y = 14.875% 10/81	7.01 10/81	7/31/76	Merrill Lynch Bond Pricing	1973
Merrill Lynch Intermediate-Term (5–9.99 years), Medium-Quality Utilities—Coupons 8–9.99 Percent 42	MV = .8 PV = 1.1	A/BBB	Total return Market value Arithmetic	12/31/72 = 100	c = 8.859% y = 15.213% 10/81	8.40 10/81	12/31/72	Merrill Lynch Bond Pricing	1973
Merrill Lynch Intermediate-Term (5–9.99 years), Medium-Quality Utilities—Coupons 10–11.99 Percent 15	MV = .8 PV = 1.0	A/BBB	Total return Market value Arithmetic	6/30/74 = 100	c = 10.840% y = 16.262% 10/81	7.99 10/81	6/30/74	Merrill Lynch Bond Pricing	1973

N/A = not available.
* MV = market value; PV = par value. Unless otherwise indicated, amount represents MV.
† YTM = yield-to-maturity.

Exhibit 1 (*continued*)

Index Name	Number of Securities	Total MV, PV* ($ billions)	Securities Included	Type (yield, total return, etc.)†	Weighting	Calculation	Period and Base Amount	YTM or Coupon and Period	Number of Years to Maturity	Beginning Date of Index	Source of Bond Prices	Historical Information and Frequency
Merrill Lynch Intermediate-Term (5–9.99 years), Medium-Quality Industrials............	96	MV = 4.4 PV = 5.7	A/A	Total return	Market value	Arithmetic	12/31/72 = 100	c = 10.321% y = 15.664% 10/81	7.94 10/81	12/31/72	Merrill Lynch Bond Pricing	1973
Merrill Lynch Intermediate-Term (5–9.99 years), Medium-Quality Industrials—Coupons 6–7.99 Percent	7	MV = .2 PV = .3	A/A	Total return	Market value	Arithmetic	6/30/74 = 100	c = 7.317% y = 15.340% 10/81	5.32 10/81	6/30/74	Merrill Lynch Bond Pricing	1973
Merrill Lynch Intermediate-Term (5–9.99 years), Medium-Quality Industrials—Coupons 8–9.99 Percent	8	MV = .3 PV = .4	A/A	Total return	Market value	Arithmetic	6/30/74 = 100	c = 9.047% y = 16.127% 10/81	7.72 10/81	6/30/74	Merrill Lynch Bond Pricing	1973
Merrill Lynch Intermediate-Term (5–9.99 years), Medium-Quality Industrials—Coupons 10–11.99 Percent	24	MV = 1.7 PV = 2.1	A/A	Total return	Market value	Arithmetic	9/30/74 = 100	c = 10.831% y = 15.874% 10/81	7.60 10/81	9/30/74	Merrill Lynch Bond Pricing	1973

Merrill Lynch Intermediate-Term (5–9.99 years), Medium-Quality Finance..........	83	MV = 4.3 PV = 6.0	A/A	Total return	Market value	Arithmetic	12/31/72 = 100	c = 9.951% y = 16.668% 10/81	12/31/72	7.26 10/81	Merrill Lynch Bond Pricing	1973
Merrill Lynch Intermediate-Term (5–9.99 years), Medium-Quality Finance—Coupons 6–7.99 Percent	11	MV = .4 PV = .6	A/BBB	Total return	Market value	Arithmetic	12/31/72 = 100	c = 7.645% y = 16.635% 10/81	12/31/72	6.95 10/81	Merrill Lynch Bond Pricing	1973
Merrill Lynch Intermediate-Term (5–9.99 years), Medium-Quality Finance—Coupons 8–9.99 Percent	40	MV = 1.9 PV = 2.8	A/BBB	Total return	Market value	Arithmetic	12/31/73 = 100	c = 8.819% y = 16.721% 10/81	12/31/73	6.72 10/81	Merrill Lynch Bond Pricing	1973
Merrill Lynch Intermediate-Term (5–9.99 years), Medium-Quality Finance—Coupons 10–11.99 Percent	9	MV = .4 PV = .5	A/A	Total return	Market value	Arithmetic	12/31/74 = 100	c = 11.140% y = 16.300% 10/81	12/31/74	7.98 10/81	Merrill Lynch Bond Pricing	1973
Merrill Lynch Short Term (1–2.99 years)	238	MV = 13.5 PV = 15.5	AA/A	Total return	Market value	Arithmetic	12/31/75 = 100	c = 8.024% y = 15.842% 10/81	12/31/75	1.93 10/81	Merrill Lynch Bond Pricing	1973

N/A = not available.
* MV = market value; PV = par value. Unless otherwise indicated, amount represents MV.
† YTM = yield-to-maturity.

Exhibit 1 (concluded)

Index Name	Number of Securities	Total MV, PV* ($ billions)	Securities Included	Type (yield, total return, etc.)†	Weighting	Calculation	Period and Base Amount	YTM or Coupon and Period	Number of Years to Maturity	Beginning Date of Index	Source of Bond Prices	Historical Information and Frequency
Merrill Lynch Short Term (1–2.99 years), High-Quality	99	MV = 7.6 PV = 8.7	AA/AAA	Total return	Market value	Arithmetic	12/31/75 = 100	c = 7.785% y = 15.611% 10/81	1.93 10/81	12/31/75	Merrill Lynch Bond Pricing	1973
Merrill Lynch Short Term (1–2.99 years), Medium-Quality	139	MV = 5.9 PV = 6.7	A/BBB	Total return	Market value	Arithmetic	12/31/75 = 100	c = 8.336% y = 16.144% 10/81	1.94 10/81	12/31/75	Merrill Lynch Bond Pricing	1973
Merrill Lynch Intermediate-Term (3–4.99 years)	292	MV = 17.5 PV = 21.9	AA/A	Total return	Market value	Arithmetic	12/31/75 = 100	c = 8.625% y = 15.651% 10/81	3.97 10/81	12/31/75	Merrill Lynch Bond Pricing	1973
Merrill Lynch Intermediate-Term (3–4.99 years) High Quality	128	MV = 11.2 PV = 13.8	AA/AAA	Total return	Market value	Arithmetic	12/31/75 = 100	c = 8.743% y = 15.439% 10/81	3.97 10/81	12/31/75	Merrill Lynch Bond Pricing	1973
Merrill Lynch Intermediate Term (3–4.99 years), Medium Quality	164	MV = 6.4 PV = 8.1	A/A	Total return	Market value	Arithmetic	12/31/75 = 100	c = 8.423% y = 16.012% 10/81	3.96 10/81	12/31/75	Merrill Lynch Bond Pricing	1973

Merrill Lynch Intermediate Term (10–14.99 years) 633	MV = 15.6 PV = 28.6	A/AA	Total return	Market value	Arithmetic	12/31/75 = 100	c = 7.152% y = 15.531% 10/81	12.72 10/81	12/31/75	Merrill Lynch Bond Pricing	1973
Merrill Lynch Intermediate Term (10–14.99 years), High Quality 192	MV = 6.4 PV = 11.9	AA/AAA	Total return	Market value	Arithmetic	12/31/75 = 100	c = 6.711 y = 15.007% 10/81	12.73 10/81	12/31/75	Merrill Lynch Bond Pricing	1973
Merrill Lynch Intermediate Term (10–14.99 years), Medium Quality 441	MV = 9.2 PV = 16.7	A/BBB	Total return	Market value	Arithmetic	12/31/75 = 100	c = 7.468% y = 15.907% 10/81	12/71 10/81	12/31/75	Merrill Lynch Bond Pricing	1973

N/A = not available.
* MV = market value; PV = par value. Unless otherwise indicated, amount represents MV.
† YTM = yield-to-maturity.

Exhibit 2
U.S. Government Bond Indices

Index Name	Number of Securities	Total MV, PV* ($ billions)	Securities Included	Type (yield, total return, etc.)†	Weighting	Calculation	Base Amount and Period	YTM or Coupon and Period	Number of Years to Maturity	Beginning Date of Index	Source of Bond Prices	Historical Information and Frequency
Salomon Brothers—Long-Term Govts.	N/A	N/A	All but flower bonds	Total return	Par value	Arithmetic	1978 = 100	c = 9.51% 11/1/81	12 years	1/1/78	Salomon Brothers	3 months monthly
Salomon Brothers—Medium-Term 3–5	N/A	N/A	All but flower bonds	Total return	Par value	Arithmetic	1978 = 100	c = 10.09 11/1/81	3–5 years	1/1/78	Salomon Brothers	3 months monthly
Salomon Brothers—Medium-Term 6–8	N/A	N/A	All but flower bonds	Total return	Par value	Arithmetic	1978 = 100	c = 9.44 11/1/81	6–8 years	1/1/78	Salomon Brothers	3 months monthly
Salomon Brothers—Medium-Term 9–11	N/A	N/A	All but flower bonds	Total return	Par value	Arithmetic	1978 = 100	c = 10/46 11/1/81	9–11 years	1/1/78	Salomon Brothers	3 months monthly
Salomon Brothers—U.S. Govt. Index	36	N/A	U.S. Treasury bonds	Total return	N/A	Arithmetic	12/31/77 = 100	N/A	14 years	12/77	Salomon Brothers	12/77 monthly
Salomon Brothers—U.S. Treasury Bill Index	N/A	N/A	U.S. Treasury bills	Total return	N/A	Arithmetic	12/31/77 = 100	N/A	3 months	12/77	Salomon Brothers	12/77 monthly
Standard & Poor's Long-Term Govt. Bond Yield Average	4	N/A	N/A	YTM	Equally	Arithmetic	N/A	y = 14.63% 10/21/81	10 years 10/81	1/42	The Wall Street Journal (YTM)	1942 monthly 1971 weekly

196

Standard & Poor's Long-Term Govt. Bond Price Index.........	4	N/A	N/A	Price	Equally	Assume 3 percent coupon for historical purposes 15 years to maturity + 7½ years to maturity	N/A	c = 3% 10/21/81 p = 30.05 10/21/81	15 years 10/81	1/42	*The Wall Street Journal* (convert yields into price)	1942 monthly 1971 weekly
Standard & Poor's Intermediate-Term Govt. Bond Yield Average	4	N/A	N/A	YTM	Equally	Arithmetic	N/A	y = 14.89% 10/21/81	6–9 years 10/81	1/42	*The Wall Street Journal* (YTM)	1942 monthly 1971 weekly
Standard & Poor's Intermediate-Term Govt. Bond Price Index.........	4	N/A	N/A	Price	Equally	YTM is converted into a price assuming 3 percent coupon + 3½ years to maturity	N/A	p = 47.30 10/21/81	7½ years 10/81	1/42	*The Wall Street Journal* (convert yields into price)	1942 monthly 1971 weekly
Standard & Poor's Short-Term Govt. Bond Yield Average	4	N/A	N/A	YTM	Equally	Arithmetic	N/A	y = 14.79% 10/21/81	2–4 years 10/81	1/42	*The Wall Street Journal* (YTM)	1942 monthly 1971 weekly
Standard & Poor's Short-Term Govt. Bond Price Index.........	4	N/A	N/A	Price	Equally	YTM is converted into a price assuming 3 percent coupon	N/A	p = 68.62 10/21/81	3½ years 10/81	1/42	*The Wall Street Journal* (convert yields into price)	1942 monthly 1971 weekly
Lehman Brothers Kuhn Loeb Treasury Bond Index	104	280.396	AAA	Total return	Market value	Arithmetic	N/A	y = 12.52%	1 year+	12/72	Lehman Brothers Kuhn Loeb	N/A

N/A = not available.
* MV = market value; PV = par value. Unless otherwise indicated, amount represents MV.
† YTM = yield-to-maturity.

Exhibit 2 (*concluded*)

Index Name	Number of Securities	Total MV, PV* ($ billions)	Securities Included	Type (yield, total return, etc.)†	Weighting	Calculation	Base Amount and Period	YTM or Coupon and Period	Number of Years to Maturity	Beginning Date of Index	Source of Bond Prices	Historical Information and Frequency
Lehman Brothers Kuhn Loeb Intermediate Treasury Bond Index	71	230.362	AAA	Total return	Market value	Arithmetic	N/A	$y = 12.44\%$	1 year+	12/72	Lehman Brothers Kuhn Loeb	N/A
Lehman Brothers Kuhn Loeb Long-Term Treasury Bond Index	33	50.033	AAA	Total return	Market value	Arithmetic	N/A	$y = 12.89\%$	10 year+	12/72	Lehman Brothers Kuhn Loeb	N/A
Merrill Lynch Govt. Master	322	MV = 398.1 PV = 458.8	AAA/AAA	Total return	Market value	Arithmetic	12/31/72 = 100	$c = 10.706\%$ $y = 14.482\%$ 10/81	6.94 10/81	12/31/72	Merrill Lynch Bond Pricing	1973
Merrill Lynch U.S. Treasury Long-Term (15+)	19	MV = 41.7 PV = 58.9	AAA/AAA	Total return	Market value	Arithmetic	3/31/73 = 100	$c = 9.829\%$ $y = 14.105\%$ 10/81	24.77 10/81	3/31/73	Merrill Lynch Bond Pricing	1973
Merrill Lynch Govt.-U.S. Treasury Intermediate Term (3 to 4.99 years)	15	MV = 53.5 PV = 59.4	AAA/AAA	Total return	Market value	Arithmetic	12/31/72 = 100	$c = 11.286\%$ $y = 14.519\%$ 10/81	3.93 10/81	12/31/72	Merrill Lynch Bond Pricing	1973
Merrill Lynch Govt.-U.S. Treasury Intermediate Term (5 to 6.99 years)	9	MV = 25.3 PV = 29.2	AAA/AAA	Total return	Market value	Arithmetic	12/31/72 = 100	$c = 11.004\%$ $y = 14.408\%$ 10/81	5.85 10/81	12/31/72	Merrill Lynch Bond Pricing	1973

Merrill Lynch Govt.-U.S. Treasury Intermediate Term (7 to 9.99 years)........ 7	MV = 20.8 PV = 24.8	AAA/AAA	Total return	Market value	Arithmetic	12/31/72 = 100	c = 11.090% y = 14.501% 10/81	5.23 10/81	12/31/72	Merrill Lynch Bond Pricing	1973
Merrill Lynch Govt.-U.S. Treasury Short Term (1 to 2.99 years) 35	MV = 130.5 PV = 137.5	AAA/AAA	Total return	Market value	Arithmetic	12/31/75 = 100	c = 11.260% y = 14.479% 10/81	1.80 10/81	12/31/75	Merrill Lynch Bond Pricing	1973
Merrill Lynch Govt.-U.S. Treasury Intermediate Term (10 to 14.99 years) 13	MV = 14.6 PV = 20.8	AAA/AAA	Total return	Market value	Arithmetic	7/31/77 = 100	c = 9.240% y = 14.554% 10/81	12.44 10/81	7/31/77	Merrill Lynch Bond Pricing	1973

N/A = not available.
* MV = market value; PV = par value. Unless otherwise indicated, amount represents MV.
† YTM = yield-to-maturity.

Exhibit 3
U.S. Government/Agencies Bond Indices

Index Name	Number of Securities	Total MV, PV* ($ billions)	Securities Included	Type (yield, total return, etc.)†	Weighting	Calculation	Base Amount and Period	YTM or Coupon and Period	Number of Years to Maturity	Beginning Date of Index	Source of Bond Prices	Historical Information and Frequency
Lehman Brothers Kuhn Loeb Govt.-Agency Bond Index	513	$395.290	AAA	Total return	Market value	Arithmetic	N/A	12.71% 11/81	1 year+	12/72	Lehman Brothers Kuhn Loeb	12/72 monthly
Lehman Brothers Kuhn Loeb Govt.-Agency Intermediate Bond Index	349	337.364	AAA	Total return	Market value	Arithmetic	N/A	12.67% 11/81	1 year+	12/72	Lehman Brothers Kuhn Loeb	12/72 monthly
Lehman Brothers Kuhn Loeb Govt.-Agency Long-Term Bond Index	164	57.926	AAA	Total return	Market value	Arithmetic	N/A	12.97% 11/81	10 years+	12/72	Lehman Brothers Kuhn Loeb	12/72 monthly
Lehman Brothers Kuhn Loeb GNMA Pass-Through Bond Index	14	N/A	AAA	Total return	Market value	Arithmetic	N/A	N/A 11/81	N/A	12/72	Lehman Brothers Kuhn Loeb	12/72 monthly
Merrill Lynch Govt.-Federal Agencies Intermediate Term (10 to 14.99 years)	6	MV = .8 PV = 1.4	AAA/AAA	Total return	Market value	Arithmetic	12/31/75 = 100	$c = 7.576\%$ $y = 15.174\%$ 10/81	12.82 10/81	12/31/75	Merrill Lynch Bond Pricing	1973

				Total return	Market value	Arithmetic					
Merrill Lynch Govt.-Federal Agencies Long Term (15 years+)	25	MV = 2.5 PV = 4.4	AAA/AAA	Total return	Market value	Arithmetic	12/31/75 = 100	c = 8.050% y = 14.828% 10/81	22.45 10/81	12/31/75	Merrill Lynch Bond Pricing	1973
Merrill Lynch Govt.-Federal Agencies Short Term (1 to 2.99 years)	83	MV = 52.8 PV = 56.6	AAA/AAA	Total return	Market value	Arithmetic	12/31/75 = 100	c = 11.283% y = 15.235% 10/81	2.03 10/81	12/31/75	Merrill Lynch Bond Pricing	1973
Merrill Lynch Govt.-Federal Agencies Intermediate Term (3 to 4.99 years)	57	MV = 28.9 PV = 32.4	AAA/AAA	Total return	Market value	Arithmetic	12/31/75 = 100	c = 11.539% y = 15.413% 10/81	3.84 10/81	12/31/75	Merrill Lynch Bond Pricing	1973
Merrill Lynch Govt.-Federal Agencies Intermediate Term (5 to 6.99 years)	29	MV = 12.7 PV = 15.7	AAA/AAA	Total return	Market value	Arithmetic	12/31/75 = 100	c = 10.041% y = 15.201% 10/81	5/71 10/81	12/31/75	Merrill Lynch Bond Pricing	1973
Merrill Lynch Govt.-Federal Agencies Intermediate Term (7 to 9.99 years)	15	MV = 5.1 PV = 6.6	AAA/AAA	Total return	Market value	Arithmetic	12/31/75 = 100	c = 10.431% y = 15.211% 10/81	8.62 10/81	12/31/75	Merrill Lynch Bond Pricing	1973

N/A = not available.
* MV = market value; PV = par value. Unless otherwise indicated, amount represents MV.
† YTM = yield-to-maturity.

Exhibit 4
U.S. Governments/Agencies/Corporates and Corporates/Governments Bond Indices

Index Name	Number of Securities	Total MV, PV* ($ billions)	Securities Included	Type (yield, total return, etc.)†	Weighting	Calculation	Base Amount and Period	YTM or Coupon and Period	Number of Years to Maturity	Beginning Date of Index	Source of Bond Prices	Historical Information and Frequency
Lehman Brothers Kuhn Loeb Long-Term, High-Quality Govt.-Agency Corp. Bond Index	1195.5	117.456	AAA	Total return	Market value	Arithmetic	N/A	$y = 13.47\%$	1 year+	12/72	Lehman Brothers Kuhn Loeb	12/72 monthly
Lehman Brothers Kuhn Loeb Intermediate Govt.-Agency Corp. Bond Index...............	1833.5	399.508	AAA	Total return	Market value	Arithmetic	N/A	$y = 12.89\%$	1 year+	12/72	Lehman Brothers Kuhn Loeb	12/72 monthly
Lehman Brothers Kuhn Loeb Long-Term Govt.-Agency Corporate Bond Index............	2949.5	177.090	AAA	Total return	Market value	Arithmetic	N/A	$y = 13.93\%$	1 year+	12/72	Lehman Brothers Kuhn Loeb	12/72 monthly
Lehman Brothers Kuhn Loeb Govt.-Agency Corporate Bond Index...............	4783.0	576.599	AAA	Total return	Market value	Arithmetic	N/A	$y = 13.21\%$	1 year+	12/72	Lehman Brothers Kuhn Loeb	12/72 monthly
Merrill Lynch Corp. and Govt. Master.................	4305.0	MV = 582.1 PV = 745.6	AA/AA	Total return	Market value	Arithmetic	12/31/72 = 100	$y = 14.988\%$ 10/81	11.086 10/81	12/72	Merrill Lynch Bond Pricing	1973

N/A = not available.
* MV = market value; PV = par value. Unless otherwise indicated, amount represents MV.
† YTM = yield-to-maturity.

Exhibit 5
Municipal Bond Indices

Index Name	Number of Securities	Total MV, PV* ($ billions)	Securities Included	Type (yield, total return, etc.)†	Weighting	Calculation	Base Amount and Period	YTM or Coupon and Period	Number of Years to Maturity	Beginning Date of Index	Source of Bond Prices	Historical Information and Frequency
Lipper General Municipal Bond Fund Index	10	2.356	Representative general bond funds	Price	Equally	Arithmetic	12/31/80 = 100	N/A	N/A	12/31/80	Bond fund prices—*The Wall Street Journal*	12/31/80 daily
Lipper Short-Term Municipal Bond Fund....	10	3.046	Representative short-term munibond funds	Average of 7-day and 30-day yields	Unweighted	Arithmetic	N/A	N/A	N/A	9/2/81	Call funds directly	9/2/81 daily
Dow Jones Municipal Bond Yield Index	20	N/A	General obligation bonds	YTM	Par	Arithmetic	N/A	N/A	20	1928	Bond dealers	No
Bond Buyer Rev. Bond Index	Potential issuers 25	N/A		YTM	Equally	Arithmetic	Coupon-par in 30 years	N/A	N/A	Thursday to Thursday	Traders from 10–15 firms are asked their yield values each Thursday	9/20/79 weekly
Bond Buyer 20—Bond Index	20	N/A		YTM	By rating	Arithmetic	Coupon-par in 20 years	N/A	N/A	Thursday to Thursday	"	Weekly— 1946 1917— monthly 1917–45

N/A = not available.
* MV = market value; PV = par value. Unless otherwise indicated, amount represents MV.
† YTM = yield-to-maturity.

Exhibit 5 (*concluded*)

Index Name	Number of Securities	Total MV, PV* ($ billions)	Securities Included	Type (yield, total return, etc.)†	Weighting	Calculation	Base Amount and Period	YTM or Coupon and Period	Number of Years to Maturity	Beginning Date of Index	Source of Bond Prices	Historical Information and Frequency
Bond Buyer 11—Bond Index	11	N/A		YTM	By rating	Arithmetic	Coupon-par in 20 years	N/A	N/A	Thursday to Thursday		Weekly—1946 to present 1917 monthly—1917–45
Standard & Poor's Municipal Bond Yield Average	15	N/A	General Obligation Bonds AAA, AA, A	YTM	Equally	Arithmetic	N/A	y = 12.82% 10/81	20 years	N/A	Phone survey	1900 monthly 1971 weekly
Standard & Poor's Municipal Bond Price Index	15	N/A	AAA, AA, A	Price	Equally	Convert YTM into price assuming 4% coupon, 20 years to maturity.	N/A	p = 36.93 10/81	20 years	N/A	Phone survey	1900 monthly 1971 weekly

N/A = not available.
* MV = market value; PV = par value. Unless otherwise indicated, amount represents MV.
† YTM = yield-to-maturity.

Exhibit 6
Yankee Bond Indices

Index Name	Number of Securities	Total MV, PV* ($ billions)	Securities Included	Type (yield, total return, etc.)†	Weighting	Calculation	Period and Base Amount	YTM or Coupon and Period	Number of Years to Maturity	Beginning Date of Index	Source of Bond Prices	Historical Information and Frequency
Lehman Brothers Kuhn Loeb Yankee Bond Index	81	$6.858	AAA	Total return	Market value	Arithmetic		YTM = 14.06% 11/81	1 year+	12/72	Lehman Brothers Kuhn Loeb	12/72 monthly
Lehman Brothers Kuhn Loeb Yankee Intermediate Bond Index..........	46	4.628	AAA	Total return	Market value	Arithmetic		YTM = 14.04% 11/81	1 year+	12/72	Lehman Brothers Kuhn Loeb	12/72 monthly
Lehman Brothers Kuhn Loeb Yankee Long-Term Bond Index............	35	2.230	AAA	Total return	Market value	Arithmetic		YTM = 14.10% 11/81	10 years+	12/72	Lehman Brothers Kuhn Loeb	12/72 monthly
Merrill Lynch Corp.— Yankee Bonds ALL............	100	MV = 9.354 PV = 12.719	AAA/AAA	Total return	Market value	Arithmetic	12/31/75 = 100	c = 8.956 y = 15.555%	8.88 10/81	12/75	Merrill Lynch Bond Pricing	1973

N/A = not available.
* MV = market value; PV = par value. Unless otherwise indicated, amount represents MV.
† YTM = yield-to-maturity.

Exhibit 7
Eurodollar and Foreign Bond Indices

Index Name	Number of Securities	Total MV, PV* ($ billions)	Securities Included	Type (yield, total return, etc.)†	Weighting	Calculation	Base Amount and Period	YTM or Coupon and Period	Number of Years to Maturity	Beginning Date of Index	Source of Bond Prices	Historical Information and Frequency
Lehman Brothers Kuhn Loeb Int'l. Global Index	748	$30.823	Publicly traded	Total return	Market value	Arithmetic	N/A	14.64% 11/81	1 year+	12/76	AIBD quotations	12/72 monthly
Lehman Brothers Kuhn Loeb Int'l. Short-Term Global Index	600	23.583	Publicly traded	Total return	Market value	Arithmetic	N/A	14.62% 11/81	1–7 years	12/76	AIBD quotations	12/72 monthly
Lehman Brothers Kuhn Loeb Int'l. Long-Term Global Index	148	7.240	Publicly traded	Total return	Market value	Arithmetic	N/A	14.71% 11/81	7 years+	12/76	AIBD quotations	12/72 monthly
Lehman Brothers Kuhn Loeb Int'l. High-Grade Public Sector Index	202	10.445	AAA	Total return	Market value	Arithmetic	N/A	14.34% 11/81	1 year+	12/76	AIBD quotations	12/72 monthly
Lehman Brothers Kuhn Loeb Int'l. Short-Term, High-Grade Public Sector Index	151	7.809	AAA	Total return	Market value	Arithmetic	N/A	14.31% 11/81	1–7 years	12/76	AIBD quotations	12/72 monthly
Lehman Brothers Kuhn Loeb Int'l. Long-Term, High-Grade Public Sector Index	51	2.636	AAA	Total return	Market value	Arithmetic	N/A	14.43% 11/81	7 years+	12/76	AIBD quotations	12/72 monthly
Lehman Brothers Kuhn Loeb Int'l. U.S. Corp. Index	184	9.390	Obligations of U.S. corp.	Total return	Market value	Arithmetic	N/A	14.99% 11/81	1 year+	12/76	AIBD quotations	12/72 monthly

206

Lehman Brothers Kuhn Loeb Int'l U.S. Short-Term Corp. Index	165	7.988	Obligations of U.S. corp.	Total return	Market value	Arithmetic	N/A	14.98% 11/81	1–7 years	12/76	AIBD quotations	12/72 monthly
Lehman Brothers Kuhn Loeb Int'l. U.S. Long-Term Corp. Index	19	1.403	Obligations of U.S. corp.	Total return	Market value	Arithmetic	N/A	15.02% 11/81	7 years+	12/76	AIBD quotations	12/76 monthly
Lehman Brothers Kuhn Loeb Int'l European Corporate Index	177	3.970	European, Australia, and New Zealand com-mercial banks	Total return	Market value	Arithmetic	N/A	14.59% 11/81	1 year+	12/76	AIBD quotations	12/76 monthly
Lehman Brothers Kuhn Loeb Int'l European Corp. Short-Term Index	140	2.761	European, Australia, and New Zealand com-mercial banks	Total return	Market value	Arithmetic	N/A	14.52% 11/81	1–7 years	12/76	AIBD quotations	12/76 monthly
Lehman Brothers Kuhn Loeb Int'l European Corp. Long-Term Index	37	1.210	European, Australia, and New Zealand com-mercial banks	Total return	Market value	Arithmetic	N/A	14.74% 11/81	7 years+	12/76	AIBD quotations	12/76 monthly
Lehman Brothers Kuhn Loeb Int'l Canadian Public Sector Index	77	4.277	Obligations of Canadian providences	Total return	Market value	Arithmetic	N/A	14.37% 11/81	1 year+	12/76	AIBD quotations	12/76 monthly

N/A = not available.
* MV = market value; PV = par value. Unless otherwise indicated, amount represents MV.
† YTM = yield-to-maturity.

Exhibit 7 (*continued*)

Index Name	Number of Securities	Total MV, PV* ($ billions)	Securities Included	Type (yield, total return, etc.)†	Weighting	Calculation	Period and Base Amount	YTM or Coupon and Period	Number of Years to Maturity	Beginning Date of Index	Source of Bond Prices	Historical Information and Frequency
Lehman Brothers Kuhn Loeb Int'l. Short-Term Canadian Public Sector Index	55	2.786	Obligations of Canadian providences	Total return	Market value	Arithmetic	N/A	14.26% 11/81	1–7 years	12/76	AIBD quotations	12/76 monthly
Lehman Brothers Kuhn Loeb Int'l. Long-Term Canadian Public Sector Index	22	1.490	Obligations of Canadian providences	Total return	Market value	Arithmetic	N/A	14.57% 11/81	7 years+	12/76	AIBD quotations	12/76 monthly
Lehman Brothers Kuhn Loeb Int'l. Short-Term Japanese Index	16	337	Japanese private sector banks	Total return	Market value	Arithmetic	N/A	14.92% 11/81	1–7 years	12/76	AIBD quotations	12/76 monthly
Handelsblatt Bond Fund Index	N/A	N/A	German F. I. mutual funds—bond and cash equivalents	Price	N/A	N/A	12/31/66 = 100	N/A	N/A	1966	Redemption prices	N/A
Financial Times Govt. Securities Index	11	N/A	U.K. govt. securities	Price	Equally	Geometric	10/15/26 = 100	N/A	N/A	10/15/26	London Stock Exchange	N/A
Financial Times Actuaries Fixed Interest Index	87	70.453	Govt. bonds	Price	Market value	Geometric	12/31/75 = 100	N/A	N/A	12/31/75	London Stock Exchange	N/A
Nikkei Bond Index	N/A	N/A	Long-, medium- and short-term bonds	YTM	Equally	Arithmetic	N/A	N/A	N/A	N/A	N/A	N/A

Index	Number	MV/PV	Description				12/31/xx = 100	c = 9.546 y = 16.082% 10/81	Maturity	Date	Pricing Source	Frequency
Merrill Corporate—Canadian (U.S. Payable) ALL	142	MV = 8541.668 PV = 13935.367	AA/AA	Total return	Market value	Arithmetic	12/31/75 = 100	c = 9.546 y = 16.082% 10/81	22.17 10/81	12/31/75	Merrill Lynch Bond Pricing	N/A
Salomon Brothers World Bond Index (weighted)	448	N/A	Prime quality, publicly traded	Total return	Market value	Arithmetic	12/31/77 = 100	N/A	9 years	12/77	Salomon Brothers Index	12/77 monthly
Salomon Brothers World Bond Index (unweighted)	448	N/A	Prime quality, publicly traded	Total return	N/A	Arithmetic	12/31/77 = 100	N/A	9 years	12/77	Salomon Brothers Index	12/77 monthly
Salomon Brothers World Money Mkt. Index (unweighted)	N/A	N/A	Money market instruments	Total return	N/A	Arithmetic	12/31/77 = 100	N/A	N/A	12/77	Salomon Brothers Index	12/77 monthly
Salomon Brothers Foreign Dollar Bond Index	38	N/A	Prime foreign $ bonds (yankees)	Total return	N/A	Arithmetic	12/31/77 = 100	N/A	18 years	12/77	Salomon Brothers Index	12/77 monthly
Salomon Brothers Eurodollar Bond Index	75	N/A	Prime quality Euro$ bonds	Total return	N/A	Arithmetic	12/31/77 = 100	N/A	7 years	12/77	Salomon Brothers Index	12/77 monthly
Salomon Brothers Euro$ FRN Index	32	N/A	Prime quality Euro$ FRNs (3 and 6 months)	Total return	N/A	Arithmetic	12/31/77 = 100	N/A	7 years	12/77	Salomon Brothers Index	12/77 monthly
Salomon Brothers Canadian Govt. Index	11	N/A	Canadian Treasury bonds	Total return	N/A	Arithmetic	12/31/77 = 100	N/A	17 years	12/77	Salomon Brothers Index	12/77 monthly

N/A = not available.
* MV = market value; PV = par value. Unless otherwise indicated, amount represents MV.
† YTM = yield-to-maturity.

209

Exhibit 7 (continued)

Index Name	Number of Securities	Total MV, PV* ($ billions)	Securities Included	Type (yield, total return, etc.)†	Weighting	Calculation	Period and Base Amount	YTM or Coupon and Period	Number of Years to Maturity	Beginning Date of Index	Source of Bond Prices	Historical Information and Frequency
Salomon Brothers Euro Canadian$ Bond Index............	8	N/A	Prime quality, Euro C$ Bonds	Total return	N/A	Arithmetic	12/31/77 = 100	N/A	8 years	12/77	Salomon Brothers Index	12/77 monthly
Salomon Brothers German Govt. Index............	15	N/A	Bundesrepublics and Bundesposts	Total return	N/A	Arithmetic	12/31/77 = 100	N/A	7 years	12/77	Salomon Brothers Index	12/77 monthly
Salomon Brothers Euro Deutsche Mark Bond Index............	48	N/A	Prime quality, Euro DM bonds	Total return	N/A	Arithmetic	12/31/77 = 100	N/A	7 years	12/77	Salomon Brothers Index	12/77 monthly
Salomon Brothers Japanese Govt. Index............	10	N/A	Japanese govt. bonds	Total return	N/A	Arithmetic	12/31/77 = 100	N/A	7 years	12/77	Salomon Brothers Index	12/77 monthly
Salomon Brothers Samurai Bond Index............	24	N/A	Prime quality, Samurai bonds	Total return	N/A	Arithmetic	12/31/77 = 100	N/A	9 years	12/77	Salomon Brothers Index	12/77 monthly
Salomon Brothers Euroyen Bond Index............	6	N/A	Prime quality, Euroyen bonds	Total return	N/A	Arithmetic	12/31/77 = 100	N/A	8 years	12/77	Salomon Brothers Index	12/77 monthly
Salomon Brothers U.K. Gilts Index............	19	N/A	U.K. gilt-edged stocks	Total return	N/A	Arithmetic	12/31/77 = 100	N/A	16 years	12/77	Salomon Brothers Index	12/77 monthly

210

Index												
Salomon Brothers Eurosterling Bond Index............	10	N/A	Prime quality, Eurosterling bonds	Total return	N/A	Arithmetic	12/31/77 = 100	N/A	8 years	12/77	Salomon Brothers Index	12/77 monthly
Salomon Brothers Swiss Govt. Index	9	N/A	Swiss confederation bonds	Total return	N/A	Arithmetic	12/31/77 = 100	N/A	8 years	12/77	Salomon Brothers Index	12/77 monthly
Salomon Brothers Foreign Sfr. Bond Index............	50	N/A	Prime quality foreign Sfr. bonds	Total return	N/A	Arithmetic	12/31/77 = 100	N/A	9 years	12/77	Salomon Brothers Index	12/77 monthly
Salomon Brothers Dutch Govt. Index	18	N/A	Netherlands govt. bonds	Total return	N/A	Arithmetic	12/31/77 = 100	N/A	6 years	12/77	Salomon Brothers Index	12/77 monthly
Salomon Brothers Foreign Dfl. Bond Index............	11	N/A	Prime quality foreign Dfl. bonds	Total return	N/A	Arithmetic	12/31/77 = 100	N/A	6 years	12/77	Salomon Brothers Index	12/77 monthly
Salomon Brothers Euro Dfl. Bond Index............	13	N/A	Prime quality Euro Dfl. bonds	Total return	N/A	Arithmetic	12/31/77 = 100	N/A	5 years	12/77	Salomon Brothers Index	12/77 monthly
Salomon Brothers French Govt. Index	7	N/A	French Govt. bonds	Total return	N/A	Arithmetic	12/31/77 = 100	N/A	6 years	12/77	Salomon Brothers Index	12/77 monthly
Salomon Brothers Euro Ffr. Bond Index............	10	N/A	Prime quality Euro Ffr. bonds	Total return	N/A	Arithmetic	12/31/77 = 100	N/A	5 years	12/77	Salomon Brothers Index	12/77 monthly

N/A = not available.
* MV = market value; PV = par value. Unless otherwise indicated, amount represents MV.
† YTM = yield-to-maturity.

211

Exhibit 7 (*continued*)

Index Name	Number of Securities	Total MV, PV* ($ billions)	Securities Included	Type (yield, total return, etc.)†	Weighting	Calculation	Period and Base Amount	YTM or Coupon and Period	Number of Years to Maturity	Beginning Date of Index	Source of Bond Prices	Historical Information and Frequency
Salomon Brothers Domestic U.S.$ CD Index	N/A	N/A	Domestic $ CD	Total return	N/A	Arithmetic	12/31/77 = 100	N/A	3 months	12/77	Salomon Brothers Index	12/77 monthly
Salomon Brothers Euro$ CD Index	N/A	N/A	Euro$ CD	Total return	N/A	Arithmetic	12/31/77 = 100	N/A	3 months	12/77	Salomon Brothers Index	12/77 monthly
Salomon Brothers Euro$ Deposit Index	N/A	N/A	Euro$ deposit	Total return	N/A	Arithmetic	12/31/77 = 100	N/A	3 months	12/77	Salomon Brothers Index	12/77 monthly
Salomon Brothers Canadian Treasury Bill Index	N/A	N/A	Canadian Treasury bill	Total return	N/A	Arithmetic	12/31/77 = 100	N/A	3 months	12/77	Salomon Brothers Index	12/77 monthly
Salomon Brothers Euro-Canadian$ Deposit Index	N/A	N/A	Euro C$ deposit	Total return	N/A	Arithmetic	12/31/77 = 100	N/A	3 months	12/77	Salomon Brothers Index	12/77 monthly
Salomon Brothers Domestic Yen CD Index	N/A	N/A	Domestic yen CD	Total return	N/A	Arithmetic	12/31/77 = 100	N/A	3 months	12/77	Salomon Brothers Index	12/77 monthly
Salomon Brothers Yen Gensaki Index	N/A	N/A	Yen Gensaki	Total return	N/A	Arithmetic	12/31/77 = 100	N/A	3 months	12/77	Salomon Brothers Index	12/77 monthly

Salomon Brothers Euroyen Deposit Index.........	N/A	N/A	Euroyen deposit	Total return	N/A	Arithmetic	12/31/77 = 100	N/A	3 months	12/77	Salomon Brothers Index	12/77 monthly
Salomon Brothers U.K. Treasury Bill Index.........	N/A	N/A	U.K. Treasury bill	Total return	N/A	Arithmetic	12/31/77 = 100	N/A	3 months	12/77	Salomon Brothers Index	12/77 monthly
Salomon Brothers Domestic L CD Index	N/A	N/A	Domestic L CD	Total return	N/A	Arithmetic	12/31/77 = 100	N/A	3 months	12/77	Salomon Brothers Index	12/77 monthly
Salomon Brothers Eurosterling Deposit Index.........	N/A	N/A	Domestic L CD	Total return	N/A	Arithmetic	12/31/77 = 100	N/A	3 months	12/77	Salomon Brothers Index	12/77 monthly
Salomon Brothers Domestic Sfr. Deposit Index.........	N/A	N/A	Domestic Sfr. deposit	Total return	N/A	Arithmetic	12/31/77 = 100	N/A	3 months	12/77	Salomon Brothers Index	12/77 monthly
Salomon Brothers Euro Sfr. Deposit Index.........	N/A	N/A	Euro Sfr. deposit	Total return	N/A	Arithmetic	12/31/77 = 100	N/A	3 months	12/77	Salomon Brothers Index	12/77 monthly
Salomon Brothers Domestic Ffr. Deposit Index.........	N/A	N/A	Domestic Ffr. deposit	Total return	N/A	Arithmetic	12/31/77 = 100	N/A	3 months	12/77	Salomon Brothers Index	12/77 monthly
Salomon Brothers Euro Ffr. Deposit Index.........	N/A	N/A	Euro Ffr. deposit	Total return	N/A	Arithmetic	12/31/77 = 100	N/A	3 months	12/77	Salomon Brothers Index	12/77 monthly

N/A = not available.
* MV = market value; PV = par value. Unless otherwise indicated, amount represents MV.
† YTM = yield-to-maturity.

PART 2

Securities and Instruments

Money Market Instruments

8 **MARCIA STIGUM, Ph.D.**
Stigum & Associates, New York

In this chapter we examine money market instruments (negotiable short-term debt securities) in which individuals and business firms invest. Treasury bills, issued by the U.S. Treasury, are the most important class of such securities in the United States, but there are others: commercial paper, bankers' acceptances, and negotiable certificates of deposit. Short-term obligations of federal agencies and municipal notes are discussed in Chapters 10 and 15, respectively.

OVERVIEW OF THE MONEY MARKET

The U.S. money market is a huge and significant part of the nation's financial system in which banks and other participants trade hundreds of billions of dollars every working day. Where those billions go and the prices at which they are traded affect how the U.S. government finances its debt, how business finances its expansion, and how consumers choose to spend or save.

The money market is a wholesale market for low-risk, highly liquid, short-term IOUs. It is a market for various sorts of debt securities rather than equities. The stock in trade of the market includes a large chunk of the U.S. Treasury's debt and billions of dollars worth of federal agency securities, negotiable bank certificates of deposit, bankers' acceptances, municipal notes, and commercial paper. Within the confines of the money market each day, banks, both domestic and foreign, actively trade in multimillion-dollar blocks billions of dollars of federal funds and Eurodollars, and banks and nonbank dealers are each day the recipients of billions of dollars of secured loans through the *repo market*. State and municipal governments also finance part of their activities in this market.

The heart of the activity in the money market occurs in the trading rooms of dealers and brokers of money market instruments. During the time the market is open, these rooms are characterized by a frenzy of activity. Each trader or broker sits in front of a battery of direct phone lines linking him or her to other dealers, brokers, and customers. The phones never ring; they just blink at a pace that makes, especially in the brokers market, for some of the shortest phone calls ever recorded. Despite the lack of ringing phones, a dealing room is anything but quiet. Dealers and brokers know only one way to hang up on a direct-line phone; they BANG the off button. And the more hectic things get, the harder they bang. Banging phones like drums in a band beat the rhythm of the noise generated in a trading room. Almost drowning that banging out at times is the constant shouting of quotes and tidbits of information.

Unless one spends a lot of time in trading rooms, it's hard to get a feel for what is going on amid all this hectic activity. Even listening in on phones is not very enlightening. One learns quickly that dealers and brokers swear a lot (it's said to lessen the tension), but the rest of their conversations is unintelligible to the uninitiated. Money market people have their own jargon, and until one learns it, it is impossible to understand them.

Once adjusted to their jargon and the speed at which traders converse, one observes that they are making huge trades—$5 million, $20 million, $150 million—at the snap of a finger. Moreover, nobody seems to be particularly awed or even impressed by the size of the figures. A federal-funds broker asked to obtain $100 million in overnight money for a bank might reply contemptuously about the size of the trade, "The buck's yours from the B of A," slam down the phone, and take another call. Federal-funds brokers earn only $1 per $1 million on overnight funds, so it takes a lot of trades to pay the overhead and let everyone in the shop make some money.

Despite its frenzied and incoherent appearance to the outsider, the money market efficiently accomplishes vital functions every day. One function is shifting vast sums of money between banks. This shifting is required because the major money market banks, with the exception of the Bank of America, all need a lot more funds than they obtain in deposits, and many smaller banks have more money deposited with them than they can profitably use internally.

The money market also provides a means by which the surplus funds of cash-rich corporations and other institutions can be funneled to banks, corporations, and other institutions that need short-term money. In addition, in the money market the U.S. Treasury can fund huge quantities of debt with ease. And the market provides the Federal Reserve System (also known as the Fed) with an arena in which to carry out open-market operations destined to influence interest rates and the growth of the money supply. The varied activities of money market participants also determine the structure of short-term interest rates, for example, what the yields on Treasury bills of different maturities are and how much commercial paper issuers have to pay to borrow. The latter rate is an important cost to many corporations, and it influences in particular the interest rate that a consumer who buys a car on time will have to pay on the loan. Finally, one might mention that the U.S. money market is becoming increasingly an international short-term capital market. In it the oil imports of the nationalized French electric company, Electricité de France, as well as the oil imports of Japan and a lot of other non-U.S. trade are financed.

Anyone who observes the money market soon picks out a number of salient features. First and most obviously, it is not one market but a collection of markets for several distinct and different instruments. What makes it possible to talk about *the* money market is the close interrelationships that link all these markets.

A second salient feature is the numerous and varied cast of participants. Borrowers in the market include foreign and domestic banks, the Treasury, corporations of all types, the Federal Home Loan Banks and other federal agencies, dealers in money market instruments, and many states and municipalities. The lenders include almost all of the above plus insurance companies, pension funds—public and private—and various other financial institutions. And often standing between borrower and lender is one or more of a varied collection of brokers and dealers.

Another key characteristic of the money market is that it is a wholesale market. Trades are big and the people who make them are almost always dealing for the account of some substantial institution. Because of the sums involved, skill is of the utmost importance, and money market participants are skilled at what they do. In effect the market is made by extremely talented specialists in very narrow professional areas. A bill trader extraordinaire may have only vague notions as to what the Euromarket is all about, and the Eurospecialist may be equally vague on other sectors of the market.

Another principal characteristic of the money market is honor.

Every day traders, brokers, investors, and borrowers do hundreds of billions of dollars of business over the phone, and however a trade may appear in retrospect, people do not renege. The motto of the money market is: *My word is my bond.* Of course, because of the pace of the market, mistakes do occur, but no one ever assumes that they are intentional, and mistakes are always ironed out in what seems the fairest way for all concerned.

The most appealing characteristic of the money market is innovation. Compared with our other financial markets, the money market is very unregulated. Someone who wants to launch a new instrument or to try brokering or dealing in a new way in existing instruments *does it*. And when the idea is good, which it often is, a new facet of the market is born.

TREASURY BILLS

Treasury bills (known more familiarly as T bills or bills) represent about 40 percent of the total marketable securities issued by the Treasury. These securities are held widely by financial business firms, nonfinancial corporations, and to some extent, by individuals. Nevertheless, despite their huge volume and wide distribution among different investor groups, T bills were relatively unknown to the average investor until the late 1960s, when the growing disparity between bill yields and savings deposit rates began drawing small investors into the bill market.

All T bills are negotiable, noninterest-bearing securities with an original maturity of one year or less—usually 13, 26, or 52 weeks. Bills are currently offered by the Treasury in denominations of $10,000, $15,000, $50,000, $100,000, $500,000, and $1 million. Bills used to be issued by the Treasury in the form of *bearer certificates.* Accordingly, to prove ownership of a bill, the owner had to produce it. The Treasury and the Federal Reserve System then made it possible to hold bills in *book-entry form.* Since 1977 the Treasury has offered bills *only* in book-entry form.

Bills are always issued at a discount from face value, and the amount of the discount is determined in bill auctions held by the Fed each time the Treasury issues new bills. At maturity, bills are redeemed by the Treasury for full face value. Thus investors in bills earn returns because they receive more for the bills at maturity than they paid for them at issue. This return is treated for federal tax purposes as ordinary interest income and, as such, is subject to full federal taxation at ordinary rates; it is, however, specifically *exempt* from state and local taxation.

In addition to normal bill issues, the Treasury periodically issues *tax-anticipation bills.* TABs, as they are called, are special-issue T bills that mature on corporate quarterly income tax payment dates and can be used at face value by corporations to pay their tax liabilities.

Determining the Yield on Bills

Bill dealers measure yield on a *bank discount basis*; that is, they quote yield as the percentage amount of the discount on an annualized basis. As an illustration, consider an investor who buys a bill maturing in one year at a price of $9,300 for each $10,000 of face value. The discount on this bill is $700, so yield on a bank discount basis works out to be 7 percent ($700/$10,000). In general, the formula for the yield on a bank discount basis for a bill *maturing in one year* is as follows.[1]

$$d = \frac{D}{F}$$

where

d = yield on a bank discount basis
F = face value in dollars
D = discount from face value in dollars

Alternatively, if the price in dollars is known, d can be calculated as follows:

$$d = \left(1 - \frac{P}{F}\right)$$

where

P = Price in dollars

On a bill maturing in less than one year, the discount is earned more quickly. So to get the correct annualized yield on a bank discount basis, the two general formulas above are modified as follows:

$$d = \left(\frac{D}{F}\right) \frac{360}{t_{sm}} \quad \text{or} \quad \left(1 - \frac{P}{F}\right) \frac{360}{t_{sm}}$$

where

t_{sm} = number of days from settlement to maturity

Thus, if the bill selling at $9,300 had 300 days from settlement to maturity, the annual yield on a bank discount basis would be 8.4 percent, found as follows:

---

[1] The formulas presented in this section are derived in Marcia Stigum, *Money Market Calculations: Yields, Break-Evens, and Arbitrage* (Homewood, Ill.: Dow Jones-Irwin, 1981), Chapter 4. © Dow Jones-Irwin, Inc., 1981.

$$d = \left(\frac{\$700}{\$10,000}\right) \frac{360}{300} = 8.4 \text{ percent}$$

or equivalently,

$$d = \left(1 - \frac{\$9,300}{\$10,000}\right) \frac{360}{300} = 8.4 \text{ percent}$$

The simple annual interest rate that an investor earns by buying a bill is found as follows:

$$i = \left(\frac{D}{P}\right) \frac{365}{t_{sm}}$$

where

$$i = \text{equivalent simple interest yield}$$

For example, the bill with 300 days from settlement to maturity and which can be purchased for \$9,300 for each \$10,000 of face value would have an equivalent simple interest yield of 9.16 percent, as shown below:

$$i = \left(\frac{\$700}{\$9,300}\right) \frac{365}{300} = 9.16 \text{ percent}$$

Alternatively, given the yield on a bank discount basis (d), the equivalent simple interest yield can be computed using the following formula:

$$i = \frac{365d}{360 - (dt_{sm})}$$

Applying this formula to our example and recalling that the yield on a bank discount basis is 8.4 percent, we find

$$i = \frac{365 \, (.084)}{360 - .084 \, (300)} = 9.16 \text{ percent}$$

Notice that the yield on a bank discount basis understates the equivalent simple interest rate that an investor would realize by holding a bill. This holds for all securities offered on a discounted basis. Moreover, as Exhibit 1 shows, the discrepancy between the two rates is greater the higher the rate of discount (i.e., higher the yield on a bank discount basis) and the longer the time to maturity.

In the secondary market, bids for and offerings of coupon securities are quoted not in terms of yields (as in the case of discount securities) but in terms of dollar prices.[2] On a coupon quote sheet, however, there is always a number for each security stating what its yield to

---

[2] An exception is municipal bonds. See Chapter 15.

Exhibit 1
Comparisons at Different Rates and Maturities between
Rates of Discount and the Equivalent Simply Interest Rates
on a 365-Day-Year Basis

Rate of Discount (Percent)	Equivalent Simple Interest (Percent)		
	30-Day Maturity	182-Day Maturity	364-Day Maturity
4	4.07	4.14	4.23
6	6.11	6.27	6.48
8	8.17	8.45	8.82
10	10.22	10.68	11.27
12	12.29	12.95	13.84
14	14.36	15.28	16.53
16	16.44	17.65	19.35

maturity would be if it were purchased at the quoted asked or offered price. However, the yield to maturity figure on a quote sheet for coupon securities *understates* the effective yield to maturity because it ignores the fact that interest is paid *semiannually*; that is, whatever investors do with coupon interest, it is worth something to them to get semiannual interest payments rather than a single year-end interest payment.

In converting the yield on a discount security to an add-on interest rate, various approaches are possible. One is to convert to an equivalent simple interest rate as explained above. However, in putting together quote sheets, "the street" takes a slightly different tack. *It restates yields on discount securities on a basis that makes them comparable to the yield to maturity quoted on coupon securities.* A rate so computed is called a *coupon yield equivalent* or *equivalent bond yield.*

"The street's" decision to restate bill yields on a coupon yield equivalent basis creates a need to distinguish between discount securities that have six months (182 days) or less to run and those that have more than six months to run. When a coupon security is on its last leg (i.e., when it will mature on the next coupon date and thus offers no opportunity for further compounding), its stated yield to maturity equals its yield on a simple interest basis. For this reason, *on discount securities with six months or less to run, equivalent bond yield is taken to be the equivalent simple interest rate offered by the instrument.* Letting d_b equal the equivalent bond yield, then d_b can be found from the rate of discount (d), or the yield on a bank discount basis, by the following formula:

$$d_b = \frac{365d}{360 - dt_{sm}}$$

However, when a discount security has more than six months to maturity, the equivalent bond yield, denoted d_b', is computed by the following formula:

$$d_b' = \frac{\left(\frac{-2t_{sm}}{365}\right) + 2\sqrt{\left(\frac{t_{sm}}{365}\right)^2 - \left(\frac{2t_{sm}}{365} - 1\right)\left(1 - \frac{1}{P}\right)}}{\frac{2t_{sm}}{365} - 1}$$

where

$$P = \text{Price per \$1 of face value}$$

To illustrate how to use the foregoing formula for a bill with more than six months to run, consider a bill with an asked price of 95.0653 percent of face value and 190 days to run. The equivalent bond yield is 9.95 percent as shown below:

$$d_b' = \frac{\left[\frac{-2(190)}{365}\right] + 2\sqrt{\left(\frac{190}{365}\right)^2 - \left(\frac{2(190)}{365} - 1\right)\left(1 - \frac{1}{0.950653}\right)}}{\frac{2(190)}{365} - 1}$$

$$= 9.95 \text{ percent}$$

Bill Quotes

Exhibit 2 reproduces Discount Corporation's T bill quote sheet for Friday, April 6, 1979. Notice that the quotes are closing rates on Thursday, April 5, and the assumed settlement date is regular settlement on Monday, April 9. The bid and asked price are quoted in terms of a "rate of discount," which is the same as the yield on a bank discount basis discussed earlier. The coupon equivalent yield (or bond equivalent yield) for each bill is also shown on the quote sheet.

Of particular interest on the quote sheet is the column "Value of .01 Per M." Investors and dealers in bills would like to know how much the price of a given bill would fluctuate if its yield changes by one basis point. The column shows the change in the price of the bill for a one-basis-point change per $1 million of face value of bills. Exhibit 3 gives these values for discount securities that mature from 1 to 365 days.[3]

---

[3] The formula used to find the "value of an 01 per $1 million" face value on a discount security is

$$V_{.01} = 0.0001(1,000,000)\left(\frac{t_{sm}}{360}\right)$$

Exhibit 2
Bill Quotes from a Dealer's Quote Sheet for Use on April 6, 1979

DISCOUNT CORPORATION OF NEW YORK

58 Pine Street, New York, N.Y. 10005
Telephone 212-248-8900 • WUI Telex 620863 Discorp • WU Telex 125675 Discorp - NYK

QUOTATIONS FOR U.S. TREASURY SECURITIES

Closing APR. 5, 1979
Ylds. for Dely. APR. 9, 1979

U. S. TREASURY BILLS(1)

Issue	Days to Mat.	Rate of Discount Bid	Rate of Discount Asked	Chge.	Coupon Yield Equiv.	Value of .01 Per M	Amount of Issue ($ millions)
4/12/79	3	9.85	9.75	--	9.89	.83	6201
4/19/79	10	9.85	9.75	--	9.91	2.78	14200
4/26/79	17	9.85	9.75	--	9.93	4.72	12205
5/01/79	22	9.55	9.45	+ .05	9.64	6.11	3022
5/03/79	24	9.50	9.40	--	9.59	6.67	6300
5/10/79	31	9.60	9.50	+ .05	9.71	8.61	6307
5/17/79	38	9.65	9.55	--	9.78	10.56	6200
5/24/79	45	9.65	9.55	--	9.80	12.50	5900
5/29/79	50	9.65	9.55	--	9.81	13.89	2477
5/31/79	52	9.65	9.55	--	9.82	14.44	5900
6/07/79	59	9.65	9.55	+ .05	9.84	16.39	5800
6/14/79	66	9.65	9.55	+ .05	9.86	18.33	5900
6/21/79	73	9.65	9.55	--	9.87	20.28	5800
6/26/79	78	9.65	9.55	--	9.89	21.67	2781
6/28/79	80	9.50	9.40	--	9.73	22.22	5900
7/05/79 ##	87	9.50	9.46	- .01	9.82	24.17	5900
7/12/79	94	9.54	9.50	- .01	9.88	26.11	2900
7/19/79	101	9.54	9.50	- .02	9.90	28.06	2900
7/24/79	106	9.57	9.53	- .05	9.94	29.44	3377
7/26/79	108	9.56	9.52	+ .02	9.94	30.00	3000

Issue	Days to Mat.	Rate of Discount Bid	Rate of Discount Asked	Chge.	Coupon Yield Equiv.	Value of .01 Per M	Amount of Issue ($ millions)
8/02/79	115	9.49	9.45	--	9.88	31.94	3000
8/09/79	122	9.52	9.48	+ .03	9.93	33.89	3000
8/16/79	129	9.50	9.46	+ .01	9.93	35.83	2900
8/21/79	134	9.48	9.44	- .02	9.92	37.22	3539
8/23/79	136	9.50	9.46	--	9.95	37.78	3001
8/30/79	143	9.48	9.44	- .02	9.94	39.72	1001
9/06/79	150	9.45	9.41	- .01	9.93	41.67	3000
9/13/79	157	9.46	9.42	--	9.96	43.61	3000
9/18/79	162	9.44	9.40	- .01	9.95	45.00	3348
9/20/79	164	9.45	9.41	--	9.97	45.56	3001
9/27/79	171	9.43	9.39	- .02	9.96	47.50	3000
10/04/79 ##	178	9.40	9.36	- .01	9.95	49.44	3003
10/16/79	190	9.39	9.35	- .02	9.95	52.78	3469
11/13/79	218	9.38	9.34	--	9.96	60.56	3893
12/11/79	246	9.34	9.30	- .02	9.94	68.33	4023
1/08/80	274	9.29	9.25	- .02	9.92	76.11	3698
2/05/80	302	9.28	9.24	- .02	9.96	83.89	3536
3/04/80	330	9.18	9.14	- .02	9.90	91.67	3320
4/01/80 ##	358	9.18	9.14	--	9.95	99.44	3343

Source: Marcia Stigum, Money Market Calculations: Yields, Break-Evens, and Arbitrage (Homewood, Ill.: Dow Jones-Irwin, 1981), p. 30. © Dow Jones-Irwin, Inc., 1981.

Exhibit 3
Value of an 01(.01 Percent) per $1 Million

Days to mat.	.01% equiv.	Days to mat.	.01% equiv.	Days to mat.	.01% equiv.	Days to mat.	.01% equiv.	Days to mat.	.01% equiv.	Days to mat.	.01% equiv.
1	$ .28	31	$8.61	61	$16.94	91	$25.28	121	$33.61	151	$41.94
2	.56	32	8.89	62	17.22	92	25.56	122	33.89	152	42.22
3	.83	33	9.17	63	17.50	93	25.83	123	34.17	153	42.50
4	1.11	34	9.44	64	17.78	94	26.11	124	34.44	154	42.78
5	1.39	35	9.72	65	18.06	95	26.39	125	34.72	155	43.06
6	1.67	36	10.00	66	18.33	96	26.67	126	35.00	156	43.33
7	1.94	37	10.28	67	18.61	97	26.94	127	35.28	157	43.61
8	2.22	38	10.56	68	18.89	98	27.22	128	35.56	158	43.89
9	2.50	39	10.83	69	19.17	99	27.50	129	35.83	159	44.17
10	2.78	40	11.11	70	19.44	100	27.78	130	36.11	160	44.44
11	3.06	41	11.39	71	19.72	101	28.06	131	36.39	161	44.72
12	3.33	42	11.67	72	20.00	102	28.33	132	36.67	162	45.00
13	3.61	43	11.94	73	20.28	103	28.61	133	36.94	163	45.28
14	3.89	44	12.22	74	20.56	104	28.89	134	37.22	164	45.56
15	4.17	45	12.50	75	20.83	105	29.17	135	37.50	165	45.83
16	4.44	46	12.78	76	21.11	106	29.44	136	37.78	166	46.11
17	4.72	47	13.06	77	21.39	107	29.72	137	38.06	167	46.39
18	5.00	48	13.33	78	21.67	108	30.00	138	38.33	168	46.67
19	5.28	49	13.61	79	21.94	109	30.28	139	38.61	169	46.94
20	5.56	50	13.89	80	22.22	110	30.56	140	38.89	170	47.22
21	5.83	51	14.17	81	22.50	111	30.83	141	39.17	171	47.50
22	6.11	52	14.44	82	22.78	112	31.11	142	39.44	172	47.78
23	6.39	53	14.72	83	23.06	113	31.39	143	39.72	173	48.06
24	6.67	54	15.00	84	23.33	114	31.67	144	40.00	174	48.33
25	6.94	55	15.28	85	23.61	115	31.94	145	40.28	175	48.61
26	7.22	56	15.56	86	23.89	116	32.22	146	40.56	176	48.89
27	7.50	57	15.83	87	24.17	117	32.50	147	40.83	177	49.17
28	7.78	58	16.11	88	24.44	118	32.78	148	41.11	178	49.44
29	8.06	59	16.39	89	24.72	119	33.06	149	41.39	179	49.72
30	8.33	60	16.67	90	25.00	120	33.33	150	41.67	180	50.00

Buying Bills

There is no way for an individual to invest in bills unless he or she has a minimum of $10,000 available or is willing and able to pool funds with other investors. For an individual with more than $10,000 to invest, it is possible to acquire bills in amounts equal to any multiple of five by buying an appropriate mix of bills in $10,000 and $15,000 denominations. Bills can be purchased from a bank or at auction.

Buying Bills at a Bank. The easiest way for a small investor to acquire bills is to buy them from a bank. If your bank is a major bank in a large financial center, such as Chicago or New York, it may well act as a dealer in government securities; in that case it will sell bills to you directly out of its inventory. If your bank is not a dealer bank, it will purchase the required amount of bills from a larger bank with which it has a correspondent relationship.

Exhibit 3 (*concluded*)

Days to mat.	.01% equiv.	Days to mat	.01% equiv.	Days to mat.	.01% equiv.	Days to mat.	.01% equiv.	Days to mat.	.01% equiv.	Days to mat.	.01% equiv.
181	$50.28	212	$58.89	243	$67.50	274	$76.11	305	$84.72	336	$93.33
182	50.56	213	59.17	244	67.78	275	76.39	306	85.00	337	93.61
183	50.83	214	59.44	245	68.06	276	76.67	307	85.28	338	93.89
184	51.11	215	59.72	246	68.33	277	76.94	308	85.56	339	94.17
185	51.39	216	60.00	247	68.61	278	77.22	309	85.83	340	94.44
186	51.67	217	60.28	248	68.89	279	77.50	310	86.11	341	94.72
187	51.94	218	60.56	249	69.17	280	77.78	311	86.39	342	95.00
188	52.22	219	60.83	250	69.44	281	78.06	312	86.67	343	95.28
189	52.50	220	61.11	251	69.72	282	78.33	313	86.94	344	95.56
190	52.78	221	61.39	252	70.00	283	78.61	314	87.22	345	95.83
191	53.06	222	61.67	253	70.28	284	78.89	315	87.50	346	96.11
192	53.33	223	61.94	254	70.56	285	79.17	316	87.78	347	96.39
193	53.61	224	62.22	255	70.83	286	79.44	317	88.06	348	96.67
194	53.89	225	62.50	256	71.11	287	79.72	318	88.33	349	96.94
195	54.17	226	62.78	257	71.39	288	80.00	319	88.61	350	97.22
196	54.44	227	63.06	258	71.67	289	80.28	320	88.89	351	97.50
197	54.72	228	63.33	259	71.94	290	80.56	321	89.17	352	97.78
198	55.00	229	63.61	260	72.22	291	80.83	322	89.44	353	98.06
199	55.28	230	63.89	261	72.50	292	81.11	323	89.72	354	98.33
200	55.56	231	64.17	262	72.78	293	81.39	324	90.00	355	98.61
201	55.83	232	64.44	263	73.06	294	81.67	325	90.28	356	98.89
202	56.11	233	64.72	264	73.33	295	81.94	326	90.56	357	99.17
203	56.39	234	65.00	265	73.61	296	82.22	327	90.83	358	99.44
204	56.67	235	65.28	266	73.89	297	82.50	328	91.11	359	99.72
205	56.94	236	65.56	267	74.17	298	82.78	329	91.39	360	100.00
206	57.22	237	65.83	268	74.44	299	83.06	330	91.67	361	100.28
207	57.50	238	66.11	269	74.72	300	83.33	331	91.94	362	100.56
208	57.78	239	66.39	270	75.00	301	83.61	332	92.22	363	100.83
209	58.06	240	66.67	271	75.28	302	83.89	333	92.50	364	101.11
210	58.33	241	66.94	272	75.56	303	84.17	334	92.78	365	101.39
211	58.61	242	67.22	273	75.83	304	84.44	335	93.06	366	101.67

Value of an 01 per $1 million $= \left(\dfrac{.01\% \times t}{360} \right)$ $1 million

Where t = Days to maturity

Source: Marcia Stigum, *Money Market Calculations: Yields, Break-Evens, and Arbitrage* (Homewood, Ill.: Dow Jones-Irwin, 1981). © Dow Jones—Irwin, Inc., 1981.

Although buying bills from a bank is convenient, it has one disadvantage: most banks impose a service charge on bill purchases for amounts less than $100,000. The only exceptions are a few small country banks that can buy bills from their respective correspondent banks without paying a fee. The size of purchase charges varies considerably from bank to bank. Typically it is in the range of $20 to $35. Higher rates are usually charged by smaller banks because to acquire bills for their customers, they have to go through another bank that charges them a fee. Moral: If you are going to buy bills through a bank, shop around and find out where you can get the lowest service charge.

Obviously the imposition of a service charge on bill purchases reduces the investor's yield, since the charge in effect raises the price paid for the bills. Since bank service charges on bill purchases generally are on a per-transaction basis—the same whether $10,000 or $60,000 of bills are purchased—the effect of such a charge on the yield will be smaller, the larger the amount invested. Also the effect will be smaller, the longer the maturity of the securities bought.

When buying bills from a bank, rate-quote shopping may also be beneficial. Because of the highly competitive conditions that prevail in the bill market, dealer banks normally quote very close if not identical rates on bills of a given maturity. However, this is not always the case. Occasionally money market banks in the same financial center quote rates to the public that differ by as much as 20 or even 40 basis points on very short issues. Thus, if you live in a financial center and you are investing a substantial amount (say, $100,000 or more), it might be worthwhile to call around and find out what rates different dealer banks are quoting. The investor who shops around can either buy bills directly from the bank quoting the best rate or can direct his or her own bank to buy bills from that source. Generally, suburban and country banks place all customer orders for bills with their correspondent bank but, if requested, they can and will buy from another source.

Bills can also be purchased from any brokerage house. How that compares with buying from a bank depends on which brokerage house you pick. Some large houses, such as Merrill Lynch, are active dealers in government securities and will fill small orders for a $25 service charge. Other brokerage houses that don't have a dealer operation have to go through a bank to purchase bills, with the result that you can end up paying a $50 purchase commission—$25 to the broker and another $25 to cover the bank's service charge to the broker.

Buying Bills at Auction.   If you are willing to put yourself out a little, you can escape the service charge that banks impose on bill purchases by buying bills directly from the Fed during one of the periodic auctions at which the Fed sells new issues of T bills.

Naturally, a small investor can't be expected to arrive panting at the Fed just before the bid window closes with a tender tuned to the morning's developments in the money market. That is no problem, however, since the Fed has made provision for the small investor who is unsophisticated and, worse still, has no runner at his or her disposal. To service such investors, the Fed accepts what are called *noncompetitive* bids for amounts up to $500,000 per investor per auction. A person submitting a noncompetitive bid gets bills at a price equal to the average of the competitive bids accepted by the Treasury. Generally the spread in competitive bids is not very wide, so the noncompetitive bidder does not fare badly.

To submit a noncompetitive bid, the first thing you must do is write to the Federal Reserve bank in your district and ask for information on bill offerings and forms for tendering bids. In response, the Fed will send a circular describing the next bill issue to be auctioned and *tender forms* for bidding on these specific securities. An investor does not really need a detailed circular on a planned T bill offering to submit a noncompetitive bid. All the investor needs to know is when to submit the bid (something that can be determined from the issuing schedule) and roughly the rate of discount at which to expect to get the bills (something that can be estimated by looking in a newspaper at yield quotes on existing bills of comparable maturity).[4]

All this may sound a bit complicated, but once you go through the process of buying bills at auction and learn the ropes, the trouble involved in making subsequent purchases is minimal. However, one caveat is in order. If you are thinking of buying bills at auction, bear in mind that money market rates are at times subject to sharp and unanticipated fluctuations. Thus, an investor who puts in a bid two days before an auction expecting to get a 9 percent return might find that rates had fallen substantially by the day of the auction. How great the danger of a sharp and unanticipated break in interest rates is depends on economic conditions. During the midst of a boom, when employment is high and inflationary pressures are the main worry, the Fed is unlikely to make a sudden switch to an easy monetary policy, which would cause short-term rates to drop. On the other hand, when the Fed has been fighting inflation with tight money for a lengthy period and employment is finally beginning to fall, as was the case in late 1974, the danger of a sudden and precipitous drop in rates is real.

For the investor who wants to avoid uncertainty and lock in a rate, the best alternative is to buy existing bills from a bank. Note in this respect that a bank buying bills through its correspondent may offer you a choice—a telephone order that locks in the rate you get versus a cheaper mail order in which you get the rate prevailing when the order is processed. Generally, the secured rate is worth a few extra dollars.

One final note: You can always ask your bank to submit in your name a noncompetitive bid for bills. This procedure is simpler than sending in your own tender form, *but* the bank will impose its normal bill-purchase fee on such transactions.

---

[4] One method of paying for T bills is to send along with the tender form full payment for the face amount of the bills applied for. Such payments can be made in cash or by sending a cashier's check, bank money order, or certified personal check. Another method of paying in full is to send with the tender T bills equal in face value to the bills applied for and maturing not later than the date on which the new bills are to be issued. If you *roll over* bills in this fashion, the Treasury will send you on the day the new bills are issued a check equal to the difference between the face amount of your maturing bills and the discounted price you must pay for your new bills.

Selling Bills

If you are investing small amounts, because of transactions costs, you will get the best yield on your bills if you hold them to maturity. However, a person investing in bills can never be sure that he or she will not experience some unexpected need for cash before the bills mature. So the natural next question is: How does one sell bills and what sort of price can one expect to get?

The answer to how to sell is simple. Go to a bank or broker. They handle bill sales as well as purchases, and their service charge on a sale is normally the same as their charge for a purchase.

Determining the price you get on your bills requires a simple calculation, since bills are quoted in terms of yield rather than price. First find the yield on a bank discount basis, d, at which the bills you hold are currently quoted. Then use the following formula to determine roughly the discount, D, from face value at which your bills are currently trading per $100 of face value:

$$D = d \times 100 \times \left(\frac{t}{360}\right)$$

The price you get is face value minus total discount.

Normally, if you have held your bills for any length of time, the price at which you can sell them will be higher than the price at which you bought them. The reason is that the price a bill commands will gradually rise over time (assuming the rate of discount at which it sells doesn't change); the dollar amount of the discount at which it sells will fall as the bill approaches maturity. For example, for a six-month bill to yield 9 percent on a bank discount rate basis, it must be priced at $95.45 per $100 of face value. For the same bill three months later to yield 9 percent, its price must have been bid up to $97.72 per $100 of face value.

Of course the rate at which a bill sells typically does not stand still over time. With an upward-sloping yield curve, this rate will tend to fall over the holding period, which means that the bill's price will be bid up even more during the holding period, enough more so that its current yield equals the rate of discount quoted on bills of shorter maturity.

To illustrate, let's look again at our six-month bill selling initially at a 9 percent rate of discount. If after three months, this bill were still quoted at 9 percent, its price would have risen by $2.26. If, however, over these three months, the rate at which the bill was quoted had fallen to 7 percent, then the bill's price would have risen from $95.45 to $98.23, or by an extra $0.51 per $100 of face value.

Movement along the yield curve is not the only factor that will alter the rate at which a bill is quoted. So, too, will changes in the general level of short-term interest rates. Moreover, the possible effects of such changes on a bill's price form a two-way street. Although a *fall* in interest rates will cause a bill's price to *rise*, a *rise* in rates will cause a bill's price to *fall*. The latter possibility adds an element of *risk* for the individual who invests money in bills he or she might not hold to maturity. If rates rise sharply while one holds the bills, the yield on the investment will be substantially below anticipated earning, maybe even negative. Notice, however, that the effect of changes in the level of interest rates on a bill's price will be smaller as the bill gets closer to maturity, and so the price risk inherent in selling a bill before maturity declines as the bill approaches maturity.

The preceding paragraphs can be summed up quite neatly. How high a price you get for bills you sell before maturity depends on how close they are to maturity, on the shape of the yield curve, and on the general level of interest rates prevailing at the time of the sale. Specifically, the price you get will be higher the closer your bills are to maturity, the steeper the yield curve, and the lower the level of short-term interest rates.

Bills Held to Maturity

If you hold a bill until maturity, cashing it in poses no problem. If you buy bills through a bank, you never see them unless you request possession; instead the money market bank through which the bills are purchased holds them and issues to you a safekeeping receipt. When the bills mature, this bank automatically cashes them in and you get your funds on the day of maturity at no charge.

If you purchased bills at auction, on the other hand, you will have physical possession of them. To collect, you have several options. One is to send your bills several days before maturity via registered, insured mail to the Fed, which will send you a check on the maturity date. A less time-consuming alternative is to ask your bank to cash in the bills. To avoid any loss of interest on your funds, be sure to give your bills to the bank several days before maturity so that the bank has time to get the bills physically to the Fed by the date of maturity. The Fed will not redeem a bill until it has possession of the bill, and the Treasury pays no additional return on bills held beyond maturity. When a bank cashes in bills, there is generally no charge except perhaps for postage, and you should get the money due you on the day the bill matures. A banker who says collection takes several days is asking for an interest-free loan.

A third alternative open to the investor who buys bills at auction and who wants to keep the money in the bill market is to roll over the bills at maturity—a procedure described earlier. In this respect, notice that the Treasury periodically issues bills in maturities other than 13,

26, and 52 weeks. One problem with investing in bills that do not have
normal maturities is that they cannot be immediately rolled over at
maturity. You can obtain information on offerings of bills that do not
have normal maturities, as well as on the specific dates for auctions of
52-week bills, by requesting the Fed to put you on its permanent
mailing list for bill issues.

COMMERCIAL PAPER

Commercial paper, whoever the issuer and whatever the precise
form it takes, is an unsecured promissory note with a fixed maturity. In
plain English, the issuer of commercial paper (the borrower) promises
to pay the buyer (the lender) some fixed amount on some future date.
But issuers pledge no assets—only liquidity and established earning
power—to guarantee that they will make good on their promises to
pay. Traditionally, commercial paper resembled in form a Treasury
bill; it was a negotiable, noninterest-bearing note issued at a discount
from face value and redeemed at maturity for full face value. Today,
however, a lot of paper is interest bearing. For the investor the major
difference between bills and paper is that paper carries some small
risk of default because the issuer is a private firm, whereas the risk of
default on bills is zero for all intents and purposes.

Firms selling commercial paper frequently expect to roll over their
paper as it matures; that is, they plan to get money to pay off maturing
paper by issuing new paper. Since there is always the danger that an
adverse turn in the paper market might make doing so difficult or
inordinately expensive, most paper issuers back their outstanding paper with *bank lines of credit;* they get a promise from a bank or banks
to lend them at any time an amount equal to their outstanding paper.
Issuers normally pay for this service in one of several ways: by holding at their line banks compensating deposit balances equal to some
percentage of their total credit lines; by paying an annual fee equal to
some small percentage of their outstanding lines; or through some mix
of balances and fees.

Issuers of Paper

The large open market for commercial paper that exists in the
United States is a unique feature of the U.S. money market. Its origins
trace back to the early 19th century, when firms in need of working
capital began using the sale of open-market paper as a substitute for
bank loans. Their need to do so resulted largely from the unit banking
system adopted in the United States. Elsewhere, it was common for
banks to operate branches nationwide, which meant that seasonal demands for credit in one part of the country, perhaps due to the move-

ment of a crop to market, could be met by a transfer of surplus funds from other areas to that area. In the United States, where banks were restricted to a single state and more often to a single location, this was difficult. Thus firms in credit-scarce, high-interest-rate areas started raising funds by selling commercial paper in New York City and other distant financial centers.

For the first 100 years or so, borrowers in the commercial paper market were all nonfinancial business firms: textile mills, wholesale jobbers, railroads, and tobacco companies, to name a few. Most of their paper was placed for a small fee by dealers, and the principal buyers of paper were banks. Then in the 1920s the character of the market began to change. The introduction of autos and other consumer durables vastly increased consumers' demands for short-term credit, and that in turn led to the creation and rapid growth of consumer finance companies.

One of the first large consumer finance companies was the General Motors Acceptance Corporation (GMAC), which financed consumer purchases of General Motors autos. To obtain funds, GMAC ("Gee Mack," in Wall Street argot) began borrowing in the paper market, a practice that other finance companies followed. Another innovation by GMAC was to short-circuit paper dealers and place paper directly with investors, a practice that made sense because GMAC borrowed such large amounts that it could save money by setting up in-house facilities to distribute its paper.

Despite the advent of finance company paper, the paper market shrank during the 1920s, stagnated during the 1930s, and then slumped again during World War II, with the result that by 1945 paper was a relatively unimportant instrument. Since then the volume of commercial paper outstanding has grown steadily and rapidly due both to the tremendous postwar increase in sales of consumer durables and to the long-term upward trend in interest rates. After 1968, when the Federal Reserve began pursuing tight money on a severe and prolonged basis, the growth of commercial paper became nothing short of spectacular.

Today, nonfinancial firms—everything from public utilities to manufacturers to retailers—still issue paper, and their paper, which is referred to as industrial paper, accounts for about 23 percent of all paper outstanding. Such paper is issued, as in the past, to meet seasonal needs for funds and also as a means of interim financing (i.e., to obtain funds to start investment projects that are later permanently funded through the sale of long-term bonds). In contrast to industrial borrowers, finance companies have a continuing need for short-term funds throughout the year; they are now the principal borrowers in the commercial paper market, accounting for roughly 59 percent of all paper.

In the recent years of tight money, bank holding companies have also joined finance companies as borrowers in the commercial paper market. Many banks are owned by a holding company, an arrangement offering the advantage that the holding company can engage in activities in which the bank itself is not permitted. Commercial paper is sold by bank holding companies primarily to finance their nonbank activities in leasing, real estate, and other lines. However, funds raised through the sale of such paper can also be funneled into the holding company's bank, if the latter is pinched for funds, through various devices, such as the sale of bank assets to the holding company.

Issuing Techniques

All industrial paper is issued through paper dealers. Currently there are about eight major paper dealers in the country; their main offices are in financial centers—New York, Chicago, and Boston—but they have branches throughout the country. Also there are a number of smaller regional dealers. Typically, dealers buy up new paper issues directly from the borrower, mark them up, and then resell them to investors. The current going rate of markup is very small, an eighth of 1 percent per annum. Generally, paper issues are for very large amounts, and the minimum round lot in which most dealers sell is $250,000. Thus the dealer market for commercial paper is a meeting ground for big corporate borrowers and for large investors (the latter including financial corporations, nonfinancial corporations, and pension funds).

Finance companies and banks occasionally place their paper through dealers, but most such paper (more than 80 percent) is placed directly by the issuer with investors. A big finance company, for example, might place $1 million or more of paper with an insurance company or with a big industrial firm that had a temporary surplus of funds. In addition to these large-volume transactions, some finance companies and banks also sell paper in relatively small denominations directly to small business firms and individual investors, as will be discussed later in this section.

Paper Maturities

Maturities on commercial paper are generally very short—one to three months being the most common on dealer-placed paper. Generally, dealers prefer not to handle paper with a maturity of less than 30 to 45 days because, on paper of such short maturity, their markup (which is figured on a percent per annum basis) barely covers costs. However, to accommodate established borrowers, they will do so.

Paper with a maturity of more than 270 days is rare because issues of such long maturity have to be registered with the SEC.

Finance companies that place their paper directly with large investors generally offer a wide range of maturities—3 to 270 days. Also they are willing to tailor maturities to the needs of investors and will often accept funds for very short periods, for example for a weekend. Finance companies that sell low-denomination paper to individual investors generally offer maturities ranging from 30 to 270 days on such paper. These companies also issue longer maturity short-term notes that have been registered with the SEC.

Paper Yields

Some paper bears interest, but much does not. Investors who buy noninterest-bearing paper get returns on their money because they buy their paper at a discount from face value, whereas the issuer redeems the paper at maturity for full face value. Yields on paper are generally quoted in eighths of 1 percent, for example, at 7⅛ percent per annum. Paper rates, whether the paper is interest-bearing or not, are quoted on a *bank discount basis,* as in the case of bills.

Bill rates vary over time, rising if business demand for credit increases or if the Fed tightens credit, falling in the opposite cases. The yields offered by paper issuers follow much the same pattern of bill yields except that paper yields are, if anything, even more volatile than bill yields.

The reason paper rates fluctuate up and down in step with the yields on bills and other money market securities is simple. Paper competes with these other instruments for investors' dollars. Therefore, as yields on bills and other money market securities rise, paper issuers must offer higher rates in order to sell their paper. In contrast, if bill yields and other short-term rates decline, paper issuers can and do ease the rates they offer.

The volatility of paper rates has important consequences for the investor. First, it means that the attractiveness of paper as an investment medium for short-term funds varies over the interest-rate cycle. It also means that the rate you get on paper bought today tells you relatively little about what rate you would get if you were to roll over that paper at maturity. Paper yields offered in the future may be substantially higher or lower than today's rates, depending on whether money is tightening or easing.

Risk and Ratings

If you are thinking of buying paper, you should consider not only the *return* it yields, but also whether there is any *risk* that you will not get timely payment on your paper when it matures. Basically there are two situations in which an issuing company might fail to pay off its maturing paper: (1) It is solvent but lacks cash, and (2) it is insolvent. How great are the chances that either situation will occur? Fortunately, today the chances are quite small, in fact, negligible, for companies with top-rated paper.

Since the early 1930s, the default record on commercial paper has been excellent. In the case of dealer paper, one reason is that after the 1920s the many little borrowers who had populated the paper market were replaced by a much smaller number of large, well-established firms. This gave dealers, who were naturally extremely careful about whose paper they handled, the opportunity to examine much more thoroughly the financial condition of each issuer with whom they dealt.

Although the payments record on paper is good, the losses that have occurred make it clear that an individual putting money into paper has the right—more strongly, the responsibility—to ask: How good is the company whose paper I am buying? Because of the investor's very real need for an answer, and because of the considerable time and money involved in obtaining one, rating services have naturally developed. Today a large proportion of dealer and direct paper is rated by one or more of three companies: Standard & Poor's, Moody's, and Fitch.

Paper issuers willingly pay the rating services to examine them and rate their paper, since a good rating makes it easier and cheaper for them to borrow in the paper market. The rating companies, despite the fact that they receive their income from issuers, basically have the interests of the investor at heart for one simple reason: The value of their ratings to investors and thereby their ability to sell rating services to issuers depend on their accuracy. The worth to an issuer of a top rating is the track record of borrowers who have held that rating.

Each rating company sets its own rating standards, but their approaches are similar. Every rating is based on an evaluation of the borrowing company's management and on a detailed study of its earnings record and balance sheet. Just what a rating company looks for depends in part on the borrower's line of business; the optimal balance sheet for a publishing company would look quite different from that of a finance company. Nonetheless, one can say in general that the criteria for a top rating are strong management, a good position in a well-established industry, an upward trend in earnings, adequate liquidity, and the ability to borrow to meet both anticipated and unexpected cash needs.

Since companies seeking a paper rating are rarely in imminent danger of insolvency, the principal focus in rating paper is on *liquidity*—can the borrower come up with cash to pay off the maturing paper? Here what the rating company looks for is ability to borrow elsewhere than in the paper market and especially the ability to borrow short term from banks. Today, for a company to get a paper rating, its paper must be backed by bank lines of credit.

Different rating firms grade borrowers according to different classifications. Standard & Poor's, for example, rates companies from A for highest quality to D for lowest. It also subdivides A-rated companies into four groups according to relative strength, A–1+ down to A–3. Fitch rates firms F–1 (highest grade) to F–4 (lowest grade). Moody's uses P–1, P–2, and P–3, with P–1 being their highest rating.

Buying Dealer Paper

All industrial and some finance company paper is sold through dealers. Dealers are essentially wholesalers operating on very small margins. Consequently, they are willing to sell only in large amounts; the minimum round lot that most dealers sell is $250,000 to $350,000. Generally, to buy paper in smaller amounts, the buyer has to be lucky enough to pick up the tag end of an issue. For example, a buyer might get $150,000 of paper from a dealer who had bought up a $5 million issue and was left with $150,000 on the shelf after cutting off for large buyers four $1 million pieces, a $600,000 piece, and a $250,000 piece.

Unfortunately, few individuals are going to have $150,000 to put into a tag end; *and* even if they do, they would not be able to buy it from a dealer. The reason is that the SEC has ruled that paper should not be sold to "unsophisticated" buyers. Just which buyers are "unsophisticated" is left up to the seller to determine. Dealers generally take the position that individuals, no matter how rich or financially savvy they may be, are unsophisticated; and consequently dealers will not sell paper to individuals.

To get dealer paper, an individual has to go to a broker. A number of brokerage houses operate on the assumption that an individual who trades stocks, has a respectable net worth, and owns a reasonably diversified holding of assets is sufficiently sophisticated to buy paper. The reason for the divergence between dealers' and brokers' interpretation of "sophisticated" lies in their contrasting positions. To dealers, who are accustomed to making large transactions with knowledgeable investors on the basis of a brief phone call, sales to individuals would be a time-consuming, money-losing proposition. So dealers are happy to accept a rule that keeps out a few well-heeled, sophisticated investors and a horde of others who would want all sorts of information and would buy in small lots. Brokers are in a different position. They are accustomed to dealing at a retail level, and they set a pricing structure that allows them to profit by doing so. A big part of a broker's role in the financial structure is to assist customers in making stock investments. But at times when the stock market looks unpromising or has badly burned investors, some of the broker's customers may choose to pull their money out of the market. To keep that cash in-house, so to speak, until stocks regain their allure, the broker needs an alternative instrument to offer—one that is safe, yields a good return, and is liquid. Paper meets these requirements, so some brokers sell paper to individuals who are established customers.

Retail brokerage houses that sell paper get it in several ways. One is to buy large lots from dealers and have them cut up into small pieces—say, a mix of $25,000, $50,000, and $100,000 denominations. Another way is for the brokerage house itself to set up facilities to act as a dealer in paper. Merrill Lynch, which sells paper to individuals, set out to capture the dealer's wholesale margin by doing exactly that.

The retail brokerage house with the widest menu of commercial paper to offer the *small* investor is Merrill Lynch.[5] Currently this firm is the primary dealer through which about 100 firms issue paper. Naturally not all of the paper issued by these 100 firms is sold by Merrill Lynch in small lots to individual investors. Out of, say, $5 million issued, $4 million might be in large blocks to big investors, and the rest might be cut up into small pieces for individual investors. Besides the paper issued through it, Merrill Lynch also obtains paper originated by other dealers through Wall Street purchases.

The minimum amount in which Merrill Lynch will sell paper is $25,000; above that, it will sell in any increment of $1,000. The charge for paper purchases under $100,000 is $25. For purchases above $100,000 there is no charge; on such sales the firm earns its profit on its dealer spread. All the paper carried by Merrill Lynch is rated. The principal paper they sell to individual investors is paper issued by the Chase Manhattan Corporation, the holding company behind the Chase Manhattan Bank.

Buying dealer paper from a broker has several disadvantages from the investor's point of view: Not all brokerage houses are prepared to sell paper to individuals; on small purchases transaction costs are significant; and maturities of less than 30 to 45 days generally are unavailable. Fortunately, there is an alternative, *direct paper.*

Buying Direct Paper

A number of large, well-known finance companies sell commercial paper in relatively small denominations directly to individual investors and/or through commercial banks. Their ranks include the General Motors Acceptance Corporation (GMAC), Chrysler Financial

---

[5] Other brokerage houses that are much more important as paper dealers—for example, Goldman Sachs, Salomon Brothers, Lehman Brothers, The First Boston, and A. G. Becker—sell only to institutional customers.

Corporation, C.I.T. Financial Corporation, Associates Corporation of North America, and other perhaps less familiar names.

Some of these companies (e.g., Associates and C.I.T. Financial) are *independent* finance companies that specialize in providing various types of short-term financing to consumers and/or business firms—making installment loans to consumers, buying up accounts receivable from business firms, and so forth. Obviously, these independent finance companies need a lot of funds to carry out their operations. One way they get them is by selling paper, mostly direct, but sometimes through dealers.

Other direct paper issuers are *captive* finance companies; that is, they specialize in financing installment and credit sales by their parent company. For example, GMAC uses the money it raises through the sale of paper to buy from GM dealers the installment loan contracts generated when consumers finance car purchases directly through a GM dealer. Similarly, the captive finance companies set up by Sears and Montgomery Ward sell paper to finance the credit sales made at their parent company's retail stores.

To get an idea of what is available in direct paper, let's look at GMAC's menu. GMAC offers investors *paper* ranging in maturity from 30 to 270 days and *notes* registered with the SEC ranging in maturity from nine months to five years. The minimum denomination in which they issue paper or notes is $25,000; above that amount they will accept funds in $100 increments.[6] Also, on investments of $100,000 or more, GMAC will write paper with a maturity as short as three days. GMAC issues its notes and paper in either bearer or registered form, as the buyer desires. Also it will issue either noninterest-bearing securities sold at a discount or interest-bearing securities sold at full face value. As you can discover by making a few phone calls to direct issuers, rates, maturities, and terms of issue vary considerably from issuer to issuer. Sears, for example, sets a minimum denomination of $150,000 and issues only paper (not notes). Because of the differences in practice between issuers, shop around. Also, in comparing yields on finance company paper with yields on other instruments, remember that paper yields are quoted on a bank discount basis. Finally, check paper ratings before you buy.

The cheapest way to buy direct paper is from the company issuing it. In the case of GMAC, this can be done in person, by phone, or by mail. To buy GMAC paper, first contact their nearest office and find out what rates, maturities, and minimum denominations they are offering. Then when you have decided what paper to buy, visit the company's office, write a check, and pick up your paper; *or* mail the company a check and have them send your paper or note. Whether

---

[6] Associates sells notes to consumers in much smaller denominations.

you deal by mail or in person, have the security you buy registered in your name. This will protect against loss if you misplace the security or it is stolen. Even with this precaution, keep paper and notes in safe-deposit box.

When your paper matures, there are several ways to redeem it. If you want to stay in paper, it is easy to roll over maturing paper. Any direct paper you bought was probably accompanied by a renewal form when you got it; if not, you can get one by mail. Simply fill out this form and send it with your maturing paper to the issuing company *before* the maturity date. On the maturity date, they will issue you new paper *and* send you a check for interest due if your paper was interest bearing. If your paper was not interest bearing, the check will be for the difference between the face value of your maturing paper and the discounted price of your new paper.

To redeem maturing paper for cash, a few days before maturity send it to the bank that handles collections on the paper you purchased. On the day of maturity, this bank will send you a check for the amount owed you (or issue you a check if you present the security personally).

As you have probably noted, a do-it-yourself purchase of direct paper requires little time and effort on the part of the investor and involves minimal transaction costs—a few phone calls and some postage stamps. An alternative procedure is to have your local bank buy direct paper for you, a route some direct issuers require that you take. This procedure calls for slightly (very slightly) less effort, but you incur a service charge that can easily run to $35 for a purchase. If your local banker buys commercial paper for you, the banker will probably buy it not directly from the issuing company but through a correspondent bank, which in turn purchases the paper from the issuer. By doing so, your banker incurs a service charge at that bank, which is passed on to you as part of the banker's fee. In return for the correspondent bank's service charge (which you in effect pay), your banker obtains convenience. The correspondent bank holds your paper in safekeeping and automatically redeems it for cash at maturity, relieving your banker from the trouble of taking delivery on the paper, keeping track of it, and then returning it for collection at maturity.

Even if you buy finance company paper directly from the issuer, your bank can cash it in for you. If you use your bank, give them the paper several days before maturity so that they have time to present it for collection on the maturity date. If you are a good customer, the bank may not charge for this service. Paper bought through a bank is automatically redeemed by the bank at maturity, and there is no charge. Either way, you should ask for and get payment from your bank on the day your paper matures.

Since buying paper from a bank saves little (if any) effort, you should calculate the reduction in return that the bank's service charge is going to entail. For example, paying your banker $35 to buy $25,000 worth of 30-day paper yielding 6 percent will reduce your yield to 4.32 percent. Obviously the yield reduction will be smaller the larger the amount invested and the longer the maturity of the paper purchased.

Buying Bank Paper

As noted earlier, many banks obtain funds by having their *holding company* issue commercial paper. Most bank paper sold is direct paper, purchased at the bank whose holding company issues it.

Most large city banks that issue paper set minimum denominations at $100,000. They are interested in catering to large investors and firms rather than to small investors. However, there are suburban and country banks that offer paper in maturities ranging from less than a month to 270 days and in minimum denominations as low as $5,000 or $10,000. You might wonder why small banks would do so, since their paper will obviously compete with bank demand and time deposits for their customers' savings dollars. The answer is that a bank following this practice realizes that when money market rates are high, some of its sophisticated depositors are going to put their liquid funds into money market instruments. If the bank itself offers them such an instrument, then chances are greater that when open-market rates fall, these depositors will again place their funds on deposit at the bank.

One big advantage of bank paper is that if your bank happens to offer paper in small denominations, the transaction costs—both monetary and in terms of effort expended by you—are reduced to near zero. To buy such paper, you simply write your banker a check for the amount of the purchase. Naturally there is no bank fee on either purchase or redemption.

If you consider buying bank paper, bear in mind that bank paper is *paper* (i.e., unsecured promissory notes). It is not bank deposits, and it is not covered by deposit insurance. If your bank fails, you are likely to lose money. Therefore, before buying bank paper, check the condition of the company issuing it. As we said, banks don't fail often these days, but when they do, it is only depositors, not paper holders, who are protected.

If you buy bank paper in small denominations, don't count on always being able to roll it over. When money is tight and interest rates are high, a bank holding company may bid aggressively for money through the sale of paper in small denominations both because it wants money and because it knows that its bank's depositors have attractive alternatives to bank deposits. When money eases, the situation is quite different. For the small investor, alternatives to bank deposits are less attractive, and the bank is likely to be less strained for funds. Therefore it will bid less aggressively for paper sales and may, besides cutting rates, also increase minimum denominations and lengthen minimum maturities.

BANKERS' ACCEPTANCES

The *Banker's acceptance* (*BA*) is an unknown instrument outside the confines of the money market. Moreover, explaining BAs isn't easy because they arise in a variety of ways out of a variety transactions. The best approach is to use an example.

Suppose a U.S. importer wants to buy shoes in Brazil and pay for them four months later, after she has had time to sell them in the United States. One approach would be for the importer to simply borrow from her bank; however, short-term rates may be lower in the open market. If they are, and if the importer is too small to go into the open market on her own, then she can go the bankers' acceptance route.

In that case she has her bank write a letter of credit for the amount of the sale and then sends this letter to the Brazilian exporter. Upon export of the shoes, the Brazilian firm, using this letter of credit, draws a time draft on the importer's U.S. bank and discounts this draft at its local bank, thereby obtaining immediate payment for its goods. The Brazilian bank in turn sends the time draft to the importer's U.S. bank, which then stamps "accepted" on the draft; that is, the bank guarantees payment on the draft and thereby creates an *acceptance*. Once this is done, the draft becomes an irrevocable primary obligation of the accepting bank. At this point, if the Brazilian bank did not want cash immediately, the U.S. bank would return the draft to that bank, which would hold it as an investment and then present it to the U.S. bank for payment at maturity. If, on the other hand, the Brazilian bank wanted cash immediately, the U.S. bank would pay it and then either hold the acceptance itself or sell it to an investor. Whoever ended up holding the acceptance, it would be the importer's responsibility to provide her U.S. bank with sufficient funds to pay off the acceptance at maturity. If the importer should fail for any reason, her bank would still be responsible for making payment at maturity.

Our example illustrates how an acceptance can arise out of a U.S. import transaction. Acceptances also arise in connection with U.S. export sales, trade between third countries (e.g., Japanese imports of oil from the Middle East), the domestic shipment of goods, and domestic or foreign storage of readily marketable staples. Currently most BAs arise out of foreign trade; the latter may be in manufactured goods, but more typically is in bulk commodities, such as cocoa, cotton, coffee, or crude oil, to name a few. Because of the complex nature of acceptance operations, only large banks that have well-staffed foreign departments act as accepting banks.

Bankers' acceptances closely resemble commercial paper in form. They are short-term (270 days or less), noninterest-bearing notes sold at a discount and redeemed by the accepting bank at maturity for full face value. The major difference between bankers' acceptances and paper is that payment on paper is guaranteed by only the issuing company, but payment on bankers' acceptances is also guaranteed by the accepting bank. Thus bankers' acceptances carry slightly less risk than commercial paper. The very low risk on acceptances is indicated by the fact that to date no investor in acceptances has ever suffered a loss.

Yields on bankers' acceptances are quoted on a bank discount basis, as in the case of commercial paper. Yields on bankers' acceptances closely parallel yields on paper. Also, both rates are highly volatile, rising sharply when money is tight and falling in an equally dramatic fashion when conditions ease. This means that when money is tight, yields on bankers' acceptances are very attractive.

The big banks through which bankers' acceptances originate generally keep some portion of the acceptances they create as investments. The rest are sold to investors through dealers or directly by the bank itself. Major investors in bankers' acceptances are other banks, foreign central banks, and Federal Reserve banks.

Many bankers' acceptances are written for very large amounts and are obviously out of the range of the small investor; certainly this includes all acceptances that pass through the hands of dealers. However, acceptances in amounts as low as $5,000 or even $500 are not uncommon. Some accepting banks offer these low-denomination acceptances to their customers as investments. An individual investing in a $25,000 acceptance may in fact be buying a single small acceptance arising out of one transaction, or be buying a bundle of even smaller acceptances that have been packaged together to form a round-dollar amount. Frequently, bankers' acceptances are available in still smaller odd-dollar amounts. The investor who puts money into an odd-dollar acceptance should be prepared to experience some difficulty in rolling over the funds. Also the availability of bankers' acceptances varies both seasonally and over the cycle. Generally, availability is greatest when money is tight and banks prefer not to tie up funds in acceptances.

The easiest and cheapest way to buy a bankers' acceptance is from an accepting bank. In that case, service charges will be zero. The rate you get will, of course, be less than the rate that a $1 million investor gets, but when money is tight, it may nevertheless be quite good—as much as twice the rate you would get on a savings account. If you don't live in the vicinity of an accepting bank, you can have your bank purchase acceptances for you through its correspondent bank. Here you are likely to run into a service charge, and its effect on yield should be carefully calculated.

The rates offered on bankers' acceptances, like those on paper, vary from day to day. Also they may vary slightly on a given day from one accepting bank to another. Thus a few calls to shop for rates are in order if you decide to invest in acceptances.

An easy way to get some idea of the general level of rates on bankers' acceptances and to see how they compare with yields on competing instruments is to check the "Money Rate" quotes in *The Wall Street Journal*, or *Barron's* "Economic and Financial Indicators." As Exhibit 4 shows, rates on bankers' acceptances are normally quoted for maturities of 30, 60, 90, 120, and 180 days. Some dealers quote rates in eighths of 1 percent, but rate quotes to two decimal points are also common.

Since payment on acceptances is guaranteed by both the accepting bank and the ultimate borrower, investing in acceptances exposes an individual to minimal risk. For small acceptances, as for paper, there is no secondary market. Thus an investor who needs cash cannot sell a bankers' acceptance to another investor but can use it as collateral for a bank loan. Also, if the investor's need for cash is really pressing, chances are that the accepting bank will be willing to buy back the acceptance early.

To sum up, bankers' acceptances are a little known, but at times very attractive, investment for the small investor.

NEGOTIABLE CERTIFICATES OF DEPOSIT

In the early post-World War II period, when interest rates were low, bankers were not inclined to accept corporate time deposits on which they would have to pay interest. However, in the late 1950s and early 1960s, things changed for several reasons. First, corporate treasurers, who had customarily met their liquidity needs by holding large balances of noninterest-bearing demand deposits, began to manage their money in a more sophisticated manner as short-term rates rose; they switched funds where possible out of demand deposits into liquid, income-yielding, money market instruments, such as T bills and commercial paper. Second, the large New York money market banks, who had historically enjoyed a dominant position on the national banking scene, found that their competitive position was eroding. As a result of industrial decentralization and the rapid growth of population outside the Northeast, their share of total deposits had declined by almost 50 percent between 1940 and 1960.

Money Rates

Thursday, January 7, 1982

The key U.S. and foreign annual interest rates below are a guide to general levels but don't always represent actual transactions.

PRIME RATE: 15¾%. The base rate on corporate loans at large U.S. money center commercial banks.

FEDERAL FUNDS: 12¾% high, 12% low, 12¼% near closing bid, 12⅜% offered. Reserves traded among commercial banks for overnight use in amounts of $1 million or more. Source: Mabon, Nugent & Co., N.Y.

DISCOUNT RATE: 12%. The charge on loans to member commercial banks by the New York Federal Reserve Bank.

CALL MONEY: 13½% to 14%. The charge on loans to brokers on stock exchange collateral.

COMMERCIAL PAPER: placed directly by General Motors Acceptance Corp.: 12¼%, 30 to 119 days; 12%, 120 to 270 days.

COMMERCIAL PAPER: high-grade unsecured notes sold through dealers by major corporations in multiples of $1,000: 12⅝%, 30 days; 12⅝%, 60 days; 12¾%, 90 days.

CERTIFICATES OF DEPOSIT: 12.60%, one month; 12.65%, two months; 13%, three months; 13.75%, six months; 14.50%, one year. Typical rates paid by major banks on new issues of negotiable C.D.'s, usually on amounts of $1 million and more. The minimum unit is $100,000.

BANKERS ACCEPTANCES: 12.50%, 30 days; 12.50%, 60 days; 12.45%, 90 days; 12.70%, 120 days; 12.90%, 150 days; 12.90%, 180 days. Negotiable, bank-backed business credit instruments typically financing an import order.

EURODOLLARS: 13 5/16% to 13 3/16%, one month; 13 11/16% to 13 9/16%, two months; 13 13/16% to 13 11/16%, three months; 14⅜% to 14¼%, four months; 14 11/16% to 14 9/16%, five months; 14 13/16% to 14 11/16% six months. The rates paid on U.S. dollar deposits in banks in London, usually on amounts of $100,000 or more. The higher rate for each maturity is LIBOR, the London Interbank Offered Rate.

FOREIGN PRIME RATES: Canada 16½%; Germany 13%; Japan 7.15%; Switzerland 8%; Britain 14½%. These rate indications aren't directly comparable; lending practices vary widely by location. Source: Morgan Guaranty Trust Co.

TREASURY BILLS: Results of the Monday, January 4, 1982, auction of short-term U.S. government bills, sold at a discount from face value in units of $10,000 to $1 million: 11.658%, 13 weeks; 12.282%, 26 weeks.

SAVINGS RATES: on instruments offered to individuals; minimum amounts vary. Money market fund-a 10.59%; six month money market certificate, 12.532%; 30-month savings institution small-saver certificate (accounts 2½ to less than 4 years) b-13.75%; one-year "all savers" tax exempt certificates, 10.16%; savings institution passbook deposit-c 5.5%; U.S. savings bond, 9%.

a-Annualized average rate of return after expenses for past 30 days on Merrill Lynch Ready Assets Trust, the largest of such funds; this isn't a forecast of future returns. b-Commercial bank rate. Savings and loan associations and savings banks are permitted to pay .25% more than commercial banks. c-Commercial banks are limited to paying .25% less than savings and loan associations and savings banks.

In response to these trends, the First National City Bank of New York announced in 1961 that it would issue large-denomination *negotiable certificates of deposit* and that a large, well-known government securities dealer, The First Boston Corporation, had agreed to create a secondary market (act as a dealer) in these securities. *A negotiable CD is simply a receipt from a bank for funds deposited at that bank for some specified period of time at some specified rate of return.*

Negotiable CDs were not a new instrument in 1961; they had been around in small volume for a long time. What made First National City's announcement the beginning of a phenomenal expansion in outstanding CDs was not its willingness to issue this instrument, but rather First Boston's intent to act as a dealer in CDs. To the corporate treasurer looking for liquidity, what is important is not *negotiability* per se, but rather *marketability*. The marketability of an instrument, which is measured in degrees, depends on the existence of a secondary market for that instrument and on the level of activity in that market. Bills and paper are both negotiable, but bills have high marketability, whereas paper does not. Thus, corporations typically use bills to provide first-line liquidity, and they use paper and other less liquid instruments to provide second-line liquidity.

Once First National City made its announcement, the other major banks quickly followed suit, and a number of other dealers joined The First Boston Corporation in the secondary market. From essentially a zero base in 1961, the volume of negotiable CDs outstanding grew rapidly. Today, the major issuers of negotiable CDs are large, nationally known money market banks, principally in New York and Chicago. In addition to these prime borrowers, there are also a number of less well known regional banks that issue CDs.

Since some investors in Eurodollars wanted liquidity, banks that accepted time deposits in London began to issue Eurodollar CDs. A *Eurodollar CD* resembles a domestic CD except that instead of being the liability of a domestic bank, it is the liability of the London branch of a domestic bank or of a British bank or some other foreign bank with a branch in London. Although many of the Eurodollar CDs issued in London are purchased by other banks operating in the Euromarket, a large portion of the remainder are sold to U.S. corporations and other domestic institutional investors. Many Euro CDs are issued through dealers and brokers who maintain secondary markets in these securities.

The Euro CD market is younger and smaller than the market for domestic CDs, but it has grown rapidly since its inception. The most recent development in the "Eurodollar" CD market is that some large banks have begun offering such CDs through their Caribbean branches.[7]

---

[7] A CD issued, for example, in Nassau is technically a Euro CD because the deposit is held in a bank branch outside the United States.

Foreign banks issue dollar-denominated CDs not only in the Euro market, but also in the domestic market through branches established there. CDs of the latter sort are frequently referred to as Yankee CDs; the name is derived from Yankee bonds, which are bonds issued in the domestic market by foreign borrowers.[8]

CDs can have any maturity longer than 30 days, and some 5- and 7-year CDs have been sold (these pay interest semiannually). Most CDs, however, have an *original maturity* of one to three months. Generally the CD buyer, who may be attempting to fund a predictable cash need—say, provide for a tax or dividend payment—can select his or her own maturity date when making the deposit.

Until May 1973, the Fed, under Regulation Q, imposed lids on the rates that banks could pay on large-denomination CDs of different maturities. Today these lids are past history, and the general level of yields on negotiable CDs is determined by conditions of demand and supply in the money market. Since holding a CD exposes the investor to a small risk of capital loss (the issuing bank might fail), prime-name negotiable CDs, in order to sell, have to be offered at rates approximately one eighth of a point above the rate on T bills of comparable maturity. Of course, in actual practice there is no one CD rate prevailing at any one time. Each issuing bank sets a range of rates for different maturities, normally with an upward-sloping yield curve. On a given day a bank at which loan demand is especially strong, and which therefore needs money, may set rates slightly more attractive than those posted by other banks. Posted rates are not fixed rates; big investors can and do haggle with banks over the rate paid.

Generally prime-name banks can attract funds more cheaply than other banks, the rate differential being one percentage point or less. Foreign banks pay still higher CD rates. In comparing CD rates with yields on other money market instruments, note that CDs are *not* issued at a discount. It takes $1 million of deposits to get a CD with a $1 million face value. CDs typically pay interest at maturity. Thus rates quoted on CDs correspond to yield in the terms in which the investor normally thinks—what we call equivalent bond yield.

Recently banks have introduced on a small scale a new type of negotiable CD, *variable-rate CDs*. The two most prevalent types are six-month CDs with a 30-day *roll* (on each roll date, accrued interest is paid and a new coupon is set) and one-year paper with a 3-month roll. The coupon established on a variable-rate CD at issue and on subsequent roll dates is set at some amount (12.5 to 30 basis points, depending on the name of the issuer and the maturity) above the average rate (as indicated by the composite rate published by the Fed) that banks are paying on new CDs with an original maturity equal to the length of the roll period.

---

[8] Yankee bonds are discussed in Chapter 25.

We can sum up our discussion of risk, liquidity, and return on negotiable CDs by saying that CDs are slightly riskier than T bills. They are also slightly less liquid, since the spread between bid and asked prices is narrower in the bill market than in the secondary CD market; the reason for this difference is that in the bill market the commodity traded is homogeneous and buying and selling occur in greater volume.

CDs, however, compensate for these failings by yielding a somewhat higher return than do bills. Euro CDs offer a higher return than do domestic CDs. The offsetting disadvantages are that they are less liquid and expose the investor to some extra risk because they are issued outside the United States. Yankee CDs expose the investor to the extra (if only in perception) risk of a foreign name, and they are also less liquid than domestic CDs. Consequently Yankee CDs trade at yields close to those on Euro CDs. Although variable-rate CDs offer the investor some interest-rate protection, they have the offsetting disadvantage of illiquidity because they trade at a concession to the market. During their last *leg* (roll period) variable-rate CDs trade like regular CDs of similar name and maturity.

How precisely does an investor buy and sell CDs? Since the minimum denomination for readily marketable CDs is $1 million, it is probably safe to ignore that question here. The market for negotiable CDs is one sector of the money market in which the individual investor certainly is not going to participate *directly*. The investor may, however, become an *indirect* participant, which is why we have discussed negotiable CDs here. One of the most attractive liquid, high-yielding investments available to the individual investor is putting money into a money market fund, an institution that is likely to invest heavily, in some cases exclusively, in bank CDs.[9]

Computing the Yield of a CD, Given Its Price

Almost all CDs issued in the domestic market have a maturity at issue of less than one year and pay simple interest on a 360-day basis.[10] The rate of interest paid is the coupon rate, and interest is paid at maturity. In the formulas presented for CDs, the following convention will be adopted. *Price P is always taken to be price per $1 of face value, with accrued interest, if any, included.*[11]

CDs are always quoted, at issue and in the secondary market, in terms of yield on a simple interest basis. The following formula is for the rate of return that a CD offered at a price P will yield an investor.

---

[9] Money market funds are described in Chapter 20.

[10] As noted above, the exceptions are variable-rate CDs and a few long-term issues that have been floated at various times.

[11] The formulas presented in this section are derived in Stigum, *Money Market Calculations*, pp. 71–80.

$$y = \left(\frac{1 + c\,\dfrac{t_{im}}{360}}{P} - 1 \right) \frac{360}{t_{sm}}$$

where

y = yield on the CD
c = coupon rate
t_{sm} = days from settlement to maturity
t_{im} = days from issue to maturity

For example, suppose that an investor buys a CD that carries a coupon rate of 10 percent and has an original maturity of 90 days and a current maturity of 60 days. If the price P is 1.009024, the yield is 9.5 percent as shown below.

$$y = \left(\frac{1 + .100\,\dfrac{90}{360}}{1.009024} - 1 \right) \frac{360}{60} = .095$$

There are two points to note about the formula for computing the yield on a CD. First, if a CD is bought on its issue date, then P = 1, and the expression for the yield reduces to the coupon rate (c), as would be expected. Second, the fact that CDs pay interest on the basis of a 360-day year should not be forgotten when CD yields are compared with those on other interest-bearing securities, such as government notes and bonds, that pay interest on a 365-day basis. To convert from a 365- to a 360-day basis, the yield on a CD must be multiplied by 1.014.[12] Therefore, getting a year's interest over 360 days is worth 1.4 extra basis points for every 1 percent interest.

Computing Price, Given Yield

Using the formula for the yield on a CD, a formula for the price at which a CD will trade in the secondary market if it is offered at a yield y can be determined. Solving, we have

$$P = \left(\frac{1 + c\,\dfrac{t_{im}}{360}}{1 + y\,\dfrac{t_{sm}}{360}} \right)$$

Let's use the CD from the yield formula example, given the price, to show how the foregoing formula is applied. The price P is 1.009024, as shown below:

---

[12] The conversion factor is found by dividing 365 by 360.

$$P = \left(\frac{1 + 0.100\,\dfrac{90}{360}}{1 + 0.095\,\dfrac{60}{360}} \right) = 1.009024$$

Breaking Out Accrued Interest

Separating the price P paid for a CD into principal and interest is easily done. Let

a_i = accrued interest
t_{is} = days from issue to settlement

On a CD accrued interest is given by the expression

$$a_i = c\,\frac{t_{is}}{360}$$

and

$$\text{Principal per \$1 of face value} = P - c\,\frac{t_{is}}{360}$$

Applying these formulas to the preceding example, we find that

$$a_i = 0.10\,\frac{30}{360} = 0.083333$$

and

$$\begin{aligned}
\text{Principal} &= 1.009024 - 0.083333 \\
&= 1.000691
\end{aligned}$$

Notice that the CD in our example is selling at a premium. This is to be expected since it was traded at a *yield well below* its coupon.

Holding Period Yield

Intuition, which seems to be invariably wrong in money market calculations, suggests that an investor who bought a CD at 10 percent and sold it before maturity at the same rate would earn 10 percent over the holding period. In fact, the investor would earn *less*. The reason is our old friend, compounding. It crops up because interest is not paid by the issuer on the CD until some period after the investor sells it; the CD is priced at sale, however, so that the buyer will earn the offered yield on an amount equal to the principal paid *plus* accrued interest.

Consider first a CD that is bought by an investor at issue and later sold before maturity. The rate of simple interest (i) earned by the investor over the holding period is

$$i = \left(\frac{1 + c \, \dfrac{t_{im}}{360}}{1 + y \, \dfrac{t_{sm}}{360}} - 1 \right) \frac{360}{t_{is}}$$

where

t_{is} = days from issue to settlement on the sale
y = rate at which the CD is sold

For example, an investor buys a 90-day CD carrying a 10 percent coupon at issue and sells it 30 days later at a 10 percent yield. The return earned is not 10 percent but a lower figure, 9.83 percent. The calculation is:

$$i = \left(\frac{1 + 0.10 \, \dfrac{90}{360}}{1 + 0.10 \, \dfrac{60}{360}} - 1 \right) \frac{360}{60} = 9.83 \text{ percent}$$

A Secondary CD

The yield on a CD purchased in the secondary market and sold before maturity can be calculated using a similar but slightly more complex formula shown below:

$$i = \left(\frac{1 + y_1 \, \dfrac{t_1}{360}}{1 + y_2 \, \dfrac{t_2}{360}} - 1 \right) \frac{360}{t_1 - t_2}$$

where

y_1 = purchase rate
y_2 = sale rate
t_1 = days from purchase to maturity
t_2 = days from sale to maturity

Sensitivity of Return to Sale Rate and Length of Holding Period

The figures in Exhibit 5, show what return (i) an investor would earn by selling a six-month CD purchased at 9 percent after various holding periods and at various rates. Notice first the column labeled 9 percent. It shows that if the investor resells the CD at the purchase rate, the return earned will be higher the longer the holding period is (that is, the closer the sale date is to the date on which the CD matures and accrued interest is paid out).

Exhibit 5
The Rate of Return (i) Earned by an Investor on a 9 Percent, Six-Month CD when
Sold at Various Rates after Various Holding Periods

Holding Period (Days)	Sale Rate, y				
	11 Percent	10 Percent	9 Percent	8 Percent	7 Percent
30	−0.96%	3.84%	8.67%	13.55%	18.46%
60	4.82	6.77	8.74	10.71	12.70
90	6.81	7.80	8.80	9.80	10.81
120	7.86	8.36	8.87	9.38	9.88
150	8.59	8.73	8.93	9.14	9.35
179	8.99	8.99	9.00	9.00	9.01

Suppose an investor sells a CD at a rate below the rate at which he bought it, he will receive a capital gain and earn over the holding period a return higher than the yield at which he bought the CD. As the columns labeled 8 percent and 7 percent show, this effect becomes smaller the longer the holding period is. If, conversely, the investor sells the CD at a rate *above* that at which he purchased it, the effect is the opposite and also decreases as the holding period is lengthened.

The reason the impact of the sale rate on the return earned by the investor diminishes as the holding period increases is: The longer the holding period, the shorter is the time in which the buyer of the CD will earn the rate at which he or she buys the CD, and therefore the smaller will be the impact of that rate on the principal amount the investor pays for the CD.

Compounding

We have noted that selling a CD before maturity tends to reduce the yield earned by the investor over the holding period. If the investor *fully* reinvests the proceeds (principal *plus* accrued interest) from the sale of the CD, this effect will be offset by the opportunity for compounding of interest earnings created by the sale and subsequent repurchase.

To illustrate, an investor who purchased at issue a 182-day CD at 9 percent and sold it 91 days later at 9 percent would earn a yield of 8.80 percent over that period. If the investor immediately fully reinvested the sale proceeds ($1.022750 per $1 of face value) in a 9 percent, 91-day CD, total earnings over the 182-day investment period would be identical with what would have been earned by holding to maturity the 182-day, 9 percent CD originally bought.

U.S. Treasury Obligations

9

MARCIA STIGUM, Ph.D.
Stigum & Associates, New York

FRANK J. FABOZZI, Ph.D., C.F.A., C.P.A.
Professor of Economics
Fordham University

INTRODUCTION

Treasury securities, commonly referred to as governments, offer the investor a number of attractive features. They expose the investor to zero credit risk, and although they yield less than other market instruments except for municipals, they are much more liquid instruments. In fact Treasury obligations are the most liquid instruments traded in the money market. Governments owe their liquidity to the fact that most individual issues are extremely large, and governments are thus not discrete heterogeneous instruments, as are bankers' acceptances and certificates of deposits. Another advantage of Treasury securities is that interest earned on them is not subject to state and local taxation. A final attraction is the wide array of these issues available.

However, like other fixed income marketable instruments, governments (other than nonmarketable issues discussed later) are subject to interest-rate risk—the risk of an adverse movement in the price of the issue as interest rates rise. Moreover, Treasury obligations, like other fixed income instruments, are subject to purchasing-power risk.

The U.S. Treasury issues marketable and nonmarketable securities. Treasury bills, notes, and bonds are marketable securities; nonmarketable securities available to investors include U.S. savings bonds, retirement-plan bonds, and individual retirement bonds.

MARKETABLE SECURITIES

Currently the Treasury issues three types of marketable securities.[1]

Bills. Treasury bills are currently issued in three-month, six-month, and one-year maturities. T bills, as they are commonly called, are issued in denominations of $10,000, $15,000, $50,000, $100,000, $500,000, and $1 million. They are issued on a discounted basis. T bills are discussed in Chapter 8.

Notes. Treasury notes are coupon securities that may be issued with a maturity of not more than 10 years but not less than 1 year. Interest is paid semiannually. Notes are available in registered, bearer, and book-entry form. When the Treasury wants to encourage individuals to invest in a new note issue, it sets the minimum denomination at $1,000. At other times it sets it at $5,000. Notes are also available in $10,000, $100,000, and $1 million denominations. The note market is a wholesale market, except for sales to individuals and small portfolio managers, who typically buy to hold to maturity. Treasury notes are not callable.

Bonds. Because Congress has granted the Treasury only minor exemptions from the 4.25 percent lid it imposes on the rate the Treasury may pay on bonds, the Treasury relies relatively little these days on the sale of new bond issues to fund the federal debt. It does, however, typically offer some bonds at quarterly refunding dates, often by reopening an old issue. Also, because of past bonds sales, there are a large number of government bonds outstanding.

Treasury bonds are issued in bearer, registered, and book-entry form. They come in denominations of $1,000, $5,000, $10,000, $100,000, and $1 million. Like the note market, the bond market is largely a wholesale market in which institutions buy and sell. About half the government bond issues outstanding are callable. Generally the call date is five years before maturity. On old low-coupon issues, the call provision is of small importance, but some new high-coupon issues might conceivably be called someday.

In Chapter 5 an overview of the primary and secondary markets for government securities is presented.

Exhibit 1 is an excerpt taken from *The Wall Street Journal* of Treasury note and bond price quotations. The coupon rate, year of maturity, and month of maturity are indicated in the first three columns, respectively. When an issue is callable, two years will be indicated in the "Mat" column. The first year is the year in which the Treasury may begin to call the issue. The second year is the year of maturity.

---

[1] The Treasury used to issue interest-bearing certificates with an original maturity of one year or less. It has not done so since 1967.

Exhibit 1
Sample Page from *The Wall Street Journal* Showing Quotations on Treasury Bonds and Notes

Wednesday, January 20, 1982

Mid-afternoon Over-the-Counter quotations; sources on request.

Decimals in bid-and-asked and bid changes represent 32nds; 101.1 means 101 1/32. a-Plus 1/64. b-Yield to call date. d-Minus 1/64. n-Treasury notes.

Treasury Bonds and Notes

Rate	Mat. Date		Bid	Asked	Bid Chg.	Yld.
11½s,	1982	Jan n	99.30	100	.....	10.91
6⅛s,	1982	Feb n	99.15	99.19	.....	12.08
6⅜s,	1982	Feb	99.15	99.19	+ .1	12.32
13⅞s,	1982	Feb n	100.1	100.5	.....	11.68
7⅞s,	1982	Mar n	98.31	99.3	.....	12.54
15s,	1982	Mar n	100.8	100.12	.....	12.36
11⅜s,	1982	Apr n	99.12	99.16	.....	12.95
7s,	1982	May n	97.29	98.1	− .2	13.40
8s,	1982	May n	98.5	98.9	− .1	13.53
9¼s,	1982	May n	98.18	98.22	− .2	13.40
9⅜s,	1982	May n	98.12	98.16	.....	13.63
8¼s,	1982	Jun n	97.22	97.26	− .1	13.46
8⅝s,	1982	Jun n	97.22	97.24	− .3	13.90
8⅞s,	1982	Jul n	97.12	97.16	.....	13.97
8⅛s,	1982	Aug n	96.26	96.30	− .4	13.93
9s,	1982	Aug n	97.6	97.10	− .2	14.09
11⅛s,	1982	Aug n	98.4	98.8	− .2	14.25
8⅜s,	1982	Sep n	96.2	96.6	− .4	14.37
11⅞s,	1982	Sep n	98.6	98.10	− .4	14.52
12⅛s,	1982	Oct n	98.6	98.10	− .2	14.52
7⅛s,	1982	Nov n	94.21	94.25	− .3	14.11
7⅞s,	1982	Nov n	95	95.4	− .2	14.41
13⅞s,	1982	Nov n	99.18	99.20	.....	14.36
9⅜s,	1982	Dec n	95.27	95.31	− .3	14.09
15⅛s,	1982	Dec n	100.16	100.20	− .4	14.38
13⅝s,	1983	Jan n	98.28	99	− .3	14.69
8s,	1983	Feb n	93.28	94.4	− .6	14.11
13⅞s,	1983	Feb n	98.28	99	− .5	14.89
9¼s,	1983	Mar n	94.9	94.13	− .3	14.52
12⅝s,	1983	Mar n	97.16	97.20	− .6	14.86
14½s,	1983	Apr n	99.14	99.18	− .4	14.88
7⅞s,	1983	May n	92.7	92.15	− .3	14.35
11⅝s,	1983	May n	96.18	96.26	− .3	14.36
15⅝s,	1983	May n	100.20	100.24	− .4	14.99
3¼s,	1978-83	Jun	87.31	88.15	− .9	12.49
8⅞s,	1983	Jun n	92.21	92.29	− .3	14.50
14⅝s,	1983	Jun n	99.16	99.20	− .4	14.92
15⅞s,	1983	Jul n	101.2	101.6	− .5	14.98
9¼s,	1983	Aug n	92.16	92.24	− .4	14.59
11⅞s,	1983	Aug n	95.30	96.2	− .5	14.77
16¼s,	1983	Aug n	101.16	101.20	− .4	15.06
9¾s,	1983	Sep n	92.22	92.26	− .4	14.70
16s,	1983	Sep n	101.4	101.12	− .4	15.04
15½s,	1983	Oct n	100.15	100.23	− .5	15.02
7s,	1983	Nov n	88.12	88.20	− .2	14.33
9⅞s,	1983	Nov n	92.10	92.18	− .4	14.69
12⅛s,	1983	Nov n	95.20	95.24	− .5	14.81
10½s,	1983	Dec n	93.2	93.10	.....	14.58
13s,	1983	Dec	96.26	96.28	− .8	14.87
7¼s,	1984	Feb n	87.6	87.14	− .1	14.50
14¼s,	1984	Mar n	98.25	99.1	− .12	14.78
9¼s,	1984	May n	89.11	89.19	− .11	14.71
13¼s,	1984	May n	96.30	97.6	− .10	14.73
15¾s,	1984	May n	101.23	101.28	− .9	14.76
8⅞s,	1984	Jun n	88.8	88.16	− .7	14.64
6⅜s,	1984	Aug	83.4	84.4	− .6	13.94
7¼s,	1984	Aug n	84.26	85.2	− .10	14.42
13¼s,	1984	Aug n	96.10	96.18	− .10	14.94
12⅛s,	1984	Sep n	93.27	94.3	− .11	14.86
14⅜s,	1984	Nov n	98.18	98.22	− .14	14.96
16s,	1984	Nov n	101.29	102.1	− .11	15.08
14s,	1984	Dec n	97.30	98.6	− .6	14.78
8s,	1985	Feb n	83.26	84.2	− .8	14.63
13⅜s,	1985	Mar n	95.30	96.6	− .10	14.91
3¼s,	1985	May	82.22	83.22	.....	9.06
4¼s,	1975-85	May	82.30	83.30	− .4	10.07
10⅜s,	1985	May n	88.24	89	− .6	14.68
14⅜s,	1985	May n	99.5	99.13	− .7	14.61
14s,	1985	Jun n	97.20	97.24	− .8	14.87
8¼s,	1985	Aug n	82.18	82.26	− .4	14.60
9⅝s,	1985	Aug n	86.14	86.22	− .1	14.54
15⅞s,	1985	Sep n	102	102.4	− .13	15.11
11¾s,	1985	Nov	91.8	91.16	− .12	14.74
14⅛s,	1985	Dec n	97.2	97.30	− 1	14.83
13½s,	1986	Feb n	95.30	96.6	− .4	14.78
7⅞s,	1986	May n	78.28	79.4	− .3	14.55
13¾s,	1986	May n	96.20	96.28	− .6	14.75
8s,	1986	Aug n	78.22	78.30	− .4	14.46
6⅛s,	1986	Nov	74.15	75.15	− .1	12.82
13⅞s,	1986	Nov n	96.23	96.28	− .9	14.81
16⅛s,	1986	Nov n	103.14	103.18	+ .26	15.07
9s,	1987	Feb n	80.8	80.16	+ .1	14.50
12¾s,	1987	Feb n	92.30	93.2	− .9	14.72
12s,	1987	May n	90.26	91.2	− .8	14.47
7⅝s,	1987	Nov n	73.24	74.8	.....	14.29
12⅜s,	1988	Jan n	91	91.8	− .2	14.62
13¼s,	1988	Apr n	93.30	94.6	− .1	14.71
8¼s,	1988	May n	74.14	74.22	+ .4	14.50
14s,	1988	Jul n	96.18	96.26	− .6	14.79
15⅜s,	1988	Oct n	101.9	101.13	− .5	15.04
8¾s,	1988	Nov n	75.3	75.19	− .3	14.51
14⅝s,	1989	Jan	99	99.4	− .4	14.83
9¼s,	1989	May n	76.4	76.20	− .2	14.55
10¾s,	1989	Nov n	81.16	82.2	− .16	14.68
3½s,	1990	Feb	82.22	83.22	+ .12	6.10
8¼s,	1990	May	69.29	70.13	+ .2	14.49
10¾s,	1990	Aug n	80.28	81.4	− .4	14.69
13s,	1990	Nov n	91.18	91.26	+ .3	14.68
14½s,	1991	May n	98.7	98.11	− .1	14.84
14⅞s,	1991	Aug n	99.19	99.23	− .5	14.93
14¼s,	1991	Nov n	97.4	97.8	− .3	14.79
4¼s,	1987-92	Aug	82.29	83.29	+ .7	6.36
7¼s,	1992	Aug	60.23	61.7	+ .3	14.56
4s,	1988-93	Feb	80.16	81.16	− 1.1	6.35
6¾s,	1993	Feb	58.12	59.12	− .6	14.11
7⅞s,	1993	Feb	63.4	63.20	+ .8	14.59
7½s,	1988-93	Aug	61.9	61.20	+ .3	14.41
8⅝s,	1993	Aug	66.12	66.28	− .2	14.65
8⅝s,	1993	Nov	66.2	66.10	.....	14.73
9s,	1994	Feb	68.2	68.10	+ .1	14.68
4⅛s,	1989-94	May	82.26	83.26	− .8	6.00
8¾s,	1994	Aug	66.4	66.12	+ .2	14.68
10⅛s,	1994	Nov	73.30	74.6	+ .4	14.64
3s,	1995	Feb	82.25	83.25	+ .11	4.67
10½s,	1995	Feb	76	76.8	.....	14.63
10⅜s,	1995	May	75.4	75.12	+ .4	14.63
12⅝s,	1995	May	88.10	88.18	+ .8	14.59
11½s,	1995	Nov	81.10	81.18	+ .8	14.64
7s,	1993-98	May	55.6	55.22	+ .7	13.95
3½s,	1998	Nov	83.4	84.4	+ .8	4.90
8½s,	1994-99	May	63.20	64.4	+ .16	14.08
7⅞s,	1995-00	Feb	58.24	59	+ .20	14.25
8⅜s,	1995-00	Aug	61.4	61.12	.....	14.38
11¾s,	2001	Feb	81.6	81.14	− .6	14.67
13⅛s,	2001	May	90	90.8	+ .7	14.65
8s,	1996-01	Aug	60.6	60.14	+ .23	13.94
13⅜s,	2001	Aug	91.24	92	− .4	14.62
15¾s,	2001	Nov	105.20	105.28	+ .6	14.82
14¼s,	2002	Feb	97.6	97.14	+ .12	14.64
8¼s,	2000-05	May	60.24	61	+ .9	13.93
7⅝s,	2002-07	Feb	57.10	57.18	− .2	13.62
7⅞s,	2002-07	Nov	59.4	59.20	+ .6	13.53
8⅜s,	2003-08	Aug	60.30	61.6	+ .4	13.94
8¾s,	2003-08	Nov	63.4	63.12	+ .4	14.03
9⅛s,	2004-09	May	65.20	65.28	+ .6	14.03
10⅜s,	2004-09	Nov	73.16	73.24	+ .8	14.18
11¾s,	2005-10	Feb	82.16	82.24	+ .2	14.26
10s,	2005-10	May	70.30	71.6	+ .2	14.17
12¾s,	2005-10	Nov	89.10	89.18	+ .8	14.26
13⅞s,	2006-11	May	96.20	96.28	+ .3	14.34
14s,	2006-11	Nov	97.26	98.2	+ .8	14.28

The *n* appearing after the month indicates that the issue is a Treasury note. The bid and the asked-price quotation are expressed as a percentage of par value plus fractional 32nds of a point. For example, the asked price for the Treasury note that matures May 1987 with a coupon rate of 12 percent, referred to as the "12s of May 1987," is "91.2."

The 2 following the decimal point represents ²⁄₃₂, or 0.0625 percent. Therefore the asked price is 91.0625 percent of par. For a $10,000 par value, the asked price is $9,106,250 ($10,000 times 0.910625). (Exhibit 2 gives the decimal equivalent of each 8th, 16th, 32nd and 64th.) The

Exhibit 2
Decimal Equivalents

8ths	16ths	32nds	64ths	Decimal equivalent	8ths	16ths	32nds	64ths	Decimal equivalent
			1	.015625				33	.515625
		1	2	.031250			17	34	.531250
			3	.046875				35	.546875
	1	2	4	.062500		9	18	36	.562500
			5	.078125				37	.578125
		3	6	.093750			19	38	.593750
			7	.109375				39	.609375
1	2	4	8	.125000	5	10	20	40	.625000
			9	.140625				41	.640625
		5	10	.156250			21	42	.656250
			11	.171875				43	.671875
	3	6	12	.187500		11	22	44	.687500
			13	.203125				45	.703125
		7	14	.218750			23	46	.718750
			15	.234375				47	.734375
2	4	8	16	.250000	6	12	24	48	.750000
			17	.265625				49	.765625
		9	18	.281250			25	50	.781250
			19	.296875				51	.796875
	5	10	20	.312500		13	26	52	.812500
			21	.328125				53	.828125
		11	22	.343750			27	54	.843750
			23	.359375				55	.859375
3	6	12	24	.375000	7	14	28	56	.875000
			25	.390625				57	.890625
		13	26	.406250			29	58	.906250
			27	.421875				59	.921875
	7	14	28	.437500		15	30	60	.937500
			29	.453125				61	.953125
		15	30	.468750			31	62	.968750
			31	.484375				63	.984375
4	8	16	32	.500000	8	16	32	64	1.000000

Source: Marcia Stigum, *Money Market Calculations: Yields, Break-Evens, and Arbitrage* (Homewood, Ill.: Dow Jones-Irwin, 1981). © Dow Jones-Irwin, 1981.

last column. "Yld," is the yield-to-maturity for a noncallable issue. For an issue that is callable and selling at a discount, the yield-to-maturity is shown. When the callable issue is selling at a premium over par value, the yield shown is the yield to the first call date. Yields are based upon the asked price.

The prices quoted in *The Wall Street Journal* are over-the-counter quotes as of the midafternoon of the date shown. This is not necessarily the price at which an investor can purchase or sell a particular issue. (Exhibit 9 of Chapter 5 provides an illustration of dealer quotes.)

The difference between the bid and asked price is the spread. The size of the spread depends upon several factors. Because there is less uncertainty about the price at which a dealer may buy or sell an actively traded issue, the size of the spread is lower for actively traded coupon issues compared with inactively traded ones. As uncertainty about future interest rates increases, the size of the spread widens. Since the price of an issue with a longer term to maturity is subject to greater price volatility compared with shorter term issues, the size of the spread is directly related to term to maturity. The spread also depends upon the size of the transaction: The smaller the dollar volume of the transaction, the larger the spread.

REALIZED YIELDS ON LONG-TERM U.S. GOVERNMENT OBLIGATIONS

As explained in Chapter 4, the quoted yield-to-maturity is a promised yield. It reflects the yield to the investor if the security is held to maturity and if coupon interest payments are reinvested at the yield-to-maturity. Exhibit 3 presents the *realized* annual total returns on long-term U.S. government bonds from 1926 to 1980. The total return is the sum of the coupon income and capital appreciation (loss), each of which are shown in Exhibit 3.

Exhibit 3
Annual Returns on Long-Term Government Bonds

Year	Total Return	Income	Capital Appreciation	Inflation-Adjusted Total Return
1926	0.0777	0.0373	0.0391	0.0937
1927	0.0893	0.0337	0.0539	0.1112
1928	0.0010	0.0332	−0.0313	0.0103
1929	0.0342	0.0363	−0.0021	0.0318
1930	0.0466	0.0334	0.0128	0.1127
1931	−0.0531	0.0342	−0.0847	0.0458
1932	0.1684	0.0351	0.1292	0.2999
1933	−0.0008	0.0316	−0.0314	−0.0071
1934	0.1002	0.0308	0.0676	0.0777
1935	0.0498	0.0279	0.0214	0.0193
1936	0.0751	0.0275	0.0464	0.0621
1937	0.0023	0.0277	−0.0248	−0.0285
1938	0.0553	0.0263	0.0283	0.0850
1939	0.0594	0.0238	0.0348	0.0623
1940	0.0609	0.0224	0.0377	0.0507
1941	0.0093	0.0197	−0.0102	−0.0807
1942	0.0322	0.0247	0.0073	−0.0560
1943	0.0208	0.0247	−0.0038	−0.0109
1944	0.0281	0.0249	0.0032	0.0069

Exhibit 3   *(concluded)*

Year	Total Return	Income	Capital Appreciation	Inflation-Adjusted Total Return
1945	0.1073	0.0229	0.0827	0.0831
1946	−0.0010	0.0209	−0.0215	−0.1595
1947	−0.0263	0.0216	−0.0470	−0.1083
1948	0.0340	0.0242	0.0096	0.0059
1949	0.0645	0.0222	0.0414	0.0837
1950	0.0006	0.0216	−0.0207	−0.0547
1951	−0.0394	0.0248	−0.0627	−0.0933
1952	0.0116	0.0268	−0.0149	0.0027
1953	0.0363	0.0295	0.0067	0.0299
1954	0.0719	0.0273	0.0435	0.0771
1955	−0.0130	0.0288	−0.0407	−0.0167
1956	−0.0559	0.0311	−0.0846	−0.0824
1957	0.0745	0.0352	0.0381	0.0429
1958	−0.0610	0.0343	−0.0923	−0.0772
1959	−0.0236	0.0418	−0.0620	−0.0371
1960	0.1378	0.0414	0.0929	0.1211
1961	0.0097	0.0393	−0.0286	0.0030
1962	0.0689	0.0400	0.0278	0.0560
1963	0.0121	0.0401	−0.0270	−0.0043
1964	0.0351	0.0425	−0.0072	0.0229
1965	0.0071	0.0430	−0.0345	−0.0120
1966	0.0365	0.0476	−0.0106	0.0027
1967	−0.0919	0.0499	−0.1355	−0.1190
1968	−0.0026	0.0553	−0.0551	−0.0478
1969	−0.0508	0.0639	−0.1083	−0.1058
1970	0.1210	0.0696	0.0484	0.0628
1971	0.1323	0.0625	0.0660	0.0955
1972	0.0568	0.0606	−0.0035	0.0221
1973	−0.0111	0.0712	−0.0773	−0.0913
1974	0.0435	0.0807	−0.0346	−0.0708
1975	0.0919	0.0841	0.0073	0.0205
1976	0.1675	0.0810	0.0807	0.1143
1977	−0.0067	0.0785	−0.0795	−0.0701
1978	−0.0116	0.0864	−0.0908	−0.0942
1979	−0.0122	0.0942	−0.0979	−0.1295
1980	−0.0395	0.1124	−0.1377	−0.1470

Source: Roger G. Ibbotson and Rex A. Sinquefield, *Stocks, Bonds, Bills and Inflation: The Past and the Future (1981 Edition)*, (Charlottesville, Va.: Financial Analysts Research Foundation, 1981).

Recall that although holders of U.S. government obligations do not face credit (default) risk, they are still exposed to interest-rate risk. The negative total returns between 1977 and 1980 shown in Exhibit 3 reflect the increase in interest rates over that time period. Moreover, holders are also exposed to purchasing-power risk. This can be seen in Exhibit 3, which presents the annual inflation-adjusted total returns.

Exhibit 4 shows the total returns for all yearly holding periods from 1926 to 1980.

Exhibit 4

Total Returns on Long-Term Government Bonds for all Yearly Holding Periods from 1926 to 1980 (percent per annum compounded annually)

TO THE END OF	FROM THE BEGINNING OF 1926	1927	1928	1929	1930	1931	1932	1933	1934	1935	1936	1937	1938	1939	1940	1941	1942	1943	1944	1945
1926	7.8																			
1927	8.3	8.9																		
1928	5.5	4.4	0.1																	
1929	5.0	4.1	1.7	3.4																
1930	4.9	4.2	2.7	4.0	4.7															
1931	3.1	2.2	0.6	0.8	-0.5	-5.3														
1932	5.0	4.5	3.7	4.6	5.0	5.2	16.8													
1933	4.4	3.9	3.1	3.7	3.7	3.4	8.1	-0.1												
1934	5.0	4.6	4.0	4.7	4.9	5.0	8.7	4.9	10.0											
1935	5.0	4.7	4.1	4.7	5.0	5.0	7.8	4.9	7.5	5.0										
1936	5.2	4.9	4.5	5.1	5.3	5.4	7.7	5.5	7.5	6.2	7.5									
1937	4.8	4.5	4.1	4.5	4.7	4.7	6.4	4.5	5.6	4.2	3.8	0.2								
1938	4.8	4.6	4.2	4.6	4.8	4.8	6.3	4.6	5.6	4.5	4.4	2.8	5.5							
1939	4.9	4.7	4.3	4.7	4.9	4.9	6.3	4.8	5.7	4.8	4.8	3.9	5.7	5.9						
1940	5.0	4.8	4.5	4.9	5.0	5.0	6.2	5.0	5.7	5.0	5.0	4.4	5.9	6.0	6.1					
1941	4.7	4.5	4.2	4.5	4.6	4.6	5.7	4.5	5.1	4.4	4.3	3.7	4.6	4.3	3.5	0.9				
1942	4.6	4.4	4.2	4.5	4.5	4.5	5.5	4.4	4.9	4.3	4.2	3.6	4.3	4.0	3.4	2.1	3.2			
1943	4.5	4.3	4.0	4.3	4.4	4.3	5.2	4.2	4.6	4.0	3.9	3.4	3.9	3.6	3.1	2.1	2.6	2.1		
1944	4.4	4.2	4.0	4.2	4.3	4.2	5.0	4.1	4.4	3.9	3.8	3.3	3.8	3.5	3.0	2.3	2.7	2.4	2.8	
1945	4.7	4.6	4.3	4.6	4.6	4.6	5.4	4.6	5.0	4.5	4.5	4.1	4.6	4.5	4.3	3.9	4.7	5.1	6.7	10.7
1946	4.5	4.3	4.1	4.3	4.4	4.3	5.0	4.2	4.6	4.1	4.0	3.7	4.1	3.9	3.6	3.2	3.7	3.8	4.4	5.2
1947	4.1	4.0	3.7	3.9	4.0	3.9	4.5	3.8	4.0	3.6	3.5	3.1	3.4	3.2	2.8	2.4	2.6	2.5	2.6	2.5
1948	4.1	4.0	3.7	3.9	3.9	3.9	4.5	3.7	4.0	3.6	3.5	3.1	3.4	3.2	2.9	2.5	2.7	2.6	2.7	2.7
1949	4.2	4.1	3.8	4.0	4.1	4.0	4.6	3.9	4.1	3.8	3.7	3.4	3.6	3.5	3.2	2.9	3.2	3.2	3.4	3.5
1950	4.0	3.9	3.7	3.8	3.9	3.8	4.3	3.7	3.9	3.5	3.4	3.1	3.4	3.2	2.9	2.6	2.8	2.8	2.9	2.9
1951	3.7	3.6	3.3	3.5	3.5	3.4	3.9	3.3	3.4	3.1	3.0	2.7	2.8	2.6	2.4	2.0	2.1	2.0	2.0	1.9
1952	3.6	3.5	3.3	3.4	3.4	3.3	3.8	3.1	3.3	3.0	2.8	2.6	2.7	2.5	2.3	1.9	2.0	1.9	1.9	1.8
1953	3.6	3.5	3.3	3.4	3.4	3.3	3.8	3.2	3.3	3.0	2.9	2.6	2.8	2.6	2.4	2.1	2.2	2.1	2.1	2.0
1954	3.7	3.6	3.4	3.5	3.5	3.5	3.9	3.4	3.5	3.2	3.1	2.9	3.0	2.9	2.7	2.4	2.5	2.5	2.5	2.5
1955	3.6	3.4	3.2	3.4	3.4	3.3	3.7	3.1	3.3	3.0	2.9	2.6	2.8	2.6	2.4	2.2	2.3	2.2	2.2	2.2
1956	3.3	3.1	2.9	3.0	3.0	2.9	3.3	2.8	2.9	2.6	2.5	2.2	2.3	2.1	1.9	1.7	1.7	1.6	1.6	1.5
1957	3.4	3.3	3.1	3.2	3.2	3.1	3.5	2.9	3.1	2.8	2.7	2.5	2.6	2.4	2.2	2.0	2.1	2.0	2.0	1.9
1958	3.1	3.0	2.8	2.9	2.8	2.8	3.1	2.6	2.7	2.4	2.3	2.1	2.1	2.0	1.8	1.5	1.6	1.5	1.4	1.3
1959	2.9	2.8	2.6	2.7	2.7	2.6	2.9	2.4	2.5	2.2	2.1	1.9	1.9	1.8	1.6	1.3	1.4	1.2	1.2	1.1
1960	3.2	3.1	2.9	3.0	3.0	2.9	3.2	2.8	2.9	2.6	2.5	2.3	2.4	2.3	2.1	1.9	2.0	1.9	1.9	1.8
1961	3.2	3.0	2.9	3.0	2.9	2.9	3.2	2.7	2.8	2.6	2.5	2.3	2.4	2.2	2.1	1.9	1.9	1.9	1.8	1.8
1962	3.3	3.1	3.0	3.1	3.1	3.0	3.3	2.9	3.0	2.7	2.6	2.5	2.5	2.4	2.3	2.1	2.2	2.1	2.1	2.1
1963	3.2	3.1	2.9	3.0	3.0	2.9	3.2	2.8	2.9	2.7	2.6	2.4	2.5	2.4	2.2	2.1	2.1	2.1	2.1	2.0
1964	3.2	3.1	2.9	3.0	3.0	3.0	3.2	2.8	2.9	2.7	2.6	2.4	2.5	2.4	2.3	2.1	2.2	2.1	2.1	2.1
1965	3.2	3.0	2.9	3.0	2.9	2.9	3.2	2.8	2.9	2.6	2.6	2.4	2.5	2.4	2.2	2.1	2.1	2.1	2.1	2.0
1966	3.2	3.1	2.9	3.0	3.0	2.9	3.2	2.8	2.9	2.7	2.6	2.4	2.5	2.4	2.3	2.1	2.2	2.1	2.1	2.1
1967	2.9	2.7	2.6	2.6	2.6	2.6	2.8	2.4	2.5	2.3	2.2	2.0	2.1	2.0	1.8	1.7	1.7	1.7	1.6	1.6
1968	2.8	2.7	2.5	2.6	2.6	2.5	2.7	2.4	2.4	2.2	2.1	2.0	2.0	1.9	1.8	1.6	1.6	1.6	1.6	1.5
1969	2.6	2.5	2.3	2.4	2.4	2.3	2.5	2.1	2.2	2.0	1.9	1.7	1.8	1.7	1.5	1.4	1.4	1.3	1.3	1.2
1970	2.8	2.7	2.5	2.6	2.6	2.5	2.7	2.4	2.5	2.3	2.2	2.0	2.1	2.0	1.9	1.7	1.7	1.7	1.7	1.6
1971	3.0	2.9	2.8	2.8	2.8	2.8	3.0	2.7	2.7	2.5	2.5	2.3	2.4	2.3	2.2	2.1	2.1	2.1	2.1	2.0
1972	3.1	3.0	2.8	2.9	2.9	2.8	3.1	2.7	2.8	2.6	2.6	2.4	2.5	2.4	2.3	2.2	2.2	2.2	2.2	2.2
1973	3.0	2.9	2.8	2.8	2.8	2.8	3.0	2.6	2.7	2.5	2.5	2.3	2.4	2.3	2.2	2.1	2.1	2.1	2.1	2.1
1974	3.0	2.9	2.8	2.8	2.8	2.8	3.0	2.7	2.7	2.6	2.5	2.4	2.4	2.4	2.3	2.1	2.2	2.1	2.1	2.1
1975	3.1	3.0	2.9	3.0	3.0	2.9	3.1	2.8	2.9	2.7	2.7	2.5	2.6	2.5	2.4	2.3	2.4	2.4	2.4	2.3
1976	3.4	3.3	3.2	3.2	3.2	3.2	3.4	3.1	3.2	3.0	3.0	2.9	3.0	2.9	2.8	2.7	2.8	2.8	2.8	2.8
1977	3.3	3.2	3.1	3.2	3.2	3.1	3.3	3.0	3.1	3.0	2.9	2.8	2.9	2.8	2.7	2.6	2.7	2.7	2.7	2.7
1978	3.2	3.1	3.0	3.1	3.1	3.0	3.2	2.9	3.0	2.9	2.8	2.7	2.8	2.7	2.6	2.5	2.6	2.5	2.6	2.5
1979	3.1	3.0	2.9	3.0	3.0	2.9	3.1	2.9	2.9	2.8	2.7	2.6	2.7	2.6	2.5	2.4	2.5	2.4	2.5	2.4
1980	3.0	2.9	2.8	2.9	2.8	2.8	3.0	2.7	2.8	2.6	2.6	2.5	2.5	2.4	2.3	2.3	2.3	2.3	2.3	2.3

Source: Roger G. Ibbotson and Rex A. Sinquefield, *Stocks, Bonds, Bills and Inflation: The Past and the Future* (1981 Edition), (Charlottesville, Va.: Financial Analysts Research Foundation, 1981).

Exhibit 4 (*concluded*)

TO THE END OF   FROM THE BEGINNING OF

TO THE END OF	1946	1947	1948	1949	1950	1951	1952	1953	1954	1955	1956	1957	1958	1959	1960	1961	1962	1963	1964	1965
1946																				
1947																				
1948																				
1949																				
1950																				
1951																				
1952																				
1953																				
1954																				
1955																				
1956																				
1957																				
1958																				
1959																				
1960																				
1961																				
1962																				
1963																				
1964																				
1965																				

FROM THE BEGINNING OF

TO THE END OF	1966	1967	1968	1969	1970	1971	1972	1973	1974	1975	1976	1977	1978	1979	1980
1966															
1967															
1968															
1969															
1970															
1971															
1972															
1973															
1974															
1975															
1976															
1977															
1978															
1979															
1980															-4.0

BUYING AND SELLING TREASURY NOTES AND BONDS

The investor may purchase an outstanding Treasury note or bond in the secondary market or purchase a new issue. Outstanding or seasoned issues may be acquired through banks and brokers. A new issue may be purchased at auction, or through banks and some brokers. An advantage of purchasing an issue in the secondary market is that the investor has a wider choice of maturities; also, the investor may find a discount security that is more attractive than a current issue.

Buying in the Secondary Market

Very little trading in Treasury notes and bonds occurs on organized exchanges. The New York Stock Exchange lists a few issues, and the American Stock Exchange (AMEX) offers odd-lot trading in a few others, but neither exchange moves much volume. The real secondary market is the dealer-made market. In this market, huge quantities of notes and bonds are constantly being traded under very competitive conditions and at very small margins. For the investor, this means that there is always an active liquid market in which to buy and sell outstanding issues.

Since notes and bonds have long maturities, the effect on yield of a small purchase commission is minimal, and avoiding it should not be an important consideration for the investor. An investor who decides to acquire a security with a long current maturity, should be sure to get a dealer's quote sheet from a banker or broker and study what is available. An investor should not expect every banker or broker to be keenly aware of what is available or to be necessarily able or willing to advise as to what securities best fit the investor's needs.

Settlement on a round-lot transaction is usually the next business day for coupon issues. Round-lot transactions are those involving securities that have a par value of $100,000 or multiples thereof. Arrangements for settlement other than the next business day can also be made. For example, "cash" settlement requires settlement the same day, and a "skip-day" settlement delays settlement until two business days following the day of trade. Securities that have been auctioned but not yet issued are traded on a when-issued basis.[2] For an odd-lot transaction, settlement is typically five business days following the trade.

Buying a New Issue at Auction

For a new issue the cheapest method of acquisition is to buy through auction. To sell new notes and bonds, the Treasury currently

---

[2] There typically exists a lag of 10 days between the time a new Treasury security is auctioned and the time the securities are actually issued. When-issued settlements are denoted by "w.i." on quote sheets.

relies on auctions carried out by the Federal Reserve System. Prior to September 1974 the Treasury always set coupons on new note and bond issues and then auctioned them off on the basis of price bids. Naturally, the higher the price bid, the lower the yield-to-maturity for the buyer, and vice versa. The *stop-out* price—below which bids were not accepted—was determined by the bids received and by the amount of securities the Treasury wanted to sell. Typically, each successful bidder paid the price he or she bid, but the Treasury did hold two *Dutch auctions* in which all successful bidders paid the stop-out price. In all price auctions, noncompetitive bids were accepted; and with the exception of the Dutch auctions, noncompetitive bidders paid a price equal to the average of the competitive bids accepted.

Under the *price-auction* system, at the time a new issue was announced, the Treasury set the coupon on the issue in line with market rates, so that the new issue's price, determined through auction, would be at or near par. Naturally, if rates moved away from the levels prevailing on announcement day, the prices bid on auction day would move correspondingly away from par. For example, if rates fell in the days between the announcement of the issue and the auction, bid prices would be above par; whereas a rise in rates would bring in bids below par. As interest rates became increasingly volatile, deviations of bid prices from par became more and more of a problem. In August 1974, for example, one Treasury issue was sold at 101, and another failed to sell out because the Treasury did not receive an adequate quantity of bids at or above the minimum price it would accept. The Treasury feared that above-par prices would discourage some bidders and that below-par prices would place purchasers in an unanticipated tax position (the amount of the discount at issue being taxable at maturity as ordinary income). To solve this problem and to ensure that its issues sold out, in late 1974 the Treasury moved to a new technique in which would-be buyers bid *yields* instead of prices.

Under the *yield-bid* system the Treasury announces what amount of securities it is going to issue, when they will mature, and what denominations will be available. Competitive bidders bid yield to two decimal points (e.g., 8.53) for specific quantities of the new issue. After bids are received, on the basis of both the bids and the amount it wishes to borrow, the Treasury determines the stop-out bid. It then sets the coupon on the security to the nearest one eighth of 1 percent necessary to make the average price charged to successful bidders equal to 100.00 or less. Once the coupon on the issue is established, each successful bidder is charged a price (discount, par, or premium) for the securities; the price is determined so that the yield-to-maturity on a bidder's securities equals the bidder's yield bid. Noncompetitive bids are also accepted for amounts up to $500,000. The noncompetitive bidder pays the average price of the accepted competitive tenders.

Although the yield-bid auction is now the prevailing practice, there are exceptions. For one thing, the Treasury sometimes *reopens* (sells more of) an already outstanding note or bond issue. In that case the coupon on the issue has already been determined in a previous auction; therefore the new securities offered must carry that coupon and must be sold through a *price-bid* auction. Another exception to yield bidding occurs in the case of very long issues. On such issues the Treasury may decide that it has to set a coupon in order to generate interest and publicity sufficient to ensure that the issue will sell out. For example, in April 1976 the Treasury offered $3.5 billion of new 7⅞ percent 10-year notes at par. This was an innovation, since notes had previously had a maximum maturity of seven years.

There are three ways to ascertain when an issue is coming out: (1) look for an announcement in *The Wall Street Journal* or the financial section of major metropolitan dailies, (2) telephone the Federal Reserve Bank 24-hour information number on scheduled auctions, or (3) request that the Federal Reserve bank in the district in which you reside place your name on its mailing list for note and bond issues.[3]

The Treasury currently auctions two-year notes on a monthly basis. Usually, the announcement of the offering is made about the middle of each month. The sale generally takes place the week following the announcement. Quarterly refinancing plans by the Treasury are generally made public at the end of January, April, July, and October. Auctions generally take place in the first week of the month following the month of the announcement of the Treasury's refinancing plans. Although three-year notes are not issued on a regular cycle, they are frequently included as part of the Treasury's midquarter refinancing package, that also includes an intermediate-term note and a long-term bond. Four- and five-year notes are usually issued in the last month and first month of each quarter, respectively.

Once an issue is announced, an investor can get a good idea of the yield at which it will be sold by consulting quotes on Treasury issues of comparable maturity. Unless something dramatic happens between the announcement and the auction, the yield on comparable securities will be very close to what the investor will get. To submit a competitive or noncompetitive bid, a tender offer must be obtained from a Federal Reserve Bank.

If an investor is not in touch with the pulse of the market, the investor's best bet is to submit a noncompetitive bid. By doing so, the investor agrees to accept the average yield and equivalent price based upon the competitive tenders that have been accepted by the Treasury. Usually, the Treasury accepts all noncompetitive tenders; hence the investor does not risk the rejection of the bid by the Treasury, as would be the case in a competitive tender in which too high a yield is

---

[3] The mailing list is for notes with a maturity of at least three years.

specified. Moreover, the investor avoids the risk of bidding a yield that is so low that he or she will be paying too high a price for the issue (given interest-rate conditions prevailing at the time).

Payment of the full amount of the purchase must be submitted with the tender form.[4] The payment can be made in U.S. currency, check (personal, cashiers, S&L), or Treasury securities maturing on or before the issue date. If the price paid ends up being less, the Treasury will refund the difference.

On the tender form or in a letter submitted with the tender form, the investor must specify the method of delivery of the securities. The delivery date is announced by the Treasury. Bearer securities can be picked up at the Federal Reserve Bank where the tender was submitted or mailed at the Treasury's expense to the investor. When the latter option is taken, the securities will usually be received by mail 10 days after the delivery date announced by the Treasury. The Treasury usually processes registered securities for delivery within four weeks of the issue date. The certificate that witnesses ownership can be mailed to the investor, or the investor can request notification by mail so that the certificate can be picked up.

Redemption or Sale of Treasury Notes and Bonds

When an issue matures, it can be redeemed at a Federal Reserve Bank. There is no service charge for redeeming an issue. Alternatively, an issue may be redeemed through a commercial bank or securities dealer, which may impose a charge. As noted earlier, a maturing issue may be used to tender a bid for a new Treasury issue.

The Treasury obligations discussed in this section are marketable securities. Therefore they can be sold prior to maturity at the prevailing market price. The services of a commercial bank or securities dealer are required to sell a security in the secondary market.

TAX ASPECTS OF TREASURY NOTES AND BONDS

In Chapter 3 the Federal income tax law applicable to interest and capital transactions is discussed. Treasury notes and bonds are capital assets, and, as such, the rules applicable to capital assets apply to these securities. Although the redemption of a Treasury obligation is a taxable event, the Secretary of the Treasury is authorized to provide a tax-free exchange of such securities for other Treasury obligations. The offering circular for the new issue will state whether the exchange is a tax-free exchange and the conditions thereof.

There are two unique nonfederal tax aspects of Treasury obligations. First, interest is exempt from all taxes imposed by any state or

---

[4] Partial payments are no longer accepted.

possession of the U.S. and from any local taxation, except estate or inheritance taxes.[5] Second, a number of Treasury bonds have a favorable tax treatment for Federal estate-tax purposes.[6] These bonds, nicknamed flower bonds because they are suggestive of funerals, are valued for federal estate-tax purposes at par value, and when tendered for payment of federal estate taxes the bonds are valued at par regardless of their market price. Since these bonds carry a coupon rate of between 3 and 4¼ percent, they sell at a deep discount. Therefore, using these bonds to pay off federal estate taxes will result in a lower effective tax bite.[7]

The redemption of flower bonds at par in order to pay federal estate taxes is subject to conditions imposed by the Treasury Department. These include:

1. At the time of the decedent's death, the bonds must actually be owned by the decedent.
2. The par value plus accrued interest of the issues redeemed may not exceed the amount of the federal estate taxes. When the denomination does exceed the federal estate-tax liability, a denominational exchange is permitted.
3. The decedent's representative must submit the securities to the Division of Securities of the Treasury Department at least three full weeks before the date credit for redemption is sought.

The yield provided by a flower bond is less than that offered by comparable current coupon Treasury issues with the same maturity and call protection. Therefore, if the investor does not intend to use flower bonds for federal estate tax planning, they should be avoided because of the yield disadvantage.

NONMARKETABLE SECURITIES

The Treasury issues nonmarketable bonds that individuals can purchase. The four nonmarketable bonds currently issued are Series EE savings bonds, Series HH current-income bonds, retirement-plan

---

[5] However, the interest and principal (or market value) may be included in determining any franchise tax imposed by a state or municipality for doing business in the state or political subdivision.

[6] The issues, listed below, were floated between 1953 and 1963:

4¼%—May 15, 1975–85	4⅛%—May 15, 1989–94
3¼%—June 15, 1978–83	3½%—February 15, 1990
3¼%—May 15, 1985	3%—February 15, 1995
4¼%—August 15, 1987–92	3½%—November 15, 1998
4%—February 15, 1988–93	

[7] Any gain realized at the time of the holder's death is taxed as a capital gain. Prior to the 1976 Tax Reform Act, such a gain was not taxable.

Exhibit 5
Redemption Values and Investment Yields on Series EE and Series HH Savings Bonds (based on $1,000 bonds)

Period after Issue Date	Series EE Redemption Values during Each Half-Year Period*	Series HH Redemption Values during Each Half-Year Period†	Approximate Investment Yield (percent)			
			Series EE		Series HH	
			On Purchase Price from Issue Date to Beginning of Each Half-Year Period	On Current Redemption Value from Beginning of Each Half-Year Period to Maturity	On Face Value from Issue Date to Each Interest Payment Date	On Current Redemption Value from Each Interest Date to Maturity
Issue price...	$ 500.00	$1,000.00				
½ year...	510.00	987.50	4.00	7.14	4.00	6.68
1 year...	522.80	979.88	4.51	7.25	4.51	6.80
1½ years...	536.00	972.20	4.69	7.37	4.69	6.94
2 years...	549.20	963.74	4.75	7.50	4.75	7.10
2½ to 3 years...	563.60	956.70	4.85	7.64	4.85	7.26
3 to 3½ years...	578.80	950.22	4.94	7.78	4.94	7.42
3½ to 4 years...	594.80	944.14	5.02	7.93	5.02	7.61
4 to 4½ years...	616.80	948.16	5.32	7.97	5.32	7.59
4½ to 5 years...	646.80	964.58	5.80	7.83	5.80	7.29
5 to 5½ years...	688.40	1,000.00	6.50	7.42	6.50	6.50
5½ to 6 years...	710.80	1,000.00	6.50	7.50	6.50	6.50
6 to 6½ years...	734.00	1,000.00	6.50	7.60	6.50	6.50
6½ to 7 years...	757.60	1,000.00	6.50	7.73	6.50	6.50
7 to 7½ years...	782.40	1,000.00	6.50	7.87	6.50	6.50
7½ to 8 years...	808.00	1,000.00	6.50	8.06	6.50	6.50
8 to 8½ years...	834.00	1,000.00	6.50	8.34	6.50	6.50
8½ to 9 years...	861.20	1,000.00	6.50	8.70	6.50	6.50
9 to 9½ years...	889.20	1,000.00	6.50	9.26	6.50	6.50
9½ to 10 years...	918.00	1,000.00	6.50	10.19	6.50	6.50
10 to 10½ years...	948.00	1,000.00	6.50	12.04	6.50	6.50
10½ to 11 years...	978.80	1,000.00	6.50	17.74	6.50	6.50
Maturity value...	$1,065.60	$1,000.00	7.00	—	6.50	6.50

* Maturity value reached at 11 years after issue.

† Each semiannual check would be for $32.50. HH bonds purchased with cash would be subject to the redemption penalties shown in the table. HH bonds purchased via E or EE exchanges are not subject to a penalty for early redemption.

bonds, and individual retirement bonds. Only the first two bonds are discussed in this chapter.

Series EE Savings Bonds

On January 1, 1980, the Treasury began issuing Series EE savings bonds. These bonds replaced the Series E savings bonds. The maturity of a Series EE and E savings bond is 11 and 5 years, respectively. Both bonds are accrual-type bonds (i.e., no interest is actually paid). The difference between the redemption value and the amount of the purchase price is the interest earned by the holder. The redemption schedule for Series EE savings bonds are shown on Exhibit 5.

Exhibit 6 provides pertinent information about Series EE bonds. Note the tax election available to the holder concerning the reporting of interest income. Since the increment in the redemption value constitutes interest, it is subject to federal income taxes.[8] However, a cash-basis taxpayer may elect to recognize the increase in the redemption value in the tax year it accrues or accrue the interest until the savings bond is redeemed.[9] The investor should be aware of the consequences of electing the former option. In the year the taxpayer elects to report the increment in redemption value, all such obligations held by the taxpayer at the time of the election and all subsequent securities acquired must be reported in the same manner.[10]

The election adopted by the investor will depend upon the circumstances. An investor currently in a high marginal tax bracket and who finds it prudent to hold the bonds until retirement will find it best to elect the deferral option. The bonds would then be redeemed when the investor retired and when presumably the investor expects to be in a lower marginal tax bracket. For investors who do not expect to be in a lower marginal tax bracket when the bond is redeemed, the interest should be reported annually to avoid the "bunching" of interest income in the year of redemption. Another important consideration that weighs in favor of postponing the recognition of interest is that the tax liability on the interest earned is a tax-free loan from the Treasury until the bond is redeemed.

Should an investor anticipate needing the funds before maturity, the investor should realize that the yield to the date of redemption increases as the holding period increases. As can be seen from Exhibit 5, although the yield-to-maturity of a newly issued Series EE savings

---

[8] Like other U.S. Treasury obligations, interest is not taxable at the state and local level.

[9] This option is not available to an accrual-basis taxpayer. They must recognize the increase in the annual increment each year.

[10] Once the election is made, a change in reporting is possible with permission from the Internal Revenue Service.

Exhibit 6
General Information about Series EE and HH Savings Bonds

	Series EE Bonds	Series HH Bonds
Offering date	Begin January 2, 1980.	Begin January 2, 1980.
Denominations..........	$50, $75, $100, $200, $500, $1,000, $5,000, $10,000.	$500, $1,000, $5,000, $10,000
Issue price...............	50 percent of face amount.	Face amount.
Maturity................	11 years.	10 years.
Interest.................	Accrues through periodic increases in redemption value to maturity.	Payable semiannually by check.
Yield curve	See Exhibit 5.	See Exhibit 5.
Retention period	Redeemable anytime after six months from issue date.	Redeemable anytime after six months from issue date.
Annual limitation	$15,000 issue price.	$20,000 face amount.
Tax status...............	Accruals subject to federal income and to estate, inheritance and gift taxes—federal and state—but exempt from all other state and local taxes. Federal income tax may be reported (1) as it accrues or (2) in year bond matures, is redeemed, or is otherwise disposed.	Interest is subject to federal income tax reporting in year it is paid. Bonds subject to estate, inheritance, and gift taxes—federal and state—but exempt from all other state and local taxes.
Registration.............	In names of individuals in single, coownership, or beneficiary form; in names of fiduciaries or organizations in single ownership only.	In names of individuals in single, coownership or beneficiary form; in names of fiduciaries or organizations in single ownership only.
Transferability	Not eligible for transfer or pledge as collateral.	Not eligible for transfer or pledge as collateral.
Rights of owners	Coownership: either owner may redeem, both must join reissue request. Beneficiary: only owner may redeem during lifetime. Consent of beneficiary to reissue not required.	Coownership: either owner may redeem; both must join reissue request. Beneficiary: only owner may redeem during lifetime. Consent of beneficiary to reissue not required.
Exchange privilege.......	Eligible, alone or with Series E bonds or savings notes, for exchange for Series HH bonds in multiples of $500, with tax deferral privilege.	Issuable on exchange from Series E, EE, and savings notes, in multiples of $500, with continued tax deferral privilege.

bond is 6½ percent, the yield earned on the purchase price is only 4 percent if the bond is held for one year. If held for just over three years, it will yield 4.94 percent. Series EE savings bonds must be held for more than five years to yield 6.5 percent on the purchase price.

When deciding whether to redeem an issue, the yield-to-maturity based upon the remaining life of the savings bond must be compared with comparable Treasury obligations. For example, suppose an investor owns a Series EE savings bond with two years remaining to maturity (i.e., the savings bond has been held for nine years). The approximate yield if the savings bond is held two years to maturity is 9.26 percent. Should prevailing yields for two-year Treasury obligations be less than 9.26 percent, then it is to the advantage of the investor to hold the issue to maturity rather than purchase a two year marketable Treasury obligation.

Series HH Savings Bonds

Whereas Series EE savings bonds are accrual-type bonds, Series HH savings bonds pay current interest. Series HH savings bonds replaced Series H savings bonds. General information about the former savings bonds are given in Exhibit 6.

Series HH savings bonds have a 10-year maturity and offer 6½ percent yield if held at least five years from the date of acquisition. As in the case of Series EE savings bonds, the yield from date of purchase to date of redemption increases with the holding period. The yield by holding period is presented in Exhibit 5. This should be considered by an investor who may have to dispose of the bond within five years after purchase.

When deciding whether to continue to hold a Series HH savings bond or redeem it and invest the proceeds in a Treasury obligation with the same time to maturity, the yield to maturity on the redemption value if the bond is held to maturity must be considered. These yields are shown on Exhibit 5.

Unlike Series EE savings bonds, holders of Series HH savings bonds must report the current interest paid, $65 per $1,000 denomination, in their federal income tax return in the year the interest is received; the option of deferring the recognition of interest is not available.

Securities of Federal
Government Agencies and
Sponsored Corporations

10 MARCIA STIGUM, Ph.D.
Stigum & Associates, New York

Securities of federal government agencies and sponsored corporations, commonly referred to in Street lingo as simply *agencies*,[1] have not been around in significant volume for very long—just slightly over two decades—but during their brief existence, the outstanding volume of these securities has grown rapidly to $227 billion by February 1982.

Federal agency securities are attractive to a wide range of investors for a number of reasons. First, most agency issues are backed either *de jure* or *de facto* by the federal government, so the credit risk attached to them is zero or negligible. Second, many agency issues offer the tax advantage that interest income on them, like interest income on governments, is exempt from state and local income taxation.

A third advantage of many agency issues is liquidity. Agency issues are smaller in size than Treasury issues, so they do not have the same liquidity Treasury issues do; but relative to other money market instruments they are highly liquid.

Normally, agencies trade at some spread to Treasury issues of the same maturity. This spread varies considerably depending on supply

---

[1] In this chapter the securities of federal government agencies and sponsored corporations are simply referred to as federal agency, or just agency, securities.

conditions and the tightness of money. In recent years agencies with a two-year maturity have offered investors a yield advantage over governments that ranged from 3 to 87 basis points. For agencies with a 10-year maturity, the highs and lows of the yield advantage over governments were 134 and 7 basis points, respectively. The spread at which agencies trade in relation to governments appears to reflect differences in the liquidity of the two sorts of instruments, since such capital-rich institutions as the Federal Home Loan banks have to pay to borrow at the same rates as more poorly capitalized federal agencies.

ISSUING TECHNIQUES

The Treasury, as we have seen in Chapters 8 and 9, issues securities through competitive auctions held by the 12 Federal Reserve banks. Through the auctions the Treasury is able to obtain a very wide distribution of its securities at yields at or near those prevailing in the market at the time of issue. The Treasury is able to do this because of its unique position: Its securities are well-known, the number of its outstanding issues is large, the dollar volume of these outstanding issues is huge, trading in governments is very active, and the size of new Treasury issues is always substantial. Also, primary dealers in government securities are major participants in Treasury auctions and act in effect as partial underwriters of Treasury issues.

For almost all other issuers of new debt securities, the auction technique would be less successful in securing both a wide distribution of the issuer's securities and a borrowing rate that compared favorably with prevailing market yields on similar securities. The reason is that other security issuers are less well known, they have fewer outstanding issues, the volume of any issues they have outstanding is small compared with that of Treasury issues, trading in such issues is light relative to that in governments, and the size of their new issues may be quite small. Thus auctions of non-Treasury new issues would simply not generate the level and breadth of interest that exists in auctions of Treasury new issues.

Underwriting of Agency Securities

To distribute their new issues of notes and bonds, all issuers other than the Treasury rely on *investment banking* firms. Many investment bankers are securities dealers who have nothing to do with banking. Some banks do act as investment bankers, but only for federal agency and municipal issues.

Just how a new issue handled by investment bankers reaches the market depends in part on the type of security being issued—federal agency, municipal, or corporate. In the case of agency securities, the agency itself selects the firms that participate in its selling group. Then when the agency wants to borrow, it may go to the syndicate for advice on what coupon to offer, or it may make this decision itself. Either way, once the coupon is set, the syndicate buys up the issue at par minus a selling concession and then retails it to investors. Generally, syndicate participants are picked so that the agency issue will have a wide geographic distribution and thus the broadest possible market.

In setting the coupon on a new agency issue, the agency's fiscal agent, who is responsible for new issues, looks at the bid and asked prices for comparable securities and at the yields-to-maturity implied by these prices. Generally the agent will set the coupon on the new issue, which is always sold at par, so that its yield will equal approximately the yield-to-maturity implied by the bid rather than the asked price on a comparable security. In other words, new agency issues are priced somewhat cheaply compared to the market. There are several reasons for this. On longer term issues, market trading may be quite thin so that dealers' bid quotes represent a price at which a few hundred bonds, but not a whole new issue, could be sold. Also the agency wants to ensure that each new issue is priced realistically and does not fall to an immediate discount in the aftermarket. If that occurred, investors might be less willing to buy up the agency's next new issue. The underwriters too have an interest in cheap pricing because the more favorably an issue is priced, the more rapidly they can sell it and the smaller their risk.

Generally, for agency securities, the scenario of a new issue runs as follows. The issue is first announced by the fiscal agent as forthcoming; then about three days later the coupon is announced. While the coupon is being determined, syndicate members begin to find buyers. In the case of agency securities, it is quite common for an issue to be sold out by the time the coupon announcement is actually made, that is, for the issue to be *presold* (in Wall Street jargon).

Once an agency issue passes into investor's hands, trading in it moves to the secondary market, which is an over-the-counter market made by securities dealers and dealer banks. This market requires little comment, since it resembles closely the secondary market for governments and is made by and large by the same dealers.

Because of the tendency for most agency issues to be priced at issue not on, but slightly below, the market, it is not uncommon for new agency issues to rise to a small premium in the after-market. Generally, bid and ask prices on agency issues straddle par right after issue, so that the premium is not large enough for a buyer to turn around and make a profit on an immediate sale; but right after issue the buyer has to pay more (a few 32nds) than the buyer at issue did. Like governments, agency issues are first traded on a when-issued basis, normally for a period of 5 to 10 days.

One final comment: We noted above that the federal government is the only major issuer of securities that does not rely on underwriters for the distribution of its securities. This is true but perhaps requires some qualification. In auctions of Treasury issues, the major dealers in government securities typically bid for large amounts of the securities auctioned. Some of these securities go to fill preauction customer orders. Others are added to inventory and later resold to investors. Thus dealers in government securities in a sense perform real underwriting services for the Treasury, but the arrangement of sale through auction is quite different from the normal type of underwriting agreement on non-Treasury issues.

The Federal Financing Bank

As federal agencies proliferated, their borrowings from the public caused several problems. One had to do with calendar scheduling. Each year federal agencies issue substantial quantities of new debt. Agency issues compete with each other and with Treasury issues for investors' funds, and an uneven flow of agency and Treasury issues to the market could result in rates being driven up one week and down the next. To avoid this, the Treasury schedules the timing and size of both its own agency issues to ensure a reasonably smooth flow of federal issues to the market. In 1973 minor federal agencies made 75 separate offerings, so many that it made Treasury calendar scheduling of new issues difficult. Another problem resulting from the proliferation of federal agencies was that the new small agencies constantly being created by Congress were not well known to investors; and because of their small size, their issues were less liquid than Treasury issues. Consequently, small agencies had to pay relatively high borrowing rates.

To deal with these problems, in 1973 Congress set up the *Federal Financing Bank (FFB)*. The FFB is authorized to acquire any obligation that is issued, sold, or guaranteed by a federal agency—except those obligations of the Farm Credit System, the Federal Home Loan Banks, the Federal Home Loan Mortgage Corporation, and the Federal National Mortgage Association.[2]

---

[2] The FFB was supposed to obtain funds by issuing securities fully backed by the government in a fashion similar to the way the Treasury issued its securities. It tried this approach once with an offering of short-term bills. This offering was bid for by dealers and others at yields close to those prevailing on T-bills, but the issue fell in price in the secondary market, which was discouraging to both dealers and the Treasury. Some dealers thought that if the FFB had continued to issue its securities, they would—after five or six issues—have been accepted by investors as equal to Treasury issues and would have sold at yields no higher than those on Treasury issues. The Treasury, however, seems to have doubted this; one reason was that the FFB offerings would have been small relative to Treasury offerings and consequently less liquid. In any case, the FFB discontinued its public offerings and now borrows from the Treasury.

Exhibit 1
Federal and Federally Sponsored Credit Agencies Debt Outstanding
($ millions)

	Agency	February 28, 1982
1	Federal and federally sponsored agencies*	$226,539
2	Federal agencies	30,806
3	Defense Department†	460
4	Export-Import Bank‡§	12,861
5	Federal Housing Administration‖	397
6	Government National Mortgage Association participation certificates#	2,165
7	Postal Service**	1,538
8	Tennessee Valley Authority	13,187
9	United States Railway Association**	198
10	Federally sponsored agencies*	195,733
11	Federal Home Loan Banks	57,743
12	Federal Home Loan Mortgage Corporation	2,604
13	Federal National Mortgage Association	9,018
14	Federal Land Banks	8,717
15	Federal Intermediate Credit Banks	1,388
16	Banks for Cooperatives	220
17	Farm Credit Banks*	61,041
18	Student Loan Marketing Association††	5,000
19	Other	2
20	Federal Financing Bank debt *‡‡	112,367
	Lending to federal and federally sponsored agencies:	
21	Export-Import Bank§	12,741
22	Postal Service**	1,288
23	Student Loan Marketing Association††	5,000
24	Tennessee Valley Authority	11,462
25	United States Railway Association**	198
	Other Lending:§§	
26	Farmers Home Administration	49,081
27	Rural Electrification Administration	13,989
28	Other	18,608

*In September 1977 the Farm Credit Banks issued their first consolidated bonds, and in January 1979 they began issuing these bonds on a regular basis to replace the financing activities of the Federal Land Banks, the Federal Intermediate Credit Banks, and the Banks for Cooperatives. Line 17 represents those consolidated bonds outstanding, as well as any discount notes that have been issued. Lines 1 and 10 reflect the addition of this item.

†Consists of mortgages assumed by the Defense Department between 1957 and 1963 under family housing and homeowners assistance programs.

‡Includes participation certificates reclassified as debt beginning October 1, 1976.

§Off-budget August 17, 1974, through September 30, 1976; on-budget thereafter.

‖Consists of debentures issued in payment of Federal Housing Administration insurance claims. Once issued, these securities may be sold privately on the securities market.

#Certificates of participation issued prior to fiscal 1969 by the Government National Mortgage Association acting as trustee for the Farmers Home Administration; Department of Health, Education, and Welfare; Department of Housing and Urban Development; Small Business Administration; and the Veterans Administration.

**Off-budget

††Unlike other federally sponsored agencies, the Student Loan Marketing Asso-

AGENCY SECURITIES

The dollar value of the outstanding securities of each federal government agency and sponsored corporations as of February 1982 is shown in Exhibit 1. Among the agencies still issuing securities to the public, practices and types of securities issued vary considerably. However, one can make a few generalizations. Each federal agency establishes a fiscal agent through which it offers its securities, all of which are negotiable.

Agency securities come in several forms: short-term notes sold at a discount and interest-bearing notes and bonds. Agency bonds are frequently issued with the title *debenture*. Any bond is an interest-bearing certificate of debt. A *mortgage bond* is secured by a lien on some specific piece of property. A debenture is a bond secured only by the general credit of the issuer.

Interest on agency securities and principal at maturity are usually payable at any branch of the issuing agency, at any Federal Reserve bank or branch, and at the Treasury. Agency bonds are typically not callable.

Like Treasury securities, agency securities are issued under the authority of an act of Congress. Therefore, unlike private offerings, they are exempt from registration with the Securities and Exchange Commission (SEC). Typically, agency issues are backed by collateral in the form of cash, U.S. government securities, and the debt obligations that the issuing agency has acquired through its lending activities. A few agency issues are backed by the full faith and credit of the United States. A number of others are guaranteed by the Treasury or supported by the issuing agency's right to borrow funds from the Treasury up to some specified amount. Finally, there are agency securities with no direct or indirect federal backing.

The major federal agencies still offering securities differ considerably in mission and method of operation, so we have organized our survey of them by function: first the mortgage-related agencies and then the farm credit agencies.

---

ciation may borrow from the Federal Financing Bank (FFB) since its obligations are guaranteed by the Department of Health, Education, and Welfare.

The FFB, which began operations in 1974, is authorized to purchase or sell obligations issued, sold, or guaranteed by other federal agencies. Since FFB incurs debt solely for the purpose of lending to other agencies, its debt is not included in the main portion of the table in order to avoid double counting.

§§Includes FFB purchases of agency assets and guaranteed loans; the latter contain loans guaranteed by numerous agencies with the guarantees of any particular agency being generally small. The Farmers Home Administration item consists exclusively of agency assets, while the Rural Electrification Administration entry contains both agency assets and guaranteed loans.

Source: *Treasury Bulletin.*

Housing Credit Agencies[3]

Federal Home Loan Banks. Behind the nation's commercial banks stands the Federal Reserve System, which regulates member banks, acts as a lender of last resort, and otherwise facilitates a smooth operation of the banking system. Behind the nation's S&Ls stands a somewhat similar institution, the Federal Home Loan Bank system. The FHLB, created in 1932, is composed of 12 regional banks and a central board in Washington.

S&Ls, savings banks, cooperative banks, homestead associations, and insurance companies may all become members of the FHLB system; federally chartered S&Ls are required to do so. Currently about 4,140 S&Ls belong to the FHLB system; these S&Ls hold more than 98 percent of the total assets of all S&Ls in the country.

The Federal Home Loan banks are owned by the private S&Ls that are members of the system, just as the 12 Federal Reserve banks are owned by their member banks. The private ownership is, however, only nominal, since the FHLB, like the Fed, operates under federal charter and is charged by Congress with regulating member S&Ls and with formulating and carrying out certain aspects of government policy with respect to the savings and loan industry. Thus the Federal Home Loan banks are in fact an arm of the federal government.

In addition to overseeing member S&Ls, the FHLB also lends to member S&Ls, just as the Fed lends to commercial banks. Here, however, the similarity ends. The Fed obtains money to lend to banks at the discount window by monetizing debt. The Federal Home Loan banks have to borrow the money they lend to member S&Ls. Most of the money S&Ls provide to home buyers comes from their depositors. The FHLB lends to member S&Ls primarily to augment this source of funds. In a nutshell, the FHLB borrows money in the open market, then relends it to S&Ls, which in turn relend it to home buyers. One purpose of this involved operation is to aid S&Ls with a temporary liquidity problem. A more important function is to channel money into the S&Ls when money is tight and rate lids cause a slowdown of the inflow of funds into S&Ls or even generate a net outflow of funds from such institutions.

The main security issued by the FHLB is consolidated *bonds, consolidated* referring to the fact that the bonds are the joint obligation of all 12 Federal Home Loan banks. FHLB bonds have a maturity at issue of one year or more, pay interest semiannually, and are not callable. They are issued only in book-entry form and are sold in a minimum denomination of $10,000, with $5,000 increments thereafter. There are seven regularly scheduled sales of consolidated bonds a

---

[3] The tax-exempt project notes of the Department of Housing and Urban Development are discussed in Chapter 15.

year, although more frequent sale dates may occur if FHLB needs funds. Obligations maturing in less than one year are called consolidated notes. These obligations once were interest-bearing notes, but in mid-1974 FHLB began issuing consolidated discount notes to raise short-term money. Maturities on consolidated discount bonds range from 30 to 360 days, at the discretion of the buyer. These obligations have denominations of $100,000, $150,000, and $1 million.

FHLB securities are backed by qualified collateral in the form of secured advances to member S&Ls, government securities, insured mortgages, etc. FHLB securities are *not* guaranteed by the U.S. government. However, they are the obligation of the FHLB system, which plays a key federal role in regulating and assisting the S&L industry. Given this role and the importance of the S&L industry to the economy, it is inconceivable that the U.S. government would ever permit the FHLB to default on outstanding securities.

Interest income from FHLB securities is subject to full federal taxes but is specifically exempt from state and local income taxation.

Federal National Mortgage Association. Most money market instruments are extremely liquid (commercial paper being the main exception). The reason is not simply that these securities are *negotiable*, but more important that they have a broad and active secondary market. One of the major factors contributing to the existence of this secondary market is the homogeneity (one unit is just like another) of bills, bonds, and notes. Because mortgages lack homogeneity, a wide secondary market for mortgages has never developed in the United States. The lack of a secondary market for mortgages makes these instruments illiquid, which in turn tends to diminish the flow of funds into the mortgage market.

The Federal National Mortgage Association (FNMA), popularly known as *Fannie Mae*, was set up in 1938 by Congress to create a secondary market in FHA mortgages (mortgages insured by the Federal Housing Administration). Initially Fannie Mae was wholly government owned and its funds came from the Treasury. Later, in 1954, Fannie Mae was split into three separate divisions: secondary market operations, special assistance functions, and management and liquidating functions.

The secondary market division was supposed to attract money to the mortgage market by providing liquidity for government-insured mortgages. To do so, it bought and sold mortgages insured or guaranteed by the Federal Housing Administration, the Veterans Administration, and the Farm Home Administration. Institutions dealing as buyers or sellers in mortgages with Fannie Mae were required to buy small amounts of Fannie Mae stock, thereby permitting the secondary market division of Fannie Mae to be converted from government ownership to private ownership.

In 1968, Congress completed its partition of Fannie Mae by putting its special assistance and management and liquidating functions into a new government-owned corporation, the *Government National Mortgage Association*. The remaining secondary market division of Fannie Mae, which retained the title Federal National Mortgage Association, was converted into a privately owned corporation. The corporation's private ownership is, however, to some degree nominal, since the government retains broad powers to direct and regulate the operations of Fannie Mae through the Secretary of Housing and Urban Development (HUD). In 1977 the question of just how much control HUD could exercise over Fannie Mae was actively disputed by both parties. HUD sought more control, suggested that Fannie Mae's profits were perhaps too high, and attempted to force the agency to funnel more funds into mortgages on inner-city housing.

Currently, Fannie Mae's function is to buy mortgages that are insured or guaranteed by the government (as well as conventional mortgages since 1970) when mortgage money is in short supply and to sell them when the demand for mortgage money slacks off. It does this through auctions at which it buys and sells some preannounced total of mortgages. For a fee, Fannie Mae also extends advance commitments to buy mortgages. In the recent years of tight money and recurring shortages of mortgage funds, Fannie Mae has been more often a buyer than a seller of mortgages. Nevertheless, this agency and others created to serve the same purpose have made significant progress toward increasing the liquidity of mortgages and attracting into mortgages funds that would otherwise have flowed elsewhere.

To finance its mortgage purchases, Fannie Mae relies primarily on the sale of debentures and short-term discount notes. The latter, whose maturities range from 30 to 360 days, are sold at published rates. Fannie Mae adjusts periodically the rates it offers on its discount notes so that they are in line with Treasury bill rates. Short-term discount notes are issued in denominations of $5,000, $25,000, $100,000, $500,000, and $1 million, with a minimum purchase order of $50,000 at the time of offering. Fannie Mae debentures are issued in book-entry form only. They pay interest semiannually, and are available in denominations starting at $10,000 and multiples of $5,000 thereafter. Fannie Mae debentures are not backed by the federal government; but given the association's role as a government policy tool and its government supervision, it seems highly improbable that the government would permit a default on Fannie Mae obligations.

Interest income on Fannie Mae securities is subject to full federal taxation and is not exempt from state and local income taxation. The large volume of Fannie Mae securities outstanding makes availability and marketability in the secondary market excellent.

Government National Mortgage Association. The 1968 partition of the old Federal National Mortgage Association spawned yet another financial lady, *Ginnie Mae,* more formally known as the Government National Mortgage Association (GNMA). Ginnie Mae, a wholly government-owned corporation within the Department of Housing and Urban Development, took over the special assistance and the management and liquidating functions that had formerly been lodged in FNMA. These functions involve activities that could not be profitably carried out by a private firm. Ginnie Mae's mission is also to make real estate investment more attractive to institutional investors, which it has done by designing and issuing—partly in conjunction with private financial institutions—new mortgage-backed securities for which an active secondary market has developed.

Under its management and liquidating functions, Ginnie Mae sold mortgages—some inherited from FNMA's earlier operations as a three-division organization and some acquired in the mid-1960s from other governmental agencies. It did this by creating pools of mortgages and selling participations in these pools to private investors. Currently there are about 15 issues of GNMA participation certificates still outstanding (none has been issued since 1968). These were issued in bearer and registered form and have minimum denominations of $5,000 and $10,000, depending on the issue. All participation certificates are guaranteed by Ginnie Mae with respect to payment of both principal and interest; they also carry the full faith and credit backing of the U.S. government.

Under its special assistance function, Ginnie Mae provides financing for selected types of mortgages through mortgage purchases and commitment to purchase mortgages. Under one program, for example, Ginnie Mae provides funds for the rehabilitation of deteriorating housing, which is subsequently resold to low-income families. Ginnie Mae finances its special assistance operations partly with funds obtained from the Treasury. To limit its borrowings from this source, Ginnie Mae currently operates most special assistance projects under a *tandem* plan. As Ginnie Mae acquires mortgages or mortgage purchase commitments, it resells them at market prices to other investors. Typically, under its special assistance function, Ginnie Mae buys mortgages at prices above prevailing market levels. Thus, to resell under the tandem plan, it has to absorb some loss, making it in effect a source of subsidy for certain types of mortgages.

Under the *pass-through* approach, private mortgage lenders assemble pools of mortgages acquired through Ginnie Mae auctions or from other sources and then sell certificates backed by these mortgages to investors. These certificates are referred to as pass-through securities because payment of interest and principal on mortgages in the pool is

passed on to the certificate holders after deduction of fees for servicing and guarantee.[4] Pass-through certificates have stated maturities
equal to those of the underlying mortgages. However, actual maturities tend to be much shorter because of prepayments. On pass-through
securities, principal and interest are paid *monthly* to the investor.
Because payments are made monthly and because the amount passed
through varies from month to month due to mortgage prepayment,
pass-throughs are issued in registered form only. Pass-through certificates have a minimum denomination of $25,000. They carry Ginnie
Mae's guarantee of timely payment of both principal and interest and
are backed in addition by the full faith and credit of the U.S. government.

Federal Home Loan Mortgage Corporation. The Federal Home
Loan Mortgage Corporation (FHLMC) was created in July 1970
through enactment of Title III of the Emergency Home Finance Act of
1970. The organization's purpose is to promote the development of a
nationwide secondary market in conventional residential mortgages.
To accomplish this, the FHLMC buys residential mortgages and then
resells them via the sale of mortgage-related instruments. The
FHLMC's operations are directed by the Federal Home Loan Bank
system, which provided the new agency with its initial capital.

To some extent the FHLMC duplicates the activities of Fannie
Mae. But it has a special feature: It may purchase mortgages only from
financial institutions that have their deposits or accounts insured by
agencies of the federal government. The requirement that it deal with
only regulated institutions (whereas Fannie Mae also buys mortgages
from mortgage bankers) permits the FHLMC to cut documentation
and paper requirements on mortgage purchases and thereby operate
at lower cost. Unlike Fannie Mae, which has borrowed to finance its
mortgage holdings, the FHLMC has pursued a course similar to that of
Ginnie Mae—namely, selling its interest in the mortgages it purchases through mortgage-backed, pass-through securities.

Specifically, the FHLMC sells two types of pass-through securities,
mortgage participation certificates (PCs) and *guaranteed mortgage
certificates* (GMCs). PCs resemble Ginnie Mae pass-throughs. Each
PC represents an undivided interest in a pool of conventional residential mortgages underwritten and previously purchased by the
FHLMC. Each month, the certificate holder receives a prorated share
of the principal and interest payments made on the underlying pool.
The FHLMC guarantees timely payment of interest on PCs and the
full return of principal to the investor. Although PCs technically have
a maturity at issue of 30 years, their average weighted life is assumed
to be 12 years or less.

---

[4] Pass-through securities are discussed in greater depth in Chapter 18.

Guaranteed mortgage certificates also represent an undivided interest in conventional residential mortgages underwritten and previously purchased by the FHLMC. These certificates pay interest semiannually and return principal once a year in guaranteed minimum amounts. The final payment date on GMCs is 30 years from the date of issue, but the expected average weighted life of these securities is about 10 years. Certificate holders may require the FHLMC to repurchase certificates at par 15 to 25 years (the put date varies with the issue) after they are issued.

PCs are sold only in registered form, in original unpaid balances of $100,000, $200,000, $500,000, $1 million, and $5 million. GMCs are also sold only in registered form. The initial principal amounts GMCs are sold at are $100,000, $500,000, and $1 million.

All securities issued by and through the FHLMC are subject to full state and federal taxation on income.

Farm Credit Agencies

The production and sale of agricultural commodities require large amounts of credit. So, too, does the acquisition by farmers of additional land and buildings. To assure an adequate supply of credit to meet these needs, the government has put together over time the Farm Credit Administration. This administration, which operates as an independent agency of the U.S. government, oversees the Farm Credit System, which operates in all states plus Puerto Rico. Under this system, the country is divided into 12 farm credit districts. In each of these, there is a Federal Land Bank, a Federal Intermediate Credit Bank, and a Bank for Cooperatives, each supplying specific types of credit to qualified borrowers in its district. To obtain funds, these 37 banks plus a Central Bank for Cooperatives all issue securities through a common fiscal agency in New York City.

Before discussing the obligations of the Bank for Cooperatives, Federal Land Banks, and Federal Intermediate Credit Banks, let's first discuss the Consolidated Systemwide obligations of the Federal Credit Banks.

Consolidated Systemwide discount notes and bonds of the Farm Credit Banks were first introduced in January 1975 and August 1977, respectively. These obligations are the secured joint and several obligations of the 37 Farm Credit Banks. The smallest denomination for the discount notes is $50,000 and is issued in bearer form. The maturities on these obligations range from 5 to 270 days. Consolidated Systemwide bonds are issued each month with maturities of six and nine *months*. About six times a year, longer term bonds are issued. For maturities of less than 13 months, they are issued in multiples of $5,000. For longer maturities, bonds are issued in multiples of $1,000.

Bonds are issued in book-entry form. Interest income from Consolidated Systemwide discount notes and bonds is subject to full federal income taxation but is specifically exempt from state and local income taxes.

Banks for Cooperatives The 12 district Banks for Cooperatives, organized under the Farm Credit Act of 1933, make seasonal and term loans to cooperatives owned by farmers, engage in purchasing farm supplies, provide business services to farmers, and market farm output. These loans may provide working capital or finance investments in buildings and equipment. The Central Bank for Cooperatives participates in large loans made by individual district banks. Initially the Banks for Cooperatives were owned by the U.S. government. Since 1955, however, government capital has been replaced by private capital, and ownership is now private.

The major means by which the Banks for Cooperatives finance new loans is through the sale of consolidated collateral trust debentures (*co-ops*). These debentures, which are not callable, are typically offered to investors once a month. They are available in bearer and book-entry form, and the smallest denominations available are $5,000 and $10,000; however, new issues are available in book-entry form in multiples of $1,000. Many recent issues have had an original maturity of six months and pay interest at maturity, but longer term (two to five years) co-ops have also been issued.

All debentures issued by the Banks for Cooperatives must be secured by acceptable collateral in the form of cash, Treasury securities, and notes or other obligations of borrowers from the banks. Also, each bank is examined at least annually by the Farm Credit Administration. Obligations of these banks are not, however, guaranteed either directly or indirectly by the U.S. government. Nevertheless, given the semiofficial status of the Banks for Cooperatives and the government's high degree of concern for agriculture, it seems unlikely, to say the least, that the government would permit these banks to default on their securities.

Interest income from debentures issued by the Banks for Cooperatives is subject to full federal income taxation but is specifically exempt from state and local income taxes.

Federal Land Banks. The 12 Federal Land Banks were organized under the Federal Farm Loan Act of 1916. These banks extend first mortgage loans on farm properties and make other loans through local Federal Land Bank (FLB) associations. Mortgage loans must be made on the basis of appraisal reports and may not exceed 65 percent of the appraised value of the mortgaged property. Maturities on FLB loans may run from 5 to 40 years, but most have original maturities of around 20 years. Although the Federal Land Banks were set up under government auspices, all government capital in these banks has been replaced by private capital, and they are now owned by the FLB associations, which in turn are owned by the farmers who have obtained FLB loans through these associations.

The Federal Land Banks obtain funds to lend out primarily by issuing Consolidated Federal Farm Loan bonds and by occasional short-term borrowings between bond issues. Since 1963, all FLB bond issues have been noncallable. These securities range in maturity from a few years to 15 years. Most have an original maturity of longer than one year. Securities with a maturity of less than five years are available in bearer and book-entry form. Those with a maturity of more than five years are also available in registered form. Interest on FLB bonds is payable semiannually. The smallest denominations available are $1,000, $5,000, and $10,000. All new issues, however, are available in book-entry form only, in multiples of $1,000.

S&Ls are placed in an uncomfortable position whenever interest rates rise because the nature of their business is to borrow short and lend long. Federal Land Banks are in a somewhat similar situation since maturities on the loans they extend tend to be longer than the original maturities of the bonds they issue. To avoid the danger inherent in this position, Federal Land Banks now write only *variable-rate* mortgages. This approach enables them to keep loan income in line with borrowing costs whether interest rates rise or fall.

FLB bonds must be backed with collateral in the form of cash, Treasury securities, or notes secured by first mortgages on farm properties. Federal Land Banks are examined at least annually by the Farm Credit Administration. Their securities are not guaranteed either directly or indirectly by the U.S. government. However, their semiofficial status makes it extremely unlikely that the government would ever permit default on their securities.

Income from FLB bonds is subject to full federal income taxation but is exempt from state and local income taxation.

Federal Intermediate Credit Banks.   The 12 Federal Intermediate Credit Banks (FICB) were organized under the Agricultural Credit Act of 1923. Their job is to help provide short-term financing for the seasonal production and marketing of crops and livestock and for other farm-related credit purposes. These banks do not lend directly to farmers. Instead they make loans to and discount agricultural and livestock paper for various financial institutions that lend to farmers.[5] These institutions include commercial banks, production credit associations organized under the Farm Credit Act of 1933, agricultural credit corporations, and incorporated livestock loan companies. Originally, Federal Intermediate Credit Banks were government owned,

---

[5] *Discounting agricultural paper* means buying up farmers' loan notes at a discount.

but like the other farm credit banks discussed above, today their ownership is wholly private.

Although FICBs are authorized to borrow from commercial banks
and to rediscount agricultural paper with the Fed, the principal source
of their funds is monthly sales of consolidated collateral trust debentures. These debentures are available in bearer and book-entry form
and come in denominations of $5,000, $10,000, $50,000, $100,000 and
$500,000. New issues are available in book-entry form only, in multi-
ples of $1,000. The Federal Intermediate Credit Banks are authorized
to issue securities with a maturity of up to five years, but many of their
obligations are issued with nine-month maturities with interest payable at maturity. Farmers may order and purchase FICB securities
directly from the production credit associations of which they are
members. Otherwise FICB securities are sold through dealers, as in
the case of other agency securities.

FICB debentures are backed by collateral in the form of Treasury
securities, other farm credit agency securities, cash, and the notes,
discounted obligations, and loans that these banks acquire through
their lending activities. Federal Intermediate Credit Banks are regularly examined by the Farm Credit Administration. *Their securities
are not guaranteed by the government, but as in the case of the
institutions discussed above, their semiofficial status offers considerable assurance to the investor that the government would not permit
default on FICB debentures.*

Interest income on FICB debentures is subject to full federal income taxation but exempt from state and local income taxation.

BUYING AND SELLING AGENCY SECURITIES

The cheapest way to buy agency securities, and the best way if you
buy short-term issues, is to buy at issue through a syndicate member.
The syndicate handling a new agency issue always sells the securities
at par and with no commission. The syndicate makes its profit on the
selling concession (roughly $3 per $1,000 of face value), which it is
granted by the issuing agency. Because of the tendency for new
agency issues to be priced generously and consequently presold, if
you want to buy agency securities at issue, you should get in your
subscription for whatever quantity you wish to buy *before* the pricing
announcement is made. Determining approximately what coupon the
new issue will carry is not difficult; all you need do is to look up *yields-
to-maturity* on comparable securities on a dealer's quote sheet or in
The Wall Street Journal. Or you can ask the selling dealer to estimate
the probable coupon; the dealer's informed guess is sure to be quite
close to the mark.

Selling syndicates usually include in their membership several securities dealers with nationwide sales organizations and a number of major money market banks. If it is not convenient to deal with a syndicate member, you can order agency issues from your bank, which in turn will purchase them through its correspondent bank. The latter route is likely to involve a charge equal to that on the purchase of Treasury securities. In this respect, it is worth noting that agency issues are a surprisingly unknown commodity to some small bankers. Consequently, if you intend to buy through a small bank, plan to know exactly what you want.

You can also buy outstanding agency issues in the secondary market. Such purchases can be made through any bank or securities dealer. On small purchases in the secondary market, the seller will charge a fee or commission. The commission will depend in part on how many hands the securities being purchased have to pass through. A dealer bank that trades agencies might charge only $25, whereas a suburban bank or broker who had to go through a bank to obtain agency securities might charge $35 or more. Such charges naturally reduce yield to the investor, especially if the amount purchased is small or the maturity short. Thus, unless the secondary market has something especially attractive to offer (say, a desired maturity or a deep-discount bond for the long-term investor) buying at issue is preferable.

Agency securities can always be sold before maturity through any bank or securities dealer. The investor making such a sale will incur a sales charge comparable to the charge on the purchase of agencies. Spreads between bid and ask prices are slightly wider for agency issues than for governments, so the argument for being a hold-until-maturity investor is even stronger in the case of short-term agencies than for governments.

WHICH AGENCIES TO BUY

Which agency securities you should consider buying depends on your particular position. If you have only a few thousand dollars to invest, Federal Land Bank bonds, which are available in a wide range of current maturities, are the obvious choice. For the investor who has a minimum of $5,000 to invest and wants a short coupon, co-op debentures are worth looking into. These are issued on a regular monthly basis and are the most actively traded of the three farm credit agency issues. FICB debentures are also available in quite short maturities.

For the investor looking for deep-discount bonds, Fanny Mae debentures, Ginny Mae participation certificates, and Federal Land Bank bonds should all be considered. Fanny Mae and Ginny Mae have the longest maturities outstanding and consequently the widest selection of securities selling at substantial discounts from par.

To the investor who is retiring and wants to turn a given amount of capital into a stream of monthly payments, Ginny Mae pass-throughs, which are fully backed by the federal government and thus expose the investor to a zero risk of default, offer a unique and attractive possibility. Purchasing a pass-through resembles putting together a do-it-yourself, 12-year annuity—the main hitch being that the amount payable each month is subject to variation because of prepayments.[6]

CONCLUSIONS ABOUT AGENCIES AS INVESTMENT VEHICLES—RISK, LIQUIDITY, AND RETURN

With respect to the risk and liquidity of agency securities, most of what we said in Chapters 8 and 9 about U.S. Treasury securities applies. Agencies are actively traded and consequently have good marketability. However, on short maturities, because of purchase and sales commissions, you should attempt to buy at issue and hold to maturity. Long-coupon agencies, like long-coupon Treasuries, fluctuate considerably in price over time as interest rates rise and fall. This price variability makes long agencies less liquid or more risky than short agencies. Risk of default is zero on all federal agency issues backed by the full faith and credit of the U.S. government. Most other federal agency issues possess de facto government backing so the actual risk of default is negligible to zero on them, too.

The return on agencies is typically slightly more than on governments, which makes them especially attractive to the conservative investor. Corporate issues offer still higher yields, but at the expense of at least some small risk of default.

The exemption of interest income on many agencies from state and local income taxes may be an important consideration for some investors.

---

[6] For a further discussion of Ginny Mae pass-throughs see Chapter 18.

Nonnegotiable Investment Vehicles Offered by Deposit-Accepting Institutions

11

LAURA NOWAK, Ph.D.
Assistant Professor of Economics
Fordham University

This chapter will focus on nonnegotiable investment instruments offered by deposit-accepting institutions. Generally, this type of investment is offered to small investors by banks, savings and loan institutions, and credit unions. Banks, savings and loan institutions, and credit unions have many similarities, but there are important differences as well.

Depository Institutions

The commercial bank is the most important type of deposit-accepting institution because such banks hold the majority of the nation's deposits. In the first quarter of 1980, commercial banks held over $1 trillion in deposits. The deposits are obtained from businesses, governments, other financial institutions, and consumers. The funds are used to extend loans to business firms and consumers and to invest in high-quality government securities. Most banks are members of the FDIC (Federal Deposit Insurance Corporation), which insures each depositor's account up to $100,000.

Savings and loans (S&Ls) are also important depository institutions. They hold more than $500 billion in deposits. S&Ls began as mutual saving societies. The members of the society deposited their savings, and the funds were loaned to members who wanted to finance the construction or purchase of a home. Later the societies accepted deposits from other consumer savers, and they now accept deposits from individuals for business use as well. S&Ls have always focused on extending loans for home mortgages, and their deposits have traditionally been regular savings and time deposits. Deposits at all nationally chartered S&Ls are insured by FSLIC (Federal Savings and Loan Insurance Corporation). Most state-chartered S&Ls have also elected to carry FSLIC insurance. Deposits are insured up to $100,000.

The mutual savings bank is another important type of depository institution. Mutual savings banks hold more than $150 billion in deposits. These institutions are not federally chartered, and most are located in the Northeast. Mutual savings banks accept deposits and use most of their funds to invest in home mortgages. The deposits are generally insured by FDIC or a state system of deposit insurance.

The smallest type of institution for savings in the United States is the credit union. Credit unions hold deposits of more than $65 billion. These nonprofit institutions were organized both to encourage thrift among their members and to offer low-cost loans to members. Technically, credit unions do not accept deposits. They sell shares and pay dividends to their shareholders. The credit unions use their funds to extend short-term consumer loans to their members.Credit unions do not ordinarily extend long-term mortgage loans. Shareholders often receive higher returns on their deposits than do depositors in banks or S&Ls, and the shares in almost all credit unions are protected by share insurance.

Congress set many restrictions on depository institutions after the massive bank failures that occurred during the Great Depression. During the 1930s more than 9,000 banks closed, and depositors lost about $1.3 billion in deposits. It was generally believed then that the high interest rates that were offered to attract depositors and the reckless investing on the part of banks precipitated the collapse.

In the 1930s, Congress empowered the Federal Reserve to set ceilings on interest rates that banks could offer, and no interest at all could be offered on checking accounts (demand deposits). The Federal Reserve's Regulation Q set the limits on interest paid for passbook savings and longer term time deposits offered by commercial banks. The FHLB (Federal Home Loan Bank) set the ceilings for S&Ls. Mutual savings banks had the same rate ceilings as S&Ls, and credit unions offered slightly higher rates. The Depository Institutions Deregulation and Monetary Control Act of 1980 will gradually lift the ceilings.

The act required the interest-rate ceiling to be lifted gradually during the period 1980–86 and to be completely lifted by 1986 so that banks and thrift institutions could make the adjustments to the higher cost for their deposits that higher interest rates entail. Another provision of the act allowed banks, S&Ls, savings banks, credit unions, and all depository institutions nationwide to offer checking services. Until 1981 only commercial banks were legally permitted to offer checking accounts, but they were not permitted to offer interest on the checking account balances. Even before 1981, however, banks were sidestepping the law in various technical ways, such as offering free services or lower rates on loans for depositors with substantial checking account balances. Similarly, the thrift institutions had sidestepped the restriction on offering checking services by inventing the NOW (negotiable order of withdrawal) account concept. Since the account was not technically a checking account, thrifts were legally able to offer interest on the balances in these accounts. There developed a situation in which many banks and thrift institutions were offering interest-bearing checking accounts by the time the practice became legalized in January 1981. The act raised the cost of funds for banks and thrift institutions, but on the other hand, it made them more competitive with other financial institutions.

DESCRIPTION OF NONNEGOTIABLE INVESTMENT INSTRUMENTS AVAILABLE

The highly competitive environment among banks, thrifts, and securities houses, the legal loopholes, and the new rules appearing on a weekly basis make it hard for the investor to figure out what is actually available. The following is a compilation and description of the nonnegotiable investment instruments that are currently offered to savers by depository institutions.

Regular Savings Accounts. The regular savings account, one of the most liquid forms of fixed income, nonnegotiable investments, is a type of time deposit. Banks and thrift institutions allow their depositors to withdraw funds "on demand," but they can legally require 30 days notice for a withdrawal of funds.[1] During the first quarter of 1982, regular savings accounts offered 5¼ percent interest on deposits at commercial banks and 5½ percent interest on deposits at savings banks. The one-fourth percentage point difference permitted by law is a way to attract funds to the savings institutions, which normally provide home mortgage loans. Originally, savings accounts were available only in passbook form. Now, they are also available in statement form. Some banks pay a lower rate on passbook accounts than on statement accounts because the passbook accounts require manual servicing, which is more costly than the automated statement accounts.

---

[1] If a personal check is deposited, the institution will require a week or two for the check to clear before they allow those funds to be withdrawn from the account.

In spite of the low yield on regular savings accounts compared with other fixed income instruments, there were still more than $300 billion deposited in regular savings accounts at the beginning of 1980. There are a variety of reasons for their persistent popularity. First of all, they are a familiar form of saving, and many people are reluctant to try new savings instruments. For some people, savings accounts are used for "mad money" or fast liquidity. Others, especially the elderly, remember the Great Depression and the bankruptcy of many financial institutions. They are genuinely afraid to place all their savings in any noninsured savings instrument, such as money market funds.

Regular savings accounts are insured up to $100,000 by either the Federal Deposit Insurance Corporation (FDIC), the Federal Savings and Loan Insurance Corporation (FSLIC), or a state-sponsored insurance corporation. There are very few exceptions. Each institution displays the type of deposit insurance that it carries so that savers can be assured of the safety of their deposits.

Club Savings. Club savings, such as Christmas and vacation clubs, is a popular way to save. Participants are required to make weekly deposits of $1 or $20 or any amount they decide. There is a penalty for missing a payment, and the yields are comparatively low, but many depositors prefer this structured type of saving plan.

Checking and NOW Accounts. Checking and NOW accounts are the most liquid types of fixed income, nonnegotiable investment. These deposits can be withdrawn on demand either in cash or by writing a check against the account. Funds placed in a checking account are not usually considered a form of investment, but when interest is paid on the balance, the account can be considered a fixed income instrument. Most consumers and firms use checking accounts for the convenience of making their payment transactions rather than as an investment instrument. For these reasons such accounts are sometimes called demand deposits or transactions balances.

Commercial banks as well as thrift institutions are now authorized to offer checking services. Some banks and thrifts offer interest on checking balances, and others do not. Banks and thrifts sometimes charge fees for checking privileges, and sometimes they offer free checking privileges. Most institutions require a minimum balance for free checking services, and some allow the depositor to keep a minimum balance in a savings account to qualify for checking privileges. The interest rate on checking and NOW accounts was 5¼ percent in 1982.

Time Deposits. Time deposits are deposits that have a fixed maturity date. The depositor agrees in writing to keep the funds on deposit for a certain amount of time. If the money is not withdrawn, some institutions will automatically renew the account. The interest rate paid on time accounts is higher than for regular savings accounts, but there is a minimum deposit required and a penalty for early withdrawals.[2] A common example of this type of account is a three-month (90-day) account from which funds may be withdrawn after 90 days; or if the account is renewed, the funds can be withdrawn during the first 10 days of each calendar quarter.

For years the ceiling interest rate on time deposits was set by law. Ceilings will be completely lifted by the Depository Institutions Deregulation and Monetary Control Act. Rates on time deposits are now based on an index of Treasury securities.

Money market certificates, small-saver certificates, retail repurchase agreements, and all-saver certificates are types of time deposits. Each is discussed below. Tax-deferred-savings retirement accounts (Individual Retirement Accounts and Keough Plans) are also available. However, they will not be discussed in this chapter, since they are covered in Appendix B of this book.

Money Market Certificates. Sometimes called six-month savings certificates, money market certificates were authorized by Congress on June 1, 1978, to help banks, especially the thrifts, attract deposits. The minimum deposit is $10,000, and the interest rate is tied to the six-month U.S. Treasury bill rate. The interest rate once established for the account is fixed for the six months. The maximum rate that may be paid is the higher of (1) the most recent auction discount rate on six-month Treasury bills plus one fourth of 1 percent or (2) an average of the discount rates on six-month Treasury bills for the four auctions immediately prior to the date of the deposit plus one fourth of 1 percent. To prevent a depositor from withdrawing funds from a money market certificate when interest rates increase shortly after an account is opened, and then opening a new money market certificate at the higher rate, there are substantial penalties for early withdrawal.

Originally, the thrifts were allowed to pay one fourth of 1 percent more than the Treasury bill rate, and commercial banks could only offer the Treasury bill rate. The one fourth of 1 percent difference had its advantages and disadvantages. On the one hand, the thrifts' rate was more attractive than the commercial bank rate; but on the other hand, the cost of funds for thrifts was higher than for the commercial banks. In March 1979, to lower the cost of attracting funds to thrift institutions and to prevent deposit attrition from small commercial banks, the regulators discontinued the one fourth of 1 percent interest-rate advantage whenever the Treasury bill rate exceeded 9 percent. As market interest rates continued to rise way beyond 9 percent, the banks and thrifts competed furiously for funds. They could not

---

[2] The interest-rate penalty for early withdrawal consists of a loss of three-months interest, if the amount has been on deposit for less than one year. If the amount has been on deposit for more than one year, the penalty is a loss of six-months interest.

compete on the basis of yields, since these were set by law, so they tried to compete on some other basis.

For example, the banks and thrifts found ways to sidestep the $10,000 minimum denomination requirement. They offered six-month savings certificates at substantially less than the $10,000 minimum deposit required by law. The loophole consists of the institution lending the saver the difference. For example, if a saver can invest only $3,000, the bank contributes $7,000 toward a $10,000 certificate. This technique is legitimate since the bank lends the money to the saver, and the saver purchases the certificate for $10,000. Of course, the bank charges a fee for the loan of $7,000, but the result may be advantageous to the depositor, depending on how much is borrowed and the current market rate of interest.[3]

The banks and thrifts also devised a way to avoid the prohibition against early withdrawal of six-month deposits. Instead of withdrawing the deposit, savers are permitted to borrow money based on their six-month certificate or to write a check on a portion of the deposit. In this way, the high interest return on the six-month saving certificate is not jeopardized, and no penalty is incurred. Of course, there is an interest charge on the money borrowed, but this technique is advantageous to the saver and attracts those who are concerned about losing access to their money during the six-month period.

When banks and thrifts advertise the current rate on six-month savings certificates, they show two rates. One is the actual annual rate paid for the first six months of the deposit. The higher rate indicates the annual return if the money is left on deposit for a full year, assuming the interest earned over the first six months is reinvested and assuming the rate remains the same during the second six months of the year.

Money market certificates are quite popular. The volume of money market certificates outstanding rose enormously as market interest rates kept rising, and in many cases the inflow of funds into the certificates was greater than the outflow of funds from savings and time deposits. Although the banks and thrifts have experienced a transfer of some funds from such lower yielding accounts as regular savings accounts to this higher yielding type of account, most bankers believe that they would have lost much of these funds altogether (to U.S. Treasury bills and notes or to money market funds) if the six-month money market certificate did not exist.

Comparisons are usually made between money market certificates and money market funds as investment vehicles. Money market funds

---

[3] An individual who does not itemize deductions on his or her Federal income tax return may find this plan unattractive because, although the interest earned is taxable, the interest expense charged by the bank can not be deducted if the standard deduction is taken.

do *not* guarantee a specified rate of interest. However, money market certificates do guarantee a rate for the six-month period. This does not necessarily make one investment vehicle more attractive than the other. Locking-in a rate is advantageous to an investor if the investor anticipates a decline in interest rates. On the other hand, if interest rates rise, the investor is saddled with the lower rate. Therefore, whether the locked-in feature of interest rates offered by money market certificates is best for an investor depends upon the investor's expectations about the movement of interest rates during the following six months. Many investors like the safe approach and simply accept the guaranteed rate offered. Since money market certificates are insured, many investors prefer certificates to money market funds because funds are not insured. However, because money market funds invest in high quality short-term instruments, there is only a small risk associated with the ownership of fund shares. Some attractive features of money market funds compared to money market certificates are that (1) the minimum investment for funds is much less than $10,000 (usually, $1,000); (2) liquidity is high for funds since shares can be redeemed at any time with no penalty, whereas early withdrawal from a money market certificate will result in a penalty; and (3) funds offer a temporary investment in which money can be invested for a period of less than six months until uncertainty concerning future interest rates and/or individual circumstances are resolved. A drawback of both investment vehicles is that if interest rates decline substantially, there is the problem of reinvestment of the proceeds at a lower rate when the certificate matures or when the fund shares are redeemed.

Small-Saver Certificates. Small-saver certificates are 2½- to 4-year time deposits that offer a fixed rate of interest. The ceilings of 12 percent for thrifts and 11.75 percent for banks were lifted in 1981, and the certificates now offer an opportunity for small savers to obtain market interest rates. The interest rate varies and is tied to an index of Treasury securities of similar maturity. The law does not require any minimum deposit on the small-saver certificates, but banks and thrifts usually place a relatively low minimum required deposit.

When banks and thrifts advertise the rate on 2½-year savings certificates, they show two rates. The first is the annual interest rate, and the higher rate is the effective annual yield when the interest is compounded daily. The rate is guaranteed for 30 months.

The small-saver certificate is currently popular among investors because market yields on Treasury securities exceed the rate on a regular savings account. The higher yield can be realized by investors who have less money to invest than would be required if Treasury securities were acquired. The minimum investment is also less than that required on money market certificates and offers the advantage of locking-in a rate for a longer period of time if investors expect a decline in interest rates. A disadvantage of a small-saver certificate compared with the ownership of Treasury securities maturing in 30 months is that the interest on Treasury securities is exempt from state and local income taxes, whereas interest on small-saver certificates is not exempt.

Retail Repurchase Agreements. Sometimes called retail repos's, investor funds, or money funds, retail repurchase agreement programs are not funds at all. Repos are simply loans that customers make to financial institutions for a specified amount of time at a fixed interest rate. They are actually a type of time deposit. The duration of the loan can be anywhere from one week to three months. The rates change daily and they vary among financial institutions. Investors must shop around for the best rates and also decide when is the best time to make the loan.

Repos are secured by a portfolio of U.S. government securities and U.S. government agency securities. Each bank or thrift institution has a different portfolio of securities and is therefore prepared to offer different rates. The repos are *not* covered by deposit insurance. Repos are not risky investments, but investors must be aware that financial institutions that borrowed the funds can fail. If they do fail, the depositors are paid first, and the creditors—those who extended loans to the institution—have to negotiate to retrieve their funds. Investors who enter into repos with a financial institution are creditors *not* depositors.

All-Savers Certificates. Initiated in October 1981, the all-saver certificate experiment was devised for one year only. Banks, S&Ls, and credit unions were permitted to offer a one-year certificate at a fixed interest rate, which was set at 70 percent of the rate on one-year U.S. Treasury notes. Since this rate fluctuates, the banks and thrifts can change the rate on *newly* issued certificates; they can do this once a month. The minimum denominations are relatively low—$500— and the deposits are covered by federal deposit insurance.

The main attraction of these certificates is that the interest up to specified limits is exempt from federal income taxation and income taxation of certain states. The interest exemption is a lifetime exemption: For individuals the exemption is $1,000, and for married couples it is $2,000.

Investors contemplating this form of investment must determine whether the tax-exempt yield is higher than the aftertax yield that can be earned by owning a one-year Treasury note. Issuers of these certificates usually provide a table that shows the yield that must be earned on a taxable instrument to produce the tax-exempt yield offered on the certificate for taxpayers with different taxable incomes. Generally, investors in a 30 percent marginal tax bracket would benefit from the all-savers certificate.[4] Of course, if the investor cannot afford the substantially higher investment required to purchase a one-year Treasury note, purchasing these certificates provides an excellent means for obtaining tax relief.

CONCLUSIONS

Investors who are comparing opportunities to invest in nonnegotiable investment instruments offered by banks and thrift institutions will notice more similarities than differences. Many of the offers at particular institutions are complex, but they operate under strict government regulations. Special bonus offers must adhere to the guidelines discussed below.

For deposits less than $5,000, the Federal Depository Institutions Deregulation Committee limits the bonus permitted to $10 in cash or in merchandise for each deposit. For each deposit of $5,000–$100,000, institutions may only offer up to $20 in cash or in merchandise.[5] For deposits of more than $100,000, there are no regulations governing the amount of interest that can be paid. Institutions can offer large cash bonuses for these deposits as well as high rates of interest, and the offers will differ significantly between institutions.

Institutions differ with respect to minimum cash balances required on free-checking or NOW accounts. They also differ with respect to the penalties that they charge when balances fall below the minimum. Sometimes savers do better without free-checking privileges. If the minimum balance required is too high, they might consider paying for check privileges and keeping the bulk of their savings in a higher yielding account.

---

[4] The formula for determining the equivalent taxable yield given the rate offered on the certificate and the marginal tax rate of the investor is as follows:

$$\text{Equivalent taxable yield} = \frac{\text{Rate offered on the certificate}}{(1 - \text{investor's marginal tax rate})}$$

For example, if the rate offered on the certificate is 12 percent and the investor's marginal tax rate is 35 percent, the equivalent taxable yield is

$$\frac{.12}{1 - .35} = .185 \text{ or } 18.5 \text{ percent}$$

[5] Because of the restrictions imposed on the cash bonus payment for accounts between $5,000 and $100,000, the investor would be better off opening multiple accounts. For example, if an investor has $15,000 to deposit in a small-savers certificate requiring a $500 minimum and the institution pays a $5 cash bonus for deposits up to $5,000 and $20 for deposits between $5,000 and $100,000, then the investor is better off opening 30 $500 accounts. In that case, the cash bonus will be $150 compared with $20 if a $15,000 account is opened. Opening more accounts requires more paperwork, but it will probably be worth the investor's time. If the institution has a policy of restricting multiple accounts, find another institution that does not impose any restrictions. The cash bonus received by the investor is taxable.

In sum, although there are more similarities than differences among banks and thrift institutions, the smart investor interested in nonnegotiable investment instruments offered by these institutions will have to investigate the opportunities available. Generally, interest rates and cash bonuses will not differ among institutions, but service charges, minimum deposit requirements, special fees, and penalties will be the factors that differ among the institutions.

Corporate Bonds

12   **FRANK J. FABOZZI, Ph.D, C.F.A., C.P.A.**
Professor of Economics
Fordham University

HARRY C. SAUVAIN, D.S.C.
University Professor Emeritus of Finance
Indiana University

Corporate debt obligations are classified by type of issuer. The three general classes are public utilities, transportations, and industrials. Public utility bonds constitute the largest portion of corporate debt obligations.

Classification by type of corporate issuer is helpful to investors because of the similar investment characteristics (e.g., default risk) of bonds within a class; however, corporate issuers within a class are not homogeneous with respect to investment characteristics. Within the three general classes, therefore, a finer breakdown of corporate issuers is generally made by market participants. Public utilities are subdivided into electric power companies, gas distribution companies, gas transmission companies, and telephone companies.[1] Telephone companies include the American Telephone & Telegraph Company and its subsidiaries as well as a number of so-called independent telephone companies. Transportation debt obligations generally available to the investing public are those of airlines and railroads organized as common carriers. Like public utilities, airlines and railroads are regu-

---

[1] Water companies are also utilities; however, they are generally municipally owned.

lated by state and/or federal government agencies. Industrials are the catchall class and therefore are the most heterogeneous class with respect to investment characteristics. Issuers that are neither public utilities nor transportation companies are referred to as industrials. Industrials include all kinds of manufacturing and merchandising companies. Banks and finance companies may be considered to make up still another category.

Corporate bondholders are creditors of the business. Bonds are evidence of a legally complex contract between the corporate issuers, or debtor, and the bondholder. Anyone who invests in corporate bonds must be familiar with the usual provisions of that contract. In bond contracts bondholders are given a legal right to be paid interest periodically by the debtor, usually every six months, at an annual percentage of the principal amount of the bond.[2] The principal amount is the sum that the debtor promises to pay at a defined date in the future.

Corporate bonds are usually issued in denominations of $1,000 and multiples thereof. In common usage, a *corporate bond* means one of $1,000 denomination. A securities dealer who says he or she has five bonds to sell means five bonds each of $1,000 principal amount. If the promised rate of interest is 6 percent, the annual amount of interest on each bond is $60 and the semiannual interest is $30. The rights of bondholders are summarized on nicely engraved pieces of paper, which are generally tucked away in safe deposit boxes. Most corporate bonds are *registered bonds*.

THE CORPORATE TRUSTEE

The promises of corporate bond issuers and the rights of investors who buy them are set forth in great detail in contracts generally called *bond indentures*. If bondholders were handed the complete indenture, they would have trouble understanding the legalese, and even greater difficulty in determining from time to time whether the corporate issuer is keeping all the promises made. These problems are solved for the most part by bringing in a corporate trustee as a third party to the contract. The indenture is made out to the corporate trustee as a representative of the interests of bondholders.

A corporate trustee is a bank or trust company with a corporate trust department and officers who are experts in performing the functions of a trustee. In legal practice the indenture is made out to the trustee, who acts in a fiduciary capacity for investors who own a bond issue. This is no small task. The corporate trustee must, at the time of issue, authenticate the bonds issued—that is, keep track of all the bonds sold

---

[2] Income bonds are exceptions to this general statement. They are discussed later.

and make sure that they do not exceed the principal amount authorized by the indenture. It must then be a sort of watchdog for the bondholders by seeing to it that the issuer complies with all the covenants of the indenture. These covenants are many and technical, and they must be watched during the entire period that a bond issue is outstanding. We will describe some of these covenants in subsequent pages.

It is very important that corporate trustees be competent and financially responsible. To this end we have a federal statute known as the Trust Indentures Act, which requires that for all corporate bond offerings in the amount of $5 million or more sold in interstate commerce there must be a corporate trustee. The indenture must include adequate requirements for performance of the trustee's duties on behalf of bondholders; there must be no conflict between the trustee's interest as a trustee and any other interest it may have; and there must be provision for reports by the trustee to bondholders. If a corporate issuer fails to pay interest or principal, the trustee must declare a default and take such action as may be necessary to protect the rights of bondholders. If the corporate issuer has promised in the indenture always to maintain an amount of current assets equal to two times the amount of current liabilities, the trustee must watch the corporation's balance sheet and see that the promise is kept. If the issuer fails to maintain the prescribed amounts, the trustee must take action on behalf of the bondholders.

The terms of bond issues set forth in bond indentures are always a compromise between the interests of the bond issuer and those of investors who buy bonds. The issuer always wants to pay the lowest possible rate of interest and to be tied up as little as possible with legal convenants. Bondholders want the highest possible interest rate, the best security, and a variety of covenants to restrict the issuer in one way or another. As we discuss the provisions of bond indentures, keep this opposition of interests in mind and see how compromises are worked out in practice.

SECURITY FOR BONDS

Shylock demanded a pound of flesh as his security. Investors who buy corporate bonds don't go quite that far, but they do like some kind of security. In fact the kind of security, or the absence of a specific pledge of security, is usually indicated by the title of a bond issue. If you are a reader of *The Wall Street Journal,* you may have seen an advertisement for "$50,000,000 issue of Metropolitan Edison, First Mortgage Bonds, 9 percent Series, due September 1, 2008." That title tells you several things about this bond issue.

It tells you that the issuer has granted the bondholders a first-mortgage lien on substantially all of its properties. That is good from the viewpoint of bondholders. But in return, the issuer got a relatively low rate of interest on the bonds. (Nine percent was relatively low at the time of issue.) A *lien* is a legal right to sell mortgaged property to satisfy unpaid obligations to bondholders. In practice, foreclosure of a mortgage and sale of mortgaged property is unusual. If a default occurs, there is usually a financial reorganization of the issuer in which provision is made for settlement of the debt to bondholders. The mortgage lien is important, though, because it gives the mortgage bondholders a very strong bargaining position relative to other creditors in determining the terms of a reorganization.

Often first-mortgage bonds are issued in series with bonds of each series secured equally by the same first mortgage. The title of the bond issue mentioned above includes "9 percent Series," which tells you that the issue is one of a series. Many companies, particularly public utilities, have a policy of financing part of their capital requirements continuously by long-term debt. They want some part of their total capitalization in the form of bonds because the cost of such capital is ordinarily less than that of capital raised by sale of stock. So, as a principal amount of debt is paid off, they issue another series of bonds under the same mortgage. As they expand and need a greater amount of debt capital, they can add new series of bonds. It is a lot easier and more advantageous to issue a series of bonds under one mortgage and one indenture than it is to create entirely new bond issues with some different arrangements for security.

When a bond indenture authorizes the issue of additional series of bonds with the same mortgage lien as those already issued, the indenture imposes certain conditions that must be met before an additional series may be issued. Bondholders do not want their security impaired; these conditions are for their benefit. It is common for a first-mortgage bond indenture to provide that property acquired by the issuer subsequent to granting of the first mortgage lien shall be subject to the first-mortgage lien. This is termed the *after-acquired clause*. Then the indenture usually permits the issue of additional bonds up to some specified percentage of the value of the after acquired property, such as 60 percent. The other 40 percent, or whatever the percentage may be, must be financed in some other way. This is intended to assure that there will be additional assets with a value significantly greater than the amount of additional bonds secured by the mortgage. Another customary kind of restriction on issue of additional series is a requirement that earnings in an immediately preceding period must be equal to some number of times the amount of annual interest on the new series plus interest on all outstanding series. For this purpose, *earnings* are usually defined as earnings before income tax. The number of times interest must be earned may be one and a half, two, or some other number. Still another common provision is that additional bonds may be issued to the extent that earlier series of bonds have been paid off.

You seldom see a bond issue with the term *second mortgage* in its title. The reason is that this term has a connotation of weakness. Sometimes companies get around that difficulty by using such words as *first and consolidated mortgage bonds,* or *first and refunding.* Usually this language means that a bond issue is secured by a first mortgage on some part of the issuer's property, but by a second or even third lien on other parts of its assets.

Collateral Trust Bonds

Some companies do not own fixed assets or other real property and so have nothing on which they can give a mortgage lien to secure bondholders. Instead, they own securities of other companies; they are *holding companies* and the other companies are *subsidiaries.* To satisfy the desire of bondholders for security, they pledge stocks, notes, bonds, or whatever other kind of obligations they own. These assets are termed *collateral,* and bonds secured by such assets are *collateral trust bonds.* Some companies own both real property and securities. They may use real property to secure mortgage bonds and use securities for collateral trust bonds.

The legal arrangement for collateral trust bonds is much the same as that for mortgage bonds. The issuer delivers to a corporate trustee under a bond indenture the securities pledged, and the trustee holds them for the bondholders. When voting common stocks are included in the collateral, the indenture permits the issuer to vote the stocks so long as there is no default on its bonds. This is important to issuers of such bonds because usually the stocks are those of subsidiaries, and the issuer depends on the exercise of voting rights to control the subsidiaries.

Indentures usually provide that, in event of default, the right to vote stocks included in the collateral are transferred to the trustee. Loss of the voting right would be a serious disadvantage to the issuer because it would mean loss of control of subsidiaries. The trustee may also sell the securities pledged for whatever prices they will bring in the market and apply the proceeds to payment of the claims of collateral trust bondholders. These rather drastic actions, however, are not usually taken immediately upon an event of default. The corporate trustee's primary responsibility is to act in the best interests of bondholders, and their interests may be served for a time at least by giving the defaulting issuer a proxy to vote stocks held as collateral and thus preserve the holding company structure. It may also defer sale of collateral when it seems likely that bondholders would fare better in a financial reorganization than they would by sale of collateral.

Collateral trust indentures contain a number of provisions designed to protect bondholders. Generally, the market or appraised value of the collateral must be maintained at some percentage of the amount of bonds outstanding. The percentage is greater than 100 so that there will be a margin of safety. If collateral value declines below the minimum percentage, additional collateral must be provided by the issuer. There is almost always provision for withdrawal of some collateral provided other acceptable collateral is substituted.

Collateral trust bonds may be issued in series in much the same way that mortgage bonds are issued in series. The rules governing additional series of bonds require that adequate collateral must be pledged, and there may be restrictions on the use to which the proceeds of an additional series may be put. All series of bonds are issued under the same indenture and have the same claim on collateral.

Equipment Trust Certificates

The desire of borrowers to pay the lowest possible rate of interest on their obligations generally leads them to offer their best security and to grant lenders the strongest claim on it. Many years ago the railway companies developed a way of financing purchase of cars and locomotives called *rolling stock* in a way that enabled them to borrow at just about the lowest rates in the corporate bond market.

Railway rolling stock has for a long time been regarded by investors as excellent security for debt. This equipment is sufficiently standardized that it can be used by one railway as well as another. And it can be readily moved from the tracks of one railroad to those of another. There is generally a good market for lease or sale of cars and locomotives. The railroads have capitalized on these characteristics of rolling stock by developing a legal arrangement for giving investors a legal claim on it that is different from, and generally better than, a mortgage lien.

The legal arrangement is one that vests legal title to railway equipment in a trustee, which is better from the standpoint of investors than a first-mortgage lien on property. A railway company orders some cars and locomotives from a manufacturer. When the job is finished, the manufacturer transfers the legal title to the equipment to a trustee. The trustee leases it to the railroad that ordered it and at the same time sells *equipment trust certificates* in an amount equal to a large percentage of the purchase price. Money from sale of certificates is paid to the manufacturer. The railway company makes an initial payment of rent equal to the balance of the purchase price, and the trustee gives that money to the manufacturer. Thus the manufacturer is paid off. The trustee collects lease rental money periodically from the railroad and uses it to pay interest and principal on the certificates. The amounts of lease rental payments are worked out carefully so that they are enough to pay the equipment trust certificates. At the end of some period of time, such as 15 years, the certificates are paid off, the trustee sells the equipment to the railroad for some nominal price, and the lease is terminated.

The beauty of this arrangement from the viewpoint of investors is that the railroad does not legally own the rolling stock until all the certificates are paid. In the event the railroad does not make the lease rental payments, there is no big legal hassle about foreclosing a lien. The trustee owns the property and can take it back because failure to pay the rent breaks the lease. The trustee can lease the equipment to another railroad and continue to make payments on the certificates from new lease rentals.

This description emphasizes the legal nature of the arrangement for securing the certificates. In practice, these certificates are regarded as obligations of the railway company that leased the equipment and are shown as liabilities in its balance sheet. In fact, the name of the railway appears in the title of the certificates. In the ordinary course of events, the trustee is just an intermediary who performs the function of holding title, acting as lessor, and collecting the money to pay the certificates. It is significant that even in the worst years of depression, railways have paid their equipment trust certificates, though they did not pay bonds secured by mortgages.

Although the railway companies developed the equipment trust device, it has also been used by companies engaged in providing other kinds of transportation. The trucking companies, for example, finance purchase of huge fleets of trucks in the same manner; air transportation companies use this kind of financing to purchase transport planes; and international oil companies use it to buy the huge tankers that bring oil from over the oceans.

Debenture Bonds

After all the emphasis upon security, you might think that Shylock-minded investors would not buy bonds without something to secure them. But not so! Investors often buy large issues of unsecured bonds just as they buy first-mortgage bonds. These unsecured bonds are termed *debentures*. However, investors generally get higher rates of interest on debentures than on well-secured bonds, or they get the privilege of converting them into common stock of the issuer.

Debenture bonds are not secured by a specific pledge of designated property, but that does not mean that they have no claim on property of issuers or on their earnings. Debenture bondholders have the claim of general creditors on all assets of the issuer not pledged specifically to secure other debt. And they even have a claim on pledged assets to the extent that these assets have value greater than necessary to satisfy secured creditors. In fact, if there are no pledged assets and no secured creditors, debenture bondholders have first claim on all assets along with other general creditors.

These unsecured bonds are sometimes issued by companies that are so strong financially and have such a high credit rating that to offer security would be gilding the lily. Such companies can simply turn a deaf ear to investors who want security and still sell their debentures at relatively low interest rates. But debentures are sometimes also issued by companies that have already sold mortgage bonds and given liens on most of their property. These debentures rank below the mortgage bonds or collateral trust bonds in their claim on assets, and investors may regard them as relatively weak. This is the kind that bears the higher rates of interest.

Even though there is no pledge of security, the indentures for debenture bonds contain a variety of provisions designed to afford some protection to investors. Frequently the amount of a debenture bond issue is limited to the amount of the initial issue. This limit is to keep issuers from weakening the position of debenture holders by running up additional unsecured debt. Sometimes additional debentures may be issued, provided that the issuer has earned its bond interest on all existing debt plus the additional issue, a specified number of times in a recent accounting period. If a company has no secured debt, it is customary to provide that debentures will be secured equally with any secured bonds that may be issued in the future. Some provisions of debenture bond issues are intended to give the corporate trustee early warning of deterioration in the issuer's financial condition. The issuer may be required always to maintain a specified minimum amount of net working capital—the excess of current assets over current liabilities—equal to not less than the amount of debentures outstanding. The corporate trustee must watch the issuer's balance sheets and, upon failure to maintain the required amount of net working capital, take whatever action is appropriate in the interest of debenture holders. Another common restriction is one limiting the payment of cash dividends by the issuer. Another limits the proportion of current earnings that may be used to pay dividends.

Subordinated and Convertible Debentures

You might think that debenture bonds have about the weakest possible claim on assets and earnings of a corporate issuer, but that is not so. Some companies have issued *subordinated debenture bonds*. The term *subordinated* means that such an issue ranks after secured debt, after debenture bonds, and often after some general creditors in its claim on assets and earnings. Owners of this kind of bond stand last in line among creditors when an issuer fails financially.

Because subordinated debentures are so weak in their claim on assets, issuers would have to offer a very high rate of interest unless they also offer some special inducement to buy the bonds. The inducement is an option to convert bonds into stock of the issuer at the discretion of bondholders. If the issuer prospers and the market price of its stock rises substantially in the market, the bondholders can convert bonds to stock worth a great deal more than they paid for the bonds. This conversion privilege may also be included in the provisions of debentures that are not subordinated. Convertible securities are discussed in Chapter 22.

The bonds may be convertible into something other than the common stock of the issuer. For example, the convertible subordinated debentures of Hi-G, Inc. 13½s due 4/15/2001 are convertible into shares of its subsidiary, Computer Magnetics. The Sun Company, Inc., subordinated exchangeable debentures 10¾s due 4/1/2006 are exchangeable into common stock of Becton, Dickinson and Company. Sun had acquired 32 percent of Becton in 1978. There are also issues convertible into silver or its cash equivalent at the time of conversion. Sunshine Mining Company sold two such offerings in 1980, and HMW Industries floated an issue in 1981.

Guaranteed Bonds

Sometimes a corporation may guarantee the bonds of another corporation.[3] Such bonds are referred to as guaranteed bonds. The guarantee, however, does not mean that these obligations are free of default risk. The safety of a guaranteed bond depends upon the financial capability of the guarantor to satisfy the terms of the guarantee, as well as the financial capability of the issuer. The terms of the guarantee may call for the guarantor to guarantee the payment of interest and/or repayment of the principal. A guaranteed bond may have more than one corporate guarantor. Each guarantor may be responsible for not only its pro rata share, but also the entire amount guaranteed by the other guarantors.

The debentures of Phillips Chemical Company due 2011 are unconditionally guaranteed by Phillips Petroleum Company and as such

---

[3] There are debt obligations in which the guarantor is a federal agency. For example, certain mortgage-backed issues, discussed in Chapter 17, are guaranteed by a federal agency. As another example, the Chrysler Corporation Loan Board was authorized by Congress to guarantee the payment of principal and interest on loans to Chrysler Corporation.

carry the triple-A rating of its guarantor. The joint venture of Gulf Oil and Texaco, called Pembroke Capital Company, is guaranteed by the two partners. The offering of $200 million, which represented the first public offering of a project-financed venture, received a triple-A rating because of its guarantors. Guaranteed bonds in which the guarantor is another corporation are prevalent in the railroad field. In order to lease the road of another company, a railroad company may have to agree to guarantee the debt of the company from whom it is leasing the road.

PROVISIONS FOR PAYING OFF BONDS

What would you pay for a bond that promises to pay interest in the amount of $50 or $60 a year from now to eternity but does not promise ever to repay principal? The right to receive interest in perpetuity may very well be worth $1,000, depending upon the current level of interest rates in the market, but investors generally dislike the absence of a promise to pay a fixed amount of principal on some specified date in the future; therefore, there is no such thing as a "perpetual bond" in the U.S. financial markets.

Most corporate bonds are *term bonds;* that is, they run for a term of years and then become due and payable. The term may be long or short. Generally, obligations due in about five years from date of issue are called *notes.* Most corporate borrowing takes the form of bonds due in 20 to 30 years. Term bonds may be retired by payment at final maturity, or retired prior to maturity if provided for in the indenture. Serial bonds mature periodically.

Call and Refund Provisions

One important question in negotiation of terms of a new bond issue is whether the issuer shall have the right to redeem the *entire amount* of bonds outstanding on a date before maturity. Issuers generally want to have this right, and investors do not want them to have it. Both sides think that at some time in the future the general level of interest rates in the market may decline to a level well below that prevailing at the time bonds are issued. If so, issuers want to redeem all of the bonds outstanding and replace them with new bond issues at lower interest rates. But this is exactly what investors do not want. If bonds are redeemed when interest rates are low, investors have to take their money back and reinvest it at a low rate.

The usual practice is a provision that denies the issuer a right to redeem bonds during the first 5 or 10 years following date of issue, but permits redemption at a premium over par after that initial period. The verb *to call* is commonly used with the same meaning as *to redeem,* and bonds are said to be *callable* or *not callable.* When the right to call is denied for a specified period of time after issuance, the bond is said to have a *deferred call.*

Paying off a bond issue with the proceeds of a new bond issue is termed *refunding.* Bond indentures sometimes provide that bonds shall not be callable at all for refunding for a specified period but may be called before maturity when the money to pay them off comes from a source other than a refunding source. Long-term industrial bonds usually may not be redeemed for refunding purposes for 10 years but are immediately callable for reasons other than refunding. For long-term public utility bonds, refunding protection is usually for 10 years. These bonds may either have a deferred call for 10 years when issued during periods of extremely high interest rates or are immediately callable except for refunding. Generally, intermediate-term debt obligations are either noncallable or possess a deferred call until the year before maturity.

As a rule, corporate bonds are callable at a premium above par. Generally, the amount of the premium declines as the bond approaches maturity. The initial amount of the premium may be as much as one year's interest or as little as interest for half a year. When less than the entire issue is called, the specific bonds to be called are selected randomly or on a pro rata basis. If the bonds selected on a random basis are bearer bonds, the serial number of the certificates is published in *The Wall Street Journal* and major metropolitan dailies.

Sinking-Fund Provision

Term bonds may be paid off by operation of a *sinking fund.* Those last two words are often misunderstood to mean that the issuer accumulates a fund in cash, or in assets readily sold for cash, that is used to pay bonds at maturity. It had that meaning many years ago, but too often it happened that the money supposed to be in a sinking fund was not all there when it was needed.[4] In modern practice there is no fund, and *sinking* means that money is applied periodically to redemption of bonds before maturity. Corporate bond indentures require the issuer to retire a specified portion of an issue each year. This kind of provision for repayment of corporate debt may be designed to liquidate all of a bond issue by maturity date, or it may be arranged to pay only a part of the total by the end of the term. If only a part is paid, the remainder is called a *balloon maturity.*

The issuer may satisfy the sinking-fund requirement in one of two ways. A cash payment of the face amount of the bonds to be retired

---

[4] For a brief history of sinking funds, see F. Corine Thompson and Richard L. Norgaard, *Sinking Funds: Their Use and Value* (New York: Research Foundation of Financial Executives Institute, 1967).

may be made by the corporate debtor to the trustee. The latter then calls the bonds by lot for redemption. Bonds have serial numbers, and numbers may be randomly selected for redemption. Owners of bonds called in this manner turn them in for redemption; *interest payments stop at the redemption date*. Alternatively, the issuer can deliver to the trustee bonds with a total face value equal to the amount that must be retired. The bonds are purchased by the *issuer* in the open market. This option is elected by the issuer when the bonds are selling below par. Some corporate bond indentures, however, prohibit the open market purchase of the bonds by the issuer.

The issuer is granted a special call price to satisfy any sinking-fund requirement. Usually, the sinking-fund call price is the par value if the bonds were originally sold at par. When issued at a price in excess of par, the sinking-fund call price generally starts at the issuance price and scales down to par as the issue approaches maturity.

There are two advantages of a sinking-fund requirement from the bondholder's perspective. First, default risk is reduced due to the orderly retirement of the issue before maturity. Second, if bond prices decline as a result of an increase in interest rates, price support will be provided by the issuer or its fiscal agent, since it must enter the market on the buy side in order to satisfy the sinking-fund requirement. However, the disadvantage is that the bonds may be called at the special sinking-fund call price at a time when interest rates are lower than rates prevailing at the time of issuance. In that case, the bonds will be selling in the market above par but may be retired by the issuer at the special call price that may be equal to par value.

Usually, the periodic payments required for sinking-fund purposes will be the same for each period. However, some indentures permit variable periodic payments, where the periodic payments vary based upon prescribed conditions set forth in the indenture. The most common condition is the level of earnings of the issuer. In such cases, the periodic payments vary directly with earnings. An issuer prefers such flexibility; however, an investor may prefer fixed periodic payments because of the greater default risk protection provided under this arrangement.

Many corporate bond indentures include a provision that grants the issuer the option to retire double the amount stipulated for sinking-fund retirement.[5] This *doubling option* effectively reduces the bondholder's call protection since when interest rates decline, the issuer may find it economically advantageous to exercise this option at the

---

[5] Martin L. Leibowitz, "An Analytic Approach to the Bond Market," in *Financial Analysts Handbook I: Methods, Theory and Portfolio Management,* ed. Sumner N. Levine (Homewood, Ill. Dow Jones-Irwin, 1975), p. 233. © Dow Jones-Irwin, Inc., 1975.

special sinking fund call price to retire a substantial portion of an outstanding issue.

With the exception of finance companies, industrial issues almost always include sinking-fund provisions. Finance companies, on the other hand, almost always do not. The inclusion or absence of a sinking-fund provision in public utility debt obligations depends upon the type of public utility. Pipeline issues almost always include sinking-fund provisions, whereas telephone issues do not. For electrical utilities a "blanket" sinking-fund requirement is generally included. This provision gives the issuer the option to spend a specified amount of funds to (1) retire either the issue in question, (2) retire any other issue of the issuer, or (3) make improvements to existing facilities.[6]

Serial Bonds

Some corporate obligations are so arranged that specified principal amounts become due on specified dates. Such issues are called serial bonds. Equipment trust certificates, discussed earlier, are structured as serial bonds. The advantage of a serial bond issue from the investor's point of view is that the repayment schedule will match the decline in the value of the equipment used as collateral. Hence, default risk is reduced. In addition, the potential investor can select from a spectrum of maturity dates.

As an example of a serial bond, consider the Equipment Trust certificates of the Union Pacific Railroad Company carrying a coupon rate of 13⅛ percent and maturing annually beginning September 1, 1981, and ending September 1, 1995. The total amount of the issue is $25.5 million. The amount maturing annually is $1.7 million. The yields at the time of issuance, May 20, 1981, varied by maturity as shown below.

September 1	Yield (percent)
1981	13.45
1982	13.45
1983	13.55
1984	13.45
1985	13.40
1986	13.35
1987	13.20
1988–1995	13.15

---

[6] Andrew J. Kalotay, "On the Management of Sinking Funds," *Financial Management*, Summer 1981, pp. 34–39.

OTHER FEATURES OF BONDS

The high interest rates that prevailed in the U.S. capital market in the late '70s and early '80s made the cost of borrowing for issuers of even the highest quality rating expensive. To reduce the cost of debt funds for their corporate clients, investment bankers designed packages to make long-term debt instruments more attractive to investors. Original-issue deep-discount bonds were first offered. These issues were attractive to certain institutional investors who anticipated that interest rates would decline and sought to lock in the then existing rate of interest. Variable rate notes, which were pioneered in 1974, were revived for investors who sought protection against further advances in interest rates. For issuers with lower quality ratings, equity kickers and exchange offerings were included in some issues. Other features, such as warrants to purchase additional bonds from the issuer and "put" bonds made their debut.[7] Despite the tax advantages offered to issuing corporations of income bonds, this form of financing has been rare.

Original-Issue Deep-Discount Bonds

As noted earlier in this chapter, as interest rates decline below the coupon rate, the likelihood that an issuer will call an issue increases. A deferred-call provision on a new issue sold near par permits the bondholder to lock in the prevailing interest rate for a limited period of time. But there is still the problem of reinvesting coupon interest payments if interest rates decline even if the issue is not called. As explained in Chapter 4, the interest-on-interest component constitutes a substantial portion of the bond's total return.

Original-issue deep-discount bonds overcome these two drawbacks.[8] First, it is highly improbable that the issuer will call such an issue because the coupon rate is set sufficiently low that it would take a major decline in rates to make early redemption economical for the issuer. Second, less of the bond's total return depends upon the interest-on-interest component. There is also another advantage to the investor who anticipates a decline in interest rates. As illustrated in Chapter 4, as interest rates decline, the price of a deep-discount bond will appreciate more in value than a comparable debt obligation selling at par or at a premium.

---

[7] Warrants to purchase additional bonds are examined in Chapter 23. In Chapter 24, "put" bonds are analyzed.

[8] Original-issue deep-discount bonds are different from seasoned bonds that become deep discount by reason of a coupon rate far below the market yield. In the case of original-issue deep-discount bonds, at the time of offering the issuer intentionally sets the coupon rate below prevailing rates so that the bonds sell at a deep discount.

The first original-issue deep-discount bonds offered by a corporation in the United States were offered by Martin Marietta Corporation.[9] Its $175 million of 7 percent, 30-year debentures was offered in March 1981. The issue, rated A by Moody's, was offered to the public at a price of 53.835 to yield 13.25 percent.[10] Later that month, General Motors Acceptance Corporation became the first high-grade finance company to offer a deep-discount bond. Other corporate issuers quickly jumped on the bandwagon.

The ultimate in corporate original-issue deep-discount notes was brought to the public marketplace on April 22, 1981. J. C. Penney Company, Inc., issued $200 million A-rated zero-coupon notes due May 1, 1989.[11] The issue was priced at 33.427 to yield 14.25. It has been estimated that if the offering had been a standard one, the cost to J. C. Penney would have been 165 basis points higher. Shortly thereafter, General Motors Acceptance Corporation and IBM Credit Corporation issued zero-coupon notes.[12]

Although the holder of an original-issue deep-discount bond and note realizes protection from call, a reduction (or elimination in the case of zero-coupon note) of reinvestment risk during the life of the issue, and greater price appreciation should interest rates decline, *there is a very important tax disadvantage that makes such issues unattractive for portfolio of individual investors and institutions subject to taxation.* As explained in Chapter 3, the original-issue discount must be amortized each year. The amount of the amortization or implicit interest is treated as ordinary income and taxed as such each year. Thus, in the extreme case of a zero-coupon note, a taxable entity will pay taxes on the amount of the amortization even though not a penny in interest may be received![13] This tax aspect of original-issue

---

[9] There were new offerings of moderate discount bonds sold prior to the issuance of the deep-discount bonds by Martin Marietta. For example, in December 1980 Leasco Corporation issued a bond due in 1997 with a coupon rate of 11½ percent and priced at 70 to yield 16.92.

[10] The popularity of the offering made Martin Marietta's management increase the size of its offering from $150 million to $175 million. To get some idea of the cost savings of this type of financing to the issuer, consider the two issues offered by Archer Daniels Midland Co. on May 12, 1981. Both issues matured on May 15, 2011, and were rated A by Moody's. The deep-discount debentures, which carried a 7 percent coupon rate, were priced at 46.25 to yield 15.35 percent. The sinking-fund debentures carried a 16 percent coupon rate and were priced slightly below par to yield 16.08 percent.

[11] A private offering of zero-coupon bonds was made by PepsiCo prior to this offering.

[12] According to The First Boston Corporation, in the first five months of 1982 approximately 40 percent, or $4 billion, of all publicly sold corporate bonds were either zero-coupon bonds or mini-coupon bonds. (Edward P. Foldessy and Jill Bettner, "Tax Break Involving 'Zero-Coupon' Bonds Is Attacked by Treasury, Backed by Issuers," *The Wall Street Journal*, May 19, 1982, p. 56.)

[13] Prior to the Tax Equity and Fiscal Responsibility Act of 1982, there was a tax advantage to corporate issuers because the issuer could deduct the discount ratably as an interest expense. This meant a larger interest expense deduction in the earlier years

deep-discount bonds and notes makes these obligations attractive only to such entities as tax-qualified pension funds that are *not* subject to income taxation from the earnings realized on the portfolios they manage and are *not* concerned with current income.[14] Another advantage of such obligations for pension funds is that if a new original-issue deep-discount bond is selling at a favorable spread over prevailing deep-discount bonds held in their portfolio, a swap can be undertaken without having an adverse impact on the financial statements of the portfolio.[15] This is because bookkeeping practices of many pension funds inhibit the fund's manager from realizing capital losses. Bond swaps that improve a portfolio's return without incurring any additional risk or simply improve the quality of the portfolio may be shunned by a portfolio manager if it means that a capital loss must result. Yet a capital loss may not arise or may be negligible if the newly acquired bond is an original-issue deep-discount bond.

Variable-Rate Notes

Variable-rate notes possess two features. First, the coupon rate changes at prescribed intervals of time based upon the interest rate offered on some specified kind of investment medium, such as the average yield on a category of Treasury obligations. The second feature of variable-rate notes is that an option is granted to the noteholder to require the issuer to redeem the issue at par prior to maturity. Usually, this option is referred to as a put option.

Variable-rate notes are usually referred to as either floating-rate notes or adjustable-rate notes, distinguished by the frequency by which the coupon rate may be changed. For floating-rate notes, the coupon rate may be changed at least every six months. In April 1979 Manufacturers Hanover Corporation issued a seven-year note with a coupon rate that could change weekly.[16] The coupon rate on an adjustable-rate note changes less frequently than semiannually, usually after two or three years have passed. For example, in November 1980 General Motors Acceptance Corporation sold a 10-year adjustable note with a rate fixed at 13.45 percent for the first two years but ad-

---

than if interest expense had been computed on an accrual basis. The new tax law requires that interest expense be computed on an accrual basis. Therefore, in the earlier years the interest expense deduction is smaller, but gradually increases over the life of the bond on a compounding basis. The holder of the bond must now follow the same procedure in computing the interest income.

[14] Zero-coupon bonds are attractive to certain investors because the tax law of certain countries does not require that the investor compute implicit interest, and allows the accrued interest to be treated as a capital gain upon sale or maturity.

[15] Bond swaps are discussed in Chapter 30.

[16] Interest on this issue is paid monthly.

justed annually thereafter. Usually, there is a floor and ceiling placed on the movement of the coupon rate for all variable rate notes.

There is no uniform investment vehicle to which the coupon rates on variable-rate notes are pegged. The Manufacturers Hanover Corporation's floating-rate notes are pegged to the interest rate on one-month, double-A commercial paper. GMAC's 10-year notes are married to the rate on 10-year Treasury obligations. There are even offerings tied to commodity prices. For example, the coupon rate of a 20-year Petro-Lewis Corporation issue varies with the price of sweet crude oil from West Texas. The initial and minimum coupon rate is 13 percent. However, if in a given year the price of sweet crude oil from West Texas increases by more than 10 percent, the coupon rate is increased, up to a maximum of 15.5 percent.

Variable-rate notes made their debut in the U.S. financial market during the high interest-rate environment of 1974.[17] At the time, market participants believed that interest rates would continue to increase. Hence these new instruments were well received by investors. However, investor enthusiasm faded as interest rates declined. No variable-rate notes were issued in 1976 and 1977. In 1979 corporations once again began issuing variable-rate notes. During the first half of 1981, many market participants thought that rates had peaked. Consequently, there were only two offerings during this period.[18]

An investor who purchases a variable-rate note is betting that the present value of the future interest-rate stream from such an offering will be greater than that on a fixed-coupon rate note for the same quality and remaining maturity.

Equity Kickers

As a sweetener to attract investors so that their bonds may be floated at a reduced cost, *equity kickers* have been included in offerings. The various forms of equity kicker are: options to convert the issue to common stock of the issuer or another entity related to the issuer, warrants to acquire common stock from the issuer, and unit packages of debt issues and common stock.

Convertible and exchangeable bonds were briefly described earlier in this chapter, and the analysis of these securities is explained in Chapter 22. Convertible securities have been around a long time and

---

[17] The first such offering was by Citicorp in July 1974. This type of security was available for decades in Europe.

[18] One of these offerings was an original-issue discount, 20-year variable-rate bond priced at 70. This issue by General Felt Industries received a rating of B by Moody's. There was a private placement of adjustable rate bonds by Pacific Gas & Electric Co. during the summer of 1981. This seems to be the first use of this type of financing vehicle by a big utility.

do not represent a new investment vehicle. Neither do common stock warrants, which grant the holder the option to acquire from the issuer a specified number of shares at a specified price within a designated period of time. Common stock warrants are also discussed in Chapter 22. As an example of the last form of equity kicker, consider the Pettibone Corporation 20-year subordinated debentures carrying a coupon of 12.375 percent. When this issue, rated double-A by Moody's, was sold in August 1980, it included six shares of its issuer's common stock for each $1,000 par value bond.

Income Bonds

Bonds contain a promise to pay a stipulated amount of interest periodically to bondholders. The amount may be fixed or may vary according to some specified index. Ordinarily, failure to make an interest payment in full is a default, or breach of contract. Income bonds, on the other hand, contain a promise to pay a stipulated interest, but payment is contingent on earnings being sufficient for the purpose. The bond indenture sets forth the items to be deducted from revenue in determining earnings for purposes of interest payments to the holders of income bonds. Repayment of the principal, however, is not subject to sufficient earnings.

The interest payments are declared by the board of directors, just as dividends are declared on preferred stock and common stock. The discretion allowed the board of directors in declaring interest varies. Some bond indentures require that the board must declare and pay interest if earned. Other indentures permit the board to allocate a portion of the earnings that the board considers appropriate for capital expenditures or other purposes before determining the amount of interest to declare.[19]

Interest may be cumulative or noncumulative. In the former case, the issuer contracts that interest not paid on schedule, or any unpaid part of the interest, must be paid in the future. Usually, there is a limitation to the amount that may be accumulated of three times the annual coupon rate.[20] If interest payments are noncumulative, interest not paid on scheduled dates is just forgotten. Income bonds may be convertible. They may be callable and require sinking-fund payments. They may or may not be subordinated to other debt incurred by the issuer.[21] Because interest is contingent on earnings, income bonds are traded flat (i.e. without accrued interest).

---

[19] Benjamin Graham, David L. Dodd, and Sidney Cottle, *Security Analysis*, 4th ed. (New York: McGraw-Hill, 1962) pp. 393–94.

[20] Ibid., p. 331.

[21] John J. McConnell and Gary G. Schlarbaum, "Another Foray Into the Backwaters of the Market," *The Journal of Portfolio Management*, Fall 1980, p. 62.

Initially, income bonds were the product of the reorganization of bankrupt railroads. Income bonds issued in this way, known as adjustment bonds, were considered highly speculative because of the uncertainty surrounding the issuer's ability to repay the principal and make the scheduled interest payments. However, in the 1950s, some firms began issuing income bonds because of the tax advantage of this form of financing to the issuer. The tax advantage is that interest, unlike dividends, is a tax-deductible expense thereby reducing the aftertax cost of funds to the issuer. Although there were a few cases in which new money was raised by issuing income bonds, most of these bonds were issued in exchange for preferred stock.

Surprisingly, corporations have shunned the use of income bonds in spite of recommendations by some members of the investment community calling for greater use.[22] The late Benjamin Graham suggested that the reluctance of corporations to issue income bonds occurs because management may believe such offerings are associated with financially weak companies, since historically these bonds often arise out of reorganization. In a 1974 study Sidney Robbins found that the professional money managers he surveyed were reluctant to acquire income bonds for their portfolios.[23] In fact, he found a number of professional money managers who had never heard of income bonds!

Income bonds have more of the characteristics of preferred stock than of a bond.[24] Therefore, they should be evaluated in the same way preferred stock is evaluated. Before leaving our discussion of income bonds, however, it is worth noting the conclusions of a recent empirical study by John McConnell and Gary Schlarbaum of the performance of income bonds:

> One moral that may be derived from this study is that those institutional portfolio managers that have shunned income bonds as an inferior investment may wish to rethink their position. Although investments in income bonds are unlikely to provide superior performance, they may add a dimension of diversification not currently present in institutional portfolios. In an age of "market funds" and optimal diversification strategies, this added element of diversification may merit consideration. Our results would certainly support such a conclusion.[25]

---

[22] See for example: Leo Barnes, "A Do-It-Yourself Way to Cut Taxes," *Business Week*, May 5, 1975, pp. 21–22; and Harold Bierman and B. Brown, "Why Corporations Should Consider Income Bonds," *Financial Executive*, October 1967, pp. 74–78.

[23] Sidney Robbins, *An Objective Look at Income Bonds* (Boston: Envision Press, 1974).

[24] Preferred stock is discussed in Chapter 13.

[25] McConnell and Schlarbaum, "Another Foray Into the Backwaters of the Market," pp. 64–65.

SOURCES OF INFORMATION ABOUT CORPORATE BOND OFFERINGS

For a new corporate bond offering, an investor can obtain a prospectus. The prospectus is a statement filed by the issuer with the Securities and Exchange Commission containing all of the pertinent information about the security being offered and the company offering the security.

Summary information about a new offering is provided in *Moody's Bond Survey*. This service is published weekly and provides information on the business of the issuer, how the issuer will use the proceeds, the quality rating of the issue as assigned by Moody's, denominations available, the form of the security (registered or bearer), exchange options, security for the bonds, guarantees, call provisions, sinking-fund requirements, restrictions on management, and statistical highlights about the issuer. Exhibit 1 is a sample write-up of a new offering taken from *Moody's Bond Survey*. This service not only provides information on new offerings, but also on proposed offerings. The *Bond Outlook*, published weekly by Standard & Poor's, provides similar information. These weekly publications are usually carried by local libraries.

For seasoned issues, major contractual provisions are provided in *Moody's Manuals*. To obtain basic information about a seasoned corporate issue, the investor can check the monthly publication by either Moody's (*Moody's Bond Record*) or Standard & Poor's (*Standard & Poor's Bond Guide*). Exhibit 2 is a sample page taken from the former, and Exhibit 3 is taken from the latter.

YIELDS ON CORPORATE BONDS

Differences in Yields by Bond Ratings

At any one time, the yields that investors obtain by purchasing bonds in the market vary according to how investors' estimate the uncertainty of future payment of dollar amounts of interest and principal exactly as set forth in bond indentures. This uncertainty is often called *financial risk* because it depends upon the financial ability of issuers to make those payments. If an issuer can pay, it will. Failure by a company to pay usually means intervention of a court of law on behalf of bondholders and court supervision of conduct of the business. In any event, a default is a disaster for an issuer.

Professional bond investors have ways of analyzing information about companies and bond issues to estimate the uncertainty of future ability to pay. These techniques are explained in Chapter 14. However, most individual bond investors and many institutional bond in-

Exhibit 1
Write-Up of a New Issue from Moody's Bond Survey

Cleveland Electric Illuminating Company

. . . has filed an S-16 registration statement covering $75 million of first mortgage bonds. due March 1, 2012, to be offered on February 24, through Morgan Stanley & Co. Inc., Merrill Lynch White Weld Capital Markets Group, and Salomon Brothers Inc.

Quality & Rating: Upper medium grade; A.

In July 1981, Moody's reduced Cleveland Electric's first mortgage bond rating to **A** to reflect the deterioration in debt-protection measurements which had occurred over the prior three years. The principal causes of the deterioration were reduced sales, particularly industrial sales, rising operating costs, and an ambitious construction program in a period of high capital costs.

In January 1980, the company, along with the other participants in the CAPCO projects, canceled four of the seven planned CAPCO nuclear units. Although the Ohio commission allowed the company to write off its investment in these units over ten years and to recover its investment through rates, a recent Ohio Supreme Court decision reversed that position, based on the intent of the controlling statute. The company appealed to the U.S. Supreme Court but was denied a hearing for procedural reasons. However, the company may file further appeals. Although the cancellations reduced the company's construction program, cost increases have been announced for the remaining three units. Additionally, Cleveland as one of the stronger participants, has increased its share of the Perry plant to 31% from about $24. The company thus continues to face an extensive construction and financing program.

As evident in *Statical Overview*, 1981's operating results improved modestly over the prior three years'. Return on equity increased to 12.6%, but is still far from the 16.22% allowed in May of 1981. Further rate relief should provide some improvement in financial strength or at least stabilization at more recent levels. The company anticipates a decision within six weeks on its $130 million rate case filed in May 1981. The case incorporates a projected test-year and requests at least a 17% return on equity. Additionally, Cleveland has filed with the commission a notice of intent to file for additional revenue of $221 million.

Purpose: The net proceeds from the sale will be used to pay a portion of outstanding short-term debt incurred to finance the company's construction program and for general corporate purposes. Short-term debt is expected to aggregate $90 million immediately before the sale.

Construction expenditures for the period 1982-1986 are estimated at $1,775 million, including AFUDC but excluding nuclear fuel. Refundings and preferred requirements could total $473.3 million during the period.

Form: The bonds will be issued in fully registered form only, in denominations of $1,000 and multiples thereof. They will bear interest as set forth in their title, payable semiannually on March 1 and September 1, beginning September 1, 1982.

Call Feature: Nonrefundable at lower interest cost to the company before March 1, 1987; otherwise, callable at prices to be supplied by amendment.

Replacement and Sinking Fund: Not applicable to this issue.

Security: The new bonds will rank equally with outstanding series of bonds issued under the mortgage which constitute a first lien on all fixed property now owned or hereafter acquired, other than specified exceptions, and subject to permissable encumbrances.

Additional bonds may be issued under the lien of the mortgage on the basis of: (a) 70% of net property additions; (b) bonds retired; (c) deposit of cash; provided all pro forma interest requirements will have been covered at least two times in a recent 12-month period.

Business: The company furnishes electric service to approximately 710,600 customers in a 1,700-square-mile area in northeastern Ohio, including Cleveland. The company derives about 70% of its total electric revenue from customers outside Cleveland. The company also provides steam service for heating and other purposes in Cleveland's downtown area. Approximately 99% of operating revenue comes from the sale of electric energy. In 1980, 31% of total electric revenue of $878.5 million came from residential sales, 25% from commercial sales, 37% from industrial sales, 5% from sales to utilities, and 2% from other sales.

The net system capability expected to be available to the company during the summer of 1981 is 4,567 mw. The net 60-minute peak load of the company's service area, excluding interruptible load, which occurred on July 20, 1977, was 3,350 mw. The company owns and operates all or a portion of five fossil-fuel plants, a 457-mw share of Davis-Besse, and a 305-mw share of a pumped storage hydroelectric plant. In 1980, approximately 92% of the company's electric generation was produced through the operation of its coal-fired and pumped storage hydroelectric units, 7% from its nuclear Davis-Besse Unit, and the remainder from the oil-fired units. The CAPCO group of which the company is a member has three nuclear units under construction: two 1,205-mw Perry units and an 833-mw unit, Beaver Valley 2, scheduled for completion in 1984, 1988, and 1986, respectively. The company's ownership in the Perry units and the Beaver Valley Unit 2 is 31.11% and

24.47%, respectively. This construction program is designed to provide the company with adequate capacity through 1990 based on a 3% compound growth in demand annually in the 1981-83 period and growth of about 2% compounded annually for 1983-90.

Regulation: The company is subject to regulation by the Public Utility Commission of Ohio (PUCO), the FERC, the NRC, and various environmental protection agencies. The company also is subject to the jurisdiction of the Pennsylvania Public Utility Commission with respect to its ownership interests in generating facilities in Pennsylvania.

On May 4, 1981, the PUCO granted the company a $143.4 million increase in rates to be effective on May 6, 1981. The new rates were based on a 11.76% return on rate base and a 16.22% return on common equity. On June 3, 1981, a $4.5 million additional increase was granted by the PUCO, correcting certain errors in the PUCO's computation of the initial increase. The $147.8 million total increase is approximately 88% of the $168.1 million the company had requested. Although the PUCO approved the concept of determining rates on the basis of a forecast test-year, it denied the company's request for a future test-year because it concluded that more information was necessary to ensure that the interests of all parties were considered. On May 1, 1981, the company filed an application with the PUCO requesting an electric rate increase of $135 million, or 13%, which, if approved, would be effective in the first quarter of 1982. As a result of the additional $4.5 million increase received in June 1981, the requested increase has been lowered to approximately $130 million. Hearings concluded on February 1, 1982, and a decision is pending. The company filed documentation for a projected test-year ended December 31, 1982, and an historical test-year ended September 15, 1982.

On November 13, 1981, the company filed a notice of intent to file an application for an additional $221 million electric rate increase. The company anticipates filing in the first quarter of 1982.

Statistical Overview (dollars in millions):

	1981	1980	1979	1978	1977
Revenue	$1,012.9	$893.6	$824.3	$717.1	$659.3
Interest expense	146.7	112.6	85.3	72.1	67.9
Net income	155.7	125.4	117.7	99.0	111.7
[1] SEC cover. incl. AFUDC	2.37x	2.33x	2.67x	2.59x	3.16x
SEC coverage excl. AFUDC	1.82x	1.76x	2.11x	2.05x	2.45x
[2] Return on common equity	12.6%	11.2%	12.0%	11.2%	15.5%
[3] Margin of safety	20.4	17.1	17.8	16.6	22.7
Construction expenditure	$409.3	$398.1	$385.9	$300.8	$286.7
[4] Less AFUDC	83.0	65.9	49.2	40.9	49.0
Net construction expend.	$326.3	$332.2	$336.7	$259.9	$237.7
Maturities & sinking fund	13.0	31.8	. . .	56.0	. . .
Working capital requirements	(14.6)	51.7	(6.1)	(104.5)	29.7
Total cash needs	$324.7	$415.7	$330.6	$211.4	$267.4
[5] Internal cash generated	$68.6	$41.7	$52.1	$50.8	$77.0
as a percentage of:					
Net construction expend.	21%	12.6%	15.5%	19.5%	32.4%
Total cash needs	21.1	10.0	15.8	24.0	28.8
Total debt	4.8	3.1	4.7	5.4	8.5
Depreciation rate	3.4%	3.4%	3.3%	3.3%	3.3%
Effective tax rate	26.0	18.0	19.7	16.8	25.5
AFUDC/Net income	53.3	52.6	41.8	41.3	43.9
Dividend payout ratio	82.0	88.5	79.3	83.6	60.5
Total capital	$2,868.8	$2,656.9	$2,266.8	$1,979.9	$1,823.3
Short-term debt	4.0%	6.7%	6.4%	1.2%	1.3%
Long-term debt	46.3	45.6	43.0	46.5	48.6
Total debt	50.3	52.3	49.4	47.7	49.9
Preferred & preference	14.7	13.4	14.4	16.5	15.4
Common & surplus	35.0	34.3	36.2	35.8	34.7
Construction expend./					
Total capital	14.3%	15.0%	17.0%	15.2%	15.7%
Current ratio	0.74	0.64	0.57	0.83	1.34

[1] Fixed-charge coverage. Pro forma, 2.13. [2] Average. [3] Net income plus income taxes divided by revenue. [4] Allowance for funds used during construction. [5] Net income plus deferred taxes plus deferred investment tax credit plus depreciation minus dividends minus AFUDC.

Capitalization: As of December 31, 1981, and pro forma reflecting the proposed sale of $75 million of first mortgage bonds the sale of common stock in January ($60.8 million) and the partial payment of short-term debt estimated to be $90 million immediately before the sale.

	Actual (000)	% of Total	Pro Forma (000)	% of Total
[1] Short-term debt	$115,108	3.7	$35,145	1.1
Mortgage bonds	1,092,291	35.2	$1,167,291	36.9
Term bank loans	134,000	4.3	134,000	4.3
Pollution control	57,945	1.9	57,945	1.8
[2] Other debt	44,168	1.4	44,168	1.4
Total debt	$1,443,512	46.5	$1,438,549	45.5
[3] Preferred stock	366,071	11.8	366,071	11.6
Preference stock	57,000	1.8	57,000	1.8
[4] Common & surplus	1,002,206	32.3	1,063,006	33.6
Def. tax & inv. credit	236,481	7.6	236,481	7.5
Total capital	$3,105,270	100.0	$3,161,107	100.0

[1] Includes $20,145,000 of long-term debt due within one year. [2] Consists of $23. million collateralized pledge, $20 million of promissory notes, and $268,000 of oth debt. [3] Outstanding 496,000 shares of redeemable preferred in eight series an 950,710 shares of nonredeemable preferred in two series. [4] Outstanding 51,054,5(shares of common stock without par value; pro forma 55,054,503 shares.

Exhibit 2
Sample Page from *Moody's Bond Record*

MOODY'S BOND RECORD — Cons-Dams 17

Issue	Interest Dates	Current Call Price	Moody's Rating	Current Price		Yield to Mat.	Price Range 1981 High	1981 Low	1946-80 High	1946-80 Low	Amt. Outst. Mil.$	Sink. Fund Prov.	Legal Status	Fed. Tax	(Mil. Dol.) Current Assets Liab. — Times Charges Earned — Annual 1978 1979 1980 Interim
• Consumers Power Co. 1st9.75 2006	J&J 1	108.07▲	Baa r	58	sale	17.04	71	56¾	108½	62½	60.0	Yes	1	N	Issued 7-7-76 @ 100.00 -yield 9.75
• do 1st 9.00 2006	A&O 1	107.45▲	Baa r	55	sale	16.63	66	52⅛	103⅛	60	60.0	Yes	1	N	Issued 5-24-77 @ 99.50 -yield
• do 1st 8.875 2007	J&D 1	§107.66▲	Baa r	53½	bid	16.83	67½	50⅜	103	58⅛	85.0	Yes	1	N	Refundable from 6-1-82 @ 107.35
• do 1st 8.625 2007	A&O15	§107.44▲	Baa r	50⅜	sale	17.36	63	50	98¼	55	100	Yes	1	N	Refundable from 10-15-82 @ 107.14
• do 1st 9.00 2008	M&S15	§108.07▲	Baa r	56	sale	16.27	65	51	97½	62½	75.0	Yes	1	N	Refundable from 9-15-83 @ 107.45
do 1st10.375 2009	M&N 1	§109.03▲	Baa r	59	bid	17.70	69½	60	103	67½	100	Yes	1	N	Refundable from 5-1-84 @ 108.03
do 1st12.375 2010	J&D15	§110.99▲	Baa r	70½	bid	17.61	84	68	103	78⅜	75.0	Yes	1	N	Refundable from 6-15-85 @ 109.42
do 1st12.50 2010	J&J15	§110.94▲	Baa r	71½	bid	17.54	83	70	102½	80	100	Yes	1	N	Refundable from 1-15-85 @ 109.73
do s.f.deb. 4.625 1994	M&S 1	102.77▲	Ba r	----		-----	38	32	103¼	36	33.4	101.23	1	N	Issued 9-10-64 @ 102.046-yield 4.50
Container Corp. s.f.deb.4.40 1987 [1]	J&D 1	100.60▲	A	58	bid	16.56	63⅜	56½	103¾	48½	10.1	100.00	3	N	Issued 6-13-62 @ 100.00 -yield 4.40
do s.f.deb. 6.625 1993	M&S15	102.25▲	A r	49	bid	16.97	59	49⅛	102	59¼	19.7	100.00	3	N	Issued 3-19-68 @ 100.00 -yield 6.63
Continental Bank (Pa.) cap.nts.7.50 1983 [2]	A&O 1	[3] 100.00	— r	91⅛	bid	16.18	90⅝	85½	99¾	80	25.0	No	-------	N	Issued 4-5-73 @ 99.25 -yield 7.61
• Continental Can deb.5.75 1985 [4]	A&O 1	100.63▲	A	71⅜	bid	16.46	75¼	74⅜	105	68⅝	13.8	100.00	13	N	1,214 853.8 3.98 4.39 3.96 --------
• Continental Grp. Inc. deb.8.50 1990	F&A 1	102.50▲	A r	69½	sale	14.95	76⅛	65	110½	69	32.9	Yes	3	N	Issued 7-22-70 @ 99.50 -yield 8.55
• do s.f.deb. 8.85 2004	M&N15	§106.37▲	A r	60	ask	15.15	66	58	104⅞	63	75.0	100.00	3	N	Refundable from 5-15-84 @ 105.31
• do s.f.deb.12.30 2005	M&N 1	§111.69▲	A r	---		-----	82	82	103½	103½	100	Yes	3	N	Refundable from 5-1-90 @ 106.15
• do s.f.deb. 8.85 2008	M&N 1	§107.79▲	A r	---		-----	66¼	59	101	60⅛	75.0	Yes	3	N	Refundable from 5-1-88 @ 105.31
Continental Grp. Over. gtd.nts.9.625 1986	JUL 1	[5] 101.00▲	A	k 83⅛	bid	14.99	85⅞	78¾	100	83¼	100	No	-------	F	Issued 6-25-79 @ 100.00 -yield 9.625
• Continental Ill. Corp. nts.8.50 1985	M&N 1	[6] 100.00	Aaa r	82	sale	14.94	85⅛	74¾	100¾	76	100	No	23	N	Issued 5-3-78 @ 99.75 -yield 8.55
• do nts.13.625 1985 [7]	M&N 1	N.C.	Aaa r	----		-----	100	100	---	---	100	No	-------	N	Issued 11-4-81 @ 100.00 -yield 13.625
• do flt.rt.nts.15.35 1987 [8,10]	M&N 1	[9] 100.00	Aaa r	95¾	sale	16.59	98	88¾	100⅛	88¼	200	No	23	N	Issued 4-19-79 @ 100.00 -yield 10.60
• do flt.rt.nts.16.80 1989 [11]	M&S15	[12] 100.00	Aaa r	100⅛	bid	16.77	102	97½	103¾	95⅜	31.9	No	3	N	Issued 8-29-74 @ 99.50 -yield 6.352
Continental Ill.O/S gtd.euronts.14.75 1984 [13]	SEPT 7	100.00	Aaa	----		-----	---	---	---	---	------	No	-------	F	Issued 8-19-81 @ 99.75 -yield 14.50
• Continental Oil s.f.deb.3.00 1984 [14]	M&N 1	100.29▲	Aa	----		-----	80⅛	80	101½	60	12.0	100.12	123	N	3,424 2,491 10.5 15.8 25.3 --------
• do s.f.deb. 4.50 1991	M&N 1	101.25▲	Aa	54¼	sale	13.21	59¼	48⅜	104¾	56	38.0	100.00	13	N	Issued 5-3-61 @ 99.25 -yield 4.53
• do s.f.deb. 7.50 1999	J&J15	103.25▲	Aa r	54¼	sale	14.93	64¾	48⅛	105	61	87.9	Yes	23	N	Issued 6-26-69 @ 99.75 -yield 7.45
• do s.f.deb. 9.125 1999	M&N 1	§105.77▲	Aa r	64	sale	14.96	75¾	60½	108⅝	67	150	Yes	23	N	Refundable from 11-1-84 @ 104.44
• do s.f.deb. 8.875 2001	J&D 1	§106.47▲	Aa r	---		-----	72	60	107	70	200	Yes	23	N	Refundable from 6-1-86 @ 104.32
• **CONTINENTAL TEL.** nts.10.50 1983	M&N 1	100.00	Baa r	95	sale	15.05	96¼	89	111	86½	75.0	No	------	N	Issued 5-6-75 @ 99.75 -yield 10.55
Continental Tel. Cal. 1st8.00 I 1996	M&N 1	104.96▲	A r	52	bid	16.94	60	52½	107½	55	12.0	Yes	3	N	Issued 11-17-71 @ 100.50 -yield 7.95
do 1st 7.625 J 1997	[15] J&J 1	104.77▲	A r	49	bid	16.98	56½	49½	99	51	10.0	Yes	3	N	Issued 1-10-73 @ 100.00 -yield 7.625
CONTROL DATA s.f.deb.5.00 1985	M&N 1	100.90▲	Baa r	---		-----	70	61	100⅝	60	18.0	100.14	------	N	1,219 684.6 3.96 4.83 4.52 -------
• do s.f.deb. 5.50 1987	J&D 1	101.30▲	Baa r	66¾	sale	14.03	65⅞	55⅛	90	58¼	30.8	Yes	------	N	Issued 12-12-67 @ 90.00 -yield 6.39
Conwood Corp. sub.deb.6.00 1991	J&D 1	101.80▲	Baa r	54	bid	15.14	64	54	72	60	2.41	Yes	------	N	73.2 17.7 26.0 22.7 36.8 [16]-----------
• **COOPER LAB.** deb.10.50 1992 [17]	J&J 1	100.00	— r	68⅝	bid	17.03	79	65⅛	105	66	6.16	Yes	------	N	Issued 8-27-76 @ -yield
• Copperwld. Corp. s.f.deb.7.875 2001	J&D15	§105.34▲	A r	----		-----	---	---	99¼	71½	27.0	Yes	23	N	Refundable from 12-15-86 @ 103.56
CORDIS CORP. s.f.sub.deb.12.25 1999	J&D15	§109.60▲	B r	58	bid	21.58	74	58	99½	71	19.9	Yes	------	N	Refundable from 6-15-84 @ 106.00
• Corn Prod Co. s.f.deb.5.75 1992 [18]	F&A15	101.58▲	Aa r	54¾	bid	14.13	61	54¾	100	52¼	56.6	Yes	123	N	Issued 6-20-67 @ 99.50 -yield 5.79
• do sub.deb. 4.625 1983	A&O 1	100.00	A	88	sale	12.86	86	80	106¼	64	27.4	Alt	3	N	1,223 803.5 7.97 8.07 5.29 ------
• Corning Glass s.f.deb.7.75 1998	M&N15	§104.65▲	Aa r	52⅛	bid	16.06	67	50⅛	101	65	50.0	Yes	23	N	Refundable from 11-15-83 @ 103.875
Corning Int'l gtd.s.f.eurodeb.8.50 1986 [19]	[20] MAR 15	101.50▲	Aa	k 87¾	bid	12.38	88¼	84	106⅞	86	10.5	Yes	------	F	Issued 3-16-71 @ 100.00 -yield 8.50
CP National Corp. deb.10.375 1991	[21] MJS&D	[22] 105.00▲	Ba r	68	bid	17.40	76½	62½	96¼	60⅛	14.8	No	------	N	23.0 35.9 1.47 2.32 2.26 -----------
do deb.16.50 1996 [23]		[24] 100.00	Ba	----		-----	100	100	---	---	15.0	No	------	N	Issued 9-11-81 @ 100.00 -yield 16.50
CPC Finance N.V. gtd.nts.16.75 1986 [25]			Aa	----		-----	---	---	---	---	50.0		------	F	Issued 9-10-81 @ 100.00 -yield 16.75
• **CRANE CO.** s.f.deb.6.50 1992	J&D 1	102.30▲	Baa r	60	bid	13.91	63	60	102⅞	58	20.1	100.00	------	N	Issued 8-17-67 @ 100.00 -yield 6.50
• do s.f.sub.deb. 8.00 1985 [17]	J&D 1	100.00	— r	84½	bid	13.29	88	78¼	98	76	30.7	Yes	------	N	Issued Dec 1975 @ -yield
• do sub.deb. 7.00 1993	A&O 1	100.00	Ba r	53¼	sale	16.18	57	48½	100	52⅛	11.9	Yes	------	N	462.8 209.2 2.69 2.56 2.44 --------
• do s.f.sub.deb.10.50 1994 [17]	F&A 1	100.00	— r	71½	bid	15.88	80	65	98½	73	54.4	No	------	N	Issued 12-27-78 @ -yield
• do sub.deb. 7.00 B 1994 [26]	J&J 1	100.00	Ba r	49⅞	sale	16.69	57	48	85	51	48.3	No	------	N	Issued 1969 @ -yield
• Credithrift Fin. zero cpn. 1990 [27]	[28]	100.00	A r	28	bid	-----	28¾	28	---	---	28.8	No	------	N	Issued 11-20-81 @ 28.75 -yield 14.34
• do sr.nts.15.50 1991	J&D1	[29] 100.00	A r	98¼	sale	15.86	100	100	---	---	75.0	No	------	N	Issued 11-20-81 @ 100.00 -yield 15.50
• do sr.deb. 8.00 1992	F&A 1	[30] 103.30▲	A r	60	sale	16.21	71¼	52¼	103½	58	22.4	Yes	3	N	Issued 2-8-72 @ 99.50 -yield 8.05
• do sr.nts. 9.00 1986	J&D15	[31] 100.00	A r	80⅞	sale	14.63	85	70⅛	104½	71	30.0	No	3	N	Issued 12-10-76 @ 99.375 -yield 9.10
• do sr.nts. 8.20 1987	J&D15	[32] 100.00	A r	67	bid	17.39	73	65	101	64¼	50.0	No	3	N	Issued 6-21-77 @ 99.80 -yield 8.23
• do sr.nts. 8.75 1988	M&N 1	[33] 100.00	A r	71¼	sale	15.83	76	68	100¾	72	35.0	No	3	N	Issued 10-25-77 @ 99.625 -yield 8.80
• do sr.nts.10.25 1989	A&O15	[34] 100.00	A r	73	bid	16.86	83	69	99¾	72⅛	35.0	No	3	N	Issued 4-24-79 @ 99.40 -yield 10.35
• do sub.nts. 9.375 1992	M&N 1	[35] 102.62▲	Baa r	62½	bid	17.12	71	59⅝	99¾	63⅛	15.0	Yes	------	N	Issued 10-25-77 @ 99.80 -yield 9.40
• do sub.nts.10.50 1994	A&O15	[36] 102.79▲	Baa r	66	bid	17.26	73	73	99¼	78	15.0	Yes	------	N	Issued 4-24-79 @ 99.25 -yield 10.60
Crocker Cit. Nat'l. cap.nts.4.60 1989	A&O 1	100.69▲	— r	47	bid	18.09	57½	47	99⅛	51	38.8	Yes	------	N	Issued 3-26-64 @ 100.00 -yield 4.60
• **CROCKER NAT'L** deb.8.60 2002	J&D 1	[37] 104.05▲	Aa r	56¾	sale	15.69	68½	53	99½	60	100	Yes	23	N	Issued 12-13-77 @ 99.50 -yield 8.65
• do flt.rt.nts.10.00 1994 [38]	F&A 1	[39] 100.00	Aa r	97	sale	10.43	99	93⅛	103¼	96	7.64	No	3	N	Issued 8-23-74 @ 100.00 -yield 7.45
• Crown Cork & Seal s.f.deb.4.375 1988	M&S15	101.41▲	A	69	bid	11.59	69	68½	101¼	60	7.48	100.51	23	N	496.3 358.0 12.0 8.44 9.50 --------
Crown Ind. Inc. sub.deb.12.00 1993 [40]	[41]	[42] 106.00▲	— r	75	bid	17.01	77	69½	100	77	6.00	Yes	------	N	Issued 9-15-78 @ 100.00 -yield 12.00
do sub.deb.12.00 1994 [40]	[43]	[39] 106.00▲	— r	75	bid	16.85	77	69½	100	80½	4.00	Yes	------	N	Issued 7-26-79 @ 100.00 -yield 12.00
• Crown Zellerbach s.f.deb.8.875 2000	M&S15	105.11▲	A r	57⅛	sale	16.29	74	54	112¼	65⅛	95.0	Yes	3	N	858.2 472.3 4.68 5.54 4.44 ---------
• do s.f.deb. 9.25 2005	M&S15	§107.03▲	A r	58	sale	16.27	75	58⅛	109¼	68	75.0	Yes	3	N	Refundable from 3-15-85 @ 105.55
• Crucible Inc. 1st6.875 E 1992 [44]	J&D15	101.99▲	A r	57¼	sale	14.95	61	50	103⅛	55	13.2	Yes	3	N	Issued 1-10-68 @ 99.75 -yield 6.90
• **CRYSTAL OIL CO.** sub.deb.12.625 1990	J&D15	§108.84▲	B r	77½	bid	17.91	89¾	76¼	107	81	20.0	Yes	------	N	Refundable from 6-15-88 @ 100.00
• do sub.deb.13.75 2000	J&J15	§112.38▲	B r	75	sale	18.57	88	69⅝	94¾	85	35.0	Yes	------	N	Refundable from 7-15-85 @ 106.875
• CTI Int'l. Inc. nts.15.00 1987	M&S15	[45] 100.00	Ba r	90⅛	sale	17.85	98	85⅛	---	---	50.0	No	------	N	Issued 9-10-80 @ 100.00 -yield 15.00
• Cuba (Rep. of) ext.4.50 1977 [46]	[47] †12-31-60		—	10½	bid	flat	18	10	118	9⅞	44.4	Yes	------	F	Issued 12-31-53 @ -yield
• Culbro Corp. sub.deb.11.50 2005 [17]	A&O 1	108.10▲	— r	65	sale	17.87	75	62	110⅛	65	4.02	Yes	------	N	Issued 11-10-75 @ -yield
• Cummins Engine s.f.deb.8.875 1995	A&O15	103.44▲	Baa r	55⅛	bid	17.66	66	55	111	67½	26.9	Yes	3	N	632.4 327.5 12.0 4.62 1.03 ---------
do s.f.deb. 7.40 1997	A&O 1	§104.07▲	Baa r	48	bid	17.09	56	48	100⅜	58	20.0	Yes	3	N	Refundable from 4-1-82 @ 103.70
Curtis Pub. sub.inc.deb.6.00 1986 [48]	A&O 1	104.00▲	Caa	50	bid	flat	26	20	88	20	0.95	No	-------	N	Issued 1956 @ -yield
Cutler-Hammer s.f.deb.5.75 1992 [49]	M&N 1	101.50▲	A r	60	bid	12.89	80	54¾	100⅝	60	11.3	100.41	3	N	Issued 5-9-67 @ 100.625-yield 5.70
• Cyprus Mines s.f.deb.8.50 2001 [50]	A&O15	§106.38▲	Aaa r	53⅜	bid	16.63	---	---	100¾	96¾	100	Yes	3	N	Refundable from 4-15-86 @ 104.25
• do nts. 8.75 1985	J&J15	[51] 100.00	Aaa r	85	sale	15.24	89	79⅛	106⅛	77¼	100	No	3	N	Issued 1-14-75 @ 99.50 -yield 8.83
• Czechoslovakia (Gov't) ext.6.00 1960	†10-1-52			49¾	bid	flat	53	43	56	7	0.93	No	-------	F	Issued 4-1-22 @ 96.50 -yield
Dallas Pwr. & Lt. 1st3.50 1983	M&S 1	100.00▲	Aaa	85⅝	bid	18.87	87	80½	105	60	9.00	100.00	123	N	64.9 133.3 3.11 3.21 4.00 12mJun4.36
do 1st 4.25 1986	J&D 1	100.81▲	Aaa	60⅜	bid	16.45	64	59	104⅛	58⅞	10.0	100.23	123	N	Issued 12-4-56 @ 100.848-yield 4.20
do 1st 3.125 1986	F&A 1	100.39▲	Aaa	60½	bid	17.18	63	59	100⅝	52½	10.0	100.14	123	N	Issued 2-16-56 @ 100.68 -yield 3.09
do 1st 4.25 1993	F&A 1	101.82▲	Aaa	41	bid	15.66	47	40½	101	42	25.0	100.53	123	N	Issued 1-30-63 @ 101.019-yield 4.19
do 1st 4.875 1996	J&J 1	102.53▲	Aaa	39	bid	15.86	46	38½	---	43	20.0	100.49	123	N	Issued 1-18-66 @ 100.75 -yield 4.83
do 1st 5.375 1997	F&A 1	103.72▲	Aaa	40¾	bid	15.80	48	40	111	45	16.0	101.60	123	N	Issued 1-26-67 @ 102.33 -yield 5.22
do 1st 9.375 2000	J&D 1	106.93▲	Aaa r	61¾	bid	15.82	71½	61½	114⅛	70	30.0	101.56	123	N	Issued 5-25-70 @ 101.774-yield 9.21
do 1st 7.375 2001	M&N 1	105.98▲	Aaa r	48¾	bid	15.97	57	48½	101¾	56	30.0	101.51	123	N	Issued 11-3-71 @ 101.75 -yield 7.23
do 1st 7.625 2002	M&S 1	106.54▲	Aaa r	50	bid	15.95	58½	50	102⅛	57	30.0	101.64	123	N	Issued 9-21-72 @ 101.845-yield 7.47
do 1st 8.875 2005	M&S 1	107.50▲	Aaa r	57⅛	bid	15.89	66½	57	107½	65	50.0	100.94	123	N	Issued 2-26-75 @ 101.00 -yield 8.80
do 1st15.125 2011	J&D1	§114.50▲	Aaa r	----		-----	99⅜	94	---	---	50.0	Yes	3	N	Refundable from 6-1-86 @ 112.00
do s.f.deb. 4.50 1989	F&A 1	101.66▲	Aa	53	bid	15.85	58	52½	102½	49	10.9	100.84	13	N	Issued 2-12-64 @ 102.125-yield 4.36
do s.f.deb. 6.75 1993	F&A 1	103.58▲	Aa	----		-----	60	56	104¼	56	12.0	101.16	13	N	Issued 2-14-68 @ 101.824-yield 6.60
• Damson Oil Corp. sub.deb.13.20 2000 [52]	F&A 1	§111.88▲	B r	68	sale	19.70	82	64½	85¼	75¼	20.0	Yes	-------	N	Refundable from 8-1-85 @ 106.60

[1]Sub. of Mobil Corp. [2]Norristown. [3]Fr. 4-15-82. [4] Now Continental Group(Coupon formerly 4.625). [5]Fr. 7-1-82. [6]Fr. 6-1-85. [7]Issued w.w. to purch. $200 mill. zero cpn. deb. due 11-1-89. [8]Int. fr.11-1-81 thru 4-30-82. [9]Fr.5-1-86. [10]Conv. prior to 5-1-86 into 8.50s deb. due 2004. [11]Int. Fr.9-15-81 to 3-14-82. [12]Fr.8-15-84. [13]Gtd. by Cont'l Ill. Corp; eurodollar financing, w.w. to purchase 200 mill. dollars zero coupon bonds due 9-7-88. [14]Now Conoco Inc. [15]Due 12-31-97. [16]Exchange for preferred. [17]Exchange offer. [18]Now CPC Int'l Inc. [19]Sub. of Corning Glass Works. [20]Due 3-15-86. [21]Int. payable at end of month; Due 6-30-91. [22]Fr. 7-1-84. [23]Int. dates: D31, M31, J30 & S30. Due 9-30-96. [24]Fr. 9-30-83. [25]Gtd. by CPC Int'l, Inc. [26]Exchange 1969. [27]Zero cpn. sr. nts. [28]Due 12-1-90. [29]Fr. 12-1-88. [30]Fr. 2-1-82. [31]Fr. 12-15-83. [32]Fr. 12-15-84. [33]Fr. 11-1-85. [34]Fr. 4-15-86. [35]Fr. 11-1-87. [36]Fr. 4-15-89. [37]Fr. 12-1-87. [38]Int. rate fr. 8-1-81 thru 1-31-82. [39]Fr. 8-1-84. [40]Int. pd. monthly. [41]Due 9-1-93. [42]Fr.9-1-83. [43]Int. pd. monthly. Due 8-1-94. [44]Now Colt Ind. [45]Fr. 9-15-85. [46]Issd. in exch. for Pub. Wks. 5 1/2s '45. [47]Due 6-30-77. [48]Ser. 56(Exch. offer). [49]Acquired by Eaton Corp. [50]Sub. of Standard Oil Co. of Ind. [51]Fr. 1-15-82. [52]Issued with 200,000 shs. of common stk.

Note: Moody's ratings are subject to change. Because of the possible time lapse between Moody's assignment or change of a rating and your use of this monthly publication, we suggest you verify the current rating of any security or issuer in which you are interested.

Source: *Moody's Bond Record*, February 1982, p. 17.

vestors make no such elaborate studies. In fact, they rely largely upon bond ratings published by several organizations that do the job of bond analysis and express their conclusions by a system of ratings.[26]

[26] Some bond market observers believe that the rating agencies tend to be overly conservative. See Gordon Pye, "Gauging the Default Premium," *Financial Analysts Journal*, January-February 1974, pp. 49–52.

Exhibit 3 Sample Page from *Standard & Poor's Bond Guide*

STANDARD & POOR'S CORPORATION

Title-Industry Code & Co. Finances (In Italics) / Individual Issue Statistics, Exchange	Ind / Interest Dates	Chgs. 1979 / S&P Quality Rating	Eligible	Times Earn. 1980 / Bond Form	1981 / Legality (C t, M a, N H, N J, N Y)	Yr. End	Cash & Eqv / Redemption Provisions: Refund Earliest/Other	Current Assets (Million $) / Call Price For S.F.	Liabs (Million $)	Date / Call Price Regular	L. Term Debt (Mil $) / Out-st'd'g (Mil $)	Debt % Prop / Underwriter Firm	Underwriter Year	Interim Times Earn. Period / Price Range 1960-80 High	1960-80 Low	1980 / 1981 High	1981 / 1981 Low	1982 High	1982 Low	Mo. End Price Sale(s) or Bid	Curr Yield	Yield to Mat.
May Department Stores	***58f***	***3.41***		***3.38***	....	***Ja***	***64.6***	***1370***	***744***	***10-81***	***546***	***58.0***										
• SF Deb 7.95s 2002	jJ15	AA	X	R	- - √ - -		[1]103.73	[2]100		±105.96	50.0	G2	'77	99½	90¾	58⅛	56	No Sale		50⅛	15.86	16.54
May Dept. Stores Credit	***26a***	***1.55***		***1.54***	....	***Ja***	***0.01***			***10-81***	***153***			***9 Mo Oct***		***1.56***	***1.54***					
• SF Deb 9s '89	mN15	AA	X	R	- - √ - -		z±101.66	100		±103.32	33.2	G2	'69	110	70⅝	79¼	67⅛	74⅞	68	71⅛	12.65	15.61
Mayer (Oscar) & Co.	***27e***	***Subsid of & Gtd by Gen'l Foods, see***																				
• SF Deb 7.85s '96	Jj15	AA	X	R	- - √√ -		....	100		±103.45	29.3	S7	'71	102	60	63⅝	59½	60⅞	59⅛	58¼	13.48	15.15
• SF Deb 11⅝s 2010	Mn15	AA	X	R	- - √√ -		[3]106.975	[4]100		±111.16	50.0	M9	'80	100	98	85	70	No Sale		70¼	16.55	16.62
[5]McCrory Corp	***17***	***2.16***		***1.92***	....	***Ja***	***9.70***	***433***	***357***	***10-81***	***286***	***125***		***9 Mo Oct***		***1.49***	***1.44***					
• Sub SF Deb 10½s '85	fA15	CCC	Y	R	- - - - -		....	100		100	6.50	Exch	'70	108¾	50	87	77⅜	81½	80⅝	81½	12.88	18.06
• Sub SF Deb 7½s '94	Mn 15	CCC	Y	R	- - - - -		....	100		100	55.5	Exch	'69	85¼	25½	50	40	50½	45¼	s47	15.96	18.68
• Sub SF Deb 7¾s '95	mS15	CCC	Y	R	- - - - -		....	100		100	62.4	Exch	'73	71¼	27	52	43⅛	50	45⅜	48	16.15	18.23
• Sub SF Deb 7⅝s '97	jD15	CCC	Y	R	- - - - -		....	[6]100		100	55.6	Exch	'72	82½	26⅛	50	42⅛	49⅞	43½	46¼	16.49	17.98
McCulloch Prop Credit	***26e***	***1.73***		***2.40***	....	***Dc***	***8.52***	***24.1***	***2.38***	***9-81***	***15.5***			***9 Mo Sep***		***2.71***	***3.32***					
◆SF Deb 7.70s '82	jD	BB	Y	R	- - - - -		....	100		100	12.5	B1	'72	100½	66⅛	92½	80	93⅛	91	92¼	8.35	20.87
◆SF Deb 11½s '84	mS	BB	Y	R	- - - - -		z100	100		[7]100	4.85	Exch	'75	110	88⅝	88⅝	85	86	86	85	13.53	19.60
McDermott (J.Ray)& Co[8]	***49e***	***2.82***		***2.78***	....	***Mr***	***456***	***2433***	***1605***	***12-81***	***466***	***39.4***		***9 Mo Dec***		***2.41***	***3.65***					
• SF Deb[9] 10.20s '99	jD	A	X	R	- - √ - -		[10]104.85	100		±106.31	47.5	S7	'74	106½	92	72½	66¼	No Sale		64	15.94	16.53
• SF Deb 9⅝s 2004	Ms15	A	X	R	- - √ - -		[11]104.675	[12]100		±107.965	150	S7	'79	99¾	94	65	60	57⅜	57⅜	A64¼	14.98	15.32
• Notes[13] 9.40s '84	jD	A	X	R	- - √ - -		....	....		100	35.0	S7	'74	106½	83	87⅞	79⅝	89	83½	86⅛	10.91	16.00
McDonald's Corp	***28b***	***3.60***		***3.43***	....	***Dc***	***52.3***	***170***	***284***	***9-81***	***928***	***38.8***		***9 Mo Sep***		***3.54***	***3.97***					
• Notes 9⅝s '82	aO15	AA	X	R	- - √ - -		....	....		100	59.9	P1	'74	108⅜	89	96.656	91	97.406	96½	97¼	9.90	15.22
• Notes 9s '85	Mn	AA	X	R	- - √ - -		....	....		100	68.0	P1	'75	108	78⅛	89	75	87⅝	83	86	10.47	14.82
• SF Notes 8⅝s '88	Jd15	AA	X	R	- - √ - -		....	100		[14]100	67.6	P1	'78	100½	68	82	78	82¾	81½	s81⅝	10.57	13.03
• SF Notes 10¼s '89	aO	AA	X	R	- - √ - -		....	[15]100		[16]100	50.0	P1	'79	100	80½	88⅛	75	79⅞	75⅝	79⅞	12.83	14.77
[17]McDonough Co.	***39b***	***9.48***		***[18]7.47***	***N/A***	***Sp***	***5.16***	***17.3***	***3.05***	***12-81***	***13.3***											
◆Sub Deb 7½s '85	Mn	NR		R	- - - - -		....	....		100	11.3	Mgr	'70	93	52¾	75½	65½	73½	73	74	10.14	19.04
◆Sub Deb 8s '85	Mn	NR		R	- - - - -		....	....		100	1.43	Mgr	'70	94½	54	80	65¼	72¼	70	71	11.27	21.31
◆Sub Deb 6s '86	aO	NR		R	- - - - -		....	....		100	2.00	Mgr	'71	83½	53	65	60	58¾	58¾	61	9.84	19.37
McGraw-Edison[19]	***24***	***2.44***		***1.53***	....	***Dc***	***9.50***	***1044***	***461***	***9-81***	***p535***	***104***										
• SF Deb 7½s '96	Mn	A-	X	R	- √√√ -		....	100		103.04	28.4	D1	'71	102¼	55	59¼	49¼	50½	49⅛	49⅛	15.27	17.20
MCI Communications	***67***	***N/A***		***N/A***	....	***Mr***	***166***	***234***	***131***	***12-81***	***409***	***78.2***										
• Sub SF Deb 15s 2000	fA	B+	Y	R	- - - - -		[20]100	[20]100		±113½	52.5	S5	'80	100½	92	98½	76½	89	81	s86½	17.34	17.47
• Sub SF Deb 14⅛s 2001	Ao	B+	Y	R	- - - - -		[21]100	[22]100		100	125	S5	'81	....	....	89¾	72¼	83⅞	77	s81¾	17.28	17.44
[23]MCO Holdings	***49a***	***2.29***		***1.67***	....	***Dc***	***15.8***	***86.7***	***46.2***	***9-81***	***p158***	***121***		***9 Mo Sep***		***2.61***	***2.16***					
◆Sub SF Deb 12½s '99	jD15	NR		R	- - - - -		....	[24]100		100	44.1	Exch	'79	93	63	82	62	71½	65	63¼	19.76	20.16
Mead Corp	***50***	***4.57***		***4.26***	***3.53***	***Dc***	***16.6***	***613***	***403***	***12-81***	***739***	***65.4***										
SF Deb[25] 4¾s '83	jJ	A	X	CR	- - √√ -		....	100		100	4.40	D9	'58	95	60	85⅞	82	89⅝	85	89⅝	5.30	14.09
SF Deb[26] 5¼s '86	Ao15	A	X	CR	- - √√ -		....	100		100¼	7.90	D9	'61	101¼	60¼	70⅝	66	73⅞	69⅛	73⅞	7.11	13.94
• SF Deb 8½s '95	jD 15	A	X	R	- - √√ -		....	100		±103.825	31.8	G2	'70	107½	59¼	71¼	56½	63	62¾	57⅞	14.69	16.26
• SF Deb 9⅞s 2000	mN	A	X	R	- - √√ -		[27]104⅜	100		±106⅜	86.9	S7	'75	109¼	79½	72⅛	58	66	60⅜	66½	14.85	15.37
Means Services	***62***	***58.35***		***41.20***	***3.29***	***Dc***	***2.42***	***28.4***	***13.6***	***12-81***	***14.3***	***39.3***										
◆Sub SF Deb 11s '96	Jj	NR		R	- - - - -		....	[28]100		[29]111	12.2	Exch	'80	....	....	69	62	67	60	64	17.19	18.21
MEDIQ Inc	***43***	***2.06***		***2.62***	***1.47***	***Sp***	***3.13***	***18.9***	***16.5***	***9-81***	***★38.6***	***189***										
◆Sub SF Deb 14⅞s '97	Fa	NR		R	- - - - -		....	[30]100		100	15.0	D9	'82	....	....	....	....	77	77	80	18.59	18.94
Mego Int'l	***40h***	***1.26***		***d2.55***	....	***Fb***	***0.68***	***47.0***	***46.9***	***11-81***	***25.2***	***330***										
◆Sub SF Deb[31] 12⅞s '94	§Fa	D	Z	R	- - - - -		Default 2-1-82 int				14.1		'79	98⅞	47	63½	22	27½	15½	s18½	...	Flat
Mellon Nat'l. Corp	***10a***	***1.13***		***1.10***	***1.07***	***Dc***					***462***											
• [32]Cv[33]FltRt[34]Nt [35]11.85s '89	Jd15	AAA	X	R	- - √ - -		....	....		[36]100	120	G2	'79	100⅛	84⅞	93⅞	87¼	89	86¼	89	13.31	....
• [37]FltRtNts[38] 13.90s '89	Jd	NR	X	R	√ - - - -		z100	....		[39]100	26.4	F2	'74	104½	98⅛	102	97¼	101	99⅜	99¾	13.93	....

Uniform Footnote Explanations—See Page 1. Other: [1]Fr 7-15-87. [2]Fr 7-15-88. [3]Fr 5-15-90. [4]Fr 5-15-91. [5]Subsid of Rapid-American. [6]Fr 2-1-83. [7]Fr 9-1-82. [8]Now McDermott Inc. [9]Incr fr:9.70% 2-1-80,9.95% 4-1-80. [10]Fr 12-1-84. [11]Fr 3-15-89. [12]Fr 3-14-90. [13]Incl fr 8.90% 4-1-80. [14]Fr 6-15-85. [15]Fr 10-1-85. [16]Fr 10-1-86. [17]Subsid of Hanson Trust Ltd. [18]Fiscal Jan'81 & prior. [19]See Studebaker-Worthington,Wagner Elec. [20]Fr 8-1-90. [21]Fr 4-1-86. [22]Fr 4-1-91. [23]Was McCulloch Oil. [24]Fr 12-15-89. [25]Incr fr 4 3/8% 11-1-77. [26]Incr fr 4 7/8% 11-1-71. [27]Fr 11-1-85. [28]Fr 1-1-88. [29]Fr 1-1-86. [30]Fr 2-1-88. [31]Offer $800 zero coupon Deb for par to Apr 16. [32]Cv by holder into 8 1/2%Deb'09 thru 6/14/88. [33]Cv by Co into Fix Rt Deb'09 to 6/15/88. [34]Thru 6-14-82,adj aft for T-Bill rate,etc. [35]Minimum int. 6%. [36]Fr 6-30-86. [37]Hldr's option to mat. ea. Jun&Dec 1 at 100. [38]Thru 5-31-82,then 1% above T-bill rate,etc. [39]Fr 6-1-84.

Source: *Standard & Poor's Bond Guide*, April 1982, p. 82.

Two widely used systems of bond ratings are those of Moody's Investors Service and Standard & Poor's Corporation. In both systems the term *high-grade* means low in financial risk, or, conversely, high in probability of future payments. The highest grade bonds are designated by Moody's by the letters *Aaa,* and by Standard & Poor's by *AAA.* The next highest grade is *Aa* or *AA;* then for the third grade both agencies use *A.* The next three grades are designated *Baa* or *BBB, Ba* or *BB,* and *B.* There are also *C* grades. Bonds assigned ratings in the triple-A to single-A categories are generally regarded as of good investment quality, the triple-B rated bonds are said to be *medium grade;* lower rated bonds are said to have speculative elements or to be *distinctly speculative.* Exhibit 26 of Chapter 5 provides more information about these bond ratings.

Both Moody's and Standard & Poor's publish periodically average yields at market prices on a number of long-term corporate bond issues grouped by ratings. These average yields by category always show the lowest yields on triple-A bonds, somewhat higher yields on double-A bonds, then still higher yields on single-A bonds. There is a relatively large differential between the average yield on single-A and triple-B bonds. Exhibit 4 presents the average promised yields[27] from 1976 to 1981 as reported by Moody's for its top four quality ratings.

Exhibit 4
Average Promised Yields on Corporate Bonds by Quality Rating: 1976–1981*

Year	Aaa	Aa	A	Baa
1976	8.43%	8.75%	9.09%	9.75%
1977	8.02	8.24	8.49	8.97
1978	8.73	8.92	9.20	9.49
1979	9.63	9.94	10.20	10.69
1980	11.94	12.50	12.89	13.67
1981	14.17	14.75	15.29	16.04

* The annual yields are the average of the monthly averages as reported in *Moody's Bond Record.*

These data on bond yields by rating categories provide empirical evidence that bond investors demand and obtain higher promised rates of return for higher levels of financial risk. The differences in average yields between rating categories are measures of how much more they demand. The principle is that investors are averse to risk; they can be induced to take a little more risk only by the probability of a little more return on investment.

---

[27] Recall from Chapter 4 the difference between promised yields and realized yields.

There is also empirical evidence that the yields actually realized by investors in corporate bonds over long periods of time vary in size according to rating categories. The classic study of realized yields to maturity on bonds was made a long time ago for the period 1900 through 1943. The study included issues in initial amounts of $5 million or more publicly offered during that period. It showed that realized yields on bonds rated in the first three rating categories at the time of issue were approximately 5 percent, but yields on triple-B bonds averaged 5.7 percent and on even lower rated bonds it rose to higher levels.[28] The flatness of the curve for the three highest rating categories may be attributed chiefly to defaults on even highly rated bonds during the Great Depression of the 1930s. For the past several decades there have been relatively few defaults on bonds initially rated in the first three rating categories, which means that yields at time of issue have been approximately realized.

Yields and Call Provisions

The right of the issuer to call all or part of the issue is advantageous from the issuer's perspective but potentially harmful to the bondholder's economic interests. To induce an investor to purchase a callable corporate bond, the issuer must offer a yield above that of otherwise comparable noncallable corporate bonds. After the initial offering, market participants in the secondary market will continue to price a callable bond so that its yield is greater than that of noncallable bonds that are otherwise comparable.

The size of the yield premium between callable and noncallable bonds depends upon several factors. Most important is the expectations of market participants as to the course of future interest rates. If market participants expect interest rates to decline sufficiently below the coupon rate on the issue so that it would be economical for the corporate issuer to refund it, there will be a substantial yield premium between callable and noncallable bonds. On the other hand, if interest rates are anticipated to rise or not fall appreciably below the coupon rate on the issue, the amount of the yield premium will be negligible. Empirical studies that examined yields on callable and noncallable public utility bonds support this view.[29]

The nature of the call provision of an issue also determines the amount of the yield premium. As noted earlier, the corporate bond

---

[28] W. Braddock Hickman, *Statistical Measures of Corporate Bond Financing Since 1900* (Princeton, N.J.: National Bureau of Economic Research, 1960), pp. 394, 579, and 580.

[29] Frank Jen and James E. Wert, "The Effect of Call Risk on Corporate Bond Yields," *Journal of Finance* (December 1967), pp. 637–651, and Gordon Pye, "The Value of Call Deferment on a Bond: Some Empirical Results," *Journal of Finance* (December 1967), pp. 623–636.

indenture may include a deferred-call provision. One would expect that, other things equal, the longer the deferment period, the lower the yield premium to compensate for the issuer's right to call. This belief is supported by empirical studies that examined yields on utility bonds.[30] A more recent study, however, found that the length of deferment per se is not an important determinant of the yield premium; instead, it is the kind of early protection provided[31]—that is, whether there is protection against both noncallability and nonrefundability.

As explained earlier, the inclusion of a sinking-fund requirement has advantages and disadvantages to the bondholder. During a period of relatively high interest rates, one study found that the disadvantage (the loss of income if the issue is called for sinking-fund purposes) dominated the advantages of a sinking-fund requirement.[32] As a result, a yield premium on corporate bond issues in which a sinking fund requirement is included in the indenture was observed.

The call price can be expected to influence the yield premium between callable and noncallable bonds because it is an important determinant of the cost to the corporate issuer of refunding the issue. The greater the dollar premium over the par value to call the issue, the more expensive it will be for the issuer to refund the issue for a given drop in interest rates. Therefore, the less likely it will be that the issuer will call the issue the higher the call price.[33]

The yield premium between callable and noncallable bonds is also found to be influenced by the number of years to maturity (the longer the maturity the higher the yield premium) and the quality of the issuer (the yield premium increases as quality decreases).[34]

Realized Total Returns on High-Quality Long-Term Corporate Bonds: 1926–80

Recall that the yields offered in the market only reflect promised yields. A recent study, however, estimated the total return (coupon

---

[30] Pye, "Gauging the Default Premium"; and Mark Frankena, "The Influence of Call Provisions and Coupon Rate on the Yields of Corporate Bonds," in *Essays on Interest Rates*, vol. 2, ed. Jack Guttentag (New York: National Bureau of Economic Research, 1971).

[31] Michael G. Ferri, "How Do Call Provisions Influence Bond Yields?" *The Journal of Portfolio Management*, Winter 1979, pp. 55–57. His study is based upon a sample of newly issued industrial and public utilities in 1976, a period of high interest rates. His finding agrees with a survey of Arleigh P. Hess, Jr., and Willis J. Winn conducted of bond fund managers—*The Value of the Call Privilege* (University of Pennsylvania, 1962.)

[32] Ferri.

[33] Ferri uses the ratio of the coupon rate to the call price as a measure of protection against the issuer calling the issue. He finds this measure, which he calls the refunding rate, to be the most important determinant of the yield premium of the various call-protection measures he examines.

[34] Pye, "Gauging the Default Premium."

interest plus the change in market value) for high-quality long-term corporate bonds from 1926 to 1980.[35] The results, along with the total return for long-term U.S. government bonds, are presented in Exhibit 5.[36] The total returns adjusted for inflation are also presented for the two instruments.

Exhibit 5
Year by Year Total Returns for High-Quality Long-Term
Corporate Bonds and Long-Term U.S. Government Bonds:
1926–1980

	Unadjusted Total Returns		Inflation-Adjusted Total Returns	
Year	Long-Term Government Bonds	Long-Term Corporate Bonds	Long-Term Government Bonds	Long-Term Corporate Bonds
1926	0.0777	0.0737	0.0937	0.0896
1927	0.0893	0.0744	0.1112	0.0963
1928	0.0010	0.0284	0.0103	0.0380
1929	0.0342	0.0327	0.0318	0.0304
1930	0.0466	0.0798	0.1127	0.1480
1931	−0.0531	−0.0185	0.0458	0.0837
1932	0.1684	0.1082	0.2999	0.2330
1933	−0.0008	0.1038	−0.0071	0.0973
1934	0.1002	0.1384	0.0777	0.1154
1935	0.0498	0.0961	0.0193	0.0644
1936	0.0751	0.0674	0.0621	0.0545
1937	0.0023	0.0275	−0.0285	−0.0039
1938	0.0553	0.0613	0.0850	0.0912
1939	0.0594	0.0397	0.0623	0.0442
1940	0.0609	0.0339	0.0507	0.0240
1941	0.0093	0.0273	−0.0807	−0.0644
1942	0.0322	0.0260	−0.0560	−0.0618
1943	0.0208	0.0283	−0.0109	−0.0036
1944	0.0281	0.0473	0.0069	0.0257
1945	0.1073	0.0408	0.0831	0.0177
1946	−0.0010	0.0172	−0.1595	−0.1439
1947	−0.0263	−0.0234	−0.1083	−0.1056
1948	0.0340	0.0414	0.0059	0.0129
1949	0.0645	0.0331	0.0837	0.0517
1950	0.0006	0.0212	−0.0547	−0.0351
1951	−0.0394	−0.0269	−0.0933	−0.0816
1952	0.0116	0.0352	0.0027	0.0261
1953	0.0363	0.0341	0.0299	0.0277
1954	0.0719	0.0539	0.0771	0.0590
1955	−0.0130	0.0048	−0.0167	0.0010

[35] Roger G. Ibbotson and Rex A. Sinquefield, *Stocks, Bonds, Bills and Inflation: The Past and the Future* (Charlottesville, Va.: Financial Analysts Federation, 1981).

[36] The total returns for corporate bonds are measured for high-quality bonds with approximately 20 years to maturity. For the U.S. government bond portfolio, the target maturity is also 20 years. Ibbotson and Sinquefield try to control for factors that might produce abnormal returns in U.S. government bonds due to favorable tax benefits, impaired marketability, or special call or redemption features.

Exhibit 5 (*concluded*)

	Unadjusted Total Returns		Inflation-Adjusted Total Returns	
Year	Long-Term Government Bonds	Long-Term Corporate Bonds	Long-Term Government Bonds	Long-Term Corporate Bonds
1956	−0.0559	−0.0681	−0.0824	−0.0944
1957	0.0745	0.0871	0.0429	0.0550
1958	−0.0610	−0.0222	−0.0772	−0.0391
1959	−0.0226	−0.0097	−0.0371	−0.0243
1960	0.1378	0.0907	0.1211	0.0747
1961	0.0097	0.0482	0.0030	0.0412
1962	0.0689	0.0795	0.0560	0.0665
1963	0.0121	0.0219	−0.0043	0.0054
1964	0.0351	0.0477	0.0229	0.0354
1965	0.0071	−0.0046	−0.0120	−0.0235
1966	0.0365	0.0020	0.0027	−0.0308
1967	−0.0919	−0.0495	−0.1190	−0.0779
1968	−0.0026	0.0257	−0.0478	−0.0206
1969	−0.0508	−0.0809	−0.1058	−0.1345
1970	0.1210	0.1837	0.0628	0.1225
1971	0.1323	0.1101	0.0955	0.0742
1972	0.0568	0.0726	0.0221	0.0373
1973	−0.0111	0.0114	−0.0913	−0.0706
1974	0.0435	−0.0306	−0.0708	−0.1373
1975	0.0919	0.1464	0.0205	0.0717
1976	0.1675	0.1865	0.1143	0.1324
1977	−0.0067	0.0171	−0.0701	−0.0477
1978	−0.0116	−0.0007	−0.0942	−0.0841
1979	−0.0122	−0.0418	−0.1295	−0.1558
1980	−0.0395	−0.0262	−0.1470	−0.1349

Source: Roger G. Ibbotson and Rex A. Sinquefield, *Stocks, Bonds, Bills and Inflation: The Past and the Future* (Charlottesville, Va.: Financial Analysts Research Foundation, 1981).

The results support the expected risk-return relationship between the two securities. The total return holding long-term corporates exceeded that for long-term U.S. governments. This is expected because the latter are free of default risk. The average default premium between long-term corporate and long-term governments is .17 percent.

Exhibit 6 shows the total rate of return on high-quality, long-term corporate bonds for all yearly holdings from 1926 to 1980.

THE BOND MARKETS

It is easy to buy bonds. All you need to know at a minimum is the telephone number of a broker-dealer firm with whom you have established an account. It is better, though, if you know something about the bond markets and how they operate. Familiarity with markets may

Exhibit 6

Long-Term Corporate Bonds: Total Returns (rates of return for all yearly holding periods from 1926 to 1980–percent per annum compounded annually)

TO THE END OF	FROM THE BEGINNING OF 1926	1927	1928	1929	1930	1931	1932	1933	1934	1935	1936	1937	1938	1939	1940	1941	1942	1943	1944	1945
1926	7.4																			
1927	7.4	7.4																		
1928	5.9	5.1	2.8																	
1929	5.2	4.5	3.1	3.3																
1930	5.8	5.4	4.7	5.6	8.0															
1931	4.4	3.9	3.0	3.1	2.9	-1.9														
1932	5.3	5.0	4.5	4.9	5.5	4.3	10.8													
1933	6.0	5.8	5.5	6.0	6.7	6.3	10.6	10.4												
1934	6.8	6.7	6.6	7.3	8.1	8.1	11.7	12.1	13.8											
1935	7.1	7.0	7.0	7.6	8.3	8.4	11.2	11.3	11.7	9.6										
1936	7.1	7.0	7.0	7.5	8.1	8.1	10.3	10.1	10.0	8.2	6.7									
1937	6.7	6.6	6.5	7.0	7.4	7.4	9.0	8.6	8.2	6.3	4.7	2.7								
1938	6.6	6.6	6.5	6.9	7.3	7.2	8.6	8.2	7.8	6.3	5.2	4.4	6.1							
1939	6.4	6.4	6.3	6.6	6.9	6.8	8.0	7.6	7.1	5.8	4.9	4.3	5.0	4.0						
1940	6.2	6.2	6.1	6.3	6.6	6.5	7.5	7.0	6.6	5.4	4.6	4.1	4.5	3.7	3.4					
1941	6.0	5.9	5.8	6.1	6.3	6.1	7.0	6.6	6.1	5.0	4.3	3.8	4.0	3.4	3.1	2.7				
1942	5.8	5.7	5.6	5.8	6.0	5.8	6.6	6.2	5.7	4.7	4.0	3.6	3.8	3.2	2.9	2.7	2.6			
1943	5.6	5.5	5.4	5.6	5.8	5.6	6.3	5.8	5.4	4.5	3.9	3.5	3.6	3.1	2.9	2.7	2.7	2.8		
1944	5.6	5.5	5.4	5.5	5.7	5.5	6.1	5.8	5.3	4.5	4.0	3.6	3.8	3.4	3.3	3.2	3.4	3.8	4.7	
1945	5.5	5.4	5.3	5.5	5.6	5.4	6.0	5.6	5.2	4.5	4.0	3.7	3.8	3.5	3.4	3.4	3.6	3.9	4.4	4.1
1946	5.3	5.2	5.1	5.3	5.4	5.2	5.7	5.3	5.0	4.3	3.8	3.5	3.6	3.3	3.2	3.1	3.2	3.3	3.5	2.9
1947	5.0	4.9	4.7	4.8	4.9	4.7	5.2	4.8	4.4	3.7	3.3	2.9	3.0	2.6	2.4	2.3	2.2	2.2	2.0	1.1
1948	4.9	4.8	4.7	4.8	4.9	4.7	5.1	4.8	4.4	3.8	3.3	3.0	3.1	2.8	2.6	2.5	2.5	2.5	2.4	1.9
1949	4.9	4.8	4.6	4.7	4.8	4.6	5.0	4.7	4.3	3.7	3.3	3.1	3.1	2.8	2.7	2.6	2.6	2.6	2.6	2.2
1950	4.8	4.7	4.5	4.6	4.7	4.5	4.9	4.5	4.2	3.6	3.2	3.0	3.0	2.8	2.6	2.6	2.6	2.6	2.5	2.1
1951	4.5	4.3	4.2	4.3	4.3	4.2	4.5	4.1	3.8	3.2	2.9	2.6	2.6	2.3	2.2	2.1	2.0	2.0	1.8	1.4
1952	4.4	4.3	4.2	4.2	4.3	4.1	4.4	4.1	3.8	3.3	2.9	2.7	2.7	2.4	2.3	2.2	2.2	2.1	2.0	1.7
1953	4.4	4.3	4.2	4.2	4.3	4.1	4.4	4.1	3.8	3.3	2.9	2.7	2.7	2.5	2.4	2.3	2.3	2.2	2.2	1.9
1954	4.4	4.3	4.2	4.3	4.3	4.2	4.4	4.1	3.8	3.4	3.1	2.9	2.9	2.7	2.6	2.5	2.5	2.5	2.5	2.2
1955	4.3	4.2	4.1	4.1	4.2	4.0	4.3	4.0	3.7	3.2	2.9	2.7	2.7	2.5	2.4	2.4	2.4	2.3	2.3	2.1
1956	3.9	3.8	3.7	3.7	3.7	3.6	3.8	3.5	3.2	2.8	2.4	2.2	2.2	2.0	1.9	1.8	1.7	1.6	1.6	1.3
1957	4.1	4.0	3.8	3.9	3.9	3.7	4.0	3.7	3.4	3.0	2.7	2.5	2.5	2.3	2.2	2.2	2.1	2.1	2.1	1.9
1958	3.9	3.8	3.6	3.7	3.7	3.5	3.7	3.5	3.2	2.8	2.5	2.3	2.3	2.1	2.0	1.9	1.9	1.8	1.8	1.6
1959	3.7	3.6	3.5	3.5	3.5	3.4	3.6	3.3	3.0	2.6	2.3	2.2	2.1	1.9	1.8	1.8	1.7	1.7	1.6	1.4
1960	3.9	3.8	3.7	3.7	3.7	3.6	3.7	3.5	3.3	2.9	2.6	2.4	2.4	2.3	2.2	2.1	2.1	2.1	2.0	1.8
1961	3.9	3.8	3.7	3.7	3.7	3.6	3.8	3.5	3.3	2.9	2.7	2.5	2.5	2.4	2.3	2.2	2.2	2.2	2.2	2.0
1962	4.0	3.9	3.8	3.8	3.9	3.7	3.9	3.7	3.5	3.1	2.9	2.7	2.7	2.6	2.5	2.5	2.5	2.5	2.5	2.3
1963	4.0	3.9	3.8	3.8	3.8	3.7	3.9	3.6	3.4	3.1	2.9	2.7	2.7	2.6	2.5	2.5	2.5	2.5	2.5	2.3
1964	4.0	3.9	3.8	3.8	3.8	3.7	3.9	3.7	3.5	3.1	2.9	2.8	2.8	2.7	2.6	2.6	2.6	2.6	2.6	2.5
1965	3.9	3.8	3.7	3.7	3.7	3.6	3.8	3.6	3.3	3.0	2.8	2.7	2.7	2.5	2.5	2.5	2.4	2.4	2.4	2.3
1966	3.8	3.7	3.6	3.6	3.6	3.5	3.7	3.5	3.2	2.9	2.7	2.6	2.6	2.5	2.4	2.4	2.4	2.3	2.3	2.2
1967	3.6	3.5	3.4	3.4	3.4	3.3	3.4	3.2	3.0	2.7	2.5	2.3	2.3	2.2	2.1	2.1	2.1	2.0	2.0	1.9
1968	3.5	3.4	3.3	3.4	3.4	3.2	3.4	3.2	3.0	2.7	2.5	2.3	2.3	2.2	2.2	2.1	2.1	2.1	2.0	1.9
1969	3.3	3.2	3.1	3.1	3.1	2.9	3.1	2.9	2.7	2.4	2.2	2.0	2.0	1.9	1.8	1.7	1.7	1.7	1.6	1.5
1970	3.6	3.5	3.4	3.4	3.4	3.3	3.4	3.2	3.1	2.8	2.6	2.5	2.5	2.3	2.3	2.3	2.2	2.2	2.2	2.1
1971	3.7	3.6	3.6	3.6	3.6	3.5	3.6	3.4	3.3	3.0	2.8	2.7	2.7	2.6	2.6	2.5	2.5	2.5	2.5	2.4
1972	3.8	3.7	3.6	3.7	3.7	3.6	3.7	3.5	3.4	3.1	2.9	2.8	2.8	2.7	2.7	2.7	2.7	2.7	2.7	2.6
1973	3.7	3.7	3.6	3.6	3.6	3.5	3.6	3.5	3.3	3.0	2.9	2.8	2.8	2.7	2.6	2.6	2.6	2.6	2.6	2.5
1974	3.6	3.5	3.4	3.4	3.5	3.4	3.5	3.3	3.1	2.9	2.7	2.6	2.6	2.5	2.5	2.4	2.4	2.4	2.4	2.3
1975	3.8	3.7	3.7	3.7	3.7	3.6	3.7	3.6	3.4	3.2	3.0	2.9	2.9	2.8	2.8	2.8	2.8	2.8	2.8	2.7
1976	4.1	4.0	3.9	4.0	4.0	3.9	4.0	3.9	3.7	3.5	3.4	3.3	3.3	3.2	3.2	3.2	3.2	3.2	3.2	3.2
1977	4.0	4.0	3.9	3.9	3.9	3.9	4.0	3.8	3.7	3.5	3.3	3.2	3.2	3.2	3.2	3.1	3.2	3.2	3.2	3.1
1978	4.0	3.9	3.8	3.8	3.9	3.8	3.9	3.7	3.6	3.4	3.2	3.2	3.2	3.1	3.1	3.1	3.1	3.1	3.1	3.0
1979	3.8	3.7	3.7	3.7	3.7	3.6	3.7	3.6	3.4	3.2	3.1	3.0	3.0	2.9	2.9	2.9	2.9	2.9	2.9	2.8
1980	3.7	3.6	3.5	3.6	3.6	3.5	3.6	3.4	3.3	3.1	2.9	2.8	2.9	2.8	2.7	2.7	2.7	2.7	2.7	2.7

Exhibit 6 (*concluded*)

FROM THE BEGINNING OF

TO THE END OF	1946	1947	1948	1949	1950	1951	1952	1953	1954	1955	1956	1957	1958	1959	1960	1961	1962	1963	1964	1965
1946	1.7																			
1947	-0.3	-2.3																		
1948	1.1	0.8	4.1																	
1949	1.7	1.7	3.7	3.3																
1950	1.8	1.8	3.2	2.7	2.1															
1951	1.0	0.9	1.7	0.9	-0.3	-2.7														
1952	1.4	1.3	2.0	1.5	0.9	0.4	3.5													
1953	1.6	1.6	2.3	1.9	1.6	1.4	3.5	3.4												
1954	2.0	2.1	2.7	2.5	2.3	2.4	4.1	4.4	5.4											
1955	1.9	1.9	2.4	2.2	2.0	2.0	3.2	3.1	2.9	0.5										
1956	1.1	1.0	1.4	1.0	0.7	0.5	1.1	0.5	-0.4	-3.2	-6.8									
1957	1.7	1.7	2.1	1.8	1.7	1.6	2.3	2.1	1.8	0.6	0.7	8.7								
1958	1.4	1.3	1.7	1.4	1.2	1.1	1.7	1.4	1.0	-0.1	-0.3	3.1	-2.2							
1959	1.2	1.2	1.5	1.2	1.0	0.9	1.3	1.0	0.6	-0.3	-0.5	1.7	-1.6	-1.0						
1960	1.7	1.7	2.0	1.8	1.7	1.7	2.2	2.0	1.8	1.2	1.4	3.5	1.8	3.9	9.1					
1961	1.9	1.9	2.2	2.1	2.0	2.0	2.4	2.3	2.2	1.7	1.9	3.8	2.6	4.2	6.9	4.8				
1962	2.2	2.3	2.6	2.5	2.4	2.4	2.9	2.9	2.8	2.5	2.8	4.5	3.6	5.1	7.3	6.4	7.9			
1963	2.2	2.3	2.6	2.5	2.4	2.4	2.9	2.8	2.7	2.4	2.7	4.1	3.4	4.5	6.0	5.0	5.0	2.2		
1964	2.4	2.4	2.7	2.6	2.6	2.6	3.0	3.0	2.9	2.7	2.9	4.2	3.6	4.6	5.7	4.9	4.9	3.5	4.8	
1965	2.2	2.3	2.5	2.4	2.4	2.4	2.8	2.7	2.6	2.4	2.6	3.7	3.1	3.8	4.7	3.8	3.6	2.1	2.1	-0.5
1966	2.1	2.1	2.4	2.3	2.2	2.2	2.6	2.5	2.4	2.2	2.4	3.3	2.7	3.4	4.0	3.2	2.9	1.7	1.5	-0.1
1967	1.8	1.8	2.0	1.9	1.8	1.8	2.1	2.0	1.9	1.6	1.7	2.5	1.9	2.4	2.9	2.0	1.5	0.3	-0.2	-1.8
1968	1.8	1.8	2.0	1.9	1.9	1.8	2.1	2.0	1.9	1.7	1.8	2.5	2.0	2.4	2.8	2.1	1.7	0.7	0.4	-0.7
1969	1.4	1.4	1.6	1.4	1.3	1.3	1.5	1.4	1.3	1.0	1.1	1.7	1.1	1.4	1.7	0.9	0.4	-0.6	-1.1	-2.2
1970	2.0	2.0	2.2	2.1	2.1	2.1	2.3	2.3	2.2	2.0	2.1	2.8	2.4	2.7	3.1	2.5	2.3	1.6	1.5	0.9
1971	2.4	2.4	2.6	2.5	2.5	2.5	2.8	2.7	2.7	2.5	2.7	3.3	3.0	3.4	3.7	3.3	3.1	2.6	2.6	2.3
1972	2.5	2.6	2.8	2.7	2.7	2.7	3.0	2.9	2.9	2.8	2.9	3.6	3.2	3.6	4.0	3.6	3.5	3.0	3.1	2.9
1973	2.5	2.5	2.7	2.6	2.6	2.6	2.9	2.9	2.8	2.7	2.8	3.4	3.1	3.5	3.8	3.4	3.3	2.9	2.9	2.7
1974	2.3	2.3	2.5	2.4	2.4	2.4	2.6	2.6	2.5	2.4	2.5	3.1	2.7	3.0	3.3	2.9	2.8	2.4	2.4	2.1
1975	2.7	2.7	2.9	2.9	2.8	2.9	3.1	3.1	3.1	3.0	3.1	3.6	3.4	3.7	4.0	3.7	3.6	3.3	3.3	3.2
1976	3.2	3.2	3.4	3.4	3.4	3.4	3.7	3.7	3.7	3.6	3.8	4.3	4.1	4.5	4.8	4.5	4.5	4.3	4.4	4.4
1977	3.1	3.2	3.3	3.3	3.3	3.4	3.6	3.6	3.6	3.5	3.7	4.2	4.0	4.3	4.6	4.4	4.3	4.1	4.2	4.2
1978	3.0	3.1	3.2	3.2	3.2	3.2	3.5	3.5	3.5	3.4	3.5	4.0	3.8	4.1	4.4	4.1	4.1	3.8	4.0	3.9
1979	2.8	2.8	3.0	3.0	2.9	3.0	3.2	3.2	3.2	3.1	3.2	3.6	3.4	3.7	3.9	3.7	3.6	3.4	3.4	3.3
1980	2.6	2.7	2.8	2.8	2.8	2.8	3.0	3.0	2.9	2.8	2.9	3.4	3.1	3.4	3.6	3.3	3.3	3.0	3.1	3.0

FROM THE BEGINNING OF

TO THE END OF	1966	1967	1968	1969	1970	1971	1972	1973	1974	1975	1976	1977	1978	1979	1980
1966	0.2														
1967	-2.4	-5.0													
1968	-0.8	-1.3	2.6												
1969	-2.7	-3.6	-2.9	-8.1											
1970	1.2	1.5	3.7	4.3	18.4										
1971	2.8	3.3	5.5	6.5	14.6	11.0									
1972	3.4	4.0	5.8	6.7	12.1	9.1	7.3								
1973	3.1	3.6	5.0	5.6	9.3	6.4	4.2	1.1							
1974	2.4	2.7	3.9	4.1	6.7	3.9	1.7	-1.0	-3.1						
1975	3.6	4.0	5.1	5.5	8.0	6.0	4.8	4.0	5.4	14.6					
1976	4.9	5.4	6.6	7.1	9.4	8.0	7.4	7.5	9.7	16.6	18.6				
1977	4.6	5.0	6.1	6.5	8.4	7.1	6.4	6.3	7.6	11.4	9.9	1.7			
1978	4.2	4.6	5.5	5.8	7.5	6.2	5.5	5.2	6.0	8.4	6.4	0.8	-0.1		
1979	3.6	3.9	4.7	4.8	6.2	5.0	4.2	3.8	4.3	5.8	3.7	-0.9	-2.1	-4.2	
1980	3.2	3.4	4.1	4.2	5.4	4.2	3.4	3.0	3.2	4.3	2.4	-1.3	-2.3	-3.4	-2.6

Source: Roger G. Ibbotson and Rex A. Sinquefield, *Stocks, Bonds, Bills and Inflation: The Past and The Future* Charlottesville, Va.: Financial Analysts Research Foundation, 1981.

affect your choice of bond issues and enable you to minimize the cost of buying and selling.

Billions of dollars of new corporate bonds are sold each year in the primary market—the market for new issues. As soon as a new bond issue is publicly offered, investors begin to buy and sell in the secondary market—the market for outstanding issues.

The secondary market for bonds is a big one. You may not hear as much about it as about the stock markets, but there are more corporate bond issues listed on the New York Stock Exchange than there are stock issues. The dollar value of daily bond trading on the exchanges and in the over-the-counter market appears to be not much less than the value of trading in stocks on the exchanges. The reason the bond market is inconspicuous to the public is that it is mostly an institutional market wherein life insurance companies, pension funds; and savings institutions quietly buy and sell large amounts of bonds with little or no publicity.

There are really two bond markets. One is the *exchange market,* where certain members make a market in listed issues. The other is the *over-the-counter market,* which is a market made by dealer firms in their offices. The exchange market for bonds is chiefly the New York Stock Exchange. The over-the-counter market is chiefly in New York City, but there are many firms all over the country who buy and sell securities as dealers.

In discussing the bond markets one must differentiate clearly between brokers and dealers. Brokers execute orders for accounts of customers; they are agents and get a commission for their services. Dealers buy and sell for their own accounts. When they buy, they take the risk of reselling at a loss. Dealers "make a market" when they quote a bond continuously. A *quote* is a bid and an offer. The *bid* is the price a dealer will pay for bonds of an issue to whomever may want to sell to the dealer; and the *offer* is the price at which a dealer will sell bonds to whomever may want to buy from the dealer. The offer is always higher than the bid; that is, the dealer buys at a lower price than that at which he or she sells, and so makes a profit. The difference between bid and offer prices is the dealer's *spread.*

The Exchange Market

If you look only at the number of bond issues listed on the New York Stock Exchange—about 2,800 to 2,900—and at the market value of listed bonds—approximately $500 billion—you would likely conclude that the exchange market is the big market. In fact, it is not. A very large percentage of all bond trading, including listed issues, is over the counter. We cannot be precise about this because there are no published data on the volume of over-the-counter trading.

The difference between the size of the two markets is partly a matter of historical development and partly of adaptation to the requirements of institutional investors. The organized security markets developed chiefly as stock markets because, during a long period of history, there was a broad public interest in stocks. However, it has long been the custom for the larger corporate bond issues to be listed on the New York Stock Exchange (NYSE), and a number of member firms do business as specialists in bonds. Dealers in the over-the-counter market have developed a larger and broader market chiefly because they have the capital required to assume the risk of buying and selling large amounts of bonds for their own accounts. They have benefited by the great growth in bond investment by institutional investors during the past several decades.

The government of the New York Stock Exchange assists its bond specialists by requiring that member firms execute customers' orders for nine bonds or fewer on the floor of the exchange unless a better price can be obtained off the floor. The exchange market has also been aided by installation of the Automated Bond System, which provides quotes by its bond specialists in all listed issues to broker-dealer firms that subscribe to the service. Leading newspapers publish daily a record of prices at which NYSE-listed bond issues were traded on the preceding business day. Examination of this information is a good way to learn more about the bond market. Exhibit 7 shows part of the record of trading in NYSE bond issues on a randomly selected day.

The first task is to identify corporate issuers. Most of us can read "ATT" to mean American Telephone and Telegraph Company, but what is the name of the issuer abbreviated to "Oakin"? You may have to refer to one of the bond-rating booklets published monthly by Moody's or Standard & Poor's to get the full name. The particular bond issue is indicated by the interest rate and year of maturity; thus, "ATT 7s01" means an issue bearing interest at 7 percent and due in the year 2001. In the next column reading from left to right is the current yield on the issue. *Notice that this is not the yield to maturity.* In some instances you find the letters *cv* instead of current yield. The letters mean that the bond is *convertible.* The conversion option affects market price and distorts current yield. Sometimes the letter *f* appears in the column for current yield. This means that the bond is *traded flat*; that is, a purchaser does not have to pay a seller accrued interest from the bond's last interest payment date to date of purchase. All other bonds are traded with accrued interest. Bonds traded flat are in default, or for some other reason the next interest payment is particularly uncertain. Moving on to the right, you see a number that indicates the total volume of trading in an issue during the day. Scan that column and you see that trading in some issues has been only 5 or 10 bonds and that many listed issues do not appear in this table of prices because there was no trading during the day. Then you come to the

Exhibit 7
Sample Page from *The Wall Street Journal*

high, low, and closing prices for the day. For some issues these three numbers are all the same, which usually means that only one transaction took place during the day. In the last column is the net change in closing price on the day of the report relative to the closing price on the most recent previous day the bond issue was traded.

The OTC Market

The over-the-counter (OTC) market is hard to describe in precise language because it does not exist in a particular place, it has no listed issues, and there is no published information about the prices at which bonds are traded or about the volume of trading. Any dealer can make a market for a bond issue without having to be a member of an exchange or even a member of the National Association of Securities Dealers (the organization to which most broker-dealer firms belong).

The heart of the over-the-counter market is a group of perhaps two dozen large dealer firms located in New York City that make *wholesale* markets in large numbers of bond issues. Their market is called wholesale because for the most part they deal only with other wholesalers and with broker-dealer firms that have *retail* orders from their own customers to execute as brokers. Wholesalers also deal directly with large institutional investors, who buy and sell in large lots, such as 100 bonds or more.

Some years ago the National Association of Securities Dealers (NASD)—which is both a trade association and a governing organization—developed a computerized system by which dealers may enter their bids and offers for issues in which they make a market and subscribers can read these quotations on cathode-ray tubes in their offices. The system is called *NASDAQ* (for National Association of Security Dealers Automated Quotation service). A broker-dealer firm with an order to execute for a customer can learn instantly the highest bid and lowest offer for the issue in which he or she is interested and then execute the order by telephone. This is much more efficient than the old system of telephoning around to several dealers for quotes.

DIFFERENCES IN THE QUALITY OF MARKETABILITY

Any bond that is quoted continually by a dealer is a *marketable bond*; there is a market for it. But sophisticated investors want to know much more than that; they want to know how good is the market. It may be inferred that a bond quoted by only one dealer in Kansas City has a poor market and that one quoted by half a dozen large wholesalers in New York City has an excellent market. There are gradations between poor and excellent. It is useful to recognize differences in the quality of markets for different bond issues.

The principal basis for grading securities in marketability is the size of the spread between dealers' bid and asked prices. A narrow spread—say, three eighths to one half of 1 percent—indicates an excellent market. A wide spread—such as 2 or 3 percent—means a poorly marketable issue. The principal determinant of the size of spread is not so much the number of dealers, as suggested above, but the usual volume of trading in an issue. The number of dealers is more or less proportionate to volume of trading. If there is a lot of business in a bond issue, there are a lot of dealers seeking the business. The size of the spread, too, is related to the volume of trading. A large volume of trading and a large number of dealers make a highly competitive market in which spreads are pressed downward. In the actively traded issues, dealers take less risk when they buy bonds and carry them in inventory. Usually, price changes in any short period are small, and a dealer who wishes to do so can unload bonds. In addition, active trading distributes the dealer's cost per transaction over many transactions.

The easiest and most direct way to learn the size of dealers' spreads on bond issues is to ask a broker-dealer who subscribes to NASDAQ to tell you the quotes on some bond issues, and also the number of dealers quoting an issue. Short of access to NASDAQ, you can learn something from the data on daily trading in NYSE-listed bonds. Look at the volume of trading for some of the bonds listed in Exhibit 7. You can see that the volume in most issues was less than 25 bonds, but volume in American Telephone and Telegraph 8¾s, due 2000, was 116 bonds. This suggests a small spread in dealers' quotes. In fact that issue is usually quoted with a spread of only three eighths of 1 percent. Another issue with a volume of 10 bonds is usually quoted with a spread of more than 1 percent.

The reason for differentiating between bond issues in grades of marketability is that high marketability costs money. Other things being equal, investors prefer the highly marketable issues, and accordingly will pay slightly more for them. A slightly higher price means a slightly lower yield. An investor who buys in the bond market and expects to sell in the market after some period of time needs high marketability. Only by trading in highly marketable issues can the investor minimize transaction costs. Consider, for example, the cost of buying and selling a bond that is usually quoted with a spread of one half of 1 percent. The cost of a *round trip*—that is, a purchase and a sale—is only 1 percent for the dealer. In addition, a broker's commission on a round trip is likely to be about 0.5 percent. The sum is about 1.5 percent. In comparison, the cost of a round trip in a poorly marketable issue might be twice as much.

Many investors do not need high marketability. They buy new corporate bond issues when they are first offered to the public at the public offering price. The cost of public distribution is paid by the issuer. Then they usually hold bonds until they are redeemed at par or a premium over par when bonds are called before maturity. Thus they pay no dealer's spread and no commission. The round trip is free. On exceptional occasions such investors elect to sell bonds in the market and have to pay for a one-way trip back.

There is also another category of corporate bond investors who buy in the secondary market and seek to realize capital gains by sale in the market at a higher price; there is speculation in bonds just as there is in stocks. Clearly this category of investors needs highly marketable issues in order to minimize the transaction costs.

SUMMARY

The category of securities described by the term *corporate bonds* includes a great variety of investment instruments. Under this heading you find bond issues generally regarded as bearing very little risk of payments in dollar amounts and others that are distinctly speculative. You find a wide range of obligations in length of the period to maturity from those due within a few days to issues that may have as much as 30 to 40 years to maturity. There are bonds secured by first mortgages on issuers' plant and equipment and those that have no specific pledge of security. There are obligations designed for particular categories of issuers, such as equipment-trust obligations for transportation companies and collateral-trust bonds for holding companies. Provisions for redemption vary widely. There are bonds that are not callable before maturity and those that are callable at any time after a specified period of notice. Most, but not all, corporate bonds have sinking funds to retire bonds from time to time during the period to maturity.

It is not surprising, then, that corporate bonds of all these varieties appeal to investors of many varieties. Life insurance companies buy more corporate obligations than any other category of investors, but other institutions, such as pension funds, trust funds, mutual funds, and casualty insurance companies, are important on the demand side of the market. Although financial institutions make up the principal market, many individuals find corporate issues of one kind or another suitable for their personal investment portfolios.

Preferred Stock

13 **HARRY C. SAUVAIN, D.C.S.**
University Professor Emeritus of Finance
Indiana University

THE ESSENTIAL NATURE OF PREFERRED STOCKS

Preferred stock is a class of stock with preferences over common stock of the issuer. It is an equity-type security and not a debt instrument. Why, then, do we call it a fixed income security? The reason is that the amount of annual dividend is almost always paid—no more and no less—but a fixed amount of dividend.

The chief preference of preferred stock over common stock is the preference to dividends. Preferred stock is always entitled to dividends at a fixed rate on par value or a fixed dollar amount per share annually before any dividend can be paid on the issuer's common stock. However, the amount of dividend on preferred stock is ordinarily limited to that fixed amount or rate of dividend. It is as though the preferred stockholders say to the common stockholders, "Let us have dividends up to the stipulated amount per share before you receive dividends, and regardless of whether you receive them, and we will agree that our dividends shall be limited to that stipulated amount per share. You common stockholders can have dividends limited in amount only by the financial ability of the company to pay them." There are always investors who will accept this kind of bargain as preferred stockholders.

There are of course differences between the terms of different issues of preferred stock and differences in the financial ability of corporate issuers to pay preferred dividends. Thus there are differences in the riskiness of preferred stocks. Investment information services provide a shortcut to initial appraisal of preferred stocks by publishing ratings for them in much the same manner as they do for bonds. The highest grade preferreds (least uncertainty about future dividends) are rated AAA or by some similar designation. Such a rating indicates a strong capacity of the issuer to pay the preferred dividend. The ratings decline to double A and single A and so on down into B ratings. As the ratings decline, riskiness increases. Investors seeking fixed income preferreds would normally limit their selections to stocks in the three highest rating categories. Preferred stock ratings, it should be noted, are not comparable with bond ratings. A triple-A-rated preferred stock is more risky than a triple-A-rated bond.

You may be surprised to see that average dividend yields on good preferred stocks obtainable in the market at any particular time are lower than yields on investment-grade bonds. This does not mean that the preferred stocks are less risky; it is due to a difference in taxation of preferred dividends to be presently described. It is important, though, to know that changes in rates of yield in the market on investment-grade preferreds are highly correlated with changes in yields on long-term investment-grade corporate bonds. When market rates of yield on bonds rise, market rates of yield on preferred stocks rise. Preferred yields decline when bond yields decline. Thus the price of a preferred stock may decline markedly during a period of rising long-term bond yields. Such a price decline does not mean that a preferred stock has become riskier as far as payment of future dividends is concerned, but only that the market is demanding higher yields, and sellers of preferred stocks have to accept lower prices to provide the higher dividend yields.

THE TERMS OF THE BARGAIN WITH INVESTORS

There are many terms in the contract between a corporate issuer and those who own its preferred stock. These terms influence the riskiness of the stock. In the bargaining between a corporation that proposes a public offering of a preferred stock issue and the investment bankers who buy the issue for resale to the public, the prospective issuer wants to give away no more in terms favorable to investors than necessary to raise capital at an acceptable cost. In a broad sense the investment bankers do the bargaining for investors. They want the most favorable terms for investors because they have to sell the stock to them.

Nonparticipating Preferred Stock

Almost all preferred stocks that can be bought in the market today are nonparticipating. This means that owners of preferred stocks are entitled to the rate or amount of dividend stipulated in the legal provisions describing a class of stock and no more. This limitation, as we have suggested above, is the big thing that is bargained away by purchasers of preferred stock. A company may become very profitable and realize earnings many times the amounts necessary to pay the regular preferred dividend. But this does preferred stockholders no good, other than to get a higher rating for their stock. The big earnings go to the common stockholders as dividends.

In the history of use of investment instruments there are instances of issue of participating preferred stocks. The terms have varied, but the general idea may be illustrated by a provision that after the preferred has received its stipulated dividend and the common has received the same amount of dividend per share as the preferred, money remaining available for dividend payments is distributed in equal amounts per share among both the common and the preferred stocks. Such an arrangement is too good for preferred stock from the standpoint of corporate management. It lets preferred shareholders have their cake and eat it, too. Their cake is the preference to dividends; the eating of it is participation with common in larger dividends per share.

Cumulative Preferred Stock

A lop-sided deal in favor of corporate management is noncumulative preferred stock. The legal language would say, in effect, "If the issuer does not pay the preferred dividend in any dividend period, you just forget about it because you are not going to get it." That would be a very weak preference; management could skip a dividend payment, and the only important adverse consequence would be that no dividend could be paid on the common stock in the same period. In our financial history there have been a few noncumulative preferred stocks.

Cumulative means that when a preferred dividend is not paid, it accumulates and no dividend may be paid on common stock of the issuer until all dividend arrears have been paid on the preferred or on any other stock of the issuer ranking junior to the preferred. The prohibition of dividend payments on common stock when dividends on preferred stock are in arrears is a serious restriction. Common stockholders like their dividends. When common dividends are stopped and cannot be resumed until some sizable amount of preferred dividends in arrears is paid, they direct some very sharp questions to management. They also express their disfavor by selling their stock and driving the market price down.

Usually failure to pay preferred dividends results in other financial restrictions on management. It is common to provide that while preferred dividends are in arrears the issuer may not redeem any shares of stock junior to the preferred. This is to prevent management from sneaking around left end and using money that should be used for payment of preferred dividends in arrears to benefit owners of stocks junior to the preferred. Generally, the terms of preferred stocks also provide that when dividends are in arrears sinking-fund payments on the preferred and on any junior preferred are suspended and no money may be used to redeem preferred or common stock.

A thorough study of a preferred stock would include examination of the terms of any bond issues and bank loans of the issuer and of any class of preferred senior to the one being studied. Sometimes these senior securities have provisions prohibiting payment of dividends on junior securities when the issuer's financial condition falls below standards set in these agreements, such as a minimum current ratio or a minimum amount of surplus available for the payment of dividends.

Preference to Assets

At the time a preferred stock is issued hardly anyone thinks about the possibility that at some time in the future the issuing corporation may be liquidated, except the lawyers who draw up the terms of security issues. They write in provisions about what happens to a preferred stock in the event the issuer is liquidated either voluntarily or involuntarily in financial failure. A simple preference is that preferred stockholders are entitled to receive, after settlement has been made with creditors and holders of any senior issue of preferred, the par value of the preferred before any distribution is made to common stock or to any junior preferred stock. In the case of stock without par value, an amount per share is stipulated. Sometimes preferred holders are entitled to a larger amount in voluntary liquidation than in involuntary liquidation under a bankruptcy statute.

The preference to an amount per share in liquidation is not worth much to preferred stockholders. Seldom is a company voluntarily liquidated. In case of liquidation due to financial failure, there is seldom very much left for them after settlement with bondholders and owners of other credit instruments.

Voting Rights

Corporate issuers of preferred stocks are inclined to the view that as long as preferred stockholders receive their dividends regularly, there is no need for them to have voting rights. Investment bankers who underwrite new issues, however, think that the right to vote makes a preferred stock more attractive to investors. Sometimes one view prevails and sometimes another.

However, it is common practice to give nonvoting stock a right to elect some number of directors when preferred dividends have been in arrears for some number of dividend periods. This is *contingent voting* stock; the voting right is contingent upon the preferred stockholders not getting their dividends. The most common kind of contingent voting right is the right of owners of a class of preferred stock voting as a class to elect two directors. Thus they are assured of representation on the board of a company experiencing financial difficulties. This kind of provision has become common because the New York Stock Exchange requires it as a condition for listing nonvoting preferred stocks. Another kind of contingent voting provision is one that gives preferred stockholders one vote per share along with common stock when dividends are in arrears. Whenever arrears of dividends on contingent voting stock have been paid or settled, the conditional voting right ceases.

Another variation that appears in the terms of some voting preferred stock is one that requires approval of specified corporate acts by preferred stockholders voting as a class whenever dividends have been in arrears for some period of time. For example, agreement by two thirds of a class of preferred stock voting as a class may be required for approval of such management proposals as (1) increasing the authorized amount of any class or series of stock that ranks ahead of the preferred as to dividends or as to assets upon liquidation, (2) altering the provisions of the issuer's articles of incorporation, or (3) merging or consolidating with another company in such manner as to adversely affect the rights and preferences of the preferred stock. Preferred stock with such a provision is called vetoing stock because it can veto action proposed by management by withholding approval. The power to veto ceases when arrears of dividends are paid.

Redemption Provisions

Companies that issue preferred stocks think that raising capital in this way is a good idea at time of issue. It provides capital at a lower cost of capital than an issue of common stock and does not create debt as would an issue of bonds. But circumstances change, and a time may come when an issuer of preferred stock finds it desirable to eliminate preferred stock from its capitalization. Voting rights, for example, might impair control of a preferred stock issuer by owners of its common stock. Or circumstances might change in such a manner that it would become advantageous to refund a preferred stock with bonds to increase earnings on common stock. Interest on bonds is a deductible expense in calculating corporate income subject to the income tax, but preferred dividends are not. Such a refunding would change a nondeductible expense (preferred dividends) to a tax-deductible expense (bond interest). So virtually all issuers of preferred stock make provision for periodic redemption by a sinking-fund arrangement, redemption of stock in whole or in part by call, or by conversion into common stock.

Sinking-fund provisions are desirable, too, from the viewpoint of investors. Preferred stockholders may benefit by redemption or repurchase of stock at prices greater than the issue price. There is also the benefit of a gradual reduction in number of preferred shares outstanding by operation of a sinking fund. The smaller the number of shares, the less the amount required to pay preferred dividends. An important consideration for corporate investors is that a rule of the Financial Accounting Standards Board permits preferred stocks with sinking funds to be valued by financial institutions for published financial statements at cost rather than at current market price.

Sinking-fund provisions for preferred stocks are similar to those of bonds. It is common practice to provide that there shall be no redemption by sinking fund until several years have elapsed from date of issue. Then some percentage of the number of shares initially issued must be retired each year; the percentage may be from 2 to 8 percent. Prices for sinking-fund redemption are related to par value or to issue price. For example, the sinking-fund prices for a preferred stock of the Detroit Edison Company issued at $100 per share are: $115.68 in 1982, $113.72 in 1983, $111.76 in 1984, and so on down to $100 in 1990. Shares to be redeemed by the sinking fund are selected by lot. When the market price for stock is less than the sinking-fund redemption price, stock may be purchased in the market to satisfy the sinking-fund requirement. This is of course to the advantage of the issuer, but it also tends to support the market price, which is to the advantage of the investors.

Besides sinking-fund redemption there is almost always a clause that authorizes an issuer to call all or part of a preferred issue for redemption at one time. In many instances, call for redemption is not permitted in the first five years, or some similar period, after initial issue. Then the redemption price is fixed somewhat higher than the initial issue price for some number of years, and it declines as time passes in much the same manner as sinking-fund prices decline. Sometimes the provision for redemption in whole or in part may not be used for refunding of a preferred stock with another issue of securities.

Convertible Preferred Stock[1]

The conversion feature for preferred is about the same as it is in convertible bonds. A share of preferred is convertible into some number of shares of common stock. This gives the convertible preferred a speculative quality as well as its investment value as a fixed income security. The ratio of exchange is subject to adjustment in the event of a common stock split or stock dividend that would reduce the value of the common stock.

The language of the conversion right is illustrated by the following statement from a prospectus, dated May 8, 1981, of the Allis Chalmers Corporation: "Holders of the Series C Convertible Preferred Stock will have the right at their option to convert their stock into shares of Common Stock at any time, initially at the conversion rate of 1.6667 shares of Common Stock for each share of Series C Preferred subject to adjustment under certain conditions. This is equivalent to a conversion price of $30.00 per share of Common Stock relative to the issue price of $50 per share for the Series C Preferred Stock."

From the standpoint of a corporate issuer of convertible preferred, this kind of security has the advantage that the dividend rate is less than it would be without the conversion feature. Thus the cost of capital is less. Conversion by redemption of preferred is also a way to eliminate a convertible preferred stock from the capital structure when the market value of the common stock that may be obtained by conversion is greater than the redemption price of the convertible preferred. Conversion is not forced upon the preferred stockholders. It is simply to their advantage to convert rather than to accept the redemption price. When the market value of the common stock obtainable by conversion is greater than the redemption value of the preferred, the preferred sells at about its conversion value. Thus an individual preferred stockholder may sell stock in the market and realize the benefit of the conversion privilege. But preferred stockholders in the aggregate must convert or accept the lower redemption price.

In this case of the Allis-Chalmers convertible preferred stock, the preferred is callable at redemption prices that begin at $55.975 per share. When the market value of 1.6667 shares of common is more than that amount, it is advantageous to the preferred stockholders to take stock instead of cash if the preferred stock is called for redemption. At the date of this writing the Allis-Chalmers common stock was selling in the market at $21.875. Thus the market value of 1.6667 common shares was $36.46. At this price it would be disadvantageous for the preferred stockholders to convert. But if the market price of the

---

[1] See Chapter 22 for a more detailed discussion of convertible securities.

common rises to, say, $35, the value of the common stock obtainable by conversion would be $58.33, which is more than the redemption price of $55.975.

MULTIPLE ISSUES OF ONE CLASS OF PREFERRED

Some companies have more than one class of preferred stock. They sold one class at one time and another class at another time. The terms of the two or more classes are determined separately at time of issue. When there is more than one class, the question important to investors is: Which stock is senior to another in claim for dividends? A senior preferred may receive dividends when a junior preferred does not. Other rights and limitations of the two or more classes of preferred may differ. This system of multiple classes of preferred makes things complicated both for an issuer and for investors.

Companies that use preferred stock continually in their capitalizations as a matter of financial policy find that it is easier both for them and for investors to authorize one class of preferred stock with a defined preference as to dividends and to provide that it may be issued in series from time to time. Thus there may be Series A, Series B, and so on. It is not uncommon for public utility companies to have six or eight series of one class of preferred stock outstanding.

What makes this arrangement attractive to investors is that all of the terms of preferred stock that we have been discussing may be different for the different series. Thus they can choose the series that best suits them. One series may have one stipulated rate of dividends and another series a different rate. For example, the Cincinnati Gas & Electric Company has eight series of preferred stock with dividend rates ranging from 4 percent to 12.52 percent. The issuer has simply established the dividend rate on each issue at the amount necessary to obtain buyers at different points in time.

All of the other terms of a class of preferred stock may differ among the series. One series may be voting and another nonvoting. The terms for sinking-fund redemption and for redemption in whole or in part may differ. One series may be convertible and another not convertible. Each series is tailored to conditions in the securities market at time of issue.

TAXABILITY OF PREFERRED STOCK DIVIDENDS[2]

For individual investors the story about taxability of dividends on preferred stocks is short with very little sweetness. Individuals may exclude from taxable income no more than $100 of dividends received

---

[2] For a more detailed discussion see Chapter 3.

during a tax year on all common and preferred stock; a married couple filing a joint tax return may exclude $200 when both taxpayers have dividend income.

For corporate investors it is a different story. A corporation may exclude from gross income 85 percent of dividends received from other domestic corporations. This exclusion is justified on the ground that it mitigates double taxation of dividends paid by one company to another and then paid to the stockholders of the second company. Dividends by one company are paid after its earnings have been taxed under the federal corporate income tax. Then when received by a second company they would be taxed again as income to that company. This 85 percent exclusion leaves only 15 percent to be taxed in the hands of a corporate owner of preferred stock. This rule applies only to preferred stocks issued after October 1, 1942. For stocks issued before that date the exclusion is 60.2 percent. When you consider these tax provisions, you understand why preferred stocks are owned chiefly by corporate investors and why they sell in the market at current dividend yields less than those on good-grade corporate bonds.

THE MARKETABILITY OF PREFERRED STOCKS

Preferred stocks that have been publicly distributed are marketable in the sense that they are traded on the stock exchanges and in the over-the-counter market. There is always a dealer or a stock exchange specialist who is willing to quote a bid price (what he or she will pay if you want to sell) and an offered price (what he or she will ask if you want to buy). But there are marked differences in the quality of marketability among preferred stocks, and these differences are important to investors who buy and sell these stocks.

The quality of marketability is measured by the size of the spread quoted by a dealer or specialist, that is, by the difference between the bid and offer prices expressed as a percentage of the bid price. For example, a preferred stock is quoted by a dealer at 50 bid and 52 offered. The spread is two points, or $2 per share, and it is 4 percent of the bid price. This is what a dealer charges for his services in making a market in a security. It is a transaction cost to an investor. Another part of the transactions cost is the commission charged by the broker who handles a transaction. It would be a fraction of 1 percent of the value. When you buy and sell you pay these costs twice. In the example above the total cost for the services of brokers and dealers is 4 to 5 percent of the $50 bid price. It might, however, be only 1 or 2 percent for a highly marketable issue. The principal variable is the dealer's spread.

The size of the dealer's spread is largely a function of the volume of trading in a stock. The larger the volume, the less the spread. The spread has to cover the dealer's costs of doing business and the dealer's profit. These costs vary somewhat with the volume of trading. A dealer who trades 10,000 shares of a stock a day will quote a spread much lower than one who trades only 1,000 shares a day. The dealer's costs are not much more for trading 10,000 shares than 1,000 shares and can be distributed over a much larger number of shares. Competition of other dealers presses downward on the spread. Other things being equal, the size of the spread in a market where 10 dealers are quoting a stock is less than in a market where only two dealers are competing for business.

INFORMATION ABOUT PREFERRED STOCKS

The best source of information about preferred stocks is the prospectuses published at the time they are first issued and, incidentally, this is the best time to buy preferreds because there is no brokerage commission on such purchases. Prospectuses contain very complete information about the terms of new preferred issues and about the issuers. Ordinarily there are financial statements for the preceding five years, a description of the kind of business conducted with data on sales for different product lines, and managements' discussion and analysis of financial condition and results of operations. The limitation of this information source is that it is soon out of date for all but the most basic types of data. Then you have to turn to the usual investment information sources.

You can get information about preferred stocks from much the same sources as for common stocks and bonds. There are the investors' manuals published by the two principal agencies that rate stocks and bonds. The manuals provide detailed information about corporate issuers and about their securities.[3] These manuals are particularly useful for information about the provisions of preferred stocks such as we have been discussing.

One of the investment information services, Standards & Poor's, publishes monthly a *Stock Guide*, which provides condensed information about preferred and common stocks as well as ratings for most of them. You can compare a number of preferred stocks quickly using this publication. It provides in abbreviated form information about the principal terms of issues as well as historical information about prices and about earnings. The dividend rate is indicated and so is the annual amount currently being paid, so you can learn quickly whether dividends are in arrears.

An indication of the financial ability of an issuer to pay its preferred dividend is provided by reported earnings per share on the preferred

---

[3] These manuals were described in the previous chapter.

for the past five years. This amount is calculated by taking the amount of an issuer's earnings after bond interest and taxes and dividing by the number of preferred shares outstanding. If the annual amount of dividend is, say, $5, and the earnings per share on the preferred is $50, the issuer seems to have abundant ability to pay the dividend. However, that amount per share is at the margin. When earnings shrink, the earnings per share shrink to an even greater extent because of the leverage provided by bond interest. Many analysts prefer to divide the amount of earnings before bond interest and taxes by the sum of interest, taxes, and preferred dividends. By this calculation, you may determine that earnings cover preferred dividends plus all prior charges in the ratio of 2:1, or 4:1, or some other ratio.

SUMMARY

A preferred stock is a peculiar kind of security. Generally it provides a fixed income—the stipulated annual amount—no more or no less. But it is not a bond; it is a right of ownership in a company. There are many possible variations in the terms of different preferred issues. A very few have a right to receive larger dividends per share than the stipulated amount. A great many more afford an opportunity for capital gains by being convertible into common stock of the issuer. They are distinctly unlike common stock in that dividends not paid accumulate and must be paid before dividends may be paid on the common. But unlike bonds, failure to pay dividends on preferred is not a default as failure to pay bond interest would be. Although not a default, failure to pay preferred dividends may result in imposition of serious financial restrictions upon the issuer. Like bonds, many preferred issues have no voting power as long as dividends are being paid, but they usually gain some limited voting power when dividends are in arrears. A company may have one class of preferred stock and issue it in series with different terms for different series of the stock. So it is peculiar because it has some of the characteristics of bonds and some of the characteristics of common stocks. It is also peculiar because the exclusion from taxable income of most of the amount of preferred dividends received by corporations causes it to be owned very largely by corporations rather than individuals.

Credit Analysis for Corporate Bonds*

14 JANE TRIPP HOWE, C.F.A.
The First National Bank of Chicago

Traditionally, credit analysis for corporate bonds has focused almost exclusively on the default risk of the bond. That is, what is the chance that the bondholder will not receive the scheduled interest payments and/or principal at maturity. This one dimensional analysis concerned itself primarily with straight ratio analysis. This approach was deemed appropriate during the time when interest rates were stable and investors purchased bonds with the purpose of holding them to maturity. In this scenario fluctuations in the market value of the bonds due to interest-rate changes were minimal, and fluctuations due to credit changes of the bonds were mitigated by the fact that the investor had no intention of selling the bond before maturity. During the past decade, however, the purpose of buying bonds has changed dramatically. Investors still purchase bonds for security and thereby forego the higher expected return of other assets such as common stock. However, an increasing number of investors buy bonds to actively trade them with the purpose of making a profit on changes in interest rates or in absolute or relative credit quality. The second dimension of

* I wish to thank Richard S. Wilson, vice president, fixed income research, Merrill Lynch, Pierce, Fenner, & Smith, for his helpful comments and suggestions.

corporate bond credit analysis addresses the latter purpose of buying a bond. What is the likelihood of a change in credit quality that will affect the price of the bond? This second dimension of corporate bond analysis deals primarily with the ratios and profitability trends, such as return on equity, operating margins, and asset turnover, generally associated with common stock analysis. In practice, both dimensions of analysis should be applied in corporate bond analysis. In a sense, both dimensions are addressing the same issue—default or credit risk. However, only by using both dimensions of credit analysis will the analyst address the dual purpose of a bondholding: security of interest and principal payments and stability or improvement of credit risk during the life of the bond.

Historically, common stock and bond research areas have been viewed as separate. However, with the development of the options theory, the two disciplines are beginning to be viewed as complementary.

The value of the option is a direct function of the company's aggregate equity valuation. As the market value of a company's stock increases, the value of the option increases. Conversely, as the market value of a company's stock declines, so does the value of the option. The practical implication of this theory for corporate bonds analysis is that the perceptions of both markets should be compared before a final credit judgment is rendered. For the analyst who believes that there is a higher level of efficiency in the stock market than in the bond market, particular attention should be paid to the stock price of the company being analyzed. Of interest will be those situations in which the judgment of the two markets differ substantially. For example, in early 1981 the market to book values of the major chemical companies ranged from .77 to 2.15. The bond ratings of these same companies ranged from Baa/BBB to Aaa/AAA. The interesting point is not the range of either the market to book values or bond ratings, but rather the fact that although there was some correlation between the market/book ratios and bond ratings, there were instances in which there was little or no correlation. The options theory would suggest that there should be more of a relationship between the two. When the relative valuation of the bond as measured by the rating is low compared with the equity valuation as measured by market/book, one or both markets may be incorrectly valuing the company. Given the evidence that bond-rating changes generally lag market moves, it is likely in this case that the bond market is undervaluing the company.

Although there are numerous types of corporate bonds outstanding, three major issuing segments of bonds can be differentiated: industrials, utilities, and finance companies. This chapter will primarily address industrials in its general description of bond analysis and then discuss the utility and finance issues.

INDUSTRY CONSIDERATIONS

The first step in analyzing a bond is to gain some familiarity with the industry. Only within the context of an industry is a company analysis valid. For example, a company growing at 15 percent annually may appear attractive. However, if the industry is growing at 50 percent annually, the company is competitively weak. Industry considerations can be numerous. However, an understanding of the following eight variables should give the general fixed income analyst a sufficient framework to properly interpret a company's prospects.

Economic Cyclicality

The economic cyclicality of an industry is the first variable an analyst should consider in reviewing an industry. Does the industry closely follow GNP growth, as does the retailing industry, or is it recession resistant but slow growing, as is the electric utility industry? The growth in earnings per share (EPS) of a company should be measured against the growth trend of its industry. Major deviations from the industry trend should be the focus of further analysis. Some industries may be somewhat dependent on general economic growth but be more sensitive to demographic changes. The nursing home industry is a prime example of this type of sensitivity. With the significant aging of the U.S. population, the nursing home industry is projected to have above average growth for the foreseeable future. Other industries, such as the banking industry, are sensitive to interest rates. When interest rates are rising, the earnings of banks with a high federal funds exposure underperform the market as their loan rates lag behind increases in the cost of money. Conversely, as interest rates fall, banking earnings outperform the market because the lag in interest change works in the banks' favor.

In general, however, the earnings of few industries perfectly correlate with one economic statistic. Not only are industries sensitive to many economic variables, but often various segments within a company or an industry move countercyclically, or at least with different lags in relation to the general economy. For example, the housing industry can be divided between new construction and remodeling and repair. New construction historically has led GNP growth, but repair and remodeling has exhibited less sensitivity to general trends. Therefore, in analyzing a company in the construction industry, the performance of each of its segments must be compared with the performance of the subindustry.

Growth Prospects

A second industry variable related to that of economic cyclicality is the growth prospects for an industry. Is the growth of the industry projected to increase and be maintained at a high level, such as in the nursing industry, or is growth expected to be stable? Each growth scenario has implications for a company. In the case of a fast-growth industry, how much capacity is needed to meet demand, and how will this capacity be financed? In the case of slow-growth industries, is there a movement toward diversification and/or a consolidation within the industry, such as in the brewing industry? A company operating within a fast-growing industry often has a better potential for credit improvement than does a company whose industry's growth prospects are below average.

Research and Development Expenses

The broad assessment of growth prospects is tempered by the third variable—the research and development expenditures required to maintain or expand market position. The technology field is growing at an above-average rate, and the companies in the industry should do correspondingly well. However, products with a high technological component can become dated and obsolete quickly. Therefore, although a company may be situated well in an industry, if it does not have the financial resources to maintain a technological lead, or at least expend a sufficient amount of money to keep technologically current, its position is likely to deteriorate in the long run. In the short run, however, a company whose R&D expenditures are consistently below industry averages may produce above-average results because of expanded margins.

Competition

Competition within an industry also directly relates to the market structure of an industry and has implications for pricing flexibility. An unregulated monopoly is in an enviable position in that it can price its goods at a level that will maximize profits. Most industries encounter some free market forces and must price their goods in relation to the supply and demand for their goods as well as the price charged for similar goods. In an oligopoly, a pricing leader is not uncommon. General Motors Corporation, for example, performs this function in the automobile industry. A concern arises when a small company is in an industry that is trending toward oligopoly. In this environment, the small company's costs of production may be higher than those of the industry leaders, and yet it may have to conform to the pricing of the industry leaders. In the extreme, a price war could force the smaller companies out of business. This situation is present now in the brewing industry. For the past decade, as the brewing industry has become increasingly concentrated, the leaders have gained market share at the expense of the small, local brewers. Many small, local brewers have either been acquired or have gone out of business. These local brewers have been at dual disadvantage: They are in an industry whose structure is moving toward oligopoly, and yet their weak competitive position within the industry largely precludes pricing flexibility.

Sources of Supply

The market structure of an industry and its competitive forces have a direct impact on the fifth industry variable—sources of supply of major production components. A company in the paper industry that has sufficient timber acreage to supply 100 percent of its pulp is preferable to a paper company that must buy all or a large percentage of its pulp. A company that is not selfsufficient in its factors of production but is sufficiently powerful in its industry to pass along increased costs is also in an enviable position. Nabisco Brands is an example of the latter type of company. Although Nabisco Brands has major exposure to commodity prices for ingredients in its baked goods, Nabisco's strong market position has enabled it historically to pass along increased costs of goods sold.

Degree of Regulation

The sixth industry consideration is the degree of regulation. The electric utility industry is the classic example of regulation. Nearly all phases of a utility's operations are regulated. The analyst should not be as concerned with the existence or absence of regulation per se, but rather with the direction of regulation and the effect it has on the profitability of the company. For the elecric utility industry, regulation generally places a cap on earned returns. On the other hand, the most recent trend of regulation within the electric utility industry indicates a growing awareness on the part of commissioners of the need for adequate and timely rate relief. Other industries, such as the drug industry, also have a high though less pervasive degree of regulation. In the drug industry, however, the threat of increased regulation has been a negative factor in the industry for some time.

Labor

The labor situation of an industry should also be analyzed. Is the industry heavily unionized? If so, what has been the historical occurence of strikes? When do the current contracts expire, and what is the likelihood of timely settlements? The labor situation is also important in nonunionized companies, particularly those whose labor situation is tight. What has been the turnover of professionals and management in the firm? What is the probability of a firm's employees, such as highly skilled engineers, being hired by competing firms? The more labor intensive an industry, the more significance the labor situation assumes.

Accounting

A final industry factor to be considered is accounting. Does the industry have special accounting practices, such as those in the insurance industry or the electric utility industry? If so, an analyst should become familiar with industry practices before proceeding with a company analysis. Also important is whether a company is liberal or conservative in applying the generally accepted accounting principles. The norm of an industry should be ascertained, and the analyst should be sure to analyze comparable figures.

FINANCIAL ANALYSIS

Once having achieved an understanding of an industry, the analyst is ready to proceed with a financial analysis. The financial analysis should be conducted in three phases. The first phase consists of traditional ratio analysis for bonds. The second phase, generally associated with common stock research, consists of analyzing the components of a company's return on equity (ROE). The final phase considers such nonfinancial factors as management and foreign exposure and includes an analysis of the indenture.

Traditional Ratio Analysis

There are numerous ratios that can be calculated in applying traditional ratio analysis to bonds. Of these, eight will be discussed in this section. Those selected are the ratios with the widest degree of applicability. In analyzing a particular industry, however, other ratios assume significance and should be considered. For example, in the electric utility industry, allowance for funds used in construction as a percent of net income is an important ratio that is inapplicable to the analysis of industrial or financial companies.

Pretax Interest Coverage. Generally, the first ratio calculated in credit analysis is pretax interest coverage. This ratio measures the number of times interest charges are covered on a pretax basis. Fixed-charge coverage is calculated by dividing pretax income plus interest charges by total interest charges. The higher the coverage figure, the safer the credit. If interest coverage is less than 1X, the company must borrow or use cash flow or sale of assets to meet its interest payments. Generally, published coverage figures are pretax as opposed to after-tax because interest payments are a pretax expense. Although pretax interest coverage ratio is useful, its utility is a function of the company's other fixed obligations. For example, if a company has other significant fixed obligations, such as rents or leases, a more appropriate coverage figure would include these other fixed obligations. An example of this is the retail industry, in which companies typically have significant lease obligations. A calculation of simple pretax interest coverage would be misleading in this case because fixed obligations other than interest are significant. The analyst should also be aware of any contingent liabilities, such as a company's guaranteeing another company's debt. Although the company being analyzed may never have to pay interest or principal on the guaranteed debt, the existence of the guarantee diminishes the quality of the pretax coverage.

Once pretax interest coverage and fixed-charge coverage are calculated, it is necessary to analyze the ratios' absolute levels and the numbers relative to those of the industry. For example, pretax interest coverage for an electric utility of 6X is consistent with an "AAA" rating, whereas the same coverage for a drug company would indicate a lower rating.

Standard & Poor's 1980 pretax interest coverage ranges for the senior debt of industrial companies were as follows:

Rating Classification	Pretax Interest Coverage
AAA	12X and higher
AA	7.5–12X
A	5–8.5X
BBB	3.5–6X

Leverage. A second important ratio is leverage, which can be defined in several ways. The most common definition, however, is long-term debt as a percent of total capitalization. The higher the level of debt, the higher the percentage of operating income that must be used to meet fixed obligations. If a company is highly leveraged, the analyst should also look at its margin of safety. The margin of safety is defined as the percentage that operating income could decline and still be sufficient to allow the company to meet its fixed obligations. Standard & Poor's 1980 leverage ranges for the senior debt of industrial companies were as follows:

Rating Classification	Long-Term Debt/Capitalization
AAA	20 percent or lower
AA	20–30 percent
A	25–35 percent
BBB	33–45 percent

The most common way to calculate leverage is to use the company's capitalization structure as stated in the most recent balance sheet. In addition to this measure, the analyst should calculate capitalization using a market approximation for the value of the common stock. When a company's common stock is selling significantly below book value, leverage will be understated by the traditional approach.

The degree of leverage and margin of safety varies dramatically among industries. Finance companies have traditionally been among the most highly leveraged companies, with debt to equity ratios of 10/1. Although such leverage is tolerated in the finance industry, an industrial company with similar leverage would have a difficult time issuing debt.

In addition to considering the absolute and relative level of leverage of a company, the analyst should evaluate the debt itself. How much of the debt has a fixed rate, and how much has a floating rate? A company with a high component of debt tied to the prime may find its margins being squeezed as interest rates rise if there is no compensating increase in the price of the firm's goods. Such a debt structure may be beneficial during certain phases of the interest-rate cycle, but it has the disadvantage of precluding a precise estimate of what interest charges for the year will be. In general, a company with a high percentage of floating-rate debt is less preferable than a similarly levered company with a small percentage of floating-rate debt.

The maturity structure of the debt should also be evaluated. What is the percentage of debt that is coming due within the next five years? As this debt is refinanced, how will the company's embedded cost of debt be changed? In this regard, the amount of original-issue discount (OID) debt should also be considered. High quality OIDs were first issued in sizable amounts in 1981, although lower quality OIDs have been issued for some time. This debt is issued with low or zero coupons and at substantial discounts to par. Each year the issuing company expenses the interest payment (coupon times the total principal amount due at maturity) as well as the amortization of the discount. At issuance only the actual bond proceeds are listed as debt on the balance sheet. However, as this debt payable will increase annually, the analyst should consider the full face amount due at maturity when evaluating the maturity structure and refinancing plans of the company.

Cash Flow. A third important ratio is cash flow as a percent of total debt. Cash flow is often defined as net income plus depreciation, depletion, and deferred taxes. In calculating cash flow for credit analysis, the analyst should also subtract noncash contributions from subsidiaries. In essence, the analyst should be concerned with cash from operations. Any extraordinary sources or uses of funds should be excluded when determining the overall trend of cash flow coverage.

Cash dividends from subsidiaries should also be questioned in terms of their appropriateness (too high or too low relative to the subsidiary's earnings) and also in terms of the parent's control over the upstreaming of dividends. Is there a legal limit to the upstreamed dividends? If so, how close is the current level of dividends to the limit? Standard & Poor's 1980 cash flow/long-term debt ranges for the senior debt of industrial companies were as follows:

Rating Classification	Cash Flow/Long-Term Debt
AAA	90 percent and higher
AA	55–90 percent
A	40–60 percent
BBB	25–40 percent

Net Assets. A fourth significant ratio is net assets to total debt. In analyzing this facet of a bond's quality, consideration should be given to the liquidation value of the assets. Liquidation value will often differ dramatically from the value stated on the balance sheet. At one extreme, consider a nuclear generating plant that has had operating problems and has been closed down and whose chance of receiving an operating license is questionable. This asset is likely overstated on the balance sheet, and the bondholder should take little comfort in reported asset protection. At the other extreme is the forest products company whose vast timber acreage is significantly understated on the balance sheet. In addition to the assets' market value, some consideration should also be given to the liquidity of the assets. A company with a high percentage of its assets in cash and marketable securities is in a much stronger asset position than a company whose primary assets are illiquid real estate.

In addition to the major variables discussed above, the analyst should also consider several other financial variables including intangibles, unfunded pension liabilities, the age and condition of the plant, and working capital adequacy.

Intangibles. Intangibles often represent a small portion of the asset side of a balance sheet. Occasionally, however, particularly with companies that have or have had an active acquisition program, intangibles can represent a significant portion of assets. In this case, the analyst should estimate the actual value of the intangibles and determine whether this value is in concert with the balance sheet valuation. A carrying value significantly higher than market value indicates a potential for a write down of assets. The actual write down may not occur until the company actually sells a subsidiary to which the intangibles are identified. However, the analyst should recognize the potential and adjust capitalization ratios accordingly.

Unfunded Pension Liabilities. Unfunded pension liabilities can also affect a credit decision. Although a fully funded pension is not necessary for a high credit assessment, a large unfunded pension liability that is 10 percent or more of net worth can be a negative. Of concern is the company whose unfunded pension liabilities are sufficiently high to interfere with corporate planning. For example, a steel company with high unfunded pension liabilities might delay or decide against closing an unprofitable plant because of the pension costs involved. The analyst should also be aware of a company's assumed rate of return on its pension funds and salary increase assumptions. The higher the assumed rate of return, the lower the contribution a company must make to its pension fund, given a set of actuarial assumptions. Occasionally, a company having difficulty with its earnings will raise its actuarial assumption and thereby lower its pension contribution and increase earnings. The impact on earnings can be dramatic.

Age and Condition of Plant. The age of a company's plant should also be estimated, if only to the extent that its age differs dramatically from industry standards. A heavy industrial company whose average plant age is well above that of its competitors is probably already paying for its aged plant through operating inefficiencies. In the longer term, however, the age of net plant is an indication of future capital expenditures for a more modern plant. In addition, the underdepreciation of the plant significantly lowers inflation-adjusted earnings.

Working Capital. A final variable in assessing a company's financial strength concerns the strength and liquidity of its working capital. Working capital is defined as current assets less current liabilities. Working capital is considered a primary measure of a company's financial flexibility. Other such measures include the current ratio (current assets divided by current liabilities) and the acid test (cash, marketable securities, and receivables divided by current liabilities). The stronger the company's liquidity measures, the better able it is to weather a downturn in business and cash flow. In assessing this variable, the analyst should consider the normal working capital requirements of a company and industry. The components of working capital should also be analyzed. Although accounts receivables are considered to be liquid, an increase in the average days a receivable is outstanding may be an indication that a higher level of working capital is needed for the efficient running of the operation.

Analysis of the Components of Return on Equity

Once the above financial analysis is complete, the bond analyst traditionally examines the earnings progression of the company and its historical return on equity (ROE). This section of analysis often receives less emphasis than the traditional ratio analysis. It is equally important, however, and demands equal emphasis. An analysis of earnings growth and ROE is vital to necessary in determining credit quality because it gives the analyst necessary insights into the components of ROE and indications of the sources of future growth. Equity analysts devote a major portion of their time examining the components of ROE, and their work should be recognized as valuable resource material.

A basic approach to the examination of the components of return on equity is presented in a popular investment textbook by Jerome B. Cohen, Edward D. Zinbarg, and Arthur Zeikel.[1] Their basic approach breaks down return on equity into four principal components: pretax margins, asset turnover, leverage, and the tax rate. These four variables multiplied together equal net income/stockholders' equity, or return on equity.

$$\left(\frac{\text{Nonoperating pretax income}}{\text{Sales}} + \frac{\text{Operating pretax income}}{\text{Sales}} \right) \times \frac{\text{Sales}}{\text{Assets}} \times \frac{\text{Assets}}{\text{Equity}}$$
$$\times (1 - \text{Tax rate}) = \text{Net Income/Equity}$$

In analyzing these four components of ROE, the analyst should examine their progression for a minimum of five years and at least through a business cycle. The progression of each variable should be compared with the progression of the same variables for the industry, and deviations from industry standards should be further analyzed. For example, perhaps two companies have similar ROE's, but one company is employing a higher level of leverage to achieve its results, whereas the other company has a higher asset-turnover rate. As the degree of leverage is largely a management decision, the analyst should focus on asset turnover. Why have sales for the former company turned down? Is this downturn a result of a general slowdown in the industry, or is it that assets have been expanded rapidly and the company is in the process of absorbing these new assets? Conversely, a relatively high rise in the asset-turnover rate may indicate a need for more capital. If this is the case, how will the company finance this growth, and what effect will the financing have on the firm's embedded cost of capital?

The analyst should not expect similar components of ROE for all companies in a particular industry. Deviations from industry norms are often indications of management philosophy. For example, one company may emphasize asset turnover, and another company in the

---

[1] *Investment Analysis and Portfolio Management* (Homewood, Ill.: Richard D. Irwin, 1977). © Richard D. Irwin, Inc., 1977.

same industry may emphasize profit margin. As in any financial analysis, the trend of the components are as important as the absolute levels.

In order to give the analyst a general idea of the type of ratios expected by the major rating agencies for a particular rating classification, Standard & Poor's medians of key ratios for 1978–1980 by rating category are outlined in Exhibit 1. The analyst should only use this table in the most general applications, however, for two reasons. First, industry standards vary considerably. Second, financial ratios are only one part of an analysis.

Exhibit 1
Three-Year (1978–1980) Medians of Key Ratios by Rating Category

	AAA	AA	A	BBB	BB	B
Pretax interest coverage..	12.82X	9.50X	6.65X	4.41X	3.14X	2.13X
Pretax interest and full rental coverage........	7.08	5.41	4.25	3.25	2.34	1.61
Cash flow/long-term debt.	134.06%	90.93%	62.98%	45.96%	27.96%	17.96%
Cash flow/total debt......	107.38	70.46	54.31	37.63	24.54	15.68
Pretax return on average long-term capital employed...............	27.04	24.90	21.14	18.81	17.44	13.20
Operating income/sales ..	16.48	15.65	13.62	12.21	11.49	9.20
Long-term debt/capitalization...................	17.11	21.66	27.70	33.94	45.16	56.17
Total debt/capitalization including short-term debt	20.73	25.53	31.82	38.47	49.39	60.47
Total debt/capitalization including short-term debt (Including 8X rents) ...	33.39	37.10	40.99	47.98	57.99	67.58
Total liabilities/tangible shareholders' equity and minority interest.......	83.54	96.64	106.07	131.52	198.42	282.15

Note: These are not meant to be minimum standards.
Source: Standard & Poor's Corporation, 1980.

Nonfinancial Factors

After the traditional bond analysis is completed, the analyst should consider some nonfinancial factors that might modify the evaluation of the company. Among these factors are the degree of foreign exposure and the quality of management. The amount of foreign exposure should be ascertainable from the annual report. Sometimes, however, specific country exposure is less clear because the annual report often lists foreign exposure by broad geographic divisions. If there is concern that a major portion of revenue and income is derived from potentially unstable areas, the analyst should carefully consider the total revenue and income derived from the area and the assets committed.

Further consideration should be given to available corporate alternatives should nationalization of assets occur. Additionally, the degree of currency exposure should be determined. If currency fluctuations are significant, has management hedged its exposure?

The quality and depth of management is more difficult to evaluate. Earnings progress at the firm is a good indication of the quality of management. Negative aspects would include a firm founded and headed by one person who is approaching retirement and has made no plan for succession. Equally negative is the firm that has had numerous changes of management and philosophy. On the other hand, excessive stability is not always desirable. If one family or group of investors owns a controlling interest in a firm, they may be too conservative in terms of reacting to changes in markets. Characteristics of a good management team should include depth, a clear line of succession if the chief officers are nearing retirement, and a diversity of age within the management team.

INDENTURE PROVISIONS

An indenture is a legal document that defines the rights and obligations of the borrower and the lender with respect to a bond issue. An analysis of the indenture should be a part of a credit review in that the indenture provisions establish rules for several important spheres of operation for the borrower. These provisions, which can be viewed as safeguards for the lender, cover such areas as the limitation on the issuance of additional debt, sale and leasebacks, and sinking-fund provisions.

The indentures of bonds of the same industry are often similar in the areas they address. Correlation between the quality rating of the senior debt of a company and the stringency of indenture provisions is not perfect. For example, the debt test is more severe in A securities than in BBB securities. However, subordinated debt of one company will often have less restrictive provisions than will the senior debt of the same company. In addition, more restrictive provisions are also generally found in private placement issues. In analyzing a company's indenture, the analyst should look for the standard industry provisions. Differences in these provisions (either more or less restrictive) should be examined more closely. In this regard, a more restrictive nature is not necessarily preferable if the provisions are so restrictive as to hinder the efficient operation of the company.

Outlined below are the provisions most commonly found in indentures. These provisions are categorized by industry because the basic provisions are fairly uniform within an industry. A general description of the indenture is found in a company's prospectus. However, notification is generally given that the indenture provisions are only summarized. A complete indenture may be obtained from the Trustee who is listed in the prospectus.

Utility Indentures

Security. The security provision is generally the first provision in a utility indenture. This provision specifies the property upon which there is a mortgage lien. In addition, the ranking of the new debt relative to outstanding debt is specified. Generally, the new bonds rank equally with all other bonds outstanding under the mortgage. This ranking is necessary, but it has created difficulty for the issuing companies because some mortgage indentures were written more than 40 years ago. Specifically, because all bondholders must be kept equal, companies must often retain antiquated provisions in their indentures. Often these provisions hinder the efficient running of a company due to structural changes in the industry since the original writing of the indenture. Changes in these provisions can be made, but changes have occurred slowly because of the high percentage of bondholders that must approve a change and the time and expense required to locate the bondholders.

Issuance of Additional Bonds. The "Issuance of Additional Bonds" provision establishes the conditions under which the company may issue additional first mortgage bonds. Often this provision contains a debt test and/or an earnings test. The debt test generally limits the amount of bonds that may be issued under the mortgage to a certain percentage (often 60 percent) of net property or net property additions, the principal amount of retired bonds, or deposited cash. The earnings test, on the other hand, restricts the issuance of additional bonds under the mortgage unless earnings for a particular period cover interest payments at a specified level.

Although both of these tests may appear straightforward, the analyst must carefully study the definitions contained in the tests. For example, net property additions may be defined as plant that has operating licenses. Over the past decade, although there has been a great deal of nuclear construction, few operating licenses have been granted. Therefore, there is a significant backlog of construction work in progress (CWIP) that has had to be financed and yet may not be operational for some time. This situation can present problems for the company whose indenture requires net plant additions to be licensed and/or used and useful assets. In the extreme case, a company with a heavy nuclear construction program may find itself unable to issue bonds under its mortgage agreement.

In a similar circumstance, a company whose regulatory commission requires a substantial write-down related to nuclear construction may find itself unable to meet a debt test for several years if the write-down is taken in one quarter.

Maintenance and Replacement Fund. The purpose of a maintenance and replacement fund (M&R) is to assure that the mortgaged property is maintained in good operating condition. To this end, electric utility indentures generally require that a certain percentage of gross operating revenues, a percentage of aggregate bonded indebtedness, or a percentage of the utility's property account be paid to the trustee for the M&R fund. A major portion of the M&R requirement has historically been satisfied with normal maintenance expenditures. To the extent there is a remaining requirement, the company may contribute cash, the pledge of unbonded property additions, or bonds.

The rapid escalation of fuel costs during the 1970s has greatly raised the required levels of many M&R funds which are tied to operating revenues. This situation precipitated a number of bond calls for M&R purposes. Bonds can still be called for this purpose, but investors are more cognizant of this risk and are less likely to pay a significant premium for bonds subject to such a call. Furthermore, M&R requirements are slowly being changed toward formulas that exclude the large portion of operating income attributable to rises in fuel costs. Finally, a number of companies have indicated that they have no intention of using M&R requirements for calling bonds because of the original intent of the provision and also because of the disfavor such an action would generate among bondholders. However, the intent of companies in this regard would certainly be secondary if a call for M&R requirements were ordered by a commission.

Redemption Provisions. The redemption, or call, provision specifies during what period and at what prices a company may call its bonds. Redemption provisions vary. Long-term bonds are generally currently callable but nonrefundable for five years. Exceptions to this statement are the longer term issues of the AT&T System, which are noncallable for five years. In the case of intermediate and short-term issues, the noncall provisions generally extend to a year or two prior to maturity. Refunding is an action by a company to replace outstanding bonds with another debt issue sold at a lower interest expense. (Refunding protection does not protect the bondholder from refunding bonds with equity or short-term debt.) The refunding protection is a safeguard for bondholders against their bonds being refunded at a disadvantageous time.

Sinking Fund. A sinking fund is an annual obligation of a company to pay the trustee an amount of cash sufficient to retire a given percentage of bonds. This requirement can often be met with actual bonds or with the pledge of property. In general, electric utilities have 1 percent sinking funds that commence at the end of the refunding period. However, there are several variations of the sinking-fund provision with which the analyst (and bondholder) should be familiar in that they could directly affect the probability of bonds being called for sinking-fund purposes. Some companies have nonspecific, or funnel, sinkers. This type of sinker often entails a 1 or 1½ percent sinking fund applicable to all outstanding bonds. The obligation can be met by the stated percentage of each issue outstanding, by cash, or by applying (or funneling) the whole requirement against one issue or several issues.

Other Provisions.   In addition to the provisions discussed above, the indenture covers the events of default, modification of the mortgage, and the powers and obligations of the trustee. In general, these provisions are fairly standard. However, differences occur that should be evaluated.

Industrial Indentures

Many of the provisions of an industrial indenture are similar to those of a utility's indenture, although specific items may be changed. For example, sinking-fund and redemption provisions are part of an industrial indenture. However, refunding protection for an industrial is generally 10 years (as opposed to 5 years for an electric utility), and sinking funds often have the option to double or more than double their requirements on an annual basis at the option of the company.

In general, there are four indenture provisions that have historically been significant in providing protection for the industrial bondholder.

Negative Pledge Clause.   The negative pledge clause provides that the company cannot create or assume liens to the extent that more than a certain percentage of consolidated net tangible assets (CNTA) is so secured without giving the same security to the bondholders. This provision is important to the bondholders because their security in the specific assets of the company establishes an important protection for their investment. The specific percentage of CNTA that is exempted from this provision is referred to as exempted indebtedness, and the exclusion provides some flexibility to the company.

Limitation on Sale and Lease-Back Transactions.   The indenture provision limiting sale and lease-back transactions parallels the protection offered by the negative pledge clause, except that it provides protection for the bondholder against the company selling and leasing back assets that provide security for the debt holder. In general, this provision requires that assets or cash equal to the property sold and leased back be applied to the retirement of the debt in question or used to acquire another property for the security of the debt holders.

Sale of Assets or Merger. The sale of assets or merger provision protects the debt holder in the event that substantially all of the assets of the company are sold or merged into another company. Under these circumstances, the provision generally states that the debt be retired or be assumed by the merged company.

Dividend Test. The dividend test provision establishes rules for the payment of dividends. Generally, it permits the company to pay dividends to the extent that they are no greater than net income from the previous year plus the earnings of a year or two prior. Although this provision allows the company to continue to pay dividends when there is a business decline, it assures the debt-holders that the corporation will not be drained by dividend payments.

Debt test. The debt test limits the amount of debt that may be issued by establishing a maximum debt/assets ratio. This provision is generally omitted from current public offerings. However, there are numerous indentures outstanding that include this provision. In addition, private placements often include a debt test. When present, the debt test generally sets a limit on the amount of debt that can be issued per dollar of total assets. This limitation is sometimes stated as a percentage. For example, a 50 percent debt/asset limit restricts debt to 50 percent of total assets.

Financial Indentures

Sinking-Fund and Refunding Provisions. Similar to industrial indentures, indentures for finance issues specify sinking-fund and refunding provisions. In general, finance issues with a short maturity are noncallable, whereas longer issues provide 10-year call protection. Occasionally, an issue can be called early in the event of declining receivables. Sinking funds are not as common in finance issues as they are in industrial issues, although they are standard for some companies.

Dividend Test. Perhaps the most important indenture provision for a debtholder of a finance subsidiary is the dividend test. This test restricts the amount of dividends that can be upstreamed from a finance subsidiary to the parent and thereby protects the debtholder against a parent draining the subsidiary. This provision is common in finance indentures, but it is not universal. (One notable exception is International Harvester Credit.)

Limitation on Liens. The limitation on liens provision restricts the degree to which a company can pledge its assets without giving the same protection to the bondholder. Generally, only a nominal amount may be pledged or otherwise liened without establishing equal protection for the debtholder.

Restriction on Debt Test. The debt test limits the amount of debt the company can issue. This provision generally is stated in terms of assets and liabilities, although an earnings test has occasionally been used.

UTILITIES

Utilities are regulated monopolies. These companies generally operate with a high degree of financial leverage and low fixed-charge coverage (relative to industrial companies.) These financial parameters have been historically accepted by investors due to the regulation of the industry and the belief that there is minimal, if any, bankruptcy risk in those securities because of the essential services they provide. The changing structure of the electric utility industry brought about by increasing investment in nuclear generating units and their inherent risk has caused some questioning of this belief. In particular, the faltering financial position of General Public Utilities precipitated by the Three Mile Island nuclear accident and the regulatory delays in making a decision regarding the units has highlighted the default risk that does exist in the industry.

Segments within the Utility Industry

There are three major segments within the utility industry: electric companies, gas companies, and telephone companies. This chapter will deal primarily with the electric utilities. This segment encompasses most of the variables affecting the industry in general.

Financial Analysis

There are three major financial ratios that should be considered in analyzing an electric utility: leverage, pretax interest coverage, and cash flow/spending.

Leverage in the electric utility industry is high relative to industrial concerns. This degree of leverage is accepted by investors because of the historical stability of the industry. However, due to the declining prospects of the industry over the past decade, there remains only a few AAA electric utilities. Evidencing this fact, Standard & Poor's does not include AAAs in its synopsis of financial parameters for the industry. The expected ranges for AA, A, and BBB companies are outlined below:

Rating Classification	Debt Leverage
AA	Less than 47 percent
A	45–55 percent
BBB	More than 53 percent

In calculating the debt leverage of an electric utility, long-term debt/capitalization is standard. However, the amount of short-term debt should also be considered because this is generally variable-rate debt. A high proportion of short-term debt may also indicate the possibility of the near-term issuance of long-term bonds. In addition, several companies guarantee the debt of subsidiaries (regulated or nonregulated). The extent of these guarantees should be considered in calculating leverage.

Fixed-charge coverage for the electric utilities is also low relative to coverage for industrial companies. Standard & Poor's expected ranges for coverage are as follows:

Rating Classification	Expected Pretax Fixed Charge Coverage
AA	3.25X and higher
A	2.50–3.50X
BBB	Under 3.00

These ranges are accepted by investors because of the stability of the industry. However, due to the changing fundamentals of the industry discussed above, perhaps less emphasis should be placed on the exact coverage figures and more on the trend and quality of the coverage.

The utility industry is unique in that its earnings include allowance for funds used during construction (AFUDC). AFUDC is an accounting treatment that allows utilities to recognize income (at a rate determined by individual regulatory commissions) on the amount of funds employed in construction. The percentage that AFUDC represents of total earnings varies significantly from almost zero to well in excess of 70 percent of earnings. Obviously, the higher the percentage that AFUDC represents of net earnings, the lower the quality of earnings. This becomes evident when the cash flow of a utility is calculated. Often, the cash flow of a utility with substantial AFUDC is less than the dividend requirements of the company. In this instance, the company is returning the capital of the shareholders!

In calculating fixed-charge coverage, the analyst should calculate two sets of coverage figures—fixed-charge coverage including AFUDC and fixed-charge coverage excluding AFUDC.

A third important ratio is cash flow/spending. This ratio should be approximated for three years (the general range of an electric company's construction forecast.) The absolute level as well as the trend of this ratio gives important insights into the trend of other financial parameters. An improving trend indicates that construction spending is probably moderating, whereas a low cash flow/spending ratio may indicate inadequate rates being approved by the commissions and a heavy construction budget. Estimates for construction spending are published in the companys' annual reports. Although these are subject to revision, the time involved in building a generating unit makes these forecasts reasonably reliable.

Standard & Poor's expected ranges for cash flow/spending are as follows:

Rating Classification	Expected Cash Flow/Spending
AA.....................	More than 40 percent
A.....................	20–50 percent
BBB.....................	Less than 30 percent

In calculating cash flow, the standard definition outlined above should be followed. However, AFUDC should also be subtracted, and any cash flow from nonregulated subsidiaries should be segregated and analyzed within the total context of the company. The regulatory commissions take divergent views on nonutility subsidiaries. Some commissions do not regulate these subsidiaries at all, whereas other commissions give inadequate rate relief to an electric utility with a profitable nonutility subsidiary under the premise that the company should be looked at as a whole. In the extreme, the latter view has encouraged companies to sell or spin off some subsidiaries.

Nonfinancial Factors

Although financial factors are important in analyzing any company, nonfinancial factors are particularly important in the electric utility industry and may alter a credit assessment. The five nonfinancial factors outlined below are of particular importance to the utility industry. These are in addition to the nonfinancial factors discussed earlier.

Regulation is perhaps the most important variable in the electric utility industry. All electric companies are regulated. Most are primarily regulated by the state or states within which they operate. If a company operates in more than one state, the analyst should weigh the evaluation of the regulatory atmosphere by revenues generated in each state. In addition, the Federal Energy Regulatory Commission (FERC) regulates interstate operations and the sale of wholesale power. Currently, FERC regulation is considered to be somewhat more favorable than that of the average state regulatory commission.

Regulation is best quantified by recent rate decisions and the trend of these decisions. Although a company being analyzed may not have had a recent rate case, the commission's decisions for other companies operating within the state may be used as a proxy. Regulatory commissions are either appointed or elected. In either case, the political atmosphere can have a dramatic effect on the trend of decisions.

The regulators determine innumerable issues in a rate decision, although analysts often mistakenly only focus on the allowed rate of return on equity or the percentage of request granted. In particular, the commissions determine how much of construction work in progress (CWIP) is allowed into the rate base. A company may appear to have a favorable allowed ROE but be hurt by the fact that only a small portion of the company's capital is permitted to earn that return, while the CWIP earns nothing. Due to the high construction budgets for nuclear generating plants and the length of time these plants are under construction, allowance of CWIP in the rate base is of critical importance. Some companies have more than half of their capital in CWIP that is not permitted to earn a return.

In addition, regulators have a high degree of control over the cash flow of a company through the allowance or disallowance of accounting practices and the speed with which decisions are made on cases.

The source of a company's energy is a second important variable. Currently, a company with a heavy nuclear construction budget is viewed negatively relative to a company with coal units under construction. Not only are the lead times for nuclear construction much longer than for other generating plants, but the risk of licensing delays are significant in nuclear construction. The energy source variable relates to a third variable, the growth and stability of the company's territory. Although above-average growth is viewed positively in an industrial company, it is viewed negatively with respect to an electric utility. An electric utility with above-average growth must necessarily have a high construction budget. To the extent that CWIP is disallowed or only partially allowed in the company's rate base, the company is likely to have declining financial parameters until the unit is operational. A fourth variable, whether a company is a subsidiary of a holding company, should also be considered. Holding company status permits nonutility subsidiaries, but it is not universal that these subsidiaries (if successful) will improve the overall credit quality of the company. This depends on the regulatory atmosphere. Furthermore, when there are several electric utility subsidiaries, the parent is more likely to give relatively large equity infusions to the relatively weak subsidiaries. The stronger subsidiary may have to "support" the other subsidiaries. Finally, holding companies should be analyzed in terms of consolidated debt. Although a particular subsidiary may have relatively strong financial parameters, off-balance sheet financing may lower the overall assessment.

A final nonfinancial factor is the rate structure of a utility. An electric utility with a comparatively low rate structure is generally in a stronger position politically to request rate increases than one with rates higher than national averages, and particularly one with rates higher than regional averages.

FINANCE COMPANIES

Finance companies are essentially financial intermediaries. Their function is to purchase funds from public and private sources and to lend it to consumers and other borrowers of funds. Finance companies earn revenue by maintaining a positive spread between what the funds cost and the interest rate charged to customers. The finance industry is highly fragmented in terms of type of lending and type of ownership. This section will briefly outline the major sectors in the industry and then discuss the principal ratios and other key variables used in the analysis of finance companies.

Segments within the Finance Industry

The finance industry can be segmented by type of business and ownership. Finance companies lend in numerous ways in order to accommodate the diverse financial needs of the economy. Five of the major lending categories are: (1) sales finance, (2) commercial lending, (3) wholesale or dealer finance, (4) consumer lending, and (5) leasing. Most often, companies are engaged in several of these lines rather than one line exclusively. Sales finance is the purchases of third-party contracts that cover goods or services sold on a credit basis. In most cases, the sales finance company receives an interest in the goods or services sold. Commercial finance is also generally on a secured basis. However, in this type of financing, the security is most often the borrower's account receivables. In factoring, another type of commercial lending, the finance company actually purchases the receivables of a company and assumes the credit risk of the receivables.

Dealer or wholesaler finance is the lending of funds to finance inventory. This type of financing is secured by the financed inventory and is short term in nature. Leasing, on the other hand, is intermediate to long-term lending—the lessor owns the equipment, finances the lessee's use of it, and generally retains the tax benefits related to the ownership.

Consumer lending has historically involved short-term, unsecured loans of relatively small amounts to individual borrowers. In part because of the more lenient bankruptcy rules and higher default rates on consumer loans, consumer finance companies have dramatically expanded the percentage of their loans for second mortgages. The lower rate charged individuals for this type of loan is offset by the security and lower default risk of the loan.

There are numerous other types of lending in addition to those described above. Among these are real estate lending and export/import financing.

The ownership of a finance company can significantly impact evaluation of the company. In some instances, ownership is the most important variable in the analysis.

There are three major types of ownership of finance companies: (1) captives, (2) wholly owned, and (3) independents. Captive finance companies, such as General Motors Acceptance Corporation and J. C. Penney Financial, are owned by the parent corporation and are engaged solely or primarily in the financing of the parent's goods or services. Generally, maintenance agreements exist between the parent and the captive finance company under which the parent agrees to maintain one or more of the finance company's financial parameters, such as fixed-charge coverage, at a minimum level. Because of the overriding relationship between a parent and a captive finance subsidiary, the financial strength of the parent is an important variable in the analysis of the finance company. However, captive finance companies can have ratings either above or below those of the parent.

A wholly-owned finance company, such as Associates Corporation of North America, differs from a captive in two ways. First, it primarily finances the goods and services of companies other than the parent. Second, maintenance agreements between the parent and the subsidiary are generally not as formal. Frequently, there are indenture provisions that address the degree to which a parent can upstream dividends from a finance subsidiary. The purpose of these provisions is to prevent a relatively weak parent from draining a healthy finance subsidiary to the detriment of the subsidiary's bondholders.

Independent finance companies are either publicly owned or closely held. Because these entities have no parent, the analysis of this finance sector is strictly a function of the strengths of the company.

Financial Analysis

In analyzing finance companies, several groups of ratios and other variables should be considered. There is more interrelationship between these ratios and variables than for any other type of company. For example, a finance company with a high degree of leverage and low liquidity may be considered to be of high investment quality if it has a strong parent and maintenance agreements. No variable should be viewed in isolation but rather within the context of the whole finance company/parent company relationship.

Loan Loss. The most important ratio in analyzing a finance company is the relationship of the company's loan loss experience and related variables. Net loan losses are defined as loans deemed uncollectible and therefore written off, less recoveries of loans previously written off. The importance of this ratio is twofold. First, the net loan loss is a major and unpredictable expense variable. Second, a company with an above-average loan loss record has the necessary business expertise to create a loan portfolio of above-average quality. A related variable that should also be evaluated is the company's provision for these losses. A company whose loss provisions are consistently inadequate should be further explored for other indications of liberal accounting.

In evaluating the company's loan loss experience, the analyst must also necessarily consider the quality of the portfolio. Diversification is one measure of portfolio quality. Is the portfolio diversified across different types of loans? If the company is concentrated in or deals exclusively in one lending type, is there geographic diversification? A company that deals exclusively in consumer loans in the economically sensitive Detroit area would not be as favorably viewed as a company with broad geographic diversification. Accounting quality is also an important factor in assessing portfolio quality. The more conservative the accounting for recognition of income, revenue, and loan losses, the better. The security for the loans is also an important variable in portfolio quality. The stronger the underlying security, the higher the loan quality. The analyst should be primarily concerned with the level of loans compared with levels of similar companies and the risk involved in the type of lending. For example, the expected loan loss from direct unsecured consumer loans is higher than for consumer loans secured by second mortgages. However, the higher fees charged for the former type of loan should compensate the company for the higher risk.

Leverage. Leverage is a second important ratio used in finance company analysis. By the nature of the business, finance companies are typically and acceptably more highly leveraged than industrial companies. The leverage is necessary to earn a sufficient return on capital. However, the acceptable range of leverage is dependent on other factors, such as parental support, portfolio quality, and type of business. The principal ratio to determine leverage is total debt to equity, although such variations as total liabilities to equity may additionally be used. In a diversified company with high portfolio quality, a leverage ratio of 5 to 1 is acceptable. On the other hand, a ratio of 10 to 1 is also acceptable for a captive with a strong parent and maintenance agreements. The analyst should always view the leverage of a finance company in comparison with similar companies.

Liquidity. The third important variable in finance company analysis is liquidity. Because of the capital structure of finance companies, the primary cause of bankruptcies in this industry is illiquidity. If for some reason a finance company is unable to raise funds in the public or private market, failure could quickly result. This inability to raise funds could result from internal factors, such as a deterioration in earnings, or from external factors, such as a major disruption in the credit markets. Whatever the cause, a company should have some liquidity cushion. The ultimate liquidity cushion, selling assets, is only a last resort because these sales could have long-term, detrimental effects on earnings. The traditional liquidity ratio is cash, cash equivalents, and receivables due within one year divided by short-term liabilities. The higher this ratio, the higher the margin of safety. Also to be considered are the liquidity of the receivables themselves and the existence of bank lines of credit to provide a company with short-term liquidity during a financial crisis. In general, the smaller and weaker companies should have a higher liquidity cushion than those companies with strong parental backing who can rely on an interest-free loan from the parent in times of market stress.

Asset Coverage.   A fourth important variable in the analysis of finance companies that is related to the three variables discussed above is the asset coverage afforded the bondholder. In assessing asset protection, the analyst should consider the liquidation value of the loan portfolio.

Earnings Record.   The fifth variable to be considered is the finance company's earnings record. The industry is fairly mature and is somewhat cyclical. The higher the annual EPS growth, the better. However, some cyclicality should be expected. In addition, the analyst should be aware of management's response to major changes in the business environment. The recent more lenient personal bankruptcy rules and the fact that personal bankruptcy is becoming more sociably acceptable have produced significantly higher loan losses in direct, unsecured consumer loans. Many companies have responded to this change by contracting their unsecured personal loans and expanding their portfolios invested in personal loans secured by second mortgages.

Size.   A final factor related to the finance company or subsidiary is size. In general, the larger companies are viewed more positively than the smaller companies. Size has important implications for market recognition in terms of selling securities but also in terms of diversification. A larger company is more easily able to diversify in terms of type and location of loan than is a smaller company, and thereby to lessen the risk of the portfolio.

In addition to an analysis of the financial strength of the company according to the above variables, the analyst must incorporate the net effect of any affiliation the finance company has with a parent. If this affiliation is strong, it may be the primary variable in the credit assessment. The affiliation between a parent company and a finance subsidiary is straightforward; it is captive, wholly owned, or independent. However, the degree to which a parent will support a finance subsidiary is not as straightforward. Traditionally, the integral relationship between a parent and a captive finance subsidiary has indicated the highest level of potential support. However, it is becoming increasingly clear that a wholly owned finance subsidiary can have just as strong an affiliation. For example, General Electric Credit Corporation (GECC) finances little or no products manufactured by its parent, General Electric Company. However, General Electric receives substantial tax benefits from its consolidation of tax returns with GECC. Additionally, General Electric has a substantial investment in its credit subsidiary. Therefore, although there are no formal maintenance agreements between General Electric and GECC, it can be assumed that General Electric would protect its investment in GECC if the finance subsidary were to need assistance. In other instances it may be that the affiliation and maintenance agreements are strong, but the parent itself is weak. In this case, the strong affiliation would be discounted to the extent that parent profitability is below industry standards.

In addition to affiliation, affiliate profitability, and maintenance agreements, the analyst should also examine any miscellaneous factors that could affect the credit standing of the finance company. Legislative initiatives should be considered to determine significant changes in the structure or profitability of the industry.

THE RATING AGENCIES AND BROKERAGE HOUSES

There is no substitute for the fundamental analysis generated by the fixed income analyst. The analyst has many sources of assistance, however. The major sources of assistance are the public rating agencies and brokerage houses that specialize in fixed income research.

Rating Agencies

Three major rating agencies provide public ratings on debt issues: Standard & Poor's Corporation, Moody's Investors Service, and Fitch Investors Service. In addition, Duff & Phelps, Inc., a Chicago-based research house, has *recently* begun to offer public ratings.

Standard & Poor's (S&P) and Moody's are the most widely recognized and used of the services, although Duff & Phelps and Fitch are frequently cited. S&P and Moody's are approximately the same size, and each rates the debt securities of approximately 2,000 companies. If a company desires a rating on an issue, it must apply to the rating agency. The agency, in turn, charges a one-time fee of generally $5,000 to $20,000. For this fee, the issue is reviewed periodically during the life of the issue and at least one formal review is made annually.

Each of the three rating agencies designate debt quality by assigning a letter rating to an issue. Standard & Poor's ratings go from AAA to D, with AAA obligations having the highest quality investment characteristics and D obligations being in default. In a similar fashion,

Moody's ratings extend from Aaa to C, and Fitch's, from AAA to D. Duff & Phelps, on the other hand, assigns numerical ratings from 1 to 14, with 1 analogous to a AAA.

Public ratings are taken seriously by corporate managements, since a downgrade or an upgrade by a major agency can cost or save a corporation thousands of dollars in interest payments over the life of an issue. In the event of downgrade below the BBB or Baa level, the corporation may find its bonds ineligible for investment by many institutions and funds, either by legal or policy constraints. Corporations therefore strive to maintain at least an investment-grade rating (Baa or higher) and are mindful of the broad financial parameters that the agencies consider in deriving a rating.

Many factors promote the use of agency ratings by investors, bankers, and brokers. Among these strengths are the breadth of companies followed, the easy access to the ratings, and the almost universal acceptance of the ratings. On the other hand, the ratings are criticized for not responding quickly enough to changes in credit conditions and for being too broad in their classifications.

The slow response time of the agencies to changes in credit conditions is certainly a valid criticism. There are few instances in which the lag is significant in terms of a dramatic change, but the market generally anticipates rating changes. The rating agencies have become increasingly sensitive to this criticism and have been quicker to change a rating in light of changing financial parameters. On the other hand, the agencies recognize the financial impact of their ratings and their obligation to rate the long-term (as opposed to the short-term) prospects of companies. They therefore have a three- to five-year perspective and purposefully do not change a rating because of short-term fluctuations.

Standard & Poor's has addressed this criticism directly by creating *Creditwatch*, a weekly notice of companies whose credit ratings are under surveillance for rating changes. These potential rating changes can be either positive or negative. The basis for potential change can emanate from a variety of sources, including company and industry fundamentals, changes in the law, and mergers. Duff & Phelps also has a "Watch List" of companies that are potential upgrades or downgrades. Additionally, subscribers to the agencies' services have access to agency analysts to discuss individual companies or industries.

The criticism of too broad classifications in the ratings is directed primarily at Fitch, which has no pluses or minuses attached to its ratings. (However, credit summaries do indicate whether the credit is in the higher or lower end of the rating.) Investors who are concerned with this circumstance can refer to several brokerage-house services that offer more continuous ratings.

Brokerage-House Services

Numerous brokerage houses specialize in fixed income research. Generally, these services are available only to institutional buyers of bonds. The strength of the research stems from the in-depth coverage provided, the statistical techniques employed, and the fine gradations in rating. On the other hand, the universe of companies that these firms follow is necessarily smaller than that followed by the agencies.

Of particular interest is the methodology employed by Kidder Peabody to quantify risk. Kidder Peabody performs Financial Quality Profiles (FQP) on approximately 200 nonoil industrial companies as well as on a universe of oil companies. The FQP analysis concentrates on inflation-adjusted financial parameters. In particular, FQP quantifies the "unit growth fundable" of a company, which is the real growth rate of unit production that a company can sustain without a significant deterioration in its balance sheet. The result of an FQP analysis is a numerical rating ranging from 0 to 125 (93–125 is roughly equivalent to an AAA). The numerical ratings are the quantitative assessment of the firm's financial parameters. Kidder Peabody tempers these ratings with its assessment of other nonfinancial factors, such as management and the outlook for the industry. In 1981 FQP analysis was extended to include forecasted FQP scores. Although several firms will qualitatively discuss the longer term outlook for a company, only FQP quantifies the evaluation.

CONCLUSION

This chapter has emphasized a basic methodology in analyzing corporate bonds. A format for analysis is essential. However, analysis of securities cannot be totally quantified, and the experienced analyst will develop a second sense about whether to delve into a particular aspect of a company's financial position or whether to take the financial statements at face value. All aspects of credit analysis, however, have become increasingly important as rapidly changing economic conditions and increasingly severe business cycles change the credit quality of companies and industries.

Tax-Exempt Securities

15 **SYLVAN G. FELDSTEIN, Ph.D.***
Vice President and Bond Analyst
Moody's Investor Service, Inc.

FRANK J. FABOZZI, Ph.D., C.F.A., C.P.A.
Professor of Economics
Fordham University

Tax-exempt, fixed income debt instruments, or municipal bonds as they are commonly known, come in a variety of types, redemption features, credit risks, and market liquidities. Most recent available information indicates that approximately 37,000 different states, counties, school districts, special districts, towns, and other public issuing bodies have issued municipal bonds. By year-end 1980, it was estimated by the Federal Reserve Board that a total of $325 billion in municipal bond and note debt was outstanding. In this chapter we describe the basic characteristics of municipal bonds as well as the municipal bond industry. In the following chapter, guidelines for evaluating the creditworthiness of municipal bonds are discussed.

THE TAXATION OF MUNICIPAL BONDS[1]

Some individuals buy municipal bonds as a way of supporting public improvements such as schools, playgrounds and parks, but the vast majority of municipal bond buyers do so because of the tax-exempt

---

* This chapter was written while the author was Vice President and Analyst at Smith Barney, Harris Upham & Co., Inc. The views expressed in this chapter are those of the author and not necessarily those of Moody's Investors Service.

[1] For a more detailed discussion of the federal income tax treatment of municipal bonds, the reader is referred to Chapter 3.

feature of these debt instruments. Municipal bonds, in general, are exempt from Federal income taxes. It should be noted that although interest income on municipal bonds is exempt from federal income taxes, capital gains are not exempt. The maximum capital gains tax rate for individuals at the time of this writing is 20 percent. Consequently, the investor comparing municipal bonds available at discount prices in the marketplace must consider the tax implications of any capital gains tax on the aftertax return.[2] Later in this chapter, we shall explain how this tax effect can be recognized.

The tax treatment of municipal bonds varies by state.[3] There are three types of tax that can be imposed: (1) an income tax on coupon income, (2) a tax on realized capital gains, and (3) a personal property tax.

There are 43 states that levy an individual income tax, as does the District of Columbia. Six of these states exempt coupon interest on *all* municipal bonds, whether the issue is in state or out of state. Coupon interest from obligations by in-state issuers is exempt from state individual income taxes in 32 states. Five states levy individual income taxes on coupon interest whether the issuer is in state or out of state.

State taxation of realized capital gains is often ignored by investors when making investment decisions. In 42 states, a tax is levied on a base that includes income from capital transactions (i.e., capital gain or losses). Only one state at the time of this writing, Connecticut, levies a capital gains tax. In many states where coupon interest is exempt if the issuer is in state, the same exemption will not apply to capital gains involving municipal bonds.

There are 20 states that levy a personal property tax. Of these 20 states, only 11 apply this tax to municipal bonds. The tax resembles more of an income tax than a personal property tax. For example, in Kansas, Michigan and Ohio, personal property taxes are measured on the annual income generated by a bond.

In determining the effective tax rate imposed by a particular state, an investor must consider the impact of the deductibility of state taxes on federal income taxes. Moreover, in 13 states, *federal* taxes are deductible in determining state income taxes.

The total effective state and local tax rate in most states appears to be minimal. There are only eight states in which the total effective state and local tax rate exceeds 5 percent for investors in the highest tax bracket. Consequently, an investor must be sure that he or she is

---

[2] Recall that for taxable bonds, there is a tax advantage when a bond sells at a discount, since the long-term capital gains tax rate is lower than the ordinary income tax rate.

[3] The source of information for the remainder of this section is from Steven J. Hueglin, *Guide to State and Local Taxation of Municipal Bonds* published by the firm of Gabriele, Hueglin & Cashman, Inc., 1981.

not sacrificing too much in yield by purchasing an in-state bond rather than an out-of-state bond.

EQUIVALENT TAXABLE YIELD

An investor interested in purchasing a municipal bond must be able to compare the promised yield on a municipal bond with that of a comparable taxable bond. The following general formula is used to determine the equivalent taxable yield for a tax-exempt bond:

$$\text{Equivalent taxable yield} = \frac{\text{Tax-exempt yield}}{(1 - \text{marginal tax rate})}$$

For example, suppose an investor in the 50 percent marginal tax bracket is considering the acquisition of a tax-exempt bond that offers a tax-exempt yield of 12.8 percent. The equivalent taxable yield is 25.6 percent, as shown below.

$$\text{Equivalent taxable yield} = \frac{.128}{(1 - .5)} = .256$$

When computing the equivalent taxable yield, the traditionally computed yield-to-maturity is not the tax-exempt yield if the issue is selling below par (i.e., selling at a discount) because only the coupon interest is exempt from federal income taxes.[4] Instead, the yield-to-maturity after an assumed capital gains tax is computed and used in the numerator of the formula.

The yield-to-maturity after an assumed capital gains tax is calculated in the same manner as the traditional yield-to-maturity. However, instead of using the redemption value in the calculation, the net proceeds after an assumed capital gains tax is used. For example, suppose that on November 1, 1981, an investor purchased $5,000 New York State Housing Agency (NYSHFA) State University 8 percent bonds maturing November 1, 1999, at 66.50, or $3,325 per bond (.6650 times $5,000). The issue has a $5,000 redemption value at maturity, 18 years from November 1, 1981. The yield-to-maturity for this issue is approximately 12.80 percent. Recall from Chapter 3 that the yield-to-maturity is the interest rate that makes the present value of the 36 semiannual interest payments of $200 plus the redemption value of $5,000 equal to the purchase price of $3,325. Assuming the maximum capital gains tax of 20 percent,[5] the net proceeds after the capital gains

---

[4] An investor who purchases a tax-exempt bond at a premium will not be entitled to a capital loss if the bond is held to maturity because the premium must be amortized. See Chapter 3.

[5] The maximum capital gains tax is 20 percent because the maximum marginal tax rate is 50 percent and only 40 percent of long-term capital gains are taxed.

tax is $4,665.[6] The interest rate that equates the present value of the 36 semiannual interest payments of $200 each and the net proceeds of $4,665 to the purchase price of $3,325 is 12.66 percent.[7] Therefore, 12.66 percent is the yield-to-maturity after a capital gains tax of 20 percent.

There is a major drawback in employing the equivalent taxable yield formula to compare the relative investment merits of a taxable and tax-exempt bond. Recall from the discussion in Chapter 4 that the yield-to-maturity measure assumes that the entire coupon interest can be reinvested at the computed yield. Consequently, taxable bonds with the same yield-to-maturity cannot be compared because the total dollar returns may differ from the computed yield. The same problem arises when attempting to compare taxable and tax-exempt bonds, especially since only a portion of the coupon interest on taxable bonds can be reinvested, although the entire coupon payment is available for reinvestment in the case of municipal bonds. A framework that should be employed to compare taxable and tax-exempt bonds is provided in Chapter 28. The framework is based upon the concept of realized compound yield, which was discussed in Chapter 4.[8]

DESCRIPTION OF THE INSTRUMENTS

Bonds

In terms of municipal bond security structures, there are basically two different types. The first type is the general obligation bond, and the second is the revenue bond.

General obligation bonds are debt instruments issued by states, counties, special districts, cities, towns, and school districts. They are secured by the issuers' general taxing powers. Usually, a general obligation bond is secured by the issuer's unlimited taxing power. For smaller governmental jurisdictions, such as school districts and towns, the only available unlimited taxing power is on property. For larger general obligation bond issuers, such as states and big cities, the tax revenues are more diverse and may include corporate and individual income taxes, sales taxes, and property taxes. The security pledges for these larger issuers are sometimes referred to as being full faith and credit obligations.

---

[6] The long-term capital gain is $1,675 ($5,000 minus the purchase price of $3,325). The assumed applicable capital gains tax is $355 (20 percent of $1,675). Therefore, the net proceeds after the assumed capital gains tax is $4,665 ($5,000 minus $335).

[7] More accurately, the interest rate is 6.33 percent. Since the interest payments are semiannual, it is traditional to double the rate to obtain the yield. See Chapter 4.

[8] See also Martin L. Leibowitz, "Total Aftertax Bond Performance and Yield Measures for Tax-Exempt Bonds Held in Taxable Portfolios," in *The Handbook of Municipal Bonds*, Vol. 1, ed. Frank J. Fabozzi, Sylvan Feldstein, Irving M. Pollack, and Frank G. Zarb (Homewood, Ill.: Dow Jones-Irwin, 1983). © Dow Jones-Irwin, Inc., 1983.

Additionally, certain general obligation bonds are secured not only by the issuer's general taxing powers to create revenues accumulated in the general fund, but also from certain identified fees, grants, and special charges, which provide additional revenues from outside the general fund. Such bonds are known as being double barreled in security because of the dual nature of the revenue sources.

Also, not all general obligation bonds are secured by unlimited taxing powers. Some have pledged taxes that are limited as to revenue sources and maximum millage amounts. Such bonds are known as limited-tax general obligation bonds.

The second basic type of security structure is found in a revenue bond. Such bonds are issued for either project or enterprise financings in which the bond issuers pledge to the bondholders the revenues generated by the operating projects financed. Below are examples of the specific types of revenue bonds that have been issued over the years.

Airport Revenue Bonds.   The revenues securing airport revenue bonds usually come from either traffic-generated sources—such as landing fees, concession fees, and airline apron-use and fueling fees—or lease revenues from one or more airlines for the use of a specific facility, such as a terminal or hangar.

College Revenue Bonds.   The revenues securing college revenue bonds usually include dormitory room rental fees, tuition payments, and sometimes the general assets of the college or university as well.

Hospital Revenue Bonds.   Hospital revenue bonds are usually secured by federal and state reimbursement programs (such as Medicaid and Medicare), third-party commercial payers (such as Blue Cross), and individual patient payments.

Single-Family Mortgage Revenue Bonds.   Single-family mortgage revenue bonds are usually secured by the mortgages and mortgage loan repayments on single-family homes. Security features vary but can include Federal Housing Administration (FHA), Federal Veterans Administration (VA), or private mortgage insurance.

Housing Revenue Bonds.   Housing revenue bonds are issued for multifamily housing projects for senior citizens and low-income families. Some housing revenue bonds are secured by mortgages that are federally insured; others receive federal government operating subsidies, such as under section 8, or interest-cost subsidies, such as under section 236; and still others receive only local property tax reductions as subsidies.

Industrial Development and Pollution-Control Revenue Bonds. Bonds are issued for a variety of industrial and commercial activities that ranges from manufacturing plants to shopping centers. They are usually secured by payments to be made by the corporations or businesses that use the facilities.

Public Power Revenue Bonds. Public power revenue bonds are secured by revenues produced from electrical operating plants. Some bonds are for a single issuer, who constructs and operates power plants and then sells the electricity. Other public power revenue bonds are issued by groups of public and private investor-owned utilities for the joint financing of the construction of one or more power plants. This last arrangement is known as a "joint power" financing structure.

Resource Recovery Revenue Bonds. A resource recovery facility converts refuse (solid waste) into commercially saleable energy, recoverable products, and a residue to be landfilled. The major revenues for a resource recovery revenue bond usually are (1) the *tipping fees* per ton paid by those who deliver the garbage to the facility for disposal; (2) revenues from steam, electricity, or refuse-derived fuel sold to either an electric power company or another energy user; and (3) revenues from the sale of recoverable materials, such as aluminum and steel scrap.

Seaport Revenue Bonds. The security for seaport revenue bonds can include specific lease agreements with the benefitting companies or pledged marine terminal and cargo tonnage fees.

Sewer Revenue Bonds. Revenues for sewer revenue bonds come from hookup fees and user charges. For many sewer bond issuers, substantial portions of their construction budgets have been financed with federal grants.

Sports Complex and Convention Center Revenue Bonds. Sports complex and convention center revenue bonds usually receive revenues from sporting or convention events held at the facilities and, in some instances, from earmarked revenues, such as local motel and hotel room taxes.

Student Loan Revenue Bonds. Student loan repayments under student loan revenue bond programs are sometimes 100 percent guaranteed either directly by the federal government—under the Federal Insured Student Loan program for 100 percent of bond principal and interest—or by a state guaranty agency under a more recent federal insurance program, the Federal Guaranteed Student Loan program. In addition to these two federally backed programs, student loan bonds are also sometimes secured by the general revenues of the specific colleges involved.

Toll-Road and Gas Tax Revenue Bonds. There are generally two types of highway revenue bonds. The bond proceeds of the first type are used to build such specific revenue-producing facilities as toll roads, bridges, and tunnels. For these pure enterprise-type revenue bonds, the pledged revenues usually are the monies collected through the tolls. The second type of highway bond is one in which the bond-holders are paid by earmarked revenues outside of toll collections, such as gasoline taxes, automobile registration payments, and driver's license fees.

Water Revenue Bonds. Water revenue bonds are issued to finance the construction of water treatment plants, pumping stations, collection facilities, and distribution systems. Revenues usually come from connection fees and user charges paid by the users of the water systems.

Hybrid and Special Bond Securities

Though having certain characteristics of general obligation and revenue bonds, there are some municipal bonds that have more unique security structures as well. They include the following:

Lease-Backed Bonds. Lease-backed bonds are usually structured as revenue-type bonds with annual rent payments. In some instances the rental payments may only come from earmarked tax revenues, student tuition payments, and patient fees. In other instances the underlying lessee governmental unit is required to make annual appropriations from its general fund.

Letter of Credit-Backed Bonds. Some municipal bonds, in addition to being secured by the issuer's cash flow revenues, also are backed by commercial bank letters of credit. In some instances the letters of credit are irrevocable, and if necessary, can be used to pay the bondholders. In other instances, the issuers are required to maintain investment worthiness before the letters of credit can be drawn upon.

Life-Care Revenue Bonds. Life-care bonds are issued to construct long-term residential facilities for older citizens. Revenues are usually derived from initial lump-sum payments made by the residents.

Moral Obligation Bonds. A moral obligation bond is a security structure for state-issued bonds that indicates that if revenues are needed for paying bondholders, the state legislature involved is legally authorized, though not required, to make an appropriation out of general state-tax revenues.

Municipal Utility District Revenue Bonds. These are bonds that are usually issued to finance the construction of water and sewer systems as well as roadways in undeveloped areas. The security is usually dependent on the commercial success of the specific development project involved—which can range from the sale of new homes to the renting of space in shopping centers and office buildings.

New Housing Authority Bonds. These bonds are secured by a contractual pledge of annual contributions from HUD. Monies from Washington are paid directly to the paying agent for the bonds, and the bondholders are given specific legal rights to enforce the pledge.

Tax Allocation Bonds. These bonds are usually issued to finance the construction of office buildings and other new buildings in formerly blighted areas. They are secured by property taxes collected on the improved real estate.

"Territorial" Bonds. These are bonds issued by United States territorial possessions, such as Puerto Rico, the Virgin Islands, and Guam. The bonds are tax exempt throughout most of the country. Also, the economies of these issuers are influenced by positive special features of the United States corporate tax codes that are not available to the states.

"Troubled-City" Bailout Bonds. There are certain bonds that are structured to appear as pure revenue bonds but in essence are not. Revenues come from general purpose taxes and revenues that otherwise would have gone to a state or city's general fund. Their bond structures were created to bail out underlying general obligation bond issuers from severe budget deficits. Examples are the New York State *Municipal Assistance Corporation for the City of New York Bonds* (*MAC*) and the state of Illinois *Chicago School Finance Authority Bonds*.

Refunded Bonds. These are bonds that originally may have been issued as general obligation or revenue bonds but are now secured by an "Escrow Fund" consisting entirely of direct U.S. government obligations that are sufficient for paying the bondholders. The bonds are usually rated in the highest investment categories by the credit-rating agencies.

Notes

Tax-exempt debt issued for periods ranging not beyond five years are usually considered to be short term in nature. Below are descriptions of some of these debt instruments.

Tax, Revenue, and Bond Anticipation Notes: TANs, RANs, and BANs. These are temporary borrowings by states, local governments, and special jurisdictions. Usually, notes are issued for a period of 12 months, though it is not uncommon for notes to be issued for periods of as short as 3 months and for as long as three years. TANs and RANs (also known as TRANs) are issued in anticipation of the collection of taxes or other expected revenues. These are borrowings to even out the cash flows caused by the irregular flows of income into the treasuries of the states and local units of government. BANs are issued in anticipation of the sale of long-term bonds.

Construction Loan Notes: CLNs. CLNs are usually issued for periods up to three years to provide short-term construction financing for multifamily housing projects. The CLNs generally are repaid by the proceeds of long-term bonds, which are sold after the housing projects are completed.

Tax-Exempt Commercial Paper. This short-term borrowing instrument is used for periods ranging from 30 to 270 days. Generally the tax-exempt commercial paper has backstop commercial bank agreements, which can include an irrevocable letter of credit, a revolving credit agreement, or a line of credit.

Project Notes of Local Housing Authorities: PNs. Project notes are secured by a contractual pledge from the United States Department of Housing and Urban Development. Monies from Washington are paid directly to the paying agent for the PNs, and the noteholders are given specific legal rights to enforce the pledge. These notes are usually given the highest available investment grade ratings by the credit-rating agencies.

Specific Description Source. It should be noted that each year Moody's Investors Service publishes the "Municipal & Government Manual." This two volume publication, known as the bible of the municipal bond industry, has over 4,000 pages and covers the security provisions, call features, and maturity schedules of over 16,000 issuers and 1.5 million separate bond and note issues.

Newer Market Sensitive Debt Instruments

Municipal bonds are usually issued with one of two debt retirement structures or a combination of both. Either a bond has a "serial" maturity structure (wherein a portion of the loan is retired each year), or a bond has a "term" maturity (wherein the loan is repaid on a final date). Usually term bonds have maturities ranging from 20 to 40 years and have retirement schedules (which are known as sinking funds) that begin 5 to 10 years before the final term maturity.

Because of the sharply upward-sloping yield curve that has existed in the municipal bond market since 1979, many investment bankers have introduced innovative financing instruments priced at short or intermediate yield levels. These debt instruments are intended to raise money for long-term capital projects at reduced interest rates. Below are descriptions of some of these more innovative debt structures.

Put or Option Tender Bonds. A "put" or "option tender" bond is one in which the bondholder has the right to return the bond at a price of par to the bond trustee prior to its stated long-term maturity. In some instances the bondholder has the right to put the bond as early as the third anniversary date of the original issuance. In other instances, the bondholder has to wait up to 10 years before returning the bond. Usually put bonds are backed by either commercial bank letters of credit in addition to the issuer's cash flow revenues or entirely by the cash flow revenues of the issuers.

Super Sinkers.   A "super sinker" is a specifically identified maturity for a single-family housing revenue bond issue to which all funds from early mortgage prepayments are used to retire bonds. A super sinker has a long stated maturity but a much shorter, albeit unknown, actual life. Because of this unique characteristic, investors have the opportunity to realize an attractive return when the municipal yield curve is upward sloping on a bond that is priced as if it had a maturity considerably greater than its anticipated life.

Variable-Rate Coupon Bonds.   Variable-rate coupon bonds have floating interest rates that change on a weekly or monthly basis. The interest rates are tied to various indices, such as Treasury bill rates, the weekly Bond Buyer Index, or combinations of these and other indices.

Minicoupon and Zero-Coupon Bonds.   The coupon interest on a minicoupon bond is below the prevailing yield in the market. The bonds are sold at issuance at a substantial discount from par. If the bonds are held to maturity, the difference between the original-issue discount price and the par value is not taxable, since it represents tax-free income.

A zero-coupon bond is one in which no interest coupons are paid to the bondholder. Instead, the bond is purchased at a very deep discount and matures at par. The difference between the original-issue discount price and par represents a specified compounded annual yield.

The reasons investors may prefer minicoupon and zero-coupon bonds are explained in Chapter 12. Minicoupon bonds reduce reinvestment risk. With zero-coupon bonds, there is no reinvestment risk. That is, the effective yield is assured, provided the issuer is able to make the payment at the time of the bond's maturity.

THE BUYERS OF MUNICIPAL BONDS[9]

The three categories of investors that have dominated the municipal securities market are commercial banks, property and casualty insurance companies, and households. Exhibit 1 shows the percentage held by each category for selected years from 1955 to 1980. Although these three investor categories have dominated the market since the mid-1950s, there has been a shift in the relative participation in each category.

---

[9] This section draws from David S. Kidwell, Frank J. Fabozzi, and Craig Moore, "Investors in Municipal Securities," in Fabozzi et al., *The Handbook of Municipal Bonds,* Vol. 1.

Exhibit 1
Holders of State and Local Government Debt*—December 31, 1971–1980 ($ billions)

	1980	1979	1978	1977	1976	1975	1974	1973	1972	1971
Total state and local debt outstanding	$325.5	$305.1	$291.4	$263.2	$239.5	$223.8	$207.7	$191.2	$176.5	$161.8
Percentage held by:										
Households............................	19.3%	21.8%	25.7%	27.8%	29.5%	30.5%	29.9%	28.1%	27.5%	28.6%
Commercial Banks	46.4	44.4	43.2	43.8	44.3	44.8	48.8	50.1	51.1	51.4
Casualty Insurance Companies............	25.6	24.6	21.4	18.7	16.1	14.9	14.8	14.9	14.0	12.7
Others................................		9.2	9.7	9.7	10.1	9.8	6.5	6.9	7.4	7.3

Source: Data from "The Bond Buyer 1980 Municipal Financial Statement."

Commercial Banks

In terms of dollar amounts held, commercial banks have become the largest holders of municipal securities. At the end of the fourth quarter of 1955, commercial banks held $12.9 billion of municipals, the least amount held by this category over the 25-year period spanning from 1955 to 1980. Commercial bank participation reached its zenith during the second quarter of 1972, when this category held 50.5 percent of all outstanding municipal securities.

Several studies of the investment behavior of banks indicate that their demand for municipal securities can best be described as a "residual demand."[10] After commercial banks have met their reserve obligations, remaining funds are placed either in loans or income-producing taxable and tax-exempt securities. If loan demand is sufficiently strong, banks may sell portions of their municipal holdings to avert potential liquidity problems. Conversely, when loan demand is weak, banks will tend to increase their purchases of municipals. In this instance, commercial banks attempt to balance reduced borrowing needs with a less cost intensive investment portfolio consisting of taxable and tax-exempt securities.

Besides shielding income from federal taxation, commercial banks hold the obligations of state and local governments for a variety of other reasons. Most state and local governments mandate that public deposits at a bank be collateralized. Although Treasury or federal agency securities may be utilized as collateral, the use of municipal bonds and notes is favored. Obligations of state and local governments also may be used as collateral when commercial banks borrow at the discount window of the Federal Reserve. Furthermore, banks frequently serve as underwriters or market makers of municipal securities, and these functions require maintaining inventories of tax-exempt bonds and notes.

As noted earlier, commercial bank participation in the municipal market peaked during the early 1970s and since that period has been trending downward. Declining profitability and lower tax liabilities apparently are the primary explanations for this reduced participation. Indeed, during the period spanning from 1960 to 1974, the average corporate tax rate of banks insured by the FDIC fell from 33.6 percent to 14.2 percent. By utilizing foreign tax credits, larger commercial banks have offset domestic tax liabilities with taxes paid to foreign governments on income generated from international banking activities. Tax-sheltered leasing operations have also helped commercial

---

[10] Donald R. Hodgman, *Commercial Bank Loan and Investment Policy* (Urbana, Ill.: University of Illinois Bureau of Economic and Business Research, 1963), pp. 38–40; and Stephen M. Goldfeld, *Commercial Bank Behavior and Economic Activity* (Amsterdam: North Holland Publishing, 1966).

banks reduce their corporate tax rates. The Economic Recovery Tax Act of 1981 will make it even easier for commercial banks to shelter taxable income via "safe harbor" leases. Liberalization of the provisions for cost recovery (depreciation) further reduce the effective tax rate. Thus the increased use of tax-sheltered leasing operations and the increased use of foreign tax credits will reduce the future demand for municipals by larger commercial banks.

Insurance Companies

By the end of 1980, property-casualty insurance companies were the second largest holders of tax-exempt securities. Purchases of municipal securities by property and casualty insurance companies are primarily a function of their underwriting profits and investment income. Claims on property and casualty companies are difficult to anticipate. Varying court awards for liability suits, the effects of inflation upon repair costs, and the unpredictability of weather are the chief factors that affect the level of claims experienced by property and casualty insurance companies. The profitability of property and casualty insurance companies, in turn, is primarily dependent upon the revenues generated from insurance premiums and investment income and the cost of claims filed. It is important to note that the premiums for various types of insurance are subject to competitive pressures and to approval from state insurance commissioners.

As can be expected then, the profitability of property and casualty companies is very cyclical. Normally, intense price competition follows highly profitable years. During these high-income periods, property and casualty companies typically step up their purchases of municipals in order to shield taxable income. Furthermore, lower rate increases are usually granted by state commissioners during this time. Underwriting losses traditionally begin to exact a toll as premium and investment income fails to keep pace with claims settlement costs. As underwriting losses mount, property and casualty insurance companies begin to curtail their investment in tax-exempt securities. The profitability cycle is completed when property and casualty companies win rate increases from state commissioners after sustaining continued underwriting losses.

Households (Individual Investors)

Retail investor participation in the municipal securities market has fluctuated widely since 1955 as reflected by the data contained in Exhibit 1. With some interruptions, retail investors' market share has been trending downward; however, in 1981 the trend was reversed.

Individual investors may purchase municipal bond and notes directly or through bond funds and tax-exempt unit investment trusts.[11] The $5,000 piece denominations for municipal securities have made unit investment trusts and bond funds very popular investments among those individuals who are unable to purchase securities in large increments. According to data compiled by the Investment Company Institute, the market value of open-end, long- and short-term municipal bond funds amounted to $2.9 billion and $1.9 billion, respectively, at the end of 1980. The first half of 1981 witnessed the market value of long- and short-term funds jump dramatically to $3.4 and $3.3 billion, respectively. Sales of unit investment trust, essentially closed-end bond funds, amounted to $4.4 billion during 1980, up 47 percent from the $3 billion sold during 1979. By the end of June 1981, $22.8 billion of unit investment trusts remained outstanding.

As a new decade began, the extent of future retail investor participation in the municipal marketplace remained uncertain. Increasing interest rates spawned by a restrictive Federal Reserve Board monetary policy and inflation cut sharply into the amount of municipals held by individuals. The interest-rate environment did not improve significantly during 1980, and individuals kept their holdings of tax exempts at a relatively constant $63 billion throughout the year. However, as yields on municipal securities reached new highs during 1981, retail investors were once again drawn back into the market and stepped up their purchases of tax-exempt securities.

Reductions of personal income tax rates, the maximum tax rate, and the maximum long-term capital gains rate should make municipal securities less attractive relative to alternative taxable investments.[12] Beginning in 1985, personal income tax rates will be indexed to inflation. This will eliminate the "artifical" demand for municipals created by "bracket creep."[13] In addition, beginning January 1, 1985, individual taxpayers will be entitled to a 15 percent interest exclusion of "qualified interest income" over "qualified interest expense."[14]

THE CREDIT-RATING AGENCIES

Many investors do not perform their own credit risk analysis, but instead rely upon credit risk ratings and written reports provided by

---

[11] Bond funds are discussed in Chapters 20 and 21.

[12] The Economic Recovery Tax Act of 1981 included a provision that granted individuals a lifetime exclusion from gross income of $1,000 for a single return ($2,000 for a joint return) of interest income earned on certain savings certificates. The certificates are known as *all savers* certificates and must be issued before January 1, 1983, in order to qualify for the special treatment. Since these certificates mature in one year from the date of issuance, they are not directly competitive with long-term municipals.

[13] "Bracket creep" is a consequence of inflation increasing the nominal incomes of individuals, which in turn force them into increasingly higher tax brackets.

[14] The maximum exclusion is $450 for a single return and $900 for a joint return.

rating services or underwriters. In this section we discuss the rating categories of the two major rating companies, Moody's Investors Service and Standard & Poor's and in what ways their respective analytical methods differ. This is particularly in regard to general obligation bonds, "moral obligation" bonds, state-aid-backed bonds, and municipal bond insurance. We have also included in this section a discussion of Moody's and Standard's credit ratings for municipal notes and tax-exempt commercial paper.

Moody's Investors Service

The municipal bond rating system used by Moody's grades the investment quality of municipal bonds in a nine-symbol system that ranges from the highest investment quality, which is Aaa, to the lowest credit rating, which is C.

The respective nine alphabetical ratings and their definitions are the following:

Moody's Municipal Bond Ratings

Rating	Definition
Aaa	Best quality; carry the smallest degree of investment risk.
Aa	High quality; margins of protection not quite as large as the Aaa bonds.
A	Upper medium grade; security adequate but could be susceptible to impairment.
Baa	Medium grade; neither highly protected nor poorly secured—lack outstanding investment characteristics and sensitive to changes in economic circumstances.
Ba	Speculative; protection is very moderate.
B	Not desirable investment; sensitive to day-to-day economic circumstances.
Caa	Poor standing; may be in default but with a workout plan.
Ca	Highly speculative; may be in default with nominal workout plan.
C	Hopelessly in default.

Municipal bonds in the top four categories (Aaa, Aa, and A, and Baa) are considered to be of investment-grade quality. Additionally, bonds in the Aa through B categories that Moody's concludes have the strongest investment features within the respective categories are designated by the symbols Aa1, A1, Baa1, Ba1, and B1, respectively. Moody's also may use the prefix *Con.* before a credit rating to indicate that the bond security is dependent on (1) the completion of a construction project, (2) earnings of a project with little operating experience, (3) rentals being paid once the facility is constructed, or (4) some other limiting condition.

It should also be noted that, as of April 1982, Moody's applies numerical modifiers 1, 2, and 3 in each generic rating classification from Aa through B to municipal bonds that are issued for industrial development and pollution control. The modifier 1 indicates that the security ranks in the higher end of its generic rating category; the modifier 2 indicates a midrange ranking, and the modifier 3 indicates that the bond ranks in the lower end of its generic rating category.

The municipal note rating system used by Moody's is designated by four investment-grade categories of Moody's Investment Grade (MIG):

Moody's Municipal Note Ratings

Rating	Definition
MIG 1.............	Best quality
MIG 2.............	High quality
MIG 3.............	Favorable quality
MIG 4.............	Adequate quality

Moody's also provides credit ratings for tax-exempt commercial paper. These are promissory obligations (1) not having an original maturity in excess of nine months and (2) backed by commercial banks. Moody's uses three designations, all considered to be of investment grade, for indicating the relative repayment capacity of the rated issues:

Moody's Tax-Exempt Commercial Paper Ratings

Rating	Definition
Prime 1 (P–1).............	Superior capacity for repayment
Prime 2 (P–2).............	Strong capacity for repayment
Prime 3 (P–3).............	Acceptable capacity for repayment

It should also be noted that Moody's, in addition to its credit ratings, produces for investors individual written reports on the specific issues it rates.

Standard & Poor's

The municipal bond rating system used by Standard & Poor's grades the investment quality of municipal bonds in a 10-symbol system that ranges from the highest investment quality, which is AAA, to the lowest credit rating, which is D. Bonds within the top four categories (AAA, AA, A, and BBB) are considered by Standard & Poor's as being of investment-grade quality. The respective 10 alphabetical ratings and definitions are the following:

Standard & Poor's Municipal Bond Ratings

Rating	Definition
AAA..................	Highest rating; extremely strong security.
AA	Very strong security; differs from AAA in only a small degree.
A.....................	Strong capacity but more susceptible to adverse economic effects than two above categories.
BBB..................	Adequate capacity but adverse economic conditions more likely to weaken capacity.
BB	Lowest degree of speculation; risk exposure.
B.....................	Speculative; risk exposure.
CCC	Speculative; major risk exposure
CC...................	Highest degree of speculation; major risk exposure.
C	No interest is being paid.
D	Bonds in default with interest and/or repayment of principal in arrears.

Standard & Poor's also uses a plus (+) or minus (−) sign to show relative standing within the rating categories ranging from AA to BB. Additionally, Standard & Poor's uses the letter p to indicate a provisional rating that is intended to be removed upon the successful and timely completion of the construction project. A double dagger (‡) on a mortgage-backed revenue bond rating indicates that the rating is contingent upon receipt by Standard & Poor's of closing documentation confirming investments and cash flows. An asterisk (*) following a credit rating indicates that the continuation of the rating is contingent upon receipt of an executed copy of the escrow agreement.

The municipal note rating system used by Standard & Poor's uses the same 10 rating categories as used for bonds, ranging from AAA to D. Additionally, Standard & Poor's also rates tax-exempt commercial paper in the same four categories as taxable commercial paper. The four tax-exempt commercial paper rating categories are:

Standard & Poor's Tax-Exempt Commercial Paper Ratings

Rating	Definition
A−1+	Highest degree of safety
A−1.................	Very strong degree of safety
A−2.................	Strong degree of safety
A−3.................	Satisfactory degree of safety

How the Rating Agencies Differ

Although there are many similarities in how Moody's and Standard & Poor's approach credit ratings, there are certain differences in their respective approaches as well. As examples we shall present below some of the differences in approach between Moody's and Standard & Poor's when they assign credit ratings to general obligation bonds.

The credit analysis of general obligation bonds issued by states, counties, school districts, and municipalities initially requires the collection and assessment of information in four basic categories. The first category includes obtaining information on the issuer's debt structure so that the overall debt burden can be determined. The debt burden usually is composed of (1) the respective direct and overlapping debts per capita as well as (2) the respective direct and overlapping debts as percentages of real estate valuations and personal incomes. The second category of needed information relates to the issuer's ability and political discipline for maintaining sound budgetary operations. The focus of attention here is usually on the issuer's general operating funds and whether or not it has maintained at least balanced budgets over the previous three to five years. The third category involves determining the specific local taxes and intergovernmental revenues available to the issuer, as well as obtaining historical information on both tax-collection rates, which are important when looking at property tax levies, and on the dependency of local budgets on specific revenue sources, which is important when looking at the impact of federal revenue sharing monies. The fourth and last general category of information necessary to the credit analysis is an assessment of the issuer's overall socioeconomic environment. Questions that have to be answered here include determining the local employment distribution and composition, population growth, and real estate property valuation and personal income trends, among other economic indices.

Although Moody's and Standard & Poor's rely on these same four informational categories in arriving at their respective credit ratings of general obligation bonds, what they emphasize among the categories can result at times in dramatically different credit ratings for the same issuer's bonds.

There are major differences between Moody's and Standard & Poor's in their respective approaches toward these four categories, and there are other differences in conceptual factors the two rating agencies bring to bear before assigning their respective general obligation credit ratings. There are very important differences between the rating agencies, and although while there are some zigs and zags in their respective rating policies, there are also clear patterns of analysis that exist and that have resulted in split credit ratings for a given issuer. The objective here is to outline what these diferences between Moody's and Standard & Poor's actually are. Furthermore, although the rating agencies have stated in their publications what criteria guide their respective credit-rating approaches, the conclusions here about how they go about rating general obligation bonds are not only derived from these sources, but also from reviewing their credit reports and rating decisions on individual bond issues.

How Do Moody's and Standard & Poor's Differ in Evaluating the Four Basic Informational Categories? Simply stated, Moody's tends to focus on the debt burden and budgetary operations of the issuer, and Standard & Poor's considers the issuer's economic environment as the most important element in its analysis. Although in most instances these differences of emphasis do not result in dramatically split credit ratings for a given issuer, there are at least two recent instances in which major differences in ratings on general obligation bonds have occurred.

The general obligation bonds of the Chicago School Finance Authority are rated only Baa1 by Moody's, but Standard & Poor's rates the same bonds AA–. In assigning the credit rating of Baa1, Moody's bases its rating on the following debt- and budget-related factors: (1) The deficit funding bonds are to be retired over a 30-year period, an unusually long time for such an obligation; (2) the overall debt burden is high; and (3) the school board faces long-term difficulties in balancing its operating budget because of reduced operating taxes, desegregation program requirements, and uncertain public employee union relations.

Standard & Poor's credit rating of AA– appears to be based primarily upon the following two factors: (1) Although Chicago's economy has been sluggish, it is still well diversified and fundamentally sound; and (2) the unique security provisions for the bonds in the opinion of the bond counsel insulate the pledged property taxes from the school board's creditors in the event of a school-system bankruptcy.

Another general obligation bond wherein split ratings have occurred is the bond issue of Allegheny County, Pennsylvania. Moody's rates the bonds Baa1, whereas the Standard & Poor's rating is AA.

Moody's Baa1 credit rating is based primarily upon four budget-related factors: (1) above-average debt load with more bonds expected to be issued for transportation related projects and for the building of a new hospital, (2) continued unfunded pension liabilities, (3) past unorthodox budgetary practices of shifting tax revenues from the county tax levy to the county institution district levy, and (4) an archaic real estate property assessment system, which is in the process of being corrected.

Standard & Poor's higher credit rating of AA also appears to be based upon four factors: (1) an affluent, diverse, and stable economy with wealth variables above the national medians, (2) a good industrial mix with decreasing dependence on steel production, (3) improved budget operations having accounting procedures developed to conform to generally accepted accounting principles, and (4) a rapid debt retirement schedule that essentially matches anticipated future bond sales.

Are State General Obligation Bonds Fundamentally Different from Local Government General Obligation Bonds?   There is also another difference between the credit rating agencies in how they apply their analytical tools to the rating of state general obligation bonds and local government general obligation bonds. Moody's basically believes that the state and local bonds are not fundamentally different. Moody's applies the same debt- and budget-related concerns to state general obligation bonds as they do to general obligation bonds issued by counties, school districts, towns, and cities. Moody's has even assigned ratings below A to state general obligation bonds. When the state of Delaware was having serious budgetary problems in the period beginning in 1975 and extending through 1978, Moody's gradually downgraded its general obligation bonds from AA to Baa1. It should be noted that when Moody's downgraded Delaware general obligation bonds to Baa1 and highlighted its budgetary problems, the state government promptly began to address its budgetary problems. By 1982 the bond rating was up to Aa. In May of 1982 Moody's downgraded the state of Michigan's general obligation bonds from A to Baa1 on the basis of the weak local economy and the state's budgetary problems. Another example of Moody's maintaining a state credit rating below A was in Alaska, where until 1974 the state general obligation bonds were rated Baa1. Here, Moody's cited the heavy debt load as a major reason for the rating.

Unlike Moody's, Standard & Poor's seems to make a distinction between state and local government general obligation bonds. Because states have broader legal powers in the areas of taxation and policy making that do not require home-rule approvals, broader revenue bases, and more diversified economies, Standard & Poor's seems to view state general obligation bonds as being significantly stronger than those of their respective underlying jurisdictions. Standard & Poor's has never given ratings below A to a state. Additionally, of the 37 state general obligation bonds that both Moody's and Standard & Poor's rated in 1982, the latter agency had given ratings of AA or better to 35 states and ratings of A to only two states. On the other hand, Moody's had given ratings of AA or better to only 30 states, and ratings of A to 6 states, and even a rating below A to one state, Michigan, as noted above. On the whole for reasons just outlined, it seems that Standard & Poor's tends to have a higher credit assessment of state general obligation bonds than does Moody's. Furthermore, it should be noted that Moody's views these broader revenue resources as making states more vulnerable in difficult economic times to demands by local governments for increased financial aid.

How Do the Credit-Rating Agencies Differ in Assessing the Moral Obligation Bonds? In more than 20 states, state agencies have issued housing revenue bonds that carry a potential state liability for making up deficiencies in their one-year debt service reserve funds (backup funds), should any occur. In most cases if a drawdown of the debt reserve occurs, the state agency must report the amount used to its governor and the state budget director. The state legislature, in turn, may appropriate the requested amount, though there is no legally enforceable obligation to do so. Bonds with this makeup provision are the so-called moral obligation bonds.

Below is an example of the legal language in the bond indenture that explains this procedure.

> In order to further assure the maintenance of each such debt service reserve fund, there shall be annually apportioned and paid to the agency for deposit in each debt service reserve fund such sum, if any, as shall be certified by the chairman of the agency to the governor and direct or of the budget as necessary to restore such fund to an amount equal to the fund requirement. The chairman of the agency shall annually, on or before December first, make and deliver to the governor and director of the budget his certificate stating the sum or sums, if any, required to restore each such debt service reserve fund to the amount aforesaid, and the sum so certified, if any, shall be apportioned and paid to the agency during the then current state fiscal year.

Moody's views the moral obligation feature as being more literary than legal when applied to legislatively permissive debt service reserve makeup provisions. Therefore, it does not consider this procedure a credit strength. Standard & Poor's, to the contrary, does. It views moral obligation bonds as being no lower than one rating category below a state's own general obligation bonds. Its rationale is based upon the implied state support for the bonds and the market implications for that state's own general obligation bonds should it ever fail to honor its moral obligation.

As for the result of these two different opinions of the moral obligation, there are several municipal bonds that have split ratings. As examples, the Nonprofit Housing Project Bonds of the New York State Housing Finance Agency, the General Purpose Bonds of the New York State Urban Development Corporation, and the Series A Bonds of the Battery Park City Authority have the Moody's credit rating of Ba, which is a speculative investment category. Standard & Poor's, because of the moral obligation pledge of the state of New York, gives the same bonds a credit rating of A−, which is a strong investment-grade category.

How Do the Credit-Rating Agencies Differ in Assessing the Importance of Withholding State Aid to Pay Debt Service?   Still another difference between Moody's and Standard & Poor's involves their respective attitudes toward state-aid security-related mechanisms. Since 1974 it has been the policy of Standard & Poor's to view as a very positive credit feature the automatic withholding and use of state aid to pay defaulted debt service on local government general obligation bonds. Usually the mechanism requires the respective state treasurer to pay debt service directly to the bondholder from monies due the local issuer from the state. Seven states have enacted security mechanisms that in one way or another allow certain local government general obligation bondholders to be paid debt service from the state-aid appropriations, if necessary. In most instances the state-aid withholding provisions apply to general obligation bonds issued by school districts.[15]

Although Standard & Poor's does review the budgetary operations of the local government issuer to be sure there are no serious budgetary problems, the assigned rating reflects the general obligation credit rating of the state involved, the legal base of the withholding mechanism, the historical background and long-term state legislative support for the pledged state aid program, and the specified coverage of the state aid monies available to maximum debt-service requirements on the local general obligation bonds. Normally, Standard & Poor's applies a blanket rating to all local general obligation bonds covered by the specific state-aid withholding mechanism. The rating is one or two notches below the rating of that particular state's general obligation bonds. Whether the rating is either one notch below or two notches below depends on the coverage figures, the legal security, and the legislative history and political durability of the pledged state-aid monies involved. It should also be noted that, although Standard & Poor's stated policy is to give the blanket ratings, a specified rating is only granted when an issuer or bondholder applies for it.

Although Moody's recognizes the state-aid withholding mechanisms in its credit reviews, it believes that its assigned rating must in the first instance reflect the underlying ability of the issuer to make timely debt-service payments. Standard & Poor's, to the contrary, considers a state-aid withholding mechanism that provides for the payment of debt service equally as important a credit factor as the underlying budget, economic, and debt-related characteristics of the bond issuer.

---

[15] The states involved are Indiana, Kentucky, New Jersey, New York, Pennsylvania, South Carolina, and West Virginia.

How Do the Credit-Rating Agencies Differ in Assessing the Importance of Municipal Bond Insurance?[16]   Since Moody's policy is to base its rating only on the merits of the underlying bond issuer, Moody's does not reflect the existence of insurance in its municipal ratings. Standard & Poor's considers bond insurance as a credit factor that allows for the timely payment of debt service. In assigning credit ratings to insured bonds, it looks at the strength of the insurance programs and resources and how diversified the risk is. There are three bond insurance programs. Standard & Poor's gives automatic AAA ratings to bonds issued either by the Municipal Bond Insurance Association (MBIA), or by the American Municipal Bond Assurance Corporation (AMBAC). In the case of MBIA, the AAA is based upon the strength and successful track record of the underlying five insurance companies. In the case of AMBAC, the "AAA" is based upon the strength of the 14 insurance companies participating in the reinsurance program with AMBAC. Prior to the reinsurance program, which began in 1979, Standard gave blanket AA ratings to bonds insured by AMBAC.

The third bond insurance program is quite unique in that the insurance program is funded by a state for the benefit of local school district general obligation bondholders.

In July 1980 the state of New Jersey pledged a portion of the existing New Jersey Fund for the Support of Free Public Schools for paying debt service on local government general obligation bonds. The school bond reserve is administered by the state treasurer, who is required to maintain an amount of U.S. securities in it equal to at least 1.5 percent of all outstanding local general obligation school bonds. Viewing this reserve as basically an insurance fund, Standard & Poor's has concluded that "from the actuarial insurance aspects, the fund and the reserve provide ample protection to meet a potential call upon said resources." As the result of this assessment, Standard & Poor's now gives a minimum of AA credit ratings to all school district general obligation bonds in New Jersey.

Moody's has stated that its policy is to weigh this security feature on a case-by-case basis as issuers come to market. Because of Moody's concern (1) that the school bond reserve is only reviewed annually, on September 15 of each year, to determine if its holdings equal at least 1.5 percent of the outstanding local school bonds, (2) that responsibility for notification of a potential default rests with the issuer, and (3) that the monies available to the reserve are relatively small when compared to the total debt service payable on the eligible bonds ($24 million in the reserve versus $1.6 billion in general obligation bonds outstanding), Moody's credit assessments of the individual general obligation bonds is influenced less by the reserve and more by the

---

[16] Municipal bond insurance is discussed in the next section.

budgetary operations and related factors of the local issuers themselves. As the result of this divergence in approach, Standard & Poor's rates the Newark, New Jersey, general purpose and school general obligation bonds BBB and AA, respectively, and Moody's rates both bonds Baa.

What Is the Difference in Attitudes toward Accounting Records? Another area of difference between Moody's and Standard & Poor's concerns their respective attitudes toward the accounting records kept by general obligation bond issuers. In May 1980 Standard & Poor's stated that if the bond issuer's financial reports are not prepared in accordance with generally accepted accounting principles (GAAP) it will consider this a "negative factor" in its rating process. Standard & Poor's has not indicated how negative a factor it is in terms of credit rating changes but has indicated that issuers will not be rated at all if either the financial report is not timely (i.e., available no later than six months after the fiscal year-end) or is substantially deficient in terms of reporting. Moody's policy here is quite different. Because Moody's reviews the historical performance of an issuer over a three- to five-year period, requiring GAAP reporting is not necessary from Moody's point of view, although the timeliness of financial reports is of importance.

MUNICIPAL BOND INSURANCE

Municipal bond insurance is an unconditional contractual guaranty by a property and casualty insurance company to pay the bondholder any bond principal and/or coupon interest that is due on a stated maturity date but for whatever reason has not been paid by the bond issuer. Once issued, this municipal bond default insurance extends for the term of the bond issue, and it cannot be cancelled by the insurance company. A one-time insurance premium (generally paid at the time of original bond issuance) is paid for the insurance policy and is nonrefundable.

The bondholder or trustee who has not received payments for bond principal and/or coupon interest on the stated due dates for the insured bonds must notify the insurance company and surrender to it the unpaid bonds and coupons. Under the terms of the policy, the insurance company is obligated to pay the paying agent sufficient monies for the bondholders. These monies must be enough to cover the face value of the insured principal and coupon interest that was due but not paid. Once the insurance company pays the monies, the company becomes the owner of the surrendered bonds and coupons and can begin legal proceedings to recover the monies that are now due it from the bond issuer.[17]

---

[17] In 1975, the IRS reversed a stand it took in 1973 and ruled that interest paid by insurers is exempt to investors.

The Insurers

Municipal bond insurance has been available since 1971, but only two groups of property and casualty insurance companies have entered this market. However, because of the use of risk reinsurance by one of the insurance issuers and the use of pool insurance by the other, some of the largest and financially strongest insurance companies in the United States are participants in this industry. Additionally, it should be noted that both groups of insurers are based in New York State and therefore are regulated in terms of reserve and capital requirements by the New York State insurance department, which is considered one of the most consumer-protection oriented among the states.

Since 1971, the American Municipal Bond Assurance Corporation (known as AMBAC), which is a subsidiary of the MGIC Investment Corporation, has been insuring municipal bonds. In 1982 MGIC was acquired by the Baldwin United Corporation. At June 30, 1981, there were more than 2,100 policies on AMBAC's books covering total principal and interest in force of $12.4 billion. Debt service for the fiscal year ending June 30, 1981, was $290,839,657. This included municipal bond portfolios held by individuals and bank trust departments as well as by tax-exempt bond funds and unit trusts, which AMBAC through an affiliate (MGIC Indemnity Corporation) has been insuring since 1973.

From 1972 through 1979 the backing for AMBAC's insurance had been the assets and net worth of AMBAC and its affiliate, MGIC Indemnity Corporation. In 1979 AMBAC established a reinsurance program with other insurance companies, which was designed to supplement its own assets and to provide additional protection.[18] The aggregate liability of the reinsurers is $75 million. Under the terms of the reinsurance contracts, the reinsurers can cancel their contracts. However, their contractual obligations cover a six-year runoff period after the first year in which they may be required to pay losses.

Since 1974 the Municipal Bond Insurance Association (known as MBIA), which represents a pool of insurers, has been insuring municipal bonds.[19] At June 30, 1981, there were some 993 policies issued, covering total principal and interest in force of $11.2 billion.

---

[18] Insurance companies participating in the AMBAC reinsurance program with at least a 5 percent interest are: Allstate Insurance Company, Continental Casualty Company (CNA), Fremont Indemnity Company, Home Insurance Company, INA Reinsurance Company, Kemper Reinsurance Company, Travelers Indemnity Company, Unigard Mutual Insurance Company. In addition to those listed above, there are six other insurance companies with respective reinsurance agreements whose participations range from 0.5 percent to 2 percent.

[19] Below are the five members of the MBIA pool of insurers and their respective percentage participations in MBIA as of mid-1981:

The pool of insurers now includes five property and casualty insurance companies, which participate in predetermined proportions. MBIA municipal bond insurance policies are "several obligations" of the participating companies—that is, the individual insurance company's liability is limited only to its beforehand agreed upon percentage share of the risk. Similarly, if a participating insurance company decides to withdraw from MBIA, its existing liabilities remain in force.

Underwriting Criteria Used by Insurers

Besides the needs for geographic diversification and for avoiding concentration in one name or type of bond, both AMBAC and MBIA only insure municipal bonds that meet their credit standards. They both carry out their own in-house credit reviews and require in general that the bonds be at least of investment-grade quality. If the bonds are rated by credit-rating companies as well, the ratings generally would not be lower than a Baa by Moody's or a BBB by Standard & Poor's. These two ratings are in the lowest investment-grade categories of the two respective credit-rating companies.

In fact, a large portion of the bonds that AMBAC and MBIA have insured have had credit ratings above these categories. Perhaps the most meaningful indications of the careful underwriting guidelines of AMBAC and MBIA are the relatively small number of insured bonds that have defaulted. In the case of AMBAC, out of more than 2,100 policies issued since 1971 (covering total principal and interest due of $12.4 billion as of June 30, 1981) there have been only 11 defaults. Since the first bond default in 1976, the total amount paid by AMBAC has been $1,080,080. Of this amount, $181,000 already has been recovered by AMBAC through foreclosure and salvage proceedings.

In the case of MBIA, since the program began in 1974 there have been 993 policies issued covering total principal and interest due of $11.2 billion. As of September 1, 1981, there have been no defaults. In summary, both AMBAC and MBIA try to be very selective about the

The Aetna Casualty & Surety Company	33%
Fireman's Fund Insurance Company	30
The Travelers Indemnity Company	15
Aetna Insurance Company (an affiliate of the Connecticut General Insurance Corporation)	12
The Continental Insurance Company	10
Total	100%

It should be noted that between 1974 and 1978 the St. Paul Fire and Marine Insurance Company also participated in MBIA. In 1978 it was replaced by the Fireman's Fund Insurance Company, which assumed St. Paul's 30 percent share of MBIA insurance obligations from the beginning of MBIA in 1974. Also, in 1980 the United States Fire Insurance Company withdrew and was replaced by the Travelers Indemnity Company and the Continental Insurance Company.

municipal bonds they insure. Likely default candidates, speculative bonds, or even "businessperson's risk" municipal bonds are clearly avoided by both AMBAC and MBIA.

Credit-Rating Agencies View of Municipal Bond Insurance

As noted in the previous section, of the two major credit-rating companies only one, Standard & Poor's, views the municipal bond insurance as the determinant credit factor in assigning ratings to the insured bonds. The other credit rating company, Moody's Investors Service, assigns credit ratings based only on the underlying merits of the specified municipal bonds involved.

In regard to AMBAC-insured municipal bonds, Standard & Poor's assigned them in 1979 its highest credit rating of AAA, when the risk reinsurance program was established. Prior to this, the bonds had been rated AA. The new AAA rating reflects the conclusion of Standard & Poor's that the structure of the reinsurance program provides adequate protection for the bondholders.

In regard to MBIA-insured municipal bonds, Standard & Poor's has assigned them its highest credit rating of AAA since the MBIA program began in 1974. This rating is based upon the combined and individual strengths of the five participating insurance companies, all of which have successful track records and excellent dispersions of risk.

Market Pricing of Insured Municipal Bonds

In general, although the AAA-rated AMBAC- and MBIA-insured municipal bonds sell at yields lower than they would without the insurance, they tend to have yields substantially higher than other Aaa/AAA-rated noninsured municipal bonds. Municipal bond traders generally price the insured bonds as double-A credits. Most recently, the pricing difference between individual insured bonds and other Aaa/AAA-rated municipal bonds has ranged from approximately 25 to 65 basis points, whereas when the insurance programs first began, the spread was as high as 75 to 130 basis points.

For example, in Exhibit 2 are shown the respective average annual yields of 20-year, Moody's Aaa-rated general obligation bonds and MBIA-insured, Standard & Poor's AAA-rated bonds. It is quite clear from this table that since the MBIA insurance began in 1974, the MBIA bonds have sold at yields at least 35 basis points higher than the Aaa general obligation bonds.

It is worth noting that the high yields on the MBIA-insured bonds in 1974 (7.19 percent versus 5.89 percent for the triple-A-rated general obligation bonds) may have occurred because 1974 was the first year

Exhibit 2
Comparison of Yields on 20-Year Insured Bonds to Moody's Aaa-Rated General Obligation Bonds, 1974–1981

Year	Average Yield on Aaa G.O. Bonds	Average Yield on MBIA-Insured Bonds	Basis Point Spread	Insured Yield as Percent
1981 (January–June)	9.58%	10.21%	63	107%
1980	7.84	8.63	79	110
1979	5.92	6.42	50	108
1978	5.52	5.98	46	108
1977	5.20	5.57	37	107
1976	5.65	6.22	57	110
1975	6.42	7.05	63	110
1974	5.89	7.19	130	122

Sources: Moody's Investors Service and MBIA.

of the MBIA insurance program. Many investors may have stayed away from purchasing the MBIA-insured bonds because of the lack of familiarity with the municipal bond insurance concept.

There are two reasons the insured municipal bonds, although rated AAA by Standard & Poor's, sell and trade at yields closer to double-A-rated bonds. First, although the insurance programs have been in existence for more than 10 years, municipal bond insurance still is a relatively new security concept for investors. The second reason for the high yields may be the fact that the insured bonds have a triple-A rating from only one of the credit-rating companies. As a result, very often bonds come to market with split ratings, such an AAA rating by Standard & Poor's given because of the bond insurance and only a Baa or A rating by Moody's.

YIELD RELATIONSHIPS WITHIN THE MUNICIPAL BOND MARKET

Differences within an Assigned Credit Rating

Major institutional bond buyers primarily use the credit ratings assigned by Moody's and Standard & Poor's as a starting point for the pricing of an issue. The final market-derived bond price is composed of the assigned credit rating and adjustments by market participants to reflect their own perceptions of credit and marketability. For example, as we noted earlier, AAA-rated AMBAC- and MBIA-insured municipal bonds tend to have yields substantially higher than noninsured Aaa/AAA-rated municipal bonds. Many market participants also have geographical preferences among bonds, in spite of identical credit ratings and otherwise comparable investment characteristics.

Also, not all issues are assigned the same credit ratings by the major rating agencies. In the case of split ratings, the issue has generally had a yield closer to the lower rating than to the higher one.

Differences between Credit Ratings

Like taxable bonds, the differences in yield between credit ratings, often referred to as quality spreads, is not constant over time. For example, on September 25, 1981, the quality spread between A-rated and Aaa-rated, 30-year general obligation bonds was roughly 150 basis points. The quality spread declined to 75 basis points on May 7, 1982.

Reasons for the change in spreads are the outlook for the economy and its anticipated impact on issuers, federal budget financing needs, and municipal market supply and demand factors. During periods of relatively low interest rates, investors sometimes increase their holdings of issues with lower credit ratings in order to obtain additional yield. During periods in which market participants anticipate a poor economic climate, there is often a "flight to quality" as market participants pursue a more conservative credit-risk posture.

Another factor that causes shifts in quality spreads is the temporary oversupply of issues within a market sector. For example, substantial new-issue volume of high-grade state general obligation bonds may tend to decrease the quality spread between high-grade and lower grade revenue bonds. Obviously, in a weak market environment it is easier for high-grade municipals to come to market than for weaker credits. Therefore, it is not uncommon for high grades to flood weak markets while at the same time there is a relative scarcity of medium-grade and lower grade municipals.

Differences between In-State, General Market, and Territorial Issues

Bonds of municipal issuers located in certain states (for example, New York, California, Arizona, Maryland, and Pennsylvania) yield considerably less than identically rated issues with similar investment characteristics that come from other states that trade in the "general market." There are three reasons for the existence of such spreads. As noted earlier in this chapter, states often exempt interest from in-state issues from state and local personal income taxes, and interest from out-of-state issues is generally not exempt. Consequently, in states with high income taxes (for example, New York and California), strong investor demand for in-state issues will reduce their yields relative to bonds of issues located in states where state and local income taxes are not important considerations (for example, Illinois, Florida, and New Jersey). Second, in some states, public funds deposited in banks must be collateralized by the bank accepting the deposit. This requirement is referred to as pledging. Acceptable collateral for pledging will typically include issues of certain in-state issuers. For those issues qualifying, pledging tends to increase demand (particularly for the shorter maturities) and reduce yields relative to nonqualifying comparable issues. The third reason is that investors in some states (South Carolina, for example) exhibit extreme reluctance to purchase issues from issuers outside of their state or region. In-state parochialism tends to decrease relative yields of issues from states in which investors exhibit this behavior.

Territorial bonds such as those issued by Puerto Rico are tax exempt throughout most of the country, and therefore are usually very marketable. Because of this feature, their yields tend to be lower than their respective credit ratings would indicate.

Differences between Maturities

The relationship between yields and term to maturity is referred to as the *maturity structure* or *term structure of interest rates*. The graphical representation of this relationship for bonds that are identical in every other way is called the *yield curve*. In the taxable market, Treasury obligations are usually used to construct a yield curve.

At any given time, a yield curve can have a positive slope or inverted slope. Three theories for explaining the shape of the yield curve are discussed in Chapters 5 and 46—liquidity preference, expectations, and market segmentation.

Two characteristics of the municipal yield curve should be noted. First, the municipal yield curve almost always has a positive slope. Exhibit 3 shows the prime municipal yield curve for July 1, 1980.

Exhibit 3
Prime Municipal Yield Curve (July 1, 1980)

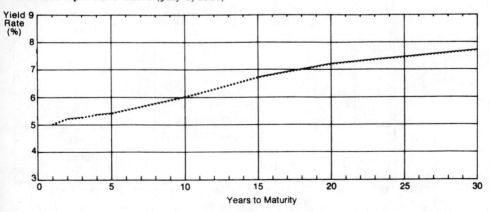

Source: Martin L. Leibowitz, "The Municipal Rolling Yield: A New Approach to the Analysis of Tax-Exempt Yield Curves," in *The Handbook of Municipal Bonds*, vol. 1, ed. Frank J. Fabozzi, Sylvan Feldstein, Irving M. Pollack, and Frank G. Zarb (Homewood, Ill.: Dow Jones-Irwin, 1983). © Dow Jones-Irwin, Inc., 1983.

Exhibit 4
Yield Curve Spreads (30-year/1-year spreads within municipal and Treasury markets)

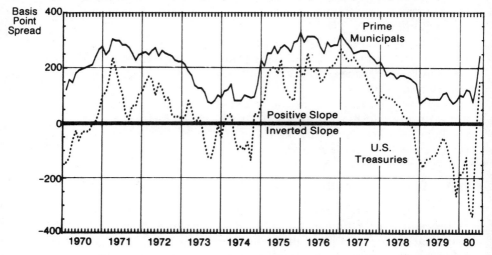

Exhibit 5
Yield Curve Spreads as Percentage (30-year/1-year spreads as percentage of 1-year rate)

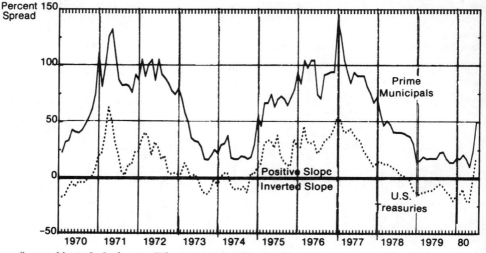

Second, the yield spreads between maturities are usually wider in the municipal market compared with maturity spreads in the Treasury market. That is, the positive slope of the municipal yield curve is usually greater than that for treasuries.[20] This is illustrated in Exhibit 4, which contrasts the historical maturity spreads between bonds with 30 years and 1 year remaining to maturity for Treasuries and high-grade municipals. These historical maturity spreads were even more dramatic when viewed in terms of percentages, as can be seen in Exhibit 5.

FORECASTING MUNICIPAL BOND YIELDS BY MONITORING TRENDS IN OTHER MARKETS

Since the 1970s, the municipal market has reacted more slowly than other fixed income markets to economic information and other information that exert influence on interest rates. Consequently, some market observers believe that tracking money market conditions and certain interest rates can be useful in forecasting the direction of future municipal bond yields.

Alan Lerner and Philip Nathanson,[21] for example, have documented the relationship between municipal bond yields and both the federal funds rate[22] and discount rate.[23] They find that since 1971 these two rates have predicted the cyclical turning points in municipal bond yields.

In particular, their analysis indicates that "[i]f historical relationships are maintained, then the behavior of funds in the most recent 15 months can aid in predicting the general movement in the BBI (*Bond Buyer Index*) over the subsequent 15-month period." Since the discount rate is almost exclusively a confirming action of Federal Reserve policy, and not a leading overt indicator of policy as is the federal funds rate, they expected a shorter lag between movements in the discount rate and municipal bond yields. They did, in fact, find that municipal bond yields lagged movements in the discount rate by 10 months compared with 15 months for the federal funds rate.

Lerner and Nathanson conclude: "The surprisingly long lags found in this study obviously may or may not be realized in the future. There

[20] Martin L. Leibowitz, "The Municipal Rolling Yield: A New Approach to the Analysis of Tax-Exempt Yield Curves," in *The Handbook of Municipal Bonds*, vol. 1., ed. Fabozzi et al.

[21] Alan C. Lerner and Philip D. Nathanson, "Forecasting Municipal Rates and Spreads by Monitoring Trends in Other Markets," in *The Handbook of Municipal Bonds*, vol. 1., ed. Fabozzi et al.

[22] The federal funds rate is the interest rate at which federal funds are traded by commercial banks. It is pegged by the Federal Reserve through open-market operations. See Chapter 45 for a discussion of the federal funds rate.

[23] The discount rate is the interest rate charged by the Federal Reserve to member banks that borrow at the discount window.

are some indications, however, that participants in the municipal market already are more sensitive to conditions in other markets than previously. This alone may cause the lags to shrink, but the relationships we have analyzed could still remain an important key to the future behavior of municipal bond rates."

THE PRIMARY AND SECONDARY MARKETS

The Primary Market

A substantial number of municipal obligations are brought to market each week. A state or local government can market its new issue by offering them publicly to the investing community or by placing them privately with a small group of investors. When a public offering is selected, the issue is usually underwritten by investment bankers and municipal bond departments of commercial banks. Public offerings may be marketed by either competitive bidding or direct negotiations with underwriters. When an issue is marketed via competitive bidding, the issue is awarded to the bidder submitting the lowest best bid.

Most states mandate that general obligation issues be marketed via competitive bidding; however, this is generally not required for revenue bonds. Usually state and local governments require that a competitive sale be announced in a recognized financial publication, such as *The Bond Buyer,* which is the trade publication of the municipal bond industry. *The Bond Buyer* also provides information on upcoming competitive sales and most negotiated sales as well as the results of the sales of previous weeks.

When an underwriter purchases a new bond issue, it relieves the issuer of two obligations. First, the underwriter is responsible for the distribution of the issue. Second, the underwriter accepts the risk that investors might fail to purchase the issue at the expected prices within the planned time period. The second risk exists because the underwriter may have incorrectly priced the issue and/or because interest rates rise, resulting in a decline in the value of unsold issues held in inventory. The underwriter spread (that is, the difference between the price it paid the issuer for the issue and the price it reoffered the issue to the public) is the underwriter's compensation for undertaking these risks as well as for other services it may have provided the issuer.[24]

An official statement describing the issue and issuer is prepared for new offerings. Exhibits 6 and 7 are cover pages of an official statement for a general obligation and revenue bond, respectively.

---

[24] For example, in the case of negotiated offerings there is the value of the origination services provided by the underwriter. Origination services represent the structuring of the issue and planning activities surrounding the offering.

Exhibit 6
Cover Page of a General Obligation Bond Official Statement

<u>NEW ISSUE</u>

In the opinion of Bond Counsel, interest on the Bonds will be exempt under existing law from Federal income taxes and from New York State and New York City personal income taxes.

$$\$75,000,000$$

The City of New York
General Obligation Bonds

Dated: March 15, 1982   Due: September 15, as shown below

Interest is payable semi-annually, beginning September 15, 1982 and on each March 15 and September 15 thereafter until maturity or redemption prior to maturity. The Bonds will be issued as bearer bonds, with coupons attached, in the denomination of $5,000 each. Bearer bonds may be converted into fully registered bonds in the denomination of $5,000 each, or any integral multiple thereof, and fully registered bonds may be converted into bearer bonds in the denomination of $5,000 each. Principal of and interest on the Bonds are payable at Manufacturers Hanover Trust Company, Corporate Trust Division, 40 Wall Street, New York, New York, the Paying Agent. The Term Bonds are subject to redemption prior to maturity as described herein.

Maturity	Amount	Interest Rate	Maturity	Amount	Interest Rate
1983	$10,000,000	9 %	1988	$2,000,000	11½%
1984	10,000,000	9½	1989	2,000,000	12
1985	10,000,000	10	1990	2,000,000	12½
1986	2,000,000	10½	1991	2,000,000	12¾
1987	2,000,000	11	1992	3,000,000	13

$30,000,000 14½% Term Bonds due September 15, 2007

Price of all Bonds: 100%

(Accrued interest to be added)

The Bonds are offered subject to prior sale, when, as and if issued by the City and accepted by the Underwriters, subject to the approval of the legality of the Bonds by Rogers & Wells, New York, New York, Bond Counsel to the City, and subject to certain other conditions. Certain legal matters in connection with the preparation of this Official Statement will be passed upon for the City by Lord, Day & Lord, New York, New York. Certain legal matters will be passed upon for the Underwriters by Brown, Wood, Ivey, Mitchell & Petty, New York, New York. It is expected that the Bonds will be available for delivery in New York, New York, on or about March 30, 1982.

Goldman, Sachs & Co.	**Merrill Lynch White Weld Capital Markets Group** Merrill Lynch, Pierce, Fenner & Smith Incorporated	
Morgan Guaranty Trust Company of New York	**The Chase Manhattan Bank, N.A.**	**Citibank, N.A.**
Bache Halsey Stuart Shields Incorporated	**Bank of America NT & SA**	**Bear, Stearns & Co.**
Blyth Eastman Paine Webber Incorporated	**Chemical Bank**	**Continental Bank** Continental Illinois National Bank and Trust Company of Chicago
Ehrlich-Bober & Co., Inc.	**First Chicago** The First National Bank of Chicago	**E. F. Hutton & Company Inc.**
L. F. Rothschild, Unterberg, Towbin	**Salomon Brothers Inc**	**Security Pacific National Bank**
Shearson/American Express Inc.		**Smith Barney, Harris Upham & Co.** Incorporated

March 18, 1982

Exhibit 7
Cover Page of a Revenue Bond Official Statement

NEW ISSUE

$400,000,000
North Carolina Eastern Municipal Power Agency
Power System Revenue Bonds, Series 1982 A

Dated: April 1, 1982   Due: January 1, as shown below

The 1982 A Bonds are issuable as coupon Bonds in the denomination of $5,000, registrable as to principal only, or as fully registered Bonds without coupons in the denomination of $5,000 or any integral multiple thereof. Principal and semiannual interest (January 1 and July 1, first coupon for nine months due January 1, 1983) will be payable at the principal corporate trust office of The Chase Manhattan Bank (National Association), New York, New York, Bond Fund Trustee and Paying Agent, or, at the option of the holder, at the principal office of Wachovia Bank and Trust Company, N.A., Winston-Salem, North Carolina, Paying Agent, or The Northern Trust Company, Chicago, Illinois, Paying Agent, unless registered or paid prior to maturity at the option of the holder.

The 1982 A Bonds are subject to redemption prior to maturity as described herein.

In the opinion of Bond Counsel, interest on the 1982 A Bonds is exempt from Federal income taxation under existing laws and regulations and, under the existing laws of the State of North Carolina, the 1982 A Bonds, their transfer and the income therefrom (including any profit made on the sale thereof) are free from taxation by the State of North Carolina or any political subdivision or any agency of either thereof, excepting inheritance or gift taxes.

The 1982 A Bonds are payable solely from and secured by the Revenues of Power Agency derived from its ownership and operation of the Power System, subject to prior payment therefrom of Operating Expenses, and other moneys and securities pledged under the Resolution. Such Revenues include payments received by Power Agency from the 32 Participants pursuant to Project Power Sales Agreements, which provide that each Participant is required to pay its share of Monthly Project Power Costs of the Initial Project (including Debt Service on all Bonds issued for the Initial Project) as an operating expense of its electric system, but solely from the revenues thereof, regardless of the completion or operational status of any of the units included in the Initial Project.

The 1982 A Bonds and additional Bonds for the Initial Project will be issued to finance primarily the acquisition from Carolina Power & Light Company of ownership interests in three coal-fired units, one in commercial operation and two under construction, and four nuclear-fueled units, two in commercial operation and two under construction. Carolina Power & Light Company is responsible for the construction and operation of such units.

AMOUNTS, MATURITIES, COUPON RATES AND PRICES
$46,000,000 Serial Bonds

Amount	Maturity	Coupon Rate	Price	Amount	Maturity	Coupon Rate	Price
$ 895,000	1985	8¾%	100%	$3,100,000	1992	12 %	100%
1,030,000	1986	9¼	100	3,615,000	1993	12.20	100
1,310,000	1987	9¾	100	4,130,000	1994	12.40	100
1,490,000	1988	10¼	100	4,710,000	1995	12.60	100
2,090,000	1989	10¾	100	5,365,000	1996	12¾	100
2,385,000	1990	11	100	6,150,000	1997	12.90	100
2,715,000	1991	11½	100	7,015,000	1998	13	100

$ 33,000,000 13¼% Term Bonds due January 1, 2002 — Price 100%
$175,000,000 13¾% Term Bonds due January 1, 2011 — Price 100%
$ 53,000,000 10% Term Bonds due January 1, 2014 — Price 75%
(Yield Approximately 13.40%)
$ 93,000,000 10½% Term Bonds due January 1, 2017 — Price 100%

(Accrued interest to be added)

The Series 1982 A Bonds due January 1, 2017 will be payable at par at the option of the holders thereof on January 1, 1987, or on any January 1 thereafter, upon notice given by the holders as described herein.

The 1982 A Bonds are offered when, as and if issued and received by the Underwriters, subject to the approval of legality by Wood & Dawson, New York, New York, Bond Counsel. Certain legal matters in connection with the 1982 A Bonds are subject to the approval of Spruill Lane McCotter & Jolly, Rocky Mount, North Carolina, North Carolina counsel to Power Agency, Spiegel & McDiarmid, Washington, D.C., Washington, D.C. counsel to Power Agency, and Brown, Wood, Ivey, Mitchell & Petty, New York, New York, counsel to the Underwriters. It is expected that the 1982 A Bonds in definitive form will be ready for delivery in New York, New York on or about April 21, 1982.

Smith Barney, Harris Upham & Co.
Incorporated

Merrill Lynch White Weld Capital Markets Group   **Salomon Brothers Inc**
Merrill Lynch, Pierce, Fenner & Smith Incorporated

The First Boston Corporation   **Dillon, Read & Co. Inc.**

Carolina Securities Corporation   **First Charlotte Corporation**

Interstate Securities Corporation   **J. Lee Peeler & Company, Inc.**

April 1, 1982   **Wheat, First Securities, Inc.**

Exhibit 8
Cover Page of *The Blue List*

The Blue List
of Current Municipal Offerings
(A Division of Standard & Poor's Corporation)

Published every weekday except Saturdays and Holidays by
The Blue List Publishing Company, 25 Broadway, New York, N. Y. 10004
Telephone 212 248-3111
Reg U S Patent Office • Printed in U S A

The bonds set forth in this list were offered at the close of business on the day before the date of this issue by the houses mentioned, subject to prior sale and change in price. Every effort is made by The Blue List Publishing Company and the offering houses whose offerings are shown in this list to avoid mistakes and inaccuracies, but due to the fact that many offerings come in by wire and that the list is subject to error both before and after the offering houses have closed for the day, occasional errors are unavoidable. Neither The Blue List Publishing Company nor the offering houses take responsibility for the accuracy of the offerings listed herein.

+ Items so marked did not appear in the previous issue of The Blue List.
‡ Items so marked are changed from previous issue.
• Prices so marked changed after the offering houses...
c Items so marked are reported to have call or option features. Consult offering house for full details.

ANNUAL SUBSCRIPTION RATE (approximately 250 issues); Hand Delivery (Wall Street Area) $300.00; First Class Mail $996.00

AMT. M	SECURITY	PURPOSE	RATE	MATURITY	YIELD OR OFFERED PRICE	OFFERED BY
	ALABAMA					
+ 70	ALABAMA	(SEAPORT FACILITY)	3.20	3/1/83	6.75	KIDDERAT
90	ALABAMA		7.25	3/1/83	7.50	IRVTRUST
590	ALABAMA		7.25	3/1/83	7.50	MERRILNV
75	ALABAMA		6.25	3/1/83	10.00	IRVTRUST
500	ALABAMA		7.50	9/1/83	7.75	MERRILNV
100	ALABAMA		7.40	9/1/83	7.40	SNISBAM
50	ALABAMA		8.50	9/1/85	7.75	BLYTHMY
+ 50	ALABAMA		8.25	9/1/85	8.25	CENTERBRM
100	ALABAMA		8.50	9/1/85	8.30	REPMOKAL
280	ALABAMA		8	3/1/86	8.50	FCNBHOUS
5	ALABAMA		5	3/1/87	10.60	SIMSNJ
25	ALABAMA		9.90	6/1/87	8.90	COMMBKKC
450	ALABAMA		9	3/1/90	9.40	NCND
10	ALABAMA		10.25	3/1/90	101 1/2	BEARSTER

AMT. M	SECURITY	PURPOSE	RATE	MATURITY	YIELD OR OFFERED PRICE	OFFERED BY
	ALABAMA—CONTINUED					
10	ALABAMA		10.25	3/1/92	10.40	MARRICCH
15	ALABAMA		10.50	3/1/92	10.00	CENTERRE
915	ALABAMA		10.50	3/1/91	9.65	REPMOKAL
+ 620	ALABAMA		10.75	3/1/91	10.10	REPMOKAL
+ 1555	ALABAMA		10.75	9/1/92	10.35	CONTILNO
450	ALABAMA		10.70	3/1/92	10.30	ROGERSLD
15	ALABAMA		10.70	9/1/95	10.40	MARRICCH
440	ALABAMA	C 8 103	10.00	3/1/95	C92 10.75	BANCMNCO
500	ALABAMA		10.00	3/1/93	10.75	MANUFHAN
230	ALABAMA		10.00	3/1/93	10.75	SEABGNBT
470	ALABAMA		10.00	3/1/93	10.75	BARNETJX
290	ALABAMA		10.00	9/1/93	10.75	CONTILNO
340	ALABAMA		10.00	3/1/93	10.75 •	MANUFHAN
500	ALABAMA		10.00	9/1/93	10.70	MADOWWUG

THE BLUE LIST
OF CURRENT MUNICIPAL OFFERINGS

Volume
187
Number
38

May
26
1982
Wednesday

The Secondary Market

Although municipal bonds are not listed and traded in formal institutions, such as are certain common stocks and corporate bonds on the New York and American stock exchanges, there are very strong and active billion-dollar secondary markets for municipals that are supported by about a thousand municipal bond dealers across the country. Markets are maintained on local credits by regional brokerage firms and local banks. General market names are supported by the larger brokerage firms and banks, many of whom have investment banking relationships with the issuers. Buying and selling decisions are often made over the phone and through municipal bond brokers. For a small fee these brokers serve as intermediaries in the sale of large blocks of municipal bonds among dealers and large institutional investors. These brokers are primarily located in New York City and include Chapdelaine & Company, Drake & Company, the J. J. Kenny Company, and Titus & Donnelly, Inc., among others.

In addition to these brokers and the daily offerings sent out over *The Bond Buyer's* "munifacts" teletype system, many dealers advertise their municipal bond offerings for the retail market in what is known as *The Blue List*. This is a 100 + -page booklet which is published every weekday by the Standard & Poor's Corporation. In it are listed state municipal bond and note offerings and prices. A sample page from *The Blue List* is shown in Exhibit 8.

In the municipal bond market, an odd lot of bonds is $25,000 (five bonds) or less in par value for retail investors. For institutions, anything below $100,000 in par value is considered an odd lot. Dealer spreads—the difference between the dealers bid and ask prices—depend on upon several factors. For the retail investor, the dealer spread can range from as low as one quarter of one point ($12.50 per $5,000 of par value) on large blocks of actively traded bonds to four points ($200 per $5,000 of par value) for odd lot sales of an inactive issue. The average spread for retail investors seems to be around two points ($100 per $5,000 of par value). For institutional investors, the dealer spread rarely exceeds one half of one point ($25 per $5,000 of par value).

REGULATION OF THE MUNICIPAL SECURITIES MARKETS[25]

As an outgrowth of abusive stock market practices, Congress passed the Securities Act of 1933 and the Securities Exchange Act of 1934.

---

[25] This discussion is drawn from the following two chapters that will appear in Fabozzi et al., *The Handbook of Municipal Bonds*, vol. 1: Thomas F. Mitchell, "Financial Disclosure and the Municipal Bond Industry," and Nancy H. Wojtas, "Federal Regulation of Municipal Securities."

The 1934 act created the Securities and Exchange Commission (SEC), granting it regulatory authority over the issuance and trading of *corporate* securities. Congress specifically exempted municipal securities from both the registration requirements of the 1933 Act and the periodic reporting requirements of the 1934 Act. However, antifraud provisions did apply to offerings of or dealings in municipal securities.

The reasons for the exemption afforded municipal securities appear to have been due to (1) the desire for governmental comity, (2) the absence of recurrent abuses in transactions involving municipal securities, (3) the greater level of sophistication of investors in this segment of the securities markets (that is, institutional investors dominated the market), and (4) the fact that there were few defaults by municipal issuers. Consequently, from the enactment of the two federal securities acts in the early 1930s to the early 1970s, the municipal securities market can be characterized as relatively free from federal regulation.

In the early 1970s, however, circumstances changed. As incomes rose, individuals participated in the municipal securities market to a much greater extent. As a result, public concern over selling practices occurred with greater frequency. For example, in the early 1970s, the SEC obtained seven injunctions against 72 defendants for fradulent municipal trading practices. According to the SEC, the abusive practices involved both disregard by the defendants as to whether the particular municipal bond offered to individuals were in fact appropriate investment vehicles for the individuals to whom they were offered and misrepresentation or failure to disclose information necessary for individuals to assess the credit risk of the municipal issuer, especially in the case of revenue bonds. Moreover, the financial problems of some municipal issuers, notably New York City, made market participants aware that municipal issuers have the potential to experience severe and bankruptcy-type financial difficulties.

Congress passed the Securities Act Amendment of 1975 to broaden federal regulation in the municipals market. The legislation brought brokers and dealers in the municipal securities market, including banks that underwrite and trade municipal securities, within the regulatory scheme of the Securities Exchange Act of 1934. In addition, the legislation mandated that the SEC establish a 15-member Municipal Securities Rule Making Board (MSRB) as an independent, self-regulatory agency, whose primary responsibility is to develop rules governing the activities of banks, brokers, and dealers in municipal securities.[26] Rules adopted by the MSRB must be approved by the SEC. The MSRB has no enforcement or inspection authority. This authority is

---

[26] For a detailed discussion of the MSRB, see Frieda K. Wallison, "Self-Regulation of the Municipal Securities Industry," in Fabozzi et al., *The Handbook of Municipal Bonds*, vol. 1.

vested with the SEC, the National Association of Securities Dealers, and certain regulatory banking agencies, such as the Federal Reserve Bank.

The Securities Act Amendment of 1975 does *not* require that municipal issuers comply with the registration requirement of the 1933 act or the periodic-reporting requirement of the 1934 act. There have been, however, several legislative proposals to mandate financial disclosure.[27] Although none has been passed, there is clearly pressure to improve disclosure.[28] Even in the absence of federal legislation dealing with the regulation of financial disclosure, underwriters began insisting upon greater disclosure as it became apparent that the SEC was exercising stricter application of the antifraud provisions. Moreover, underwriters recognized the need for improved disclosure to sell municipal securities to an investing public that has become much more concerned about credit risk by municipal issuers. Thus it is in the best interest of all parties—the issuer, the underwriter and the investor—that meaningful disclosure requirements be established.

---

[27] Senator Thomas Eagleton proposed a bill that would repeal the provision exempting municipal securities from registration and other requirements. In mid-1979 and early 1981, a bill was introduced to amend the 1934 act to assure the availability of nationally recognized accounting and financial reporting standards for municipal issuers. In 1976 the Treasury proposed legislation that would have established a system of mandatory, uniform accounting standards.

[28] In the SEC study concerning transactions of the city of New York and related matters, the staff report states that the "commission's mandate is to assure that investors in securities, whether issued by municipalities or others, receive the protections afforded by the federal securities laws." The staff report concludes that investors did not receive these protections and that the key participants had the responsibility to assure adequate disclosure that investors could rely upon for investment decisions. Yet the SEC did not institute enforcement proceedings against any of the key participants. Instead, the SEC believed that it would better serve the public interest by supporting legislative solutions to the problem of inadequate disclosure.

Guidelines in the Credit Analysis of General Obligation and Revenue Municipal Bonds

16 SYLVAN G. FELDSTEIN, Ph.D.
Vice President and Bond Analyst
Moody's Investors Service, Inc.

INTRODUCTION

Although historically the degree of safety of investing in municipal bonds has been considered second only to that of U.S. Treasury bonds, beginning in the 1970s there has developed among many investors and underwriters ongoing concerns about the potential default risks of municipal bonds.

The First Influence: Defaults and Bankruptcies

One concern resulted from the well-publicized, billion-dollar general obligation note defaults in 1975 of New York City. Not only were specific investors threatened with the loss of their principal, but also the defaults sent a loud and clear warning to municipal bond investors in general. That warning was that regardless of the supposedly iron-clad legal protections for the bondholder, when issuers, such as large cities, have severe budget-balancing difficulties, the political hues, cries, and financial interests of public employee unions, vendors, and community groups may be dominant forces in the initial decision-making process.

This reality was further reinforced by the new federal bankruptcy law, which took effect on October 1, 1979, and which makes it easier for municipal bond issuers to seek protection from bondholders by filing for bankruptcy. One by-product of the increased investor concern is that since 1975 the official statement, which is the counterpart to a prospectus in an equity or corporate bond offering and which is to contain a summary of the key legal and financial security features, has become more comprehensive. As an example, prior to 1975 it was common for a city of New York official statement to be only 6 pages long, whereas for a bond sale in 1981 it was close to 100 pages long.

The Second Influence: Strong Investor Demand for Tax Exemption

The second reason for the increased interest in credit analysis was derived from the changing nature of the municipal bond market. For most of the decade of the 1970s, the municipal bond market was characterized by strong buying patterns by both private investors and institutions. The patterns were caused in part by high federal, state, and local income tax rates. Additionally, as inflation pushed many investors into higher and higher income tax brackets, tax-exempt bonds increasingly became an important and convenient way for sheltering income. One corollary of the strong buyers' demand for tax exemption has been an erosion of the traditional security provisions and bondholder safeguards that had grown out of the default experiences of the 1930s. General obligation bond issuers with high tax and debt burdens, declining local economies, and chronic budget-balancing problems had little difficulty finding willing buyers. Also, revenue bonds increasingly were rushed to market with legally untested security provisions, modest rate covenants, reduced debt reserves, and weak additional-bonds tests. Because of this widespread weakening of security provisions, it has become more important than ever before that the prudent investor carefully evaluate the creditworthiness of a municipal bond before making a purchase.

In analyzing the creditworthiness of either a general obligation or revenue bond, the investor should cover five categories of inquiry. They are questions related to (1) legal documents and opinions (2) politics/management, (3) underwriter/financial advisor, (4) general credit indicators and economics, and (5) red flag, or danger signals.

The purpose of this chapter is to set forth the general guidelines that the investor should rely upon in asking questions about specific bonds.

THE LEGAL OPINION

The popular notion is that much of the legal work done in a bond issue is boiler plate in nature, but from the bondholder's point of view the legal opinions and document reviews should be the ultimate security provisions. This is because, if all else fails, the bondholder may have to go to court to enforce his or her security rights. Therefore, the integrity and competency of the lawyers who review the documents and write the legal opinions that usually are summarized and stated in the official statements are very important.

The relationship of the legal opinion to the analysis of municipal bonds for both general obligation and revenue bonds is threefold. First, the lawyer should check to determine if the issuer is indeed legally able to issue the bonds. Second, the lawyer is to see that the issuer has properly prepared for the bond sale by having enacted the various required ordinances, resolutions, and trust indentures and without violating any other laws and regulations. This preparation is particularly important in the highly technical areas of determining whether the bond issue is qualified for tax exemption under federal law and whether the issue has not been structured in such a way so as to violate federal arbitrage regulations. Third, the lawyer is to certify that the security safeguards and remedies provided for the bondholders and pledged either by the bond issuer or by third parties, such as banks with letter-of-credit agreements, are actually supported by federal, state, and local government laws and regulations.

General Obligation Bonds

General obligation bonds are debt instruments issued by states, counties, towns, cities, and school districts. They are secured by the issuers' general taxing powers. The investor should review the legal documents and opinion as summarized in the official statement to determine what specific *unlimited* taxing powers, such as those on real estate and personal property, corporate and individual income taxes, and sales taxes, are legally available to the issuer, if necessary, to pay the bondholders. Usually for smaller governmental jurisdictions, such as school districts and towns, the only available unlimited taxing power is on property. If there are statutory or constitutional taxing power limitations, the legal documents and opinion should clearly describe how they impact the security for the bonds.

For larger general obligation bond issuers, such as states and big cities that have diverse revenue and tax sources, the legal opinion should indicate the claim of the general obligation bondholder on the issuer's general fund. Does the bondholder have a legal claim, if necessary, to the first revenues coming into the general fund? This is the case with bondholders of state of New York general obligation bonds. Does the bondholder stand second in line? This is the case with bondholders of state of California general obligation bonds. Or are the laws silent on the question altogether? This is the case for most other state and local governments.

Additionally, certain general obligation bonds, such as those for water and sewer purposes, are secured in the first instance by user charges and then by the general obligation pledge. (Such bonds are popularly known as being double barreled) If so, the legal documents and opinion should state how the bonds are secured by revenues and funds outside the issuer's general taxing powers and general fund.

Revenue Bonds

Revenue bonds are issued for either project or enterprise financings that are secured by the revenues generated by the completed projects themselves, or for general public-purpose financings in which the issuers pledge to the bondholders tax and revenue resources that were previously part of the general fund. This latter type of revenue bond is usually created to allow issuers to raise debt outside general obligation debt limits and without voter approvals. The trust indenture and legal opinion for both types of revenue bonds should provide the investor with legal comfort in six bond-security areas:

1. The limits of the basic security.
2. The flow-of-funds structure.
3. The rate, or user-charge, covenant.
4. The priority-of-revenue claims.
5. The additional-bonds test.
6. Other relevant covenants.

Limits of the Basic Security. The trust indenture and legal opinion should explain what are the revenues for the bonds and how they realistically may be limited by federal, state, and local laws and procedures. The importance of this is that although most revenue bonds are structured and appear to be supported by identifiable revenue streams, those revenues sometimes can be negatively impacted directly by other levels of government. As an example, the Mineral Royalties Revenue Bonds that the state of Wyoming sold in December 1981 have most of the attributes of revenue bonds. The bonds have a first lien on the pledged revenues, and additional bonds can only be issued if a coverage test of 125 percent is met. Yet the basic revenues, themselves, are monies received by the state from the federal government as royalty payments for mineral production on federal lands. The U.S. Congress is under no legal obligation to continue this aid program. Therefore the legal opinion as summarized in the official statement must clearly delineate this shortcoming of the bond security.

Flow-of-Funds Structure. The trust indenture and legal opinion should explain what the bond issuer has promised to do concerning the revenues received. What is the order of the revenue flows through the various accounting funds of the issuer to pay for the operating expenses of the facility, to provide for payments to the bondholders, to provide for maintenance and special capital improvements, and to provide for debt-service reserves. Additionally, the trust indenture and legal opinion should indicate what happens to excess revenues if they exceed the various annual fund requirements.

The flow of funds of most revenue bonds is structured as *net revenues* (i.e., debt service is paid to the bondholders immediately after revenues are paid to the basic operating and maintenance funds, but before paying all other expenses). A *gross revenues* flow-of-funds structure is one in which the bondholders are to be paid even before the operating expenses of the facility are paid. Examples of gross revenue bonds are those issued by the New York Metropolitan Transportation Authority. However, although it is true that these bonds legally have a claim to the fare-box revenues before all other claimants, it is doubtful that the system could function if the operational expenses, such as wages and electricity bills, were not paid first.

Rate, or User-Charge, Covenants. The trust indenture and legal opinion should indicate what the issuer has legally committed itself to do to safeguard the bondholders. Do the rates charged only have to be sufficient to meet expenses, including debt service, or do they have to be set and maintained at higher levels so as to provide for reserves? The legal opinion should also indicate whether or not the issuer has the legal power to increase rates or charges upon users without having to obtain prior approvals by other governmental units.

Priority-of-Revenue Claims. The legal opinion as summarized in the official statement should clearly indicate whether or not others can legally tap the revenues of the issuer even before they start passing through the issuer's flow-of-funds structure. An example would be the Highway Revenue Bonds issued by the Puerto Rico Highway Authority. These bonds are secured by the revenues from the Commonwealth of Puerto Rico gasoline tax. However, under the commonwealth's constitution, the revenues are first subject to being applied to the commonwealth government's own general obligation bonds if no other funds are available for them.

Additional-Bonds Test. The trust indenture and legal opinion should indicate under what circumstances the issuer can issue additional bonds that share equal claims to the issuer's revenues. Usually, the legal requirement is that the maximum annual debt service on the new bonds as well as on the old bonds be covered by the projected net revenues by a specified minimum amount. This can be as low as one times coverage. Some revenue bonds have stronger additional-bonds tests to protect the bondholders. As an example, the state of Florida Orlando-Orange County Expressway Bonds have an additional-bonds test that is twofold. First, under the Florida constitution the previous year's *pledged historical revenues* must equal at least 1.33 times maximum annual debt service on the outstanding and to-be-issued bonds. Second, under the original trust indenture *projected revenues* must provide at least 1.50 times estimated maximum annual debt service on the outstanding and to-be-issued bonds.

Other Relevant Covenants. Lastly, the trust indenture and legal opinion should indicate whether there are other relevant covenants for the bondholder's protection. These usually include pledges by the issuer of the bonds to have insurance on the project (if it is a project-financing revenue bond), to have the accounting records of the issuer annually audited by an outside certified public accountant, to have outside engineers annually review the condition of the capital plant, and to keep the facility operating for the life of the bonds.

In addition ot the above aspects of the specific revenue structures of general obligation and revenue bonds, two other developments over the recent past make it more important than ever that the legal documents and opinions summarized in the official statements be carefully reviewed by the investor. The first development involves the mushrooming of new financing techniques that may rest on legally untested security structures. The second development is the increased use of legal opinions provided by local attorneys who may have little prior municipal bond experience. (Legal opinions have traditionally been written by recognized municipal bond attorneys.)

Legally Untested Security Structures and New Financing Techniques

In addition to the more traditional general obligation bonds and toll road, bridge and tunnel revenue bonds, there are now more nonvoter-approved, innovative, and legally untested security mechanisms. These innovative financing mechanisms include lease-rental bonds, moral obligation housing bonds, take-and-pay power bonds with step-up provisions requiring the participants to increase payments to make up for those that may default, medicaid-backed hospital bonds, commercial bank-backed letter of credit "put" bonds, and tax-exempt commercial paper. What distinguishes these newer bonds from the more traditional general obligation and revenue bonds is that they have no history of court decisions and other case law to firmly protect the rights of the bondholders. For the newer financing mechanisms, the legal opinion should include an assessment of the probable outcome if the bond security were challenged in court. It should be noted, however, that in most official statements this is not provided to the investor.

The Need for Reliable Legal Opinions

For many years before the 1970s, concern over the reliability of the legal opinion was not as important as it is now. As the result of the numerous bond defaults and related shoddy legal opinions in the 19th century, the investment community demanded that legal documents and opinions be written by recognized municipal bond attorneys. As a consequence, over the years a small group of primarily Wall Street-based law firms and certain recognized firms in other financial centers dominated the industry and developed high standards of professionalism.

In the 1970s, however, more and more issuers began to have their legal work done by local law firms, a few of whom had little experience in municipal bond work. This development, along with the introduction of more innovative and legally untested financing mechanisms, has created a greater need for reliable legal opinions. An example of a specific concern involves the documents the issuers' lawyers must complete so as to avoid arbitrage problems with the Internal Revenue Service. On negotiated bond issues, one remedy has been for the underwriters to have their own counsels review the documents and to provide separate legal opinions.

THE NEED TO KNOW WHO *REALLY* IS THE ISSUER

Still another general question to ask before purchasing a municipal bond is just what kind of people are the issuers? Are they conscientious public servants with clearly defined public goals? Do they have histories of successful management of public institutions? Have they demonstrated commitments to professional and fiscally stringent operations? Additionally, issuers in highly charged and partisan environments in which conflicts chronically occur between political parties and/or among factions or personalities within the governing bodies are clearly bond issuers to scrutinize closely, and possibly to avoid. Such issuers should be scrutinized regardless of the strength of the surrounding economic environment.

For General Obligation Bonds

For general obligation bond issuers the focus is on the political relationships that exist on the one hand among chief executives, such as mayors, county executives, and governors, and on the other hand their legislative counterparts. Issuers with unstable political elites are of particular concern. Of course, rivalry among political actors is not necessarily bad. What is undesirable is competition so bitter and personal that real cooperation among the warring public officials in addressing future budgetary problems may be precluded. An example of an issuer that was avoided because of such dissension is the city of Cleveland. The political problems of the city in 1978 and the bitter conflicts between Mayor Kucinich and the city council resulted in a general obligation note default in December of that year.

For Revenue Bonds

When investigating revenue bond issuers, it is important to determine not only the degree of political conflict, if any, that exists among the members of the bond-issuing body, but also the relationships and conflicts among those who make the appointments to the body. Additionally, the investor should determine whether the issuer of the revenue bond has to seek prior approval from another governmental jurisdiction before the user-fees or other charges can be levied. If this is the case, then the stability of the political relationships between the two units of government must be determined.

An example of the importance of this information can be seen when reviewing the creditworthiness of the water and electric utility revenue bonds and notes issued by Kansas City, Kansas. Although the revenue bonds and notes were issued by city hall, it was the six-member board of public utilities, a separately elected body, that had the power to set the water and electricity utility rates. In the spring of 1981, because of political dissension among the board members caused by a political struggle between a faction on the board of public utilities and the city commissioners (including the city's finance commissioner), the board refused to raise utility rates as required by the covenant. As a result of the political conflict and confusion, the ratings of the revenue bonds and notes were suspended by Moody's. The situation only came under control when a new election changed the makeup of the board in favor of those supported by city hall.

In addition to the above institutional and political concerns, for revenue bond issuers in particular an assessment of the technical and managerial abilities of the staff should be made. The professional competency of the staff is a more critical factor in revenue bond analysis than it is in the analysis of general obligation bonds. This is because unlike general obligation bonds, which are secured in the final instance by the full faith and credit and unlimited taxing powers of the issuers, many revenue bonds are secured by the ability of the revenue projects to be operational and financially self-supporting.

The professional staffs of authorities that issue revenue bonds for the construction of nuclear and other public power-generating facilities, apartment complexes, hospitals, water and sewer systems, and other large public works projects, such as convention centers and sports arenas, should be carefully reviewed. Issuers who have histories of high management turnovers, project cost overruns, or little experience should be avoided by the conservative investor, or at least considered higher risks than their assigned credit ratings may indicate. Additionally, it is helpful, although not mandatory, for revenue bond issuers to have their accounting records annually audited by outside certified public accountants, so as to ensure the investor of a more accurate picture of the issuer's financial health.

ON THE FINANCIAL ADVISOR AND UNDERWRITER

Shorthand indications of the quality of the investment are (1) who the issuer selected as its financial advisor, if any, (2) its principal underwriter if the bond sale was negotiated, and (3) its financial advisor if the bond issue came to market competitively. Additionally, since 1975 many prudent underwriters will not bid on competitive bond issues if there are significant credit-quality concerns. Therefore, it is also useful to learn who was the underwriter for the competitive bond sales as well.

Indentifying the financial advisors and underwriters is important for two reasons.

The Need for Complete, Not Just Adequate, Investment Risk Disclosures

The first reason relates to the quality and thoroughness of information provided to the investor by the issuer. The official statement, or private placement papers if the issue is placed privately, is usually prepared with the assistance of lawyers and a financial advisor or by the principal underwriter. There are industry-wide disclosure guidelines that are generally adhered to, but not all official statements provide the investor with complete discussions of the risk potentials that may result from either the specific economics of the project or the community settings and the operational details of the security provisions. It is usually the author of this document who decides what to either emphasize or downplay in the official statement. The more professional and established the experience of the author to provide the investor with unbiased and complete information about the issuer, the more comfortable the investor can be with information provided by the issuer and in arriving at a credit-quality conclusion.

The Importance of Firm Reputation for Thoroughness and Integrity

By itself, the reputation of the issuer's financial advisor and/or underwriter should not be the determinant credit-quality factor, but it is a fact the investor should consider. This is particularly the case for marginally feasible bond issues that have complex flow-of-funds and security structures. The securities industry is unique as compared with other industries, such as real estate, in that trading and investment commitments are usually made verbally over the phone with a paper trail following days later. Many institutional investors, such as banks, bond funds, and casualty insurance companies, have learned to judge issuers by the "company" they keep. Institutions tend to be conservative, and they are more comfortable with financial information provided by established financial advisors and underwriters who have recognized reputations for honesty. Individual investors and analysts would do well to adopt this approach as well.

GENERAL CREDIT INDICATORS AND ECONOMIC FACTORS IN THE CREDIT ANALYSIS

The last analytical factor is the health or viability of the economics of the bond issuer or specific project financed by the bond proceeds. The economics cover a variety of concerns. When analyzing general obligation bond issuers, one should look at the specific budgetary and debt characteristics of the issuer as well as the general economic environment. For project-financing, or enterprise, revenue bonds, the economics are primarily limited to the ability of the project to generate sufficient charges upon the users to pay the bondholders. These are known as pure revenue bonds.

For those revenue bonds that rely not upon user charges and fees, but instead upon general purpose taxes and revenues, the analysis should take basically the same approach as for general obligation bonds. For these bonds the taxes and revenues diverted to the bondholders would otherwise have gone to the state's or city's general fund.

As examples of such bonds, the New York State Municipal Assistance Corporation for the City of New York Bonds (MAC), secured by general New York City sales taxes and annual state-aid appropriations, and the state of Illinois Chicago School Finance Authority Bonds, secured by unlimited property taxes levied within the city of Chicago, are bonds structured to appear as pure revenue bonds; but in essence they are not. They both incorporate bond structures created to bail out the former, New York City, and the latter, Chicago's board of education, from severe budget deficits. The creditworthiness of these bonds is tied to that of their underlying jurisdictions, which have given or have had portions of their taxing powers and general fund revenues diverted to secure the new revenue-type bail-out bonds. Besides looking at the revenue features, the investor therefore must look at the underlying jurisdictions as well.

For General Obligation Bonds

For general obligation bonds, the economics include asking questions and obtaining answers in four specific areas: debt burden, budget soundness, tax burden, and the overall economy.

Debt Burden. Concerning the debt burden of the general obligation bond issuer, some of the more important concerns include the determination of the total amount of debt outstanding and to be issued that is supported by the general taxing powers of the issuer as well as by earmarked revenues.

For example, general obligation bonds issued by school districts in New York State and certain general obligation bonds issued by the city of New York are general obligations of the issuer and are also secured by state-aid to education payments due the issuer. If the issuer defaults, the bondholder can go to the state comptroller and be made whole from the next state-aid payment due the local issuer. An example of another earmarked-revenue general obligation bond is the state of Illinois General Obligation Transportation, Series A Bond. Besides being state general obligations, debt service is secured by gasoline taxes in the state's transportation fund as well.

The debt of the general obligation bond issuer includes, in addition to the general obligation bonds outstanding, leases and "moral obligation" commitments, among others. Additionally, the amount of the unfunded pension liabilities should be determined. Key debt ratios that reveal the burden on local taxpayers include determining the per capita amount of general obligation debt as well as the per capita debt of the overlapping or underlying general obligation bond issuers. Other key measures of debt burden include determining what are the amounts and percentages of the outstanding general obligation bonds as well as the outstanding general obligation bonds of the overlapping or underlying jurisdictions to real estate valuations. These numbers and percentages can be compared to Moody's most recent year medians, as well as with the past history of the issuer, to determine whether the debt burden is increasing, declining, or remaining relatively stable.

Budgetary Soundness. Concerning the budgetary operations and budgetary soundness of the general obligation bond issuer, some of the more important questions include how well the issuer over at least the previous five years has been able to maintain balanced budgets and fund reserves. How dependent is the issuer on short-term debt to finance annual budgetary operations? How have increased demands by residents for costly social services been handled? That is, how frugal is the issuer? How well have the public-employee unions been handled? They usually pressure for higher salaries, liberal pensions, and other costly fringe benefits. Clearly, it is undesirable for the pattern of dealing with the constituent demands and public-employee unions to result in raising taxes and drawing down nonrecurring budget reserves. Last, another general concern in the budgetary area is the reliability of the budget and accounting records of the issuer. Are interfund borrowings reported? And who audits the books?

Tax Burden.   Concerning the tax burden, it is important to learn two things initially. First, what are the primary sources of revenue in the issuer's general fund? Second, how dependent is the issuer on any one revenue source? If the general obligation bond issuer relies increasingly upon either a property tax, wage and income taxes, or a sales tax to provide the major share of financing for annually increasing budget appropriations, taxes could quickly become so high as to drive businesses and people away. Many larger northern states and cities with their relatively high income, sales, and property taxes appear to be experiencing this phenomenon. Still another concern is the degree of dependency of the issuer on intergovernmental revenues, such as federal or state revenue sharing and grants-in-aid to finance its annual budget appropriations. Political coalitions on the state and federal levels that support these financial transfer programs are not permanent and could undergo dramatic change very quickly. Therefore, a general obligation bond issuer that currently has a relatively low tax burden but receives substantial amounts of intergovernmental monies should be carefully reviewed by the investor. If it should occur that the aid monies are reduced, as has been occurring under many of President Reagan's legislative programs, certain issuers may primarily increase their taxes, instead of reducing their expenditures to conform to the reduced federal grants-in-aid.

Overall Economy.   The fourth and last area of general obligation bond analysis concerns the issuer's overall economy. For local governments, such as counties, cities, towns, and school districts, key items include learning the annual rate of growth of the full value of all taxable real estate for the previous 10 years and identifying the 10 largest taxable properties. What kinds of business or activity occur on the respective properties? What percentage of the total property tax base do the 10 largest properties represent? What is the building permit trend for at least the previous five years? What percentage of all real estate is tax exempt, and what is the distribution of the taxable ones by purpose such as residential, commercial, industrial, railroad, and public utility? Last, who are the five largest employers? Concerning the final item, those communities that have one large employer are more susceptible to rapid adverse economic change than communities that have more diversified employment and real estate bases. Additional information that reveals either economic health or decline include determining whether the population of the community over the previous 10 years has been increasing or declining by age, income, and ethnicity and how the monthly and yearly unemployment rates compare with the comparable national averages as well as to the previous history of the community.

For state governments that issue general obligation bonds, the economic analysis should include many of the same questions applied to local governments. In addition, the investor should determine the annual rates of growth on the state level for the previous five years of personal income and retail sales and how much the state has had to borrow from the Federal Unemployment Trust Fund to pay unemployment benefits. This last item is particularly significant for the long-term economic attractiveness of the state, since under current federal law employers in those states with large federal loans in arrears are required to pay increased unemployment taxes to the federal government.

For Revenue Bonds

Airport Revenue Bonds.   For airport revenue bonds, the economic questions vary according to the type of bond security involved. There are two basic security structures.

The first type of airport revenue bond is one based upon traffic-generated revenues that result from the competitiveness and passenger demand for the airport. The financial data on the operations of the airport should come from audited financial statements going back at least three years. If a new facility is planned, a feasibility study prepared by a recognized consultant should be reviewed. The feasibility study should have two components: (1) a market and demand analysis to define the service area and examine demographic and airport utilization trends and (2) a financial analysis to examine project operating costs and revenues.

Revenues at an airport may come from landing fees paid by the airlines for their flights, concession fees paid by restaurants, shops, newsstands and parking facilities, and from airline apron and fueling fees.

Also, in determining the long-term economic viability of an airport, the investor should determine whether or not the wealth trends of the service area are upward; whether or not the airport is either dependent on tourism or serves as a vital transfer point; whether or not passenger enplanements and air cargo handled over the previous five years have been growing; whether or not increased costs of jet fuel would make such other transportation as trains and automobiles more attractive in that particular region; and whether or not the airport is a major domestic hub for an airline, which could make the airport particularly vulnerable to route changes caused by schedule revisions and changes in airline corporate management.

An example of this last concern can be found in the St. Louis Airport Revenue Bonds issued by the city of St. Louis. The revenues of the airport have been substantially higher than the rate covenant requires. As an example, in 1981 debt service was covered by available revenues 2.52 times, although the rate covenant only required a one-times coverage. On the one hand this appears to show a strong revenue base, but on the other hand the source of the revenues is of concern. At the time of this writing, the airport serves as the passenger-transfer hub for both Trans World Airlines and Ozark Airlines, who together are the major users of the airport. Corporate mergers of these companies with others outside the region could result in shifts of flights to other airports, and thus a significant reduction in revenues.

The second type of airport revenue bond is secured by a lease with one or more airlines for the use of a specific facility, such as a terminal or hangar. The lease usually obligates them to make annual payments sufficient to pay the expenses and debt service for the facility. For many of these bonds, the analysis of the airline lease is based upon the credit quality of the lessee airline. Whether or not the lease should extend as long as the bonds are outstanding depends on the specific airport and facility involved. For major hub airports it may be better not to have long term leases, since without leases fees and revenues can be increased as the traffic grows regardless of which airline uses the specific facility. Of course, for regional or startup airports, long-term leases with trunk (i.e., major airline) carriers are preferred.

Highway Revenue Bonds.   There are generally two types of highway revenue bonds. The bond proceeds of the first type are used to build specific revenue producing facilities, such as toll roads, bridges, and tunnels. For these pure enterprise revenue bonds, the bondholders have claims to the revenues collected through the tolls. The financial soundness of the bonds depend on the ability of the specific projects to be self-supporting. Proceeds from the second type of highway revenue bond generally are used for public highway improvements, and the bondholders are paid by earmarked revenues, such as gasoline taxes, automobile registration payments, and driver's license fees.

Concerning the economic viability of a toll road, bridge, or tunnel revenue bond, the investor should ask a number of questions.

1. What is the traffic history, and how inelastic is the demand? Toll roads, bridges, and tunnels that provide vital transportation links are clearly preferred to those that face competition from interstate highways, toll-free bridges, or mass transit.
2. How well is the facility maintained? Has the issuer established a maintenance reserve fund at a reasonable level to use for such repair work as road resurfacing and bridge painting?

3. Does the issuer have the ability to raise tolls to meet covenant and debt-reserve requirements without seeking approvals from other governmental actors, such as state legislatures and governors? In those few cases where such approvals are necessary, a question to ask is how sympathetic have these other power centers been in the past in approving toll-increase requests?
4. What is the debt-to-equity ratio? Some toll-road, bridge, and tunnel authorities have received substantial nonreimbursable federal grants that have helped to subsidize their costs of construction. This, of course, reduces the amount of debt that has to be issued.
5. What is the history of labor-management relations, and can public employee strikes substantially reduce toll collections?
6. When was the facility constructed? Generally, toll roads financed and constructed in the 1950s and 1960s tend now to be in good financial condition. This is because the cost of financing was much less than it is today. Many of these older revenue bond issuers have been retiring their bonds ahead of schedule by buying them at deep discounts to par in the secondary market.
7. If the facility is a bridge that could be damaged by a ship and made inoperable, does the issuer have adequate "use and occupancy" insurance?

Those few toll-road and bridge revenue bonds that have defaulted have done so because of either unexpected competition from toll-free highways and bridges, poor traffic projections, or substantially higher than projected construction costs. An example of one of the few defaulted bonds is the West Virginia Turnpike Commission's Turnpike Revenue Bonds issued in 1952 and 1954 to finance the construction of an 88-mile expressway from Charleston to Princeton, West Virginia. The initial traffic-engineering estimates were overly optimistic, and the construction costs came in approximately $37 million higher than the original budgeted amount of $96 million. Because of insufficient traffic and toll collections, between 1956 and 1979 the bonds were in default. By the late 1970s with the completion of various connecting cross-country highways, the turnpike became a major link for interstate traffic. Since 1979 the bonds have become self-supporting.

Concerning the economics of highway revenue bonds that are not pure enterprise type but instead are secured by earmarked revenues, such as gasoline taxes, automobile registration payments, and driver's license fees, the investor should ask the following questions.

1. Are the earmarked tax revenues based on either state constitutional mandates, such as the state of Ohio's Highway Improvement Bonds, or are they derived from laws enacted by state legislatures, such as the state of Washington's Chapters 56, 121, and 167 Motor Vehicle Fuel Tax Bonds? A constitutional pledge is usually more permanent and reliable.

2. What has been the coverage trend of the available revenues to
    debt service over the previous 10 years? Has the coverage been
    increasing, stable, or declining?
3. If the earmarked revenue is a gasoline tax, is it based either on a
    specific amount of cents per gallon of gasoline sold, or as a per-
    centage of the price of each gallon sold? With greater conservation
    and more efficient cars, the latter tax structure is preferred be-
    cause it is not as susceptable to declining sales of gasoline and
    because it benefits directly from any increased gasoline prices at
    the pumps.

Hospital Revenue Bonds.   Two unique features of hospitals make
the analysis of their debt particularly complex and uncertain. The first
concerns their sources of revenue, and the second concerns the basic
structure of the institutions themselves.

During the past 15 years, the major sources of revenue for most
hospitals have been (1) payments from the federal (Medicare) and
combined federal-state (Medicaid) hospital reimbursement programs
and (2) appropriations made by local governments through their taxing powers. It is not uncommon for hospitals to receive at least two
thirds of their annual revenues from these sources. How well the
hospital management markets its service to attract more private-pay
patients, how aggressive it is in its third-party collections, such as
from Blue Cross, and how conservatively it budgets for the governmental reimbursement payments are key elements for distinguishing
weak from strong hospital bonds.

Particularly for community-based hospitals (as opposed to teaching
hospitals affiliated with medical schools), a unique feature of their
financial structure is that their major financial beneficiaries, physicians, have no legal or financial liabilities if the institutions do not
remain financially viable over the long term. An example of the problems that can be caused by this lack of liability is found in the story of
the Sarpy County, Nebraska, Midlands Community Hospital Revenue
Bonds. These bonds were issued to finance the construction of a hospital three miles south of Omaha, Nebraska, that was to replace an
older one located in the downtown area. Physician questionnaires
prepared for the feasibility study prior to the construction of the hospital indicated strong support for the replacement facility. Many doctors
had used the older hospital in downtown Omaha as a backup facility
for a larger nearby hospital. Unfortunately, once the new Sarpy hospital opened in 1976, many physicians found that the new hospital could
not serve as a backup because it was 12 miles further away from the
major hospital than the old hospital had been. With these physicians
not referring their patients to the new Sarpy hospital, it was soon
unable to make bond principal payments and was put under the jurisdiction of a court receiver.

The above factors raise long-term uncertainties about many community-based hospitals, but certain key areas of analysis and trends reveal the relative economic health of hospitals that already have revenue bonds outstanding. The first area is the liquidity of the hospital as measured by the ratio of dollars held in current assets to current liabilities. In general, a five-year trend of high values for the ratio is desirable because it implies an ability by the hospital to pay short-term obligations and thereby avoid budgetary problems. The second indicator is the ratio of long-term debt to equity, as measured in the unrestricted end-of-year fund balance. In general, the lower the long-term debt to equity ratio, the stronger the finances of the hospital. The third indicator is the actual debt-service coverage of the previous five years as well as the projected coverage. The fourth indicator is the annual bed-occupancy rates for the previous five years. The fifth is the percentage of physicians at the hospital who are professionally approved (board certified), their respective ages, and how many of them use the hospital as their primary institution. These ratios and indices should also be compared to Moody's most recent hospital enterprise medians.

For new or expanded hospitals, much of the above data is provided to the investor in the feasibility study. One item in particular that should be covered for a new hospital is whether or not the physicians who plan to use the hospital actually live in the area to be served by the hospital. Because of its importance in providing answers to these questions, the national reputation and experience of the people who prepare the feasibility study is of critical concern to the investor.

Housing Revenue Bonds. For housing revenue bonds the economic and financial questions vary according to the type of bond security involved. There are two basic types of housing revenue bonds— each with a different type of security structure. One is the housing revenue bond secured by *single-family* mortgage repayments, and the other is the housing revenue bond secured by mortgage repayments on *multifamily* housing projects.

Concerning single-family housing revenue bonds, the strongly secured bonds usually have five characteristics.

1.   The single-family home loans are insured by the Federal Housing Administration (FHA), Federal Veterans Administration (VA), or an acceptable private mortgage insurer. If the individual home loans are not insured, then they should have a loan-to-value ratio of 80 percent or less.

2.   All conventional home loans are covered by no less than a 10 percent mortgage-pool insurance policy.

3.   In addition to a debt reserve that has an amount of monies equal at least to six months interest on the single-family housing revenue bonds, there is a mortgage reserve fund that has an amount equal at least to 1 percent of the bond issue outstanding.

4. The issuer of the single-family housing revenue bonds is in a region of the country that has either stable or strong economic growth as indicated by increased real estate valuations, personal income, and retail sales, as well as low unemployment rates and relatively low state and local government overall tax burdens.

In addition to looking for the four characteristics mentioned above, the investor should review the retirement schedule for the single-family mortgage revenue bonds to determine whether or not the issuer has assumed large, lump-sum mortgage prepayments in the early year cash flow projections. And if so, how conservative are the prepayment assumptions, and how dependent is the issuer on the prepayments to meet the annual debt-service requirements?

It should be noted that single-family housing revenue bonds issued by local governments, such as towns, cities, and counties usually have conservative bond-retirement schedules that do not include any home-mortgage prepayment assumptions. Single-family housing revenue bonds issued by states do use prepayment assumptions. This positive feature of local government-issued bonds is balanced somewhat by the fact that the state-issued bonds usually are secured by home mortgages covering wider geographic areas. Additionally, the state issuing agencies usually have professional in-house staffs that closely monitor the home-mortgage portfolios, whereas the local issuers do not.

For multifamily housing revenue bonds, there are three specific, though overlapping, security structures. The first type of multifamily housing revenue bond is one in which the bonds are secured by mortgages that are federally insured. Usually the federal insurance covers all but the difference between the outstanding bond principal and collectible mortgage amount (usually 1 percent), and all but the *non-asset* bonds (i.e., bonds issued to cover issuance costs and capitalized interest). The attractiveness of the federal insurance is that it protects the investor against bond default within the limitations outlined. The insurance protects the bondholders regardless of whether or not the projects are fully occupied and generating rental payments.

The second type of multifamily housing revenue bond is one in which the federal government subsidizes under the federal Section 8 program all annual costs, including debt service, of the project not covered by tenant rental payments. Under Section 8 the eligible low-income and elderly tenants pay only 15 to 30 percent of their incomes for rent. Since the ultimate security comes from the Section 8 subsidies, which escalate annually with the increased cost of living in that particular geographic region, the bondholder's primary risks concern the developer's ability to complete the project, find tenants eligible under the federal guidelines to live in the project, and then maintain high occupancy rates for the life of the bonds. The investor should carefully review the location and construction standards used in building the project, as well as the competency of the project manager in selecting tenants who will take care of the building and pay their rents. In this regard, state agencies that issue Section 8 bonds usually have stronger in-house management experience and resources for dealing with problems than do the local development corporations that have issued Section 8 bonds.

The third type of multifamily housing revenue bond is one in which the ultimate security for the bondholder is the ability of the project to generate sufficient monthly rental payments from the tenants themselves to meet the operating and debt-service expenses. Many of these projects receive governmental subsidies (such as interest cost reductions under the federal Section 236 program and property tax abatements from local governments), but the ultimate security is the economic viability of the project. Key information includes the location of the project, its occupancy rate, whether large families or the elderly will primarily live in the project, whether or not the rents necessary to keep the project financially sound are competitive with others in the surrounding community, and whether or not the project manager has proven records of maintaining good services and of establishing careful tenant selection standards.

Other financial features desirable in all multifamily housing bonds include a debt-service reserve fund, which should contain an amount of money equal to the maximum annual debt service on the bonds, a mortgage reserve fund, and a capital repair and maintenance fund.

Still another feature of many multifamily housing revenue bonds, and particularly of those issued by state housing agencies, is the state moral obligation pledge. Several state agencies have issued housing revenue bonds that carry a potential state liability for making up deficiencies in their one-year debt-service reserve funds, should any occur. In most cases if a drawdown of the debt reserve occurs, the state agency must report the amount used to its governor and state budget director. The state legislature, in turn, may appropriate the requested amount, though there is no legally enforceable obligation to do so. Bonds with this makeup provision are the so-called moral obligation bonds.

The moral obligation only provides a state legislature with permissive authority—*not mandatory authority*—to make an appropriation to the troubled state housing agency. Therefore the analysis should determine (1) whether the state has the budgetary surpluses for subsidizing the housing agency's revenue bonds and (2) whether or not there is a consensus within the executive and legislative branches of that particular state's government to use state general fund revenues for subsidizing multifamily housing projects.

Industrial Revenue Bonds.   Generally, industrial revenue bonds are issued by state and local governments on behalf of individual corporations and businesses. The security for the bonds usually depends on the economic soundness of the particular corporation or business involved. If the bond issue is for a subsidiary of a larger corporation, one question to ask is whether or not the parent guarantees the bonds. Is it only obligated through a lease, or does it not have any obligation whatsoever for paying the bondholders? If the answer is that the parent corporation has no responsibility for the bonds, then the investor must look very closely at the operations of the subsidiary in addition to those of the parent corporation. Here the investor must determine also whether the bond is guaranteed by the company or is a lease obligation.

For companies that have issued common stock that is publicly traded, economic data is readily available either in the annual reports, or in the 10-K reports that must be filed annually with the Securities and Exchange Commission. For privately held companies, financial data is more difficult to obtain. However, such credit information services as Dun & Bradstreet have financial information available for many smaller companies and businesses.

In assessing the economic risk of investing in an industrial revenue bond, another question to ask is whether the bondholder or the trustee holds the mortgage on the property. Although holding the mortgage is not an important economic factor in assessing either hospital or low-income, multifamily housing bonds where the properties have very limited commercial value, it can be an important strength for the holder of industrial development revenue bonds. If the bond is secured by a mortgage on a property of either a fast-food retailer, such as MacDonalds, or an industrial facility, such as a warehouse, the property location and resale value of the real estate may provide some protection to the bondholder, regardless of what happens to the company that issued the bonds. Of course, the investor should always avoid possible bankruptcy situations regardless of the economic attractiveness of the particular piece of real estate involved. This is because the bankruptcy process usually involves years of litigation and numerous court hearings, which no investor should want to be concerned about.

Lease-Rental Bonds. Lease-rental bonds are usually structured as revenue bonds, and annual rent payments, paid by a state or local government, cover all costs including operations, maintenance, and debt service. The public purposes financed by these bond issues include the construction of public office buildings, fire houses, police stations, university buildings, mental health facilities, and highways, as well as the purchase of office equipment and computers. In some instances the rental payments may only come from student tuition, patient fees, and earmarked tax revenues, and the state or local government is not legally obligated to make lease-rental payments beyond the amount of available earmarked revenues. However, for many lease-rental bonds the underlying lessee state, county, or city is required to make annual appropriations from its general fund. For example, the Albany County, New York, Lease Rental South Mall Bonds were issued to finance the construction of state office buildings. Although the bonds are technically general obligations of Albany County, the real security comes from the annual lease payments made by the state of New York. These payments are annually appropriated. For such bonds, the basic economic and financial analysis should follow the same guidelines as for general obligation bonds.

Public Power Revenue Bonds.   Public power revenue bonds are issued to finance the construction of electrical generating plants. An issuer of the bonds may construct and operate one power plant, buy electrical power from a "wholesaler" and sell it "retail," construct and operate several power plants, or join with other public and private utilities in jointly financing the construction of one or more power plants. This last arrangement is known as a joint-power financing structure. Although there are revenue bonds that can claim the revenues of a federal agency (for example, the Washington Public Power Supply System's Nuclear Project No. 2 Revenue Bonds, which if necessary can claim the revenues of the Bonneville Power Administration) and many others that can require the participating underlying municipal electric systems to pay the bondholders whether or not the plants are completed and operating (for example, the Massachusetts Municipal Wholesale Electric Company's Power Supply System Revenue Bonds), the focus here is how the investor determines which power projects will be financially self-supporting without these backup security features.

There are at least five major questions to ask when evaluating the investment soundness of a public power revenue bond.

1.   Does the bond issuer have the authority to raise its electric rates in a timely fashion without going to any regulatory agencies? This is particularly important if substantial rate increases are necessary to pay for either new construction or plant improvements.
2.   How diversified is the customer base among residential, commercial, and industrial users?
3.   Is the service area growing in terms of population, personal income, and commercial/industrial activity so as to warrant the electrical power generated by the existing or new facilities?
4.   What are the projected and actual costs of power generated by the system, and how competitive are they with other regions of the country? Power rates are particularly important for determining the long-term economic attractiveness of the region for those industries that are large energy users.
5.   How diversified is the fuel mix? Is the issuer dependent on one energy such as hydro dams, oil, natural gas, coal, or nuclear fuel?

Concerning electrical generating plants fueled by nuclear power, the aftermath of the Three Mile Island nuclear accident in 1979 has resulted in greater construction and maintenance reviews and costly safety requirements prompted by the Federal Nuclear Regulatory Commission (NRC). The NRC oversees this industry. In the past, although nuclear power plants were expected to cost far more to build than other types of power plants, it was also believed that, once the generating plants became operational, the relatively low fuel and maintenance costs would more than offset the initial capital outlays. However, with the increased concern about public safety brought about by the Three Mile Island accident, repairs and design modifications are now expected to be made even after plants begin to operate. This of course increases the ongoing costs of generating electricity and reduces the attractiveness of nuclear power as an alternative to the oil, gas, and coal fuels. For ongoing nuclear plant construction projects, the investor should review the feasibility study to see that it was prepared by experienced and recognized consulting engineers and that it has realistic construction, design schedule, and cost estimates.

Resource Recovery Revenue Bonds.   A resource recovery facility converts refuse (solid waste) into commercially saleable energy, recoverable products, and a residue to be landfilled. The major revenues for a resource recovery bond usually are the "tipping fees" per ton paid monthly by those who deliver the garbage to the facility for disposal; revenues from steam, electricity, or refuse-derived fuel sold to either an electric power company or another energy user; and revenues from the sale of recoverable materials, such as aluminum and steel scrap.

Resource recovery bonds are secured in one of two ways or a combination thereof. The first security structure is one in which the cost of running the resource recovery plant and paying the bondholders comes from the sale of the energy produced (steam, electricity, or refuse-derived fuel) as well as from fees paid by the haulers, both municipal and private, who bring the garbage to the facility. In this financing structure the resource recovery plant usually has to be operational and self-supporting for the bondholders to be paid. The second security structure involves an agreement with a state or local government, such as a county or municipality, which contractually obligates the government to haul or to have hauled a certain amount of garbage to the facility each year for the life of the facility and to pay a tipping fee (service fee) sufficient to operate the facility. The tipping fee must include amounts sufficient to pay bondholders regardless of whether or not the resource recovery plant has become fully operational.

When deciding to invest in a resource recovery revenue bond, one should ask the following questions. First, how proven is the system technology to be used in the plant? *Mass burning* is the simplest method, and it has years of proven experience, primarily in Europe. In mass burning the refuse is burned with very little processing. Prepared fuels and shredding, the next most proven method, requires the refuse to be prepared by separation or shredding so as to produce a higher quality fuel for burning. More innovative and eclectic approaches require the most detailed engineering evaluations by qualified specialists. Second, how experienced and reliable are the construction contractors and facility operators (vendors)? Third, are there adequate safeguards and financial incentives for the contractor/vendor to complete and then maintain the facility? Fourth, what are the estimated tipping fees that will have to be charged, and how do they compare with those at any available nearby landfills? One way for a state resource recovery revenue bond issuer to deal with the latter concern occurred with the Delaware Solid Waste Authority's Resource Recovery Revenue Bonds, Series 1979. The state of Delaware enacted a law requiring that all residential garbage within a specified geographic region be hauled to its plant. Fifth, is the bondholder protected during the construction stage by reserves and by fixed-price construction contracts? Sixth, are the prices charged for the generated energy fixed, or instead are they tied to the changing costs of the fuel sources such as oil and gas in that particular market place?

Because of the uniqueness of the resource recovery technology, there are additional questions that should be asked. First, even if the plant-system technology is a proven one, is the plant either the same size as others already in operation, or is it a larger-scale model that would require careful investor review? Second, if the system technology used is innovative and eclectic, is there sufficient redundancy, or low-utilization assumptions, in the plant design to absorb any unforeseen problems once the plant begins production? Last, in addition to the more routine reserves and covenants—such as debt, maintenance, and special capital improvement reserves along with covenants that commercial insurance be placed on the facility and that the contractor (or vendor) pledge to maintain the plant for the life of the bonds—there should also be required yearly plant reviews by independent consulting engineers. The vendor should be required to make the necessary repairs so that the facility will be operational for the life of the bonds.

For resource recovery revenue bonds that have a security structure involving an agreement with a local government, additional questions for the investor to ask are the following: Is the contractual obligation at a fixed rate, or is the tipping fee elastic enough to cover all the increasing costs of operations, maintenance, and debt service? Would strikes or other *force majeure* events prevent the contract either from being enforceable or preclude the availability of an adequate supply of garbage? Last, the investor should determine the soundness of the budgetary operations and general fund reserves of the local government that is to pay the tipping or service fee. For these bonds, the basic economic analysis should follow the same guidelines as for general obligation bonds.

Student Loan Revenue Bonds. Student loan revenue bonds are usually issued by statewide agencies and are used for purchasing either new guaranteed student loans for higher education, or existing guaranteed student loans from local banks.

The student loans are 100 percent guaranteed. They are either guaranteed directly by the federal government—under the Federal Insured Student Loan (FISL) program for 100 percent of principal and interest—or by a state guaranty agency—under a more recent federal insurance program, the Federal Guaranteed Student Loan (GSL) program. This latter program provides federal reimbursement for a state guaranty agency on an annual basis for 100 percent of the payment on defaulted loans up to approximately 5 percent of the amount of loans being repaid, 90 percent for claims in excess of 5 percent but less than 9 percent, and 80 percent for claims exceeding 9 percent. The federal commitments are not dependent on future congressional approvals. Loans made under the FISL and GSL programs are contractual obligations of the federal government.

Although most student loans have federal government support, the financial soundness of the bond program that issues the student loan revenue bonds and monitors the loan portfolio is of critical importance to the investor. This is because of the unique financial structure of a student loan portfolio. Although loan repayments from the student or, in the event of student default, repayments from the guaranty agency are contractually assured, it is difficult to precisely project the actual loan repayment cash flows. This is because the student does not begin repaying the loan until he or she leaves college or graduate school and all other deferments, such as military service, have ended. Before the student begins the loan repayments, the federal government pays the interest on the loans under prescribed formulas. Therefore the first general concern of the investor should be to determine the strength of the cash flow protection.

The second general concern is the adequacy of the loan guaranty. Under all economic scenarios short of a depression, in which the student loan default rate could be 20 percent or greater, the GSL sliding federal reinsurance scale of 100–90–80 should provide adequate cash flow and bond default protection as long as the student loan revenue bond issuer effectively services the student loan repayments, has established and adequately funded loan-guaranty and debt-reserve funds, employs conservative loan-repayment assumptions in the original bond-maturity schedule, and is required to call the bonds at par if the student loan repayments are accelerated. This latter factor prevents a reinvestment risk for the bondholder.

There are eight specific questions for the investor to ask. (1) What percentage of the student loans are FISL and GSL backed, respectively? (2) Has a loan-guarantee fund been established and funded? Usually a fund that is required to have an amount at least equal to 2 percent of the loan principal outstanding is desirable. (3) Is the issuer required to maintain a debt-reserve fund? Usually, for notes a fund with at least six-months interest, and for bonds a fund with a one-year maximum annual debt-service are desirable. (4) If the bond issuer has purchased portfolios of student loans from local banks, are the local lenders required to repurchase any loans if there are either defaults or improperly originated loans? (5) What in-house capability does the issuer have for monitoring and servicing the loan repayments? (6) What is the historic loan-default rate? (7) How are the operating expenses of the agency met? If federal operating subsidies are received under the "Special Allowance Payment Rate" program, what are the rate assumptions used? In this program the issuer receives a supplemental subsidy, which fluctuates with the 91-day U.S. Treasury bill rate. (8) If a state agency is the issuer, is it dependent on appropriations for covering operating expenses and reserve requirements?

Water and Sewer Revenue Bonds. Water and sewer revenue bonds are issued to provide for a local community's basic needs and as such are not usually subject to general economic changes. Because of the vital utility services performed, their respective financial structures are usually designed to have the lowest possible user changes and still remain financially viable. Generally, rate covenants requiring that user charges cover operations, maintenance, and approximately 1.2 times annual debt-service and reserve requirements are most desirable. On the one hand, a lower rate covenant provides a smaller margin for either unanticipated slow collections or increased operating and plant maintenance costs caused by inflation. On the other hand, rates that generate revenues in excess of 1.2 times could cause unnecessary financial burdens on the users of the water and sewer systems. A useful indication of the soundness of an issuer's operations is to compare the water or sewer utility's average quarterly customer billings to those of other water or sewer systems. Assuming that good customer service is given, the water or sewer system that has a relatively low customer billing charge generally indicates an efficient operation, and therefore strong bond-payment prospects.

Key questions for the investor to ask include the following. (1) Has the bond issuer through local ordinances required mandatory water or sewer connections? Also, local board of health directives against well water contaminations and septic tank usage can often accomplish the same objective as the mandatory hookups. (2) In regard to sewer revenue bonds in particular, how dependent is the issuer on federal grants either to complete ongoing construction projects or to supplement the cost of future expansions of the sewer system? The level of dependence is particularly important in light of President Reagan's efforts in Congress to reduce the multibillion dollar federal sewage treatment grant program for states and local governments. (3) What is the physical condition of the facilities in terms of plant, lines, and meters, and what capital improvements are necessary for maintaining the utilities as well as for providing for anticipated community growth? (4) For water systems in particular, it is important to determine whether the system has water supplies in excess of current peak and projected demands. An operating system at less than full utilization is able to serve future customers and bring in revenues without having to issue additional bonds to enlarge its facilities. (5) What is the operating record of the water or sewer utility for the previous five years? (6) If the bond issuer does not have its own distribution system, but instead charges other participating local governments that do, are the charges or fees either based upon the actual water flow drawn (for water revenue bonds) and sewage treated (for sewer revenue bonds), or upon gallonage entitlements? (7) For water revenue bonds issued for agricultural regions, what kind of produce is grown? An acre of oranges or cherries in California will provide the grower with more income than will an acre of corn or wheat in Iowa. (8) For expanding water and sewer systems, does the issuer have a record over the previous two years of achieving net income equal to or exceeding the rate covenants, and will the facilities to be constructed add to the issuer's net revenues? (9) Has the issuer established and funded debt and maintenance reserves to deal with either unexpected cash flow problems or system repairs? (10) Does the bond issuer have the power to place tax liens against the real estate of those who have not paid their water or sewer bills? Although the investor would not want to own a bond for which court actions of this nature would be necessary before the investor could be paid, the legal existence of this power usually provides an economic incentive for water and sewer bills to be paid promptly by the users.

Additional bonds should only be issued if the need, cost, and construction schedule of the facility have been certified by an independent consulting engineer and if the past and projected revenues are sufficient to pay operating expenses and debt service. Of course, for a new system that does not have an operating history, the quality of the consulting engineer's report is of the uppermost importance.

RED FLAGS FOR THE INVESTOR

In addition to the areas of analysis described above, certain red flags, or negative trends, suggest increased credit risks.

For General Obligation Bonds

For general obligation bonds, the signals that indicate a decline in the ability of a state, county, town, city, or school district to function within fiscally sound parameters include the following:

1. Declining property values and increasing delinquent taxpayers.
2. An annually increasing tax burden relative to other regions.
3. An increasing property tax rate in conjunction with a declining population.
4. Declines in the number and value of issued permits for new building construction.
5. Actual general fund revenues consistently falling below budgeted amounts.
6. Increasing end-of-year general fund deficits.
7. Budget expenditures increasing annually in excess of the inflation rate.
8. The unfunded pension liabilities are increasing.
9. General obligation debt increasing while property values are stagnant.
10. Declining economy as measured by increased unemployment and declining personal income.

For Revenue Bonds

For revenue bonds, the general signals that indicate a decline in credit quality include the following:

1. Annually decreasing coverage of debt service by net revenues.
2. Regular use of debt reserve and other reserves by the issuer.
3. Growing financial dependence of the issuer on unpredictable federal and state-aid appropriations for meeting operating budget expenses.
4. Chronic lateness in supplying investors with annual audited financials.
5. Unanticipated cost overruns and schedule delays on capital construction projects.
6. Frequent or significant rate increases.
7. Deferring capital plant maintenance and improvements.
8. Excessive management turnovers.
9. Shrinking customer base.
10. New and unanticipated competition.

Mortgages

17 **DEXTER SENFT**
Vice President, Fixed Income Research
The First Boston Corporation

In order to understand and analyze mortgage-related securities, it is necessary to understand how mortgages operate. In this chapter we examine the types of mortgage loans in existence today, their cash flow, and certain other aspects relevant to the analysis of pass-through securities.

WHAT IS A MORTGAGE?

By definition, a mortgage is a "pledge of property to secure payment of a debt." Typically, property refers to real estate, which is often in the form of a house; the debt is the loan given to the buyer of the house by a bank or other lender. Thus a mortgage might be a "pledge of a house to secure payment of a bank loan." If a homeowner (the *mortgagor*) fails to pay the lender (the *mortgagee*), the lender has the right to foreclose the loan and seize the property in order to ensure that it is repaid.

The form that a mortgage loan takes could technically be anything the borrower and lender agree upon. Traditionally, however, most mortgage loans were structured similarly. There was a fixed rate of interest on the loan for its entire term, and the loan was repaid in monthly installments of principal and interest. Each loan was structured in such a way that the total payment each month (the sum of the principal and interest) was equal, or *level*. We shall refer to this type of loan arrangement as a *traditional* mortgage loan. (There is a growing trend away from this traditional structure, but this is getting ahead of the story.) In a traditional mortgage loan, the terms to be negotiated are the interest rate and the period to maturity. Interest rates vary with the general economic climate, and maturities range from 12 to 40 years, depending on the type of property involved. Most mortgages on single-family homes carry 30-year maturities.

Exhibit 1 illustrates the breakdown of monthly payments between

Exhibit 1

Monthly Mortgage Payments-Interest/Principal (30-year 10 percent conventional loan)

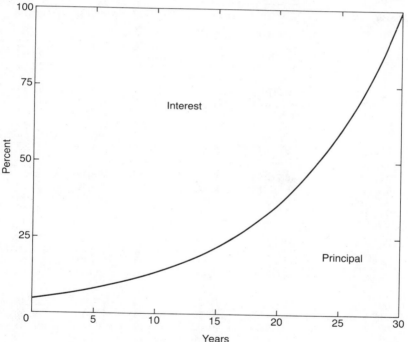

principal and interest on a 30-year, 10 percent traditional mortgage. At first, the mortgage payment is mostly interest. The principal portion increases over time until, at maturity, the payment is almost entirely principal. At all times, however, the sum of the principal and interest payments is the same. Notice that over the course of the loan the borrower pays more dollars as interest than as principal—in fact, total interest is more than twice total principal in this example.

The principal portion of each monthly payment is used to reduce the amount of the loan outstanding. In mortgage terms, the loan is *amortized* over 30 years, and the principal payments each month are known as amortization payments. The amount of the loan that is outstanding at any time is known as the *mortgage balance.* In any month the interest payment equals the interest rate (expressed monthly) times the mortgage balance at the beginning of the month (see Exhibit 2). Often the mortgage balance is expressed as a ratio or percentage of

Exhibit 2
Sample Payment Schedule: Traditional Mortgage (10 percent interest rate, 30-year [360-month] term)

Month	Mortgage Balance Dollars	Decimal	Monthly Payment	Interest	Principal
0	50000.00	1.00000			
1	49977.88	.99956	438.79	416.67	22.12
2	49955.58	.99911	438.79	416.48	22.30
3	49933.09	.99866	438.79	416.30	22.49
4	49910.41	.99821	438.79	416.11	22.68
5	49887.55	.99775	438.79	415.92	22.87
6	49864.49	.99729	438.79	415.73	23.06
7	49841.24	.99682	438.79	415.54	23.25
8	49817.80	.99636	438.79	415.34	23.44
9	49794.16	.99588	438.79	415.15	23.64
10	49770.33	.99541	438.79	414.95	23.83
. . .	. . .	. . .	. . .	. . .	. . .
100	46567.88	.93136	438.79	388.48	50.30
101	46517.16	.93034	438.79	388.07	50.72
102	46466.02	.92932	438.79	387.64	51.14
103	46414.45	.92829	438.79	387.22	51.57
. . .	. . .	. . .	. . .	. . .	. . .
200	38697.88	.77396	438.79	323.44	115.34
201	38581.57	.77163	438.79	322.48	116.30
202	38464.30	.76929	438.79	321.51	117.27
203	38346.05	.76692	438.79	320.54	118.25
. . .	. . .	. . .	. . .	. . .	. . .
300	20651.61	.41303	438.79	174.30	264.48
301	20384.93	.40770	438.79	172.10	266.69
302	20116.01	.40232	438.79	169.87	268.91
303	19844.86	.39690	438.79	167.63	271.15
. . .	. . .	. . .	. . .	. . .	. . .
355	2140.13	.04280	438.79	21.31	417.47
356	1719.18	.03438	438.79	17.83	420.95
357	1294.72	.02589	438.79	14.33	424.46
358	866.72	.01733	438.79	10.79	428.00
359	435.16	.00870	438.79	7.22	431.56
360	0.00	.00000	438.79	3.63	435.16

Note: Each month, the interest payment is $\frac{1}{12}$ of 10 percent of the mortgage balance. The principal payment is the total payment less the interest due. The principal balance is reduced by the amount of the principal payment.

Exhibit 3
Examples of Mortgage Balances for Various Loans

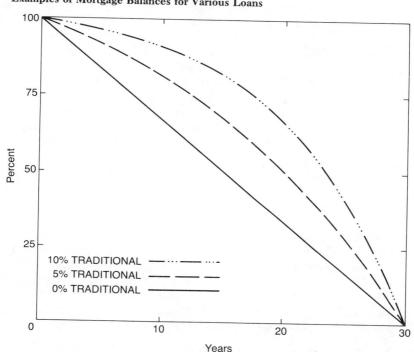

Percent

Years

10% TRADITIONAL ——···——····-
5% TRADITIONAL —— —— —
0% TRADITIONAL ——————

the original loan amount, in which case the mortgage balance runs from 1 (or 100 percent) initially to 0 at maturity. Exhibit 3 shows how the mortgage balance for several possible loans would decline over time. Another way to view the mortgage balance is as the amount of the house value the home buyer does not yet own. The amount of a home's value that is owned is referred to as the homeowner's *equity*. Equity can be defined as the difference between the current value of the home and the mortgage balance; as the mortgage balance declines, the equity rises. Equity also increases if the current value of the home increases, due to home improvements, inflation, etc.

Sometimes a mortgagor may want to make a monthly payment that is greater than the amount actually due, with the idea of applying the excess payment to further reducing the loan. Such excess principal payments are called *prepayments* and may be made for several reasons (these reasons will be discussed in detail later). Prepayments result in a direct reduction of the mortgage balance and a direct increase in the amount of equity. Another way to define mortgage balance is that it equals the original loan amount less the total amount of amortization and prepayments to date.

A mortgagor who fails to make a mortgage payment is said to be *delinquent*. Delinquencies can have a variety of causes—the homeowner may have died, become unemployed, bounced a check, or simply forgotten to make the payment. The mortgagee then reminds the homeowner that the payment is overdue and attempts to collect the money. If the matter is not resolved quickly the mortgagee may assess the mortgagor with a late payment charge. Sometimes there is no quick solution, and the mortgagor may become more than one month in arrears. Although most lenders are willing to allow a borrower a few months leeway, in extreme cases it may be necessary for the bank to foreclose the loan, in which case the property is taken from the mortgagor and sold in order to pay off the loan.

QUALIFYING FOR A MORTGAGE

Borrowers who are interested in obtaining mortgage loans must meet certain standards set by the lender in order to be considered creditworthy. The first thing a lender checks is whether the borrower has any other loans or obligations outstanding; if so, these will diminish the borrower's ability to make mortgage payments. Next the lender determines the income and net worth of the borrower. Many mortgage lenders use these classical rules of thumb to determine whether or not a borrower's income is adequate for the mortgage:

1. The total mortgage payment (principal and interest) should not exceed 25 percent of the borrower's total income less any payments owed for other obligations.
2. Total mortgage payments plus other housing expenses should not exceed 33 percent of the borrower's income less payments for other obligations. Other housing expenses include such items as taxes, insurance, utilities, and normal maintenance costs.

Of course, these percentages may vary depending on the lender and the circumstances. In particular, borrowers with relatively high net worth and/or liquid assets will find lenders to be more flexible. Also, in times of high interest rates and tight money, lenders have been known to bend these rules somewhat in order to maintain a certain level of business.

The buyer is usually required to make a down payment on the property in order to qualify for the mortgage. The down payment might range anywhere from 5 to 25 percent of the purchase price. The reason for requiring a down payment is that, in the event the lender is forced to foreclose the loan and sell the property, the mortgage balance will be more easily recovered. In other words, there is room for error if the property is sold—even if it cannot bring the original purchase price on the market, there can still be enough to cover the debt.

Lenders use the term *loan to value ratio,* or LTV, to express the amount of protection on the mortgage. LTV is calculated as the ratio of the mortgage balance to the market value of the property and is expressed as a percentage. The lower the LTV, the less the loan amount relative to the property value, and the greater the safety.

The LTV ratio tends to decrease over time. For example, if a buyer makes a 10 percent down payment on a property and mortgages the rest, the LTV is initially 90 percent. Over time, the mortgage balance declines from amortization and prepayments, while the property value tends to increase due to inflation. Both of these changes serve to lower the LTV.

As with income requirements, down payment and LTV requirements depend on certain circumstances. These include not only the net worth of the borrower but the condition and marketability of the property and the availability of credit. Higher LTV ratios are associated with newer, more marketable properties and with easier credit and lower interest rates.

An important (if not obvious) conclusion about qualifying for a mortgage is that it becomes harder when interest rates rise. Because of the income and LTV requirements, smaller mortgage balances are affordable when rates rise, and yet this is also the time when inflation and therefore home purchase prices are rising. As a consequence, all but those buyers with large amounts of cash or equity are squeezed from the market.

MORTGAGE INSURANCE

There are two types of mortgage insurance that may be used when borrowers obtain mortgage financing. One type is originated by borrowers and the other by lenders. Although both have a beneficial effect on the creditworthiness of the borrowers, the latter is of greater importance from the lender's point of view.

The first type of mortgage insurance is taken out by the borrower (borrowers) usually with a life insurance company. The policy provides for the continuing payment of the mortgage after the death of the insured person, thus enabling the survivors to continue living in the house. In the sense that the mortgage might just as well have been paid off with part of the proceeds of ordinary life insurance, this form of mortgage insurance is really only a special form of life insurance. It is cheaper than ordinary life insurance, however, because the death benefit, which is equal to the mortgage balance, declines over time.

The other type of mortgage insurance is taken out by the lender, although borrowers pay the insurance premiums. This policy covers some percentage of the loan amount and guarantees that in the event of a default by the borrower/s the insurance company will pay the amount insured or pay off the loan in full.

An example of how this type of mortgage insurance works is shown in Exhibit 4. Suppose a borrower finances $60,000 of property with a

Exhibit 4

Situation initially:

$$LTV = \frac{55,000}{60,000} = 91.7\%$$

$11,000 Mortgage insurance obtained

Mortgage:	$55,000	Property
Down payment:	5,000	value:
Total	$60,000	$60,000

Situation after 5 years:

Borrower defaults
Property value falls

Mortgage balance:
$52,000

Property value:
$50,000

Option 1: Insurance company pays claim

Lender has	$50,000	Property	Insurance company has
	11,000	Insurance	($11,000) Loss
	(52,000)	Bad debt	
	$ 9,000	Net profit	

Option 2: Insurance company takes title to property

Lender has	$52,000	From insurer	Insurance Company has
	(52,000)	Bad debt	50,000 Property
	0	Net profit	(52,000) Payment to lender
			(2,000) Net loss

$5,000 down payment and a $55,000 mortgage. The initial LTV ratio is fairly high (91.7 percent), so mortgage insurance is obtained in the amount of $11,000 (20 percent of the loan). Suppose the borrower defaults after five years (the mortgage balance having been paid down to $52,000 by then). Suppose further that the property has deteriorated in condition (or perhaps has been partially destroyed), and its market value falls to $50,000. The bank then turns to the insurance company.

Several options are open to the insurance company, perhaps the simplest of which is that it can assist the borrower financially so that the amount in arrears can be paid and no foreclosure is necessary. Assuming this fails, there are two other alternatives. First, the insurance company could pay the claim of $11,000 and let the bank foreclose. The bank, which gets $50,000 for the property and $11,000 insurance, actually makes a profit of $9,000 over the mortgage balance outstanding. A better alternative for the insurance company, however, is to pay off the mortgage balance ($52,000), take title of the property, and sell it (for $50,000). The insurance company thereby loses only $2,000, instead of $11,000. Of course, the insurer could hold the property or even make improvements to it in hope of making a future gain instead of selling it immediately.

The net effect of mortgage insurance from the lender's standpoint is to reduce its risk. The exposure of a lender to loss equals the amount loaned less property value and mortgage insurance. In a sense, the insurance has an effect similar to having a higher down payment because both reduce the lender's exposure to loss. Mortgage insurance is advantageous to borrowers who do not have enough money for a large down payment but who can afford enough down payment and insurance to satisfy the lender.

The cost of the insurance can be passed on to the borrower in several ways. Traditionally, the cost was added to the mortgage rate as an extra one-eighth percent or one-fourth percent, depending on the amount of coverage. As mortgage rates escalated, however, increasing the rate further became less attractive. (In a sense, the insurance company would be increasing the chance of the default it was insuring against.) It has become increasingly common to pay for mortgage insurance in one lump sum at the time of mortgage origination.

It is not necessary to have mortgage insurance in effect for the entire term of a loan. Because the mortgage balance amortizes and the LTV tends to fall over time, the lender may deem mortgage insurance to be unnecessary when the mortgage balance has declined to some predetermined level. At that point, the policy is either cancelled or allowed to expire.

SERVICING

Among the jobs that mortgage lenders must perform in order to ensure that borrowers make timely and accurate payments are sending payment notices, reminding borrowers when payments are overdue, recording prepayments, keeping records of mortgage balances, administering escrow accounts for payment of property taxes or insurance, sending out tax information at year end, and initiating foreclosure proceedings. These functions are collectively known as *servicing* the loans. Many times the original lender, known as the mortgage *originator*, is the one who services the loan, but this is not always the case. Sometimes the mortgage is sold to someone else, and the servicing of the loan may or may not go along with the mortgage.

In the event that one party owns a mortgage and another services it, the servicer receives a fee (the *servicing fee*) for the trouble. Servicing fees usually take the form of a fixed percentage of the mortgage balance outstanding. Although the percentage may vary from one servicer to the next, it is usually in the area of .25 percent to .50 percent. Small servicing fee percentages are usually associated with larger commercial property loans, and larger percentages with smaller residential loans. From the point of view of the owner of the mortgage, the servicing fee comes out of the interest portion of the mortgage payment. For example, if party A owns a 10 percent mortgage being serviced by party B for a three eighths of 1 percent fee, then A is really earning 95⁄8 percent (10 percent minus three eighths of 1 percent) on the loan.

In addition to servicing fees, there are occasionally other fees that the servicer may keep. For example, some servicers are entitled to keep late-payment penalties paid by the borrower, foreclosure penalties, and certain other penalty fees. The specific types and amounts of fees that servicers are entitled to receive are set forth in a servicing agreement between the mortgage owner and the servicer.

WHERE DOES MORTGAGE MONEY COME FROM?

Exhibit 5 shows the originators of mortgage loans in the United States in 1978, in order of importance. The largest single originating group is the Savings and Loan industry, which contributed more than half of the $192 billion in mortgage money that year. Savings and loans, together with savings banks and credit unions constitute the "thrift industry"—so-called because its funds come from the savings accumulated by thrifty depositors. Commercial banks make up the second largest group of originators, and like thrift institutions, the money they put into mortgages comes primarily from deposits. The third major source of mortgage loans is the mortgage company sector, or mortgage banks. Unlike savings banks or commercial banks, mortgage banks do not have depositors. They are in the business of finding other sources of mortgage money, such as thrifts or insurance companies, and making it available for housing construction and ownership; mortgage bankers' profits come from servicing the loans they originate, plus any profit that can be made from buying and selling the mortgages. The lesser originators of mortgages are the insurance companies, pension funds, and various federal, state, and local entities empowered to make mortgage loans.

Knowing who originates mortgages, however, does not really answer the question of where mortgage money comes from. The real

Exhibit 5
Originators of U.S. Mortgage Loans as of October 1981

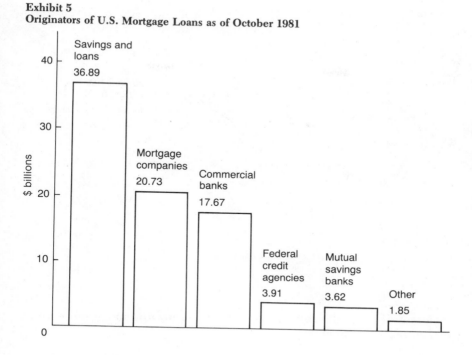

lenders of mortgage money are those who *own* mortgages, who are somewhat different from those who create them. Mortgage bankers, for example, generally do not want to own mortgages at all—once they create them, they sell the mortgages to someone else. Exhibit 6 breaks down the ownership of mortgages in the United States by type of holder over the past 10 years. The thrifts and commercial banks prove to be the major holders of mortgages, but there are several other notable ones. Life insurance companies, for example, have owned between 9 percent and 16 percent of all mortgages over the past decade, with a trend toward holding less. Individuals and others have owned 13–16 percent fairly consistently. The owner category with by far the largest growth over the past 10 years is Mortgage Pools and Trusts, which went from almost zero in 1970 to 7.4 percent in 1978.

What are these pools and trusts? Essentially, they are collections of mortgages of which shares, or participations, are resold to someone else. (In this sense, Mortgage Pools and Trusts as an ownership category is not very informative.) Mortgage trusts can be created by securities dealers or investment advisors who offer shares in the trust as a form of investment for their clients. Mortgage pools, however, have the lion's share of this category, and will be the subject under analysis in the next chapter. Suffice it to say for now that by 1978 approxi-

Exhibit 6
Mortgages by Type of Holder (1970–1980)

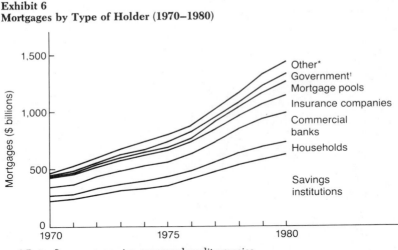

* Reits, finance companies, sponsored credit agencies.
† State, local, and U.S.

mately 1 of every 10 new mortgages ended up in a mortgage pool of one form or another.

WHAT TYPES OF PROPERTIES ARE MORTGAGED?

Virtually all forms of real estate have been mortgaged, but these properties fall into several categories. First, property (and the mortgage on it) can be classified as either residential or nonresidential, depending on whether or not people use the property primarily for living. Residential properties include houses, apartments, condominiums, cooperatives, and mobile homes. These do not necessarily have to be someone's primary residence—for example, summer homes and skiing condominiums are classified as residential properties. Residential properties are subdivided into one- to four-family dwellings and multifamily dwellings for the purposes of Federal Reserve statistics.

Nonresidential properties are subdivided into commercial properties and farm properties. The commercial category encompasses a wide variety of properties, such as office buildings, shopping centers, hospitals, and industrial plants.

Exhibit 7 shows the outstanding amounts of mortgage debt in various years broken out by type of property. For the past 30 years, roughly three of every four mortgage dollars went to finance residential property, and of that amount, more than 80 percent went to one- to four-family dwellings.

Exhibit 7
Mortgages by Type of Property (1970–1980)

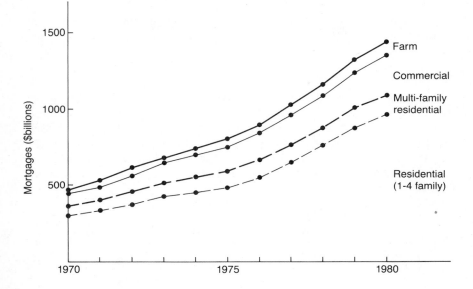

NONTRADITIONAL MORTGAGES

The decade of the 1970s saw the advent of many new and different varieties of mortgages. Unlike traditional mortgages, most of these alternative mortgage instruments (AMIs) do not have level monthly payments, but employ some other (often complicated) scheme. One AMI even provides a way for the homeowner to continually take cash out of equity, as opposed to continually putting cash into it.

What was the impetus for the creation of AMIs, and in what ways are they superior to traditional mortgages? The answers to these questions are related to level and behavior of mortgage interest rates. In the 15 years ending in 1979, mortgage rates doubled from roughly 6 percent levels to 12 percent levels, and by 1981 they had almost tripled to 17 percent. More importantly, the volatility of these rates increased tremendously. Moves of 1 percentage point between the time a loan application was made and the time the loan was closed were not unheard of in 1979. The interest climate resulted in a great deal of risk to both borrower and lender that the rate that seemed plausible one week might be out of line the next week. (Not to mention the next 30 years.) High interest rates combined with the rapid inflation in housing prices to make home financing difficult in general and all but impossible for the first-time buyer. AMIs were created as a way of coping with these problems.

There are literally dozens of different types of AMIs, each with its own peculiar twist. Their names, which are often abbreviated, include GPMs, VRMs, ROMs, RRMs, ARMs, PAMs, FLIPs, WRAPs, and SAMs. The remainder of this chapter will discuss some of the salient features of the more popular AMIs.

Graduated-Payment Mortgages (GPMs)

The only essential difference between the GPM and the traditional mortgage is that the payments on a GPM are not all equal. Graduated payment refers to the fact that GPM payments start at a relatively low level and rise for some number of years. The actual number of years that the payments rise and the percentage increase per year depend on the exact type or plan of the GPM. The five major GPM plans work as follows:

Plan	Term to Maturity (years)	Years That Payments Rise	Percentage Increase per Year
I.	30	5	2.5%
II.	30	5	5.0
III.	30	5	7.5
IV.	30	10	2.0
V.	30	10	3.0

At the end of the graduation period, the monthly payment is held at its existing level for the remainder of the mortgage term. Exhibit 8 shows the payment schedule on a $50,000, 10 percent, Plan III GPM.

The attraction of a GPM is the small payment in its early years. A first-time home buyer who might not be able to afford payments on a

Exhibit 8
Mortgage Payment Schedule for a $50,000 Plan III GPM (30-year term, 10 percent mortgage rate)

Year(s)	Monthly Payment
1	$333.52
2	358.53
3	385.42
4	414.33
5	445.40
6–30.	478.81

Note: Plan III GPMs call for monthly payments that increase by 7.5 percent at the end of each of the first five years of the mortgage.

traditional mortgage might be able to afford the smaller payments of the GPM, even if both loans were for the same principal amount. Eventually, when the graduation period has ended, homeowners with GPMs make up the difference by paying larger monthly amounts than the traditional mortgages require. The originators of GPMs reason that most home buyers, particularly young, first-time home buyers, have incomes that will increase at least as rapidly as the mortgage payments increase. Thus they should always be able to afford their monthly payments. Exhibit 9 compares the initial and final payments of a tradi-

Exhibit 9
Comparison of Initial and Final Payments:
Traditional Mortgages versus GPMs ($50,000, 10 percent, 30-year mortgages)

Loan Type	Initial Payment	Final Payment
Traditional	$438.79	$438.79
GPM Plan I	400.29	452.88
GPM Plan II	365.29	466.22
GPM Plan III	333.29	478.81
GPM Plan IV................	390.02	475.43
GPM Plan V.................	367.29	493.60

tional mortgage with the five GPM plans, assuming all mortgages have a $50,000 balance and a 10 percent interest rate. Notice that the lowest initial payment is on the Plan III GPM, and in this example it is about $100 less per month than the traditional mortgage in the first year. It is perhaps not surprising that Plan III GPMs are the most popular and accounted for more than 80 percent of all the GPMs originated in late 1978 and early 1979. The Plan III GPM is the only plan to offer a 7.5 percent graduation rate; this is the maximum graduation rate that federally chartered banks can currently offer.

Because GPMs have smaller initial payments than do traditional mortgages, they do not pay down their mortgage balances as quickly. The interesting feature of GPMs is that in their early years they do not pay down any principal at all—in fact their mortgage balances actually *increase* for a short period of time. Technically, we would say that they experience "negative amortization" at the outset. To see how this works, consider the first-month payment on the GPM in Exhibit 8.

Interest due for month one is 10 percent per year for one-twelfth year on $50,000 balance.
= $50,000 × $\frac{1}{12}$ × $\frac{10}{100}$ = $416.67
Payment on GPM = $333.52
Principal paid = $333.52 − $416.67 = −83.15
New mortgage balance = $50,000 − (−83.15) = $50,083.15

Another way of viewing this situation is as follows: The amount paid on the mortgage ($333.52) was insufficient to cover even the interest due on the loan ($416.67), so the shortfall ($83.15) is lent to the mortgagor. Thus the new mortgage balance is the sum of the original balance plus the new loan:

$$\$50,000 + \$83.15 = \$50,083.15$$

Of course, the mortgage balance must eventually be reduced to zero. The annual increases in the mortgage payment eventually catch up to and overtake the amount of interest due, and at that time the mortgage balance begins to decrease. In Exhibit 10 the mortgage balances (expressed as ratios to the original loan amount) are shown at the end of each year, for all five GPM plans as well as for a traditional

Exhibit 10
Graduated Payment Mortgage (GPM) Factor Comparison for 10 Percent, 30-Year Loans

Year-End Factors	Ordinary Mortgage	Plan I 5-Year 2.5 Percent	Plan II 5-Year 5.0 Percent	Plan III 5-Year 7.5 Percent	Plan IV 10-Year 2.0 Percent	Plan V 10-Year 3.0 Percent
0.........	1.00000	1.00000	1.00000	1.00000	1.00000	1.00000
1.........	.99444	1.00412	1.01291	1.02090	1.00670	1.01241
2.........	.98830	1.00615	1.02258	1.03769	1.01214	1.02335
3.........	.98152	1.00582	1.02845	1.04949	1.01614	1.03258
4.........	.97402	1.00281	1.02987	1.05526	1.01853	1.03985
5.........	.96574	.99678	1.02612	1.05383	1.01909	1.04484
6.........	.95660	.98734	1.01640	1.04385	1.01759	1.04725
7.........	.94649	.97691	1.00567	1.03282	1.01376	1.04669
8.........	.93533	.96539	.99381	1.02064	1.00732	1.04277
9.........	.92300	.95266	.98071	1.00719	.99796	1.03504
10.........	.90938	.93860	.96623	.99233	.98532	1.02299
11.........	.89433	.92307	.95025	.97591	.96902	1.00606
12.........	.97771	.90591	.93258	.95777	.95101	.98736
13.........	.85934	.88696	.91307	.93773	.93111	.96670
14.........	.83906	.86602	.89151	.91559	.90913	.94388
15.........	.81665	.84289	.86770	.89113	.88484	.91867
16.........	.79189	.81733	.84140	.86412	.85802	.89082
17.........	.76454	.78910	.81233	.83427	.82838	.86005
18.........	.73432	.75792	.78023	.80130	.79564	.82606
19.........	.70094	.72347	.74477	.76488	.75948	.78851
20.........	.66407	.68541	.70559	.72464	.71953	.74703
21.........	.62333	.64336	.66230	.68019	.67539	.70120
22.........	.57833	.59692	.61449	.63108	.62663	.65058
23.........	.52862	.54561	.56167	.57684	.57277	.59466
24.........	.47370	.48892	.50332	.51691	.51326	.53288
25.........	.41303	.42631	.43885	.45071	.44752	.46463
26.........	.34601	.35713	.36764	.37757	.37491	.38924
27.........	.27197	.28071	.28897	.29678	.29468	.30595
28.........	.19018	.19629	.20207	.20752	.20606	.21394
29.........	.09982	.10303	.10606	.10892	.10816	.11229
30.........	.00000	.00000	.00000	.00000	.00000	.00000

mortgage. Notice that a Plan III GPM has a balance that rises through the end of the fourth year, at which point it declines to zero over the next 26 years. It is interesting to note that the mortgage balance does not go below 1.0 until some time in the 10th year. Exhibit 11 is a graph of the mortgage balances for a traditional mortgage and a Plan III GPM.

Exhibit 11
Comparison between Plan III GPM and a Traditional Mortgage

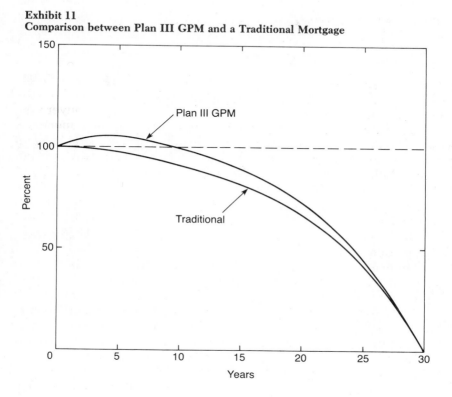

GPMs were first introduced by the Federal Housing Administration (FHA) in November 1976, although various legal and technical matters prevented any large-scale issuance until late 1978. In April 1979 GPMs became eligible for pooling into GNMA pass-through securities, and since that time GPMs have accounted for roughly 25–30 percent of all FHA-insured mortgages. In early 1979 the Mortgage Bankers Association of America had predicted that by the end of 1981 GPMs could grow to half of the FHA-insured mortgages; the disarray of the mortgage market since 1979 has postponed such an event, but it still appears feasible.

As interest rates continue to rise, the need for GPMs and similar vehicles becomes increasingly important to the first-time home buyer or those with low cash flows. New varieties and plans of GPMs have been proposed that increase the period that payments rise and/or the graduation rate, thereby making the initial payment progressively smaller. One GPM proposal called for delaying the time at which payments would begin to rise—making the payments have a flat-rising-flat pattern. Such a scheme called for a mortgage balance that would rise for nine years and not become less than 1.0 until half of the term to maturity had elapsed.

Pledged-Account Mortgages (PAMs)

Pledged-account mortgages are structured so as to resemble GPMs from the borrower's point of view and traditional mortgages from the lender's point of view. This is engineered by using some or all of the down payment on the property to create a pledged savings account that not only becomes collateral on the loan but also is used to pay off the mortgage. The borrower makes mortgage payments that are initially small; withdrawals from the savings account are then made to supplement the payments. The bank, which receives the sum of the two amounts, gets a level stream of payments, just as it would with a traditional mortgage. PAMs are sometimes referred to as FLIPs (for flexible loan-insurance program), in recognition of the FLIP Mortgage Corporation, which was a pioneer of this type of loan.

Exhibit 12 shows a sample PAM mortgage scheme for a buyer who is interested in a $55,000 house and who has down payment money of $8,767.50. With a traditional mortgage, the buyer would get a mortgage for $46,232.50 (the house price less the down payment); assuming a 10 percent interest rate, this would require a monthly payment of $405.73. In the PAM example, $5,000 of the down payment money is applied to the house directly (leaving $50,000 to be mortgaged), and the remaining $3,767.50 is used to create the pledged savings account, which returns the passbook savings rate (assumed to be 5¼ percent in this example). In the first year of the PAM mortgage, the homeowner pays only $327.89 per month, and an additional $110.90 is taken from the savings account each month. The out-of-pocket expense during the first year is $77.84 less than the traditional mortgage, a saving of 19.2 percent. After each of the first five years of this PAM mortgage, the payment from the borrower rises (6 percent in this case), and the saving relative to the traditional mortgage decreases. As with a GPM, when the graduation period is over, the monthly PAM payment is greater than the payment on the traditional mortgage. (The savings in the early years are paid for in the later years.)

While all of this goes on at the borrower's level, the bank receives a constant monthly sum of $438.79—precisely the amount that the monthly payments on a traditional mortgage for $50,000 would be

Exhibit 12
Conventional Mortgage

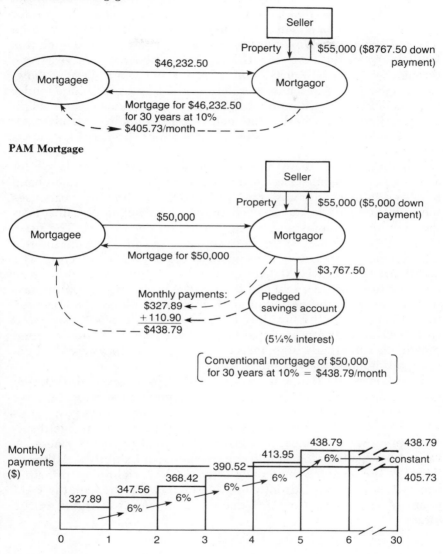

PAM Mortgage

(also the amount the homeowner pays out of pocket in years 6 through 30, after the savings account is exhausted). From the bank's point of view, the total indebtedness of the borrower equals the mortgage balance less whatever money is in the savings account. Because money is withdrawn from the savings account faster than the mortgage balance is paid down, the total indebtedness of the borrower rises for the first five years. This is analogous to the rise in the mortgage balance of a GPM during the period of negative amortization. If, in this example, we assume that the property value remains at $55,000 (no inflation or improvement), the LTV ratio of the mortgage will rise for five years. If the bank had a maximum LTV ratio of 85 percent, then this FLIP mortgage would not be feasible because, even though it is low enough in the first year, the LTV rises above .85 in years two through nine. An LTV maximum of 90 percent would be met, however. In making PAM loans, therefore (and GPMs as well), the lender must examine the maximum possible LTV that the loan can reach in order to determine whether the loan meets the lender's standards or whether additional cash for a down payment or mortgage insurance is called for.

The PAM loan is really an ingenious way of trading net worth (or assets) against income. The borrower who has sufficient cash on hand but faces an income or cash flow shortage for the first few years uses the cash to create the savings account, which subsequently subsidizes the monthly payments and lowers the out-of-pocket cost. The price the borrower pays for this privilege is that the savings account interest rate generally does not yield as much as the mortgage rate costs. The additional cost of a PAM loan over 30 years equals the difference between the mortgage rate and the savings passbook rate on the savings balances for the period of graduation. As with GPMs, however, the PAM could be the best buy in the long run despite these added costs because the costs are repaid in the later years of the mortgage; if inflation is sufficiently high, then the homeowner repays current benefits with inflated future dollars.

Like GPMs, PAMs come in a variety of packages with different terms to maturity, graduation periods, and graduation rates. Because PAMs are designed to meet constraints on income to expense ratios and LTV ratios and take into account such factors as mortgage insurance, property insurance, and taxes, the actual payment schedules vary somewhat from the simple pattern shown in Exhibit 12. Although PAMs do not have the same popularity as GPMs right now (primarily because they are not currently eligible for FHA insurance), the PAM is an interesting form of AMI that deserves closer attention in the future.

Buydown Loans

The buydown loan is extremely similar to the PAM loan described previously, except that it is the seller, not the buyer, who places cash in a segregated account that is subsequently used to augment the buyer's mortgage payments. When newly constructed property is financed in this fashion, the loans may be referred to as builder buydowns, since the seller is the home builder. In general, these loans derive their name from the fact that the seller is using cash to buy down the mortgage rate from a high level to a lower level for some period of time.

The buydown loan is very attractive from the buyer's point of view because it provides the benefit of a PAM loan or a GPM at someone else's expense. It might seem that the seller could pass along the cost of the buydown to the buyer by increasing the price of the house; although this may occur to some small extent, it is not true in general because the mortgage lender places constraints on the maximum LTV ratio. The seller of the home cannot arbitrarily hike the price of the property lest there be a difference of opinion with the lender, who bases the LTV ratio on the appraised value of the property.

What motivation does the seller have, then, to give up part of the profit on the sale in order to create a buydown loan? And would it not be simpler just to reduce the price of the property? The answer to both these questions is that the buydown loan is very often the only financing vehicle that can get the property sold because it is the only type of loan that potential buyers may qualify for. Consider a comparison of two possible ways of financing a $60,000 house (see Exhibit 13), using as alternatives a 30-year traditional loan and a buydown loan. In both cases it is assumed that the prevailing mortgage interest rate is 16 percent, that the home buyer has $10,000 down payment money, and that the home builder is willing to give up $3,000 of its profit. The buydown loan shown in the exhibit is of the "3–2–1" variety, meaning that the buyer pays 3 percent less interest the first year (13 percent in this case), 2 percent less the second year, 1 percent less the third year, and all of the mortgage payment thereafter.

If the builder contributes no money to the sale, the monthly payment (on a $50,000 traditional loan) is $672.38. If the builder simply contributes $3,000 to the purchase (by selling the house for $57,000) the monthly payment on the $47,000 loan is reduced to $632.04. If the $3,000 is used to buy down the interest rate from 16 percent according to the 3–2–1 plan, however, the initial monthly payment is only $547.37 and graduates to $672.38 after three years. The buyer of the house can now apply for the loan based on a monthly payment that is roughly 14 percent less than the payment would have been if the price of the property had simply been lowered, and since the seller is the one who is buying down the rate, no increase in down payment is required. Furthermore, if the escrow account in which the seller's funds are placed pays some rate of interest, then not all of the $3,000 will be necessary to buy down the rate (e.g., if the account pays 8 percent, then only about $2,700 would be needed). Thus the buydown loan can be a cheaper alternative for the seller as well.

Exhibit 13
Conventional: LTV = .0833

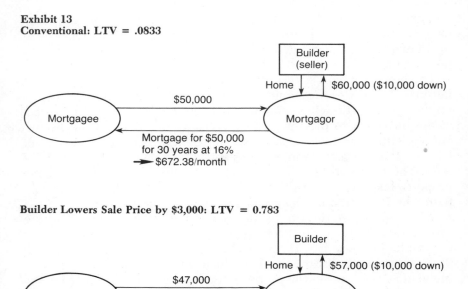

Builder Lowers Sale Price by $3,000: LTV = 0.783

Builder Buys Down Interest Rate:

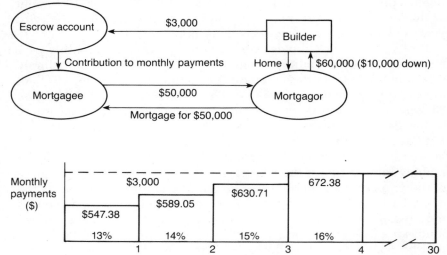

Variable-Rate Mortgages (VRMs)

The VRM was one of the first AMIs to emerge and is one of the most popular today because of the advantages it affords to both borrowers and lenders. The chief difference between a VRM and a traditional mortgage is that the VRM has no fixed interest rate. Instead, the rate is variable and depends on the level of interest rates in general. This type of mortgage is accomplished by tying the mortgage rate to some index related to government borrowing, cost of funds, inflation, and so on. Sometimes one will see the term *ARM* (adjustable-rate mortgage) used to describe a loan with similar features.

There are various rules governing how often and by how much the mortgage rate on a VRM may change. These rules may vary slightly from one lender to the next, although they are basically similar in design. As an example of a typical VRM, let us consider the provisions of those initially issued by Home Savings and Loan Association in California, the first lender to issue a pass-through security backed by VRMs:

1. The mortgage rate is based on the weighted average cost of savings index published by the Federal Home Loan Bank of San Francisco. In general, the "spread" between the mortgage rate and the index rate is held constant (when the index changes, the VRM changes equally). However, the provisions that follow may prevent this from happening all the time.

2. The mortgage rate may change (up or down) only once in any six-month period and may not be changed at all during the first six months.

3. The mortgage rate may not change (up or down) more than 0.25 percent (25 basis points) at a time, no matter how much the index changes. Combined with provision number 2 above, this means that the VRM rate may not change more than 0.5 percent per year.

4. The rate must change at least 0.1 percent (10 basis points) at a time, except to bring the rate to a level previously impossible because of the 25-basis-point limitation. For example, suppose the index rises five basis points from its initial level. The VRM rate does not rise because it cannot rise by 10 basis points. However, suppose the index rises 30 basis points from its initial level. The VRM will rise 25 basis points (the maximum rise) after six months, and may then rise another 5 basis points in another six months.

5. The VRM rate may not rise more than 2.5 percent higher than its initial level, no matter how much the index rises. In addition, state usury laws may prevent the VRM rate from exceeding a certain rate.

6. Increases in the VRM rate are optional on the part of the lender. Decreases, however, are mandatory.

7. Within 90 days of any time of the VRM rate is increased, or at any time the VRM rate exceeds its initial level, the borrower may prepay the loan in whole or in part with no prepayment penalty.

8. Whenever the VRM rate is increased to a rate higher than its initial level, the borrower may elect to keep his monthly payment con-

stant by extending the maturity of the mortgage. However, the new maturity may not be more than 40 years from the origination date (i.e., if the original VRM had a term of 30 years, it cannot be extended more than another 10 years). If a borrower extends the maturity of his loan and if the VRM rate is subsequently decreased, the lender may decrease the maturity by a comparable amount.

As the last provision indicates, VRMs may have maturities that vary as well as rates. For example, suppose a borrower obtains a $50,000 VRM for 30 years with an initial rate of 10 percent. This requires monthly payments of $438.79. Suppose the rate rises after six months to 10¼ percent. By doing nothing, the borrower will have a new monthly payment of $447.99. On the other hand, electing to keep paying $438.79 (which is the buyer's option), extends the mortgage maturity an additional five years and one month to assure repayment of the debt. Should the VRM rate rise to 10½ percent in another six months, the borrower could no longer keep paying the same monthly amount because that change would add another 11 years and 9 months to the maturity, making a total of 46 years, 10 months from origination, which is too long. The borrower could extend the mortgage to a total of 40 years from origination, but no further.

It is impossible to calculate the exact amortization schedule for a VRM because it depends on the patterns that the rate and maturity follow. Exhibit 14 shows one possible course that a VRM might take and footnotes the various decisions made by the lender and the borrower along the way. Even with the same origination date, initial rate, and index, two VRMs may follow different courses if either the lender *or* the borrower is different because each affects the payment pattern. In deciding whether or not a borrower meets the qualifications of creditworthiness on a VRM, lenders usually examine the "worst case" scenario—that is, the case in which the VRM rate rises as much as possible as soon as possible.

With all of these complexities, it may not be immediately obvious why the VRM is so popular. The reason lies in the fact that it reduces risk for the lender, who passes on some of the benefit via a lower initial mortgage rate. In making mortgage loans, lenders face the risk that interest rates will rise. Since mortgage lenders usually have short-term liabilities (deposits) matched against their long-term assets (mortgages), rising interest rates mean greater costs and no offsetting increase in revenues. The VRM serves as a hedge against rising rates by permitting revenues (mortgage payments) to fluctuate with the lender's costs. Without the VRM hedge, lenders tack on a premium to the mortgage rate to compensate for the greater risk they face. Thus the VRM reduces the lender's risk, and the borrower can get a preferential rate, often as much as one fourth to three fourths of 1 percent less than a traditional mortgage.

Exhibit 14
VRM: An Example

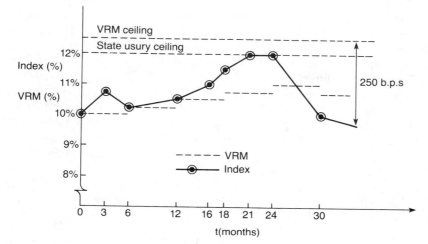

Month

0 . . . .   Index = 10 percent
 VRM of $50,000 for 30 years at 10 percent = $438.79/month

3 . . . .   Index = 10¾ percent
 VRM rate does not change (since less than six months since
 settlement).

6 . . . .   Index = 10¼ percent
 Borrower may elect to (*a*) pay $477.99/month (rate increases to
 10¼ percent—maximum allowed) or (*b*) pay $438.79/month
 and extend maturity by five years, one month (i.e., term increases from 360 to 415 months).
 [Assume (*a*) is chosen.]

12 . . . .   Index = 10½ percent
 Borrower may elect to (*a*) pay $443.14 *and* extend mortgage by
 only 4 years, 11 months (to bring mortgage to 40 years past settlement) or (*b*) pay $448.33/month.
 [Assume (*a*) is chosen.]

16 . . . .   Index = 11 percent
 VRM rate cannot increase (since it increased less than six
 months previously)

18 . . . .   Index = 11½ percent
 Borrower has no option (since maturity is at 40 years). Lender
 elects to increase VRM rate by 25 b.p. maximum to 10¾ percent. Monthly payment is $452.94.

21 . . . .   Index = 12 percent
 VRM/usury ceilings apply to VRM rate only.

24 . . . .   Index = 12 percent
 Notice that VRM rate increased to 11 percent, even though the
 index decreased in the ensuing time period. Monthly payments are $462.75.

30 . . . .   Index = 10 percent
 VRM rate decreases to 10¾ percent. Borrower decides to prepay $5,000. However, lender decides to reduce maturity to 30
 years (past settlement). Hence, payments are now $419.87/
 month (instead of $406.96 with a 40-year maturity).

. . . and so on.

VRMs are especially attractive to lenders in periods of rising interest rates because this is what enables them to raise the mortgage rate.
Because high interest rates go hand-in-hand with tight money, borrowers often take loans in the form in which they are most readily
available. Therefore, we would expect VRMs to have increased in
popularity in a year in which interest rates were high and rising for the
entire year. This is exactly what happened in 1979. In California,
where VRMs first gained widespread acceptance, VRMs grew from
roughly 20 percent of originations in early 1978 to more than 40 percent in 1979, based on surveys by the Federal Home Loan Bank of San
Francisco. Nationwide acceptance of the VRM continued to grow in
the years that followed as interest rates moved to record highs and
their wild fluctuations encouraged both lenders and borrowers to minimize risk.

Rollover Mortgages (ROMs)

The ROM is one of the more recent AMIs to be used in the United
States and is seen by many economists and mortgage-market analysts
to be the trend of the future for the domestic mortgage market. The
ROM is hardly a U.S. innovation, since it has been a major financing
vehicle in Canada for at least 50 years. In fact ROMs are often referred
to as Canadian-type mortgages or Canadian rollover mortgages. Occasionally these loans are called RRMs, for "renegotiated-rate mortgages."

In essence ROMs offer long-term amortization with short-term financing. This means that the lender gives money to the borrower to
be repaid over a long period (e.g., 30 years) at an interest rate that is
periodically renegotiated (e.g., every three to five years). Because
ROMs are just now making headway into the United States, there is
no one model one can refer to as the typical ROM. It seems certain,
however, that ROMs will develop the same sorts of "bells and whis-
tles" seen on VRMs regarding the renegotiation of the mortgage rate.
One prototype ROM proposed by the Federal Home Loan Bank Board
in January 1980 called for the renegotiation of rates every three to five
years (to be determined at the time of origination), a maximum change
in mortgage rate of one half of 1 percent for each year in the renegotiation period (e.g., 2½ percent for five-year periods) and a guarantee by
the lender to provide new financing to the borrower each period at
either the going rate on similar loans or at a rate based on an index,
such as with VRMs. Other proposals call for guaranteeing the borrower a new loan only for one additional period and not thereafter.

As with VRMs, there is no way to predict the amortization schedule
of a ROM ahead of time, since it will depend on the mortgage rates to
be negotiated in the future. Exhibit 15 shows a possible ROM over the

Exhibit 15
Possible $50,000 Rollover Mortgage (ROM)

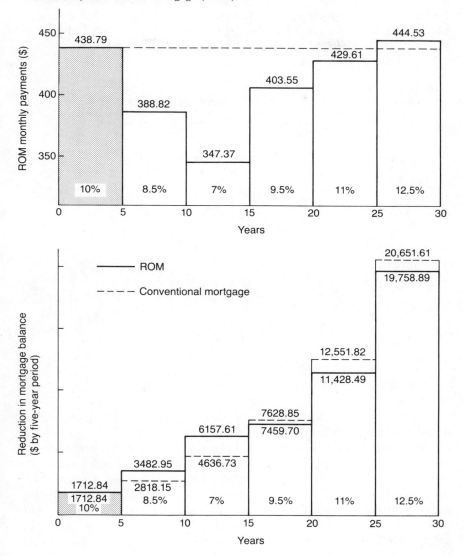

course of 30 years. It begins at a 10 percent mortgage rate with renegotiation to occur every five years. In years one through five the payment
schedule on the ROM exactly corresponds to a traditional 30-year, 10
percent mortgage from both borrower's and lender's points of view.
After five years we assume that interest rates have declined, and the
new mortgage rate is negotiated to be 8½ percent. At this point and

until year 10 the payment schedule exactly matches that of a 25-year, 8½ percent mortgage. Over its 30-year term the ROM always resembles a traditional mortgage, but the particular mortgage that it resembles changes five times. Exhibit 16 graphs the mortgage balance of this hypothetical ROM versus that of a traditional mortgage.

Exhibit 16
Comparison between a ROM and a Traditional Mortgage

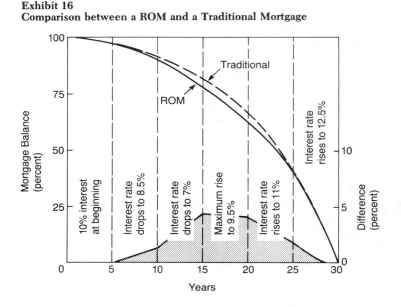

Notice that the mortgage rate on the ROM is always described as negotiated rather than determined (as with a VRM). *This is because the borrower has no obligation to keep the loan with the same lender after each period elapses,* but is free to find a new lender who can provide a lower mortgage rate and/or superior services. It would be common, however, for the borrower to use the same lender for the entire mortgage term. Not only would this be more convenient, but taking the loan elsewhere would probably mean paying a mortgage origination fee, whereas keeping the same lender would probably cost only a small amount for the paperwork involved.

As with the VRM, the ROM has the advantage of reducing interest-rate risk to both borrower and lender (most especially to the lender). Unlike the VRM, however, the ROM takes on the flavor of a short-term asset, which is so badly needed to offset the short-term liabilities of the banks. Indeed, ROMs have been described as the key to the survival of the thrift industry in the United States in the coming years.

Reverse-Annuity Mortgages (RAMs)

The key word to remember when discussing RAMs is *reverse* because, unlike any of the mortgages discussed so far, RAMs do not call for the homeowner to make payments to the bank. Rather, the homeowner (who is still the borrower) receives monthly payments *from* the bank, while the equity in his or her home *decreases*.

Young and first-time borrowers are not the only groups that tend to have cash flow problems from lack of income. Another such group is the elderly, often retired and on a fixed income. In the event that such a person owns (or has substantial equity in) a house, then a RAM provides a way of converting that equity into an income stream. Traditionally this equity could be converted to cash in one of two ways: (1) By selling the house and paying off any outstanding mortgage balance, the homeowner realizes the entire equity in the home in cash; or (2) by taking out a new or second mortgage, the homeowner realizes part of the equity in cash. The RAM goes one step further by allowing homeowners to realize part of their equity in a cash stream, paid to them in monthly installments.

Exhibit 17 illustrates a possible RAM. It involves a homeowner who originally bought her home for $25,000—with a $5,000 down payment and $20,000 mortgage, which has been paid down to a $5,000 balance. The price of the house has risen, due to inflation, to $60,000. The equity in the home is $60,000 less the $5,000 mortgage balance, or $55,000. The homeowner decides to get a RAM for $40,000 for 10 years at an interest rate of 10 percent. The RAM provides her with a monthly payment of $195.27, which she then uses for food, utilities, home improvements, and/or other expenses. Each year the mortgage balance on the RAM rises to reflect additional payments to the homeowner plus interest on the money lent so far; at the end of 10 years, the mortgage balance is precisely $40,000. Of course, monthly payments on the original mortgage must still be made until it matures. (Often there is no outstanding mortgage when the RAM is originated, so this proviso would not apply.)

From the bank's point of view, the RAM is a continuous series of loans to a homeowner against which the house serves as collateral. Assuming the property keeps the same value, the LTV ratio is continually increasing because the mortgage balance is continually rising. Banks would probably not allow the LTV to get as high as they would for traditional mortgages (i.e., the RAM could not be made for a very high amount relative to the equity) because of the uncertainty of the property value at the end of the RAM's term; as far as the bank is concerned, the property could decline in value and/or deteriorate in condition and marketability.

Exhibit 17
Example of a RAM

Original Mortgage:

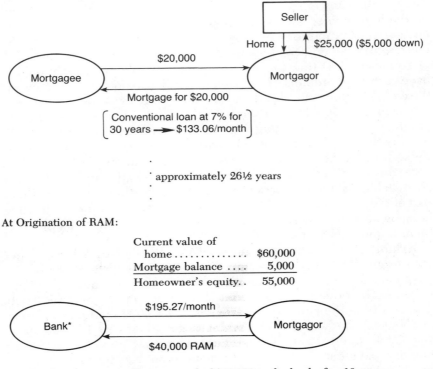

. approximately 26½ years

At Origination of RAM:

Current value of
     home $60,000
Mortgage balance   5,000
Homeowner's equity.. 55,000

The mortgagor will owe a total of $40,000 to the bank after 10 years.

Cash flows associated with mortgage and RAM:

Before Ram: −133.06   (outflow = monthly mortgage payment)
For 3½ years after RAM: +62.21   (net inflow)
For remaining 6½ years of RAM: +195.77   (RAM monthly payment received)

   * The "Bank" may or may not be the original mortgagee.

Shared-Appreciation Mortgages (SAMs)

The SAM loan is another innovation of the early 1980s brought about by high interest rates, and it uses inflation as a way of paying for part of the property. The basic terms are fairly simple. The mortgage lender agrees to provide funds at a greatly reduced rate of interest. In return, the borrower agrees to share part of the increase in the property value with the lender when the loan matures, when the property is sold, or at some other specified time.

At the inception of the SAM program, a one-third participation was popular—the lender would reduce the interest rate by a third (e.g., in a period of 15 percent interest rates the home buyer would obtain a loan at 10 percent) in return for one third of the appreciation in the property value. Over time, the formulas behind SAMs have varied somewhat from the one-third mix. In periods such as 1981 when interest rates were rising in concert with inflation falling, SAM lenders needed to compensate for the imbalance by lowering the percentage reduction in the interest rate, raising the percentage of property appreciation to be shared, or some combination of both.

Exhibit 18 shows the consequences of a SAM loan, assuming the home buyer remains in the home for five years. If the actual percent-

Exhibit 18
Traditional Loan versus Shared-Appreciation Mortgage (SAM)

- Traditional loan: $50,000 for 30 years @ 15 percent
- One-third SAM: $50,000 for 30 years @ 10 percent one third of appreciation due on sale

Assume: Inflation rate = 12 percent (1 percent per month).
Homeowner sells after five years.
Original down payment = $10,000.

		Traditional Loan	SAM	SAM Benefit
A.	Monthly payment	($632.22)	($438.79)	$193.43
B.	Total value of payments for five years (assuming 15 percent time value)	(55,998.58)	(38,865.61)	17,132.97
C.	Value of house today	60,000.00	60,000.00	—
D.	Value of house in five years	109,001.80	109,001.80	—
E.	Mortgage balance in five years	(49,360.31)	(48,287.16)	1,073.15
F.	One third of appreciation due to bank on SAM	—	(16,333.93)	(16,333.93)
G.	Net benefit of SAM in five years (B + E − F)			1,872.19

age increase in the property value (the inflation rate) is close to the prevailing level of interest rates, the cumulative savings over the first five years for the home buyer are roughly the same as the value surrendered at the end of the period. (This example assumes the one-third-type SAM and expresses all costs and benefits in comparable terms.) If inflation turns out to be lower, the homeowner wins in the long run because there is less appreciation in value to surrender; if actual inflation is greater, the homeowner loses. Of course, the homeowner will never have a problem coming up with the funds to pay the lender if the property is sold because they can be taken from the proceeds of the sale. In the event that the SAM matures or whenever the lender must be repaid without the property being sold, it may be necessary for the homeowner to obtain new financing on the property in order to obtain the required funds.

The attractions of the SAM loan are great to both borrower and lender; the borrower is able to purchase the otherwise unaffordable home, and the lender has the potentially lucrative equity kicker, depending on the rate of inflation. Two factors, though have prevented SAMs from becoming more popular than they already are. First, although the SAM is simple in concept, the fine print can be onerous. The complications created by property additions or home improvements, for example, can cloud the issue of which portion of the overall increase in property value is really due to inflation and shareable with the lender. Second, SAMs are difficult to package into units and sell as securities because there is such a broad range of formulas and other parameters being used to create them. It is difficult to have mass production of an item for which there is no standardization of parts. Access to the securities markets, which is vital as a liquidity source for mortgage originators, is effectively denied without a fungible product.

The process of creating mortgage securities and the ways of analyzing them are the subjects of the next chapter.

Pass-Through Securities

18 DEXTER SENFT
Vice President, Fixed Income Research
The First Boston Corporation

As we saw in the previous chapter, the holders of mortgages and the originators of mortgages are not always the same groups. For different reasons, a holder of a mortgage may want to sell all or part of his or her interest to someone else. In the past, the only way to do this was to sell "whole loans," which meant transferring the title and various other legal documents to the buyer. Even though the servicing may have remained with the originator of the mortgage, buyers of whole loans faced many of the legal complications and paperwork of mortgage ownership. Perhaps more importantly, there was not a great deal of liquidity in the whole-loan market, and buyers ran the risk of potential losses if they were ever forced to quickly sell their mortgages. Finally, there were very few small buyers of whole loans, because the details and paperwork involved made larger holdings more economical. The introduction of the pass-through security brought about a means of buying and selling mortgages that was "cleaner" and in many respects superior to the whole-loan market.

A pass-through security is created when one or more mortgage holders from a collection, or "pool" of mortgages and sell shares or participations in the pool. The pool may consist of as little as one to as many as several thousand mortgages. Each mortgage continues to be serviced by its originator or other servicer, not by the security holders. A trustee is assigned to hold the titles of all mortgages in the pool and to ensure that all mortgages and properties are in acceptable form and that payments are properly made. Essentially the cash flow from the pool of mortgages, which consists of principal and interest less servicing and other fees, is distributed to the security holders in a pro rata fashion. These securities get their name from the fact that the cash flow from the pool is "passed through" to the security holders by the mortgage servicers.

Although all pass-through securities have the same basic structure described above, there is a wide variety of pass-throughs available that differ substantially in their fine print. Aside from the fact that there are different issuers of pass-throughs, the securities may vary in one or more of the following ways:

1. The nature of the component mortgages.
2. The method for determining and distributing payments to security holders.
3. The guarantees on the security and the mortgages.

We will discuss each of these in general, occasionally using an actual security as an example. The reader should consult Appendix A at the end of this chapter for the specific attributes of each type of pass-through.

THE UNDERLYING MORTGAGES

Because a purchaser of a pass-through owns a share of the cash flow from the mortgages in the pass-through pool, the nature of those mortgages is of paramount importance in determining the value of the security. In particular, the following factors should be examined when analyzing the components of a pool:

1. Types of mortgages or AMIs.
2. Distribution of mortgage rates versus pass-through coupon.
3. Distribution of mortgage maturities.
4. Number and size of mortgages.
5. Geographic distribution of mortgages.
6. Creditworthiness of mortgages.

The first three factors directly affect the amount of monthly cash flow from a pool and the breakdown between principal and interest. The last three factors contribute to the regularity, predictability, and risk of that cash flow. A key word in the above factors is *distribution*. It is not enough to know only the level (or average level) of the mortgage rates, maturities, etc.; one must also know the range and diversity of levels on the individual mortgages. For example, there may be two pools with average mortgage rates of 11 percent. In one pool this could mean that all mortgages have 11 percent rates, although in the other there could be a range of rates from 10 percent to 14 percent. The actual pattern affects the amount of cash flow as well as its predictability.

Type of mortgage is an important determinant of cash flow because different types of mortgages have different amortization patterns. A pass-through pool consisting of GPMs, for example, would have negative principal amortization in its early years. In general, the more progressive the AMIs in a pool (meaning the more they lower the initial payments from that on a traditional mortgage), the less principal gets passed through in the early years of the security (with more principal in the later years).

The mortgage interest rates, curiously, do not affect the amount of interest passed through to the security holders because the holders earn the coupon rate on the security at all times. The mortgage rates usually vary from the coupon rate, with any excess of mortgage rate above coupon rate being kept by the mortgage servicer and/or the security issuer. Mortgage interest rates are important to the investor because they affect the principal amortization schedule. Higher mortgage rates mean slower amortization of the loan (less principal in the early years, more in the later years). This is true regardless of the mortgage type or maturity. Servicers generally like high mortgage rates and/or low coupon rates so as to maximize the difference, which is their servicing fee. Investors, on the other hand, tend to want higher coupon rates (more interest paid to them) and lower mortgage rates (faster amortization).

The distribution of mortgage maturities is important in the same regard as the mortgage types and interest rates. The longer the maturity, the more time over which the principal is amortized and therefore the less amortization is passed through in the early years of the security. The maturity date of a pass-through is generally stated to be the date on which the last component mortgage is fully repaid. The investor must not assume that all of the mortgages in the pool mature on the same date. Each issuer has its own limitations as to the allowable distribution of mortgage maturities in a pool—typically the maturities must all lie in a one-year time span. Nonetheless, the average maturity of the component mortgages, and therefore the average maturity of the pool, is almost always shorter than the stated maturity of the pool. Any difference that does exist becomes increasingly important over time.

The greater the number of mortgages in a pool, the more regular and predictable its cash flow. If it were not for prepayments, predicting pass-through payments would be easy as long as one knew the components of the pool. Prepayments are often voluntary (and occasionally unanticipated) payments of principal that vary with each individual mortgage. The greater the population of mortgages, the more the law of averages applies and historical behavior can be used as a standard. Although issuers rarely disclose the exact number of mortgages in a pool, it can be estimated by dividing the size of the pool by the average size of the mortgages. The size of the mortgages is often indicated by issuers, and in many cases there is a maximum size that allows one to establish a minimum number of mortgages for the pool.

Geographic distribution is important because it affects the likelihood and predictability of prepayments. Certain areas of the country are popular (and others unpopular) among pass-through investors, so pools that are highly concentrated in a particular region will be evaluated accordingly. From the standpoint of predictability, however, the more geographical diversification the better. This is because certain events that precipitate prepayments and defaults, such as natural disasters or factory closings, are local in nature and would have a greater impact on regionalized pools than on diversified pools.

Finally, there is the matter of creditworthiness. The creditworthiness of a pool can be greater than that of the mortgages because of pool insurance and payment guarantees that go beyond mortgage insurance alone. (These will be explained more fully later.) Still, the strength of the mortgages determines in large part the strength of the pool. In the absence of payment guarantees, the stronger the individual mortgage's credit, the more valuable the security. However, payment guarantees can alter this perspective. For example, if an issuer agrees to pay off in full any loan that defaults, the investor may begin to hope for defaults and prize pools consisting of low-quality mortgages.

By far the biggest problem in evaluating the underlying mortgages of a pass-through pool is obtaining information on them. The information available and the ease with which it can be obtained varies from issuer to issuer. Suffice it to say that in general there is never enough information available to the investor. In time, securities investors and dealers may persuade issuers to make more detailed data available.

PAYMENTS TO INVESTORS

The methods by which pass-through issuers collect, determine, and distribute payments to security holders is a somewhat complicated topic. It involves closely examining who pays what to whom and when, as well as who is entitled to which part of the payments. Rather than discuss this subject in general, we shall choose an actual type of pass-through as a model. The most obvious choice for the model is the GNMA (Government National Mortgage Association) arrangement because GNMAs have consistently constituted more than 75 percent of all outstanding pass-throughs. Information on other pass-throughs is detailed in Appendix A at the end of this chapter.

The flow of money in a GNMA pass-through security is fairly simple and is illustrated in Exhibit 1. Each pool has one originator and

Exhibit 1
The Pass-Through Process for GNMA Securities

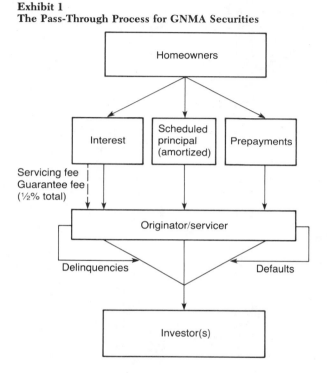

servicer, who each month collects principal and interest payments from the mortgagors. The originator/servicer sends checks to investors and reports payments and principal balances to GNMA. The servicer keeps .5 percent (50 basis points) of the outstanding principal balance each month as a gross servicing fee (this comes out of the interest passed through to the investors). From the .5 percent fee, the servicer remits .06 percent (6 basis points) to GNMA as a guarantee fee, thereby leaving .44 percent (44 basis points) as the net servicing fee.

The timing of payments is shown in Exhibit 2. Mortgage payments are due from the homeowners on the 1st of each month and are sent to investors on the 15th of the month. Prepayments might be made by homeowners at any time during the month, so a cutoff date must be established. For GNMAs, any prepayments received by the servicer up to the 25th day of a month will be passed through on the 15th of the following month. Because GNMAs are securities that are routinely

Exhibit 2
Timing of Payments for GNMA Securities

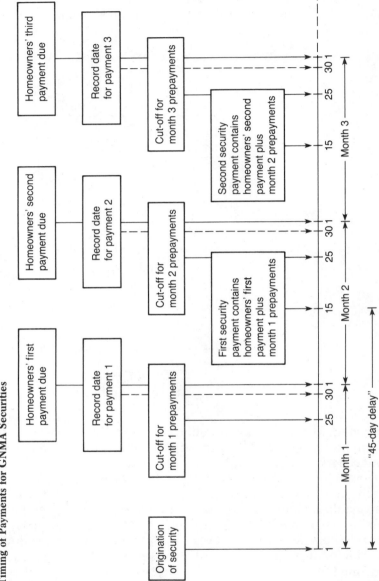

bought and sold in the secondary market, the servicer must have some way of determining whom to pay. The method used is to remit a check each month to the owner of the securities registered as of the 30th day of the prior month. This date is known as the record date because payments are received by holders of record on that date.

Notice that an investor who buys a GNMA on the first of a month (or who buys a new GNMA) does not receive the first payment until the 15th day of the following month. How many days does such an investor have to wait before receiving the payment? Let us assume that the month is 30 days long; this is the standard assumption made by Wall Street dealers with regard to all corporate, agency, and municipal securities, no matter how many days are really in the month. The number of days that elapse from the 1st of one month to the 15th of the next month is therefore 44. Because pass-throughs are a monthly payment security, the investor would expect to receive a payment after 30 days, and every 30 days thereafter. Clearly, then, the first payment on a GNMA is delayed by 14 additional days. The only problem is that many a GNMA trader, salesperson, or investor will tell you that GNMAs have a 45-day payment delay. It is difficult to imagine how this phrase was started—even if you count the first 30 days, the total wait is only 44 days. The real shame is that this misconception was subsequently inherited by all other types of pass-throughs. As a result, the analyst must always subtract 31 from the stated payment delay in order to obtain the real delay or penalty. For example, the pass-throughs issued by the Federal Home Loan Mortgage Corporation (FHLMC, or "Freddie Mac") are said to have a 75-day delay in receipt of the initial payment. For analytical purposes (computing yields, etc.) this equates to a penalty of 75−31 = 44 days.

GUARANTEES

To date there are four types of guarantees that have been placed on pass-through securities in order to elevate their creditworthiness from that of whole loans. These are:

1. Guarantees on interest payments.
2. Guarantees on principal payments.
3. Mortgage guarantee insurance.
4. Hazard insurance.

Not all types of guarantees apply to each type of pass-through, and investors should determine the exact nature of any guarantees before purchasing these securities.

A guarantee on interest payments is a promise that investors will receive interest earned on the outstanding principal balance of the security on a timely basis. This means that investors are assured of collecting interest due whether or not it was actually collected by the servicer (i.e., whether or not the homeowner actually paid it). It also means that if principal payments fall in arrears, the investor is guaranteed to receive interest due on the entire unpaid principal balance, despite the fact that the mortgage balance would have been less if the principal payments were up to date. Pass-throughs that have guarantees of timely interest payments are said to be *modified* pass-throughs.

Some pass-throughs guarantee the timely payment of principal as well as interest. Such securities are said to be *fully modified*. A fully modified pass-through therefore assures investors that they will always receive payments as if there were no delinquencies.

Certain private issuers of pass-throughs are effectively prevented from offering modified or fully modified securities because of a legal technicality: Although the issuance of a pass-through normally constitutes a sale of assets (which is what is desired), the existence of any guarantees as to principal or interest keeps the mortgages on the issuer's balance sheet as a contingent liability. In order to avoid this problem, private pass-through issuers have purchased one or more types of insurance to compensate the investor for the absence of direct guarantees.

Mortgage guarantee insurance, or pool insurance, is a policy that insures against defaults on the part of the homeowners. It is limited in scope, typically to 5 percent of the initial principal amount of the mortgage pool. Hazard insurance, on the other hand, covers certain physical risks, such as earthquakes and floods, which may not be covered by the insurance policies of the property owners. Hazard insurance is also limited in scope, often to 1 percent of the initial pool size.

Guarantees, either outright or in the form of insurance, can only benefit a security's creditworthiness, although it should be remembered that a guarantee is only as strong as the guarantor. GNMA securities have by far the strongest guarantee, since they are fully modified and guaranteed by the U.S. government. (At present, GNMAs are the only government-guaranteed pass-throughs.) The types of guarantees for other pass-throughs are detailed in Appendix A at the end of this chapter.

PREPAYMENTS

The analysis of pass-through securities would be fairly straightforward if it were not for the existence of prepayments. If no prepayments took place, the cash flow generated by a pass-through security would be the aggregate cash flow from all of the underlying mortgages less the servicing and guarantee fees kept by the originator and/or issuer. Although there might be some degree of uncertainty as to the exact composition of a pool in terms of mortgage interest rate and maturity mix, these would usually be known accurately enough to forecast pass-through payments with a high degree of precision. With cash flow out of the way, the analyst's sole concern would be creditworthiness of the security.

A prepayment occurs whenever a monthly mortgage payment is made in excess of the amount actually due. The amount of the excess payment is applied directly to the outstanding principal balance, and therefore serves to extinguish the loan earlier than its original maturity date. Usually a prepayment means that an entire mortgage loan was repaid. It is rare that a property owner decides to prepay only a portion of an outstanding loan, especially in a climate of rising interest rates and/or tight money. There are several possible causes for prepayments, among which are the following:

1. *Sale of the property*—the original property owner uses part of the proceeds from the sale to repay the mortgage loan.
2. *Refinancing*—if interest rates fall, the property owner may obtain a new mortgage loan at a more favorable rate and use the proceeds to retire the original mortgage.
3. *Disaster*—in the event the property is destroyed by fire, flood, or other disaster, insurance proceeds may be used to repay the mortgage. A homeowner may die, and the survivors may repay the mortgage from life insurance proceeds.

In addition to the above, investors of fully modified or insured pass-throughs will receive prepayments in the event of a default on one or more of the underlying mortgages. In general, an investor is unaware of whether any principal prepayments were caused by mortgage retirements or defaults. On average, though, defaults have accounted for a relatively small percentage of total pass-through prepayments.

Some mortgage lenders discourage property owners from prepaying their loans by imposing a prepayment penalty. This often takes the form of an additional six months of interest charges and may decline to zero over some period of time. Depending on the exact structure of a pass-through security, prepayment penalties may be distributed to the security holders or kept by the mortgage servicer or issuer. This question does not arise with GNMA securities, however, since neither the FHA-insured nor the VA-guaranteed mortgages comprising GNMAs permit prepayment penalties to be charged.

It is tempting to assume that a prepayment would always be desireable from the point of view of the security holder. However, this is not the case. The security holder should compare the investment opportunities available with any prepaid dollars to the coupon rate being earned by the dollars that are not prepaid. When the coupon is higher, prepayments are undesireable. An equivalent analysis is the comparison of the market value of the security to par. If the security is valued at a premium, then each dollar of principal value is worth more in security form than as cash (when it is prepaid). One form of prepayment that is almost always detrimental to the investor is refinancing. The property owner will generally not refinance unless interest rates are low enough to make it worthwhile; however, this is precisely the case in which the prevailing interest rate is lower than the coupon rate (i.e., the security is selling at a premium), and therefore the prepayment is undesireable.

One final point concerning the fine print on pass-through prepayments regards the interest on prepaid principal. Suppose a homeowner prepays the mortgage on the second day of the month. The mortgage lender ceases to earn interest on the prepaid amount but does not pass through this payment until the end of the month. Depending on the particular security, the investor may or may not earn a full month's interest on the prepaid amount. This problem is less significant for larger pools and/or pools with fewer prepayments, since the percentage of mortgages experiencing this problem will tend to be lower.

MEASURING PREPAYMENTS

The cash flow to an investor from a pass-through security consists of three parts: coupon income, principal amortization, and prepayments. The first two of these are predictable quantities, since they are determined by the characteristics of the mortgages making up the pool. Prepayments, however, are inherently unpredictable, since they depend on the actions of individual property owners. Nonetheless, if large numbers of mortgages are aggregated, the prepayments that do occur tend to become spread out over time. Although a prepayment tends to be an all-or-none event at the individual mortgage level, it may represent the return of only a small percentage of total principal at the pool level. Thus a mortgage pool may have prepayment activity ongoing over its entire period to maturity. The level of this prepayment activity is referred to as the *prepayment experience rate* of the pool, and it may be measured in several different ways. In any event, the prepayment experience rate as measured by any standard need not be constant over time. In fact, prepayment experience tends to fluctuate in conjunction with various economic indicators.

Before explaining how prepayments are measured, some terminology is required. We already know that *mortgage balance* is the ratio of the remaining principal amount on an individual mortgage loan to the original loan amount. This ratio generally runs from 0 to 1, although certain AMIs (e.g., GPMs) may permit it to exceed 1. In an analogous fashion, we define the *pool factor* of a pass-through security to be the ratio of its outstanding principal balance to the original principal amount.

If a mortgage pool had no prepayments, then at any point in time its pool factor would be the same as the mortgage balance on the underlying mortgages. (If the component mortgages were of different types, interest rates, or origination dates, then the pool factor would represent a weighted average of the individual mortgage balances.) On the other hand, if prepayments did occur, the pool factor would be less than the mortgage balance. In effect, the mortgage balance measures the remaining principal on loans that have not prepaid, whereas the pool factor accounts for prepaid loans as well.

Exhibit 3 illustrates this distinction between mortgage balance and

Exhibit 3
Sample Pool Factor Computation

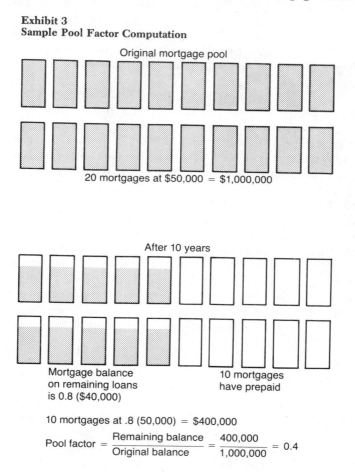

Original mortgage pool

20 mortgages at $50,000 = $1,000,000

After 10 years

Mortgage balance on remaining loans is 0.8 ($40,000)

10 mortgages have prepaid

10 mortgages at .8 (50,000) = $400,000

$$\text{Pool factor} = \frac{\text{Remaining balance}}{\text{Original balance}} = \frac{400,000}{1,000,000} = 0.4$$

pool factor. It assumes a pool is originally constructed of 20 identical mortgages for $50,000 each, giving a pool size of $1 million. At the end of 10 years, half of the loans are assumed to have prepaid, and the balance on each remaining loan is $40,000. Thus the pool contains $.4

million principal at that time. The mortgage balance is 0.4 million/0.5 million, or 0.8, whereas the pool factor is 0.4 million/1 million, or 0.4. A measurement for prepayments now suggests itself; prepayment experience may be expressed as the amount by which the pool factor has declined relative to the mortgage balance. In other words, it is the amount by which the pool factor is different from what its value would have been if no prepayments had occurred. We define the overall prepayment rate for the 10-year period as the ratio of the pool factor to the mortgage balance: 0.4/0.8 = 0.5, or 50 percent. This of course merely reiterates what we already knew—that half of the loans had prepaid. In practice, however, we are neither given the number of loans composing a pool nor the sizes of the individual loans, so that the prepayment rate must be imputed by dividing the pool factor (which is always known) by the mortgage balance (which can be computed based on the known or assumed characteristics of the underlying mortgages).

A subtle problem arises with mortgage pools containing a mixture of mortgage types, interest rates, and/or maturity dates. In order to perform the calculation described above, it is necessary to know the average mortgage balance on the loans in the pool. If the pool originally contained a mixed bag of loans, this average mortgage balance would vary depending on exactly which loans survived (i.e., did not prepay). For example, if a pool originally contained half 8 percent loans and half 10 percent loans, the average mortgage balance would depend on how much of each type prepaid. Unfortunately, this information may not be available. For better or worse, it is commonplace to assume that all of the loans in a pool have common characteristics (e.g., the above pool could be viewed as if it were entirely composed of 9 percent loans). These characteristics would be viewed as immutable until such time as information to the contrary become available. This assumption causes the calculation of prepayment rates to be somewhat imprecise, although with long periods to maturity it is rarely a problem.

SMM Experience

In examining the prepayment rate of a pool, it is not enough to know simply the number of mortgages that prepaid. One must also consider the amount of time involved. In the previous example, we could say that since 50 percent of the mortgages terminated over a 10-year period, the average prepayment rate was 5 percent per year. A similar prepayment measurement is the Single Monthly Mortality, or SMM, prepayment rate of the pool. SMM differs from the above calculation in two respects:

1. The SMM rate reflects average prepayments per month rather than per year.
2. SMM expresses the amount of mortgages that prepay relative to the amount of mortgages outstanding, not the original amount.

The second point is worth elaborating. If a mortgage pool had 75 percent of its mortgages prepay after only two months, it would be tempting to compute the SMM rate as 37.5 percent. In fact though, the SMM rate would be 50 percent. After one month at 50 percent SMM, half the loans would prepay. In the second month, half the *remaining* loans would prepay, leaving 25 percent of the original pool, which is the desired result. In the first example, in which half the loans in a pool prepay in the first 10 years, the SMM rate works out to roughly 0.58 percent. Typical SMM experience rates for mortgage pools are 1 percent or less.

Notice that the SMM experience for a pool is an average prepayment rate and does not imply that prepayments take place every month. In fact pools containing relatively few mortgages will rarely have prepayments, and when prepayments do occur they will tend to be for a relatively large percentage of the pool. Investors should be careful to notice any difference between the *cumulative* prepayment rate (the average rate of prepayments since the pool's inception) and the *interim* experience rates (e.g., the prepayments during the past six months, prepayments for each calendar quarter, etc.).

Exhibit 4 graphs the pool factor for a pass-through security containing 30-year, 10 percent mortgages at various SMM prepayment rates. The higher the prepayment rate, the more quickly the pool factor declines. Notice that the line labeled 0 percent SMM represents no prepayments (i.e., it is the schedule for the mortgage balance).

SMM is an appealing way to measure prepayments because of its simplicity, but it is not in any way a predictive model. In other words, there is no basis (yet) for supposing that the historical prepayment rate should be continued into the future. Certain studies of mortgage termination behavior have resulted in the discovery of prepayment patterns. These patterns can be built into a prepayment model, and individual pools can be evaluated *relative* to this norm. The best known prepayment model and the measurement employed by most institutional investors is known as FHA-experience.

FHA Experience

The Federal Housing Administration (FHA) was established in 1934 to encourage the improvement of housing standards and to provide a system at the national level for mortgage insurance as an aid to

Exhibit 4
Mortgage Balances at Various SMM-Experience Rates (10 percent mortgage,
30-year maturity)

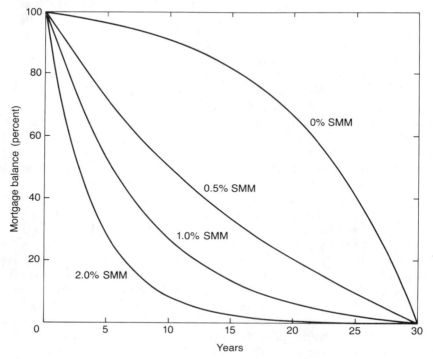

home builders, buyers, and mortgage lenders. In the process of performing these tasks, FHA has accumulated a wealth of historical information on the mortgages it insures, including data on mortgage terminations. Each year the Actuarial Division of the Department of
Housing and Urban Development (HUD) performs a statistical analysis of the FHA data going back to 1957. The results of this analysis
have become the basis for the FHA-experience model.

Technically, there are several varieties of FHA experience corresponding to mortgages insured under different sections of the National Housing Act. Each section applies to loans for different property types and calls for various terms to maturity, and so on. In fact the
full HUD analysis breaks down prepayments by mortgage type and by
state. The most commonly insured FHA loan, though, is the Section
203 single-family loan, and when the term *FHA experience* is used
without further qualification, it generally means the most recent HUD
study on Section 203 loans for the United States as a whole.

FHA experience takes the form of a decimal-balance table, which
indicates for each year in the life of a mortgage what the probability is

Exhibit 5
Historical FHA-Experience Decimal Balances (U.S. total section 203 30-year original term)

FHA-Exp as of Year	1974	1975	1977	1978	1979	1980	1981
0	1.00000	1.00000	1.00000	1.00000	1.00000	1.00000	1.00000
1	.99191	.99161	.99187	.99186	.99163	.98993	.98880
2	.96707	.96360	.96246	.96246	.96063	.95036	.95172
3	.93425	.92884	.92207	.92253	.91892	.89668	.90090
4	.89564	.88920	.87666	.87740	.87289	.84139	.84965
5	.85425	.84692	.82972	.82978	.82380	.78728	.79839
6	.81060	.80291	.78252	.78267	.77424	.73430	.74676
7	.76702	.75907	.73765	.73746	.72756	.68304	.69785
8	.72598	.71727	.69570	.69490	.68357	.63459	.65191
9	.68712	.67760	.65710	.65566	.64264	.58952	.61100
10	.65033	.63991	.62084	.61921	.60480	.54752	.57486
11	.61292	.60122	.58638	.58432	.56885	.50836	.53998
12	.57933	.56710	.55449	.55128	.53486	.47196	.50748
13	.54425	.53168	.52325	.51945	.50245	.43794	.47715
14	.51381	.50038	.49416	.48841	.47118	.40612	.44880
15	.48959	.47585	.46766	.45781	.44062	.37635	.42227
16	.46484	.45116	.44448	.42724	.41034	.34810	.39540
17	.44151	.42569	.42482	.39639	.37997	.32085	.36842
18	.41619	.40123	.40754	.36496	.34940	.29436	.34156
19	.39159	.37756	.38276	.33247	.31866	.26865	.31504
20	.36869	.35508	.35881	.30121	.28761	.24400	.28910
21	.34821	.33585	.33574	.27130	.25808	.22061	.26394
22	.32618	.31176	.31357	.24286	.23015	.19842	.23973
23	.30415	.29154	.29230	.21598	.20390	.17776	.21663
24	.28212	.21732	.27197	.19075	.17940	.15861	.19745
25	.26010	.25110	.25256	.16724	.15669	.14092	.17418
26	.23808	.23088	.23410	.14548	.13580	.12465	.15499
27	.21606	.21066	.21657	.12551	.11673	.10975	.13720
28	.19404	.19044	.19997	.10734	.09948	.09618	.12083
29	.17202	.17022	.18429	.08464	.07767	.07880	.09990
30	.15000	.15000	.17000	.06200	.05590	.06140	.07900
Data through	1971	1972	1975	1976	1977	1979	1980

that it will survive (i.e., not prepay or default) to that point. For example, consider the figures from Exhibit 5, which shows the standard FHA-experience balances used during each of the years 1974 through 1981. According to the 1981 data, a Section 203 mortgage had a 98.88 percent chance of surviving until the end of 1 year, a 57.49 percent chance of lasting 10 years, and so on. Notice that only 7.9 percent of all such mortgages are expected to reach their 30-year maturity. From the decimal balance table, one can compute the percentage of mortgages expected to terminate in any given year. By spreading these terminations out over the entire year, one can then compute expected terminations per month. (In fact the HUD study allows one to differentiate between terminations due to prepayments and terminations due to defaults. For the purposes of pass-through analysis, though, these can be lumped together and are usually referred to simply as prepayments.)

It should be mentioned that not all of the decimal balances are based on actual mortgage prepayment data. Exhibit 5 shows the year through which the mortgage data were taken. For instance, the 1981 study used data through the end of 1980. Since the data started in 1957, the latest study had only 24 years of information on which to base 30 years of prepayment estimates. Therefore, the last six years of data in the 1981 study are extrapolations of the earlier data.

Historically, there has been some controversy as to the exact interpretation of FHA-experience multiples. In fact the investment community reversed itself in 1979 and changed the standard computation. To illustrate with an example, suppose we are given a four-year-old mortgage pool and asked to determine the proportion of mortgages that would prepay during the next year at a 200 percent FHA-experience rate. We know that at 100 percent FHA experience the decimal balance table goes from .84965 after four years to .79839 after five years—a decrease of .05126. According to the old (and currently obsolete) computation, at 200 percent FHA we would have expected to see a decline of 2(0.05126), or 0.10252, in the mortgage population. The accepted procedure currently is somewhat more sophisticated. To begin with, we look at the proportion of mortgages normally expected to survive between years 4 and 5. This is given by the ratio of the decimal balances: $0.79839/0.84965 = 0.9397$ (or 93.97 percent). Now at an arbitrary prepayment rate we compute the ratio of survivors by raising this number to the power of the FHA multiple—in this case, we square it. Thus we have $(0.9397)^2$, which is roughly 88 percent of the mortgages expected to survive. Therefore, 12 percent of the outstanding mortgages would be expected to prepay in year 5. Note that these two procedures will give equivalent results at 0 percent FHA and at 100 percent FHA, but different results for everything else.

Unlike SMM experience, which merely quantifies prepayments, FHA experience represents a normal rate of prepayments as measured on actual mortgages. It allows for different paydown rates depending on how old the mortgage is. For example, the number of terminations in the second year can be seen to be roughly three times the rate in the first year. This is an appealing notion, since the circumstances leading to a default, refinancing, or other reason for termination would seem rather unlikely to crop up in the first 12 months of a mortgage. It turns out that the FHA-experience data imply a generally increasing conditional probability of termination with time. More simply stated, the older the mortgage, the more likely it is to terminate.

Mortgage market participants measure the prepayment rates of pass-through pools in terms of percentages or multiples of FHA expe-

rience. A pool conforming to the FHA prediction is said to prepay at
100 percent FHA experience. Pools prepaying at twice the normal rate
are said to be 200 percent FHA pools, and so on. A pool experiencing
no prepayments at all is said to be a 0 percent FHA pool. Exhibit 6

Exhibit 6
Mortgage Balances at Various FHA-Experience Rates (10 percent mortgage,
30-year maturity)

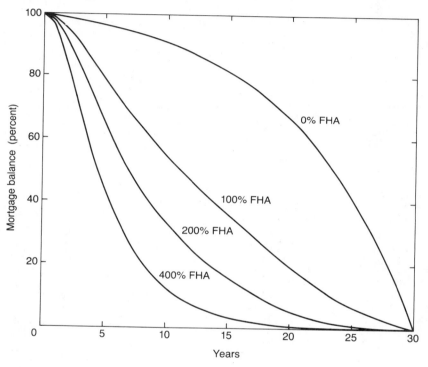

graphs the pool factor of a new 10 percent pool as a function of time for
various FHA-experience rates. Notice that the 0 percent FHA line is
identical to the 0 percent SMM line in Exhibit 4.

   As with SMM experience, FHA experience can be measured either
cumulatively or as an interim prepayment rate for some specific time
period. Pools with cumulative prepayment rates that are above average are often referred to as *fast-pay* securities, and slower than average
cumulative prepayments indicate a *slow-pay* pool. Surprisingly, the
average prepayment rate for most pass-through securities does not
turn out to be 100 percent FHA. Exhibit 7 is a graph of the monthly
average (interim) prepayment rates, expressed as multiples of FHA
experience for three large sectors of the pass-through market: GNMA
Single-Family securities (Section 203), GNMA Graduated-Payment

Exhibit 7
Monthly Interim FHA-Experience Rates

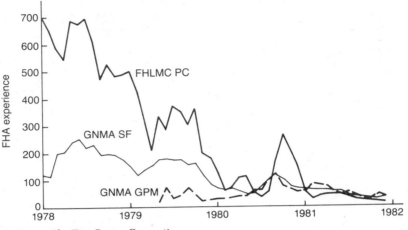

Source: The First Boston Corporation.

securities (Section 245), and FHLMC Participation Certificates (conventional mortgages). The graph shows that the prepayment rate for the market as a whole can vary substantially with time. Except for GPMs, the securities on the exhibit have prepaid faster than 100 percent FHA in some periods and slower than 100 percent FHA in others. This is why the concepts of fast pay and slow pay are (or should be) relative to the universe of securities outstanding and not the 100 percent FHA standard.

Exhibit 8 is a graph similar to Exhibit 7 but expressed in SMM terms. The GNMA Mobile Home sector is also shown on this chart. Again, there is considerable fluctuation in historical rates of prepayment, and no one number suggests itself as "the" appropriate prepayment rate. One cannot help noticing the obvious prepayment pattern in both exhibits. As interest rates in general (and mortgage rates in particular) skyrocketed in the late 1970s and early 1980s, the housing market was "crunched." The low volume of home construction and turnover led to a drastically reduced level of prepayment activity from the levels prevailing in the mid-70s.

Pros and Cons of FHA Experience

Perhaps the greatest asset of FHA experience is the fact that it is widely accepted and utilized among pass-through dealers and institutional investors. The introduction of any alternative model for prepayments must first combat the traditional usage of FHA experience, and if the pass-through market is anything, it is a market of tradition.

Exhibit 8
Monthly Interim SMM-Experience Rates

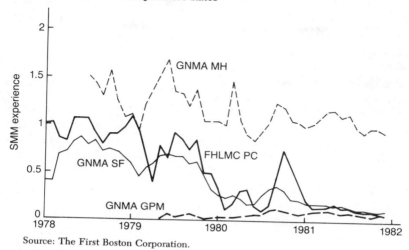

Source: The First Boston Corporation.

The best mathematical selling point for FHA experience is the fact that it is founded on the basis of actual historical behavior of mortgage prepayments and therefore embodies a pattern of increasing termination probabilities known to be representative. This underlying pattern is preserved even if multiples of FHA experience are being used to quantify or predict a pool's behavior.

This is not to say that FHA experience is without its drawbacks, however. One disadvantage, which is probably better described as an abuse, is that the original HUD study quantified prepayments on Section 203 loans, but FHA experience is being applied as a predictor for prepayments on virtually all types of 30-year loans. The applicability of termination data computed for level-payment mortgages to graduated-payment mortgages (to choose one example) is at best questionable and at worst seriously misleading when employed in a predictive capacity.

A second disadvantage to FHA experience is the fact that the data upon which it is based are old. Since the HUD study utilizes information beginning in 1957, most of the mortgages in the study carried relatively low interest rates in comparison with today's levels. Furthermore, the prepayment trends that are built into the decimal balance table are largely a reflection of mortgage behavior in the 1950s and 1960s, when the economic and social climate were vastly different from that of the 1980s. One outcropping of this age problem can be seen in the HUD analyses of terminations by state. In the late 1970s it became evident to most mortgage analysts that certain regions of the country—most notably the Southwest, California, and Florida—were experiencing faster mortgage prepayments than the rest of the country by virtue of their strong economic growth and population influx. The FHA-experience data, however, would have indicated just the reverse. In fact, the HUD figures showed the fastest prepaying states to be Maine, Vermont, and New Hampshire.

A third problem often cited with regard to FHA experience is its ignorance of variables that are known to have significant influences on prepayments. The only parameter considered by the FHA-experience model is the age of the mortgages. The most notable parameter *not* in the HUD study is the mortgage interest rate. As one might expect, mortgages carrying higher interest rates tend to be more likely candidates for prepayments, especially during periods of declining interest rates, when refinancing becomes attractive. Several other variables, including the level of interest rates (yields) in general, the level of housing activity (e.g., housing starts), and seasonal factors are known to play an important part in determining prepayment activity. These too are absent from the FHA-experience model, although for predictive purposes that may actually be considered an advantage. If one's goal is to calculate a yield based on assumed prepayments, it is less than appealing to have to forecast interest rates and/or housing starts in order to obtain an answer.

One final complaint about FHA experience is that it gets revised every year. This requires new yield tables to be printed and distributed each time the updated decimal balances become available, resulting in a short period of confusion by some market participants as to which numbers are correct. Since the alternative (of having no future updates) is even less palatable than the problem itself, this is a problem most investors are willing to live with.

The ultimate test of any prepayment model is its ability to successfully describe the historical prepayment behavior known to have taken place and the ease with which it can be used to predict future prepayments. On these grounds, FHA experience is about as good as most alternative models. It is interesting, though, that the SMM model, which is obviously simpler than FHA experience (no parameters versus one), is actually more effective in describing the behavior of certain mortgage pools. In fact SMM was conceived in 1978 by The First Boston Corporation as an attempt to more accurately quantify yields on FHLMC PCs.

Exhibit 9 is a scatter diagram of age versus FHA-experience rate for all of the FHLMC PCs that has been outstanding at least six months in mid-1978. There was a rather strong indication from the data that FHA experience (measured cumulatively) tended to decline on PCs over time. Because the FHA-experience data have a built-in acceleration of expected prepayments, the idea that PCs might simply have constant paydown rates in absolute percentage terms suggested itself. The dotted line on the exhibit is where pools would lie if they were to prepay

Exhibit 9

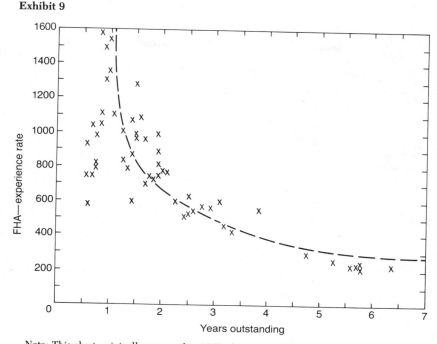

Note: This chart, originally prepared in 1978, shows how the idea for the SMM prepayment model was conceived. Each *x* represents a FHLMC PC; the FHA-experience rate of the PC is plotted versus its age. The older pools were the slower prepaying pools. The dotted line shows where the *x*s would be if all pools prepaid at a rate of 1 percent SMM. The fit to the actual data was tantalizingly close.

at a constant 1 percent SMM rate; the correlation was obvious and tantalizing. The final test of SMM came when First Boston measured its "standard error" in describing the pattern of FHLMC PC factors versus the error from FHA experience. SMM was found to reduce total squared error by anywhere from 50 percent to 75 percent for various PC pools. As a consequence, SMM gained popularity as a prepayment measurement, especially for FHLMC issues, and is used today as an alternative approach to FHA experience for the production of yield tables.

AVERAGE LIFE VERSUS HALF-LIFE

Buyers of mortgages and pass-through securities are generally interested in two statistics that summarize the nature of their investments. The first of these is the yield, or rate of return, of the investment, which is a subject we shall address shortly. The other is the life of the investment, or the span of time over which the rate of return is realized.

One could argue (correctly) that since the cash flow of a 30-year pass-through security extends all the way to 30 years (barring complete extinction of the pool beforehand), the life of the security is 30 years. However, as Exhibits 4 and 6 showed, most of the principal amount in a mortgage pool is retired, due to amortization and prepayments, well before that time. Investors found it desireable to quantify the effective lifetime of a pool in a way that accounted for its principal paydowns. There are two traditional approaches to this problem, known as *average life* and *half-life.*

Half-life is probably the easier of the two measurements to explain. The half-life of a security is the number of years that must elapse before half of the principal is repaid. Exhibit 10 illustrates the half-life

Exhibit 10
Half-Life of a $1 Million GNMA Security (200 percent FHA experience assumed)

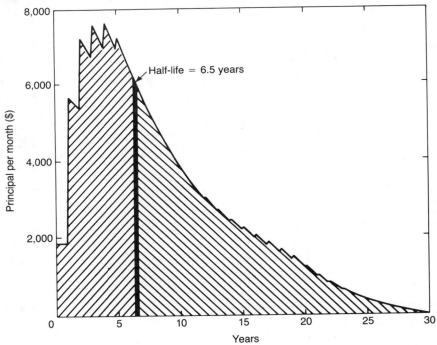

concept by graphing the total principal payments (amortization plus prepayments) that would be received from a 30-year, 9½ percent GNMA security at 200 percent FHA experience. The half-life of the security is 6.5 years and is indicated by a vertical line. When depicted in this fashion, half-life has a simple geometric interpretation: It is the vertical line that divides the graph into equal portions. In other words, the two shaded regions on the exhibit have areas that are equal.

One of the drawbacks of half-life is that it fails to consider the actual timing of principal payments. Suppose for example, that in the previous exhibit all of the principal outstanding in year 7 was prepaid at that time. This would have the effect of squeezing the portion of the graph lying to the right of the half-life line into a tall, narrow band. Most investors would agree that such a cash flow has a shorter life than it did before. However, the half-life statistic would not change. Because all of the squeezing occurs after the halfway point, nothing happened to affect the half-life measurement; half of the issue is still retired by the end of 6.5 years. Although this example is somewhat perverse, it does indicate the need for a more sensitive measurement of the effective term, and average life provides such a measurement.

The average life of a security is the average number of years that each principal dollar will be outstanding. Stated differently, it is the number of years that each dollar in a pass-through pool can be expected to survive. Mathematically, the computation of average life is somewhat more difficult than of half-life. Average life is computed as the weighted average time to repayment of all of the principal paydowns, using as weights the dollar amounts of the paydowns. Like half-life, average life has a geometric interpretation, which is shown in Exhibit 11. The graph shows the same cash flow as does Exhibit 10,

Exhibit 11
Average Life of a $1 Million GNMA Security (200 percent FHA experience assumed)

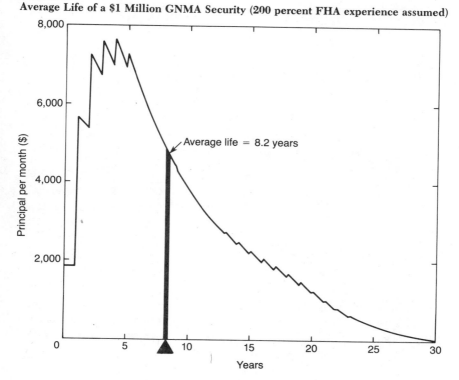

but this time we consider the horizontal axis to be a seesaw. Each payment is a weight on the seesaw; the greater the payment, the heavier the weight. Average life turns out to be that location on the axis where the fulcrum of the seesaw must be placed in order to make it balance. In this example, average life works out to about 8.2 years.

Unlike half-life, average life is sensitive to any shifts in the timing of principal repayments. For example, if the security were to prepay in year 7 as previously supposed, the seesaw would become imbalanced to the left. In order to restore balance, the fulcrum would have to be shifted left to compensate. This is equivalent to saying that average life decreased, as expected.

It should be noted that both average life and half-life tend to decrease as the mortgage pool ages. At each point in time, average life and half-life measure the term of the *remaining* dollars in the pool. Obviously, each measurement must go to zero by the time the pass-through matures. Exhibit 12 graphs the average lives of a GNMA 9½

Exhibit 12
Average Life of a GNMA 9½ (assuming various prepayment rates, over first 15 years)

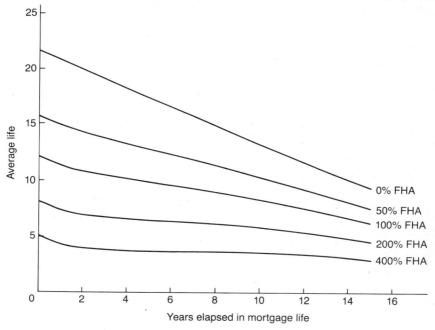

percent pass-through over time at various assumed rates of FHA experience. The higher the prepayment rate, the shorter the average life, although as time elapses the differences in average life (for different prepayment rates) become smaller.

Average life is typically longer than half-life for pass-through securities because of the nature of the cash flow. Pass-throughs generally return more dollars in their early years than in their later years. This keeps the half-life short, but the leverage on the seesaw provided by the few dollars going out to the later years keeps the average life from getting as small.

Despite its greater difficulty in computation, average life is generally regarded to be superior to half-life as an estimate of the effective period over which returns are generated. Average life is quite sensitive to changes in a pass-through's prepayment assumption and/or its age. Although average life is not as accurate a measure of volatility as it is purported to be, it should continue to be used in conjunction with yield to arrive at an overall evaluation of an investment.

YIELD MEASUREMENT

There is very likely no market as rich in controversy as the pass-through securities market when it comes to the subject of yield. The selection of the correct yield for a given pass-through at a given price is virtually the name of the game. Yet for all of the possible yields a security might have, there is really only one way to mathematically arrive at that yield. The various models, prepayment rates, and other assumptions determine the amount and timing of the cash flow received by the investor. Given the cash flow, however, there is very little freedom in determining the corresponding yield.

The yield of any investment is a measurement of its equivalent rate of return. Mathematically, yield should be viewed as a discounting rate used to compute present value. An investor who buys a security spends some amount of money in order to receive a series of future payments. In the case of pass-throughs, these future payments may not be known with certainty. In any event, when these future payments are converted to present value equivalents and summed, the result should be the known market price. Yield (or more properly, yield to maturity) is the discount rate that makes this relationship true. For a more detailed discussion of how yield is computed, consult Chapter 4.

The yields that are quoted for pass-through securities fall into two general categories: mortgage yield and cash flow yield. Mortgage yield is based on certain simplifying assumptions that force a definite cash flow into the yield calculation, and as such it is useful only for very rough comparison purposes and should not be viewed as a true rate of return. Conversely, cash flow yield, which is often referred to as HTG yield, is based on cash flow assumptions chosen by the investor as being appropriate for the particular security and is generally more difficult to compute.

Mortgage Yield

Mortgages were bought and sold as whole loans by mortgage bankers and thrift institutions long before high-speed computers made the computation of yields easy. Fifty years ago one did not have the luxury of being able to speculate as to the yield impact of the future prepayment rate of a mortgage or a mortgage pool. In fact such prepayment models as FHA experience and SMM did not even exist. As a result, yields on mortgages were obtained by looking up the instrument in a yield book—often having to interpolate between available results to compensate for fractional coupon rates or prices.

Most yield books for mortgages contained columns of numbers corresponding to various years to prepayment. (See Exhibit 13.) It was assumed that a mortgage or mortgage pool would experience no pre-

Exhibit 13
Pass-Through Yields and Corporate Bond Equivalents

GNMA 15

PREPAID IN	8 YEARS		10 YEARS		12 YEARS		15 YEARS		18 YEARS		20 YEARS		25 YEARS	
PRICE	GNMA YIELD	FOR CBE	GNMA YIELD	FOR CBE	GNMA YIELD	FOR CBE	GNMA YIELD	FOR CBE	GNMA YIELD	FOR CBE	GNMA YIELD	FOR CBE	GNMA YIELD	FOR CBE
75	21.44	+98	20.88	+93	20.55	+90	20.27	+88	20.13	+86	20.08	+86	20.02	+85
76	21.11	+95	20.58	+90	20.26	+87	20.00	+85	19.86	+84	19.81	+84	19.76	+83
77	20.80	+92	20.29	+88	19.99	+85	19.73	+83	19.60	+82	19.55	+81	19.50	+81
78	20.49	+89	20.00	+85	19.71	+82	19.47	+81	19.35	+80	19.30	+79	19.25	+79
79	20.19	+87	19.73	+83	19.45	+81	19.22	+79	19.10	+78	19.05	+77	19.00	+77
80	19.89	+84	19.45	+81	19.19	+78	18.97	+77	18.85	+76	18.81	+75	18.76	+75
81	19.60	+82	19.18	+78	18.94	+76	18.72	+75	18.61	+74	18.57	+73	18.53	+73
82	19.31	+79	18.92	+76	18.69	+74	18.49	+73	18.38	+72	18.34	+72	18.30	+71
83	19.03	+77	18.65	+74	18.44	+72	18.25	+71	18.15	+70	18.12	+70	18.07	+69
84	18.75	+75	18.41	+72	18.20	+70	18.02	+69	17.93	+68	17.89	+68	17.85	+68
85	18.48	+73	18.16	+70	17.97	+69	17.80	+67	17.71	+67	17.68	+66	17.64	+66
86	18.21	+71	17.92	+68	17.74	+67	17.58	+66	17.50	+65	17.47	+65	17.43	+65
87	17.95	+68	17.67	+66	17.51	+65	17.37	+64	17.29	+63	17.26	+63	17.22	+63
88	17.69	+66	17.44	+65	17.29	+63	17.15	+62	17.08	+62	17.06	+62	17.02	+62
89	17.44	+65	17.21	+63	17.07	+62	16.95	+61	16.88	+61	16.86	+60	16.83	+60
90	17.18	+63	16.98	+61	16.85	+60	16.74	+60	16.69	+59	16.66	+59	16.64	+59
91	16.94	+61	16.75	+60	16.64	+59	16.54	+58	16.49	+58	16.47	+58	16.45	+57
92	16.69	+59	16.52	+58	16.43	+57	16.35	+57	16.30	+56	16.28	+56	16.26	+56
93	16.46	+57	16.32	+56	16.23	+56	16.16	+55	16.12	+55	16.10	+55	16.08	+55
94	16.22	+56	16.10	+55	16.03	+55	15.97	+54	15.93	+54	15.92	+54	15.90	+54
95	15.99	+54	15.89	+54	15.83	+53	15.78	+53	15.75	+53	15.74	+53	15.73	+52
96	15.76	+53	15.69	+52	15.64	+52	15.60	+52	15.58	+51	15.57	+51	15.56	+51
97	15.53	+51	15.48	+51	15.45	+51	15.42	+50	15.41	+50	15.40	+50	15.39	+50
98	15.31	+50	15.28	+49	15.26	+49	15.25	+49	15.24	+49	15.23	+49	15.23	+49
99	15.09	+48	15.08	+48	15.08	+48	15.07	+48	15.07	+48	15.07	+48	15.07	+48
100	14.88	+47	14.89	+47	14.90	+47	14.90	+47	14.91	+47	14.91	+47	14.91	+47
101	14.66	+46	14.70	+46	14.72	+46	14.73	+46	14.74	+46	14.75	+46	14.75	+46
102	14.45	+44	14.51	+45	14.54	+45	14.57	+45	14.59	+45	14.59	+45	14.60	+45
103	14.24	+43	14.32	+43	14.37	+44	14.41	+44	14.43	+44	14.44	+44	14.45	+44
104	14.04	+42	14.14	+42	14.19	+43	14.25	+43	14.28	+43	14.29	+43	14.30	+43
105	13.84	+41	13.95	+41	14.03	+42	14.09	+42	14.13	+42	14.14	+42	14.16	+42
106	13.64	+39	13.78	+40	13.86	+41	13.94	+41	13.98	+41	13.99	+41	14.02	+42
107	13.44	+38	13.60	+39	13.70	+40	13.78	+40	13.83	+40	13.85	+41	13.88	+41
108	13.25	+37	13.42	+38	13.53	+39	13.62	+39	13.69	+40	13.71	+40	13.74	+40
109	13.06	+36	13.25	+37	13.38	+38	13.48	+38	13.55	+39	13.57	+39	13.60	+39
110	12.87	+35	13.08	+36	13.22	+37	13.34	+38	13.41	+38	13.43	+38	13.47	+38
111	12.68	+34	12.92	+35	13.06	+36	13.20	+37	13.27	+37	13.30	+37	13.34	+38
112	12.49	+33	12.75	+34	12.91	+35	13.05	+36	13.13	+36	13.17	+37	13.21	+37
113	12.31	+32	12.59	+33	12.76	+34	12.91	+35	13.00	+36	13.04	+36	13.08	+36
114	12.13	+31	12.43	+33	12.61	+34	12.78	+34	12.87	+35	12.91	+35	12.96	+35

Source: The First Boston Corporation.

payments at all for the indicated number of years, at which time it would prepay in full. The yield obtained would depend on how much time elapsed before the pool terminated. Exhibit 14 depicts this situation for a 30-year mortgage assumed to prepay in 12 years. Two things

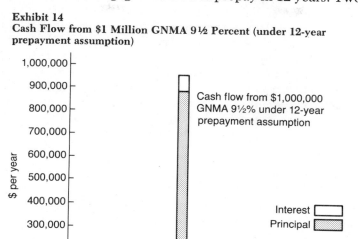

Exhibit 14
Cash Flow from $1 Million GNMA 9½ Percent (under 12-year prepayment assumption)

should be noticed in this exhibit. First, we are no longer dealing with a 30-year investment; the cash flow shown goes out no farther than 12 years. Second, this pattern is similar to that of an ordinary 12-year bond, which suggests that mortgage yields might be approximated using existing yield computations for corporate or government bond issues. Unfortunately, the cash flow in Exhibit 14 is different from that on straight debt in three respects, which are strong enough in combination to render the traditional bond yield books unusable:

1. The cash flow for the mortgage yield is monthly as opposed to the semiannual cash flow on ordinary bonds.
2. The mortgage cash flow returns some principal (in the form of amortization) over the entire period, whereas for straight debt all principal is repaid at maturity.
3. The existence of any servicing fee prevents the mortgage cash flow from being level up to its termination date, whereas straight debt pays level coupons.

In the event that the mortgage yield is being computed for a pass-through security, a fourth difference exists—payment delay. The longer the investor must wait to begin receiving payments, the lower the investor's net yield will be, other things being equal. This effect is not quantified in traditional bond yield tables, since bonds ordinarily have no payment delays.

Exhibit 13 makes it clear that the choice of the number of years to prepayment is critical in determining the mortgage yield when the price is significantly different from par. Unfortunately, there was no way to know a priori when a mortgage investment was going to terminate, so some type of assumption had to be made. Over time, the mortgage industry evolved certain standard assumptions, which would be used in deciding the years to prepayment when there was no compelling reason to choose another number. These standards, still in use today, are displayed in Exhibit 15. The exhibit shows that

Exhibit 15
Standard Assumptions behind Mortgage Yield

Security Type	Years to Maturity	Years to Prepayment	Servicing Fee	Payment Delay (days)*
GNMA:				
Single family	30	12	½%	45
Graduated payment	30	12	½	45
Buydown	30	12	½	45
Mobile home A	12	5	2½	45
Mobile home B	15	7	2½	45
Mobile home C	18	9	2½	45
Mobile home D	20	10	2½	45
Project Loan	40	20	¼	45
FHLMC PC	30	12	0	75
FNMA	30	12	0	55
Private Issuers	30	12	⅜	55

* Notice that the actual time penalty for each security is 31 days less than the stated payment delay.

for 30-year mortgages, 12 years was the accepted standard prepayment assumption. Generally, mortgages with shorter original terms had shorter prepayment assumptions.

The pass-through securities market adopted mortgage yield as its standard from its inception in the early 1970s. The standard assumptions regarding the term to prepayment have been left intact. Of course pass-throughs require additional assumptions regarding servicing fee and payment delay in order to determine yield; each type of security has its own particular parameters for the yield formula, and these parameters are detailed in Appendix B.

What does it mean when we say the mortgage yield is the pass-through market standard? Essentially there are three ways that mortgage yield is used as a standard. First, because mortgage yield is the accepted norm, it is often referred to using the security name itself. For example, *GNMA yield* means mortgage yield on GNMA securities (using the parameters appropriate for GNMAs), and *FHLMC yield* means mortgage yield for FHLMC PCs. Second, mortgage yield is the standard for quotations among securities dealers. This means that trades done on a yield basis will be billed by computing a price using mortgage yield formulas. It also means that yields appearing in newspaper quotations or other market literature are mortgage yields. The third way in which mortgage yield is used as a standard is in "yield maintenance" trades. In the pass-through securities market, buyers often purchase securities for forward delivery, meaning that the trades will settle at some future date, usually from one to four months later. In some cases it is not possible to guarantee to the buyer receipt of the exact coupon requested; this is because the securities the buyer receives may not have been created yet. In these situations, the buyer and seller agree that if another coupon is substituted, the price of the trade will be adjusted to maintain the original yield to the buyer. It is the mortgage yield that is referred to. In other words, the actual delivered coupon at the adjusted price has the same mortgage yield as the original coupon at the original price.

DRAWBACKS IN MORTGAGE YIELD

Before discussing cash flow yield, or HTG yield, it is appropriate to point out two problems with mortgage yield. It was these problems that led to the need for an alternative yield mechanism.

First, the cash flow assumptions underlying mortgage yield are viewed as unrealistic. The possibility of all the remaining principal balance prepaying on just one date may be reasonable for individual mortgage loans, but it is not reasonable for a mortgage pool. Because the pool has large numbers of mortgages contributing to the cash flow, its prepayments will tend to be spread out over time.

The second problem is more serious and yet is not realized by many market participants. Mortgage yield for a given type of security is always based on the same assumption as to years to prepayment and years to maturity, regardless of the actual age of the underlying mortgages. For example, GNMA 8 percent single-family securities, which were issued primarily in the mid-1970s, have mortgage yields based on 30 years to maturity and 12 years to prepayment, regardless of the fact that many of these issues have only 25 years or less of remaining term. In fact, according to the rules, these issues' yields would still be quoted based on this 30/12 system, even when they are 20 years old and have only 10 years remaining term. This ignorance of mortgage age has the effect of seriously understating the true yield of older deep-discount securities. In fact, if left unchecked this problem will be magnified every year as the existing population of pass-throughs continues to age. The market will undoubtedly be forced at some point to reevaluate its standards, but for those who prefer not to wait there is another solution.

HTG YIELD

Cash flow yield, or HTG yield, differs from mortgage yield in that the underlying cash flow is made to be as realistic as possible. This means accounting for all known factors, such as the age of the underlying mortgages, as well as projecting reasonable estimates for future prepayments. Prepayments are usually specified in the form of a percentage FHA- or SMM-experience rate. The name HTG is short for "honest-to-God" and was coined in 1977 by The First Boston Corporation; it was intended to suggest, if somewhat unsubtly, a superior estimate to the true yield of a pass-through. Unlike mortgage yield, there is more than one HTG yield for a given pass-through at a given price. In fact there are infinitely many HTG yields depending on the prepayment assumption used; no one prepayment model or experience multiple is cast as the "standard," although market conditions inevitably make some assumptions appear to be more reasonable than others. Perhaps the greatest asset of HTG yield is its ability to evolve with a changing market environment.

Exhibit 16 is an example of an HTG yield table for a GNMA security. Separate sections are produced for each age assumption on the underlying mortgages. In this particular format, yields at various FHA-experience rates are calculated in addition to the GNMA yield (mortgage yield). Also, each column of yields is followed by the average life of the security under the given assumptions.

Several points can be made using this one exhibit. First, notice that as FHA experience increases, average life decreases. This serves to raise the HTG yield at discount prices and to lower it for premium prices. Second, notice that increasing the mortgage age (thereby decreasing remaining term) has the same effect because this too decreases remaining average life. Finally, notice that GNMA yield is insensitive to either of these effects. There is only one GNMA yield at a given price because neither age nor assumed prepayment rate enter into the mortgage yield computation.

The investor or analyst who has been accustomed to mortgage yield might find a quite different world in terms of HTG yield. The values of pass-throughs, both relatively and absolutely, are subject to change in the HTG analysis, particularly for older securities, higher assumed prepayment rates, and/or deeper discount prices. As an example, Exhibit 17 shows how the GNMA market looked in both GNMA yield and HTG yield perspectives at the end of 1981. The prices used are actual bid side quotations, ages are approximate average values for

Exhibit 16
Example of an HTG Yield Table

GNMA 9 1/2   SERVICING FEE 1/2   MORTGAGE AGE (YRS) 4
MORTGAGE RATE 10   YEARS TO MATURITY 26
PAYMENT DELAY 45 DAYS

PRICE	GNMA YIELD	0	50	100	150	200	250	300	400	500	600	800	1000
		--- HTG YIELDS FOR VARIOUS FHA-EXPERIENCE RATES ---											
70.000	15.01	14.36	15.57	16.82	18.09	19.37	20.66	21.94	24.50	27.02	29.51	34.36	39.07
75.000	13.86	13.31	14.24	15.20	16.19	17.18	18.18	19.18	21.16	23.13	25.07	28.85	32.53
80.000	12.82	12.33	13.07	13.78	14.51	15.25	16.00	16.74	18.23	19.70	21.16	24.00	26.77
85.000	11.87	11.54	12.02	12.52	13.03	13.55	14.07	14.59	15.64	16.67	17.70	19.70	21.65
90.000	11.00	10.78	11.08	11.39	11.70	12.02	12.35	12.67	13.32	13.97	14.60	15.86	17.07
95.000	10.20	10.09	10.22	10.36	10.51	10.65	10.80	10.95	11.24	11.54	11.83	12.40	12.96
100.000	9.45	9.46	9.45	9.44	9.42	9.41	9.40	9.39	9.37	9.35	9.32	9.28	9.24
105.000	8.75	8.87	8.73	8.58	8.44	8.28	8.13	7.97	7.66	7.35	7.05	6.44	5.85
110.000	8.09	8.33	8.07	7.80	7.53	7.25	6.97	6.68	6.11	5.54	4.97	3.86	2.77
115.000	7.48	7.83	7.46	7.08	6.70	6.30	5.90	5.50	4.69	3.88	3.08	1.49	-.06
AVG LIFE (YEARS)		18.15	13.19	10.08	8.02	6.59	5.56	4.79	3.73	3.05	2.58	1.97	1.61

COPYRIGHT 1982 THE FIRST BOSTON CORPORATION
FHA DATA AS OF 9/81 ON S203 MTGES THRU 12/80

GNMA 9 1/2   SERVICING FEE 1/2   MORTGAGE AGE (YRS) 6
MORTGAGE RATE 10   YEARS TO MATURITY 24
PAYMENT DELAY 45 DAYS

PRICE	GNMA YIELD	0	50	100	150	200	250	300	400	500	600	800	1000
		--- HTG YIELDS FOR VARIOUS FHA-EXPERIENCE RATES ---											
70.000	15.01	14.55	15.74	16.99	18.26	19.55	20.86	22.18	24.83	27.48	30.12	35.33	40.42
75.000	13.86	13.46	14.38	15.34	16.32	17.32	18.33	19.35	21.41	23.46	25.51	29.56	33.53
80.000	12.82	12.49	13.18	13.89	14.62	15.36	16.11	16.87	18.40	19.94	21.47	24.50	27.48
85.000	11.87	11.62	12.10	12.60	13.11	13.63	14.15	14.68	15.75	16.83	17.90	20.03	22.13
90.000	11.00	10.83	11.13	11.44	11.75	12.07	12.40	12.73	13.39	14.06	14.72	16.05	17.36
95.000	10.20	10.11	10.25	10.39	10.53	10.68	10.82	10.97	11.27	11.58	11.88	12.49	13.08
100.000	9.45	9.45	9.44	9.43	9.42	9.41	9.40	9.39	9.37	9.34	9.32	9.27	9.23
105.000	8.75	8.84	8.70	8.56	8.41	8.26	8.10	7.95	7.63	7.32	7.00	6.36	5.74
110.000	8.09	8.28	8.02	7.76	7.48	7.20	6.92	6.64	6.06	5.47	4.89	3.72	2.56
115.000	7.48	7.76	7.39	7.01	6.63	6.23	5.84	5.43	4.61	3.79	2.96	1.30	-.34
AVG LIFE (YEARS)		16.46	12.23	9.51	7.66	6.36	5.40	4.67	3.66	2.99	2.53	1.92	1.55

COPYRIGHT 1982 THE FIRST BOSTON CORPORATION
FHA DATA AS OF 9/81 ON S203 MTGES THRU 12/80

Exhibit 17
GNMA Market Analysis as of December 31, 1981

Coupon	Price 12/31/81	GNMA Yield	Assumed Age (years)	HTG Yield
6½	55¾	14.79	9	18.57
7¼	57¾	15.26	6	18.12
8	60⅞	15.41	5	17.74
9	65¼	15.57	3	17.19
10	70⅜	15.55	2	16.68
11	75⅜	15.57	1	16.28
12½	83¼	15.55	1	15.98
13½	88⅜	15.58	1	15.85
15	94¾	15.88	0	15.95
16	98⅜	16.19	0	16.21
17	102⅞	16.32	0	16.28

Notes: GNMA yield and HTG yield calculated based on monthly compounding. HTG yield assumes mortgages have ages as shown and that prepayments are at 75 percent FHA.

each coupon, and the prepayment assumption of 75 percent FHA experience was moderately bullish in posture at that time.

The investor or analyst who looked only at GNMA yields would see a pattern of generally increasing yields as coupon rates rise. This might seem appropriate, since it is typical in the fixed income markets for higher coupon issues to yield more, due primarily to tax considerations, reinvestment potential for incoming cash flow, and/or call protection. In the pass-through market, however, one would not always expect these traditional relationships to hold. It is true that GNMAs (or other pass-throughs) priced over par should carry a substantial yield premium as compensation for the risk that the issue could be prepaid and the investor would suffer a loss in market value. However, it is also reasonable to expect very low coupon pass-throughs to carry high yields to compensate for a risk specific to such securities, known as prepayment risk. As Exhibit 16 demonstrates, the HTG yield of a deep-discount pass-through is highly sensitive to the precise prepayment assumption used. For example, a 4-year-old GNMA 9½ at par has a difference in yield of only one basis point between the assumptions of 50 percent FHA experience and 100 percent FHA. However, if the security were priced at 70, the difference in yield between the two assumptions is 125 basis points. The penalty for guessing wrong as to future prepayment rate is therefore far greater for low-coupon pass-throughs that carry deep-discount prices.

Returning to Exhibit 17, notice that the pattern of HTG yields (using 75 percent FHA and ages appropriate for each coupon level) is closer to the way one might expect to see it. It is the intermediate coupons that yield the least. High coupons yield more due to risk of prepayments speeding up when their prices go above par, and lower coupons yield more to compensate for the risk that prepayments may be less than predicted.

Obviously the GNMA yield and HTG yield columns paint very different pictures of the world in both absolute level of returns and relationships between coupon sectors. One always prefers to go with the picture that makes the most sense to the observer, and for this reason HTG-yield analysis has become very popular.

CORPORATE BOND EQUIVALENT YIELD

Pass-through securities have a built-in advantage over traditional corporate or government debt in that they make monthly payments of principal and interest as opposed to semiannual payments. Investors always prefer payments to be more frequent and/or begin sooner, since this gives them more time to reinvest the payments to earn additional income.

Both pass-through yield and HTG yield are computed on the basis of monthly compounding, and as such they do not reflect this advantage over other securities. If one wishes to compare pass-throughs with corporate or government bonds, it is necessary to put all yields on an equal footing with respect to compounding. This is usually accomplished by adjusting the pass-through's yield upward to compute its "corporate bond equivalent" yield, or CBE.

Exhibit 18 is a table of CBE adjustments for monthly pay securities. The entries in the table are in the form of basis point add-ons. As an

Exhibit 18
Yield Adjustments for Corporate Bond Equivalents

Yield Range	BP	Yield range	BP
8.02– 8.30	+14	13.84–14.00	+41
8.31– 8.58	+15	14.01–14.17	+42
8.59– 8.85	+16	14.18–14.33	+43
8.86– 9.11	+17	14.34–14.49	+44
9.12– 9.37	+18	14.50–14.65	+45
9.38– 9.62	+19	14.66–14.81	+46
9.63– 9.86	+20	14.82–14.97	+47
9.87–10.10	+21	14.98–15.12	+48
10.11–10.33	+22	15.13–15.28	+49
10.34–10.55	+23	15.29–15.43	+50
10.56–10.77	+24	15.44–15.58	+51
10.78–10.99	+25	15.59–15.73	+52
11.00–11.20	+26	15.74–15.88	+53
11.21–11.41	+27	15.89–16.03	+54
11.42–11.62	+28	16.04–16.17	+55
11.63–11.82	+29	16.18–16.31	+56
11.83–12.01	+30	16.32–16.46	+57
12.02–12.21	+31	16.47–16.60	+58
12.22–12.40	+32	16.61–16.74	+59
12.41–12.59	+33	16.75–16.88	+60
12.60–12.77	+34	16.89–17.01	+61
12.78–12.96	+35	17.02–17.15	+62
12.97–13.13	+36	17.16–17.29	+63
13.14–13.31	+37	17.30–17.42	+64
13.32–13.49	+38	17.43–17.55	+65
13.50–13.66	+39	17.56–17.69	+66
13.67–13.83	+40	17.70–17.82	+67

Example: If GNMA yield is 16.32 percent, adjustment is 57 basis points. Therefore the corporate bond equivalent is

$$16.32 + .57 = 16.89 \text{ percent}$$

example, let us consider GNMA 17s at a price of 102⅞, which is where they were at year-end 1981. (See Exhibit 17.) The table in Exhibit 18 indicates that for the GNMA yield of 16.32 percent the adjustment is 57 basis points, giving the GNMA-CBE yield of 16.89 percent. Similarly, the HTG yield of 16.28 percent (based on 30-year term, 75 percent FHA) has a CBE adjustment of 56 basis points, giving an HTG-CBE yield of 16.84 percent.

Notice that the adjustment does not depend on whether the starting yield is a mortgage yield or an HTG yield. All that matters is the absolute level of the initial yield. The mathematics are such that any monthly pay security will use the same table of adjustments for comparison to any semiannual-pay security. The exact formula for computing CBE values can be found in Appendix B.

The amount of the CBE adjustment rises very quickly as yield levels increase. The additional yield value in pass-through securities versus corporate bonds is therefore substantially more than it first appears during periods of high interest rates. Investors must remember to make this adjustment (or to use yield tables with the adjustment already built in) when operating in more than one market.

PARITY PRICE

Bond investors are accustomed to the fact that at a price of par the yield to maturity of a bond is equal to its coupon rate. They are probably also aware that for pass-through securities this relationship does not hold true. As Exhibit 16 shows, at a price of par both mortgage yield and HTG yield are less than the coupon rate, and in fact HTG yield decreases for higher prepayment rates. The cause of this phenomenon is the payment delay. It can be shown mathematically that at a price of par, yield equals coupon only if there is no payment delay. (This is why the relationship is true for ordinary bonds.)

As it turns out, there is a unique price for which yield (both mortgage and HTG) equals coupon regardless of prepayment rate. This price, known as the *parity price* of the security, is always less than par and typically in the range from about 98½ to 99½. The parity price will be lower for higher coupon rates and/or greater payment delays.

Parity price is the analog to par in the pass-through market. Since a price of par is over the parity price, yields are less than the coupon rate and will decline as average life decreases, which accounts for the pattern in Exhibit 16. An exact formula for parity price can be found in Appendix B.

TAXATION

Like corporate and government bonds, pass-through securities are generally taxable. (The small quantity of pass-throughs issued in the municipal sector should be disregarded for the purposes of this section.) One does not often find a discussion of the tax aspects of pass-throughs, though, for two reasons. First, most pass-through buyers are tax-exempt institutions, such as pension funds, for whom the topic is not relevant. Second, there is some ambiguity as to exactly how pass-throughs should be taxed, which sections of the tax code apply, and so on. What follows here, therefore, is First Boston's present understanding of the tax aspects of pass-throughs, which at the very least should be checked with the reader's tax counsel.

There is no question that the coupon income from a pass-through represents ordinary income and is taxed as such. The controversy arises in the treatment of gains or losses on the return of principal due to amortization or prepayments. With ordinary bonds such gain or loss would represent capital gain or loss, and would be long term if the holding period (i.e., the time from purchase to the date of the principal payment) was more than one year. It seems that this capital gains treatment is not afforded to pass-throughs, on the grounds that to qualify for such treatment the obligor of the security (the party responsible for making the payment) must be a corporation or government-related body. The thinking is that the obligor of a pass-through is the collection of property owners whose mortgages compose the pool, and since property owners are usually individuals, the capital gains treatment does not apply. Therefore any gains on amortized or prepaid principal are ordinary income, regardless of holding period. This is definitely a tax disadvantage for pass-throughs and perhaps explains why so few taxable investors own them. It may be some consolation that this adverse treatment applies only while the security is being held. If the security is sold, any gain or loss in the remaining principal balance once again becomes capital gain or loss, long term for holding periods of more than one year.

As if the tax treatment of pass-throughs were not complicated enough, it gets worse for GPM pass-throughs. As we have seen, GPMs experience negative amortization over their first few years, so their monthly payments are substantially smaller than for traditional mortgages. Taxable buyers of GPMs who are on an accrual basis must pay income taxes on the entire amount of interest that would have been paid on a traditional loan, even though only part of that interest was actually received. In other words, taxes are due on monies not received. The interest shortfall is treated as a deferred interest item by the tax payer. Since taxes have already been paid on it, it is not taxed
id. Should a GPM pool exhibit prepayments, the first
ments are used to reduce any deferred interest out-
ld come as no surprise that GPMs are even less attrac-
ry pass-throughs to taxable buyers.

CONSISTENCY

you are an investor trying to choose between two
r purchase into your portfolio. Both are GNMA 8s,
3½ years old, both were issued by Philadelphia mort-
and both are offered at a price of 65 (14.33 percent

GNMA yield) in May 1981. An investigation of the historical prepayment rates reveal that although both pools are above average in speed, one pool has prepaid at an average of about 200 percent of FHA experience and the other at a truly fast-pay pace of more-than 600 percent FHA. Which pool would you choose?

Because the pools appear identical in most other respects, many investors would automatically choose the fast-pay pool. Some investors, noting that at 600 percent FHA the HTG yield of such a security is more than 33 percent, would pay a substantial premium for the fast-pay pool. Other investors would take the position that future prepayments might not be as good as 600 percent FHA, but they would still favor the fast-pay pool because of its established trend of high prepayments. However, a recent study by The First Boston Corporation has revealed that the historical performance of a GNMA pool is in general a poor indication of its future performance, and it is entirely possible that the 200 percent FHA pool described above would be the superior investment.

Exhibit 19 details the payment history of two actual GNMA pools that have the characteristics just described. The total payment each month consists of three components: coupon (mortgage interest less servicing and guarantee fees), amortization, and prepayments (including defaults). Coupon payments and amortization for a month are predictable from the pool factor at the beginning of the month. Prepayments are the only unknown component, and it is the prepayments that ultimately make pass-through investments attractive or unattractive. (Usually, buyers of discount pass-throughs want prepayments, and buyers of premium securities do not.) Notice that the prepayments of the 200 percent FHA pool are strikingly regular through May 1981. The numbers from month to month are still unpredictable, but in 41 of the 43 periods the dollar amount of prepayments was at least $1000 (per million dollars original principal amount). The fast-pay pool, on the other hand, had more than 99.9 percent of its prepayments occur in the first three months following its issuance; an investor who purchased the pool after April 1978 in expectation of fast prepayments would have been very unpleasantly surprised. Most people who could see the actual prepayment records would conclude that, if anything, the 200 percent FHA pool has the better chance for future prepayments. Both pools in this example are extreme cases, and by no means do all comparisons work out this way. Nevertheless, examples like this are not so rare either, and the possibility of this phenomenon should be cause for concern among investors.

Because it would be extremely cumbersome for an investor to examine the detailed prepayment history of every pass-through pool before buying or selling it, it would be nice if there were some way of summarizing the *consistency* of historical prepayments into a single

Exhibit 19
Prepayment Histories of Two Actual GNMAs

		Cash flow from $1 mil GNMA 8 (No. 19886)				Cash flow from $1 mil GNMA 8 (No. 17730)				
		Pool Factor	Amort	Prepay	Coupon	Total Payment	Pool Factor	Amort	Prepay	Coupon	Total Payment
1977	OCT	1.00000	$644	$1,078	$6,667	$8,389					
	NOV	.99828	648	4,540	6,655	11,843					
	DEC	.99309	650	6,147	6,621	13,417					
1978	JAN	.98629	650	8,593	6,575	15,819	1.00000	$634	$60	$6,667	$7,361
	FEB	.97705	649	6,823	6,514	13,986	.99931	639	84,661	6,662	91,962
	MAR	.96958	649	2,298	6,464	9,411	.91401	589	489,030	6,093	495,712
	APR	.96663	652	9,215	6,444	16,312	.42439	284		2,829	3,113
	MAY	.95676	651	3,024	6,378	10,053	.42410	286		2,827	3,114
	JUN	.95309	653	7,070	6,354	14,077	.42382	288		2,825	3,114
	JUL	.94537	653	3,697	6,302	10,652	.42353	290		2,824	3,114
	AUG	.94102	655	10,398	6,273	17,326	.42324	292		2,822	3,114
	SEP	.92996	652	12,679	6,200	19,531	.42295	294	22	2,820	3,136
	OCT	.91663	648	10,648	6,111	17,407	.42263	296		2,818	3,114
	NOV	.90534	645	7,850	6,036	14,530	.42233	298	22	2,816	3,136
	DEC	.89684	644	20,228	5,979	26,851	.42201	300	24	2,813	3,137
1979	JAN	.87597	634	11,079	5,840	17,553	.42169	302	24	2,811	3,137
	FEB	.86426	630	3,291	5,762	9,683	.42136	305	24	2,809	3,138
	MAR	.86034	632	5,506	5,736	11,874	.42103	308		2,807	3,115
	APR	.85420	633	5,466	5,695	11,794	.42073	310		2,805	3,115
	MAY	.84810	633	11,483	5,654	17,770	.42042	312		2,803	3,115
	JUN	.83598	629	6,822	5,573	13,024	.42010	315		2,800	3,115
	JUL	.82853	628	9,417	5,524	15,569	.41979	315	26	2,799	3,140
	AUG	.81849	625	8,302	5,457	14,384	.41945	318	25	2,796	3,140
	SEP	.80956	623	8,212	5,397	14,232	.41910	321		2,794	3,116
	OCT	.80072	621	9,604	5,338	15,563	.41878	324	25	2,792	3,141
	NOV	.79050	618	7,238	5,270	13,126	.41843	327		2,790	3,116
	DEC	.78264	617	12,506	5,218	18,340	.41811	329		2,787	3,116
1980	JAN	.76952	611	11,339	5,130	17,081	.41778	331		2,785	3,116
	FEB	.75757	607	5,659	5,050	11,316	.41745	334		2,783	3,116
	MAR	.75130	606	21	5,009	5,636	.41711	336		2,781	3,116
	APR	.75068	611	1,553	5,005	7,168	.41678	338		2,779	3,117
	MAY	.74851	614	3,047	4,990	8,651	.41644	340		2,776	3,117
	JUN	.74485	616	1,219	4,966	6,801	.41610	343		2,774	3,117
	JUL	.74302	619	3,728	4,953	9,300	.41576	345		2,772	3,117
	AUG	.73867	620	4,637	4,924	10,182	.41541	347		2,769	3,117
	SEP	.73341	621	1,917	4,889	7,427	.41506	351		2,767	3,117
	OCT	.73088	623	6,655	4,873	12,151	.41471	353		2,765	3,118
	NOV	.72360	622	2,231	4,824	7,677	.41436	355		2,762	3,118
	DEC	.72074	625	3,377	4,805	8,807	.41401	358		2,760	3,118
1981	JAN	.71674	626	29	4,778	5,433	.41365	360		2,758	3,118
	FEB	.71609	630	8,030	4,774	13,434	.41329	363		2,755	3,118
	MAR	.70743	628	5,054	4,716	10,398	.41293	365		2,753	3,118
	APR	.70175	628	5,752	4,678	11,058	.41256	368		2,750	3,118
	MAY	.69537					.41219				

FHA- experience rate	208%	FHA- experience rate	637%
Prepay. consistency	84	Prepay. consistency	15
Original pool size	$14.8 mil	Original pool size	$1.0 mil
Mortgage banker in Philadelphia		Mortgage banker in Philadelphia	

index. First Boston devised just such an index, which is referred to simply as C. This is not a perfect substitute for the detailed history, but it is a step in that direction. The possible values of C range from 0 to 100, where low numbers mean inconsistent prepayments, and high numbers mean consistent ones. In Exhibit 19, the first pool has a C-value of 84, and the second pool (the fast-paying pool) a value of only 15. Our experience with C indicates that values of 80 or more should be considered very consistent, and pools with C-values under 20 should have their prepayment rates viewed skeptically. C is based on a computation that considers the standard deviation of a pool's monthly prepayment record in relation to the maximum possible deviation the pool could have had. Also, C is adjusted for the effect of time.

Exhibit 20
Consistency Patterns

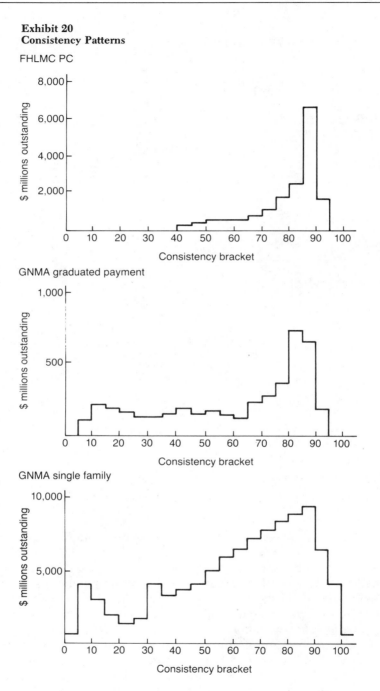

Pools that have not been outstanding very long can hardly be viewed as having established much of a trend, and their C-values will be mathematically constrained to being close to 50. Conversely, a pool with a very high or a very low consistency must by definition be a pool that has been outstanding for a reasonably long time. The precise definition of C appears in Appendix B.

Exhibit 20 displays the pattern of consistency as of May 1981 for the three largest sectors of the pass-through market: GNMA single-family (fixed payment), GNMA graduated payment, and FHLMC PC pools. In each case, the bracket with the single largest amount of pools has C of about 85—apparently an optimistic note. Notice, however, that each of the GNMA securities has a significant amount of pools with lower consistencies, whereas the FHLMCs are all clustered at the high end of the scale. What is the reason for this?

THE LAW OF AVERAGES

There are two major differences in the composition of GNMA and FHLMC pools. First, FHLMCs are composed of conventional loans instead of the FHA/VA loans in GNMAs. It is not clear why this would make any difference as far as consistency is concerned. The other difference is pool size, and this can indeed make a difference. The average GNMA single-family or GPM pool is issued with an original balance of about $2 million, which means the pool contains about 50 loans (assuming an average loan size of around $40,000). Freddie Mac pools, though, contain several thousand mortgages, generally totaling more than $100 million, which gives PCs an advantage as far as consistency is concerned—the law of averages.

Mortgage prepayments and defaults, although influenced by seasonal and cyclical factors, are essentially random events. If a single homeowner whose mortgage is in a GNMA pool of 50 loans should move and prepay the loan, say after living in the home for about three years, the GNMA will show a prepayment rate of about 550 percent FHA for that month. (If the prepayment occurs before three years, the FHA multiple is even higher.) The statistical value of a forecast for the other 49 loans based on this one event is dubious. In a FHLMC pool, however, single events are not statistically significant; and in order to establish a prepayment trend, large numbers of mortgages must be involved. The law of averages makes a forecast based on this trend more reliable, and as a consequence the consistency of month-to-month prepayments should be higher.

Referring to Exhibit 19 again, it should come as no surprise that the first (consistent) pool had an original principal amount of $14.8 million, large by GNMA standards, and the second pool had an original size of only $1.0 million. There is another cause for high consistency

in mortgage prepayments, and that is the lack of prepayments altogether. Obviously, if a pool never has any prepayments, it is behaving
as consistently as possible. A statistical analysis of the pass-through
universe reveals a negative correlation between consistency and average prepayment rate for all sectors of the market. In other words, the
more consistent pools tend to be the slower paying ones. This does
not mean that every fast-pay pool is going to be inconsistent, but it
does mean that a fast-pay consistent pool is relatively hard to find.

ARGUMENTS AGAINST CONSISTENCY

Though there are several possible flaws in the consistency concept,
consistency has withstood these challenges in most cases. First, it can
be argued that inconsistency results from having a poor prepayment
model—in this case, FHA experience. Obviously, if a prepayment
model could perfectly predict future prepayments, all pools would
behave consistently, and if a model were terrible, pools would tend to
prepay randomly. The reason consistency is meaningful under FHA
experience is not because FHA experience is a great model (it is not),
but because it is the premier model being used by investors and
dealers. It is FHA experience that makes pools "fast-pay" in people's
minds, so it is the FHA consistency that counts.

Another argument is that one-month periods are too short for pools
to behave consistently and that more consistent patterns would
emerge if longer periods were examined. This is reasonable, but un-
true. We repeated the consistency measurement on all pass-throughs
using three-month, six-month, and one year periods, and in most cases
consistency actually was worse. Part of the reason for this is that high
consistency mathematically requires many time periods—a pool's prepayment history has only one-twelfth the number of annual periods as
monthly periods. But the fact that most six-year and older pools have
lower quarterly consistency than monthly consistency shoots down
this argument quite clearly.

A third argument is that interest rates and seasonal factors have
caused prepayments to fluctuate to a degree that destroys consistency.
Again, this is a good possibility, but there is evidence against it. We
took several thousand pools at random and ranked their prepayments
relative to one another for each period. In other words, the prepayment rates were expressed as percentiles instead of absolute paydown
rates. (The pools, in effect, were graded on a curve.) It turned out that
the average change in the pool's percentile from one period to the
next and the standard deviation of such changes were close to the
values one would have obtained with a series of random numbers.
This implies that no information is added (indeed, little even seems to
be present) by accounting for overall market behavior.

One good argument against consistency is its failure to discriminate among pools based on the times at which prepayments occurred. In other words, two pools with all features alike except that one had gradually increasing prepayments and the other gradually decreasing prepayments would show the same value for C. By the same token, the fast-pay pool in Exhibit 19 would be equally inconsistent (but no doubt more attractive to investors) if its large prepayments had occurred in the most recent three months instead of the first three months. All that can be said is that no one index can fully describe a series of numbers. We do not believe that this type of behavior is common or that is poses a serious problem, but of course some sort of "prepayment acceleration index" could be invented. A more attractive alternative is to examine recent prepayment experience in addition to overall consistency.

THE ALTERNATIVE

If consistency proves that historically fast-paying pools should not be relied upon to provide high future prepayments (in the absence of other information), how should they be viewed? Based on a statistical theorem proved by Charles Stein in the early 1960s, it can be shown that for most GNMA pools a better guess for future prepayments is the average prepayment rate for the market, or even better, the average rate for similar pools of the same coupon. In other words, historical prepayment rates of individual pools are of little of no value in detecting the fast-pay GNMA pools of the future. First Boston advocates that investors obtain more information about specific pools before considering any trade at a price other than the going price for "ordinary" pools of the same type and coupon. Exhibit 21 shows the sort of information First Boston generates on every GNMA and FHLMC pool. In addition to the pool's overall prepayment rate and consistency, prepayment rates for the past three months, six months, and one year are shown (other periods could be chosen) to provide a feel for whether the prepayments have been coming or going. In conjunction with consistency, these prepayments give a good picture of the pool's behavior and get around the last problem cited earlier. The pools circled on the exhibit are the ones appearing in Exhibit 19.

As long as there are pass-throughs, there will be pools that prepay faster or slower than average. However, a pool's historical prepayment rate alone is not a good indicator of which pools will be the fast-pay pools of the future. The consistency index is a useful tool in making more reliable forecasts for individuals pools. In the absence of a consistency index, investors are advised to concentrate primarily on pool size because there tends to be safety in large numbers. In any event, the concept of the fast-paying GNMA should be taken with several grains of salt.

Exhibit 21
Prepayment Consistency Report for Pass-Through Securities Data as of May 1981

Pool Number	Coupon	Type	Dated	$MM Outstanding	FHA-EXP for past			FHA to Date	C
					3 Months	6 Months	1 Year		
7071..........	8	SF	9/75	.82	2	2	2	57	45
8655..........	8½	SF	4/76	.82	0	113	58	93	65
12337..........	8	SF	10/76	.88	2	2	2	45	45
15569..........	7½	SF	2/77	.72	2	1	158	155	68
17730..........	8	SF	1/78	.41	0	0	0	637	15
17993..........	7½	SF	12/77	2.40	0	15	49	146	65
19662..........	8	SF	9/77	3.26	77	121	109	115	69
19886..........	8	SF	10/77	10.29	168	109	102	208	84
20013..........	8	SF	1/78	1.73	2	2	45	92	64
20995..........	8	SF	11/77	1.72	0	71	109	85	54
27754..........	9	SF	2/79	3.74	1	116	64	81	53
28005..........	8½	SF	12/78	.86	24	427	308	197	46
29336..........	9	SF	6/79	.96	283	142	76	61	6
38892..........	11	SF	1/80	.98	3	3	157	137	20
39112..........	11	SF	2/80	.97	0	266	200	178	7

Source: The First Boston Corporation.

RISK VERSUS REWARD

We have shown that pass-through securities are more complex in nature than the typical corporate or government bond and are capable of posing formidable problems to the back office of an institutional investor. Not only are payments routinely composed of odd amounts of principal and interest, making it difficult to simply round off to the nearest million, but payments are received monthly. Furthermore, the prospect of calling individual mortgage bankers to track down errant checks for those issuers that have no central payment mechanism is less than appealing. Finally, the challenge of negative amortization on GPMs or (Heaven forbid!) of taxation is sufficient to scare off many a would-be buyer.

The pass-through market compensates investors for their trouble by offering relatively high yields in comparison with comparable-quality corporate or government issues. Exhibit 22 is a graph of the yield of U.S. Treasury 8¼ percent due 1990 versus the yield of GNMA 8s, both as GNMA yield and HTG yield (100 percent FHA assumed) since 1975. Both issues are virtually risk-free from a credit point of view, since the GNMAs are government guaranteed. Both have similar coupons and reasonably similar average lives. Yet the difference in yield (using the HTG figures) has averaged 130 basis points and has been as wide as 550 basis points.

There is more to the high yield of GNMAs than mere compensation for difficulties in bookkeeping. High reward in the securities markets almost always spells high risk. All pass-throughs embody five different forms of risk, which are as follows:

1. Market risk.
2. Credit risk.
3. Liquidity risk.
4. Reinvestment risk.
5. Prepayment risk.

Market risk is the risk that the market price of a security may change adversely in the future on either an absolute or a relative basis. As such, market risk embodies the volatility of the security's price as well as the yield relationship, or spread, to other issues. Pass-throughs historically have nearly as much volatility as long-term Treasury bonds, and the spreads in the pass-through market are influenced by traditional factors in the fixed income market as well as external factors, such as housing turnover and mortgage issuance. Thus, the market risk of pass-throughs is relatively high as debt instruments go.

Credit risk, or the risk of default, is not a factor for GNMAs but is a consideration for FHLMC, FNMA, and privately issued pass-throughs. Each issuer must be evaluated much like any other corporate issuer, but for FHLMC and FNMA there are certain indirect

Exhibit 22
Historical Relationship of GNMAs versus Treasuries

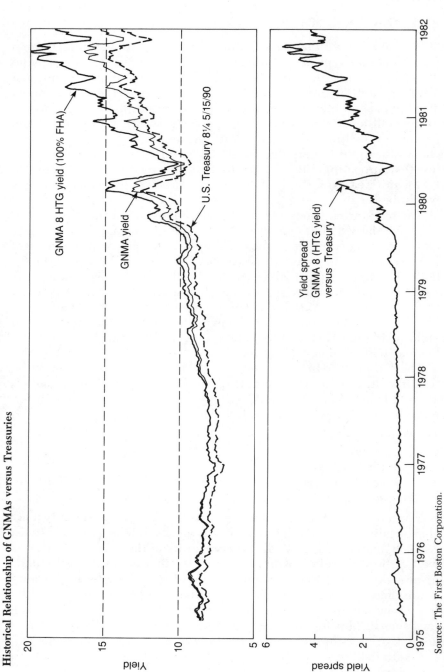

Source: The First Boston Corporation.

government ties that make these analyses somewhat more uncertain. Uncertainty is risk.

Liquidity risk is the risk that an investor may sustain a loss if forced to quickly sell an asset. In the fixed income market, liquidity risk is often quantified in terms of the spread between the bid and offered sides of the market (i.e., the difference between the prices at which dealers will buy and sell the security). Treasury issues are generally the most liquid, with bid-offer spreads ranging from as little as 1/16 of 1 percent or less for short maturities to about one-fourth point on long bonds. GNMAs typically fall in the one fourth to one half point range depending on the particular coupon, and other pass-throughs are in the one half point plus range depending on the issuer. On average, then, liquidity is not as good as for Treasury issues and is sometimes comparable to corporate issues.

Reinvestment risk describes the uncertainty pass-through investors face in being able to put incoming cash flow to work at a favorable rate. Mathematically, one cannot realize a rate of return equal to the yield unless the cash flow can be reinvested at that rate on average. Pass-throughs are not the only securities with reinvestment risk—indeed, most securities have some degree of reinvestment risk. However, pass-throughs do tend to have high degrees of reinvestment risk for two reasons. First, pass-throughs tend to provide much of their return in the early part of their life. More cash flow up front is desirable only when it can be put to work favorably. Thus the pass-throughs' realized returns have a greater dependence on reinvestment potential than do the returns for many other issues. Second, and perhaps more important, is the double-whammy effect in pass-throughs—the fact that prepayments tend to be negatively correlated to interest rates. This means that the investor is most likely to receive the greatest cash flow from a pass-through at precisely the time when reinvestment opportunities are the worst.

Finally, there is prepayment risk, which is unique to the pass-through market. The previous exhibits have demonstrated that yields on pass-throughs can be extremely sensitive to the actual prepayment rate; at the same time, our consistency studies show that historical prepayment rates often do not count for much. Investors demand extra return from pass-throughs, especially those at deep discounts or high premiums, largely to compensate for the uncertainty in yield created by the need to forecast future prepayments.

Obviously any security will look attractive at the right price, and pass-through investors seem to have been rewarded adequately for their risk more often than not. The pass-through market has been and remains the most imperfect of the fixed income markets; it is a market with many possible pitfalls, but at the same time a market with large rewards for those willing to take the trouble to understand it.

Appendix A: Issuers of Pass-Through Securities

GOVERNMENT NATIONAL MORTGAGE ASSOCIATION

The Government National Mortgage Association (GNMA) is a wholly owned U.S. government corporation within the Department of Housing and Urban Development. GNMA is authorized to guarantee the timely payment of principal and interest on securities issued by approved institutions and backed by pools of FHA-insured or VA-guaranteed mortgages. GNMA was created in 1968 as a spin-off from FNMA.

Nickname: GNMA or "Ginnie Mae."

Originators: Mortgage bankers, savings and loan associations, savings banks, and commercial banks.

Servicer: The originator is responsible for servicing and otherwise administering all component mortgages in a pool.

Types of Mortgage Securities Issued:
GNMA Single-Family securities (SF).
GNMA Graduated-Payment Mortgage securities (GPM).
GNMA Mobile Home securities (MH).
GNMA Project Loan securities (PL).
GNMA Buydown securities (BD).
GNMA Construction Loan securities (CL).
GNMA Serial Note securities (SN).

Component Mortgages in General: All mortgages in GNMA pools must be insured under the National Housing Act, guaranteed under Title V of the Housing Act of 1949 or insured or guaranteed under the Servicemen's Readjustment Act of 1944 or Chapter 37 of Title 38, United States Code.

Payments
Frequency: Monthly.
Made by: Originator direct to holder(s) for each pool.
Record date: 30th day of each month.
Cutoff date: 25th day of each month for prepayments.
Prepayment penalties: None.
Interest on prepayments: The holder is due a full 30 days interest at the coupon rate on the unpaid principal balance at the beginning of the month, regardless of any prepayments up to the cutoff date.
Payment delay: Payments due on the 1st of the month are passed through on the 15th day of that month (14-day penalty, 45-day stated delay).

Guarantees: Fully modified. Timely payment of interest and amortized principal is unconditionally guaranteed by GNMA. A decision of a U.S. assistant attorney general on December 9, 1969, states that such guarantees constitute general obligations of the U.S. government and are backed by its full faith and credit.

Insurance: No pool or hazard insurance is used.

Minimum Pool Size: $1 million for SF and GPM securities, $.5 million for other types.

Form and Denomination: Fully registered, $25,000 minimum, $5,000 increments thereafter. For pools with odd principal amounts, one certificate per pool may reflect such odd amount, but this certificate must still be for at least $25,000.

Transfer: Certificates are freely and fully transferable. Transfer agent is Chemical Bank in New York.

How Issued: Originator obtains commitment from GNMA to guarantee a pool of mortgages. Upon completion of such pool, a GNMA certificate is issued, and the originator is free to sell it.

Geographic Distribution: Narrow. Most pools contain 50 mortgages or fewer from one originator, so pools tend to be highly regionalized.

Comment: GNMA was the first pass-through issuer, is certainly the largest issuer, and offers the only mortgage securities that are government guaranteed. Questions on specific pools or on the programs in general should be referred to GNMA in Washington at (202) 755–5926.

GNMA Single-Family (SF) Pass-Throughs

Component Mortgages: Single-family, level-payment loans insured by FHA or guaranteed by VA or the Farmers Home Administration (FmHA). VA guarantees must cover at least 25 percent of the property value. FmHA-guaranteed loans must be made under the Section 502 (Guaranteed Single-Family Rural Housing) Program, and only the fully guaranteed loan portions may be included. Each pool must contain at least 12 loans, and no loan may represent more than 10 percent of the original principal amount.

Maturity: Mortgages may have any maturity allowable under the various FHA, VA, and FmHa programs eligible for inclusion, but at least 90 percent of the loans must have a minimum of 20 years to maturity originally. Most GNMA SF pools contain 30-year mortgages. All loans must be pooled within one year of origination. Maturity of the pool is stated to be that of the longest component mortgage.

Interest Rate: Mortgages all carry interest rates 0.5 percent higher than the stated coupon rate on the security. From this .5 percent, 44 basis points go to the servicer as a servicing fee, and 6 basis points go to GNMA as a guarantee fee.

Yield Calculation: Assumes 30-year maturity, 12-year prepayment, 0.5 percent servicing fee, 45-day delay.

Securities Outstanding: As of January 1, 1982, there were approximately 45,200 pools representing $116 billion original principal amount and $95 billion outstanding principal amount. The table below summarizes data for certain of the more common coupons.

SF Coupon	Approximate Total Pools	Approximate Amount Issued ($ billions)	Approximate Amount Outstanding as of 1/1/82 ($ billions)
6½	1,271	$ 5.27	$ 2.56
7¼	873	3.40	2.24
7½	4,394	10.26	7.69
8	10,369	25.61	18.60
8¼	2,346	4.85	3.71
8½	2,696	5.29	3.98
9	6,479	16.75	14.76
9½	3,745	11.28	10.69
10	1,138	2.86	2.75
11	3,458	9.37	8.93
11½	1,155	2.64	2.54
12½	2,186	4.95	4.76
13	1,284	3.16	3.06
13½	941	1.99	1.84
14	477	1.11	1.09
15	958	2.37	2.31
16	440	0.94	0.90
17	253	1.46	1.45

Comment: GNMA Single-Families, often called regular GNMAs, are the premier mortgage security and constitute 80 percent of the pass-through market. They are highly liquid and are the only mortgage securities with an established futures market. There should shortly be listed options on them as well.

GNMA Graduated-Payment Mortgage (GPM) Pass-Throughs

Component Mortgages: Graduated-Payment Mortgages insured by FHA under Section 245 of the National Housing Act, which call for graduations in each of the first 5 years only. At present, there are three such GPM plans, which have payments that increase either 2.5 percent, 5 percent or 7.5 percent annually. More than 80 percent of all GNMA GPM mortgages have the 7.5 percent graduation rate.

Maturity: Mortgages have 30-year original terms and must be pooled within one year of origination. Maturity of pool stated to be that of the longest component mortgage.

Interest Rate: Mortgages all carry interest rates 0.5 percent higher than the stated coupon rate on the security. From this 0.5 percent, 44 basis points go to the servicer as a servicing fee, and 6 basis points go to GNMA as a guarantee fee.

Yield Calculation: Assumes 30-year maturity, 12-year prepayment, 0.5 percent servicing fee, 45-day delay, 5-year graduation period, 7.5 percent graduation rate.

Securities Outstanding: As of January 1, 1982, there were approximately 3,400 pools representing $6 billion original principal amount and $6 billion outstanding principal amount. The table below summarizes data for certain of the more common coupons.

GPM Coupon	Aproximate Total Pools	Approximate Amount Issued ($ billions)	Approximate Amount Outstanding as of 1/1/82 ($ billions)
9	103	$0.32	$0.30
9½	683	1.44	1.45
10	195	0.33	0.33
11	663	1.17	1.16
12	165	0.27	0.27
12½	263	0.43	0.43
13	246	0.39	0.38
13½	409	0.62	0.62
14	120	0.19	0.19
14½	109	0.20	0.20
15½	219	0.36	0.36
16½	93	0.12	0.12
17½	45	0.06	0.05

Comment: GNMA GPMs are a smaller and less liquid market than the SF securities; this plus their complex cash flows and negative amortization features have caused GPMs to trade at higher yields than regular GNMAs. Investors should remember that after five years elapse, a GPM becomes mathematically identical to a regular GNMA.

GNMA Mobile Home (MH) Pass-throughs

Component Mortgages: Loans secured by mobile homes or by "combination" mobile home units and developed lots. For VA-guaranteed loans, the amount of the guarantee must be at least 50 percent of the loan balance at the time it is placed in the pool (except 35 percent for combination loans).

Maturity: Mortgage maturities may be mixed in a pool—provided that at least 50 percent of the component mortgages have an original term equal to the longest original term in the pool and that the shortest original term is within 60 months of the longest original term. Combination loans have minimum original terms of 18 years. Stated maturity is that of the longest component mortgage. Mobile Home securities are classified into four types depending on the longest original term to maturity:

Type A: 12 years
     B: 15 years
     C: 18 years
     D: 20 years

Interest Rate: Mortgages may carry mixed interest rates but must all produce the same coupon rate when netted of servicing. The servicing percentage may run from 3 to 3½ percent on FHA-insured loans and from 2¾ to 3¼ percent on VA-guaranteed loans, except for combination loans for which these ranges are 0.5 percent lower. From the servicing fee, GNMA receives a guarantee fee of 0.3 percent.

Yield Calculation: Assumes 2½ percent servicing fee and 45-day delay. Maturity and prepayment assumptions depend on security type, as follows:

Type A: 12-year maturity,   5-year prepayment
     B: 15-year maturity,   7-year prepayment
     C: 18-year maturity,   9-year prepayment
     D: 20-year maturity, 10-year prepayment

Securities Outstanding: As of January 1, 1982, there were approximately 2,100 pools representing $2.1 billion original principal amount and $1.7 billion outstanding principal amount. Of the pools outstanding, more than 85 percent are type B, and the bulk of the remainder are type A. The table below summarizes data for some of the more common coupons.

MH Coupon	Approximate Total Pools	Approximate Amount Issued ($ millions)	Approximate Amount Outstanding as of 1/1/82 ($ millions)
6	106	$ 79	$ 21
8½	217	242	177
8¾	477	431	342
9¼	156	157	134
9½	187	180	97
10¼	115	103	90
11¼	91	87	81
11¾	61	52	50
12¼	176	144	136
13¾	183	193	187
14¾	143	171	167
15¾	61	56	55

Comment: Despite the relatively small size of the Mobile Home GNMA program, these securities enjoy a great deal of popularity among longer term investors due to their high rate of prepayments, which has been less affected by the housing crunch and tight credit conditions than other pass-through sectors.

GNMA Project Loan (PL) Pass-throughs

Component Mortgages: Each Project Loan pool consists of one mortgage with an original balance of at least $500,000 and insured by FHA under any section of the National Housing Act except Title X and Section 244.

Maturity: No specific restrictions, although most mortgages carry 40-year original maturities. Loans must be pooled within one year of origination.

Interest Rate: The coupon rate on the security is set 0.25 percent below the mortgage rate. From this 0.25 percent, GNMA receives between 0.1 percent and 0.2 percent as a guarantee fee (depending on initial balance), and the remainder constitutes the servicing fee.

Yield Calculations: Assumes 40-year maturity, 20-year prepayment, 0.25 percent servicing fee and 45-day delay.

Securities Outstanding: As of January 1982 there were roughly 583 Project Loan pools representing $2.9 billion original principal amount and $2.6 billion outstanding. Only 7 coupons have 10 or more pools outstanding; these are summarized in the table below.

PL Coupon	Approximate Total Pools	Approximate Amount Issued ($ millions)	Approximate Amount Outstanding as of 1/1/82 ($ millions)
8.00%	11	$ 71	$ 68
8.15	23	64	58
8.20	20	221	161
8.25	117	550	514
8.50	32	125	114
8.75	126	626	577
9.25	72	253	233

Other GNMA Pass-through Programs

There are three additional GNMA pass-through security programs, but they are less known by investors due to their small size. The first of these is the GNMA Construction Loan (CL) pool, which is a loan made to a project developer and which eventually becomes a GNMA Project Loan. Second is the Serial Note (SN) program, in which pools of at least $5 million of single-family mortgages are used to collateralize 200 consecutively numbered notes. Each note pays a guaranteed rate of interest, but principal payments from the pool are used to retire the notes in sequence. Finally, there is the GNMA Buydown (BD) security, whose component mortgages provide for level debt service to the mortgage lender but for which the borrower's payments are subsidized by funds drawn from an escrow account (same arrangement as PAM loans). The following table indicates the size of these programs as of January 1982.

GNMA Program	Approximate Total Pools	Approximate Amount Issued as of 1/1/82 ($ billions)
Construction Loan (CL)	171	$1.257
Serial Note (SN)	28	0.014
Buydown (BD)	43	0.048

FEDERAL HOME LOAN MORTGAGE CORPORATION

The Federal Home Loan Mortgage Corporation (FHLMC) is a corporate instrumentality of the United States and was created by Congress in 1970 for the purpose of increasing the availability of mortgage credit for housing. Its stock is owned by the 12 Federal Home Loan Banks.

Nickname: FHLMC, or "Freddie Mac."

Originators: FHLMC may purchase mortgages from any Federal Home Loan Bank, the Federal Savings and Loan Insurance Corporation, a member of any Federal Home Loan Bank, any financial institution whose deposits or accounts are insured by an agency of the United States, certain institutions whose accounts are insured under state law, and any mortgage approved by the Secretary of HUD for participation in any mortgage insurance program under the National Housing Act.

Servicer: Sellers of mortgages to FHLMC agree to service such loans under FHLMC's supervision. Subject to FHLMC approval, servicing may be contracted to other eligible sellers or to servicing agents not eligible to sell to FHLMC.

Types of Mortgage Securities Issued:
  FHLMC Participation Certificates (PC).
  FHLMC Guarantor Program Participation Certificates.
  FHLMC Guaranteed Mortgage Certificates (GMC).
Payments: (except for GMCs).
  Frequency: monthly.
  Made by: FHLMC. One check per holder with itemized statement regardless of number of pools or certificates held.
  Record date: last day of each month.
  Cutoff date: Each month's pool factor is based on an estimated level

of prepayment activity and is published on the 25th day of the preceding month. Actual prepayment data through the 20th day of the second preceding month are used in this computation. Should future data show that an estimated factor was too low or too high, subsequent principal payments are adjusted to compensate for such error.

Prepayment Penalties: passed through to security holders.

Interest on prepayments: The holder is due a full 30 days interest at the coupon rate on the unpaid principal balance at the beginning of the month, regardless of any prepayments during the month.

Payment delay: Payments due on the first of a month are passed through on the 15th day of the next month (44-day penalty, 75-day stated delay).

Guarantees: Modified pass-through. Timely payment of interest is guaranteed by FHLMC. Principal is passed through as collected, and FHLMC guarantees payment of all principal no later than one year after it becomes payable. These guarantees do not constitute a debt or obligation of the United States or any Federal Home Loan Bank.

Insurance: No pool or hazard insurance is used. Mortgage insurance is required on loans purchased by FHLMC whose LTV ratios exceed 80 percent. (This insurance must be sufficient to reduce liability to 75 percent of appraised value.)

Minimum Pool Size: $100 million, except for guarantor program PCs, which must be at least $5 million.

Form and Denomination: Fully registered, in denominations of $25,000, $100,000, $200,000, $500,000, $1 million and $5 million.

Transfer: Freely transferable. Transfer agent is Chemical Bank in New York.

How Issued: In its regular PC program, FHLMC purchases mortgages from eligible sellers in weekly auctions. These mortgages may be held in the FHLMC portfolio or put into pools and sold as PCs in weekly auctions directly or through a dealer group. In the guarantor program, FHLMC swaps a certificate for mortgages directly with the mortgage originator, who is then free to sell the PC.

Geographic Distribution: Regular PC pools consist of mortgages from FHLMC's entire national portfolio. Although FHLMC tends to purchase mortgages more heavily in certain parts of the country, the pools are generally broad based geographically and contain thousands of loans. Guarantor program PCs, though, are smaller and usually concentrated with a single mortgage originator.

Comment: FHLMC is the second largest pass-through issuer and was the first to offer pools containing conventional mortgages. Prepayments are more consistent than GNMAs due to larger pool sizes. Itemized statement and single monthly check appeals to institutional investors. Information on pools, paydowns, and the PC program in general can be obtained from the FHLMC Marketing Department in Washington at (202) 789–4900. Securities tend to yield more than GNMAs due to lack of government guarantee.

FHLMC Participation Certificates

Component Mortgages: Each pool consists of whole loans and/or participations in loans. At least 95 percent of a pool consists of mortgages on 1–4 family dwellings. At least 97.5 percent of the loans are traditional (fixed-payment) loans. Maximum loan size for single-family mortgages is $75,000 for LTV ratios between 90 percent and 95 percent and $93,750 for those with an LTV ratio of 90 percent or less. (Higher amounts are allowed for Alaska and Hawaii.)

Maturity: Maximum maturity of PC mortgages is 30 years, and loans are generally pooled within one year from purchase. FHLMC can purchase conventional loans more than one year old only if the seller is engaged in mortgage lending or investing and only to the extent of 20 percent of the total conventional portfolio. In practice more than 95 percent of all conventional loan purchases are less than one-year old. Stated maturity is that of the longest component mortgage.

Interest Rate: Mortgage interest rates may be mixed in a pool. Mortgage rates must be higher than the coupon rate except when FHLMC retains an interest in the loan sufficient to pay PC holders any difference between mortgage rate and coupon rate from its own proceeds. The seller/servicer of each mortgage retains a minimum three eighths of 1 percent servicing fee, and any remaining excess of mortgage rate over coupon rate is kept by FHLMC.

Yield Calculation: Assumes 30-year maturity, 12-year prepayment, no servicing fee, and 75-day delay.

Securities Outstanding: As of January 1, 1982, there were approximately 232 PCs outstanding, of which 74 were guarantor program PCs. Total amount issued is roughly $19 billion with roughly $15 billion still outstanding. Only six coupons have more than $1 billion outstanding, as follows:

PC Coupon	Approximate Total Pools	Approximate Amount Issued ($ billions)	Approximate Amount Outstanding as of 1/1/82 ($ billions)
8	56	$2.7	$1.7
8¼	12	2.1	1.4
8½	17	1.8	1.3
8¾	10	1.4	1.1
9¼	9	1.3	1.1
10	27	1.8	1.7

Comment: In addition to its PC programs, FHLMC also offers guaranteed mortgage certificates, or GMCs. The GMC is not a pass-through security, but a corporate bond with semiannual payments of interest and annual principal payments. Each of the 14 outstanding GMCs has a minimum principal reduction schedule, with the provision that if the mortgage pool that collateralizes the GMC should experience prepayments in excess of the minimum guaranteed payment, FHLMC will pass through such excess. The GMC program has been small relative to PCs ($3 billion issued), and FHLMC·has not issued any GMCs since 1979.

FEDERAL NATIONAL MORTGAGE ASSOCIATION

The Federal National Mortgage Association (FNMA) is a government-sponsored corporation owned entirely by private stockholders. It is subject to regulation by the Secretary of Housing and Urban Development. It was originally chartered in 1938, and in 1968 it was partitioned into two corporations—the privately owned FNMA as it is today and the government-owned GNMA. FNMA was originally authorized to render assistance to the secondary market in federally guaranteed or insured mortgages, but as of 1970 FNMA has also been empowered (subject to HUD approval) to buy, sell, service, and issue debt backed by conventional mortgages as well.

Nickname: FNMA or "Fannie Mae."

Originators: FNMA purchases mortgages from a list of approved seller/servicers, including state and federally chartered savings and loan associations, mutual savings banks, commercial banks, credit unions, and similar institutions whose deposits or accounts are insured by the FDIC, FSLIC, or the National Credit Union Administration. FNMA may also determine other institutions, such as mortgage bankers, to be eligible on an individual basis by examining their mortgage origination experience, servicing experience, and financial capacity.

Servicer: FNMA is responsible for servicing its mortgages but is permitted to contract servicing to the originator or other eligible servicer under FNMA's supervision.

Types of Mortgage Securities Issued
Guaranteed mortgage pass-through certificates.

Payments:
Frequency: monthly.
Made by: FNMA. One check per holder with itemized statement regardless of number of pools or certificates held. Central paying agent is Chemical Bank in New York.
Record date: last day of each month.
Cutoff date: Two possible cases. Most loans in a pool do not come

from the FNMA portfolio, and for these the prepayment cutoff
date is anywhere from the 25th to the last day of the month preceding payment. Loans that do come from the portfolio have a
cutoff date of the end of the second month preceding payment.

Prepayment penalties: The holder is due a full 30 days interest at
the coupon rate on the unpaid principal balance at the beginning
of the month, regardless of any prepayments during the month.

Payment delay: Payments due on the first of a month are passed
through on the 25th day of that month (24-day penalty, 55-day
stated delay.)

Guarantees: Fully modified pass-through. FNMA guarantees timely
payment of principal and interest whether or not collected. These
guarantees do not constitute a debt or obligation of the United
States.

Insurance: No pool or hazard insurance is used. Mortgage insurance is
required for mortgages with LTV ratios in excess of 80 percent. (The
insurance must be sufficient to reduce liability to 75 percent of
appraised value.)

Minimum Pool Size: $1 million.

Form and Denomination: Fully registered only, minimum denomination $25,000 original principal amount. There are no restrictions as
to increments above this minimum.

Transfer: Freely transferable. Transfer agent is Chemical Bank in
New York.

How Issued: Several possibilities. While FNMA is the issuer of the
security, sales may be direct from the originator of the pool to the
investor. FNMA may contribute loans from its portfolio to a pool.
Where more than one originator is involved, a pool may be offered
through a dealer group.

Geographic Distribution: Variable. This will depend on the size of
the pool and the number of originators. The first FNMA security
had a pool of $250 million face amount and contained mortgages
from 25 states.

Component Mortgages: Each pool consists of level-payment mortgages on single-family or 2–4 family residential property. The maximum loan size for single-family property is $98,500, except in
Alaska and Hawaii where it is $147,500. Mortgages must either be
due on sale of the property, or the originator must provide FNMA
the option to force repayment at the end of seven years. For underwritten pools, FNMA provides a prospectus supplement detailing
the location of mortgaged properties, and the average size and term
of the loans.

Maturity: Substantially all component mortgages have 30-year original maturities and at least 20 years remaining term. The first FNMA

offering of $250 million had loans averaging four years old. Stated maturity is that of the longest component mortgage.

Interest Rate: Mortgage rates may be mixed in a pool. All component mortgages must have interest rates from 0.5 percent to 2.5 percent higher than the coupon rate. Any difference between the mortgage and coupon rates is kept by the seller/servicer, from which a 0.25 percent fee will be paid to FNMA. The first FNMA offering consisted of mortgages averaging 1.33 percent higher than the coupon rate.

Yield Calculation: Assumes 30-year maturity, 12-year prepayment, no servicing fee, 55-day delay.

Securities Outstanding: As of January 1, 1982, there was only one pool issued for $250 million. It carried a coupon of 8.5 percent and was backed by mortgages with an average 9.88 percent interest rate and 26 years to maturity.

Comment: FNMA is the newest pass-through issuer and offers a security similar in many respects to FHLMC PCs. The distinguishing feature of the FNMA pass-through has been its low coupon rate and discount price, which in conjunction with its older mortgages produces attractive HTG yields to investors with moderately bullish expectations on future prepayments.

PRIVATELY ISSUED PASS-THROUGHS

As of the end of 1981, a half dozen banks and mortgage bankers had publicly offered pass-through certificates backed by pools of mortgages they had originated. These pass-throughs are known collec-

Issuer	Coupon	Amount Offered ($ millions)	Year(s) Offered
Bank of America.............................	8⅜	$150	1977
	9	346	1978
	9½	316	1978–79
	10½	27	1979
	11⅞	102	1980
	12	50	1980
First Federal Savings and Loan of Chicago.....	8¾	100	1977
Home Savings and Loan Association of California	VRM	307	1978–79
Glandale Federal Savings and Loan Association................................	9⅛	100	1978
	11	61	1980
Washington Mutual Savings Bank	9	50	1978
PMI Mortgage Corporation...................	10¼	27	1979
Total 27 separate issues		$1.636 billion issued	

tively as Connie Macs. In general, Connie Macs are backed by 30-year traditional loans, although Home Savings and Loan Association is the only issuer to offer pass-throughs backed by variable rate mortgages. Mortgage pool and hazard insurance is typically used to compensate for the lack of any direct payment guarantees. Specific information on each type of security should be obtained from a prospectus or offering circular. For yield calculations, Connie Macs assume a 30-year maturity, 12-year prepayment, three eights of 1 percent servicing fee, and 55-day delay. A brief summary of the securities issued as of January 1982 appears at the bottom of page 525.

Appendix B: Formulas Relating to Mortgages and Pass-Throughs

The following formulas are provided for those who wish to calculate cash flows, average life, or yield for mortgages and pass-throughs. The following symbols are used (variables preceded by an asterisk [*] apply only to GPMs).

C = Coupon rate on security, as a percentage   e.g.,   9.5
S = Servicing fee (total), as a percentage   0.5
D = Stated payment delay, in days   45
P = Security price, as a percentage   80.484
Y = Pass-through yield, as a percentage   12.5
N = Term to maturity, in years   30
M = Term to prepayment, in years   12
$*R$ = Percentage rate of payment graduation   7.5
$*A$ = Number of times payment graduates   5
$*B$ = Number of years between graduations   1

Definitions

Certain variables are now defined in terms of the inputs and/or other variables. We use lowercase letters to denote basic quantities (such as conversions of annual percentages to monthly decimals) and uppercase letters for more abstract quantities. (Again, asterisks denote variables necessary only for GPMs.)

$$i = \frac{C + S}{1200} \qquad n = 12N \qquad *r = \frac{R}{100}$$

$$s = \frac{S}{1200} \qquad m = 12M \qquad *a = A$$

$$y = \frac{Y}{1200} \qquad d = (1 + y)^{\frac{D-31}{30}} \qquad *b = 12B$$

$$F = \frac{1 + i}{1 + y}$$

$$*K = \frac{(1 + y)^b - 1}{y}$$

$$*U = (1 + i)^m$$

$$*G = \frac{1 + r}{(1 + y)^b}$$

$$*L = (1 + r)^a$$

$$*V = (1 + i)^{ab}$$

$$*H = \frac{G^a - 1}{G - 1}$$

$$*Q = \frac{1 + r}{(1 + i)^b}$$

$$W = (1 + y)^m$$

$$*J = \frac{(1 + i)^b - 1}{i}$$

$$T = (1 + i)^n$$

$$*Z = (1 + y)^{ab}$$

Formulas

1. Monthly mortgage payment.

    Let X = monthly payment per \$1 original mortgage amount. This formula applies only to traditional (level-payment) mortgages. For the formula on GPMs (initial payment only) see formula 5.

$$X = \frac{iT}{T - 1}$$

2. Mortgage balance.

    Let X = amount of mortgage remaining after k months per \$1 original mortgage amount (traditional mortgage only).

$$X = \frac{T - (1 + i)^k}{T - 1}$$

3. Principal payment.

    Let X = amount of principal paid in month k per \$1 original mortgage amount (traditional mortgage only).

$$X = \frac{i(1 + i)^{k-1}}{T - 1}$$

4. Interest payment.

    Let X = amount of interest paid in month k per \$1 original mortgage amount (traditional mortgage only).

$$X = \frac{i[T - (1 + i)^{k-1}]}{T - 1}$$

5. Mortgage yield.

    a. Yield to price for non-GPMs.

$$P = \frac{100}{d(T - 1)} \left[\frac{T(i - s)(W - 1)}{yW} + \frac{s}{1 + y} \left(\frac{F^m - 1}{F - 1} \right) + \frac{T}{W} - F^m \right]$$

Special cases:

(1)   If $y = i - s$, then $P = \dfrac{100}{d}$.

(2)   If $y = i$, then $F = 1$. Substitute the value m in place of $(F^m - 1)/(F - 1)$ in the formula to avoid division by zero.

(3)   If $y = 0$, then substitute m for $(W - 1)/y$ in the formula to avoid division by zero.

(4)   If $i = 0$, then $P = \dfrac{100}{dn}\left[\dfrac{W - 1 + y(n - m)}{yW}\right]$.

b.   Yield to price for GPMs.

For the sake of simplicity, we define four more quantities X, E_1, E_2, and E_3. The price is then computed in terms of these. For those who might be interested, X is the initial GPM monthly payment (per \$1 principal), E_1 is the portion of the price attributable to gross principal and interest, E_2 is the value of servicing (to be subtracted out), and E_3 is the value of the residual security after m months. Note: This formula is valid only for the case in which the security is prepaid after all graduations have taken place ($m \geq ab$).

$$X = \dfrac{iV}{V + L + \dfrac{iLJ - rV}{1 + r - (1 + i)^b} - \dfrac{LV}{T}}$$

$$E_1 = \dfrac{XKH}{(1 + y)^b}$$

$$E_2 = \dfrac{sE_1}{i} + \left[\dfrac{s(F^b - 1)}{(1 + y)(F - 1)}\right] \times$$

$$\left[\dfrac{F^{ab} - 1}{F^b - 1} + \dfrac{XQJ}{(1 + r)(Q - 1)}\left(\dfrac{F^{ab} - 1}{F^b - 1} - H\right) - \dfrac{XH}{i}\right]$$

$$E_3 = \left[\dfrac{V}{T - V}\right] \times \left[1 - \dfrac{XJ(Q^a - 1)}{(Q - 1)(1 + i)^b}\right] \times$$

$$\left[\dfrac{(i - s)T(W - Z)}{yWZ} + \dfrac{s(F^m - F^{ab})}{(1 + y)(F - 1)} + \dfrac{T - U}{W}\right]$$

Now $P = \dfrac{100}{d}(E_1 - E_2 + E_3)$

Special cases:

(1)   If $y = i - s$, then $P = \dfrac{100}{d}$.

(2)   If $y = i$, three substitutions are necessary to avoid division by zero, as follows:

Replace	With	In Definition of
$\dfrac{F^b - 1}{F - 1}$	b	E_2
$\dfrac{F^{ab} - 1}{F^b - 1}$	a	E_2
$\dfrac{F^m - F^{ab}}{F - 1}$	$m - ab$	E_3

(3)   If r and i have values such that $1 + r = (1 + i)^b$, then $Q = 1$ and two substitutions are necessary to avoid division by zero, as follows:

Replace	With	In Definition of
$\dfrac{iLJ - rV}{1 + r - (1 + i)^b}$	$L\left(\dfrac{ar}{1 + r} - 1\right)$	X
$\dfrac{XQJ}{(1 + r)(Q - 1)}\left(\dfrac{F^{ab} - 1}{F^b - 1} - H\right)$	$\dfrac{XJ}{(1 + y)^b}\left(\dfrac{G^a - 1 - aG^{a-1}(G - 1)}{(G - 1)^2}\right)$	E_2
$\dfrac{XJ(Q^a - 1)}{(Q - 1)(1 + i)^b}$	$\dfrac{aXJ}{(1 + i)^b}$	E_3

(4)   If *both* $y = i$ and $1 + r = (1 + i)^b$, then in place of

$$\frac{XQJ}{(1 + r)(Q - 1)}\left(\frac{F^{ab} - 1}{F^b - 1} - H\right)$$

in the expression for E_2 substitute

$$\frac{XJa(1 - a)}{2(1 + r)}$$

(5)   If $y = 0$, two substitutions are necessary to avoid division by zero.

Replace	With	In Definition of
K	b	E_1
$\dfrac{(i - s)T(W - Z)}{yWZ}$	$(i - s)T(m - ab)$	E_3

(6)   If $i = 0$, then use the formula

$$P = \frac{100}{d}\left[\frac{rKH}{(1 + y)^b[bL - b + rL(n - ab)]} + \frac{W - Z + yZ(n - m - ab)}{yW(n - ab)}\right]$$

c.   Price to yield computations.
    There is no way to compute a pass-through yield directly from a price, so a technique known as iteration must be used to

estimate the yield via successive approximation. Each yield estimate is converted to a price (based on the foregoing), which is compared to the known price. As an initial (but very crude) approximation with which to begin the process one can use

$$Y = \frac{2C + \dfrac{12(100 + Pd)}{5M}}{1 + \dfrac{Pd}{100}}$$

The second approximation can be taken as some small difference from the first one. Now suppose we have two yield approximations, Y_1 and Y_2, and prices for each of these, P_1 and P_2, respectively. Then

$$Y = Y_2 + \frac{(Y_1 - Y_2)(P_2 - P)}{P_2 - P_1}$$

This approximation is tested, and if it is not sufficiently close to the known price, the process is repeated until the yield has been determined to the desired degree of accuracy.

d.   Standard assumptions.

Several of the input parameters take on "standard" values for the purposes of computing "street practice" pass-through yields. For non-GPMs, these parameters are servicing fee, payment delay, term to maturity, and term to prepayment. At the present time, the values assumed for various non-GPMs are as follows:

Type of Security	Value to Assume for			
	S	D	N	M
GNMA:				
Single-family	.50	45	30	12
Mobile home, type A	2.50	45	12	5
Mobile home, type B	2.50	45	15	7
Mobile home, type C	2.50	45	18	9
Mobile home, type D	2.50	45	20	10
Project loan	.25	45	40	20
FHLMC—PC	0	75	30	12
FNMA	0	55	30	12
Privately issued (Connie Macs)....	.375	55	30	12

At present, the only GPM security is issued by GNMA. The assumptions for GPMs are the same as for GNMA. Single-family securities plus values of 7.5 for **R**, 5 for **A** and 1 for **B**.

6. Corporate bond equivalent yield.

Let Y be any yield (in percentage terms) computed on the basis of monthly compounding. Then the corporate bond equivalent (CBE) yield for Y is

$$\text{CBE} = \left[\left(1 + \frac{Y}{1200}\right)^6 - 1\right] \times 200$$

7. Parity price.

The Parity Price (PP) for a pass-through security is the price at which the yield (mortgage yield or HTG yield) equals the coupon rate.

$$\text{PP} = \left(1 + \frac{C}{1200}\right)^{\frac{31-D}{30}} \times 100$$

8. Calculation of prepayment rate.

Suppose we want to calculate the prepayment on a pass-through between months m and n ($0 \le m < n$). Let

F_m = pool factor in month m
F_n = pool factor in month n
B_m = mortgage balance (per \$1) in month m
B_n = mortgage balance (per \$1) in month n

(See Formula 2 for a calculation of mortgage balance.)

$$\text{Define } R_m = \frac{F_m}{B_m} \text{ and } R_n = \frac{F_n}{B_n}$$

The decimals R_m and R_n represent the number of mortgages in the pool that have not yet terminated (been prepaid).

a. FHA experience.

Let $\{G_i\}$ represent the fraction of mortgages in a pool expected to survive (not be prepaid) at the beginning of year i. These values are given by the FHA-experience decimal balance table. Now we define for K = 0, 1, . . . , 360.

$$i = \frac{K}{12} \text{ truncated to an integer (i is a year number)}$$

$$j = K - 12i \text{ (j is the month number within the year)}$$

$$g_K = G_i \left(\frac{G_{i+1}}{G_n}\right)^{j/12}.$$

The values $\{g_K\}$ are the values $\{G_i\}$ "filled in" by month; g_K is the predicted amount of mortgages expected to survive K months. Now, the FHA-experience percentage is given by

$$\text{FHA} = \frac{100 \ (\log R_n - \log R_m)}{\log g_n - \log g_m}$$

b. SMM model.

The percentage SMM paydown is given by

$$\text{SMM} = 1 - \left(\frac{R_n}{R_m}\right)^{\frac{1}{n-m}}$$

Among the advantages of the SMM model are its simplicity and the fact that it can be computed for mortgages of any original term to maturity.

9. Prepayment consistency.

Suppose P is a pass-through pool that has been outstanding for K periods ($K \geq 2$). Let Y_i denote the interim prepayment rate in the ith period, $i = 1$ to K. Mean interim prepayment for pool P is

$$M_p = \frac{1}{K} \sum_{i=1}^{K} Y_i$$

Standard deviation of prepayments for pool P is

$$\sigma_p = \left[\frac{1}{K} \sum_{i=1}^{K} (Y_i - M_p)^2\right]^{1/2}$$

Note that prepayment rate (by any model) is never negative in a period. Therefore, the series $\{Y_i | i = 1,K\}$ is a series of K nonnegative numbers with mean M_p. In general, the maximum standard deviation for a series of K nonnegative numbers with mean M_p is the series $\{KM_p, 0, 0, \ldots, 0\}$, where there are $K - 1$ zeros. Define the standard deviation of this series as σ_{max}. Then

$$\sigma_{max} = M_p \sqrt{K - 1}$$

The lumpiness, L, of a series is its standard deviation divided by the maximum possible standard deviation for a nonnegative series with the same number of elements and the same mean. Thus

$$L_p = \frac{\sigma_p}{\sigma_{max}} = \frac{\sigma_p}{M_p \sqrt{K - 1}}$$

Consistency, or C, is given by the formula

$$C_p = \frac{(K - 1) - L_p(K - 2)}{K} \cdot 100$$

What this means is although L_p ranges from 0 to 1, C_p runs from 100 to 0 (respectively), but C_p is bounded by 100/K below and $100(K - 1)/K$ above. Thus, C_p can only approach 0 or 100 as K becomes infinite.

The Historical Performance of Mortgage Securities: 1972–1981*

19

MICHAEL WALDMAN
Vice President
Salomon Brothers Inc

STEVEN P. BAUM Ph.D.
Vice President
Salomon Brothers Inc

The tremendous growth of mortgage pass-through securities in the 1970s, and their acceptance as an investment vehicle by not only thrift institutions, but also by a wide variety of institutional investors, led Salomon Brothers Inc to introduce a total rate-of-return index for these securities in March 1979. This index allows investors to compare the performance of mortgage pass-throughs with alternative fixed income investments and to compare the performance of their pass-through portfolios with the "market average" return. The index covers periods beginning with January 1, 1972, for GNMA pass-throughs, January 1, 1977, for FHLMC PCs, and January 1, 1978, for conventional pass-throughs.[1]

---

* A previous version of this study appeared in the *Mortgage Banker*, October 1980, published in New York by Salomon Brothers Inc. The authors wish to express their appreciation to Lucille Corcione and Donna Gialanella for their assistance in the preparation of this study.

Although the information in this chapter has been obtained from sources which the authors believe to be reliable, Salomon Brothers Inc cannot guarantee its accuracy, and such information may be incomplete or condensed. All opinions and estimates included in this chapter constitute judgment as of this date and are subject to change without notice.

[1] Conventional mortgage pools issued by "private sector" institutions.

The purpose of this chapter is to present the rate-of-return results and to analyze these results over the various market cycles between 1972 and the present. Comparisons are made between the mortgage index and the Salomon Brothers High-Grade Corporate Bond Index, as well as long and 10-year Treasury securities. Finally, some of the relative performance differences within the mortgage pass-through market are discussed.

The results show that the mortgages outperformed the three alternative investments: corporate bonds by 15 percent over the period January 1972 through June 1981; long Treasuries by 24.7 percent over the period September 1974 through June 1981; and 10-year Treasuries by 2.6 percent over the period January 1977 through June 1981.[2] The main reasons for this return advantage of the mortgage pass-throughs are their shorter maturity (versus the corporates and long Treasuries) during a period of generally rising rates, and their higher yield (versus both the long and 10-year Treasuries), especially when the full value of prepayments for discount pass-throughs is taken into account.

THE MORTGAGE PASS-THROUGH INDEX

The mortgage index covers single family GNMA, FHLMC, and conventional mortgage pools. The total return of the mortgage index is made up of three parts: principal return, interest return, and reinvestment return. The principal return component is further divided into price move and the return resulting from the principal paydown (including any prepayments). Since prepayments on mortgages are statistically uncertain, Salomon Brothers maintains a data base of monthly paydowns on all mortgage pass-throughs. Thus, the paydown return over any holding period reflects the actual principal payments on all pools covered by the index. Reinvestment is "back into the market"; that is, each month's payment of principal and interest is reinvested into the pass-through market in amounts weighted by the overall composition of the market that month.

The dimensions of the index are shown in Exhibit 1. The index currently covers about 43,000 pools, representing approximately $128 billion in original face amount. (This is about 90 percent of the total of all outstanding mortgage pass-through pools—the difference arises in large part because the index does not cover "odd coupon" pass-throughs for which there are no regularly available price quotes, or nonsingle-family pass-throughs.)

The index covers GNMAs from the beginning of calendar year 1972. Since paydown figures for GNMAs were not available until

---

[2] The reason for the shorter comparison periods versus the Treasuries is the lack of comparable Treasury issues during the first part of the 1970s.

Exhibit 1
Dimensions of Salomon Brothers Mortgage Pass-through Index ($ billions)

January 1	GNMA	FHLMC	Conventional
1972	$ 2.6	—	—
1973	4.0	—	—
1974	6.2	—	—
1975	9.5	—	—
1976	16.7	—	—
1977	27.2	$ 0.5	—
1978	46.6	5.5	$0.2
1979	59.6	11.1	1.0
1980	69.3	15.0	1.4
1981	98.8	17.3	1.6

March 1972, it was assumed that the paydowns for January and February of that year were at the same rate as in March. With this exception, the mortgage index is based entirely on historical paydowns, prices, and market compositions. FHLMC PCs are first included in the index in January 1977, when FHLMC started using a dealer network to distribute its PCs, thus generating an active secondary market in these securities. The first (private sector) conventional pass-throughs were issued in the fall of 1977; the index picks them up at the start of 1978.

The yearly total returns are summarized in the table below. Although the monthly returns are not shown, we will analyze them in the remainder of this chapter and compare them with those of some other fixed income investments.

	Annual Total Returns			
	GNMA	FHLMC	Conventional	All Mortgage Securities
1972	6.13%	—	—	6.13%
1973	2.55	—	—	2.55
1974	3.85	—	—	3.85
1975	10.39	—	—	10.34
1976	16.32	—	—	16.32
1977	1.53	2.93%	—	1.56
1978	2.19	3.97	1.60%	2.39
1979	0.18	0.06	0.62	0.15
1980	0.42	0.72	0.50	0.52
1981	1.54	−0.89	0.79	1.19

ANALYSIS OF THE RESULTS

A natural starting point for comparisons with the mortgage index is the Salomon Brothers High-Grade Corporate Bond Index, an index similar to the mortgage index, covering long-term AAA and AA utility and industrial bonds. For the period from January 1972 through June 1981, the mortgage index shows a net advantage in total return of 15 percent over the High-Grade Corporate Bond Index (Exhibits 2 and 3). Almost all of this advantage accrued during the market decline years of 1973–1974 and 1978–1980. On the other hand, the bond index significantly outperformed the mortgage index during the rally

Exhibit 2
Historical Returns over Calendar Years

	SB H-G Corporate Bond Index	SB Mortgage Pass-through Index	Advantage of Mortgage Index
1972.............................	7.26%	6.13%	−1.13%
1973.............................	1.14	2.55	1.41
1974.............................	−3.04	3.85	6.89
1975.............................	14.64	10.39	−4.25
1976.............................	18.64	16.32	−2.32
1977.............................	1.70	1.56	−0.14
1978.............................	−0.10	2.39	2.49
1979.............................	−4.18	0.15	4.33
1980.............................	−2.62	0.51	3.13
January–June 1981..............	−3.30	−3.78	−0.48
Entire period*	31.17%	46.17%	15.00%

* All returns result from compounding monthly returns; nonannualized.

Exhibit 3
Historical Returns over Calendar Years

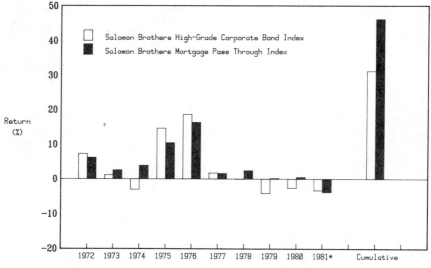

* 1981 returns are for the first half.

years of 1975–1976. An overall widening in yield spreads between the mortgage market and other fixed income securities contributed to a slight return advantage for the corporates in the continuing bear market of the first half of 1981.

That the mortgage index should enjoy an overall advantage during this period is not surprising; the bond index represents an average maturity of approximately 25 years, and mortgage pass-throughs are traded to a 12-year average life. Thus one would expect the (shorter) mortgage index to do better during the significant upward trend in interest rates of the past eight years. Exhibit 4 shows the cumulative

Exhibit 4
Comparative Rate-of-Return Indexes (January 1972–July 1981)

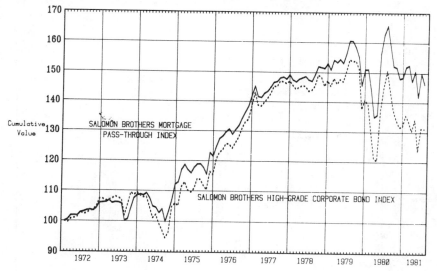

value of the two indexes (January 1, 1972 = 100). Here, one can clearly see the mortgage index gaining its advantage during the bear bond market of 1973–1974—an advantage that it maintains to the present— although it was somewhat narrowed in the 1975–1976 rally.

The performance characteristics of mortgage pass-throughs relative to other fixed income investments can be seen even more clearly when one breaks the period under consideration into market cycles. Exhibits 5 and 6 give the rates-of-return for long Treasury and 10-year Treasury securities, as well as for the mortgage and corporate bond indexes, for eight cycles. (The long rise in interest rates from January 1977 through March 1980 is broken into the periods before and after the Fed initiatives of October 6, 1979.)

The long Treasuries first are analyzed for the rally period starting in

Exhibit 5
Historical Returns over Market Cycles

	Corporate Bond Index	Long Treasuries	10-Year Treasuries	Mortgage Index
Beginning of Month				
January 1972–September '74, decline.....	−5.41%	—	—	−0.05%
September 1974–March '75, rally.........	19.45	14.23%	—	18.80
March 1975–October '75, decline.........	−2.28	−3.17	—	−2.64
October 1975–January '77, rally..........	29.58	26.56	—	25.54
January 1977–October '79, decline	5.69	1.08	4.32%	6.92
October 1979–April '80, decline..........	−20.34	−19.34	−12.63	−12.50
April 1980–July '80, rally	25.05	24.80	18.99	22.15
July 1980–July '81, decline	−12.95	−15.86	−9.50	−11.84
Overall				
9.5 years................................	31.17%			46.17%

Exhibit 6
Historical Returns over Market Cycles

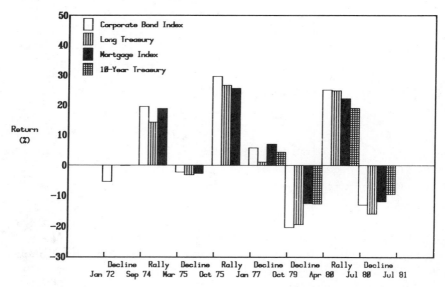

September 1974, shortly after the issuance of the Treasury 8½s of May 15, 1999. The analysis of 10-year Treasuries starts with the cycle beginning in January 1977, about half a year after the 7⅞ percent notes of May 15, 1986, were issued.

COMPARISON VERSUS TREASURY MARKET

Let us focus now on the comparison between mortgage pass-throughs and long Treasury securities in the period September 1974

Exhibit 7
Historical Returns over Market Cycles—Long Treasuries versus Mortgage Securities

Beginning of Month	Long Treasuries	Mortgage Index	Advantage of Mortgage Index
September 1974–March '75, rally	14.23%	18.80%	4.57%
March 1975–October '75, decline	−3.17	−2.63	0.54
October 1975–January '77, rally	26.56	25.54	−1.02
January 1977–October '79, decline	1.08	6.92	5.84
October 1979–April '80, decline	−19.34	−12.50	6.84
April 1980–July '80, rally	24.80	22.15	−2.65
July 1980–July '81, decline.................	−15.86	−11.84	4.02
Overall			
6.8 years	21.55	46.24	24.69

Exhibit 8
Historical Returns over Market Cycles—Long Treasuries versus Mortgage Securities

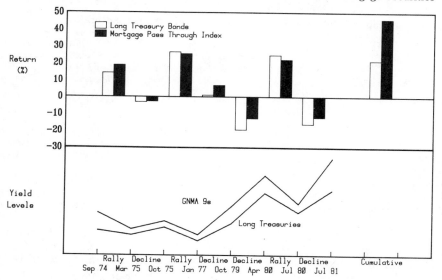

through June 1981 (Exhibits 7 and 8). Over this nearly seven-year period, the mortgage pass-throughs provided a substantial net 24.7 percent greater total return. Again, the mortgage securities were ahead in all the market decline cycles, as would be expected given their much shorter average maturity. However, the pass-throughs also outperformed the long Treasuries in the 1974–1975 rally by a considerable 4.57 percent. How is this explained?

The answer is that there are two important factors determining the relative performance of these securities other than their maturity differences. One is that the mortgages provide a "yield cushion" over the Treasuries, both in quoted yield (and more appropriately for comparisons, its bond equivalent) and even more so when the actual prepayment characteristics (i.e., cash flows) of the pass-throughs in this period are used as the basis for yield calculations. Mortgage pass-through pools have traditionally been quoted to a 12-year prepayment, an assumption that often proved too conservative during the 1970s (though prepayment levels have dropped severely during the 1980–81 housing recession). These faster prepayments can provide a considerable "yield kicker" over the quoted yield for pass-throughs trading at a discount, thereby widening their yield advantage over the Treasuries beyond that which is apparent when simply comparing market quoted yields.

The other main factor influencing the return of the pass-throughs vis-à-vis the long Treasuries is the changing relationship of the yield spread between these two instruments (Exhibit 9). This largely ac-

Exhibit 9
Changing Yield Spread Relationships—Treasuries versus Mortgage Securities

Beginning of Month	Long Treasuries Yield	10-Year Treasuries Yield	GNMA 9s Yield*	Basis-Point Spread of Long Treasuries	Basis-Point Spread of 10-Year Treasuries
September 1974	8.70%	—	9.89%	119 b.p.	—
March 1975	7.83	—	8.38	55	—
October 1975	8.55	—	9.13	58	—
January 1977	7.30	6.79%	7.86	56	107 b.p.
October 1979	9.23	9.42	10.49	126	107
April 1980	12.27	12.60	13.40	113	80
July 1980	9.94	9.98	10.76	82	78
July 1981	13.30	13.84	14.99	169	115

* Mortgage yield to a 12-year life.

counted for the surprisingly strong showing of the mortgage index during the September 1974–March 1975 rally. For this period, the yield spread of the pass-throughs (as represented by GNMA 9s) over the Treasuries narrowed from approximately 119 basis points to 55 basis points. This narrowing, combined with the pass-throughs' natural yield cushion, more than overcame the greater positive price volatility of the longer Treasuries in a rally. Spreads then remained relatively stable until the beginning of 1977. Predictably, the mortgages did better in the two declines in this period; the Treasuries did better in the late 1975–1976 rally. In 1977 the spreads widened to somewhat over 100 basis points again, but the magnitude of the general market decline (again together with the yield cushion) more than offset the effect of the widening spread and still left the pass-throughs well ahead in return.

The "narrowing yield spread" effect could be seen again in the initial sharp drop in interest rates in April 1980. The yield spread between long Treasuries and GNMA 9s collapsed from 113 basis points at the end of March to 41 basis points at the end of April, allowing the mortgage securities (15.06 percent) to outperform the long Treasuries (13 percent) by a substantial margin in April 1980. As in the October 1974–March 1975 rally, yield spreads to the long Treasuries widened in the last stage of the market decline and then snapped down as recession took hold and interest rates fell. Several factors common to both periods contributed to the narrowing in spreads. The yield curve returned to a positive slope, improving the relative position of intermediate issues vis-à-vis longer securities in general. Mortgage supply dried up in a depressed housing market. At the same time, Treasury financing needs increased, and the corporate bond calendar greatly expanded as a result of the lower level of rates. Finally, in both periods, thrift institutions reentered the market as buyers of mortgage securities when their savings flows shifted from negative to positive.

However, under the continuing decline in interest rates in May–June 1980, the higher volatility of the long bonds, along with some widening in yield spreads, resulted in the longer Treasuries outperforming mortgage securities for these months. Overall, long Treasuries had a return of 24.80 percent to the mortgage securities' 22.15 percent for the April–June 1980 rally.

The continuing bear market since July 1980 has seen yield spreads between mortgage instruments and long Treasuries widen to record levels. However, the shorter average maturity of the mortgages has proved to be the dominating force in the long, steep rise in interest rates of the past year, and the return of the mortgage securities (−11.84 percent) was about 400 basis points better than that of the long Treasuries (−15.86 percent) during the period from July 1980 to June 1981.

COMPARISON VERSUS 10-YEAR TREASURIES

Turning our attention to the 10-year Treasuries, we see that over the two market decline cycles from January 1977 through March 1980, the mortgage index had a net return advantage of 2.4 percent (Exhibits 10 and 11). This may be a little unexpected, in view of the fact that the mortgages are traded to a 12-year life and in this sense represent a slightly longer investment than the 10-year Treasuries. However, the sizable yield advantage of the mortgage securities and a slight narrowing in the spread between mortgage investments (again represented by GNMA 9s) and the Treasuries (Exhibit 9) once more predominated, and the pass-throughs provided a higher total return. The April–June 1980 rally saw the mortgages continue to provide a return advantage over the 10-year Treasuries, 22.15 percent to 18.99 percent.

Exhibit 10
Historical Returns over Market Cycles—10-Year Treasuries versus
Mortgage Securities

Beginning of Month	10-Year Treasuries	Mortgage Index	Advantage of Mortgage Index
January 1977–October '79, decline...........	4.32	6.92	2.60
October 1979–April '80, decline.............	−12.63	−12.50	0.13
April 1980–July '80, rally	18.99	22.15	3.16
July 1980–July '81, decline.................	−9.50	−11.84	−2.34
Overall 4.5 years	−1.84	0.72	2.56

Exhibit 11
Historical Returns over Market Cycles—10-Year Treasuries versus Mortgage
Securities

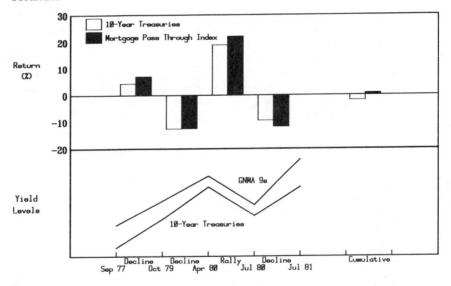

In the July 1980–June 1981 decline, widening yield spreads and the shorter nominal maturity of the Treasuries resulted in a return for the 10-year Treasuries (−9.50 percent), which was 2.34 percent higher than that of the mortgages (−11.84 percent). The spread between GNMA 9s and the 10-year Treasuries widened from 78 to 115 basis points during this period.

PERFORMANCE WITHIN THE MORTGAGE SECURITIES MARKET

In general, the returns of the individual mortgage securities have followed the overall mortgage market returns. However, there have been significant relative performance differences within the market. Exhibit 12 outlines the calendar-year performance record for the three mortgage security categories (GNMAs, FHLMCs, and conventional pass-throughs) and for selected coupon sectors. Particular comparisons over various periods are highlighted below.

GNMA 7½s versus 9s: 1976–1978

	Total Return			Yield Spread Relationship			
	GNMA 7½	GNMA 9	Advantage of 7½s	First of Month	GNMA 7½s Yield	GNMA 9 Yield	Basis Point Spread
1976	17.86%	14.50%	+3.36%	January 1976	8.53%	8.60%	7
1977	0.25	2.71	−2.46	January 1977	7.41	7.86	45
1978	2.43	0.56	+1.87	January 1978	8.46	8.56	10
				January 1979	9.40	9.78	38

As GNMA 9s traded at premium prices in the 1976 rally, they became less attractive to many investors because of the potential losses on prepayments. As a result, prices on 9s rose less than those on the discount GNMAs—they stalled out in the rally. The yield spread versus 7½s widened to 45 basis points at the end of the year, and the 9s underperformed the 7½s by 3.36 percent in total return.

As rates increased in the second half of 1977, the 9s traded closer to par, the yield spread reverted back to a narrower 10 basis points, and the 9s outperformed the 7½s for calendar 1977.

GNMA 9s performed well in the first half of 1978 but deteriorated later in the year. (Overall, the return on 9s was 1.87 percent lower than on 7½s.) A large supply of the 9s became available following the FHA/VA rate change in June 1978, which made the 9s the GNMA current coupon. At the same time, investor interest shifted toward the lower coupons because of a heightened awareness of the value of fast principal paydowns, together with a fear of sluggish performance for the 9s (then the highest GNMA coupon) in a possible rally. Demand for the discounts also derived from standby contracts coming due.

FHLMCs versus GNMAs: 1977–1978

	Total Return			Yield Spread Relationship			
	All GNMAs	All FHLMCs	Advantage of FHLMCs	First of Month	GNMA 8 Yield	FHLMC 8 Yield	Basis Point Spread
1977	1.53%	2.93%	+1.40%	January 1977	7.59%	7.83%	24
1978	2.19	3.97	+1.78	January 1978	8.46	8.60	14
				January 1979	9.43	9.25	−18

Exhibit 12
Returns for Selected Sectors

GNMA Coupon

Year	6½%	7½%	8%	9%	11%	13½%	All
1972	6.63%	—	5.98%	—	—	—	6.13%
1973	2.15	—	3.27	—	—	—	2.55
1974	3.99	—	4.09	—	—	—	3.85
1975	10.38	—	10.18	11.34%	—	—	10.39
1976	18.42	17.86%	15.91	14.50	—	—	16.32
1977	1.12	0.25	1.76	2.71	—	—	1.53
1978	2.29	2.43	2.20	0.56	—	—	2.19
1979	2.17	-0.14	0.12	0.21	—	—	0.18
1980	-2.61	-1.22	-0.66	0.38	1.99%	—	0.42
January-June 1981	-0.21	-3.23	-3.26	-4.89	-4.20	-3.01%	-3.92

FHLMC PC Coupon

Year	8%	8½%	10%	12½%	14¾%	All	Conventional
1977	2.90%	—	—	—	—	2.93%	—
1978	5.12	3.39%	0.41%	—	—	3.97	1.60%
1979	-1.18	-0.17	0.42	4.65%	—	0.06	0.62
1980	-0.52	-0.53	-2.67	-2.31	—	0.65	0.56
January-June 1981	-3.06	-3.35			-1.49	-2.98	-3.41

A dealer group was established to distribute and trade FHLMC PCs in January 1977. Over the following two years, FHLMCs outperformed GNMAs, as shown by the yield spread from GNMA 8s to FHLMC 8s, which narrowed in 1977 and then turned negative in 1978. These yield spread improvements relate primarily to the relationship between the discount sectors rather than the current coupons. A key factor in this development was the recognition of fast FHLMC paydowns, which implied higher yields on discount PCs than represented by the standard yield to 12-year life. This perception tended to raise the prices of discount PCs relative both to GNMAs and current coupon PCs. Also contributing to the strong FHLMC performance over this period were an increase in the FHLMC investor base as the security became more familiar to nontraditional mortgage investors, and a limited supply of discount PCs, which were free to trade because of loss constraints on certain institutional holders (primarily thrifts) of these securities.

Market Decline: First Quarter 1980
(FHLMC current coupon outperformed discount FHLMCs)

	Total Return			Yield Spread Relationship			
	FHLMC 8½	*FHLMC 12½*	*Advantage of 12½s*	*First of Month*	*FHLMC 8½ Yield*	*FHLMC 12½ Yield*	*Basis Point Spread*
January–March 1980	−9.93%	−5.77%	+4.16%	January 1980	11.10%	12.31%	121
				April 1980	13.19	13.85	66

In the market decline in the first quarter of 1980, the FHLMC current coupon 12½s outperformed discount FHLMCs, for example the 8½s, by more than 4 percent.

Two factors contributed to this strong performance. First, principal paydowns fell to low levels in the depressed housing market, thus reducing the attractiveness of the discounts. Second, the high level of rates attracted certain buyers who focused on the highest yielding current-coupon issues. At the same time, the volume of FHLMCs created was extremely low, resulting in a scarcity of the current-coupon issue and in some cases problems in covering shorts.

As the market rallied in April and May, total return investors shifted support to the discounts in the belief that the lower coupon issues would show better price performance. The perception was that issues priced over par would stall out in a rally (as in 1976) because of potential loses on prepayments. Subsequently, the discounts did move further up in price than the high-coupon issues. For example, FHLMC 8½s outperformed FHLMC 12½s by 6 percent in total re-

Market Rally: Second Quarter 1980 (discounts outperformed high-coupon issues)

	Total Return			Yield Spread Relationship			
	GNMA 9	GNMA 12½	Advantage of 9s	First of Month	GNMA 9 Yield	GNMA 12½ Yield	Basis Point Spread
April–June 1980	21.86%	16.12%	5.74%	April 1980 July 1980	13.40% 10.76	13.85% 11.88	45 112
	FHLMC 8½	FHLMC 12½	Advantage of 8½s	First of Month	FHLMC 8½ Yield	FHLMC 12½ Yield	Basis Point Spread
April–June 1980	21.76%	15.79%	5.97%	April 1980 July 1980	13.19% 10.63	13.85% 11.96	66 133

turn. The yield spread between these issues widened by 67 basis points.

The same factors applied in the GNMA market, where the 9s outperformed the 12½s by 5.7 percent. In the earlier part of the rally in April and May, the situation was moderated by a certain amount of demand for the GNMA high-coupon issues. Mortgage bankers bought these issues when they could not create enough loans to cover prior sales. Also, high-coupon GNMAs were used to deliver against futures contracts on the Chicago Board of Trade.

Market Decline: July 1980–June 1981 (high coupons outperformed discount issues)

	Total Return			Yield Spread Relationship			
	GNMA 9	GNMA 13½	Advantage of 13½s	First of Month	GNMA 9 Yield	GNMA 13½ Yield	Basis Point Spread
July 1980–June 1981	−12.71%	−5.20%	7.21%	July 1980 July 1981	10.76% 14.99	12.05% 15.52	131 53
	FHLMC 8½	FHLMC 12½	Advantage of 12½s	First of Month	FHLMC 8½ Yield	FHLMC 12½ Yield	Basis Point Spread
July 1980–June 1981	−12.30%	−6.31%	5.99%	July 1980 July 1981	10.63% 15.03	11.96% 15.65	133 62

Coupon yield spreads narrowed dramatically during the July 1980–June 1981 period, resulting in large return advantages for higher coupon issues versus the deeper discounts, as shown above. The severe housing recession of 1980–81 led to much slower mortgage turnover than had been characteristic of the late 1970s. Accordingly, the market adjusted its average life estimates on the lower coupon issues upward, thus detracting from their relative attractiveness. For instance, the yield spread between GNMA 13½s and GNMA 9s fell from 131 basis points at the beginning of July 1980 to 53 basis points at the beginning of July 1981, and the 13½s had a huge 7.21 percent return advantage over the 9s during this period.

CONCLUSION

Overall, mortgage securities have outperformed each of the other sectors examined (high-grade corporate bonds, long Treasuries, and 10-year Treasuries). As we have seen, the main reasons for this are the shorter average maturity of the mortgages during a period of generally rising rates and the high relative yield levels of the mortgages.

In past market rallies, pass-throughs have shown surprising strength versus longer issues. For instance, narrowing spreads and the "yield cushion" enabled pass-throughs to outperform long Treasuries in both the September 1974–March 1975 rally and in the initial sharp drop in interest rates in April 1980. On the other hand, in the absence of an offsetting narrowing in yield spreads, greater price volatility produced advantages for the longer issues in the October 1975–January 1977 rally and in May–June 1980.

Within the market, the key factors affecting relative performance in the past must have been these: the supply of liquidity of the specific issues or sectors, the preference by total return investors for discounts in a rising market and by thrift institutions for current coupon issues, and the changing perception of the value of prepayments.

In summary, the yield advantage of mortgage securities provides return benefits over the course of time. These investments offer particular advantages in an environment of rising interest rates. In market rallies, long bonds have the advantage of greater price volatility for a given yield move. However, mortgage securities may still provide favorable relative performance if yield spreads narrow sufficiently.

Fixed Income Funds

20   **A. MICHAEL LIPPER, C.F.A.**
Lipper Analytical Services, Inc.

INTRODUCTION

By the time you have reached this point in expanding your knowledge of fixed income securities, you probably have learned the following lessons:

1. Fixed income securities are characterized by reasonably predictable income, known credit quality, and maximum maturity.
2. The price one pays for these features does not guarantee any specific investment return prior to maturity, nor does it guarantee the relative attractiveness of returns under conditions of changing interest rates.
3. There are substantial credit and interest-rate risks inherent in the character of fixed income securities.
4. The opportunity to buy any particular bond at a known price and in reasonable quantity is rare after the initial offering.
5. Collecting and reinvesting interest to produce the fabled interest-on-interest return is a time-consuming bore for many investors who are not organized to perform these functions.
6. Basic to the security of all investments in common-law countries is the ability (and willingness) to assert one's right through legal action, which requires expertise and expense.

However, as is often the case, a lesson is nothing more than an identification of problems, the solution of which requires expert and timely action. Many fixed income investors lack the knowledge, resolve, facilities, and most important the buying power, to bring about an orderly solution to their problems. One alternative for individuals and institutions who have this view is the use of fixed income funds. In this chapter we will examine some of the critical elements of funds for the fixed income investor and the types of fixed income funds.

FIXED INCOME FUNDS IN GENERAL

Because of the expertise required for the intelligent selection and management of a fixed income portfolio, it seemed reasonable to set up fixed income funds. Fixed income funds provide diversity by owning a variety of issues. Each fund provides for the safekeeping of cash and securities, the collection of income either for distribution or reinvestment, and income management. These types of funds have all the indication of ownership including specific legal rights of action.

LEGAL FORMS OF FIXED INCOME INVESTMENT COMPANIES

There are three types of fixed income funds regulated by the Investment Company Act of 1940. All three are subject to regulations prescribed by the Securities and Exchange Commission and to rules of the various states' securities commissions. The distinctions among the three types involve whether the fund has a fixed portfolio of issues and whether it has a fixed number of shares outstanding.

The three types of funds, in terms of their corporate and legal structure, are unit trusts, open-end funds, and closed-end funds. Any one of these types of funds could be the most appropriate for an investor, depending upon the investor's particular requirements. Also, each type of fund has some specific drawbacks in terms of flexibility and exact portfolio focus in terms of maturities, coupons, and quality.

Unit Investment Trusts

Unit investment trusts are fixed portfolios of securities not subject to continuous management. Unit trust portfolios are assembled by an underwriter sponsor, usually a brokerage firm and underwriter of fixed income issues. Upon completion of the sponsors' and fellow unit trust underwriters' selling efforts, the sponsor deposits the portfolio with an independent trustee, usually a bank. The trustee holds these issues until they are redeemed, unless their agreement with the fund requires a sale for some very specific reason, for example, a material downgrade in the issue's credit rating.

The trustee collects the income and remits either to shareholders or to the fund sponsor for reinvestment as directed by the shareholder. Unit trusts have a definite termination date, usually between 6 months and 10 years from the offering date. The principal feature of unit trusts is that they are passive investors with a known and preselected portfolio not subject to subsequent management.

The remaining sections of this and subsequent chapters will not deal further with unit investment trusts. Readers who are interested in learning more about these trusts should contact the sponsors of these trusts: John Nuveen & Co. and Merrill Lynch Pierce, Fenner & Smith, among others, in addition to their regular securities broker.

Open-End Funds

Open-end fixed income mutual funds, including money market instrument funds, as of June 30, 1982, had total net assets of $221 billion. There are three essential characteristics of an open-end mutual fund, which can be summarized as follows:

1. An open-end fund stands ready on any business day to sell and redeem any of its shares. (In contrast, unit trusts or closed-end funds do not sell additional shares after their initial offering.)

2. Most open-end funds employ an investment adviser who is responsible for making appropriate changes in the portfolio. (This produces a changing or dynamic portfolio as compared with the static portfolio of a unit trust.)

3. There is a board of directors for each open-end fund. Except in very rare cases these boards have a majority of directors who are not affiliated with the fund or its adviser. These directors, particularly the outside directors, must annually approve the investment advisory contract and other key arrangements for the fund on behalf of its shareholders. (Unit investment trusts have no such safeguards because many of these continuous problems and potential conflicts of interest apparently do not arise.)

Closed-End Funds

The original type of fund, which began in England after the Napoleonic Wars and in the early stages of the Industrial Revolution, was what we in this country call a closed-end fund. In England, however, they are known as investment trusts.

The closed-end investment company, similar to the unit trust, has an initial offering (occasionally followed by subsequent new securities offerings). Following the offering, however, investors who wish to transact in these shares must find through their brokers a willing counterparty (buyer or seller) in order to consumate a trade. Very often such transactions take place at prices below the current underlying proportionate asset value of the shareholders interest in the portfolio. This proportionate interest in the portfolio is calculated by adding up all the current market value of the portfolio holdings, deducting any liabilities including accrued expenses, and dividing by the number of shares to determine the net asset value per share. Sales below net asset value are said to be at a discount, and sales above net asset value are said to be at a premium.

The reasons closed-end funds often sell at discounts have been subject to extensive study, but there is no general agreement as to the answer. We take the position that the discount is the bargain rate required to entice a buyer to make a purchase. Because most brokers are not interested in the additional work of finding a new buyer, the discount price mechanism must create the inducement. The brokerage commissions charged in such transactions are at the normal rates for equity trades of similar dollar value for the similar type of customer.

SHAREHOLDER SERVICES

The share owner of an investment company share is not only a proportionate owner in the portfolio, but also is recipient of a number of shareholder services imbedded in the ownership rights. Some of these rights are of particular value to a share owner of fixed income funds.

Safekeeping

Most fixed income securities are in bearer form and thus offer opportunities for theft. However, investment companies are required to have independent custodians of securities and cash. Both the custodians, usually major banks, and the registered investment adviser (the investment company's manager) are required to carry fidelity bonds (insurance) at prescribed levels to protect shareholders against losses due to theft, embezzlement, and so on. Fund managements and directors are held responsible for protecting the fund shareholder against frauds or defalcations. Further, the independent auditor is required to physically count the securities belonging to the fund periodically. This in turn, in the case of managed funds, is backed up by a periodic review by the fund's board of directors.

Income Collection

Income collection of interest is an administrative function provided by a fund's custodian included in its charges to the fund. The fund custodian working with an investment adviser is likely to be diligent in efforts to collect at the earliest possible date, permitting immediate reinvestment of these proceeds and producing the highest possible interest-on-interest consistent with the fund's investment policy. In the case of long maturities, interest-on-interest is the largest component of the total return to the bond holder.

Securities and Portfolio Valuations

Information concerning the value of securities and portfolio valuations is another important benefit shareholders in fixed income funds receive. Since fixed income issues are largely traded by dealers in the over-the-counter market, transaction prices are not publicly available, and representative quotations do not reflect true market value, especially in large size. Quite often particular issues of fixed income securities become very inactively traded as long-term holders remove the issue from the dealers' trading inventory. Hence the owner of a portfolio of fixed income securities may have some difficulty in determining the value of holdings before an actual sale.

Without periodic valuation of portfolios, investors cannot compare their results with those of other investors or with relevant standards of performance or, perhaps more important, with other alternative opportunities. Investment companies are skilled in developing valuation studies of their portfolios. In the case of open-end-funds, pricing the portfolio valuation is of particular importance because this determines the price that purchasing and redeeming shareholders pay or receive. Errors are to be avoided at all costs, since they may entail significant commercial and legal risks. Both the fund's independent auditors and the various regulatory authorities periodically check and verify the calculations. Fund directors are held responsible for supervision of the valuation process.

Reports to Shareholders

Reports to shareholders are issued to shareholders periodically. All funds issue them semiannually and annually, and some funds issue them monthly or quarterly. Depending upon the type of fund and type of report, the information provided usually includes the net asset value and income generated by the fund for the period. Other information often provided are a complete portfolio showing current market value (and often historic cost) and a rather complete income statement of the fund. Perhaps the information of greatest value in shareholder reports is the investment adviser's commentary on the performance and characteristics of the portfolio. In some cases the commentary is excellent and can be of material aid to the investor both as an educational device and a guide for investment policy generally.

Information for Tax Reporting

Form 1099 is a report to the Internal Revenue Service issued by each fund in January every year indicating the level of taxable income and its composition for each of its shareholders. A copy is supplied to each shareholder. This is required for preparation of the shareholder's income tax return.

Exchange Privileges

The exchange privilege between one fund and another at zero or nominal cost is an especially valuable service available to shareholders of most funds. Such exchanges are usually, but not always, limited to other funds managed by the same investment adviser but having different investment objectives. Many funds permit such exchanges to be arranged by telephone, subject to prior written authority.

Check-Writing Privilege

Check-writing is a privilege available on many short-term funds. This permits the shareholder to sign a draft payment order for larger bills (typically in excess of $500). For all practical purposes the draft is a check that is processed through normal banking channels and is presented to the fund's custodian bank for payment through an automatic preauthorized redemption procedure. A particular advantage of the check-redemption feature is that the shareholder continues to earn income until the draft is finally presented (i.e., the shareholder is working the "float" rather than the bank).

SOURCES OF INFORMATION ON INVESTMENT COMPANIES

The best sources of information for most purposes are the individual fund report and prospectus (an offering document). Information on no-load funds (funds that do not have a sales charge) should be sought direct from the fund. Most brokerage firms will be happy to provide information on load funds, from which they earn a sales commission.

The No-Load Mutual Fund Association publishes regularly an extensive description, including the addresses and phone numbers of its members, and other sources of information are available.[1]

---

[1] No-Load Mutual Fund Association, Valley Forge, PA 19481, (215) 783-7600. Twice a year the Investment Dealers Digest (212) 227–1200, 150 Broadway, New York 10038, publishes a mutual fund directory with addresses, phone numbers, and other information on funds. Other sources of information include Investment Company Institute, 1775 K Street, Washington, DC 20006; United Mutual Fund Selector, 210 Newbury Street, Boston, MA 02116; Weisenberger Investment Company Services, 210 S. Street, Boston, MA 02111; and Donoghue's Money Fund Report, Holliston, MA 01746.

TYPES OF FIXED INCOME FUNDS

Thus far we have identified funds in terms of their legal and organizational characteristics—unit trusts, open-end funds, and closed-end funds. In this section, we will discuss the various types of long-term funds. In the next section, we will discuss short-term funds that are used for liquidity or short-term reserve functions.

The shareholder usually chooses a fund based on its investment characteristics. The main characteristics of a fund are determined by the type of securities in its portfolio. Other investment characteristics result from the portfolio manager's use of the individual securities and the expenses to the shareholder of producing the expected returns.

Exhibit 1 sets forth the criteria used by Lipper Analytical Services, Inc. to assign a particular fund to an investment objective category. Notice that the criteria reflect particularly the type of issues that represent the bulk of the securities in the portfolios. The criteria for short-term funds are included for completeness; such funds are discussed more completely in the next section.

Uses, Advantages, and Disadvantages of Different Types of Funds

United States Government Funds. These funds should be utilized by investors whose primary objective is absolute highest quality,with virtually no risk of default. Securities of the U.S. government are considered to be the highest credit quality available in the marketplace. This is due to the U.S. government history of no defaults, combined with its virtually unlimited ability to print money. Although there may be theoretical risks associated with U.S. government obligations, very few analysts apply credit analysis to the U.S. government financial status.

Subject only to congressional approval of the debt limit, the government always has the ability to pay. One caveat to remember is that the U.S. government cannot be sued without its permission. Due to the very high perceived quality of U.S. government securities, investors usually accept on U.S. government investments somewhat less yield than available from comparable maturities of the highest quality corporate debt.

Although U.S. government securities pose no credit risk, there is a sizeable interest-rate risk during the life of the investment. Further, the interest is wholly subject to federal income taxes, although exempt from state taxes. These issues are most appropriate for extremely credit-risk-adverse investors, often as a permanent reserve element for the investor's portfolio. The major disadvantage of these funds is their relatively smaller yield compared with portfolios of corporate bonds.

Exhibit 1
Criteria for Assignment of Fixed Income Funds to Investment Objectives

Our assignment of funds to a specific investment objective is often a matter of judgement rather than pin-point precision. When a fund is initially offered, the prospectus' statement of policy and intent are initially used in assigning it to one of the various groups. As the fund matures and develops a clearly discernible investment policy, the intent, practices, and preferences of the fund management become clear and then assume paramount importance in assigning the fund to a specific category. Once assigned, funds are not again changed without clear evidence of further change in the portfolio-management policy. Such change may become more subtly evident from close observation and analysis of changes in the portfolio and the style of management. Our *Lipper Portfolio Analysis Report on Fixed Income Funds* is one of the most useful tools for this purpose. Below are the symbols and definitions we use for each of the fixed income objectives.

Open-End Short-Term Funds

Money Market Instrument Funds—invest in financial instruments with short maturities. In order to be allowed to use amortized prices and/or dollar rounding, funds must have an average weighted maturity of no more than 120 days. Most funds restrict their longest maturity to one year. However, longer maturity issues with shorter term optional maturities of under one year have been used by these funds.

U.S. Government Short-Term Funds—invest in U.S. treasury and agency issues with maturities mostly below one year. Some of these issues may be the underlying security in holdings of repurchase agreements.

Short-Term Municipal Bond Funds—a type of money market instrument fund which invests primarily in tax-exempt securities with the bulk of their maturities below one year.

Open- and Closed-End Long-Term Funds

U.S. Government Funds—invest in U.S. Treasury and agency issues usually not limited as to maturity.

Funds of GNMA Issues—invest in a minimum of 50 percent of their portfolio in Government National Mortgage Association securities.

Corporate Bond Funds, A-Rated—invest 60 percent of their corporate holdings in A-rated issues or better.

Corporate Bond Funds, BBB-Rated—invest 60 percent of their corporate holdings in the top four grades of bonds.

Open and Closed-End Long-Term Funds (Continued)

Corporate Bond Funds BBB/Trading—similar to the BBB funds except their prospectus permits turnover rates in excess of 100 percent.

High Current Yield Funds—managed with an emphasis on high current (relative) yield. There are no quality or maturity restrictions.

General Bond Funds—do not have restrictions other than to keep the bulk of their portfolio in corporate bonds.

Convertible Securities Funds—invest the bulk of their portfolios in convertible bonds and convertible preferred shares.

Private Placement Bond Funds—invest in excess of 25 percent of their portfolio in issues that have been placed privately rather than sold to the public via registered offerings.

Flexible Income Funds—emphasize income generation by investing in bonds, preferreds, convertibles, and/or common stocks with warrants.

General Municipal Bond Funds—invests 60 percent or more of their assets in the top four tax-exempt credit ratings.

Intermediate Municipal Bond Funds—generally restrict their holdings of municipal bonds to those with maturities between 2 and 20 years.

High-Yield Municipal Bond Funds—may utilize lower rated municipal bonds for 50 percent of their portfolio.

Preferred Stock Funds—invest 50 percent or more of their assets in preferred shares.

Source: Lipper Analytical Services, Inc.

Funds of Government National Mortgage Association (GNMA) Issues. GNMA issues are utilized by investors for many of the same reasons that attract investors to other U.S. government issues. The main difference is that GNMA issues are guaranteed by a specific agency of the U.S. government, rather than directly by the Treasury. Second, because they are mortgage bonds, there is amortization of principal during the holding period. Third, when the owners of homes mortgaged under a GNMA mortgage sell their homes prior to the final maturity date of the mortgage, they must pay the remaining principal value of their debt under the mortgage in full. This money is then transmitted to the owner of the mortgage, who receives cash at an earlier date than expected, and this in turn changes the yield to maturity calculations.

The amortization of principal and liquidation of mortgage prior to termination give GNMA mortgages a more rapid return of borrowed funds than other types of fixed income securities. This is an advantage during periods of rising interest rates but a disadvantage in periods of declining rates. As the decision to sell a home and thus repay in full a mortgage is the homeowner's decision, there is no certainty of early repayment. Also, sales may accelerate in periods of easy money, and this may be a disadvantage. From a fund investor's viewpoint, another disadvantage of these funds is that there are only three small funds of this type available.

A-Rated Corporate Bond Funds. A-rated corporate bond funds are invested primarily in high-quality corporate bonds. For investors willing to take some modest credit risk, these funds usually offer somewhat higher yields than funds invested exclusively in government issues. Experience over many years suggests that these funds provide a better strategic reserve element than do government bond funds.

BBB-Rated Corporate Bond Funds. Investors who wish the bulk of their portfolios to be investment-grade issue and can accept some additional credit risk as compared with higher credit-rated bond portfolios may invest in BBB-rated corporate bond funds. In general, these funds have performed better than the A-rated issue funds because of higher interest returns. In portfolios of less than AAA credit, there are the opportunities for the credit ratings to be upgraded, which in turn usually leads to higher prices over the ensuing two years. Any downgrading of credit rating often has an immediate impact of lowering the price of the issues. To take advantage of potential or actual credit upgrades and to avoid potential cuts in credit ratings, these funds experience a higher degree of portfolio trading (turnover) than the A-rated issue funds in general.

BBB/Trading Corporate Bond Fund. In the early part of the 1970s, a number of managers believed that by aggressively trading their portfolios, taking advantage of imperfections in the market, they could add significantly to the total returns of their portfolios. Thus when a number of new closed-end bond funds were launched during this period, their policy statements permitted portfolio turnover rates as high as 100 percent annually. In some markets this can create a worthwhile advantage, but in other markets high turnover has not worked. Generally, the most favorable environment for the BBB/trading funds is a market with gradual interest rate trends and with different portions of the market reacting slowly and at different rates of change.

High Current Yield Funds. When high current income is of primary importance high current yield funds are used. Although entailing high principal risk, such funds might be appropriate for a relatively impoverished individual with little or no other source of taxable income. In the past, a number of these funds were sold by sales people without regard to the risk of principal, which is greater on the high current yield frontier. At times yields that are high relative to others signify perceived additional risk by investors.

General Bond Funds. General bond funds can have strategies and tactics ranging over the whole spectrum of the bond market. This type of fund is appropriate for investors who do not want to restrict their fixed income investment managers.

Convertible Securities Funds. The investment manager of convertible securities invests in hybrid securities that have some characteristics of both fixed income and equity issues. The success of most convertible funds has been attributable to selection of issues convertible into what later proved to be equities that rise in price. In declining equity markets, eventually, convertible issues decline at a slower rate than does common stock in the same company. Most of the time they also go up at a somewhat slower rate.

Private Placement Funds. Private placement funds offer to the investor a chance to participate in a select portfolio of securities that were not offered to the public. Often these issues can have more attractive terms than those available in the public market of similar companies. These advantages may be higher income, stronger covenants, better conversion privileges, warrants, and so on.

Flexible Income Funds. Flexible income funds can select any publicly traded securities that pay an income. Thus they have an even broader field of maneuver than the general bond funds. The key to success for such funds is an ability to balance their attempts between income production and capital preservation.

Municipal Bond Funds. Municipal bond funds come in many different sizes and shapes with the same general breakdowns as corporate bond funds in terms of quality and maturity. We believe our description of the three categories of municipal bond funds are self-explanatory. Municipal bond funds may be broken down into subcategories of short-term funds (which will be discussed later in this chapter with money market funds) and intermediate-term funds (maturities

2 to 20 years). High-yield municipal bond funds may utilize lower rated municipal bonds, and general municipal bond funds keep 60 percent of their assets in the top four tax-exempt credit ratings.

Investors in municipal bond funds should recognize that these funds may have up to 20 percent of their income from taxable sources and still maintain their designation as tax-exempt funds. Therefore investors should examine carefully the portfolios of these funds if there is a desire for nontaxable income.

Investors in tax-exempt securities should remember that inflation attacks their principal at the same rate as it reduces the purchasing power of money invested in taxable securities. With a lower interest rate on tax-exempt securities than available on taxable securities, there is a smaller income earned to offset the deterioration of the principal value caused by inflation. In the past one could not earn a "real" tax-exempt income due to the purchasing power decline of the principal value. In an environment of lower inflation and higher interest rates, one may be able to earn a real inflation-adjusted rate-of-return on tax exempts.

Preferred Stock Funds. Funds specializing in preferred stock are attractive to corporate buyers due to the 85 percent tax exemption feature on intercompany dividends on the portfolio of preferred shares they own. Some of these issues are convertible into common stock.

Exhibit 2
Fixed Income Fund Industry as of June 30, 1982

Type of Funds	Number of Funds*	Total Net Assets ($ millions)
Money market instrument funds	154	$167,598.1
Short-term U.S. government funds	69	32,556.6
Short-term municipal bond funds	30	8,270.4
U.S. government funds	13	225.8
GNMA funds	2	36.2
Corporate bond funds A rated	21	1,960.4
BBB rated	17	1,024.7
BBB rated/trading	16	910.6
General bond funds	12	1,180.7
High-current-yield bond funds	24	3,238.0
Private placement bond funds	6	377.9
Convertible securities funds	6	262.7
Preferred funds	2	29.5
Flexible income funds	26	1,081.5
General municipal bond funds	42	3,475.9
Intermediate-term municipal bond funds	6	134.3
High-yield municipal bond funds	5	783.9
	451	$223,147.2

* Includes both open- and closed-end funds.
Source: Lipper-Fixed Income Fund Performance Analysis.

THE STRUCTURE OF THE FIXED INCOME
FUND INDUSTRY

Exhibit 2 shows the breakdown of the fixed income fund industry in terms of number of funds and total net assets in each category. As of June 30, 1982 there were 45 fixed income funds with total net assets of $223 billion.

SHORT—TERM MONEY MARKET INSTRUMENT FUNDS

Starting in 1971 a new phenomenon hit both the investment company and fixed income scenes—the short-term money market instrument funds. These funds, generally called money funds, offer a combination of cash management (liquidity) services and near money market instrument yields. They make available to small investors the economies and high returns of large-scale money market investment and so have become major competitors to the more traditional savings institutions.[2]

Definitions

Three important elements of the money fund industry should be identified:

1. *General money market instrument funds*—open-end funds that invest in financial instruments with short maturities. In order to

---

[2] In order to compete with savings institutions, the marketers of money market instrument funds convinced the Securities and Exchange Commission that their funds should have a fixed net asset value. Income was to be the only variable similar to the experience in bank accounts in which the principal is nominally level. After considerable discussion and rancor, the fund industry and the Securities and Exchange Commission agreed that if funds followed one of two procedures called penny-rounding or amortized cost, it would permit funds to attempt to keep their net asset value at a predetermined level, normally $1 per share.

Valuing a fund's securities by the amortized cost method means that all of the securities in the fund's portfolio will be valued at their amortized cost. Amortized cost is an approximation of market value determined by systematically increasing the carrying value of a security if acquired at a discount, or systematically reducing the carrying value if acquired at a premium, so that the carrying value is equal to maturity value on the maturity date. It does not take into consideration unrealized capital gains or losses.

A penny-rounding fund's net asset value per share will remain constant if all net income that includes interest and similar plus net changes in the value of the portfolio is declared as a dividend each day and net asset value per share is computed to the nearest penny. The latter procedure prevents any net realized gains or losses on portfolio securities from being reflected in net asset value per share unless their accumulation over time would amount to more than a one-half cent per share variance from the fund's central value of $1 per share. The opportunity for such a sizable accumulation to occur is considered minimal due to the fund's portfolio and valuation policies, including the fund's commitment to maintaining a dollar-weighted average portfolio maturity that does not exceed 120 days.

be allowed to use amortized prices and dollar rounding, funds must have an average weighted maturity of no more than 120 days. Most funds restrict their longest maturity to one year, with average maturities tending to be 30 days or less. However, longer maturity issues with short term optional maturities of under one year have been used by these funds.

2. *U.S. government short-term funds*—open-end funds that invest in U.S. Treasury and agency issues with maturities mostly below one year. Some of these issues may be the underlying security in holdings of repurchase agreements.

3. *Short-term municipal bond funds*—open-end funds that invest largely, if not exclusively, in fixed income securities paying interest exempt from federal income tax. The maturities in the portfolio are normally limited to one year or less. Most of the short-term municipal bond funds are modeled after the money market funds in that they are priced continuously at a fixed price, normally of $1 per share. The Securities and Exchange Commission will grant the request to use penny rounding and/or amortized cost, which in effect keeps the net asset value even, only to those funds which make an undertaking to keep their average maximum maturity of the portfolio under 120 days.

During periods of increasing credit crisis threat, the U.S. government short-term funds tend to attract a major part of the new investment in money funds.

From a beginning in 1971, the money market funds industry has had incredible growth. On Exhibit 3 one can see that by June 30, 1982 the short-term funds (money market funds, short-term U.S. Government funds, and short-term municipal bond funds) had total net assets of $208 billion as compared with total fixed income fund assets (including closed-end funds) total net assets of $223 billion. Notice that there were several distinct periods of growth for the industry. The industry was tiny through 1973; it mushroomed in 1974, grew by 50 percent in 1975, plateaued essentially in 1976 and 1977, tripled in 1978, grew four-fold in 1979, grew by 70 percent in 1980, and another 140 percent in 1981. The pattern established by the money market funds was followed by the short-term U.S. government funds, and at a later date the short-term municipal bond funds. This growth was in response to needs. The principal needs served by money market funds are interest-bearing liquidity accounts and above-average yields.

Usefulness of Money Funds

Development of the money fund industry has proven of great service not only to the small investor (who never or rarely before had access to the high returns and the conveniences offered by the indus-

Exhibit 3
Total Net Assets and Number of Short-Term Funds Compared with Total Universe of Fixed Income Funds

	Money Market Funds		Short-Term U.S. Government Funds		Short-Term Municipal Bond Funds		Total Fixed Income Funds*	
	Total Net Assets ($ millions)	Number of Funds	Total Net Assets ($ millions)	Number of Funds	Total net Assets ($ millions)	Number of Funds	Total Net Assets ($ millions)	Number of Funds
June 30, 1982	$167,598	154	$32,557	69	$8,270	30	$223,147	451
1981	158,904	121	22,893	39	5,223	26	200,260	380
1980	67,157	84	8,143	25	2,161	13	90,672	305
1979	40,686	67	4,243	13	363	5	58,005	254
1978	9,067	50	1,262	7	31	2	22,081	218
1977	3,028	41	559	7	3	2	14,253	190
1976	2,971	34	335	6	—	—	10,992	148
1975	3,156	23	101	5	—	—	8,692	120
1974	2,178	14	27	2	—	—	6,602	105
1973	79	1	2	2	—	—	4,809	83
1972	0	1	0	1	—	—	3,423	63

* Includes closed-end funds.
Source: Lipper—Fixed Income Fund Performance Analysis.

try), but also to large investors, especially institutional, who have become extensive users of money funds. The wide scope of usefulness of these funds is indicated by the following examples:

1. To obtain approximately the money market instrument rate of return, otherwise available only to large institutional investors.
2. To completely avoid the administrative problem of continuously reinvesting maturing instruments.
3. To obtain broad diversification and competent professional screening of credit risks.
4. To keep funds fully and efficiently invested at all times, via the automatic investment of income and the check-writing privileges offered by nearly all money funds.

We believe that these many conveniences and economies have become so widely appreciated that the money fund industry is here to stay in an important way. It probably will retain a major part of its present assets, even when short-term interest rates fall below the NOW account and savings bank rates.

Short-Term Municipal Bond Funds

Due to the success of the original short-term funds, which invested in taxable instruments, funds investing in short-term tax-exempt instruments began to attract the reserve funds of investors in high tax brackets. By mid-1981 the total net assets of the short-term tax-exempt funds was in excess of $3 billion. The annualized yield was about 7 percent, compared with 16 percent for funds investing exclusively in short-term U.S. government funds and 17 percent for other money market instrument funds.

Although the gap between taxable and tax-exempt long-term bond fund yields narrowed considerably in 1981, the spread between taxable and tax-exempt money fund yields remained about 10 percent. In the future we would expect this spread to contract. Part of this change in expected relative yields is that investors are less interested in tax exemption in a period of high inflation and uncertain taxable incomes. In addition, the changes in the tax law in late 1981—the lowering of the maximum tax on all forms of income to 50 percent from 70 percent—considerably reduced the attractiveness of tax-exempt income, even for quite wealthy investors.

Selection of a Money Market Fund

As with any investment, the selection criteria for money market funds must satisfy the primary requirements of the investor. Following are some major elements to be considered in the selection process:

1. *The fund managements's structure, degree of experience, and capabilities.* A breadth of experience in money management and strong research capabilities should be sought. We particularly favor funds equipped to perform their own independent credit research.

2. *Character and scope of the fund's areas of investment.* Investment area may spread broadly across the following alternatives or may be closely limited to a few of them:

   U.S. Treasury
   U.S. government agencies
   Issuers guaranteed by U.S. government
   Foreign governments
   Domestic U.S. banks
   Foreign branches of U.S. banks
   Foreign banks U.S. branches
   Foreign banks' foreign branches
   Bankers Acceptances
   Commercial paper issuers
   State and municipal governments
   Revenue authorities

   The investor may wish to avoid certain of these areas due to quality preferences, tax problems, or for other personal reasons.

3. *The investor's own interest-rate expectations.* This should influence the choice between funds with relatively short or long average maturities. A money fund will provide the investor with the average market yield available over the length of its average maturity, typically less than 60 days, but possibly longer.

4. *The investor's own income tax shelter.* This is of obvious importance in the selection between taxable and nontaxable types of funds. Some close calculations should be made because it is sometimes most economical to chose taxable funds.

5. *The investor's degree of risk tolerance.* There are wide differences in average quality among the funds, with the U.S. government funds unquestioned by most as having the highest quality. The investor who is apprehensive about credit risks should adhere either to U.S. government or to the very highest quality corporate or municipal funds.

6. *Ease of investment and prompt liquidation.* Some funds have ascertainable reputations for back-office foul-ups, due to poor organization and/or to excessively large size. A major purpose of money fund investment is instant liquidity, and the investor should be reassured as to that expectation.

Sources of Information on Money Funds

There are numerous sources of information on money funds. Generally, they fall into three categories—funds, newspapers, and specialized publications. The funds themselves will provide a great deal of historic information in terms of yields, performance, periodic portfolios, policies, and so on. This information is found in prospectuses, and annual and interim reports. Yield information for most funds is usually available on a prerecorded message reached by calling a designated phone number.

Although funds produce primary information about themselves, the funds do not provide comparative information about competitors. *The Wall Street Journal* and other major newspapers at least once a week publish 7-day and 30-day yields plus the number of days of average maturity for each portfolio. These lists are usually for funds with total net assets in excess of $100 million.

A third source of data, specialized publications, includes the following:

Donoghue's Money Fund Report
Box 540
770 Washington Street
Holliston, MA 01746
Money Market Fund Survey
51East 42nd Street
New York, NY 10017
United Mutual Fund Selector
210 Newbury Street
Boston, MA 02116
Wiesenberger Investment Companies Service
870 Seventh Avenue
New York, NY 10019

The first two cover short-term funds exclusively. The second two publications are more general mutual fund publications. (The various Lipper Analytical Services publications are not in general distribution but are utilized exclusively by professional financial organizations (e.g., banks, insurance companies, independent counselors, pension plans.)

Limited Significance of Past Investment Performance and Yields

Money funds investors should recognize that past investment performance and/or yields do not provide a useful means for selecting funds. Although past results may be a useful clue to fund-management expertise under similar future market conditions, it affords no guarantee of future performance, either absolute or relative to other funds or to the market.

The volatility of the money market is so great that today's successful strategy, in terms of instruments and maturities, may well prove wrong for tomorrow's markets.

Investors in short-term funds should not be overly concerned with performance rank of the various funds for two reasons. First, the spread between the highest return fund and the lowest return fund are relatively small as shown in Exhibit 4. Not only are these spreads too

Exhibit 4
Spread in Total Reinvested Returns between the Highest and Lowest Return Short-Term Funds as of June, 1982

	Money Market Funds		Short-Term U.S. Government Funds		Short-Term Municipal Bond Funds	
			One month			
Highest return............	1.34%		1.22%		0.68%	
Lowest return	0.95		0.91		−0.54	
Average	1.12		1.04		0.53	
Number of funds...........		145		58		29
			Three months			
Highest return............	4.97%		3.45%		2.23%	
Lowest return	2.11		2.22		1.55	
Average	3.44		3.22		1.82	
Number of funds...........		134		49		28
			Twelve months			
Highest return............	17.47%		15.20%		8.63%	
Lowest return	14.19		13.52		6.22	
Average	15.48		14.43		7.52	
Number of funds...........		101		25		23

Source: Lipper—Fixed Income Performance Analysis

narrow for investors to give much credence to the ranking, but also the policies that may have led to a performance extreme in one period may be reversed in some subsequent period. An example of this type of reversal is the efficacy of having the shortest possible portfolio versus the longest. Clearly, different portfolio compositions in terms of quality will produce different results.

Some Concluding Remarks About Short-Term Funds

The proliferation of short-term funds and publications that follow them is testimony to their growth and significance. Initially for the investor the choice is whether to continue to leave money where it was or to utilize a short-term fund. In the past the practice of leaving large balances in checking accounts, brokerage accounts, or low-interest savings accounts was acceptable, since there were no perceived alternatives except for the choices available to the very wealthy and financially sophisticated. With the introduction of money funds in which idle money could receive higher interest rates than in savings accounts and could be accessed through a check-writing account, all that has changed. The money fund has probably won a permanent place in the portfolio of most investors. The size of the commitment to money funds will be determined by numerous variables; but not the least of these variables will be the interest rates afforded on the funds compared with other perceived alternatives. We suggest that even if the money funds did not yield a competitive rate, some money would stay in the funds, both for convenience and due to inertia.

For most investors the concern for perceived risk should play a higher role than should maximization of return. As already noted, the spread between the highest and lowest returns is not substantial enough to be the first concern of the investor. The key elements are the interest-rate (maturity) risk and the credit risk. The interest-rate risk (and opportunity) is a function of being locked into a portfolio when the market is moving the other way. For example, assume that the average fund has an average maturity in its portfolio of 20 days, and interest rates begin to rise. A particular fund with an average maturity of 60 days would not be able to take advantage of the higher yielding paper as quickly as could most of the other funds. (If this were an extreme case in which the fund with a 20-day average is small and a significant number of its shareholders redeem to go to higher yielding funds, the small fund might have to sell some of its assets below their portfolio value. If that were to happen, a minor loss could be sustained.)

The second risk is credit risk. In this case the fear is that the issuer fails to pay principal or interest in a timely fashion as required by its promise or indenture. This is a much smaller risk than the interest-rate risk.

Further, we would not expect any substantial risk to short-term fund investors to be sustained at any time. However, if a risk were to occur, it would be most likely to come in a period of very low interest rates when some funds for competitive reasons extend maturities and accept lower credits. These funds would typically be small or have great competitive pressures placed on them.

Despite the cautionary notes expressed, we believe that short-term funds are a good place for idle funds awaiting longer term use. In periods of volatile short-term rates, they may very well be among the very best of investments.

Performance and Portfolio Analysis of Fixed Income Funds

21 A. MICHAEL LIPPER, C.F.A.
Lipper Analytical Services, Inc.

INTRODUCTION

The fixed income fund investor who wants to investigate fixed income funds is interested in measuring a number of different attributes. Although past performance is no guarantee of future performance, it is a useful guide to thinking about specific future periods, provided that both the portfolio characteristics and the conditions that created performance are similar to the specific past periods measured. There are three significant performance-related items to be measured: income production, capital progress, and some mixture of the first two into a combined return. Calculating these three items often reveals a repeating pattern in the fund's performance. The patterns are most likely to repeat in fixed income funds if the portfolio structure (maturities, quality, and sector) and turnover rates are reasonably constant.

INCOME PRODUCTION

Income production for a fund is normally measured by the amount of net investment income produced per share. Net investment income is the gross income of the fund (interest, dividends, and other income generated) less the expenses of the fund, including management fees.

567

Most funds choose to qualify as a conduit for tax purposes and, thus pay no income taxes. In order to do this they must qualify under Subchapter M of the Internal Revenue Code, which requires among other things that they distribute at least 90 percent of their net investment income. As a practical matter, most funds pay out essentially all of their investment income. The method of payment is the declaration of an income dividend. Most funds have a policy of paying income dividends regularly, and they may choose to pay out dividends daily, monthly, quarterly, semiannually, or annually. In most cases the shareholder has the option of receiving the dividend in cash or in additional shares of the fund. if the dividend is paid in the form of additional shares, this does not relieve the shareholder of the obligations of reporting the income and paying taxes on the dividends.

To determine income production, the four elements to be measured are as follows:

1. Yield. Yield is the income generated over each 12-month period divided by the ending net asset value generating the income. (Variations on this measure use beginning or an average net asset value.) The most current net asset value yield is the easiest measure of income generation efficiency for comparison purposes among alternatives.

2. Growth in income generation. Shifting levels of interest rates, change in nature of assets, and change in funds's expenses will cause income generated to fluctuate. Investors should be aware of the changing level of income because for many investors a low-yielding fund with growing dividends may fill their needs better than a high-yielding fund with no growth.

3. Volatility of income. Income volatility is important for the many investors who need the predictability of their income. In a period of widely fluctuating interest rates, different strategies may produce wide changes in income dividends. To determine income production, we want to know whether income will be stable or will vary widely.

4. Compostion of income. Knowing the income composition is also important. Income may come from unreliable sources (bonds of companies close to bankruptcy) or those with different tax implications.

CAPITAL PROGRESS

Capital progress is the performance of the principal of an account—the difference between the beginning cost and the current price. Measuring capital progress works very well for a security or a portfolio of securities, but the measurement is not particularly useful for investment companies because of tax considerations.

Exhibit 1
A-Rated Corporate Bond Fund Performance for Periods Ending October 31, 1981

Investment Company	Total Reinvestment						Principal Only					
	Percent Change 9/81 to 10/81	Rank	Percent Change 12/80 to 10/81	Rank	Percent Change 10/80 to 10/81	Rank	Percent Change 9/81 to 10/81	Rank	Percent Change 12/80 to 10/81	Rank	Percent Change 10/80 to 10/81	Rank
Fidelity Thrift Trust	4.50	10	7.17	1	8.87	1	3.28	11	-4.75	2	-5.36	2
Safeco Special Bond	4.58	9	6.42	2	7.50	2	4.58	6	-1.86	1	-0.87	1
Merrill Lynch High Quality	3.06	18	5.25	3	—		1.78	17	-7.39	4	—	
Dreyfus A Bonds Plus	3.48	16	2.58	4	4.12	4	2.34	15	-7.94	5	-8.37	4
Sentinel Bond Fund	7.50	1	1.35	5	7.06	3	6.33	2	-8.88	6	-5.78	3
Bond Fund of America	4.29	13	1.02	6	3.39	5	4.29	7	-8.94	7	-9.64	6
Security Bond Fund	1.16	20	0.98	7	2.97	7	-2.55	20	-11.47	9	-9.72	7
Bond Portfolio for Endowments	3.76	15	0.47	8	3.25	6	3.76	9	-5.97	3	-8.91	5
Pro Income Fund	2.71	19	-0.24	9	1.01	8	-0.98	19	-12.25	11	-11.15	9
Keystone B-1	3.42	17	-1.35	10	-0.09	12	2.28	16	-11.31	8	-11.93	11
John Hancock Bond	4.29	14	-1.72	11	0.92	9	2.65	14	-12.29	12	-11.64	10
United Bond Fund	4.31	12	-2.29	12	-0.15	13	2.97	13	-13.29	18	-13.29	16
North Star Bond Fund	4.87	7	-2.38	13	0.50	10	1.46	18	-12.71	14	-10.14	8
Bunker Hill Income Securities	5.21	5	-2.64	14	-1.65	15	5.21	4	-12.21	10	-14.00	17
Montgomery Street Income	4.77	8	-3.23	15	-2.18	18	3.67	10	-13.21	16	-14.10	18
Kemper Income & Cap. Pres.	5.27	4	-3.41	16	0.38	11	4.06	8	-13.39	19	-12.07	12
Sigma Income Shares	6.93	2	-4.28	17	-1.92	17	6.93	1	-12.57	13	-12.81	13
Excelsior Income Shares	5.17	6	-4.31	18	-1.34	14	5.17	5	-13.12	15	-12.96	15
Investors Selective	4.47	11	-4.74	19	-2.44	19	3.24	12	-15.01	20	-14.77	19
Fort Dearborn Income Securities	5.91	3	-4.86	20	-1.76	16	5.91	3	-13.29	17	-12.91	14
Average	4.48	20	-0.51	20	1.49	19	3.31	20	-10.59	20	-10.54	19

Note: The rank order of funds changes depending on which method of calculation is applied. This is very dramatically shown if one focuses on the rank order of the funds for the first 10 months of 1981. The rank order for the total return calculation is the 4th column from the left and the 10th column for the principal-only calculation. Out of 20 funds not a single fund has the same rank in both columns. What is even more remarkable is that one fund, Bond Portfolio for Endowments, ranks number 8 on a total return basis and number 8 on a principal-only basis.

Source: Lipper—Fixed Income Fund Performance Analysis, 10/31/81.

As previously mentioned, most funds choose to avoid paying taxes by qualifying under Subchapter M of the Internal Revenue Code. These provisions cover not only investment income generated, but also capital gains from securities transactions. Funds each year have a single opportunity to declare a capital gains dividend. Shareholders have the option of taking the dividend in cash or in additional shares of the fund. In either case the shareholders have a tax liability for the taxes due on the capital gains. After declaring a dividend, the fund calculates the percentage change from the beginning net asset value to the *adjusted* ending net asset value (after the dividend). Note that the preferred technique uses reinvestment rather than adding back the distributions to net asset value at the end of the period. The reinvestment method gives the investor the benefit of the dividend being reinvested from the "ex-date" to the end of the period. In a period of rising prices, this will improve the performance over the add-back methodology, and the reverse is true for declining markets.

Although for most comparison purposes fixed income funds should be measured by the use of the total (reinvested) return methodology, certain trust accounts may find a hybrid method useful. Often personal trusts require income generated to go to one class of beneficiaries and the ultimate beneficiaries to eventually receive the remaining principal or capital. To aid the analysis for the remainderman class in the Lipper—Fixed Income Fund Performance Analysis, performance data are shown for both total return and principal only. In this report, the principal-only calculation reinvests the capital gains only. Exhibit 1 shows both total reinvestment and principal-only performance for a sample of funds keeping the bulk of their assets in A or better credits.

PERIODS TO BE MEASURED

One looks at performance data, in part, to develop an understanding of the past and to aid in looking at the future. As the past is made up of discrete if not overlapping periods, past records should be measured in a similar fashion. In Exhibit 1 three periods with different beginning dates and the same ending dates are measured. Even though this particular table covers a maximum period of 12 months, examine the variability in the ranking columns. Out of 20 funds shown, review the top and bottom 2 funds for each period shown. Below is a further extract from the table utilizing only the total return calculation data for October and the 10 months ending in October.

Month of October	*10 Months*
1 Sentinel Bond	1 Fidelity Thrift Trust
2 Sigma Income	2 Safeco Special
19 Pro Income	19 Investors Selective
20 Security Bond	20 Fort Dearborn Income

Out of a 20-fund universe, not one of the 4 funds on the extremities of the performance array was found at either extreme for the other time period. Thus one must select carefully which periods to measure. If there is a sufficient number of funds operating, one should measure fixed income funds for at least three periods: 1, 5, and 10 years. Also each significant part of a market cycle should be examined.

PATTERNS

As we indicated earlier, the purpose of performance analysis is to identify the historical patterns that may have some undetermined but probably significant value in thinking about the future. We have already demonstrated that it is unusual to find in any large universe of performers, be they funds or others, consistency of outstanding performance. To a large extent those funds who desire to be at the top of any performance league, particularly short-term periods, will accept the risk of being on the bottom. This comes from the strategy of taking extreme positions relative to competition. Nevertheless, performance analysis can be extremely valuable in identifying periods when specific funds perform well or poorly versus competition and seeing whether these periods have common characteristics (e.g., rising interest rates, increase in supply of new issues, etc.).

Another pattern one looks for is whether over longer periods of time a fund is showing an above-average return in periods that contain a number of rising and falling markets. For many long-term investors, funds that go down less than average and show some gains in rising markets are better investments than ones that have a better performance in rising markets but a substantially greater than average decline in falling markets. The reason for this belief is that investors very often lose their courage in falling markets and exit at absolutely the wrong time and price, and therefore the funds with the greatest decline during that period do the most damage to the investors' capital.

Another use of pattern analysis is to reveal a sharp break in the fund's past performance patterns. This can be caused by a change in portfolio manager, a change in portfolio strategy, or a sructural change in the fund's principal investment arena, for example the decline in perceived quality of electric utility issues relative to industrial issues.

Perhaps the most important pattern to look for is the performance of a group of funds based on their investment characteristics. In Exhibit 2 we have shown the relative performance of 11 fixed income fund groups, 1972–1981.

Based upon Exhibit 2, the following significant observations should be noted:

Exhibit 2
Relative Performance of 11 Fixed Income Funds (cumulative performance December 1972 = 100.00)

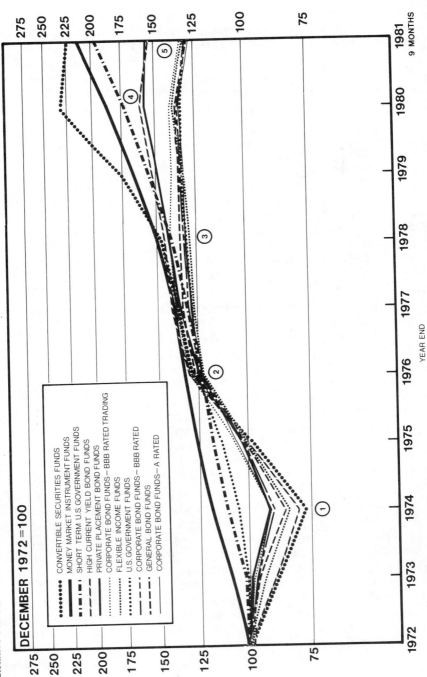

• • • • •	CONVERTIBLE SECURITIES FUNDS
▬▬▬	MONEY MARKET INSTRUMENT FUNDS
▬ · ▬ · ▬	SHORT TERM U.S. GOVERNMENT FUNDS
▬ ▬ ▬	HIGH CURRENT YIELD BOND FUNDS
	PRIVATE PLACEMENT BOND FUNDS
· · · · · ·	CORPORATE BOND FUNDS – BBB RATED TRADING
	FLEXIBLE INCOME FUNDS
● ● ● ●	U.S. GOVERNMENT FUNDS
▬ ▬ ▬	CORPORATE BOND FUNDS – BBB RATED
▬ · · ▬	GENERAL BOND FUNDS
▬▬▬	CORPORATE BOND FUNDS – A RATED

DECEMBER 1972 = 100

YEAR END

9 MONTHS

1972 1973 1974 1975 1976 1977 1978 1979 1980 1981

Source: Lipper—Fixed Income Fund Performance Analysis, 10/31/81

1. From 1972 to 1974 only money market funds, U.S. government short-term funds and U.S. government long-term funds increased in their total reinvested cumulative reinvested performance.
2. All funds showed gains from 1974 to 1977, and the corporation funds showed the biggest gains between 1974 and 1976.
3. In 1978 convertible funds, money market funds, and U.S. government short-term funds began a period of increasing performance.
4. In 1978 through the third quarter of 1981, private placements and high current yield funds generally rose, but gently.
5. Corporate bond funds, private placement funds, and general bond funds plateaued and showed minor declines from the end of 1977 through the end of the third quarter of 1981.

PORTFOLIO ANALYSIS

Within each type of fixed income fund category, there are funds that display different performance characteristics than the others in the same category. Often the cause for the different results is a significant difference in the structure of the portfolio. Structural analysis of a fixed income fund focuses on type of instrument, maturity, quality, and coupon. In general, structural portfolio analysis is more useful with fixed income funds than with equity funds. In the latter case the collection of individual issues may have significantly different characteristics than the average characteristics of their class of security.

Each quarter Lipper Analytical Services examines the portfolio structure of the fixed income funds. Exhibits 3 and 4 examine the structure of the A-rated bond fund group.

From Exhibit 3, notice the following points:

1. In total reinvested performance there was a dispersion of 392 basis points for the quarter from +2.01 to −1.91.
2. Twelve-month yields did not array themselves in the same order as performance, suggesting that a yield-only orientation did not produce performance.
3. The number of holdings divided by the total net asset gives the average holding per security. Although the average holding is around $1.5 million, there is significant variation—some funds have very concentrated portfolios with an average commitment to an issue of 5 percent of total net assets and others have an average commitment of about 0.5 percent.
4. Cash usage varies from 2 percent to 31 percent of total net assets.

From Exhibit 4, notice the following points:

1. In general the higher the coupon, the better the performance in this particular quarter.

Exhibit 3
Corporate Bond Funds A Rated Second Quarter 1981—Performance, Yield and Portfolio Structure

Total (Reinvested) Performance	12-month Yield	Number of Holdings	Total Net Assets ($ Millions)	Investment Company Name	Percent of Total Net Assets							
					Cash and Money Market Instruments	U.S. Government Bonds	Canadian Bonds	Other International Bonds	Corporate Bonds	Corporate Preferreds	Convertible Bonds and Preferreds	Common Stock and Other
2.01	13.6	38	51.9	Fidelity Thrift Trust	3	57	0	0	40	0	0	0
1.11	12.7	27	8.9	Bond Portfolio for Endowments	18	11	4	0	67	0	0	0
1.11	11.9	20	20.6	Pro Income Fund	31	4	0	1	65	0	0	0
1.06	13.1	137	164.7	Bond Fund of America	23	11	9	1	55	0	1	0
0.85	12.3	53	46.4	Keystone B-1	3	16	0	4	77	0	0	0
0.71	12.2	27	16.9	Dreyfus A Bonds Plus, Inc.	14	31	0	3	52	0	0	0
0.70	12.8	26	26.0	Security Bond Fund	0	12	0	0	88	0	0	0
0.68	12.5	152	286.7	John Hancock Bond	17	1	3	4	75	0	0	0
0.65	9.9	15	1.3	Safeco Special Bond	17	49	0	3	31	0	0	0
0.51	12.9	32	8.7	Sentinel Bond Fund	11	11	6	0	72	0	0	0
0.30	13.5	39	40.5	Bunker Hill Inc. Securities	2	10	2	8	78	0	0	0
0.09	13.7	114	218.4	United Bond Fund	8	11	2	2	77	0	0	0
-0.24	10.8	36	6.9	North Star Bond Fund	6	22	3	3	65	0	1	0
-0.34	13.3	191	517.8	Investors Selective	3	28	0	3	62	1	3	0
-0.35	13.1	97	121.2	Montgomery Str. Inc. Fund.	6	0	1	1	92	0	0	0
-0.48	12.5	28	33.0	Excelsior Inc. Shares Inc.	10	8	7	0	75	0	0	0
-1.91	12.1	39	15.2	Sigma Income Shares	4	43	0	0	50	2	1	0
0.38	12.5	63	93.2	Average	10	19	2	1	65	0	0	0

Source: Lipper—Portfolio Analysis Report on Fixed Income Funds, 6/81.

Exhibit 4
Corporate Bond Funds A Rated Second Quarter 1981—Portfolio Diversification and Maturity Schedule

Rated Percent of Total Net Assets	Average Coupon	Investment Company Name	Percent of Total Net Assets										
			Ratings					Years to Maturity					
			AAA and AA	A	BBB	BB	B and Under	<1	1–5	6–10	11–15	16–20	20+
N.A.	N.A.	Fidelity Thrift Trust	N.A.	N.A.	N.A.	N.A.	N.A.	N.A.	N.A.	N.A.	N.A.	N.A.	N.A.
67	12.5	Bond Portfolio for Endowments	32	24	11	0	0	0	10	21	0	6	45
69	11.9	Pro Income Fund	25	32	12	0	0	0	0	19	8	3	39
64	11.9	Bond Fund of America	26	16	11	7	4	1	7	16	3	11	39
81	N.A.	Keystone B-1	57	24	0	0	4	3	12	16	8	16	42
52	13.3	Dreyfus A Bonds Plus, INC.	23	14	10	0	5	15	10	26	0	1	34
100	14.4	Security Bond Fund	46	39	15	0	5	0	8	34	0	1	50
82	10.4	John Hancock Bond	19	31	29	1	2	0	9	15	5	8	35
31	9.8	Safeco Special Bond	15	13	3	0	0	3	52	31	5	16	0
75	11.8	Sentinel Bond Fund	23	34	18	0	0	2	15	32	9	0	21
98	10.4	Bunker Hill Inc. Securities	47	22	22	3	4	0	5	8	5	23	57
75	11.4	United Bond Fund	23	24	28	0	0	0	0	9	6	12	65
72	10.4	North Star Bond Fund	54	18	0	0	0	1	28	11	5	6	43
65	10.9	Investors Selective	13	26	18	3	5	0	5	9	4	31	48
94	9.6	Montgomery Str. Inc. Fund	45	32	12	5	0	0	1	3	11	38	41
82	10.0	Excelsior Inc. Shares Inc.	70	12	0	0	0	0	0	8	2	7	72
50	9.2	Sigma Income Shares	18	20	4	6	2	0	6	2	5	19	62
72*	11.1*	Average	33*	23*	12*	1*	1*	1*	10*	16*	4*	12*	43*

* Excludes issues for which data is not available (N.A.).

Source: Lipper—Portfolio Analysis Report on Fixed Income Funds.

Exhibit 5
Variations Report: Corporate Bond Funds—A Rated from First Quarter 1981 to Second Quarter 1981 (performance, yield, and portfolio structure)

Total (Reinvested) Performance	12-Month Yield	Number of Holdings	Total Net Assets ($ millions)	Investment Company Name	Percent of Total Net Assets							
					Cash and Money Market Instruments	U.S. Government Bonds	Canadian Bonds	Other International Bonds	Corporate Bonds	Corporate Preferreds	Convertible Bonds and Preferreds	Common Stock and Other
2.01	0.2	8	-0.7	Fidelity Thrift Trust	-22	21	0	0	1	0	0	0
1.11	0.1	0	-0.2	Bond Portfolio for Endowments	-1	5	4	0	-8	0	0	0
1.11	0.6	-6	0.2	Pro Income Fund	27	0	-4	0	-23	0	0	0
1.06	0.5	-5	-1.1	Bond Fund of America	5	-3	7	-1	-8	0	0	0
0.85	0.1	-2	-2.1	Keystone B-1	-1	-2	0	4	-1	0	0	0
0.71	0.1	4	3.1	Dreyfus A Bonds Plus, Inc.	9	-11	0	3	-1	0	0	0
0.70	0.4	-2	-0.7	Security Bond Fund	-1	-6	0	0	7	0	0	0
0.68	0.2	7	11.8	John Hancock Bond	2	0	0	0	-2	0	0	0
0.65	0.4	1	-0.1	Safeco Special Bond	-9	9	0	0	0	0	0	0
0.51	0.4	-2	0.0	Sentinel Bond Fund	5	0	0	0	-5	0	0	0
0.30	0.6	1	-1.2	Bunker Hill Inc. Securities	-12	10	0	1	2	0	0	0
0.09	0.6	2	-5.5	United Bond Fund	0	-5	2	1	2	0	0	0
-0.04	0.6	3	0.8	North Star Bond Fund	-2	2	0	-1	2	0	-1	0
-0.34	0.4	-5	-7.7	Investors Selective	0	3	0	0	-4	1	0	0
-0.35	0.5	0	-4.4	Montgomery Str. Inc. Fund	2	-5	-8	-8	21	0	-2	0
-0.48	0.6	N.A.	-1.1	Excelsior Inc. Shares Inc.	N.A.	N.A.	N.A.	N.A.	N.A.	1	N.A.	N.A.
-1.91	0.6	-1	-1.5	Sigma Income Shares	-2	1	0	0	0	0	0	0
0.38	0.4	0*	-0.6	Average	0*	1*	0*	-0*	-1*	0*	-0*	0*

* Excludes issues for which data is not available (N.A.).
Source: Lipper—Portfolio Analysis Report on Fixed Income Funds.

Exhibit 6

Variations Report: Corporate Bond Funds—A Rated from First Quarter 1981 to Second Quarter 1981 (portfolio diversification and maturity schedule)

| | | | Percent of Total Net Assets | | | | | | | | | | | |
| | | | Ratings | | | | | Years to Maturity | | | | | |
Rated Percent of Total Net Assets	Average Coupon	Investment Company Name	AAA and AA	A	BBB	BB	B and Under	<1	1-5	6-10	11-15	16-20	20+
N.A.	N.A.	Fidelity Thrift Trust	N.A.	N.A.	N.A.	N.A.	N.A.	N.A.	N.A.	N.A.	N.A.	N.A.	N.A.
-3	0.3	Bond Portfolio for Endowments	-2	2	-3	0	0	0	0	6	0	0	-5
-27	0.3	Pro Income Fund	-12	-10	-5	0	0	0	0	-1	-6	-4	-16
0	0.2	Bond Fund of America	2	-3	-1	2	0	0	-2	1	-2	2	-4
3	N.A.	Keystone B-1	4	-1	0	0	0	2	-2	5	-4	2	-2
3	0.5	Dreyfus A Bonds Plus, Inc.	6	-3	2	-3	1	2	2	6	0	-3	-6
1	0.9	Security Bond Fund	46	-60	15	0	0	-7	-6	-4	-4	1	14
-3	-0.6	John Hancock Bond	-2	1	-3	-1	2	3	-1	0	2	1	-5
0	0.6	Safeco Special Bond	0	0	0	0	0	0	12	-3	0	0	0
-5	0.4	Sentinel Bond Fund	-3	-2	0	0	2	0	8	-1	-6	-4	-2
12	-0.2	Bunker Hill Inc. Securities	5	6	-3	2	2	0	5	4	1	-3	5
-12	0.2	United Bond Fund	-10	-3	2	-1	0	0	0	3	1	-1	-3
0	0.3	North Star Bond Fund	-3	3	0	0	0	-4	1	-5	-3	0	7
-1	0.1	Investors Selective	-1	-4	4	0	0	0	-1	2	0	4	-3
-2	N.A.	Montgomery Str. Inc. Fund	1	-6	2	1	0	0	0	0	0	-1	-1
N.A.	N.A.	Excelsior Inc. Shares Inc.	N.A.	N.A.	N.A.	N.A.	N.A.	N.A.	N.A.	N.A.	N.A.	N.A.	N.A.
-2	-2.4	Sigma Income Shares	1	-3	0	0	0	0	-3	2	1	2	-1
-2*	0.0*	Average	2*	-5*	0*	0*	0*	-0*	0*	1*	-1*	-0*	-1*

* Excludes issues for which data is not available (N.A.).

Source: Lipper—Portfolio Analysis Report on Fixed Income Funds.

2. Within a group of funds that keep more than 60 percent of their assets in A or better corporates and government securities, the commitments to various credit ratings varies substantially from 28 percent A or better combined corporate commitment to 81 percent.

3. With higher quality portfolios the management of the maturity schedule is critical to the performance results. In this quarter the funds that had a significant portion of their portfolios in the 1- to 10-year maturities on average did better than other funds.

In examining the historic record of any fund, it is important to identify substantial portfolio structure changes. The changes on a quarter-to-quarter basis for the funds previously shown are found in Exhibit 5.

In Exhibit 5 notice that most of the changes involve the switch into or out of cash. Exhibit 6 highlights the quality and maturity schedule switches, which were less dramatic, on average, than the cash commitment switches.

Exhibit 7
Turnover Rates

Fund Name	Fiscal 1980	Fiscal 1979	Fiscal 1978
Alpha Income	132	52	33
American General Capital Bond	11	45	61
Axe-Houghton Income	15	41	4
Bond Fund of America	89	62	51
Bond Portfolio for Endowments	52	61	40
Delchester Bond Fund	59	52	57
Dreyfus A Bonds Plus	141	77	76
Fidelity Corporate Bond	169	165	77
Fidelity Thrift Trust	164	112	91
Financial Bond Shares	36	96	—
John Hancock Bond	2	2	5
Investors Selective	73	47	41
Kemper Income & Cap. Pres.	113	104	29
Keystone B-1	51	32	18
Mass Finl Bond	120	140	68
Monthly Income Shares	40	15	12
North Star Bond Fund	25	76	—
Pliyield Fund	18	68	27
T. Rowe Price New Income	105	135	23
Pro Income Fund	97	169	54
Putnam Income	89	90	283
St. Paul Income	243	103	106
Security Bond Fund	100	29	6
Sentinel Bond Fund	86	75	68
Sigma Income Shares	14	4	31
United Bond Fund	84	9	14
Vanguard FI Investors Grade	161	91	—
Average	84.78	72.30	47.22

Another useful portfolio analysis tool is to follow the turnover rate of investments within the portfolio. The particular measure used is the smaller of sales or purchases of securities divided into the average total net assets. Exhibit 7 shows that between 1978 and 1980 corporate bond funds in general have significantly increased turnover.

CONCLUSIONS

Performance analysis of fixed income funds is a useful historical tool to get an understanding as to what funds and policies worked well in specific time periods. Portfolio analysis is useful in understanding performance results.

For most investors a fund that continues to follow a basic policy in terms of structure and turnover rate is likely to produce a more predictable result than one that shifts policy frequently and rapidly even if the more changeable fund produces a better result. Another reason for the preference for the more sedate fund is that the chances are greater that the fund that demonstrates more flexibility will probably change its policy after the new trend has already gotten underway and thus will be playing catch-up ball. On the other hand, a fund that has a consistent policy that has recently had a period of poor relative performance is probably much closer to the point in time it will have relatively good performance unless it changes its policy, which unfortunately happens too often at the absolutely wrong time.

For most investors who have a need to invest in fixed income securities, fixed income funds will offer a distinct advantage of buying into an existing portfolio with a known policy and expense structure. Often the fixed income shareholder will, quite inexpensively, have some of the best managers in the institutional investment world working for him or her. The funds are likely to do a good job for their investors.

Convertible Bonds and Warrants

22   JOHN C. RITCHIE, JR., Ph.D.
Professor of Finance
Temple University

A bond or preferred stock may have warrants attached or offer a conversion privilege. In either case, the holder has the right to acquire the common stock of the issuing corporation under specified conditions rather than by direct purchase in the market. One can, however, pay what later proves to be an excessive price for the privilege conferred.

This chapter clarifies the nature of each of these securities, discusses their advantages and disadvantages, and develops an analytical framework aimed at assessing the desirability of acquiring either security by an investor. The investor's point of view, rather than that of the issuer, is emphasized.

CONVERTIBLE SECURITIES

The holder of a convertible bond or preferred stock can exchange the security, at his or her option, for the common stock of the issuer in accordance with terms set forth in the bond indenture. The option to convert is solely at the discretion of the holder and will only be exercised when and if the holder finds such an exchange desirable.[1]

---

[1] We will later discuss the possibility of the corporation forcing conversion through exercising a call privilege.

Convertible bonds are typically subordinated debentures; this means that the claims of "senior" creditors must be settled in full before any payment will be made to holders of subordinated debentures in the event of insolvency or bankruptcy. Senior creditors typically include all other long-term debt issues and bank loans. Subordinated debentures do, of course, have a priority over common and preferred stockholders. Convertible preferred stocks are equity securities with a priority to dividend payments over common stockholders but typically offer little opportunity to share in corporate growth.

Although our discussion will consistently refer to convertible bonds, the comments and the approach to analysis of such securities is in general equally applicable to convertible preferred stocks.

Who Issues Convertibles?

The issuers of convertible bonds are classified in Exhibit 1 in terms of broad groupings commonly used by bond analysts and the rating services, such as Standard & Poor's Corporation. It is interesting to note that although utility issues account for the largest portion of total bond issues outstanding in the United States, utilities have chosen not to issue convertible bonds, except for a relatively small amount in 1976. Industrial, finance and real estate, and commercial are the largest issuers of convertible bonds.

New cash offerings tend to be greater during periods of rising stock prices, such as in 1972, 1975–76, and 1980–81. The right to share in future price rises for the common stock is likely to be most highly valued during such a period of bullish expectations, allowing the corporation to offer such securities on favorable terms.

Smaller and more speculative firms, especially when a new venture is being undertaken, often issue convertible bonds in the form of subordinated debentures. The risks inherent in such issues tend to make it difficult to sell straight bonds or common stock at a reasonable cost. Management sweetens the debt issue by giving purchasers a chance to participate in potential profits (which may be large), while having a priority over equity securityholders in the event of financial difficulty.

Advantages and Disadvantages to Issuing Firms

Convertible issues offer two basic potential advantages to the issuer. First, a lower interest cost is incurred and generally less restrictive convenants need be included in the indenture than for a nonconvertible bond issue. In other words, the investor pays for the privilege of speculating on future favorable price changes in the underlying common stock by accepting a lower interest return and a less restrictive debt agreement.

Exhibit 1
Convertible Bond Issues 1972–1981 ($ billions)

Issuing Classification	1972	1973	1974	1975	1976	1977	1978	1979	1980	1981
Public utility	$ 0.0	$ 0.0	$ 0.0	$ 0.0	$ 0.0	$ 0.1	$ 0.0	$ 0.0	$ 0.0	$ 0.0
Communications	0.1	0.0	0.0	0.0	0.0	0.0	0.0	0.0	0.0	0.0
Transportation	0.1	0.1	0.0	0.0	0.1	0.1	0.3	0.2	0.2	0.3
Industrial	0.8	0.1	0.3	0.7	0.8	0.5	0.3	0.4	3.3	3.9
Sales finance	N.A.	N.A.	N.A.	0.0	0.0	0.0	0.1	0.0	0.2	0.1
Other finance and real estate	0.8	0.4	0.0	0.5	0.0	0.0	0.1	0.2	0.3	0.3
Commercial and miscellaneous	0.5	0.0	0.2	0.1	0.1	0.1	0.0	0.0	0.3	0.4
Total cash offerings	$ 2.3	$ 0.6	$ 0.5	$ 1.3	$ 1.0	$ 0.8	$ 0.4	$ 0.8	$ 4.3	$ 5.0
Plus exchange, net of conversion	−1.8	−1.3	0.1	−0.8	−0.5	−0.3	−0.5	−0.3	−0.5	−1.0
Less calls and other retirements	−0.2	−0.1	−0.2	−0.2	−0.2	−0.1	−0.1	−0.1	−0.1	−0.2
Net issuance convertible debt	$ 0.3	$−0.8	$ 0.4	$ 0.3	$ 0.3	$ 0.4	$−0.2	$ 0.4	$ 3.7	$ 3.8
Net issuance all corporate bonds	$18.9	$ 13.2	$26.9	$34.0	$33.0	$32.2	$ 27.6	$24.8	$40.5	$37.7
Convertible issues as a percent of all corporate issues based on:										
Total cash offerings	12.17%	4.55%	1.86%	3.82%	3.03%	2.48%	1.45%	3.23%	10.62%	13.26%
Net issuance	1.59	N.M.	1.49	0.88	0.91	1.24	N.M.	1.61	9.14	10.08

Source: Henry Kaufman, James McKeon, and David Foster, *1981 Prospects for Financial Markets* (New York: Solomon Brothers, December 8, 1980), p. 22. Figures for 1972–74 were obtained from the issue covering 1978.

The required yield to sell a convertible relative to that of a nonconvertible issue varies over time and with the issuer. A nonconvertible issue might require a yield-to-maturity that could range from 50 basis points (one half of 1 percent) to 4 percent or more higher than that offered by a convertible issue.[2] Convertible bonds, moreover, are typically subordinated debt issues. The rating agencies, therefore, have usually rated convertible issues one class below that of a straight debenture issue.[3] This would suggest even higher relative interest-cost savings than suggested by the differentials noted above. The interest-cost saving to a firm will, of course, be highly related to market expectations for the common stock.

Second, a firm may be able to sell common stock at a better price through a convertible bond than by a direct issue. To illustrate, assume a firm is currently earning $5 a common share and that the common stock is selling at $50 per share. The firm believes it can utilize new capital effectively and that it would be preferable to raise equity rather than debt capital. The firm foresees, however, a potential fall in earnings per share if common stock is sold directly because it will take time to bring the new facilities, acquired with the funds raised, on stream. The market might well also fear potential dilution of earnings per share and might not be as optimistic as management about the future of the planned investments. For these reasons, the firm might well have to sell new common stock at less than $50 a share. On the other hand, the firm might be able to sell a convertible bond issue at par that can be converted into 20 shares of the firm's common stock. The required interest rate might result in less dilution in earnings per share currently than would a direct stock issue, since the number of shares outstanding would not increase. Further assume that the bonds would be callable at 105 ($1,050 per bond).

If the new capital investments raised earnings per share to $6.50 two years hence, the price of the common stock in the market would increase to $65 a share, assuming a price-earnings ratio of 10 continued to exist. The firm could then call the bonds, forcing conversion. The value of stock received in conversion is $1,300 ($65 per share times 20 shares), which is greater than the cash ($1,050) that would be received by allowing the issuer to call the stock. In effect, the firm sold stock for $50 a share, less issuance costs, through the convertible bonds. The firm, therefore, received a greater price per share than by a direct issue of common stock, at that time, since the market price for a direct issue is expected to be lower and the issuance cost of a common issue is typically higher than for a convertible bond issue. The firm, in

[2] For example, see Eugene F. Brigham, "An Analysis of Convertible Debentures: Theory and Some Empirical Evidence," *Journal of Finance* March 1966), pp. 35–54.

[3] George E. Pinches and Kent A. Mingo, "A Multivariate Analysis of Industrial Bond Ratings," *Journal of Finance* (March 1973), pp. 1–18.

other words, would have to issue fewer common shares to raise a given amount by selling convertibles and forcing conversion than by directly selling common stock. Also, interest cost is lowered, sometimes substantially, by offering the convertible privilege.

Convertible securities do have possible disadvantages to the issuer. If the underlying common stock does increase markedly in price, the issuer might have been better off had the financing been postponed and a direct issue made. Moreover, if the price of the common stock drops after the issue of the convertible instrument, conversion cannot be forced and will not occur. The firm, therefore, cannot be sure it is raising equity capital when a convertible issue is made.

Advantages to the Investor

An investor purchasing a convertible security supposedly receives the advantages of a senior security; that is, safety of principal in terms of a prior claim to assets over equity security holders and relative income stability at a known rate. Furthermore, if the common stock of the issuer rises in price, the convertible instrument will usually also rise to reflect the increased value of the underlying common stock. Upside potential can be realized through sale of the convertible bond, without conversion into the stock. On the other hand, if the price of the underlying common stock declines in the market, the bond can be expected to decline only to the point where it yields a satisfactory return on its value as a straight bond. A convertible offers the downside protection that bonds can offer during bad economic times, while allowing one to share in the upside potential for the common stock of a growing firm.

In terms of their dividend yield, convertible bonds also typically offer higher current yield than do common stocks. If the dividend yield on the underlying common stock surpassed the current yield on the convertible bond, conversion would tend to be attractive.

Convertible bonds may have special appeal for financial institutions, notably commercial banks. Commercial banks are not permitted to purchase common stocks for their own account and, therefore, lose the possibility of capital gains through participation in corporate earnings growth. In 1957 approval was given for the purchase of eligible convertible issues by commercial banks if the yield obtained is reasonably similar to nonconvertible issues of similar quality and maturity and they are not selling at a significant conversion premium. Admittedly, commercial banks hold relatively few convertibles, and convertibles typically do sell at a conversion premium.

Convertible bonds have good marketability, as shown by active trading in large issues on the New York Exchange; whereas nonconvertible issues of similar quality are sometimes difficult to follow, since they are traded over the counter.

Disadvantages to the Investor

The investor pays for the convertible privilege by accepting a significantly lower yield-to-maturity than that currently offered by non-convertible bonds of equivalent quality. Also a call clause can lessen the potential attractiveness of a convertible bond, since the firm may be able to force conversion into the common stock as previously discussed. The possibility of forced conversion limits the speculative appeal.

If anticipated corporate growth is not realized, the purchaser will have sacrificed current yield and may well see the market value of the convertible instrument fall below the price paid to acquire it. A rise in the price of the underlying common stock is necessary to offset the yield sacrifice. For example, prices of convertible bonds rose to very high levels in 1965, but in 1966, when both stock and bond markets declined, many convertible issues declined even more than the stocks into which they were convertible. It appears a speculative premium was built into the price of convertibles in 1965, and the market no longer believed that this premium was justified in 1966.

Investor risk can be markedly heightened by purchasing convertibles on margin. If interest rates rise after purchase, bondholders may receive margin calls, reflecting falling prices of convertible bonds, as happened during the 1966–70 period. Many bonds had to be sold, depressing the market further than purchasers had thought possible based on their estimate of a floor price at which the bonds would sell on a pure yield or straight investment basis.

Analysis of Convertible Bonds

The following factors must be considered when evaluating convertible securities:

1. The appreciation in price of the common stock that is required before conversion could become attractive. This is measured by the *conversion premium ratio.*
2. The prospects for growth in the price of the underlying stock.
3. The downside potential in the event that the conversion privilege proves valueless.
4. The yield sacrifice required to purchase the convertible.
5. The income advantage offered through acquiring the convertible bond, rather than the number of common shares that would be obtained through conversion.
6. The quality of the security being offered.
7. The number of years over which the conversion premium paid to acquire the convertible will be recouped by means of the favorable income differential offered by the convertible relative to the underlying common stock. This is the *break-even time.*

The discussion that follows will concentrate on calculations typically used by analysts to evaluate points 1, 3, 4, 5, and 7 above. The grading of bonds in terms of quality, both by the rating agencies and in terms of financial analysis, is discussed in Chapter 14. Assessing the prospects for growth in the price of the underlying common stock is the work of fundamental analysis. The techniques of fundamental analysis are reviewed in several well-accepted books.[4]

Convertible Bonds: An Illustrative Analysis

Exhibit 2 contrasts the 87⁄8 percent convertible debentures issued by Boeing Corporation that mature in the year 2006 with the 95⁄8

Exhibit 2
Comparative Data for Two Convertible Bonds As of September 11, 1981

	Boeing Corp. 87⁄8s, 2006	Holiday Inns 95⁄8s, 2005
Known data:		
Conversion ratio	23.67 Shares	50 Shares
Market price of convertible	$ 740.00	$1300.00
Market price of common stock	$ 24.00	$ 25.00
Dividend per share—common	$ 1.40	$ 0.74
Call price.	$1065.10	$1055.00
Yield to maturity, equivalent.	17.70%*	17.90%*
Quality Nonconvertible.		
Calculated data:		
Market conversion price†	$ 31.26	$ 26.00
Conversion premium per common share	$ 7.26	$ 1.00
Conversion premium ratio‡	30.25%	4.00%
Current yield—convertible	12.00%	7.40%
Dividend yield—common	5.80%	3.00%
Yield sacrifice on convertible§	5.70%	10.50%
Bond income differential‖	$ 55.61	$ 59.25
Estimated floor price#	$ 509.89	$ 546.59
Break-even time	3.09 Years	0.85 Years

* The average yield-to-maturity for 25-year corporate bonds rated AA to A by Standard & Poor's in September 1981, and the writer's judgement.
† Market price of the convertible instrument divided by the conversion ratio.
‡ The conversion premium per common share divided by the market price of the common stock.
§ The yield-to-maturity offered by equivalent nonconvertible bonds less the yield-to-maturity offered by the convertible bond.
‖ The interest income paid by the convertible bond less the annual dividend income that would be received by converting into the underlying common shares. This figure expresses the income advantage in holding the convertible bond rather than the equivalent number of shares of the underlying common stock.
The price at which the convertible would have to sell to offer the yield currently being offered by nonconvertible bonds of equivalent risk.

[4] For example, see Douglas H. Bellemore, Herbert E. Phillips and John C. Ritchie, *Investment Analysis and Portfolio Selection: An Integrated Approach* (Cincinnati: South-Western Publishing, 1979), Chapters 6, 15–20, and 22–26.

percent convertible debentures issued by Holiday Inns that mature in the year 2005. Pertinent calculations, contained in the exhibit, are explained below.

A few basic definitions are in order before we begin to discuss Exhibit 2. The convertible bond contract will either state a conversion ratio or a conversion price. A *conversion ratio* directly specifies the number of shares of the issuing firm's common stock that can be obtained by surrendering the convertible bond. Alternatively, the conversion rate may be expressed in terms of a *conversion price*—the price paid per share to acquire the underlying common stock through conversion. The conversion ratio may then be determined by dividing the stated conversion price into the par value of the bond:

$$\text{Conversion ratio} = \frac{\text{Par of bond}}{\text{Conversion price}}$$

For example, if the conversion price were $20, a holder of such a bond would receive 50 shares of common stock in conversion, assuming a typical par value of $1,000 for the bond.

In some cases, the bond indenture may provide for changes in the conversion price over time. For example, a conversion price of 20 might be specified for the first five years, 25 for the next five years, 30 for the next five years, and so on. This of course means that a holder of the instrument will be able to obtain fewer shares through conversion each time the conversion price increases. For example, 50 shares can be obtained when the conversion price is 20, but only 40 shares when the conversion price rises to 25. Such a provision forces investors to emphasize early conversion if they intend to convert, and the provision would be reasonable if corporate growth had generally led to a rising value for the common stock over time.

Conversion Premium.   The *market conversion price* of a convertible instrument represents the cost per share of the common stock if obtained through the convertible instrument, ignoring commissions. For example, the market conversion price of $31.26 calculated for the Boeing Corporation convertible bond is obtained by dividing the market price of the convertible bond ($740) by the number of common shares that could be obtained by converting that bond (23.67 shares). Since the market conversion price per common share is higher than the current market price of a common share, the bond is selling at a *conversion premium*, represented by the excess cost per share to obtain the common stock through conversion.

The *conversion premium ratio* shows the percentage increase necessary to reach a *parity price* relationship between the underlying common stock and the convertible instrument. *Conversion parity* is that price relationship between the convertible instrument and the common stock at which neither a profit nor loss would be realized by purchasing the convertible, converting it, and selling the common shares that were received in conversion, ignoring commissions. At conversion parity the following condition would exist:

$$\frac{\text{Par of bond}}{\text{Conversion price}} = \frac{\text{Market price of the convertible}}{\text{Market price of the common}}$$

When the price of the common stock exceeds its conversion parity price, one could feel certain that the convertible bond would fluctuate directly with changes in the market price of the underlying common stock. In other words, gains in value of the underlying common stock should then be able to be realized by the sale of the convertible instrument rather than conversion and sale of the stock itself. The market conversion price, incidentally, is the parity price for a share of common stock obtainable through the convertible instrument.

At the time of this comparative analysis, both instruments sold at a premium, but the premium on the Boeing Corporation convertible was substantially greater in both relative and absolute terms. If one assumes that the appreciation potential of the common stocks of both companies were equal (a feeling the market appeared not to hold), the Holiday Inns bond had a substantial advantage. An increase of only 4 percent in the common stock of Holiday Inns was needed to ensure that further increases in the underlying common would be reflected in the price of the convertible bond. Boeing Corporation common stock, on the other hand, would have to rise 30.25 percent before the conversion had an assured value.

There is usually, although not always, some conversion premium present on convertible instruments, which reflects the anticipation of a possible increase in the price of the underlying common stock beyond the parity price. Professional arbitrageurs are constantly looking for situations in which the stock can be obtained more cheaply (allowing for commissions) by buying the convertible instrument than through direct purchase in the market. For example, assume a bond is convertible into 20 shares and can be purchased for $1,000. If the common stock were currently selling at $55 a share, an arbitrageur would buy the convertible and simultaneously short sell the common stock. The arbitrageur would realize a gross profit (before transaction costs) of $375 calculated as follows:

Short sale of 25 shares at $55/share..........	$1375
Less purchase cost of bond	1000
	$ 375

The demand by arbitrageurs for the convertible would continue until the resultant rise in price of the convertible no longer made such actions profitable.

Yield Sacrifice. At the time of this analysis, nonconvertible bonds of equivalent quality to the convertible issued by Boeing Corporation offered a yield of 17.7 percent, or 5.7 percent higher than that offered by the convertible. This yield sacrifice would have to be overcome by a rise in the price of the underlying common stock, or the investor would have been better off to purchase the nonconvertible instrument. The yield sacrifice for the Holiday Inns bonds was approximately twice that for the Boeing Corporation bonds, thereby requiring much more attractive appreciation potential for their common stock during the holding period to make the convertible attractive. Although the Boeing Corporation instrument offered an advantage in terms of the lower yield sacrifice required, this could have been offset by a more attractive price appreciation potential for the common stock of Holiday Inns, if that was in fact the case.

Downside Risk Potential.   The *floor price* for a convertible is typically estimated as that value at which the instrument would sell in the market to offer the yield of an equivalent nonconvertible instrument. Boeing Corporation bonds were rated AA by Standard and Poor's Corporation at the time of this analysis, and Holiday Inns bonds were rated a bit lower. Present value calculations were used to determine the estimated floor prices in Exhibit 2.

The analysis suggests a substantially greater downside risk for Holiday Inns convertible bonds than for the Boeing Corporation convertibles.

One should not place too much emphasis on the estimated floor prices, however. The calculations assume that current yield levels will continue, and this may well not be correct. If yields rise to even higher levels, and the conversion privilege proves worthless, the price of the bonds could fall below the estimated floor price. On the other hand, if yield levels fall, the loss will not be as great as suggested. More importantly one should not be purchasing convertibles (remember the yield sacrifice) unless they believe the probability is relatively high that the market price of the underlying common will rise and eventually exceed the parity price for that common stock.

Break-even Time.   Break-even time represents the number of years it will take for the favorable income differential over the common stock offered by the convertible instrument to equal the total dollar conversion premium paid to acquire that convertible instrument. For example, the break-even time for the Boeing Corporation bonds is 3.09 years, calculated as follows:

Interest paid on each $1,000 bond at 8⅞ percent	$88.75
Dividend income offered by 23.67 shares into which each bond is convertible (23.67 shares × 1.40/share)........................	33.14
Favorable bond income differential	55.61
Favorable income differential per common share (55.61 − 23.67 shares)	$ 2.35
Break-even time equals the conversion premium per share divided by the favorable income differential per share (7.26 ÷ 2.35)	3.09 years

A break-even time exceeding five years is widely regarded by analysts as excessive, other things being equal. The Holiday Inns bonds have a definite advantage in terms of break-even time, though neither bond suggests an excessive break-even time.

Dilution of the Convertible Privilege

A large common stock split or stock dividend could markedly dilute the value of the conversion privilege, unless adjustment of the number of shares received in conversion is made. For example, assume a bond is convertible into 20 shares, and the company undergoes a two-for-one stock split. Recognizing this, the conversion privilege is typically protected by a provision in the bond identure providing for a pro rata adjustment of the conversion price and/or the conversion ratio, so that the exchange ratio would increase to 40 shares after the stock split.

When Should a Convertible Be Converted or Sold?

If the prospects for favorable growth in the underlying common stock or the relative prices and yields of the convertible security and the common stock change significantly, a sale or conversion may be suggested. For example, the dividend obtainable by converting into the common stock of AT&T from the $4 convertible preferred rose to $4.20 a share during 1977. A conversion was then desirable, assuming the investor still wished to retain a claim on the further potential growth of AT&T, since current yield would be increased through conversion by 20 cents per share.

Summary of Convertibles

Some fixed income securities are convertible into common stock, offering the basic advantages of a senior security (bond or preferred stock) while allowing the holder to participate in potential corporate growth. The investor pays for the conversion privilege by accepting a significantly lower yield than could be obtained by purchasing nonconvertible bonds or preferred stocks. A convertible, moreover, usually sells at a premium over the value of the underlying common stock. If the anticipated growth in the value of the common stock is not realized, the purchaser will have sacrificed yield and may well also see the value of the convertible instrument fall sharply.

There are three distinct areas of analysis that should be undertaken when evaluating a convertible security:

1. The quality of the security should be assessed in the same way as for other nonconvertible senior securities. This requires assessing the ability of the issuing company to meet the fixed charges man-

dated by the issue under reasonably conceivable adverse economic circumstances.

2. The growth potential for the underlying common stock must be evaluated, since that growth potential offers the basis for generating the added yield necessary to offset the yield sacrifice incurred at the time of purchase and provide a return that makes purchase attractive.

3. Special calculations developed in the illustrative analysis in this chapter should be used to assess the relative attractiveness of the many convertible securities available in the market.

Conversion should be considered when the annual total dividends that would be received from the common shares obtained through conversion exceeds the annual coupon payments offered by the convertible bond. Sale of the convertible security should also be considered when the price of that security exceeds the estimated value of the underlying stock into which it is convertible and/or the prospects for favorable growth in the underlying common stock deteriorate.

COMMON STOCK WARRANTS

A warrant is usually a long-term option, at least when issued, that conveys to the holder the privilege of buying a specified number of shares of the underlying common stock at a specified exercise price at any time on or before an expiration date. The typical warrant originates by attachment to a bond or preferred stock issue, with the intent to lower the cost of capital for the issuing firm and/or make an issue more attractive to investors, thereby improving its marketability. Warrants may also be added to make possible the sale of a marginal-quality issue. In addition, warrants may be issued to corporate employees under a bonus plan or could even be offered as a security in a direct sale.

A warrant that is attached to a bond or preferred stock can only be exercised by the holder of that financial instrument. Such warrants, however, may typically be detached as of a particular date and subsequently traded on their own merits. A number of warrants are now listed by the New York Stock Exchange, and trading in warrants can be expected to increase in volume in the years ahead.[5]

Warrants and Stock Rights Distinguished

Stock purchase rights are created by corporations who issue them to existing common stockholders when making a privileged subscription offering. Stock rights typically allow subscription to new shares

---

[5] The first warrant to be listed on the NYSE was an AT&T warrant that expired April 1975. Other warrants have since been listed there. Most existing warrants, however, trade over the counter or are listed on the American or Pacific Coast Stock Exchanges.

on a pro rata basis at a price below the current market price for the common stock, and warrants at the time of issue offer the holder the option to buy the common stock at a price substantially *above* the current market price. Warrants, however, have a long life, often exceeding five years; and stock rights usually have a life of one month or less.

The value of a warrant is usually defined in terms of the probabilities that the future price of the common stock will exceed the option price. The value of stock rights, on the other hand, is measured in terms of the dollar savings per right that can be realized by purchasing the common stock at the preferential price, which is below the current market price.

Warrants and Call Options Distinguished

A call option gives the buyer the right to purchase the underlying common stock from the option seller at a fixed price within a given period. Therefore, it is similar to a warrant. Call options also trade independently from the common stock, as do warrants.

However, call options are written by investors, who will purchase and deliver already outstanding shares of common stock if the option is exercised. Warrants, on the other hand, are issued by business corporations, and the corporation utilizes the instrument as a means of selling a new issue and thereby raising additional capital. Also, warrants may well have a life of many years, but a call option typically expires within nine months. Finally, warrants are often attached to bonds (or other financial instruments) to make them more attractive when being initially sold.

Leverage and Minimum Values

The price of a warrant is usually quite small in comparison with the current market price of the common stock of the issuer. A given percentage increase in the common stock's price, therefore, may have a magnified percentage effect on the price of the warrant.

For example, assume the common stock of company X is now selling for $50 a share, and an investor expects the price to rise to $100 a share within a few years. Further assume a warrant is outstanding that gives the holder the right to buy a share of common stock of company X for $65 a share at any time during the next 10 years. A warrant currently sells for $10.

An investor who bought the common stock at $50 a share would realize a 100 percent gain (ignoring commissions) plus any dividend income received if the stock rose to $100 in a year. The *minimum value of the warrant* when the stock rises to $100, however, is about $35 ($100 − $65), the saving that can be realized by acquiring the stock through exercise of the warrant rather than by direct purchase. If it were much less than this, arbitrageurs would buy the warrant and short sell the stock to take advantage of the assured gain, thereby forcing the price of the warrant to the minimum value.[6] An investor who had bought a warrant at $10 and sold it at $35 would have realized a gain of 250 percent, substantially exceeding the gain offered by direct purchase of the common stock. Actually, the warrant is likely to be selling for more than $35 when the stock reaches $100 per share because of the speculative enthusiasm such a price rise would tend to generate.

But the value of the warrant may fall sharply, even to zero, if the common stock does not rise in value. Notice that at any price below $65 a share for the common stock, the warrant has no assured minimum value. Suppose the price of the common stock merely stayed at $50 a share, and reduced expectations for future growth in the market reduced the price of a warrant to $5. An investor in the warrants would have lost 50 percent of his or her capital, but an investor in the stock would have no potential current loss and would receive any dividend income paid by the corporation. Furthermore, if the stock does not rise above $65 a share before expiration, the warrant will be worth $0.

Like any leveraged situation, the potential return is increased by purchasing warrants, but risk is also increased.

Warrant Premiums

Warrants tend to sell at a premium over minimum value, reflecting expectations of future increases in the price of the common stock and the leverage potential. The speculative leverage possibilities diminish, however, as the price of the underlying stock rises relative to the exercise price of the warrant and/or as the warrant approaches expiration. This is because the expectation of further substantial gains in the price of the common stock is likely to become less probable in terms of market expectations, leading to lower leverage potential that may not seem worthwhile when one realizes that direct purchase of the common stock would generate dividend income that will not be realized through purchase of the warrant.

The factors affecting the size of the warrant premium have been explored in the financial literature,[7] and are briefly summarized below:

---

[6] In the event a warrant entitles the holder to purchase more or less than one share, the formula for calculating the minimum value is $N(MP - EP)$, where N is the number of shares that can be purchased through exercise of the warrant, MP is the market price of a share of the common stock, and EP is the exercise price, or price at which a share of the common stock can be acquired through the warrant.

[7] See, for example, J. P. Shelton, "The Relation of the Price of a Warrant to the Price of Its Associated Stock," *Financial Analysts Journal*, May–June and July–August 1967; S. T. Kassonf, "Warrant Price Behavior, 1945–1964, *"Financial Analysts Journal*, January–February 1968; and J. D. Miller, "Longevity of Stock Purchase Warrants," *Financial Analysts Journal*, November–December 1971.

1. The most important factor, of course, is the market's expectations regarding the future price of the underlying common stock. The greater the growth expectations, the larger the premium will be, other things equal.
2. The longer the warrant has to go before reaching the expiration date, the higher the premium is likely to be. Once the life of a warrant exceeds five years, however, it has less chance of further increasing the premium paid.
3. A higher dividend yield offered by the underlying common stock will tend to lower the premium paid, since the sacrificed dividend yield makes purchase of the warrant less attractive.
4. Empirical studies suggest that warrants trading on organized exchanges tend to have higher premiums than those trading over the counter. For similar reasons, the warrants of small companies or those of companies whose stocks are inactively traded tend to have smaller premiums.
5. As the expiration date of the warrant nears, the premium tends to shrink, and the price of the warrant approaches minimum value or zero, whichever is the lower bound.

Summary of Warrants

The purchase of a warrant, essentially a means of obtaining a call on a common stock, offers attractive leverage possibilities. A warrant typically sells at a premium over the value represented by the savings that could be made by acquiring the common stock through exercise. If the expected appreciation is not realized on the common stock, an investor in warrants may lose a greater percentage of the capital invested than would have been lost by direct investment in the common stock. On the other hand, investment in warrants may produce a greater percentage gain on the capital committed when the stock does increase in value, than could have been realized by direct investment in the underlying common stock.

Contingent Takedown Options on Fixed Income Securities*

23

ROBERT W. KOPPRASCH, Ph.D., C.F.A.
Vice President
Salomon Brothers Inc

Contingent takedown options (CTOs)—options to buy fixed income securities—have received widespread attention recently in the fixed income market. Recent bond issues with contingent takedown options attached, as well as the prospect of exchange-tradable options have directed investor interest toward these new securities.[1] This interest is heightened by the continuing evidence of a new level of market volatility. In such a volatile environment, there is a natural attraction to the CTOs' potential for almost full participation in an appreciating debt market, coupled with a limited loss (i.e., the premium paid) in the event of a market decline. This profit pattern offers the prospect of a return pattern compatible with the risk averse posture of the traditional fixed income investor.

Another attractive feature of contingent takedown options is that they are usually issued as part of an investment unit through the

* This chapter is adapted from an earlier paper, "Contingent Takedown Options on Fixed Income Securities," Salomon Brothers Inc, January 1981, coauthored with Martin L. Leibowitz. The author would like to acknowledge Dr. Leibowitz's role in the development of this chapter.

Although the information in this chapter has been obtained from sources that the author believes to be reliable, Salomon Brothers Inc cannot guarantee its accuracy, and such information may be incomplete or condensed. All opinions and estimates included in this chapter constitute judgment as of this date and are subject to change without notice.

[1] For a discussion of the prospect of exchange-tradable options, see Chapter 39.

normal debt market mechanisms. The investment "unit" (bond and attached option) will typically be considered an appropriate investment vehicle even if warrants or options per se are not. The CTO may usually be "detached" and sold separately, or may be held with or without the original bond. Additionally, because CTOs are traded through the traditional bond market, familiar to the investor, there is no need to open new accounts and learn new trading procedures or margin requirements as is necessary with some other new investment vehicles.

In the perception of many investors, options are classified together with financial futures as a new but specialized innovation in the debt market. In fact, these options represent a fundamentally different vehicle.[2] Although interest-rate futures offer the investor a highly leveraged profit in a volatile market, they also expose the investor to considerable risk, as well as to daily mark-to-market margin requirements.[3] The limited loss feature of CTOs allows the investor to maintain a position through market swings without the worry of greater loss or the complications of variation margin.

Naturally, the attraction of a particular option is a function of its cost, possible profit, liquidity, and the new structure of returns now made available to the investor. This chapter will suggest a framework for analyzing debt options and will discuss their role as a component of specific investment strategies.

HYPOTHETICAL CTO EXAMPLE

In the discussion that follows, frequent reference will be made to a specific example of a hypothetical option with the following characteristics:

1. The option allows the holder to buy, at any time until expiration, an 11 percent coupon bond that has 20 years to maturity (as of the option's expiration). This bond is known as the deliverable bond.
2. The option allows the holder to buy the deliverable bond at par (i.e., 100). This is known as the exercise price or strike price.
3. The option has a life of one year from issue until expiration.

Further, we will assume that the option was issued as part of an investment unit consisting of the option and a 21-year, 11 percent coupon bond (which we will call the issue bond) sold at par. If the market yield for a 21-year, 11 percent bond of the same quality were 12 percent at the time of issue, the 100-basis-point give-up in yield

---

[2] See Chapter 39 for a discussion of the differences between options and futures.

[3] The futures markets incorporate a mechanism to protect a party to a trade from any credit risk that would arise from the accumulation of large, unrealized losses by the opposite party. This mechanism involves daily settlement of any change in the contract's value, so that profits and losses are settled in cash every day. This is known as "marking to the market."

represents the cost of the option, known as the premium. A 21-year, 11 percent bond would be priced at 92.39 to yield 12 percent. Hence the premium paid for the option is 7.61.

The option described above is sometimes called a double-up option because the deliverable bond is identical to the issue bond in terms of coupon and maturity date. Thus the investor can double up on the original issue if it is advantageous to do so. Although there are some special advantages to the double-up option (to be mentioned later), the discussion that follows is based on general option considerations and not on the specific double-up feature.

THE INTRINSIC VALUE OF AN OPTION

The value of the option is obviously derived from the fact that it allows the purchase of the deliverable bond for 100 regardless of prevailing market price. If the bond is worth less than 100, the holder will let the option expire. If the bond is worth more than 100, however, the investor can exercise the option and thereby acquire the bond at par. One of the key elements of value, therefore, is the expected price at expiration relative to the exercise price. For any price of the deliverable security, the "intrinsic" value of an option can be quickly determined. For any price below the exercise price, the intrinsic value of the option is zero because the deliverable security can be purchased more cheaply in the open market than by exercising the option. For any price above the exercise price, the option's intrinsic value is the difference between market price and exercise price, as shown in Exhibit 1. If, for example, the deliverable bond is worth 110, the option's intrinsic value is 10.

Exhibit 1
The Intrinsic Value Pattern

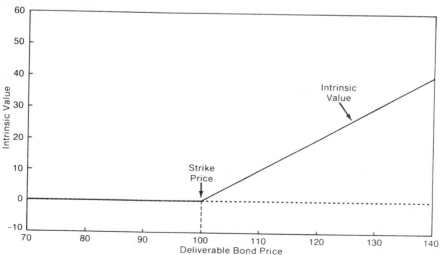

THE OPTION'S PROFIT

The intrinsic value in Exhibit 1 does not include consideration of the premium paid for the option. When the 7.61-point premium is subtracted from the intrinsic value, the result is the profit, as shown in Exhibit 2.

Exhibit 2
The Option's Profit Pattern

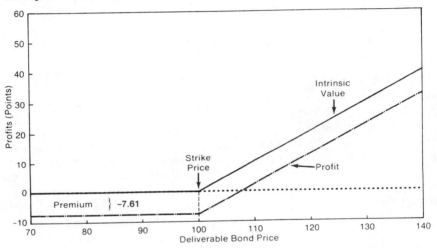

Exhibit 3
Intrinsic Value as Function of Yield

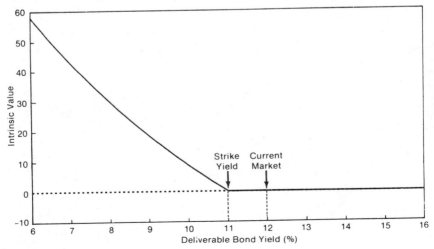

To put this in a more familiar framework for the fixed income investor, the intrinsic value and profit charts in Exhibits 1 and 2 have been translated to a yield basis in Exhibits 3 and 4, respectively. (The left-to-right reversal of the shapes results from the inverse nature of prices and yields. The slight curvature in Exhibits 3 and 4 results from the nonlinear relationship between price and yield.) The strike price can be translated into a "strike yield," that is, the yield of the security if purchased at the strike price. In this example, the strike yield is 11 percent.

Exhibit 4
Option Profit as Function of Yield

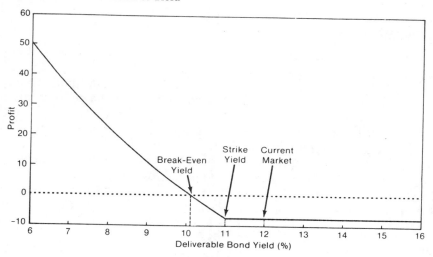

THE BREAK-EVEN PRICE AND YIELD

In Exhibit 2 the price at which the option profit line crosses the horizontal axis—zero—is the break-even price. The analogous point in Exhibit 4 is the break-even yield. At any lower yield, the option holder would have a profit, and at any higher yield, would suffer a loss.

The break-even yield for the CTO is a function both of the premium paid, which determines how much intrinsic value is necessary to recover the premium, and the relationship between yield and price, which determines how large a yield move is necessary to produce the required intrinsic value. Thus, for the same premium, shorter maturity bonds would require larger favorable yield moves to reach the break-even point.

For a given deliverable bond, the break-even yield can easily be determined: It is the yield on the bond that results in a price equal to the exercise price plus the premium. The break-even yield can be compared with current yields and the projected volatility of yields to determine whether such an outcome is likely. But although the breakeven yield is a useful measure, it captures only one facet of the valuation problem. It does not explicitly indicate what a "fair" price for the option would be.

Most option valuation models developed for equities have as their starting point some probability distribution of expected future prices. This general approach, oriented toward the fixed income market, will be discussed in the next section.

PROBABILITY MODELS

When considering the possible future yield (and price) levels, it is useful to think in terms of the most likely outcome, taking into account some range of uncertainty. The analysis is greatly simplified if the uncertainty range is equal in both directions from the most likely outcome.

One distribution that meets this condition is known as the normal probability distribution, the familiar bell-shaped curve shown in Exhibit 5. In this example, the expected yield is 11 percent. The uncertainty measure usually used with the normal distribution is known as the standard deviation. The wider the range of uncertainty, the greater the standard deviation, and vice versa. Without delving any deeper

Exhibit 5
The Normal Probability Distribution (expected yield = 11 percent)

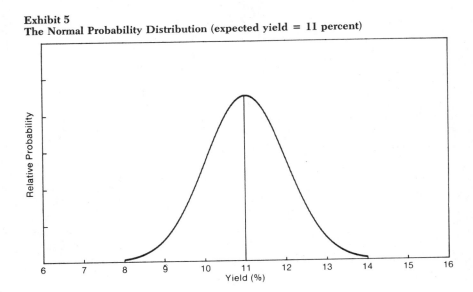

into statistical theory, the normal distribution has the following properties: 68 percent of the outcomes fall in a range that is one standard deviation in each direction from the expected value; 95 percent falls within two standard deviations on each side; and almost 99.75 percent falls within three standard deviations on each side. This quality is illustrated in Exhibit 6, which shows a normal distribution with a standard deviation of 100 basis poins.

Exhibit 6
Probability Intervals for the Normal Distribution (expected yield = 11 percent, standard deviation = 1 percent)

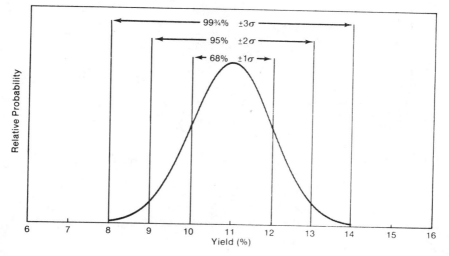

The height of the curve indicates the relative probabilities of the various outcomes. Exhibit 6 shows that there is little probability of a final yield of 8 percent. Yields in the 10 to 12 percent range are considered much more likely, with 11 percent naturally having the greatest likelihood of occurrence.

With a forecast of the expected yield and the associated uncertainty (standard deviation), one can determine the option's intrinsic value at expiration for all of the possible yields (from Exhibit 2). This intrinsic value is superimposed upon the probability of each yield in Exhibit 7. As shown, yields just below 11 percent, although likely, produce little exercise value; and yields below 9 percent are unlikely but worth considerably more if they do occur. One approach to valuing the option is to calculate its "expected value." This figure is derived by determining a probability-weighted average of the intrinsic values for each yield level.

A series of diagrams like that in Exhibit 7 will enable the reader to visualize how the option's expected value will vary with changes in

Exhibit 7
Intrinsic Value and Relative Probability (expected yield = 11 percent; standard deviation = 1 percent)

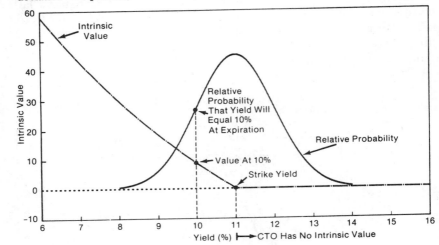

the width (standard deviation) and location (expected yield) of the estimated probability distribution.

Exhibit 8 illustrates the case in which the expected yield has been increased to 12 percent. The curve is thus shifted to the right (while the standard deviation is unchanged). In this scenario, a 10 percent

Exhibit 8
Impact of Higher Expected Yield (expected yield = 12 percent; standard deviation = 1 percent)

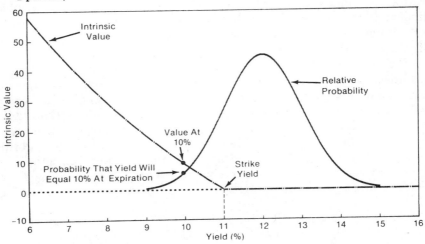

final yield would still produce the same value, but its likelihood is lower. This is also true for all yield values below 11 percent. Thus the investor with a 12 percent expected yield would not value the option as highly as the investor in Exhibit 7 who had an expected yield of 11 percent. On the other hand, for an investor who has an expected yield lower than 11 percent, the option will be worth even more.

The effect of greater uncertainty—a wider standard deviation—is shown in Exhibit 9. This repeats Exhibit 7, but with a higher standard

Exhibit 9
Impact of Increased Uncertainty (expected yield = 11 percent; standard deviation = 1½ percent)

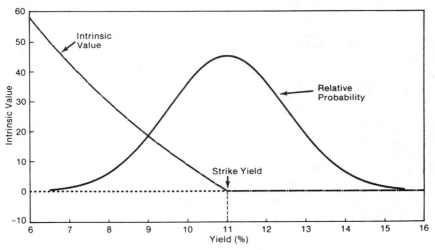

deviation. In this case, a final yield of 8 percent produces the same intrinsic value for the option at expiration, but it has a higher probability of occurrence than in Exhibit 7. As in Exhibit 7, only 50 percent of the expected distribution produces a profit, but the range that produces a profit is wider, and the extreme of the reasonable range produces a larger profit. Note that the extreme of the right side of the yield distribution is also higher, producing lower *bond* prices, but the option holder is indifferent to the amount by which the price goes below the exercise price. It is precisely this asymmetry that produces value because large downward yield moves produce more value, but large upward moves cannot drop the value below zero. The increased uncertainty is valuable to the investor because it enhances the possibility of large profits, and the possible loss remains limited to the premium paid for the option. Thus a wider range of uncertainty around the expected yield provides higher expected value.

It should be recognized that assuming a symmetric distribution of expected yield is not equivalent to assuming an equal probability of an increase or decline in rates. If the expected yield in a symmetric distribution is lower than today's rate, the probability of a decline in rates is greater than that of an increase. Moreover, in certain situations, an investor's expectations may suggest a probability distribution that is itself asymmetric about the expected yield. It is possible to fit virtually any probability distribution into a valuation framework.

THE BLACK-SCHOLES OPTION VALUATION APPROACH

Most popular option valuation models in the stock market are variants of the model first published by Black and Scholes in 1973.[4] This model is based upon constructing a neutral or riskless hedge. In the neutral hedge, a particular number of options are sold short per 100 shares of stock held long, so that small stock price moves are exactly offset by changes in the value of the option position. If such a riskless hedge can be constructed and maintained, Black and Scholes argue that the combined long and short position has little or no risk and that the return earned on the invested funds should therefore equal the T-bill or other short-term, low-risk rate.[5] The inputs necessary for the Black-Scholes formula are the option strike price, the security's current price, cash flows (dividends or interest) prior to the expiration of the option, the variance of the rate of return, the length of time to expiration, and the short-term rate. All of these items are readily available or can be estimated when considering CTOs and, therefore, the Black-Scholes values can be calculated.

APPLYING OPTION MODELS TO "FIXED INCOME" OPTIONS

Several structural differences between the equity and fixed income markets suggest that a departure from the Black-Scholes model may be appropriate when valuing CTOs. First, the neutral hedge may not be relevant for CTOs because it is the issuer who is short the option, and other investors cannot construct the riskless hedge. Issuers are unlikely to "hedge" their option position by purchasing the securities originally sold with the options. Nor can investors safely "write" or sell their own options, for reasons relating to marketability, performance guarantees, and the possible nonexistence of deliverable securities.

In the absence of the riskless hedge approach, market expectations become more important in option valuations. For many fixed income

---

[4] Fischer Black and Myron Scholes, "The Pricing of Options and Corporate Liabilities," *Journal of Political Economy*, (May–June, 1973), pp. 637–59.

[5] For further explanation of the Black-Scholes model, see Clifford Smith, "Option Pricing: A Review," *Journal of Financial Economics* 3 (1976), pp. 3–51.

investors, expectations regarding future yields play a large role in portfolio construction. These expectations may be based on economic or technical factors, the rate structure implied in the yield curve itself, or roll-down yields in the absence of yield curve movement.[6] Appropriate adjustments can be made to the Black-Scholes model, and CTO values consistent with investor expectations and uncertainty regarding rates can be determined. Salomon Brothers Inc, for example, has developed computer programs that will provide discounted expected values for CTOs under a variety of projected yield distributions. The Black-Scholes values then emerge as a special case.

The option values thus determined can be used in several ways. The investor can compare the actual option cost with its estimated value to determine its attractiveness. In addition, the model can be fit to today's CTO price and can produce insights into the combinations of expectations and uncertainty that would imply such a value. This may be useful in determining other market participants' expectations and provides another input in the investment decision-making process.

PROFIT ANALYSIS

By combining CTOs with other debt market instruments, new patterns of return become available. In this section, several will be graphically depicted to explore these opportunities. Exhibit 10 shows the basic price-yield curve of a 20-year, 11 percent bond (on which Exhibits 3 and 4 are based).

Exhibit 10
Price Yield Curve for 20-year 11 Percent Coupon Deliverable Bond

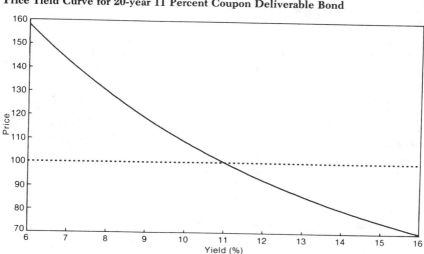

---

[6] See Chapters 5, 32 and 46 for a further discussion.

By comparing Exhibits 10 and 4, it is apparent that the bond investor is subject to an almost symmetric return pattern, and the CTO holder is not. This is the benefit of CTOs that was mentioned earlier (i.e., limited loss and the potential of highly leveraged profits). Now let us combine the CTO and bond into a CTO "unit" to consider its profit possibilities.

AGGRESSIVE STRATEGY: THE CTO UNIT "DOUBLE-UP"

If yields decline sufficiently, the CTO unit holder is doubly rewarded, with profits on both the bond and CTO. If yields increase, the premium is lost along with the consequent loss on the bond. The total dollar return for the unit, including coupon income (but ignoring reinvestment for simplicity), is shown in Exhibit 11. In Exhibit 12 this

Exhibit 11
Total Dollar Return of a "CTO Unit"

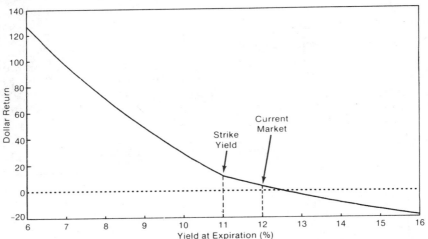

total dollar return pattern is shown along with that of a bond investor with an equal dollar investment in bonds alone. The magnified gains available to the unit holder are readily apparent. For the investor deciding between debt only or the CTO unit, the crossover yield is easily computed.

DEFENSIVE STRATEGY: CTO PLUS CDs

As an alternative, a defensive posture may be struck, with investment in CDs, for example, complementing the option purchase. This

Exhibit 12
Total Dollar Return of a "CTO Unit" versus Bond Alone (assumes equal dollar investment)

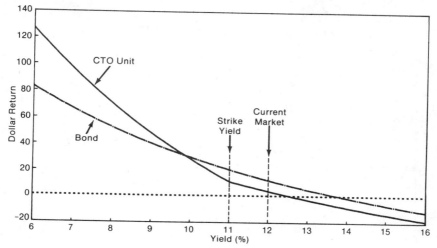

Exhibit 13
Total Dollar Return of CD versus CTO + CD Combination (assumes equal dollar investment)

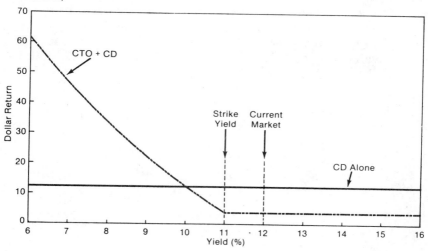

allows the investor to participate in an appreciating market without the potential for large loss if yields increase. The total dollar returns for the combined CTO + CD purchase are shown with a 12 percent CD alone in Exhibit 13. For comparative purposes the bond, unit, and CTO + CD combination are shown together in Exhibit 14.

Exhibit 14
Comparison of Returns of Fixed Income and CTO Combination Investments
(assumes equal dollar investment)

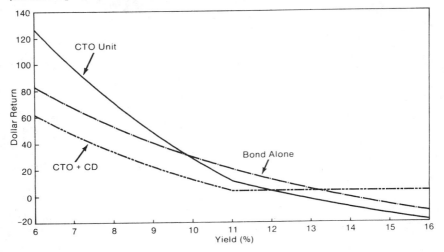

AVERAGE YIELD

Many investors' cash flows are such that regular periodic investments are normally made. In this case, it may be useful to consider the
average yield for two sequential investments. Exhibit 15 depicts the
purchase yield (to maturity) on the first issue, the subsequent issue,
and the average in the case where CTOs are not used. Exhibit 16

Exhibit 15
Purchase Yields without CTOs

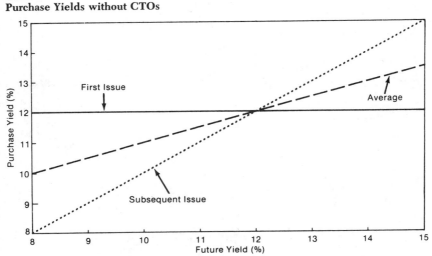

Exhibit 16
Purchase Yields with CTOs

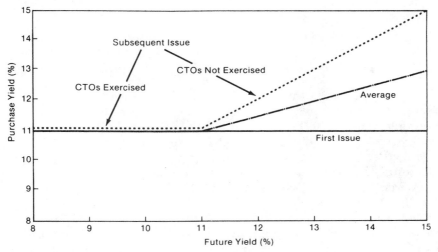

shows these yields when a CTO unit is purchased as the first investment. Exhibit 17 compares the two average yields and indicates the
yield range for which the CTO purchase is more advantageous. (For
the issuer, the average yield becomes the average cost of both issues.
The advantage to the option holder is a cost to the issuer, and the area
of loss to the investor is an area of profit for the issuer.)

Exhibit 17
Comparison of Average Purchase Yields with and without CTOs

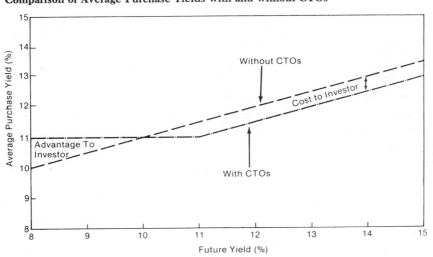

CTO VARIATIONS

The "double-up" option has several advantages to the potential purchaser. Because the deliverable bond is identical to the issue bond, exact prices for the deliverable bond can be determined. This would not be the case if the deliverable bond were not yet outstanding and prices were based on estimated yields for the particular quality and maturity of the yet-to-be-issued security.

More importantly, the existing market for the issue bond provides ready liquidity for any investor who exercises his or her option early and then wants to sell the deliverable bond. If the deliverable bond were a new instrument, any early exerciser would not have a liquid aftermarket because of the small number of deliverable bonds outstanding. If prices subsequently dropped so that no other options were exercised, the early exercisers would face this liquidity problem for the life of the bond.

Nevertheless, there may be advantages to the issuer and purchaser in structuring the CTO differently than a double-up. For example, a five-year bond "unit" might include a CTO with a 10- or 20-year maturity bond as the deliverable security. The shorter term of the issue bond provides greater price stability, and the volatility of the longer deliverable security provides good upside potential if yields decline.

As another example, the firm may reopen an existing issue (or use a new bond with terms identical to an existing issue) as the deliverable security, with a strike price chosen so as to offer a close-to-market yield at the time of the CTO issue. This may avoid the liquidity problem described above.

Still another variation is to allow delivery of any of a group of bonds for which the strike price is set in terms of a specific yield. Such "yield maintenance CTOs" may be useful to municipalities or utilities that are faced with special constraints on coupon levels. Zero-coupon bonds are deliverable against several CTOs, and these have strike "prices" defined in terms of yield because of the natural accretion to par as time elapses.

In December 1980, the Kingdom of Sweden sold the first CTO unit: a five-year note with a warrant attached that allowed the holder to purchase another five-year note (with an identical coupon) at par. The warrant expired (worthless, as it turned out) six months later. In the first 12 months after that date, a number of issues with CTOs came to the market. Exhibit 18 lists the domestic corporate and municipal bonds that had warrants attached, and Exhibit 19 lists the Eurodollar and yankee bonds with warrants issued in 1981. Different underwriting regulations in the international market have contributed to the popularity of warrant issues overseas.

Exhibit 18
Domestic Corporate and Municipal Bonds with Warrants

Issuer	Issue Bond	Delivery Bond	Warrant Terms
Corporate:			
Continental Illinois	13⅝, '85 issued 11/4/81	0 percent due 11/1/89	Two warrants attached; each allows purchase of one delivery bond at a yield of 14.25 percent; expires 10/31/82.
Manufacturers Hanover	12¾, '85 issued 11/16/81	0 percent due 12/18/89	Two warrants; each allows purchase of one delivery bond to yield 12.875; expires 11/28/82.
Commercial Credit	14¼, '85 issued 12/3/81	0 percent due 12/1/90	Two warrants; each allows purchase of one delivery bond to yield 15⅛; expires 11/30/82.
Municipal:			
Municipal Assistance Corporation for the City of New York	10⅝, '08 dated 12/1/81	10⅝ percent due 7/1/07	One warrant; allows purchase of one delivery bond at par until 1/18/83.
Municipal Assistance Corporation for the City of New York	12¾, '08 dated 11/1/81	12¾ percent due 7/1/08	One warrant, allows purchase of one delivery bond at par until 1/18/83.

Exhibit 19
Eurodollar and Yankee Bonds with Warrants Offered in 1981

Date of Issue	Borrower	Warrant	Expiration Date
Fixed-rate Bonds:			
January 1981	**GTE Finance** U.S.$50 million, 13¾%, 1986	One warrant for 13¾% (later increased to 16¼%) bonds due 1988	Aug 81
January 1981	**Hydro-Quebec (GG)** U.S.$100 million, 13%, 1991	One warrant for 13% bonds due 1991	Sep 81
March 1981	**American Airlines O/S Finance (PG)** U.S.$55 million, 15¼%, 1986 (collateral trust bonds)	One warrant for 15¼% bonds due 1988	Dec 81
August 1981	**Continental Illinois O/S Finance (PG)** U.S.$100 million, 14 3/4%, 1984	Two warrants for 0% bonds due 1988, yielding 14½%	Sep 82
August 1981	**Wells Fargo Int'l Finance (PG)** U.S.$75 million, 15%, 1985	Two warrants for 0% bonds due 1988, yielding 14¾%	Sep 82
August 1981	**Hiram Walker Holdings (PG)** U.S.$65 million, 15¾%, 1984	Two warrants for 0% bonds due 1989, yielding 15½%	Sep 82
September 1981	**GTE Finance** U.S.$50 million, 16¼%, 1985	One warrant for 16% bonds due 1988	Sep 82
October 1981	**BFCE (GG)** U.S.$100 million, 16%, 1986	Two warrants for 16% bonds due 1986	Oct 82
Original Issue Discount Bonds:			
August 1981	**Citicorp O/S Finance (PG)** U.S.$100 million, 0%, 1984	Two warrants for 0% bonds due 1988, yielding 14½%	Aug 82
August 1981	**Transamerica Finance Corp (PG)** U.S.$75 million, 7%, 1986	Two warrants for 0% bonds due 1991, yielding 15¼%	Sep 82
December 1981	**Transamerica Finance Corp (PG)** U.S.$75 million, 0%, 1986	Two warrants for 0% bonds due 1989, yielding 14½%	Dec 82
Floating Rate Notes:			
February 1981	**Citicorp O/S Finance (PG)** U.S.$250 million, E$ bid (3 Mo) 1984	One warrant for 12⅝% bonds due 1991	Sep 81
Convertible Bonds:			
January 1981	**Anacomp Int'l (PG)** U.S.$12.5 million, 9%, 1996	One warrant for 9% bonds due 1996 (non-detachable)	Sep 81
Yankee Bonds:			
April 1981	**Kingdom of Sweden** U.S.$200 million, 14⅝%, 1988	One warrant for 14⅝% bonds due 1988	Oct 81

(GG) Government Guarantee; (PG) Parent Guarantee.

Source: Adapted from Tran Q. Hung and Karen A. Johnson, "Eurowarrants: The Potential for Capital Gains with Limited Risk," Salomon Brothers Inc (December 1981).

CONCLUSION

It should be apparent that the introduction of CTOs has provided the fixed income investor with a new instrument that offers risk-return patterns new to the debt market. The warrants alone provide downside protection and upside potential and "unit" investments provide enhanced upside return. Thus, although the CTO can be an appealing individual tool, it may also be used for the control of the portfolio's overall-risk level in uncertain markets. CTOs should be seriously considered by all investors whose objective is to participate in appreciating markets with limited downside risk.

Early Redemption (Put) Options on Fixed Income Securities*

24

ROBERT W. KOPPRASCH, Ph.D., C.F.A.
Vice President
Salomon Brothers Inc

An early redemption option on a fixed income security can remove much of the risk associated with investment in such securities. The purpose of this chapter is to discuss the factors and variables involved in analyzing and valuing early redemption options. These options are frequently referred to as puts, although they may not be puts in the traditional sense because they cannot be detached and traded separately. Nevertheless, the term *put* is descriptive and has become accepted Street usage; therefore, we will also use the term *put*.

EARLY PUT ISSUES

Although a number of recent issues have included puts, they are not an entirely new development. In 1974 Citicorp sold a floating-rate issue that included a put provision, and recently the company sold

* The author would like to express his appreciation to Martin L. Leibowitz for assisting in the development of this chapter.

Although the information in this chapter has been obtained from sources that the author believes to be reliable, Salomon Brothers Inc cannot guarantee its accuracy, and such information may be incomplete or condensed. All opinions and estimates included in this chapter constitute judgment as of this date and are subject to change without notice.

another. Beneficial Corporation now has several fixed coupon issues outstanding that give the holders early redemption options.

In Canada, bonds known as extendables and retractables have long been common. A 30-year bond "retractable" to a 10-year maturity has, in essence, a put attached with an effective exercise date 10 years after issue. An extendable technically incorporates a call option, but a 10-year bond extendable to 30 years is, practically speaking, indistinguishable from a 30-year bond retractable to 10 years. Either can be redeemed after 10 years, or after 30 years. Thus both extendables and retractables may be included under the broad category of puts.

Recent interest-rate volatility has increased investor awareness of the vulnerability of bond portfolios to increases in rates. Because of the early redemption feature, issues with puts will generally experience less downside fluctuation, thus making them attractive to investors. If the recent level of interest-rate volatility continues, one would not be surprised to see a resurgence of interest in issues with various types of put provisions.

BASICS OF A PUT

A number of factors must be known to assess the attractiveness, or risk-reducing ability, of a put. These factors, each of which will be considered later in detail, are the following:

1. The early redemption price, known as the *strike price*. (This assumes that the redemption is for cash, although there are other possibilities.) The strike price may be defined in terms of dollar price or yield.
2. How often the early redemption privilege is "active" (e.g., every coupon date).
3. The first date when the put may be exercised (first exercise date).
4. The last date the put may be exercised (expiration date).

Two factors, external to the put itself, will also have some impact: the maturity of the bond and, especially, the shape of the yield curve. In fact, the yield curve has a major impact on putable bond pricing.

The consideration of the yield curve will be deferred until a later section and will be ignored in the early examples. We will assume here that yield curve effects are not significant, thus implicitly assuming a flat curve.

The primary value of an early redemption option is the privilege of selling the bond back to the issuer at the strike price. This privilege should tether the price of the bond to a level close to the strike price near "active" dates, thus reducing downside price risk.

AN EXAMPLE

Assume that straight debt with a 30-year maturity and 12 percent coupon could be issued at par. If a bond with identical terms but incorporating a one-year put at par could be sold to yield 11.5 percent (price = 104.20), the put premium would be 4.20. (Most issues are not structured in this way but rather have a reduced coupon and are sold at par. However, as considerations of an "in the money" strike price and coupon differential would complicate the example and charts, this technique allows us to concentrate on the explicit cost of the put alone, without either implied costs due to lower coupons or exercise prices that differ from the original issue price. We will alter the example to "real world" specifications in a later section.)

The price yield curve for the bond one year later when the put can be exercised is shown in Exhibit 1. Obviously the bond that includes a

Exhibit 1
Price-Yield Curve for 30-Year 12 Percent Coupon Bond

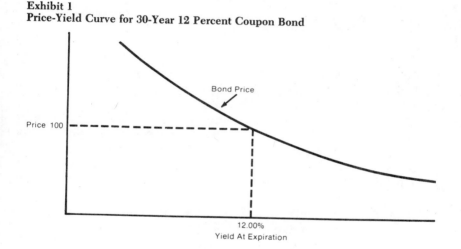

put with a strike price at par will sell for par at all market yields above 12 percent because of the put. Straight bonds will sell below par as shown in the figure. If we compute the profit or loss for the two types of bonds, we will see that the put-bond holder can lose a maximum of 4.2—the premium paid for the put—but the straight-bond holder's loss will depend upon how much yields move above 12 percent. If yields decline, both straight and putable bonds will be priced along the price yield curve on the put's expiration date, with the profit depending upon whether the investor paid 100 (straight debt) or 104.2 (putable) for the bond. Profits and losses for various yields are shown in Exhibit 2.

Exhibit 2
Profit Pattern of Putable Bond versus Straight Bond

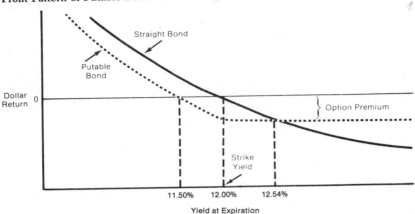

Note: Chart assumes investment in one bond and one option, as opposed to equal dollar investments. Coupon income is ignored.

Two points in Exhibit 2 are likely to be of interest to the investor. If yields decline to 11.5, the bond will sell for 104.20, and the investor who bought a putable bond will break even. If yields increase instead to 12.54, both the straight-bond holder and the putable-bond holder will show a loss of 4.2, thus establishing an indifference point. At any higher yield, the straight-bond holder will have a greater loss. At any lower yield, he or she will have a lower loss or higher profit. (The problem of different initial investments will be remedied when the example is changed.)

The profit patterns in Exhibit 2 make clear the risk and return trade-off of the buyer of the putable bond. The maximum possible loss—the premium paid—is limited and known in advance, but the potential profits are reduced only by the amount of the premium.

THE VALUE OF THE PUT

Although most puts cannot be detached from the underlying bonds, we can strip the put from the bond for analytical purposes and look only at the value of the put. At market yields below 12 percent, the put clearly has no intrinsic value because the bond can be sold for more than the strike price in the open market. At yields above 12 percent, the put (if exercisable immediately) has an intrinsic value equal to the strike price less the normal (nonputable) price for that yield. The intrinsic value derived from the price yield curve shown in Exhibit 1, is shown in Exhibit 3.

Exhibit 3
Intrinsic Value Pattern of a Put

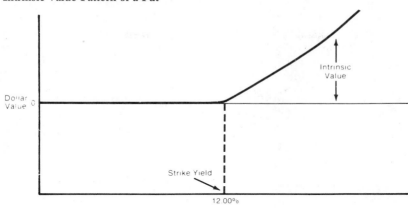

Dollar Value 0

Intrinsic Value

Strike Yield

12.00%

Yield At Expiration

Exhibit 4
A Probability Distribution

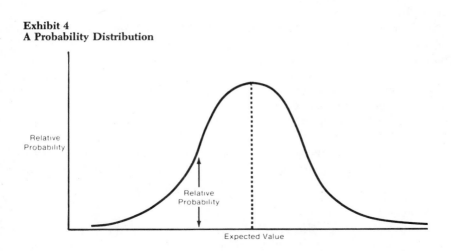

Relative Probability

Relative Probability

Expected Value

Before buying a put issue, an investor will probably consider the value likely to be realized at expiration. One method of valuation for a put would be to consider the range of likely yields at expiration and to assign some subjective probabilities to these yields. A symmetrical probability distribution, such as the one shown in Exhibit 4, provides a good starting example.[1]

The center (highest point) of the distribution is placed over the investor's expected yield at the put date. The width of the distribution

---

[1] See the previous chapter for a more detailed description of fixed income option valuation.

recognizes that there is some potential error in the predicted yield. Statistically, the measure of dispersion (a width measure) usually used is the standard deviation. If the standard deviation of the prediction is large, the investor perceives that there is a possibility that the put may be very valuable (toward the right in Exhibit 4). Without going any deeper into option valuation theory that can be found in the previous chapter, the following observations will be made.

1. Higher expected yields lead to higher put values.
2. Higher standard deviations lead to higher put values.
3. Longer maturity of the bond itself leads to higher put values because of increased sensitivity to yield changes.

IN-THE-MONEY PUTS

The basic example used earlier assumed that the put premium was paid in addition to the par amount for the purchase of the bond. In the more likely case, the issue will carry a lower coupon than the market yield for that type of instrument, but will nevertheless sell at par to reflect the inclusion of the put. This presents some pricing problems that need to be discussed.

When a *call* option is included with a bond issued at par, the par price includes both the value of the option and the value of the bond. Thus the bond's value, based on its coupon, maturity, and other features, is less than par, and the option to buy another *at par* is "out of the money"; that is, the bond must move in a favorable direction just to reach the exercise price. This option is worth less than an "at the money" option because the option holder does not participate in the initial price appreciation of the bond.

Similarly, when a putable bond sells at par, the put value is the difference between the bond's straight price and par. In contrast to the call option, however, the put option is in the money because the bond can be sold (redeemed) at par, although its straight value is less than par. In fact, it would be difficult to correctly price such an issue if the put were exercisable immediately because the price being paid for the put is simply its intrinsic value, with no value attached to its potential for a large payoff in the future. Obviously this type of put cannot be struck at par at the outset if the bond-put unit is issued at par.

ALTERING THE EXAMPLE FOR AN ISSUE AT PAR

Let us consider the earlier example, amended as follows: the putable 30-year bond will be issued at par in a 12 percent market but will carry an 11.5 percent coupon. Thus the bond's value is 95.96, and the put premium is 4.04 (100 − 95.96). The strike price, as before, is 100.

Notice that the premium paid for the put is equal to its immediate exercise value of 4.04. That is, the bond that is worth 95.96 can be sold (to the issuer) immediately for 100, for a gross gain of 4.04. Thus the buyer is paying no time-value premium, and the advantage to the issuer is minimized.

There are several ways to rectify the pricing problem. One method would be to lower the strike price to the actual bond value (without put) at issue. In the example above, then, the strike would be 95.96. This approach is very similar to the earlier example except on a scaled-down basis. Although theoretically clean, it is not the approach taken in most of the putable bonds available today.

Another method is to defer activation of the put for several years. In this case, the 4.04 value would not be available immediately, but perhaps five years later. Thus today's value of the 4.04 is its discounted present value, and the buyer is paying up for the option.

The example above will be used in later sections as a reference point. For the next section, however, we will again assume a near-term exercise possibility for the purpose of illustrating another pricing dilemma: the yield curve.

THE IMPORTANCE OF THE YIELD CURVE

An early redemption option on a bond makes it more difficult to place the issue on the yield curve because of the possibility of early "maturity." This section will address pricing considerations for short-term puts and deferred puts in light of the shape of the yield curve.

Let us assume that the yield curve is positively sloped, rising from about 10 percent in the 1-year maturity area to 12 percent for 30 years. If the putable bond were given a coupon of 11.5 percent as in the earlier example, it would clearly dominate all other one-year securities that yielded 10 percent. It would be quickly purchased by one-year investors as a superior investment, and they would intend to put the bond in one year. The bond would quickly trade to a premium to yield a return competitive with other 1-year investments, but this would leave it uncompetitive with other 30-year instruments. Although adjustments to the strike price could potentially solve this problem, the example illustrates the basic dual maturity nature of putable bonds with a single put date.

Market forces will cause the putable bond to trade to the maturity point at which it is most competitive. Thus the yield levels at both the early redemption and normal maturity must be considered as important in the pricing of putable bonds. Additionally, because the bondholder has the option of electing the other maturity if it becomes more advantageous to do so (i.e., the option still has value), the bond should trade at a slightly higher price/lower yield than a bond at the selected maturity without this option.

For example, consider the 11.5 percent, 30-year bond with an early redemption option (exercisable after one year) that is trading at 101.39 so as to have a 10 percent yield that is competitive with 1-year instruments. If the yields in the 30-year area dropped, the bond would be worth more as a 30-year bond and would perhaps trade to 110. Similarly, if restrictive monetary policy caused short rates to rise sharply, the bond might simply be priced at the 30-year point because that became the higher price. This option to change maturities will command a premium in price and result in some reduction in yield. The magnitude of the premium will probably reflect market participants' aggregate sense not only of the probability that a switch in optimum maturity will occur, but also whether that switch would produce extra profit or soften a loss.

THE YIELD CURVE AND MULTIMATURITY BONDS (MULTIPLE EXERCISE DATES)

If a putable bond has several exercise dates for early redemption, the yield at each potential maturity becomes important in pricing the bond. The bond's price should be the maximum price obtained by pricing it to the yield at each relevant redemption date. As with dual-maturity bonds, if the bond's price does not reflect its maximum value, arbitrage or normal bond swapping would force it to the maximum price, *plus* the premium to reflect the multimaturity option.

Although it is theoretically possible to construct a probabilistic model for valuing the maturity switch option, practical considerations, involving conditional probabilities at dates long into the future, make this approach unwieldy. In order to provide some market evidence regarding putable bond pricing, let us consider the seven putable bonds described in Exhibit 5.

Exhibit 5
Terms of Putable Corporate Bonds*

Name	S & P Rating	Coupon	Issued Amount	Maturity	Put Date, Terms
Avco Financial Services	A	9.75%	$125	8/1/99	12/1/87
Beneficial Corporation	AA-	8.00	150	6/15/01	every 6/15, from 1982-2001
Beneficial Corporation	AA-	8.40	150	5/15/08	every 12/15, from 1986-2008
Beneficial Corporation	AA-	11.50	250	1/15/05	1/15/84, then coupon drops to 9%
Ford Motor Credit	A	16.25	250	1/15/87	1/15/85
Transamerica Financial	A+	8.50	50	7/1/01	every 7/1, from 1984-2001
ITT Financial	A	8.875	125	6/15/03	6/15/87, 6/15/92, 6/15/97

* Excludes floating rate issues. There are also some municipal bonds with puts.

Exhibit 6
Putable Corporate Bonds: Yield to First Put versus Yield to Maturity

Name	Coupon	Price	Maturity	Yield to Maturity	First Put Date	Yield to First Put
Avco Financial Services	9.75%	79⅜	8/1/99	12.67	12/1/87	14.805
Beneficial Corporation	8.00	88⅛	6/15/01	9.32	6/15/83	15.116
Beneficial Corporation	8.40	76	5/15/08	11.25	12/15/86	14.931
Beneficial Corporation	11.50	92⅝	1/15/05	10.49	1/15/84	15.007
Transamerica Financial	8.50	84½	7/1/01	10.35	7/1/84	14.980
ITT Financial	8.875	77½	6/15/03	11.75	6/15/87	14.619

Note: Ford Motor Credit 16¼ was issued after the pricing date of this table. Its yield to put would probably not differ significantly from yield to maturity because the put date is only two years prior to maturity.

Exhibit 7
U.S. Treasury Yield Curve versus Putable Bond Yield Curves (as of the close of Friday, May 29, 1981)

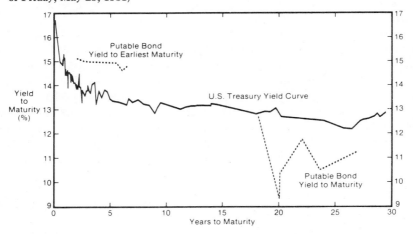

Exhibit 6 provides prices as of May 29, 1981, with corresponding yields to maturity and yields to first redemption.

In order to place these yields in a more meaningful perspective, they are plotted in Exhibit 7 against the Treasury yield curve for the same date. It can be seen that the yields to maturity all lie below the Treasury curve, indicating that these bonds are certainly not priced on a yield-to-maturity basis. When viewed as intermediate-term bonds, however, their yield levels are more appropriate. It is obvious that the early redemption option has not gone unnoticed by investors.

MULTIMATURITY BONDS AS INVESTOR CALL OPTIONS

The maturity switch option that gives a putable bond its multimaturity nature can also be thought of as a call option. Consider the 11.5
percent, 30-year bond mentioned earlier that is putable in one year
and is now trading as if it were a 1-year bond. This bond can be
thought of as a bond with a 1-year maturity, with a call on a 29-year
bond exercisable at the end of 1 year. That is, at the redemption of the
"1-year" bond, the investor can, at his or her option, reinvest the funds
in a 29-year, 12 percent bond. The bond's current price should reflect
the value of this call option. If, at the 1-year date, the 29-year bond is
worth more than the redemption price, the investor can "exercise" the
call option by *not* redeeming the bond early. The investor has in effect
rolled the redemption proceeds into the long maturity bond (purchased the bond at the strike price). If, on the other hand, the 29-year
bond were trading below the redemption price, the option could be
allowed to "expire" by the act of early redemption. An investor who
desires a 29-year, 12 percent bond in his or her portfolio can buy one
in the open market for less than the redemption proceeds. In option
parlance, we would say that the option was "out of the money" and
thus worthless at "expiration."

Consider the Avco 9.75 of 99 listed in Exhibit 5 as having a single
put date of 12/1/87. This bond is worth more than others maturing later
in 1987 with similar quality and coupon because the Avco includes a
"call" on "another" bond maturing 8/1/99. If the call is close to "at the
money," the bond should sell at a premium and lower yield.

If a put has many exercise dates, the value of the "call" option is
more difficult to determine. Assume that the bond is trading as a one-
year instrument. The option allows the investor to "purchase" at the
redemption strike price another bond, the value of which depends
upon whether it is considered a one-year bond, a five-year bond, and
so on. Each of the feasible maturity bonds includes another call option
on a bond, or a string of bonds, whose last maturity is 29 years later.
Although a precise value is difficult to determine, some value is obviously inherent in such an option. The Beneficial Corporation's 8s and
8.40s provide examples of this variable maturity structure.

The next several sections will deal with variations in the terms of
the put, with the modified example being used as the reference point.
Before proceeding with the changes, however, it is necessary to establish some benchmark value. Although there are probably a number of
ways to measure the value, we have chosen to use the present value of
the cash flows over the next 30 years associated with the original
investment. The bond's yield at the time of the analysis is used as the
discount rate. Thus, if the bond is not redeemed early, the cash flows
consist of coupon payments and normal redemption. If the bond is

put, the cash flows consist of the early coupons, redemption at the strike, and coupons and redemption of the subsequent investment. The put will be considered active at the five-year point for one time only unless otherwise specified.

One advantage of using the present value approach is that it is equally applicable to the issuer and the bondholder because they are on opposite sides of each cash flow. Thus the present value of future receipts (assuming reinvestment if the bond were put) is the same as the cost to the issuer of future payments (assuming refinancing if the bond were put) if we ignore taxes. In the examples that follow, a 12 percent discount rate will be applied to all future cash flows. Thus a 12 percent, 30-year straight bond would have a present value of 100. This then is the benchmark. A lower figure represents a savings to the issuer and a cost to the investor and vice versa.

Naturally, if the yield for straight debt on the expiration date exceeds the strike yield, the bonds will be put back to the issuer. The investor will receive the strike price and reinvest this amount at the new higher market yield, thus increasing the investor's return. The issuer will have to refinance at the higher market yield, resulting in higher cost thereafter. The present value profile of the putable bond is shown versus straight debt in Exhibit 8.

Exhibit 8
Present Value Pattern of Putable Bond versus Straight Bond

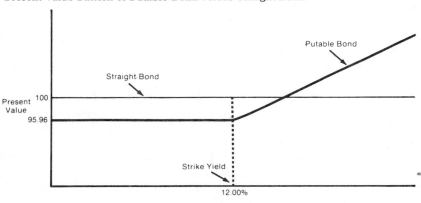

Notice that we have ignored the possibility of the bond being called if yields decline. This would naturally lower the investor's return and issuer's cost if yields declined. A detailed treatment of the effect of the call feature can be found elsewhere.[2]

---

[2] Martin L. Leibowitz, *The Maturity Decision: The Issuer's Choice between the Intermediate and Long-Term Debt Markets* (New York: Salomon Brothers Inc, 1980).

THE STRIKE YIELD

The strike yield is an important parameter because it effectively sets the early redemption price. If the market yield is above the strike yield (i.e., the market price is below the strike price), it is reasonable to expect that the bond will be put back to the issuer for early redemption. By setting a strike yield above the yield at the time of issue, the put options are effectively out of the money, and the issuer can establish some cushion of downward price movement necessary before the bonds will be put for early redemption. The present value patterns for the benchmark example and several higher strike yields are shown in Exhibit 9.

Exhibit 9
Present Value Patterns for Different Strike Yields

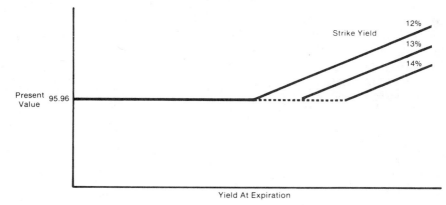

One can see that higher strike yields (lower strike prices) result in lower returns for investors and lower costs for issuers than the benchmark if yields increase and the bonds are put. (Recognizing this, however, investors would probably demand a higher coupon to offset the lower level of price protection. This would have little effect if the bonds were put after a year but would have more significant impact on return if the issue remained outstanding for the entire 30 years.)

PUT RATIO

One of the areas of concern to the issuer is the need to have the cash available on exercise dates if it appears that the bonds will be put. Normally this would involve refinancing in a higher yield environment. Because the issuer may want to limit the risk of refinancing the entire issue when yields are high and capital potentially scarce, the entire issue may not be subject to early redemption. The holder may be allowed, for example, to have one half of his or her bonds redeemed early. Thus two puts may be necessary to redeem one bond, much as several "rights" are necessary to purchase new shares in an equity rights offering.

Exhibit 10 compares the present values of issues with different put ratios, the ratio being defined as the number of bonds redeemable per number of bonds in the original issue. It is assumed in Exhibit 10 that

Exhibit 10
Present Value Patterns for Different Put Ratios

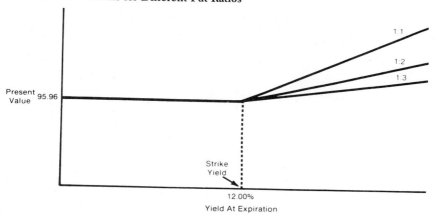

the terms of the various issues are identical except for the put ratio. In practice, if a 1 : 1 ratio resulted in a 50-basis-point concession, a 1 : 2 ratio issue would presumably have a higher coupon to reflect the diluted put value.

CONCLUSION

The debt market has seen the introduction of a number of new investment vehicles and sweeteners in recent years as issuers have found it necessary to entice buyers into a volatile market. Warrants to buy additional bonds capitalize on upside price volatility, and puts provide protection from downside volatility. The dollar-for-dollar downside protection is not linked with dollar-for-dollar upside losses, and the new pattern of return and risk makes these bonds an excellent hedging vehicle.

If downside volatility is perceived as a continuing threat, we would not be surprised to see additional issues of this form. They provide a special benefit to portfolios that are constrained from taking losses, and when trading as intermediates, they provide "call options" to long-term investors.

Puts should receive strong consideration from both issuers and investors as they search for investments with features that are attractive in the rapidly changing debt market of the 1980s.

Perspectives on International Bond Investing*

25 **MARGARET DARASZ HADZIMA, C.F.A.**
Vice President, Bonds
Scudder, Stevens & Clark

CORNELIA M. SMALL
Vice President, Economics
Scudder, Stevens & Clark

INTRODUCTION

In the five years from 1976 to 1980, the total amount of funds raised by all issuers in the Eurobond market equalled approximately two thirds of the new-issue volume in the U.S. public corporate bond market. In this same period, the volume of nondollar foreign bonds sold by issuers outside their own domestic market was nearly as large, totaling about one half the U.S. new-issue public corporate bond volume. Although complete statistics on the entire size of the various worldwide domestic bond markets are not readily available, the total outstanding size of the U.S. bond market is now less than half the size of the sum of all bond markets[1] compared to a larger proportion in

* The authors would like to express gratitude to their colleagues at Scudder, Stevens and Clark for their editing assistance and many insightful comments. Special thanks go to Mary Spyropoulos for her valuable contribution in the computer development of the statistical analysis.

[1] This conclusion is supported by a study prepared by Jeffrey D. Hanna and David Johnson published October 15, 1981, by Salomon Brothers Inc, entitled "How Big is the World Bond Market?" According to this study, which is based on 1980 figures, the United States represents 39 percent of the total government bond markets in eight major countries including Japan, Germany, the United Kingdom, France, Canada, Switzerland, the Netherlands, and the United States. When agencies, municipals, cor-

earlier years. Whether or not international bonds in any of their various forms have a place in U.S. portfolios, their sheer volume suggests that a general understanding of their characteristics is in order.

The term *international bonds* is often used to describe a number of different types of bonds with a variety of characteristics relating to issuer domicile, the nature of the underwriting syndicate, the location of the primary trading market, the domicile of the primary buyers, and/or currency denomination. Insofar as price movements are concerned, the most important characteristic is currency denomination. Regardless of the domicile of the issuer, the buyer, or the trading market, prices of issues denominated in U.S. dollars ("U.S. pay") are affected principally by the direction of U.S. interest rates, whereas prices of issues denominated in other currencies ("foreign pay") are determined primarily by movements of interest rates in the country of the currency denomination. Thus, analysis of international bond investing must be separated into two parts—U.S. pay and foreign pay.

U.S.-PAY INTERNATIONAL BOND INVESTING

The U.S.-pay international bond market can in turn be divided into issues for which the primary trading market is in the United States ("Yankees") and issues for which the primary trading market is abroad ("Eurodollar").

Eurodollar Bonds

The latter has come to be known as the *Eurodollar market*, and Eurodollar bonds are described as securities that are:

1. Denominated in U.S. dollars.
2. Underwritten by an international syndicate.
3. Sold at issue to non-U.S. investors.

Since offerings of Eurodollar bonds are not registered with the SEC, the expenses of bringing an issue to market are less than in the domestic U.S. bond market. However, because the securities are not registered, underwriters are legally prohibited from selling new issues to the U.S. public until the issue has come to rest and a cooling-off or seasoning period has expired. Most underwriters' counsels judge this period to range from three to nine months, depending on their legal interpretations. As a result, although U.S.-based investors may buy Eurodollar bonds after the seasoning period, the market re-

---

porates, and other domestic public issues are included, the United States represents 50.4 percent of the total; and when foreign and Eurobonds are added, the United States represents 51 percent of the total.

mains dominated by foreign-based investors, and the primary trading center remains in London.

The size of the Eurodollar bond market has grown dramatically from a nominal new-issue volume in the early 1960s to more than $16 billion of new issues in 1980. Marketability of Eurodollar bonds has improved over the years but is still limited. Although the size of recent Eurodollar issues has been about $100 million, most of the older issues are less than $50 million. In recent issues, trades of $2–5 million sometimes occur, but $1 million is normally a large trade. In older issues, trading volume of $200,000 per trade is considered good size. Eurodollar bonds pay interest only annually, so adjustment in the yield calculation must be made for comparison to domestic issues that pay interest semiannually. New-issue Eurodollar bonds must generally be an obligation of a foreign entity to be exempt from U.S. withholding taxes, which are discussed later in this chapter. Thus many U.S. corporations sell Eurodollar issues through a foreign subsidiary and then guarantee payment of principal and interest.

Like the U.S. domestic market, which has seen a number of creative financing techniques over the last few years, the Eurodollar market has spawned a number of innovations, including floating rate notes, original issue discounts, index-linked securities, and convertibles. When convertible into the stock of a foreign-based company, Eurodollar convertibles provide opportunities for currency gain related to prospects for increased conversion value while maintaining their bond-related denomination in U.S. dollars.

Yankee Bonds

The other portion of the U.S.-pay international bond market encompasses those foreign-domiciled issuers who register with the SEC and borrow U.S. dollars via issues underwritten by a U.S. syndicate for delivery in the United States. The principal trading market is in the United States, although foreign buyers can and do participate. Unlike the Eurodollar market, interest is paid semiannually. Marketability of these "foreign bonds" in the United States is usually better than in the Euromarket but can at times be limited depending largely on the quality of the issuer. This market has loosely been termed the *Yankee bond market*, although technically Yankee bonds are issues that would have been subject to the interest equalization tax (IET) prior to its elimination in 1974.[2] Canadian bonds, some South American issues, and issues of some supranational agencies (such as the World

---

[2] The interest equalization tax was imposed on purchases of foreign securities by U.S. residents during the years 1963 to 1974. The intent and affect of the tax was to discourage foreign borrowing in the United States by increasing the cost of capital. In order to make returns after the I.E.T. competitive with rates on domestic issues, gross rates on foreign borrowings had to be higher than would otherwise have been the case.

Bank, Inter American Development Bank, and Asian Development Bank) were not subject to the IET and therefore are not formally considered Yankee bonds.

Since removal of the IET in 1974, sale of "foreign bonds" in the United States has been significant, although recent years have seen a decline in volume, coming in part as a response to the high borrowing rates in the United States compared with alternative markets. Annual new-issue volumes are shown in Exhibit 1.

Exhibit 1
New-Issue Foreign Bonds Sold in the United States ($ millions)

	1973	1974	1975	1976	1977	1978	1979	1980
Canadian entities	$865	$1,962	$3,074	$ 6,138	$3,022	$3,142	$2,193	$2,136
International organizations	—	610	1,900	2,275	1,917	459	1,100	550
Other	95	719	1,488	2,191	2,489	2,194	1,222	743
Total	$960	$3,291	$6,462	$10,604	$7,428	$5,795	$4,515	$3,429

Source: *World Financial Markets*, (New York: Morgan Guaranty).

U.S.-pay international bonds are generally more attractive to foreign buyers than are U.S. Treasury or corporate issues. The primary reason is that interest on these bonds—Eurodollar, Yankee, Canadian, and supranational agency bonds—is exempt from U.S. withholding tax. In contrast, interest on domestic bonds, including U.S. Treasury obligations, is subject to a 30 percent withholding tax unless that rate is reduced by a U.S. tax treaty with the holder's domicile country. In practice, the United States has tax treaties with most major countries, and thereby the effective withholding tax on interest received on domestic bonds by residents of these countries is signficantly less than 30 percent, as shown in Exhibit 2. These treaties also apply to the withholding tax rate on dividends of U.S. corporations and generally provide that any withholding tax paid can be used as a partial offset to the investor's domestic income tax bill. Certain foreign institutions with tax-exempt status in their own country are subject to reduced or eliminated withholding tax rates, and foreign central banks are exempt from all taxes. However, even when a purchaser can offset or reclaim the 30 percent withholding tax on domestic bond interest, it is often a tedious and time-consuming task, since a filing must be made to the U.S government in order to reclaim the withholding tax paid. Perhaps even more important, the filing process eliminates anonymity, which is an important concern for some foreign buyers. Thus securities that are themselves exempt from the withholding tax have an advantage to foreigners, an advantage that has no value to domestic buyers.

Periodically, bills have been filed in Congress to eliminate the withholding tax on interest paid to foreigners. If the tax is ever elimi-

Exhibit 2
Withholding Taxes on Dividends and Interest

Investor Resident in*	Dividend-Paying Company or Interest-Paying Debtor In									
	S. Africa		Belgium		France		Germany		Hong Kong	
Belgium	15	10			25	25	25	25	—	15
	—	—			25†	13–15	10	10	—	—
France	15	10	20	20			25	25	—	15
	—	—	5	5			10	25	—	—
Germany	15	10	20	20	25	25			—	15
	—	—	5	5	25†	25			—	—
Hong Kong	15	10	20	20	25	25	25	25		
	—	—	—	—	—	—	—	—		
Italy	15	10	20	20	25	25	25	25	—	15
	—	—	5	5	10†	13–15	—	—	—	—
Japan	15	10	20	20	25	25	25	25	—	15
	—	—	5	5	10	15	10	15	—	—
Netherlands	15	10	20	20	25	25	25	25	—	15
	—	—	5	10	25†	13–15	10	25	—	—
Switzerland	15	10	20	20	25	25	25	25	—	15
	7.5	—	—	—	25†	13–15	10	25	—	—
United Kingdom	15	10	20	20	25	25	25	25	—	15
	—	—	5	5	25†	13–15	10	25	—	—
United States	15	10	20	20	25	25	25	25	—	15
	—	—	5	5	10†	13–15	10	25	—	—

* S. Africa has been excluded, since residents are prohibited from purchasing foreign securities.
† Plus avoir fiscal.
‡ Plus tax credit less 15 percent withholding tax.
§ Some gilts free of withholding taxes to nonresidents.
Source: Compiled by Vickers da Costa Securities, Inc. Reprinted by permission.

nated, the withholding-tax-free nature of Eurodollar and Yankee bonds themselves will have no benefit to nonresident buyers. Particularly in the case of the Eurodollar market, where foreign buyers predominate, this could well affect the future of the market, or at least the pricing of these securities relative to U.S. domestic issues.

There are a number of other less important factors that explain the preference of foreign buyers for U.S.-pay international bonds over Treasury or domestic corporate issues. One factor is the familiarity foreign buyers have with Yankee bond credits when coupled with yields that are generally higher than U.S. governments or corporates. Yankee and Eurodollar bond maturities are usually shorter than many U.S. domestic issues, and call protection is sometimes longer—both characteristics traditionally appeal to foreign bond buyers. Finally, although Canadians and some supranational agency issues are often issued in registered form only, Eurodollar and Yankee bonds are generally available in coupon form, which assures anonymity.

Italy‡		Japan		Nether-lands		Switzer-land		United Kingdom§		U.S.A.	
30	0–20	20	20	25	—	35	35	—	30	30	30
15	0–15	5	5	10	—	—	—	—	15	15	15
30	0–20	20	20	25	—	35	35	—	30	30	30
15	0–15	5	10	10	—	30	25	‡	20	15	20
30	0–20	20	20	25	—	35	35	—	30	30	30
—	—	5	10	10	—	20	35	—	30	15	30
30	0–20	20	20	25	—	35	35	—	30	30	30
—	—	—	—	—	—	—	—	—	—	—	—
		20	20	25	—	35	35	—	30	30	30
		5	10	25	—	—	—	—	—	15	—
30	0–20			25	—	35	35	—	30	15	10
15	—			10	—	20	25	—	20	—	—
30	0–20	20	20			35	35	—	30	30	30
—	—	5	10			20	30	‡	30	15	30
30	0–20	20	20	25	—			—	30	30	30
—	—	5	10	10	—			‡	30	15	25
30	0–20	20	20	25	—	35	35			15	—
15	—	5	10	10	—	20	35			—	—
30	0–20	20	20	25	—	35	35	—	30		
15	—	5	10	10	—	20	30	‡	30		

A	C
B	D

A Withholding tax on dividends.
B Reclaimable part of A.
C Coupon tax on interest.
D Reclaimable part of C.

All of these factors generally lead foreign buyers to prefer U.S.-pay international bond issues—Eurodollar, Yankee, Canadian, or suprana-tional agencies—to domestic issues. As a result of this preference, the degree of interest of foreign buyers in U.S.-pay securities, or lack thereof, is often reflected in a narrowing or widening in the spread between U.S.-pay international bond yields and U.S. domestic yields. This is particularly true of Eurodollar bonds, since foreign interest governs this market to a greater extent than in the other types of international issues that are more broadly distributed in the United States. The attraction of Eurodollar bonds to foreigners is most often related to judgements on the prospects for the U.S. dollar, the level of interest rates in the United States relative to other foreign markets, and expectations for capital changes. Since the structure of bond mar-kets in most other countries is geared to short or intermediate maturi-ties (out to 10 years), foreign participants in the U.S. market usually prefer this range. Thus fluctuations in yield spreads of U.S.-pay international bonds versus Treasury obligations can be more pronounced in intermediate maturities than in longer term bonds.

There are of course exceptions to this general preference by foreigners for U.S.-pay international bonds. Since there is no capital gains tax in some countries, residents of these countries sometimes prefer discount U.S. domestic bonds, depending on price relationships. Central banks are exempt from withholding tax, so the tax-free nature of the international securities is not a factor in their purchases. Of late, the volatility of the U.S. bond market has occasioned some foreign buyers to look to the U.S. market for short-term capital plays with little regard to the income flow or tax thereon. In these situations U.S. Treasury obligations have been preferred because of their high liquidity.

FOREIGN—PAY INTERNATIONAL BOND INVESTING

From the standpoint of the U.S. investor, foreign-pay international bonds encompass all issues denominated in currencies other than the dollar. There is a variety of types of issues available to the U.S. investor, but in all cases the primary trading market is outside the United States.

The Markets

Securities sold by a particular issuer within its own country and in that country's currency are typically termed *domestic issues*. These may include direct government issues, government agencies sometimes called semigovernments, or corporates. Corporate bonds clearly carry an additional risk beyond the currency, interest rate, and sovereign risks—that of company credit risk. Although a yield advantage to governments may be available from corporates, this margin relative to the total return expected must always be measured against their lesser marketability and additional credit concern. If a withholding tax is imposed by a particular country, all securities in the domestic bond market of that country are subject to withholding tax on interest when sold to nonresidents unless the rate is reduced or eliminated by a tax treaty with the country of the buyer. The withholding tax rates imposed by countries with the most developed bond markets are shown in Exhibit 2.

Another market is termed the *foreign bond market*, which includes issues sold primarily in one country and currency by a borrower of a different nationality. The Yankee market is the U.S.-dollar version of this market. Other examples are the Samurai market, which consists of yen-denominated bonds issued by non-Japanese issuers, and the Bulldog market, which is comprised of United Kingdom sterling-denominated bonds issued by non-British entities. Relative to the size of the domestic bond markets, these foreign bond markets are quite small, and liquidity can be limited. However, to the nonresident investor, these issues have the advantage of freedom from withholding taxes.

This tax advantage is shared by securities called *Eurobonds,* of which Eurodollar bonds are the U.S.-pay version. These securities are typically underwritten by international syndicates and are sold in a number of national markets simultaneously. They may or may not be obligations of or guaranteed by an issuer domiciled in the country of currency denomination, and the issuer may be a sovereign government, a corporation, or a supranational agency. Eurodollar bonds have consistently been the largest sector of this market, representing about 60 percent of the total over the last 10 years, and Euro deutsche mark issues have regularly been second, averaging above 20 percent of the total. Like the foreign bond market, liquidity of Eurobond issues is typically less than in domestic government issues.

Components of Return

To the dollar-based investor, there are only two components of return in U.S.-pay bond investing: income, and capital change resulting from interest-rate movements. In foreign-pay investing, a third component of return must be considered: foreign currency movements. Thus the U.S. investor must couple the domestic or internal price movement with income and then translate the total domestic return into dollars to assess the total return in U.S. dollars.

For the U.S. investor in foreign currency bonds, the prospects for return should not only be viewed in an absolute sense, but also be analyzed relative to returns expected in the U.S. market. The analysis can be separated into three different questions.

1.   **What is the starting yield level relative to yield levels on U.S. bonds?**   Where this spread is positive, the income advantage will, over time, provide a cushion against adverse movements of the foreign bond price relative to U.S. bonds or against deterioration in the value of the foreign currency. The longer the time horizon, the greater the cushion provided by this accumulating income advantage. If, on the other hand, the starting income level of the foreign currency issue is below that provided by U.S. bonds, this income deficiency must be offset continually by an appreciating currency or positive internal price movement relative to U.S. bonds in order to provide comparable returns. This may appear to be a difficult challenge, but the decade of the 1970s as a whole saw the best converted U.S. dollar total returns accruing to bond investments with the lowest income levels. The underlying rationale for this result was that bonds with low yields were denominated in currencies of countries with low inflation rates, which were ultimately translated to currency appreciation relative to the U.S. dollar.

2.   What are the prospects for internal price movements relative to expectations for U.S. bond prices?   This factor can be broadly discussed in terms of changing yield spreads of foreign pay bonds versus U.S. issues in the same way that changing yield spreads within the domestic U.S. market are discussed when describing changes in relative prices. However, several points should be considered in regard to this analogy. In the U.S. market, all bond prices generally move in the same direction, although not always to the same extent; whereas domestic price movements of foreign-pay bonds may move in a direction opposite to that of the U.S. market. Second, although yield spread relationships within the U.S. market may fluctuate broadly, in many cases there is a normal spread that has some repetitive meaning. However, changing economic, social, and political trends between the United States and other countries suggests that there are few normal relationships to serve as useful guidelines.

Finally, although both U.S. and international investors must be aware of differing price movements emanating from equal yield movements in securities of differing maturities, international bond investors must also be aware of the impact a given basis point change in yield has on the price movements of bonds with significantly different starting yield levels. For example, a 100-basis-point movement in a 10-year United Kingdom government issue starting at a 15 percent yield is about 5 percent, whereas the same 100-basis-point move equates to about a 7 percent price change for a 10-year Swiss Franc issue with a starting yield of 7 percent. When the more commonly analyzed effects of varying maturities and differing yield changes are added to the impact of different starting yield levels, the resulting changes in relative price movements are not intuitively obvious. For example, the various combinations of starting yield, maturity, and yield change shown in Exhibit 3 all result in the same 10 percent capital price increases.

3.   What are the prospects for currency gain or loss versus the dollar?   The debate on whether or not foreign currency changes can be predicted and, if so, what factors determine such changes has been a continuing one. In many ways this debate is little different from that

Exhibit 3
Impact of Maturity and Starting Yield on Yield and Price Change Relationships

Starting Yield	Maturity (years)	Yield Change	Price Change
15 percent	10	−1.83%	+10%
15	5	−2.73	+10
7	10	−1.32	+10
7	5	−2.27	+10

regarding the predictability of stock market movements or interest rates. Like the stock and bond markets, a number of factors can be identified as exerting a direct influence on foreign exchange rates. The common problems faced by forecasters are whether these factors have already been fully discounted in prices—be they stock, bond, or foreign exchange—and which factor will predominate at any given time. Those factors generally regarded to affect foreign currency movements include the following:

1. The balance of payments and prospective changes in that balance.
2. Inflation and interest differentials between countries.
3. The social and political atmosphere, particularly with regard to the impact on foreign investment.
4. Central bank intervention in the currency markets.

Some people have questioned whether returns for international bond investing are almost entirely a function of currency movements. Exhibit 4 shows that for the 15 year period 1966–1980 and for the

Exhibit 4
Average Annual Returns of International Bond Index* by Components

		Contribution to Return		
	Income	Domestic Capital Gain	Foreign Currency	Total Dollar-Converted Average Annual Return
1966–70	+6.5%	−2.8%	−0.2%	+3.5%
1971–75	+8.4	−3.1	+4.0	+9.3
1976–80	+9.3	−1.9	+3.8	+11.2
1966–80	+8.0	−2.6	+2.6	+8.0

* Equally weighted in government bonds of Australia, Canada, France, Germany, Japan, Netherlands, Switzerland, United Kingdom. Rebalanced monthly.

three interim 5-year periods the income component of return has proven to be the largest of the three portions, as measured by an index of international bonds equally weighted in eight foreign countries.

However, for specific years, domestic capital change and/or foreign exchange at times played significantly larger roles, as shown in Exhibit 5. Domestic capital changes ranged from −10.3 percent in 1973 to +9 percent in 1977, and currency returns varied from −5.9 percent in 1975 to +11.9 percent in 1978. For individual countries, the variation in components of return was even greater. The greatest capital price changes occurred in the United Kingdom, where losses and gains were about 28 percent in 1974 and 1977, respectively. Currency changes for specific countries ranged from nearly +28 percent for the

Exhibit 5
Annual Returns of International Bond Index* by Components

		Contribution to Return		
	Income	*Domestic Capital Gain*	*Foreign Currency*	*Total Dollar-Converted Annual Return*
1966	+6.0%	−2.1%	−0.2%	+3.7%
1967	+6.1	−1.0	−1.5	+3.6
1968	+6.3	−1.9	−0.1	+4.3
1969	+6.5	−7.0	−0.3	−0.8
1970	+7.6	−2.0	+1.1	+6.7
1971	+7.8	+4.3	+9.2	+21.3
1972	+7.1	−2.9	+1.6	+5.8
1973	+7.4	−10.3	+10.0	+7.1
1974	+9.3	−10.2	+5.0	+4.1
1975	+10.4	+4.8	−5.9	+9.3
1976	+9.9	+2.9	−0.9	+11.9
1977	+9.6	+9.0	+11.5	+30.1
1978	+8.2	−3.3	+11.9	+16.8
1979	+8.4	−10.1	+0.3	−1.4
1980	+10.2	−6.5	−2.1	+1.6

* Equally weighted in government bonds of Australia, Canada, France, Germany, Japan, Netherlands, Switzerland, United Kingdom. Rebalanced monthly.

Swiss franc in 1974 to −19 percent for the Japanese yen in 1979. These data show clearly that all three factors of return—income, capital change, and currency movement—are important and must be considered both absolutely and relative to U.S. alternatives.

THE RATIONALE FOR INTERNATIONAL BOND INVESTING

The rationale for foreign-pay international bond investing is twofold. First, international bonds can enhance an investor's total rate of return relative to what is available from alternative U.S. domestic bond investments. The composition of return will, however, be variable as between income, domestic price change, and foreign currency change. Second, international bonds can reduce the risk or the volatility of return relative to a portfolio invested solely in U.S. fixed income securities.

In analyzing the case for international bonds, there is no a priori reason why one rationale for international bond investing should receive more emphasis than the other. The relative emphasis on these rationales is properly a function of the investment objectives of the investor, and these objectives should be reflected in the composition of an international bond portfolio. To some investors with long-term time horizons, the impact of international bonds on interim volatility of returns is unimportant. For these investors, embarking on a program of international bond investing is not appropriate unless international bonds can improve the rate of return. To others, particularly those with shorter time horizons who have been seared by the recent roller coaster in the U.S. fixed income markets, the attraction of international bonds may be their potential for a reduction in the volatility of overall portfolio returns.

Superior Rates of Return

One of the cornerstones of the rationale for international equity investing is that a portfolio of foreign equities should, over time, provide a higher return than a portfolio of U.S. equities, since many areas of the world are growing more rapidly than the United States and are experiencing higher rates of investment spending and productivity growth. Ultimately these superior growth characteristics should translate into more rapid increases in corporate profits and, in turn, stock prices assuming a degree of comparability in starting valuations.

No such strong fundamental arguments exist for international bonds. If the United States were to continue to experience higher unanticipated rates of inflation than other industrialized nations, international bonds would probably continue to provide a higher rate of return than their U.S. counterparts as translated through both foreign currency appreciation and better domestic bond price behavior. Indeed, as inflation has increased and eroded both nominal and real rates of returns on traditional investments, one inflation haven for the U.S. investor has been foreign currency-denominated investments. Although there are many factors that determine currency relationships, differential inflation rates have explained much of the movement over long periods of time.

Alternatively, if one could identify countries where, after deducting an expected inflation rate, the real or inflation-adjusted rate of interest is historically high, a selection of foreign bonds would provide the potential for superior performance. Although a high real rate of interest derived in this fashion is not synonomous with a true, or economic, real-interest rate, a positive differential between these two concepts can provide a signal of undervaluation of long-term fixed income securities and the opportunity for superior foreign bond price action. These propositions may be valid, but they are not persuasive; indeed such fundamental arguments are not required to establish the basis for international bonds.

The best case for international bonds lies in the continual array of opportunities and risks provided by the constant shifting of international exchange rate and interest rate relationships. The range of start-

ing yields is continuously changing; some foreign rates provide a
yield cushion against a U.S. interest rate bogey, and others provide a
disadvantage. At any time, different countries will be at different
points in their economic and interest rate cycles. Similarly, foreign
currency relationships are continuously shifting, sometimes moving
with interest rates and sometimes against them.

Over time it should be possible to capitalize on these shifting relationships, which will, in the aggregate, supply a greater number of
opportunities than can any one individual and relatively homogeneous market. This rationale is an opportunistic and selective one,
which has at its heart the cyclicality of economic behavior worldwide.

In the analysis that follows, eight foreign bond markets are analyzed in relationship with the U.S. market. Included are the government bond markets of Australia, Canada, France, Germany, Japan, the
Netherlands, Switzerland, and the United Kingdom. In the absence of
published price data extending back historically, price movements
have been imputed from monthly yield series.[3]

A comparison of eight foreign bond markets with the U.S. market
shows that over the period 1966–80, foreign bonds provided a supe-
rior rate of return to that produced by a U.S. long-bond average.[4]
Exhibit 6 shows the total rates of return from nine bond markets in
U.S.-dollar terms over the 15-year period. In that period the return on
U.S. bonds was exceeded by every other foreign market. In the subpe-

Exhibit 6
International Bond Markets Compound Annual Rates of Return—1966–1980

	Total Return in U.S. Dollars	Components of Return			
		Domestic Capital Change	Income	Total Domestic Return	Foreign Exchange Change
Australia	3.26%	−4.89%	7.77%	2.88%	.40%
Canada	2.71	−4.75	8.19	3.44	−.71
France	5.62	−3.77	8.82	5.05	.54
Germany	12.58	−0.68	8.02	7.34	4.88
Japan	10.77	−1.19	7.79	6.60	3.91
Netherlands	9.71	−2.02	7.93	5.91	3.59
Switzerland	11.09	−0.37	5.01	4.64	6.16
United Kingdom	4.98	−4.65	10.77	6.12	−1.07
United States	2.06	−5.03	7.09	2.06	

---

[3] Domestic Government Bond Yields from 1966 to 1977 were compiled by Morgan
Guaranty and published in their *World Financial Markets*. Yields for 1978–1980 were
compiled by Scudder, Stevens and Clark.

[4] U.S. bond returns were calculated in a manner consistent with all other foreign
markets. Returns were extrapolated from the government yield series described in
footnote 3, and maturities were either 10 or 20 years based on the typical long-bond
convention in each market.

riods of 1966–70 and 1971–75, the return on U.S. bonds ranked seventh out of nine, outperforming the United Kingdom and France in the first instance and the United Kingdom and Canada in the latter period. In 1976–80 it ranked eighth out of nine, just ahead of Canada.

Over the 15-year period, the superior performance of most foreign bond markets relative to the U.S. market was attributable to all three components of return: an income advantage, more favorable relative price trends, and positive currency changes. The period has been one of rising interest rates worldwide and declining bond prices in domestic price terms in all nine markets analyzed. The percentage drop, however, was the least in the relatively low inflation countries of Germany, Switzerland, and Japan. The price performance was the worst in Australia, Canada, and the United Kingdom, but even these drops were exceeded by that of the U.S. bond market. With the exception of Switzerland, the return attributable to income was greater in each of the eight foreign markets than in the United States. Although long U.S. interest rates were among the highest by 1980, they were exceeded by many foreign rates during the first 10 years of the period when annual income from U.S. bonds averaged from 70 to 370 basis points less than that provided by foreign bonds. Combining these two variables, the return in local currency terms in each foreign market exceeded that of the U.S. bond market. When foreign exchange movements are factored in, the relative advantage of foreign bonds widens. Of eight foreign currencies considered, six appreciated against the dollar by amounts ranging from .4 percent to 6.16 percent per annum. Only the Canadian dollar and British pound declined relative to the U.S. dollar, but not by enough to offset the relative advantages of price and income.

The higher rate of return from foreign bond markets over the 1966–80 period relative to the U.S. market has, of course, no necessary repetitive significance. This 15-year period was obviously unique in many respects: the Vietnam War, the impact of the oil price rise in both 1973–74 and 1979–80, and a variance in political trends here and abroad that contributed to important differences in economic priorities and policy in the United States and in other industrial nations. The almost uniform decline in the dollar will not necessarily be repeated in the next 15 years. The relative trend in inflation and interest rates could well prove quite different.

What is important to notice about the data is the variability of the source of return. For example, in the case of Switzerland, the rise in the value of the Swiss franc more than offset the relative income disadvantage of Swiss franc bonds. In contrast, although the value of pound sterling declined by 1 percent per annum, the 368-basis-point income advantage underwrote the higher return on United Kingdom bonds.

The variability of the sources of return is even more evident in a comparison of annual data. The components of return for the two years 1976 and 1980 are shown in Exhibit 7. In both cases, the U.S. bond market ranked fifth out of nine markets as measured by total return in

Exhibit 7
The Variability of the Components of Returns

1976

	Total Return (Dollars)	Components of Return		
		Capital Change	Income	Foreign Exchange Change
Germany.........................	32.24%	10.07%	9.07%	11.00%
Switzerland	24.96	11.12	5.75	6.92
Netherlands.....................	20.98	1.12	9.45	9.41
Canada..........................	20.98	9.62	10.51	0.71
United States....................	17.70	8.84	8.86	
Japan	16.90	2.84	9.33	4.22
France..........................	−5.11	−5.29	10.43	−9.75
United Kingdom.................	−6.02	−2.37	14.08	−15.87
Australia	−8.45	−4.34	10.28	−13.58

1980

	Total Return (Dollars)	Components of Return		
		Capital Change	Income	Foreign Exchange Change
United Kingdom..................	28.11%	3.84%	15.62%	7.24%
Japan	25.16	−3.20	9.20	18.07
Canada..........................	−0.52	−10.29	12.04	−2.23
Australia	−1.44	−18.03	10.31	6.80
United States....................	−3.77	−14.14	10.37	
France..........................	−7.24	−8.62	12.82	−10.98
Switzerland	−8.54	−2.62	4.56	−10.28
Netherlands.....................	−9.14	−7.92	9.46	−10.52
Germany.........................	−10.30	−6.55	8.04	−11.62

U.S.-dollar terms. In 1976 the three top performers were the major hard currency countries of Europe: Germany, Switzerland, and the Netherlands. In 1980 these three countries trailed the list, and the United Kingdom, Japan, and Canada provided the best returns. In the case of the United Kingdom, the positive return in 1980 was accounted for by all three components of return; whereas the 18 percent rise in the value of the yen contributed 70 percent of the return on Japanese bonds, and in Canada the cushion of a higher income advantage accounted for half of the 3 percent excess return over U.S. long bonds. In 1976 the superior performance of German bonds was due to all three components of return; while in Switzerland currency and price movements offset the 300-basis-point income disadvantage; and in the Netherlands higher income and foreign exchange appreciation offset a lower capital change than in the United States.

This variability in the components of return is one answer to the frequent challenge to international bond investing that the favorable foreign bond returns of the past decade are due primarily to the weak dollar. It is argued that to embark on foreign bond investing just as the United States begins to put its economic house in order and the dollar has begun to strengthen is tantamount to "aiming where the rabbit was." Although there is merit to this argument, the historical contribution of return from currency appreciation should not be overemphasized. Exhibit 8 shows the contribution in basis points of currency

Exhibit 8
Average Annual Contribution of Foreign Currency Changes to
International Bond Returns (basis points)

	1966–80	1966–70	1971–75	1976–80
Australia....................	38	−6	247	−132
Canada....................	−73	126	−11	−333
France	57	−241	448	−15
Germany	524	202	735	644
Japan.....................	417	20	340	915
Netherlands	380	8	636	509
Switzerland...............	645	1	1111	878
United Kingdom	−114	−315	−346	376

movements to returns. In the 1966–80 period, in six out of eight cases the impact was favorable, with the positive contribution to returns ranging from 38 to 645 basis points. The data for the three five-year time periods show that the positive contribution of foreign currency changes to returns increased over the period, particularly after the 1971 watershed in the foreign exchange markets marking the beginning of floating exchange rates. The trend was strongest in the case of the low-inflation, hard currency countries (Japan, Germany, Switzerland, and the Netherlands). However, although the impact of foreign currency changes on returns was significant, the more favorable performance of foreign bonds versus U.S. bonds was not dependent on exchange-rate movements. Exhibit 9 shows a comparison of bond returns in domestic currency and in dollar terms for the 1966–80 period. In all cases but the United Kingdom and Canada, the domestic currency returns were lower than in dollar-denominated terms but were still above returns generated by U.S. long bonds.

A second challenge relating to foreign currency exposure relates to the fact that the foreign currency factor adds to the volatility of foreign

Exhibit 9
Comparison of International Bond Returns

	Average Annual Return of Long Bonds Converted to U.S. Dollars 1966–1980	Average Annual Return of Long Bonds in Domestic Currency 1966–1980
Australia	3.3%	2.9%
Canada	2.7	3.4
France	5.6	5.1
Germany	12.6	7.3
Japan	10.8	6.6
Netherlands	9.7	5.9
Switzerland	11.1	4.6
United Kingdom	5.0	6.1
United States	2.1	2.1

bond returns. On a market-by-market basis, this has been true. Exhibits 10 and 11 show the standard deviation of monthly total returns in nine bond markets in both local currency and dollar-denominated terms. The data are presented for the 1966–80 period and are also broken down into five-year segments. In the period 1966–80, the volatility of returns in the United States was greater than in any other market in local currency terms except for the United Kingdom. In all cases except Australia, the volatility increased during the period; but the volatility of U.S. returns continued to exceed all other markets except the United Kingdom. When foreign exchange movements are factored in, the volatility of foreign bond returns increased substantially, and in fact for the 1966–80 period the standard deviation of the U.S. return is the lowest after Canada. The increase in volatility was particularly marked in the 1971–75 and 1976–80 periods after the introduction of floating exchange rates.

The fact that foreign currency movements add to the volatility of individual market returns suggests (and other evidence lends some

Exhibit 10
Standard Deviation of Monthly Domestic Total Returns

	1966–80	1966–70	1971–75	1976–80
Australia	2.162	1.420	3.126	1.527
Canada	2.416	1.951	2.416	2.837
France	1.380	1.085	1.417	1.588
Germany	1.768	1.156	1.917	2.115
Japan	1.720	.090	1.497	2.588
Netherlands	1.851	1.043	1.811	2.451
Switzerland	1.340	.809	1.162	1.835
United Kingdom	4.030	2.156	4.540	4.853
United States	2.872	2.342	2.752	3.457

Exhibit 11
Standard Deviation of Monthly Total Return Converted to U.S. Dollars

	1966–80	1966–70	1971–75	1976–80
Australia........................	3.054	1.431	3.778	3.454
Canada..........................	2.757	2.184	2.535	3.441
France	3.056	1.561	3.551	3.593
Germany	3.429	1.295	3.614	4.560
Japan...........................	3.478	.142	3.088	5.167
Netherlands	3.496	1.105	3.755	4.636
Switzerland.....................	3.573	.828	3.674	4.863
United Kingdom	4.998	2.887	5.240	6.218
United States	2.872	2.342	2.752	3.457

credence to this theory) that foreign exchange movements reinforce returns in domestic price terms over long periods of time. This is not surprising considering the common long-term fundamental factors affecting both domestic prices and foreign exchange rates.

As discussed in the next section, however, the increase in volatility of individual market returns due to foreign exchange movements is not reflected in the volatility of a diversified international bond portfolio.

Diversification

A second rationale for international bond investing is diversification. The inclusion of foreign bonds in a portfolio should reduce the risk or volatility of returns of a portfolio otherwise invested solely in U.S. fixed income securities. The fundamental reason for this is that foreign bond markets do not move with, or are not perfectly correlated with, the U.S. bond market. Intuitively this is obvious. The dynamics of the business cycle differ by country. The role of monetary policy in the arsenal of a government's economic weapons varies among countries. Institutional or structural forces, government financing practices, and tradition mean that the role of buyers and sellers differs between fixed income markets. The trend of inflation, a nation's tolerance of inflation, and the sources of inflationary pressure differ among countries, as does the impact of inflation on the trend and structure of interest rates.

Finally, there is a host of geopolitical, foreign policy, and societal forces that ensure that the movements of foreign bond prices are not perfectly correlated. Consequently, when foreign currency bonds are added to a portfolio of U.S. fixed income securities, the price movements often offset each other, and the overall volatility of returns can be reduced.

Exhibit 12 shows the correlation coefficients of monthly changes in bond prices in local currency terms between nine major bond mar-

Exhibit 12
Correlation Coefficients of Domestic Capital Change in Major Foreign Bond Markets—1966–1980 (based on monthly data)

	United States	Australia	Canada	France	Germany	Japan	Netherlands	Switzerland	United Kingdom
United States	1.00								
Australia	.04	1.00							
Canada	.68	.05	1.00						
France	.17	.09	.30	1.00					
Germany	.31	.22	.28	.13	1.00				
Japan	.31	.09	.32	.33	.41	1.00			
Netherlands	.35	.10	.36	.34	.45	.34	1.00		
Switzerland	.20	.07	.24	.25	.35	.45	.36	1.00	
United Kingdom	.12	.04	.20	.17	.17	.17	.04	.17	1.00

kets, including the United States, over the 1966–80 period. The highest correlation with the U.S. market is Canada—not a surprising occurrence in view of the multilateral relationships between the two
economies. The correlation is practically zero with Australia, which
once again is reasonable in view of the lack of interdependence between the two economies. Between these two extremes lie the European markets and Japan. It should be noted that in most cases the
correlation among the continental European markets is higher than
that between those markets and the United States, reflecting the high
degree of interdependence between the European economies and the
existence of informal currency blocs.

Exhibit 13 shows the correlation coefficients of monthly domestic
capital changes between the United States and foreign markets bro-

Exhibit 13
Correlation Coefficient between U.S. and Foreign Bond Markets Domestic
Capital Change (based on monthly data)

	1966–80	1966–70	1971–75	1976–80
Australia	.04	.06	−.03	.17
Canada	.68	.68	.45	.84
France	.17	.08	.12	.24
Germany	.31	.23	.09	.50
Japan	.31	−.04	.16	.45
Netherlands	.35	.14	.02	.62
Switzerland	.20	−.07	.21	.29
United Kingdom	.12	.40	.10	.06

ken down by five-year time periods. In all cases except the United
Kingdom, the degree of correlation or interdependence rose over the
period. This is one more statistical manifestation of the degree to
which the world is getting smaller and the increased synchronization
of economic behavior resulting from growing trade and capital flows.
More specifically, it reflects the heavy and uniform impact of the sharp
rise in oil prices in all industrialized countries in 1973–75 and
1979–80, particularly on the trend of inflation and interest rates. To
the extent the industrialized world succeeds in better coordinating
national financial and economic policies, it is possible that the trend
toward a somewhat higher interdependence between markets will
continue. For reasons discussed above, however, international bond
price trends should remain less than perfectly correlated.

Exhibits 14 and 15 show the correlation coefficients of the change
in bond prices converted to U.S. dollars between the U.S. and foreign
markets and the total return, including income, converted to U.S. dollars for the 1966–80 period overall, and again broken down into five-
year segments. The inclusion of income had only a modest impact on

Exhibit 14
Correlation Coefficients between U.S. and Foreign Bond Markets Capital
Change Converted to U.S. Dollars (based on monthly data)

	1966–80	1966–70	1971–75	1976–80
Australia..........................	.05	.06	−.02	.11
Canada............................	.62	.67	.45	.71
France	.21	.09	.11	.32
Germany	.29	.16	.08	.46
Japan.............................	.24	.04	.11	.36
Netherlands	.32	.12	.09	.53
Switzerland.......................	.22	−.08	.05	.38
United Kingdom	.16	.38	.10	.14

Exhibit 15
Correlation Coefficient between U.S. and Foreign Bond Markets Total Return
Converted to U.S. Dollars (based on monthly data)

	1966–80	1966–70	1971–75	1976–80
Australia..........................	.05	.06	−.02	.11
Canada............................	.62	.67	.45	.70
France	.20	.09	.11	.32
Germany	.28	.17	.08	.45
Japan.............................	.25	.05	.11	.36
Netherlands	.32	.13	.09	.53
Switzerland.......................	.22	−.08	.05	.37
United Kingdom	.16	.38	.09	.14

the degree of correlation between markets. Comparison of Exhibits 13 and 14 shows that the impact of currency movements on the correlation of returns was, however, more substantial but not tremendous by any means and varied significantly by country. In the 1966–80 period, in four cases (Australia, Switzerland, the United Kingdom, and France) the degree of correlation was increased, and in four cases (Canada, Germany, Japan, and the Netherlands) it was reduced. The impact of currency movements was much more substantial in the post-1971 period once exchange rates started to float. The divergent effects of currency movements on the degree of correlation is understandable given the volatility of foreign exchange rates in the post-1971 period and the complexity of factors underlying foreign exchange-rate movements.

THE IMPACT OF FOREIGN BONDS ON A U.S.
BOND PORTFOLIO

Given the risk/return characteristic of foreign bond investing outlined above, it is natural to question the impact of foreign bonds on a

U.S. fixed income portfolio. Although the magnitude of future effects is uncertain, some guidance may be provided by analyzing, albeit somewhat hypothetically, what the impact of foreign bond investing would have been on a U.S. bond portfolio in the past.

In order to gauge the overall magnitude of the impact of a broad international bond commitment, two indices have been constructed. International Index I is the equally weighted index of the eight major government bond markets (Australia, Canada, Japan, United Kingdom, Germany, Netherlands, Switzerland, France), rebalanced monthly. International Index II is weighted by the annual proportion of government domestic currency debt outstanding in each country, rebalanced monthly.

Exhibit 16 shows the comparison of the compound rates of return of these two indices and the U.S. bond market together with two portfo-

Exhibit 16
Compound Annual Rates of Return

	1966–80	1966–70	1971–75	1976–1980
International Index I	7.96	3.46	9.34	11.24
International Index II	7.40	.30	6.35	14.27
United States	2.06	.80	3.46	1.95
Portfolio I (80 percent United States, 20 percent International Index I)	3.31	1.37	4.72	3.86
Portfolio II (80 percent United States, 20 percent International Index II)	3.22	.74	4.15	4.46

lios assumed to be invested 80 percent in the U.S. market average and 20 percent in each of the two international bond indices. In the 1966–80 period, the international indices returned three to four times the return of the U.S. bond market average. In 1966–70, the results were mixed; in the 1971–75 period the indices averaged two to three times the U.S. average; and in the 1976–80 period the returns were five- to sevenfold greater than in the U.S. market. Consequently, assuming a 20 percent commitment, international bonds would have increased the compound annual return of the portfolio by roughly 55–60 percent or about 1 percent annually for the 15-year period as a whole. Although there were several years in which the U.S. market outperformed the two international indices (1970, 1972, 1974, 1976, 1979), an international bond commitment would also have added an increment to return in each of the five-year periods shown by anywhere from 20 percent to 125 percent or .6 percent to 2.5 percent annually except in the case of International Index II in the 1966–70 period.

Exhibit 17
Standard Deviations of Monthly Returns (in U.S. dollars)

	1966–80	1966–70	1971–75	1976–80
International Index I	2.408	.714	2.449	3.293
International Index II	2.868	1.549	2.782	3.760
United States	2.872	2.342	2.752	3.457
Portfolio I				
(80 percent United States, 20 percent				
International Index I).................	2.514	1.955	2.329	3.143
Portfolio II				
(80 percent United States, 20 percent				
International Index II)................	2.559	2.050	2.369	3.165

Exhibit 17 shows the comparison of standard deviation of returns. Although Exhibit 11 demonstrated that dollar denominated returns from individual foreign bond markets were significantly more volatile than U.S. bond returns, Exhibit 17 indicates that the standard deviation of an international bond portfolio was relatively low by comparison, reflecting the relatively low degree of correlations between foreign markets. In the case of International Index I, the volatility was less than the U.S. market in every time period, but the standard deviation of International Index II was only slightly above the U.S. market in the more recent years. When international bonds are included in a portfolio, the volatility of returns is reduced relative to a portfolio invested 100 percent in the U.S. market average. Over the 1966–80 period as a whole and in each of the five-year periods, the variability of monthly returns of both Portfolios I and II was 10–15 percent below that of the U.S. market average. Underlying these diversification characteristics, which were nominally more pronounced in the case of the equally weighted index than for the index weighted by outstanding debt, are correlation coefficients of .37 and .36 for the two indices respectively, converted to U.S. dollars relative to the U.S. market.

This historical record suggests that international bonds were successful in reducing the volatility and raising the level of returns even when only 20 percent of the portfolio was invested in international bonds. For practical purposes, however, the bond investor always has the option of achieving the same objectives by going short. Would shortening maturities have been a more efficient strategy? Exhibit 18 shows the risk-return characteristics of the U.S. market and Portfolios I and II (taken from Exhibits 16 and 17) together with a portfolio composed 80 percent of the long U.S. market and 20 percent one-month U.S.-dollar CD's (Portfolio III). For the period overall, the use of short-term dollar instruments produced virtually the same return as use of international bonds but reduced the volatility of return by an additional 9–10 percent. In the most recent period, 1976–80, the effi-

Exhibit 18
Risk-Return Characteristics of International Bonds versus Short-term
Maturities

	Compound Annual Return			
	1966–80	*1966–70*	*1971–75*	*1976–80*
United States	2.06	.8	3.46	1.95
Portfolio I*	3.31	1.37	4.72	3.86
Portfolio II†	3.22	.74	4.15	4.46
Portfolio III‡...............	3.17	1.92	4.24	3.37

	Standard Deviation of Monthly Returns			
	1966–80	*1966–70*	*1971–75*	*1976–80*
United States	2.872	2.342	2.752	3.457
Portfolio I*	2.514	1.955	2.329	3.143
Portfolio II†	2.559	2.050	2.369	3.165
Portfolio III‡	2.301	1.877	2.202	2.770

* Eighty percent United States, 20 percent International Index I.
† Eighty percent United States, 20 percent International Index II.
‡ Eighty percent United States, 20 percent one-month CDS.

ciency of the use of shorts versus international bonds was indeterminate—it also reduced the volatility but produced a meaningfully lower level of return than the use of international bonds. In that period the optimum course would have been a function of the degree of emphasis the investor assigned to total return as opposed to risk reduction.

SUMMARY

International bonds, both U.S. pay and foreign pay, represent a significant portion of the world's fixed income markets, and an understanding of their characteristics is important for all bond investors.

Since U.S.-pay foreign bonds have particular appeal to non-U.S. buyers, knowledge of the reasons for this preference and an ongoing familiarity with the investment posture of non-U.S. buyers toward U.S.-pay bonds is necessary in order to effectively participate in that market.

Not only must investors in foreign-pay bonds consider income levels and prospective price movements both absolute and relative to U.S. alternatives, but the outlook for foreign currency changes must also be evaluated. The evidence indicates that over the 1966–80 period, foreign-pay bonds converted to U.S. dollars would have both reduced the overall volatility of a portfolio invested solely in U.S. issues and increased the returns. Although this fact has by itself little repetitive significance, many of the factors leading to the low correlation in returns between the U.S.- and foreign-pay markets continue. It is more difficult to conclude that the factors that generally led to superior foreign-pay bond returns relative to U.S. returns still persist, but the variance of social, political, monetary, and fiscal trends and policies between countries suggest that there will often be particular markets that offer better values than the U.S. market.

International Fixed Income Securities and Instruments

26

MORRIS W. OFFIT
Chief Executive Officer
Julius Baer Securities Inc.

FRANCESCO ANDINA
Vice President
Julius Baer Securities Inc.

INTRODUCTION

The international financial system serves basically the function of collecting savings and allocating credits on an international basis. Thus conceptually it does not differ from a domestic financial system. In practice, however, the existence of unregulated external financial markets and the use of different currencies in different jurisdiction areas does require careful analysis before using any of the services offered by the international financial system.

For the purpose of the U.S. investor, *domestic* markets in foreign countries, rather than their *external* counterparts, frequently offer a better opportunity to diversify internationally because of liquidity considerations. This chapter will therefore first describe some of the most widely used fixed income instruments of the foreign domestic markets and then address the instruments of the so-called external markets.

DOMESTIC INSTRUMENTS

United Kingdom

Gilt-Edged Securities. Gilt-edged securities are bonds issued by the British government through the United Kingdom Treasury (that is, their principal and interest are guaranteed by the British government). The gilt market is extremely liquid and offers from the marketability point of view the best opportunity for investing in non-U.S. domestic bonds.

Interest payments on gilts are subject to withholding taxes; however, a large number of gilts are so-called FOT-stocks, which stands for "free of tax." The foreign investor has to apply for the exemption from withholding taxes at least six weeks before coupon payment. For non-FOT-stocks the withholding tax can be reclaimed by investors residing in a country that has concluded a double-taxation agreement with the United Kingdom, as it is the case, for example, for the United States.

There is a large selection of different maturities: long gilts with maturities of 10 and more years, medium gilts with maturities of 5 to 10 years, and short gilts with maturities of less than 5 years. *This difference is particularly important because medium and long gilts are traded on a flat basis (i.e., the price is inclusive of the accrued interest). Short gilts are traded on the basis of price plus accrued interest, which is computed as actual days accrued divided by a year of 365 days.*

United Kingdom Treasury Bills. Every week the British Treasury tenders Treasury bills to cover its short-term financing needs and at the same time to regulate the liquidity of the banking system. The largest portion of the Treasury bills are subscribed to by the London discount houses, which enjoy a special position within the British banking system. In fact, money deposited on call with them by other banks is considered to cover the legal reserve requirement for these banks. Furthermore, discount houses are able to borrow from the Bank of England (equivalent to the U.S. Federal Reserve System)

Exhibit 1
United Kingdom Domestic Market, Outstanding Bonds (nominal value, £ millions)

End of Period	Government Bonds (Gilts)	Local Authority Bonds*	Corporate Bonds
1970	20,960	360	5,502
1975	34,296	1,060	6,610
1976	40,632	1,145	6,571
1977	51,822	1,183	6,288
1978	56,973	1,167	5,983
1979	68,205	1,101	5,570
1980	81,721	1,167	5,348

* Comprehensive figures do not exist for this category of issues; the best available data are obtained from government surveys and are shown here.
Source: Salomon Brothers Inc, *International Bond Market Analysis*, October 15, 1981.

whenever they need funds to cover demands by the banks. Thus discount houses, in order to match their liabilities, like to invest their funds in Treasury bills and maintain a very active secondary market. The holder of a bill cannot resell it to the Bank of England before due date but always will find a discount house ready to buy it at the going rate. The virtually secured liquidity usually entails a lower yield than that obtainable from other short-term instruments.

Treasury bills are always issued on a discount basis at a maturity of 91 days, in denominations ranging from £ 5000 up to £ 1,000,000.

The nominal value of outstanding bonds in the United Kingdom is shown in Exhibit 1.

Germany

Public Authority Bonds. Several public authorities issue bonds, such as the Laender (states) and the municipalities. For foreign investors the only public authority bonds of interest are bonds issued by the federal government, the federal railways and the federal postal service. These are the so-called Bundbahnpost bonds; they are all guaranteed by the government and enjoy therefore the same credit rating. They are issued by the Federal Bond Syndicate led by the Deutsche Bundesbank. They have excellent marketability primarily caused by the large amount of debt outstanding. On the coupon payment, the German withholding tax of 25 percent is levied, which can be reclaimed by U.S. investors under the double-taxation treaty. The maturity range is 5 to 12 years.

Schuldscheindarlehen.

> Under German law, Schuldscheindarlehen ("Schuldscheine") are loan agreements which are documented in the form of a promissory letter issued by the borrower. This document contains the terms and conditions of the loan. The terms normally provide that the loan may be assigned in whole or in part to other lenders.[1]

The maturity range is 1 to 15 years, but only issues with maturities above 4 years can currently be sold to foreign investors. Because Schuldscheine are formally not securities, their coupons are not subject to withholding taxes.

The secondary market is rather illiquid, because of transfer procedures that require a written assignment. Depending on the borrower, the number of the assignments can be restricted. The main advantage of the Schuldscheindarlehen to the investor is that the yield is generally higher than the yield for other comparable domestic instruments.

---

[1] M. S. Dobbs-Higginson, *Investment Manual for Fixed Income Securities in the International and Major Domestic Capital Markets,* Credit Suisse First Boston Limited, 1980, p. 82.

Exhibit 2
German Domestic Market, Outstanding Bonds (nominal value, billions of deutsche marks)

End of Period	Federal Government (Bundbahnpost) Total*	Provinces and Municipalities	Bank Bonds	Schuldscheine Total
1970	24.6	6.9	117.8	76.4
1975	54.9	12.6	239.7	176.2
1976	70.4	14.1	271.8	203.5
1977	91.9	13.9	302.7	216.5
1978	106.2	14.1	334.1	248.3
1979	112.8	13.0	372.0	284.7
1980	118.2	12.5	413.3	338.1

* Bund, Bahn, and Post are considered equivalent from the investor's viewpoint and are grouped together as central government bonds.
Source: Salomon Brothers Inc, *International Bond Market Analysis*, October 15, 1981.

Exhibit 2 presents the amount of the outstanding obligations in the German domestic market.

Netherlands

The most important feature for domestic Dutch fixed income securities (see Exhibit 3) is that they are not subject to withholding taxes and are therefore attractive investment vehicles for foreign investors. Furthermore, Dutch domestic instruments have all mandatory early redemption provisions. Therefore, when considering investments in Dutch bonds, average life and yield to average life are important information.

Dutch Government Bonds. Dutch Government bonds are issued by the Dutch government by tender. The secondary market is very

Exhibit 3
Dutch Guilder Domestic Bonds Outstanding (nominal value, billions of Dutch guilders)

End of Period	Government Bonds	Provincial and Municipal Bonds*	Corporate Bonds
1970	12.8	N.A.	N.A.
1975	14.8	N.A.	17.0
1976	16.6	13.0	18.9
1977	18.1	13.5	23.4
1978	20.2	13.1	28.3
1979	22.9	12.5	33.4
1980	28.8	12.0	37.6

* Includes issues of the BNG, the Nederlands Polder Board Bank and individual local governments.
Source: Salomon Brothers Inc, *International Bond Market Analysis*, October 15, 1981.

active, both on the Amsterdam Exchange and over the counter. Maturities usually range from 10 to 25 years.

Bank voor Nederlandsche Gemeenten (BNG) Bonds.   The BNG is the finance authority for most of the Dutch municipalities. The bonds are offered through a selling group of Dutch banks. The secondary market is less active than the one for government bonds. BNG bonds are traded on the Amsterdam Exchange and over the counter. The maturities range from 8 to 25 years. Their credit rating is excellent, and their yield is slightly higher than the yield on government bonds.

Corporate Bonds.   The largest segment of the Dutch domestic borrowers is made up of the corporations and banks, often very well known "internationals," rated as prime debtors. These bonds are also issued with maturities of up to 25 years and generally offer good marketability.

Switzerland

Swiss franc domestic bonds (see Exhibit 4) are issued by the federal cantonal, and local governments and by nongovernment institutions, such as banks and industrial companies.

Exhibit 4
Swiss Franc Domestic Bonds Outstanding (nominal value, billions of Swiss francs)*

End of Period	Federal Government	Cantons and Municipalities	Banks and Mortgage Institutions†	Nonbank Corporate
1970	9.9	4.9	9.8	10.2
1975	12.0	11.3	13.5	19.2
1976	14.6	12.4	14.4	21.2
1977	15.0	12.7	15.6	22.2
1978	15.0	12.4	16.0	22.8
1979	14.6	12.0	17.7	23.0
1980	15.1	12.1	21.9	23.9

* The pre-1980 figures in this table were derived from net new issues and the total volume of bonds in each category outstanding at the end of 1980. The net new-issue figures were calculated from Swiss National Bank data by subtracting conversions and redemptions from gross new public issues.

† Includes issues of cantonal banks and Emissionszentrale (joint issuing associations, which may issue bonds on behalf of a group of municipalities) as well as issues of commercial banks and mortgage institutions. At the end of 1980 the first two types of issue accounted for about one third of the total.

Source: Salomon Brothers Inc, *International Bond Market Analysis,* October 15, 1981.

Swiss Government Bonds.   Swiss government bonds can be of interest to foreign investors, since their marketability is quite good. These bonds are listed in Zurich, Geneva, and Basle (the major Swiss exchanges) and other regional stock exchanges.

The Swiss banks and occasionally also the Swiss National Bank maintain an active market on these issues. Because of the excellent quality of the debtor, their yield is usually 0.5 percent to 1 percent lower than that for other comparable bonds. Their coupon payments are subject to a 35 percent withholding tax, of which 30 percent can be reclaimed by U.S. investors. The maturity for Swiss government bonds usually ranges from 8 to 15 years.

Kassaobligationen. Kassaobligationen are medium-term notes issued by Swiss banks and have maturities of three to eight years. Generally the banks use Kassaobligationen to finance parts of their mortgage portfolios and some medium-term commercial loans as well. Kassaobligationen are not quoted on any exchange; a market in these securities (for denominations of Sfr. 100,000 and multiples thereof) is, however, maintained by the Swiss banks. Their interest income is subject to a 35 percent withholding tax, 30 percent of which can be reclaimed by U.S. investors.

Canada

Most Canadian debt instruments are not subject to withholding taxes and are therefore quite attractive for foreign investors. Government securities are totally exempt from withholding taxes (except the government bonds issued between December 1960 and April 1966). Corporate bonds are not subject to withholding taxes if their maturity at issue is five years or longer.

The debt quality coupled with the variety of maturities available and the liquidity of the market have attracted considerable amounts of foreign investment capital. The size of the Canadian debt market is shown in Exhibit 5.

Exhibit 5
Canadian Dollar Domestic Bonds Outstanding (nominal value, billions of Canadian dollars)

End of Period	Government Bonds	Provinces and Municipalities*	Corporate Bonds (Including Conventional Bonds)†
1970.............	13.8	20.9	10.4
1975.............	15.7	35.7	19.1
1976.............	17.5	40.8	20.3
1977.............	21.3	46.5	23.0
1978.............	24.7	52.7	25.7
1979.............	31.5	57.8	27.1
1980.............	38.7	66.4	29.1

* Includes a substantial portion of nonmarketable provincial issues. At the end of 1980, the marketable portion of provincial bonds amounted to Can. $20.6 billion.
† Includes some private placements.
Source: Salomon Brothers Inc, *International Bond Market Analysis*, October 15, 1981.

Federal Government Bonds. Federal government bonds are issued by the Canadian government with maturities of 1 to 25 years. The Bank of Canada auctions these bonds to a group of banks forming a selling group. The secondary market is quite active and the liquidity of these securities has improved considerably during the 1970s.

Treasury Bills. Treasury bills are tendered every week by the Bank of Canada on a discount basis and have maturities of 91 to 182 days. No withholding taxes are due, since the income is considered capital gain.

Provincial Governments and Bonds of Municipalities. Generally, these debt instruments are long-term bonds with maturities of up to 30 years. The quality is considered to be almost as good as that of the Canadian government bond; therefore these bonds offer only a small yield advantage compared to government bonds.

Corporate Bonds. The Canadian domestic corporate bonds are not subject to withholding taxes if their maturity at issue is longer than five years. These bonds are issued at maturities of up to 25 years.

Japan

The Japanese domestic bond market (see Exhibit 6) consists of basically two sectors of bonds: public bonds and private bonds. The

Exhibit 6
Japanese Yen Domestic Bonds Outstanding (nominal value, billions of yen)

End of Period*	Government Bonds	Government Guaranteed Bonds and Associated Organizations	Municipal Bonds	Banks Debentures	Corporate (Including Convertible Bonds)
1970.......	3,597	6,006	1,748	6,174	2,980
1975.......	13,911	12,803	6,346	15,510	6,477
1976.......	21,720	14,833	8,613	17,779	7,105
1977.......	30,351	17,336	10,874	20,165	7,741
1978.......	42,140	19,804	13,228	22,429	8,449
1979.......	53,637	22,397	15,637	24,254	9,307
1980.......	67,336	25,464	17,093	26,049	9,818

* Amounts outstanding at the end of the fiscal year (March of the year following the year indicated; for example, fiscal year 1970 ended on March 31, 1971).
Source: Salomon Brothers Inc, *International Bond Market Analysis*, October 15, 1981.

public bonds are subdivided into three categories: (1) government bonds (long, medium, and short term, the latter called bills), (2) local government bonds, and (3) government-related organization bonds.

The private sector covers the industrial bonds and the bank debentures.

Long-Term Government Bonds. The Japanese Government usually issues 10-year bonds every month.[2] The terms of the bonds including the maturity date are identical for a series of bonds issued over a period of three months. The government maintains a sinking fund, which may be used to repurchase these bonds before they mature. Government bonds have coupons attached, and their payments are subject to a 20 percent withholding tax—10 percent reclaimable for U.S. investors. There is a very liquid market for these bonds with an amount of over $300 billion outstanding at the end of fiscal 1980.[3]

Medium-Term Government Bonds. Medium-term bonds are issued as discount bonds with five-year maturities or as coupon bonds with maturities of two to four years. For nonresident investors, coupon bonds are taxed like the long-term government bonds; on the discount bonds a 16 percent withholding tax is imposed when issued on the expected redemption gain (tax on redemption). Residents of a country with a tax treaty with Japan providing for a lower tax rate than 16 percent (the U.S. rate is 10 percent) can claim a tax reduction. As of the end of fiscal 1980 $26.2 billion were outstanding.[4]

Short-Term Government Bills. Short-term government bills are discount bills issued by the Japanese government with maturities of 60 to 64 days. No withholding tax or tax on redemption gains is levied. The amount outstanding as of the end of fiscal year 1980 was $65.4 billion.[5]

Local Government Bonds (Municipal Bonds). Local government bonds are mostly issued as private placements and are therefore less attractive to foreign investors. However, an active secondary over-the-counter market does exist. As of the end of fiscal 1980 the amount of $87.1 billion of local government bonds was outstanding.[6]

Government-Related Organization Bonds. Government-related organization bonds are issued by corporations owned by the government and have therefore a government guarantee.[7] The maturity is always 10 years, and they are issued with a coupon attached. The interest income is subject to withholding taxes as long-term govern-

---

[2] There have been periods in the past during which no new bonds were issued for several months, either for reasons relating to the general capital market situation or in anticipation of more advantageous conditions at a later date.

[3] *Introduction to Japanese Bonds*, Daiwa Securities Co. Ltd., 1981.

[4] Ibid.

[5] Ibid.

[6] Ibid.

[7] The following 19 corporations have issued bonds with a government guarantee: Japanese National Railways, Nippon Telegraph & Telephone Public Corporation, Japan Highway Public Corporation, Tokyo Expressway Public Corporation, Japan Housing Corporation, Hanshin Expressway Public Corporation, Finance Corporation of Lo-

ment bonds. As of the end of fiscal 1980, the market size of this sector amounted to $37.1 billion.[8]

Corporate Bonds. Corporate bonds are issued by private corporations, typically electric power companies, but also industrial corporations. The latter bonds are secured by mortgages. Unsecured bonds have only been issued as convertible bonds. The commercial code of Japan limits the amount of bonds that can be issued by a corporation. As of the end of fiscal 1980, $44.0 billion of industrial bonds and $5.8 billion of convertible bonds were outstanding.[9]

Bank Debentures. Bank debentures are issued by a number of specified institutions. There are three kind of debentures: five-year debentures (coupon bonds), three-year debentures (coupon bonds), and one-year debentures (discounted notes).

For all three kinds of debentures there is an active secondary market. Withholding tax and tax on redemption gains are applicable as explained earlier in the discussion of long- and medium-term government bonds. Only the six following banks can issue such debentures: The Industrial Bank of Japan, The Long-Term Credit Bank of Japan, The Nippon Credit Bank, The Bank of Tokyo, The Norin-Chukin Bank, and The Shoko-Chukin Bank.

Gensakis. The Gensaki is a "repurchase agreement" for a bond, and it is used as a short-term financing instrument. The seller of the bond (borrower) agrees to repurchase the bond at an agreed date and price from the buyer (lender) of the bond. The repurchase date has to be within 12 months of the selling date but is usually within 3 months. Gensakis are traded over the counter by major securities houses, which act as principal or intermediaries for their clients.

When the security house acts as an intermediary, the Gensaki is referred to as "commissioned." To the buyer the brokerage house appears as the seller even for commissioned Gensakis. Consequently Gensaki buyers have the guaranty from the brokerage house that their contracts will be repurchased, and they do not need to worry about the creditworthiness of the original seller.

Until 1979 foreign investors were not permitted to participate in the Gensaki market; today foreign investors, particularly affiliates of foreign corporations in Japan, are active market participants.

---

cal Public Enterprise, Hokkaido Tohoku Development Corporation, Water Resources Development Public Corporation, Japan Petroleum Resources Exploration Co., Ltd., Small Business Finance Corporation, Maritime Credit Corporation, Japan Railway Construction Public Corporation, Small Business Promotion Corporation, Tohoku Development Co., Ltd., Japan Air Lines Co., Ltd., Electric Power Development Co., Ltd., Nihon Airplane Manufacturing Co., Ltd., Japan Regional Development Corporation.

[8] *Introduction to Japanese Bonds.*

[9] Ibid.

FOREIGN INSTRUMENTS

Bonds

Eurobonds. Eurobonds are bonds issued and traded in markets that are not subject to the jurisdiction of the country in which currency the bonds are denominated.[10] Eurobonds are used by borrowers and lenders on a worldwide basis; they are traded in an "external" market (i.e., the market is not tied to any national regulatory agency or particular location). The main participants and market makers are large institutionally oriented banks and brokerage houses. The birth and subsequent rapid growth of the Euromarket was initiated mainly by the interest equalization tax and the voluntary foreign credit restraints (both introduced by the United States in 1963 and 1965, respectively), which forced U.S. corporations until 1974 to finance their foreign expansion by borrowing in foreign markets. However, other reasons have also contributed and are continuing today to favor the growth of the Euromarkets. These reasons are related to the relatively control-free environment in which the Eurobanks can operate and therefore generally offer more competitive rates than their national counterparts.[11]

The special characteristics of Eurobonds are:

1. Eurobonds are placed in several countries at the same time by multinational syndicates of underwriting banks and brokerage companies.
2. Most Eurobonds are quoted on at least one or more exchanges, but trading volume on the exchange is in most cases insignificant. They are mainly traded over the counter, whereby large banks and brokerage houses in various financial centers act as major market makers. The spread between bid and asked prices in an active secondary market is usually one half of 1 percent. In times of pronounced market uncertainty larger spreads reading 1 percent or more are not infrequent.
3. Eurobonds are only issued in bearer form.
4. Interest payments on Eurobonds are not subject to withholding taxes. For this purpose the issuing company has to be a subsidiary of the parent company, formed in a country that does not charge withholding taxes on interest paid to nonresidents, such as Holland, Luxembourg, the Netherlands Antilles, and so on.

---

[10] Some Eurobonds are also traded within the country in which currency the bonds are denominated, notably some Dutch guilder Eurobonds.

[11] For a detailed description of the Euromarket, see: Gunter Dufey and Ian H. Giddy, *The International Money Market* (Englewood Cliffs, N.J.: Prentice-Hall, 1978), and M. S. Dobbs-Higginson, *Investment Manual for Fixed Income Securities in International and Domestic Capital Markets*, Credit Suisse First Boston Limited, 1980.

Primary Market. Eurobonds are placed in a large number of countries simultaneously. The initial offering is controlled by the lead-managers and co-managers. The manager selects an underwriting syndicate and a selling group. Members of the underwriting syndicate take a firm commitment to place a predetermined number of bonds, which they have to buy for their own account in case they are unable to sell them to their customers. The selling group members, on the other hand, do not have the same commitment; they are only involved in the placement of the issue (i.e., they only participate to the extent that they are capable of placing the issue with their clients.

Private Placements. Private placements are bonds that are usually placed through small syndicates involving only one or few managers. This form of placement is frequently used during times of favorable market conditions. Private placements are issued in larger denominations than are public offerings ($5000 or more), have shorter maturities (5 to 8 years versus 15 to 20 years), and generally offer a somewhat higher yield than comparable public offerings. However, the disadvantage of many private placements is their limited liquidity because most of them are not traded broadly in the secondary market.

Payment of Principal and Interest. The accrued interest is calculated on the basis of 30 days per month, 360 days per year. Payments are made through the paying agent, a bank in the country of origin of the denominating currency. Interest payments are generally made on an annual basis.

Clearing and Custodian Procedures. The following two clearing systems exist for the Eurobond Market:

1. Euroclear, owned by a large number of banks worldwide, but mainly of European and North American origin, is domiciled in Brussels at the offices of Morgan Guaranty Trust, which also provides safe custody facilities in various financial centers.
2. Cedel, owned by a large number of European banks, located in Luxembourg.

Settlement is usually seven days after the trade date. Both Euroclear and Cedel perform the custodian function.

Currencies. For practical and comparative reasons, Exhibit 7 also lists the market size of so-called foreign bonds, which we will discuss later. In addition to the currencies shown in Exhibit 7, Eurobonds are also issued in several other currencies in much smaller amounts (Australian dollars, Hong Kong dollars, Norwegian kroner, Luxembourg francs, Kuwait dinars, Bahrain dinars) and in "European Units of Account" (EUA's) and "Special Drawing Rights" (SDRs).

Foreign Bonds. Foreign bonds are bonds that are issued by a foreign borrower in the country in which currency the bond is denominated. This enables the regulatory bodies of the country in which the

Exhibit 7
Market Size at the End of 1980 (nominal value, billions of local currency)

Currencies	Eurobonds	Foreign Bonds
U.S. dollar.........	63.200	47.6
Canadian dollar....	3.300	0.3
Sterling...........	0.724	0.673
Deutsche mark.....	79.200*	—
Dutch guilder......	5.400	3.1
Yen	125.000	1784.0
French franc.......	8.700	3.9
Swiss franc	—	52.0†

Source: Salomon Brothers Inc, *International Bond Market Analysis*, October 15, 1981.
* Eurobonds and foreign bonds.
† Consists of Sfr. 26.0 billion foreign bonds and Sfr. 26.0 billion foreign notes. There are no Euro Swiss franc bonds.

bond is issued to control the volume of foreign bonds issued. Except for this factor, the foreign bonds are almost identical to the Eurobonds. Foreign bonds are issued in the countries shown in Exhibit 8.

Foreign Notes. Foreign notes have the same characteristics as foreign bonds, except that they are frequently issued as private placements and have maturities of three to eight years. In Switzerland,

Exhibit 8
Issuers of Foreign Bonds

Japan	Samurai bonds—relatively small market, low liquidity.
Holland	Well-developed market; maturities up to 15 years; under normal market conditions good liquidity. Marketplace is the Amsterdam Stock Exchange. (The market size for Dutch guilder foreign bonds is only hfl. 3.1 billion as of December 31, 1980. However, since Dutch domestic bonds also are not subject to withholding taxes, the Dutch guilder market has to be viewed as a whole—composed of government bonds, provincial and municipal bonds, corporate bonds and foreign bonds. The size of this market is hfl. 81.5 billion).
Switzerland	Well-developed market; maturities usually of 8 to 15 years; under normal market conditions good liquidity. Most bonds are traded on the Zurich, Geneva, and Basle exchanges.
United States	Yankee bonds—bonds issued by a foreign borrower in the United States after registering with the SEC. Maturities up to 25 years; liquidity varies, but has been rather poor in recent years; it is currently improving as the volume of new issues has started to increase again.
Germany	Foreign DM bonds and Euro DM bonds enjoy a well-developed market and normally good liquidity, which can depend on the syndicate manager who usually acts as the main market maker. After U.S.-dollar bonds, DM bonds are the most widely used instruments in the international bond market. This is due to their availability and also the fundamental strength of the German mark.

foreign notes are issued as private placements for which the Swiss National Bank has established a special set of rules. The volume of new private placements has at times been larger than the volume of new foreign bonds. There is, however, no regular secondary market for those notes. The Swiss National Bank recently liberalized the provisions which restricted the trading of these securities. However these notes are still rather illiquid, especially in adverse market conditions. The market size is difficult to assess, since the Swiss banks are reluctant to give information for reasons related to "bank secrecy." Salomon Brothers estimates the size to be Sfr. 26.0 billion,[12] equally as large as the Swiss francs foreign bond market.[13]

Floating-Rate Notes

Floating-rate notes are similar to Euro straight bonds, except that their coupon rate is variable in intervals of three or six months. Most floating-rate notes offer a minimum interest rate, below which the coupon may not be fixed. An agent bank determines every three or six months the new coupon rate, which in most cases is fixed at one eighth to one fourth of 1 percent above the London Interbank Offered Rate (LIBOR), unless the rate is lower than the minimum interest rate stipulated at the issuing.

Convertible Bonds and Bonds with Warrants

Convertible Bonds. Convertible Eurobonds or convertible foreign notes offer all characteristics of a domestic convertible bond, except that the interest is paid free of withholding taxes, whereas dividends of the underlying shares are always subject to withholding taxes that normally can only be partially offset. The bondholders have the privilege to convert their bonds into common stocks at a specified price, within a given time and under stated terms and conditions. These convertible bonds are often issued by a foreign subsidiary of the company in which shares the bonds can be converted. Some Euro convertible bonds have call and sinking-fund provisions. The call feature provides that the company can call the bond for redemption at an initially stated price before maturity. When a convertible bond is called for redemption, the bondholder can either convert the bonds into stocks or turn in the bonds to the company against payment of the redemption price. (Of course, the bondholder can also sell it in the

---

[12] Salomon Brothers Inc, *International Bond Market Analysis*, October 15, 1981.

[13] The certificates (always in the form of bearer securities) for Swiss francs foreign notes and foreign bonds have to be kept physically in Switzerland, and there are no paying agents for these securities outside of Switzerland.

market.) If a bond is selling above the redemption price, the company can "force" conversion by calling bonds for redemption.

Convertible bonds can also be issued in currency other than the one of the underlying common stocks. These are the so-called *multi-currency convertible bonds*. The value of the convertible bond does not only reflect the value of the underlying shares or its intrinsic yield value, but it is also influenced by exchange-rate changes of the currencies involved. If the exchange rate of the currency in which the bond is denominated and the currency of the underlying common stock have been fixed, then the conversion price must be adjusted as follows:

Adjusted conversion price

$$\frac{\text{Original conversion price} \times \text{Present exchange rate}}{\text{Fixed exchange rate}}$$

If the exchange rate of the currency in which the bond is denominated and the currency of the underlying common stock have not been fixed, then both the conversion price and the current share price have to be converted into the currency in which the bond is denominated by applying the current exchange rate.

Most international convertible bonds have been issued in U.S. dollars, Deutsche marks, and Swiss francs. The Swiss francs convertible notes have been issued mostly by Japanese companies as private placements.

Bonds with Warrants. Bonds with warrants are less frequently issued than convertible bonds. The warrant, which can be detached from the bond and traded separately, gives the holder the right to buy a specified number of shares of the issuing company[14] during a specified period of time at a predetermined price. The value of the warrant (W) equals the number of shares (N_s) that can be purchased with one warrant times the current market price per share (M_p) minus the exercise price per share (E_p):

$$W = N_s (M_p - E_p)$$

Normally, the exercise price is denominated in the currency of the underlying shares. In a few cases the exercise price is stated in the currency of the bond, which (as explained in the case of convertible bonds) opens additional possibilities for currency gains or losses.

Lately Eurobonds have been issued with a new type of warrant attached. The warrant does not give the right to the holder to purchase shares of the underlying company; instead, it gives the right to sub-

---

[14] Frequently the issuing company is a foreign subsidiary of the parent company. The warrants give the right to buy shares of the parent company. (See also convertible bonds).

scribe to an issue of Eurobonds of the same company at a predetermined interest rate and maturity and during a specified period of time. These are the so-called debt warrants, as opposed to equity warrants discussed above. The investor who anticipates lower interest rates may be attracted by this instrument because the warrants will rise in value if the level of interest rates declines. For example, in September 1981 G.T.E. Finance N.V. issued $50 million notes with warrants at 16¼ percent due 1985. Each U.S. $1,000 note has one detachable warrant entitling the holder to purchase at par one U.S. $1,000 note due 1988 with an annual coupon of 16 percent. The warrant may be exercised at any time during a 12-month period commencing at the offering date.[15]

MONEY MARKET INSTRUMENTS

In this section we describe a variety of short-term investment vehicles that have one common characteristic—they have a secondary market and are therefore liquid to varying degrees. We do not concern ourselves with a widely used substitute, namely, time accounts or fixed-term deposits—which are issued by banks in the widest variety of currencies at usually attractive rates but are not marketable.

Certificates of Deposits[16]

In order to obtain short-term money, the leading commercial banks in the United States created at the beginning of the 1960s a new money market paper, which, being easily converted into cash, has met with great interest and today occupies an important position in the international money market. The certificate of deposit, or CD for short, is essentially an acknowledgment by a particular bank that it has received a specified dollar sum and will repay it on expiration of the time specified by the lender, together with an interest fixed at the time of the issuance. This acknowledgment or receipt is negotiable; thus an active secondary market has developed.

CDs issued in the United States are subject to Regulation Q, which used to limit the interest-rate level payable. When rates started to increase sharply, the banks in the United States were not able to raise the interest rate on CDs to the prevailing market rate, with the result that the inflow of money for CDs, from abroad particularly, stopped. The U.S. banks operating in this line consequently instructed their London branches, which were not subject to Regulation Q, to issue

---

[15] See Chapter 23.

[16] The source for the material that appears in this section and the section on Bankers' acceptances and promissory notes is Bank Julius Baer & Co., Ltd., *The Money Market Paper—An Investment without Fluctuations*, Zurich, 1975.

Cds at Euro-market rates. The London Eurodollar Cd market has since assumed considerable volume, and currently U.S. banks in London pay more attractive rates than the respective home offices. Non-U.S. banks operating in London are also issuing these instruments. Some British banks also began issuing certificates of deposits denominated in pound sterling.

There is a ready market for London CDs of primary banks so that they can be sold at any time before maturity. The maturity range is 1 month to 5 years, and maturities up to 12 months are most frequent.

Floating-Rate CDs (FRCDs)

FRCDs are issued with maturities of 1½ to 5 years at a variable interest rate. The rate is set every six months at levels of one eighth to one fourth of 1 percent above the London Interbank Offered Rate (LIBOR). It should be noted that FRCDs in contrast to floating-rate notes do not provide for a minimum interest rate and are therefore characterized as money market instruments.

Asian-Dollar CDs

Since the late 1970s, branches of U.S. and Japanese banks have issued conventional short-term CDs as well as FRCDs. These CDs are based on the Singapore Interbank Offered Rate (SIBOR).

Bankers' Acceptances[17]

Bankers' acceptances are bills of exchange running for 90 days, sometimes for 180 days, which are drawn on a bank and accepted by it. Initially such bills of exchange were accepted by leading U.S. banks and were therefore made out for U.S. dollars. In London such instruments are known as banks bills. Such bills are accepted by British banks and are made out for pounds sterling. In addition, many bills made out for dollars and accepted by European banks are reaching the London market. Both kinds, American as well as European acceptances, are traded on a discount basis in New York and London, and the discount is not subject to withholding tax. Such bankers' acceptances may be considered first-rate liquidity, being easily converted into cash at any time.

How does a bankers' acceptance arise? The following example will illustrate the process. A firm in the United States buys goods abroad, in Switzerland, for instance. Payment for those goods is due within 90 to 180 days from receipt of the shipping documents. The U.S. importer

---

[17] Ibid.

arranges with a banker for the issuance of an irrevocable letter of credit in favor of the Swiss exporter, who in turn, in conformity with the terms of the letter of credit, draws a draft on the U.S. bank and negotiates the draft with a local Swiss bank, receiving payment. The Swiss bank forwards the draft for presentation to the U.S. bank that issued the letter of credit. This bank stamps the draft "accepted"; that is, the American bank has accepted an obligation to pay the draft at maturity. An acceptance has been created. The acceptance is either returned to the Swiss bank or it is sold to an acceptance dealer and the products credited to the account of the Swiss bank. The shipping documents are released to the U.S. importer thus allowing the importer to process and sell the goods. The sale proceeds are deposited at the accepting bank to honor at maturity the acceptance.

Promissory Notes[18]

The method of fund raising that the leading U.S. finance and industrial companies have for decades employed by issuing commercial paper began to be adopted by large non-U.S. corporations in the late 1960s and early 1970s. Very frequently, internationally known firms raise short-term funds on the European money market by means of the promissory note. Such papers are taken over on a firm basis by the leading banks operating in the international money market and subsequently tendered to individual investors. A welcomed aspect is that such bills are issued for various currencies, such as Swiss francs, Deutsche marks, U.S. dollars, etc. enabling the investor to achieve a better risk distribution in terms of currency. These finance bills are as a rule traded on a discount basis, and the discount is not subject to withholding tax. However, the market for such papers is rather limited, so that they do not perhaps have the same degree of liquidity as do bankers' acceptances and Treasury bills.

Treasury Bills[19]

Treasury Bills are an exception in this context, since they do not represent a part of the Eurocurrency market, even though they are widely used for the purpose of international liquidity management. United Kingdom and Canadian T bills have already been discussed in this chapter. To facilitate the overview of international money market instruments the essential characteristics for Treasury bills are summarized below.

Treasury bills are essentially debt acknowledgment issued by the government to cover its short-term financial needs. So it is a short-

---

[18] Ibid.
[19] Ibid.

Exhibit 9
International Money Market Instruments

Money Market Instruments	Currency	Maturity Range of Issue	Yield Basis	Advantages*	Disadvantages
Certificates of deposit	London Eurodollar CDs Pound Sterling	1 to 36 months 3 to 6 months	Interest Interest	Relatively high yield; large variety of maturities.	Lower quality than T bills
	Yen	3 to 6 months	Interest		Yen CDs—withholding tax
Floating rates certificates of deposit	Dollar	1½ to 5 years	Interest, adjusted all 3 to 6 months annually ⅛ to ¼ above LIBOR rate	Highly liquid secondary market; high yield	Lower quality than T bills; long commitment; large denomination.

Instrument	Currency	Maturities	Basis	Advantages	Disadvantages
Bankers' acceptances (bank bills)........	Dollar	3 to 6 months	Discount	Good liquidity through rediscounting; relatively high yield, higher than CDs.	Lower quality than T bills; limited range of maturities; often only odd amounts available.
	Pound Sterling	Usually 3 months	Discount		
Treasury bills	Dollar	3 to 12 months	Discount	Highest quality; large variety of maturities (except United Kingdom); good marketability.	Lower yield; maturities above 6 months cause a withholding tax liability for U.S. T bills.
	Canadian Dollar	3 to 12 months	Discount		
Promissory notes	All major currencies	1 to 6 months	Discount or interest	Great variety of maturities; excellent liquidity—most widely used instrument in the Euromarket; relatively high yield; available in all major currencies.	Lower quality than T bills.

* Of all the instruments listed above, none are subject to withholding taxes except yen CDs.

term government paper, normally running for terms from 3 to 12 months (United Kingdom T bills are always issued for 91 days). Notably the United States, Canada, and Britain use this facility to obtain their short-term resources on their money markets by auctioning such papers weekly. Those bills, which are made out for the currency of the issuing state, doubtless constitute an excellent liquidity reserve, since they have a ready market and can thus be converted into cash at any time. Trading is on a discount basis, and the discount is not subject to withholding tax.

Exhibit 9 provides summary information about money market instruments.

PART 3

Bond Investment
Management

Introduction to Bond Investment Management

27

H. GIFFORD FONG
President
Gifford Fong Associates

This section of the book is concerned with describing some of the new approaches to bond investment management—new in the sense of analytical innovation, but not new in the sense of the conceptual framework generally followed by the practitioner. In other words, the emphasis will be on defining analytical frameworks that draw upon current practice and that offer the promise of better decision making. The intent is to describe techniques that are extensions and complements to most traditional practice.

There is a significant evolution going on in both active and passive fixed income strategies. Although there are some parallels with the evolution going on in the equity area, bond portfolio analysis offers a unique opportunity for fulfilling a number of investor needs. As the diversity of investment requirements of participants in the financial markets expands, additional strategies responsive to these needs become highly desirable. In following chapters a number of approaches that may provide assistance in this area are described. It is the blending of the traditional with the modern techniques that promises to expand the capability of bond management to better serve the investor.

NATURE OF BOND PORTFOLIO ANALYSIS[1]

Portfolio management can be viewed as a two-level process: The macro decision is the proportion of the portfolio to be held in various asset classes (stocks, bonds, Treasury bills, etc.), and the micro decision is which individual securities to be held will make up the respective components. Both steps have similar concerns relating to return and risks, but the first step, or macro decision, usually deserves special attention. In fact, this is probably the most important portfolio decision in terms of maximizing return and minimizing risk. Another name for this process is *asset allocation*.[2] Our interest in the following discussion will be in the role that bonds can play in the macro analysis.

For those who find less volatility more emotionally acceptable or for those who realize their investment needs are more modest than those promised by an all-equity portfolio (over the long term), bonds represent an important investment alternative for the portfolio asset-allocation decision. If minimizing risk is the only objective, then investment in Treasury instruments will achieve a return that is accepted as being risk free. If maximizing return is the only objective, then investment in the highest expected return asset is the answer. Given the usual range of alternatives, this is common stock. The real problem occurs when a trade-off is desired between return and risk. This can be expressed as maximizing expected return at a given level of risk or minimizing risk at a given level of expected return. Any departure from the lowest or highest return alternatives confronts the problem of the best trade-off and consequently the best mix of the alternatives. In evaluating the trade-off between return and risk, return is merely the weighted average of the assets included in the portfolio, but risk requires additional analysis.

The total risk of a portfolio may be thought of as the individual risk of each investment and their covariance, or tendency to move relative to each other.[3] For example, if an investor had two assets of the same return and same individual risk, there would be benefits to holding both assets if they had a negative covariance, or tendency for one asset to counteract the volatility of the other. Exhibit 1 provides some indication of the characteristics of stocks, bonds, and Treasury bills.

There has been a historical positive covariance relationship between stocks and bonds. Since Treasury bills have only nominal price

---

[1] The following discussion is drawn from H. Gifford Fong, *Bond Portfolio Analysis* (Charlottesville, Va.: The Financial Analysts Research Foundation, 1980), Chapter 2. The tables presented here are updated from those in the monograph.

[2] This process is described in H. Gifford Fong, "An Asset Allocation Framework," *The Journal of Portfolio Management* (Winter 1980), pp. 58–66.

[3] Harry M. Markowitz, *Portfolio Selection* (New York: John Wiley & Sons, 1959).

Exhibit 1
Common Stocks and Bonds Return and Risk Comparison—1926–1980

	Return	Risk (Standard Deviation)	Coefficient of Variation*
Common stock...............	9.5%	21.1%	2.2%
Long-term bonds	3.7	5.7	1.5
Treasury bills	2.8	.8	.3

* Coefficient of variation is risk divided by return.
Source: Roger G. Ibbotson and Rex A. Sinquefield, *Stocks, Bonds, Bills and Inflation: The Past and the Future* (Charlottesville, Va.: The Financial Analysts Research Foundation, 1981 edition).

risk, there has not been a strong relationship between Treasury bills and changes in returns on stocks or on bonds.

These relationships measure the tendency for comovement or correlation. In simple terms, as each asset fluctuates over time, the correlation measures the tendency of the relative direction of return to be similar. The returns of one asset moving in one direction are a measure of the expectation by investors of the future return of the other asset. Ideally, assets would be combined having a positive return expectation with the tendency of their respective interim fluctuations over the horizon to be negatively correlated. The net result would be the realization of the return sought with dispersion or fluctuation minimized in the process. Exhibit 2 schematically illustrates this concept. Assets A and B have positive returns expected and some fluctuation

Exhibit 2
Schematic Illustration of Comovements of Assets

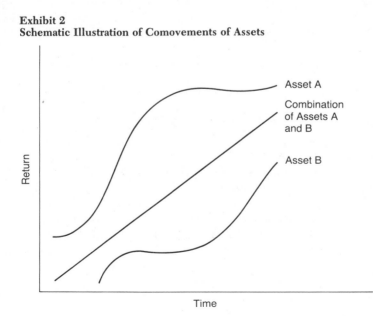

associated with those returns. However, because of the negative correlation between the two assets, a combination of the two results in an expected return with fluctuation minimized.

Over time the magnitude and in some cases even the sign of the covariance may change. However, there may be an economic basis for this characteristic. For example, as interest rates rise, the return from Treasury bills will increase, and there may be a tendency for the stock market return to decrease. Interest-rate changes can become a fundamental cause of both the magnitude and sign of the covariance. For stocks, increased interest rates increase the discount factor on the stream of future cash flows resulting in a lower intrinsic value unless offset by increased earnings or other changes resulting from inflation; for Treasury bills, increased interest rates will increase the return, assuming the instrument is held to maturity and rolled over. These tendencies over subperiods within the time horizon contribute to the relative fluctuation in return. For the entire time horizon, both assets will presumably have a positive return, and by taking into account short run tendencies, the interim portfolio fluctuations can be minimized.

Of course, if one always held the portfolio to the end of the horizon, and all the return expectations were met, the problem would become academic. In the face of uncertainty, however, and the prospect that the portfolio will not be held for the entire period, minimizing portfolio return fluctuation is desirable.

Because there is an underlying economic rationale, there is a tendency, as in the Treasury bill and stock market example, for the relative relationships to persist. Exhibit 3 shows the correlation coefficients (stated as percentages) between bonds and treasury bills for various combinations of years from 1966 to 1980. The data show that covariance between the series is weak and, maybe, negative. This fact tends to add to the problem of forecasting covariance without detracting from the need to do so.

One of the fundamental principles of optimal asset allocation is the combination of assets to take advantage of the existence of low or negatively correlated assets to minimize overall portfolio risk.[4] Bonds and Treasury bills with their low or negatively correlated returns are therefore attractive candidates for portfolio inclusion.

Another dimension one should consider is the absolute risk-return characteristics of asset alternatives. With the standard deviation as a proxy for risk, the ratio achieved from dividing the historical risk by return reveals some interesting relationships. Exhibit 1 reveals the results for the three asset types commonly used.

---

[4] Fong, "An Asset Allocation Framework."

Exhibit 3
Correlation of Monthly Returns (percent)

High-Grade Corporate Bond Indexes—Composite: Total Returns
U.S. Treasury Bills: Total Returns
Based on Monthly Returns from January 1 to December 31 of Years Shown

From: To:	1966	1967	1968	1969	1970	1971	1972	1973	1974	1975	1976	1977	1978	1979	1980
1966	43.4														
1967	39.3	37.1													
1968	33.8	32.1	24.9												
1969	5.1	4.6	-8.2	10.5											
1970	15.9	14.8	2.4	-3.9	-12.6										
1971	14.9	13.4	4.4	1.9	20.5	61.7									
1972	11.4	10.0	3.2	2.1	24.0	43.6	29.0								
1973	9.5	8.2	2.0	0.8	9.3	5.6	-2.7	18.0							
1974	0.1	-1.2	-7.1	-8.6	-7.3	-10.8	-15.1	-10.0	-26.2						
1975	3.6	2.3	-3.0	-4.4	-2.4	-4.2	-7.6	-8.4	-15.6	55.0					
1976	2.5	0.9	-4.7	-6.2	-3.7	-5.6	-10.6	-15.6	-20.3	38.5	27.9				
1977	2.7	1.3	-3.7	-5.0	-2.3	-4.4	-8.4	-10.5	-13.3	34.1	8.8	1.1			
1978	0.8	-0.6	-5.6	-6.8	-5.1	-7.2	-10.7	-12.3	-15.8	1.9	-21.4	-10.9	-16.4		
1979	-3.0	-4.1	-3.2	-9.3	-9.4	-10.3	-12.2	-12.5	-15.1	-11.5	-17.2	-4.6	0.0	15.1	
1980	21.8	21.6	20.7	20.9	21.3	22.9	25.3	28.3	28.7	33.5	37.8	48.5	57.5	67.7	77.3

Source: Roger G. Ibbotson and Rex A. Sinquefield, *Stocks, Bonds, Bills and Inflation: The Past and the Future* (Charlottesville, Va.: The Financial Analysts Research Foundation, 1981 edition).

It can be seen that as higher returns are achieved, the amount of risk per unit of return (coefficient of variation) increases. The implication is that, although the expectations over sufficiently long periods of time are for stocks to outperform bonds and bonds to outperform Treasury bills, the associated risk over a one-year time frame rises rapidly as higher return assets are held. For every rule there is an exception. Whether the risk preference of the investor can tolerate the associated short-term risk of equity's ownership is a significant issue. This issue has helped stimulate the concern in the asset allocation process and the role bonds can play.

In summary, the characteristics of bonds in a portfolio reveal a number of causes for the continued interest in this asset class. More modest risk and return preferences suit the fundamental characteristics of bonds. In addition, the argument for minimizing the role of bonds in favor of higher expected return from stock is countered by a more realistic appraisal of investment need and the associated risk of seeking higher return. The performance of bonds during the period of October 1979 through May 1980 illustrates this point.

Aside from the return that can be achieved, the relative and absolute risk characteristics of bonds make them an attractive investment. Turning to the micro case of what individual bonds should be held, the same type of issue remains: how to acheive the most return with the least amount of risk. Given a portfolio with a bond component, the question becomes which individual instruments to hold. To evaluate this, a framework for understanding the genesis of bond returns and risk is also explained in the following chapters of this section.

Total Aftertax Bond Performance and Yield Measures for Taxable Bonds Held in Taxable Portfolios*

28

MARTIN L. LEIBOWITZ, Ph.D.
Managing Director, Bond
Portfolio Analysis Group
Salomon Brothers Inc

The conventional yield-to-maturity,[1] both in its pretax and aftertax forms, leaves much to be desired as a comprehensive tool for investment analysis and the comparison of relative values. In *Inside the Yield Book*,[2] it was suggested that a total return measure called the realized compound yield could prove useful in evaluating prospective bond purchases and bond swaps.[3] We have since explored the total

---

* Adapted from Martin L. Leibowitz, *Total After-Tax Bond Performance and Yield Measures* (New York: Salomon Brothers Inc, 1974). Although this chapter will explain ways of integrating different tax structures into an analytic investment framework, there will be no attempt to discuss any corporation's specific situations. All tax examples presented here are used strictly for the purpose of illustrating the various analytic techniques and should not be interpreted as necessarily applicable to any given individual or corporate entity. Moreover, the author does not wish to represent himself as being qualified to provide advice relating to tax matters, and neither the author nor Salomon Brothers Inc is in the business of providing such advice.

Although the information in this chapter has been obtained from sources that the author believes to be reliable, Salomon Brothers Inc cannot guarantee its accuracy, and such information may be incomplete or condensed. All opinions and estimates included in this chapter constitute judgment as of this date and are subject to change without notice.

[1] See Chapter 4 for the definition of yield-to-maturity.

[2] Sidney Homer and Martin L. Leibowitz, *Inside the Yield Book* (New York: Prentice-Hall and New York Institute of Finance, 1972).

[3] Bond swaps are discussed in Chapter 30.

return to taxable portfolios in some detail. We have found that our realized compound yield approach could be properly extended, in ways that are far from obvious, into the complex world of the taxed portfolio. Once the key concepts of "effective par rate" and "opportunity dollars" were identified, it became clear that this extension was not only possible but could indeed prove to be a most valuable investment tool. In fact, in certain taxed environments this extension proves more informative and provides more counter-intuitive surprises than in the comparable tax-free case.

The purpose of this chapter is to describe how the realized compound yield can be translated into a consistent and useful concept for taxable bonds in taxed bond portfolios and to provide some examples of its application to certain important bond investment situations.[4]

TAX-FREE PORTFOLIOS

Realized Compound Yield for the Tax-Free Portfolio

Before proceeding to the taxed cases, we shall summarize some of the main features of realized compound yield in the tax-free case.

A bond has three basic elements of return: (1) coupon income, (2) principal appreciation, and (3) interest-on-interest. The first two elements are self-explanatory. Interest-on-interest is the indirect return that arises from the compounded reinvestment of the bond's coupon payments at the then available market rates. Since interest-on-interest may well account for more than 70 percent of the overall return for a long-term bond, no evaluation of a bond investment can be complete without giving due consideration to this important factor.

Exhibit 1 shows how a $1 million holding of a 30-year, 7.5 percent par bond generates interest-on-interest from reinvestment of its coupons at an arbitrarily assumed compounding rate of 6 percent. Each semiannual coupon payment will be $37,500. The first such payment is received after six months. It is assumed to be immediately reinvested at 6 percent so that it earns 3 percent over the next six months, or

$$\$37,500 \times .03 = \$1,125$$

Together with the second $37,500 coupon payment, this means that there would be a total accrual of $76,125 available for reinvestment at the end of the first year. At 3 percent over the next six months, these total accrued funds would earn an additional interest-on-interest of

$$\$76,125 \times .03 = \$2,284$$

---

[4] A discussion of tax-exempt bonds in taxable bond portfolios is presented in Frank J. Fabozzi, Sylvan G. Feldstein, Irving M. Pollack, and Frank G. Zarb, *The Handbook of Municipal Bonds* (Homewood, Ill.: Dow Jones-Irwin, 1983). © Dow Jones-Irwin, Inc, 1983.

Exhibit 1
Accrual Schedule for $1 million Par Amount of 25-Year 7.5 Percent Bonds with All Coupons Reinvested at a 6 Percent Rate Compounded Semiannually

Period Start Date	Total Amount Accrued at Start of Period		Reinvestment Rate over Period		Interest on Interest	Coupon Payment at End of Period	Total Amount Accrued by End of Period
0 Years 0 Months	$ 0	×	.03	=	$ 0	$ 37,500	$ 37,500
0 Years 6 Months	37,500	×	.03	=	1,125	37,500	76,125
1 Year 0 Months	76,125	×	.03	=	2,284	37,500	115,909
1 Year 6 Months	115,909	×	.03	=	3,477	37,500	156,886
2 Years 0 Months	156,886	×	.03	=	4,707	37,500	199,093
23 Years 6 Months	3,764,869	×	.03	=	112,946	37,500	3,915,315
24 Years 0 Months	3,915,315	×	.03	=	117,459	37,500	4,070,274
24 Years 6 Months	4,070,274	×	.03	=	122,108	37,500	4,229,883
Totals at maturity	$4,229,883				$2,354,883	$1,875,000	
Plus redemption of principal	1,000,000						
Total future value	$5,229,883						

Continuing in this fashion, the interest-on-interest and total amount
accrued would grow as shown on Exhibit 1. At the bond's maturity in
25 years, the investor would have received a total of $1,875,000 in
direct coupon payments. By reinvesting each of these coupons at the 6
percent rate, compounded semiannually, the investor would have realized an additional $2,354,883 of interest-on-interest. In other words,
of the total return of $4,229,883 on the $1 million invested, the factor
of interest-on-interest would account for about 56 percent.

The amount of interest-on-interest expected depends on the assumed rate at which coupons are reinvested and compounded over
the bond's life. Exhibit 2 shows the dollars of interest-on-interest ac-

Exhibit 2
**Effect of the Reinvestment Rate on the Total Dollar Return over the Life of 25-Year, 7.5
Percent Par Bond**

Assumed Reinvestment Rate (Semiannual Basis)	Dollars per $1,000 Bond			Interest-on-Interest as Percent of Total Return	Realized Compound Yield
	Coupon Income	Interest-on-Interest	Total Return		
0.0%	$1,875	$ 0	$1,875	0%	4.27%
5.0	1,875	1,781	3,656	49	6.25
6.0	1,875	2,355	4,230	56	6.73
7.0	1,875	3,037	4,912	62	7.24
7.5*	1,875*	3,426*	5,301*	65*	7.50*
8.0	1,875	3,850	5,725	67	7.77
9.0	1,875	4,819	6,694	72	8.33
10.0	1,875	5,976	7,851	76	8.91

* Reinvestment at the conventional yield rate.

cumulated from compounding at various fixed rates over the bond's
life (e.g., at a 7 percent fixed reinvestment rate, the interest-on-interest would accumulate to $3,037,000 or 62 percent of the bond's total
return). At an 8 percent reinvestment rate, the accumulated interest-
on-interest becomes $3,850,000, or 67 percent of the total dollar re-
turn.

Many investors are surprised by the magnitude of these interest-on-
interest figures. Since every bond investment forces a certain cash
flow schedule upon the investor, which must either be reinvested or
used in some time-valued fashion, this interest-on-interest must be
considered in comparing alternative fixed income investments.

Without an assumption on the reinvestment of the coupons, a dollar-and-cents analysis of a bond swap over time will give inconsistent
results. In fact, it is literally impossible to determine the compounded
dollar-and-cents return from a bond investment without making at
least an implicit judgment regarding reinvestment rates.

The concept of realized compound yield as tabulated in Exhibit 2 is one convenient way of characterizing the total return provided by any investment under a given set of reinvestment assumptions. For example, as shown in Exhibit 1, a $1 million investment in a 7.5 percent, 25-year bond, when all coupons are reinvested at 6 percent, will lead to a total dollar return of $4,229,883, above and beyond the repayment of the original $1 million investment. This corresponds to a return of $4.23 for every $1 invested over a period of 25 years, which in turn corresponds to full semiannual compounding at a uniform rate of 6.73 percent. The procedure for computing this rate is explained in Chapter 4. Thus the 7.5 percent, 25-year bond investment can be said to provide a realized compound yield of 6.73 percent at the assumed reinvestment rate of 6 percent. The realized compound yield will always be between the conventional yield-to-maturity and the reinvestment rate.

The realized compound yield is a convenient yardstick for consistently evaluating alternative investments over a range of assumed market conditions. Exhibit 2 shows the realized compound yields associated with the 7.5 percent, 25-year par bond for one such range of reinvestment conditions. This table demonstrates the sensitivity of bond returns to changes in the reinvestment rate assumption. It is also interesting to note that, when the reinvestment rate is the same as the bond's conventional yield, (i.e., 7.5 percent, the bond's realized compound yield then also coincides with the bond's 7.5 percent *conventional yield-to-maturity*. This equality holds quite generally because the conventional yield computation, when interpreted as the rate of dollars-and-cents accrual of funds, carries the tacit assumption that all cash flows are reinvested (or "time-valued") at the conventional yield rate itself.

Up to this point, we have only discussed "par" bonds. However, all of these concepts hold true for bonds priced at either a premium above par, or at a discount below par.

For example, consider a 25-year, 4 percent bond priced at 60.739 to provide a conventional yield-to-maturity of 7.5 percent. Over its 25-year life, each $1000 bond would have a return consisting of the locked-in capital gain of $392.61, plus $1,000 in coupon payments (= 25 × $40), plus interest-on-interest arising from the compounded reinvestment of these coupon payments. At a fixed 6 percent reinvestment rate, this interest-on-interest would amount to $1,255.94, so that the total return would become $2,648.55. Since the bond cost $607.39, this would amount to a total return of $4.36 per dollar invested, which corresponds to a fully compounded 6.83 percent rate. Thus this bond investment can be said to provide a prospective realized compound yield of 6.83 percent.

Exhibit 3 shows the discount bond's return per invested dollar and

Exhibit 3
**A Comparison of Various Investment Measures (for two bonds with the same 7.5 percent
conventional yield-to-maturity—a 25-year, 7.5 percent par bond priced at 100 and a 25-year, 4
percent discount bond priced at 60.739)**

Assumed Reinvestment Rate	Conventional Yield-to-Maturity		Total Dollar Return per $1.00 Invested		Realized Compound Yield		Effective Par Rate	
	7.5	4s	7.5s	4s	7.5s	4s	7.5s	4s
0.0%............	7.5%	7.5%	$1.88	$2.92	4.27%	4.82%	7.5%	9.17%
5.0.............	7.5	7.5	3.66	3.86	6.25	6.42	7.5	7.91
6.0.............	7.5	7.5	4.23	4.36	6.73	6.83	7.5	7.73
7.0.............	7.5	7.5	4.92	4.96	7.24	7.27	7.5	7.57
7.5*............	7.5*	7.5*	5.30*	5.30*	7.50*	7.50*	7.5*	7.50*
8.0.............	7.5	7.5	5.72	5.66	7.77	7.74	7.5	7.43
9.0.............	7.5	7.5	6.66	6.53	8.33	8.24	7.5	7.31
10.0	7.5	7.5	7.84	7.55	8.91	8.77	7.5	7.20

* Reinvestment at the conventional yield rate.

realized compound yield for a range of reinvestment rates. Once
again, we see that the realized compound yield coincides with the
conventional yield-to-maturity only when reinvestment takes place at
the 7.5 percent yield rate. As reinvestment rates fall below or rise
above this 7.5 percent yield rate, the realized compound yields also
drop or fall. The same observation holds, of course, for the total return
per invested dollar.

In fact, since the realized compound yield is just a mathematical
restatement of the total return per invested dollar, every swap improvement in realized compound yield will correspond to an improvement in dollars-and-cents return. This is a critically important characteristic for an investment measure. *As Exhibit 3 illustrates, the
conventional yield-to-maturity fails to possess this critical property
of accurately reflecting the investment's dollars-and-cents payoff.* In
fact, it turns out that for reasonable reinvestment rates, the spread in
conventional yields-to-maturity almost always *overstates* the actual
difference in this dollars-and-cents return.

By comparing the realized compound yields (or total returns per
dollar invested) for the two bonds as shown in Exhibit 3, we see that
the discount bond has somewhat less sensitivity than the par bond to
variations in reinvestment rate. This reduced variability results from
the discount bond's capital gain contribution, which is fixed in advance and hence totally insensitive to reinvestment conditions.

A New Concept: The Effective Par Rate

Conventional judgments of relative long-term investment values
are often based upon "yield spreads" between a given security or

sector and some benchmark "yield level." This benchmark is often taken to be the new-issue rate for the particular market in question. Since most market movements are communicated in terms of new-issue rates, this capability to "benchmark" yields against new-issue rates has great practical significance. The problem is that such benchmarking comparisons tacitly imply that the conventional yield-to-maturity corresponds to the long-term return provided by a given coupon rate on a par bond. In fact, one might argue further that this benchmarking forms the intuitive basis for the conventional yield-to-maturity (i.e., many investors interpret a conventional yield value as saying that the bonds' dollars-and-cents return is equivalent to that from a par bond having the same yield and maturity. Thus, a 4 percent bond selling on a 7.5 percent conventional yield is taken to be equivalent to a 7.5 percent par bond with regard to long-term return. As Exhibit 3 shows, this will be strictly true only when coupon reinvestment also takes place at 7.5 percent. At reinvestment rates other than the 7.5 percent yield value, the discount 4 percent bond's dollars-and-cents return differs significantly from that of the 7.5 percent par bond.

By its very definition, the realized compound yield values will correctly reflect the differences in dollars-and-cents return. However, the realized compound yield neither fits the intuitively comfortable scale of par bond returns nor can it be conveniently benchmarked against new-issue levels. The "effective par rate" is a new concept that has these two very desirable properties and yet retains the accuracy of the realized compound yield as a consistent measure of dollars-and-cents return.

Put very simply, *the "effective par rate" for a given bond is the coupon rate for that par bond that would produce the same dollars-and-cents return* (and hence the same realized compound yield) *as the given bond under the assumed reinvestment conditions.* Taking an example from Exhibit 3, with reinvestment at 6 percent, the 25-year, 4 percent bond priced at 60.739 (to yield 7.5 percent) provides $4.36 of return for every dollar invested, or a realized compound yield of under 7.5 percent (i.e., 6.83 percent). To obtain this same return from a 25-year par bond, a coupon rate of 7.73 percent would be required. Stated another way, in considering a swap out of the discount 4 percent bond and into the new-issue market, an investor with a 6 percent reinvestment assumption would have to obtain a new-issue rate of at least 7.73 percent in order to break even in terms of the long-term dollars-and-cents return. For this reason, the effective par rate of 7.73 percent can be viewed as the breakeven par bond yield for the 4 percent bond under a 6 percent reinvestment assumption.[5]

---

[5] Martin L. Leibowitz, "New Tools in Bond Portfolio Management," *Trusts and Estates,* January 1973).

As we see from this example, the effective par rate provides a measuring tool for the investment manager to immediately benchmark the bonds in his or her portfolio against new-issue levels. It also provides an intuitively comfortable scale for defining long-term investment value in a manner consistent with dollars-and-cents return. Thus, for a given investor and his or her reinvestment assumptions, all bonds with the same effective par rate over a specified time horizon are completely equivalent in terms of dollars-and-cents return. All such bonds are equivalent not only to each other, but also to the hypothetical par bond having a coupon rate equal to the effective par rate and a maturity spanning the specified time horizon.

The question of yield spread deserves some further discussion. In *Inside the Yield Book,* we observed that the conventional yields-to-maturity tend to overstate the difference in dollars-and-cents return between two bonds. This arises because two bonds at different conventional yields carry the implication of two distinct (and naturally inconsistent) reinvestment-rate assumptions, with the higher rate being ascribed to the higher yielding bond. At a common reinvestment rate, the difference in realized compound yields would usually be less than the conventional yield spread. The magnitude of this contraction depends critically on the investment horizon, but for long-term bonds it would not be surprising to see a 40-basis-point conventional yield spread shrink by a factor of 2 to a 20-basis-point spread in terms of realized compound yields. Although this contraction in the yield spread is indeed an accurate reflection of the basic rate of return, it does require a double shift on the part of the portfolio manager. Not only must the portfolio manager change his or her orientation toward dealing with an explicit reinvestment rate, but must also shift from a conventional scale of values. Thus a 40-basis-point increase in new-issue rates or a 40-basis-point improvement on a swap package now only corresponds to a 20-basis-point improvement in realized compound yield. Hence the meaning of *basis point* in the everyday marketplace would have to differ from the meaning of *basis point* in terms of the personalized realized compound yield measure.

This shift of scale could naturally lead to many problems. For example, a portfolio manager whose market judgment suggests that a 14-basis-point pickup should be attainable might reject a portfolio action resulting in a 7-basis-point pickup in realized compound yield. Yet the 7 basis points of realized compound yield might well correspond to well over 14 basis points in terms of the conventional yield scale ingrained in the manager's past experience and forming the basis for the market judgment.

The effective par rate concept can help resolve this problem of the shifting meaning of a basis point. A given basis point change in conventional yield for a given bond will result in much the same basis-point change in the bond's effective par rate. The level of the effective par rate will, of course, differ from the conventional yield to reflect the impact of the reinvestment assumption on the dollars-and-cents return. These effects are illustrated in Exhibit 4.

Exhibit 4
Required Increases in Various Investment Measures to Provide Given Levels of Total Dollar Return (for a 25-year 4 percent bond under a fixed 6 percent reinvestment assumption)

Total Dollar Return per $1 Invested	Required Purchase Price	Required Conventional Yield-to-Maturity		Required Realized Compound Yield		Required Effective Par Rate	
		Level	Increase	Level	Increase	Level	Increas
$4.36	60.739	7.50%		6.83%		7.73%	
4.46	59.591	7.65	+15 B.P.	6.91	+8 B.P.	7.91	+18
4.56	58.585	7.89	+14	6.98	+7	8.08	+17
4.66	57.333	7.93	+14	7.06	+8	8.26	+18
4.76	56.509	8.08	+15	7.13	+7	8.44	+18

The effective par rate thus has many appealing characteristics as a measure of investment value—consistency with dollars-and-cents return, preservation of the interpretation of a yield *level*, maintenance of the intuitive scale for *basis-point spreads* and *changes,* and the convenience of benchmarking against the new-issue market. For all these reasons, it might be argued that it is the effective par rate that should be taken as the natural analogue of the conventional yield value as a consistent and correct measure of dollars-and-cents investment return.

As we shall soon see, this argument in behalf of the effective par rate becomes strongly reinforced when dealing with portfolios subject to taxation.

Realized Compound Yields over the Short Term

Over investment horizons encompassing a bond's maturity, the realized compound yield (or the effective rate) has the great advantage of providing a consistent measure of the dollars-and-cents return. The one uncertainty here is, of course, that of future reinvestment rates. The realized compound yield approach forces the portfolio manager to openly confront this real-life uncertainty and to render explicit judgments as to future level(s) of reinvestment rates consistent with the manager's portfolio structure and purpose. Over investment periods that are shorter than the bond's maturity, a second key element of uncertainty enters the scene: Where will the bond be priced at the end of the review period? Here again, the portfolio manager can use the realized compound yield to confront this uncertainty by exploring the effect of one or more *explicit* assumptions regarding future price (or yield) levels. Once again, the realized compound yield will provide a consistent measure of the dollars-and-cents return that would be obtained under the fulfillment of each of the manager's assumptions.

Exhibit 5 illustrates the computation of realized compound yields for the 25-year, 7.5 percent and 4 percent bonds under the assumption of a conventional yield move from 7.5 percent to 7.4 percent over the first one-year period. It also shows the corresponding effective par rates. It should be noted that the standard par bond in this computation always has a maturity matched to the review period, no matter what the maturity of the original bond. Thus, under the assumed yield decline over one year, the 4 percent discount bond produces a realized compound yield of 8.71 percent. This in turn corresponds to the realized compound yield of a par bond with a coupon rate of 8.77 percent (the effective par rate) and a maturity of *one year*. Even this simple computation shows a number of more general results. First, over a period as short as one year, the reinvestment effects do not have a chance to develop. Consequently, the realized compound yield and the effective par rate essentially coincide. Moreover, as long as there

Exhibit 5
Realized Compound Yields over the Short Term (One Year) under the Assumption of a 10-Basis-Point Yield Decline

	25-Year 7.50s	25-Year 4.00s
Original investment per bond (@ 7.50 percent conventional yield)	$1,000.00	$607.39
Two coupons during year	75.00	40.00
Interest-on-interest on one coupon @ 6 percent for ½ year	1.13	.60
Year-end principal appreciation at constant 7.50 percent conventional yield	0.00	5.66
Total dollar gain—without yield move	$ 76.13	$ 46.26
Dollar return per $1.00 invested—without yield move	$ .07613	$ .07616
Realized compound yield—without yield move	7.47%	7.48%
Effective par rate—without yield move	7.50%	7.50%
Year-end principal value at 7.40 percent conventional yield	$1,011.15	$620.86
less year-end principal value at 7.50 percent—without yield move	$1,000.00	$613.05
Principal appreciation due to 10 b.p. yield move	$ 11.15	$ 7.81
Dollar return per $1.00 invested due to 10 b.p. yield move	$ .01115	$ .01286
Total dollar return per $1.00 invested—with yield move	$ .08728	$ .08902
Realized compound yield—with yield move	8.55%	8.71%
Effective par rate—with yield move	8.60%	8.77%
Incremental realized compound yield due to 10 b.p. yield move	+108 b.p.	+123 b.p.
Incremental effective par rate due to 10 b.p. yield move	+110 b.p.	+127 b.p.

is no change in yield (i.e., as long as all price changes are due only to amortization at a constant conventional yield), then the conventional yield value will closely approximate the realized compound yield and come even closer to the effective par rate. However, even a relatively small 10-basis-point decline in the conventional yield of a long-term bond will lead to well over 10 times that magnitude of change in both the realized compound yield and the effective par rate. Finally, even with two bonds having the exact same maturity and starting yield value, the bond with the lower coupon will undergo a somewhat greater response to a given yield move.

TAXABLE BONDS IN TAXED PORTFOLIOS

Taxed Portfolios: Sources of Return

The sources of bond return in taxed portfolios include the three basic elements described earlier for the tax-free case—coupons, capital gains or losses, and interest-on-interest. These elements must be adjusted, of course, for the direct effects of taxation. However, most taxed portfolios are subject to a number of other indirect statutory and/ or tax factors that can have a significant effect upon the net return derived from a given bond holding or bond purchase. We shall first discuss the three basic elements of return and then later turn to a review of some of the more important indirect factors.

Aftertax Coupon Return

The treatment of coupon return is theoretically straightforward, but can actually present some serious estimation problems in practice. For all bonds purchased at par or at a discount, there is some appropriate marginal income tax rate that can be directly charged against the coupon payments. This marginal tax rate will, of course, depend on both the type of institution, the type of the bond (i.e., fully taxable, state tax exempt, federal tax exempt, federal and state tax exempt, etc.) as well as on the intricacies of the particular institution's operating structure. In fact, determination of the appropriate marginal income tax rate is often a much more complex process than might first appear, and many portfolio managers will confess that they are sometimes hard pressed to obtain usable official estimates for their funds. This problem is, of course, greatly compounded by the fact that most prospective coupon payments will be received—and taxed—in future fiscal years. Ideally, one should develop a sequence of future-estimated income tax rates over the life of the bond. Of course, this is rarely possible except in certain cases where a progressive change in the tax laws is already on the books. In practice, this partial uncertainty is usually dealt with in somewhat the same simplifying manner as the uncertainty regarding future reinvestment rates (i.e., the same fixed tax rate is assumed over the entire life of all of the bonds held in the same tax status). This fixed rate may then be varied over the range of uncertainty in order to explore the effects of various taxation scenarios.

The interaction of the coupon cycle with the tax payment cycle will have some minor impact upon the effective tax rate, but this is one complication that can usually be neglected in practice.

When bonds have been purchased in the secondary market at a premium above par, most institutions have an option regarding their tax treatment. The coupon income can either be taxed fully and directly, and a capital loss taken at maturity, or the purchase premium can be written down year by year, with each year's write-off acting as an offset to the taxable income. When they have such an option, most institutions will elect to obtain the immediate write-off at the more highly taxed income rate. The effect of this write-off option must be correctly treated in analyzing the aftertax coupon flows from premium bonds.[6]

For purposes of our analyses here, we shall assume that an appropriate marginal income tax rate has been chosen for the bond in question. The net coupon rate will then be considered to be the gross coupon flow, with each coupon payment directly reduced by the amount of the tax liability incurred. This is tantamount to treating the bond as possessing an aftertax coupon rate determined by the pretax coupon rates times the income tax "pull-through rate." For example, a 48 percent income tax rate implies a 52 percent pull-through rate. At this tax level, the aftertax coupon rate for the 7.5 percent par bond in Exhibit 5 would be 3.9 percent (= .52 × 7.5 percent), and the discount 4 percent would have an aftertax coupon rate of 2.08 percent (= .52 × 4 percent).

Aftertax Interest-on-Interest

The stream of aftertax coupons will have a time value that can be represented either figuratively or literally by reinvestment at some specified rate. However, the reinvestment rate will itself be subject to taxation. Depending on the nature of the presumed reinvestment process and its relationship to the bond in question, the tax rate for reinvestment might be quite different from the tax rate applied to direct-coupon income. For example, in an insurance company, the bond may be a fully taxable corporate issue, but if envisioned future investments involve a heavy mixture of tax-exempts and preferred stocks, then the reinvestment rate selected as well as the applicable

---

[6] The tax treatment of bonds is discussed in Chapter 3.

tax rate will differ considerably from the values for the bond itself. In fact, wide differences between the average portfolio return and the reinvestment rates may be relatively common in taxed portfolios. Such portfolios frequently exist, at least in part, to meet statutory reserve requirements of some form or another. Consequently, the bond portfolio may not be representative of the highest rates of return available among investment alternatives within the corporate structure. Some portion of the aftertax coupon receipts may, therefore, gravitate toward higher return investment alternatives outside the portfolio. This process would tend to lead toward considerably higher aftertax reinvestment rates.

In any case, a practical point of departure is to once again assume a fixed reinvestment rate, and a fixed tax rate applicable to the reinvestment rate. Although it is usually a good idea to identify these two rates as constituting two distinct assumptions, the net effect is readily seen to be the determination of a single aftertax reinvestment rate.

The same tax rates have a surprisingly disproportionate impact upon the different sources of return. For example, one might at first glance expect that a 48 percent tax rate applied to both coupon and reinvestment income would lead to a comparable reduction in the bond's dollars-and-cents return from these two sources. In fact, although the total coupon return will indeed be reduced by precisely 48 percent, there will be a much more severe reduction in the total interest-on-interest figure. For example, for a pretax reinvestment rate of 6 percent over a 25-year maturity period, the imposition of a 48 percent tax rate will slash the interest-on-interest by 79 percent. At higher pretax reinvestment rates, taxation will have an even more dramatic effect. At a 10 percent reinvestment rate, there will be an 84 percent reduction in the amount of interest-on-interest return.

These results are quite surprising at first, but they are closely related to a well-known property of the compounding process. When the compounding rate is doubled, the total accrual of compound interest over any given period will more than double. Similarly, when the compounding rate is halved, the total interest accrual will undergo a greater than 50 percent reduction. For this reason, reduction of the reinvestment rate through taxation leads to a generally far greater reduction in the total net accrual of interest-on-interest.

This disproportionate impact of taxation dramatically changes the character of the bond's return. Exhibit 6 illustrates these changes for our earlier examples of the 25-year, 7.5 percent par bond and 25-year, 4 percent discount bond, both priced to have a pretax conventional yield of 7.5 percent. A 6 percent pretax reinvestment rate is assumed. Without taxation, the 7.5 percent par bond derives 56 percent of its total return from interest-on-interest. Taxation of both the coupon and the reinvestment rate at 48 percent leads to 48 percent reduction in coupon income and a 79 percent reduction in interest-on-interest.

Exhibit 6
The Disproportionate Impact of Taxation on the Components of Return—a 25-Year 7.5
Percent Par Bond and a 25-Year 4 Percent Discount Bond Priced at 60.739 to Yield 7.5
Percent with an Assumed Reinvestment Rate of 6 Percent

	Dollars of Return per $1,000 Bond			As Percent of Total Return	
	Without Taxes	48 Percent Tax Rate	Change	Without Taxes	48 Percent Tax Rate
7.5 percent par bond					
Coupon income	$1,875	$ 975	−48%	44%	67%
Interest-on-interest	2,355	485	−79	56	33
Capital gain..................	0	0	0	0	0
Total return..............	$4,230	$1,460	−65%	100%	100%
Total return per $1 invested......	$4.23	$1.46	$−2.77		
Realized compound yield	6.73%	3.63%	−310 B.P.		
4 percent discount bond					
Coupon income	$1,000	$ 520	−48%	38%	53%
Interest-on-interest	1,256	259	−79	47	26
Capital gain..................	393	204	−48	15	21
Total return..............	$2,649	$ 983	−63%	100%	100%
Total return per $1 invested......	$4.36	$1.62	$−2.74		
Realized compound yield	6.83%	3.89%	−294 B.P.		

This results in a cut in the total return of more than 65 percent. Thus the impact of taxation on overall return is greatly magnified through its "leveraged" effect on the reinvestment compounding process.

The structure of the return is, of course, also strongly affected. Without taxation, interest-on-interest accounts for more than half the total return. With the 48 percent tax, the disproportionately reduced interest-on-interest provides only 33 percent of the total aftertax return.

These results suggest that the ultimate "cost of taxation" in dollars and cents may greatly exceed the direct effects of the tax rate.

Aftertax Capital Gain on a Proposed Purchase

We will use the term *capital gain* to refer to any return derived from principal appreciation realized upon a bond's sale or maturity.[7]

---

[7] We make this point because commercial banks and thrift institutions technically classify all such returns as "*income* derived from security transactions." Since such returns have the same tax rate as fully taxable coupon payments, these institutions sometimes view themselves as not being subject to capital gains tax. This is a matter of terminology, and we wish to make it clear at the outset that our reference to a capital gain and a capital gains tax relates to the structure of the return as a realized principal appreciation. For purposes of our *terminology*, it does not matter whether or not this realized principal appreciation is taxed at a special capital gains tax rate. Even if it is taxed at the regular income rates, we will still refer to such appreciation as a capital gain and to the relevant tax rate as the capital gains tax rate. As we shall see, it is the structure of the capital gain that counts in the investment analysis.

For bonds purchased at par or in the secondary market at a discount, the capital gain is generally measured from the purchase price to the sale price. The bond's maturity has the same effect as a sale at a price of par. For a bond purchased at a premium in the secondary market, the capital gain may be defined in terms of the "adjusted tax cost" or "adjusted tax basis" rather than the purchase cost. This arises when the premium is being amortized year by year as an offset to coupon income. The bond's amortized cost at the time of sale will then be used as an adjusted tax cost in determining the capital gain.[8]

The tax liability associated with principal appreciation becomes due and payable only when the capital gain is realized through the bond's sale or maturity. There may be accounting tax reserves set aside year by year to match a bond's book accretion, but the actual tax liability is triggered by the act of sale.

Apart from maturity, it is the portfolio manager's choice to select the time of sale. Consequently, the manager can theoretically determine, in part, the timing of the flow of capital gains. This capital gains flexibility can prove a primary resource in the management of overall tax liabilities.

For the moment, we shall discuss capital gains in the context of a bond that is being proposed for purchase. Such a bond will be called a P bond, as distinguished from an H bond, which is already held in the portfolio. In terms of our discussion of capital gains, the important point is that the tax cost of a P bond (other than a premium bond) will always be its current market price. Consequently, the capital gain realized over the life of such a P bond will then just coincide with its original price discount from par. The capital gains tax, at the appropriate tax rate, then becomes payable at maturity.

Exhibit 6 illustrates how capital gains taxation at the same 48 percent rate affects the total return from a 4 percent discount bond. The 48 percent taxation reduces the dollars-and-cents value of the capital gain by exactly 48 percent. While this is the same reduction as for coupon income, their effects are quite different. An increased proportion of return from coupon income always means an increased proportion of interest-on-interest. Since interest-on-interest is always reduced by more than the tax rate itself, increased coupon income tends to magnify the impact of taxation because of the associated increase in interest-on-interest. An increased capital gain component, on the other hand, reduces the percentage of return due to coupon income and consequently to interest-on-interest. This acts as a cushion to soften the overall impact of the 79 percent reduction in interest-on-interest. In the extreme limit, for a pure discount bond with a 0 percent coupon, all of the return would be capital gain, and a 48 percent taxation rate would just reduce the overall return by 48 percent. For real-life bonds with only a part of their return due to capital gains, this

---

[8] See Chapter 3.

capital gain component helps to keep the reduction in total return closer to the 48 percent level.

This effect can be seen in Exhibit 6. The 4 percent taxable discount bond has a pretax capital gain component amounting to 15 percent of the total dollar return. Because of this capital gain component, interest-on-interest accounts for only 47 percent of the total return, as opposed to 56 percent of the total return for a 7.5 percent par bond. Consequently, when taxation is imposed, there is a disproportionately greater reduction in the total return of the par bond relative to that of the discount bond.

Thus, even when capital gains are taxed at the same rate as coupons, a discount bond will tend to have a greater aftertax return than a par bond with the same pretax conventional yield. Perhaps a more intuitive view of this effect is that the coupon income is taxed at the point of receipt *prior* to compounding, but the capital gain is taxed only *after* it has already compounded to its full value at maturity.

This added value of the discount bond reveals itself in the conventional yields as well. Under the same tax rate for income and capital gains, a discount bond will have a greater aftertax conventional yield than a par bond with the same pretax conventional yield.[9]

Aftertax Realized Compound Yields

Once there has been a determination of tax rates to be applied to income, reinvestment, and capital gains, one can readily compute the aftertax cash flow and total return over the life of a given P bond. Because we are dealing with a P bond, the original dollar investment clearly corresponds to the bond's current market cost. By dividing the total aftertax return by the market cost, we can determine, as before, the dollars of return per invested dollar. The compound interest tables will then tell us what semiannually compounded interest rate would generate this same level of growth. The result is the aftertax realized compound yield.

Exhibit 6 illustrates the interim steps in this computation for our two sample bonds. As we would expect from the earlier discussion, the advantage in realized compound yields of the taxable discount bond over the par bond is increased by the impact of uniform taxation.

Exhibit 7 shows the effect of varying reinvestment-rate and tax-rate assumptions on the realized compound yields of the two sample bonds.[10] Several points of interest emerge from this presentation. The

---

[9] Many practitioners may not be fully aware of this fact. This is one of the many excellent points made by William M. Cox in "Aftertax Compounded Yields for Corporate Bonds" (Fort Wayne, Ind.: The Lincoln National Life Insurance Co., 1974).

[10] Some of the tax structures in Exhibit 7 may appear a little odd at this point, but the rationale behind their selection will be presented later. The selection of the specific tax rates used in Exhibit 7 is purely for illustration purposes. The maximum federal tax rate applicable to capital gains is presently 20 percent for individuals and 28 percent for corporations. (See Chapter 3.)

Exhibit 7
Comparison of Aftertax Realized Compound and Conventional Yields (for a 25-year 7.5 percent par bond and a 25-year 4 percent discount bond, both priced to provide a conventional pretax yield of 7.5 percent)

Tax Rates		Reinvestment Rate		7.5 Percent Par Bond			4 Percent Discount Bond			Discount Bond's Advantage	
Coupon and Reinvestment	Capital Gains	Pretax	Aftertax	Realized Compound Yield	Aftertax Conventional Yield	Difference	Realized Compound Yield	Aftertax Conventional Yield	Difference	As Realized Compound Yield	As Conventional Yield
0%	0%	6.0%	6.00%	6.73%	7.50%	+77 B.P.	6.83%	7.50%	+67 B.P.	+10 B.P.	0 B.P.
		7.5	7.50	7.50	7.50	0	7.50	7.50	0	0	0
		9.0	9.00	8.33	7.50	−81	8.24	7.50	−74	−7	0
48	48	6.0	3.12	3.63	3.90	+27	3.89	4.19	+30	+26	+29
		7.5	3.90	3.90	3.90	0	4.11	4.19	+8	+21	+29
		9.0	4.68	4.18	3.90	−28	4.35	4.19	−16	+17	+29
	30	6.0	3.12	3.63	3.90	+27	4.07	4.43	+36	+44	+53
		7.5	3.90	3.90	3.90	0	4.28	4.43	+15	+38	+53
		9.0	4.68	4.18	3.90	−28	4.51	4.43	−8	+33	+53
	0	6.0	3.12	3.63	3.90	+27	4.35	4.79	+44	+72	+89
		7.5	3.90	3.90	3.90	0	4.54	4.79	+25	+64	+89
		9.0	4.68	4.18	3.90	−28	4.76	4.79	+3	+58	+89
30	30	6.0	4.20	4.81	5.25	+44	5.02	5.47	+45	+21	+22
		7.5	5.25	5.25	5.25	0	5.39	5.47	+8	+14	+22
		9.0	6.30	5.72	5.25	−47	5.80	5.47	−33	+8	+22
	0	6.0	4.20	4.81	5.25	+44	5.25	5.79	+54	+44	+54
		7.5	5.25	5.25	5.25	0	5.60	5.79	+19	+35	+54
		9.0	6.30	5.72	5.25	−47	5.98	5.79	−19	+26	+54

realized compound yields of both bonds are far less sensitive to the reinvestment-rate assumption in the taxed environments than in the portfolios of tax-free owners. This is to be expected in light of the reduced net rate of interest-on-interest. For each tax structure illustrated, except for the tax-free case, the discount bond has a spread advantage over the par bond in terms of realized compound yield. This spread advantage occurs even in the two cases where both income and capital gains are taxed at the same rate. (As would be expected, the discount advantage is largest in those tax structures having the greatest disparity between the income and the capital gains tax rate.) We also observe that the discount bond's spread advantage declines with increasing reinvestment rate. Again, this is to be expected for the same reason as in the tax-free case—higher reinvestment rates place a greater time value on the par bond's relatively larger coupon flow.

The Conventional Aftertax Yield-to-Maturity

To put the aftertax realized compound yield in perspective, we must briefly touch the conventional aftertax yield. This yield is based upon exactly the same principles as the pretax conventional yield, except that it deals with the bond's aftertax cash flow to maturity. Formally, the aftertax conventional yield will be that discount rate that, when applied to the bond's aftertax cash flow, produces a present value equal to the bond's market cost. In terms of the growth of total dollars-and-cents return, the conventional aftertax yield coincides with the realized compound yield only when the aftertax coupon receipts are assumed to be compounded at an *aftertax* reinvestment rate equal to the aftertax yield value itself. Thus, exactly as in the tax-free situation, the conventional aftertax yield-to-maturity carries its own implicit reinvestment-rate assumption. This will create a discrepancy between the conventional yield and the realized compound yield whenever the appropriate explicit reinvestment-rate assumption differs significantly from the conventional yield level. As noted earlier, such significant differences are not uncommon in taxed portfolios. In such cases, the conventional aftertax yield will be a particularly unreliable guide, with respect to both absolute as well as relative investment value.

Exhibit 7 shows the relationship between the realized compound yield and the conventional yield for a range of reinvestment rates and tax structures. For example, at a common 48 percent tax rate for both income and capital gains, the conventional aftertax yield turns out to be 3.9 percent for the 7.5 percent par bond and 4.19 percent for the 4 percent bond selling to yield 7.5 percent. By comparison, at an aftertax reinvestment rate of 4.68 percent, the respective realized compound yields are 4.18 percent and 4.35 percent, or 28 and 16 basis points above the conventional yields. This discrepancy would widen further at higher investment rates.

With respect to relative values, the discount bond has a 29-basis-point spread advantage in terms of conventional yields. As in the tax-free case, the conventional aftertax yield tends to exaggerate the rate of return difference between the two bonds. The higher yielding discount bond gets an added advantage through the higher implicit reinvestment rate of 4.19 percent. The magnitude of this effect can be seen in Exhibit 7 when both bonds are subject to a common reinvestment rate of 3.9 percent. The discount bond's spread advantage in terms of realized compound yield then shrinks from 29 to 21 basis points.

Exhibit 7 shows that the conventional yield's overstatement of the discount bond's advantage is highly dependent on the tax structure and reinvestment rate. The most grievous exaggeration of this discount advantage is 31 basis points for the 48 percent income tax rate, 0 percent capital gains tax, and the 4.68 percent reinvestment rate.

The "Coupon" Approximation for the Aftertax Yield

There is occasionally some confusion as to how to compute the conventional aftertax yield. Although the above definition corresponds to the "true yield" in the conventional sense, there is a much simpler computation that is often used to approximate this true yield value. In fact, this approximation technique has become so popular in certain circles that it is sometimes thought to be the standard rather than the approximation. We will illustrate this computation for the case of the discount 4 percent bond with 48 percent income tax and a 30 percent capital gains tax:

1. Subtract pretax coupon rate from pretax yield.

$$7.50 \text{ percent} - 4 \text{ percent} = 3.5 \text{ percent}$$

2. Multiply result by capital gain pull-through rate.

$$3.5 \text{ percent} \times .7 = 2.45 \text{ percent}$$

3. Compute the aftertax coupon rate and add to the above figure.

$$4 \text{ percent} \times .52 = 2.08 \text{ percent}$$
$$2.08 \text{ percent} + 2.45 \text{ percent} = 4.53 \text{ percent}$$

The true yield is 4.43 percent, 10 basis points lower than the approximation.

The approximation works remarkably well for the "48 percent, 30 percent" tax structure, especially for short maturities and relatively modest discounts or premiums. However, the disparities become quite severe for long discount bonds in other tax structures. Exhibit 8 illustrates the problems with pushing this technique too far.

Effective Par Rates in Taxed Portfolios

In the tax-free case, the effective par rate for a given bond was defined to be the coupon (or yield) rate of that par bond that, under the same reinvestment conditions, would match the given bond's total dollars-and-cents return over a specified review period. This same definition extends to the taxed case if we simply add the phrase "under the same reinvestment *and tax conditions.*"

The calculation of the effective par rate is actually quite simple. Taking the example of the 4 percent discount bond illustrated in Exhibit 6, the total aftertax return per dollar invested is $1.62, or a return of $1,618.40 for each $1,000 par bond purchased. The assumed aftertax reinvestment rate is 3.12 percent. The compound interest tables would then tell us that for each $1 of a semiannual aftertax coupon payment, reinvested and compounded semiannually at this 3.12 percent (annual) rate, we would accumulate a total return of $74.896 by the end of the 25-year review period. Dividing $74.896 into the required return of $1,618.40, we see that each coupon payment from the hypothetical par bond must provide $21.61 of aftertax income. Since the tax rate assumed was 48 percent, this would require a pretax coupon payment of

$$\$21.61 \div (.52) = \$41.56$$

or an annual payment of $83.11 per $1,000 par bond. The effective par rate would thus have to be 8.31 percent. In other words, we have a 25-year, 4 percent discount bond selling on the basis of a 7.5 percent conventional pretax yield, a 4.19 percent aftertax conventional yield (from Exhibit 7), and a 3.89 percent aftertax realized compound yield. However, from its effective par rate, we now know that this discount bond will provide the better long-term investment value as long as the comparable new issue market only offers rates below 8.31 percent.

As noted earlier for the taxfree case, the effective par rate provides major advantages in terms of a yardstick with an intuitively comfortable scale which can be readily benchmarked against the new issue market. With this extended definition, the added complications of taxation can be consistently integrated with the reinvestment effects and represented through this one simple measure with its direct market significance. Thus the benefits of the "effective par rate" concept are preserved and even enhanced in the case of portfolios subject to taxation.

Exhibit 8

The Limitations of a Popular Technique for Approximating the True Conventional Aftertax Yield—(all bonds priced for a pretax yield of 7.5 percent)

Maturity	Coupon	Income Tax: 48% / Capital Gains Tax: 30%		Income Tax: 48% / Capital Gains Tax: 48%		Income Tax: 48% / Capital Gains Tax: 0%	
		Approximation	True Yield	Approximation	True Yield	Approximation	True Yield
1 Year	4.0%	4.53%	4.52%	3.90%	3.91%	5.58%	5.53%
	6.0	4.17	4.16	3.90	3.90	4.62	4.59
	7.5	3.90	3.90	3.90	3.90	3.90	3.90
5 Years	4.0%	4.53%	4.54%	3.90%	4.02%	5.58%	5.40%
	6.0	4.17	4.16	3.90	3.95	4.62	4.51
	7.5	3.90	3.90	3.90	3.90	3.90	3.90
10 Years	4.0%	4.53%	4.55%	3.90%	4.11%	5.58%	5.24%
	6.0	4.17	4.15	3.90	3.98	4.62	4.42
	7.5	3.90	3.90	3.90	3.90	3.90	3.90
25 Years	4.0%	4.53%	4.43%	3.90%	4.19%	5.58%	4.79%
	6.0	4.17	4.09	3.90	4.00	4.62	4.22
	7.5	3.90	3.90	3.90	3.90	3.90	3.90

As set forth in our definition, the effective par rate is a useful new tool that is extremely simple both in conception and computation.

The Taxable Equivalent Yield

There is one closely analogous computation commonly used in hopes of obtaining the same benchmarking objectives. This is the conventional notion of the "taxable equivalent yield" (or, as it is sometimes called, the corporate equivalent yield).

The taxable equivalent yield is the coupon rate of a par bond that would provide the same conventional aftertax yield as the given bond. But the conventional aftertax yield of par bonds is always just the aftertax coupon rate (i.e., the coupon rate times the pull-through rate). Hence the taxable equivalent is simply determined by dividing the specified conventional aftertax yield by the pull-through rate. For the above example of the 4 percent discount bond with a conventional aftertax yield of 4.19 percent, the taxable equivalent is simply

$$4.19 \text{ percent} \div (.52) = 8.07 \text{ percent}$$

Exhibit 9 compares the effective par rates and the taxable equivalent yields for the same range of cases as Exhibit 8. For the 7.5 percent par bond, the effective par rate and the taxable equivalent yield coincide at 7.5 percent for all tax structures and all reinvestment rates. This is because both computations, while providing different estimates of aftertax return, relate their respective return estimates to that provided by a par bond. Consequently, both computations will always lead to the original par bond as being its own effective par rate as well as its own taxable equivalent.

On the other hand, the discount bond in Exhibit 9 shows variations as wide as 70 basis points between the effective par rate and the corresponding taxable equivalent. This variation arises from the reinvestment-rate effect. The greatest discrepancy occurs when the explicit reinvestment-rate assumption differs most significantly from the taxable equivalent yield value. This is because the taxable equivalent, like the conventional aftertax yield upon which it is based, carries with it the implicit assumption that reinvestment takes place at a rate equal to its own value.

The Tax-Exempt Effective Par Rate

In taxed portfolios, bonds are benchmarked not only against the new issue market of fully taxable issues, but also against markets of bonds having various degrees of tax exemptions. In particular, the fully tax-exempt municipal market almost always serves as an important reference point for taxed portfolios. The common practice is to

Exhibit 9
Comparison of Effective Par Rates and Conventional Taxable Equivalent Yields for Various Tax Structures and Reinvestment Rates (for a 25-year 7.5 percent par bond and a 25-year 4 percent discount bond both priced to provide a conventional pretax yield of 7.5 percent)

| Tax Rates | | Reinvestment Rate | | 7.5 Percent Par Bond | | | 4 Percent Discount Bond | | | Discount Bond's Advantage | |
Coupon and Reinvestment	Capital Gains	Pretax	Aftertax	Effective Par Rate	Conventional Taxable Equivalent	Difference	Effective Par Rate	Conventional Taxable Equivalent	Difference	As Effective Par Rate	As Conventional Taxable Equivalent
0%	0%	6.0%	6.00%	7.5%	7.5%	0 B.P.	7.73%	7.50%	−23 B.P.	+ 23 B.P.	0 B.P.
		7.5	7.50	7.5	7.5	0	7.50	7.50	0	0	0
		9.0	9.00	7.5	7.5	0	7.31	7.50	+19	− 19	0
48	48	6.0	3.12	7.5	7.5	0	8.31	8.07	−24	+ 81	+ 57
		7.5	3.90	7.5	7.5	0	8.14	8.07	− 7	+ 64	+ 57
		9.0	4.68	7.5	7.5	0	7.97	8.07	+10	+ 47	+ 57
48	30	6.0	3.12	7.5	7.5	0	8.91	8.53	−38	+141	+103
		7.5	3.90	7.5	7.5	0	8.67	8.53	−14	+117	+103
		9.0	4.68	7.5	7.5	0	8.45	8.53	+ 8	+ 95	+103
48	0	6.0	3.12	7.5	7.5	0	9.91	9.21	−70	+241	+171
		7.5	3.90	7.5	7.5	0	9.57	9.21	−36	+207	+171
		9.0	4.68	7.5	7.5	0	9.26	9.21	− 5	+176	+171
30	30	6.0	4.20	7.5	7.5	0	8.07	7.81	−26	+ 57	+ 31
		7.5	5.25	7.5	7.5	0	7.87	7.81	− 6	+ 37	+ 31
		9.0	6.30	7.5	7.5	0	7.68	7.81	+13	+ 18	+ 31
30	0	6.0	4.20	7.5	7.5	0	8.71	8.27	−44	+121	+ 77
		7.5	5.25	7.5	7.5	0	8.41	8.27	−14	+ 91	+ 77
		9.0	6.30	7.5	7.5	0	8.15	8.27	+12	+ 65	+ 77

use the conventional aftertax yield as a yardstick for comparisons with the par market for fully tax-exempt bonds. However, as in all the preceding instances, this comparison can prove highly erroneous when the relevant reinvestment rate differs significantly from the conventional yield value.

The general concept of the effective par rate can overcome this problem by adapting the characteristics of the underlying standard par bond to the new-issue market in question.

A *tax-exempt effective par rate* for a given bond can be defined as the coupon rate of that tax-exempt bond that would produce the same aftertax return as the given bond under the same reinvestment and tax conditions. In the earlier example of the 4 percent discount bond at a 6 percent reinvestment rate and 48 percent taxation, it was found that the aftertax return would be matched by an 8.31 percent fully taxable par bond. The return from such a par bond is identical to that from a tax-exempt par bond with a coupon rate of

$$8.31 \text{ percent} \times .52 = 4.32 \text{ percent}$$

The analogous tax-exempt effective par rate would, therefore, be 4.32 percent. This value can be used to benchmark the taxable discount bond against the level of the tax-exempt market.

In effect, an equivalent definition for *tax-exempt effective par rate* would be the corresponding fully taxable effective par rate multiplied by the pull-through rate on coupon income. This is just the relationship between the taxable equivalent and the conventional aftertax yield. One might, therefore, reverse the definitions and say that the fully taxable effective par rate is just the taxable equivalent of the tax-exempt effective par rate, which in turn is itself based on the aftertax realized compound yield.

As noted earlier, the current practice is to use the conventional aftertax yield for comparison with the tax-exempt market. Therefore, the tax-exempt effective par rate should be compared with this conventional yield. This is done in Exhibit 10 for the same tax structures and reinvestment assumptions as in Exhibits 7 and 9. As would be expected, the two measures coincide in the special case of the 7.5 percent par bond. For the 4 percent discount bond, on the other hand, there are significant discrepancies, ranging up to 36 basis points. Actually Exhibit 10 is just a tax-deflated image of Exhibit 9, since the effective par rate and the conventional taxable equivalent yield can both be viewed as taxable equivalents of Exhibit 10s tax-exempt effective par rate and conventional aftertax yield, respectively.

Aftertax Capital Gain on a Proposed Portfolio Sale

A bond holding in a portfolio subject to taxation has a fundamentally different investment value from the exact same issue not held in

Exhibit 10

Comparison of Tax-Exempt Effective Par Rates and Conventional Aftertax Yields for Various Tax Structures and Reinvestment Rates (for a 25-year 7.5 percent par bond and a 25-year 4 percent discount bond both priced to provide a conventional pretax yield of 7.5 percent)

Tax Rates		Reinvestment Rate		7.5 Percent Par Bond			4 Percent Discount Bond			Discount Bond's Advantage	
Coupon and Reinvestment	Capital Gains	Pretax	Aftertax	Tax Exempt Effective Par Rate	Conventional Aftertax Yield	Difference	Tax Exempt Effective Par Rate	Conventional Aftertax Yield	Difference	As Effective Par Rate	As Conventional Aftertax Yield
0%	0%	6.0%	6.00%	7.50%	7.50%	0 B.P.	7.73%	7.50%	−23 B.P.	+ 23 B.P.	0 B.P.
		7.5	7.50	7.50	7.50	0	7.50	7.50	0	0	0
		9.0	9.00	7.50	7.50	0	7.31	7.50	+19	− 19	0
48	48	6.0	3.12	3.90	3.90	0	4.32	4.19	−13	+ 42	+29
		7.5	3.90	3.90	3.90	0	4.23	4.19	− 4	+ 33	+29
		9.0	4.68	3.90	3.90	0	4.14	4.19	+ 5	+ 24	+29
48	30	6.0	3.12	3.90	3.90	0	4.63	4.43	−20	+ 73	+53
		7.5	3.90	3.90	3.90	0	4.51	4.43	− 8	+ 61	+53
		9.0	4.68	3.90	3.90	0	4.40	4.43	+ 3	+ 50	+53
48	0	6.0	3.12	3.90	3.90	0	5.15	4.79	−36	+125	+89
		7.5	3.90	3.90	3.90	0	4.98	4.79	−19	+108	+89
		9.0	4.68	3.90	3.90	0	4.82	4.79	− 3	+ 92	+89
30	30	6.0	4.20	5.25	5.25	0	5.65	5.47	−18	+ 40	+22
		7.5	5.25	5.25	5.25	0	5.51	5.47	− 4	+ 26	+22
		9.0	6.30	5.25	5.25	0	5.38	5.47	+ 9	+ 13	+22
30	0	6.0	4.20	5.25	5.25	0	6.10	5.79	−31	+ 85	+54
		7.5	5.25	5.25	5.25	0	5.89	5.79	−10	+ 64	+54
		9.0	6.30	5.25	5.25	0	5.71	5.79	+ 8	+ 46	+54

that portfolio. This is because the bonds in the portfolio have their unique tax cost. The principal appreciation subject to capital gains taxation will always be measured using this tax cost as a basis. Hence, this tax cost must enter as a critical element in any rational investment decision relating to such a portfolio bond.

For the moment, we shall focus on par and discount bonds and put aside the somewhat more complex case of premium bonds. Then we can say that it is the historical tax cost of the portfolio bond (or H bond, for bond now held) that differentiates it from P bond whose tax cost always coincides with its current market value. Actually, there is a related but even more fundamental difference between the investment analysis of an H bond and that of a P bond. With the P bond, the question of capital gains liability becomes pertinent only at the future review point of possible sale or maturity. For the H bond, on the other hand, there are two times when the capital gains liability becomes relevant: (1) the future point of sale or maturity that would result from continued holding, and (2) the present, in terms of the capital gains liability that would become payable *immediately* if the H bond were to be sold today at its current market value. As we shall soon see, it is the relationship between these two capital gains that determines the total aftertax return over a specified review period.

For given tax and reinvestment assumptions, we can readily compute the H bond's aftertax return from coupon income and from interest-on-interest that would be earned over a review period. The aftertax capital gain at maturity will also be well defined, but it will be based on the bond's tax cost (i.e., its historical purchase price). Consequently, this unadjusted aftertax capital gain figure will reflect the net principal appreciation that took place over the bond's *literal* holding period (i.e., stretching back before the present time to the original date of purchase). However, for comparison with other investment alternatives, our purpose is to identify the capital gains return accruing from holding the bond from *today's* decision point to its future maturity or point of review. Thus we must separate the bond's total capital gains figure into (1) one portion already accrued from its purchase date to today's decision point and (2) a second portion that will accrue from today forward over the review period. Only this second portion of the capital gains return should enter into our total-return computations for purposes of evaluating investment alternatives.

Actually, this separation is readily performed. The H bond's total pretax capital gain does, after all, consist of the sum of its *past* capital gain from the purchase price to today's market value *plus* its future capital gains from today's market value to its future sale price or maturity value. The capital gains tax liability can be assigned accordingly to each of these components. The net aftertax capital gain can also be divided up in this fashion. Consequently, the H bond's aftertax capital gain over the review period can be taken as the gross principal appreciation from its market value today to its value at the end of the review period, *less* the *increase* in the capital gains tax liability.

For bonds purchased at a discount, this definition will coincide with the net aftertax capital gains from a P bond (as long as there are no anticipated changes in the effective capital gains tax rate). This coincidence arises because the incremental capital gains tax liability for both H bonds and P bonds will always be the same fraction of the incremental capital gain associated with the review period. In particular, when there is no principal appreciation, there will be no increase in the capital gains tax liability, and so the net aftertax capital gain will be zero.

With bonds purchased in the secondary market at a premium, a different situation arises when the tax cost is amortized year by year. In this case, even when the bond's market price remains at the same level, the capital gains tax liability will increase as a result of the dropping tax cost, thus leading to an aftertax capital loss. The rate of amortization of the tax cost will vary with the original time and cost of purchase. Consequently, even for the same change in market value over the review period, the capital gains tax liability accrued for an H bond will generally differ from that accrued for a P bond. In accordance with our definition, this will lead to different aftertax capital gains for premium H bonds and P bonds.

With this general definition of the aftertax capital gain, all sources of aftertax return from an H bond can be computed, and so an H bond's total dollars-and-cents return can be determined for any review period.

In our earlier analysis for P bonds, the next step then consisted in dividing this dollar return by the P bond's market value to determine the return per dollar invested. In the case of the H bond, however, the market value does not constitute directly investable dollars because of the capital gains liability incurred through the act of sale. Therefore, there is some question as to how to proceed with our computation of the return per dollar invested for H bonds, and this leads us to the key concept of "opportunity dollars."

Opportunity Dollars

When an H bond is sold, the portfolio receives its market value in dollars, and it theoretically could use these dollar receipts as a medium of exchange to purchase other bonds in the marketplace. However, when such an H-bond sale also incurs a capital gains tax liability, then some of the immediate dollar receipts must in effect be put aside to pay the added tax liability. This leaves the portfolio with a reduced amount of free dollars available for the pursuit of new investment opportunities. In fact, the funds freely available for new investment would consist of just the market value receipts from the H bond's sale *less* the capital gains tax liability incurred by this act of sale. We will use the term *opportunity dollars* to denote this figure.

This concept of opportunity dollars can be immediately generalized to represent the dollars that *would* be freed for new investment if a given H bond with an "embedded" capital gain *were* to be sold at any given time. Thus, with this more general interpretation, every such H bond in a portfolio has an associated opportunity-dollar value at every point in time.

As an example, suppose a portfolio had purchased our 25-year 4 percent discount bond 5 years ago at a price of 50.739. Today, this H bond would have an embedded capital gain of $100 per bond. If the capital gains tax liability were to be triggered by a sale today, this liability would amount to $48 at a 48 percent capital gains tax rate. Thus the opportunity dollars per bond that would be freed by such a sale today would amount to

$$\$607.39 - \$48.00 = \$559.39$$

Up to this point, we have only discussed the somewhat more cheerful case of bonds with embedded capital gains. What about bonds selling at capital losses relative to their historical tax cost? When such bonds are sold, a capital loss is realized. This loss may in turn be usable as an offset to capital gains in current or future fiscal years. If this offset does in fact lead to a real marginal savings in the portfolio's capital gains tax liability, then this loss will have a concrete positive value. This marginal value of each dollar of loss offset can be represented through an appropriate "capital loss tax rate." The actual value assignable to this capital loss rate will depend critically on several factors relating to the portfolio's overall tax status. This whole subject will be discussed in some detail later. For the moment, however, let us assume that the portfolio has already realized an overwhelming surplus of capital gains in this fiscal year and that any contemplated capital losses may be fully usable as offsets against the existing tax liability. In such a case, the capital loss tax rate will coincide with the assumed capital gain tax rate.

As a concrete example, let us again take the 4 percent discount bond, but now assume that it had been purchased five years earlier at a price of 70.739. Its sale today at a price of 60.739 would then create a capital loss of 10 points, or $100 per bond. At a capital loss tax rate of 48 percent, $48 of this loss would be usable as an offset against existing tax liabilities. Under the presumed conditions, this $48 loss offset would actually free $48 in additional funds that the portfolio could use this fiscal year for new investment purposes. Putting aside the question of the timing of the sale relative to the tax liability cycle, this $48 loss offset then *adds* to the opportunity dollars freed by the H bond's sale. In other words, this H bond's sale would generate an opportunity-dollar value of

$$\$607.39 + \$48.00 = \$655.39$$

This example provides the key to extending the concept of opportunity dollars to include H bonds with embedded tax losses. The opportunity dollar value of such an H bond is its current market value *plus* the product of the embedded capital loss multiplied by the appropriate capital loss tax rate. With this extension, *every* H bond can now be viewed as always having a certain opportunity-dollar value determined by the interplay of market forces with the portfolio's overall tax status.

Up to this point, we have defined the opportunity dollars associated with an H bond as funds that would be freed by its sale. However, every such sale can be considered as a decision between the options of selling the bond, on the one hand, or its continued holding, on the other hand. A decision for continued holding can in turn be viewed as a sort of purchase decision (i.e., the H bond is "purchased" in exchange for the funds that would have been freed by its sale. This means that it is the opportunity dollars that reflect the current "cost" of a decision to continue holding a given H bond. Thus an H bond's opportunity-dollar value can be interpreted in several related ways: (1) as the net usable funds that would be freed by its sale, (2) as the net usable funds that are tied up by its continued holding, and/or (3) as the cost in terms of taxfree exchangeable funds given a decision to purchase its continued holding. Thus, for H bonds, the opportunity-dollar value serves almost precisely the same functions as does the market value for P bonds.

It will be recalled that the preceding section raised the question of how to define the dollars invested in an H bond. It should be clear now that an H bond's opportunity dollars provide a consistent measure for this investment base.

The concept of opportunity dollars also clarifies the determination of an H bond's capital gain over a future review period. Consider the above example of a 4 percent H bond purchased five years earlier at 50.739. At the bond's maturity in 25 years, the total realized capital gain will be

$$\$1,000.00 - \$507.39 = \$492.61$$

or an aftertax gain of

$$\$492.61 \times .52 = \$256.16$$

at a 48 percent capital gains tax rate. However, in accordance with the discussion in the preceding section, the investment return should include only that portion of the capital gain accrued over the *next* 25 years. Since the bond's price today is 60.739, this will amount to

$$\$1,000.00 - \$607.39 = \$392.61$$

for an aftertax capital gains return of

$$\$392.61 \times .52 = \$204.16$$

This calculation can also be expressed in terms of the H bond's opportunity dollars today and at maturity. At its maturity, the H bond will realize a total capital gain amounting to $492.61 and a consequent tax liability of

$$\$492.61 \times .48 = \$236.45$$

The H bond's opportunity value per bond at maturity will therefore be

$$\$1,000.00 - \$236.45 = \$763.55$$

The same H bond's opportunity dollar value today was computed above to be $559.39. Hence, the increase in opportunity dollars over the 25-year period is just

$$\$763.55 - \$559.39 = \$204.16$$

This is the exact same value as the appropriate contribution to the H bond's aftertax return from capital gains over the 25-year review period.

This relationship holds quite generally (for P bonds as well as H bonds): The change in a bond's opportunity-dollar value precisely measures its aftertax capital gain return over any given review period. This relationship holds for premium bonds as well as for discount bonds. It even holds true under the more general case when the effective capital gains (and/or loss) tax rates are expected to undergo changes during the review period.

The Opportunity Yield

With the opportunity dollars as an investment base, we can now proceed to compute an aftertax return per dollar invested for both H bonds and P bonds.

As noted above, the expression "return per dollar invested" is slightly ambiguous for the case of an H bond. However, this ambiguity can be overcome by interpreting an H bond's opportunity dollars as the dollar amount "invested" in its continued holding. Since a P bond's opportunity dollars coincide with its market cost at the time of purchase, we can employ this concept of return per opportunity dollar for *both* H bonds and P bonds. We can then proceed to compute the aftertax return per (opportunity) dollar invested, and move toward the other return measures developed earlier for P bonds.

Staying with the above example of a 4 percent H bond purchased earlier at a price of 50.739, we first determine the total dollars of return over the 25-year review period. The aftertax contributions from coupon income and interest-on-interest will be identical with the $520 and $259 given in Exhibit 6 for the 4 percent P bond. Moreover, the H bond's aftertax capital gain return, when properly allocated to the next 25 years, will also coincide with the $204 associated with the 4 percent P bond. The H bond's total aftertax return will therefore be $983, which in this case of a discount bond is exactly the same value as for the comparable P bond. This equality will not hold for premium bonds or in the face of changes in the structure of capital gains taxation over the review period. The H bond's opportunity dollars was computed earlier to be

$$\$607.39 - \$48.00 = \$559.39$$

Using this amount of opportunity dollars as an investment base, the total aftertax return per invested dollar becomes

$$\$983 \div \$559.39 = \$1.76$$

in comparison with $1.62 for the comparable P bond.

We can now proceed to ask, as before, what fully compounded rate of interest would be needed to provide this same level of return over 25 years of semiannual compounding? For a return per invested dollar of $1.76, the compound interest tables would then supply the rate of 2.05 percent per semiannual period, or 4.1 percent on an annual bond basis. For H bonds, this figure of 4.1 percent is the analogue of the aftertax realized compound yield. However, it does seem useful to distinguish this realized compound yield value as reflecting an investment base measured in opportunity dollars. For this reason, we shall refer to this figure as the opportunity yield.

The opportunity yield as defined here can be applied to both P bonds and H bonds, and hence it can be viewed as a generalization of the aftertax realized compound yield.

Exhibit 11 shows the opportunity yield values for four 25-year 4 percent discount bonds, each identical except for their historical cost basis. The tax and reinvestment structures are the same as used before in Exhibits 7, 9, and 10. As we would expect, Exhibit 11 shows that the historical purchase price is irrelevant when the capital gains and loss are untaxed. It becomes most relevant in those cases where this capital gains taxation is strongest—in the 48 percent case, there is almost a 90 basis point variation in opportunity yields depending only on the historical purchase cost. For this tax case at a 6 percent reinvestment rate, the 10-point capital gain pushes the opportunity yield 21 basis points above the P bond case, 40 basis points above the 10-point loss case, and 86 basis points above the opportunity yield for the bond that had been purchased at par.

Exhibit 11
Opportunity Yields under Various Tax Structures and Reinvestment Rates (for a 25-year 4 percent bond selling today at 60.739 but purchased earlier)

Tax Rates		Reinvestment Rate		Bond's Price at Earlier Purchase Date			
Coupon and Reinvestment	Capital Gain and Loss	Pretax	Aftertax	50.739 (H bond with capital gain)	60.739 (P bond)	70.739 (H bond with capital loss)	100.00 (H bond with real capital loss!)
0%	0%	6.00%	6.00%	6.83%	6.83%	6.83%	6.83%
		7.50	7.50	7.50	7.50	7.50	7.50
		9.00	9.00	8.24	8.24	8.24	8.24
48	48	6.00	3.12	4.10	3.89	3.70	3.24
		7.50	3.90	4.33	4.11	3.91	3.44
		9.00	4.68	4.57	4.35	4.15	3.66
48	30	6.00	3.12	4.20	4.07	3.94	3.62
		7.50	3.90	4.41	4.28	4.15	3.82
		9.00	4.68	4.65	4.51	4.38	4.03
48	0	6.00	3.12	4.35	4.35	4.35	4.35
		7.50	3.90	4.54	4.54	4.54	4.54
		9.00	4.68	4.76	4.76	4.76	4.76
30	30	6.00	4.20	5.17	5.02	4.89	4.52
		7.50	5.25	5.55	5.39	5.25	4.87
		9.00	6.30	5.95	5.80	5.65	5.25
30	0	6.00	4.20	5.25	5.25	5.25	5.25
		7.50	5.25	5.60	5.60	5.60	5.60
		9.00	6.30	5.98	5.98	5.98	5.98

All four of these bonds actually provide the exact same aftertax return *per bond*. The higher opportunity yield for the bond with the 10-point embedded capital gain is derived from the fact that the same return *per bond* is earned on a smaller investment base of opportunity dollars. This reduction in the opportunity-dollar base occurs because of the tax liability inherent in the embedded capital gain. Hence this bond is a much more valuable "hold" than the other three bonds. The greater opportunity yield reflects this higher holding value. In other words, selling any of the four bonds would entail giving up the same dollars of return, but the opportunity dollars freed would be considerably greater for the bonds with embedded losses.

The H bonds in Exhibit 11 appear to follow the P bond with respect to their opportunity yields' sensitivity to reinvestment-rate effects. In other words, the spreads between the H bond's and the P bond's opportunity yields seem to remain fairly constant as the reinvestment rate varies. In fact, this spread seems to be primarily dependent on the capital gains (and loss) tax rate. Thus for the 48 percent, 30 percent tax structure, the H bond with the 10-point embedded gain and the one with the 10-point embedded loss keep close to a spread of 13–14 basis points above and below the P bond opportunity yield. Very nearly the same spread relationship is maintained for the 30 percent, 30 percent tax structure across all three reinvestment rates.

It should perhaps be reemphasized at this point that the opportunity yield is a completely consistent representation of the aftertax dollars-and-cents return under the assumed tax and reinvestment conditions. Thus, under the same assumptions, an H bond with an opportunity yield of 4.1 percent will always provide a greater aftertax return per invested dollar than a P bond with a smaller opportunity yield, and vice versa. Another way of saying the same thing is to envision the sale of this H bond and the reinvestment of all released opportunity dollars into a new P bond. Unless this new P bond has an opportunity yield exceeding the H bond's 4.1 percent, the swap will turn out to be a loser in terms of dollars-and-cents return under the assumed conditions. Similarly, in comparing any two H bonds, the one with the smaller opportunity yield will prove the better sale, and the one with the higher opportunity yield will always prove the better hold. For a dollars-and-cents comparison of two H bonds, one can always take the model of swapping each of them into a given P bond. The H bond with the lower opportunity yield will always prove the better sale under such a dollars-and-cents evaluation.

Thus the opportunity yield simply, compactly, and consistently integrates the effects of several different elements that affect a bond's investment value: the portfolio's explicit reinvestment rate assumption; its anticipated future tax rates on coupon income, reinvestment, and capital gains and losses; the portfolio's present capital gains tax status; the given bond's position as an H bond or a P bond; and if an H bond, its adjusted tax-cost basis.

The Opportunity Par Rate

The opportunity yield will by its nature have the same problem of intuitive scaling and market benchmarking as the realized compound yield. Once again, to overcome these problems, we can turn to the same device of a hypothetical par bond that would match the bond's level of opportunity yield. This leads us to the effective par rate or, if we wish to stress the fact that the underlying rate of return is based upon an investment base of opportunity dollars, what we might call the opportunity par rate.

Exhibit 12 presents the opportunity par rate values corresponding to the opportunity yield situations of Exhibit 11. Thus, for the 48 percent, 48 percent tax case and a 6 percent reinvestment rate, the H bond with the 10-point capital gain is seen to have an opportunity par rate of 9.03 percent. This means that this bond will provide the portfolio with the same aftertax return per invested (opportunity) dollar as a

Exhibit 12
Opportunity Par Rates under Various Tax Structures and Reinvestment Rates (for a 25-year 4 percent bond selling today at 60.739 but purchased earlier)

Tax Rates		Reinvestment Rate		Bond's Price at Earlier Purchase Date			
Coupon and Reinvestment	Capital Gain and Loss	Pretax	Aftertax	50.739 (H bond with capital gain)	60.739 (P bond)	70.739 (H bond with capital loss)	100.00 (H bond with real capital loss)
0%	0%	6.0%	6.00%	7.73%	7.73%	7.73%	7.73%
		7.5	7.50	7.50	7.50	7.50	7.50
		9.0	9.00	7.31	7.31	7.31	7.31
48	48	6.0	3.12	9.03	8.31	7.70	6.34
		7.5	3.90	8.83	8.14	7.54	6.21
		9.0	4.68	8.66	7.97	7.39	6.09
48	30	6.0	3.12	9.37	8.91	8.49	7.46
		7.5	3.90	9.12	8.67	8.26	7.26
		9.0	4.68	8.89	8.46	8.06	7.08
48	0	6.0	3.12	9.91	9.91	9.91	9.91
		7.5	3.90	9.57	9.57	9.57	9.57
		9.0	4.68	9.26	9.26	9.26	9.26
30	30	6.0	4.20	8.49	8.07	7.69	6.76
		7.5	5.25	8.27	7.87	7.49	6.59
		9.0	6.30	8.08	7.68	7.32	6.43
30	0	6.0	4.20	8.71	8.71	8.71	8.71
		7.5	5.25	8.41	8.41	8.41	8.41
		9.0	6.30	8.15	8.15	8.15	8.15

25-year par bond with a fully taxable 9.03 percent coupon rate. To state it more precisely, any swap out of this H bond and into a new 25-year par bond with any coupon rate below 9.03 percent will turn out to be a loser in terms of dollars-and-cents return.

The opportunity par rate can be a remarkably compact and convenient tool. Suppose that we compute the opportunity par rate for every bond in a given portfolio. Whenever the level of the *comparable* new-issue market exceeds the opportunity par rate of any of the H bonds, then this is an immediate signal that a swap into the new issue would work out profitably in terms of dollars-and-cents return. Moreover, we know that the best swap would, everything else being equal, entail sale of that bond with the lowest opportunity par rate. However, a word of caution is in order. Although it is a convenient point of comparison, the new-issue par market may not represent the best possible P bond sector for a given portfolio.

A tax-exempt opportunity par rate can be computed in the now obvious fashion for benchmarking against the tax-exempt market.

The incorporation of an H bond's capital gains tax liability or loss offset into its investment base dates back to the idea of the "give-up yield," which has long been used in the management of many commercial bank portfolios. The give-up yield was usually computed as a conventional aftertax yield determined at a price corresponding to what we have called the bond's opportunity dollars. However, this give-up yield failed to include any treatment of explicit reinvestment-rate assumptions.

The opportunity yield concept presented here can be viewed as an integration of the old bank give-up yield with the more recent work on explicit reinvestment rates and realized compound yield.[11]

Tax Losses and Tax Offsets

The estimation of the effective capital gains tax rate for a given portfolio is usually a far more difficult process than it might first appear, even when the tax rate for an isolated capital gain is quite well defined. The actual capital gains tax that can be fairly charged against a contemplated H bond sale depends critically on the overall gain or loss status of the portfolio, not only in the present fiscal year, but over future years as well.

For example, suppose the portfolio carries unrealized losses of such huge proportions as to far outweigh any foreseeable capital gains, and further suppose that the portfolio is blessed with the flexibility to freely realize these losses, as needed, to offset capital gains. In such a situation, the effective capital gains tax rate will be 0 percent! There is no real need for the portfolio to pay a capital gains tax, since by assumption every such gain can be readily offset without depleting the portfolio's resource of losses. By the same token, any particular capital loss realized during this period conveys no special benefit (i.e., it simply adds to an already more-than-abundant resource). Hence the capital loss tax rate would also correspond to 0 percent! It was just this type of situation that motivated the inclusion of the 0 percent capital gains tax cases in Exhibits 7, 9, 10, 11, and 12.

On the other hand, suppose the portfolio has a mountain of unrealized losses, but is unable to take additional tax or book losses in the current fiscal year. Then, any further transactions in the current year should be taxed at the full capital gains rate. However, in future years,

---

[11] Published references to the give-up yield appear to be rather slim, but there is a mathematically elegant discussion in Robert I. Komar, "Developing a Liquidity Management Model," *Journal of Bank Research* (Spring 1971). On the other hand, there are many references dealing with explicit reinvestment rates and their effects on a bond's total return. (In particular, see: J. Peter Williamson, "Computerized Approaches to Bond Switching," *Financial Analysts Journal* (July–August 1970); and the monograph by Robert H. Cramer and Stephen L. Hawk, *The Consideration of Coupon Levels, Taxes, Reinvestment Rates, and Maturity in the Investment Management of Financial Institutions* (Madison, Wis.: University of Wisconsin-Madison, 1973). These studies explored the area of aftertax cash flows but stopped short of relating these results to the bond's opportunity dollars in terms of an opportunity yield figure.

if capital losses were to become more freely realizable, then the effective capital gains tax rate might decline to 0 percent.

Another situation would be a portfolio having substantial *realized* losses that have reached the end of their carry-forward period. In other words, the losses will be lost forever unless they are used as offsets in the current fiscal year. If the portfolio does not have an overabundance of *unrealized* losses, then this situation might correspond to a 0 percent effective capital gains tax this year followed by a full capital gains rate next year.

Of course, if a portfolio has already taken an excess of realized capital gains in the current year, and if there is a limited amount of unrealized losses, then any loss taken will be a truly marginal offset and should be valued at the full rate.

In all the above situations, the effective tax rates for capital gains and capital losses were symmetric (i.e., gains and losses both had the same rate in any given year). Moreover, this rate corresponded to either the full capital gains tax rate or to 0 percent. Now one can also envision situations where asymmetric and partial tax rates would be appropriate.

For example, suppose a portfolio has relatively few unrealized losses relative to its unrealized capital gains. However, in terms of *realized* gains and losses, the situation is just the opposite: There is a huge body of capital losses for which the carry forward limit ends in the current fiscal year. The magnitude of these losses far outweighs both the realized and unrealized gains. An incremental capital gain realized this year will therefore be taxed at a marginal rate of 0 percent. An incremental capital loss realized this year would not be marginally useful in the current fiscal year. However, such a loss would be carried forward into subsequent years when the embedded gains would outweigh the available losses. Hence, such a loss might be viewed as having an opportunity-dollar value in excess of 0 percent but below the full capital gains rate that would apply to a needed offset in the present year. In such a case, the marginal-gains rate would be less than the marginal-loss rate. This asymmetry in tax rates creates a corresponding asymmetry in the risk/reward balance. The implications of such an asymmetry for investment policy are fairly evident.

In fact, it could be argued that whenever the unrealized capital gains are out of balance with the losses available as potential offsets, that this creates an "asymmetry of resources" with significant implications for portfolio strategy.

In this connection, it is sometimes quite suggestive to look at the portfolio in terms of its overall value in opportunity dollars. This overall value should correspond to the funds remaining following a hypothetical liquidation of the entire portfolio and the payment of any resulting tax liabilities. For example, take the preceding example of a portfolio with carry forward losses that are about to expire. Since the current realized losses outweigh both the realized and unrealized capital gains, the portfolio's current opportunity-dollar value would coincide with its market value. However, in the next fiscal year, if no further action had been taken, the carry-forward losses would have expired and the unrealized capital gains would then exceed the available loss offset. Consequently, liquidation of the portfolio would then result in some net capital gains liability and the opportunity-dollar value would fall below the portfolio's market value. Thus, even if the portfolio's market value remains unchanged over the year, there would be a definite decline in the opportunity-dollar value. This would have the exact same effect as a market decline, and the portfolio would show a reduced opportunity yield over the one-year period. This loss in opportunity yield, of course, reflects the opportunity foregone by not realizing all possible capital gains in the current fiscal year when they could be fully offset against the expiring pool of capital losses.

This whole area of the management of capital gains and losses can obviously become quite intricate and can lead to some thorny estimation problems. However, its difficulty should not lead to its neglect. Theoretically, the subject has many fascinating facets. Practically, it would seem that correct strategic decisions at this level might well have an enormous (and relatively risk-free) impact on the portfolio's total performance.

Indirect Factors Influencing Aftertax Return

The foregoing development of the opportunity yield approach focused on the relatively direct tax factors affecting income, reinvestment, and capital gains or losses. However, there are many indirect factors that can have a powerful and frequently overwhelming influence on the portfolio's return and management strategy. Some of these factors can be readily measured and incorporated into an opportunity yield. Other factors are of a more qualitative nature and probably would defy any effort to introduce them into a formal analytic framework.

One of the more important measurable factors is the "asset tax," which arises in connection with life insurance company portfolios. Many major insurance companies believe that, through the complexities of their taxation structure, they become subject to what amounts to an implicit tax on their portfolio's asset value. Estimates of the magnitude of this asset tax range up to 1 percent. Such an asset tax can readily be incorporated into the opportunity yield measure, and would have a major effect on a bond portfolio strategy. For example, consider a 25-year, 4 percent H bond purchased earlier at a price of par, but selling now at 60.739. At a 30 percent income tax rate, the 4 percent coupon would provide an annual payment of $40 pretax or

$$\$40 \times .70 = \$28$$

aftertax for an aftertax coupon rate of 2.8 percent. The presence of an additional 1 percent asset tax applied to the bond's book value of par would constitute a further tax charge of $10 per bond per year. This would reduce the net aftertax coupon income to

$$\$28 - \$10 = \$18$$

per year, or an after-coupon rate of only 1.80%! Moreover, this asset tax is based on the H-bond's inflated book asset value. Suppose the H-bond were sold and then repurchased and put on the books at its present market value of 60.739. The 1.00% asset tax would then amount to $6.07 per year, or a savings of $3.93 per year per bond. In terms of market value, this would constitute a savings of

$$100 \text{ percent} \times (\$3.93 \div \$607.39) = .65 \text{ percent}$$

or 65 basis points of "unnecessary" taxation per year.

Many important but less measurable factors surround the whole issue of realizing book and/or tax losses. As we have seen, it often makes sense to take losses in terms of the direct dollars-and-cents effects. However, the taking of losses can have powerful effects that may reach beyond the confines of the portfolio and have great impact upon the corporation's overall reporting and statutory status. Profits may be adversely affected. The various measures of corporate returns on assets may be reduced. There may be an encroachment upon the level of needed reserves. There are many such circumstances, all of which tend to place limits on the freedom to realize portfolio losses or gains. From the narrower vista of the portfolio, it may seem that such restrictions are purely artificial and have little to do with the true financial realities of the corporation. However, it should be remembered that the financial reporting structure ultimately does have a real economic impact on overall corporate operations regardless of the realities that they may or may not reflect. Obviously, a corporate policy is needed that balances the very real benefits of portfolio loss realization against their possible adverse "reporting" effects. Unfortunately, many taxed portfolios labor under an unexamined and unmeasured dictum that arbitrarily restricts or often prohibits any form of loss realization.

INVESTMENT IMPLICATIONS

The investment implications of the results presented in this chapter are as follows:

1. *Conventional pretax yields and yield spreads can be deceptive for taxed portfolios and can result in apparent yield pickup swaps that actually turn out to be dollars-and-cents losers.*

Consider a swapout of 25-year taxable 4s at 7.5 percent into 25-year taxable 8.5 percent par bonds. Even at a 48 percent, 0 percent tax structure and a 6 percent reinvestment rate, the 100-basis-point yield pickup would appear to be large enough to overwhelm all the fine points and lead to substantial profit. However, Exhibit 9 shows that the 4s have a taxable effective par rate of 9.91 percent. Hence this swap would actually entail a loss of 141 basis points in terms of effective par rate. In terms of dollars-and-cents, this would amount to a loss of $274,000 on a $1,000,000 market value holding over the 25-year period.

2. *The conventional aftertax yields and yield spreads, when computed using the common approximation formulas can prove very unreliable.*

For a 48 percent, 0 percent tax structure, the common "coupon" approximation formula for taxable bonds works out to an aftertax yield estimate of 5.58 percent for a 25-year 4 percent bond priced to yield 7.5 percent. The true *conventional* aftertax yield is 4.79 percent, a discrepancy of 79 basis points. (See Exhibit 8.) For tax-exempts, it can be shown that the popular current yield approximation becomes highly inaccurate for the deeper discount bonds.[12]

3. *The conventional aftertax yields and yield spreads (even when computed exactly) can either overstate or understate or even reverse the actual dollars-and-cents relationship between two bonds.*

In a 48 percent, 48 percent tax structure, suppose a 25-year taxable 4 percent bond is offered at 7.5 percent, and a 25-year taxable new issue is offered at 8.125 percent. The conventional aftertax yields on the 4s is 4.19 percent, leading to a conventional taxable equivalent yield of 8.07 percent. Thus, by the conventional aftertax calculations, the 8.125 percent par bond appears to have a modest yield advantage over the 4s. Actually, at a 9 percent pretax reinvestment rate, using the opportunity yield approach, the 4s would be seen to equate to a 7.97 percent par bond, so that the choice of the par bond would actually lead to a more significant pickup of 16 basis points in effective par rate. On the other hand, at a 6 percent reinvestment rate, the 4s would equate to an 8.31 percent par bond, so that selecting the 8.125 percent par bond would lead to a *loss* of 18 basis points, or about $36,000 on a $1 million investment. (See Exhibit 9.) Even worse, suppose the 4s

---

[12] See Fabozzi et al., *The Handbook of Municipal Bonds* for the investment implications of tax-exempts.

had been purchased earlier at 10 points below their current market
value. Then a swap into the 8.125 percent par bond would actually
entail a giveup of 90 basis points in terms of the opportunity par rate,
or $175,000 over the next 25 years for each $1 million of net opportunity proceeds (See Exhibit 12).

The conventional aftertax yields of tax-exempt bonds can also lead
to similar important distortions of their investment relationship.

4. *Unlike the conventional yields, the opportunity yield and the opportunity par rate provide investment measures that will be consistent with the dollars-and-cents return to be received under
   specified portfolio and market conditions.*

The interaction of the effects of taxation, coupon reinvestment, realized and unrealized capital gains and losses, and market actions
create quite a complex decision-making environment for the manager
of a bond portfolio subject to taxation. The opportunity yield is designed to integrate these factors into a relatively simple and intuitive
yardstick that can be readily benchmarked against the marketplace.
The validity of the resulting measurements, of course, still depends
totally on the validity of the assumptions relating to the portfolio and
to market conditions. However, at least the role of these conditions
becomes clearer through the need to make these assumptions explicit.

Although the opportunity yields and par rates can be computed
manually, they do not represent trivial calculations when performed
for large bond portfolios. However, with the assistance of modern
computers, opportunity yields can be quickly and accurately determined. Moreover, the use of the computer permits the extension of
the opportunity yield approach into the high payoff areas, such as
various forms of swap analyses, determination of breakeven yields,
yield spread studies, loss recovery times, as well as the more complex
cash flows resulting from sinking-fund bonds and mortgagelike securities.

5. *Discount bonds have an intrinsic aftertax advantage over par
   bonds priced at the same conventional pretax yield—even when
   capital gains are taxed at the same rate as coupon income.*

This is true for conventional aftertax yields and for realized compound yields at virtually any reasonable reinvestment rates. (See Exhibit 10.) Of course, this advantage may well be offset by the yield
spread relationships existing in the market at any given time.

6. *A portfolio with a large reservoir of unrealized losses relative to
   gains* and *the freedom to realize these losses can, up to a certain
   point, reduce its effective capital gains tax to 0 percent by offsetting gains with losses.*

No portfolio willingly seeks losses, but once they have occurred, they constitute a valuable resource for tax liability management.

7. *For portfolios with large, usable loss reservoirs, discount bonds with their locked-in capital gain have an even greater structural advantage.*

As always, for any given portfolio, this structural advantage must be evaluated in the context of existing market levels, spreads, and prospects.

8. *Taxation leads to a much greater erosion in dollars-and-cents return than is indicated by the magnitude of the tax rates or any of the aftertax yields.*

A 48 percent, 48 percent tax structure can lead to 65 percent reduction in total aftertax return of taxable bonds, while the conventional yields are reduced by only 48 percent. (See Exhibit 6.) Because of the very nature of the compounding process, the conventional aftertax yields of both taxable and tax-exempt bonds will not fully reflect this dollars-and-cents reduction.

9. *Any tax structure on income greatly reduces the incremental dollars-and-cents return from pure yield pickup swaps (no matter how accurately the yields are figured).*

Without taxes, a swap from a 25-year effective par rate of 7.5 percent to 8 percent would, on a $1 million investment amount to an increased return of $446,000 with reinvestment at a 9 percent rate. Under a 48 percent tax rate on coupon income and reinvestment, this same swap would only provide an additional return of $121,000, a reduction of more than 73 percent of the added return in the tax-free case.

10. *Income taxation renders pure yield pickup swaps far more vulnerable to adverse market moves in yields and/or yield spreads.*

Income taxation reduces the dollars-and-cents accumulation of benefits from pure yield pickup swaps. (See Exhibit 6.) At the same time, it aggravates the aftertax impact of an adverse yield move, particularly in those tax structures where capital gains are taxed at a lower rate than coupon income.

The following, although not demonstrated in this chapter, are other investment implications of the tools discussed in this chapter:[13]

1. *Short and intermediate discounts have a very special advantage, all else being equal, in taxed structures favoring capital gains.*

---

[13] See Martin L. Leibowitz, *Total After-Tax Bond Performance and Yield Measures.*

2. *In selecting potential sale candidates within the discount portion of a portfolio with a tax structure favoring capital gains, there is a strong incentive to focus on the longer maturity bonds.*

3. *The effective volatility of a taxable bond's net return under changes in yields and/or yield spreads is greatly enhanced by any tax structure favorable to capital gains.*

Horizon Analysis: An Analytical Framework for Managed Bond Portfolios*

29

MARTIN L. LEIBOWITZ, Ph.D.
Managing Director, Bond
Portfolio Analysis Group
Salomon Brothers Inc

The fundamental variables of the bond market are interest-rate levels, yield curves, and yield spread relationships. The changing structure of values among these variables forms the sources of investment return. However, as shown in *Inside the Yield Book*[1] and in Chapters 4 and 28 of this book, the conventional yields that the market quotes, observes, and tracks on an everyday basis are very different from the usual portfolio objective of total return. This chapter presents a simple analytic framework for relating the portfolio objective of total return over a given investment horizon to the sources of that return—the basic market variables of interest-rate levels, yield curves, and yield spread relationships. How *horizon analysis* can be applied to yield

* This chapter draws from Martin L. Leibowitz, "Horizon Analysis: A New Analytic Framework for Managed Bond Portfolios," *The Journal of Portfolio Management* (Spring 1975); © Institutional Investor, Inc., 1975.

Although the information in this chapter has been obtained from sources that the author believes to be reliable, Salomon Brothers Inc cannot guarantee its accuracy, and such information may be incomplete or condensed. All opinions and estimates included in this chapter constitute judgment as of this date and are subject to change without notice.

[1] Sidney Homer and Martin L. Leibowitz, *Inside the Yield Book* (New York: published jointly by The New York Institute of Finance and Prentice-Hall, 1972).

curve analysis and bond-swap analysis are discussed in Chapters 30 and 32, respectively.[2]

THE MIDDLE GROUND OF BOND INVESTMENT

The full impact of the passage of time upon bond investment decisions is often overlooked.

Basically, two vantage points are common among bond market participants: the long view based on some measure of yield-to-maturity and the very short term view with a primary focus on day-to-day price movements. Surprisingly few investors consistently explore investment horizons extending beyond the current calendar year but earlier than the shortest maturity bond under consideration. At the same time, the most comfortable projections of bond market relationships often imply workout periods extending beyond the immediate months ahead, but rarely further than a few years into the future. This middle ground "between tomorrow and maturity" offers a relatively unscrutinized arena for uncovering new relationships, new values, and consequently, fresh opportunities.

However, there are few convenient analytic tools to aid the investor who wishes to explore this middle ground. The conventional yield book really indicates the levels of return for holders to maturity, and even there, it has its limitations.[3] On the other hand, most studies of price volatility have really dealt with price and yield moves concentrated at a single instant in time. Relatively little has been done to explore the problem of a bond's volatility and return *over time*.

THE THREE BASIC SOURCES OF RETURN

A bond investment provides value from three basic sources—coupon income, interest-on-interest, and capital gains.

---

[2] Horizon analysis turns out to have an interesting interpretation in terms of the swap classification system described in *Inside the Yield Book* and in Chapter 30 of this book. Using this framework, a given bond swap can be viewed, at each point in time, as a well-defined mixture of components from idealized swap categories. A given swap may thus have different quantifiable components reflecting the effects of pure yield pickup, rate anticipation, changing sector spreads, quality spreads, yield curve effects, and substitution relationships. This enables the bond portfolio manager to associate a proposed portfolio action with the primary sources of its expected return. The manager can then explore the vulnerabilities of this expected return over a range of feasible market conditions. By pursuing this route in a more formal fashion, he or she can begin to define and quantify the various dimensions of risk. Horizon analysis simplifies the computation of certain risk measures, such as breakeven points for yield levels and yield spreads. It also suggests a role for "sensitivity ratios" to quantify the risk associated with each market force conflicting with the "target" factor motivating the swap. Horizon analysis also clarifies how the very passage of time leads to dramatic changes in risk structure. See "Horizon Analysis: A New Analytical Framework for Managed Bond Portfolios," *The Journal of Portfolio Management*, Spring 1975, for illustrations.

[3] See Chapter 4.

Coupon income is taken here to include coupon payments and any accrued interest received should the bond be sold prior to maturity.

Interest-on-interest is the return earned through reinvestment and compounding of this coupon income. Since neither the vehicle nor the rates for this reinvestment process can be specified in advance, the level of accumulation of interest-on-interest is necessarily uncertain. However, interest-on-interest can account for more than 70 percent of the total return for a long-term bond and should therefore be included in every comprehensive evaluation of a bond investment. One convenient, although admittedly simplistic, approach is to assume the availability of a reinvestment rate that is constant over time. The impact of the uncertainty associated with reinvestment can then be explored by varying this rate assumption across some range of feasible values.

The capital gains component of return relates to the increase in the bond's market value. For tax-free portfolios, $1 of capital gains enters into the total return in as direct and as valuable fashion as $1 of coupon income or $1 of interest-on-interest.

These three components of total return apply to any investment medium. As a long-term investment vehicle, bonds are characterized by deriving a significant proportion of their *long-term* return from relatively predictable coupon and redemption flows together with the reinvestment of these flows. On the other hand, over short- and intermediate-term time periods, the more uncertain elements of the capital gain or loss can represent a much more significant proportion of the bond's total return. Consequently, these relatively predictable and relatively uncertain factors must be differentiated in order to develop a good handle on the bond's return over short- to intermediate-term investment horizons. As we shall see, this differentiation leads to an important refinement in the capital gains component.

THE GROWTH OF RETURN OVER TIME

As an example, consider a 10-year 4 percent bond purchased at a price of 67.48 for a conventional yield-to-maturity of 9 percent. One such bond would generate coupon income of $40 over the first year, $80 over a two-year period, and so on. Upon dividing these figures by the original purchase price of $674.80, the cumulative percentage return becomes

$$100 \text{ percent} \times (\$40/\$674.80) = 5.93 \text{ percent}$$

(i.e., just the bond's current yield) over the first year, 11.86 percent over a two-year period, and so forth, as shown in Exhibit 1.

Interest-on-interest results from the reinvestment and compounding of the $20 semiannual coupon payment at the assumed semiannual rate of 3.75 percent (i.e., 7.5 percent annually). For an investment horizon consisting of 10 semiannual compounding periods (i.e., five years), the compound interest tables show that each $1 of periodic payment would grow to a total future value of $11.868. This future value consists of the 10 payments plus the resulting interest-on-interest. Since the bond's semiannual payment is $20, the total future value for this example would be:

$$\$20 \times 11.868 = \$237.36$$

The pure interest-on-interest here is this future value less the 10 coupon payments totaling $200:

$$\$237.36 - \$200 = \$37.36$$

This is the interest-on-interest earned over the five-year investment horizon for each bond. To find the percentage figure shown in Exhibit 1, the above dollar amount must be divided by the cost per bond:

$$100 \text{ percent} \times (\$37.36/\$674.80) = 5.54 \text{ percent}$$

The third component of the bond's return, capital gains, cannot really be viewed solely in terms of some continuous process of growth. The capital gain component has two very different facets, and all bond market participants would be well advised to distinguish between them.

THE ACCUMULATION PORTION OF A BOND'S CAPITAL GAIN

A high-grade discount bond provides a specified capital gain over its life (presuming that there is no danger of default). However, this capital gain does not materialize in a flash at the bond's maturity. Rather it accrues in some fashion on a year-by-year basis throughout the bond's life. Consequently, at each point, prior to a discount bond's maturity, some portion of its capital gain must be attributed to an accretion process, which will ultimately bring the bond's price up to par at maturity. The nature of this *accumulation capital gain* makes it fundamentally different from the *market capital gain* derived through interest-rate movements.

Any formal scheme for distinguishing between these two facets of capital gain must necessarily contain arbitrary features. Nevertheless, as a practical method of analysis, one can make a useful distinction based upon the bond's conventional yield-to-maturity. *Accumulation capital gain* would then be defined as the price appreciation that would take place if the bond's yield-to-maturity remained constant throughout the investment period. Any deviation from this amortized price level can then be ascribed as the market changes affecting the bond's yield value.

Return now to the example of the 10-year 4 percent bond purchased at a 9 percent yield-to-maturity. At the end of a five-year horizon, the bond's remaining life would be five years. From the yield book, a five-year 4 percent bond at the "amortizing" yield of 9 percent would be priced at 80.218, i.e., an accumulation capital gain of

$$\$802.18 - \$674.80 = \$127.38$$

per bond or a cumulative percentage of

$$100 \text{ percent} \times (\$127.38/\$674.80) = 18.88 \text{ percent}$$

Exhibit 1 shows how this accumulation capital gain grows over time.[4]

THE YIELD ACCUMULATION RETURN

By adding this accumulation capital gain component to the coupon income and interest-on-interest, one obtains an approximate measure of the bond's accumulating return which is *relatively* free from the uncertainties of day-to-day movements in market rates. Consequently, this sum may be called the yield accumulation return.

Exhibit 1 shows how the yield accumulation return and its components grow over longer and longer investment horizons. In the early

Exhibit 1
Growth of Cumulative Percentage Return with Constant Yield Amortization (10-year 4 percent bond purchased at 67.48 for a yield-to-maturity of 9 percent)

	Cumulative Percentage Return			
Investment Horizon	*Coupon Income*	*Interest-on-Interest (at 7.5%)*	*Accumulation Capital Gain*	*Total "Yield Accumulation" Return*
0.0 Years	0.00%	0.00%	0.00%	0.00%
1.0..........	5.93	0.11	3.14	9.18
2.0..........	11.86	0.68	6.57	19.11
3.0..........	17.78	1.75	10.32	29.85
4.0..........	23.71	3.36	14.41	41.48
5.0..........	29.64	5.54	18.88	54.06
6.0..........	35.57	8.34	23.76	67.67
7.0..........	41.49	11.80	29.08	82.37
8.0..........	47.42	15.98	34.90	98.30
9.0..........	53.35	20.94	41.25	115.54
10.0..........	59.28	26.73	48.19	134.20

Note: Accumulation capital gains based on constant-yield ("scientific") amortization at 9 percent assumed reinvestment rate = 7.5 percent.

---

[4] This constant-yield amortization might, at first, appear to be related to the so-called "scientific amortization" technique used for writing up the book value of a bond purchased at a discount. However, the resemblance is superficial on many counts. Basically, our intent here is to analyze projected market prices at future horizons, and the

years, the coupon income provides almost twice as much return as the accumulation capital gain; and the interest-on-interest component is virtually negligible at the outset. As the investment horizon lengthens, the coupon income maintains its constant pace, the interest-on-interest grows in the expected fashion, and the capital gain provides an ever-increasing contribution.

Exhibit 2 provides a clearer view of these growth patterns. Each column here represents the increment to the cumulative percentage

Exhibit 2
Annual Increments to Cumulative Percentage Return with Constant-Yield Amortization
10-year 4 percent bond purchased at 67.48 for a yield-to-maturity of 9 percent

For Annual Period Ending After	Annual Increment to Cumulative Percentage Return			
	Coupon Income	Interest-on-Interest (at 7.5%)	Accumulation Capital Gain	Total "Yield Accumulation" Return
1st Year	5.93%	0.11%	3.14%	9.18%
2nd	5.93	0.57	3.43	9.93
3rd...................	5.93	1.07	3.75	10.74
4th..................	5.93	1.61	4.09	11.63
5th..................	5.93	2.18	4.47	12.58
6th..................	5.93	2.80	4.88	13.61
7th..................	5.93	3.46	5.32	14.70
8th..................	5.93	4.18	5.82	15.93
9th..................	5.93	4.96	6.35	17.21
10th.................	5.93	5.79	6.94	18.66
Total..............	59.28%	26.73%	48.19%	134.20%

Note: Accumulation capital gains based on constant-yield ("scientific") amortization at 9 percent assumed reinvestment rate = 7.5 percent.

return resulting from extending the investment horizon by one additional year. In particular, it is interesting to note how the accumulation capital gain grows to the point of becoming the largest source of incremental return in the last two years of the bond's life.

It should be noted that the key yardstick is the *cumulative* percentage return (i.e., the net gain in future value represented as a percentage of the current investment base). For various reasons, we have decided to use the cumulative total return figures throughout rather than to translate them into the corresponding annualized *rates* of return.

---

purpose of scientific amortization is to provide a consistent accounting treatment over portfolio holding periods presumed to cover the bond's remaining life. Thus scientific amortization is always based upon the bond's yield at the time of its original purchase. On the other hand, our accumulation capital gain is based upon the bond's yield at the point of investment decision—which is always *today*.

THE "MARKET" PORTION OF A BOND'S CAPITAL GAIN

The yield accumulation return captures a bond's total return as long as there are no changes in the conventional yield-to-maturity. However, as we know, there are *constant changes* in interest rates, in the relationship between different market sectors, and in the precise relative value attached to individual securities. Apart from all of these factors, a specific bond's character and its role in the general fixed-interest market change with just the simple passage of time. For all these reasons, the investor must carefully study the effects of bond price and yield movements and their contribution to total return.

As it is buffeted by all the dynamics of the marketplace, a bond's actual price may weave many strange patterns indeed over time. However, once a given investment horizon has been selected, there are only two prices that matter for purposes of computing the bond's capital gain over that period—the starting price and the ending price.

Returning to the earlier example of a 10-year, 4 percent bond, Exhibit 3 illustrates a possible price pattern across the page on an abbre-

Exhibit 3
An Abbreviated Yield Book for 4 Percent Bonds Showing How a Bond's Price Movement Can Be Represented as a Constant-Yield Accumulation over Time Plus an Instantaneous Future Yield Move

Yield-to-Maturity	10 Years	9 Years	. . .	5 Years	. . .	1 Year	0 Years
7.00%	78.68	80.22		87.53		97.15	100.00
7.50	75.68	77.39		85.63		96.69	100.00
8.00	72.82	74.68		83.78		96.23	100.00
8.50	70.09	72.09		81.98		95.77	100.00
					Market capital gain		
9.00	67.48	69.60		80.22		95.32	100.00
	Accumulation capital gain						
9.50	64.99	67.22		78.51		94.87	100.00
10.00	62.61	64.92		76.83		94.42	100.00
10.50	60.34	62.74		75.21		93.98	100.00
11.00	58.17	60.64		73.62		93.54	100.00

Actual price pattern over time

viated yield book. Starting at its purchase price of 67.48 when the bond has a life of 10 years, Exhibit 3 shows the price varying over time and finally winding up five years later at 83.78, resulting in a total capital gain of

$$83.78 - 67.48 = 16.30$$

points, or a cumulative percentage capital gain of

$$100 \text{ percent} \times (16.30/67.48) = 24.16 \text{ percent}$$

Now in determining this bond's yield accumulation return of 54.06 percent over these 5 years, a process of constant-yield amortization was assumed. As shown in Exhibit 3, this amortization process is tantamount to a hypothetical lateral movement across the "9 percent row" in the yield book. Over the five-year investment horizon, this hypothetical amortization process would, by itself, carry the bond's price to 80.22. There, of course, remains the price gap of 3.56 points between this amortized price and the bond's actual price of 83.78. This gap could be theoretically ascribed to a sudden (in fact, a hypothetically instantaneous) jump in yields carrying the bond's price from 80.22 *up* the five-year column to its actual price level of 83.78.

This example can, of course, be generalized. Any price movement over a specified horizon can be theoretically represented as the result of a simple two-step process: (1) a constant-yield amortization over the horizon period (i.e., a lateral movement across one row in the yield book) and (2) an instantaneous yield change taking place at *the end of the* investment horizon period (i.e., a vertical movement up or down one column in the yield book).

Obviously, this two-step representation will *not* provide an accurate description of how the price movement actually took place over time. However, it will provide a mathematically correct result for the total capital gains contribution resulting from any given actual price movement.

The big advantage of this two-step model is that it clearly differentiates the two facets of a bond's capital gain. The first step corresponds to the accumulation capital gain accruing as a result of the passage of time and the bond's consequent march toward its maturity date. The second step corresponds to the effects of any change in the bond's yield. Since most market participants associate such yield changes with market actions, this portion of capital gain component may be referred to as the *market capital gain*.

In terms of cumulative percentage return, the market capital gain is simply added to the yield accumulation return to find the total return. For the example illustrated by price movement in Exhibit 3, the market capital gain of

$$100 \text{ percent } (3.56/67.48) = 5.28 \text{ percent}$$

can be added to the five-year yield accumulation return of 54.06 percent shown in Exhibit 1 to obtain the total cumulative return of 59.34 percent.

With this approach, the total returns can easily be computed over a range of possible yield moves. Exhibit 4 provides such a presentation for yield moves of −100, 0, and +100 basis points by the end of each investment horizon.

MEASURES OF VOLATILITY

Over short-term investment horizons, price changes can often overwhelm all other sources of return. Exhibit 4 illustrates this effect. Every bond market participant needs some sort of handy guide for linking the market yield movements (which he or she follows) to the resulting bond price changes (which he or she feels).

Many practitioners use various simple rules of thumb, for example, "a 10-basis-point move in a 30-year bond corresponds to 1⅜ point change." One of the problems with such rules of thumb is that they tend to become dangerously inaccurate in today's dynamic marketplace. The rule just cited, for example, is really correcct only at a 6 percent yield level.

In *Inside the Yield Book* and in Chapter 4 of this book, a series of tabulations were developed to illustrate how the percentage price volatility increased with (1) increasing maturity, (2) higher yield levels, and (3) lower coupon rates. A given bond's volatility was also shown to depend upon the direction and magnitude of the yield move.

Many key aspects of these volatility relationships can be read directly from the pages of the yield book itself. For example, Exhibit 3 shows that a five-year, 4 percent bond with a 9 percent yield carries a price of 80.22. As observed above, a yield decline to 8 percent would result in a price rise of

$$83.78 - 80.22 = 3.56$$

points or

$$100 \text{ percent } (3.56/80.22) = 4.44 \text{ percent}$$

relative to the starting price of 80.22. On the other hand, an increase in yield to the 10 percent level results in a price decline of

$$80.22 - 76.83 = 3.39$$

points, or a percentage drop of

$$100 \text{ percent } (3.39/80.22) = 4.23 \text{ percent}$$

In other words, an upward yield move leads to a somewhat smaller percentage price change than a downward yield move of the same magnitude.

Exhibit 3 illustrates another aspect of price volatility. Suppose the yield of the five-year, 4 percent bond dropped to 8.5 percent. This would lead to a percentage change of

$$100 \text{ percent } \times \left(\frac{81.98 - 80.22}{80.22} \right) = 2.19 \text{ percent}$$

Dividing this figure by the 50 basis points of yield move, one gets a value of

Exhibit 4
Growth of Cumulative Percentage Return with Market Yield Moves (10-year 4 percent bond purchased at 67.48 for a yield-to-maturity of 9 percent)

Investment Horizon	Total Yield Accumulation Return	Percentage Return from Market Capital Gain Given Yield Move of			Total Cumulative Percentage Return Given Yield Move of		
	0%	−100 B.P.	0 B.P.	+100 B.P.	−100 B.P.	0 B.P.	+100 B.P.
0 years	0%	7.91%	0%	−7.21%	7.91%	0%	−7.21%
1	9.18	7.53	0	−6.92	16.71	9.18	2.26
2	19.11	7.09	0	−6.56	26.20	19.11	12.55
3	29.85	6.57	0	−6.13	36.42	29.85	23.72
4	41.48	5.97	0	−5.62	47.45	41.48	35.86
5	54.06	5.27	0	−5.02	59.33	54.06	49.04
6	67.67	4.48	0	−4.30	72.15	67.67	63.37
7	82.37	3.57	0	−3.46	85.94	82.37	78.91
8	98.30	2.53	0	−2.47	100.83	98.30	95.83
9	115.54	1.34	0	−1.33	116.88	115.54	114.21
10	134.20	0	0	0	134.20	134.20	134.20

Note: Total yield accumulation return based on 7.5 percent reinvestment rate and constant-yield amortization at 9 percent.

$$\frac{2.19 \text{ percent}}{50 \text{ B.P.}} = .0439 \text{ percent/B.P.}$$

as the percentage price change per basis-point move. Upon comparing this value with the .0444 percent B.P. obtained with a move of -100 basis points, we further see that it is not possible to *precisely* determine percentage price changes by multiplying the yield move by some constant volatility factor (i.e., each yield move would correspond to a different value for this volatility factor.)

At the same time, this volatility factor approach can provide a fairly close approximation to percentage price changes across a range of different yield moves. For example, averaging the percentage price changes for yield moves of -100 basis points and $+100$ basis points leads to a figure of

$$\frac{1}{2} \times (4.44) \text{ percent} + \frac{1}{2} \times (4.23) \text{ percent} = 4.33 \text{ percent}$$

or an average volatility factor of .0433 percent per basis-point move. By applying this average factor to the yield move from 9 percent to 8.5 percent, the approximate percentage price change is found to be

$$-0.433 \text{ percent/B.P.} \times (-50 \text{ B.P.}) = +2.17 \text{ percent}$$

that is, fairly close to the exact value of 2.19 percent found above.

Now there are a number of more sophisticated techniques for finding volatility factors. One such technique is based on the concept of *duration* introduced by Macaulay in 1938.[5] A bond's duration is the weighted average life of all its coupon and principal payments, where the weighting factors consist of present values of each payment. As a measure of average life, duration has many advantages over conventional techniques that only consider principal repayments and even then ignore the time value of different repayment dates. It turns out that, with a simple adjustment, a bond's duration provides a very useful indication of the bond's price volatility. In fact, for small yield moves the (adjusted) duration provides a mathematically *exact* volatility factor.

However, for most investors, Duration is not the easiest thing to compute. For our expository purposes here, the simple average of up and down moves of 100 basis points provides adequate volatility factors. As we shall see, even these approximate volatility factors can fulfill a valuable function in relating projected market movements to the total return expected from different sectors of the bond market. When fine tuning is needed in these computations, there are various computer programs available that can refine the results by incorporating the exact percentage price change associated with each projected yield move.

---

[5] Duration is the topic of Chapter 35.

THE HORIZON VOLATILITY FACTOR

As with most discussions of price volatility, the preceding section focused on *instantaneous* price changes. However, when one wants to determine a bond's total return over an extended investment horizon, then the concept of price volatility must itself be extended beyond the immediate moment. We must proceed from instantaneous volatility to the idea of a *volatility over time*.

This idea of a volatility over time can actually be incorporated quite simply into our two-step representation of capital gains. In this model, all price movements derived from yield changes are relegated to the market capital gain component. Recalling Exhibit 3, all such market price changes are treated *as if* they occurred at the end of the investment horizon. Moreover, they are treated *as if* they began from a future price level obtained through a constant-yield amortization process.

For example, we just found an instantaneous percentage price change of 4.44 percent for a five-year, 4 percent bond moving from 9 percent to 8 percent. However, this percentage price change was measured relative to an investment base of 80.22 (i.e., the price corresponding to a 9 percent yield level for the 5-year bond). For the investment problem analyzed in Exhibit 4, the original investment base is the 10-year bond's starting price of 67.48. Over a five-year investment horizon, the constant-yield amortization would carry the bond to a price of 80.22. At this point five years hence, a *future* yield move from the 9 percent to the 8 percent level would then produce the price move of

$$83.78 - 80.22 = 3.56$$

points. In terms of points of price, this move is identical to that generated by the same *instantaneous* yield move in a five-year bond. However, as we noted, the investment base is different in these two cases. Suppose we wished to make use of the five-year bond's instantaneous percentage price change of 4.44 percent to help determine the market capital gain return for the 10-year bond over a five-year horizon. Then the investment base must be shifted from the amortized price of 80.22 "backward" to the original price of 67.48. Multiplying the instantaneous percentage price change by the ratio of the two prices will achieve this backward translation, that is,

$$100 \text{ percent} \times (3.56/67.48) = 100 \text{ percent} \times \frac{3.56}{80.22} \times \frac{80.22}{67.48}$$
$$= 4.44 \text{ percent} \times (80.22/67.48)$$
$$= 4.44 \text{ percent} \times (1.1888)$$
$$= 5.28 \text{ percent}$$

This figure coincides with the market capital gain return shown in Exhibit 4 for a −100 basis point yield move over a five-year horizon.

The price ratio used in the above translation, 1.1888, can also be expressed as

$$\frac{100 \text{ percent} + 18.88 \text{ percent}}{100 \text{ percent}}$$

where 18.88 percent is the accumulation capital gain return shown in Exhibit 1 for the five-year horizon. This result can be generalized. The accumulation capital gain return over any horizon period can be used to translate an instantaneous percentage price change at the horizon backward into a figure for the market capital gain return.

Moreover, any measure of instantaneous price *volatility* can be translated backward over an investment horizon in exactly the same manner to obtain a volatility factor for the market capital gain. To differentiate it from the instantaneous volatilities, this figure will be referred to as the *horizon volatility*. As a numerical example, the simple average instantaneous volatility figure of .0433 percent per basis-point move, computed above for the five-year bond, translates into a horizon volatility of

$$\left(\frac{100 \text{ percent} + 18.88 \text{ percent}}{100 \text{ percent}}\right) \times .0433 \text{ percent/B.P.}$$
$$= (1.1888) \times .0433 \text{ percent/B.P.}$$
$$= .0515 \text{ percent/B.P.}$$

Referring to the five-year horizon in Exhibit 4, this horizon volatility of .0515 percent/B.P. would approximate market capital gain resulting from a minus or plus 100 basis-point yield move by plus or minus 5.15 percent, compared with the actual figures of 5.27 percent and −5.02 percent.

The accumulation capital gain is thus seen to act as a magnifier of the instantaneous volatility at the end of the horizon period. Generally speaking, for discount bonds, this effect will boost the horizon volatility above the instantaneous volatility value. Consequently, the longer the horizon period and the larger the accumulation capital gain, the greater will be this magnification effect. On the other hand, for premium bonds, the accumulation capital gain will, of course, be negative, and the horizon volatility will be smaller than the instantaneous volatility, whose own value shrinks with increasing horizon and the consequent shorter maturity.

These volatility factors can also be expressed in terms of the more dramatic scale of "basis points of price move per basis point of yield move." For example, the preceding volatility factor of .0515 percent/B.P. could be restated as 5.15 B.P./B.P., meaning that each basis point of yield move produces approximately 5.15 basis points of incremental return.

The great advantage of the horizon volatility is that it enables a bond's return over a given horizon to be characterized by two readily computed numbers: (1) a yield accumulation return, which depends only upon the selected reinvestment rate, and (2) a horizon volatility factor, from which market capital gain figures can be quickly approximated across any range or combination of projected yield moves.

Bond Swaps

30   CHRISTINA SEIX, C.F.A.
Director of Bond Management
MacKay-Shields Financial Corporation

Horizon analysis is a sound analytical framework for bond-swap decisions. In volatile markets, it is more important than ever to focus on the sources of expected benefits from a proposed swap and thus identify its potential vulnerabilities. The purpose of this chapter is to present several bond transactions that are common in today's market and to analyze them within the framework of *horizon analysis* (discussed in Chapter 29).

GENERAL COMMENTS

The bond market has undergone a profound change over recent years. Bond prices, which fluctuated in an average daily range of ±1/16 point prior to November 1978, now average ±1/2 to ±3/4 point on a typical trading day. In the past, volatility would heighten as the market was approaching a cyclical turn in interest rates. Currently, whether the market is close to a cyclical turning point or not, managing bond assets is a treacherous exercise. Not only has the market's volatility increased, but many of the key determinants of interest-rate behavior have changed. Interest-rate cycles in the past, for example, were very much related to the disintermediation process in the banking and thrift industries. With recent innovations in the banking system, some of the old barometers are less effective in determining interest-rate pressures.

Monitoring the federal funds rate to gauge the intentions of the Federal Reserve Board has become considerably less important than measuring actual "money" growth. And defining *money* or *transactions balances* in today's economy, which is the commodity whose price we are interested in forecasting, has become a near impossible feat.

The adjustment to this new market has brought with it subtle changes in professional bond management. Among the most apparent are: a general shortening of the performance measurement period (horizon period), larger required-return expectations for executing a given swap, and in some cases, larger percentage moves into and out of the market. That is, a 1- to 2-year measurement period has become more prevalent than the 5- to 10-year horizons of the past. The expected portfolio improvement of holding one bond versus another has to be more significant than in the past to generate a swap action.

Finally, market actions entailing 1 or 2 percent of the portfolio have generally been replaced by 3 and 5 percent commitments. Each of these subtle changes is management's response to the new level of price volatility in today's bond market. A general resetting of priorities in the professional manager's portfolio activities has been an outgrowth of this new environment.

PREPARATION FOR ANALYSIS

One thing that has not changed over this period is the proper measure of portfolio performance. In 1966 The Bank Administration Institute published a comprehensive study on performance measurement that concluded that *total return* was the best measure of overall portfolio growth. Total return is the sum of all investment income plus changes in capital values in a portfolio. It continues to be the critical measure of portfolio improvement.

Moreover, the *realized compound yield* of a specific bond, which is the direct analogy to total return of an entire portfolio, continues to be the best yardstick for a bond-swap decision. This measure was defined in *Inside the Yield Book* by Sidney Homer and Martin L. Leibowitz and is explained in Chapters 4 and 28 of the *Handbook*.

Bond performance has always been determined by three basic factors: (1) position on the *yield curve*, (2) *sector* of the market, and (3) *quality* of the securities held. As of late, position on the yield curve has vastly overridden the other two factors in determining performance. Nevertheless, bond portfolio managers are continually faced with swap decisions involving all three factors. Maintaining a solid analytical framework for day-to-day portfolio decisions is critical during these hectic times. Horizon analysis, as defined in Chapter 29, provides precisely such a framework.

To use horizon analysis, the portfolio manager needs no more information than the standard tools already at hand to manage bond portfolios, namely:

1. Time frame for measuring results (horizon).
2. Today's market levels.
3. Forecast of yield curve (at end of horizon).
4. Forecast of sector spreads (at end of horizon).
5. Forecast of quality spreads (at end of horizon).

It is important to notice that interest-rate projections must be made, implicitly or explicitly, by the bond manager whether or not horizon analysis is to be used. These projections should be internally consistent with an overall economic forecast.

APPLICATION OF HORIZON ANALYSIS TO BOND SWAPS

For ease of classification, we will use the swap types identified in *Inside the Yield Book*.

Applying *horizon analysis* to the idea of exchanging one bond for another requires that we subdivide our expected return from each bond into three *basic* sources: (1) coupon income, (2) interest-on-interest, and (3) principal change (from accumulation plus market changes). In the two swap illustrations that follow, a one-year time horizon is assumed. Therefore, the effect of interest-on-interest and the accumulation part of the principal change will be minor.[1]

Intermarket Spread Swap

The motivation on an intermarket spread swap is to take advantage of changing yield spread relationships between various segments of the bond market. Market segments can be differentiated by quality (e.g., Aa versus A public utilities), type of issuer (GNMA versus Treasury), coupon rate, and so on.

The following assumptions are made for the purpose of illustrating an intermarket spread swap:

---

[1] The one-year time horizon is used here for illustrative purposes. This period could be shortened to a calendar quarter (three months) or lengthened to a full interest-rate cycle (approximately four to five years).

1. The time horizon is one year.
2. The bond to be sold is a U.S. Treasury bond with a 14⅞ percent coupon rate maturing August 15, 1991, selling at 99.834 to yield 14.9 percent.[2]
3. The bond to be purchased is Texas Eastern Transmission (utility with an A rating) with a 17 percent coupon rate maturing October 1, 1991, selling at 100.929 to yield 16.8 percent.
4. The projected yield for the two bonds one year hence is 11.75 percent for the Treasury bond and 13.38 percent for the utility.

This swap proposal suggests that we move out of the government sector and into the single A utility sector to take advantage of relatively wide quality and sector spreads that prevail in the current market.

We apply the tools established above in a *horizon analysis* framework as shown in Exhibit 1. This allows us to assess the sources of benefit from holding the Treasuries versus holding the utilities. It further identifies where we may be vulnerable given our projections, if we consummate the transaction.

Horizon analysis clearly reveals the sources of return in this swap. How important is our interest-rate forecast in choosing one bond over the other? In this case, the expected decline in rates only provides a 45-basis-point *increment* in total return. Spread narrowing between the utility and Treasury sectors helped to a small extent. But the return is improved by 196 basis points, close to 2 percent, by being in one sector of the market versus another. Credit analysis, that is, comfort with A utilities and Texas Eastern in particular, is the focal point for this swap and its main vulnerability. If this issue defaults or if the yield on single A utilities widens significantly versus Treasuries, this swap would hurt portfolio performance. If rates remain at the initial level, or even rise further from this point, the difference in total return will still be overwhelmingly governed by the initial differential in coupon income.

Rate Anticipation Swap

In a rate anticipation swap, the portfolio manager designs a swap to protect or benefit from projected changes in market yields. For example, if interest rates are expected to rise (fall), the portfolio manager will shorten (lengthen) maturities.

The following assumptions are made for the purpose of illustrating a rate anticipation swap:

---

[2] The market prices used in the illustrations in this chapter are those that prevailed on September 18, 1981.

Exhibit 1
Intermarket Spread Swap (Total return at end of one-year horizon)

Bond	Coupon Income	Interest on Interest at 14 Percent Reinvestment Rate	Accumulation Capital Gain	Total Yield Accumulation Return	Percentage Return from "Market" Capital Gain	Total Return
Sell:						
U.S. Treasury 14⅞ percent 8–15–91 at 14.90 percent/99.834	14.90%	.52%	.01%	15.43%	17.14%	32.57%
Buy:						
Texas Eastern Transmission 17 percent 10–1–91 (A utility) at 16.80 percent/100.929	16.84%	.59%	–.04%	17.39%	17.59%	34.98%
Basis point differential in return........	194 b.p.	7 b.p.	–5 b.p.	196 b.p.	45 b.p.	241 b.p.

	S Bond		P Bond	
	$ Return	Percent Return*	$ Return	Percent Return*
Computations:				
Initial price	$ 99.834	—	$100.929	—
Projected price	116.952	—	118.645	—
Capital gain (loss).....	17.118	17.15%	17.716	17.55%
Portion due to accumulation......	.006	.01	–.042	–.04
Portion due to change in market yield	17.112	17.14	17.758	17.59
Coupon interest	14.875	14.90	17.000	16.84
Interest on interest at 14 percent	.521	.52	.595	.59
Total return	$ 32.514	32.57%	$ 35.291	34.98%

* Percent return is derived by dividing each dollar return by the initial price.

1. The time horizon is one year.
2. The bond to be sold is a U.S. Treasury bond with a 13⅞ percent coupon rate maturing May 15, 2001, selling at 97.358 to yield 14.25 percent.
3. The bond to be purchased is a U.S. Treasury bond with a 16¼ percent coupon maturing August 31, 1983, selling at 100.378 to yield 16 percent.
4. The initial and projected interest rates for U.S. Treasury obligations are given below:

Time to maturity	Initial	Projected (one year hence)
3 months................	15.10%	10.00%
1 year	16.00	10.25
2 years..................	16.00	10.50
10 years	14.90	11.25
30 years	14.25	12.00

This swap proposal is a move to shorten maturity in order to pick up yield. In a very inverted yield curve environment, it is sometimes argued that when interest rates finally decline, the "snap-down" effect of the yield curve moving to a positive slope may result in better performance from shorter maturities. Exhibit 2 shows the performance of each bond, over a 12-month horizon, given our earlier projections.

The results of this *horizon analysis* clearly show that regardless of the 300-basis-point aggregate shift in the yield curve from a negative to positive slope, the overall decline in interest rates is the critical determinant of the success of this swap. Shortening maturity results in a healthy yield pickup of 181 basis points of income for the year, but this effect is dwarfed by the 1306-basis-point increase in total return that results from the capital gain on the longer maturity instrument.

The vulnerability of this swap is obviously the case where rates decline substantially. On the other hand, if interest rates remain at these levels or trend higher, the giveup in total return from not consummating the swap is at least 200 basis points of current yield.

Other Swaps

In the two illustrations cited above, *horizon analysis* has been used to clearly identify the sources of return from different fixed income securities. Homer and Leibowitz have categorized bond swaps into four different types including pure yield pickup swaps, substitution swaps, and the two discussed above (intermarket spread swaps and

Exhibit 2
Rate-Anticipation Swap (total return at end of one-year horizon)

Bond	Coupon Income	Interest on Interest at 14 Percent Reinvestment Rate	Accumulation Capital Gain	Total Yield Accumulation Return	Percentage Return from "Market" Capital Gain	Total Return
Sell: U.S. Treasury 13⅞ percent 5–15–11 at 14.25 percent/97.358...	14.25%	.50%	.01%	14.76%	18.14%	32.90%
Buy: U.S. Treasury 16¼ percent 8–31–83 at 16 percent/100.378	16.19%	.57%	–.19%	16.57%	5.08%	21.65%
Basis point differential in return	194 b.p.	7 b.p.	–20 b.p.	181 b.p.	–1306 b.p.	–1125 b.p.

	S Bond		P Bond	
Computations:	$ Return	Percent Return*	$ Return	Percent Return*
Initial price	$ 97.358	—	$100.378	—
Projected price	115.026	—	105.289	—
Capital gain (loss)	17.668	18.15%	4.911	4.89%
Portion due to accumulation	.007	.01	–.193	–.19
Portion due to change in market yield	17.661	18.14	5.104	5.08
Coupon interest	13.875	14.25	16.250	16.19
Interest on interest at 14 percent	.486	.50	.569	.57
Total return	$ 32.029	32.90%	$ 21.730	21.65%

* Percent return is derived by dividing each dollar return by the initial price.

rate-anticipation swaps). In pure yield pickup swaps, the portfolio manager has no expectations of market changes but is simply interested in increasing yield. In substitution swaps, the portfolio manager swaps from one bond into a similar bond (in terms of quality, coupon, and maturity) when a yield spread inducement exists. The aberration is a result of temporary market imbalances and is expected to reverse itself at some future time.

Although in this chapter we have only analyzed intermarket-spread swaps and rate-anticipation swaps within the context of *horizon analysis,* all swaps can easily be viewed within this framework.

SUMMARY

As the bond market continues to undergo massive shifts in composition, volatility, and overriding fundamentals, it is useful to have a solid analytical framework upon which to base bond swap decisions. *Horizon analysis* is precisely such a tool.

Using Yield Spreads as a Portfolio Improvement Strategy

31 **MICHAEL D. JOEHNK, Ph.D., C.F.A.**
Professor and Chairman
Department of Finance
Arizona State University

The subject of market interest rates is important to every bond investor. It is important to conservative investors, since one of their major objectives is to lock-in high yields. Aggressive bond traders also have a stake in interest rates because their programs are built on the capital gains opportunities that accompany major swings in rates. Just as there is no single bond market but a series of different market sectors, so too there is no single interest rate applicable to all segments of the market. Rather each segment has its own, somewhat unique, level of interest rates. Such rate differentials are what produce *yield spreads*. A yield spread is simply *the difference in promised yields that exists at a given point in time between one bond (or segment of the market) and another.* Granted, various market rates tend to drift in the same direction and to follow the same general pattern of behavior over time. But even so, yield spreads do still exist and as such can affect the comparative yield and price behavior of alternative debt securities. This chapter examines yield spreads and the effects that they can have on comparative short-term price and realized yield behavior. In so doing, attention will be directed not only toward explaining and illustrating the nature of yield spreads, but also toward noting the conditions under which changes in the structure of such differentials can lead to incremental profit opportunities. The objective, in short, is a better appreciation of the importance of this often overlooked market variable.

ELEMENTS OF BOND YIELD SPREADS

A yield spread may be either positive or negative—the former condition exists whenever a particular bond (identified for expository purposes as an I bond) provides a promised yield-to-maturity in excess of that offered on an alternative issue (A bond). A negative yield spread, on the other hand, exists whenever the I bond provides a yield less than the A bond. Moreover, yield spreads possess dynamic behavioral characteristics to the extent that the magnitude and/or direction of these differentials change over time. Definitionally, a yield spread "narrows" whenever the difference in yield becomes smaller, and it "widens" as the differential becomes greater.

Exhibit 1 provides average data on a variety of yield spreads that have prevailed in the recent past. As seen, yield spreads are rather common, and their size is subject to change. The ever-changing level of yield spreads is due to such market forces as changing levels of interest rates, variations in investor perceptions of risk, and the like. Moreover, analysis would indicate that the widespread occurrence of yield differentials is not necessarily a random event; instead, they generally behave in a fairly predictable manner. The structure of market rates suggests the presence of various types of yield differentials. They are:

1. Different *segments* of the bond market (e.g., governments versus agencies or governments versus corporates).
2. Different *sectors* of the same market segment (e.g., prime-grade municipals versus good-grade municipals or Aa utilities versus Baa utilities).
3. Different *coupons* within a given market segment/sector (e.g., current coupon governments versus deep discounted governments or new Aa industrials versus seasoned Aa industrials).
4. Different *maturities* within a given market segment/sector (e.g., short agencies versus long agencies or 3-year prime municipals versus 25-year prime municipals).

Irrespective of whether yield spreads come about as a result of segment, sector, coupon, and/or maturity differences, it is clear that they exist not independently, but because there are different market rates associated with different types of bonds. More specifically, because a structure of interest rates exists, there is prevalent in the market a structure of yield spreads. And just as certain market forces act to provide a whole structure of market rates, so too do these forces

Exhibit 1
Selected Mean Yield Spreads (yield spreads reported in basis points)

Comparisons*	1970	1971	1972	1973	1974	1975	1976	1977	1978	1979	1980
Short govts.: long govts.	+70	−4	+10	+23	+22	+68	+104	+107	+21	−33	−14
Short munies: long munies	+150	+192	+157	+95	+100	+192	+203	+176	+113	+72	+168
Long govts.: long corps.	+162	+173	+172	+75	+132	+126	+72	+56	+60	+85	+175
10-yr. govts: 10-yr. agencies	+70	+80	+53	+45	+85	+73	+26	+14	+21	+26	+39
Long munies: long corps.	+202	+217	+234	+254	+337	+307	+273	+297	+343	+403	+512
10-yr. munies: 10-yr. agencies	+256	+256	+261	+273	+301	+271	+301	+315	+361	+415	+493
Long prime munies: long good munies...	+15	+20	+10	+10	+10	+13	+18	+11	+11	+10	+16
Long Aa utils.: long Baa utils.	+75	+71	+41	+50	+141	+251	+117	+57	+63	+95	+152
Long Aa utils.: long Aa ind'ls.	−48	−44	−28	−29	−50	−54	−38	−31	−28	−49	−93
Long disct'd corps.: long curr. cpn. corps.	+76	+50	+34	+28	+51	+90	+57	+54	+42	+53	+146

Notes: The yield spreads are based on average market rates (monthly observations) existing for each of the respective market sectors; the "short" maturities are considered 3–5 years, and the "long" maturities are considered 20–25 years; unless otherwise noted, the municipals are rated as prime grade, and the corporates are represented by Aa-rated public utilities.

* The yield spreads are reported using the bond sector listed first as the benchmark (e.g., a + yield spread with the "Short govts: long govts" comparison means the latter type of issue is providing the higher average market yield).

Sources: *An Analytical Record of Yields and Yield Spreads* (New York: Salomon Brothers Inc); Board of Governors of the Federal Reserve System, *Federal Reserve Bulletin*, and "Security Price Index Record"; *Standard & Poor's Trade and Securities Statistics* (New York: Standard & Poor's Corp.).

vary over time and provide the basis for dynamic yield spread behavior.

EFFECTS ON COMPARATIVE PRICE BEHAVIOR

Although bond prices change inversely with interest rates, the *extent* to which prices react is a function of certain intrinsic and market variables. Such variables would include: (1) the *coupon* that the issue bears, (2) the bond's *term-to-maturity,* (3) the *level* of beginning market rates, and (4) the *direction* and *amount* of change in rates. The behavior of the *structure of yield spreads* is also important in this regard, however, as it can affect *comparative* yield-to-maturity performance—and in so doing, lead to different degrees of change in yield, different price behavior, and therefore, different profit (realized yield) opportunities. As indicated above, yield spreads possess two major dimensions, both of which are important in bond investment decisions: (1) the direction of initial yield spreads—whether they are positive or negative and (2) the change in yield spreads over time—whether they widen or narrow. When both of these dimensions exist, the behavior of yield spreads over time can be categorized according to certain, established performance patterns:

1. Prevailing yield spreads are *normal* with regard to magnitude and direction, but they are expected to:
   a. Widen over time.
   b. Narrow over time.
2. Prevailing yield spreads are subject to *magnitudinal anomalies*—that is, they are temporarily unusually narrow (or wide)—but are expected to:
   a. Widen (or narrow) to a more normal spread—the more likely alternative.
   b. Narrow (or widen) even more—least likely alternative.
3. Prevailing yield spreads are subject to *directional anomalies*—that is, they are temporarily positive (or negative), although they normally are just the opposite—but are expected to:
   a. Return to their normal directional stance—the more likely alternative.
   b. Maintain the directional anomaly—least likely alternative.

These patterns can behave in the manners indicated either (1) when market rates undergo increases or decreases or (2) when rates remain stable over a given period of time—a condition that is particularly important when temporary anomalies (patterns 2 and 3 above) exist.

When the initial yield spread equals zero, and there is no change in the differential over time, it should be clear that the relative behavior (price change and potential realized yield) of *comparable*[1] issues will be identical—irrespective of what happens to market rates. In contrast, when beginning yield spreads are greater than zero but remain unchanged over time, the comparative performance of the alternative issues is no longer identical. For even though the magnitude of the spread does not change over the investment horizon, *the presence of an initial differential is sufficient to cause differences in price and realized yield behavior.*

There are several behavior characteristics that hold regardless of the direction of change in market rates. That is, so long as the size (and direction) of the yield spread does not change, then the alternative (comparable) issues must undergo the same amount of change in promised yield, and their prices must (necessarily) move in the same direction. Most important, given two comparable issues, *the one with the lowest beginning price* (highest beginning yield) *will always provide the superior realized yield*—albeit the difference in realized yields will usually be very small (often 8–10 basis points, or less). Of course, the size of the initial yield spread is also important, since it directly determines the extent to which one issue would be more desirable than its alternative.

The More Common Case of Changing Yield Spreads

Changes in the yield spread dimension over a particular investment horizon are important, since such behavior will lead to differences in respective yield-to-maturity changes. If we assume a beginning yield spread of zero (in order to eliminate the price influence of an initial yield spread), it follows that the way the yield spread *changes over time* can, in itself, produce substantial differences in comparative bond performance, since a change in the yield spread generates more favorable yield-to-maturity changes for one bond than for the other. And like the presence of an initial yield spread, the greater the change in the yield differential, the greater the influence on comparative bond performance. However, in relation to the presence of an initial yield spread, the change component is, by far, the more powerful. This can be seen in Exhibit 2, which illustrates the impact of yield spreads on comparative bond price and realized yield behavior. Notice that when yield spreads change over time, the bond with the superior return is the one that undergoes the greatest change (drop) in yield—which, of course, was caused by the change in yield spread.

---

[1] Initially, attention will be centered on the comparative price and return performance of bonds that are similar with respect to two of the important features that affect price volatility: coupon and term-to-maturity; as a result, we can consider these bonds to be "comparable" obligations.

Exhibit 2
Effects of Yield Spreads on Comparative Bond Price Behavior

Assumptions: 1. Both issues are 10 percent, 20-year bonds.
           2. Market rates (in general) move from 14 percent to 12 percent in the course of a year.

	Now		One Year Later		Change in Promised Yield	Price Appreciation	Realized Yield
	Yield	Price	Yield	Price			
I. 1 percent initial yield spread; no change in spread over time:							
Bond A..........	14%	$735.30	12%	$850.90	−2%	$115.60	29.32%
Bond I...........	13	$789.50	11	920.30	−2%	130.80	29.24
Yield spread......	1%		1%				
II. No initial yield spread; spread widens (to 1 percent) over time:							
Bond A..........	14%	$735.30	12%	$850.90	−2%	$115.60	29.32%
Bond I...........	14	735.30	11	920.30	−3	185.00	38.76
Yield spread......	0%		1%				
III. 1 percent initial yield spread; spread widens (to 2 percent) over time:							
Bond A..........	14%	$735.30	12%	$850.90	−2%	$115.60	29.32%
Bond I...........	13	789.50	10	1000.00	−3	210.50	39.34
Yield spread......	1%		2%				

Combining the effects of beginning yield spreads with changes in such differentials, there are always but two yield spread conditions that lead to superior performance on the part of a given issue: (1) *positive* beginning yield spreads that *narrow* over time and (2) *negative* differentials that *widen*. These are universal and fundamental behavioral patterns that affect yield-to-maturity change in a positive manner and, in so doing, provide superior comparative realized yield. The best performance, in effect, is obtained with the issue under evaluation (the I bond) when yield spreads change in a direction opposite that of the beginning differential, i.e., when positive (+) spreads narrow (−), or negative (−) spreads widen (+).

The Case of Differences in Coupons and/or Maturities

The discussion thus far has assumed that the alternative issues bear identical (or comparable) nominal rates and terms-to-maturity. Yet in the vast majority of actual investment situations, differences will exist in alternative coupons and/or maturities. Thus, although the various yield spread patterns as set out above will continue to exert their influence on changes in respective yield-to-maturity, it should be clear that respective price and realized yield performance will be affected by coupon and maturity differentials.

It follows that if the I bond (or A bond) provides the best return when coupons and maturities are identical, then that same alternative obviously will generate an even more favorable return when it carries the lower coupon and longer maturity. Under all other circumstances, including the condition in which one issue carries the lower coupon but the shorter maturity, the basic rule of performance may be stated as follows: The forces of differing coupons and maturities *will predominate* **unless** the change in yield spread is sufficient to provide more than offsetting effects on change in yield-to-maturity.

INVESTOR IMPLICATIONS

Along with other market and intrinsic factors, yield spreads clearly rank as an important force within the bond investment decision. In fact, such differentials are particularly important when the investment process is properly viewed as one involving an alternative use of funds. Within the multidimensional aspects of yield spreads, the change criterion has been identified as the more powerful and therefore the more critical variable. By itself a change in the magnitude and/or direction of a yield spread can lead to substantial differences in comparative bond performance.

We can identify three market conditions in which yield spreads would be particularly important:

1. A *normal* beginning spread that is expected to become *abnormal* (i.e., the direction of the spread is expected to change to an abnormal positive or negative, and/or the size is anticipated to move to an abnormally wide or narrow position).
2. A beginning yield spread that is *abnormal* (with regard to direction and/or size) but is expected to become *normal*.
3. A *normal* beginning spread that is expected to change but remain *normal*, with an anticipated *major* drop in interest rates (i.e., with a major swing in market rates would come a major change in the size, but not direction, of the spread).

Obviously, economic and market analysis would be necessary in order to formulate the foregoing expectations. Yet each of the three conditions possesses at least one common characteristic: The potential exists for yield spreads to undergo *substantial* change.

Having identified the market conditions that can provide differences in alternative investment returns, the next step is to pin down the type of anticipated yield spread behavior. Since each of the three market conditions is based on the premise that a normal or abnormal yield spread exists initially, it follows that both dimensions of yield differentials must be considered at the point of investment. Other things being equal, so long as a positive (+) beginning yield spread exists and it is expected to narrow (−) over time, then the *higher* yielding issue would provide the greater return. Conversely, if a negative (−) yield spread exists initially and is expected to widen (+), the *lower* yielding bond would be superior. Under any other set of conditions/expectations—for example, a positive (+) yield spread is expected to widen (+)—it follows that the counterpart lower (or higher) yielding issue would be the preferable obligation.

Of course if a considerable difference exists in comparative coupons and/or maturities, the investor would have to evaluate the possible effects of such differentials on alternative price and realized yield behavior. All else the same, the above selection procedures would apply with any one of the three market conditions and in any interest-rate environment. Actually, by identifying the market condition, the investor would have a handle on the type of anticipated yield spread behavior. And with the noted selection procedures, the investor would possess the means of identifying the issue with the greatest potential. For example, if a negative spread is abnormally narrow but is expected to move to its normal relationship, such an expectation implies that the negative (−) spread should widen (+); as a result, the *lower yielding* bond(s) should be selected.

Such knowledge of yield spreads should enable the investor to capitalize on temporary yield spread anomalies, to gain the most from anticipated major swings in market rates, and to identify certain bonds (or sectors of the bond market) that, because of anticipated behavior of yield spreads, promise the greater return potential. Conversely, it allows investors to eliminate certain candidates because of their inherently undesirable yield spread attributes. In effect, by correctly determining the existing conditions and anticipated behavior of yield spreads, it is possible to specify issues that, all other things equal, possess the possibility for substantially improved investment return.

Analysis of Yield Curves*

32

MARTIN L. LEIBOWITZ, Ph.D.
Managing Director
Bond Portfolio Analysis Group
Salomon Brothers Inc

THE YIELD CURVE

The traditional "yield curve" plots the yields of fixed income securities against their respective maturities. When the securities plotted are comparable in quality and structure, then the resulting yield curve depicts the available trade-off between yield and maturity. Exhibit 1 illustrates a yield curve for Treasury securities.[1]

The yield curve has many different applications as an investment tool. Some market participants study the yield curve for clues to the market forces acting in the different maturity arenas. Some search for historical analogues by comparing the curve's current shape with sim-

---

* Reprinted from *Bond Analysis and Selection: The Proceedings of a Seminar on Bond Portfolio Management*, (Charlottesville, Va.: Financial Analysts Research Federation, 1977) pp. 1–21. (Adaptations made by the editors of the *Handbook* with permission of the author.)

Although the information in this chapter has been obtained from sources that the author believes to be reliable, Salomon Brothers Inc cannot guarantee its accuracy, and such information may be incomplete or condensed. All opinions and estimates included in this chapter constitute judgment as of this date and are subject to change without notice.

[1] The yield curve used in the illustration is that which prevailed on March 29, 1977, for Treasury securities.

Exhibit 1
The U.S. Treasury Yield Curve

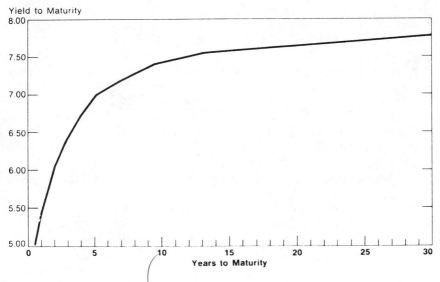

Yield to Maturity

Years to Maturity

ilar patterns obtained in the past. Some view the yield curve as reflecting the consensus expectations of the marketplace, and they use mathematical techniques to extract these implicit forecasts. Some gauge the relative value of individual securities by comparing their yield/maturity position relative to current and past yield curves. Many investment managers try to forecast the changing shape of the yield curve so that they can then position their portfolio for maximum performance. Other participants try to find "elbows" in the yield curve, *i.e.*, maturity areas which they consider to represent the most attractive short term investment.

THE YIELD CURVE AS A RETURN/RISK TRADE-OFF

The most widespread use of the yield curve is probably the one mentioned at the outset—a portrayal of the available trade-off between yield and maturity. In other words, the yield curve indicates how much additional yield can be obtained in exchange for each extension in maturity.

The basic investment problem in any market always comes down to an evaluation of the trade-off between return and risk. Since yield is a measure of total return, and since maturity is closely associated with price volatility, there is a natural temptation to accept the yield curve as depicting this return/risk trade-off. Unfortunately, this interpretation is seriously faulty on several counts.

First of all, there are a number of problems in equating maturity with risk. Maturity is not the only variable determining mathematical price volatility.[2] Price volatility is not the sole determinant of the volatility of return. And volatility of return over short-term periods is not the only (or perhaps even the primary) risk element for many bond portfolios.

With regard to equating yield with return, there is an even more fundamental problem. The concept of total return must refer to a specific investment horizon. Apart from the questions regarding coupon reinvestment,[3] a bond's conventional yield-to-maturity can be used to represent its total return—but only over an investment period coincident with the bond's remaining life.[4] The yield curve, by its very nature, consists of yields over different maturities. Since they do not refer to a common investment horizon, these yield values are not directly comparable as total returns.

As an example, consider a one-year note with a yield of 6 percent and a two-year note with a yield of 7 percent. Over a one-year investment horizon, the one-year, 6 percent note will indeed provide a total return of approximately 6 percent. However, over this same one-year period, the total return provided by the two-year note will depend greatly on its price at year's end. At that point, it will be a one-year security, and its price will then be set by the level of one-year yields. As these yields range from 5 percent to 10 percent, the note's total return will range anywhere from 4.29 percent to 8.85 percent. One can see that these total return values can depart widely from the original 7 percent yield level. In fact, the two-year note will provide a 7 percent total return over a one-year period only if one-year rates are 7 percent one year hence. In turn, this would require one-year rates to rise by 100 basis points over the course of the year.

Extrapolating from this example, the total return provided by any security on the yield curve can thus be seen to depend on the yield curve that will prevail at the end of the investment horizon.

HORIZON ANALYSIS APPLIED TO THE YIELD CURVE

Since no one can predict future yield curves with certainty, there is a corresponding uncertainty in the total returns from any security on the yield curve. However, portfolio managers must come to grips with this uncertainty in one way or another. At the very least, they must be

---

[2] For a discussion of the factors that affect bond price volatility, see Chapter 4 and Chapter 35 on duration.

[3] See Chapter 4 for a discussion of interest-on-interest and its role in computing the total return of a bond.

[4] See Chapter 4 for a discussion of the difference between a promised yield and a realized yield.

able to translate their market judgment(s) into the corresponding total return implications for the various maturity sectors along the yield curve. The technique of "horizon analysis" can prove helpful in this translation process.

Essentially, horizon analysis distinguishes the return achieved under "nominal market conditions" from the return achieved by departures from these nominal conditions. In Chapter 29, the nominal condition was defined to be that of "constant yield over time." Recalling the example of a two-year note with a yield of 7 percent, this "constant-yield" condition would imply a total return of 7 percent over a one-year horizon. If one-year rates actually fell to 6 percent, i.e., 1 percent below the nominal 7 percent level, then the total return would become 7.92 percent. In fact, for every basis point that one-year rates at the horizon fell below the nominal 7 percent level, the total return will be boosted by approximately .92 basis points. This volatility factor of .92 is called the horizon volatility.

There are several advantages in being able to break down prospective return into a "nominal-condition" return plus a return component derived through a "departure-from-the-nominal-condition." First of all, one can distinguish the returns derived through the passage of time from the return achieved through market movements. In fact, by using the horizon volatility factor, changes in market yields can be immediately translated into changes in total return. In the context of a bond or sector swap,[5] horizon analysis allows the swap's incremental return to be decomposed into three basic components:

1. A pure yield pickup component, resulting from the accumulation of the original yields over time, independent of any market changes.
2. A rate anticipation component dependent on the change in overall market levels as magnified by an increase in the horizon volatilities of the two bonds (or sectors).
3. A spread component, determined solely by the changing yield spread relationships between the two bonds or sectors.

In other words, horizon analysis facilitates the manager's ability to relate his judgment regarding conventional market variables—yields, yield spreads, and the changes in yields and yield spreads over time— to total return performance. This structuring also enables the manager to clearly see the effect of departures from his primary expectations, and this can assist in evaluating the nature and magnitude of the risks associated with a contemplated course of action.

It would be most helpful if a simple structuring, along the lines of horizon analysis, could be made applicable to the yield curve.

---

[5] A sector swap is discussed in Chapter 30.

However, at the outset, the preceding method runs into a problem with its use of the constant yield as a nominal market condition. The very nature of yield curve implies some change in a bond's yield with the passage of time. Consequently, the constant-yield approach must be revised before horizon analysis can even begin to be usefully applied to the yield curve.

The problem is to find a reasonable, convenient, and well-defined yield structure that can serve as a benchmark for nominal market conditions at the end of the investment horizon. There are a number of candidates for this nominal yield structure—the existing yield curve, the implied "forward" yield curve, the individual manager's expected yield curve, etc. However, the simplest approach is to work with the existing yield curve itself.

When the *existing* yield curve is used to define the nominal market conditions at *future* horizons, then each bond's nominal future yield is simply determined by the passage of time along the yield curve. This process is often described as "rolling down the yield curve." For that reason, we refer to this nominal total return as the bond's "rolling yield."

THE ROLLING YIELD

A security's rolling yield can be determined by a relatively simple calculation, at least in theory. Exhibit 2 provides an illustration.

Exhibit 2
Calculation of a Rolling Yield (a three-year 6.5 percent par bond rolling down to a 2.5-year yield curve value of 6.3 percent over a six-month horizon)

Coupon income (as percent of par)		3.250%
Reinvestment income (as percent of par)		0.000
Market Appreciation:		
Nominal price six months hence based on yield curve value of 6.3 percent	100.456	
Price today	(100.000)	
Price appreciation	.456	.456
Total return as percent of par		3.706%
Total return as percent of initial market value		3.706%
Annualized total return (rolling yield)		7.410%

Suppose the prevailing yield curve has yield levels of 6.5 percent for three-year maturities and 6.3 percent for 2.5-year maturities. A three-year 6.5 percent bond lying on the yield curve would then be priced at par to yield 6.5 percent. We wish to compute this bond's rolling yield over a six-month investment horizon.

The total return consists of three components—market appreciation, coupon income, and reinvestment income (or more generally, the time value of coupon payments). In this particular example, reinvestment income—usually only a negligible factor over short-term horizons—is completely eliminated.

Coupon income consists of one semiannual coupon payment of 3.25 percent.

The market appreciation is derived from the yield changes associated with rolling down the yield curve for the six-month period. At the end of this period, under the assumed nominal condition of a constant-yield curve, the bond will be priced at the curve's 2.5-year value, i.e., at 6.3 percent. At this yield, the original par bond will be priced at 100.456.[6]

The total points of return (as a percentage of par) thus sum up to 3.706 percent. Since we are dealing with a bond originally priced at par, this 3.706 percent figure also represents the total return as a percentage of initial market value.

Finally, by annualizing this return figure, we obtain the bond's rolling yield of 7.41 percent.

It is interesting to note that this rolling yield of 7.41 percent exceeds the original 6.5 percent conventional yield-to-maturity by 91 basis points!

THE ROLLING YIELD CURVE

The basic yield curve consists of a plot of conventional yield against maturity for a set of comparable securities (e.g., the U.S. Treasury market). When the conventional yield for each security is replaced by the corresponding rolling yield, the resulting plot may be called a rolling yield curve.

Exhibit 3 shows the rolling yield curve, based on a six-month investment horizon, corresponding to the basic yield curve depicted in Exhibit 1.

It is instructive to compare Exhibits 1 and 3.

The most striking characteristic of the rolling yield curve is that essentially all the rolling yield values exceed the basic yield curve values for the same maturity. This "boost" in the rolling yield is derived from the process of rolling down to lower yield values over time (see Exhibit 2). This effect will always be seen with positively sloped—i.e., ascending—yield curves. (An opposite effect will occur in the case of inverted—i.e., descending—yield curves.)

The magnitude of this boost of the rolling yield above the basic yield varies widely across the maturity scale. The basic yield curve of

---

[6] To maintain the simplicity of this example, we have purposely neglected a number of practically important problems: determining the exact shape of the yield curve, finding the location over time of individual securities relative to the curve itself, the whole question of transaction costs, etc.

Exhibit 3
The Rolling Yield Curve

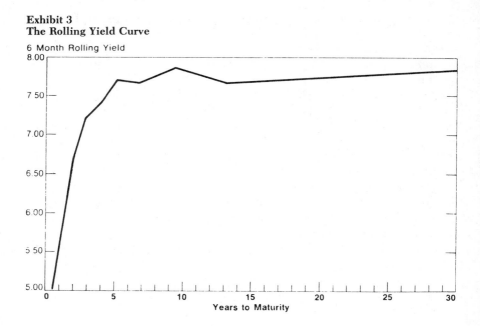

Exhibit 1 has the property that the slope is greatest for the shorter maturities. For such yield curves, the roll-down in yield—when measured in basis points—will naturally also be greatest at the shorter maturities. However, the boost in return depends on price volatility as well as the basis-point size of the roll-down. As maturity shortens, the roll-down in basis points may increase, but its effect on return will be partially offset by the decline in price volatility. For example, with a six-month security, there will be no price volatility at all at the six-month horizon. Consequently, there will of course be no boost in return regardless of the steepness of the underlying yield curve at that point.

This conflict between increasing roll-down and decreasing price volatility will often lead to the boost in return reaching its maximum value at some point among the intermediate maturities. Moreover, when this boost effect is overlaid on a typical positively sloped yield curve, one will often see a peak in the rolling yield curve itself. In Exhibit 3 we see that this peak is reached at the ninth year.

INTERPRETING ROLLING YIELD CURVES

By definition, the rolling yield curve shows the total return that will be realized by each security on the yield curve provided that the yield curve remains exactly constant over the investment horizon.

In contrast to the conventional yields, rolling yields represent total returns over a common investment horizon. Consequently, rolling yields are directly comparable with one another. This comparability of individual rolling yields makes it possible to interpret the rolling yield curve in a number of interesting ways.

The rolling yield curve can be viewed as a plot of nominal returns against maturity. For example, consider the rolling yield curve shown in Exhibit 3. Apart from any changes in the underlying yield curve, Exhibit 3 tells us that an investment in a one-year security will provide a total return of 5.62 percent, a two-year security will provide a return of 6.7 percent, etc. Thus, the rolling yield curve depicts the trade-off between comparable *nominal* returns and maturity.

Pursuing this tack one step further, the rolling yield curve also shows the compensation in (nominal) return for a given extension in maturity. Thus, Exhibit 3 shows that a one-year extension from one year to two years increases the rolling yield from 5.62 percent to 6.7 percent, a jump of 108 basis points. However, a one-year extension from four years to five years achieves an improvement in rolling yield from 7.42 percent to 7.71 percent, or 29 basis points.

Similarly, the slope of the rolling yield curve indicates the rate of nominal compensation for every month of extension. (However, as noted earlier, each month of maturity extension incurs different degrees of maturity risk.)

If the rolling yield curve reaches a maximum, then there is no compensation in *nominal* return for further extension of maturity. Any manager extending his maturity beyond this point would presumably have expectations of favorable changes in the yield curve, i.e., lower overall rates and/or a flattening of the curve in the longer maturities.

Peaks in the rolling yield curve are often associated with the so-called elbow points in the underlying yield curve. In fact, one could argue that the common market practice of searching for elbows has value precisely because of this association with maximum or near-maximum rolling yields. By making these relationships explicit, the rolling yield curve can assist in determining the relative risks and rewards of moderate departures from a given elbow point.

The rolling yield curve can also be interpreted as the sequence of short-term returns provided by a security at various points in its life. For example, the 13-year value of 7.67 percent in Exhibit 3 says that a 13-year bond would provide a return of 7.67 percent over the first six-month period—as long as the yield curve remains unchanged. Over the next six months, this same security will generate—again assuming an unchanged yield curve—a return of 7.7 percent, i.e., the rolling yield curve value associated with the 12.5-year maturity. And so on for each succeeding six-month period. This leads to the observation that the security will produce its greatest return over the six-month period that begins when its remaining life has declined to nine years. After this point, the return falls period by period until it reaches the minimum return of 5 percent in the last six-month period. Of course, all of this transpires only under the rather strong assumption that the yield curve remains unchanged over the entire 13 years.

Nevertheless, this interpretation is rather intriguing because it quantifies the concept that there is an optimal time to sell every bond as it rolls down the yield curve.

The rolling yield curve can also be useful in constructing "bridge swaps." By combining two bonds with different maturities, one can create a "bond package" having an average maturity somewhere between the two original bonds. Similarly, this bond package will have an average rolling yield lying somewhere between the rolling yields of the two bonds. In fact, by adjusting the mixture ratio, one can obtain a bond package falling anywhere on a straight line drawn between the rolling yield curve plots of the original two bonds. Suppose this straight line (i.e., the "bridge" across two maturity points) passes significantly below the plot of a third bond on the rolling yield curve. Then, as illustrated in Exhibit 4, a swap out of the appropriately mixed bond package into this third bond can result in an increase in rolling yield while maintaining the same average maturity.

Once again, we must caution that such a swap—like the rolling yield itself—depends upon a constant yield curve. In addition, bond

Exhibit 4
A Bridge Swap

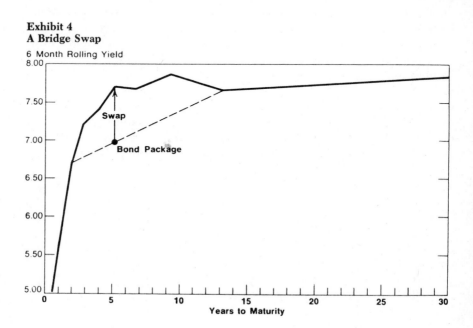

packages with the same average maturity can differ widely in their volatility characteristics.[7]

ROLLING YIELDS AND CHANGING YIELD CURVES

Of course, yield curves do change—and sometimes change rather violently. Any comprehensive approach to yield curve analysis must deal with the prospect of both expected and unexpected changes in the yield curve.

Any such change will produce realized returns for a given bond that will be higher or lower than its rolling yield. The more adverse the change in the yield curve, the more the realized return will drop below its rolling yield. The more favorable the change in the yield curve, the greater the extent by which the realized return will exceed the rolling yield.

The rolling yield thus serves as benchmark, fully capturing the total return implications of the existing yield curve. One can then focus on potential changes from the existing curve—shifts in overall level as well as sharpenings and/or flattenings at various maturity points. For each maturity, the sum of these changes will result in a given yield move away from the existing curve. Such changes in yield can readily be translated into their approximate value as increments (or decrements) of total return.[8] But the point is that each of these increments (or decrements) of total return must be added to (or subtracted from) the rolling yield.

By serving this role as a total return benchmark for the existing yield curve, rolling yields can help clarify the impact of prospective market changes that may move the yield curve away from its present level and shape.

PARALLEL SHIFTS

The simplest form of yield curve change is the "parallel shift," where all yields undergo exactly the same basis-point move. Exhibit 5 illustrates a parallel shift of +50 basis points in the U.S. Treasury yield curve shown in Exhibit 1.[9]

For any given security, a yield move leads to a corresponding change in price. In turn, this will affect the security's total return over

---

[7] This fundamental problem can be partially overcome by substituting horizon volatility for maturity as a measure of price volatility. (See Chapter 29.)

[8] The horizon volatility for each maturity point provides a handy scaling factor for this translation.

[9] It is interesting to notice that parallel shifts almost never really look "parallel" to the eye.

Exhibit 5
Yield Curves under a Parallel Shift of +50 Basis Points

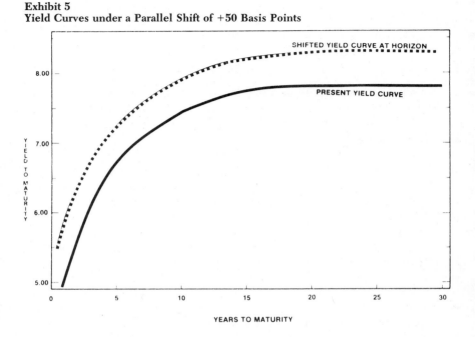

the investment horizon. For the rolling yield, this change is based upon a roll-down of the *existing* yield curve. When the yield curve itself changes, then the additional yield and price move must be incorporated into the total return calculation. This computational process is illustrated in Exhibit 6.

Exhibit 6
Calculation of Horizon Return (a three-year 6.5 percent par bond rolling down to a 2.5-year yield curve value of 6.3 percent over a six-month horizon—followed by a +50-basis-point parallel shift)

Coupon income (as percent of par).....................			3.25%
Reinvestment income (as percent of par)			0.00
Market Appreciation:			
Present yield curve value at 2.5 years..............	6.30%		
Magnitude of parallel shift	+.50		
Yield curve value six months hence at 2.5 years	6.80%		
Price six months hence based on yield curve value			
of 6.8 percent	99.32	99.32	
Price today @ 6.5 percent.......................		(100.00)	
Price appreciation		−.68	−.68%
Total return as percent of par...............			2.57%
Total return as percent of initial market			
value.....................................			2.57%
Annualized total return (rolling yield)...............			5.14%

Note: for simplicity, this example is based on rounded values and hence does not exactly correspond to Exhibit 5.

The horizon returns for all securities along the yield curve can be computed in a similar fashion. When these returns are plotted against the original maturity of each security, one obtains a graphic illustration of the effect of changing yield curves.

Exhibit 7 shows the horizon returns for the +50-basis-point parallel shift applied to the yield curve shown in Exhibit 5. Exhibit 7 also

Exhibit 7
Horizon Returns from Parallel Shift

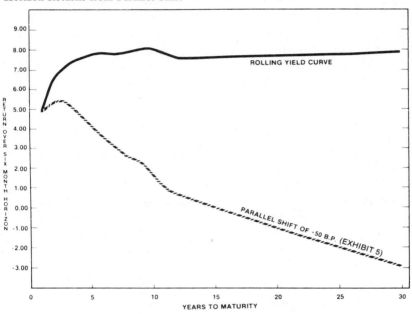

shows the rolling yield curve as a benchmark for what the horizon returns would have been without any market changes.

The pattern exhibited in Exhibit 7 can be readily explained in terms of price volatilities. The price impact of a given yield move is determined by the bond's maturity, coupon rate, and its starting yield level.[10] Among these factors, the bond's maturity usually dominates. In particular, for the "current coupon" bonds that comprise the Treasury yield curve, increasing maturity leads to increasing price volatility. In turn, this means that the parallel shift in the yield curve will have increasing price impact at the longer maturities. Consequently, the effect of any parallel shift on returns will always be greatest at the longer end of the curve.

---

[10] See Chapter 4.

By the same token, at the short end of the yield curve, the effect of a parallel shift will become smaller with decreasing maturity. In fact, for the security whose maturity coincides with the investment horizon, there will be no change whatsoever. In this study, a six-month horizon is used for all examples. The security at this point on the yield curve is the six-month Treasury bill. The rolling yield of the six-month T bill over a six-month horizon is just its original yield (on a bond equivalent basis). Moreover, the six-month T bill will obviously provide this same return over a six-month horizon no matter what changes take place in the yield curve. Consequently, this six-month maturity acts like a fixed point under all yield curve changes.

These volatility responses are clearly evident in Exhibit 7. One has the fixed point at the six-month maturity, where the rolling yield curve and the horizon return curve meet. As the maturity increases, the horizon returns depart farther and farther from the rolling yield, reflecting the increasing volatility of longer bonds. In fact, the *upward* parallel shift in the yield curve has the overall effect of a *downward* angular rotation of the rolling yield curve around the fixed point at the six-month maturity.

For an investor anticipating the parallel shifts shown in Exhibit 7, it is immediately evident that the longer maturities are to be avoided. In general, because of its simple response pattern, the investment implications of any parallel shift are usually quite obvious. There is only one problem. Actual changes in the yield curve rarely take the form of a simple parallel shift across all maturities. When the market moves, the yield curve almost always undergoes some change in shape as well as a shift in level.

CHANGING SHAPES

The reshaping that accompanies a shift movement can often have a surprisingly strong impact on the horizon returns. This is illustrated in Exhibits 8 and 9. Exhibit 8 depicts a market move where the yields in the shorter and intermediate maturities undergo a greater deterioration than yields in the longer maturities. As many investors have learned to their sorrow, such market movements are not uncommon.

Exhibit 9 shows the horizon returns resulting from this reshaping of the yield curve. One can see that in this case, the simple maxim to avoid long maturities could have led the investor astray. In Exhibit 9, the intermediate maturities are hit the hardest in terms of total return. In fact, under this market move, the very worst return is recorded at the thirteenth year, where a relatively high rolling yield value would have been obtained (i.e., if the yield curve had remained unchanged).

It is useful to contrast the effects of the shape changes shown in Exhibit 8 with the earlier examples of parallel shift. This comparison

Exhibit 8
Yield Curves under a Change in Both Shape and Level

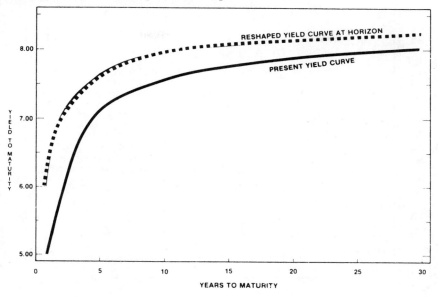

Exhibit 9
Horizon Returns from Changing Shape and Level

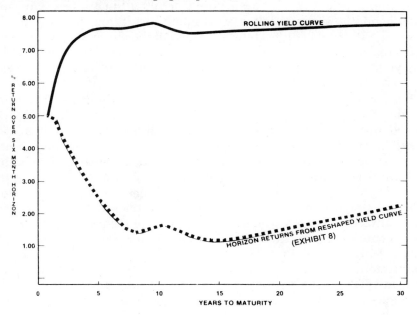

Exhibit 10
Yield Changes across Maturity

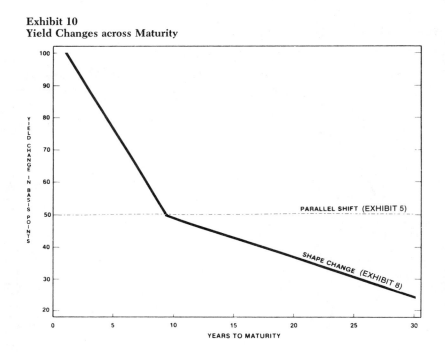

is facilitated by Exhibit 10, which depicts the respective changes in yields at each maturity. For the parallel shift, the yield change is by definition constant at +50 basis points across all maturities. On the other hand, the shape changes of Exhibit 8 result from a strong yield move of +100 basis points at the short end of the curve, with a pattern of decreasing yield changes as maturity increases. By the ninth year, this yield change declines to +50 basis points, and then decreases thereafter at a somewhat slower pace.

Exhibit 11 compares the corresponding horizon returns. One can see that there are two points of coincidence. The first of these is the six-month "fixed point," where the six-month horizon return is unaffected by any change in yields. The second point of coincidence is at the ninth year, where the +50-basis-point yield change occurs in both cases, and naturally results in the same horizon return of +1.7 percent.

Between these two intersection points, the flattening shape change provides a significantly worse horizon return than the parallel shift. This is exactly what we would expect given the respective pattern of yield changes shown in Exhibit 10. At the one-year maturity, the shape change results in a +97-basis-point yield move, over 48 basis points more than the parallel shift. However, because of the limited horizon volatility of the one-year maturity, this leads only to a small difference in horizon returns. On the other hand, at the two-year matu-

Exhibit 11
Comparison of Horizon Returns

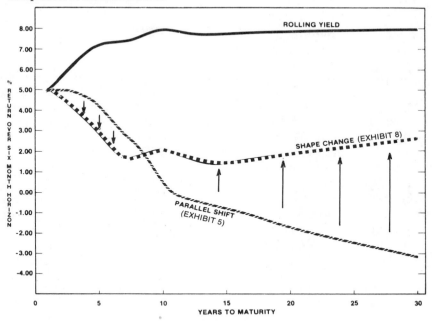

rity, the horizon volatility is sufficient to generate a −110-basis-point difference in return for the +40-basis-point difference in the yield changes. The horizon return difference grows to about −150 basis points at the third year. It remains roughly stable around this level until the seventh year. This stability is derived from the compensating effects of increasing volatility against the decreasing difference in the yield change.

At the ninth year, the horizon return curves intersect. After the ninth year, the two factors of less adverse yield changes and increasing horizon volatility work in concert. As a result, the shape change produces an increasingly better return than the parallel shift. By the 30th year, the improvement in horizon return has grown by over 5%, from −3% for the parallel shift to +2.4% for the shape change.

Thus, it is clear that changing yield curve shapes can have powerful impact on horizon returns. Consequently, there is a need for techniques to help the portfolio manager in evaluating the effect of potential shape changes. However, in trying to develop such techniques, one immediately encounters a problem in the bewildering profusion of yield curve shapes that can and do arise in the marketplace. One way to come to grips with this problem is to find a simple way for classifying yield curve movements. The first step in this direction is to break down yield curve changes into a parallel shift followed by a series of sharpenings and flattenings.

Classification of Yield Curve Changes

In Exhibit 8 the intermediate nine-year maturity undergoes a +50-basis-point change. Suppose this nine-year point is selected as a "benchmark maturity" to define the parallel shift component. Then this parallel shift of +50 basis points can be viewed as the first component in the yield curve's total process of change. The remaining changes will then consist of relative "twists" that act to sharpen or flatten the slopes along the curve.

To help visualize this process as it applies to the shape change in Exhibit 8 consider the yield changes plotted in Exhibit 10. In this particular situation, we clearly have the parallel shift of +50 basis points at the ninth year, plus two flattening twists. From the six-month point to the ninth-year benchmark, the yield change declines from +100 basis points to +50 basis points. At the six-month point, this represents a "short-end up-twist" of 50 basis points above and beyond the parallel shift of +50 basis points. Similarly, from the 9th year to the 30th year, the changes decline from +50 basis points to +25 basis points. This 25-basis-point flattening could be viewed as the result of a uniform "long-end down-twist" having a magnitude of 25 basis points when measured in the 30th year.

As Exhibit 10 illustrates, this combination of a parallel shift plus the two twists completely describes the yield curve change. This rather pat fit is, of course, a result of the particular situation chosen for Exhibit 8.

Whenever the yield curve change can be defined in this simple form, the resulting horizon return curve can be visualized as developing from a parallel shift followed by up-twists or down-twists on either side of the benchmark maturity. The parallel shift first leads to a horizon return curve that approximates the angular rotation of the rolling yield. If the shape change consists of a short-end up-twist affecting the maturities preceding the benchmark, then the horizon returns will be depressed below the return levels of parallel shift. The difference in the returns, relative to the parallel shift, will start at zero at the six-month maturity, plummet to some trough value, and then rise to zero again at the benchmark maturity. If a long-end down-twist occurs beyond the benchmark maturity, then the horizon returns will be boosted above the level of the rotated rolling yield curve. The magnitude of this boost will grow with increasing maturity.

On a relative basis, we would see these same effects from up-twists and down-twists regardless of whether the parallel shift was in a positive or negative direction. This has a number of important practical implications. For example, the return from a "bridge swap" tends to be relatively independent from the effects of parallel shifts in either direction. However, up-twists and down-twists can have a severe impact on the profitability of such swaps. Thus, in a short-end up-twist, in the maturities preceding the benchmark, the shorter securities in the bridge will undergo a greater relative upward yield move. In such situations, the horizon return from a bond package can differ significantly from the return provided by the corresponding maturity point on the yield curve.

In the many instances where yield curve changes can be approximated in terms of up-twists or down-twists on either side of an appropriately chosen benchmark security, the horizon returns can be visualized as consisting of three components:

1. The rolling yield curve.
2. An angular rotation of the rolling yield curve to match the shift at the benchmark maturity.
3. The different relative return effects of up-twists or down-twists in the maturities preceding and following the benchmark. These effects can be summarized as follows:
    a. *Short-end up-twist* (i.e., increased rates in maturities preceding the benchmark). This will create a "bulge" depression in relative return, growing in magnitude to a maximum trough level at some maturity between the relative fixed points at six months and the benchmark maturity.
    b. *Short-end down-twist* (i.e., lower relative rates in maturities preceding the benchmark). This will create an upward bulge in relative return, peaking at some interim point between six months and the benchmark.
    c. *Long-end down-twist* (i.e., decreased relative rates in longer maturities beyond the benchmark). The relative return becomes increasingly favorable with the longer maturities.
    d. *Long-end up-twist* (i.e., increased relative rates in the longer maturities beyond the benchmark). The relative return becomes increasingly negative with the longer maturities.

As illustrated in Exhibit 11, these relative return effects from up-twists and/or down-twists can override the shift changes in the overall level of rates. With this classification system for yield curve changes, we can quickly isolate the key components of return that would affect any contemplated portfolio action.

There are certain patterns of change that cannot be adequately described by a parallel shift followed by only two simple segment twist effects such as in Exhibit 10. However, even complex patterns of change can be approximated (as closely as desired) by a series of up-twists and down-twists over a sufficient number of consecutive maturity segments.

PROPORTIONAL CHANGES IN YIELDS

Up to this point, a yield curve change has been treated as a movement from the present curve to a single, well-defined future curve. In practice, there will always be a certain range of uncertainty surrounding any anticipated future yield curve. It is usually wise to consider how this range of uncertainty can affect the pattern of horizon returns. Once again, this effort can quickly become bogged down in the bewildering range of possible shapes and patterns of change that the market might thrust upon us. However, there is a way to extend the preceding classification system so that it can easily depict the evolution of a wide range of possible future yield curves.

The key assumption is that of "proportional changes" across maturities for each basis point of parallel shift in the benchmark maturity. As an example, consider the pattern of change illustrated in Exhibit 10. When the benchmark nine-year maturity shifts by +50 basis points, the six-month maturity undergoes a change of +100 basis points. Now suppose that the six-month maturity maintained this same change ratio of 2 : 1 over a range of shifts in the nine-year benchmark. For example, if the nine-year benchmark shifted by only 25 basis points, then the proportional change in the six-month maturity would be 50 basis points. More generally, whatever the benchmark shift, there would be exactly twice that move in the six-month maturity. Similarly, the 30-year maturity would also maintain the same change ratio and would move only 50 basis points for every 100-basis-point shift in the benchmark. In essence, this technique provides a way to define a relative yield response pattern. In this case, the response pattern was based on beliefs that the yield curve will flatten and sharpen in a particular way. This pattern of change could also be made to reflect beliefs regarding the differential volatilities of rates at various maturities. Thus, one could interpret this response pattern as a statement that six-month maturities are twice as volatile in yield as nine-year maturities, etc.

With proportional changes relative to the benchmark defined in this fashion, a whole spectrum of yield curves can be constructed. Exhibit 12 shows the spectrum of yield curves that would be associated with shifts of 0, +10, +20, +30, +40, and +50 basis points in the nine-year benchmark. Each benchmark shift creates a pattern of change for all maturities in accordance with the proportional changes defined in Exhibit 10.

Different patterns of proportional yield responses might be anticipated if the shift in the yield curve were downward rather than upward. To accommodate this dual pattern, two expected yield curves could be defined—one based on a pessimistic scenario (e.g., Exhibit 8) and the other based on an optimistic scenario. Each curve then

Exhibit 12
A Spectrum of Yield Curves

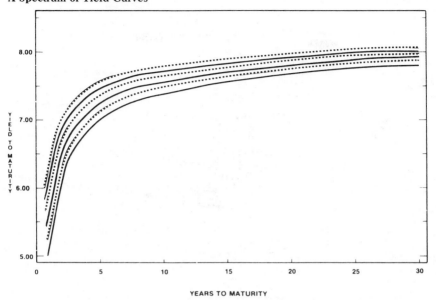

YEARS TO MATURITY

determines a pattern of change across maturities (e.g., Exhibit 10). (In fact, the revised yield curve itself can be determined by a small number of estimated changes. For example, the pessimistic yield curve in Exhibit 8 could be defined by three yield changes: +100 basis points at six months, +50 basis points at 9 years and +25 basis points at 30 years.) This pessimistic scenario can then be used to define a pattern of proportional yield change relative to any given benchmark shift in a pessimistic direction. By applying this technique to a sequence of incremental shifts, one can obtain a spectrum of yield curves that move toward and finally coincide with the originally defined pessimistic yield curve (e.g., Exhibit 12).

An identical procedure could then be taken with respect to changes in the optimistic direction.

A SPECTRUM OF HORIZON RETURNS

Each curve in the spectrum shown in Exhibit 12 corresponds to a certain change from the present yield curve. Consequently, each curve will generate a characteristic pattern of horizon returns. This corresponding spectrum of horizon returns is shown in Exhibit 13.

The yield curves of Exhibit 12 are related in an inverse sequence to the horizon returns of Exhibit 13. Thus, the present yield curve (i.e., the one reflecting a scenario of no market movement) lies at the *bot-*

Exhibit 13
A Spectrum of Horizon Returns

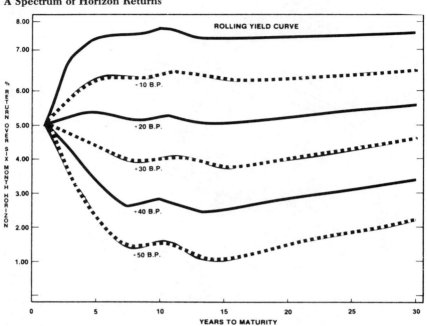

tom of the spectrum in Exhibit 12. The corresponding horizon return graph is the rolling yield curve lying at the *top* of the spectrum in Exhibit 13. By the same token, the most pessimistic yield curve lies at the top in Exhibit 12, while its corresponding horizon return curve is naturally the lowest one in Exhibit 13.

Each of these horizon return curves corresponds to the rotation from a parallel shift followed by the two twist effects. In the two- to nine-year range, the up-twist acts to first straighten out and then to reverse the strong upward slope of the rolling yield curve. In the longer maturities, the different horizon return curves are almost parallel. This is due to the down-twist almost offsetting the volatility increases at the longer maturities. For the 20-basis-point shift, these effects combine to produce a virtually flat return curve.

These spectrums must be recognized as highly simplified approximations of a very complex process. However, they do permit an investor to explore the impact of different kinds of yield curve movements on horizon returns. This exploration can often result in some surprising findings. For example, if Exhibit 13 represented an investor's beliefs, he would see that the longest maturities are not necessarily the most volatile. He would also see that the maturity where the rolling yield reaches its peak, the nine-year maturity, may actually represent quite a high risk sector.

Under the most pessimistic assumption, i.e., the bottom curve, the investor would be reluctant to extend beyond the six-month T bill. However, if his expectations were distributed more equally across all six curves, the investor would clearly extend at least to the one-year T bill and possibly to the third or fourth year. By the same token, unless he had considerable faith in the most optimistic of the six curves, he would probably be reluctant to extend beyond the fifth year. It should be remembered that this example is restricted to the essentially pessimistic spectrum represented in Exhibit 13.

In general, by selecting one or more patterns of proportional yield changes, the investor can explore a wide spectrum of horizon return curves that would result from changing yield curves. The effects of both optimistic and pessimistic changes can then be examined. The impact of various types of shape changes can be studied through alternative patterns of proportional yield changes. By associating different horizons with different degrees of shift in the benchmark maturity, one can visualize the evolution of various return curves over time.

In the final analysis, all investment decisions come down to a trade-off between risk and return. This trade-off is clearly present in decisions relating to the maturity structure of a fixed income portfolio. The current shape of the yield curve and prospective changes in its shape constitute critical factors in this trade-off. With this extension of the rolling yield technique, the investor can examine explicit representations of the risk/return trade-off over a wide range of assumed yield curve conditions.

Riding the Yield Curve to Improved Returns on Money Market Portfolios

33

MICHAEL D. JOEHNK, Ph.D., C.F.A.
Professor and Chairman
Department of Finance
Arizona State University

Without sacrificing the basic liquidity objective of a money market portfolio, it is possible for a financial manager to increase the rate of return earned from short-term securities by employing a trading technique called riding the yield curve. If all works out according to expectations, riding the yield curve enables a portfolio manager to earn a rate of return higher than prevailing holding period rates. In effect, the investor/portfolio manager purchases a security with a maturity longer than the anticipated holding period and then sells it before it matures to take advantage of the capital appreciation that results from a stable upward-sloping yield curve. For example, suppose a money manager has funds to invest for 90 days; he or she has two options: (1) to buy a 90-day security and hold it to maturity or (2) to buy a longer issue and sell it in the open market after 90 days (e.g., buy a six-month instrument and then sell it 90 days later when the issue still has three months remaining to maturity). The latter approach—of buying and selling the longer maturity—is known as riding the yield curve. The material that follows will examine riding the yield curve as a trading technique. We begin by illustrating its sources of extra return; this is followed by the development of a measure of expected return, which can be used along with potential risk exposure to assess the desirability of riding the yield curve.[1]

SOURCES OF RETURN FROM RIDING THE YIELD CURVE

The situation depicted in Exhibit 1 can be used to demonstrate the sources of extra return from riding the yield curve. This yield curve is upward sloping (a necessary condition), with two-year bonds selling to yield 9 percent and one-year bonds selling at yields of 8 percent.

Exhibit 1
Riding a Yield Curve

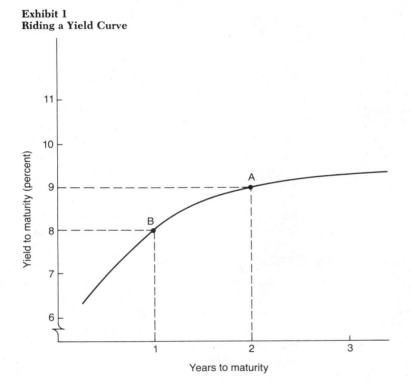

Years to maturity

To illustrate riding the yield curve, consider an investor with $1,000 in investable funds and a one-year investment horizon. He or she could meet this one year investment goal by purchasing the two-year, 9 percent bond (point A). One year later, after having received annual interest of $90, the investor could sell the bond for approximately $1,009.26—so long as the prevailing rate on one-year bonds

---

[1] This chapter was adapted from an article written, in part, by the author. See Edward A. Dyl and Michael D. Joehnk, "Riding the Yield Curve: Does it Work?" *Journal of Portfolio Management*, Spring 1981, pp. 13–17.

remains at 8 percent (point B). The price of $1,009.26 results from the fact that a one-year, 9 percent bond must sell for this amount if it is to return an 8 percent yield to maturity. Upon selling the bond, the investor would have generated capital gains of $9.26 (by selling the issue for more than he or she paid for it) and earned $90 in interest. The total earnings of $99.26 on an investment of $1,000 would thus provide a one-year return of almost 10 percent (versus the 9 percent promised yield). Clearly, by investing in the higher yielding end of the yield curve, the portfolio manager can not only invest at a *higher initial yield* (9 percent versus 8 percent), but also may be able to *realize an even higher return* (9.93 percent versus 9 percent) via the capital gains that accrue from moving down the yield curve and selling the issue (at point B) at a yield that is less than that which existed when the bond was purchased.

It is important to notice that the crucial factor in riding the yield curve is that (at the minimum) the yield curve remains the same—or approximately so—over the holding period. For if the yield curve flattens out or shifts upward, the trading profit will be smaller than anticipated or may even disappear. Indeed, with a significant upswing in interest rates, substantial losses could result. Conversely, of course, the profit would increase if the curve's slope were to steepen or if rates in general were to fall. In any event, since neither the yield curve nor the overall level of interest rates is likely to remain stable for a whole year, one would seldom attempt to ride the yield curve for a period as long as one year (as shown in our simplified illustration)—the risk of interest rate fluctuations would simply be too great.

A MEASURE OF EXPECTED RETURN

Securities held for liquidity purposes are generally default-free, short-term instruments, such as U.S. Treasury bills. Riding the yield curve with investments in short-term securities is much less risky than with long-term investments, because short-term securities are less price volatile than long-term securities. As an illustration of riding the yield curve using short-term securities, consider the pattern of Treasury bill yields shown in Exhibit 2. Since the yields on Treasury bills and other discount securities are computed on a bank discount basis, the yields shown in the table are annual rates based on a 360-day year.[2]

---

[2] Securities like T bills sell at a discount from their par value and are redeemed at par when they mature. Thus the interest earned is the difference between the price paid and the security's eventual maturity value (or what amounts to the same thing, interest earned = the size of the discount). As more fully described in Chapter 8, the price of a discount security is computed as

$$P = 100 - R(M/360)$$

where

P is the price per $100 of maturity value, R is the interest yield (stated on a bank discount basis), and M is the number of days to maturity.

Exhibit 2
Illustrative T Bill Yields

Weeks to Maturity	Yield* Bid	Yield* Ask	Weeks to Maturity	Yield* Bid	Yield* Ask
1.............	11.15%	11.09%	14.............	12.10%	11.99%
2.............	11.18	11.11	15.............	12.19	12.08
3.............	11.24	11.12	16.............	12.27	12.16
4.............	11.30	11.19	17.............	12.39	12.28
5.............	11.36	11.22	18.............	12.50	12.40
6.............	11.42	11.30	19.............	12.61	12.50
7.............	11.50	11.38	20.............	12.75	12.62
8.............	11.55	11.43	21.............	12.86	12.71
9.............	11.63	11.50	22.............	12.98	12.83
10.............	11.72	11.58	23.............	13.09	12.94
11.............	11.80	11.64	24.............	13.20	13.04
12.............	11.90	11.78	25.............	13.31	13.15
13.............	11.99	11.88	26.............	13.42	13.25

* Note: Annual yield, stated on a 360-day bank discount basis.

Assume that a financial manager plans to invest a portion of his or her portfolio in 10-week T bills, perhaps in anticipation of known future liquidity needs. The return on these 10-week T bills is seen in Exhibit 2 as 11.58 percent—the "ask" yield indicates the discount at which the security can be purchased and represents the return to the investor if the security is held to maturity. In essence, this is the return the investor would realize by following a buy-and-hold strategy. However, if the yield curve remains the same during the next 10 weeks, the money manager can earn an even higher return for the 10-week period by riding the yield curve. The expected rate of return from riding the yield curve may be computed as follows:

$$E(R_{yc}) = R_O + \left\{ [R_O - E(R_s)] \left(\frac{M - H}{H} \right) \right\}$$

where

$E(R_{yc})$ = the expected return from riding the yield curve
R_O = the original yield on the security purchased
$E(R_s)$ = the expected yield on the security when it is sold
M = the number of days to maturity when the security was purchased
H = the number of days the security was held before it was sold (i.e., the holding period)

Now, if instead of investing in the 10-week T bills, the portfolio manager purchases 24-week T bills (currently selling to yield 13.04 percent) and sells them after 10 weeks, the T bills will then sell to yield 12.10 percent if interest rates have *not* changed during the 10-week holding period [i.e., after 10 weeks, the 24-week T bills will have 14 weeks until maturity and the current (bid) yield on 14-week T bills is 12.10 percent]. In short, if we expect no change in the yield curve, the expected rate of return from riding the yield curve is

$$E(R_{yc}) = 13.04 + \left[(13.04 - 12.10)\left(\frac{168 - 70}{70}\right)\right] = 14.36 \text{ percent}$$

This 14.36 percent expected return is substantially greater than the 11.58 percent that can be earned with the buy-and-hold strategy.

Unfortunately, the 14.36 percent return is *not* a certainty, since interest rates could rise over the 10-week holding period, in which case the bills will not be able to be sold at our expected yield of 12.10 percent. Having to liquidate a position prior to maturity *always* exposes an investment to interest-rate risk and, therefore, to the risk of capital loss (or reduced capital gains). For example, if interest rates rise such that when the T bills are sold after 10 weeks, they are selling to yield 12.75 percent rather than 12.10 percent, the effective return on the investment will fall to

$$E(R_{yc}) = 13.04 + \left[(13.04 - 12.75)\left(\frac{168 - 70}{70}\right)\right] = 13.45 \text{ percent}$$

This is still substantially better than the 11.58 percent return on the buy-and-hold approach because, as we'll see below, interest rates in this particular example would have to rise by almost 2 percentage points over the 10-week period before buying and holding will provide a higher return than that earned from riding the yield curve.

Note that the portfolio manager might just as easily have used T bills with some other maturity to ride the yield curve. All other things equal, the longer the maturity of the instrument employed to ride the yield curve, the greater the extra return. If interest rates begin to rise, however, the potential for reduced profits—or even losses—is also greater on longer maturity instruments.

GETTING A HANDLE ON RISK

The crucial element in increasing portfolio returns from riding the yield curve is the yield on the security *when it is sold* (which we have denoted as R_s). The inherent risk is, of course, that interest rates will rise and that R_s will thus be so high that little profit—or even a loss—results when the manager liquidates the security at the end of the holding period.

An approach that can be used to quantify this risk is to determine the level of interest rates at the end of the holding period that would just eliminate the profit from riding the yield curve. Let us define the profit from riding the yield curve as the excess return over that available from buying a shorter T bill and holding it until maturity. For the returns from riding the yield curve to exceed those available from buying and holding, the yield on the T bills at the end of the holding period must be less than

$$R_s^* = R_O + \left[(R_O - R_{bh}) \left(\frac{H}{M - H} \right) \right]$$

where

R_s^* = the break-even level of interest rates when we sell
R_{bh} = the yield that could be obtained by buying and holding

Once R_s^* has been computed, the portfolio manager can evaluate the probability of such a move in interest rates occurring and can compare this "risk" with the potential increase in return from riding the yield curve.

As an example, consider the investment in 24-week T bills referred to in the preceding section. Since the current rate on 10-week T bills is 11.58 percent, the break-even value for R_s^* is:

$$R_s^* = 13.04 + \left[(13.04 - 11.58) \left(\frac{70}{168 - 70} \right) \right] = 14.08 \text{ percent}$$

That is, if the bid yield on 14-week T bills increases from the current 12.10 percent to 14.08 percent over the 10-week holding period, the portfolio manager will do no better by riding the yield curve than by buying and holding. If the rate goes above 14.08 percent, then the manager will earn less than the 11.58 percent certain rate of return available from buying 10-week T bills and holding them to maturity.

All other things equal, it's clear that the wider the spread between R_s^* and $E(R_s)$, the more likely that the realized rate of return from riding the yield curve will be greater than the rate available from buying a T bill of the desired maturity and holding it. Thus this spread is the investor's margin of safety (MOS) in riding the yield curve, which we may express in percentage terms as follows:

$$\text{MOS} = \frac{R_s^* - E(R_s)}{E(R_s)}$$

For our illustration:

$$\text{MOS} = \frac{14.08 - 12.10}{12.10} = .164$$

That is, the bid yield on 14-week T bills would have to rise by more than 16.4 percent for the investor to be worse off riding the yield curve than simply buying and holding. At this point, the investor can assess the possibility of such a change occurring. Obviously, if the likelihood is small, then riding the yield curve should be considered.

CONCLUSION

Available evidence indicates that although all sorts of trading positions are possible and a wide variety of market conditions can exist,
riding the yield curve *is generally profitable* so long as the margin of
safety is high, i.e., greater than 10–15 percent.[3] On average, when the
margin of safety is high (above 10 percent), returns from riding the
yield curve should exceed returns from buy-and-hold by about 25 to
30 basis points (or more, depending upon the level of interest rates).
Thus, riding the yield curve is a viable technique that can be used by
money managers to improve returns on short-term portfolios. Of
course, not all situations will end up being more profitable than the
buy-and-hold alternative, but if properly assessed, the opportunity for
extra return is certainly there: Riding the yield curve *does* result in
extra returns in about 75 percent of the cases where there is an upward-sloping yield curve and an MOS above 10 percent.

---

[3] See Dyl and Joehnk, "Riding the Yield Curve," pp. 15–17, for some interesting
empirical tests of the extra returns available from riding the yield curve.

The Use of Margining to
Enhance Aftertax Yields

34

JAMES W. JENKINS, Ph.D., C.F.A.
President
Sterling Wentworth Corporation and
Associate Professor (on leave)
Brigham Young University

Taxable bonds at times seem like the bastard son of the Internal Revenue Code. While other investment vehicles receive preferential tax treatment, taxable bonds are left with the bare pickings. Real estate investors may deduct a depreciation allowance from taxable income that exceeds economic depreciation, thereby both converting some ordinary income into capital gains and deferring taxation. In addition, real estate "at risk" rules are generous. Similarly, oil and gas exploration, livestock breeding, motion pictures, farming and forestry, and equipment rental and leasing all have been given special tax considerations.[1] The investment tax credit, the accelerated cost-recovery system, and liberal expense allowances combine to form this preferred treatment.

Taxable bonds are left with few protections from the full burden of taxation: long-term capital gains taxed at 40 percent of the marginal rate[2] and deductibility of the interest paid on funds borrowed to pur-

---

[1] For a discussion of the portfolio impact of some of these tax preferences, see Harvey Galper and Dennis Zimmerman, "Preferential Taxation and Portfolio Choice: Some Empirical Evidence," *National Tax Journal*, December 1977, pp 387–97.

[2] Although the alternative minimum tax on the excluded portion of the long-term capital gains may be important to some investors, it is ignored here for the sake of simplicity.

chase the securities.[3] Even though these tax features are modest in comparison with other investments, they are nevertheless important determinants of return and should not be ignored in bond selection. Indeed, because of them, the investor may find some taxable-bond yields to be very competitive with those from other better endowed investments, even on an aftertax basis.

This chapter explains how the use of margining alters bond yields and enhances expected aftertax performance. In particular, margining of discount bonds is shown to turn these securities into single-payment notes whose returns are taxed as capital gains. Similarly, margining of some convertible bonds transforms them into long-term options. For other convertible bonds, margining allows easier direct comparison with the related common stock, and thereby more direct analysis.

THE MECHANICS OF MARGINING

Like other securities, bonds may be purchased with cash or with partial loan financing. The terms of margin loans are determined in part by initial and maintenance margin requirements. The *initial margin requirement* defines the percentage level of equity that must be contributed when a security is purchased. The *maintenance margin* indicates the proportion of equity in the account that must at minimum be maintained after the purchase. A *margin call* will be produced when a substantial decline in the bonds' market price reduces the accounts' equity below the maintenance margin. A margin call can be met by reducing the debit balance or by placing additional securities as collateral for the margin loan.

The initial margin requirements for common stocks and other securities convertible into equities are set by the Federal Reserve Bank. At the time of this writing the level of the initial margin requirement for stocks was 50 percent. The initial margin requirements for other securities, such as bonds, are set by the individual brokerage houses, in conjunction with their banks or other financial institutions. Despite this, they must be set at least as high as the maintenance margin requirements set by the related exchange.

Minimum maintenance requirements are determined by the appropriate exchanges and the National Association of Securities Dealers. Individual firms may always set more demanding requirements, but they may never lower them. For bonds, the minimum maintenance margin requirements at the time of this writing were as follows:

---

[3] It is important to note that this interest deductibility is limited. Specifically, the deduction of investment interest is limited to $10,000 plus the level of taxable investment income. Additionally, albeit tangentially, the interest on loans to purchase municipal securities is not tax deductible.

- 25 percent on nonconvertible corporates long
- 5 percent of principal or 30 percent of market value, whichever is greater, on bonds short
- 5 percent on government obligations on the principal amount
- 15 percent of par or 25 percent of market, whichever is less, on municipals

In actuality, the margining terms vary somewhat from firm to firm. Exhibit 1 shows that typical levels of the initial margin range from 10

Exhibit 1
Typical Margin Levels for Bonds

Security	Initial Margin	Maintenance Margin
Treasury bills...........................	10%	5%
GNMAs	15	10
FNMAs................................	50	30
Municipals (rated A or better)............	25	15
Nonconvertible corporates	30	25
Convertibles...........................	50	25

percent to 50 percent, depending upon the type of bond. Maintenance margin requirements also differ considerably. They are typically somewhat below the initial requirement. Margin requirements are also influenced at times by the total dollar amount of securities held in the margin account. Interest rates on the largest margin loans are typically set a fraction of a percent above the call-money rate facing the brokerage house. For categories of smaller loans, the margin rates range up to 1 percent to 1.5 percent above the base level.

THE IMPACT OF MARGINING UPON CASH FLOWS

The composition of a bond's cash flow depends upon whether it is selling for a discount, at premium, or at face value. The bonds in Exhibit 2 have been selected to illustrate this point. In addition, the discount Cleveland Electric Illumination bond from this table will be used in later examples. Three sets of two bonds each show combinations from identical companies. Each bond has similar risk and maturity, but they promise very different types of yield. In each group of two, one of the bonds is selling for a deep discount. As a result, its yield relies heavily on capital gain. The other bond in each pair is selling for a price close to its face value. The yield for the second bond comes almost entirely from interest. The capital gain yield represents

Exhibit 2
Basic Financial Data on Selected Bonds

S & P Quality Rating	Company	Collateral Arrangement	Coupon Rate	Date of Maturity	Current Price	Years to Maturity	Yield to Maturity	Interest Yield	Capital Gain Yield
AAA	General Motors Acceptance	Debenture	6¼	9/1/88	63½	6.9	14.8%	8.1%	6.7%
AAA	General Motors Acceptance	Note	14⅝	6/15/89	94⅛	7.7	16.0	15.2	0.8
A	Cleveland Elec. Illum.	1st	2¾	9/1/85	63⅞	3.9	15.1	4.2	10.9
A	Cleveland Elec. Illum.	1st	11½	6/1/85	85	3.7	17.0	12.6	4.4
BBB−	Appalachian Power	1st	4	5/1/88	53½	6.6	15.3	5.6	9.7
BBB−	Appalachian Power	1st	14¾	2/1/87	91½	5.3	17.2	16.4	0.8

Data Source: Standard & Poor's *Bond Guide*, August 1981.

the return due to the contractual capital gain of the bond from now to maturity.[4] The interest yield is the residual interest return from the bond's income.[5]

The net impact margining has upon returns, of course, depends upon a comparison between the aftertax cost of borrowing and the aftertax return realized on the investment. If returns exceed interest cost, net returns on equity are higher with margining. Of course, the reverse is also true.

The impact of margining upon the cash flows of a bond investment depends upon the composition of the bond's cash flow. Periodic interest income can be increased or reduced. The relative importance of capital gain income, if present, can be enhanced.

With margining, all the cash flows from a bond investment are changed. The beginning *equity investment* is reduced by the amount of margin loan. The *semiannual net cash flows* are determined by the following formula:

$$\begin{matrix} \text{Semiannual interest} \\ \text{payments per bond} \end{matrix} - \left(\begin{matrix} \text{Semiannual percentage} \\ \text{interest cost of} \\ \text{margin} \end{matrix} \times \begin{matrix} \text{Percentage} \\ \text{of debt} \\ \text{employed} \end{matrix} \times \begin{matrix} \text{Initial} \\ \text{bond} \\ \text{price} \end{matrix} \right)$$

This equation finds the net interest income—the difference between the semiannual interest income and the interest expense. The *cash flow* received *at maturity* is expressed as:

$$\begin{matrix} \text{Face value} \\ \text{of bond} \end{matrix} + \begin{matrix} \text{Last semiannual} \\ \text{net cash flow} \end{matrix} - \left(\begin{matrix} \text{Percentage of} \\ \text{debt employed} \end{matrix} \times \begin{matrix} \text{Initial} \\ \text{bond price} \end{matrix} \right)$$

This second formula subtracts the debit balance from the bond's face value and last net interest payment.

Exhibit 3 shows the cash flows for the Cleveland Electric Illumination discount bond assuming (1) no margining (2) 25 percent margining, and (3) 50 percent margining. Exhibit 3 also shows the yield to maturity, interest yield, and capital gain yield before taxes for each debt level. A 15 percent margin rate (cost of the borrowed funds) is

---

[4] The capital gain yield is computed by the formula:

$$g = (F/P)^{1/n} - 1$$

where

  g = the capital gain yield
  n = the number of compounding periods
  F = the face value of the bond
  P = the current market price of the bond

[5] The interest yield is defined as the bond's yield to maturity minus the capital gain yield.

Exhibit 3
**Cash Flows with and without margining for discount bond [Cleveland Elec. Illum.
(A) 2¾s 1985]**

	100 Percent Equity 0 Percent Debt	75 Percent Equity 25 Percent Debt	50 Percent Equity 50 Percent Debt
Equity investment................	$ 638.75	$479.06	$319.38
Net interest income (semiannual, 3/1/82 through 3/1/85)	$ 13.75	$ 1.77	$ (10.20)
Net payment on maturity..........	$1,013.75	$842.08	$670.43
Yield to maturity.................	15.1%	15.1%	15.2%
Interest yield....................	4.2%	0.4%	(3.2%)
Capital gain yield................	10.9%	14.7%	18.4%

assumed.[6] Notice that the introduction of margining reduces the absolute and relative level of returns received as *interest income*. Because
the bond's yield to maturity and the margining rate are almost identical, the positive impact of the financial leverage is small. When no
leverage is employed, about one half of the total return comes in the
form of interest. With 25 percent margining, almost all of the return is
in capital gain form. With 50 percent margining, the annual cash flow
is negative.[7] The capital gain return exceeds the yield to maturity. In
this example, margining changes little the level of return. Despite
this, the composition of the cash flow shifts markedly from interest to
capital gains.

In fact, the margined bond position employing 25 percent debt can
be viewed as a single-payment note promising $842 in about four
years on a $479 original investment. Net interest cash flow is negligible. From a tax viewpoint, it is important to note that the returns on
such a single-payment note will be treated as capital gains.

THE IMPACT OF MARGINING ON AFTERTAX YIELDS

Exhibit 4 illustrates the aftertax results of margining the discount
Cleveland Electric bond. The aftertax (semiannually compounded)
yields here equate the present values of the aftertax cash flows at the
indicated marginal tax rates with the current equity investment. By
reducing the portion of the yield that is taxable as ordinary income
and by increasing the capital gain portion of the total return, margin

---

[6] The assumption here is that the average interest costs over the life of the bond is
equal to its current yield to maturity. During ordinary times, with a positively sloped
yield curve, the margin rate will likely be less than this amount. At any rate, this
assumption produces a nearly neutral before-tax impact of the financial leverage and
allows focus upon the aftertax effects. The reader could easily reproduce similar results
for different relative or absolute assumptions.

[7] This analysis assumes that this investment interest expense is deductible. (Refer to
footnote 3.)

Exhibit 4
Aftertax Yields for Margining Discount Bond [Cleveland Electric Illum.
(A) 2¾s 1985]

Tax Rate	100 Percent Equity 0 Percent Debt	75 Percent Equity 25 Percent Debt	50 Percent Equity 50 Percent Debt
0.0%	15.1%	15.1%	15.2%
20.0	13.7	14.1	14.9
40.0	12.2	13.0	14.5
60.0	10.7	11.9	14.1

ing causes the aftertax returns to decrease much less rapidly due to taxes as do the unleveraged returns. In simpler terms, margining reduces the bite of taxes.

Notice in the first case, without margining, that the aftertax yield does not drop as rapidly as tax rates increase. If there were no tax sheltering, the original 15.1 percent yield would fall proportionally as taxes were deducted. The presence of capital gains in the yield, however, reduces this potential reduction in yield due to taxes by about half. Without the capital gains yield in this bond's yield to maturity, at a 60 percent tax rate the aftertax yield would be about 6 percent, rather than the 10.7 percent in Exhibit 4.

In the second case, with 25 percent margining, the tax bite is reduced further because of the increasing concentration of returns into capital gains form. In the third case, with 50 percent margining, the negative deductible periodic cash flow almost flattens out the tax impact on the return. The tax benefits received from the early deductions in large part offset the later capital gains taxes.

RISKS ASSOCIATED WITH MARGINING

There are several dimensions to the risks created by margining. First, margining increases the volatility of the expected returns. Since margining defers the receipt of cash flows toward the maturity date, the average duration of the levered investment position,[8] and hence the volatility of the investor's position, is increased.

In fact, it can be shown that the band of possible returns increases proportionally to the debt-equity ratio.[9] A movement from no debt to

---

[8] See Chapter 35 for a discussion of duration.
[9] This relationship is specifically

$$\sigma p = \sigma (1 + D/E)$$

where

σp = standard deviation of the return distribution of the portfolio
σ = standard deviation of the return distribution of the portfolio assets
D/E = the debt-equity mix used in financing the assets.

This formula assumes, however, a fixed rate on the debt contract.

Exhibit 5
Price Changes of a Discount Bond with and without Margining [Cleveland Elec. Illum. (A)
2¾s 1985]

If Long-Term Interest Rates Move from 15.1 Percent to	Without Margining		With 50 Percent Margining		
	Market Price of Bond	Percent Return	Original Equity Investment	Remaining Equity Investment	Percent Return
19.0%	$558.53	−13%	$319.38	$239.16	−25%
17.0	598.21	−6	319.38	278.84	−13
15.1	638.75	0	319.38	319.38	0
13.0	687.95	8	319.38	368.58	15
11.0	738.70	16	319.38	419.33	31

50 percent leverage, or to a debt-equity ratio of one, will double the width of possible returns. This point is illustrated in Exhibit 5. Without debt, returns ranging from 13 percent to 16 percent are all possible, depending upon changes in market interest yields.

With 50 percent margining, the band of returns under the same set of circumstances ranges now from a low of 25 percent to a high of 31 percent. The difference between the high and low returns increases from 29 percent when no debt is used to 56 percent with margining, an approximate doubling in return variability.

The riskiness of margined bond positions deserves some additional considerations as well. First, as the market price of the bond fluctuates, there is a chance for a margin call at some point over the life of the bond. The maturity of the bond thus may not be reached, and the yield to maturity not realized. Only by maintaining a reserve of liquid assets or borrowing potential to provide additional funds when bond prices are low can an investor reduce this risk substantially. Second, the floating margin interest cost changes from month to month and tends to be highest when bond prices are their lowest; thus annual cash flows are a bit more uncertain than the above discussion suggests. Third, with margining, there is a greater maximum possible loss in the case of default, since the debit balance may potentially exceed the equity by several times. With margining, there may be more funds placed at risk.

Duration and Its Properties*

35 FRANK K. REILLY, Ph.D., C.F.A.
Dean and Bernard J. Hank Professor
of Business Administration
University of Notre Dame

RUPINDER S. SIDHU
Associate, Strategic Services Group
Merrill Lynch White Weld
Capital Markets Group

In Chapter 4, *duration of a bond* is defined and the relation between duration and price sensitivity of a bond to changes in interest rates is explained. In this chapter we explain the basic concept of duration and discuss in detail how duration is computed and how it is affected by maturity, coupon, and market yield. In Chapter 36 the role of duration in immunizing a bond portfolio is explained.

To understand the concept of duration properly, it is useful to place it in the perspective of other summary measures of the timing of an asset's cash flows. Although measurement of the timing of cash flows is important to the analysis of all investments, the ability to measure it precisely is typically limited because the investor is not certain of the timing and size of the flows. Because the cash flows from bonds are specified both as to timing and amount, however, analysts have derived a precise measure of the timing for bonds. We discuss below the principal measures and demonstrate their application for the two bonds described in Exhibit 1.

---

* This chapter is adapted with permission from pages 59–63 of Frank K. Reilly and Rupinder S. Sidhu, "The Many Uses of Bond Duration," *Financial Analysts Journal,* July–August 1980, pp. 58–72.

Exhibit 1
Specification of Sample Bonds

	Bond A	Bond B
Face value..............	$1,000	$1,000
Maturity...............	10 years	10 years
Coupon................	4%	8%
Sinking fund..........	10% a year of face value starting at end of year 5	15% a year of face value starting at end of year 5

TERM TO MATURITY

The most popular timing measure is *term to maturity (TM)—the number of years prior to the final payment on the bond.* Our two sample bonds have identical terms to maturity—10 years. Term to maturity has the advantage of being easily identified and measured, since bonds are always specified in terms of the final maturity date, and it is easy to compute the time from the present to that final year. The obvious disadvantage of term to maturity is that it ignores the amount and timing of all cash flows except the final payment. In the case of the sample bonds, term to maturity ignores the substantial difference in coupon rates and the difference in the sinking funds.

A number of years ago some bond analysts and portfolio managers attempted to rectify this deficiency by computing a measure that considered the interest payments and the final principal payment. *The weighted average term to maturity (WATM) computes the proportion of each individual payment as a percentage of all payments and makes this proportion the weight for the year (1 through 10) the payment is made.*[1] It equals

$$\text{WATM} = \frac{\text{CF}_1(1)}{\text{TCF}} + \frac{\text{CF}_2(2)}{\text{TCF}} + \cdots \frac{\text{CF}_n(n)}{\text{TCF}}$$

where

$$\text{CF}_t = \text{the cash flow in year t}$$
$$(t) = \text{the year when cash flow is received}$$
$$n = \text{maturity}$$
$$\text{TCF} = \text{the total cash flow from the bond}$$

For example, bond A (the four percent coupon, 10-year bond) will have total cash flow payments (TCF) of $1,400 ($40 a year for 10 years plus $1,000 at maturity). Thus the $40 payment in year one (CF$_1$) will have a weight of 0.02857 ($40/1,400), each subsequent interest payment will have the same weight, and the principal payment in year 10

---

[1] Although it is recognized that interest payments are typically made at six-month intervals, we assume annual payments at year-end to simplify the computations.

Exhibit 2
Weighted Average Term to Maturity (assuming annual interest payments)

(1) Year	(2) Cash Flow	(3) Cash Flow/TCF	(4) (1) × (3)
Bond A			
1...............	$ 40	0.02857	0.02857
2...............	40	0.02857	0.05714
3...............	40	0.02857	0.08571
4...............	40	0.02857	0.11428
5...............	40	0.02857	0.14285
6...............	40	0.02857	0.17142
7...............	40	0.02857	0.19999
8...............	40	0.02857	0.22856
9...............	40	0.02857	0.25713
10...............	1,040	0.74286	7.42860
Sum.............	$1,400	1.00000	8.71425

Weighted average term to maturity = 8.71 years

Bond B			
1...............	$ 80	0.04444	0.04444
2...............	80	0.04444	0.08888
3...............	80	0.04444	0.13332
4...............	80	0.04444	0.17776
5...............	80	0.04444	0.22220
6...............	80	0.04444	0.26664
7...............	80	0.04444	0.31108
8...............	80	0.04444	0.35552
9...............	80	0.04444	0.39996
10	1,080	0.60000	6.00000
Sum.............	$1,800	1.00000	7.99980

Weighted average term to maturity = 8.00 years

will have a weight of 0.74286 ($1,000/1,400). Exhibit 2 demonstrates the specific computation of the weighted average term to maturity for each sample bond.

It is apparent from Exhibit 2 that the weighted average term to maturity is definitely less than the term to maturity because it takes account of all interim cash flows in addition to the final principal payment. Furthermore, the bond with the larger coupon has a shorter weighted average term to maturity because a larger proportion of its total cash flows is derived from the coupon payments that come prior to maturity. Specifically, the interest payments constitute 28.6 percent ($400/1,400) of the total returns on bond A but 44.4 percent ($800/1,800) of the total flow for bond B. Obviously, if one were to compute a measure that included sinking-fund payments, the weighted average term to maturity would be even lower.

A major advantage of the weighted average term to maturity is that it considers the timing of all flows from the bond, rather than only the final payment. One drawback is that it does not consider the time value of the flows. The interest payment in the 1st year has the same weight as the interest payment in the 10th year, although the present value of the payment in the 10th year is substantially less. Also, the weighted average term to maturity would give the $1,000 principal the same weight whether payment was made in year 10 or year 20.

DURATION

The duration measure is similar to the weighted average term to maturity, with the exception that *all flows are in terms of present value*. Duration equals[2]

$$D = \frac{\sum\limits_{t=1}^{n} \dfrac{C_t(t)}{(1 + r)^t}}{\sum\limits_{t=1}^{n} \dfrac{C_t}{(1 + r)^t}}$$

where

C_t = the interest and/or principal payment in year t
(t) = the length of time to the interest and/or principal payment
n = the length of time to final maturity
r = the yield to maturity

In the style of our equation for weighted average term to maturity, duration is

$$D = \frac{PVCF_1(1)}{PVTCF} + \frac{PVCF_2(2)}{PVTCF} + \cdots \frac{PVCF_n(n)}{PVTCF}$$

where

$PVCF_1$ = the present value of the cash flow in year t discounted at current yield to maturity
(t) = the year when cash flow is received
$PVTCF$ = the present value of total cash flow from the bond discounted at current yield to maturity—obviously, the prevailing market price for the bond including accrued interest

Exhibit 3 shows the computations of duration for the two sample bonds. *Duration is simply a weighted average maturity in which the*

---

[2] The concept of duration was originally developed by Professor Frederick Macaulay in *Some Theoretical Problems Suggested by the Movements of Interest Rates, Bond Yields, and Stock Prices in the United States since 1865* (New York: National Bureau of Economic Research, 1938).

Exhibit 3
Duration (assuming 8 percent market yield)

(1) Year	(2) Cash Flow	(3) PV at 8 Percent	(4) PV of Flow	(5) PV as Percent of Price	(6) (1) × (5)
		Bond A			
1	$ 40	0.9259	$ 37.04	0.0506	0.0506
2	40	0.8573	34.29	0.0469	0.0938
3	40	0.7938	31.75	0.0434	0.1302
4	40	0.7350	29.40	0.0402	0.1608
5	40	0.6806	27.22	0.0372	0.1860
6	40	0.6302	25.21	0.0345	0.2070
7	40	0.5835	23.34	0.0319	0.2233
8	40	0.5403	21.61	0.0295	0.2360
9	40	0.5002	20.01	0.0274	0.2466
10	1,040	0.4632	481.73	0.6585	6.5850
Sum			$ 731.58	1.0000	8.1193

Duration = 8.12 years

		Bond B			
1	$ 80	0.9259	$ 74.07	0.0741	0.0741
2	80	0.8573	68.59	0.0686	0.1372
3	80	0.7938	63.50	0.0635	0.1906
4	80	0.7350	58.80	0.0588	0.1906
5	80	0.6806	54.44	0.0544	0.2720
6	80	0.6302	50.42	0.0504	0.3024
7	80	0.5835	46.68	0.0467	0.3269
8	80	0.5403	43.22	0.0432	0.3456
9	80	0.5002	40.02	0.0400	0.3600
10	1,080	0.4632	500.26	0.5003	5.0030
Sum			$1000.00	1.0000	7.2470

Duration = 7.25 Years

weights are stated in present value terms. Specifically, the time in the future a cash flow is received is weighted by the proportion that the present value of that cash flow contributes to the total present value or price of the bond.

Recall that we assume that interest payments are made annually; use of the more realistic semiannual payments would result in a shorter duration—7.99 versus 8.12 years and 7.07 years compared with 7.25 years. When measuring duration using semiannual payments, the resulting duration will be in half years. Therefore it is necessary to divide the computed duration by two. In general, if payments are made m times per year, duration in years is found by dividing the value for duration, assuming m periodic payments, by m.

As with weighted average term to maturity, the duration of a bond is shorter than its term to maturity because of the interim interest payments. Obviously, a zero-coupon bond yielding no interim payments would have the same duration, weighted average term to maturity, and term to maturity, since 100 percent of the total cash flow, and 100 percent of total present value, would come at maturity. Also, like weighted average term to maturity, *duration is inversely related to the coupon for the bond* (i.e., the larger the coupon, the greater the proportion of total returns received in the interim, and the shorter the duration). Exhibit 4 graphs the relation between duration and maturity for a range of coupon rates.

Exhibit 4
Relation between Duration and Term to Maturity for Alternative Coupons

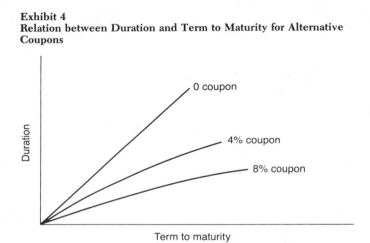

One variable that does not influence weighted average term to maturity but can affect duration is the prevailing market yield (r). Market yield does not influence weighted average term to maturity because this measure does not consider the present value of flows. Market yield affects both the numerator and denominator of the duration computation, but it affects the numerator more. As a result, *there is an inverse relation between a change in the market yield and a bond's*

Exhibit 5
How Duration Is Affected by Alternative Market Yields (assuming semiannual interest payments)

	Market Yields			
	0 Percent	*4 Percent*	*8 Percent*	*12 Percent*
Bond A	8.60*	8.34	7.99*	7.57
Bond B	7.87*	7.50	7.07*	6.61

* These durations differ from those in Exhibits 2 and 3 because of the use of semiannual interest payments.

duration. That is, an increase in the market yield will cause a decline in duration, other things being equal.

Exhibit 5 demonstrates how different market yields will affect the duration of our sample bonds. The results for the case of zero market yield indicate that duration is the same as weighted average term to maturity when there is no discounting.

EFFECT OF SINKING FUNDS

The discussion thus far has ignored the effects of sinking funds. But a large proportion of current bond issues do have sinking funds, and these can definitely affect a bond's duration. Exhibit 6 shows the computations of duration for the sample bonds with sinking funds. Inclusion of the sinking funds causes the computed durations to decline by approximately one year in both cases (i.e., from 8.12 to 7.04 for bond A and from 7.25 to 5.99 for bond B).

Exhibit 6
Impact of Sinking Fund on Duration (assuming eight percent market yield)

(1) Year	(2) Cash Flow	(3) PV at 8 Percent	(4) PV of Flow	(5) PV/Total CF	(6) (1) × (5)
		Bond A			
1..................	$ 40	0.9259	$ 37.04	.04858	.04858
2..................	40	0.8573	34.29	.04497	.08994
3..................	40	0.7938	31.75	.04164	.12492
4..................	40	0.7350	29.40	.03856	.15424
5..................	140	0.6806	95.28	.12495	.62475
6..................	136	0.6302	85.71	.11240	.67440
7..................	132	0.5835	77.02	.10101	.70707
8..................	128	0.5403	69.16	.09070	.72560
9..................	124	0.5002	62.02	.08133	.73197
10.................	520	0.4632	240.86	.31587	3.15879
Sum...............			$ 762.53	1.00000	7.04024
Duration = 7.04 Years					
		Bond B			
1..................	$ 80	0.9259	$ 74.07	.07407	.07407
2..................	80	0.8573	68.59	.06859	.13718
3..................	80	0.7938	63.50	.06350	.19050
4..................	80	0.7350	58.80	.05880	.23520
5..................	230	0.6806	156.54	.15654	.78270
6..................	218	0.6302	137.38	.13738	.82428
7..................	206	0.5835	120.20	.12020	.84140
8..................	194	0.5403	104.82	.10482	.83856
9..................	182	0.5002	91.04	.09104	.81936
10.................	270	0.4632	125.06	.12506	1.25060
Sum...............			$1,000.00	1.00000	5.99385
Duration = 5.99 Years					

The effect of a sinking fund on the time structure of cash flows for a bond is certain to the issuer of the bond, since the firm must make the payments; they represent a legal cash flow requirement that will affect the firm's cash flow. In contrast, the sinking fund may not affect the investor. Even though the money put into the sinking fund may not necessarily be used to retire outstanding bonds, even if it is, it is not certain that a given investor's bonds will be called for retirement.

EFFECT OF CALL

In contrast to a sinking fund, which reduces duration by only one year and may affect only a few investors, all bondholders will be affected if a bond is called, and the call feature can influence duration substantially. For example, consider a 30-year bond of 8 percent coupon, selling at par and callable after 10 years at 108. First, compute a crossover yield.[3] At yields above the crossover yield, the yield to maturity is the minimum yield. When the price of the bond rises to some value above the call price and the market yield declines to a value below the crossover yield, however, the yield to call becomes the minimum yield. At this price and yield, the firm will probably exercise a call option when it is available.

As Homer and Leibowitz have demonstrated, it is possible to calculate the crossover yield by deriving the yield to maturity for a bond selling at the call price for the original maturity minus the years of call protection.[4] For the above example, this would involve deriving the yield to maturity for an 8 percent coupon bond selling at $1,080 and maturing in 30 years; the implied crossover yield is 7.24 percent. In one year's time, the bond's maturity will be 29 years, with 9 years to call. Assume the market rate has declined to the point at which the yield to maturity for the bond is 7 percent (below the crossover yield of 7.24 percent). At this price ($1,123.43) the bond's yield to call will be 6.2 percent.

If a bond portfolio manager ignored the call option and computed the duration of this bond to maturity (29 years) assuming a market yield of 7 percent, he or she would arrive at a duration of 12.49 years. Recognizing the call option would mean computing the duration for a bond to be called in 9 years at a price of $1,080 and using the yield to call of 6.2 percent, for a duration of 6.83 years. Exhibit 7 summarizes this example.

The existence of a call option, which is almost universal on corporate bonds, can have a dramatic impact on the computed duration for a

---

[3] The discussion of crossover yield and its computation is drawn from Sidney Homer and Martin L. Leibowitz, *Inside the Yield Book* (Englewood Cliffs, N.J.: Prentice-Hall, 1972). In Chapter 4 of the *Handbook* the crossover yield is explained and illustrated.

[4] Ibid., pp. 58–63.

Exhibit 7
Impact of Call Options on Duration

Original bond:	8 percent coupon bond sold at par with 30 years to maturity. Callable in 10 years at 108 of par. (Computed crossover yield is 7.24 percent.)
One year later:	Market yields on bond decline from 8 to 7 percent.

Current market price:	$1,123.43
Yield to maturity (29 years):	7%
Yield to call (9 years)	6.2%
Call price:	108

Duration:	At 7 percent yield and 29 years maturity—12.49 years
	At 6.2 percent yield, 9 years to call at 108—6.83 years

bond. The above example assumed a deferred call of 10 years, which is currently the maximum period; 5 years is more typical.

DURATION OF GNMA BONDS[5]

During the past several years there has been a substantial increase in investor interest in GNMA pass-through bonds because of the inherent safety of the bonds and their higher yields relative to other government securities. Without detracting from the safety and yield characteristics of these securities, a portfolio manager should recognize the extreme difference between the initial promised term to maturity, the empirical maturity, and the probable duration, taking into account the form of cash flow and the empirical maturity.

An investor in a GNMA pass-through is basically purchasing a share of a pool of mortgages. The investor receives each month a payment from the mortgages that includes not only interest, but also partial repayment of the principal. Of course, homeowners may decide to pay off their mortgages in order to buy other houses (in which case prepayment penalties are usually waived). As a result, mortgage contracts are like bonds with sinking funds because they pay interest and principal over time, and they are also like bonds that are freely callable because they can be paid off when the house is sold. *The empirical duration of a GNMA pass-through will thus be substantially less than the stated maturity.*

The stated maturity of most home mortgages is 25 years. Given the nature of the payment stream including principal and interest, the duration of a mortgage without prepayment is substantially less than the stated maturity. For example, assuming a 10 percent market rate and annual payments at the end of the year, a 30-year mortgage has a

---

[5] GNMA pass-through bonds are discussed in Chapter 18.

duration of 9.18 years, a 25-year mortgage has a duration of 8.46 years, and a 20-year mortgage has a duration of 7.51 years. (The consideration of realistic monthly payments would reduce these durations further.)

In addition, because of numerous prepayments, the empirical maturity of most mortgage pools is actually only about 12 years, rather than the stated 25. If one assumes principal and interest payments for 12 years and a prepayment at the end of 12 years (with no call premium), the computed durations would decline further. Under these assumptions, the mortgages have the following durations—30 years, 7.22 years; 25 years, 7.04 years; 20 years, 6.71 years. Bond portfolio managers should recognize that they are acquiring relatively short duration bonds when they invest in GNMAs.

DURATION PROPERTIES

Except for very long maturity bonds selling at a discount, duration is positively related to the maturity of the bond.[6] It is inversely related to the coupon on a bond and to the market yield for the bond. Furthermore, duration can be reduced by sinking-fund or call provisions.

Weighted average term to maturity and duration will be equal to a bond's term to maturity when the coupon rate is zero—that is, when there are no interim cash flows prior to maturity. But weighted average term to maturity and duration will never exceed a bond's term to maturity. In fact, Fisher and Weil suggest that insurance companies encourage some issuers (including the government) to sell long-term, zero-coupon discount bonds that would have maturities and durations of 30 or 40 years; in this way, they could match their long-term liabilities with long-duration assets.[7] Regardless of coupon size, it is nearly impossible to find bonds that have durations in excess of 20 years; most bonds have a limit of about 15 years.

As Exhibits 2 and 3 show, weighted average term to maturity is always longer than the duration of a bond, and the difference increases with the market rate used in the duration formula. This is consistent with the observation that there is an inverse relation between duration and the market rate. Further, this relation confirms our earlier observation that weighted average term to maturity and duration are equal when the market rate is zero.

---

[6] For a discussion of this point, see James Van Horne, *Financial Market Rates and Flows* (Englewood Cliffs, N.J.: Prentice-Hall, 1978), p. 120.

[7] Lawrence Fisher and Roman L. Weil, "Coping with the Risk of Interest-Rate Fluctuations: Returns to Bondholders from Naive and Optimal Strategies," *Journal of Business*, October 1971, pp. 408–31.

ALTERNATIVE DEFINITIONS OF DURATION

Bierwag and Kaufman have pointed out that there are several speci-fications of the duration measure.[8] The measure derived by Macaulay (the one used throughout this chapter) discounts all flows by the pre-vailing average yield to maturity on the bond being measured. Fisher and Weil, for example, use future one-period discount rates (forward rates) to discount the future flows.[9] Depending upon the shape of the yield curves, these two definitions could give different results. Only if all forward rates are equal (so that the yield curve is flat) will the two definitions result in equal estimates of duration.

As will be explained in Chapter 36, duration plays a pivotal role in bond immunization strategies. Bierwag and Kaufman, however, note that the definition of duration used for bond portfolio immunization should be a function of the nature of the shock to the interest-rate structure. It is possible to conceive of an additive shock to interest rates, where all interest rates are changed by the same nominal amount (e.g., 50 basis points), or a multiplicative shock, where all interest rates change by the same percentage (e.g., all rates decline by 10 percent). Bierwag contends that the optimal definition of duration for perfect immunization of a portfolio will depend upon the nature of the shock to the interest-rate structure.[10] In the case of an additive shock, the Fisher-Weil definition is best, but a multiplicative shock requires a third measure of duration. Bierwag and Kaufman computed the duration for a set of bonds using the three definitions of duration and concluded:

> "Except at high coupons and long maturities, the values of the three definitions do not vary greatly. Thus, D_1 [Macaulay] may be used as a first approximation for D_2 and D_3 [Fisher-Weil and Bierwag-Kaufman, respectively]. The expression for D_1 has the additional advantage of being a function of the yield to maturity of the bond. As a result, neither a forecast of the stream of one-period forward rates over maturity of the bond nor a specific assumption about the nature of the random shocks is required."[11]

CONCLUSION

The most popular measure of the timing of a bond's cash flow is term to maturity—the number of years until final payment. But term to

---

[8] G. O. Bierwag and George C. Kaufman, "Coping with the Risk of Interest-Rate Fluctuations: A Note," *Journal of Business,* July 1977, pp. 364–70.

[9] Fisher and Weil, "Coping with the Risk of Interest-Rate Fluctuations: Returns to Bondholders."

[10] G. O. Bierwag, "Immunization, Duration, and the Term Structure of Interest Rates," *Journal of Financial and Quantitative Analysis,* December 1977, pp. 725–42.

[11] Bierwag and Kaufman, "Coping with the Risk of Interest-Rate Fluctuations: A Note."

maturity ignores the amount and timing of all cash flows prior to the final payment. Duration takes into account interim cash flows as well as the final payment, weighting each by its present value.

As noted in Chapter 4, the following relationship exists between duration and interest-rate changes:

Percentage change in bond's price

$$= -\ (\text{Modified duration}) \times \left(\frac{\begin{array}{c} \text{Change in market yield} \\ \text{in basis points} \end{array}}{100} \right)$$

where

$$\text{Modified duration} = \text{duration divided by } \left(1 + \frac{\text{market yield}}{m} \right)$$

$$m = \text{number of coupon interest payments per year}$$

The active bond portfolio manager will maximize the duration of his or her portfolio when expecting interest rates to decline. On the other hand, the manager who must fulfill an ending-wealth requirement at a specific investment horizon faces two kinds of risk—price risk and coupon reinvestment risk: If rates increase after the bond is purchased, the price of the bond in the secondary market will fall; if rates decrease, interim coupon payments will be reinvested at lower rates.

As will be explained in Chapter 36 the portfolio manager can immunize his or her portfolio from interest-rate risk by setting the duration of the portfolio equal to the desired horizon. The reason this is true is that it can be demonstrated that duration is the investment horizon for which the price risk and the coupon reinvestment risk of the bond portfolio have equal magnitudes but opposite signs (i.e., for which their effects on the portfolio's ending wealth cancel each other out).

Bond Portfolio Immunization

36

PETER E. CHRISTENSEN
Vice President
The First Boston Corporation

SYLVAN G. FELDSTEIN, Ph.D.*
Vice President and Bond Analyst
Moody's Investors Service, Inc.

FRANK J. FABOZZI, Ph.D., C.F.A., C.P.A.
Professor of Economics
Fordham University

The volatility of interest rates during the last decade, and particularly during the past few years, has created unprecedented risks for bond portfolio managers. Those who tried to time the cyclical downturn in interest rates by committing money to the intermediate and long ends of the bond market have seen heavy erosion at various times in their asset values. In this chapter we illustrate a bond portfolio strategy that can be employed to minimize the risk of interest-rate volatility over a predetermined horizon. The strategy, known as *immunization*, has been applied to bond portfolios by bank trust departments and pension funds and by life insurance companies as a funding vehicle for their "guaranteed" annuity products.[1] Although bond immunization

* This chapter was written while the author was Vice President and Analyst at Smith Barney, Harris Upham & Co., Inc. The views expressed in this chapter are those of the author and not necessarily those of Moody's Investors Service, Inc.

[1] For a discussion of immunization applied to specific institutions, see the following: R. M. Redington, "Review of the Principle of Life-Office Valuations," *Journal of the Institute of Actuaries* 78 (1952), pp. 286–340; Irwin T. Vanderhoof, "The Interest-Rate Assumption and the Maturity Structure of the Assets of a Life Insurance Company," *Transactions of the Society of Actuaries*, May-June 1972; G. O. Bierwag, George G. Kaufman, and Alden Toevs, "Management Strategies for Savings and Loan Associations to Reduce Interest Rate Risk," *Proceedings of the Conference on New Sources of Capital for the Savings and Loan Industry* (Federal Home Loan Bank of San Francisco, 1979); Richard Keintz and Clyde Stickney, "Immunization of Pension Funds From

may not be an appropriate strategy for all bond portfolios and particularly not for individual and pension investors with a more active risk disposition, it is attractive for those who either need to reduce their funding risks by matching at least a portion of their bond assets to anticipated liabilities or for those who just want to lock in today's prevailing rates over a predetermined time horizon.

THE NEED FOR STABLE RETURNS IN A VOLATILE INTEREST-RATE ENVIRONMENT

Is there a way to hedge against the uncertainty surrounding the enormous volatility in today's interest rates? Is there a way to minimize or control interest-rate risk? Is there a way to protect at least a portion of your assets from the unpredictable or uncontrollable? The British were the first to respond to these portfolio management problems through the development of immunization theory. The British naturally found it easier to develop these concepts, since they had related experience in reducing risk by matching assets and liabilities in varying currencies.

In the same manner that currency risk can be controlled, an immunized bond strategy can also minimize or control interest-rate risk. As such, immunization is a strategy suitable for investors who require safety for at least a portion of their assets. It is a strategy also well suited for those who wish to avoid committing themselves 100 percent to an "active position" in the bond market.

The risk an investor assumes with the purchase of a bond portfolio is related not just to security and other portfolio characteristics, but also to the investor's time horizon and the interest-rate fluctuations that occur over that horizon. Interest-rate risk, including reinvestment risk, can be effectively eliminated, however, by implementing a portfolio strategy based upon the concept of *duration*, which is the building block of immunization. Duration very simply is a mathematical measure of the *term* of a bond, taking into account all coupon and principal payments as well as the time value of money (reflecting prevailing yields).[2] As explained in Chapter 35, the price sensitivity of a bond to changes in interest rates is related to its duration.

Interest Rate Changes," Dartmouth College Working Paper (1977); D. Don Ezra, "Immunization: A New Look for Actuarial Liabilities," *Journal of Portfolio Management*, Winter 1976, pp. 50–53.

For a discussion of immunization theory, see the following: Lawrence Fisher and Roman Weil, "Coping with the Risk of Interest Rate Fluctuations: Returns to Bondholders from Naive and Optimal Strategies," *Journal of Business*, October 1971, pp. 408–431; G. O. Bierwag and George G. Kaufman, "Coping with the Risk of Interest-Rate Fluctuations: A Note," *Journal of Business*, July 1977, pp. 364–70; Seymour Smidt, "Investment Horizons and Performance Measures," *Journal of Portfolio Management*, Winter 1978, pp. 18–22.

[2] Frederick R. Macaulay, *Some Theoretical Problems Suggested by the Movements of Interest Rates, Bond Yields, and Stock Prices in the United States since 1856* (New York: National Bureau of Economic Research, 1938).

By matching the duration (or term) of a portfolio to a specific time horizon over which they would like to lock in rates, portfolio managers can hedge their portfolios, minimize the risk of repeated and unexpected changes in interest rates, and lock in prevailing yields. With immunization, managers find that assets and liabilities are equally affected by changes in interest rates. They are therefore able to achieve a highly predictable rate of return over the planning horizon, independent of the future fluctuations in interest rates that always occur in the bond market.

Knowledge of the immunized position is also of crucial value to active portfolio managers. Based on their perceptions of changes in the direction of interest rates, they must purposefully aim the duration of their portfolios away from the neutral or immunized position according to their forecast of interest rates in order to incrementally increase their holding period return.

In this instance, "active" or "contingent" immunization may be used by active managers to provide a "floor" or baseline return to a portfolio (say, 8 or 9 percent) that is a level below the immunized rate (say, 11 percent), yet allow them wide discretion in actively managing their bond portfolio. If performance is so short of target that total compounded return over the planning horizon approaches the floor or baseline, then the portfolio is immunized for the remaining time in the planning period.

Immunization and duration may also be used by active managers to assess their risk position relative to the neutral or immunized state. For instance, if we assume a planning horizon on September 1, 1982, of six and one-half years and a set of performance standards for this period, active managers cannot position themselves long with the purchase of U.S. Treasury 7⅞s of 1993. In spite of the 10½ years to maturity, the Treasury 7⅞s represent an immunized position relative to the portfolio planning period. This is because the duration of the Treasury 7⅞s is precisely equal to the planning horizon. That is, the duration is also 6½ years. To position themselves long, managers must instead purchase lower coupon or longer maturity bonds with longer durations. *The key point to remember for active or neutral managers is that bonds must be purchased for their durations, not their maturities.*

In contrast to the measured assumption of risk, the immunization strategy offers the opportunity to *control* or minimize interest-rate risk over a specific planning horizon by reducing the standard deviation of return. Clearly this is not necessarily an optimal strategy. It is however an efficient strategy and therefore one that may suit the preferences of many types of investors. It does not replace active bond management. Rather it is a strategy designed for those investors who may have a fixed sum liability due at specific periods in the future. It is also a strategy designed for those investors who wish to have a "core" of their portfolio appreciate at a fixed, assured rate over a finite period and thereby lock in prevailing rates.

WHAT IS AN IMMUNIZED BOND PORTFOLIO?

Immunization, as it is presently conceived, is a duration-matching strategy. In 1952 F. M. Redington defined immunization as "the investment of the assets in such a way that the existing business is immune to a general change in the rate of interest."[3] He also stated that the average duration of assets, when set equal to the average duration of liabilities, will immunize a portfolio from the effects of a change in interest rates. By matching durations on both sides of the ledger, we ensure that assets and liabilities are equally affected by changes in interest rates. For any change in yield, both sides of the ledger are equally affected, and therefore the relative values of assets and liabilities are not changed.

Interest-rate risk appears then as a result of assets having a longer or shorter duration than the liabilities or planning horizon. The greater the disparity between durations, the greater the risk. However, the greater the equality of average durations, the better the immunity, and the better the probability we could fully fund any fixed liabilities or meet interest-rate goals regardless of market interest-rate fluctuations. It is important to repeat at this juncture that immunization is not necessarily an optimal strategy. It is, however, an efficient strategy and therefore one that may suit the preferences of many types of investors. It is well suited for those investors who have fixed-sum liabilities due at specific points in the future. It is also well suited for those who wish to have a "core" of their bond portfolio appreciate at a fixed, assured rate over a finite period (i.e., lock in prevailing rates). Immunization maximizes the likelihood that a high fixed rate of return will be achieved over a fixed time horizon—up to eight years. It tends to minimize the degree of risk that is assumed in the portfolio over that horizon. At that same time it must be noted that it also restricts opportunities to position a portfolio to benefit from a series of unexpected, or even expected but favorable, interest-rate changes as well.

THE NONIMMUNIZED PORTFOLIO

Alternatively, a nonimmunized portfolio must bear the risk of fluctuating bond values as well as the consequent risk that the portfolio will not have earned sufficient return to fully fund its liabilities. This condition may result from quarter-to-quarter positioning of the portfolio to take maximum advantage of anticipated changes in interest

---

[3] Redington, "Life-Office Valuations."

rates. If rates do not shift according to the anticipated plan, the long-term health of the bond portfolio may be thwarted by efforts to maximize short-term performance.

For this reason, a longer term framework can serve as a better guide when managing bonds that will eventually either be matched against long-term liabilities or be used for achieving predetermined interest-rate goals. Knowing the immunized or neutral position for a portfolio will give managers a better understanding of the degree of risk they have assumed. The portfolio manager who has firm expectations about the future direction of interest rates can also use the immunized position as the reference from which to base an active position. In this way, the manager is able to gauge the degree of risk he or she is assuming and plan the returns to be expected from the directional change in interest rates.

CONSTRUCTION OF AN IMMUNIZED PORTFOLIO

Lawrence Fisher and Roman Weil have defined an immunized portfolio as follows:[4]

> A portfolio of investments in bonds is *immunized* for a holding period if its value at the end of the holding period, regardless of the course of interest rates during the holding period, must be at least as large as it would have been had the interest-rate function been constant throughout the holding period.
>
> If the realized return on an investment in bonds is sure to be at least as large as the appropriately computed yield to the horizon, then that investment is immunized."

Fisher and Weil have demonstrated that to achieve the immunized result, the average duration of a portfolio of bonds must be set equal to the remaining time in the planning horizon.

As time passes however, the bond portfolio must be rebalanced so that the duration of the bond portfolio is set equal to the remaining life in the planning period. This condition requires that coupon income, interest on coupon income, matured principal, and proceeds from possible liquidation of longer bonds be reinvested in order to continually maintain the duration equal to the remaining life in the planning period. Because of these multiple rebalancings, the bond portfolio is maintained in an immunized state throughout the planning period and should achieve its interest-rate target return in spite of periodic shifts in rates.

An immunized bond portfolio, therefore, can be constructed once a time horizon has been established. Since duration is inversely related to both the prevailing yields and the coupon rate, it may not be possi-

---

[4] Fisher and Weil, "Coping with the Risk of Interest Rate Fluctuations."

ble to immunize a portfolio beyond a certain number of years. For example, when yields in the bond market reached a historic high in 1981, it was not possible to immunize beyond 10 years in the tax-exempt markets and eight years in the taxable markets.

Of course, the actual targeted return on an immunized portfolio will depend on the level of interest rates at the time the program is initiated. An immunized portfolio hedges interest-rate risk irrespective of rate changes. Though bond values may for example decline as interest rates rise, the future value of the portfolio (or security) based on the new (higher) reinvestment rate and lower principal value will still correspond to the original targeted yield. As we demonstrate later, duration is the key control of reinvestment rates and asset values as interest rates fluctuate.

The important point to remember is: The standard deviation of return on an immunized portfolio will be much lower over a given horizon than that on a nonimmunized portfolio—whether measured around the sample mean or promised yield. With interest-rate risk minimized (when held over an assumed time horizon), the performance of the immunized portfolio is virtually assured, regardless of reinvestment rates. For example, if we wanted to achieve a target return over five years, we could purchase, say, five-year bonds and hold them to maturity. By so doing, we can be certain (assuming no defaults occur) of receiving the specified coupon payments over the five-year period as well as the principal repayment at redemption. These two sources of income are fixed in dollar amounts. The third and final source of income is the interest earned on the semiannual coupon payments. "Interest on coupon" is not fixed in dollar amounts; rather it depends upon the interest-rate environments at the various times of payment. Thus to secure a targeted level of return five years hence, one must reduce or eliminate this "reinvestment risk" associated with the interest-on-coupon source of income.

Immunization seeks to do just that. By targeting the duration of the portfolio rather than specific maturities to the prespecified investment period of five years, we again see the offsets of capital gain and reinvestment return occurring in equal measure. Moreover, by varying the maturity pattern around the time horizon while still maintaining the same duration on the portfolio (i.e., barbell, even-ladder, or bullet maturity patterns[5]—we find different risk-return characteristics. The barbell and even-ladder strategies incorporate greater reinvestment risk, since matured principal must be reinvested in future unknown yield environments.

---

[5] For a discussion of these strategies, see H. Russell Fogler, William A. Groves, and James G. Richardson, "Managing Bonds: Are "Dumbbells" Smart?" *Journal of Portfolio Management,* Winter 1976, pp. 54–60.

Ideally, the exact maturity pattern to an immunized portfolio should not be of significance to the fixed result. However, there are two simplifying assumptions used in the theoretical literature on immunization, the harmful effects of which can be neutralized or minimized if we employ the bullet (or clustered) maturity pattern. The Macaulay duration measure assumes (1) a flat yield curve, and (2) parallel shifts of a flat yield curve.[6]

Since both assumptions are wholly unrealistic, we minimize their otherwise harmful effects by compressing the maturity pattern into a bullet, thereby creating a relatively flat yield curve over the restricted range of maturities. In any conceivable yield environment therefore, we minimize our violation of these two harsh assumptions with a bullet maturity pattern. As such, we are able to lock in prevailing rates for a fixed number of years regardless of future fluctuations in interest rates.

MATURITY MATCHING: THE REINVESTMENT PROBLEM WHEN IMMUNIZATION IS NOT USED

Suppose an investor wishes to lock in prevailing interest rates for a 10-year period. Then why not buy a 10-year bond?

An investor, however will *not* be protected from changes in interest rates with the purchase of a 10-year bond. A reinvestment problem arises as the reinvestment of coupon income occurs at rates below the original target yield. Note from Exhibit 1 that as interest rates shift and remain at the new levels for a 10-year period, the total "holding period" return on a 9 percent par bond due in 10 years will vary considerably. The initial effect will appear in the value of the asset. A capital gain (or loss) will appear immediately.

As the holding period increases after a change in rates, the interest-on-coupon component of total return begins to exert a stronger influence. At 10 years, we note that the interest on coupon exerts a dominance over capital gain (or loss) in the determination of holding period returns.

Intuitively we know that these relationships make sense. Capital gains appear instantly, whereas changes in reinvestment rates take time to exert their effect on the total holding period return on a bond.

Understanding the forces operating on the total return of a bond, we may now ask at what point do the forces of capital gain and reinvestment rate *equally* offset one another in a manner similar to a break even? If rates jump from 9 percent to 11 percent and a capital loss

---

[6] For a further discussion, see G. O. Bierwag, George G. Kaufman, Robert Schweitzer, and Alden Toevs, "The Art of Risk Management in Bond Portfolios," *Journal of Portfolio Management*, Spring 1981, pp. 27–36.

Exhibit 1
Total Return on a 9 Percent, $1,000 Bond Due in 10 Years and Held through Various Holding Periods

Income Source	Interest Rate at Time of Reinvestment	Holding Period in Years					
		1	3	5	6.79*	9	10
Coupon income....	5%	$ 90	$270	$450	$611	$ 810	$ 900
Capital gain or loss....		287	234	175	100	39	–0–
Interest on interest....		1	17	54	105	191	241
Total return....		$ 378	$ 521	$679	$816	$1,040	$1,141
(and yield)....		(37.0%)	(15.0%)	(11.0%)	(9.0%)	(8.5%)	(8.2%)
Coupon income....	7%	$ 90	$270	$450	$611	$ 810	$ 900
Capital gain or loss....		132	109	83	56	19	–0–
Interest on interest....		2	25	78	149	279	355
Total return....		$224	$404	$611	$816	$1,108	$1,255
(and yield)....		(22.0%)	(12.0%)	(10.0%)	(9.0%)	(8.6%)	(8.5%)
Coupon income....	9%	$ 90	$270	$450	$611	$ 810	$ 900
Capital gain or loss....		–0–	–0–	–0–	–0–	–0–	–0–
Interest on interest....		2	32	103	205	387	495
Total return....		$ 92	$302	$553	$816	$1,197	$1,395
(and yield)....		(9.0%)	(9.0%)	(9.0%)	(9.0%)	(9.0%)	(9.0%)
Coupon income....	11%	$ 90	$270	$450	$611	$ 810	$ 900
Capital gain or loss....		–112	–95	–75	–56	–18	–0–
Interest on interest....		2	40	129	261	502	647
Total return....		$ 20	$215	$504	$816	$1,294	$1,547
(and yield)....		(2.0%)	(6.7%)	(8.5%)	(9.0%)	(9.7%)	(9.8%)

* Duration of a 9 percent bond bought at par and due in 10 years.

occurs today, at what point will that capital loss be made up because we are reinvesting those coupon income payments in a higher (11 percent) rate environment? The two offsetting forces of capital value and reinvestment return equally offset at the duration of the bond—in this case at 6.79 years. In order to earn the original 9 percent target return (the original yield to maturity at the time of purchase) in this example, it is necessary to hold that bond for the period of its duration—6.79 years. If we wanted to lock in a market rate of 9 percent for a 10-year period, we would select a bond with a duration of 10 years (not a maturity of 10 years). The maturity for such a par bond in this yield environment is roughly 23 years.

From Exhibit 1 we note that regardless of the interest-rate fluctuations (in Exhibit 1 they fluctuate from 5 to 11 percent), we are still able to earn the 9 percent total return if our holding period is 6.79 years— the duration of the bond.

Similarly, in order to control the interest-rate risk of a portfolio of bonds, we must monitor the duration of the portfolio so that the duration of the portfolio always stays on that point of break-even. Regardless of how rates fluctuate, we are able to lock in rates and effectively eliminate the reinvestment risk that is associated with the maturity matching strategy.

Finally, the duration of a portfolio will not move in lock step with the passage of time. Therefore we must monitor and adjust the "duration wandering" that takes place by rebalancing the portfolio on an annual or as-needed basis. To illustrate, suppose the remaining life in the planning period has declined by a year—from 10 years to 9 years. The duration of that bond may have declined by less than a year—to, say, 9.2 years. In order to neutralize the harmful effects of this tendency, we should rebalance the portfolio in order to match the duration of the portfolio with the remaining time in the planning period. Left unchecked, duration wandering will effect the performance of a portfolio. By monitoring and adjusting the portfolio's duration, we remain immunized in the face of multiple shifts in interest rates and eliminate in the process the so-called reinvestment problem.

A SIMULATED ILLUSTRATION OF AN IMMUNIZED BOND PORTFOLIO

The immunization strategy will be illustrated for a U.S. Treasury bond portfolio. The following assumptions are made:

1. We begin our investment initially with $18 million on September 1, 1982.
2. The investment horizon is five years.
3. The portfolio will consist of U.S. Treasury bonds in maximum initial denominations of $1 million.

Exhibit 2
Assumed Yield Curves: 1982–87

	Year 1 9/1/82	Year 2 9/1/83	Year 3 9/1/84	Year 4 9/1/85	Year 5 9/1/86	At Termination 9/1/87
Reinvestment Rate:	12%	9%	9%	10%	9%	
1982	14	–	–	–	–	–
1983	14	10	–	–	–	–
1984	14	10	8	–	–	–
1985	14	10	8.13	10	–	–
1986	14	10	8.27	10.13	10	–
1987	14	10	8.40	10.27	10	8
1988	14	10	8.53	10.40	10	8.13
1989	14	10	8.67	10.53	10	8.27
1990	14	10	8.80	10.67	10	8.40
1991	14	10	8.93	10.80	10	8.53
1992	14	10	9.07	10.93	10	8.67
1993	14	10	9.20	11.07	10	8.80
1994	14	10	9.33	11.20	10	8.93
1995	14	10	9.47	11.33	10	9.07
1996	14	10	9.60	11.47	10	9.20
1997	14	10	9.73	11.60	10	9.33
1998	14	10	9.87	11.73	10	9.47
1999	14	10	10.00	11.87	10	9.60
2000	14	10	10.13	12.00	10	9.73

4. Our target yield established on September 1, 1982, was 14 percent.

5. The specific Treasury bonds used in the simulation are shown in Exhibit 3.

6. The yield curve assumptions used in this simulation are presented in Exhibit 2. These are *not* interest-rate projections. They are used here in order to subject an immunized portfolio to a wide variety of interest rate fluctuations over the five-year horizon.

7. We assumed a transaction cost of a quarter point on bond sales and no transaction cost on bond purchases.

Exhibit 3 presents the following information for the portfolio at the beginning of each year including issues in the portfolio, market value of each issue in the portfolio, total market value, duration, average maturity, average coupon, average yield, and transaction fees. Notice that the duration of the portfolio is adjusted each year so as to approximately match the remaining period in the time horizon. Exhibits 4 through 8 summarize the actual portfolio transactions each year.

The important conclusion drawn from the above example is that immunization does work, even in the hostile yield environment envisioned in this scenario. We note from Exhibit 9 that the target yield of 14 percent and target future value of $34,565,757 were exceeded by 33 basis points and $516,581, respectively.[7] We demonstrated, therefore,

---

[7] Since the initial investment is $17,952,371 and the target yield is 14 percent, the target value is

$$(1.1400)^5 \times \$17,952,371 = \$34,565,757$$

Exhibit 3

PORTFOLIO STATUS REPORT: At beginning of Year 1, September 1, 1982

PAR (000)	Issue	Coupon	Maturity	Price	Yield	Market Value
1000	Tsy	12.375	1/15/88	93.96	14.00	$ 955,454
1000	Tsy	13.250	4/15/88	97.10	14.00	1,021,107
1000	Tsy	8.250	5/15/88	77.87	14.00	803,013
1000	Tsy	14.000	7/15/88	100.00	14.00	1,017,891
1000	Tsy	15.375	10/15/88	105.48	14.00	1,112,926
1000	Tsy	14.625	1/15/89	102.53	14.00	1,044,010
1000	Tsy	14.375	4/15/89	101.54	14.00	1,069,108
1000	Tsy	9.250	5/15/89	79.72	14.00	824,498
1000	Tsy	14.500	7/15/89	102.11	14.00	1,039,690
1000	Tsy	10.750	11/15/89	85.49	14.00	886,625
1000	Tsy	8.250	5/15/90	73.37	14.00	758,023
1000	Tsy	10.750	8/15/90	84.68	14.00	851,610
1000	Tsy	13.000	11/15/90	95.15	14.00	989,850
1000	Tsy	14.50	5/15/91	102.41	14.00	1,066,817
1000	Tsy	14.250	11/15/91	101.21	14.00	1,054,091
1000	Tsy	14.625	2/15/92	103.20	14.00	1,038,533
1000	Tsy	13.75	5/15/92	98.630	14.00	1,026,869
1000	Tsy	7.250	8/15/92	64.31	14.00	646,334
1000	Tsy	6.750	2/15/93	60.78	14.00	610,881
200	Tsy	7.875	2/15/93	66.87	14.00	134,440

Total Market Value: $17,952,371   **Average Maturity:** 4/ 7/90

Total Par Value: $19,200,000   **Average Coupon:** 12.055 percent

Duration: 4.963 years   **Average Yield:** 14.000 percent

PORTFOLIO STATUS REPORT: At beginning of Year 2, September 1, 1983

PAR (000)	Issue	Coupon	Maturity	Price	Yield	Market Value
5500	Tsy	13.750	8/15/87	111.995	10.00	$6,193,351
2000	Tsy	7.625	11/15/87	91.983	10.00	1,884,566
1000	Tsy	12.375	1/15/88	108.220	10.00	1,098,014
1000	Tsy	13.250	4/15/88	111.769	10.00	1,167,747
1000	Tsy	8.250	5/15/88	93.532	10.00	959,613
1000	Tsy	14.000	7/15/88	115.103	10.00	1,168,921
1000	Tsy	15.375	10/15/88	121.109	10.00	1,269,176
1000	Tsy	14.625	1/15/89	118.835	10.00.	1,207,040
1000	Tsy	14.375	4/15/89	118.441	10.00	1,238,718
1000	Tsy	9.250	5/15/89	96.771	10.00	994,948
1000	Tsy	14.500	7/15/89	119.594	10.00	1,214,470
1000	Tsy	10.750	11/15/89	103.375	10.00	1,065,405
1000	Tsy	8.250	5/15/90	91.572	10.00	940,013
1000	Tsy	10.750	8/15/90	103.685	10.00	1,041,630
1000	Tsy	13.000	11/15/90	115.110	10.00	1,189,380
1000	Tsy	14.500	5/15/91	123.741	10.00	1,280,107

Total Market Value: $23,913,099   **Average Maturity:** 11/ 1/88

Total Par Value: $21,500,000   **Average Coupon:** 12.285 percent

Duration: 4.007 years   **Average Yield:** 10.000 percent

Exhibit 3 (*continued*)

PORTFOLIO STATUS REPORT: At beginning of Year 3, September 1, 1984

PAR (000)	Issue	Coupon	Maturity	Price	Yield	Market Value
11800	Tsy	13.750	8/15/87	113.738	8.40	$13,493,227
2000	Tsy	7.625	11/15/87	97.788	8.42	2,000,666
1000	Tsy	12.375	1/15/88	111.318	8.44	1,128,994
1000	Tsy	13.250	4/15/88	114.622	8.47	1,196,277
1000	Tsy	8.250	5/15/88	99.261	8.48	1,016,903
1000	Tsy	14.000	7/15/88	117.766	8.51	1,195,551
1000	Tsy	15.375	10/15/88	123.268	8.55	1,290,766
1000	Tsy	14.625	1/15/89	121.629	8.58	1,234,980
1000	Tsy	14.375	4/15/89	121.536	8.62	1,269,668
1000	Tsy	9.250	5/15/89	102.333	8.63	1,050,568
1000	Tsy	14.500	7/15/89	122.789	8.66	1,246,420
1000	Tsy	10.750	11/15/89	108.453	8.69	1,116,185

Total Market Value: $27,240,204   **Average Maturity:**   3/ 8/88

Total Par Value: $23,800,000   **Average Coupon:**   12.784 percent

Duration: 2.974 years   **Average Yield:**   8.470 percent

PORTFOLIO STATUS REPORT: At beginning of Year 4, September 1, 1985

PAR (000)	Issue	Coupon	Maturity	Price	Yield	Market Value
17800	Tsy	13.750	8/15/87	106.014	10.27	$18,979,318
2000	Tsy	7.625	11/15/87	94.835	10.29	1,941,606
1000	Tsy	12.375	1/15/88	104.220	10.31	1,058,014
1000	Tsy	13.250	4/15/88	106.507	10.34	1,115,127
1000	Tsy	8.250	5/15/88	95.127	10.35	975,563
1000	Tsy	14.000	7/15/88	108.763	10.38	1,105,521
1000	Tsy	15.375	10/15/88	112.888	10.42	1,186,966
1000	Tsy	14.625	1/15/89	111.579	10.45	1,134,480
1000	Tsy	14.375	4/15/89	111.429	10.49	1,168,598

Total Market Value: $28,665,193   **Average Maturity:**   11/25/87

Total Par Value: $26,800,000   **Average Coupon:**   13.144 percent

Duration: 2.012 years   **Average Yield:**   10.300 percent

that targeted rates may be obtained over a predetermined immunization term, regardless of fluctuations in market yields.

In contrast to the measured assumption of risk, the immunization strategy offers the opportunity to *control* and *minimize* interest rate risk and to reduce the standard deviation of expected return on a

Exhibit 3 (*concluded*)

PORTFOLIO STATUS REPORT: At beginning of Year 5, September 1, 1986

PAR (000)	Issue	Coupon	Maturity	Price	Yield	Market Value
23700	Tsy	13.750	8/15/87	103.326	10.00	$24,633,159
4000	Tsy	7.625	11/15/87	97.342	10.00	3,983,492
1000	Tsy	12.375	1/15/88	102.948	10.00	1,045,294
1000	Tsy	13.250	4/15/88	104.728	10.00	1,097,337
1000	Tsy	8.250	5/15/88	97.293	10.00	997,223

Total Market Value: $31,756,506 **Average Maturity:** 9/17/87

Total Par Value: $30,700,000 **Average Coupon:** 12.712 percent

Duration: 1.013 years **Average Yield:** 10.000 percent

PORTFOLIO STATUS REPORT: At termination of portfolio, September 1, 1987

PAR (000)	Issue	Coupon	Maturity	Price	Yield	Market Value
4000	Tsy	7.625	11/15/87	99.882	8.02	$4,083,393
1000	Tsy	12.375	1/15/88	101.542	8.05	1,030,545
1000	Tsy	13.250	4/15/88	103.073	8.09	1,080,050
1000	Tsy	8.250	5/15/88	100.082	8.10	1,024,654

Total Market Value: $7,218,641 **Average Maturity:** 1/10/88

Total Par Value: $7,000,000 **Average Coupon:** 9.196 percent

Duration: 0.368 years **Average Yield:** 8.050 percent

portfolio. It is a strategy which may suit the preferences of many types of investors, particularly those who wish to have a "core" or segment of their portfolios appreciate at a fixed, assured rate over a finite period.

Exhibit 4

BOND IMMUNIZATION YEAR END TRANSACTIONS REPORT: **YEAR** 1982   **AUGUST 31, 19**83

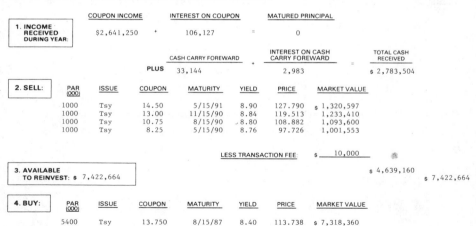

		COUPON INCOME		INTEREST ON COUPON		MATURED PRINCIPAL		
1. INCOME RECEIVED DURING YEAR:		$2,314,500	+	134,471	=	0		

				CASH CARRY FOREWARD		INTEREST ON CASH CARRY FOREWARD		TOTAL CASH RECEIVED
			PLUS	47,629	+	5,715	=	$ 2,502,315

2. SELL:

PAR (000)	ISSUE	COUPON	MATURITY	YIELD	PRICE	MARKET VALUE	
200	Tsy	7.875	2/15/93	10.00	87.189	175,078	
1000	Tsy	6.750	2/15/93	10.00	80.411	$ 807,111	
1000	Tsy	7.250	8/15/92	10.00	83.970	842,924	
1000	Tsy	13.750	5/15/92	10.00	121.423	1,254,719	
1000	Tsy	14.625	2/15/92	10.00	125.970	1,266,203	
1000	Tsy	14.250	11/15/91	10.00	123.375	1,275,711	

LESS TRANSACTION FEE: $ 13,000

$ 5,608,746

3. AVAILABLE TO REINVEST: $ 8,111,061 $ 8,111,061

4. BUY:

PAR (000)	ISSUE	COUPON	MATURITY	YIELD	PRICE	MARKET VALUE
5500	Tsy	13.750	8/15/87	10.00	111.995	$ 6,193,351
2000	Tsy	7.625	11/15/87	10.00	91.983	1,884,566

$ 7,318,360

5. CASH CARRY FOREWARD: $104,304 $ 7,318,360

$ 104,304

Exhibit 5

BOND IMMUNIZATION YEAR END TRANSACTIONS REPORT: **YEAR** 1983   **AUGUST 31, 19**84

		COUPON INCOME		INTEREST ON COUPON		MATURED PRINCIPAL		
1. INCOME RECEIVED DURING YEAR:		$2,641,250	+	106,127	=	0		

				CASH CARRY FOREWARD		INTEREST ON CASH CARRY FOREWARD		TOTAL CASH RECEIVED
			PLUS	33,144	+	2,983	=	$ 2,783,504

2. SELL:

PAR (000)	ISSUE	COUPON	MATURITY	YIELD	PRICE	MARKET VALUE
1000	Tsy	14.50	5/15/91	8.90	127.790	$ 1,320,597
1000	Tsy	13.00	11/15/90	8.84	119.513	1,233,410
1000	Tsy	10.75	8/15/90	8.80	108.882	1,093,600
1000	Tsy	8.25	5/15/90	8.76	97.726	1,001,553

LESS TRANSACTION FEE: $ 10,000

$ 4,639,160

3. AVAILABLE TO REINVEST: $ 7,422,664 $ 7,422,664

4. BUY:

PAR (000)	ISSUE	COUPON	MATURITY	YIELD	PRICE	MARKET VALUE
5400	Tsy	13.750	8/15/87	8.40	113.738	$ 7,318,360

$ 7,318,360

5. CASH CARRY FOREWARD: $104,304 $ 7,318,360

$ 104,304

Exhibit 6

BOND IMMUNIZATION YEAR END TRANSACTIONS REPORT: YEAR 1934   **AUGUST 31, 1985**

	COUPON INCOME		INTEREST ON COUPON		MATURED PRINCIPAL		
1. INCOME RECEIVED DURING YEAR:	$3,042,500	+	108,952	=	0		

			CASH CARRY FOREWARD	+	INTEREST ON CASH CARRY FOREWARD	=	TOTAL CASH RECEIVED
		PLUS	104,304		9,387		$ 3,265,143

2. SELL:	PAR (000)	ISSUE	COUPON	MATURITY	YIELD	PRICE	MARKET VALUE
	1000	Tsy	10.750	11/15/89	10.56	100.599	$ 1,037,645
	1000	Tsy	14.500	7/15/89	10.53	112.328	1,141,810
	1000	Tsy	9.250	5/15/89	10.50	96.214	989,378

LESS TRANSACTION FEE: $ 7,500

3. AVAILABLE TO REINVEST: $ 6,426,476				$ 3,161,333 $ 6,426,476

4. BUY:	PAR (000)	ISSUE	COUPON	MATURITY	YIELD	PRICE	MARKET VALUE
	6000	Tsy	13.750	8/15/87	10.27	106.014	$ 6,397,523

$ 6,397,523

5. CASH CARRY FOREWARD: $28,953	$ 6,397,523
	$ 28,953

Exhibit 7

BOND IMMUNIZATION YEAR END TRANSACTIONS REPORT: YEAR 1985   **AUGUST 31, 1986**

	COUPON INCOME		INTEREST ON COUPON		MATURED PRINCIPAL		
1. INCOME RECEIVED DURING YEAR:	$3,522,500	+	129,016	=	0		

			CASH CARRY FOREWARD	+	INTEREST ON CASH CARRY FOREWARD	=	TOTAL CASH RECEIVED
		PLUS	28,953		2,895		$ 3,683,364

2. SELL:	PAR (000)	ISSUE	COUPON	MATURITY	YIELD	PRICE	MARKET VALUE
	1000	Tsy	14.375	4/15/89	10.00	109.845	$ 1,152,758
	1000	Tsy	14.625	1/15/89	10.00	109.523	1,113,920
	1000	Tsy	15.375	10/15/88	10.00	110.019	1,158,276
	1000	Tsy	14.000	7/18/88	10.00	106.647	1,084,361

LESS TRANSACTION FEE: $ 10,000

3. AVAILABLE TO REINVEST: $ 8,182,679				$ 4,499,315 $ 8,182,679

4. BUY:	PAR (000)	ISSUE	COUPON	MATURITY	YIELD	PRICE	MARKET VALUE
	5900	Tsy	13.750	8/15/87	10.00	103.326	$ 6,132,305
	2000	Tsy	7.625	11/15/87	10.00	97.342	1,991,746

$ 8,124,051

5. CASH CARRY FOREWARD: $58,628	$ 8,124,051
	$ 58,628

Exhibit 8

BOND IMMUNIZATION YEAR END TRANSACTIONS REPORT: **YEAR**   1986   **AUGUST 31, 19**87

	COUPON INCOME	INTEREST ON COUPON	MATURED PRINCIPAL	
1. INCOME RECEIVED DURING YEAR:	$3,902,500	+ 214,792	= 23,700,000	

	CASH CARRY FORWARD	INTEREST ON CASH CARRY FORWARD	TOTAL CASH RECEIVED
PLUS	58,628	+ 5,276	= $ 27,881,197

2. SELL:

PAR (000)	ISSUE	COUPON	MATURITY	YIELD	PRICE	MARKET VALUE
1000	Tsy	8.250	5/15/88	8.10	100.082	$ 1,024,654
1000	Tsy	13.250	4/15/88	8.09	103.073	1,080,050
1000	Tsy	12.375	1/15/88	8.05	101.542	1,030,545
4000	Tsy	7.625	11/15/87	8.02	99.882	4,083,393

LESS TRANSACTION FEE: $ 17,500

3. AVAILABLE TO REINVEST: $ 35,082,338

$ 7,201,141

$ 35,082,338

4. BUY:

PAR (000)	ISSUE	COUPON	MATURITY	YIELD	PRICE	MARKET VALUE
						$

5. CASH CARRY FOREWARD:

$ _____

$

Exhibit 9
Performance Evaluation Report

Valuation Date	Market Value of Portfolio	Market Yield	Years Remaining	Compounded Future Value	Target Future Value
9/1/82	$17,952,371	14.00%	5.0	$34,565,757	$34,565,757
9/1/83	23,913,099	10.00	4.0	35,011,168	34,565,757
9/1/84	27,240,204	8.47	3.0	34,764,763	34,565,757
9/1/85	28,665,193	10.30	2.0	34,874,332	34,565,757
9/1/86	31,756,506	10.00	1.0	34,932,157	34,565,757
9/1/87	35,082,338	–	0.0	35,082,338	34,565,757

Realized Yield: 14.33%

Target Yield: 14.00%

Surplus Yield: 33 basis points

Surplus Value: $516,581

GENERAL CONCERNS WHEN IMMUNIZATION IS USED

There are four concerns that have to be considered when applying the concept of bond portfolio immunization.

1. Although an immunized portfolio is a hedge against changes in interest rates, it is not a hedge against credit risk. All bonds used in a corporate or municipal bond immunization portfolio would have to be reviewed in terms of creditworthiness.

2. Taxes must be considered in the return calculations of nonpension immunized portfolios. For taxable investors, taxes must be paid on all coupon payments except in the case of tax-exempt obligations. Moreover, if discount bonds are used and later are sold at higher prices or mature at par, the taxes to be paid on the capital gains would have to be factored into the overall yield expectations.

3. The credit quality of the portfolio must be kept constant throughout its life. If the initial portfolio is composed of A-rated bonds, and a target yield is initially determined on that basis, swapping into Aa rated or better bonds would adversely impact the performance in relation to the yield target.

4. When bonds are swapped in an immunized portfolio, the spread between bid and asked prices should be as narrow as possible. Though spreads are tight in the government market, they widen slightly in the corporate market, but can widen even more in the municipal market. Unless good execution can be obtained, the expected immunized yields could be adversely impacted.

Dealing with High Corporate, State, and Municipal Pension Costs by "Dedicating" a Bond Portfolio

37

PETER E. CHRISTENSEN
Vice President
The First Boston Corporation

SYLVAN G. FELDSTEIN, Ph.D.*
Vice President and Bond Analyst
Moody's Investors Service, Inc.

FRANK J. FABOZZI, Ph.D., C.F.A., C.P.A.
Professor of Economics
Fordham University

INTRODUCTION

Although a great deal of attention in the financial literature has focused on investment strategy from an asset management perspective, relatively little has been written about investment strategy from a "funding" perspective—that is, in relationship to the liabilities of a pension system. As a result, investment or funding strategies are typically not evaluated in terms of their inherent "funding risks." In this chapter we introduce and describe the "dedicated-pension strategy" as an investment approach that minimizes the amount of funding risk assumed by a portion of a defined benefit pension plan. Once we trace through this minimum risk strategy, we may then better evaluate the incremental funding risks assumed by current active asset management strategies. This chapter then summarizes how the dedicated pension strategy may be generalized to a broader range of portfolio objectives.

---

* This chapter was written while the author was Vice President and Analyst in the Fixed-Income Research Department at Smith Barney, Harris Upham & Co., Inc. The views expressed in this chapter are those of the author and not necessarily those of Moody's Investors Service.

The Need for a Broader Asset/Liability Focus

The need for a more complete funding perspective is best illustrated by the enormous discrepancy that exists between current actuarial rates and currently available market yields on fixed income investments. Many private and public pension systems are laboring under low actuarial investment return assumptions of 6 percent to 8 percent. Yet ironically, these low valuations occur at a time when long-term taxable yields on fixed income securities have soared to as high as 15 percent and 16 percent. Why is this enormous discrepancy allowed to exist?

A primary reason for this disparity is the current assumption of high funding risks by investment managers and plan sponsors in their deployment of plan assets. Since most plan assets are not managed in relationship to plan liabilities, great uncertainty is created by the use of both active investment management strategies and today's extremely volatile bond, stock, real estate, and commodity instruments. These two factors are certain to create a wide dispersion in possible investment returns over an extended period of time. Since future investment performance can be so unpredictable, the actuarial profession has included a wide margin of conservatism in its actuarial cost determinations and investment return assumptions.

As an example of performance uncertainty, note from Exhibit 1 that with active bond management, performance can range from very good

Exhibit 1

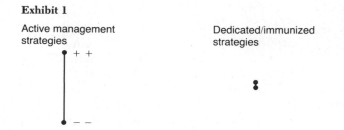

to very poor. Of course, to do very well, the pension manager must consistently forecast interest rates correctly and position his or her bond portfolio accordingly. Since there are hazards in attempting to correctly forecast interest rates, the probability is that out of the universe of all pension managers who actively manage their funds, a few should do very well, a few should do very poorly, and the rest should cluster somewhere in the middle range.

Exhibit 2 illustrates this point graphically. We assign subjective probabilities to various investment-return outcomes over an extended time horizon. We have assumed that the current level of interest rates is 15 percent—the approximate rate of an immunized or dedicated portfolio.

Exhibit 2
Expected Investment Return Outcomes with Active Strategies
(10-year horizon)

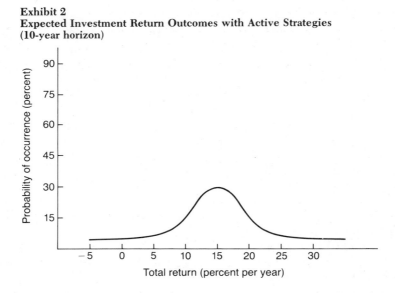

We should note that as rates fluctuate in volatile markets, the median rate (with perhaps the highest probability) might also be expected to fluctuate around market levels. Therefore such imponderables as the future course of inflation and interest rates and future "success probabilities" of an active investment manager defy accurate quantification. Since future investment performance can be so unpredictable, actuaries must build into their actuarial cost determinations and investment return assumptions a wide margin of conservatism.

As an example, who knows how much the General Motors Corporation pension plan is going to earn over the next 10, 20, or 30 years? Their actuary is currently assuming 7 percent. Unless investment managers can develop an investment strategy that can provide a *precise* answer to that question, plan sponsors still must live with the actuarial consequences of risky active management strategies.

Furthermore, as we illustrate in Exhibit 3, the dedicated strategy lends much greater *precision* to the funding of defined pension liabilities. It is probably as close as we can come, as investment managers, to the *perfect* funding of known pension liabilities.

As inferred from Exhibit 3, the risk/return distribution that results from the dedicated strategy contrasts strongly with the risk/return distribution that results from an active timing strategy as displayed in Exhibit 2.

Current Plan Sponsor Problems

The extreme importance of the investment return assumption is manifested in the following plan sponsor problems. First, a wide dis-

Exhibit 3
Expected Investment Return Outcomes Using the Dedicated Strategy

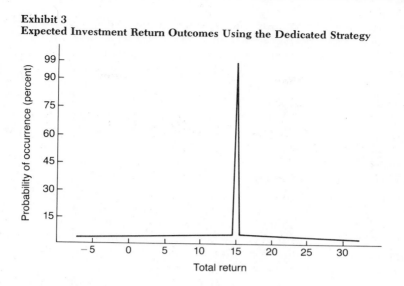

parity exists between low actuarial return assumptions and today's high yields, which is partially the result of risky active management strategies. Second, high unfunded liability positions exist due to these low actuarial valuations. And last, high and inflated pension contribution levels occur that are caused by conservative valuations and high funding risk profiles, again partially the result of risky active management strategies.

Since the high yields of between 13 percent and 15 percent available at the time of this writing cannot be perpetually assumed over an actuary's long planning horizon, actuaries must protect plan participants and assume less than current market level returns. Since funding risk can be very high using active timing strategies, most plans must labor under low return assumptions, large asset requirements, and high contribution levels to compensate for this risk.

Is there a way to reduce a plan's funding risk in order to fully fund a plan's liabilities and achieve the benefits of higher actuarial valuations? We think so.

THE DEDICATED PENSION STRATEGY

Though there is not currently available an investment strategy that can fully fund a plan's entire liabilities, there is a strategy that can minimize the funding risks for a portion of a plan's assets and, with the actuary's permission, help raise a plan's presently low actuarial valuations to higher, more current levels.

The approach is called the *dedicated pension strategy*. With the "dedicated" approach we, for the first time, match the assets of a corporate, state, or municipal pension system with a portion of its liabilities. That is, we first specify a schedule of liabilities to be funded—specifically, the expected benefit payouts for the closed block of current retirees of a plan—and then structure the assets so that the cash flow from those assets will match very closely the benefit payouts furnished by the actuary.

Once we fully fund the retired payouts and lock in the high yields of 13 to 15 percent offered at the time of this writing, the actuary may then raise the investment return assumption to a more current 13 percent.

It is understandable that an actuary would raise the assumed rate on a dedicated structure, since the dedicated plan has funded its liabilities with much greater *precision*. Although plan assets are currently managed without regard to plan liabilities for favorable quarter-to-quarter or year-to-year performance rankings, the dedicated strategy represents the first attempt in recent times to manage a plan's assets in relationship to a plan's liabilities.

Because retired liabilities can be funded with great precision using the dedicated structure, the investment and actuarial benefits of the dedicated approach can be fivefold.

1. By dedicating or matching assets to fund-retired liabilities, conservatively low investment return assumptions can, with the approval of the actuary, be dramatically raised to current market levels.
2. By raising the investment return assumption, the unfunded liabilities of the pension system (or the present value of accumulated plan benefits) can also be reduced substantially.
3. The plan sponsor now has new policy options available, such as reducing contributions or permitting greater freedom to raise benefit levels if the plan wishes a catch-up with inflation.
4. Reduced contributions can provide needed budget and earnings relief to a company, state government, or municipality in a year in which company profits and government budgets are tight.
5. By implementing the dedicated approach for the retired portion of the plan, the plan sponsor has virtually eliminated market risk or "funding risk" from a significant part of a plan's liability and thereby eliminated the problem of market value fluctuations when reporting unfunded positions associated with the liability.

AN ACTUAL EXAMPLE

Several large pension plans for which we have already applied the dedicated strategy have been able to raise their actuarial rates to 14 percent and 15 percent on the dedicated portion of their plan from levels of 6 percent and 7½ percent, reduce their annual contributions by as much as 50 percent per year, increase their reported earnings, and reduce or eliminate their unfunded liability positions as well.

In the following simulation, we illustrate how the dedicated pension strategy is specifically applied.

Determining the Liabilities

The first step in establishing a dedicated bond portfolio is to determine the exact forecast of benefit payouts for the retired lives portion of the plan. For our simulation Exhibit 4 shows by year the schedule

Exhibit 4
The Schedule of Expected Benefit Payouts

Year	Payout Amounts
1982 (9/1)	$ 8,067,461
1983	23,225,960
1984	22,444,547
1985	21,626,503
1986	20,776,913
1987	19,897,961
1988	18,994,617
1989	18,062,762
1990	17,117,618
1991	16,147,201
1992	15,163,588
1993	14,177,133
1994	13,188,631
1995	12,192,553
1996	11,224,388
1997	10,266,058
1998	9,338,069
1999	8,433,031
2000	7,575,599
2001	6,767,880
2002	5,996,468
2003	5,278,810
2004	4,604,799
2005	3,939,332
2006	3,439,599
2007	2,934,052
2008	2,497,460
2009	2,093,629
2010	1,748,721
2011	1,447,570
Total Liability	$328,568,813

of benefit payouts in dollar amounts that are expected to be paid to those vested employees who have already retired.

This payout schedule is furnished by the actuaries to the pension system. These forecasted payouts are based upon a number of variables, such as mortality projections, spouse benefit assumptions, cost-

of-living assumptions as well as the known benefit payouts at retirement for the individual employees. As shown in Exhibit 4 the total
estimated liability in nominal dollars over a 30-year time horizon for
those employees who have already retired is $328,568,813.

It should be noted that over time this liability schedule should be
reviewed by the plan's actuaries to determine that the various mortality and benefit assumptions remain accurate.

Selecting the Optimum Portfolio of Bonds

Having been provided the expected benefit payouts for the retired
portion of the plan, the next step in instituting a dedicated bond portfolio is to specify the portfolio constraint on quality, sector, and issue
selection. For example, a portfolio manager may want an optimum or
"least cost" portfolio that will satisfy all of the liability obligation and
be of Aa quality or better, having a 20 percent maximum limit in utility
paper, a 25 percent maximum in finance paper, and another 25 percent
maximum in foreign names.

The third and final step in instituting a dedicated portfolio is to
specify the assumed reinvestment rate for the plan, usually the current actuarial rate. Since the timing of cash receipts does not always
match the timing of cash disbursements, we are required to reinvest
the surplus funds at an assumed future rate until the next liability
payout date. This reinvestment rate is of vital importance because it is
often preferable to prefund future benefit payments with higher yielding issues and reinvest the prefunded amounts at the lower (assumed)
reinvestment rate than to purchase lower yielding issues that mature
closer to the liability payment dates.

Once the schedule of expected benefit payouts, the portfolio constraints, and the reinvestment rate are specified, we then structure the
least cost portfolio to fully fund or defease the expected benefit payouts specified by the actuary.

Exhibit 5 displays the specific bonds we have used in our simulation to achieve this cash flow match. We should note that assembling a
dedicated portfolio that has a very high probability of attaining its
funding objective over time does necessitate a restricted universe of
available issues. The fund manager must avoid questionable credits
and, most important, avoid issues that may be called prior to maturity
or that have large sinking funds. Defaults and loss of issues prior to
maturity would mean that the funding of the liability schedule would
not be sufficient. As a result, most current coupon bonds are not appropriate for a dedicated structure.

We would also recommend that the portfolio be reviewed periodically by the fund manager or investment advisor to reassess credit
quality, call activity, and swapping potential.

Exhibit 5
A Sample Dedicated Portfolio of U.S.
Treasury Bonds

Par Amount $000	Coupon Rate	Maturity Date
673	11.125	8/31/82
3,000	12.125	10/31/82
3,000	14.500	4/30/83
3,000	15.500	10/31/83
2,600	13.875	4/30/84
3,200	12.125	9/30/84
3,000	13.375	3/31/85
3,100	15.875	9/30/85
2,600	14.000	3/31/86
3,200	14.875	6/30/86
3,900	16.125	11/15/86
2,900	13.750	8/15/87
3,100	12.375	1/15/88
3,200	14.000	7/15/88
3,000	14.625	1/15/89
7,800	14.500	7/15/89
2,000	10.750	8/15/90
3,000	13.000	11/15/90
4,600	14.500	5/15/91
9,400	14.625	2/15/92
3,100	8.625	8/15/93
2,900	9.000	2/15/94
2,000	8.750	8/15/94
2,700	10.125	11/15/94
5,300	10.375	5/15/95
2,400	12.625	5/15/95
12,000	11.500	11/15/95
2,900	8.500	5/15/99
3,300	7.875	2/15/00
3,800	11.750	2/15/01
12,000	15.750	11/15/01
8,700	14.250	2/15/02
2,500	11.750	2/15/10

In Exhibit 5, note a caveat to our analysis: We illustrate the cash flow matching concept by using round lot purchases. In an actual portfolio, we could have used the exact number of bonds necessary to complete the match.

The Cash Flow Match

Exhibit 6 summarizes the cash flow match inherent in a dedicated structure. Note that in every year, the cash flow generated from the maturing principal when added to the cash flow generated from the coupon income will almost precisely offset the liability requirements

Exhibit 6
A Summary of the Cash Flow Match

Period Ending	Maturing Principal	Coupon Income	Reinvestment Income	Liability Payments	Surplus Deficit	Cumulative Surplus
9/ 1/82	673,000	2,503,309	8,049	−1,991,886	1,192,471	1,192,471
9/ 1/83	6,000,001	17,225,743	136,890	−23,395,126	−32,493	1,159,979
9/ 1/84	5,600,001	16,376,368	115,092	−22,639,894	−548,433	611,546
9/ 1/85	6,200,001	15,589,118	125,441	−21,831,010	83,551	695,097
9/ 1/86	8,900,001	14,747,806	139,292	−20,989,299	2,797,800	3,492,897
9/ 1/87	6,800,001	13,347,306	223,511	−20,117,685	253,133	3,746,030
9/ 1/88	6,300,001	12,442,307	181,143	−19,220,445	−296,995	3,449,036
9/ 1/89	10,800,002	11,583,120	203,721	−18,295,716	4,291,127	7,740,162
9/ 1/90	2,000,000	10,232,745	303,141	−17,353,893	−4,818,006	2,922,156
9/ 1/91	7,600,001	9,822,745	240,129	−16,389,795	1,273,081	4,195,237
9/ 1/92	9,400,002	8,273,371	419,266	−15,409,479	2,683,160	6,878,397
9/ 1/93	3,100,001	7,585,997	266,296	−14,423,738	−3,471,445	3,406,952
9/ 1/94	4,900,001	7,188,122	151,788	−13,435,751	−1,195,841	2,211,111
9/ 1/95	10,400,002	6,745,935	282,143	−12,441,571	4,986,508	7,197,619
9/ 1/96	12,000,002	5,066,373	980,330	−11,466,433	6,580,272	13,777,891
9/ 1/97		4,376,373	763,687	−10,505,644	−5,365,585	8,412,306
9/ 1/98		4,376,373	411,971	−9,570,064	−4,781,721	3,630,586
9/ 1/99	2,900,000	4,376,373	161,191	−8,659,294	−1,221,730	2,408,856
9/ 1/ 0	3,300,001	3,999,935	158,856	−7,789,960	−331,167	2,077,688
9/ 1/ 1	3,800,001	3,646,748	174,601	−6,969,810	651,539	2,729,227
9/ 1/ 2	20,700,003	1,858,624	1,076,967	−6,189,324	17,446,270	20,175,497
9/ 1/ 3		293,750	1,261,810	−5,458,227	−3,902,667	16,272,830
9/ 1/ 4		293,750	1,009,177	−4,773,300	−3,470,373	12,802,457
9/ 1/ 5		293,750	780,738	−4,105,701	−3,031,213	9,771,244
9/ 1/ 6		293,750	583,442	−3,564,531	−2,687,339	7,083,904
9/ 1/ 7		293,750	408,293	−3,060,435	−2,358,391	4,725,513
9/ 1/ 8		293,750	256,204	−2,606,610	−2,056,656	2,668,857
9/ 1/ 9		293,750	122,502	−2,194,587	−1,778,335	890,522
9/ 1/10	2,500,000	146,875	102,462	−1,834,878	914,459	1,804,981
9/ 1/11			77,319	−1,522,835	−1,445,517	359,465
12/31/11			4,150	−361,893	−357,743	1,721
TOTALS:	133,873,022	183,567,913	11,129,600	−328,568,813	1,721	

specified by the actuary in Exhibit 4. Since most coupon income is being paid out to fund the liability, the portfolio is assuming very little reinvestment risk. The plan can therefore lock in at the time of this writing the high rates of over 13 percent available using this matching structure.

In this simulation we have minimized the reinvestment risk by structuring relatively small surplus positions in every year. Again, in an actual dedicated bond portfolio, it is usually desirable and sometimes necessary to prefund some payouts with higher yielding issues than to purchase bonds with better matching characteristics, but with a lower yield to payout. Note from Exhibit 6 the large amount of prefunding in the 2002 due to the lack of available and desireable issues in subsequent years.

Pricing the Bonds

It is important to notice in Exhibit 6 that prices or yields do not appear in the analysis. The dedicated portfolio is concerned only with cash flows. As long as all coupon payments are made in a timely fashion and as long as every maturing bond is redeemed on time, then all of the retired liabilities specified by the actuary will be fully funded. Though the credit ratings on some of the bonds in a portfolio may deteriorate over time and their market prices drop markedly, the dedicated structure is still preserved as long as all cash flow payments are punctual.

Prices and yields enter the analysis in Exhibit 7. Listed in Exhibit 7 are the market values of all the bonds that were displayed in Exhibit 5. In this simulation, all bonds were priced as of August 2, 1982.

Exhibit 7
The Pricing of the Bonds in the Sample Dedicated Bond Portfolio*

Bond Name	Face Value ($100)	Coupon Rate	Maturity Date	Yield Mat/Call	Price	Market Value
U.S. Treasury.......	673	11.125	8/31/82	9.86	100.065	704842
U.S. Treasury.......	3,000	12.125	10/31/82	10.49	100.317	3101458
U.S. Treasury.......	3,000	14.500	4/30/83	12.07	101.626	3159946
U.S. Treasury.......	3,000	15.500	10/31/83	12.65	103.129	3211411
U.S. Treasury.......	2,600	13.875	4/30/84	12.97	101.313	2726329
U.S. Treasury.......	3,200	12.125	9/30/84	12.85	98.623	3287422
U.S. Treasury.......	3,000	13.375	3/31/85	13.07	100.624	3153582
U.S. Treasury.......	3,100	15.875	9/30/85	13.41	106.126	3456679
U.S. Treasury.......	2,600	14.000	3/31/86	13.36	101.748	2767790
U.S. Treasury.......	3,200	14,875	6/30/86	13.39	104.374	3382276
U.S. Treasury.......	3,900	16.125	11/15/86	13.69	107.624	4331851
U.S. Treasury.......	2,900	13.750	8/15/87	13.40	101.250	3121229
U.S. Treasury.......	3,100	12.375	1/15/88	13.29	96.501	3009648
U.S. Treasury.......	3,200	14.000	7/15/88	13.40	102.378	3297253
U.S. Treasury.......	3,000	14.625	1/15/89	13.55	104.501	3155750
U.S. Treasury.......	7,800	14.500	7/15/89	13.50	104.379	8194975
U.S. Treasury.......	2,000	10.750	8/15/90	13.22	88.002	1859778
U.S. Treasury.......	3,000	13.000	11/15/90	13.29	98.498	3038360
U.S. Treasury.......	4,600	14.500	5/15/91	13.55	104.747	4961032
U.S. Treasury.......	9,400	14.625	2/15/92	13.55	105.624	10566399
U.S. Treasury.......	3,100	8.625	8/15/93	13.15	74.001	2418066
U.S. Treasury.......	2,900	9.000	2/15/94	13.09	76.002	2325135
U.S. Treasury.......	2,000	8.750	8/15/94	13.05	74.251	1566202
U.S. Treasury.......	2,700	10.125	11/15/94	13.15	81.747	2265643
U.S. Treasury.......	5,300	10.375	5/15/95	13.23	82.563	4493456
U.S. Treasury.......	2,400	12.625	5/15/95	13.21	96.373	2377763
U.S. Treasury.......	12,000	11.500	11/15/95	13.19	89.501	11035299
U.S. Treasury.......	2,900	8.500	5/15/99	12.91	70.001	2082755
U.S. Treasury.......	3,300	7.875	2/15/ 0	13.15	64.187	2238726
U.S. Treasury.......	3,800	11.750	2/15/ 1	13.28	89.499	3608092
U.S. Treasury.......	12,000	15.750	11/15/ 1	13.53	115.000	14204267
U.S. Treasury.......	8,700	14.250	2/15/ 2	13.38	105.999	9797030
U.S. Treasury.......	2,500	11.750	2/15/10	13.19	89.375	2370645

* Prices as of 8/2/82
Market value: $135,271,091
Average maturity: 1/15/93
Average coupon: 13.059 percent
Average yield: 13.21 percent
  Internal Rate of Return: 13.08 percent

It is worth noting that the market value of the bonds in the portfolio as of August 2d, was $135,271,091, and the average yield was 13.21 percent, reflecting the market yields available at the time.

If none of the bonds in the dedicated portfolio default and if the mortality assumptions are accurate, only $135,271,091 in assets will be required to fully fund the total retired payouts of $328,568,813 that we see in Exhibit 4.

The Savings to the Pension System

Exhibit 8 summarizes the potential benefits of establishing a dedicated bond portfolio if the actuaries for the plan were to raise their actuarial rate to the higher, more current level of 13.08 percent (the internal rate of return on the portfolio).

Exhibit 8
Summary Report of Reduced Funding Requirements

	Percent	Dollar Amount
Total of expected benefit payouts................	—	$328,568,813
Present value of total benefit payouts	7.00	$190,184,656
Portfolio cost (market value)....................	13.08	$135,271,091
Potential savings..............................	—	$ 54,913,565
Percent savings...............................	29.00	

As illustrated in Exhibit 8, using the current actuarial rate of 7 percent, the plan must have on hand today $190,184,656 in order to fully fund its $328,568,813 of retired liabilities. On the basis of the August 2, 1982, pricing however, the portfolio would return 13.08 percent, requiring $135,271,091 in market value of assets to fully fund these same retired liabilities.

By raising the assumed rate from 7 percent to 14 percent on the retired portion of the plan, the plan sponsor is able to reduce the present value of the accumulated plan benefits by $54,913,552. This dramatic reduction represents a *29 percent diminution* from levels required under a 7 percent actuarial assumption.

As the present value of accumulated plan benefits are reduced by employing the dedicated design, so may pension contributions be reduced. For example, a plan that eliminated its unfunded liability position with a dedicated portfolio will now find that it no longer has to make amortization payments to pay off that unfunded position. For a dedicated plan that was originally fully funded and now enjoys a surplus position, it too may be able to reduce its contribution levels significantly in accordance with an amortization schedule worked out with the plan's actuaries.

As implied from our simulation, the reduction in plan contributions that the dedicated pension strategy can make possible is substantial. However, since every pension plan is different, and since many actuaries have differing methods of valuing the liabilities and assets of pension systems, the dedicated pension strategy has to be tailored to meet the specific requirements of the particular pension fund involved.

A FURTHER WORD ON THE DEDICATED DESIGN: VARIATIONS AVAILABLE

In addition to the simple dedicated design used in our above simulation, there is also a wide range of available variations that provide greater flexibility to the pension plan sponsor and investment manager. In broad terms, these flexibilities include:

1. Provision for more active management within the dedicated context.
2. Provision for cost-of-living adjustments (i.e., post retirement increases).
3. Provision for either a larger or smaller block of plan participants than the currently retired population.
4. Provision for the use of futures within the dedicated context.

Since each retirement system that considers a dedicated design could have a different matrix of plan characteristics as well as plan objectives, the specific dedicated design should be tailored through the use of these variations to the unique needs of the plan sponsor.

CONCLUSION

Our dedicated strategy departs from current portfolio management practice inasmuch as we structure the assets of a pension system to fund a portion of the plan liabilities rather than according to the manager's forecast of interest rates. Concerning the issue of portfolio allocation, we also note that the fixed income commitments in a dedicated plan are now deployed to fund the retired portion of that plan, and the equity and real estate investments remain outside the dedicated plan and can be used to fund the active lives. Much as investors often invest differently for their parents than for themselves or for their children, so may a pension plan fund its liabilities with greater concern for the horizons of its participants.

The dedicated pension strategy represents a major advance in pension funding. It is not the single answer to all pension funding problems. Instead, it is another available investment strategy that will allow a plan sponsor to virtually eliminate market risk or funding risk from a significant part of a plan's liability and eliminate market value fluctuations when reporting unfunded liability positions associated with that liability.

Since the summer of 1980 when we first developed this new pension funding strategy, we have been able to raise actuarial valuations to 13, 14, and 15 percent on the retired portions of plans, reduce or eliminate unfunded liabilities (or present value of accumulated plan benefits) dramatically, reduce significantly pension contributions, provide budget relief, and increase reported earnings. The investment and actuarial benefits of the dedicated strategy may be of compelling interest to corporate treasurers, governors, mayors, budget directors, and pension managers.

Though the benefits of the dedicated strategy are most applicable to "mature" industries with large retired populations and to governments, all plans may want to consider this approach regardless of their financial circumstances. It is an approach that can reduce current pension expenses and minimize market or funding risk in today's volatile capital markets.

Financial Futures: Hedging Interest-Rate Risk*

38 **ALLAN M. LOOSIGIAN**
President
A. M. Loosigian & Co.

INTRODUCTION

Commodity futures and fixed income securities traditionally have been regarded as widely disparate financial markets. But since the advent of the interest-rate, or financial futures, market in early 1976, seasoned commodity traders have had to master the intricacies of various types of debt instruments, and corporate financial executives and institutional investment managers have been thrust for the first time into what was for most of them the alien world of futures trading. The futures men and women and the securities people have since then endeavored to create a common language and become accustomed to doing business with one another.

THE DEVELOPMENT OF INTEREST-RATE FUTURES

The impetus to this new, hybrid market was the sharp increase during the 1970s and early 1980s in the volatility and absolute level of interest rates. Reacting to the debilitating effect of the 1973–74 credit crunch on the California—indeed the nationwide—thrift and construc-

---

* This chapter is adapted from Allan M. Loosigian, *Interest Rate Futures* (Homewood, Ill.: Dow Jones-Irwin, 1980).

Exhibit 1
Currently Traded Futures Contracts on Financial Instruments

	COMEX[1]	IMM[2]	Treasury Bills IMM[2]	Intermediate-Term Treasury Coupon Securities CBT[3]	IMM[2]	Treasury Bonds CBT[3]
Deliverable items	$1 million par value of Treasury bills with 90, 91, or 92 days to maturity	$1 million par value of Treasury bills with 90, 91, or 92 days to maturity	$250,000 par value of Treasury bills due in 52 weeks	$100,000 par value of Treasury notes and noncallable bonds with 4 to 6 years to maturity	$100,000 par value of Treasury notes maturing between 3½ years and 4½ years	$100,000 par value of Treasury bonds with at least 15 years to first call or to maturity
Initial margin[4] (per contract)	$800	$1,500	$600	$900	$500	$2,000[5]
Maintenance margin* (per contract)	$600	$1,200	$400	$600	$300	$1,600[5]
Daily limits[6]	60 basis points	50 basis points	50 basis points	1 point (32/32)	¾ point (48/64)	2 points (64/32)
Delivery months (each year)	February, May, August, November	March, June, September, December	March, June, September, December	March, June, September, December	February, May, August, November	March, June, September, December
Total open interest (December 31, 1979)	913	36,495	435	715	265	90,676
Date trading began	October 2, 1979	January 6, 1976	September 11, 1978	June 25, 1979	July 10, 1979	August 22, 1977

Exhibit 1 (*concluded*)

	CBT (old)[3]	Government National Mortgage Association (modified pass-through mortgage-backed certificates)	
		CBT (new)[3]	COMEX[1]
Deliverable items	Collateralized depository receipt covering $100,000 principal balance of GNMA certificates	$100,000 principal balance of GNMA certificates	$100,000 principal balance of GNMA certificates
Initial margin[4] (per contract)	$2,000	$2,000	$1,500
Maintenance margin[4] (per contract)	$1,500	$1,500	$1,125
Daily limits[6]	1½ points (48/32)	1½ points (48/32)	1 point (64/64)
Delivery months (each year)	March, June, September, December	March, June, September, December	January, April, July, October[7]
Total open interest (December 31, 1979)	88,982	4,478	64
Date trading began	October 20, 1975	September 12, 1978	November 13, 1979

All specifications are as of year-end 1979.
[1] Commodity Exchange, Inc.—New York.
[2] International Monetary Market (Chicago Mercantile Exchange).
[3] Chicago Board of Trade.
[4] The speculative margin is shown where margins vary according to whether the contracts cover speculative, hedged, or spread positions.
[5] For all contracts but those that mature in current month. Then initial margin is increased to $2,500, and maintenance margin is raised to $2,000.
[6] Exchanges frequently have rules allowing expansion of daily limits once they have been in effect for a few days (margins may change also).
[7] Principal trading months; rules allow trading for current plus two succeeding months.
Source: Marcelle Arak and Christopher J. McCurdy, "Interest Rate Futures," *Federal Reserve Bank of New York Quarterly Review*, Winter 1980.

tion industries, a group of faculty members at the University of California at Berkeley in cooperation with representatives of several of that state's large savings and loan associations sought relief from the next and subsequent squeezes in the futures market. They reasoned that the type of forward hedging that had long been practiced in the commodity and foreign exchange markets could be adapted to serve the needs of financial institutions and other organizations adversely affected by precipitous interest-rate swings. What was then lacking were instruments to accomplish such hedging and specific markets in which to trade them.

Ever receptive to new ideas that offer the prospect of increased business, the two principal Chicago futures exchanges separately developed and introduced what were generally referred to as interest-rate futures contracts. The Chicago Board of Trade introduced in October 1975 contracts for the future delivery of Government National Mortgage Association certificates, or Ginnie Maes. Several months later, a few blocks away, the Chicago Mercantile Exchange launched its first interest-rate futures contract on 90-day U.S. Treasury bills.

The next several years saw a proliferation of futures contracts on other financial instruments at the two Chicago exchanges and at other commodity and securities exchanges eager to participate in what was heralded as a potential business bonanza. Some of the new contracts, notably those on U.S. Treasury bonds and large bank 90-day certificates of deposit, flourished and attracted a wide trading interest. Others, such as 30- and 90-day commercial paper and assorted Treasury note contracts, were largely ignored. Meanwhile, a so-called second generation of financial instrument contracts, put and call options on fixed income securities, were being developed by various exchanges amid a dispute as to whether these new vehicles were securities or commodities and which regulatory agency—the SEC or the Commodity Futures Trading Commission—therefore had the primary responsibility for supervising their trading.

Exhibit 1 presents the currently traded futures contracts on financial instruments and relevant information for each contract.

WHAT IS HEDGING?

A standard textbook definition of *futures hedging* is the assumption of a futures market position, equal in size and on the opposite side of the market (i.e., long versus short or vice versa) to a related cash position for the purpose of reducing exposure to price change. An ancillary definition is the purchase or sale of futures contracts as temporary substitutes for an intended transaction in the actual commodity. The popular expression "to hedge one's bets" is a readily understood reference to this process of risk reduction.

Organized futures markets were developed more than a century ago to afford farmers and other dealers in agricultural products an alternative to relying on Providence to ensure that prices would remain unchanged or move in their favor by the time the crops were harvested, moved to market, and processed. A bond portfolio manager is essentially exercising the same option when selling Treasury bond futures as a hedge against the price depreciation that higher interest rates would inflict on bond values. Both the farmer and the portfolio manager are placing short hedges by selling futures to offset any potential reduction in the cash value of their respective commodities, be it wheat or 20-year Treasury bonds.

A *long hedge* is undertaken by a prospective purchaser—for example, a flour miller who buys futures to fix the cost of the wheat he plans to acquire for processing at a later date (the wheat futures are hence a temporary substitute for the actual wheat), or a corporate treasurer who buys 90-day Treasury bill futures to lock in a specific yield on a three-month investment she anticipates making when the cash earmarked for it becomes available.

In each instance, the farmer, portfolio manager, miller, and treasurer would assume equal and opposite positions in the cash (actual) and futures markets. And in each case, the futures transaction would anticipate a projected cash purchase or sale. When the farmer harvests his wheat, he will cover his short futures position by repurchasing the contracts he sold earlier, and at the same time sell the crop through his customary marketing channels. By the same token, the portfolio manager will buy in her short bond futures contracts when she is ready to sell the bonds out of her portfolio or decides that interest rates are more likely to decline than to continue rising. The miller and corporate treasurer would follow the reverse procedure, selling their long futures positions when their operating requirements and cash flow make it timely to buy the wheat or Treasury bills.

Using the popular phrase, all four "hedge their bets" in the futures market to protect themselves against adverse price changes in wheat or interest rates. But, as a result, they also forego any benefit from favorable fluctuations.

TEXTBOOK HEDGING VERSUS BASIS TRADING

Most descriptions of hedging start with at least one example of a hypothetical "perfect" hedge to illustrate the objective of recouping in one market the amount lost in another. Exhibit 2 summarizes the arithmetic of such a perfect short hedge in the case of the bond portfolio cited above. Notice that futures and cash prices declined by identical amounts—724/32—between June 1 and December 1, satisfying the conditions of a perfect hedge, so that the $77,500 paper loss in-

Exhibit 2
Perfect Short Hedge in U.S. Treasury Bonds

Cash Market	Futures Market
June 1:	
Owns $1 million U.S. Treasury 7⅞s of 1995 at 68–04* to yield 12.329 percent.	Sells 10 December bond contracts at 69–02 to yield 12.152 percent.
No transaction.	
December 1:	
U.S. Treasury 7⅞s of 1995 are at 60–12 to yield 13.870 percent.	Buys 10 December bond contracts at 61–10 to yield 13.705 percent.
No transaction.	
Unrealized loss:	Realized profit (before commissions):
7²⁴⁄₃₂ or $77,500	7²⁴⁄₃₂ or $77,500

* In futures quotations 68⁴⁄₃₂s is abbreviated 68–04, 69²⁄₃₂s as 69–02, and so on.

curred in the bond portfolio was offset precisely by an equivalent profit before brokerage commissions on the short futures position.

Another way to describe the situation is that the hedge was initiated on June 1 at a 30/32 difference (69–02 minus 68–04) and was "unwound" on December 1, again at 30/32 (61–10 minus 60–12). This difference between cash and futures prices, called the basis, is the controlling factor in determining the outcome of all hedged positions. In the Treasury bond short hedge example, if the basis on December 1 between the 7⅞s of 1995 and the December T bond contract was less than ³⁰⁄₃₂s, signifying that the futures price had declined by less than the cash bonds, the futures gain on the short position would not have matched the decline in market value of the 7⅞s of 1995. If, on the other hand, the basis on December 1 was greater than ³⁰⁄₃₂, the futures gain would have exceeded the cash market loss. In either instance, we would have gone beyond the textbook case of a perfect hedge and entered the "real world" condition of a changing basis. The overriding question then becomes: Did the basis grow wider or narrower between June 1 and December 1, and to what extent? A synopsis of real-world conditions during 1980 is contained in Exhibit 3, where the first-of-month yields on 20-year Treasury bonds and bond futures are listed among other cash and futures market yields for that year.

The perfect short hedge summarized in Exhibit 2 is also a straight, or pure, hedge in the sense that securities are hedged by futures contracts for which they are deliverable. In such an instance, the cash futures basis is determined by variations from the specified coupon rate and the remaining time to the contract delivery date.

Although a straight hedge is the most satisfactory sort, interest-rate futures are often employed to hedge securities that are not deliverable under the terms of the contract being used. This so-called *cross-hedging* introduces an additional (and greater) degree of basis risk, that of

Exhibit 3
1980 Selected Cash and Futures Market Yields (beginning of month, 1980)

First of Month	90-Day Bills (discount)	One-Year Bills (discount)	Three-Month CDs (discount)	90-Day Commercial Paper (discount)	GNMA 8 Percent (yield)	20-Year 8 Percent Treasury Bonds (yield)	Federal Funds (closing bid)	Prime Rate
January	12.10%	11.04%	13.25%	13.50%	10.92%	10.25%	14¼%	15 %
February	12.03	11.31	13.25	13.35	11.70	11.24	13¾	15¼
March	15.13	13.73	15.55	15.75	12.65	12.17	16½	16¾
April	15.03	13.90	18.00	17.35	12.88	12.31	19	19½
May	10.78	10.05	12.00	12.15	10.59	10.47	15½	19
June	8.03	8.20	8.65	9.65	10.61	10.43	10¾	14
July	8.15	7.90	8.15	8.75	10.40	9.98	9	12
August	8.22	8.64	9.40	9.85	11.06	10.70	10	11
September	10.12	10.10	11.00	11.50	11.96	11.33	9	11½
October	11.52	11.05	12.65	12.85	11.89	11.82	14½	13
November	13.34	12.46	14.50	14.25	12.59	12.24	13¾	14½
December	14.65	13.51	17.25	17.35	13.03	12.39	17	18
Average	11.59	10.99	12.80	13.02	11.69	11.27	13½	15

Exhibit 3 (*concluded*)

First of Month	90-Day Bill Futures		GNMA 8 Percent Futures		8 Percent Treasury Bond Futures	
	Nearby	One-Year	Nearby	One-Year	Nearby	One-Year
January	11.35	9.26	11.46	11.29	10.27	10.05
February	11.99	9.96	12.48	12.22	11.46	11.09
March	14.59	12.39	13.46	13.30	12.55	12.01
April	14.04	12.16	13.38	12.91	12.25	11.81
May	10.21	9.20	11.60	11.50	10.63	10.52
June	7.77	8.53	11.65	11.78	10.60	10.67
July	7.91	8.83	11.69	11.80	11.13	11.22
August	8.79	9.35	12.32	12.41	11.02	11.05
September	10.14	10.86	12.65	12.60	11.26	11.15
October	11.86	11.61	13.17	13.07	11.89	11.69
November	13.14	12.35	13.54	13.48	12.32	12.07
December	14.38	12.62	13.71	13.45	12.53	11.97
Average	11.34	10.59	12.59	12.48	11.49	11.27

the price/yield variations between the instrument being hedged and the security to be delivered according to the contract specifications. In addition to Treasury issues, Treasury bond futures might, for example, be sold to hedge long positions in corporate or government agency bonds. The effectiveness of such cross-hedges depends for the most part on the price correlation between Treasury bonds of contract grade and the bonds being hedged.

Futures contracts on 90-day commercial paper were introduced in 1977, followed two years later by contracts on 30-day commercial paper, on the supposition that they would provide a better hedge than a cross-hedge between commercial paper of varying maturities and 90-day Treasury bill futures. Yet the commercial paper futures languished and were finally discontinued because most users apparently were satisfied with the cross-hedge and did not feel a need to change. On the other hand, contracts on large bank certificates of deposit were well received when they were launched in 1981 because a cross-hedge between CDs and Treasury bill futures was not considered adequate.

Hedging, therefore, be it of a wheat crop or of a government bond portfolio, is not the automatic cut-and-dried type of operation suggested by the perfect hedge example. A closer look at Exhibit 3 shows that between June and December 1980, or during any other period for that matter, there were times when a hedge, short or long, would have proven to be more advantageous to the hedger than at other times. *Basis trading* is the attempt to profit from correct judgments concerning the optimum time to initiate and close out a hedge. Experienced hedgers know that although the futures market affords them an opportunity to substitute the lesser risk of a changing cash-futures price relationship for that of an exposed long or short position, that does not eliminate the need for careful planning and seasoned market judgment. Even so, after all of the critical factors have been weighed and due diligence exercised, the importance of sheer luck should not be minimized.

THE CASH-FUTURES PRICE STRUCTURE

An informed judgment regarding the basis (in other words, an opinion concerning the most favorable time to place and then to lift a hedge) begins with a study of the cash-futures price structure. In the case of the interest-rate futures complex, the structure is a representation of the yield equivalent of contract prices for successive delivery dates.[1] Until futures and cash yields start to converge as a contract's expiration approaches, futures prices often display a life of their own that can deviate sharply from cash market interest rates, a phenomenon we can identify as a variation in the basis.

As has always been true in the case of tangible commodities, the semiindependent behavior of interest-rate futures prices vis-à-vis cash market yields stems chiefly from differences in time and delivery grade. The pattern of successive delivery-month prices is generally one of increasingly greater discounts from, or premiums over, the cash price/yield, a sequence that depends in large part upon the absolute trend in interest rates and the relationship between short- and long-term rates. Moreover, as is demonstrated in Exhibit 4, the cash to futures and futures to futures relationships are in a continual state of flux due to ever-changing money market conditions.

So long as the consensus of market participants is that interest rates will continue to rise (as embodied in an upward-sloping yield curve), the contract price for each successive delivery month is lower than the one preceding it. As the expectation spreads that the cyclical peak in interest rates is within sight (as embodied in a flattening or downward-sloping yield curve), prices of contracts with deferred-delivery dates become progressively higher, reflecting the anticipation of lower yields with the passage of time. As time elapses and each contract in turn approaches its delivery date, bringing the indicated yield for that contract closer to the comparable cash market rate, these structural discounts and premiums diminish, giving the basis an upward or downward bias.

Hedgers must take the premium or discount structure of futures markets into account when making their market decisions. A short hedge ordinarily will fare better in a premium market (cash prices

---

[1] It is not the familiar cash yield curve per se that we are dealing with here, but the yield on securities of the same grade and maturity spaced at quarterly intervals over a two- to three-year period that spans a series of contract delivery dates.

Exhibit 4
Cash and Futures Discounts and (Spreads) 90-Day Treasury Bills (international monetary market beginning-of-month settlement discounts based on IMM index)

Month	Cash Discount First of Month	March 1980	June 1980	September 1980	December 1980
1980					
January	12.10	(−75) 11.35	(−3) 10.32	(−68) 9.64	(−29) 9.35
February	12.03	(−4) 11.99	(−61) 11.38	(−71) 10.67	(−45) 10.22
March	15.13	(−54) 14.59	(−58) 14.01	(−75) 13.26	(−51) 12.75
April	15.03		(−99) 14.04	(−96) 13.08	(−58) 12.50
May	10.78		(−57) 10.21	(−57) 9.64	(−38) 9.26
June	8.03		(−26) 7.77	(24) 8.01	(16) 8.17
July	8.15			(−24) 7.91	(27) 8.18
August	8.22			(57) 8.79	(8) 8.87
September	10.12			(2) 10.14	(33) 10.47
October	11.52				(34) 11.86
November	13.34				(−20) 13.14
December	14.65				(−27) 14.38

below futures) as futures prices decline relative to cash. Other considerations being equal, a discount market (cash above futures) normally favors a long hedge with futures rising toward the spot price as the contracts approach delivery date. The progression from premium or discount to parity with cash prices/yields is not always a smooth one, since imbalances occur in the current or anticipated supply and demand for deliverable securities, technical analysts respond to chart signals, and Fed watchers speculate on a change in monetary policy. All or any one of these events would cause significant, even if only temporary, changes in the basis.

WHO SHOULD HEDGE?

The basic determination by corporate management concerning any futures market involvement should be whether there is sufficient interest-rate exposure to make hedging a necessary, or desirable undertaking. What would be the impact on corporate earnings, say, of a 2 percent increase or decline in short- and long-term interest rates? What is the company's present or anticipated position in fixed income securities or, in the case of banking institutions, fixed-rate loans? What is the amount of projected borrowing and/or investment over the coming year or two, and what will be the likely net position, the so-called asset/liability "gap." Would any foreseeable adverse change in rates be an acceptable cost of doing business? If the perceived risks are insignificant, or fall within tolerable limits, and are likely to average out over time, management may see no compelling incentive to embark upon interest-rate hedging operations.

On the other hand, should the wide swings in rates that have become the norm over the past decade persist and continue to have a

March 1981	June 1981	September 1981	December 1981	March 1982	June 1982	September 1982
(−9) 9.26	(3) 9.29	(5) 9.34	(−2) 9.32			
(−26) 9.96	(−6) 9.90	(−5) 9.85	(−4) 9.81			
(−36) 12.39	(−21) 12.18	(−8) 12.18	(−2) 12.08			
(−27) 12.23	(−7) 12.16	(−5) 12.11	(5) 12.16	(−1) 12.15		
(−14) 9.12	(8) 9.20	(5) 9.25	(−5) 9.20	(−) 9.20		
(18) 8.35	(18) 8.53	(19) 8.72	(25) 8.97	(34) 9.31		
(26) 8.44	(18) 8.62	(21) 8.83	(21) 9.04	(28) 9.32	(21) 9.53	
(14) 9.01	(14) 9.15	(20) 9.35	(20) 9.55	(17) 9.72	(28) 10.00	
(17) 10.64	(14) 10.78	(8) 10.86	(9) 10.95	(12) 11.07	(11) 11.18	
(10) 11.96	(−12) 11.84	(−14) 11.70	(−9) 11.61	(−4) 11.57	(−11) 11.46	(−4) 11.42
(−21) 12.93	(−27) 12.66	(−22) 12.44	(−9) 12.35	(−8) 12.27	(−13) 12.14	(−3) 12.11
(−73) 13.65	(−58) 13.07	(−28) 12.79	(−17) 12.62	(−16) 12.46	(−12) 12.34	(−9) 12.25

marked effect on portfolio values, investment income, and/or borrowing cost, the company is vulnerable and may consider itself a hedge candidate. If such be the case, management should establish a set of policies guiding the firm's activity in this area and determine the type of hedging strategy it wishes to adopt. Should it regard itself as a straight hedger in the textbook sense, estimating its risk exposure as closely as possible and taking the prescribed action in the futures market to offset it? Or should it assume a more aggressive posture, placing a hedge when the basis appears to offer a profit opportunity over and above straight price or rate protection, and closing it out when that profit is attained?

The strategy that is selected will influence (and in turn be influenced by) the organizational fit of the hedging operation within the business structure. Some firms regard their hedge activity as a distinct profit center and expect it to be self-sustaining. Those who favor a protective, or defensive, approach usually see hedging as a support function and do not look to it to show profits per se.

CASE ONE—A BOND PORTFOLIO HEDGE

The collapse of bond prices during 1980–81 as a consequence of soaring interest rates has been amply chronicled and does not need to be recounted here. The immediate question is: How may Treasury bond futures have been employed during those years—or indeed at any time—to offset the deleterious effect on bond portfolios of such severe price declines?

As is noted in Exhibit 1, the Chicago Board of Trade U.S. Treasury bond contract specifies the delivery of $100,000 face value Treasury bonds bearing an 8 percent coupon and a call or maturity date 15 years or more beyond the delivery month of the futures contract. To execute a short hedge, therefore, a portfolio manager would sell one futures contract for every $100,000 face value of bonds held in the portfolio. If, for example, the portfolio contained $100 million of U.S. Treasury 8s of 1996–01, the manager would sell 1,000 contracts (i.e., 1,000 contracts times $100,000 contract size = $100 million Treasury 8s in portfolio).[2]

For every futures contract sold (or bought in the case of a long hedge) the hedger must deposit initial margin of approximately $2,000 with the broker carrying the futures account. The figure is approximate because the amount required varies from broker to broker and is changed from time to time by the exchange on which that particular futures contract is traded. To hedge a $100 million bond position with the sale of 1,000 futures contracts, therefore, the hedger must deposit with the broker cash or actual U.S. Treasury bills (not bill futures) on the order of $2 million.

After once establishing a short futures position, the hedger profits by $31.25 per contract for each "tick," or minimum fluctuation of 1/32nd of a point, the Treasury bond contract drops in price. That minimum price fluctuation in turn amounts to $31,250 per 1/32nd of a point on a 1,000 contract position. To the extent that interest rates decline and the contract price rises, the hedger loses money on the short futures position at the same rate. Should the contract price move against the hedger by 25 percent of the initial margin on deposit with the broker, the hedger is required to deposit additional (maintenance) margin to his or her account.

Severe tightening of monetary policy by the Federal Reserve Board to contain inflation and support the U.S. dollar in foreign exchange markets—the so-called Saturday massacre at the Fed—commenced on October 8, 1979. The U.S. Treasury 8s of 1996–01 were then quoted as 88¼ bid, giving a hypothetical $100 million portfolio consisting solely of that issue a market value of about $88 million at the then prevailing price. (See Exhibit 5.) On the same date, September 1980 Treasury bond futures contracts traded at 87¾ on the Chicago Board of Trade. Had it been possible to sell 1,000 contracts at that price, it would have been necessary for the short hedger to deposit with a broker initial margin of about $2 million. So long as the basis— the half-point spread between cash bonds at 88¼ and futures at 87¾—remained constant, the portfolio would effectively have been locked into a value per bond of 88¼. That constant basis would have provided a perfect hedge.

---

[2] For clarity of illustration, a portfolio holding of U.S. Treasury bonds is assumed in this example. A similar hedge might be employed in the case of corporate, agency, or municipal bonds. Such cross-hedging, however, exposes the hedger to a greater degree of basis variation of the sort described earlier in this chapter.

Exhibit 5
Treasury Bond Portfolio Hedge 1979–80

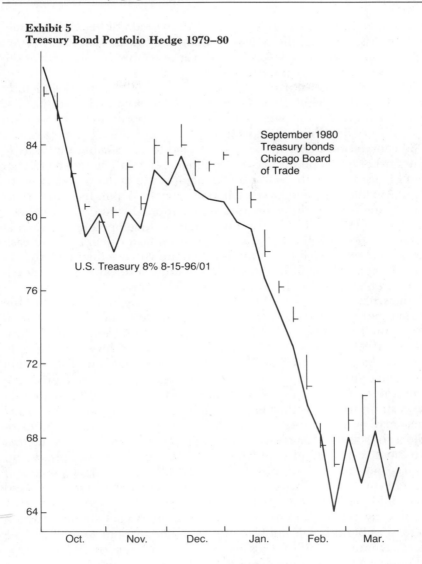

September 1980
Treasury bonds
Chicago Board
of Trade

U.S. Treasury 8% 8-15-96/01

Such was not the case. By October 25, 1979, the 8s of 1996–01 had dropped to 79, subjecting the hypothetical portfolio to a loss of 9¼ points, or $9.25 million; and the September 1980 bond futures fell 8 points to 79¾. The $9.25 million loss in the bond portfolio was only offset, therefore, by an $8 million gain on the futures side. Another way of saying the same thing is that futures (the September 1980 contract at any rate) actually went *up* relative to the cash bonds from one-half point below to three-fourths point above. That 1¼-point swing, the equivalent of $1.25 million on 1,000 contracts, is referred to as a change in the basis and is a good illustration of hedging in practice. In this instance, the hedger substituted for the risk (as it turned out) of bonds dropping 9¼ points, the appreciably smaller risk of the basis changing by 1¼ points.

The bond market staged a modest rally during November and early December. The 8s of 1996–01 moved up to about 83¼ in the first week of December, bringing the hypothetical portfolio back to within 5 points, or $5 million, of its October 8 market value. The September 1980 contract rose during the same period to 85, causing the basis to shift further to 1¾ points above cash bonds. In total, between October 8 and December 6, there was a shift against the hedger of 2¼ points, or $2,250,000, inasmuch as cash bonds were 5 points below their earlier level while the short futures position showed an unrealized gain of 2¾ (87¾ minus 85). This disparity developed as the market turned up because futures prices moved up faster than those of cash bonds. Not only are futures inherently more volatile than cash, but in early December 1979 they were anticipating a further drop in long-term interest rates by the September 1980 contracts-delivery date.

The six-week rally proved to be a false start. By mid-December the market had resumed its downward course; the 8s of 1996–01 fell in the ensuing 11-week period between December 10, 1979, and February 26, 1980, from 83 to 64. From its October 8 level, the sample portfolio had lost more than $24 million, or 27 percent of its market value, an unprecedented decline within such a brief span. During the same interval, September 1980 bond futures slid to 66½, widening the cash-futures basis further to 2½ points above cash. Under normal bond market conditions, a basis shift of one or two points is considered a substantial change. But in a crisis environment such as the first two months of 1980 clearly were, the hedger in the example would even so have managed to offset more than $22 million, or 90 percent of the $24 million decline in bond values, by means of an unrealized gain on his or her short position in futures.

Like any market operation, futures hedging is not a one-way street. So long as bond prices continue to drop, hedgers are something like heros, avoiding significant losses in their portfolios. But when a rally gets under way and unrealized losses begin to mount in the futures account, the situation is not so comfortable for them. Top managers and directors are frequently unimpressed by the argument that whatever the company is losing on its futures position, it is recouping—apart from any change in the basis—on the cash side.

As was noted earlier, initial margin is in effect the price of establishing a futures hedge. Once short hedgers deposit with the broker the required initial margin, they receive no calls for additional funds so long as the market continues to decline. The hedgers are making money on their futures position, and the equity in their trading account is thereby increasing. They are even entitled to withdraw profits from the account as profits accrue, but must subsequently replace the profits when the market turns against them.

Futures contracts are limited in the extent to which they are permitted to advance or decline from the prior day's settlement price during the course of a single trading session. These daily price limits are the futures market equivalent of a stock exchange suspending trading in a particular issue in anticipation, or in the wake of, a significant news announcement and are intended to give traders an opportunity to assess the situation before the contract price is inordinately affected. The daily price limit also circumscribes the amount of loss (and profit) individual traders and the exchange clearing house may suffer on any given day.

If buying pressure forces a contract price "up the limit" without attracting corresponding sell orders at or below the limit price, trading ceases in that particular contract until there are offers to sell within the specified limit. The same procedure is observed each succeeding day until sell orders do materialize.

The opposite sequence occurs in a declining market wherein no buyers can be found before the contract price is offered "down the limit." The daily limits that were in effect as of December 1979 are listed in Exhibit 1. Futures exchanges have the authority to reduce or increase existing limits in the event that a change in market conditions causes a change in a contract's normal price volatility.

If, in the case of the foregoing example, the short hedge had been initiated at the end of October 1979 instead of at the beginning, repeated calls for additional margin would have been issued by the broker during the November rally. Had September 1980 Treasury bond futures contracts been sold at or near the October 29 settlement price of 79¾, the hedger would have received maintenance margin calls on his or her 1,000 short contracts of about $2 million by November 15 as the contract price rallied to 81¾. By December 6 the contract price had moved yet higher to 84¾, at which point the hedger would be called for another $3 million margin.

To be sure, as interest rates once again turned upward and bond futures prices resumed their decline, these funds were recouped. But there is a point after which the burden of repeated margin calls becomes onerous and the likelihood increases that the market will not in fact reverse itself and in the process alleviate the short hedger's distress. At some juncture the hedger should determine that market conditions dictate that it is better to remain unhedged and act to preclude further losses by liquidating the futures position (i.e., by buying the short contracts in).

If, under the worst of circumstances, a portfolio manager had elected to initiate a short hedge at the February 26 market trough and accordingly sold 1,000 September 1980 bond contracts at 66½, and if the manager had not acted to reverse this decision, the manager's futures losses would have assumed staggering proportions. During the subsequent rally of Spring, 1980, cumulative margin calls on a 1,000 contract short position would have amounted to more than $20 million. Once again, a market reversal would have erased those unrealized losses had the short position been maintained through the rally's peak. Prudent managers would in all likelihood have removed their hedges during the early stages of the spring rally and sought to reinstate them after it had become clear that interest rates had resumed their upward trend.

CASE TWO—A COMMERCIAL PAPER HEDGE

Just as in the preceding case, in which a bond portfolio manager would sell futures to protect the portfolio against price decline as a consequence of rising interest rates, so too would a corporate borrower sell financial futures to limit the interest cost of prospective borrowings. In the case of a commercial paper issuer, a corporate hedger would want to sell futures at a price equivalent to a discount, say, of 10 percent to recoup the additional interest cost should commercial paper rates rise to a 20 percent discount. In that event, the hedger would accrue a gain on the short futures position substantially equal to the incremental borrowing cost between 10 percent and 20 percent. That is what is referred to as locking-in a rate. If interest rates instead declined, the short hedger would instead lose money on the short futures position as the contract price moved in inverse relation to yield. That loss would in turn be offset by a lower actual borrowing cost at the time of the commercial paper sale. As in the case of a short portfolio hedge, a perfect hedge in which the two sides are exactly matched is theoretically possible, but it is seldom realized in practice.

The contract specifications for 90-day U.S. Treasury bill futures contracts traded at the International Monetary Market affiliate of the Chicago Mercantile Exchange stipulate the delivery of $1 million face value 13-week bills on a predetermined date. A buyer of 10 December contracts, for example, will receive delivery in the third week of that month of $10 million face value in bills that mature at par the third week of the following March. The seller of those 10 contracts assumes an obligation to deliver the same amount and maturity of bills on the specified delivery date.

Treasury bill futures are quoted on an index basis to reflect the 90-day discount of the deliverable bills. The index is 100 less the applicable discount, so that the purchase or sale of contracts at an 85 index fixes the delivery price of actual Treasury bills at a 90-day discount of 15 percent. A trader would buy a contract at 85 when he or she believed the cash (actual) 90-day discount on the contract delivery date would be less than 15 percent. In that case, the contract price would have risen above the trader's purchase price by the dollar equivalent of the basis-point decline in yield. The trader would sell at 85 when he or she believed the discount would ultimately be greater than 15 percent. As with bond futures, a corporate hedger must deposit with its brokerage house initial margin of about $2,000 per contract and will be called by the broker for additional margin in the event of adverse price movement.

The dotted line in Exhibit 6 is an inverted chart of the highest quality, 90-day dealer commercial paper rate during 1980. The pur-

Exhibit 6
Basis Chart: Treasury Bill Futures versus 90-Day Commercial Paper Rates (inverted)

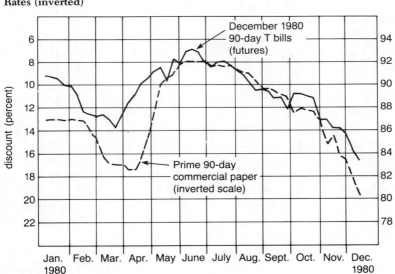

pose of inverting the scale of the chart is to compare the dollar consequences of a changing commercial paper discount with the index movement of December 1980 Treasury bill futures (solid line) throughout the year.[3]

The year opened with the 90-day dealer commercial paper discount tracing a plateau at 13 percent through January and the first half of February. There followed a rapid rate rise (shown as a price decline

---

[3] The Chicago Board of Trade introduced futures contracts on both 90-day and 30-day commercial paper, but discontinued trading in the two contracts because they failed to gain acceptance by market participants. The participants preferred the more liquid Treasury bill futures contracts as hedging vehicles, even though there is some disparity between the two rates.

on the inverted scale) that peaked in mid-April at about 17½ percent and then an even sharper drop to the 8 percent level by the end of May. The third quarter witnessed a gradual rate rise, and in the fourth quarter an accelerating rate of increase exceeded the April peak in late November and went on to end the year at about the 20 percent level.

Obviously, a corporation that sold commercial paper during the May–June 1980 period obtained a far lower rate (about 800 basis points) than a corporation that sold its paper in November and December. The question to be answered is: How may the futures market have been used to avoid paying commercial paper rates of 16 percent and above in March–April, and again during November and December?

To begin with a favorable case, a commercial paper issuer would have been able to sell futures during the final week of January at about 90, an index price reflecting a Treasury bill discount of 10 percent. By the third week of March, after the prime commercial paper rate had risen 400 basis points from 13 percent to 17 percent, it was possible to buy in (liquidate) the short futures position at an index equivalent of about 13½ percent for a gain of 350 basis points. The corporation would at that point sell its commercial paper at 17 percent, but after taking the 350-basis-point futures profit into account, it would have established an effective hedged rate of 13½ percent.

The same futures contracts, had they been sold in mid-June at 93, or 7 percent, would have realized a 950-basis-point gain when repurchased in mid-December at 83.50, or 16½ percent. For a corporation selling its commercial paper in December at 20 percent, that gain would have served to reduce its hedged borrowing cost to 10½ percent. In that instance, the basis expanded during the six-month period, so the hedge would have been in force from about 100 basis points (7 percent T bill futures to 8 percent commercial paper) to about 350 basis points (16½ percent T bill futures to 20 percent commercial paper). The net result for a corporation observing such a scenario would have been to substitute for the unhedged risk of the commercial paper rate climbing 1200 basis points from 8 percent to 20 percent, the considerably smaller risk of the basis changing adversely by 250 basis points.

Such a strategy is by no means a surefire formula for reducing borrowing cost. The market can always go the other way; that is to say, interest rates might decline. In that case, as was noted above, a hedger would incur a loss on the short futures position and in so doing lock in a hedged rate higher than the market rate prevailing when it became time to issue its commercial paper. A corporation that sold December 1980 Treasury bill futures at 87, or 13 percent, just before the Spring 1980 market rally would, if it sold commercial paper in mid-June, have covered its short futures position at about 93, or 7 percent, for a 600-basis-point *loss*. Adding that loss to the 8 percent prime 90-day commercial paper rate in mid-June would impose a hedged borrowing cost of 14 percent at a time when nonhedgers were borrowing at 8 percent.

The moral of this story, as with that of the bond portfolio hedge, is that there are times to hedge and times not to hedge. Hedging decisions should be taken with a view of the market. The objective is to take advantage of what are perceived as temporarily low interest rates (in absolute terms as well as in terms of the cash-futures basis), applying them to prospective borrowings at a time when interest rates are expected to be significantly higher. A similar approach may be taken with respect to long-term bond financing. A major drawback in the long-term sector, however, is the relatively low correlation between corporate bond yields and the prices/yields on U.S. Treasury bond or Ginnie Mae futures contracts traded at the Chicago Board of Trade.

Another drawback in both the short- and long-term markets is the need to deposit additional margin money in the hedger's brokerage account when interest rates decline and a loss is incurred on a short futures position. Barring an abnormal shift in the basis, any losses registered in the futures account will be substantially recouped on the cash side. Nevertheless, until such time as the hedged position is terminated and the commercial paper or bonds are issued at a lower rate, cash maintenance margin deposits must be made for as long as losses are incurred in the futures account. The interest income foregone on such deposits should be included when calculating the cost of hedging.

The reverse of this strategy—a long hedge—may be employed to lock in what is judged to be an acceptable rate of return on a prospective short-term investment. In this instance, Treasury bill futures are purchased at a lower index price than the price that is expected to prevail at the time the planned investment is to be made. If the hedger's expectations are realized, the lower discount on the cash investment will be substantially offset by price appreciation of the futures contract. As with the short hedge, the actual trend of interest rates may run contrary to the long hedger's expectations. In such an event, the hedger might be advised to sell out the long futures position and attempt to capture the higher yield that would result if the upward movement in interest rates were to persist until the date of the projected investment.

ORGANIZING FOR HEDGING

A corporation, fund, or financial institution that plans to implement a hedging program should follow several basic steps:

1. A plan should be committed to writing. It should explain what

the hedging function is intended to accomplish and how. It should set down limits with regard to the size of positions (number of contracts), maximum acceptable losses (in basis points and dollars), and so on. Everyone involved with the hedging program from the board of directors to its executors should understand the plan, have input to it, and be in accord with its methods and objectives.

2. A hedge manager should be designated to execute the plan. The manager may have the title of assistant treasurer, portfolio or cash manager, or some other, but an important part of the job should be to monitor hedge positions on a daily basis and be responsible for initiating and terminating such positions.

3. The hedge manager and, to a lesser extent, everyone else involved with the plan should become thoroughly familiar with the behavior of the basis—what we have defined as the relationship between futures prices and actual interest rates—under a variety of money market conditions. The basis, after all, is the real (net) price with which a hedger is concerned.

4. A corporation's brokers, bankers, and accountants should be advised of the hedge plan, and their respective areas of expertise should be utilized as circumstances dictate.

5. It is important to develop a simple system of reporting and record-keeping that everyone concerned has access to and can understand.

6. Above all, it is virtually imperative to initiate the hedging program on a limited scale. Financial futures are still an unknown quantity for most managers, and the learning process to master them can be costly if losses are not controlled. It usually is advisable to begin with a pilot position of 10 contracts or less. As the hedge manager and associates become more familiar with and adept in the futures market, the size of positions may be progressively increased.

ACCOUNTING CONSIDERATIONS

The accounting for hedge transactions is relatively straightforward. Inasmuch as futures contracts are regarded as commitments rather than investments, they are booked as a memorandum entry rather than entered in the general ledger. The initial margin deposit for a long or short position is debited to a margin debit account, and cash is credited by a like figure. Similar entries are made when adverse market action necessitates additional maintenance margin deposits. Realized profits and losses are posted to the deferred profit or loss account and accumulated or written off over the average life of the securities that were hedged.

Any unrealized gains or losses on open futures positions at the end of the accounting period are entered as maintenance margin deposits, matching the gains and losses against their related cash market transactions. When an anticipated cash transaction does not occur, the futures position is treated as a speculation, with the ensuing profit or loss reflected in the current income statement. Initial and maintenance margin deposits are carried as "other assets," and any related amounts due to or from brokers are shown as miscellaneous receivables or payables.

A major obstacle to interest-rate hedging by banks and savings and loan associations is the regulatory requirement that unrealized gains and losses on outstanding futures positions be "marked to the market" (i.e., priced daily and included in current income), while the offsetting cash market position being hedged continues to be carried at cost. This discrepancy in accounting treatment distorts the economic status of a hedge and renders it ineffective for reporting purposes. At the end of 1981 the accounting standards board was considering proposals to correct this anomaly.

WHAT IS A SPREAD?

The term *spread* has somewhat different meanings in the money and commodity markets, a cause for some initial confusion to newcomers to financial futures. An interest-rate spread is the basis-point difference between yields on similar fixed income securities, or various maturities of the same instrument. A futures market spread entails concurrent long and short positions in related futures contracts. The hedged positions discussed in the previous sections make up a particular type of spread, in which one of the two "legs" is a position in the cash market. Another source of confusion is the indiscriminate use of the terms *spread, straddle,* and *arbitrage* to describe the same thing. The first two terms are functionally synonymous; the word spread is favored in the grain trade, and straddle is heard more frequently in other futures markets within the United States and abroad. Arbitrage is in the strictest sense a different type of operation.

For the same reason that hedgers consider basis risk to be less than that of a fully exposed position, futures spreaders regard their specialty as a more conservative method of trading than speculating on outright long or short positions. The key element in both instances is the tendency of cash instruments and futures contracts with successive delivery dates to move up and down in price/yield more or less in tandem. An intermonth spread consists of simultaneous long and short positions in different delivery months of the same contract. An intermarket spread is placed between similar contracts, again long and short, traded on different futures exchanges. An example of such a spread would be contrary positions in U.S. Treasury note contracts traded at the Chicago Mercantile Exchange and at the Commodity Exchange (Comex) in New York. Interinstrument spreads are taken between contracts for different maturities of like securities (i.e., 90-day versus one-year T bills) or between different securities, such as T bills and certificates of deposit or bonds and Ginnie Mae contracts.

Exhibit 4 traces the dynamics of spread relationships among the International Monetary Market's 90-day Treasury bill contracts during 1980. The data for selected dates throughout the year are presented graphically in Exhibit 7. A comparison between the two exhibits re-

Exhibit 7
Selected T Bill Futures Curves, 1980

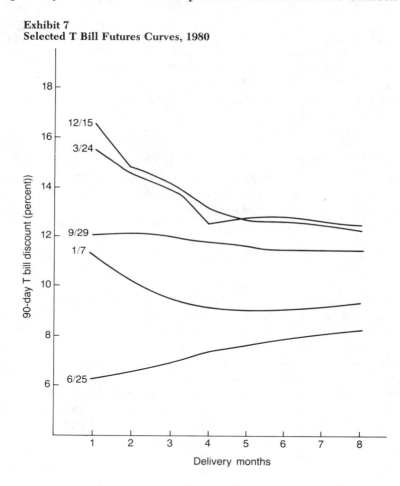

veals that as the curve of yields for successive contract deliveries assumes a sharper upward slope, the price/yield spreads between delivery months tend to expand. But as the nearby deliveries move higher up the yield axis, causing the curve to flatten out and eventually to turn into a negative or humped configuration (indicating the market's belief that short-term interest rates are at or near a peak), the spreads begin to contract, at which point the distant contracts begin moving to a price premium (yield discount) over the near and intermediate deliveries.

It is possible to reconstruct from the figures in Exhibit 4 a hypothetical 90-day T bill intermonth spread initiated in April 1980, when a short position in the December 1980 contract could have been taken at a 34-basis-point discount under a long position in December 1981 T bills (87.84 minus 87.50).[4] By the following November, the spread between the nearby and distant December contracts had widened to 79 basis points (87.65 minus 86.86), allowing the position to be "unwound" at a 45-basis-point, or $1,125, profit before commission charges on an initial margin commitment of $500. If the reverse spread had been placed in April—long December 1980, short December 1981—the position would have incurred a loss of the same magnitude during the seven-month holding period (assuming the trader made the mistake of not closing the contracts out before that point); the described situation is a demonstration that spread trading is not without its risks. An up-to-date record on the order of Exhibit 4 should be maintained by futures traders and should be studied as assiduously as traders who carry outright positions scrutinize their trend charts. Moreover, once a spread position has been established, price protection in the form of stop orders should be utilized.

WHAT IS ARBITRAGE?

The conventional definition of an arbitrage is the purchase of an asset in one market against its immediate resale at a profit in another. One example would be buying General Motors common stock on the New York Stock Exchange and selling it on the Pacific Coast Exchange. Another is the purchase of Swiss francs in Zurich against their simultaneous resale in London. A futures spread between like or different contracts is based upon an anticipated change over a period of time in the relationship between two prices, such as the short (December 1980) and long (December 1981) 90-day T bill spread described in the previous section. Since its outcome is not immediately realizable, therefore, a spread contains an element of risk that a classic arbitrage does not entail. Occasional disparities between yields prevailing in the cash money and bond markets and related futures do, however, provide opportunities to engage in so-called quasi arbitrage.

One of these quasi arbitrages is known as the "hedged yield curve ride." Riding the yield curve is a commonplace money market operation wherein investors endeavor to improve their rate of return by

---

[4] Although Exhibit 4 lists futures yields to afford ease of comparison with the cash 90-day T bill discount, the contract, as noted above, is actually quoted and traded in terms of the I.M.M. index.

purchasing a fixed income instrument with a maturity running beyond the intended term of the investment.[5] A frequently cited illustration involves purchasing a 180-day Treasury bill with the intention of re-selling it after 90 days in lieu of buying and holding to maturity an original 90-day bill. The advantage of buying the longer maturity is-sue is the incremental return it provides as the passage of time carries its discount down the steepest part of the yield curve. The risk im-plicit in this gambit is that any increase in short-term rates during the holding period would eradicate the anticipated yield advantage. If rates rose sharply enough, the investor unable to hold them to matu-rity might even be forced to sell the bills at a loss.

The investment trade-off made by a yield curve rider is one of accepting exposure to interest-rate risk and possible capital deprecia-tion in return for the chance of earning a higher rate. The sale of an appropriate futures contract(s) at the time the longer term instrument is purchased serves to offset this risk. The combined transactions con-tain some elements of an arbitrage in that they provide for the sale of an asset at a firm price in the futures market at the same time that it is purchased in the cash market. In other words, the profit or return on the bills is fixed at the time they are bought.

Another type of interest-rate arbitrage between cash and futures markets involves the short sale of Treasury bonds and the purchase of comparable futures contracts to assure coverage of the short position at a known price. if, for example, $1 million U.S. Treasury 8¾s of 2003–08 were sold short at 65 (assuming the bonds could be borrowed to make delivery on the short sale), and at the same time 10 New York Futures Exchange Treasury bond futures contracts were purchased at 63, the bonds deliverable on the futures long position could be used to reimburse the lender of the borrowed bonds. And the two-point, or $20,000, difference less interest expense and brokerage commissions would provide a virtually riskless profit on the transaction.

Apart from the problem of borrowing appropriate bonds to deliver against the original short sale, a money manager who contemplates this type of arbitrage must take into account the price adjustment required to convert to its delivery value the market price of a Treasury bond bearing a coupon other than the specified 9 percent futures contract grade. The manager should also be aware that he or she is likely to receive from the futures short seller the cheapest bond eligi-ble for delivery under the terms of the contract, which will be the least desirable issue from the manager's perspective. In other words, be-fore embarking upon such an operation the would-be arbitrageur must become thoroughly familiar with the delivery terms and other futures contract specifications. Neglecting to do so, may cause the manager to

---

[5] See Chapter 33.

be confronted with an unpleasant surprise instead of the anticipated assured profit.

HOW WELL DO FUTURES FORECAST ACTUAL INTEREST RATES?

For futures prices to forecast invariably and accurately the interest rate on a particular financial instrument as of the date it is to be delivered from the short to the long position holder, expectations must remain unchanged over a 24- to 36-month period, and market participants would need to possess perfect prescience. Both assumptions are manifestly unrealistic. If they were not, there would be no justification for futures markets in interest rates, since investors and borrowers would make their decisions on the basis of complete foreknowledge. It is precisely because short- and long-term rates have become so volatile, hence even more predictable than they were in the past, that such markets were established and very quickly became a success.

The nature of the futures delivery process requires that cash and futures prices converge to identity by the delivery date because the two are at that point interchangeable. As the element of futurity elapses during the last month or two of a contract's existence, its price becomes more closely linked to the cash counterpart.

The history of the December 1980 90-day Treasury bill contract charted in Exhibit 6 illustrates the broad swings futures prices can exhibit relative to cash rates during the life of a contract. The cash 90-day bill rate at the close of 1980 was about 15.75 percent, and the "spot" (delivery month) contract accordingly went off the board two weeks earlier on December 18 (its final trading day) at 83.5, reflecting a 16.5 discount. But throughout its 18-month life, or the approximately 360 market sessions during which the December 1980 contract was traded, it changed hands at a price of 84.25 (15.75 percent discount) on only one trading day. Between the time trading in that particular contract began in June 1979 and its expiration, the price ranged from 75 basis points below (83.5) to 875 basis points above (93) the price at which it was closed out.

The curves depicted in Exhibit 7 represent the distribution of yields on 90-day Treasury bill contracts for eight successive delivery months on five selected dates throughout 1980. The first quarter of the year saw a rise in the cash 90-day T bill discount from about 12 percent to 15 percent, a second-quarter dip to a 7 percent discount, and then a steady and ultimately accelerating climb to close the year at about the 15.75 percent level.

The T bill futures curve remained inverted during the first quarter of the year, projecting a decrease in the discount over a 24-month period of approximately 225 basis points, at a rate of about 9 basis points a month. The first marked change in the curve during 1980 took place by March 24, when it retained the same approximate slope relative to January 7 but moved about 400 basis points up the yield axis. By June 16, at the peak of the spring rally, the futures yield curve turned positive, reflecting a steadily rising discount from about 6.25 percent to 8.25 percent. By September 29 the curve had risen and turned virtually flat in the 11.5 percent to 12 percent range, and by mid-December it resumed its inverted shape from about 16.5 percent in the nearby contract to 12.5 percent in the most distant.

Evidently, the futures forecast that prevailed at the outset of 1980 underwent a continual revision throughout the year as the market responded to the same factors that shaped the course of cash market yields.

ARE FUTURES SUITABLE INVESTMENT TOOLS?

The issue of suitability of futures trading in an institutional context comes down to the matter of risk. The overriding question should be whether the use of futures increases or reduces risk under a given set of circumstances. This chapter has stressed that there are a variety of applications to which these instruments may be put. Some of them are well suited to, and can in fact contribute materially to, the realization of conservative investment objectives. Other applications are patently inappropriate. It is the responsibility of corporate financial officers or portfolio managers to acquaint themselves with the possibilities and limitations of the various trading techniques in deciding which, if any, of them are best fitted to the situation with which they are confronted.

The experience of recent years has repeatedly confirmed that we occupy a risk-ridden world, in the financial sphere as elsewhere. If it can be demonstrated that the economic risk of entering into a futures contract is measurably less than the risk of not doing so, the determination of suitability should go beyond a knee-jerk reaction that futures are highly speculative, hence beyond the pale so far as prudent money management is concerned.

Futures and Options on Fixed Income Securities: Their Role in Fixed Income Portfolio Management

39

GARY L. GASTINEAU
Manager of the Options Portfolio Service
Kidder, Peabody & Co., Inc.

OPTIONS AND FUTURES: DERIVATIVE SECURITIES

The concepts of (1) a debt obligation and (2) a fixed, often periodic, interest payment are the essence of most fixed income securities. These concepts are not difficult for most investors to grasp. The concepts of options and futures contracts on the same fixed income securities are not so simple.

An option on a fixed income security is a right or privilege to buy (a call option) or to sell (a put option) a designated face amount of a particular fixed income security or class of securities during a time period ending on the expiration date of the option. The fixed income security is purchased or sold at the price specified in the option contract, even if the price of the security has changed dramatically by the time the option is exercised. The owner or holder of an option is under no obligation to buy or sell the security and will do so only if exercising the option is preferable to letting the option expire. The seller or writer of the call (or put) option has a contingent obligation to sell (or buy) if the option is exercised. In return for acceptance of this obligation, the seller receives an option premium from the buyer. Options on some fixed income securities are traded on organized exchanges where they can be sold or purchased like any other security. Exchange-listed option positions are usually closed out on the exchange rather than exercised.

A *financial (fixed income) futures contract,* in contrast to an option contract, imposes a firm obligation on each party to buy or sell a predetermined position in a specific fixed income security or class of securities. Also, in contrast to the options market, no "premium" is paid or received by either party. More detailed descriptions of specific options and futures contracts are available from the exchanges where these contracts are traded and from members of these exchanges.

A rudimentary understanding of the key characteristics of options and futures contracts is helpful in most modern investment analysis and essential to an understanding of this chapter. A brief numerical example illustrating the economics of options and futures contracts should provide the necessary background. This example bears only a passing resemblance to any real option or futures contract. It does, however, serve to highlight some of the significant characteristics of these instruments.[1]

The underlying security that is subject to both options and futures contracts in our example is a 10-year Treasury bond bearing a 10 percent coupon and selling at 95 (or $950 per $1000 face amount.) Our hypothetical call option contract would give the owner of the call the right to buy $100,000 face amount of this security, at a price of 96, for a period ending on the expiration date of the option eight months in the future. The buyer of this call option might pay three points ($3,000 per $100,000 face amount of bonds) for the right represented by this call option. If the price of the bond does not rise above 96 by the expiration date, or if it rises above it and falls back before the holder of the call elects to exercise, the call will expire worthless. Prior to exercise or expiration, the price of the call will move up and down with the price of the underlying bond. For example, if the price of the bond rises from 95 to 97, the price of the call might rise from 3 to 4. This price change represents a change from $3,000 to $4,000 on the option covering $100,000 face amount of bonds. Early exercise of such an option would be rare. Most option holders who elect to close their positions prior to the expiration date of the option simply sell the option on the exchange where they bought it.

A futures contract on this same bond will behave quite differently from the option. The purchaser of a call option pays a premium to the

---

[1] For a more detailed discussion of differences between options, futures and forward contracts, see Fischer Black, "The Pricing of Commodity Contracts," *Journal of Financial Economics* 3 (1976), pp. 167–79. A comprehensive discussion of options is available in Gary L. Gastineau, *The Stock Options Manual* (New York: McGraw-Hill, 1979). An introduction to financial futures is presented in Chapter 38 of this handbook. More comprehensive information on interest rate futures has been prepared by Arthur Rebell, Gail Gordon, and Suzanne Ward of Wertheim & Co.

seller of the option in return for the right (but not the obligation) to buy the bond at a fixed price on a future date. In contrast, both parties to a futures contract are obligated—the buyer to pay for the bonds and the seller to deliver the bonds at the contract price. These differences between the option contract and the futures contract are important. Whereas the buyer of the option contract is not required to exercise the option, the buyer of the futures contract *is* under an obligation to purchase the securities at the agreed-upon price.

The striking price of an option is standardized by the options exchange to facilitate uniformity in option contract terms. There will rarely be more than five or six different option-striking prices. In the case we have assumed, the exercise price of the option was 96 or $96,000 per $100,000 per face amount of bonds. If the bonds are selling below this price a call option holder will simply let the option expire. The three-point premium ($3,000) will be lost.

Participants in the futures market do not pay a premium. The price at which the buyer agrees to purchase and the seller agrees to deliver is determined in the market place. In this case we assume that the futures price for delivery eight months hence is 95–17. This means that the buyer agrees to purchase and the seller agrees to sell at a price of 95 and 17/32s: ($95,531.25) eight months in the future unless their obligations are cancelled by an offsetting transaction before then.

Neither party to a futures contract pays or receives a premium. In fact, no cash passes between buyer and seller at the time of the initial transaction. The value of the transaction to each participant is reflected in the futures price they agree upon. This procedure contrasts with the option market wherein the buyer and seller of an option contract exchange a nonrefundable premium. The premium belongs to the option seller whether or not the option is exercised. Parties to a futures contract typically deposit government securities or other collateral with their broker to guarantee that they will fulfill their respective obligations under the contract.

While no cash is required initially, the futures contract must be marked to the market. As the futures price rises (falls) from the 95–17 price, the buyer (seller) will receive a cash credit to his or her account with the broker. This cash may be reinvested at interest. If the futures price falls (rises) the buyer (seller) will have to deposit additional cash with the broker, which will in turn be transferred to the seller (buyer), or interest will be charged on a debit balance. We will have more to say about the differences between options and futures-margin arrangements when we discuss the relative attractiveness of the two markets from the viewpoint of a participant.

Futures contracts are currently available on a variety of fixed income securities ranging from commercial paper, CDs, and Treasury bills on the short end of the yield curve to GNMA certificates and

Treasury bonds on the long end.[2] Option contracts on a similar range of fixed income securities will become available over the next year or two. To complicate matters, some of the new option contracts will be options on futures contracts rather than options on underlying securities.

Anyone who plans to participate in either market will need much more extensive and specific information than we have provided here. The example was designed only to help readers unfamiliar with these markets to understand the discussion that follows.

HEDGING—CLASSIC AND MODERN CONCEPTS

Most people understand hedging in options and futures markets to be a mysterious technique to reduce or eliminate risks associated with price fluctuations. Common examples include a farmer who sells futures against a prospective wheat harvest and a manufacturer who purchases copper futures contracts to cover the risks of a fixed-price contract. In contrast to popular wisdom, it is not clear that each of these parties is really eliminating major risks.

The wheat farmer, for example, might lose the crop to adverse weather or pestilence. If crop destruction is widespread and wheat prices rise, the "hedging" attempt would compound the loss of the crop with a loss in the futures market. The manufacturer trying to cover copper requirements and "hedge" the supply price might have problems with currency fluctuations, import restrictions, and political changes in Central Africa. The manufacturer's risks, like the farmer's, might be increased rather than reduced by the futures transaction.

The modern concept of hedging in the options and futures markets focuses on the use of underlying and derivative (futures and options) securities to *control* some element of portfolio or business risk. The notion of control suggests that some participants may increase risks in one way while reducing them in another. Under this very broad but useful definition, the "speculator" who has received so much attention from economists and legislators is probably a very small factor in most markets. By implication, a true speculator is someone who does not adequately understand the magnitude of the risks being taken. Under this definition a market participant would be categorized as a hedger or speculator on the basis of sophistication.

In the following discussion we will examine hedging in the modern sense—the attempted control of portfolio or business risk. Our focus will be on risks associated with interest-rate fluctuations. In thinking about the specific examples of interest rate risk control we describe, two points should be kept in mind. First, a transaction that reduces interest-rate risk for one party may reduce risk in another way for the

---

[2] See Chapter 38.

other party to the transaction. Second, and seemingly inconsistent with the first point, the total amount of interest-rate risk in the financial system cannot be changed by a transaction in a derivative security, such as a futures or options contract. The key to resolving any inconsistency between these points is that we live in a world where financial markets are derivative to the provision of goods and services and where operating and financial organizations have both asset and liability sides to their balance sheets.

DURATION AND THE CONCEPT OF BOND EQUIVALENCE

As a prelude to understanding the use of options and futures contracts in risk control, the reader needs to have a basic understanding of two important concepts. The first of these concepts, *duration*, is discussed in Chapter 35. Although duration has other functions, we use it here as a measure of relative sensitivity to interest-rate fluctuations. A long-term bond with a calculated duration of five years has approximately 10 times the interest-rate risk of a six-month Treasury bill. Although there are credit risk factors that affect the relative riskiness of government and nongovernment securities apart from differences in duration, it is useful to adjust the basic duration number for these additional risk factors and focus on a single measurement of risk. This type of adjustment may seem arbitrary, but more complex techniques for incorporating credit risks do not seem warranted.

Because most other risk factors associated with fixed income securities are correlated with interest-rate fluctuations, a single number for duration modified for differences in credit standing is probably an adequate measurement of risk for most fixed income securities. With appropriate attention to differences in coupons and principal between and among deliverable securities, duration is an adequate interest-rate risk measure in relating futures contracts to a broad range of fixed income securities.

Another concept in addition to duration is necessary to relate the risk characteristics of option contracts to underlying securities. This additional concept is the notion of *bond equivalence*.

The literature on stock options thoroughly describes and documents the concept of the *neutral hedge ratio*.[3] The neutral hedge ratio gets its name from the fact that an option position can be used to neutralize price fluctuations in the underlying security. The neutral hedge ratio is the fractional change in the value of a put or call option in response to a one-point change in the value of the underlying security. As soon as options on a fixed income security begin trading, computer services will have programs to translate option positions

---

[3] Gastineau, *The Stock Options Manual*, pp. 71–84, 97–111, and 264–267.

into bond or bill equivalents using the neutral hedge ratio. The fractional change in the option will vary as the distance between the bond price and the striking price changes, but an appropriate risk structure can be maintained by adding to or subtracting from the option position as bond prices move up and down.

The concept of bond equivalence is so important that we will take the time to illustrate it in more detail. In the example we developed earlier to describe the differences between options and futures contracts, we hypothesized a movement in the call option contract from a price of 3 to 4 ($3,000 to $4,000 in terms of the total value of that contract) in response to a move from 95 to 97 ($95,000 to $97,000) in the underlying security. In this very simple example, the value of the option contract changed by half the value of the underlying security. The fraction by which the option changes in response to a move in the underlying security will not always be one half. It could range from a very small fraction if the option is well out of the money to nearly one if the expiration date is near and the option is in the money.[4] If the value of the option in the example changes by one half the value of the underlying security, each option is the interest-rate risk equivalent of $50,000 face amount (about $48,000 market value) of the underlying bonds. Two of these call option contracts are equivalent in risk to a $100,000 face amount bond position. They can be used as a substitute for the bond position when an investor buys them or to offset the interest-rate risk of the bond position when the investor sells them.

The calculation of duration and bond equivalence for futures and options is complex. Fortunately, information and software are available through many brokerage firms and some computer services. The quality of this material is uneven, and the wary investor should not accept a computer printout at face value. Once the analytical obstacles are overcome, the incentive to use these instruments in portfolio risk control can be substantial.

USING FINANCIAL INSTRUMENT OPTIONS AND FUTURES CONTRACTS TO CONTROL INTEREST-RATE RISKS

The participants in these markets have widely differing objectives. The following examples illustrate rather than exhaust the possibilities.

---

[4] The phrases "in the money" and "out of the money" refer to the relationship between the market price of the underlying security and the striking price of the option. An in-the-money option has intrinsic value because the current market price of the bond exceeds the striking price of a call or is below the striking price of a put. For example, a call exercisable at 72 is said to be three points in the money when the bond is selling at 75. An out-of-the-money option has no intrinsic value because the current market price is below the striking price of a call or above the striking price of a put.

Securities Dealers and Underwriters

Securities dealers and underwriters have one of the most difficult interest-rate risk control problems faced by any participant in the fixed income securities markets. Several years ago it was not unusual for a major bond dealer to gain or lose $10 million or more in a relatively short period of time from changes in the value of his or her bond inventory in response to interest-rate fluctuations. Since the introduction and widespread use of financial futures, there have been fewer reported cases of huge losses by bond dealers and underwriters than most observers would have expected given recent dramatic fluctuations in interest rates.

The typical underwriting fee is much larger than the cost of hedging interest risks in the financial futures or option markets. Bond dealers and underwriters no longer need to take the kind of risks that were almost unavoidable before the introduction of these derivative markets.

Banks

An increasing volume of literature has focused on the potential use of financial futures and options markets by commercial and savings banks.[5] These new markets can be extremely useful in balancing maturities on the asset side of the balance sheet with those on the liability side. The basic risk-management problem for both commercial and savings banks is that their assets are usually of longer duration than their liabilities. Commercial banks have tried to cope with this problem by linking the interest rates on their longer term loans (assets) to the prime rate. The prime rate, in turn, is adjusted to reflect the short-term cost of funds (liabilities). Savings banks and other housing lenders have an even more severe asset-liability mismatch than commercial banks. Variable-rate and renegotiable mortgage loans are helpful, but some lenders have faced adverse reactions when they have tried to raise rates. Increasing rates on a mortgage is often not practical even when it is permitted by the contract. The focus of asset-liability management for deposit institutions has increasingly shifted from changing rates on old loans to offsetting changes in the cost of money through transactions in the financial futures and options markets.

It is probably safe to predict that increased use of options and futures markets for asset-liability matching and for controlling the risk of their municipal bond portfolios will have a profound effect on com-

---

[5] For example, Sanford Rose, "Banks Should Look to the Futures," *Fortune*, April 20, 1981, pp. 185–192; and Anthony J. Vignola, "Bank Use of Financial Futures," (New York: Kidder, Peabody & Co, October 1981).

mercial banks. When the use of options and futures is combined with the leasing provisions of the Reagan tax program, the average tax rate of money-center banks will almost certainly drop. Investors should also expect changes in the composition of loan and investment portfolios. Assets will be of longer duration, but futures and options will be used to improve the match of assets and liabilities. Other things equal, earnings should be higher and more stable.

Other Tax-Paying Entities

Nonfinancial Corporations. Two important uses of these derivative securities by nonfinancial corporations are corporate cash management and control of the corporation's cost of capital.

To the extent that the relatively long duration of a preferred stock or utility common stock portfolio can be offset with transactions in Treasury bond futures and options, most corporations that expect to have (1) significant cash balances for several years and (2) high marginal tax rates could benefit from a preferred stock or utility common stock hedging program. Corporate taxpayers receive an 85 percent dividend-received deduction.[6] If the corporation's marginal federal tax rate is 46 percent, it pays a 6.9 percent federal tax on a preferred stock or utility common stock dividend. If the interest-rate risk of preferred stocks or utility common stocks is hedged with options or futures, the interest-rate risk characteristics of the portfolio can approximate those of a portfolio of commercial paper. The aftertax return should be hundreds of basis points higher than the commercial paper return.

Several securities underwriters have begun insulating their corporate clients from interest-rate fluctuations during the period between the decision to sell a debt issue and the actual sale of securities. The underwriter establishes a futures or options position designed to fluctuate in response to interest rates much like the proposed corporate debt issue. When the issue is priced by the underwriter, any gain or loss on the futures or options position is added to or subtracted from the proceeds paid to the issuing company. The underwriter rather than the issuer carries the futures or options position on his or her books to avoid distorting a single year's reported earnings for the issuer. The underwriter offsets the gain or loss on the hedge position against the adjusted underwriting fee. If the corporate client carried the position, it might incur a short-term capital loss, which has limited deductibility for tax purposes.

Individuals. Relatively few individuals face asset-liability mismatches as severe as those that characterize some corporate entities. On the other hand, a growing group of individual participants in the

---

[6] See Chapter 3.

fixed income futures and options markets are high tax bracket individuals who wish to hedge municipal bond portfolios. These individuals want to have the high rates available on long-term municipals without taking the corresponding risk of interest-rate fluctuations. Through careful planning and execution they can achieve extraordinary aftertax returns with interest-rate risk comparable to the risks of municipal project notes.[7]

Municipal bond hedging is not yet as popular among individual investors as what are popularly called speculative uses of these contracts. These "speculative" positions express a viewpoint on interest-rate movements. Without debating the speculative label, money market participants have found these derivative securities a less costly alternative to positions in conventional securities. Only in rare circumstances would classic interest-rate plays like leveraged positions in government bonds be preferable to futures or options positions.

Individuals who can move quickly might find opportunities to exploit market anomalies through arbitrage-type transactions. The opportunities for this kind of scalping by nonprofessional investors are limited, however. Much individual arbitrage-type participation in fixed income futures and options markets is probably the result of overzealous selling or a misplaced conviction that a few back-of-an-envelope calculations are a match for the computer power and order execution skills of large traders.

Institutional Investors—Exploiting Market Anomolies

So far the groups of investors that seem most likely to benefit from financial futures and options trading are individuals and organizations that use these markets much as agribusinesses use agricultural commodity futures markets. Many corporations and high tax bracket individuals can obtain unique tax advantages as well as effective risk control. Most nontaxpaying institutions have done relatively little in these markets to date.

Mutual funds using futures and options contracts may ultimately give their corporate or individual shareholders many of the advantages of direct investment in dividend-paying stocks or municipal debt by passing income to shareholders without changing its character. It may even be possible to take advantage of one aspect of the tax treatment of registered investment companies to convert short-term capital gains into qualified dividends for corporate shareholders.

---

[7] For a description of this technique, see Gary L. Gastineau, "The Impact of Options and Financial Futures on Municipal Bond Portfolio Management," in *The Handbook of Municipal Bonds*, vol. 1, ed. Frank J. Fabozzi, Sylvan Feldstein, Irving M. Pollack, and Frank G. Zarb (Homewood, Ill.: Dow Jones-Irwin, 1983). © Dow Jones-Irwin, Inc., 1983.

For institutional investors unaffected by taxes, such as pension and profit sharing plans and endowment accounts, the advantages of financial futures and options trading are less obvious. The magnitude of market inefficiencies would have to be unusual by any standard for financial futures transactions to appear dramatically more attractive than other means of adjusting the interest-rate risk characteristics of these portfolios. The case for options in a nontaxable account is more tenable if the portfolio is in the hands of a skilled manager. There is little question that the use of options can improve results to the extent that underpriced options are purchased and overpriced options sold as part of a common stock or fixed income portfolio management effort. It should be possible through careful attention to option evaluation to add one or two percentage points to the level of return from a comparable risk, conventional fixed income portfolio.

An additional case for these derivative securities in the management of tax-free portfolios lies in meeting needs for asset-liability matching. This matching can be particularly important for pension plans. Insurance and pension actuaries have begun to work on this concept, and new products and services will undoubtedly appear over the next few years. On balance, it seems probable that the major participants in financial futures and options markets will continue to be securities dealers, banks and other savings institutions, nonfinancial corporations, and individuals. Insurance companies and tax-free institutions will gradually increase their participation.

MISUSE OF FINANCIAL FUTURES AND OPTIONS MARKETS

In our definition of hedging, we suggested that, under the modern concept of hedging, speculators were probably people who really did not understand the risks they were intent on taking. Misuse of financial futures and options markets is essentially a result of failure on the part of market participants to understand the true risk characteristics of the investment strategies and tactics they are using. For example, we suspect that a good deal of the interest in financial futures by pension and profit sharing plans is based on misunderstanding the mathematics of futures markets.

Options frequently become significantly under- or overpriced, but futures contract prices have less tendency to significant misalignment. Anomalies in the futures markets are more likely to arise out of a peculiarity in the delivery process or an unusual and only partly predictable change in government or private financing plans. Anomalies in options markets are more frequent and generally of larger magnitude. Nonetheless, a high degree of skill is required to earn superior returns. Investors seeking to exploit opportunities should expect to pay above-average brokerage commissions or investment management fees. Skill in finding and exploiting these opportunities does not come cheaply.

Apart from misunderstandings and mistaken expectations, the most serious misuse of futures and options markets is to view them as a source of leverage. In our discussion of the concept of bond equivalence, we described how every futures and option position can be translated into an equivalent bond position. Rational investors, whether they view themselves as hedgers or speculators, should translate every fixed income futures and options position into the equivalent of the underlying security. If they would not buy $10 million worth of long-term bonds with cash or by using margin debt, they should not take an equivalent position in the futures or options market.

A less frequent misuse of these markets is in fine-tuning portfolio risk. Although it is *theoretically* possible, through bond equivalence translations, to control risks with an extraordinary degree of precision, the additional transaction costs occasioned by such fine tuning will probably wipe out any advantages. Interest-rate hedging works best when large risks are offset and small risks are accepted.

One final abuse or misuse of fixed income options seems worth noting. A long-held belief that is an article of faith with many stock option market participants is that option sellers enjoy a large and systematic advantage over option buyers. The untruth of this proposition has been amply demonstrated with regard to stock options,[8] but similar demonstrations will probably be necessary with fixed income options. In the meantime, any proposal that an investor "add to income" by selling options should be rejected.

OPTIONS VERSUS FUTURES

As the options market on fixed income securities develops, much will be written and said about the relative attractiveness of options on these securities versus the established financial futures markets. In what may be the first article in the genre, Eugene Moriarty, Susan Phillips and Paul Tosini[9] argue that options and futures contracts serve different needs and it is unlikely that either instrument will dominate the other. Their conclusion that neither options nor futures

---

[8] Gastineau, *The Stock Options Manual*, pp. 282–312; and Gary L. Gastineau and Albert Madansky, "Why Simulations Are an Unreliable Test of Option Strategies," *Financial Analysts Journal*, September–October 1979, pp. 66–76.

[9] "A Comparison of Options and Futures in the Management of Portfolio Risk," *Financial Analysts Journal*, January–February 1981, pp. 61–67.

will dominate may or may not be valid. If it is valid, the reasons are quite different from the reasons they advance.

There is no precedent for *simultaneous* opening of futures and option trading on the same underlying security or commodity. The existence of entrenched vested interests and a reluctance to change established ways of doing things gives the first market established an advantage over a new financial instrument. Options, without exception, have been and will be established only after the futures market is entrenched.

Futures markets have another advantage, particularly for the small participant, in that they are *relatively* easier to participate in intelligently than the options market. Although most so-called analysis of cash-futures relationships is overly simplistic, the fact that small investors can comprehend a cash-futures relationship gives them a feeling of comfort. An appropriate analysis of option values and techniques to translate options into stock, bond, or commodity equivalents is much more complex. For the small participant this analysis is probably impractical. Sophisticated investors (and investors who believe they are sophisticated) will probably be attracted to the options market.

In "popular" investment literature and in the press, authors often cite limited risk and the small grubstake required to buy options as an advantage of the options market. These market characteristics may attract a few marginal participants, but they are highly unlikely to affect the outcome of a tug-of-war between competing options and futures markets.

Another factor that may affect the relative importance of options and futures markets is position limits. Until recently, there have been few restrictions on the positions a futures market participant may take, although large positions usually had to be reported to some regulatory authority. Position limits have been imposed from the beginning in option markets. A position limit is a restriction on the number of contracts an individual or group may buy or sell in an options or futures market. For example, the limit on GNMA options is 1000 contracts on the same side of the market (long calls *plus* short puts). Position limits probably reflect a lack of understanding of the market and lack of "comfort" on the part of regulatory authorities. To the extent that position limits inhibit participation by large investors, they could have an effect on the relative size of options and futures markets.

Options have a few things going for them, too. One very important advantage of options over futures is a function of the margin structure and the way in which positions are "marked to the market." Margin deposits in an option account are a good-faith collateral deposit to guarantee the performance of an option *seller*. The premium an option buyer pays goes to the seller and may be invested in securities or replaced in the account by a marketable security, which serves as collateral. The option seller may be required to post more collateral if the value of the position changes adversely, but no additional *cash* is required from either buyer or seller unless and until the position is closed out or exercised.

Margin serves a different function in futures markets. Whereas the option contract is a *contingent* obligation of the seller, the futures contract is a firm obligation of both buyer and seller until it is offset (closed out). If the price of a futures contract changes in an adverse direction, either buyer or seller will be called upon to deposit cash or incur a debit balance. A favorable price movement generates cash, which can be removed or invested at interest. These credits or debits change the balance *daily*. In contrast, there are no cash flows associated with maintenance margins on options.

This difference in the character of margin will work to the advantage of the options market, particularly in a high interest-rate environment. Users of options who have substantial securities holdings need not worry about borrowing short-term funds to meet a cash margin call. Users of futures contracts often are surprised when the value of the position they are trying to hedge increases and they have to borrow to cover margin calls on futures contracts. If they have a profit on the futures position, they must arrange for investment of funds generated by marking the futures position to the market or else forego part of their return. The futures margin system is appreciably more cumbersome and potentially more costly to the investor than is the option margin system.

All in all, where both options and futures markets on a given underlying security or commodity exist, the relative market share of option transactions should consistently increase. This shift will take place partly because of the margin characteristics outlined above and partly because options have slightly more flexible risk-limiting and risk-control characteristics. Through the purchase of underpriced and the sale of overpriced contracts, options can also provide an enhanced risk-adjusted return more consistently than corresponding futures contracts.

An analogy may serve to illustrate how and why options might gain market share at the expense of competing futures contracts. One of the most interesting phenomena of the financial futures markets has been the dramatic growth of Treasury bond futures. For 1981, Chicago Board of Trade Treasury bond futures contracts were more actively traded than any other futures contract series on any exchange. The Treasury bond futures contract began trading in August 1977. This

growth is particularly interesting in view of the fact that futures contracts on GNMA pass-through certificates were introduced long before
Treasury bond futures.

There are a number of reasons why GNMA futures were introduced
first. The most important reason was probably a conviction on the part
of financial futures market originators that hedging participants would
be important early market participants. Government bond dealers and
other users of long-term fixed income securities, however, found the
Treasury bond contract much more to their liking. The underlying
security on a Treasury bond contract exhibits price fluctuations comparable to those of many other fixed income securities. In contrast,
GNMA futures are not very useful in cross-hedging. The payback of
principal as well as interest over the life of the obligation is a peculiarity of the GNMA instrument not shared by most other fixed income
securities. Because the Treasury bond futures contract can be used to
hedge other interest-rate risks, the volume in Treasury bond futures
now dwarfs volume in GNMA futures.

Although the usefulness of option contracts relative to futures contracts is not nearly as dramatic as the usefulness of Treasury bond
futures contracts relative to GNMA futures contracts, the parallel is
important. To a wide variety of sophisticated individual and institutional investors who understand the basics of option evaluation and
risk equivalence, options are a more satisfactory hedging instrument
than are financial futures.

An analogy from the listed stock option market is probably even
more instructive. The number of option contracts traded on a particular stock frequently exceeds the number of round lots of the underlying stock that trade on the stock exchange. Two to 10 times as many
option contracts as round lots is a common relationship. A moment's
reflection suggests that this is appropriate because option transactions
permit an investor to adjust risk more economically than do transactions in the underlying security. Growth in stock option and financial
futures markets has been due in part to savings in transaction costs
versus equivalent transactions in the underlying security. The combination of commission costs and bid-asked trading spreads for risk
equivalent positions will probably be the single most important factor
in determining whether options or futures will dominate. Established
markets typically have narrower trading spreads than new markets.
Time and foresight on the part of market makers in a new instrument
can overcome this "Catch-22" situation, but the established market
has a definite advantage.

It is hard to generalize when options on fixed income securities are
not yet established, but there seems to be a reasonable chance that
options may dominate futures in the fixed income markets. Perhaps,

after a much longer break in period, they will dominate in the commodities market as well.

THE IMPACT OF FINANCIAL FUTURES AND FIXED INCOME OPTIONS CONTRACTS ON YIELD CURVES AND MARKET EFFICIENCY

As noted earlier, the total interest-rate risk in the financial system will be unchanged as a result of the availability of financial futures and options contracts. What these derivative securities do is provide an opportunity for a reallocation of risk among market participants. To the extent that this reallocation takes place, many anomalies in the interest-rate structure will probably be reduced.

Some theories of the term structure of interest rates focus on the notion of preferred habitats or institutional restrictions that affect the number and enthusiasm of participants in certain sectors of the market. Interest-rate futures and fixed income options will probably increase the flexibility of many market participants. Specific examples include (1) the availability of a commercial paper equivalent instrument paying qualified dividends through preferred and utility common stock hedging, (2) a higher yield on short-term equivalent hedged municipal obligations, and (3) better duration matching of assets and liabilities for many market participants.

The function of financial futures contracts and options in the elimination of market anomalies and inefficiencies could easily be exaggerated. We do not mean to suggest that these instruments alone will eliminate all pockets of market inefficiency. They should, however, help markets move in the general direction of greater efficiency. Any phenomenon that leads to increased capital market efficiency should promote greater efficiency and productivity in the economy as a whole.

CONCLUSION

The analysis and risk-control techniques used by debt and equity portfolio managers have changed dramatically in recent years. Nowhere has the change been more rapid than in the fixed income markets. Although it is not difficult to find bond portfolio managers whose current approach would have been considered "time honored" in the 1920s, the parade has passed these managers by. These traditional managers find it nearly impossible to obtain new business because they are unlikely to provide their clients with results that justify a fee.

Today's effective fixed income manager must understand duration, the nuances of credit-rating systems, bond portfolio immunization, the mathematics of bond yields, and much more. The manager who cannot adapt to new concepts and new techniques will be at a marketing and performance disadvantage. It seems safe to predict that in a few years the manager who does not understand risk-control and risk-adjusted return enhancement with futures and options contracts will be obsolete.

The Gold Spread as a Fixed Income Strategy*

40

IRA G. KAWALLER, Ph.D.
Director, New York Office
International Monetary Market

Although the term *fixed income securities* generally refers to debt
instruments, a more literal interpretation of this designation would
allow for any financial vehicle that offers a specified and predetermined return to maturity. Thus the kind of arrangement that would
qualify would be one in which an asset is bought at one time with a
concurrent agreement to be sold in the future at a price determined
simultaneously with the original purchase. This kind of transaction is
common with U.S. Treasury securities and is known as a *reverse repurchase agreement* or, more simply, a *reverse*. By doing a reverse,
the investor is simply making a loan and holding a very standardized
form of collateral. The counterpart on the opposite side of this transaction is selling the security and contracting to buy it back at a later date.
This transaction allows one to use collateral to raise cash, and it is
called a *repurchase* or *repo*. In effect, then, repos or reverses are
simply mechanisms that allow loans to be negotiated with attractive
terms (the repo rate), partly because of the standardized nature of the
collateral.

* The author wishes to acknowledge Lauri Osterland for the programming needed
to generate the charts within this paper and Kurt Dew and Jeff Nichols for their comments.

Although such transactions more commonly have Treasury issues serving as collateral, virtually any mutually acceptable asset can serve the same purpose. Gold—*as well as other precious metals*—is often used in this manner. The attractiveness of gold has to do with the durability of the metal, its wide acceptance as a store of value, and its abundant stored supply. By selling gold and simultaneously contracting to buy it back at a later time, one is using gold as collateral to create cash (i.e., creating a collateralized loan or a repo). This specific multiple transaction is commonly referred to as buying a spread.[1] Conversely, if one were to buy the physical gold in the cash (or spot) market and simultaneously short (sell) the future, it would be called selling the spread. The rate associated with spread transactions is the spread yield. Buying the spread is conceptually the same as doing a repo, and thus from this perspective the spread yield may be thought of as a borrowing rate. Selling a spread is conceptually the same as doing a reverse, and so from this perspective the spread yield may be thought of as a lending rate.

SPOT/FUTURE GOLD SPREADS

The maturity of a gold spread is the period between the settlement date (as distinguished from the purchase date) and the date at which the gold must be delivered to the futures exchange. With gold, the normal trading convention calls for two-day delivery. That is, the physical transfer of gold for cash occurs two business days after the deal is struck. Thus the settlement day is two business days after the purchase day.

Consider the following example based on prices of August 3, 1981: The physical price of gold was $392.50, as reported by Handy & Harmon; and the closing price for gold traded for delivery on September 1, 1982, on the International Monetary Market was $452.70. By buying physical gold and selling it on the IMM, the investor would have realized a profit of $60.20 per ounce if he or she were willing to hold the gold for the entire period between the settlement date (August 5, 1981) and the delivery date (September 1, 1982).[2] In this example the spread yield appropriate for these 392 days, calculated on a discount

---

[1] Spreads are alternatively called swaps or switches. Thus the transaction described may also be called buying a swap or buying a switch, as well as buying a spread. Importantly, the convention in gold that associates the "sell" or "buy" to the deferred month of the switch is just the reverse of the convention in other contracts. Buying a grain spread, for instance, means buying the nearby month and selling the deferred month.

[2] The delivery to the exchange may be made on any business day during the contract month; but no definitive benefit can be secured by the short-position holder by maintaining this position beyond the first delivery day.

basis, is equal to 12.2 percent.[3] Alternatively, instead of shorting the
September 1982 contract, the investor could have chosen to short a
contract in a different month. For example, if the investor had chosen
to short the March 1982 contract at $422.10, he or she would have
been able to obtain a return of 12.1 percent for a holding period of 208
days; or by choosing to short the June 1982 contract for $437.30, the
investor would have been able to realize a return of 12.3 percent for a
period of 300 days. At the time of this decision, whether these opportunities would have been attractive would have been based on a consideration of alternative yields and relative risks available to the investor at that time.

In order to show that gold spreads behave very much like other
fixed income securities, Exhibit 1 plots a spread yield series against
the rate on one-year Treasury bills. The similarity of the patterns
reflects this close relationship between these instruments. Despite
the closeness, the rates are not strictly comparable. The Treasury bill

Exhibit 1
Spot/Future Gold Spread Yield versus the One-Year Treasury Bill Yield

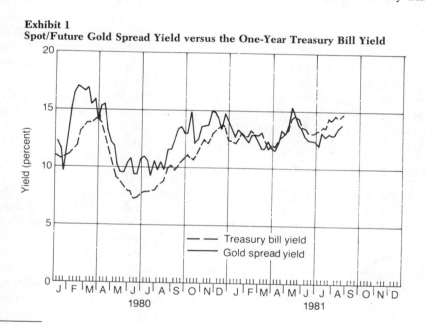

---

[3] The formula for calculating a discount rate of return is as follows:

$$r = \left(\frac{P_f - P_p}{P_f}\right) \left(\frac{360}{D}\right)$$

where

   r = discount rate of return
  P_f = futures price
  P_p = price of physical gold
  D = days between the settlement date and the delivery date on the exchange.

has a constant, one-year maturity; but by the nature of the construction of the gold spread, the spread has a maturity that varies between about 15 months and one year. The way this spread is constructed is as follows: Physical gold transactions occurring from December 1 through February 28 (or 29) are paired with the March contract of the following year; physical transactions from March 1 through May 31 are paired with the June contract of the following year; physical transactions from June 1 through August 31 are paired with the September contract of the following year; and physical transactions from September 1 through November 30 are paired with the December contract of the following year. As a result the maturity of spreads associated with a particular futures contract will decline each day. For example, consider transactions that include the September 1982 contract: For the August 3, 1981, transaction, the holding period would be 392 days; on August 4, 1981, the holding period would be 391 days, and so on. When it is time to switch to the December contract, however, the maturity is "reset" to the 15-month maximum. One other consideration concerning the two rates shown on Exhibit 1 deserves mention. Whereas the investor who buys a Treasury Bill earns the rate that is plotted, the investor who sells the gold switch does not earn the spread yield but earns somewhat less. As a consequence of buying physical gold, additional costs associated with transportation, security, storage, and insurance would be realized; but they have been ignored in this calculation. They would necessarily reduce the overall rate of return from that rate calculated in Exhibit 1.

FUTURE/FUTURE GOLD SPREADS

Both the maturity differences and the physical cost considerations are largely mitigated—or at least deferred from consideration—when attention is shifted from a comparison of current interest rates to a comparison of forward interest rates. This transition is made by constructing a "forward gold spread"[4] using two futures contract prices— the "nearby," which is the contract month with the closest delivery date, and the "next-out," which is the contract month immediately following the nearby month. At any time, the maturity of this spread will have a constant, three-month maturity, beginning on the delivery date for the closer futures contract. Therefore, this forward gold spread is essentially a forward three-month interest rate vehicle.

Several aspects of the future/future gold spread differ from the spot/ future gold spread. With the spot/future spread, one can sell physical

---

[4] The term *forward gold spread* is not commonly accepted by commodity professionals. When one uses the terms *switch, spread,* or *swap,* it is not clear whether the "closer" part of the multiple transaction is for a physical transaction or for some forward date.

gold and buy future only if one has gold in one's possession to start. Using a future/future gold switch one can sell the nearby and buy the next-out, regardless whether one holds gold or not. However, it must be emphasized that to initiate such a position, one must be prepared to liquidate the nearby short position prior to the delivery date, or one must stand ready to purchase gold in order to satisfy the delivery requirement. Another difference has to do with the margin requirements and financial exposure that is associated with futures trading. As a function of the practice of marking-to-market, whereby all losses and profits from exchange positions are settled after each business day, cash flow practicalities could seriously distort the rate of return one might anticipate when the initial spread position is put on. In a future/future gold spread position, the likelihood is that variation margin requirements would be largely offsetting for the two legs of the spread trade. In a spot/future spread, on the other hand, margin is only required on one leg of the spread, and thus variation margin calls have the potential to cause more severe distortions of the anticipated return.

In Exhibit 2, the three-month future/future gold spread yield is plotted against the three-month Treasury bill futures yield. Again, both of these interest rates are calculated on a discount basis. Like the interest rates shown in Exhibit 1, the forward interest rates in Exhibit 2 show similar patterns, although turning points for the Treasury bill future have tended to precede those of the future/future gold spread—more pronouncedly earlier in the period shown.

Exhibit 2
Future/Future Gold Spread Yield versus the Three-Month Treasury Bill Futures Yield

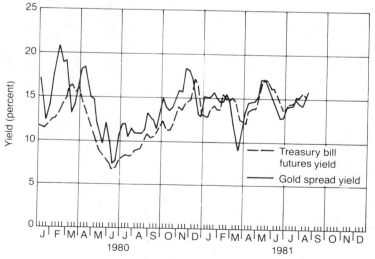

GOLD SPREAD PRICES

The previous sections have demonstrated the interest-rate aspects of gold spreads, but these vehicles have *price* considerations that should be clarified, as well. The definition of a spread price is simply the difference in the prices of the two legs of the spread. This price will be affected by (1) the spread yield, (2) the time between the delivery dates of the two legs, and (3) the base price of gold (i.e., the price of the closer leg of the spread).

It should be clear from the previous sections that, all else being equal, a rise (fall) in the spread yield will cause a widening (narrowing) of the prices of the two legs of the spread, and thus a rise (fall) in the value of the spread. Regarding point (2) concerning a spot/future spread, on a day-to-day basis the spread price will shrink as the spot and future prices converge. For future/future spreads, on the other hand, the time difference between the two legs is constant; thus, with no other factors changing, the price of the spread will remain fixed.

Finally, the effect of a change in the base price of gold can be best explained by example: Assuming a one-year spread with a base price of gold of $500/ounce[5] and a far leg priced at $580/ounce, the spread price would be $80/ounce. If the price of gold were to double instantaneously, for instance, assuming no change in interest rates (or spread yields), the base price would be $1,000/ounce, and the far-leg price would be $1160/ounce. Thus the spread price would also double (from $80 to $160).

In some cases, it may be desirable to eliminate the effects of such price moves, which can be accomplished by the use of a "tail." A tail is simply the outright purchase or sale of one leg of the spread, such that when prices change, the effect of the price move on the spread will be in the opposite direction and of the same magnitude as the effect of the price move on the tail. In the example used above, the purchase (sale) of a 100-ounce spread should be accompanied by a sale (purchase) of 16 ounces of the closer leg. With this combination, suppose one were long 100 ounces of gold spreads at $80 per ounce and short 16 ounces of base gold at $500 per ounce. When the price doubled, the gain on the spread ($80/ounce × 100 ounces, or $8,000) would be exactly equal to the loss on the tail ($500/ounce × 16 ounces, or $8,000); or if prices halved, the loss on the spread ($4,000) would be exactly equal to the gain on the tail ($4,000).

The formula appropriate for determining the tail/spread ratio is as follows:

$$T/S = \frac{P_{fl} - P_{nl}}{P_{nl}}$$

---

[5] In this example, because all changes are assumed to be instantaneous, it does not matter whether you assume the base price to be a spot price or a price of a nearby future.

where

> T = number of ounces (contracts) for the tail
> S = number of ounces (contracts) for the spread
> P_{fl} = price of the far leg
> P_{nl} = price of the near leg

It should be clear that if prices undergo any significant change, the tail spread ratio would be affected. Thus when employing a tail, a monitoring of the position would be required.

CONCLUSION

Although the focus of this paper is limited to simply demonstrating the similarity of gold spreads to fixed income securities, its implication is that spreads may be used in a variety of ways. Specifically, the gold spread may be considered as an alternative to some fixed income securities when the differential between the spread yield and the more traditional interest rate justifies the substitution. For example, instead of buying Treasury bills, one might consider selling appropriately tailed gold spreads if the gold spread yield were high relative to the Treasury bill yield. Or, if one were interested in locking-in a low forward interest rate, one could buy a future/future gold spread (again appropriately tailed) instead of shorting one of the interest-rate futures. In this case, the strategy would be most appropriate when these gold spread yields were low, relative to the interest-rate futures. In conclusion, whether hedging, investing, or employing various trading ideas, the gold spread may—when used with discretion—provide profitable alternatives to more traditional interest-rate vehicles.

A Corporate Bond
Index Fund*

41 JANE TRIPP HOWE, C.F.A.
The First National Bank of Chicago

The epitome of passive bond management—a buy-and-hold strategy—has been in existence as long as bonds have been. However, with the advent of volatile interest rates in the late 1960s, the theory and practice of active bond management became the dominant force in fixed income management. The trend of fixed income management shifted again in the late 1970s and early 1980s toward passive management. This trend closely paralleled the movement toward passive equity management in the mid-1970s. The development of passive fixed income theory was a major impetus behind this move. However, sponsors' disillusionment with the performance of their fixed income portfolios and a growing belief that interest rates cannot be predicted were perhaps the most important factors in the movement back to passive management. The increasingly unanticipated movement of interest rates and the attendant significant volatility of market values has reinforced this belief and contributed to a significant movement of funds (particularly employee benefit funds) to passive management.

---

* Reprinted in part from "A Corporate Bond Index Fund," *Proceedings*, Center for Research in Security Prices, Graduate School of Business, The University of Chicago, November 1978.

Passive fixed income management today is very different from that practiced historically. A high proportion of "passive" fixed income management has a highly theoretical base and is largely facilitated by specialized computer programs. In addition, the current trend of passive fixed income management is weighted toward portfolio immunization, a technique designed to reduce or eliminate interest-rate risk in a portfolio over a given time horizon.[1] However, to the extent that *passive* is defined as diversifying the nonmarket risk in a portfolio and only accepting the market risk of a portfolio, the immunization strategy is not a purely passive strategy, but rather a technique used to structure a portfolio to meet a given fund objective. Contingent or active immunization goes a step further in that this technique permits the active management of a fund as long as the predetermined annual rate of return can be achieved over the entire horizon period. At the point at which interest rates have moved adversely and the predetermined annual rate of return could not be achieved with further adverse interest-rate movements, the portfolio reverts to the immunization mode, and the portfolio is structured so that future interest-rate risk to the horizon will be reduced or eliminated.

The purest passive technique available today is the bond index fund. Its primary objective is to match the performance of the corporate bond universe, rather than to match the liabilities of a given employee benefit fund. This objective is achieved through the continuous matching of the fund with the characteristics of the bond universe. It cannot be achieved with a passive buy-and-hold strategy because this buy-and-hold portfolio will change over time in terms of duration, maturity, and so on. An index fund does not have the immunized fund's guarantee of a close approximation of matching an employee benefit fund's given liabilities. However, it does have the significant advantage of producing the highest level of expected return per unit of risk over a long time horizon. This advantage is similar to the diversification benefit offered by an equity index fund, although the variables used for diversification are different. In practice, because the corporate bond market is more homogeneous than the equity market, the matching of a corporate bond proxy is easier than matching a proxy for the equity market.

In selecting a bond index fund, a sponsor will benefit in at least two additional ways. First, an improvement in performance can be expected due to a reduction in fees and transaction costs. Second, any duplication of managers' efforts will be eliminated. The extent of the savings in terms of fees will depend on the sponsor's current active versus passive fees and also on the extent that fund assets are switched from the higher cost active managers to the lower cost pas-

---

[1] See Chapter 36.

sive managers. Over the life of a fund, the savings in management fees could be substantial.

A more significant savings should be realized in transaction costs. Bonds are typically traded without a commission explicitly stated. However, there is definitely a cost associated with a bond trade, which owners of bonds ultimately pay. Savings to a sponsor in lower transaction costs will be particularly significant to the sponsor of a large pension fund with several active fixed income managers. Each of these managers may report annual turnover in the area of 100 percent. However, it is possible that this estimate of turnover really represents the turning over of the highly liquid issues five or six times per year. Conceivably, the same issues could be bought and sold by the same fund with little or no time interval! It is therefore possible that a manager is doing one of two things: (1) hedging the overall composition of his or her fund by diversifying a portion of it and intensely managing only a portion of it or (2) actively managing a portion of the fund and essentially ignoring an undiversified core. In either case, the division of active versus passive (if any) fees should be questioned. In effect, the plan sponsor should examine the total composition and activity of his or her portfolio to eliminate duplication of fees and commissions.

THE SELECTION OF A PROXY FOR THE BOND UNIVERSE

Once the decision to invest in a bond index fund has been made, a benchmark or proxy for the bond universe must be selected. This selection process has two parts. First, the appropriate universe must be chosen. This decision is essentially a choice among a corporate bond market, the government market, and a combination of the two. Once this question is resolved, a specific proxy has to be chosen in order that the fund's performance can be evaluated.

The resolution of the first half of the selection process is straightforward—publicly issued corporate bonds are the logical initial step in indexing bonds for several reasons. First, a major benefit of a bond index fund is that it provides the highest level of expected return for diversification across interest rate as well as default risk. As the government market is generally perceived as presenting no default risk, the inclusion of government securities in an index fund would only increase interest-rate diversification. Therefore, if the choice is between a corporate bond index fund and a government bond index fund, the former would produce the higher level of diversification benefits. Second, if the inclusion of government bonds is desired in order to make the index more comprehensive, it is not clear what weighting they should be allotted. First, a large portion of Treasury debt is nonmarketable and therefore should be excluded from a marketable bond index. In a similar manner, corporate private placements should also be excluded. Second, even if the nonmarketable government debt can be specified and isolated, the question of what constitutes wealth must be addressed. A significant portion of Treasury debt does not represent wealth but rather represents claims on future tax revenues, such as social security. To the extent that these claims can be identified, they should be excluded from a bond index. Finally, to the extent that government issues represent a disproportionately high percentage of the total bond market, a further case can be made for their exclusion from a bond index.

Once a corporate bond index has been chosen, the selection of a specific proxy for the corporate bond market must be made. The comprehensiveness of the proxy is a key element in this process, since the purpose of a bond index is to match the risk and return of the entire public corporate bond market to the extent possible. Unfortunately (from a theoretical viewpoint), issues with ratings below BBB should be excluded due to the institutional and legal constraints involved in buying these issues. Therefore, attention should be focused on those indices covering securities rated BBB and above. Although there are numerous bond indices published, few are comprehensive.[2] Of these, the Lehman Brothers Kuhn Loeb (LBKL) Index may be the most appropriate for use in an index. The most important difference between the LBKL index and other indices is the relative comprehensiveness of the LBKL index. This index tracks all publicly issued industrial, financial, and utility bonds rated Baa or higher that have at least one year until maturity and at least $1 million principal amount outstanding. As of November 1981, this universe contained approximately 4,300 issues with a total market value in excess of $181 billion. All other well-known public indices have at least one serious drawback in terms of quality range, coupon, maturity, or industrial classification. Another important difference is ability of the LBKL to reflect changes in the market.

Since LBKL tracks all issues in its universe, its index by definition will reflect all changes in the bond market. Other indices, on the other hand, use samples of their universes and adjust these samples on an annual or less frequent basis. Therefore, on a month-to-month basis, only the LBKL index will mirror market changes. This property is important in a dynamic market whose characteristics can change significantly during the course of a year due to such occurrences as sizable calls and refundings or the issuance of a particular type of debt (such as original-issue discount bonds.) For example, if a portion of an issue is retired (such as AT&T 8.75 percent debenture due 5/15/00), such a partial retirement will be reflected in the LBKL index with

---

[2] See Chapter 7 for a discussion of bond indices.

a maximum lag of one month. The effect of such a retirement in other indices is unclear and would depend on such factors as whether the particular bond is in the index and how close the index is to a periodic adjustment. In a similar manner, the LBKL index is the only index that will exactly represent the percentage of upgrades and down-grades occurring in the market.

As of May 29, 1981, the LBKL index had an average coupon of 8.59 percent, an average maturity of 17.3 years and an average duration of 6.32. Additionally, the index had an average rating of Aa by Moody's and AA− by Standard & Poor's. Exhibit 1 further describes the LBKL

Exhibit 1
The Corporate Bond Market as of May 29, 1981 (components of the Lehman Brothers Kuhn Loeb Bond Index)

	Rating				
Characteristic	Aaa	Aa	A	Baa	Total
Percent of total market	25.00	24.40	37.50	13.20	100.00
Average coupon (percent).........	8.16	8.53	8.85	8.82	8.59
Average maturity (years)..........	20.99	16.35	16.12	15.41	17.30
Duration.......................	6.70	6.26	6.22	5.96	6.32

	Industry Classification			
Characteristic	Industrial	Utility	Finance	Total
Percent of total market.............	30.20	51.20	18.60	100.00
Average coupon (percent)	8.70	8.40	9.00	8.59
Average maturity (years)	15.82	20.48	10.96	17.30
Duration	6.40	6.70	5.14	6.32

Source: Lehman Brothers Kuhn Loeb.

universe by segmenting it according to industrial classifications and Moody's ratings. Although Baas represent approximately 13 percent of this universe, it should be noted that the additional volatility intro-duced by Baa securities (as opposed to the indices that track only Aaa, Aa, and A securities) is largely offset by the lower duration of the Baa group.

PERFORMANCE OF A CORPORATE BOND INDEX

The performance of a corporate bond index fund that matches the LBKL index should at least match the performance of "active" fixed income managers as a group over the long run. If the corporate market is viewed as a "zero-sum game" (i.e., a game in which the winnings of players are equal to the losses of other players), the long-term aggre-gate return of all bond managers should approximate the aggregate return of the market. However, to the extent that active managers have higher transaction costs and fees than do passive managers, the bond universe can be expected to perform somewhat better than the median of managed bond funds. The available data is inconclusive on this point. For the period December 31, 1972 (the date the LBKL index was begun), through December 31, 1977, the performance of the index compared favorably with the A. G. Becker median and the Salomon Brothers High Grade Index. During this five-year period, the LBKL index produced an annual compound rate of return of +6.63 percent compared with +6.22 percent for A. G. Becker and +6.25 percent for the Salomon index. On the other hand, for the eight-year period of December 31, 1972 through December 31, 1980, the A. G. Becker median produced an annual rate of return of +4.4 percent, compared with +3.8 percent for LBKL and +3.0 percent for Salomon Brothers.[3] Unfortunately, this data can only give an indication of the similarity of returns because the A. G. Becker median numbers include cash and therefore are not a pure comparison.[4] Furthermore, the nature of these statistics precludes a definitive assessment of whether a fund would increase or decrease its volatility by investing in a bond index fund. This issue has to be answered on an individual account basis.

A comparison of the rates of return and standard deviations of the LBKL index and the Salomon Brothers index does suggest, however, that the diversification advantage is significant. For the eight-year period December 31, 1972, through December 31, 1980, the LBKL index produced an annual compound return of +3.8 percent with a monthly mean and standard deviation of +.35 percent and 9.49 percent, respectively. During the same period, the Salomon Brothers index produced an annual compound return of +3.0 percent and had a lower monthly mean of +.29 percent and a higher monthly standard deviation of 10.39 percent. It therefore appears that, at least over this time period, the variability produced by the longer average maturity of the Salomon index is more of a factor than the variability produced by the lower average quality of the LBKL index. Comparable variability figures for the median performer of managed funds are unavailable. Medians can be justified as proxies for active fixed income managers. However, the median by its nature will be less volatile than the individual funds that contribute to the median. Furthermore, there will be an unmeasured bias in the median figures to the extent that a certain percent of the assets in the managed funds universe may be reported at book rather than at market value.

---

[3] For the same eight-year period, the Lehman Brothers Kuhn Loeb Government/ Corporate index slightly outperformed the median manager.

[4] This comparison difficulty could probably be most easily resolved by including a cash component in the market index.

This chapter has dealt to this point with the premise that managers collectively cannot outperform the bond market. To address the possibility that one manager or a subgroup of managers could outperform the market is to address the efficiency of the market. There is not available for investigating this subject the voluminous empirical data for bonds that exists for stocks. However, there are two major deductive reasons for concluding that the bond market is probably at least as efficient as the stock market. First, the default risk of a bond is lower than that of a stock in that bondholders' claims in bankruptcy are senior to the claims of stockholders. Second, the fixed parameters of a bond agreement are more precise than those of stocks. Therefore, inefficiencies that arise from events other than credit changes should generally be smaller and more readily identifiable.

THE OPERATIONAL PROCESS OF RUNNING A CORPORATE BOND INDEX

In establishing and running a corporate bond index fund, many of the procedures for running an equity index fund can be used. However, the operational process is more complex for bonds than for stocks, even though the homogeneity of the bond market should make the bond market easier to track. Specifically, relatively greater care should be taken in dealing with the three following areas when establishing a bond index fund.

Characteristics Used for Diversification

In indexing the equity market, only two variables—capitalization and risk decile—need to be used to provide adequate diversification and tracking, although many equity fund managers use many more characteristics. Bonds have many characteristics that affect return, including maturity, duration, quality, capitalization, coupon, industrial classification, sinking fund, and call features, to name a few. There is no precise formula to weight every possible variable. It is clear, however, that a specific assessment must be made in regard to which of these variables should be explicitly taken into consideration and which implicitly.

Trading

Because bonds are traded over the counter (unlike most stock trading, which is more centralized), there is always going to be a trader's judgment involved in buying for a bond index fund. In this situation, it is important that purchases be made from inventory to the extent possible to avoid creating a demand for a specific bond that will drive up its price. It is also important to try to eliminate prejudices a trader may have about certain credits. One possible way of alleviating this potential problem would be to use a bankruptcy screen as the primary credit guide. In this regard, all companies should be considered purchase candidates with the exception of those companies deemed to be imminent bankruptcy candidates. Because this exception list will generally contain only a few companies, the universe of purchase candidates will approximate the LBKL index. Another way of reducing a trader's prejudice is to use the options model as a trading aid.[5] The mathematics of this model have not been sufficiently developed to allow the model to act as the sole credit screen for coupon bonds of complex structures. However, the theory of the model can be used in practice if the trader follows the stock as well as the bond price of a firm.

Reinvestment of Cash Flow

The cash flow from a bond index fund is going to be several times heavier than that generated from an equity index fund. Therefore, relatively frequent and small buying programs will occur in a bond index, and distortions in the overall composition of the fund could occur. Minimization of possible distortions can be achieved through the conscious balancing of purchases among all relevant bond characteristics.

CONCLUSION

The degree to which indexing should be used by a specific fund depends on account circumstances. The fixed income portion of a fund can be viewed as being composed of several parts. Particularly for a large fund with several managers, a bond index should represent the passive core that is equal to that portion of the fund that is permanently and passively invested in bonds. The sponsor can then add a variety of complementary active and passive strategies that will determine the overall level of risk he or she wants to assume, given account circumstances.

---

[5] The model looks at the relationship of a firm's stock and bond prices and views the firm's bonds as an option to buy the firm from the equity holders. (See Fischer Black and Myron Scholes, "The Pricing of Options and Corporate Liabilities," *The Journal of Political Economy*, May–June 1973, pp. 637–54.

International Portfolio Management*

42 **CORNELIA M. SMALL**
Vice President, Economics
Scudder, Stevens & Clark

MARGARET DARASZ HADZIMA, C.F.A.
Vice President, Bonds
Scudder, Stevens & Clark

Chapter 25 presents the rationale for investment in foreign-pay bonds: superior investment returns and a reduction in the volatility of returns. Once the investor accepts the basic justification for investing in foreign-pay bonds and determines whether or not foreign-pay bonds are suitable for the portfolio objectives and requirements, the next question relates to the appropriate investment strategy. As in the U.S. stock and bond markets and in international equities, the investor must resolve the debate between active and passive investing.

PASSIVE VERSUS ACTIVE MANAGEMENT

There is little question that, with the benefit of hindsight, a strategy of active international bond portfolio management over the 15-year period beginning in 1966 could have provided a better return than a passive strategy. Exhibit 1 shows the range in international bond returns converted to U.S. dollars for each year between 1966 and 1980 in comparison with U.S. bond returns and an index equally weighted in

* The authors would like to express gratitude to their colleagues at Scudder, Stevens and Clark for their editing assistance and many insightful comments. Special thanks go to Mary Spyropoulos for her valuable contribution in the computer development of the statistical analysis.

Exhibit 1
Total Annual Return Converted to U.S. Dollars

	Best		Worst			
	Percentage	Country	Percentage	Country	U.S.	Index I
1980.......	28.1%	United Kingdom	−10.3%	Germany	− 3.8%	1.6%
1979.......	12.6	United Kingdom	−24.2	Japan	− 1.1	− 1.4
1978.......	35.5	Switzerland	− 8.8	Canada	− 1.3	16.8
1977.......	62.0	United Kingdom	− 2.4	Canada	− .3	30.1
1976.......	32.2	Germany	− 8.5	Australia	17.7	11.9
1975.......	16.6	France	− .4	Canada	9.2	9.3
1974.......	28.7	Switzerland	−17.1	United Kingdom	− .1	4.1
1973.......	21.6	Germany	− 8.3	United States	− 8.3	7.1
1972.......	20.1	Australia	−11.0	United Kingdom	5.6	5.8
1971.......	31.6	United Kingdom	12.2	United States	12.2	21.3
1970.......	31.2	Canada	− 4.7	Australia	12.8	6.7
1969.......	9.4	Germany	−10.4	France	− 4.4	− .8
1968.......	9.3	Germany	− 2.6	United Kingdom	− .5	4.3
1967.......	12.8	Germany	−11.1	United Kingdom	− 6.1	3.6
1966.......	8.3	Germany	− .5	Switzerland	3.3	3.7

Note: Index I is equally weighted in government bonds of Australia, Canada, France, Germany, Japan, the Netherlands, Switzerland, and the United Kingdom.

eight major foreign markets. Of interest is the wide range of returns for each year and the variety of countries that headed the best and worst return scales. The average percentage spread from the best to worst return in each year was 31.2 percent and ranged from 64.4 percent to 8.8 percent. In the 15-year period, six of the eight foreign markets reviewed provided the best total returns converted to U.S. dollars at least once, and seven of the eight were the worst at least once.

The crucial question, of course, is whether without such prescience an actively managed portfolio can provide an incremental return over a passive portfolio without incurring a commensurate degree of risk. Although this can only be answered empirically, it is difficult to justify a passive approach to international bond investing on either a theoretical or practical basis. This conclusion is based on several different considerations.

Assumption of Efficient Markets. Underlying the theoretical basis of a passive approach to investing is the assumption of efficient markets. This assumption may be argued to be valid in the case of the U.S. capital markets, but the assumption does not hold when the definition is extended to the international fixed income markets. For a market to be efficient, information must be freely available, all participants must use the information similarly, and capital flows between investments must be free. It is obvious that these conditions do not apply to the various constituent markets making up the international bond market. The availability of information is probably freer in the case of international bonds than of international stocks, but it is scarcely complete.

There are very different degrees of disclosure among countries regarding the various factors that influence the trend and level of interest rates: monetary policy, government financing requirements, foreign exchange policy, broad economic statistics. Furthermore, that information that is available is, for all practical purposes, not uniformly shared by all participants in the marketplace.

Use of Market Information. A variety of impediments prevent market information from being used in a similar fashion: differences in national character and tradition, legal differences, differences in tax treatment by countries and the tax situation of investors, and institutional differences between countries. Also, a number of obstacles (of which foreign exchange and capital controls are the most obvious) often impede the free flow of capital between markets.

Exchange-Rate Changes. As has been demonstrated in Chapter 25, foreign exchange-rate changes make up an important component of return. A passive approach would prevent the investor from implementing any independent judgement regarding currency movements. This consideration would be a minor one if the foreign exchange markets were, as is frequently argued, efficient. If they were, the bond returns of various countries when converted to a common currency would be roughly equivalent over time. In such a case, the interest differentials and currency changes would reflect differential inflation rates so that currency changes would equal the difference in income factors. In the 15-year period from 1966 to 1980, this did not prove to be the case. The average annual converted return ranged from about 2 percent for the U.S. market to 12.6 percent for German bonds. In fact, the variation was less in domestic prices than after conversion to a common currency, the U.S. dollar. These results are shown on Exhibit 2. In addition, it is intuitively obvious that the foreign exchange markets are not perfectly efficient. There is a myriad of special factors that

Exhibit 2
Comparison of International Bond Returns

	Average Annual Return of Long Bonds Converted to U.S. Dollars 1966–1980	Average Annual Return of Long Bonds in Domestic Currency 1966–80
Australia	3.3%	2.9%
Canada	2.7	3.4
France	5.6	5.1
Germany	12.6	7.3
Japan	10.8	6.6
Netherlands	9.7	5.9
Switzerland	11.1	4.6
United Kingdom	5.0	6.1
United States	2.1	2.1

determine exchange-rate movements; inflation differentials is only one of these factors. Official foreign exchange intervention and different perceptions of political forces are among the many factors that distort fundamental exchange-rate relationships. In view of these inefficiencies, it is to be expected that active decisions regarding foreign commitments can add incremental value to a foreign bond portfolio.

Choice of Market Portfolio. An additional factor challenging the case for a passive approach relates to the choice of a market portfolio. It can be argued that an efficient market portfolio in its purest form should include all investment assets, not just one class, such as bonds. Even if the universe is confined to bonds, what is the appropriate market index? In Chapter 25 the risk/return characteristics of two alternative indices were discussed: one weighted equally and one weighted by the amount of outstanding government debt. Exhibit 3 shows the differences between these two indices over the 1966–80

Exhibit 3
A Comparison of Two International Indexes—Dollar Denominated Total Return

	Index I	Index II	Difference
1966	3.70	3.86	−.16
1967	3.57	−2.93	6.50
1968	4.28	.87	3.41
1969	−.83	.04	−.87
1970	6.71	5.91	.80
1971	21.31	24.25	−2.94
1972	5.77	.13	5.64
1973	7.10	3.03	4.07
1974	4.08	−4.35	8.43
1975	9.27	10.99	−1.72
1976	11.86	13.29	−1.43
1977	30.12	41.15	−11.03
1978	16.77	13.91	2.86
1979	−1.39	−4.25	2.86
1980	1.64	11.71	−10.07
Average Annual Mean	7.96	7.40	
Monthly Standard Deviation of Return	2.408	2.868	

period. Because of the dominance of the Japanese and British markets in the market capitalization index (accounting for more than 50 percent combined), there are significant and frequent differences in returns, particularly on an annual basis. In view of the special circumstances that pertain in each of these countries, it is questionable whether the investor should be submitted to such a weighting on an ongoing basis. In the case of both indices, but particularly the equally weighted index, there is the additional complication of liquidity constraints in some markets that may prevent the investor from practically achieving a full investment position.

Specific Investment Objectives.   A final drawback to a passive investment approach is that it removes any incorporation of specific investment objectives. The optimum portfolio will depend on the investment requirements of the investor. In some cases there may be a desire to tailor a portfolio so as to capitalize on the risk reduction capabilities of international investing, and in other cases incremental return should be emphasized. A passive approach treats all investors uniformly.

ACTIVE MANAGEMENT

A thorough understanding of the components of total return and their interrelationships is important to any international investor, but it is particularly important if active management is selected as the international investment technique. As discussed in Chapter 25, there are three factors in the return provided by international bonds—income, capital change, and currency. Of these, only income in local currency terms and the margin over the income bogey provided by U.S. alternatives are known initially, and even they are subject to change as exchange rates fluctuate. A positive yield advantage over alternative U.S. bonds will, over time, provide a cushion for deterioration in the domestic capital price or the currency relative to U.S. issues. By the same token, with time, a negative yield spread will have to be offset by relative appreciation of the domestic bond price or currency. This requirement may suggest that investment in lower yielding foreign securities may necessitate a limited time horizon, since a longer time horizon demands continually increasing relative price or currency appreciation to offset the income disadvantage.

It is noteworthy that over the 15-year period studied, during which international bonds provided a higher return than U.S. bonds, the average income of international bonds was about 1 percent higher than in the United States. At the beginning of the period, the average yield of the eight foreign bond markets was 5.85 percent, whereas long United States rates were 4.5 percent. Over time that margin has fluctuated, but in recent years it has narrowed as shown in Exhibit 4. By the end of 1980, U.S. rates were more than 1 percent higher than international rates. For international bonds to achieve a return competitive with U.S. bonds in the future, this income disadvantage must be offset by higher currency appreciation or favorable movements in foreign domestic bond prices relative to U.S. bond prices.

The factors that have a bearing on currency fluctuation, the second component of return, are well known. By and large, most factors can be characterized as relating to one or more of the following:

Exhibit 4
Domestic Government Yield Levels

	Average of International Bond Markets at Beginning of Year	U.S. Government Yields at Beginning of Year	Yield Spread (basis points)
1966	5.85%	4.49%	136
1967	6.08	4.59	149
1968	6.14	5.48	66
1969	6.33	5.97	36
1970	7.16	6.92	24
1971	7.42	6.42	100
1972	6.93	5.92	101
1973	7.32	5.95	137
1974	8.68	7.35	133
1975	10.21	8.13	208
1976	9.44	8.05	139
1977	9.08	7.20	188
1978	7.92	8.23	−31
1979	8.34	8.98	−64
1980	9.82	10.12	−30
1981	10.78	11.94	−116

1. The balance of payments and its circular relationship with exchange rates.
2. Inflation and interest-rate differentials.
3. Social and political developments.
4. Central bank intervention.

From a practical viewpoint, there are two main problems in using these factors to project currency trends. One relates to the analyst's ability accurately to perceive trends not already efficiently reflected in the currency price. The second relates to the interaction of these factors and the ability to project which factors will predominate. As more fully pointed out in Chapter 25, the component of return provided by currency changes for an international bond index over intermediate time periods has not been large, ranging from −.2 percent to 4 percent annually for the three five-year periods in 1966–80. (See Exhibit 4 of Chapter 25.) However, for one-year periods the importance of currency changes can be significant when aggregated in an index, and they can be even more important for individual markets. Thus the international bond investor who opts for the active management approach must be willing to make judgements on foreign exchange.

The third component of return, domestic price movements, must be analyzed both absolutely and relative to expected U.S. movements. There are substantial differences between various markets regarding the extent of government influence on the level of interest rates. However, the common key variables affecting interest-rate movements are generally viewed to be the following:

1. Monetary policy, particularly with regard to exchange rates.
2. The level and direction of domestic inflation rates.
3. Demand for funds, which is often related to real GNP growth.
4. Supply of funds.
5. Fiscal policy and budget deficits.
6. Social and political developments.

The international bond investor must then assess these factors to make judgements on the likely direction of rates in each country. As in the United States, this assessment must distinguish between movements in short rates and long rates, which most often move in the same direction but not usually to the same extent. Interest-rate movements are typically magnified in the short-term area relative to long yield movements, with the degree of interest-rate movements for intermediate issues often somewhere in the middle. Projections of the extent of these movements can then be translated into possible price movements, and when coupled with income differentials, some judgements on appropriate maturity structure within each country can be made.

However, it is also important to view the maturity allocation of the portfolio as a whole. The 1980–81 experience reminds us of both the interrelationship between the interest-rate and currency levels and of the circular and interrelated nature of interest rates between countries with floating exchange rates. While domestic economic trends and apparent government desires would have suggested lower interest levels in a number of foreign economies, record high U.S. interest rates precluded lower rates abroad without precipitating even further foreign exchange deterioration. Increasingly, few projections of foreign interest-rate levels were made without reference to expectations for the United States. Only time will tell whether the increased interrelationship of all markets is a permanent change or a transitory one. A strong case can be made that it is transitory and precipated by a rare and unusual event—extraordinarily high and volatile rates and prices in the largest bond market in the world. In more normal times the pattern of differing social and political trends, monetary policy, inflation trends, and phases of the economic cycle may once again predominate.

Clearly then, an active approach to international bond management requires ongoing economic analysis and judgement to assess the prospective exchange rate and domestic price components of return. Even the most dedicated active manager is aware of the room for error in interest-rate and currency projections. Although a single economic forecast may suffice for an international economist, the portfolio manager must consider the alternatives should the preferred forecast prove to be wrong. Chapter 25 pointed out that the international bond expert had to deal not only with price changes resulting from interest-rate movements on differing maturities, but also with the impact of interest-rate movements on price for substantially different starting interest-rate levels. When currency changes and income levels are added, the problem is complicated further. For example, not even the most mathematically inclined bond specialist is likely to know intuitively whether the best one-year return is provided by a 7 percent, 10-year bond beginning at par with a 275-basis-point decline in yield and no currency change or a 14 percent, 20-year issue starting at par with a 25-basis-point decline in yield and a 10 percent currency gain. In both cases, the one-year returns are about equal at 27 percent. When the necessity for a variety of alternative currency and interest-rate forecasts is imposed, the problem is further magnified. Thus the active international bond manager quickly finds that the facility for simple computer modeling and sensitivity analysis may be required.

INTERNATIONAL BONDS—THEIR ROLE IN PORTFOLIO MANAGEMENT

The foregoing discussion focused on the case for and the techniques of active international bond management. A related issue is the role of international bonds in portfolio construction or management.

Traditionally, U.S. investors have viewed international bonds as an alternative to long U.S. bonds, if at all. There are two reasons for this. First, the U.S. investment community is bifurcated into two areas of specialization and expertise: stocks and bonds. This separation is reflected in the common division of portfolios into bonds and stocks, with the responsibility for investment management frequently divided. It is, therefore, natural that bond managers consider international bonds as part of their ken. Second, both international and domestic bonds share certain characteristics—most notably a fixed income stream. As shown in Exhibit 4 of Chapter 25, this income component proved to be the largest component of return over both intermediate and long-term periods.

Despite this frequent association, it is interesting to note the dissimilarities between international and domestic bonds. Both instruments have fixed income flows in local currency terms, but the income produced by foreign currency bonds when translated into dollars can be highly volatile. In addition, in the case of domestic bonds, their investment attraction in portfolio construction relative to stocks has traditionally been price stability and the income component of return. As was discussed in the prior section, income is only one of three components of foreign bond returns, and at any given time it may not represent the justification for purchasing foreign bonds.

It can be argued that foreign bonds at times are much more similar to international equities. Over short time periods, as seen in Exhibit 5 of Chapter 25, capital change and currency movements can dominate returns. It is these two components of return that are affected by the same economic factors the international equity manager must consider in the analysis of expected international equity returns. The exchange-rate movement is a direct common component, but those determinants of interest-rate movements—GNP growth, inflation prospects, fiscal and monetary policy, social and political developments, and supply of funds—are also considered in projecting price movements of the stock market or particular companies. In fact, the level of interest rates itself is of critical importance to the equity manager in assessing the appropriate discount rate. With all of these common denominators then, international bonds perhaps should be considered a direct alternative to international equities. This suggests that the use of international bonds should be considered within the context of an international balanced portfolio. Carrying this logic further, since both international equities and U.S. bonds are an alternative to U.S. equities, the transitive property suggests that international bonds, too, must be viewed as an alternative to U.S. equities.

The result of this argument is satisfying. In this day of investment specialization, all too often the investment process leads to acceptance of good returns relative to a particular bogey, without regard either to a broader spectrum of alternative returns or the absolute level of returns. It is not satisfactory for a long-term return on an actively managed international bond portfolio to be superior to a passively managed one if the absolute or real return over the inflation rate is not satisfactory or if alternative investment vehicles offer substantially better returns on a risk-adjusted basis. Between 1966 and 1980 international bonds provided an average annual converted dollar return of 7½–8 percent; the return on U.S. bonds was 2 percent, and the CPI was around 7%. At the same time, U.S. equity returns (including dividends) were in line with the inflation rate, and international equity returns converted to U.S. dollars were somewhat better. Relative to the alternatives, then, international bonds have provided a satisfactory return on a historical basis.

This historical record is not sufficient to bestow on international bonds a permanent role in a portfolio of U.S. and foreign securities. A number of factors have changed over this period that could have important bearing on future results. An assessment of prospective relative returns from international bonds and appropriate equity and U.S. bond alternatives must include consideration of the following:

1. In comparison with stocks, the substantially higher level of starting interest rates than in earlier years.

2. In comparison with U.S. bonds, a starting yield about 1 percent lower than U.S. bonds, as opposed to an average 1 percent higher in the prior 15-year period.
3. In comparison with inflation, the starting level of interest rates relative to the long-term expected rate of inflation.
4. In comparison with U.S. investments of all types, the long-range judgment on the outlook of the dollar.

Investors considering international bonds must have a truly worldwide scope in assessing alternative prospective returns. The conclusions are not clear, and perhaps no final opinions can be drawn. In that event, perhaps a case for some international bond investments can be made simply on the basis of diversifying out of the dollar and into a variety of asset classes. This is an acceptable rationale, as is an approach based on the reasoned belief that some of the factors leading to acceptable international bond results in the past will continue. The investor must avoid, however, blindly extrapolating these historical results into a world and investment environment that has changed dramatically in the 15-year period since 1966.

INTERNATIONAL BONDS—THEIR ROLE BY PORTFOLIO TYPE

The appropriate role of international bonds in a portfolio is in part a function of their investment characteristics relative to alternative assets (bonds or stocks) and in part a function of the investment objectives of the investor. Put simply, international bonds will play a different role in different kinds of portfolios.

Private Employee Benefit Plans. The suitability of international bonds is probably the greatest in the case of private employee benefit plans. International investments in both stocks and bonds are generally viewed to be permitted under ERISA. In cases in which individual plan agreements prohibit international investing, amendment is frequently possible. A more common obstacle to international investing is emotion—an uneasiness attached to investing in a foreign security whose credit is not as well known as a comparable U.S. security and concern with vulnerability to sharp exchange-rate changes. These obstacles can be overcome with education regarding the investment risk/return characteristics of international bonds. Although the diversification characteristic of international bonds is of value to private pension plans, the typical plan characteristics of a long-term time horizon and improved total return are probably of paramount importance. International bond investing meshes well with these objectives. The reduced reliability of income flows from foreign pay bonds, both as to level and variability, is less of a deterrent to their use in private plans than in many other kinds of portfolios. Except in cases of mature plans where there is a net cash outflow, stipulated income requirements can usually be interpreted flexibly enough to accommodate foreign-pay bond investing.

Finally, foreign bond investments can be easily adapted to the investment structure of private plans. For example, in those cases in which the total portfolio has been divided into a core portfolio and special investment situations, the bulk of the portfolio may be effectively indexed and then above market return can be provided by small satellite portfolios. In situations of in-house management, although the complexity of foreign bond analysis may be too demanding for an in-house staff, a portion of a portfolio can easily be spun off for external international bond management without duplicating investment research and management effort.

Other Pension Plans. In most cases legal or political obstacles will prevent the use of international bonds in public funds and labor management or multiemployer funds.

Endowments and Foundations. The suitability of international bonds in the investment of endowment and foundation portfolios will vary. When investment objectives focus on current income requirements, the use of international bonds will be limited, except as an equity substitute. In cases in which income requirements do not prevail, their use will depend on the same factors as in the preceding discussion under private employee benefit plans.

Individuals. In most cases international bonds will play a limited role in individual portfolios. Income requirements, tax considerations, problems of custody, execution, and liquidity are likely to preclude effective active management of international bonds. These factors, which to some extent are matters of concern to all types of potential international investors, are discussed below.

THE OBSTACLES—PERCEIVED AND REAL

One of the common arguments used against international bond investing relates to perceived and real obstacles in dealing in foreign markets. Indeed international bond investing is more difficult than limiting oneself to the domestic U.S. market, but most concerns are surmountable, particularly given the opportunities available within this broader horizon.

Once a decision is made to invest internationally and to buy a certain bond market and currency, an appropriate vehicle must be identified. Thus international bond investors must have sufficient knowledge of the alternatives to select the appropriate type of issue.

Like investment in U.S.-dollar-denominated bonds, investments in foreign-pay bonds are divided into two classes as discussed in Chap-

ter 25. One group includes domestic or internal issues that are obligations of domestic issuers, underwritten by domestic syndicates, and
sold primarily within the particular country. The second group encompasses international bonds that are the equivalent of the Eurodollar and yankee markets in the U.S. Eurocurrency issues are underwritten by international syndicates and normally sold outside of the
country of currency denomination. Foreign bonds, of which yankee
bonds are the U.S.-dollar version, are foreign issuers raising funds in a
country and currency other than their own. These types of issues
come under a variety of names ranging from the "bulldog" market for
sterling-denominated foreign bonds to the "samurai" market for yen-
denominated foreign bonds.

Like the U.S. market, a prime difference between domestic foreign-
pay issues and international Eurocurrency and foreign credit bonds is
that many domestic issues, when bought by foreigners, are subject to
withholding tax by the host country. As pointed out in Chapter 25, the
U.S. has tax treaties with a number of countries that reduce or eliminate these taxes, but they are still a factor to consider in selection of
the investment vehicle. Methods of handling the withholding tax payments differ from country to country. For example, in Japan the 20
percent withholding tax rate on interest is reduced to 10 percent for
U.S. investors by declaration of the selling dealer at the time of purchase. In Germany the 25 percent withholding tax is withheld and
must be reclaimed by U.S. investors subsequent to the interest payment. A particular interest-bearing instrument, called Schuldscheindarlehen, is exempt from German withholding taxes because it is
technically a loan, not a security. With the permission of the borrower,
the loan can be resold, but liquidity can be a problem. The Netherlands has no withholding tax on interest, and Canada has none on
government issues and most other recently issued securities with
original maturities of five or more years. Although the general rate of
withholding on interest is 30 percent in the United Kingdom, a number of previously issued government securities are exempt from withholding tax when paid to non-United Kingdom residents who have
made the appropriate filing. The withholding tax rates for most major
bond markets and the reduction for U.S. residents under tax treaties
are shown in Exhibit 2 of Chapter 25.

Although international equity investors are spared the vagaries of
various interest calculation traditions, international bond investors
must understand the variety of techniques and make adjustments to
attain comparability. In most countries, bonds are traded at price plus
accrued interest as in the U.S. In the United Kingdom, however, security prices of bonds with maturities longer than five years include the
accrued interest. Thus to calculate yield, the interest earned from the
last payment date must be "stripped" from the price as in the case of

preferred stocks. Adjustments in yield calculations are also required to equate the yields on bonds with annual coupons to the U.S. standard of semiannual payments. United Kingdom, Japanese, and Canadian interest on domestic issues is paid semiannually, but interest in most other domestic markets and in the Euromarkets is paid annually. Furthermore, yield calculations include a provision for compounding, be it annual or semiannual, but the standard Japanese method does not.

One factor that is regularly discussed as an obstacle in international equity investing is whether or not information on particular companies is adequate. This is not a real problem in the bond area, since there is a large supply of government paper available, that allows one to invest internationally without having to evaluate the credit of particular companies. Relative to the income, currency, and capital change returns emanating from interest-rate movements, the gain to be added from selection of relatively undervalued corporate issues appears small.

Another key factor in the assessment of particular securities is marketability. Without exception, government securities in the domestic markets are more liquid than either corporate issues or the foreign type of securities. The United Kingdom gilt-edged market is renowned for its liquidity, and large holdings of government securities in Japan, Canada, and Germany are easily tradable. Euro DM bonds enjoy a reasonably liquid market, but Swiss franc foreign bonds at times trade in blocks no larger than 500,000 SF.

When an understanding of the tax situation in each market coupled with knowledge of the relative marketability of the various types of issues is joined with a comparison of yields and expectations, a decision can be made as to the appropriate investment vehicle.

Three additional factors that may cause some initial concern are custody of international securities, foreign exchange controls, and trading.

1. *Custody.* Some U.S. banks have improved substantially their ability to handle foreign-pay securities. Many have branches in a number of foreign cities, and others can arrange subcustodial relationships or utilize one of two book-entry clearing facilities for most Eurocurrency and foreign securities—Euroclear, managed by Morgan Guaranty Trust, and Cedel, owned by a consortium of banks around the world.

2. *Foreign exchange controls.* Foreign exchange controls remain a philosophical concern. In practice, they have rarely been imposed on foreign investors except to limit investment in securities of strong currencies to prevent further upward pressure on the currency. Still they are a risk that the international investor must consider and be willing to accept.

3. *Execution.* As in the U.S. market, there is no substitute for years of experience in dealing in particular markets to facilitate trades efficiently. However, in the past few years a number of foreign banks and brokerage firms have opened offices in the United States to accommodate U.S. investors. Additionally, several U.S. brokerage firms have expanded their abilities in this area so that execution of foreign trades has become easier for the U.S.-based investor. The normal period of time from trade to settlement varies between countries, but alternative arrangements can often be made if discussed before the transaction.

CONCLUSION

There is no question that international investing requires special expertise and acceptance of some uncertainties and structural impediments not required in investment in U.S. securities. However, it is these same factors that allow inefficiencies to exist, thereby providing the potential for adding incremental return while reducing the overall volatility of a portfolio.

Performance Evaluation in Fixed Income Securities*

43 **ARTHUR WILLIAMS III, C.F.A.**
Vice President, Pension Fund Investments
Merrill Lynch, Pierce, Fenner & Smith, Inc.

INTRODUCTION

In past and simpler days, investors felt no need to measure fixed income investments to any great extent. It was sufficient to know the quality rating, the interest rate, and term to maturity of fixed income investments. As long as these factors suited the objectives of the investor, bonds were held to maturity rather than being actively traded; analysis was unnecessary. For better or worse, those days have long since past. Because of the huge sums invested in fixed income securities, volatility caused by high inflation and high interest rates, and the modern-world need to extract as much as possible from every asset, investors now must take a much more vigorous approach to measuring their fixed income portfolios. In short, performance must be measured. In recent years, significant steps have been made in measuring prices, developing indices against which performance could be measured, and even constructing approaches that measure not only return, but also risk. The first problem that arises in the measurement of bond portfolios is calculating the value of the fund. That is, before any

---

* For a complete discussion of performance measurement see Arthur Williams III, *Managing Your Investment Manager—The Complete Guide to Selection, Measurement, and Control* (Homewood, Ill.: Dow Jones-Irwin, 1980).

measurements of return or risk can be performed, the portfolio must be valued. This, in turn, requires an accurate and consistent method of measuring prices. Since there is not a central marketplace for trading bonds, there is no single source of transaction history that can be used for price measurement. Fortunately, as investors have become increasingly interested in measuring portfolios, computerized techniques have been developed for measuring and transmitting bond price information.

MEASURING RETURNS

Once an adequate pricing system is in effect, it is then possible to begin measuring portfolios. One way to do this is to measure a hypothetical portfolio and create an index that can be used for comparison purposes. Chapter 7 deals extensively with how such indices are created and which indices are available for use by investors.

The next step in performance measurement is to determine the rate of return earned by the portfolio. Presumably the time-weighted return is desired. For best results, frequent portfolio valuations should be used, and monthly frequency provides excellent results. The time-weighted return (as opposed to the dollar-weighted return, internal rate of return, or yield-to-maturity, all of which are synonymous) is preferred, assuming that the manager has no control over external contributions to or withdrawals from the fund. The time-weighted return is that return that would have been earned on $1 invested in the portfolio at the beginning of the period and maintained throughout. For example, if the market fell significantly and a contribution were received into the portfolio and invested in bonds, the portfolio would grow through the timeliness of the investment. However, assuming the decision to fund the portfolio was made by the owner rather than the manager of the fund, the manager's performance should be calculated independent of this contribution. The time-weighted method correctly calculates return independent of the cash flow.[1]

MEASURING RISK

As investors become more interested in the results of their portfolios, it is no longer adequate to ask how well the portfolio performed without asking how well it performed "relative to the risk taken." Risk measurement provides an entirely new set of problems for investors, since there are many possible definitions of *risk*. As an example, risk can be looked at as potential loss due to default or in terms of loss that would be incurred if interest rates rose above levels at the time of the

---

[1] See a more complete discussion in ibid., pp. 117–40.

purchase. For purposes of this chapter, *risk* will be defined as the uncertainty of the portfolio's rate of return or the uncertainty of its future value. For example, even though short-term Treasury bills have no risk of default, they have uncertainty as to rate of return for investors whose time horizon is greater than the time to maturity of the obligation. Even if the investor's time horizon is equal to the maturity of the instrument owned, the investor will have some uncertainty as to the rate of return, since it will not be known in advance what interest will be earned on the coupon income received on the portfolio. Of course, if the bond carries no coupon (i.e., it is "pure discount" or "zero coupon") then this factor does not prevail.

One might ask why investors should care about risk in fixed income portfolios, especially if the instruments owned are of high quality and the risk of default is minimal. There are several reasons. First, if a fund has a wrong policy toward risk, its chances of meeting its goal are significantly reduced. Further, since market cycles are so long, it takes many years to find out if a portfolio is successful in meeting its objectives. Consequently, it is difficult to establish a control process whereby results can be monitored and changes instituted when results are unsatisfactory. This makes it especially important to establish the proper risk policy initially in order to avoid what will almost certainly be a disastrous policy if goals are changed as the market fluctuates up and down.

A second reason for measuring risk is to find out if returns are adequate relative to results achieved. Although it is certainly more important to have good results than to have achieved bad results for good reasons, nonetheless, it is important to know whether results are adequate relative to risks, since high risk carries with it the potential for highly unsatisfactory returns.

Finally, since times of high interest rates returns are especially volatile, it is important to measure risk to be able to provide some protection against this volatility.

Why, instead of measuring risk, should not the investor merely compare returns to hoped-for return, the return of the market, or comparisons with other portfolios? Each of these comparisons is important, but none is sufficient. Absolute objectives are not particularly helpful standards in the short run, since when markets rise all funds tend to exceed these objectives, and in declining markets funds generally fall below these standards. Looking solely at comparisons relative to the market is not satisfactory, either, since in long periods of decline the fund may outperform the market but fail to have sufficient funds to meet its cash requirements. Similarly, when measuring success in relation to the performance of other portfolios, it is possible to do better than everyone else and still have insufficient funds to meet the portfolio's goal.

Sources of Risk in Bond Portfolios

Of course, the primary risk to be concerned about when looking at bond portfolios is that of default. If the issuer is unable to pay interest and principal when due, the portfolio's rate of return will suffer dramatically. Practically speaking, the overwhelming majority of bonds owned by investors are creditworthy. Consequently, the risk of default is usually more obvious in the difference in the yields among bonds of different quality than in the real potential for default. However, it should always be kept in mind that the potential exists for a depression, such as the country has witnessed on several occasions, during which a number of issuers would default.

For bonds that are unlikely to run into these difficulties, two types of uncertainty are apparent. Changes in the general level of interest rates and changes in the "spread" or difference in yield between sectors both provide opportunities for changes in rate of return. A third risk, that arising from changes in reinvestment rate, can also be observed. On one extreme, interest rates might drop sharply thus leading the issue to be called, in which case investors end up owning low-yielding bonds instead of the high-yielding bonds they formerly had. Even in a less dramatic example, the interest-on-interest earned in the portfolio can be substantially less than was originally anticipated.

It should also be noted that there are other risks deriving from special features of bonds. For instance, if a bond is subordinated or has a junior position to that of other creditors, obviously the bond's risk increases. When bonds are convertible into other securities, an additional source of uncertainty of return is introduced. In this case the bond may act more like an equity than like a fixed income security.

Changes in the Level of Interest Rates.   When viewing the impact of changes in the general level of interest rates, three laws will be noted. First, as interest rates change, bond prices change also, but in the opposite direction.[2] In other words, as interest rates rise, bond prices decline and vice versa. Second, all other things being equal, bonds with longer term maturities are more volatile than those with shorter maturities.[3] Finally, bonds with lower coupons are more volatile than those with higher coupons.[4]

Changes in Spreads between Bond Sectors.   Bonds can be characterized by their quality, coupon, maturity, and issuer type. Each of these characteristics leads to an assignment by the marketplace of a yield-to-maturity at any point in time. However, just as the overall yield levels in the marketplace can change, the spread or the differen-

---

[2] See Chapter 4.

[3] See Chapter 4 for illustrations.

[4] See Chapter 4 for illustrations.

tial in yields between bonds of different types can also change. This provides an additional uncertainty as to rate of return. The following example demonstrates this phenomenon, which holds true for each of the five characteristics: maturity, quality, coupon, issuer type, and coupon area (discount or premium). Consider bonds A and B, with initial yields of 8 percent and 8.1 percent, respectively. The spread is 10 basis points in favor of B. When the spread between the higher yielding bond (B) and the lower yield bond (A) widens, the lower yielding bond is the better performer. If the spread widens by bond B's yield rising, bond B will sustain a capital loss, making bond A, the lower yielding bond, a better performer. If the spread widens by bond A's yield declining, bond A will sustain a capital gain, making it the better performer.

Traditional Risk Measures

Historical or traditional risk measurements of bonds can be divided into two general categories. One looks at the underlying strength of the *issuer*, and the other looks at the characteristics of the *bond issue*. Measurements describing the issuer can be further subdivided into (1) those analyzing the issuer's income or cash flow relative to the amount of debt to be repaid and (2) others that view liabilities relative to assets. These measures are discussed in Chapter 14.

The analytical techniques discussed above are used primarily in looking at individual securities to determine creditworthiness or value. However, investors are typically more concerned with portfolios than with individual securities, so it is necessary to apply these measurements to portfolios as a whole. This can be done by weighting the individual securities' risk measures by the proportion of the portfolio in each security. For certain nonnumerical measures, such as quality ratings, some sort of numerical translation has to be made. For instance, the highest quality securities can be considered "one," second highest "two," and so on, and then the weighting process can be applied.

New Quantitative Techniques for Measuring Risk

In addition to the traditional measures described previously, new techniques have been developed. Three such risk measures will be considered here. The first uses standard deviation, or total variability, as a measure of risk. The second model uses the beta measurement. Finally, a third model uses "duration" or measures of sensitivity to changes in the level of interest rates.

Standard Deviation in the Market Line Analysis. A market line is a method of measuring risk and return using variability of returns as

Exhibit 1
Bond Portfolio Market Line Analysis (for period 12/75 to 12/80)

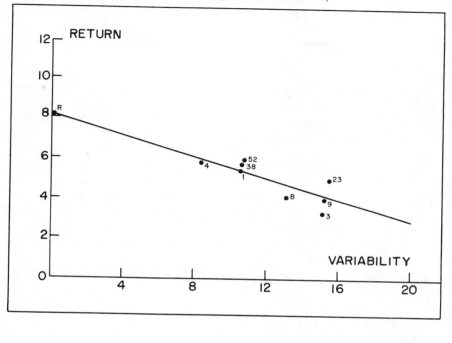

B – BOND PORTFOLIO
R – RISK-FREE 91 DAY U.S. T-BILL
3 – ML 15 YEAR AND OVER U.S. T-BOND
4 – ML 3-5 YEAR U.S. T-BOND

1 – ML CORP. AND GOVT. MASTER
9 – ML HIGH-DUAL. LONG TERM CORP.
23 – ML MED-DUAL. LONG TERM CORP.
38 – ML HIGH-DUAL. INT.-TERM CORP.
52 – ML MED-DUAL. INT.-TERM CORP.

the measure of risk. Exhibit 1 shows a market line analysis for a bond portfolio. The vertical axis of the market line shows return, and the horizontal axis shows variability as measured by the standard deviation of return. (Since standard deviation is an arithmetic, as opposed to geometric, concept, the returns shown are arithmetic rather than geometric. Although this changes the actual measurement of return somewhat, it does not in any way alter the concept of return.) It can be seen from this framework for measuring risk and return that the most desirable portfolio would be one represented by a point at the upper left part of the graph, signifying a low level of risk and a high level of return.

Utilization of the market line begins with measurement of the risk and return of Treasury bills and the overall bond market (index 1). Treasury bills (represented by R) had a return during the period of a little more than 8 percent and a variability of zero for a one-quarter time horizon. Similarly, a point is shown that represents the risk and return for the overall bond market, as measured by the Merrill Lynch Corporate and Government Master Index. This point shows a return of slightly less than 6 percent, with a variability of about 11 percent. This risk measurement indicates that about two thirds of the time during this period we would have expected the market line to have a return within eleven percentage points of its average. Put another way, the return would be between −5 percent and +17 percent about two thirds of the time. It should be noted that any return is theoretically possible but that a return above or below two standard deviations (plus or minus 22 percent, or outside the range of −16 percent to +28 percent in this case) would only occur 5 percent of the time.

We have thus described two points on the fixed income spectrum, the risk and return of Treasury bills and the risk and return of the overall bond market. We can now draw a market line showing the risk and return of "market" portfolios with a wide variety of risk levels. This is done by connecting the Treasury bill point with the bond market point and indicating that an investor could achieve a portfolio of any risk level and any return shown on that line merely by combining the appropriate proportions of Treasury bills and the bond market. In other words, a point halfway along the line would have a risk of about 5½ percent and a return halfway between that of bills and that of the market. This portfolio can be constructed by allocating half of fund assets at the beginning of the period to bills and the other half to the bond market as represented by the index. Similarly, any other point on the line can be achieved by combining the appropriate amount of bills and bonds. It must be noted that in order to achieve a point to the right of the bond market, the percentage in Treasury bills must be negative; that is, the investor must borrow money at the risk-free rate and leverage his portfolio. Although this may not be a legal alternative for most funds, it is at least a theoretical alternative and useful from an analytical point of view.

Having drawn a market line for the period December 1975 to December 1980, we note that during this period the line slants downward. This indicates that during the period there was a negative "premium" for bearing risk: The greater the risk that was taken, the worse portfolios tended to do. Although this is contrary to long-run expectations, it is certainly possible during any period, and in fact it is what happened for the five years that ended in December 1980.

Beta Analysis.   The beta measurement presents the relationship between a portfolio's historic rate of return and the market's historic rate of return, and the slope of the line indicates how volatile the portfolio is relative to the market index.[5] Exhibits 2 and 3 use the beta

---

[5] See Williams, *Managing Your Investment Manager*, pp. 163–76.

Exhibit 2
Returns-Calculated Excess of Treasury Bills for Period
12/72–12/77

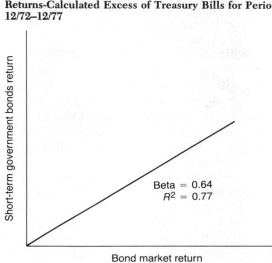

Beta = 0.64
R^2 = 0.77

Short-term government bonds return

Bond market return

model to show the relationship between short-term government portfolios and long-term corporate portfolios, both in relation to a broad-
based market index. It can easily be seen that the short-term government index has a much flatter slope than that of the long-term
corporate index, indicating its lesser volatility, or risk.

Exhibit 3
Returns-Calculated Excess of Treasury Bills, for Period
12/72–12/77

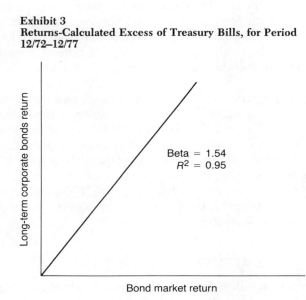

Beta = 1.54
R^2 = 0.95

Long-term corporate bonds return

Bond market return

Certain difficulties arise in using the beta measurement for bond portfolios and hoping to make judgments about them. First, the choice of index makes a great deal of difference in the results achieved. Second, the portfolio's characteristics should be stable for the measurement to be highly useful. Since bond portfolios, if no action is taken, are constantly becoming shorter term and hence less risky, this creates difficulties with the measurement. Finally, as will be discussed later, because of these problems it is highly questionable whether the beta analysis can be expanded beyond risk to measure selection and diversification, as can be done with equity portfolios.

The Duration Model.   In recent years, with the increasing emphasis on measuring fixed income portfolios, considerable importance has been attached to an old idea: the concept of duration. Duration measures the average time required for the investor to receive the investment and the interest on it. It is similar to maturity, except that maturity only considers the timing and the amount of the final payment of a bond. Duration, on the other hand, also considers the significant impact on the investor of the timing and magnitude of coupon payments. As explained in Chapter 35, long maturity high-coupon bonds have a considerably shorter duration than do long-maturity, low-coupon bonds. The significance of duration is that the greater the duration, the more volatile a portfolio's return is with respect to changes in the general level of interest rates. In fact, for small changes in rates the relationship is proportional.

As was noted earlier in the chapter, longer maturity bonds are more volatile than shorter maturity bonds because the time period over which the discounting process takes place is much longer with longer maturity bonds. With low-coupon bonds the percentage of the total return represented by the final payment is much lower, and since the final payment is obviously the longest term payment received, the volatility of the portfolio or bond with respect to changes in interest rates is increased.

The duration measure has several limitations, and these should be noted. First, there are risks to portfolios other than those associated with interest-rate changes. Second, the precise measurement of the portfolio's volatility with respect to interest-rate changes assumes a so-called parallel shift in the yield curve. In other words, if 20-year rates move 1 percent, then a similar change is assumed for 19-year bonds, 10-year bonds, 5-year bonds, and so on. Despite these limitations the duration measure is of considerable use in measuring the risk of fixed income securities.

MEASURING RISK-ADJUSTED RETURN

The rate of return adjusted for the amount of risk taken, also known as the *manager's contribution*, can be calculated by using each of the three measurements shown for calculating portfolio risk. Each of these measurements will be discussed below.

Using Standard Deviation in Market Line Analysis

In the Market Line analysis, a line was drawn representing the risk and return of portfolios consisting of various portions of Treasury bills and the market. This line can be viewed as an unmanaged or "naive" portfolio. In other words, it is possible to suggest that the line represents a market portfolio of a specific risk level and that the market return for a portfolio of that risk level is the one shown on the vertical axis (see Exhibit 1). If the return is above the line, it can be stated that the portfolio achieved a risk-adjusted return above that of the market. If the return is below the line, the portfolio did less well than an unmanaged portfolio of the same risk level. As with all measurements comparing actual performance to a market index, it must be considered that the index has no transaction costs and that real portfolios do. Consequently, all such measurements are somewhat biased against the investment manager operating in the real world.

Using Beta

Just as with equity portfolios, it is possible to use the alpha, or intercept, to measure risk-adjusted returns.[6] However, this procedure is not recommended because of the following factors: (1) the segmented nature of the bond market, (2) the impact on the portfolio of shifts in the bond yield curve, (3) the varying results that can occur, depending on which index is used to represent the overall bond market, and (4) the changing risk level of the portfolio that occurs as bonds become shorter in maturity and as coupon reinvestment and other funds added to the portfolio change its structure. All of these factors impact the measurement of risk in the portfolio and create the possibility that the alpha is showing a factor representing risk when it is supposedly demonstrating the impact of the manager over and above that indicated by the risk of the portfolio.

Using the Duration Model

With the duration measurement, it is possible to calculate the sensitivity of a portfolio to changes in the general level of interest rates. With this information, it becomes possible to attribute the sources of the portfolio's return to the market effect, the policy effect, the interest-rate anticipation effect, the analysis effect, and the trading effect. In the duration model (Exhibit 4), the rate of return is shown on the

---

[6] See Williams, *Managing Your Investment Manager*, pp. 163–76.

Exhibit 4
The Duration Model

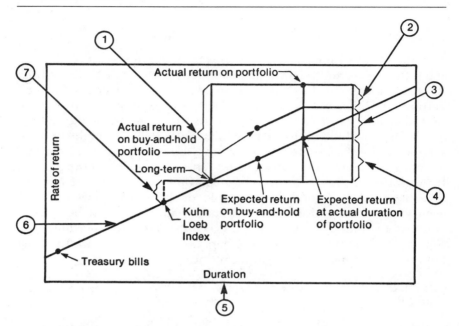

1. The management effect is the improvement in the investment performance of a passive strategy through active bond management. It is the difference between the total bond portfolio return and the expected return at the long-term average duration.
2. The trading effect is the result of the current quarter's trading, either through effective trade desk operation or short-term selection abilities. It is the difference between the total management effect and the effects attributable to analysis and interest rate anticipation.
3. The analysis effect, attributable to the selection of issues with better than average long-term prospects, is the difference between the actual return of the buy-and-hold portfolio at the beginning of the quarter and the expected return of that buy-and-hold portfolio.
4. The interest rate anticipation effect is attributable to changes in portfolio duration resulting from attempts to profit from and ability to predict bond market movements. It is the difference between the expected return at the actual portfolio duration and the expected return at the long-term average duration.
5. Duration, a measure of the average time to the receipt of cash flows from an investment, is a measure of the sensitivity of a bond's price to changes in interest rates. An increase in yields causes a percentage decrease in price equal to the duration times change in yield.
6. The bond market line is a straight line drawn through the return/duration of Treasury bills and the return/duration of the Kuhn Loeb Index.
7. The policy effect is the difference between the long-term duration of a bond portfolio and the duration of a bond market index resulting from long-term investment policy, measured as the return at the long-average less the return on the Kuhn Loeb Index.

Note: The buy-and-hold portfolio is the composition of the portfolio at the beginning of the quarter. It is used to differentiate between trading gains secured within a quarter and long-term analysis gains.
Source: Wilshire Associates, *Pension World*, June 1977.

vertical axis, and duration is shown on the horizontal axis. This is similar to the market line, except that duration rather than total variability is used as the risk measure. The *market effect* is the base point; it represents the return the market achieved during the period being measured. Moving up the line, the long-term average risk level of the portfolio is shown, the difference between the market return and the return of a market portfolio with the fund's policy being the *policy effect*. A manager who expects rates to change will probably shift the duration of the portfolio accordingly. In the example shown (Exhibit 4), higher risk was rewarded as the manager increased the duration of the portfolio above the long-run policy average and achieved a higher rate of return in the process. The difference between the return at the actual duration of the market line and the return at the policy duration, also on the line, is the *interest-rate anticipation effect*. If successful in finding undervalued bonds, the manager's favorable *analysis effect* would be shown as the difference between the rate of return of the initial portfolio—had it been held for the whole period—and a portfolio of the same duration on the market line. Finally, any difference between the actual rate of return earned and the return on the buy-and-hold portfolio is called the *trading effect*. This analysis is extremely interesting, but unfortunately it has limitations. Because measurements are attributed so minutely, it is extremely important that the portfolios be valued precisely and that they be measured whenever any significant cash flow takes place. In other words, the rate of return must be precisely measured for it to be possible to attribute return to the various effects. Also, duration is not a complete measurement of the risk in a portfolio, since it leaves out quality factors. Thus these factors will be attributed to other areas. In addition, the impact on the portfolio from sinking funds, calls, and redemptions will be attributed to trading, whereas they may be due to fortuitous causes. Naturally, since the market line is based on the return and the duration of the market index, precise measurements of the index must also be available. Finally, it should be noted that there is no generally accepted theory that suggests that a straight-line relationship should exist between return and duration. Although the analysis may be extremely ambitious, nonetheless the results being sought are entirely desirable.

Using Traditional Measurements

One recently developed approach to bond measurement uses traditional measurements (see Exhibit 5). This method compares results to the market and to a buy-and-hold portfolio. The difference between the rate of return on the market and the rate of return on the beginning or buy-and-hold portfolio is considered to be the *management differential*. The difference between the rate of return on the beginning

Exhibit 5
Measuring Manager Contribution Using Traditional Analysis

Return analysis (beginning portfolio):

	Total Return	Adjusted Beginning Yield to Maturity	Interest- Rate Effect	Sector/ Quality Return	Residual
1. Return of beginning portfolio...........	0.92% =	2.14%	+ (3.84%)	+ 0.80%	+ 1.82%
2. Market return........	(1.25) =	2.06	+ (4.13)	+ 0.87	+ (0.05)
3. Management differential	2.17% =	0.08%	+ 0.29%	+ (0.07)%	+ 1.87%

The manager static portfolio performed considerably better (+2.17 percent) than the market portfolio. This better performance was mainly attributable to 1.87 percent from "other selection effects," which occurred on several bonds. Also, about 0.29 percent additional return was experienced because of the shorter maturity of this portfolio (13.5 years) versus the market average maturity of 19.5 years.

Activity factor:

Total reported return	versus	Return on beginning portfolio	=	Activity factor
0.30%		0.92%	=	(0.62%)

Account descriptors:

	Market	Manager
Maturity	19.5 years	13.5 years
Coupon	7.9%	8.2%

Source: Russell Fogler and Peter O. Dietz, Frank Russell & Company, Inc.

portfolio and the actual portfolio is called the *activity factor.* This analysis suggests that the return on a portfolio will equal its beginning yield-to-maturity if nothing else changes. However, interest rates may change, and this impact is measured by looking at the shift in the government bond yield curve from the beginning to the end of the period. The impact of this shift is called the *interest-rate effect.* To the extent that the portfolio is weighted differently from the market, any changes in the relationship between quality and issuer type will also have an impact on the portfolio. The difference between the total rate of return of the beginning portfolio and the sum of the beginning yield-to-maturity, the interest rate effect, and the sector/quality effect, is called the *residual effect,* or *other selection effect.* Finally, the difference between the return on the beginning portfolio and the actual return is an *activity* or *swapping factor.*

COMPARISON WITH A BASELINE PORTFOLIO

Some practitioners suggest that it is inappropriate to compare a portfolio's results to a market index or to the results of other funds. Rather, a fund's results should be compared to its objective. The objective is not a simple percentage or dollar amount but a portfolio that meets the needs of the fund sponsor. Assume that a certain fund with assets of $1 million is required to pay $100,000 per year to the sponsor for 10 years. In this case the baseline portfolio might be a U.S. government bond with a 10 percent coupon and a 10-year maturity. It is then possible to compare the results of the portfolio in any period to those that would have been achieved by investing in this bond.

This method has considerable appeal, though it is not easy to put into practice. First, it is not easy for most sponsors to articulate their needs as specifically as the method requires. Second, a portfolio must be found that meets these needs. Third, this portfolio must be measured along with the real portfolio. Nonetheless, at least conceptually, there is considerable merit to this approach. If nothing else, the method forces sponsors to investigate and articulate their needs.

SUMMARY

The measurement of fixed income portfolios has undergone substantial, if not revolutionary, changes in the past 10 years, and there appears to be no letup in sight. As computers and computerized data bases proliferate, this process may even accelerate. In many senses it is long overdue. Although bonds appear to be rather straightforward instruments, the workings of compound interest and changes in relationships within the market provide considerable intricacies in analyzing fixed income instruments. The need for investors to answer the question "For the risk I took, was I amply compensated?" provides the need to measure both risk and risk-adjusted returns. Gains have been made in this area, but more work has to be done, particularly in relation to the specific requirements of individual investors. For if two investors have different time horizons, a very risky portfolio for one may in fact be an extremely conservative portfolio for another. The improvements made in bond indices and with computerized techniques provide hope that this process can be continued.

Measuring Market Timing
in Fixed Income Portfolios

44

ARTHUR WILLIAMS III, C.F.A.
Vice President, Pension Fund Investments
Merrill Lynch, Pierce, Fenner & Smith, Inc.

There are two general ways in which investment managers can add return to portfolios. The first is securities selection, and the second is market timing. In equity investment it is debatable whether securities selection is more or less important to long-run success than market timing. This is because individual securities can behave very differently from the market over time. In fixed income securities, the question is not debatable at all. Assuming securities in the portfolio do not default, all bonds tend to behave more or less similarly. Wide swings in portfolio return are, then, a function of variability of the market and the risk posture of the portfolio. This risk posture, whether measured as average maturity, duration, or cash position, is an expression of the investment manager's view of the market outlook relative to the client's ability to bear risk.

Although we all intuitively feel that we know what market timing is, nonetheless, it is a very difficult phenomenon to measure. By market timing is meant changing the allocation between cash and longer term fixed income securities in anticipation of changes in the bond market. For purposes of analysis here, three categories of measuring market timing have been established: *changes in portfolio value, use of market indices,* and *measurement of cash flow movements.*

CHANGES IN PORTFOLIO VALUE

Measuring changes in portfolio values involves looking at the portfolio at the beginning of the period and calculating the return that would have been achieved had that same portfolio been held throughout the period. That return can then be compared with the actual return achieved to see whether or not the "unmanaged" buy-and-hold portfolio would have performed better than the managed portfolio. Although this information can certainly be of interest, it is really not a satisfactory measurement of market timing. First, this type of measurement is very sensitive to the beginning point chosen. If the period chosen were one year earlier or one year later, the results might be dramatically different. Also, any aberration in the portfolio's structure at the beginning point impacts the result. More important, this measurement does not distinguish among market timing, the risk level of each asset category, and contributions through selection. Consequently, the measurement has serious deficiencies for investors who are trying to determine the contribution made by timing the market. The impacts of asset category risk level and selection are demonstrated below.

THE USE OF MARKET INDICES

In order to overcome the biases caused by differences in asset category risk level and selection, it is possible to view the portfolio as being invested not in the actual securities held but in market indices. In other words, if the portfolio were 70 percent in bonds and 30 percent in cash equivalents, we could assume that the portfolio was invested 70 percent in a bond index and 30 percent in Treasury bills. This appears to be a quite satisfactory solution to the biases introduced by measuring the actual portfolio owned. Someone might suggest that this is not appropriate, since a manager might go from cash into certain long bonds that outperform the market. According to general terminology, however, this manager would be deemed to have had success in selection, as opposed to success in market timing.

Numerous methods can be derived for measuring market timing with the use of indices.

The Beginning Allocation

It is possible to use the beginning percentage allocation between bonds and cash in order to see whether the portfolio would have performed better over time had the manager maintained the beginning allocation rather than causing or allowing the allocation to change as it did. This method is also very sensitive to the beginning point chosen. It would be possible to repeat this method for each year (or even each quarter or month) of the measurement period. That is to say, we could look at the results from a point starting five years ago, a second point starting four years ago, a third point starting three years ago, and so on. The difficulty with this approach is that the results might be positive for some years and negative for others, and there would be no obvious way of averaging the results for the entire period.

Since this method is sensitive to the beginning point chosen, an improvement can be made by making the beginning point less arbitrary. For instance, if the beginning of a market cycle is used as the beginning point and the end of the market cycle as the end point, the period being measured is both rationally determined and the same for all portfolios. In this case the performance in a market cycle would be measured for the two hypothetical portfolios, one with the average allocation during the cycle and the other with the actual allocation. If the portfolio at the average allocation exceeded the portfolio at the beginning allocation, a positive timing score would result. A drawback of this method is that it cannot be used unless the portfolio was under the manager's control for at least the full market cycle being measured.

The Average Allocation

In order to avoid dependence on the beginning point, it is possible to use the average allocation during the period rather than the allocation at the beginning point. In other words, if the average percentage in bonds and cash equivalents is 70/30, a comparison can be made of the return that would have been achieved by investing in market indices at the average allocation and comparing it to the return that would have been achieved by investing at the actual quarter-by-quarter allocation that occurred in the portfolio. This method has considerable merit. However, like all of the index methods discussed here, it suffers from two problems: The measurement is "period dependent," and it is sensitive to the level of average allocation. In other words, a manager who behaved exactly the same from 1968 to 1972 as from 1973 to 1977 would show different timing results simply because the bond and cash equivalent markets behaved differently during the two periods. Furthermore, even if we look at only a single period, two funds with significantly different allocations will have different timing measures. This makes it difficult to compare managers over a given period. Such period dependence is the result of a phenomenon that might be called the rebalancing effect. Serious students of performance measurement may wish to study this phenomenon, since it crops up in several different areas of analysis.

The measurement technique is looking at the difference between a portfolio that was rebalanced periodically to a certain allocation level and one that was not rebalanced. This means that if the market rises, the percentage in bonds increases and the rebalancing occurs by selling sufficient bonds to rebalance the desired level. If the market declines, the percentage in bonds also declines, thus making it necessary to rebalance by purchasing additional bonds. As long as the market heads in one direction, rebalancing hurts the portfolio. That is, as long as the market is rising, a policy of selling bonds obviously hurts the portfolio. Similarly, if the market is declining, a policy of purchasing bonds hurts the portfolio. Thus in periods in which the market goes straight up or straight down, the rebalancing strategy works poorly, and the unbalanced portfolio will tend to outperform the rebalanced portfolio. On the other hand, if the market has wide fluctuations but ends up roughly where it started, the rebalancing strategy is effective in increasing returns. This is because the percentage in equities in a rising market is constantly reduced, and at such time as the market declines, the lower level of bonds works to the portfolio's benefit. Consequently, in a declining market the policy of rebalancing by purchasing bonds increases the fund's return when the market rebounds to its original position. Thus the rebalancing effect is different in each period measured due to the differences in what the market did during that period. Consequently, a bias is introduced into all measurements that involve rebalancing. Unfortunately, this includes almost all measurements of timing.

A variation of the measurement of looking at the average percentage in bonds versus the actual percentage is to look at the average of a risk measure, such as standard deviation or duration, of the total portfolio in comparison with the period-by-period measures. In other words, the expected returns could be calculated for a portfolio with a duration equal to the average duration over the period, and these returns could be compared to the expected returns from the quarter-by-quarter duration of the portfolio. Again, if the average returns exceed the returns quarter by quarter, a negative timing score results.

The Trend Line Allocation

One of the most difficult problems associated with the measurement of market timing is the need to distinguish between the discretionary activity of the manager and the policies dictated by the sponsor. If the sponsor dictates or suggests a maturity maximum, the measurement of market timing must take this change in policy into account. Otherwise, an impact will be attributed to the manager that should be attributed to the sponsor. Similarly, if the manager changes the long-term policy as to percentage in equities, this change cannot easily be distinguished from attempts at timing.

Regretably, there is no simple way to measure this phenomenon unless the sponsor precisely and before the fact states an investment policy. It is insufficient for the sponsor to give general guidelines, and of course there is no way to distinguish between the impact of such policy decisions on a manager and the results of subtle comments by the sponsor, such as "I see you've been doing some buying lately; that surprises me, given the market's outlook." One means for eliminating the impact of these policy decisions involves looking not at the average allocation, but at the trend line. That is, if the average, or trend, over time is rising or declining, it is possible to measure the impact of the portfolio's being invested at a higher or lower allocation than that indicated by the trend line. Of course, there is still no way to distinguish between the sponsor's and the manager's impact.

The Perfect Allocation

It is possible to compare the results of a portfolio at actual allocation with the results of a portfolio that had perfect (or always wrong) allocation. Instead of the standard being the beginning point, the average, or the trend line, the standard would be the results obtained from having always been in the highest returning (or the worst returning) asset category. Unfortunately, this measurement is not particularly useful, since it really measures the policy rather than the deviations from the policy that result from the manager's attempts at timing. In a period in which long bonds did well, portfolios with high percentages in long bonds would show up well under this score, even if the manager's activities in deviating from this policy actually hurt the portfolio's results.

All of the measurements using the indices are affected by the frequency with which the percentage in asset categories is measured and by the stability and magnitude of cash flows. If the portfolio's structure is measured only quarterly and there are large, infrequent cash flows, the measurement of the asset allocation will be impacted. For instance, if a portfolio is normally 50 percent each in stocks and bonds, and the annual contribution (equal to 10 percent of the portfolio) is received on March 28 and temporarily put in cash equivalents, the portfolio's allocation as of March 31 will be distorted, even though the distortion lasts only a few days.

MOVEMENT OF CASH

In order to eliminate the problems associated with viewing the percentage allocation, some people feel that it is better to look at the movements of cash. This can be done in two ways: looking at purchases and sales and looking at the disposition of new cash in the portfolio.

In applying the first method, if the fund's manager in a given quarter purchased $100 of bonds and sold $30, for a net purchase of $70, this would be regarded as an indication of greater commitment to bonds, and hence the subsequent performance of bonds would be tracked. Although this idea has merit in principle, there are drawbacks. The first drawback is the difficulty of achieving sufficiently detailed information as to when the purchase took place. If the typical system of using midmonth cash flows is utilized, it is possible that the fund manager purchased securities early or late in the month when the situation was more favorable than that suggested by use of the midmonth assumption. Even if the exact timing of bond purchases and sales could be shown, there would still be a need to average purchases on the 5th of the month with sales on the 16th in some intelligent fashion. And if this problem could be solved, there would be the question of how long to track the purchases before deciding that the manager did well or poorly by making them. Should we view the change in the market over the next week, month, year, and so on? Another important limitation of this method is that heavy contributions or withdrawals may dictate making purchases or sales at times when the manager would far prefer to be doing just the opposite.

The second method, tracking new cash added to the portfolio, has two limitations. First, if there is no cash flow activity at all, there is no measurement of market timing, even though there may have been significant attempts at timing the market. Further, a contribution may be used to purchase bonds, whereas shortly before or after this purchase other, more significant sales of bonds may have been made. Obviously, the disposition of contributions does not provide a satisfactory basis for measuring timing. An effort might be made to look at the allocation of contributions as well as the impact of purchases and sales in order to determine the impact of both. However, it is not clear how this would be done, nor would doing it solve the problems of measuring the timing of purchases and sales and the appropriate period for viewing their results.

DOLLAR-WEIGHTED VERSUS TIME-WEIGHTED RETURNS FOR ASSET CATEGORIES

For an asset category (but not for the total portfolio) it is possible to look at the difference between dollar-weighted and time-weighted rates of return. The latter assumes that equal amounts were invested in the asset category during the whole period, whereas the former weights returns by the amount of money invested. Thus if money were moved in and out of the equity portfolio at propitious times, dollar-weighted returns for bonds would exceed time-weighted returns. Conversely, if the timing were poor, dollar-weighted returns would be less than time-weighted returns. It would, however, be difficult to use this method in a portfolio with several asset categories. The measurement could be carried out for each asset sector, though there appears to be no way of combining the results of various sectors unless the portfolio had no external cash flows. If there were no such cash flows, it would be possible to translate the returns into dollars and then combine the dollars in various sectors into a total portfolio measurement. However, if there were external cash flows, there is no obvious way for calculating the average amount of money impacted by the differences between dollar-weighted and time-weighted returns.

DEVIATION FROM "OPTIMUM" AND PRESCRIBED POLICIES

It is possible to establish a "market line" that shows the risk/return relationship available in the marketplace over any period. A longer period could be broken up into shorter periods, over which risk/return ratios for bonds and cash equivalents would each be calculated. The investor's bogey would then become, not the actual return of some hypothetical portfolio, but rather the portfolio with the average risk/return characteristics for the period.

Perhaps the only real method of measuring market timing can be made if the portfolio's owner prescribes a policy and then measures deviations from this policy. If the sponsor says that the policy will be to invest 70 percent in bonds at all times, it is possible to look at the return of a portfolio consisting of market indices invested at the 70 percent level and to compare its return with that of a portfolio invested at the actual quarter-by-quarter allocations of the fund. Although this method is quite satisfactory in principle, in practice few sponsors prescribe policies sufficiently to permit such a measurement.

SUMMARY

The measurement of the investment manager's contribution to return from market timing is extremely complex, and no bias-free solution appears to exist. Perhaps the only solution, then, is to choose a measurement that is easy to understand and to openly recognize its limitations, so that no one will be misled. With this viewpoint in mind, comparing the return of hypothetical portfolios invested in market indices at the average allocation with the return of similar portfolios invested at actual allocations appears to be a satisfactory approach.

PART 4

Interest Rate and Interest-Rate Forecasting

Fedwatching and the Federal Funds Market

45   **WILLIAM C. MELTON, Ph.D.***
Vice President—Senior Economist
Investors Diversified Services, Inc.

Myriad factors affect the determination of interest rates, including the pace of economic activity, the mix of fiscal and monetary policies, the financing strategies of borrowers, and the preferences of investors. This chapter discusses a small subset of these factors—those directly affecting the rate on federal funds. The object is to present the basic concepts necessary to analyze the behavior of the major participants in the market as well as to describe some analytical techniques of interest to the practitioner.[1]

    A proper understanding of the funds market is crucial to market participants, since it is the immediate locus of Federal Reserve operations to affect the availability of reserves to the banking system—and

    * Like many people, the author gets by with a little help from his friends. Critical comments and other assistance were generously provided by Irving Auerbach, Jeffrey Brummette, Louis V. B. Crandall, Kenneth D. Garbade, David Jones, William Jordan, Gerald Levy, Charles Lieberman, Jean M. Mahr, Christopher McCurdy, Paul Meek, Anne-Marie Meulendyke, Larry Ricciardelli, Madeleine D. Robinson, Marcia L. Stigum, Robert W. Stone, Thom B. Thurston, and Betsy B. White. Michele Farrano labored mightily typing the manuscript, and Olga Vidal prepared the charts. The author alone bears responsibility for any remaining errors.

    [1] Though analysis of the federal funds market generally occupies only a portion of Fedwatchers' time, space limitations preclude discussion of techniques applied in money stock forecasting, for example.

no other single factor so influences other money market interest rates as the funds rate. Moreover, in view of the substantially increased rate volatility produced by the Federal Reserve's reserves-oriented operating procedures, it is also worthwhile to consider whether—and how—the market could be made to function more efficiently.

The chapter first discusses forces affecting the funds market "in the large"—during a reserves statement week taken as a whole. Once the special character of the reserves market has been roughed out, the focus of the analysis shifts to the market "in the small"—the day-to-day behavior of market participants and the relation of that behavior to the highly volatile daily movements of the funds rate. Throughout, the emphasis is on the (in)ability of market participants to understand and quantify factors affecting the market, and thus to estimate the equilibrium funds rate. In that activity (among others) "Fedwatchers"—an apt vernacular description of the (sometimes) highly expert analysts of Fed policy—have a key role. In order to understand clearly the forecasting activities of Fedwatchers as they relate to the funds market, the next two sections discuss the major factors affecting bank reserves positions as well as the strategy of Federal Reserve open market operations. The chapter concludes with some thoughts on the inefficiencies created by the paucity of information available to market participants (relative to that in the hands of the Fed), together with suggestions as to how they might best be ameliorated.

Before proceeding to the analysis, a few definitional comments are in order. In referring to the "federal funds market," most of the discussion actually has in mind the market for loans of immediately available funds typically settled via the Fed Wire. That market comprises not only federal funds proper (i.e., typically unsecured loans of immediately available funds through which member banks may secure reserve-free balances from certain categories of financial institutions), but also the market for repurchase agreements (RPs).[2] Since the security involved in loans of immediately available funds is largely unimportant in the analysis, this distinction is ignored.

THE RESERVES MARKET: IN THE LARGE

One of the most powerful techniques in the economist's analytical toolbox is the concept of a market equilibrium defined by demand and supply functions. The simple model typically ignores all dynamic aspects of price formation, as well as risk aversion and the imperfect

---

[2] For discussions of the regulatory and other distinctions between federal funds and repurchase agreements, see Charles M. Lucas, Marcos T. Jones, and Thom B. Thurston, "Federal Funds and Repurchase Agreements," *Federal Reserve Bank of New York Quarterly Review*, Summer 1977, pp. 33–48; and Marcia L. Stigum, *The Money Market: Myth, Reality and Practice* (Homewood, Ill.: Dow Jones-Irwin, 1978). © Dow Jones-Irwin, Inc., 1978.

quality of available information—the very factors that account for some of the most interesting (and bizarre) behavior in the funds market. Nevertheless, precisely because the model is so austere, it can, if properly applied, focus the analysis on a set of fundamental determinants of the equilibrium interest rate that might otherwise be difficult to identify. In that spirit, this section uses a simple graphic model of the reserves market to illustrate some of the peculiarities of the supply and demand for reserves and to trace their consequences for the nature of equilibrium in the funds market as well as the Federal Reserve's implementation of monetary policy.

Supply of Reserves

The Federal Reserve controls the supply of reserves available to the banking system, though its control is imprecise in the very short run, principally due to the unpredictability of certain so-called operating factors (about which more later). For analytical purposes, the supply of reserves may be decomposed into two components: nonborrowed reserves and borrowed reserves. Nonborrowed reserves are those supplied by the Fed through acquisition of assets for its own account, other than through extension of accommodation credit through the discount window. Borrowed reserves are those supplied through accommodation lending.

Prior to October 6, 1979, the Fed attempted to alter the supply of nonborrowed reserves in whatever amount was required to maintain the federal funds rate at a target level. Afterward, the Fed adopted a reserves-oriented operating procedure, which, to a first approximation, requires that the supply of nonborrowed reserves be kept on a target growth path.[3] For present purposes, the nature of the growth path is of secondary importance; the key point is that unlike the period prior to October 6, 1979, the supply of nonborrowed reserves is now essentially unresponsive to the funds rate.

In contrast, the supply of borrowed reserves continues to respond to the funds rate, though in a complex fashion that is the result of the peculiar historical evolution of the Fed discount window.[4] In essence,

---

[3] As Exhibit 1 illustrates, the Fed continues to specify upper and lower bounds for the funds rate, but these differ from the pre-October 1979 bounds in that they are much wider and serve only to prompt consultations when they are breached. They do not constitute an operational constraint on the system account manager.

[4] A key purpose of the Federal Reserve Act of 1913 was to establish a "lender of last resort," a central bank function first clearly defined by Walter Bagehot, the prominent 19th-century English economist, historian, and literary critic, who is also credited with the invention of the Treasury bill and the founding of the *Economist* magazine. Bagehot viewed the central bank as the ultimate source of liquidity in a financial crisis and framed the principle that credit extended under such circumstances should be charged an above-market interest rate to ensure that the central bank would be the last resort of banks in trouble and the first of their borrowing sources to be paid off as the crisis

the Fed views borrowing as a privilege and not a right. Operationally, that principle generally means that one individual bank should not borrow too frequently, and when it does borrow, it should demonstrate an inability to secure funds in the market. The obvious way to do that is to bid aggressively for funds without successfully covering the reserves deficiency before applying to the discount window. Otherwise expressed, the willingness of a discount officer to accept a bank's request for accommodation is likely to be an increasing function of the spread of the funds rate over the discount rate.[5] However, the precise nature of that relationship depends on banks's *attitudes* toward borrowing from the Fed. For that reason, discount window borrowing has sometimes been viewed as demand determined, although it clearly is a channel for the supply of reserves.

It is now possible to assemble these two components of the Fed's supply of reserves in a diagram. As Exhibit 1 indicates, the supply schedule is vertical at lower levels of the funds rate and becomes positively sloped at higher rates.

Since borrowing is, for all practical purposes, the only channel for additions to the aggregate reserves of the banking system, the funds rate should not be above the discount rate when borrowing is at essentially "frictional" levels. Otherwise expressed, the reserves supply function begins to take on a positive slope at that approximate funds-rate level.

However, though this point is conceptually clear, a problem of interpretation arises from the fact that since March 17, 1980, a surcharge on frequent borrowings by large institutions (those with deposits of $500 million or more) has been applied intermittently.[6] Since the

---

waned. In contrast, the Federal Reserve generally has sought to maintain its discount rate below the funds rate and to empty the (implied) threat of nonaccommodation in order to maintain discipline over banks seeking assistance. The logic to this approach is that banks experiencing temporary difficulties ought not to be penalized by the Fed for their misfortune. Were Bagehot alive today, he surely would point out that such an approach also reduces the incentive of banks to take measures to forestall the occurrence of such events.

[5] Discount window borrowings fall into two categories—short-term adjustment credit and extended credit. Extended credit comprises long-term assistance provided by the Federal Reserve to certain troubled financial institutions. Since its volume is essentially unresponsive to the funds rate, it is best regarded as functionally a component of nonborrowed reserves, or the so-called operating factors. Short-term adjustment credit corresponds directly to the concept of borrowing employed in the text. In data reported by the Federal Reserve, short-term adjustment credit is disaggregated into seasonal borrowings and other borrowings. Judging solely by its name, seasonal borrowing might appear to be influenced by seasonal credit needs and to be similarly unaffected by the funds rate, but it appears to be fully as responsive to the funds rate as the "other" category. In any event, the figures for net borrowed reserves which the Federal Reserve releases to the press subtract "seasonal" borrowing (along with extended credit and excess reserves) from total borrowing.

[6] Effective March 17, 1980, through May 7, 1980, the surcharge was set at 3 percent. Thereafter, it was eliminated, only to be reinstituted at a 2 percent level effective

Exhibit 1
Federal Reserve Supply of Reserves

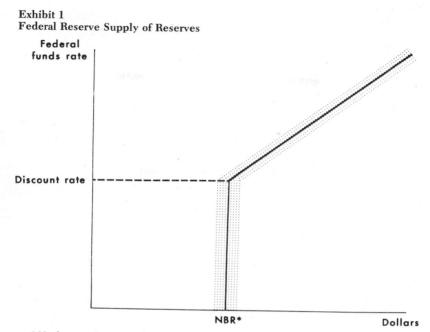

* Nonborrowed reserves path target.

rules have provided that an institution must borrow in more than a specified number of statement weeks in the recent past in order to be subjected to the surcharge, the "effective" discount rate (i.e., the rate that banks perceive as the opportunity cost of reserves) has been a complex function of the volume of borrowing in past weeks as well as banks's inherently subjective appraisal of the likelihood that they might have to borrow in the future.[7] About all that could be said in

---

November 17, 1980, subsequently raised to 3 percent on December 5, 1980, and to 4 percent on May 5, 1981. Effective October 1, 1981, the surcharge was reduced to 3 percent, reduced again to 2 percent on October 13, 1981, and then eliminated entirely effective November 17, 1981.

[7] Specifically, until October 1, 1981, the rules stipulated that the surcharge would apply to an institution borrowing during (a) two successive statement weeks or (b) more than four weeks during a *calendar* quarter. Such an arrangement had the effect that, in a quarter in which borrowing had been modest, banks found themselves possessed of excess "tickets" as the quarter end approached, with the result that their attitude toward borrowing became more aggressive, making the effective discount rate plunge toward the basic rate. That process was especially evident during the first and third quarters of 1981. The Fed responded by altering the rules effective October 1, 1981, to replace the calendar quarter with a "moving quarter" consisting of the current statement week plus the 12 prior weeks. That change meant that there could never be a glut of "tickets" unless borrowing were at essentially frictional levels for a protracted period of time.

practice was that the effective discount rate lay somewhere between the basic discount rate and that rate plus the surcharge.[8]

Finally, it is important to note that—for reasons that will be explored in more detail later on—the supply of nonborrowed reserves is not perfectly controlled by the Fed. As a result, the supply of nonborrowed reserves may actually fluctuate in a *range* around its estimated amount. In addition, though the relation of discount window borrowing to the funds rate is theoretically precise, in practice—as Exhibit 2

Exhibit 2
Relation of the Spread of the Funds Rate over the Discount Rate to Accommodation Borrowing

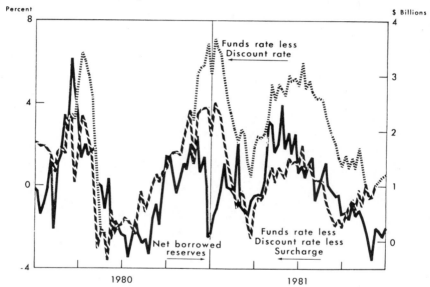

illustrates—it is at times highly variable. The uncertainty thus introduced into the supply of nonborrowed and borrowed reserves is represented in Exhibit 1 by the shaded area around the supply schedule.

---

[8] Two considerations apparently have caused the Fed to view the surcharge as a useful supplement to the basic discount rate. First, since the stringency of discount window administration varies considerably from one Federal Reserve district to another, subjecting frequent users of accommodation credit to the surcharge guarantees at least a minimum of uniformity of treatment of similar banks in different districts. In addition, with the surcharge structure in place, the "effective" discount rate tends to rise toward the full (i.e., basic plus surcharge) rate as borrowing pressure increases. Other things equal, that feature makes the funds rate more responsive to borrowing pressure and is clearly consistent with the spirit of the Fed's reserves-oriented operating procedures.

Demand for Reserves

Banks's demand for reserves is usefully decomposed into two components: required reserves and excess reserves. (*Excess reserves* is defined residually as the difference between total reserves and required reserves.) In the current statement week, the amount of reserves a bank is required to maintain is exogenously given.[9] This is because reserve requirements are calculated on the basis of weekly average deposits two weeks previous to the week in which reserves must be maintained. In other words, banks's demand for reserves with which to cover their reserve requirements is totally unresponsive to interest rates during the reserve statement week.

The second component of reserves demand, excess reserves, is generally kept at the most minimal levels consistent with the state of the art of funds transfers and management of banks's reserves positions.[10] In general, the large money-center banks, which devote substantial resources to managing their reserves positions, maintain their average excess reserves in the neighborhood of zero. The bulk of the approximately \$200–250 million weekly average of excess reserves is held by smaller banks for whom the cost savings from more precise management of reserves positions is less than the expense of staffing themselves adequately to monitor their positions. Since the Fed pays no interest on excess reserves balances, the aggregate cost thus incurred is substantial: at a 10 percent funds rate, \$250 million of excess reserves implies \$25 million of interest foregone annually. But spread out over the approximately 5000 banks that hold those balances, the average cost is only on the order of \$5000 per bank.

Although the cost incentive induces banks generally to maintain their excess reserves at "frictional" levels, a minor degree of interest sensitivity remains in their demand for excess reserves.[11] The reason

---

[9] Reserves can be maintained in two forms: collected deposits at a Federal Reserve Bank and holdings of vault cash. Deposits are measured during the current reserves statement week, but vault cash held in the statement week two weeks ago counts as reserves during the current statement week. The reason for lagging vault cash is to facilitate banks's monitoring of their reserves positions. Prior to 1968, when the practice was introduced, a drain of reserves could occur through tellers' windows, and some banks tried to gauge the likely size of the drain through such expedients as observing the length of queues in front of the tellers! Lagging vault cash makes that practice unnecessary.

[10] For a useful overview of the impact of increasing technological sophistication and reserves accounting changes on the behavior of excess reserves, see David C. Beek, "Excess Reserves and Reserves Targeting," Federal Reserve Bank of New York *Quarterly Review*, Autumn 1981, pp. 15–22.

[11] Beek, ibid., failed to detect any significant interest sensitivity in the demand for excess reserves. In a more elaborate study, Jones did find a rather small negative impact of the funds rate on the demand for excess reserves. See David S. Jones, "An Empirical Analysis of Monetary Control under Contemporaneous and Lagged Reserves Accounting," Research Working Paper 82–02, Federal Reserve Bank of Kansas City, March 1982.

is that Federal Reserve regulations permit banks to carry into the next reserve statement week a deficiency or excess in the bank's reserve position—provided that it is within 2 percent of the bank's required reserves and provided further that the bank does not post deficiencies for two weeks in succession. Although banks may have excesses in successive weeks, in such a case, the carry-over from the prior week to the current one may not be counted toward the current week's reserve position. Thus, if the funds rate is abnormally high at the end of a statement week, a bank with a small deficiency can reduce its funding cost by covering it in the following week, when (it is hoped) the rate is lower. Similarly, a soft funds rate at the end of the week may prompt potential sellers of funds to carry over small excesses rather than to sell the funds at an abnormally low rate.[12] The result is that Federal funds are not a completely perishable commodity; to a very limited extent they can be "stored" in the current statement week and "consumed" in the following week (alternatively, "consumed" this week and "replenished" next week). That imparts a minor degree of interest sensitivity to banks' demand for excess reserves.

Due to lagged reserves accounting, the amount of required reserves is known with a high degree of precision. In contrast, the demand for excess reserves can be highly erratic at times, reflecting, among other things, banks's imperfect knowledge of their true reserves positions as well as interest-rate expectations. This uncertainty is indicated in Exhibit 3 by the shaded area around the demand schedule for excess reserves.

Summing banks' demand for required reserves and excess reserves, the demand for total reserves has the shape shown in Exhibit 3. Reflecting the limited ability of banks to store excess reserves, the function has a steeply negative slope, indicating very little responsiveness of reserves demand to interest rates.

Market Equilibrium

Having defined the properties of the supply and demand for reserves during a statement week, it remains to put them together to

---

[12] Assuming a bank's reserve position in the current week is even and that it was even or deficient in the prior week, the expected profit from buying funds to carry into the next week is simply the spread of the rate expected to prevail next week over the current rate. However, if the bank carried in an excess from last week, that amount will be lost, thus reducing the expected profit. Consequently, for a bank contemplating "doubling up" in this way, the break-even funds rate (i.e., the current funds rate that makes the expected profit zero) can be found by using the following formula:

$$\text{Break-even funds rate} = \frac{\text{Carry-over from this week}}{\text{Carry-over from last week} + \text{Carry-over from this week}} \times \text{Funds rate expected next week}$$

Exhibit 3
Demand for Total Reserves

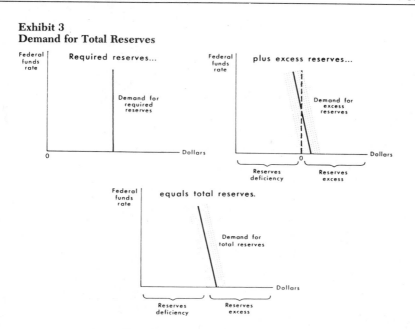

analyze the nature of the market equilibrium and, in particular, the source of the volatility of the funds rate.

Exhibit 4 shows the equilibrium funds rate determined by the intersection of the supply and demand functions discussed earlier. The equilibrium is reasonably stable so long as the amount of borrowing from the discount window remains above frictional levels. In that case, the spread of the funds rate over the discount rate is determined by banks' reluctance to borrow (alternatively, the firmness of discount window administration).[13] Unanticipated shocks to the demand for excess reserves are offset by equal movements of borrowed reserves, with relatively modest impacts on the funds rate. Of course, if something should cause the slope of the borrowing function to increase (e.g., an increase of "discipline" exerted on banks by the Fed's discount officers) then the impacts on the funds rate will be greater.

Moreover, if borrowing becomes depressed—perhaps as a result of slow growth of the money supply, and thus of required reserves rela-

---

[13] This underscores the radically different role of the discount rate in the post-October 6, 1979, period compared with the role in the earlier period. Previously, the funds-rate target set the trading range for the funds rate, and the discount rate was merely adjusted from time to time to keep it in line with the funds rate (i.e., to keep the spread from becoming enlarged). That helped enforce discipline at the discount window. In contrast, the discount rate now serves as the base for the funds-rate structure, with the spread determined by the degree of borrowing pressure. Consequently, although a discount-rate increase in the earlier period need have no impact on the funds rate, an increase now would be expected to lift the funds rate by an identical amount.

Exhibit 4
Equilibrium in the Federal Funds Market

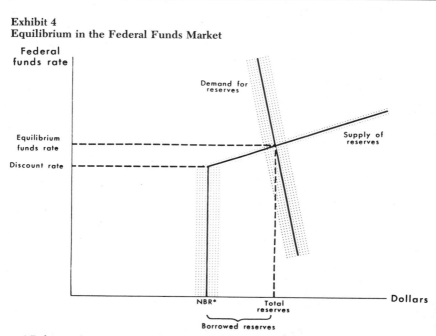

* Path target for nonborrowed reserves (actually path target plus a small, frictional amount of borrowed reserves).

tive to the target for nonborrowed reserves—then the equilibrium funds rate is determined by the intersection of the vertical supply schedule for nonborrowed reserves with the *almost* vertical reserves demand schedule. In that situation, small errors in the Fed's supply of nonborrowed reserves and small shocks to banks's demand for excess reserves can produce large movements of the funds rate. Moreover, an attempt by the Fed to keep nonborrowed reserves greater than required reserves will enlarge excess reserves while forcing borrowing to frictional levels, so that a pell-mell drop of the funds rate may well ensue, reflecting the "perishability" of the excess funds.

In other words, though the funds market is always volatile due to shocks of various sorts, it is especially so when borrowing is so low that the discount rate may cease to serve as a prop under the funds rate. The Fed, of course, is well aware of that fact and is not likely to allow a "free fall" to develop. It has several options available to forestall such a situation. Perhaps the most obvious is to revert to some kind of funds-rate targeting. That is essentially what was done in the May-June 1980 period, when borrowing was at frictional levels and the funds rate repeatedly challenged or breached the lower limit of the funds-rate band then in force. As noted earlier, targeting the funds rate causes the Fed to lose control of nonborrowed reserves, through supplying or draining whatever amount is necessary to keep the funds rate at the desired level. Another way to brake the decline of the funds rate without explicitly targeting its level is to depress the supply of nonborrowed reserves sufficiently to maintain borrowings—at least for a time—at an above-frictional level. This approach was employed during March-April 1981 and again in the autumn of that year. In terms of Exhibit 4, the policy shifts the whole supply function to the left, thereby keeping some distance between the demand function and nonborrowed reserves. Such an approach is obviously akin to funds-rate targeting, but the key difference is that the Fed does not "endogenize" its provision of nonborrowed reserves. Moreover, since the objective presumably is to allow the funds rate to decline in a reasonably restrained fashion, a simultaneous reduction of the discount rate would be appropriate. That way, the funds rate (in principle) will decline without entering the free-fall zone.

Excursus: Contemporaneous Reserves Accounting

The present system of lagged reserves accounting (LRA) was introduced in 1968 primarily in order to make reserve management less burdensome to banks and to facilitate the Fed's targeting of net free reserves (equal to excess reserves less accommodation borrowings), which was a key operating target at the time. The Fed then attached less importance to controlling the growth of monetary aggregates than it does now, and the change appeared to have few disadvantages. However, as the emphasis on achieving a stable and reduced rate of monetary growth has increased, a number of critics have suggested that LRA is an impediment to precise monetary control, at least in the very short run. The reason is that LRA severs the contemporaneous linkage between reserves and the money supply. In contrast, with contemporaneous reserves accounting (CRA), banks would have an option unavailable under LRA: They could affect their required reserves by altering the level of their deposits. That would make the demand for reserves to meet reserve requirements somewhat sensitive to interest rates, instead of being totally insensitive as depicted in Exhibit 3. In addition, proponents of CRA generally advocate a radically different role for the discount rate. Instead of serving as a prop *under* the funds rate as in Exhibit 3, a "penalty" discount rate is advocated that would be kept well above the normal trading range of the funds rate. That way, as depicted in Exhibit 5, the relevant range of the reserves supply function is vertical, while the demand for reserves is sharply negatively sloped (through not quite so sharply as under the current system of lagged reserves accounting).[14] As a result,

---

[14] For economic evidence on this point, see Jones, "An Empirical Analysis."

Exhibit 5
Market Equilibrium under Contemporaneous Reserves Accounting

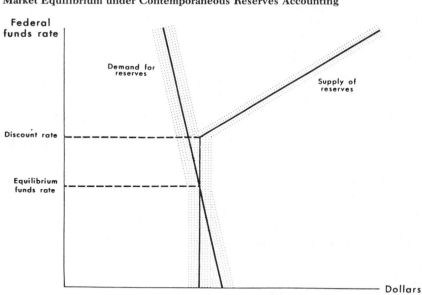

the funds rate under CRA would be more volatile than currently, not because of the contemporaneous calculation of required reserves—in fact, *despite* that feature—but because of the radically different form of the reserves supply function.[15]

Most econometric evidence suggests that CRA—even if buttressed by a penalty discount rate—would improve monetary control marginally over the span of a month or so, without affecting its precision over longer time horizons. Thus one's attitude toward CRA or LRA is importantly conditioned on the importance one attaches to short-run control as well as the greater interest-rate volatility likely to be associated with CRA. However, there is at least one channel through which the potential benefits of CRA might be diluted: the behavior of excess reserves. If banks experience difficulty monitoring their reserves positions under CRA, they are likely to compensate by maintaining larger aggregate excess reserves positions. In itself, that is no problem; but if

---

[15] To mitigate this property, it has been suggested that the bank reserves maintenance period be increased from one statement week to four statement weeks, with the maintenance periods of different banks overlapping. Essentially, this proposal has the same effect as an increase in the allowable carry-in from the current 2 percent of required reserves. Graphically, such a change would make the demand for reserves more interest sensitive than that shown in Exhibit 4, thus reducing the impact of shocks to reserves demand on the funds rate. However, the principal benefit claimed for CRA—that it would force a speedier adjustment of bank deposits to the target—would be substantially vitiated by this feature. For a proponent view, see "Interest Rate Volatility: A Way to Ease the Problem," *Morgan Guaranty Survey*, July 1981, pp. 7–10.

excess reserves becomes more volatile and difficult for the Fed to predict, then the increased precision of control resulting from the interest sensitivity of banks's demand for required reserves would be offset somewhat by the greater varability of excess reserves.[16]

Fed Tracking Paths

Up to this point, the analysis has focused on the funds market at a point in time in which the supply of nonborrowed reserves is held constant. In reality, of course, the Fed defines a short-run growth path for nonborrowed reserves thought to be consistent with the short-term monetary growth target adopted by the FOMC.[17]

It is useful to visualize graphically the tracking paths for nonborrowed and total reserves and to relate them to the funds-market model developed earlier. Exhibit 6 depicts, in two panels, a stylized tracking path for nonborrowed reserves. The difference between that path and the path of total reserves is obviously equal to borrowed reserves. In

Exhibit 6
Federal Reserve Tracking Paths for Total and Nonborrowed Reserves

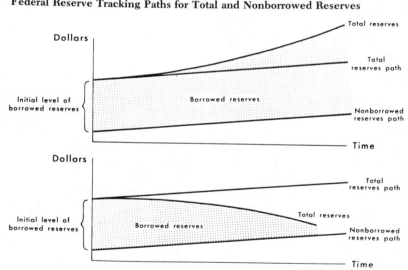

---

[16] In 1982, the Federal Reserve announced its intention to implement a system of (almost) contemporaneous reserve requirements. However, no plans were set to introduce a penalty discount rate. Consequently, the Fed's proposal seems likely to make the demand for reserves somewhat more interest sensitive, as noted earlier, *without* making the relevant range of the reserves supply schedule vertical as in Exhibit 5. Such a change is unlikely to have a major impact on the operation of the reserves market.

[17] For a detailed description of the operation of the reserves-oriented operating procedures, see E. J. Stevens, "The New Procedure," Federal Reserve Bank of Cleveland *Economic Review*, Summer 1981, pp. 1–17; and "Monetary Policy and Open Market Operations in 1980," Federal Reserve Bank of New York *Quarterly Review*, Summer 1981, pp. 56–75.

the top panel, total reserves increases rapidly, propelled by the rising levels of required reserves produced by deposit growth exceeding the short-term target rate. As a result, borrowing increases. In terms of Exhibit 4, the demand for reserves is shifting to the right, increasing borrowed reserves, and with it the funds rate. Parenthetically, it should be noted that on occasion the Fed has acted to accelerate the adjustment of interest rates by depressing the nonborrowed reserves path to increase the amount of borrowing pressure quickly. In terms of Exhibit 4, such a policy shifts the supply of reserves to the left. The trajectory of total reserves shown in the bottom panel of Exhibit 6 is produced by stagnating deposit growth. As total reserves approaches the nonborrowed reserves path (i.e., as borrowing declines toward zero), the nonborrowed reserves path must be adjusted downward if the funds rate is not to enter into the free-fall zone.

Rationale for Reserves Targets

The rationale for the Fed's adoption of the reserves-oriented operating procedures was to speed the adjustment of the funds rate to a deviation of monetary growth from target. Although the earlier operating procedures, which embodied narrow tolerance ranges for the funds rate, in principle could have been used to react equally as fast, in practice the funds rate was quite slow to respond.[18] The most likely explanation is that the Fed at the time was operating in a political environment in which sensitivity to short-run volatility was much greater than at present, while concern with the longer run problems of monetary growth and inflation was less pronounced. In addition, the FOMC is like almost any other committee in that it is cautious in reacting to new and typically tentative data; consequently, whatever its target may be, that target will probably be adjusted slowly. In a sense, the new procedure represented a middle ground between funds-rate targeting and a full-fledged total reserves targeting procedure buttressed by contemporaneous reserves accounting and a penalty discount rate. As noted earlier, the latter procedure would provide almost instantaneous adjustment of the funds rate, at the cost of a large degree of rate volatility.

The reserves-oriented procedures retain an active role for the FOMC and the staff and do not work mechanically as some monetarists have occasionally envisioned. First, the FOMC must decide the relative emphasis to be given to the various monetary aggregates. As the board has pointed out repeatedly, in a period of rapid change in

---

[18] Studies of the Fed's speed of reaction to deviations of money growth from target in the pre-1979 period uniformly found a slow response. See, for example, Gary Stern and Paul De Rosa, "Monetary Control and the Federal Funds Rate," *Journal of Monetary Economics*, February 1976.

the payments mechanism, a determination as to the appropriate transactions measure is no trivial task. Second, given the desired emphasis, the committee must set short-run paths to correct for deviations from the annual targets; moreover, adjustments must be made by the staff for the frequent short-run shifts in the reserve multiplier resulting from changes in the relative proportions of reservable components of the monetary aggregates. Third, some degree of judgment must be employed in responding to changes in an aggregate that are suspected of being transitory in nature.[19] Finally, when establishing the intermeeting reserves tracking paths, the FOMC must exercise discretion in setting the initial amount of borrowing (though as a rule it is kept close to levels prevailing before the meeting).[20] Although the FOMC thus has a large judgmental input under the reserves-oriented operating procedure, and although in all likelihood the committee's response is slow as before, there is a key difference between the new procedures and the old: under the reserves-oriented procedures, slow adjustment of the reserves path by the FOMC does not inhibit the funds rate from reacting promptly, whereas the old procedures often delayed precisely that response.

Studies by the board staff suggest that faster adjustment of the funds rate increases the likelihood of monetary targets being hit, though it is unclear whether still faster adjustment speeds—as probably would be produced through CRA—might be desirable or whether the present adjustment speed itself is too fast.[21] An attempted resolution of these issues would carry the discussion far beyond the confines of this chapter. The crucial point here is that the faster adjustment speed increases funds market participants' need for information concerning factors affecting the market equilibrium far beyond what was adequate in the past. The next section explains how funds traders attempt to solve that problem.

THE RESERVES MARKET: IN THE SMALL

This section changes the focus of the analysis from the supply and demand for reserves in the statement week as a whole to the adjustment of banks's reserves positions and the Fed's provision of reserves *during* the statement week.

---

[19] On several occasions in the past, the Fed has temporarily accommodated (through nonborrowed reserves provision) the extra reserve need created by a large increase in M–1B when, for technical reasons, the increase was thought likely to be reversed in the following week or two.

[20] For further detail on these matters, see Henry C. Wallich, "Techniques of Monetary Policy," *Financial Analysts Journal*, July–August 1981, pp. 41–56.

[21] For evidence on this question, see *New Monetary Control Procedures*, Board of Governors of the Federal Reserve System, February 1981.

Supplying Reserves: The Fed's Problem

In supplying nonborrowed reserves during the statement week, the Fed typically tries to hit its target path. That task is complicated by the at times highly erratic movements of the so-called operating factors. Easily the most variable such factor is Federal Reserve float, the weekly average of which can swing by $2 billion or so in response to seasonal interruptions in the payments system or acute operational problems. (Float and other operating factors are discussed in more detail below.) In contrast, the average weekly reserves provision needed to attain the growth path for nonborrowed reserves is only on the order of about $50 million. The upshot is that for the most part the Fed's open-market operations are "defensive" in nature; that is, they are intended to offset a swing in reserves availability produced by float or some other operating factor rather than to provide the small increment of reserves called for by the target path.

Moreover, given the overall need to add to or drain from the weekly average level of reserves, the Fed still must decide the *timing* of open-market operations during the week. Several factors influence the timing decision. First, though required reserves at present are calculated on the basis of average deposits in the statement week two weeks prior to the reserves maintenance week, the Fed's open-market desk (hereafter, desk) does not have available a final total for required reserves on Thursday, the first day of the statement week. On that day it has an estimate for required reserves, which obviously may differ from the final figure, which is typically in hand by Friday morning. Similar considerations apply to projections of some of the operating factors. All other things equal, then, the desk would probably prefer to wait until Friday before arranging any open-market operations.

Also, the desk on occasion may attempt to smooth out swings in the availability of reserves during the week so as to avoid unnecessary volatility in the funds market. Since banks must meet reserve requirements on a weekly average basis, *intra* week swings in reserve availability in principle need have no impact on the funds rate. Indeed, if banks were able to anticipate the movement in availability with confidence, they could passively allow their reserves position to mirror the swing, and there would be no impact on the funds rate. In practice, banks are highly uncertain about their reserves positions—as is discussed further below—and the funds rate is likely to respond to major daily imbalances between banks's "normal" reserve positions and actual availability. Though such funds-rate movements may mislead some market participants, the Fed now appears much less inclined than in the past to smooth out swings in availability. Nevertheless, if projections suggest a very large excess of reserves emerging prior to the weekend, the desk probably would want to offset the glut on Thursday or Friday rather than see the funds rate temporarily depressed. Similarly, if the reserves market appears generally in balance prior to the weekend, with a major excess supply expected to emerge later, then the desk's natural inclination would be to delay the reserves-draining operation until Monday. On the other hand, moderate intraweekly swings in reserves availability probably would be ignored.

Smoothing adjustments may also be necessitated by variations in the distribution of discount window borrowing during the week. The problem is rooted in the institutional phenomenon that virtually all discount window borrowing by large banks (abstracting from long-term credit extensions) is done on only two days in the statement week: Friday and Wednesday.[22] If, as is usually the case, the discount rate is below the Fed funds rate, Friday is the preferred day to borrow. This is because borrowing on that day counts for three days, thus magnifying the favorable impact of the below-market discount rate on a bank's average funds cost for the week. (Primarily regional banks can succeed with such a tactic; discount window administration at the New York Federal Reserve Bank is generally acknowledged to be more stringent than in other Federal Reserve districts.) Indeed, as Exhibit 7 illustrates, the Wednesday percentage of total borrowing is

Exhibit 7
Behavior of Federal Reserve Adjustment Borrowing: Wednesday Borrowing As a Percentage of Total Weekly Borrowing

	$ millions		Percent			
	Average Weekly Borrowing	Average Net Borrowed Reserves	Mean	Standard Deviation	Minimum	Maximum
1976	84.7	−133.9	40.6	24.4	7.8	82.1
1977	463.5	249.9	29.4	22.4	7.6	92.8
1978	868.0	671.0	20.5	9.9	7.5	56.3
1979	1338.0	1115.6	19.6	9.0	7.0	47.7
1980	1232.4	933.9	28.1	24.0	4.1	97.2
1981	1265.5	964.0	27.2	15.6	7.5	89.2

Note: Borrowing data have been adjusted to remove the extended credit advanced to certain institutions.

negatively related to the overall level of borrowing. In 1976, when banks actually averaged net free reserves and the funds rate was low relative to the discount rate, Wednesday borrowing averaged about 40 percent of the total. During 1978–1979, when borrowing traffic was

---

[22] When small banks borrow from the discount window, they frequently do so for every day of the statement week. The reason is that such banks almost always are sellers of federal funds, so that if they have sustained a reserve drain so large that it cannot be covered by reducing funds sales, there may be little alternative to seeking accomodation for a number of days.

much greater and the funds rate was correspondingly higher than the discount rate, the Wednesday percentage was about half as large, reflecting the greater attractiveness of Friday borrowing. However, during 1980–81 the Wednesday percentage on average was substantially higher than in 1978–79 and more erratic, despite the fact that average borrowing was about the same in both periods. Though the reasons for that phenomenon are not clear, it is probably related to the advent of the reserves-oriented operating procedures in late 1979 and perhaps the effect of the discount rate surcharge on banks's borrowing behavior.

The substantial variability of the distribution of borrowing traffic between Friday and Wednesday illustrated in Exhibit 8 can create

Exhibit 8
Wednesday Borrowing As a Percentage of Total Weekly Borrowing

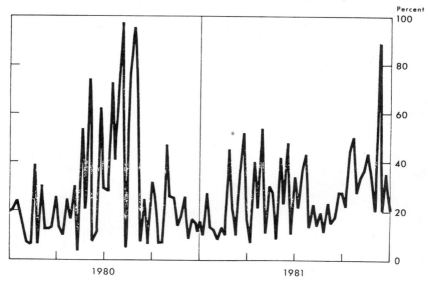

problems for the desk. For example, if for some reason Friday borrowing is unexpectedly high, then by Monday it may well be that essentially all of the week's borrowing target has been fulfilled, leaving nothing to be done on Wednesday. The result would be downward pressure on the funds rate unless the desk enters the market to drain out some of the excess.[23] Such an operation would involve a deliber-

---

[23] In a sense, Friday borrowing is "demand-determined," largely reflecting banks's efforts to take advantage of a (possibly) below-market discount rate. By Wednesday afternoon, however, the total amount of borrowing remaining to be done is almost completely determined by reserves availability earlier in the statement week. That means that on Wednesday (and perhaps somewhat earlier) the funds rate responds to the scale of borrowing and not the other way around as on Friday.

ate, though probably temporary, departure from the nonborrowed reserves path, rather than merely a decision with regard to the timing of reserves availability during the statement week.[24]

Once the desk has formed a view with regard to the desirable timing of any operations affecting reserves availability, the specific instrument to be used to accomplish the objective must be chosen. Basically, the decision involves a choice between (1) permanent reserves operations versus temporary ones and (2) various alternative kinds of temporary operations. In order to avoid interfering with the market's determination of interest rates, the desk tries to minimize its presence in the market. Thus if there is a need to add reserves over a substantial period of time (e.g., during the late-year holiday season), the natural course is to make one or more purchases of securities. One way this can be done is to buy them from the foreign central banks for whom the New York Fed acts as agent and securities custodian. Such a transaction would be arranged internally and would involve no operations in the market; it thus serves as a convenient device to reduce the Fed's presence in the market. The major limitation of that kind of transaction is that the decision to buy or sell securities is made by the foreign customers, so that the Fed can take advantage of a timely opportunity to carry out its reserve-adding task this way, but it cannot create that opportunity itself. In the event that no such opportunity appears, the Fed must instead purchase the securities in the market by asking dealers for their offers.[25] Regardless of how the outright purchase (sale) of securities is arranged, its purpose is to relieve the Fed of the necessity of repeatedly carrying out temporary additions (drains) of reserves for a protracted period of time.

In the event of a need to drain reserves over a substantial time period, a sale of securities to foreign accounts, if possible, would be convenient. But in this case, there is another nonmarket option as well: The Fed can bid to redeem some of its maturing bills at the regular weekly auction of Treasury bills. To do so, the Fed simply submits its tender for a dollar amount smaller than its holding of the maturing issues. The major limitation of this approach is that the Fed obviously can redeem only as much as it holds of the maturing issues and in practice would not want to disrupt the auction process by concentrating a large redemption in a single auction. Consequently,

---

[24] On not a few occasions, the desk has made precisely such a departure in nonborrowed reserves provision in order to offset swings of borrowing. For details, see Paul Meek and Fred J. Levin, "Implementing the New Operating Procedures: The View from the Trading Desk," in *New Monetary Control Procedures.*

[25] The Federal Reserve may not bid to increase its holdings of maturing Treasury bills or coupons in an auction. The reason is that doing so would in effect reduce the size of the offering to the public below the size announced, thus tending to produce an unexpectedly high price (low yield) on the issue. That could be disadvantageous to securities dealers and others submitting competitive bids for the issue.

only reserve drains in amounts of $500 million or so are likely to be implemented in this fashion. Larger operations will involve outright sales of securities in the market.[26]

When a reserve need is perceived to be temporary, affecting only one or a few statement weeks, the Fed's preferred action is to arrange repurchase agreements (RPs) with the dealers. That injects reserves for the duration of the RPs, and is operationally simpler and less obtrusive than would be an outright purchase of securities followed by an outright sale.

RPs can be arranged by the Fed for its own account—so-called system RPs—or by the Fed as agent for foreign central bank customers. Given the Fed's practice in figuring reserve needs, there is no difference between the reserve impact of the two kinds of transactions, though that fact is not always recognized by market participants. If they are functionally identical, then what explains the Fed's choice between them? As a rule, the Fed employs customer RPs when it estimates a reserve need to be small.[27] The largest customer RP ever arranged totaled only slightly more than $2 billion, and the average size is a bit over $1 billion. In contrast, system RPs have been executed for amounts as great as $6–7 billion. Customer RPs are fundamentally limited by the available volume of foreign investment orders, which generally average somewhat more than $2 billion. Moreover, since the foreign orders primarily constitute working cash balances of central banks, it is rather unusual for the desk to arrange multiday customer RPs, though some do occur. Thus if a multiday RP is needed, a system transaction is the most likely alternative. Finally, for institutional reasons, only Treasury and agency securities are eligible collateral for customer RPs, although those securities as well as certain bankers' acceptances are eligible for system RPs.[28] When there is an ample "floating supply" of collateral, arranging customer RPs presents no problem; but if collateral is rather scarce, a premium (i.e., a lower-than-market rate) would be expected to be charged on the customer RPs.[29] Rather than have its customers disadvantaged in such

---

[26] In practice, outright sales of securities are rather rare. They sometimes occur early in the year to implement a seasonal drain of reserves. In addition, outright sales tend to be associated with reductions of reserve requirements, which otherwise might produce a substantial reserve excess.

[27] When the Fed was targeting the funds rate, customer RPs frequently were employed to signal that the Fed had no objection to the current funds rate but wanted to add reserves to meet a modest estimated reserve need. The new operating procedures have obviated that practice.

[28] Moreover, until relatively recently, collateral for customer RPs was priced at market value, and that for system RPs was priced at par value. That meant that the dealer required more collateral per dollar of customer RPs than of system RPs. Currently, collateral for both forms of RPs is priced at market value, including any accrued interest.

[29] Before 1972, only securities owned by dealer firms recognized by the Federal Reserve Bank of New York—so-called primary dealers—were eligible collateral for RPs. Since then, securities obtained by the firms through separate transactions with their customers are also eligible.

a fashion, the Fed would probably prefer to execute the foreign orders internally and arrange system RPs in the market.[30] In fact, if the collateral shortage were severe, the desk might experience difficulty in executing the desired amount of system RPs.[31] When faced with such a situation in the past, the desk frequently has preannounced its RPs (e.g., notified dealers on Wednesday afternoon of its intention to do RPs on the following Thursday) in order to encourage dealers and their customers to keep collateral available for use with the system RPs.

A temporary reserve-draining operation is simpler in that matched sale-purchase transactions (MSPs), which are functionally equivalent to repurchase agreements, can be used to remove the temporary reserve glut.[32] Here again, however, there may be a delicate problem of choice of technique. Frequently, market participants show relatively poor proposals to the Fed for multiday MSPs for an abundantly clear reason: They are being asked to extend the Fed a fixed-rate loan when they have at least some grounds for suspecting that the rationale for the Fed's initiative was to tighten the reserves market—and thus, other things equal, to increase their costs of funding that loan.[33] Proposals are more competitive for overnight MSPs or for multiday MSPs when market participants generally recognize the need to drain reserves. As a result, the Fed may well encounter a situation in which it is simply unable to drain a sufficient amount of reserves via multiday MSPs arranged, for example, on Thursday (without, that is, accepting rates well above the going market rate) and thus must return for more on Friday. This problem can be alleviated somewhat by offering simultaneously overnight and multiday MSPs.

Finally, if inadequate proposals prevent the desk from achieving the desired reserve add (drain), the Treasury may be asked to alter the balances in its account at the Fed. Such an operation would take care

---

[30] When foreign orders are executed internally (i.e., not passed through to the market as customer RPs), the Fed pays an average rate obtained when it surveys dealers.

[31] A collateral shortage may exist when the floating supply of eligible securities in the hands of dealers and their customers is relatively small, as when widespread expectations of rising interest rates cause dealers and banks to trim their holdings of securities.

[32] Since the Federal Reserve Act prohibits the Federal Reserve Banks from borrowing from the public, reverse RPs were and are viewed as an illegal transaction for the Fed. However, in 1966 a sudden, temporary increase in float resulting from a disruption of airline service prompted the innovation of the matched (cash) sale- (forward) purchase agreement. The agreement is structured as two separate transactions, and is therefore legal under the act's authorization to buy and sell securities. Moral: There's more than one way to skin a cat! Operationally, MSPs are less time-consuming for the desk than are RPs, since the Fed controls the collateral. That is, the Fed can specify the one or two bill issues in its portfolio that are to be used in the MSPs and set the prices easily. For RPs, however, the Fed must accept whatever eligible collateral the dealers wish to offer, and the pricing task is commensurately greater.

[33] On the other hand, if the MSPs are widely perceived to be required to offset a reserve excess due to movements of the operating factors, then proposals likely will be more competitive.

of the problem if an additional drain is called for, but there can be difficulties when Treasury balances are used to inject reserves. The reason is that Treasury deposits must be collateralized, and if banks have insufficient collateral available, they will remit the balances back to the Treasury's Fed account, thus frustrating the reserve injection. In any event, manipulation of Treasury balances to adjust reserve positions is done only infrequently; in general, balances in the Treasury's Fed account are maintained close to a weekly average of $3 billion.[34]

Banks's Problem: Managing Reserve Positions

The key objective of a bank in managing its reserves position during a statement week is to maintain its weekly average level of excess reserves as close as possible to zero. The reason is that excess reserves earn no interest and are capable of being applied to a bank's reserve requirement in the subsequent statement week only to a minor degree. The two principal areas of uncertainty affecting a bank as it begins the statement week are the scale of its needs for funds and the level of the federal funds rate during the course of the week. The latter has been especially volatile since the Fed's reserves-oriented operating procedures were introduced in late 1979. The former is the result of the net flow of collected funds to the bank during the week. For the most part, it reflects transfers in and out of deposit accounts, but it is also affected by maturing securities and other sources of funds. For a small bank serving primarily retail customers, uncertainty concerning its funds need may be minor. In contrast, large money-center banks sometimes sustain net increases or decreases of 20 percent or more in their demand deposits in a single day. If such movements are so erratic as to be essentially unpredictable, then the bank faces a difficult task in controlling its reserves position.

In addition, a bank's funds trader works under several major constraints as he or she attempts to home in on the zero excess reserves target. First, as noted earlier, a reserve deficiency of up to 2 percent of required reserves may be carried in from one statement week to the next, but significant penalties will be incurred if the bank is deficient in the second week. Thus, following a deficiency, a funds trader must exercise special care to end up even or in an excess position subsequently. If an excess is carried over in two consecutive weeks, the first carry-over is lost, so that also involves a cost. Second, the Federal Reserve does not allow banks to have an overnight overdraft in their

---

[34] This procedure was reintroduced in November 1978, when new regulations were adopted governing Treasury tax and loan accounts. For details, see Joan E. Lovett, "Treasury Tax and Loan Accounts and Federal Reserve Open Market Operations," *Federal Reserve Bank of New York Quarterly Review*, Summer 1978, pp. 41–46.

reserves accounts (that would constitute a loan by the Fed). That limits the ability of a funds trader to maintain a "short" position in a reserve account. Third, it is generally rather late in the day before the funds trader can know what the closing position in his or her Fed account will be, and that operational constraint limits somewhat the trader's willingness to take a view in the funds market earlier in the day.

Most funds traders cope with these constraints by covering their reserve needs incrementally during the statement week, as available information concerning their weekly need becomes more refined with each passing day.[35] Moreover, even if the trader feels confident about his or her reserve need and the direction of the funds rate, the inability to run a deficit in the reserve account limits the trader's ability to "take a view." For example, a trader who expects the funds rate to decline will want to have a "short" position in the reserve account (i.e., to have less reserves in the account than necessary to cover that day's normal portion of the total weekly reserve need), which the trader will cover later (it is hoped) at a lower rate. But the overdraft constraint limits the trader's ability to do that. Similarly, a trader who expects the funds rate to increase will want to have a "long" position now, followed by a sufficiently short position later as to make the excess reserves average about zero over the statement week as a whole. Here again, the overdraft constraint limits the amount of funds that can be sold later and thus the size of the long position that can be taken now. In fact, even if they have a well-defined rate outlook, large money-center banks typically run deficit positions over the weekend, which they cover starting on Monday. That minimizes the risk that they may be caught with surpluses early in the week that would prevent making excess reserves average zero without running an overdraft later in the week. (The mirror image of this process is that small banks and other sellers of funds that have much less uncertainty concerning their positions run surpluses over the weekend.)

To a minor extent, the overdraft constraint has been alleviated by the development of a forward market in Federal funds. In the forward market, traders buy or sell funds today for settlement on future days when the transaction can be covered in the cash market. This device thus allows traders the possibility of realizing a large spread between the rate at which they sell funds and the rate at which they buy them (if they guess right) without having to arrange all the transactions on the same day and without running an overdraft on any day.

However, volume in the forward funds market is very small relative

---

[35] The major exception is that a funds trader consciously preparing to borrow from the Fed discount window will purposely try to stay in a deficit position before going to the window. In doing so, the trader will generally not sell funds—the Fed would frown on that—but rather will avoid buying funds by refusing to bid at the market rate.

to total transactions and is even smaller now than in the recent past. The reason for the decline in activity is the demise of so-called Euro-dollar arbitrage, a technique by which large banks were able to reduce their effective required reserves.[36] Arbitrage created an incentive for forward funds transactions to be arranged for Friday and Monday in order to lock in the profit from the transaction. Before September 1980 such forward trades frequently accounted for 10 percent or more of total funds trades on those days.[37] However, by late 1981 forward trades—though more dispersed throughout the week—generally ac-counted for only about 1 percent of total volume, and on a fair number of days there was no forward trading at all. Moreover, such trading as there was tended to be limited to a handful of banks.

Intraweekly Pattern of the Funds Rate

The preceding discussion has outlined the essential relationships a funds trader should consider when forming a view as to the likely course of the funds rate during the week. First, one needs to know the Fed's implied target for borrowing during the week. Assume also that actual borrowing closely approximates the target. Then, by solving the relationship between borrowing and the spread of the funds rate over the discount rate, a notion can be formed of the funds rate consistent with the borrowing target (given the discount rate). And *that* is the level at which a funds trader should expect to trade. Forming a view, in essence, is the process of gauging the extent to which the current funds rate differs from that equilibrium rate.

Alas, in practice it's not that simple. To start with, as the statement week begins on Thursday, the funds trader knows neither the Fed's target for borrowed reserves nor the actual level of borrowing during the preceding statement week. Add to that the fact that the relation between borrowing and the funds rate is uncertain, particularly when the "effective" discount rate is unknown (as in the case of a surcharge applied to the basic rate), and it is apparent that several layers of uncertainty obscure the funds trader's perception of the equilibrium rate.

In this setting, many funds traders rely on a second-best approach. They in effect filter recent movements of the funds rate in order to define the current equilibrium (or notionally "fair") rate.[38] This proce-

---

[36] The best description of Eurodollar arbitrage is Warren L. Coats, Jr., "The Week-end Eurodollar Game," *Journal of Finance*, June 1981, pp. 649–60.

[37] The basis for these statements is the author's inspection of the records of trades kept by one of the largest federal funds brokers.

[38] Conceptually, this process is similar to the way dealers in a thin market try to use transactions data to determine the equilibrium price of a security. For an excellent description and analysis of such behavior, see Kenneth D. Garbade, *Securities Markets* (New York: McGraw-Hill, 1982), Chapter 26.

dure makes a great deal of sense during the statement week, as an emerging reserve imbalance tends to persist for a while, causing serially correlated movements in the funds rate. From the informational point of view, the technique has much less merit in analyzing trading in two separate statement weeks, since as noted earlier reserves provision is almost totally separated between them. Nevertheless, the Thursday opening rate appears to be very strongly correlated with the rates at which funds traded on Tuesday afternoon and Wednesday morning. (Trading during Wednesday afternoon, when the market is generally thin and often erratic, seems to be ignored in setting the opening rate.)

As a result of traders' notional equilibrium, the funds rate is sometimes slow to adjust to a change in the degree of borrowing pressure in the banking system. One reason is that such a change may only begin to be evident in the reserves market in late Wednesday trading, and events at that time are erratic anyway and consequently are given little weight by funds traders. Moreover, in some cases a reserve stringency, if widespread, may be manifested initially not as an increase of borrowing, but as a negative excess reserves position. As banks seek to avoid reserve deficiencies in the subsequent week, the funds rate should belatedly increase. Finally, if borrowing has been at very low levels for some time, banks may feel little initial concern about seeking accomodation at the Fed window, and as long as that attitude persists, the full effect of increased borrowing pressure will be delayed.[39]

The notional equilibrium funds rate is obviously compatible with the incremental approach to covering reserves positions discussed earlier, in that both depend on an assumption that it is impossible to determine precisely where the funds rate ought to trade. In the absence of such well-defined knowledge, both techniques represent second-best methods with which funds traders can cope.

Nevertheless, it would be mistaken to assume that the occasional sluggishness of the funds rate is solely attributable to funds traders. The Fed's open-market desk also uses movements in the funds rate as a check on its reserves projections. The logic of the approach is to use the information contained in funds-rate movements to verify the existence of an imbalance in the reserves market. Thus, if the borrowing target has not changed appreciably, but the funds rate is moving sharply higher (lower), that suggests that some disturbance to nonborrowed reserves has created a reserves shortage (excess). The desk

---

[39] Exactly that is what appears to have happened during the August-October period of 1980. Though borrowing pressure on banks was mounting steadily, the funds rate was relatively slow to respond. As a result, the Fed undertook special measures, including increases in the discount rate, to achieve the desired effect. See Meek and Levin, "Implementing the New Operating Procedures."

probably would use this kind of information only in relation to large movements of the funds rate, ignoring smaller changes. However, such a tactic in principle should induce a tendency toward serial correlation in the funds rate, since movements of the rate away from its previous level will be more likely to prompt offsetting open-market operations. Ironically, then, the existence of such second guessing on the part of the Fed lends some credence to funds traders' notional equilibrium funds rate. The desk, for its part, has pointed to market expectations of open-market operations as reducing the usefulness of the funds rate as an indication of reserve need.[40]

During the statement week, the funds rate responds to a *perceived imbalance* in the reserves market. Such an imbalance will be only temporary because as the funds rate adjusts to a level consistent with inducing the implied amount of borrowing from the discount window, the imbalance is relieved. As noted earlier, borrowed reserves for the most part are provided at two points in the statement week. Hence, in order to increase borrowing, the Fed generally will need to create a palpable reserve shortage early in the statement week in order to put upward pressure on the funds rate in time to induce the called-for traffic at the discount window on Friday night. If the funds rate does not respond immediately, for whatever reason, then pressure should intensify by the following Wednesday. If the funds rate is rising during Tuesday and Wednesday morning, the increased tightness will generally produce a higher rate at the following Thursday opening, which could in principle induce the desired average weekly volume of borrowing. The same basic procedure operates in reverse when the Fed is in process of easing pressure on bank reserves positions.

The principal problem this convoluted procedure presents to a funds trader is that of distinguishing the weekly rate gyrations due only to unevenness of borrowing (given the weekly total) from adjustments designed to create a change in the total. It is not an easy task, but it is greatly facilitated if one has a clear conception of the pattern of open-market operations that would be most likely to produce an even distribution of borrowing at the weekly pace of the previous week. A deviation from such a pattern may signal to a funds trader a possible shift in the funds rate before the end of the statement week.

ANALYTICS OF RESERVES: A CHILD'S GUIDE TO FLOAT AND OTHER MYSTERIES

The starting point for anticipating and interpreting open-market operations is the ability to estimate the extent to which forces outside the direct control of the Fed are increasing or decreasing banks's

---

[40] For a description of the frequency and relative success with which the Fed has used this technique, see Meek and Levin, ibid.

needs for reserves. Exhibit 9 summarizes the most important such influences. The first category is those factors that create a reserve need for banks (i.e., those for which an increase implies an added need for the banking system to hold reserves in the form of deposits at the Federal Reserve Banks). They include required reserves (calculated on the basis of average deposit levels two weeks ago) as well as excess reserves. In addition, certain factors drain funds from these reserve accounts, such as Treasury deposits at the Federal Reserve Banks, currency in circulation, and a variety of other minor items. The mechanism involved is simple: An increase of Treasury deposits, for example, involves a transfer of funds from bank reserves accounts to the Treasury's account at the Fed, thus reducing reserve availability. Similarly, when the nonbank public increases its holdings of currency, banks must replenish their stocks by obtaining currency from the Fed (either directly or via a correspondent bank) in exchange for debits to their reserve accounts.

Exhibit 9
Factors Affecting Reserves (statement week ended January 20, 1982)

		$ millions
Factors creating reserve need:		
1. Required Reserves*	+2268	
2. Excess Reserves	+140	
3. Currency in Circulation	−1385	
4. Treasury Deposits at Federal Reserve Banks	+643	
5. Miscellaneous Liabilities	−191	
6. Total		+1475
Factors reducing reserve need:		
7. Vault cash†	+111	
8. Float	+2651	
9. Advances	−50	
10. Miscellaneous Assets	+165	
11. Total		+2877
12. Total Reserve Need (6 less 11)		−1402

Note: Data are changes in weekly average levels.
* Adjusted for required reserves covered through holdings of vault cash.
† Held by institutions maintaining reserve balances at a Federal Reserve Bank; data reflect holdings two weeks prior to the current statement week.

The second basic category of reserve factors comprises those for which an increase reduces banks's reserve needs. Because vault cash (held two weeks ago) counts as reserves, an increase (other things equal) reduces the need for reserves from other sources. Easily the most variable factor in this category is Federal Reserve float (essentially the discrepancy between the *scheduled* availability of checks and other cash items presented to the Fed for collection versus the *actual* volume of collections posted). Since float for the most part reflects the degree to which the check-processing system is functioning smoothly, it swings erratically in response to seasonal pressures on the collection process as well as acute disruptions of normal procedures (e.g., airport closures due to bad weather or computer malfunctions).[41] Last, but not least, borrowings from the Fed obviously reduce the reserves needed by banks from other sources.

In order to compute the amount of reserves to be supplied (drained) during the statement week, the total change of the factors reducing reserve needs is subtracted from the total change of factors increasing reserve needs. If the result is positive (negative), the Fed needs to add (drain) reserves.

Of course, as a practical matter, both the Fed and Fedwatchers rely on estimates of factors that may diverge considerably from their actual values, especially in the case of such a volatile factor as float. For example, as Exhibit 10 shows, projections of the total weekly average reserve need made by the system open market desk staff on Thursday morning of the statement week diverged from the actual by an average absolute amount of about $673 million. Exceptionally, the Thursday projections were wide of the mark by a couple of billion dollars or more. In part, however, it is misleading to judge the precision of the Fed's forecasts by the Thursday projections, since daily data streams into the Fed, allowing forecasts to be revised. For example, on Thursday morning the Fed does not have a final number for required reserves but has only an estimate; by Friday morning, the final number is in hand. Similarly, daily data for the other factors allow the Fed forecasters to update their estimates every day. The result is that by Monday the Fed generally (though by no means always!) has an accurate estimate of the reserve need for the statement week as a whole. In any event, the estimates are still more refined by Wednesday.[42]

The information available to Fedwatchers compares very poorly with that available to the Fed itself. Fedwatchers, for example, receive data on reserve factors on Friday evening following the statement week; in other words, two whole days of the new statement

---

[41] The classic description of techniques used by the Fed and Fedwatchers to predict float is Irving Auerbach, "Forecasting Float," *Essays in Money and Credit* (New York: Federal Reserve Bank of New York, 1964), pp. 7–13. A more recent, though less analytical, discussion is Arline Hoel, "A Primer on Federal Reserve Float," Federal Reserve Bank of New York *Monthly Review*, October 1975, pp. 245–53. Finally, readers wondering what the current Federal Reserve Board Chairman had to say about float some years back may find interesting Hobart C. Carr, Madeline McWhinney, and Paul A. Volcker, "Federal Reserve Float," in *Bank Reserves: Some Major Factors Affecting Them*, 2d ed. (New York: Federal Reserve Bank of New York, 1953).

[42] As Exhibit 10 shows, during 1979–80 the average absolute error of Fed projections of current-week reserve need available on Wednesday morning was $144 million—substantially lower than the error in the Thursday projections but definitely still of an order of magnitude capable of producing erratic behavior in the funds market on Wednesday afternoon.

Exhibit 10
Federal Reserve Bank of New York Reserve Projection Errors by Major Component for Selected Years* (weekly average, $ millions)

	Nonborrowed Reserves (market factors)		Float		Treasury Deposits		Currency in Circulation		Other Factors		Addendum: Required Reserves	
	$\|\bar{e}\|$	$\|\bar{\Delta}\|$	$\|\bar{e}\|$	$\|\bar{\Delta}\|$	$\|\bar{e}\|$	$\|\bar{\Delta}\|$	$\|\bar{e}\|$	$\|\bar{\Delta}\|$	$\|\bar{e}\|$	$\|\bar{\Delta}\|$	$\|\bar{e}\|$	$\|\bar{\Delta}\|$
One Week Ahead (Thursday) Forecasts												
1977–78	711	1,867	592	873	409	1,681	152	453	158	628	31	597
1978–79	887	1,435	861	1,189	334	692	140	519	221	776	65	707
1979–80	673	1,057	619	918	350	535	170	551	176	646	155	724
One Day Ahead (Wednesday) Forecasts												
1977–78	118	1,867	110	873	41	1,681	52	453	55	628	17	597
1978–79	176	1,435	182	1,189	49	692	54	519	73	776	35	707
1979–80	144	1,057	140	918	37	535	30	551	73	646	48	724

* From third statement week in October to second statement week in October of following year.
$\|\bar{e}\|$ = mean absolute forecast error.
$\|\bar{\Delta}\|$ = mean absolute change.
Source: Reprinted from Meek and Levin, "Implementing the New Operating Procedures."

week elapse before actual data are in hand for the preceding week. The only daily data received by Fedwatchers is for Treasury balances, and that is available only with a two-day lag. Nevertheless, despite these great handicaps, some of the more astute Fedwatchers maintain a forecast accuracy closely approximating the Fed staff's Thursday/ Wednesday accuracy. But even they are often in error concerning open-market operations, since they may lack crucial data on the previous statement week or on the course of developments in the current week.

Once one knows the value of the reserve need as given on line 12 of Exhibit 9, there remain two additional steps to be taken before computing the amount of open-market operations. First, if RPs (MSPs) were executed in the prior week, the runoff from their average level in that week to zero in the current week will create a reserve drain (add), in addition to that indicated on line 12. Second, as noted earlier, the Fed may execute internally the temporary investment orders of its foreign central-bank customers, or it may pass them through to the market as customer RPs. If the volume of orders executed increases, the result is an increased reserve need. In that respect, the foreign orders resemble other factors creating a need. As a matter of simplicity, the desk personnel add the change in foreign orders (i.e., the average level of orders available for execution in the current week minus the average level of orders *actually* executed in the previous week) to the reserve need given on line 12. If the Deity is disposed to ease the desk's job, the result will be zero, and no operations in the market will be necessary. That does not happen often, however.

STRATEGY OF OPEN-MARKET OPERATIONS

During the year, both the reserve need (line 12) and the reserve need adjusted for runoffs of RPs and MSPs and for changes in foreign investment orders display a pronounced seasonal movement. Currency and demand deposits follow distinct multiweek swings and also fluctuate around certain dates—for example, holidays and tax-payment dates. Float behavior is also strongly influenced by holidays. In principle, even the large swings of reserve need could be met through execution of large amounts of RPs, but a number of considerations argue against such a tactic. First, the amount of collateral required easily approaches $10 billion or so and could well exceed the floating supply of "free" collateral in the hands of dealers and other financial institutions (mainly commercial banks). The result would be that the desk would be unable to adhere to its nonborrowed reserves target. Moreover, even if the amount of collateral were adequate, the fact that banks would repeatedly commence the statement week with a severe reserve deficiency (until the need was met through RPs) would imply considerable upward pressure on the funds rate. For these reasons, provision of at least some portion of the reserve need through outright purchases of securities is desirable, and outright transactions are closely related to swings in seasonal reserve needs as well as changes in reserve requirements.

There are, of course, various ways to do outright transactions. First, as noted earlier, a suitable foreign customer order may present an opportunity for the Fed to effect the permanent addition (drain) of reserves without recourse to transactions with dealers. Such an approach is consistent with the Fed's desire to minimize its presence in the market, but it presents problems to Fedwatchers, who do not learn of the existence of the transaction until the Fed's release of reserves data in the evening of the Friday following the statement week in which it was executed. Another means by which the Fed can achieve a permanent reserve drain is to bid to reduce its holdings of maturing bills in a Treasury auction, for example, the regular Monday auction of three- and six-month bills. In such a case, Fedwatchers will learn of the redemption when the results are announced shortly after the auction. Since settlement for the auctioned bills is the following Thursday, Fedwatchers in this case will know the size of the reserves impact a couple of days before it actually occurs. In many cases, the Fed will have no choice but to execute an outright transaction in the market. Such transactions usually are arranged on Wednesday for settlement the following day, though they do occur on other days as well, sometimes for skip-day settlement. Fedwatchers can only guess at the size of the transaction, since the Fed does not announce it; typically, nine days elapse before the size of the Wednesday transaction becomes known to the market through the Friday evening data release.

Given the decision to effect a permanent addition (drain) of reserves, the Fed must decide how many securities of what type to purchase (sell). The alternatives are Treasury bills, Treasury coupon securities, and Federal agency securities. In general, bills are the preferred instrument. The bill market is more liquid than the market for any other money market instrument, so that the large transactions arranged by the Fed (frequently on the order of $1–2 billion) will not have much impact on rates in the market. Since the Fed prefers not to exercise undue influence on market rates, that is an important consideration. On the other hand, there is some incentive for the Fed to allocate at least some of its holdings to coupon securities, so as to provide a core of permanent reserves without the need repeatedly to roll over large amounts of maturing issues. Operationally, the problem with coupon purchases is that the amounts in dealer hands are frequently rather modest relative to the size the Fed requires, so that the Fed generally must solicit offers for a wide variety of issues in order to have flexibility to obtain competitive rates and to maintain the desired maturity balance.[43] That means a sizable task of computing yields for a large number of issues and extends the time required for the transaction to be processed. Otherwise expressed, a coupon "pass" is a royal pain. Even worse is an agency pass. Since supplies of agency issues in dealer hands are typically light, even for short-term issues, offers must be solicited for many maturities of each agency's issues, necessitating an arduous computation of yields, followed by comparison of spreads between the rates on issues of different agencies. Thus it comes as no surprise that agency passes are infrequent.

Though in the final analysis the desired mix of permanent and temporary reserve injections must inevitably depend on subjective judgments by the system account manager, there are certain situations for which temporary reserve injections or drains are particularly appropriate. A good example would be a two-week period in which the first statement week requires, say, a $1 billion weekly average addition to reserves, followed by a $1 billion drain in the following week. This could be accomplished easily by executing $2.3 billion three-day RPs on Friday ($2.3 billion × 3 days ÷ 7 days = $1 billion) and doing no RPs in the subsequent week, producing a $1 billion weekly average reserve drain. That approach obviously has the merit that it minimizes the need for the Fed to enter the market.

In practice, of course, matters are rarely that straightforward. In the first place, estimates of reserve need are only that—estimates. Second, at times repeated execution of temporary reserve injection (drain) operations may serve an ancillary purpose by affecting the psychological attitude of funds traders. For example, in an environment in which the funds rate has declined substantially in past weeks, funds traders may be apt to anticipate still further declines in the current statement week. One way in which the Fed may temper such expectations without departing from the nonborrowed reserves path (i.e., without temporarily forcing higher borrowing) would be to arrange open-market operations so that for several weeks RPs are necessary. Then banks would start each statement week short of reserves, and would therefore probably bid more aggressively for funds.[44]

Needless to say, to monetary policy purists such behavior smacks of the old procedure of funds-rate targeting, and some critics have suggested that the Fed should reduce the frequency with which it arranges RPs.[45] On balance, however, it appears to the author that the

---

[43] This problem is obviously less severe in the period immediately following the settlement of an auction of Treasury coupon securities when dealer holdings typically are rather ample. Not coincidentally, most of the Fed's purchases of coupon securities are made at such times.

[44] A simpler way to achieve the same objective would be to undersupply nonborrowed reserves, but that approach obviously would involve a departure from the nonborrowed reserves path.

[45] For example, Milton Friedman has criticized the Fed for an excessive amount of RP activity. See *Bondweek*, August 27, 1981, p. 1.

vast majority of temporary reserve injections (drains) are not related to the kind of expectations alteration described above but are required by very short term movements in the operating factors.

Nevertheless, there is one respect in which the frequency of execution of RPs could be reduced with only a trivial change in techniques. It is not widely appreciated among market participants that multiday system RPs typically are "withdrawable"; that is, the dealer participating in the transaction may give notice to the Fed by 1:30 P.M. on the day the dealer wishes to terminate the agreement. As a result, if the Fed arranges, say, a 7-day RP on Thursday with a "stop" rate (the lowest accepted rate) of 10 percent, but the market RP rate declines to 9½ percent by Friday, then a substantial and essentially unpredictable portion of the dealers who entered into the RPs with the Fed on Thursday now have a palpable economic incentive to withdraw, leaving the Fed with the job of coming back into the market to arrange more RPs so as to prevent a reserve scarcity from emerging. Not only that, but if rates rise after Thursday and dealers respond by lightening their positions, then their reduced financing needs may also cause them to withdraw from the RPs, putting still further pressure on the funds market.

At this point, the reader may well be wondering why the Fed would allow its RPs to be withdrawable in the first place, especially since nonwithdrawable RPs are standard among other market participants. The best explanation appears to be that the withdrawable RP is an institution that has survived the circumstances that originally made it useful. Before 1966, when the first MSPs were executed, any reserve draining was accomplished through outright sales of securities. Thus, if the Fed had done RPs early in the week in response to a perceived reserve need but had later found itself faced with a need to drain reserves, then to the extent that the soft funds rate caused RPs to be withdrawn the reserve drain would be accomplished automatically and, in particular, without requiring an outright sale of securities.[46] Obviously, however, MSPs make this particular feature of RPs redundant.

Presumably because of the interest-rate risk involved, dealers generally have participated in a smaller portion of the Fed's multiday

---

[46] Sometimes, however, the withdrawal of RPs in those days was not altogether automatic. The story is told of a system open-market account manager who was confronted with a need to drain reserves after multiday RPs had been executed earlier in the week. Though the funds rate was softening, no withdrawals were forthcoming. Upon investigation, it turned out that a large block of the RPs was held at a major dealer firm. Accordingly, the account manager called the firm's head trader and asked whether he would like to withdraw his RPs. The head trader replied that he was not interested. Then the account manager said that he would appreciate it if the RPs were withdrawn. Again the offer was declined. Before hanging up, the account manager observed that he was certain to remember this event the next time the head trader was in a jam and needed a favor. About 10 minutes later, a phone call to the Fed announced the withdrawal of the RPs.

MSPs and (very rare) multiday nonwithdrawable RPs than have their so-called customers (primarily banks). Consequently, if multiday RPs were made uniformly nonwithdrawable, a smaller volume of less attractively priced proposals generally would be submitted, and that might impair the Fed's ability to execute as many transactions as desired.[47] One way to cope with that problem would be to offer one-day and multiday RPs simultaneously, as is frequently done with MSPs.

With the exception of customer RPs, the Fed does not disclose the size of a temporary addition (drain) of reserves, and that presents problems for Fedwatchers and other market participants. Some participants attempt to cope by monitoring the stop rate on the transaction. The conventional wisdom is that a low (high) stop on an RP (MSP) relative to the market rate indicates an "aggressive" operation. But in fact, monitoring the stop is a very poor substitute for knowing the size of the transaction relative to the size of the reserve need. The reason is that the stop rate in general depends on the size of the transaction *and* the distribution of proposals submitted to the Fed. As Exhibit 11 illus-

Exhibit 11
Hypothetical Distributions of Proposals for Repurchase Agreements and Matched Sale-Purchase Agreements

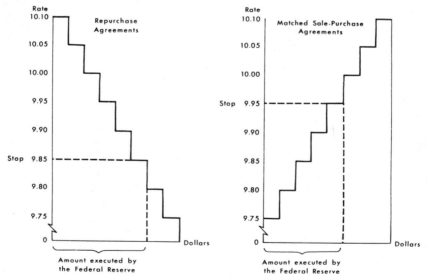

---

[47] Recall that dealers desire to do RPs primarily to finance their inventory of securities, though many do run a so-called matched book quite independently of their securities position. Consequently, if the inventory being financed by a multiday nonwithdrawable RP were liquidated, the dealer would suddenly be in a long funds position that could not be eliminated by the simple device of withdrawing from the RP. For the same reason, customers account for a larger than normal portion of multiday MSPs as well as RPs when dealers have very light or net short positions.

trates, the flatter the "tail" of the proposals (i.e., the narrower the range from the highest to the lowest rates shown to the Fed), the less responsive is the stop rate to variations in the size of the transaction. Consequently, there is no unique relation between the stop relative to the market and the aggressiveness of the operation. Moreover, as noted earlier, in some circumstances dealers and perhaps also their customers are likely to be loath to submit very competitive proposals to the Fed—for example, multiday MSPs in general and RPs when dealers are holding negligible or short positions.

DOES FEDWATCHING MATTER?

Essentially, Fedwatching comprises three analytical techniques. First, like many other economists, a Fedwatcher makes projections, whether formally or subjectively, of the level of economic activity, especially as it bears on variables in which the Fed is thought to be particularly interested (e.g., money demand). In this same general area, the federal budget may be analyzed, both for its overall macroeconomic impact as well as for the more direct impact on financial markets of the scale and timing of Treasury financing needs. The second focus is the forecasting and interpretation of bank reserves positions and the Fed's open-market operations. Most of this chapter has been devoted to explaining the objectives and techniques of such analysis. Flowing naturally from the first two is the third area of interest: the projection of interest rates in money and capital markets. As far as the operation of a financial institution in general and a securities dealer firm in particular is concerned, the latter is the most important of all.

The first and the last of these activities will always be necessary, but there is no intrinsic reason for projection of reserve positions and open-market operations to be part of the job. In performing such an analysis, Fedwatchers merely duplicate and improve upon, if possible, the projections routinely generated by the Fed staff to guide the desk. Moreover, as the preceding discussion has illustrated, the best efforts of Fedwatchers often fall short of the quality of the Fed staff's projections, primarily because of major delays in the receipt of information by market participants.

As noted earlier, the consequence of this lack of information is greater uncertainty among funds traders as to the degree of borrowing pressure being placed on banks, and thus the equilibrium funds rate, so that funds traders are impelled to be more or less aggressive in bidding for funds than they otherwise would be. Indeed, in a sense the quantity of information provided to the market has been sharply *reduced* since the advent of the reserves-oriented operating procedures in 1979. Prior to that time, by targeting the funds rate, the Fed effectively communicated all information necessary to determine the equilibrium funds rate with precision. Market participants concentrated their analytical energies on divining the next change in the funds-rate target, and had to do little more than watch the Fed's "intervention points" (the funds rate at which reserves were added or drained) to determine the equilibrium rate. Since late 1979, however, Fedwatchers and funds traders have had to process information on reserves to estimate the equilibrium rate. In principle there is nothing wrong with that, and of course the reserves-oriented procedures have advantages for monetary policy. The main disadvantage—extreme intraweek volatility of the funds rate—is due in substantial part to the unavailability of current information concerning factors affecting reserves.

Suppose that market participants were perfectly informed concerning reserve factors and the Fed's intended supplies of nonborrowed reserves. Then they would have a fairly precise idea of the equilibrium funds rate, and any change of the Fed's policy with respect to reserves supplies would be followed immediately by a change in the perceived equilibrium funds rate—and thus of the actual funds rate. The prompt implementation of such a change, when called for by the Fed's monetary aggregates targets, is of course the rationale for its operating procedures. The only question is how rapidly the change is to occur. In that context the Fed seems to be of two minds: On the one hand, its reserves-oriented operating procedures are designed to speed the adjustment of the funds rate to deviations from monetary targets, but on the other hand, the information supplied to the market is far from adequate to allow participants to estimate confidently an equilibrium rate to which they can respond. As a result, when the equilibrium is changing, the actual funds rate probably will lag behind but may even rush ahead. That kind of response is inconsistent with a fully efficient market. Moreover, even if the equilibrium rate is not changing, uncertainty caused by swings in Friday/Wednesday borrowing traffic contributes to a wide dispersion of trades around the equilibrium rate.

Needless to say, the flow of information to the market can never be perfect. But the Fed could supply to the market at almost negligible cost all daily information on factors affecting reserves, thus enhancing the ability of market participants to interpret their environment. Even better, the Fed could announce to the market its own projections of operating factors as well as the size of all open-market operations carried out. Doing so would scarcely interfere with the Fed's ability to conduct its operations. On the contrary, it could facilitate them in certain cases (such as multiday MSPs).

Several considerations in addition to the usual bureaucratic inertia may account for the Fed's reluctance to provide such data. First, the Fed may suspect (no doubt correctly in some cases) that the wealth of

data to be released would prove confusing to some market participants. Moreover, since the float data, for example, are subject to a
variety of "as of" adjustments, one could argue that on some occasions
data released might be misleading if not supplemented with background information on the continuing flow of such adjustments. Another consideration that probably influences the Fed's attitude is that
the occasional large size of revisions to factor estimates could be em-
barrassing. Finally, the Fed may believe that release of the full set of
reserves data and projections might "tie the hands" of the desk, con-
veying to the market an impression of a need for open-market operations when the desk had grounds to suspect that some other factor
(such as a prospective swing in the volume of foreign investment
orders) might invalidate a superficial interpretation of the data and
projections. In such a case, the market might be misled by the Fed's
abstaining from open-market operations.

These are not trivial considerations, but their significance is unduly
magnified when they are advanced with an implicit assumption that
the market functions efficiently now. For example, coping with the
complexity of reserves data and the revisions constantly being made
would indeed tax the patience of almost anyone, but it could hardly be
argued to be more trying than the patently inadequate techniques
currently employed for the same purpose. Similarly, revisions to projections are a source of embarrassment to all forecasters, and all
Fedwatchers (the author included!) regularly eat their humble pie in
large portions; but that is merely evidence of the job's difficulty. In
any event, the Fed regularly releases data on its major weekly forecast
errors, anyway. Finally, the "tie our hands" argument only applies
when the market is deprived of the knowledge that the Fed questions
the accuracy or interpretation of the projections; otherwise, it has no
force. In sum, the objections typically advanced against timely release
of reserves data have little merit. Ironically, they had more substance
when the Fed was targeting the funds rate.

In view of the pivotal role of the funds market in implementing
monetary policy, the market's striking inefficiencies are of major concern. Though the reserves-projecting activities of Fedwatchers make
up a logical and—under the circumstances—crucial response to the
problems, this response is not the most effective way to improve the
operation of the funds market.

The Term Structure of Interest Rates

46   **RICHARD W. McENALLY, Ph.D., C.F.A.**
Professor of Finance
University of North Carolina

INTRODUCTION

Exhibit 1 contains a three-dimensional representation of yields on U.S. Treasury securities with different terms to maturity for each calendar month since 1950. Even the most casual observer of this plot cannot help but be struck by the facts that in each month these yields vary with maturity, and this yield-maturity relationship itself varies from month to month. Such relationships are generally referred to as the *term structure of interest rates*, or more properly, the term structure of *yields*. When plots of the yield-maturity relationship are examined for a single point in time, as in Exhibit 2, such a representation is frequently called the *yield curve*. Regardless of how it is examined or what it is called, awareness and appreciation of this relationship is absolutely essential in fixed income investment analysis and management.

Some of the uses of the term structure include the following:

1. *Analyzing the returns for asset commitments of different terms.* Fixed income investment managers vary their portfolios along many dimensions, including quality, coupon level, and type of issuer. But no dimension is more important than the maturity dimension; it has the greatest influence on whether the portfolio will gain or lose in

today's volatile interest-rate environment. The yield curve shows what the rewards will be for commitments of different lengths if they are held to maturity. Properly interpreted, it can also be used to make judgments about the short-term rewards of different maturity strategies as interest rates change.

2. *Assessing consensus expectations of future interest rates.* In fixed income investment the manager who can make better predictions of future interest rates than the consensus forecast—or even the manager who can correctly identify the *direction of error* in the consensus forecast—can profit immensely. But a strategy based on this principle requires a knowledge of what the consensus expectation of future interest rates is. Analysis of the term structure can provide this information.

3. *Pricing bonds and other fixed-payment contracts.* The yield curve shows the pure price of time, a price that changes from hour to hour and day to day. In pricing financial obligations, it is essential that consideration be given to the yields available on alternative investments with a similar length of commitment. The yield curve shows what these alternative yields are. Today it is commonplace to price bonds and other contracts "off the yield curve."

4. *Arbitraging between bonds of different maturities.* As explained in Chapter 30, swaps between similar bonds whose prices appear to be out of line is a traditional fixed income portfolio management technique. Appraising the effects of term is no problem if the maturities are virtually identical. When they are not, yield curve analysis can be used to make the yields more directly comparable and thereby facilitate yield spread analysis.

In this chapter we deal principally with two questions about the term structure: What causes it to be the way it is? And how can we measure, analyze, and interpret it? However, we should acknowledge at the outset that, despite the attention that has been given to the term structure (the term structure is a prime candidate for the title of "most studied topic in financial economics"), there are no firm answers to these questions. Nowhere is the well-known disagreement among economists more pronounced than in the term structure area. Thus about the best we can hope for is more insight and understanding.

DETERMINANTS OF THE SHAPE OF THE TERM STRUCTURE

Theories

If buyers of fixed income securities were indifferent among securities of differing maturity, there would be no meaningful term structure; all yields would be equal. Therefore, the fact that yield curves

Exhibit 1a
Term Structure of Interest Rates, January 1950–December 1964

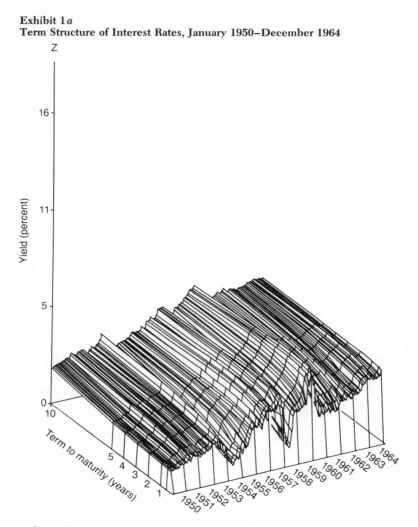

Source: Data courtesy of Salomon Brothers Inc.

are not perfectly horizontal suggests that some maturity preferences must exist. Reasons that have been advanced for the shape of the term structure are in effect theories or hypotheses about maturity preferences among investors. Three such theories are prominent: the market segmentation hypothesis, the expectations hypothesis, and the liquidity premium hypothesis. Let us examine each of these in turn.

The Market Segmentation Hypothesis. Suppose buyers of fixed income securities fall roughly into two groups, one with a strong pref-

Exhibit 1b
Term Structure of Interest Rates, January 1965–March 1981

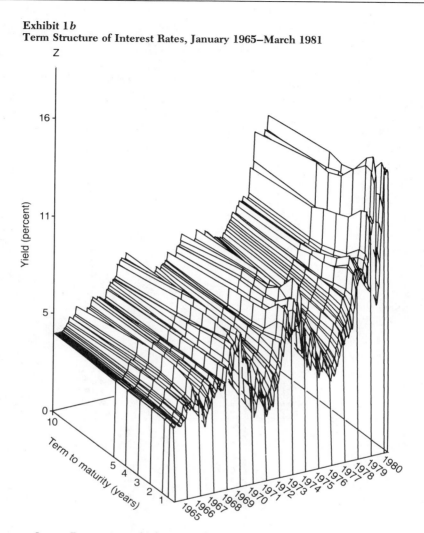

Source: Data courtesy of Salomon Brothers Inc.

erence for short-term securities and the other with a strong preference for long-term securities. If there is little overlap in the range of maturities each group considers acceptable for portfolio investment, then *the* market for fixed income securities will actually be separated or segmented into two separate submarkets. And if one group of investors gains on the other in terms of funds available for investment, then, in the absence of an offsetting response by borrowers, this group will bid up prices and thus force down security yields in its preferred sub-

Exhibit 2
Yields of Treasury Securities, December 31, 1980 (based on closing bid quotations)

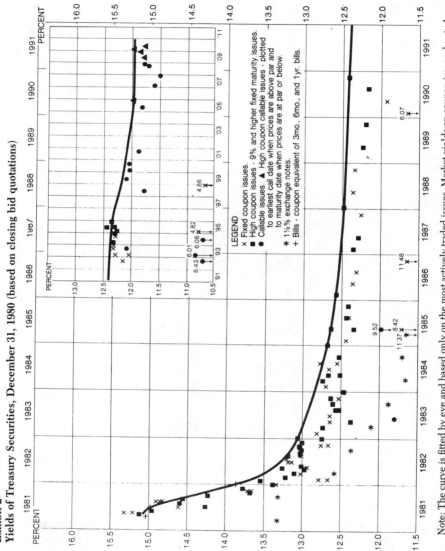

Note: The curve is fitted by eye and based only on the most actively traded issues. Market yields on coupon issues due in less than three months are excluded. Source: *U.S. Treasury Bulletin*, January 1981.

market. The same result might occur from a relative increase in the quantity of bonds issued by borrowers in one of the maturity ranges.[1]

This, in a nutshell, is the *market segmentation, preferred habitat,* or *hedging pressure* theory of the term structure. It appears to be particularly popular among practicing investments professionals. The commercial bank is usually identified as the primary source of demand for short-term securities, and the demand for long-term securities is associated with life insurance companies. Advocates of this hypothesis acknowledge that these two types of institutions do not confine their investment exclusively to one end of the maturity spectrum. Moreover, they recognize the presence of other investors, including investors who will operate in either maturity range. But they also believe that banks and life insurors are so dominant and their maturity preferences are so pronounced that short- and long-term yields behave as if the markets were segmented along these lines.

It is usually asserted that life insurance company demand for long-term bonds is reasonably stable over time. On the other hand, bank demand for short-term securities is said to be more volatile. Banks prefer to lend directly to businesses and individuals when possible, only putting funds that are left over into securities. But demand for short-term loans by businesses and individuals is also quite volatile. In periods of strong economic activity, these borrowers demand funds for business expansion and consumption, banks sell securities to accomodate their demands, and short-term yields rise compared with long-term yields. In slack periods these borrowers pay down their loans, and banks have excess funds for which they seek an outlet in short-term securities, driving their yields downward in comparison with long-term yields.

Opposition to the market segmentation hypothesis is based primarily on a belief that some other hypothesis provides a better explanation for the behavior of the term structure. Advocates of other hypotheses also believe that the segmentation hypothesis understates the willingness of banks, insurance companies, and many other investors to gravitate to the segment of the maturity structure that appears to offer the highest return, thereby arbitraging away temporary yield differentials.

The "Unbiased" or "Pure" Expectations Hypothesis: This hypothesis stands in sharp contrast to the market segmentation hypothe-

---

[1] Alternatively, issuers might offset changes in the relative position of investors in the two submarkets by shifting their borrowing to the favored, lower interest-rate market, thereby restoring equality of interest rates. In the absence of strong maturity preferences, this is what we would expect rational borrowers to do, and there is evidence that some large borrowers—such as the U.S. Treasury—tend to behave in just this way. However, typical formulations of the market segmentation hypothesis assume that borrower behavior is unaffected by interest rates, or, as it is said, is "exogenously determined."

sis, for it is based on the assumption that fixed income investors in the aggregate act to eliminate any comparative attraction of securities of a particular maturity. In effect, it acknowledges that maturity preferences may initially exist because of expectations about the future level of interest rates, but asserts that investors will respond in reasonable and rational ways to profit from these expectations. In the process they neutralize maturity preferences, but they also create yield differences among securities of different maturities.

A simple example will help us understand the expectations hypothesis. Suppose the yield curve is flat, "the" yield is 6 percent per annum, and investors are generally in agreement that yields will increase to 8 percent in one year. Under these conditions the yield curve would not remain flat but would become upward sloped. Plausible equilibrium or indifference yields to maturity are 6 percent on one-year (or short-term) securities and 7 percent on two-year (or long-term) securities.

To see why this is so, let us first consider an investor with a long-term, or two-year horizon. His objective is to earn the highest possible rate of return on his money over these two years, and yield aside he is indifferent between initially buying a two-year security and holding it for two years, or purchasing a one-year security, holding it one year, and then rolling over into another one-year security for the second year. Before yields adjust, the first alternative gives him 6 percent on his money in each year. Under the second alternative, he knows he can earn 6 percent on his money for the first year and expects that he can earn 8 percent on his money in the second year, for an average yield of approximately 7 percent per annum over the two years. Thus he will prefer the second alternative and will buy one-year securities at 6 percent rather than two-year securities at 6 percent. As he and other like-minded investors behave in this manner, prices on two-year securities will be driven down, and yields will be driven up. Only when they reach 7 percent will the investor consider their purchase as attractive as the series of two one-year securities.[2]

We can get to the same result by considering an investor who is seeking the largest total return (coupon yield plus price change) over the next year. She has a short-term horizon. Under our yield scenario she knows that her total return on the one-year security will be 6 percent, for it will pay off at par in one year. On the other hand, her expected total return on the two-year security over the next year is only 4 percent.

---

[2] In this example we are requiring that equilibrium be restored by movement in the yield of the long-term security. This is purely for expository convenience. Restoration of equilibrium might well involve both a decline in one-year yields and an increase in two-year yields.

To see this, assume the two-year security has a 6 percent coupon. At the end of one year it will be a one-year security—that is, it will have one year of life remaining. If it is then to offer the expected yield-to-maturity of 8 percent, it must sell for approximately 98. At this price a purchaser will in the second year get a coupon of 6 and a capital gain of 2, for a total return of $(6 + 2)/98 \cong 8$ percent. But if the two-year security sells at 98 at the end of a year, its total return over the first year is only 4 percent because of the loss of value of 2; that is, $(6 - 2)/100 \cong 4$ percent.

The bottom line is that the investor oriented to one-year total return and having a one-year horizon will also prefer the one-year 6 percent security and avoid the two-year 6 percent security until the yield to maturity on the latter rises to 7 percent. At this yield she is indifferent, as the following tabulation shows.

	Maturity	
	1 Year	*2 Years*
Coupon	6%	6%
Initial yield-to-maturity.	6%	7%
Initial price.	100	98
Return over life	6/100 = 6%	$6 + 6 + 2/98 \cong 14\%$
		$\cong 7\%$
		per annum
Price at end of year at 8 percent	—	98
Return, year 1.	6/100 = 6%	$6/98 \cong 6\%$
Return, year 2.	—	$(6 + 2)/98 \cong 8\%$

At an initial price of 98, the two-year security offers an average yield to maturity of 7 percent per annum, based on its 6 percent coupon each year plus a capital gain of 2 spread out over the two years on an initial investment of 98. However, if the price at the end of the first year remains at 98, consistent with a yield-to-maturity of 8 percent in the second year, then its total return in the first year is only 6 percent ($\cong 6/98$); there is no capital gain or loss. Thus, its total rate of return in the first year is exactly equal to the total rate of return on the one-year security, even though the yields to maturity are different.

This example illustrates several significant implications of the pure expectations hypothesis. First, in each period total rates of return—coupon plus capital gain or loss—are expected to be identical on all securities regardless of their term to maturity. Second, the consensus expectation of future yields can be inferred from the presently observable term structure; e.g., in our example, observing a 6 percent yield to maturity on one-year securities and a 7 percent yield to maturity on two-year securities, we know that the consensus forecast of one-year yields in one year must be 8 percent. Third, yields on long-term securities are equal to an average of the present yield on a short-term security plus an expected future yield (or yields) on short-term securities.

This last implication is believed to account for the observable tendency of short-term yields to fluctuate more than long-term yields. This tendency is readily evident in Exhibit 1; it is also shown directly in Exhibit 3, which plots the mean absolute deviation (average devia-

Exhibit 3
Mean Absolute Deviation of Monthly Changes in U.S. Government Security Yields and Prices, January 1950–March 1981*

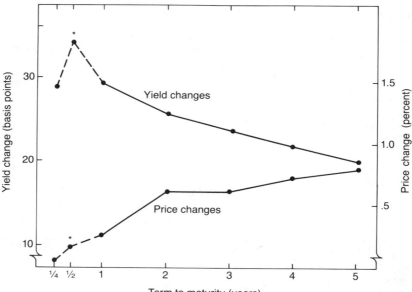

* Except for maturities of one-half year, which date from January 1959.
Source of data: Courtesy of Salomon Brothers Inc.

tion with sign ignored) of the same yields from month to month. At any given time short-term money may be cheap or dear. But the market believes it will not always be this way; tight credit periods tend to be followed by loose money periods, and conversely. And such fluctuations tend to be averaged out more and more in yields on progressively longer securities. This phenomenon leads to a common analogy of the yield curve with a person's waving arm: The arm is anchored to the shoulder (the long-maturity end), and the hand (short-term securities) moves up and down most as the arm is waved.

It is useful to formulate the pure expectations hypothesis algebraically, and over the years a somewhat standard notation has evolved for doing this. Let $_tR_n$ be the actual, observable yield on a security, with the prescript denoting the time at which it is observed and the postscript indicating term to maturity. In terms of our simple example, we have for the one-year security $_0R_1 = 6$ percent, and for the two-year security after adjustment, $_0R_2 = 7$ percent, where 0 means "now." These are frequently called *spot* rates. We also need something to represent unobservable but anticipated future yields; $_tr_{n,t}$ is used for this purpose, with the prescript representing the time at which the rate goes into effect, the first postscript indicating the term to maturity of the securities to which it applies, and the second postscript denoting the time at which the forecast is made. For example, instead of saying that "the presently expected yield on one-year securities in one year is 8 percent," we say $_1r_{1,0} = 8$ percent. Such rates are commonly referred to as *forward* rates.

Given this notation, and acknowledging the fact of interest compounding ignored in our simple example, the proposition that long rates are an average of observable and unobservable short rates can be stated as

$$(1 + {}_tR_n) = [(1 + {}_tR_1)(1 + {}_{t+1}r_{1,0})(1 + {}_{t+2}r_{1,0}) \ldots (1 + {}_{t+n-1}r_{1,0})]^{1/n} \quad (1)$$

In terms of our example

$$(1 + {}_0R_2) = [(1 + {}_0R_1)(1 + {}_1r_{1,0})]^{1/2} \quad (1a)$$

or

$$(1.07) \cong [(1.06)(1.08)]^{1/2} \quad (1b)$$

Notice that the average on the right side of this equation is a *geometric average*, in which we take the nth root of the product of n values, as opposed to an arithmetic average, in which we divide the sum of n values by n. A geometric average is necessary because, with compounding, returns combine multiplicatively rather than additively. The product of 1.06 and 1.08 is 1.1448, implying that $1 invested for one year at 6 percent and the next at 8 percent would grow in value by 14.48 percent. Because of compounding, a yield slightly less than 7 percent earned in each of the two years would give the same appreciation. The geometric mean of 1.06 and 1.08 (that is, the square root of 1.1448) is actually 1.06995, and this is the value that belongs on the left side of equation (1b).

We can use the same notation to derive the forward rate implicit in two observed spot rates. In terms of our example

$$(1 + {}_1r_{1,0}) = (1 + {}_0R_2)^2/(1 + {}_0R_1) \quad (2a)$$

or

$$(1.08) \cong (1.07)^2/1.06 \quad (2b)$$

or more generally

$$(1 + {}_{t+m}r_{n-m,t})^{n-m} = (1 + {}_tR_n)^n/(1 + {}_tR_m)^m \tag{2}$$

Thus, if we know any two points on the yield curve, we can infer the yield that connects them. We can deduce the yield that is expected to prevail at the end of the shorter term to maturity (m) for the time interval that will be remaining (n − m) until the end of the longer term to maturity (n). For instance, if we know the yield on four-year obligations and five-year obligations, we can readily determine the implied yield on one-year obligations that is expected to prevail in four years; if we know the yield on one-year obligations and five-year obligations, we can obtain the yield expected on four-year securities in one year.

The Liquidity or Interest-Rate Risk Hypothesis. For the moment, let us set aside our knowledge of the market segmentation and pure expectations hypotheses, and let us return to our simple situation in which there is a one-year bond and a two-year bond, each of which carries a 6 percent coupon in an environment in which the rate of interest is 6 percent. (Alternatively, think of this as a market in which institutional and expectations considerations are neutral.) Now, let us suppose the interest rate instantaneously goes to 7 percent: What happens to the prices of these two securities?

As we have already seen, the two-year security will drop to 98 in price. At this price it offers a capital gain of two spread over two years, or one per year, and a coupon of six each year. If the rate of interest remains at 7 percent, then the price at the end of the first year is 99; the return in the first year is $(6 + 1)/98 \cong 7$ percent and in the second year $(6 + 1)/99 \cong 7$ percent.

What about the one-year security? We would expect its price to drop immediately to 99. At this price it is like the two-year security after one year has elapsed; it offers a capital gain of 1, which when added to the coupon of 6 represents a total return $\cong 7$ percent on the initial investment of 99.

These price declines in response to a one percentage point increase in yields are 1 percent and 2 percent of the initial prices of the one- and two-year securities, respectively. For securities of even longer term, the price decline would be ever larger. Now in reality the price decline would not increase *quite* proportionately with the term to maturity. The intuition for this nonproportionality is that the more the price drops below par the smaller is the initial investment.[3]

---

[3] For example, $(6 + 1)/99$ is actually equal to 7.07 percent, and $(6 + 6 + 2)/98$ is actually equal to 14.28 percent; a price decline to 99.07 and to 98.25 are all that are necessary to give total returns of 7 percent and 14 percent respectively:

$$(6 + 100 - 99.07)/99.07 = (6 + .93)/99.07 = 7 \text{ percent}$$

$$(6 + 6 + 100 - 98.25)/98.25 = (12 + 1.75)/98.25 = 14 \text{ percent}$$

Exhibit 4
Price of a 12 Percent Coupon Bond of Various Maturities at Yields of 10 Percent and 14 Percent

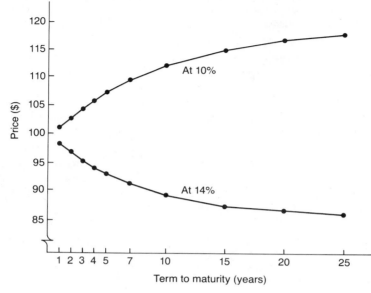

Exhibit 4 plots the actual prices at which a 12 percent coupon security must sell to yield 14 percent to maturity when it has a term to maturity of one, two, . . . twenty years. The necessary price decline does increase with maturity, but at a decreasing rate. Exhibit 4 also shows the prices needed for such securities to yield only 10 percent; compared with par, these represent increases in prices that rise with maturity but at a decreasing rate.

This price change/yield change relationship is purely mechanical in nature; it follows from the mathematics of bond price calculations. Therefore, if all yields fluctuated by the same amount, then long bonds should fluctuate more in price than short bonds. But we have already established that short-term yields fluctuate more than long-term yields; this was the message of Exhibit 3. Which of these influences is more important in terms of price fluctuation? That is, do short-term bonds actually vary more or less in price than long-term bonds? The answer, which can only be obtained by observation, turns out to be that longer term bonds have greater price volatility. Exhibit 3 also shows mean absolute deviations of monthly bond price changes derived from yield changes for 1950 to the present. Here it is evident that bond price volatility increases with maturity, at first at a very rapid rate but then at a much lower rate as bond maturity lengthens.

This observation suggests a third reason investors might not be indifferent among bonds of different maturities. If most investors are adverse to fluctuations in the value of their portfolios, they will have some preference for short-term securities simply because their values are more stable. Therefore, in order to induce them to hold progressively longer term bonds, they must expect to receive higher returns. Such a return increment is usually referred to as a *liquidity premium* on the basis that shorter term securities are more money-like, and this is a premium for bearing illiquidity. For obvious reasons it might better be described as an interest-rate risk premium. But regardless of what it is called, its implication is the same: other considerations aside, longer term bonds should offer higher yields.[4]

Because actual bond price fluctuations increase with maturity but at a decreasing rate, interest-rate risk premia should also increase with maturity but at a decreasing rate. Therefore, yields that would otherwise be equal regardless of maturity should increase but at a decreasing rate as maturity lengthens. In fact, individuals who are familiar with yield curves and yield curve analysis will recognize that the general shape of the classical textbook yield curve resembles the price volatility curve in Exhibit 3, always rising with increasing maturity but more and more gradually, so that the slope of the curve is very steep at short maturities but very gentle—almost unobservable—at long maturities.

A formal statement of the liquidity premium or interest-rate risk premium hypothesis is that the market adds increments L_t to yields that would otherwise exist, with

$$0 < L_t < L_{t+1} < L_{t+2} < \ldots < L_{t+n}$$

implying these liquidity premia are positive and rise with longer maturities. Moreover,

$$(L_{t+1} - L_t) > (L_{t+2} - L_{t+1}) > \ldots (L_{t+n} - L_{t+n-1})$$

That is, the liquidity premia increase at a decreasing rate with lengthening maturities.

An Eclectic Yield Curve Hypothesis. The market segmentation, unbiased expectations, and interest-rate risk premium hypotheses are not mutually exclusive ways of thinking about interest rates. It is probably fair to say the majority of those who watch the money and credit markets believe that at least two and possibly all three of these

---

[4] This is the conventional wisdom. A large class of fixed income investors carry their securities at cost rather than market value and are possibly more concerned about reinvestment-rate risk than price risk—life insurors being a prime example. Such investors might well *prefer* long-term securities. These issues expose them to less risk of being forced to reinvest a large portion of their portfolio when yields are low. If such long-term investors dominated the markets, then there might actually be negative liquidity premia.

influences are present in the term structure from time to time. For example, one might be of the opinion that relative yields are usually determined by supply/demand conditions in the short- and long-term securities markets with some tendency toward lower rates in the short end, yet still feel that at some particular time the expectation of sharply lower rates was also influencing the term structure.

One composite hypothesis, the *biased expectation hypothesis*, is particularly prominent. According to this theory, the yield curve reflects future interest-rate expectations of the moment and also persistent (but not necessarily stable) liquidity premia. Formally,[5]

$$(1 + {}_tR_n) = [(1 + {}_tR_1)(1 + {}_{t+1}r_{1,0} + L_2)(1 + {}_{t+2}r_{1,0} + L_3) \ldots$$
$$(1 + {}_{t+n-1}r_{1,0} + L_n)]^{1/n}$$
$$(3)$$

This hypothesis is liked by many because, in addition to incorporating two elements they find intuitively appealing, it is readily able to account for "humped" yield curves, which can be observed in Exhibit 1—situations in which rates initially rise with lengthening maturity but then reach a peak and decline at the longer maturities. This pattern can be rationalized in the following way. Interest rates are expected to decline moderately, and this alone should produce a yield curve that declines over its entire length. However, liquidity premia, which have their largest marginal effects at short maturities, overpower this tendency toward a downward-sweeping yield curve at the short end. Toward the middle of the yield curve and at its long end, the expectations component is dominant. Exhibit 5 summarizes these effects.

Classical Yield Curves and Their Rationale

The yield curve in Exhibit 5 can be explained in other ways, and in fact almost any yield curve can be accounted for in a variety of ways. Exhibit 6 portrays four different yield curves that might be described as "classics" in the sense that they are prototypes of the forms into which all yield curves are supposed to fall. It is important to observe

---

[5] This presentation follows the conventional practice of showing the liquidity premium as a series of constants that are added to the basic rates. However, many believe that such liquidity premia are more likely to be multiplicative in form, so that, for example, one term might be

$$(1 + {}_{t+1}r_{1,0})(1 + L_2)$$

The additive model implies that the incremental return for increased interest-rate risk is the same absolute amount regardless of the level of rates, whereas the multiplicative model is a constant relative to the level of rates. If L_2 is .005, we might have

additive: $1.04 + .005 = 1.045; 1.08 = .005 = 1.085$
multiplicative: $(1.04)(1.005) = 1.0452; (1.08)(1.005) = 1.0854$

Exhibit 5
Expectations and Liquidity Effects in the Yield Curve

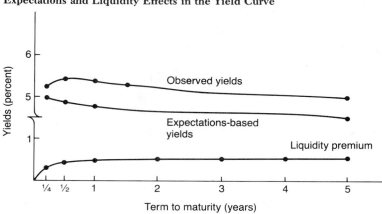

the level at which these yield curves are plotted as well as their shape, for the level of rates plays an important role in the usual stories that are told to explain the shapes.

The four forms are these:

1. *Normal.* Interest rates are at moderate levels. Yields rise continuously with increasing maturity but with a gentle and continuously decreasing slope.
2. *Rising.* Interest rates are "low" by historical or other standards. Yields rise substantially with increasing term to maturity, but possibly with some reduction in the rate of increase at longer maturities.
3. *Falling.* Yields are extremely high by historical standards and decline over the entire maturity range of the yield curve.
4. *Humped.* This is the curve in Exhibit 5. Interest rates are high by historical standards. The yield curve at first rises with increasing maturity but then peaks and declines at the longer maturities.

Exhibit 6 also summarizes the stories that can be told under a variety of theories of the term structure to account for these shapes. Notice that in several cases there is no adequate stand-alone explanation for the yield curve shape under the liquidity premium hypothesis. This is consistent with the earlier discussion to the effect that the liquidity premium hypothesis is most often regarded as an "add on" rather than a "free standing" hypothesis.

Empirical Evidence on the Term Structure Hypotheses

In principle, it should be possible to look at the numerical record and establish which of these hypotheses is most nearly valid. But in practice such validation is extremely difficult for a variety of reasons.

Exhibit 6
Alternative Classical Yield Curves and Their Explanations

Hypothetical	Actual	Market Segmentation	Unbiased Expectations	Liquidity Premium	Biased Expectations
Normal	September 1980	Banks have some excess investable funds versus insurance companies	Yields are expected to rise moderately	Liquidity premia increase with maturity at a decreasing rate	Yields are expected to remain unchanged; liquidity premia increase with maturity at a decreasing rate
Rising	June 1980	Banks have substantial excess investment funds versus insurance companies	Yields are expected to rise substantially	Liquidity premia increase with maturity	Yields are expected to rise substantially; liquidity premia increase with maturity at a decreasing rate
Falling	February 1981	Banks are in an extreme investable funds deficit compared to insurance companies	Yields are expected to fall substantially	None	Yields are expected to fall substantially; liquidity premia increase with maturity at a decreasing rate
Humped	March 1980	Banks and insurance companies have equivalent investable funds positions; there is a void between their maturity preferences	Yields are expected to first rise and then fall	None	Yields are expected to fall; liquidity premia increase with maturity at a decreasing rate

Hypothetical curves: Normal, Rising, Falling, Humped (Yield vs. Maturity)

Actual curves (Yield percent vs. Maturity in years):
- September 1980: Yield axis 8, 9, 10, 11; Maturity 1 2 3 4 years
- June 1980: Yield axis 8, 9, 10, 11; Maturity 1 2 3 4 years
- February 1981: Yield axis 12, 13, 14, 15; Maturity 1 2 3 4 years
- March 1980: Yield axis 12, 13, 14, 15; Maturity 1 2 3 4 years

First, market consensus expectations, which are needed to verify the expectations hypothesis, are not directly observable. We can actually observe future interest rates that are supposed to be predicted by forward rates embedded in the term structure, but there is nothing in the expectations hypothesis that guarantees that these forward rate predictions will come to pass.

Second, the two theories most at odds conceptually—the segmented markets and expectation hypothesis—often are both consistent with observed yield curves. For example, when the yield curve is low by historical standards but steeply upward sloping, the implication according to the expectations hypothesis is that yields are expected to rise. But periods when interest rates are low also tend to be periods of slack economic activity and low short-term loan demand, so banks are in a surplus funds position compared with life insurance companies. These conditions should produce upward-sloping yield curves according to the segmentation hypothesis. In the same manner, high but downward-sloped yield curves imply decreasing interest rates in the future. But periods when interest rates are high also tend to be characterized by strong economic activity and high demand for the type of loans that banks tend to make, so the price of short-term money should exceed the price of long-term money supplied by insurance companies. Unfortunately, if two theories can account for observed yield patterns equally well, then it is impossible to differentiate between them.

Third, and as we shall see, measurement of liquidity premia is extremely difficult in an uncertain world.

Nevertheless, it is useful to look at some of the evidence that has been brought forth on the various hypotheses.[6] This evidence does permit some general, tentative conclusions. And in a number of instances the form of the evidence should be of interest to fixed income investors in its own right.

Interest-Rate Risk or Liquidity Premia   This is the hypothesis on which the evidence is the most unequivocal, and it tends to add up to a strong case for the presence of interest-rate risk or liquidity premia.

Possibly the most obvious evidence is the behavior of yields over long periods of time. For example, analysis of the term structure numbers underlying Exhibit 1 reveals that yields on securities of the shortest term have tended to be below those on longer term securities the majority of the time over the past three decades as shown by the following tabulation:

---

[6] A standard reference source on the term structure that reviews evidence bearing on the alternative theories in much more detail is James C. Van Horne's *Financial Market Rates and Flows* (Englewood Cliffs, N.J.: Prentice-Hall, 1978), especially Chapters 4 and 5.

	Number (Proportion) of Times —	
	Short Rate ≤ Long Rate	Short Rate > Long Rate
3-month Treasury bills versus 6-month Treasury bills*	256 (.959)	11 (.041)
3-month Treasury bills versus 1-year bonds........................	349 (.931)	26 (.069)
6-month Treasury bills versus 1-year bonds*......................	223 (.835)	44 (.165)

* Six-month Treasury bill series commenced January 1959.

It is also useful to look at long-run total returns, which consider changes in value as well as coupon income on longer term securities. The well-known Ibbotson-Sinquefield total return series, which looked at monthly rates of return from the beginning of 1926 through the end of 1978, reveals an average annual rate of return on short-term bills (maturities of just over one month) of 2.5 percent per annum versus 3.4 percent per annum on long-term government bonds (maturities of 20 years).[7] This result obtains despite the general upward trend of interest rates over these years, which tended to produce capital losses on average from month to month in the long-term bond series.

The Expectations Hypotheses It is evident that if the liquidity premium hypothesis is valid, then the pure or unbiased expectations hypothesis cannot be. What about the biased expectations hypothesis, in which the term structure reflects expected future interest rates as well as liquidity premia?

A popular form of test of the biased expectations hypothesis examines the pattern of revisions in yield curves with the passage of time. Such tests accept the validity of the so-called error-learning model of the formation of economic expectations. The essence of this model is that expectations of the more distant future will be revised when expectations of the more immediate future are found to be in error, and they will be revised in the same direction. As an example of this in the present context, suppose the market routinely forecasts some rate both three months into the future and six months into the future. If after three months have elapsed the actual rate is below the forecast

---

[7] Roger G. Ibbotson and Rex A. Sinquefield, "Stocks, Bonds, Bills, and Inflation: Updates," *Financial Analysts Journal*, July–August 1979, pp. 40–44. It should be noted, however, that such higher returns for longer term securities do not always show up in the short run, even when the short run is quite long. For example, over the January 1950–March 1981 period, three-month bills had higher actual holding period returns than long-term Treasury bonds.

made three months previously, then the market might be expected to revise downward its forecast that was formerly six months into the future but is now only three months out. If this indeed seems to happen, one is justified in concluding that (1) the error-learning model captures the way in which forecasts are made, and (2) expectations of future rates are embedded in present rates.

This test was devised by David Meiselman, and his work on the subject is a standard reference.[8] However, for our purposes it may be more useful to look at a recent study utilizing a variant of this technique by Richard Worley and Stanley Diller.[9]

Their results are summarized in Exhibit 7. The upper panel of this figure shows the errors in forecasts of three-month rates made three months earlier—that is, the actual three-month rate is subtracted from the three-month rate that was implied by the term structure three months earlier (or $_tr_{3,t-3} - {}_tR_3$). Notice that an inverted scale is used, so large underestimates of actual rates are near the top of the plot, and large overestimates are near the bottom. The lower panel shows the coincident changes in forecasted future rates—the difference in three-month rates expected in three months and the same three-month rate that was implied by the term structure three months previously (or $_{t+3}r_{3,t} - {}_{t+3}r_{3,t-3}$). These values are plotted in the usual way, so for example, a positive number means that the forecast for rates three months out has been raised. The plotted values are based on monthly observations for 1966 through most of 1976.

It is evident from the figure that there is close correlation between forecast errors and revisions in the forecasts. Underestimates in prior forecasts are associated with increases in forecasts of the future, and conversely for overestimates. Although such association does not prove that the term structure is based on expectations of future interest rates, it is consistent with the expectations hypothesis.

The Market Segmentation Hypothesis. Empirical evidence hearing on this hypothesis is limited. One of the more relevant studies, by Echols and Elliott,[10] was part of a larger study of term structure influences. These authors worked with monthly data from the beginning of 1964 through the end of 1971. They first made estimates of forward rates from a model that considers macroeconomic variables—changes in the money supply, the net budgetary position, net export deficit or surplus, and the like. These estimates were refined to include the

---

[8] David Meiselman, *The Term Structure of Interest Rates* (Englewood Cliffs, N.J.: Prentice-Hall, 1962).

[9] Richard B. Worley and Stanley Diller, "Interpreting the Yield Curve," *Financial Analysts Journal* (November–December 1976), pp. 37–45.

[10] Michael E. Echols and Jon Walter Elliott, "Rational Expectations in a Disequilibrium Model of the Term Structure," *American Economic Review* (March 1976), pp. 28–74.

Exhibit 7

Worley-Diller Analysis of the Influence of Forecast Errors on Forecast Changes

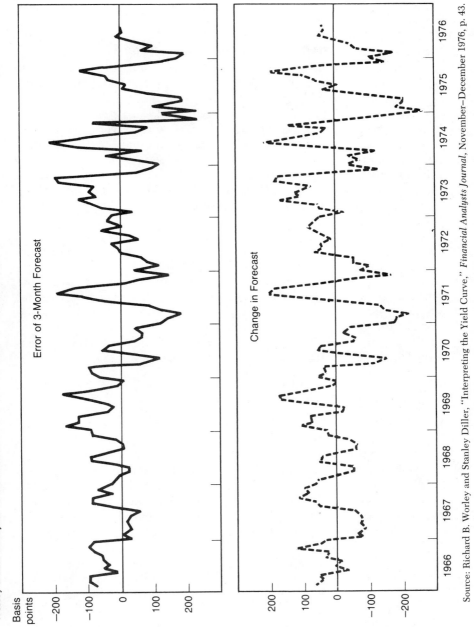

Basis points

Error of 3-Month Forecast

Change in Forecast

Source: Richard B. Worley and Stanley Diller, "Interpreting the Yield Curve," *Financial Analysts Journal*, November–December 1976, p. 43.

measured effects of a liquidity premium. An effort was then made to explain differences in these estimated forward rates and forward rates that were actually observed by use of a supply and a demand variable. The supply measure was the ratio of the quantity of government bonds outstanding with 5 or fewer years to maturity to the quantity of bonds with 10+ years to maturity. The demand measure was the ratio of the stock of bank funds invested in U.S. government securities to the stock of insurance company funds invested in this way. Echols and Elliott found that an increase in bank holdings relative to insurance company holdings did tend to push down forward rates, especially at shorter maturities. This result is as predicted by the segmentation hypothesis. Increases in the relative supply of short-term bonds also tended to raise forward rates, particularly in shorter maturities, but this effect was not statistically significant. The authors considered these results to be consistent with the operations of preferred maturity habitats for the institutions.

The same variables were also used in an effort to explain actual yield spreads, the excess of 12-year bond yields over the three-month Treasury bill rate. In this investigation the spread was negatively related to relative institutional participation—more bank funds in government securities compared with insurance company funds meant *smaller* spreads. Moreover, here they found that an increase in the relative quantity of short-term bonds outstanding actually tended to *raise* the spread. Both these results are not consistent with the segmented market hypothesis as it is usually conceived.

A Related Issue—Forecasting Efficiency

Recall that one of the implications of the expectations hypothesis is that forecasts of future interest rates are imbedded in the present term structure of interest rates, or to state the same proposition another way, the term structure prices bonds in such a way that expected holding period returns across maturities are equal (interest-rate risk premium and market segmentation considerations aside). If the expectations considered tend to dominate the slope of the yield curve *and* if the market in the aggregate possesses adequate forecasting ability, then we should find that the term structure actually does forecast future interest rates with some degree of accuracy and that actual holding period returns across maturities do tend toward equality.

If the term structure doesn't forecast future rates well or holding period returns show little similarity across maturities, we cannot conclude unequivocally that the expectations hypothesis as a theory of the term structure is not valid. Interest-rate forecasting is an activity at which it is extremely easy to be very wrong! And it may simply be that the market forecast is consistently wrong. Nevertheless, evidence bearing on the forecasting ability of the term structures is extremely important to professional investors. For if the term structure displays little forecasting ability—either because it doesn't incorporate forecasts or because those forecasts aren't very good—then the investor can come out ahead on average by simply investing in maturities from the highest yielding portion of the yield curve.[11]

Many of the early investigations of the expectations hypothesis were actually joint tests of this hypothesis and the forecasting capabilities of the market. In one of the classic papers on the term structure, J. M. Culbertson examined holding weekly period returns on Treasury bills (the longest outstanding) and Treasury bonds (Culbertson used a bond of approximately 19 years' maturity) for 1953. Culbertson detected little evidence of parallel movements in holding period returns, and as a result indicated, "The conclusion to which we seem forced to turn is that speculative activity [i.e., activity that should equate holding period returns], dominant though it can be in very short-run movements, does not determine the broad course of interest rates or of interest-rate relationships."[12]

In contrast, Jacob Michaelson looked at weekly holding period returns on U.S. government securities with maturities ranging from one week to 10+-years over the 1951–1962 period.[13] He first observed a tendency for average realized total returns to increase with terms to maturity of from 1 to 13 weeks over this overall period and in a number of subperiods typified by cyclical upturns or downturns in interest rates. Since these results conformed closely to what one would expect in a market dominated by the biased expectation theory, he concluded that the realized returns on short-term securities conformed closely to anticipations. He then looked at the correlation between total returns on the 13-week and the longer maturity series. The correlations obtained in this way were uniformly positive. On this basis he concluded that the expectations hypothesis was supported; his results also suggest that on average the market did possess some interest-rate forecasting ability.

---

[11] If this is so, then the fixed income securities markets are not efficient in the "no easy money" or "no free lunch" sense, as excess profits can be obtained by the use of readily available strategies without the investor bearing extra risk. Note also that a frequent test of efficiency in the stock market—independence of price changes over time—is not appropriate in the fixed income markets. If fixed income security prices or yields do not display some dependence over time, then excess returns are possible provided the yield curve is not horizontal. Apparently there is confusion regarding this point, for authors occasionally describe the bond market as "efficient" when they are unable to disclose yield dependencies.

[12] J. M. Culbertson, "The Term Structure of Interest Rates," *Quarterly Journal of Economics*, November 1957, pp. 485–517. This particular statement appears on pages 508 and 509.

[13] Jacob B. Michaelson, "The Term Structure of Interest Rates and Holding Period Yields in Government Securities," *Journal of Finance*, September 1965, pp. 444–63.

Another implication of the expectations hypothesis is that long-term yields should lead short-term yields in time. This relationship follows from the assumption that long-term rates have expected future short-term rates embedded in them along with a belief that the market should have some meaningful interest-rate forecasting ability. This relationship was utilized by Frederick R. Macaulay in a test reported in his landmark volume *Some Theoretical Problems Suggested by the Movement of Interest Rates, Bond Yields, and Stock Prices in the United States Since 1856.*[14] Macaulay examined the relationship for the 1890–1913 period between yields on call money and on 90-day loans and found some evidence of the latter yield series leading the former. More recently, Thomas Sargent utilized the technique of cross-spectral analysis (in essence, a technique for extracting all possible lead and lag relationships from two time series) to examine interrelationships between monthly yield series for the 1951–1960 period.[15] He also found a tendency for longer rates to lead the shorter ones.

The proposition that the market cannot forecast yield changes has recently been propounded with considerable vigor by Herbert Ayres and John Barry. As they express it, "For every real bond, the expected rate of change of yield to maturity is zero, hence the expected total rate of return for any real bond is its present yield to maturity."[16]

To test this proposition, they use the mathematical expression

$$\Delta y(m) = \Delta y(\infty) + \Delta S(m - \infty) \tag{4}$$

which says that the changes in the yield of a security with a maturity of m, $\Delta y(m)$, is equal to the change in the yield on a perpetual bond, $\Delta y(\infty)$, plus the change in the spread between yields on the security with a maturity of m and the perpetuity, $\Delta S(m - \infty)$. They then show the following:

1. On monthly observations over the 1966–1974 period, the mean change in long-term bond yields (a proxy for the perpetuity) was not statistically different from zero. In other words, and despite the considerable drift upward in yield that occurred over those years, the monthly change in long-term yields could not have been reliably predicted to be positive.

2. Over the same period, the average change in spread between yields on long bonds and bonds of shorter maturities was not significantly different from zero, meaning it could not be reliably predicted to be other than zero.

---

[14] National Bureau of Economic Research, New York, 1938.

[15] Thomas J. Sargent, "Interest Rates in the Nineteen Fifties," *Review of Economics and Statistics*, May 1968, pp. 164–72.

[16] Herbert F. Ayres and John Y. Barry, "The Equilibrium Yield Curve for Government Securities," *Financial Analysts Journal*, May–June 1979, pp. 31–39. The quotation appears on page 34.

3. Changes in the perpetuity rate and changes in the spread were uncorrelated. That is, there was no association between $\Delta y(\infty)$ and $\Delta S(m - \infty)$. This is the finding that is most at odds with the expectation hypothesis, for the hypothesis implies that there should be positive correlation between the two—that is, they should change in the same direction. For example, if short yields are initially above long yields, the yield spread $S(m - \infty)$ is positive, and the yield curve is downward sweeping; then the long yield should decline, and as it does the yield spread should become negative $[y(m) < y(\infty)]$ as the yield curve returns to its normal shape. As evidence on this point, Ayres and Barry examine changes in the five-year rate and changes in the spread on one- and five-year yields, in Exhibit 8. The data, which are standardized, display no statistically meaningful correlation.

Exhibit 8
Ayres and Barry's Correlations between Changes in Yield Spreads and Long Yields, January 1956–August 1978

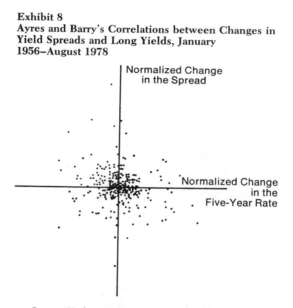

Source: Herbert F. Ayres and John Y. Barry, "The Equilibrium Yield Curve for Government Securities," *Financial Analysts Journal,* May–June 1979, p. 35.

Actually, the situation may not be quite so bleak as Ayres and Barry suggest. The relationship between $\Delta y(\infty)$ and $\Delta S(m - \infty)$ is only one of many that might be examined. Consider these additional comparisons:

$$\Delta S(m - \infty) \quad \text{and} \quad \Delta y(m)$$

This is similar to the Ayres-Barry comparison, but looks at changes in spreads and changes in short rates. The expectations hypothesis again predicts a positive correlation.

$$S(m - \infty)_t \quad \text{and} \quad \Delta y(\infty)_{t+1}$$

This comparison is actually more in the spirit of the expectations hypothesis. The expectation is for a negative correlation between an observed spread and the change in the long rate in the succeeding period. For example, if the spread is large and positive, with short rates above long rates, the implication is that long rates will decline. If the spread is large but negative, short rates are well below long rates, and long rates are expected to increase.

$$S(m - \infty)_t \quad \text{and} \quad \Delta y(m)_{t+1}$$

This is a restatement of the preceding comparison but in this statement an effort is made to predict short rates. For similar reasons the correlations should be negative.

$$S(m - \infty)_t \quad \text{and} \quad \Delta S(m - \infty)_{t+1}$$

This comparison is between observed spreads and changes in spreads in the succeeding period. The expectations hypothesis predicts a negative relationship—a downward-sloped yield curve $[S(m - \infty) > 0]$ should become less downward sloped, whereas a strongly upward-sloped yield curve $[S(m - \infty) < 0]$ should become less upward sloped.

Exhibit 9 shows the simple correlation coefficients for each of these comparisons for intervals of 1, 3, 6, and 12 months over the same January 1956–August 1978 period examined by Ayres and Barry. The correlation for the comparison suggested by Ayres and Barry is the first value shown in Exhibit 9, and the result is quite consistent with what they report. However, as the interval is lengthened, this correlation becomes significant in the proper positive direction. The other correlations are also generally significant and in the direction the expectations hypothesis predicts, except for some of the one-month interval comparisons and the comparisons that attempt to predict changes in the long rate from the preceeding month's yield spread.[17]

These results, therefore, are consistent with a market that has some forecasting ability and that incorporates these forecasts into the term structure. Thus they support many of the more traditional tests of the expectations hypothesis. But there is a substantial difference between statistical tests and economic tests. It may well be, as Ayres and Barry suggest, that *for practical purposes* one can proceed as though the best guess regarding the holding period return from a bond of any maturity is its yield to maturity. Obviously much more testing is

---

[17] For holding period intervals in excess of one month, the successive observations are not independent; for example, 11 months in a given 12-month period overlap with the preceeding period. Such nonindependence can make overlap correlation coefficients of the sort contained in Exhibit 9 and tests of other significance misleading. However, this analysis has been repeated with only nonoverlapping holding periods (e.g., January through December periods only) with similar results.

Exhibit 9
Selected Correlations between Yield Changes, Yield Spreads, and Changes in Yield Spreads, January 1956–August 1978

$\Delta y(\infty)$ versus $\Delta S(m - \infty)$:

Monthly	0.097
Quarterly	0.460*
Semiannually	0.547*
Annually	0.512*

$\Delta S(m - \infty)$ versus $\Delta y(m)$:

Monthly	0.698*
Quarterly	0.805*
Semiannually	0.839*
Annually	0.834*

$S(m - \infty)_t$ versus $\Delta y(\infty)_{t+1}$:

Monthly	.019
Quarterly	−0.044
Semiannually	−0.023
Annually	−0.028

$S(m - \infty)_t$ versus $\Delta y(m)_{t+1}$:

Monthly	0.125*
Quarterly	−0.191*
Semiannually	−0.238*
Annually	−0.281*

$S(m - \infty)_t$ versus $\Delta S(m - \infty)_{t+1}$:

Monthly	−0.222*
Quarterly	−0.324*
Semiannually	−0.460*
Annually	−0.594*

* Relationship is statistically significant at 5 percent level.

needed in this area, particularly testing that is more directly oriented toward the economic rewards of different investment strategies based on the predictive properties of the term structure.

MEASURING THE TERM STRUCTURE

For many investors an occasional rundown on yields on U.S. Treasury securities as published by *The Wall Street Journal* and other periodicals will be sufficient to keep an eye on the term structure. Others will want to be more formal in their analysis. In this section we review some of the ways for monitoring the term structures.

Published Yield Curves

Possibly the most frequently utilized representatives of the term structure are the yield curves published each month in the *U.S. Treasury Bulletin*; the yield curve in Exhibit 2 comes from this source. These curves are visually fitted to month-end yields to maturity on

U.S. government securities by Treasury analysts; that is, they are drawn in free hand or by eye without resort to statistical curve-fitting techniques. In fitting these curves only the yields on approximately current coupon bonds with no special features (e.g., flower bonds) are considered. Yields on low-coupon bonds are believed to be downward-biased representations of market yields because of the favorable taxation awarded to the capital gains component of their returns, and flower bond yields are also downward biased due to their favored treatment in payment of federal estate taxes.

The *Treasury Bulletin* yield curves provide an excellent means for keeping abreast of the general behavior of the term structure. However, for more detailed analytical purposes, they are not entirely satisfactory for two reasons. First, in the final analysis they are judgmentally derived, and there is always uncertainty about judgmental members—it is unlikely, for example, that any two analysts would usually fit exactly the same yield curve. Second, another problem arises when explicit numerical yield numbers are needed. Such numbers must be read off the yield curve, and this is an activity of uncertain precision. It is unlikely that these are serious problems, and in fact they are present to a greater or lesser degree in almost all yield curve analysis. But it has become more common to work with constructed or synthetic yield/maturity data series and to statistically fit yield curves in analyzing the term structure.

Sources of Yield/Maturity Series

A standard source of yields on U.S. government securities by maturity is a series published by Salomon Brothers Inc. The Salomon Brothers yields have been employed to construct many of the exhibits in this chapter. This series currently shows yields at 11 maturity points ranging from three months to 30 years in numerical form. It is published weekly in Salomon Brothers' *Bond Market Roundup*, and historical first-of-month (midmonth prior to 1959) yields are reported in Salomon Brothers' *An Analytical Record of Yields and Yield Spreads*. The Salomon Brothers data is prepared in much the same way as the *Treasury Bulletin* yield curves; that is, yield curves are fitted to actual bond yield data, following the yields of higher coupon bonds when a choice exists, and then the yields are read off at each maturity point. Thus the primary advantages of the Salomon Brothers series are its timeliness and that fact that the curve reading has already been done for the analyst.

In recent years the *Federal Reserve Bulletin* has contained a constant maturity yield series for U.S. government bonds and notes ranging from 1 to 30 years to maturity. This series is described as "yields on the more actively traded issues adjusted to constant maturities by the U.S. Treasury, based on daily closing bid prices." The yields are reported by calendar weeks ending on Wednesdays, by months, and by years; the weekly data represent averages of the undisclosed daily values, monthly data are averages of the weeks, and so on. Therefore, the *FRB Bulletin* numbers are not directly comparable with the Salomon Brothers data. Exhibit 10 contains the Salomon Brothers data for

Exhibit 10
A Comparison of Salomon Brothers and Federal Reserve Bulletin Yield Data

Term to Maturity	Yields, Salomon Brothers, January 2, 1981	Yields, Federal Reserve Bulletin, Week Ending January 2, 1981
3 months	15.02%	15.05%*
6 months	14.96	14.96*
1 year	13.97	13.86
2 years	13.01	13.00
3 years	12.65	12.81
4 years	12.68	—
5 years	12.57	12.54
7 years	12.47	12.43
10 years	12.43	12.36
20 years	11.96	12.05
30 years	11.94	11.95

* Treasury bill discounts converted to coupon-equivalent yields.
Source: Data courtesy of Salomon Brothers Inc and from the *Federal Reserve Bulletin,* February 1981.

January 2, 1981 (the first was a holiday) and the *FRB* data for the week ending January 2, 1981. Although the two series are not identical, they are quite similar, especially in the yield curve patterns they display.

Fitting Yield Curves

These yield series are probably more useful for investment decision making than the *Treasury Bulletin* yield curves because they have been reduced to numerical terms by someone who is experienced in doing this. The numbers themselves can be examined for yield patterns, or they can be plotted to obtain yield curves such as those in Exhibit 1, which are of the "connect the dots" variety.

Such curves are described as discontinuous. This means that they change shape at each measurement point and can do so abruptly. However, one would expect yield transitions from one maturity to another to be fairly smooth— that is, to be characterized by a continuous curve. In addition, one is often interested in maturities that lie away from measurement points. Such intermediate yields could be estimated by linear interpolation, but this is clumsy and at odds with the notion of yield curves that change shape continuously. For those

reasons it is frequently desirable to fit mathematical curves to the
yield points.

A number of models have been proposed for fitting such curves. All
use the method of least squares to actually fit the curve. Where they
differ is in the form of the equation that is fitted and its number of
terms. With too few terms the estimated yield curve is excessively
smooth—for example, with one term it would simply be a straight line.
Too many terms will "overfit" the line—with as many terms as maturity points, the line will go precisely through each point.

One model that has been proved particularly effective for such
applications is due to Stephen Bradley and Dwight Crane.[18] The
Bradley-Crane model has the form

$$\ln(1 + R_M) = a + b_1(M) + b_2\ln(M) + e \qquad (5)$$

That is, values equal to the natural logarithm of one plus the observed
yields for term to maturity of length M are regressed on two variables,
the term to maturity and the natural log of the term to maturity. The
last term represents the unexplained yield variation. Fitting this
model is well within the capability of the typical scientific calculator.
Once the estimated values of a, b_1, and b_2 are obtained, specific maturities of interest can be substituted to obtain estimated yields at these
maturity points. Exhibit 11 shows the Salomon Brothers yield series

Exhibit 11
**Bradley-Crane Yield Curve Fitted to Salomon Brothers Yield Data for January 2,
1981**

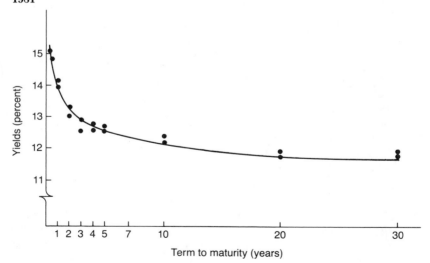

Source of data: courtesy of Salomon Brothers Inc; line estimated by author.

---

[18] Stephen P. Bradley and Dwight B. Crane, "Management of Commercial Bank
Government Security Portfolios: An Optimization Approach under Uncertainty," *Journal of Bank Research*, Spring 1973, pp. 18–30.

as of January 2, 1981, along with a yield curve fitted by this method. It can be observed that the fit is not particularly good in the shorter maturities. Fortunately, Treasury bill yields are available in weekly maturity intervals out to approximately one year, so they can readily be used instead for many purposes.

Occasionally one wishes to fit yield curves directly to yield data for individual bonds rather than to homogenized yield series. This might be desirable as a means of avoiding possible distortions created in the process of arriving at the synthetic yield series. It might also be motivated by a particular interest in individual bonds—for example, when looking for arbitrage opportunities between underpriced or overpriced bonds by examining their yields in comparison with a fitted yield curve. A model for fitting such yield curves has been proposed by Elliot and Echols.[19]

The Elliot-Echols model has the form:

$$\ln(1 + R_i) = a + b_1(1/M_i) + b_2(M_i) + b_3(C_i) + e_i \qquad (6)$$

where R_i, M_i, and C_i are the yield to maturity, term to maturity, and coupon rate of the ith bond.

Notice that yield and maturity are related in somewhat different ways than in the Bradley-Crane model. This representation also differs by the inclusion of the individual bond's coupons. As was noted previously, low-coupon bonds tend to have yields that are subnormal for their term to maturity, presumably because of the favored tax treatment of their built-in capital gain. The coupon term adjusts for this effect.

Elliott and Echols suggested that in obtaining yield curves from this model the coupon term should be set equal to zero so as to avoid confounding coupon effects and maturity effects. The author believes that a more appropriate (if more cumbersome) procedure is to search for that coupon rate at which the coupon rate and the yield to maturity of a hypothetical bond of a given term to maturity would be the same. The resulting point on the yield curve is the estimated yield at which a current coupon bond would sell if one existed. (The Elliott-Echols method gives the estimated yield at which a zero-coupon bond would sell if one existed.) Exhibit 12 shows such a yield curve fitted to individual bond and note data for this method as of the end of March 1977. Note that because of this coupon effect there is no reason for the individual bonds to be scattered evenly around the line. Of course, a bond's actual coupon should be used in estimating its appropriate yield if the objective is to determine whether it is underpriced or overpriced.

---

[19] Michael E. Echols and Jan Walter Elliott, "A Quantitative Yield Curve Model for Estimating the Term Structure of Interest Rates," *Journal of Financial and Quantitative Analysis*, March 1976, pp. 87–114.

Exhibit 12
Elliot-Echols Yield Curve Fitted to Individual U.S. Government Bond and Note Yields, March 31, 1977

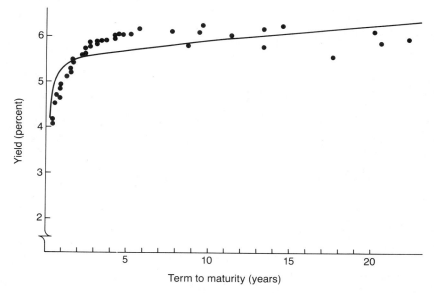

Estimating Forward Rates

Many uses of term structure or yield curve do not require the estimation of forward rates. However, there will be occasions in which it is desirable to actually extract forward rates from the yield curve or other data in order to get some idea of interest rates the market consensus in forecasting.

If suitably spaced yields on either synthetic or actual securities are available, then forward rates can be estimated directly by the use of equation (2) without the necessity for fitting yield curves. Recall that equation (2) stated

$$(1 + {}_{t+m}r^b_{n-m,t})^{n-m} = (1 + {}_tR_n)^n/(1 + {}_tR_m)^m \qquad (2)$$

Use of this formula is extremely straightforward once the data are in proper form. The equation is written on the assumption that all yields are expressed in the same units of time, per annum yields being most common. For many purposes it will be useful to measure m and n in units that have the effect of making $m - n = 1$.

A simple example may help illustrate the process and clarify this last point. On January 2, 1981, three-month and six-month coupon-equivalent Treasury bill yields as reported in *The Wall Street Journal* were 15.31 percent and 15.00 percent per annum respectively. If we use equation (2) with m and n expressed in years to estimate the three-month rate anticipated in three months, we have

$$(1 + {}_{1/4}r^b{}_{1/4,0})^{1/4} = \frac{(1.1500)^{1/2}}{(1.1531)^{1/4}} = \frac{1.0724}{1.0363} = 1.0349$$

This last value is one plus an annual rate, but is raised to the one-fourth power in accordance with it being for a quarter of a year. In order to make it apply to a whole year, we must raise it to the fourth power, or

$$[(1 + {}_{1/4}r^b{}_{1/4,0})^{1/4}]^4 = (1 + {}_{1/4}r^b{}_{1/4,0})$$

When we do we get

$$(1.0349)^4 = 1.1469, \text{ or } 14.69 \text{ percent}$$

Alternatively, we might simply express m and n in three-month periods, since we are interested in a three-month forward rate:

$$(1 + {}_{1}r^b{}_{1,0})^1 = \frac{(1.1500)^2}{(1.1531)^1} = \frac{1.3225}{1.1531} = 1.1469$$

or 14.69 percent again.

Exhibit 13 continues the estimation of three-month forward rates as of January 2, 1981. The first rate in each series is unadjusted; the second has been adjusted for liquidity premia, as will be discussed subsequently. The exhibit also shows forward rates estimated using a simplified method proposed by Worley and Diller.[20,21]

$$_{t+m}r^b{}_{n-m,t} = \frac{({}_tR_n \cdot n) - ({}_tR_m \cdot m)}{n - m} \tag{7}$$

This equation, which does not require the use of exponents or assume compounding, is quite satisfactory provided the interval n − m is not large.

Suppose suitably spaced yields are not available. Suppose, for example, we want to estimate forward rates for three-month intervals on out beyond a year in the future. This is where fitted yield curves become useful. After having estimated the appropriate coefficients, we can simply substitute in the appropriate values of m and n and use equation (5) or (6) to obtain the forward rate. For example, the Bradley-Crane model equation for January 2, 1981 (Exhibit 11), is

$$\ln(1 + R_M) = 0.129700 + 0.000425(M) - 0.008497 \ln(M)$$

If we are interested in the three-month rate one year into the future, at the beginning of January 1982, we substitute 1.0 and 1.25 (m and n, equal to 1 year and 1¼ years) in the equation, obtaining 13.8970 for R_1 and 13.6933 for $R_{1.25}$. Equation (2) gives

---

[20] Worley and Diller, "Interpreting the Yield Curve," p. 45.

[21] The values in the first four columns of Exhibit 13 are computed by reference to the actual number of days in each period because the periods are not of equal length—principally because no Treasury bill traded on January 2 matured on October 2, making it necessary to use the bill maturing October 8.

Exhibit 13
Alternative Estimates of Three-Month Forward Rates, January 2, 1981

Forward Rates for Three Months Beginning	Actual Yields, Equation (2)		Actual Yields, Equation (7)		Fitted Yields, Equation (2)	
	Unadjusted	Adjusted	Unadjusted	Adjusted	Unadjusted	Adjusted
April 2, 1981	14.69%	14.11%	14.69%	14.11%	13.88%	13.71%
July 2, 1981	13.02	12.76	13.01	12.77	13.40	13.19
October 8, 1981*	12.88	12.66	12.87	12.65	13.10	12.88
January 2, 1982					12.88	12.66
April 2, 1982					12.71	12.49
July 2, 1982					12.58	12.36
October 2, 1982					12.46	12.24
January 2, 1983					12.37	12.15
April 2, 1983					12.29	12.07
July 2, 1983					12.21	11.99
October 2, 1983					12.15	11.93

* October 2, 1981 for estimates based on fitted yields.

$$\left(_{1}r^{b}{}_{.25,0}\right)^{.25} = \frac{(1.136933)^{1.25}}{(1.138970)^{1}}$$

$$= 1.030756$$

or 12.88 percent per annum.

Exhibit 13 contains forward rates for each three-month interval beginning three months through three years into the future in addition to the forward rates for the first three of those intervals obtained earlier. The differences in the two series, which are caused by differences in data as well as method, are initially large but converge rapidly. Both sets of numbers illustrate in striking fashion the decline that was expected in interest rates during 1981 as the year began.

Liquidity Premia Adjustment

The formulas for forward rates presented in the preceding section all had a superscript b attached to the r's representing forward rates. This superscript is intended as a reminder that these are "biased" forward rates; that is, to the extent that there are liquidity premia imbedded in the term structure, then forward rates are upward-biased estimates of yields the market consensus expects in the future. For many purposes these biased forward rates are acceptable or even desirable. For example, if our interest is in monitoring the pattern of changes in expected forward rates from month to month, we need not be concerned about the liquidity premia, since they are imbedded in both the beginning and ending series and probably don't change much over such short intervals. If we are attempting to price out a bond using forward rates, we would actually *prefer* rates with imbedded liquidity premia.

This is fortunate, because entirely satisfactory liquidity premia estimates are impossible to obtain. Ideally, we could estimate liquidity premia in any of the following ways:

1. Compute differences in yields along a long-run average yield curve.
2. Compute long-run differences in average total returns on bonds of different maturities.
3. Compute long-run differences in implied forward rates and actual outcomes.

In practice none of these approaches is entirely satisfactory. The problem is that there is no reason to believe liquidity premia remain stable over long periods of time, yet for shorter periods of time it is unlikely that on average interest rates are expected to remain unchanged [which makes approach (1) unsatisfactory] or that forecasted yields actually turn out as expected [which militates against the value of approaches (2) and (3)].

Using the third approach, Worley and Diller estimated liquidity premia for the 1966–1976 period as follows:

m	$n - m$	L
3 months	3 months	58 basis points
6	3	26
9	3	22
6	6	24

where

m = time in future when rate is effective
$n - m$ = maturity of security to which rate applies
L = liquidity premium in basis points

J. Houston McCulloch has employed a variant of this approach to make liquidity premium estimates for the largely nonoverlapping period March 1951–March 1966 contained in Exhibit 14.[22] Direct comparisons with the Worley-Diller estimates are possible. For the three-month rate in three months, the estimates are dramatically different—58 basis points for Worley-Diller versus 17 basis points for McCulloch. However, premia for three-month maturities further into the future are similar—for example, 21 and 26 basis points for rates to be effective in six months, and 22 basis points for both for rates effective in nine months.

It is interesting that the incremental liquidity premia is for practical purposes zero for yields beyond about six months into the future in both series. If this property persists over time (and there is reason to believe that it should), it is good news. Even though forward rates derived from the term structures may be biased, the bias is internally consistent beyond six months or so into the future. Thus, for example, if the forward rates show 3-months money rising in price between 9 and 12 months into the future, it is likely that this reflects the market's expectation of higher future interest rates rather than effects of liquidity premia.

Exhibit 13 uses the Worley-Diller and McCulloch liquidity premia to adjust the forward rates for January 2, 1981, obtained previously.

Another Approach to Estimating the Term Structure

A problem with conventional yields to maturity and hence yield curve analysis based on such yields is that they suffer from a "coupon

---

[22] J. Houston McCulloch, "An Estimate of the Liquidity Premium," *Journal of Political Economy*, February 1975, pp. 95–119.

Exhibit 14
McCulloch Liquidity Premium Estimates, March 1951–March 1966

m \ $n-m$	0	*One Month*	*Two Months*	*Three Months*	*Six Months*	*Nine Months*	*1 Year*	*2 Years*	*3 Years*	*5 Years*	*10 Years*	*20 Years*	*30 Years*
One month	0.17	0.13	0.11	0.09	0.05	0.04	0.03	0.01	0.01	0.01	0.00	C.00	0.00
Two months	0.28	0.22	0.17	0.14	0.09	0.06	0.05	0.02	0.02	0.01	0.00	0.00	0.00
Three months	0.34	0.27	0.21	0.17	0.11	0.07	0.06	0.03	0.02	0.01	0.01	0.00	0.00
Six months	0.41	0.32	0.26	0.21	0.13	0.09	0.07	0.03	0.02	0.01	0.01	0.00	0.00
Nine months	0.32	0.34	0.27	0.22	0.13	0.09	0.07	0.04	0.02	0.01	0.01	0.00	0.00
1 year	0.43	0.34	0.27	0.22	0.14	0.09	0.07	0.04	0.02	0.01	0.01	0.00	0.00
2 years	0.43	0.34	0.27	0.22	0.14	0.09	0.07	0.04	0.02	0.01	0.01	0.00	0.00
3 years	0.43	0.34	0.27	0.22	0.14	0.09	0.07	0.04	0.02	0.01	0.01	0.00	0.00
5 years	0.43	0.34	0.27	0.22	0.14	0.09	0.07	0.04	0.02	0.01	0.01	0.00	0.00
10 years	0.43	0.34	0.27	0.22	0.14	0.09	0.07	0.04	0.02	0.01	0.01	0.00	0.00
20 years	0.43	0.34	0.27	0.22	0.14	0.09	0.07	0.04	0.02	0.01	0.01	0.00	0.00
30 years	0.43	0.34	0.27	0.22	0.14	0.09	0.07	0.04	0.02	0.01	0.01	0.00	0.00

Source: Adapted from J. Houston McCulloch, "An Estimate of the Liquidity Premium," *Journal of Political Economy*, vol. 83, no. 1 (1975), p. 113. © 1975 The University of Chicago, publisher. All rights reserved.

effect" that is independent of any tax consequences of coupons and price discounts. Because of this coupon effect, the yield to maturity on any specific bond is probably *not* equal to the market's required rate of return over the bond's term to maturity. The essence of the problem is that bonds with different coupons have different cash flow patterns that yield-to-maturity calculations do not adequately reflect. It is analogous to the difficulties that can arise in using internal rate of return in ranking projects for capital budgeting purposes.

The problem is probably best understood via an example.[23] Suppose we have two two-period bonds, Bond A with a 9 percent coupon and Bond B with a 5 percent coupon. Assume that the spot rates the market is using to price the bonds are $_0R_1 = 0.04$ and $_0R_2 = 0.09$. That is, the market presently requires 4 percent per annum on money committed for one year and 9 percent on two-year money. Then the proper prices of these bonds are

$$P_A = \frac{9}{(1.04)} + \frac{109}{(1.09)^2} = 100.397$$

$$P_B = \frac{5}{(1.04)} + \frac{105}{(1.09)^2} = 93.184$$

At these prices the bonds will each provide the one- and two-period returns the market requires. But the conventionally computed yields to maturity are 8.78 percent for Bond A and 8.87 percent for Bond B!

Now this may be an extreme example—for instance, the implied rate on one-year money in one year is 14.24 percent. Moreover, this problem does not arise with zero-coupon securities, such as Treasury bills, so it creates no difficulties for analysis of near-term forward rates. Nevertheless, the principle is valid, and there is some evidence that it can be serious in forward-rate estimation.

A way around it that has been known to academics for some years and is beginning to be applied in fixed income decision-making applications works with discount factors rather than yields.[24] Discount factors are values equal to $1/(1 + R_t)^t$; they are the factors found in the familiar present value tables.

The essence of the approach is to estimate the d coefficients in the multiple regression

$$P_{i,0} = d_1X_{i,1} + d_2X_{i,2} + \cdots + d_TX_{i,T} + e_i$$

---

[23] This example was provided to the author by James V. Jordan.

[24] Development and use of this methodology is reported in J. Houston McCulloch, "Measuring the Term Structure of Interest Rates," *Journal of Business*, January 1971, pp. 19-31; Stephen M. Schaefer, "On Measuring the Term Structure of Interest Rates," paper presented to the International Workshop on Recent Reasearch in Capital Markets, Berlin, September 1973; and Willard T. Carleton and Ian A. Cooper, "Estimation and Uses of the Term Structure of Interest Rates," *Journal of Finance*, September 1976, pp. 1067–1083. The liquidity premia estimates appearing in Exhibit 14 were estimated by McCulloch utilizing this method.

where

$$P_{i,0} = \text{the price of the } i^{th} \text{ bond at time zero}$$
$$X_{i,t} \ (t = 1, \ldots, T) = \text{the cash flows from the bond in period t}$$

In other words, prices of a number of bonds at a specific instant in time are regressed on their future coupons and maturity payments in a cross-sectional regression. The estimated values of d are discount factors, and from them yields that are free of coupon bias can be computed. For example, d_1 is an estimate of $1/(1 + R_1)$, d_2 is an estimate of $1/(1 + R_2)^2$, and so on.

Practical implementation of this approach involves dealing with some issues that are beyond the scope of this chapter, including data selection and constraints on the behavior of the d_t. However, those issues have been dealt with and largely resolved in the academic literature, and thus this method is worthy of consideration by persons contemplating serious term structure analysis.[25]

Financial Futures as a Guide to the Term Structure

The recent emergence of a viable market in interest-rate futures provides a means of observing forward interest rates that should be highly satisfactory for many purposes. There is currently an active market on the Chicago Board of Trade for Treasury bonds of 15+ years to maturity and Government National Mortgage Association mortgage pass-throughs (GNMAs) to be delivered up to 3 years in the future; futures contracts on three-month Treasury bills to be delivered as far as two years into the future trade on the International Monetary Mart. Those futures contracts trade on a price basis, but equivalent yield figures are usually provided along with price quotations. The delivery dates correspond to m, the date at which the forward rate becomes effective, and the maturities of the securities in question are the same as n − m. Thus forward rates for three-month money, money of approximately 6 to 8 years duration, and 15+ years can be read directly out of *The Wall Street Journal* or equivalent sources.[26]

---

[25] A good introduction to the implementation of this model appears in James V. Jordon, "Studies in Direct Estimation of the Term Structure," a dissertation completed at the University of North Carolina in 1980. It is unpublished, but copies are available from the author of this chapter.

[26] The life of GNMAs is not an obvious number. Conventional GNMA computations assume that all mortgages in the pool are paid down according to schedule until the 12th year of their life, at which time they are paid off entirely. Prepayment in recent years has been considerably more rapid than this. Moreover, since a mortgage is a constant paydown investment, the date of the last payment (maturity date) is much less relevant than for conventional bonds. The range of six to eight years encompasses a number of alternative measures of life estimated by Martin L. Leibowitz. These measures as well as a more general discussion of the problem appears in a memorandum entitled "Cash Flow Characteristics of Mortgage Securities," presented to the Financial Analysts Federation/Institute of Chartered Financial Analysts Symposium, Boston, 1979. It is reprinted in *CFA Readings in Financial Analysis*, 5th ed. (Charlottesville, Va.: The Institute of Chartered Finance Analysts, 1981), pp. 152–82.

Exhibit 15
Yields on Financial Futures Instruments, January 2, 1981

Delivery Month	Treasury Bills*	GNMAs	Treasury Bonds
March 1981	12.97%	12.79%	11.66
June 1981	11.85	12.66	11.52
September 1981	11.42	12.63	11.45
December 1981	11.29	12.64	11.44
March 1982	11.28	12.65	11.43
June 1982	11.09	12.66	11.42
September 1982	11.00	12.67	11.41
December 1982	11.52	12.69	11.40

* Treasury bill yields have been converted from a discount to a coupon-equivalent basis.

Such numbers as of January 2, 1981, appear in Exhibit 15. These are biased forward rates.[27] This means that the caveats that are in order for biased forward rates also apply to financial futures yields. Nevertheless, financial futures quotations provide a readily accessible means of monitoring the market's consensus of future yields and tracing changes in these consensus forecasts.

---

[27] To see this, consider the fact that the cash flows of a six-month Treasury bill can be duplicated by buying a three-month bill and a contract for delivery of another three-month bill in three months; under the latter scenario the proceeds on the maturing three month bills are used to pay for the bills delivered on the contract. Thus

$$(1 + \text{6-month bill yield})^{1/2} = (1 + \text{3-month bill yield})^{1/4}$$
$$(1 + \text{yield on three-month bill contract for delivery in three months})^{1/4}$$

If this relationship did not hold, then arbitragers would enter the market, buying the higher yielding side and shorting the lower yielding side. This relationship is the same as

$$(1 + {}_0R_{1/2})^{1/2} = (1 + {}_0R_{1/4})^{1/4}(1 + {}_{1/4}r^b{}_{1/4})^{1/4}$$

which can be written as

$$(1 + {}_{1/4}r^b{}_{1/4})^{1/4} = (1 + {}_0R_{1/2})^{1/2}(1 + {}_0R_{1/4})^{1/4}$$

a version of equation (2).

For this reason yields on the financial futures instruments are not independent of the present level of interest rates. They should tend to fall as interest rates between the observation point and the delivery date rise, all other things equal. And the liquidity premia that are imbedded in the spot three- and six-month rates will also affect these yields.

Forecasting Interest Rates

47 **W. DAVID WOOLFORD**
Vice President
The First National Bank of Chicago

INTRODUCTION

There is no shortage of interest-rate forecasts, although only a small segment of the population dares to make this the sole basis for a career. Each day individuals buy and sell money for various time periods, both for their own account and as agent or investment advisor. Whether the analyses leading to their decisions were shallow or deep, rigorous or emotional, the outcome of these myriad decisions—in the cash markets, financial futures markets, with and without the assistance of financial intermediaries—is a series of interest rates for various maturities and types of securities. This series, in turn, can be decomposed—though imperfectly—into a consensus forecast for interest rates. That consensus provides a benchmark for successful forecasting. Improve on this consensus consistently (net of transaction and opportunity costs), and the forecast has been profitable. However, not everyone can succeed, for the consensus, by definition, has been established by an equal weighting of dollars on both sides.

For many market professionals, the difficulty in consistently correctly predicting shifts in the consensus has led to a refocus of their analysis toward topics outlined elsewhere in this volume. That new focus entails a goal not so much to outguess the consensus as to exploit even momentary adjustment lags, to arbitrage cash and futures markets, and to construct portfolios that offer significant upside potential but have already built-in limits to downside risk. These adjustments are not free, however, and returns from such activity will not exceed the market average unless the professional can somehow combine this activity with better information, transaction or scale economies, or a cheaper access to financing.

This chapter, however, is intended to lay the groundwork for those daring (or foolish) enough to attempt to improve on the consensus. For those so determined, a large body of literature stands ready to prepare (and perhaps dissuade) the uninitiated. With few exceptions, methods can be catalogued in two groups.

At one extreme are multisector models, simplifications of the economy that seek to explain interest-rate behavior from the interactions of a wide range of hypothetical economic actors in a hypothetical economy containing various degrees of realism. Among the large multisector models providing users with excellent equation/sector descriptions and analyses are Wharton, Data Resources, and Chase Econometrics. Such models need not be composed of several hundred interacting equations. They may also be grossly oversimplified—a restatement of the demand for money to forecast interest rates, for example—but they share a common element that the forecast for interest rates is based on a pattern of causality from one or more economic variables that is expected to be reproduced, on average, in the future.

At the other extreme are projections that lack any causal specification but rather are based on an analysis of technical factors. Again, such technical activity may be limited to charting relationships or may be very sophisticated time series analyses. These models lack the structural specification that, say, conditions A, B, and C will be associated with result X in strength Y within time T. However, they share one commonality with structural models. Both seek to explain the future on the basis of the past. Furthermore, only a biased sample of past data can be used. When combined with the range of innovation in financial markets over the past century, and particularly in the past 25 years, this selection bias helps to explain why identical models in the hands of different forecasters can produce sharply varying results.

Just how different can be seen from a survey of interest-rate forecasters. In early 1981 a comparatively small sample of forecasters, presumably with access to roughly equivalent sources of information, reported forecasts of interest rates on federal funds at year-end 1981 that differed by 900 basis points. For most cyclical experiences over the past two centuries, that range exceeds the actual trough-to-peak and peak-to-trough movements in interest rates. (We live in interesting times!)

Consensus forecasts display considerably less variation, as might be expected from an average. One estimate of the consensus forecast, prepared roughly at the same time as the forecasts above, is shown in Exhibit 1. In retrospect, it proved to be a tough standard.

Exhibit 1
Forecast for Federal Funds for the Fourth Quarter, or Year-End, 1981
(prepared near year-end 1980, actual data rounded)

Estimate of market consensus*	12.75%
Forecast 1	8 %
Forecast 2	11
Forecast 3	14
Forecast 4	16
Forecast 5	17
Median forecast (including other projections not shown separately)	13.3 %

* Extrapolated from forward rates estimated from Treasury yield curve, assuming funds carry a 100-basis-point premium.

Estimates of the market consensus cannot be prepared directly from interest rates quoted in cash or futures markets, except in the case of pure discount instruments. The usual specification of interest rates in bond markets, however, is the conventional yield-to-maturity, an internal rate-of-return calculation that assumes that all coupon payments can be reinvested at today's rate in all future periods. Furthermore, the bond markets contain a vast heterogeneity of instruments bearing differing call, default risk, liquidity premia, and other features.

The first difficulty with the conventional yield-to-maturity specification presents largely computational difficulties. A complete description of the term structure can be created by estimating a well-defined concept, the *spot rate*. The spot rate is the rate that, compounded over the period, gives the return that the market would demand for a pure discount instrument for that period, say T. (With pure discount instruments, reinvestment risk is eliminated.) As T is varied, the sequence of spot rates traces out the term structure. Equivalently, this also describes a series of forward rates—the incremental return in varying T. Hence the spot rate, R_T, is equivalent to the geometric average of all forward rates, r_i.

$$(1 + R_T) = (1 + r_1) (1 + r_2) \ldots (1 + r_R) (1 + r_T)$$

This series of forward rates, in turn, can be decomposed into an anticipated interest rate, F and a liquidity premium, L.

$$(1 + r_k) = (1 + F_k) (1 + L_k) \quad (k = 1, 2, \ldots, T)$$

Because most spot rates must be estimated from a sample of securities (in practice, Treasury securities are used to minimize default risk
and call features), an element of error is introduced that complicates
estimation of liquidity premiums. This is further complicated by some
empirical support to the following argument: Although the postwar
average liquidity (term) premium has ranged from perhaps 15 to 20
basis points in very short bill maturities, to 50 to 75 basis points for
three-month rates six months forward, to perhaps 200 basis points or
more at longer forwards, these liquidity premia will vary procyclically
over the business cycle.[1]

With the advent of organized financial future markets, a new source
of data from which to compile the market consensus became available.
There was initially some consternation that forward cash market and
futures rates were not equal, despite their apparent theoretical equivalence. However, that apparent inconsistency has been resolved by
noting, first, differences in tax treatments in cash and futures transactions and (a more fundamental difference) the cost of guaranteeing
futures contracts in an organized market (Kane [40]).[2] Despite the reserves carried by the organized exchanges, residual risk does exist—a
future contract on a default-free security does not make the contract
default free. The price to be paid for bearing the residual risk is sufficient to generate differences in prices for forward cash market and
futures claims.

For the interest-rate forecaster, however, each of these considerations might be judged to pale by contrast to the more difficult task of
preparing an alternative to the consensus. Empirical research, particularly work by Roll [59] and Pesando [55], has shown that the consensus sets a high standard by which to be judged. Fame and fortune have
accrued to those fortunate enough to top the consensus, but forecasts
by those less fortunate lie in unmarked graves. Thus an understanding
of the consensus is important as a benchmark. The consensus is also
useful as a neutral position when other methods offer no clear strategy, which occurs more frequently than most fixed income managers
care to admit.

STRUCTURAL MODELS

The heart of all structural models used in interest-rate forecasting is
a description of the supply of funds to the credit markets and the

---

[1] The origin of the liquidity premium is itself a source of debate. It may reflect
moneyness, perceived default risk (including credit or interest-rate controls), or
changes in the volatility of interest rates. For example, Throop [66] found that the
standard deviation of rates is significantly related to a measure of the liquidity premium
for Treasury bill rates in some specifications. In general, however, there is no hard
agreement as yet on either the underlying cause(s) or the empirical size of liquidity
premiums.

[2] For clarity, numbers in brackets are used to footnote references. Corresponding
numbered references are contained in the bibliography at the end of this chapter.

demand for these funds. This equilibrium has been summarized (and embellished in numerous ways) in the so-called Hicksian Cross, or IS–LM framework.[3] Exhibit 2 shows the determination of interest rates and economic activity under this framework. This IS curve traces the locus of points along which savings (often assumed simply proportional to economic activity, although clearly responsive to interest rates as they reflect the reward for postponing expenditures, and not just anticipated inflation) is equal to investment (measured as some kind of hurdle rate derived from the marginal efficiency of capital). Clearly, both can be made conditional on various monetary and fiscal policies. This curve is downward sloping because lower interest rates would be found as higher levels of economic activity increased the flow of savings, and because increased investment reduces the marginal return on investment. (However, the slope is reversed in comparing interest rates and inflation. The anticipation of accelerated inflation rates reduce savings, forcing higher interest rates.) Similarly, LM measures the locus of points along which money supply and money demand are equal and is an upward-sloping function, reflecting a higher demand for money as economic activity increases.[4]

The intersection of the proximate determinants of increments to the flow of funds as expressed by the IS curve, and monetary factors, determines the equilibrium interest rate. Forecasting interest rates would appear to be merely a matter of forecasting determinants of IS and LM. In fact, this is the route taken by early structural models and continued up to this day (though with a significant upgrading in sophistication) by many econometric model builders.

Structural models of which IS-LM is the major form offer the only means currently available to evaluate structural changes in the economy, including changes in operating procedures for monetary and fiscal policies. Their failure to produce above-average forecasts, however (see Pesando [55] and McNees [47]), has produced a healthy skepticism directed at econometric models. Noncritical users of these models should be aware of a number of shortcomings. The following is only a partial catalogue.

Stability

Large econometric models include a substantial number and variety of feedback relations. Changes in farm prices, for example, alter trade balances and affect farm machinery sales, industrial orders and

---

[3] This is also sometimes mistakenly called the Keynesian cross. Keynes himself may have felt that a somewhat different interpretation of the interest rate was in order. See Meltzer [48].

[4] This sidesteps both the precise definition of *moneyness* to be used in forecasting interest rates and the interest elasticity of the demand for money function. Despite the wealth of empirical tests of this elasticity, its value remains a matter of dispute. Recent discussions of the "stability" of the demand for money implicitly argue that with interest-rate volatility, estimation errors have increased.

**Exhibit 2
IS-LM Relationships**

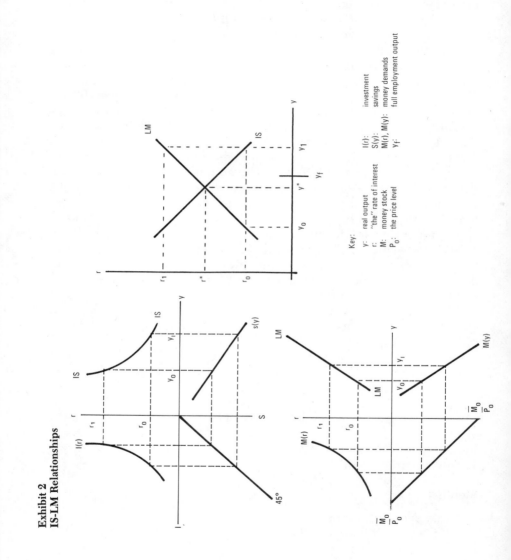

Key:

y:	real output	I(r):	investment
r:	"the" rate of interest	S(y):	savings
M:	money stock	M(r), M(y):	money demands
P_0:	the price level	y_f:	full employment output

employment, personal income, food consumption, and farm prices. Lower interest rates (for example, from an unexpectedly expansionary monetary policy) initially increase investment and economic activity, increase prices of assets (including common stocks), and spur additional borrowing, thereby forcing interest rates to reverse their initial decline. Not infrequently, specification of individual feedback relationships produces simultaneity in which model specification must be altered (*add-factored* is the professional euphemism) to produce convergence. Usual practice is for model-building entrepreneurs to permit users to interact with the ultimate system, but such a "simulation" leaves the model's response *framework* unchanged; reestimation to explore alternative specifications is not particularly user-friendly. Some modelers do report dynamic Monte Carlo simulations that provide more accurate error bounds on forecasts, but again, these projections of forecast errors are conditional on the future appropriateness of the underlying model structure.

Identification

The proverbial introductory economics examination question: "We observe a decline in interest rates. Investment demand must have fallen." In terms of Exhibit 2, a fall in investment demand (a shift to the right of $I(r)$) is consistent with a decline in interest rates, but this decline is also consistent with a host of other phenomena. Identification of the large model equivalents of IS and LM relationships usually involve simplifying assumptions on the determinants and specification of interest-sensitive relationships, in order to distinguish demand and supply.

Specification Error

Pressures for convergence and identification will lead to specification bias. Forecasts of an upturn in interest rates may be conditional on a prior upturn in inflation, for example, when there is considerable evidence that the reverse is true. Wage rates may *lead* rather than (correctly) *lag* inflation. Wealth effects may operate with unacceptably long or short lags to be consistent with other equilibrium conditions. Long-run, own-price elasticities may be estimated to be no larger than short-run responses. Of necessity, volatility will be damped. This is a necessary concomitant of regression procedures, but one that can have the unfortunate side effect of increasing the apparent explanatory power of one-factor models while failing to capture the unique characteristics that can distinguish a correct forecast from the consensus.

A full description of various models and their specific features cannot be attempted in this chapter. However, model builders and buyers should ask for some minimum requirements if the model is to be useful in answering hypotheses on the impact of structural changes on levels of interest rates:

1.   Over long periods of time, inflation is essentially a monetary phenomenon; and over that same time frame, the primary determinant of level of interest rates is inflation. Short-term relationships of money stock and inflation are highly variable. However, models should have steady-state characteristics consistent with the long-run rate of inflation having nearly a one-to-one relationship with the long run growth of the money stock. One test is to double the growth rate of the quantity of money and maintain the new growth for a sustained period of time. Does the model show the predicted response?

2.   Concerning the government budget constraint, how does the model close the identity that Treasury outlays must match receipts from taxes and debt issue, including debt sales through the intermediary of the central bank? What mechanism, if any, is there for the central bank's response to the deficit? Earlier mechanisms specified this response as one in which the central bank's willingness to absorb the deficit via open-market debt purchases was a positive function of the level of interest rates.[5] These mechanisms are perhaps appropriate so long as the central bank follows an interest-rate target, but their applicability may be sharply reduced by recent changes in operating procedures. Specification of the central bank's reaction function is not an easy task. Moreover, heightened recognition of the central bank's importance in the inflationary process has increased the focus on this reaction function. For example, the fear that deficits will ultimately be monetized because of pressures from political or economic events can lead to substantial term premiums.

3.   Under an interest-rate target, what mechanism exists to model the central bank's reaction function when the target is incompatible with price stability? Many models contain no such bridge, pretending that an infinitely elastic reserve supply procedure can nevertheless co-exist with a determinant price level. The fault generally lies in a failure to specify a clearing mechanism for *aggregate* demand, replacing this with n–1 clearing markets in a way that confuses relative prices with the aggregate price level. Such a model cannot capture interest-rate movements.

4.   Is there a monetary explanation of the exchange rate (and, if applicable, central bank intervention)? External/internal balance is particularly important because of the potential to only partly specify

---

[5] Focus on this factor assumes that there is not a high interest elasticity of demand for money. If there is—Keynes' so-called liquidity trap—interest rates are insensitive to changes in money supply, and it is immaterial how the deficit is financed. Empirically, however, a liquidity trap has not characterized the postwar period.

credit demand if the Euromarket is ignored.[6] A recent paper by Hartman [34] finds support for the hypothesis that a significant part of the variation in short-term U.S. interest rates in the 1975–78 period was attributable to foreign influences.

5. How is credit market equilibrium specified? Although money supply growth is the primary determinant of the long-term level of inflation, inflation is the rate of change of the purchasing power of money. Interest rates specify the price of credit—the rate for exchanging future claims on consumption for present claims. Clearly, their most important determinant will be the time path of anticipated price changes for these consumption claims over the period, and this explains the attention paid to projecting expectations of inflation rates and actual inflation rates in interest-rate-forecasting models. In the short run, however, other factors can combine to generate sharply different interest-rate conditions than would be projected on the basis of inflation expectations. Adjustment lags, institutional conditions (disintermediation, for example), central bank and Treasury financing activity, inventory adjustments, and other factors can all produce interest-rate environments that differ, short term, from what expectations of inflation might suggest.

Ultimately such temporary conditions will be arbitraged. Many models of credit market conditions provide such arbitrage. The user should be careful to analyze the following:

1. Analyze whether such arbitrage exists. Can interest rates permanently fail to reflect expected inflation? If so, the model is useful only for very short-term timing activities and is inconsistent with equilibrium.

2. Analyze whether or not the credit market specification closes the asset and liability sides of the relationship. For example, some flow-of-funds models contain no constraint on loan growth from funding—implicitly assuming an infinitely elastic supply of bank reserves by the central bank. In such an environment, however, no meaningful specification of the level or movement in interest rates is possible, and the entire model should be discarded. (In terms of the IS–LM framework, such a model presumes a horizontal LM function.)

Rational Expectations

Even if these checks produce a satisfactory report, model users face a potentially insurmountable obstacle in the form of rational expecta-

---

[6] In principle, Walras' Law ensures that if n−1 markets can be shown to clear, the nth market must also be in equilibrium. Domestic asset markets, however, cannot be fully specified, so Walras' law cannot be used to justify omitting consideration of foreign influences on the domestic interest-rate environment. Indeed, for small countries with open capital markets, foreign influences are the most important determinant of interest rates.

tions to improving on the consensus forecast.[7] Early models of expectations merely specified some mechanically extrapolative formation of expectations—distributed lags, for example. No attempt was made to see if this was consistent with competitive equilibrium in, say, the capital markets. When such tests of equilibrium were performed, however, it became clear that mechanical formulations of expectations (whether adaptive, regressive, inertial, extrapolative, or some combination) offered unexploited profits.[8] Market participants could consequently improve on mechanical extrapolations, and would if markets were efficient. Interest-rate forecasting in an efficient market sense would be defined as the solution to the following exercise:

1. Assume the change in interest rates, dr, is linear in the information set, S, needed to forecast changes in interest rates. Then to a first order approximation, the change in interest rates, dr, can be described by:

$$dr = f(S,V) \tag{1}$$

    where V is a serially uncorrelated error term independent of S.

2. By definition, S is not known to all or even a significant number of capital market participants, or interest rates would already reflect this information. This is equivalent to saying that data on interest-rate determinants, K, can be decomposed into two components, information already available (K_{-1}) and S:

$$K = f(K_{-1},S) \tag{2}$$

3. Statistically, an estimate for S can be derived from errors in (2). Efficient market theory would argue that estimates of S in (2) will be serially independent. Otherwise lagged values of S could be used to improve estimates in (2). These estimates of S can then be used in (1) to solve for dr. If the efficient markets hypothesis holds, lagged values of S will have no significance for dr in (1). Furthermore at the margin, the cost of collecting S and estimating its impact should roughly equal its value in estimating dr.[9]

---

[7] There is a tendency to confuse rational expectations with market efficiency because tests for these phenomena are joint tests. Market efficiency implies that prices already efficiently use available information. Forecasters cannot expect to improve on the market consensus unless they have access to new information at above-average efficiency or (what amounts to the same thing) have additional information. Efficiency can be produced with all market participants behaving irrationally—that is, in ways other than consistently in their own best interests.

[8] Adaptive expectations adjust the new forecast by a proportion of the error between forecast and actual values; regressive expectations projects the actual return will adjust to its previous level (equilibrium) over a period of time. (See, for example, Dobson, Sutch, and Vanderford [13].)

[9] For a further discussion, and some estimates, see Evans [16] and Pesando [55]. Evan's estimates, however, should be carefully reviewed because of statistical problems created by overlapping sample intervals reducing degrees of freedom.

Note that this does not preclude improving on the market consensus in forecasting short-term rates, because there is no arbitrage opportunity in serial dependence to exploit—a one-period bond matures in the same period as information is available. References elsewhere in this chapter supporting apparent improvements on the market forecast, in fact, are uniformly limited to short-term rates. Furthermore, the longer the forecast horizon, the weaker is the evidence for market efficiency, in part because term premiums will display (cyclical) variability.[10]

The difficulty that rational expectations presents to model builders is that it hypothecates that market participants will *alter* their behavior to reduce unexploited profit opportunities—in terms of the above framework that participants consistently reduce $E(S/S_{-1})$ to zero. Profitable arbitrages cannot persist. This means that the response coefficients estimated from a structural model, which has been of necessity based on past reactions, will change depending on the actual outcome.

The reader interested in pursuing this problem with respect to the term structure should always be aware that since rationality is specified in the sense that expectations must be consistent with predictions deriving from economic and statistical theory, and since the term structure is also estimated from the same data set, the test will be a joint test of rational expectations formations and the hypothecated term structure.[11]

The question of rationality also has been addressed with regard to the Fisher equation. Irving Fisher postulated that the nominal rate of interest would equal the rate of return from holding real assets together with the expected rate of inflation on these assets. The Fisher equation is easily understood in theory. Its use in practical forecasting is largely limited to longer-term asset equilibrium. The equation:

$$(1 + i_t) = (1 + r_t)(1 + p_t)(1 + g_t) \tag{3}$$

where

i_t = the nominal interest rate
r_t = the default-free real return
p_t = the anticipated rate of inflation
g_t = the "risk premium."

At this level of generality, g_t can be linked to many sources: default risk, term or other issuer options, the volatility of inflation, taxes, to name a few. Clearly, g_t can be positive or negative. Although there is no agreement on either the size or stability of r_t, Friedman and Sch-

---

[10] For a similar but more restrictive view on the potential for successful forecasting, see Pesando [55].

[11] See for example Modigliani and Shiller [50].

wartz [25], in an encyclopedic study of monetary developments in the United States and United Kingdom, argue that over the past century a 3 percent figure would have been appropriate. Accepting this figure, a portfolio manager would choose a rate of inflation that he or she expected to persist at the end of a given period, set r_t equal to 300 basis points, and add any additional premiums to solve for i_t in (3). That solution could then be compared with forward rates available given the current term structure vector consistent with (1). The excess (deficient) available return, on a risk-adjusted basis, can then be used as an input in asset allocation. The real rate cannot be stimulated from averaging ex post data. For example, Ibbotson and Sinquefield [39] found that the average real return to an investment in long-term Treasury securities was 0.7 percent between 1926 and 1978. This is an estimate of the real rate if, over the period, average errors in estimating p were zero and the average value of g was zero. Realized real returns are heavily impacted by unanticipated inflation. (From 1926 to 1950, realized real returns were 2.7 percent—much closer to the 3 percent figure of Friedman and Schwartz.)

The tenuous short-term connection between inflation and interest rates limits the practical use of this relation to longer term asset equilibrium. The Fisher equation holds so long as real assets and bonds are arbitraged by investors—in other words, an efficient market. Tests by Fama [17] supported the joint test of rationality and a constant real rate, but this result has been the subject of significant criticisms, particularly Fama's use of the CPI as an index of real asset prices. However, for those determined to forecast interest rates through forecasts of inflation, Fama's tests are disturbing because they appear to support the argument that current interest rates already contain *all* relevant information about inflation (in other words, interest rates may operate as the best predictor of inflation), but the reverse does not hold.

Such a finding would deal a harsh blow to forecasts based on projections of inflation, although it would still leave open the question of whether it was possible to develop projections of the real rate (whether the real rate should properly be treated as a constant, either in analytical or forecasting applications, remains an open question). Recent evidence questioning the cyclical constancy of the natural rate of unemployment, for example, indirectly supports the hypothesis that the real rate of interest also varies.

A different question is addressed by the preferred habitat thesis, which argues that interest rates on different instruments will reflect demand and supply by major participants in these sectors. For example, this thesis would forecast that a major determinant of changes in negotiable certificate of deposit rates will be the future path of bank loan demand, or that prices for corporate bonds will reflect demand for these securities by such typical institutional purchasers as insurance and pension fund portfolios. Such a hypothesis is often implicitly used by flow-of-funds forecasts in projecting various kinds of new issue indigestion because traditional purchasers will be unable to absorb forthcoming supply. The Fisher equation, as noted, relies for its validity on arbitrage between real goods and bonds. As an aid to short-term run forecasts, preferred habitat rests on an even more fragile reed— the lack of arbitrage, except at substantial premiums, between various sectors of the debt markets. As initially proposed by Modigliani and Sutch [51], preferred habitat reflected differences in investor time period preferences for consumption. Cox, Ross, and Ingersoll's extension [11] to differing risk preferences does not alter the fundamental difficulty that forecasting interest rates on the basis of preferred habitat requires an institutional or other rationale for the absence of arbitrageurs. It is thus a disequilibrium situation, observable at times, but extremely difficult to forecast on a systematic basis. In fact, Singleton [63, p. 612] found no evidence that maturity-specific disturbances could explain a significant part of yield movements for Treasury securities. Except for the one-year bill, he said, "the specific processes appeared to be generated by serially uncorrelated processes and, thus, [were] of no value for forecasting future interest rates." Singleton was led to conclude that "if institutional variables have an effect, then it will be through their influence on liquidity premiums and expectations."

Projecting interest-rate movements by ascribing future twists in the yield curve to "preferred habitat" remains a popular, if questionable, practice. Some examples:

1. Bank portfolios tend to purchase Treasury securities in 2- to 7- (occasionally 10-) year maturities to speculate on interest-rate movements (by mismatching asset and liability durations) when loan demand weakens. If the hypothesis were valid, one would expect to find, other things equal, upward pressure on these maturities when loan demand is very strong.

2. Insurance companies and pension fund managers are traditional buyers of longer term fixed income securities. Their asset allocation and available funding, then, should twist the yield curve up or down for these instruments relative to other maturities. (The author knows of no valid evidence for this statement.)

3. Many analysts view short-term interest rates as purely demand determined, arguing that the aggregate supply of short-term credit will be insensitive to interest rates because of a lack of liquid investment alternatives. The statement has been used to justify forecasts of short-term rates well below inflation rates. Though perhaps valid for some investors, it neglects the ability of other

investors to alter their asset/liability structure. For example, inordinately high short-term interest rates will encourage borrowing long to lend short; the reverse will be true levels of short-term rates viewed as excessively low.

4.   The Euromarkets are typically financial markets with overnight to 15-year maturities. Strong foreign demand for dollars will reduce domestic interest rates. The last statement is true, other things equal, but there is no reason to expect that particular maturities purchased will not be arbitraged by other investors. However, there is evidence that new Eurodollar instruments—floating-rate instruments, for example—have temporarily offered above-average returns, presumably partly because nonbank institutions in this country and elsewhere have tended to underemphasize international dollar vehicles.

Recap

This brief review of structural models may appear to have been a uniformly negative one. In fact, the scale of criticism that can be brought to bear is testimony to the wealth of knowledge that has been accumulated in this area. Future work directed at liquidity premia and rational expectations can pay further dividends in expanding knowledge, although it is clear that profitable forecasts are dependent on use of unprocessed or normally unavailable information, or as a side benefit to necessary participation in risk-bearing. There are several directions that this may take:

1.   Improved processing of information. Time-series analysis has produced, in some instances, forecasts that improve on implicit forward rates. One recent states/space improvement on ARIMA is the contribution by Fildes and Fitzgerald [21]. Improved time-series models have become increasingly available to serious portfolio managers. Their appeal should be particularly strong to forecasters interested in constructing benchmark forecasts independent of their personal interpretation of history. There remains the hurdle of quantifying changing response patterns to new information. This is a fertile and, to some extent, productive field for Bayesian analysis.

2.   There has now been sufficient empirical evidence to question the applicability of the simple one-factor capital asset pricing model in equity markets. Bond price variability has increased to reflect the increased variability of inflation. (This was predictable. With the acceleration of inflation, either yields could remain low and price variability low, giving bonds the character of a nominal option with a suboptimal return, or returns and risks could both rise.) Despite the more univariate character of bonds, this has spurred interest in an application of the arbitrage pricing theory [60] in which compensation for

bearing risk is composed of several premia. Elsewhere in this volume, work reported on the respective values for call options, sinking funds, warrants, and other extendable/retractable features all can be expressed in the framework of the price of an individual bond as the result of several risk premia. In turn, the term structure can be viewed as a piecewise continuous set of risk premia for capital and reinvestment risks.

3. Improvement in quantitative research into business cycles. A review of current methodology in the following pages makes the gaps in this area readily apparent. However, the need to estimate rational expectations models incorporating predictable response coefficients stands as a major stumbling block to useful forecasting improvements to this area.[12]

BUSINESS-CYCLE MODELS

A charitable view of less-than-perfect performance of large-scale forecasting models would be that their useful features are already incorporated in the term structure, as market efficiency would suggest. Of course, this has also had the impact of maintaining interest in other forecasting procedures having various levels of naivete.

Any examination of the term structure over the business cycle should begin with Phillip Cagan's three intensive studies of cyclical movements in interest rates (in [31] and [32]) augmented by his exhaustive examination of trends and cycles in the quantity of money [8]. There has been a clear tendency for interest-rate cycles to better anticipate business cycles in more recent times, although this undoubtedly reflects the improved frequency and quality of economic information. Just as noticeable is a tendency for the lag in cyclical swings in long- to short-term rates to tighten. Long-term rates now exhibit peaks and troughs coincident with or in advance of swings in short-term rates. Growth in sophistication and activity of financial markets may be one explanation for this observation; another is the increased attention to monetary policy and attempts by portfolio managers to anticipate shifts in policy intent. To the extent these consensus expectations prove to be correct and shifts in policy intent are consistent with the economy's cyclical character, long-term rates can lead short-term rates. To the extent they are incorrect, rate movements will display a jagged trend, and each successive error in the direction of long-term rates will lead the market to extract greater risk premiums varying with the duration (interest sensitivity) of the security and

---

[12] This point has been made in another context by Al Wojnilower [72, p. 278]: "Because of the major structural changes in finance between most successive cycles, the behavior of financial data, including monetary aggregates, also is likely to have different implications from cycle to cycle."

produce a steeper (or for initially inverted cases, a flatter) yield curve. Forecasting interest-rate cycles in this formulation is thus a joint forecast of (1) the economy's underlying strength and (2) the reaction function of policymakers.

Studies of the term structure over the business cycle have noted some general similarities, of which the following is a sampling.

1. Since business cycles incorporate an adjustment of actual inventory to desired inventory positions that typically involves some inventory liquidation (or at least a sharp reduction in accumulation), the cessation of the liquidation stage at or near the cycle trough typically produces a relatively sharp rebound in production activity and temporary sharp upward pressure on interest rates as working capital needs expand. This pressure relaxes for two reasons: The translation of raw materials into finished products reduces the pressure on cash flow, and initial inflation expectations generated by the contemporaneous rebound in raw material and intermediate product prices (as these inventories contract to and below target levels) are softened by the evidence of more moderate price increases at the finished goods level. With the gain in productivity as capacity utilization begins to climb, expanded profit margins are possible, further contributing to moderating pressures to raise prices while improving cash flow.

2. This upward pressure on interest rates around and following the trough typically lasts at most 6 to 12 months. It is then followed by a sharp rally that will carry bond prices back to near (or through) previous highs and yields to near (or below) their previous cyclical lows. At this point, the postwar history has been one of rising demand for funds producing a fundamental inconsistency between the interest-rate targets sought by the central bank and economic reality. Since this result is perceived only with a lag, the result is a succession of policy adjustments until policy ultimately succeeds in either pricing sufficient participants out of the market or engages in direct allocation (via disintermediation, for example) to achieve this goal.

So long as the Federal Reserve persisted on pursuing an interest-rate target that permitted credit demands to continue to be met at prices that were generally below inflationary expectations, projections of interest-rate turning points at peaks were equivalent to finding evidence of the onset of disintermediation. In this respect, it is important to remember that financial institutions make forward commitments and, until recently, had no organized markets in which to offset this risk.[13]

Among the tools the author has found useful in the past is one that monitors sources and uses of funds by insured savings and loan associ-

---

[13] Furthermore, since the commitments have some probability of not being exercised, no market for state-contingent claims yet exists to perfectly offset commitment risk.

Exhibit 3
Changes in Liquidity and Mortgage Commitments of Insured Savings and Loan Associations

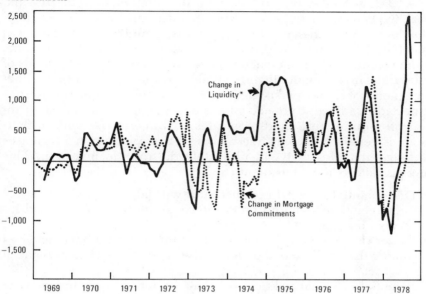

* Net savings, interest, loan repayments, and borrowings less funds extended for mortgages, and loans and participations (three-month moving average).

ations (the choice of institution is partly because of an extensive commitment series). Exhibit 3 summarizes this analysis. Sources of funds are measured including and excluding FHLB/other advances and borrowing. Periods of net deficiencies tend to lead or be coincident with interest-rate peaks. However, the increased availability of market-priced sources of funds to thrifts changed this relationship, and in the 1979–80 period, the measure failed to anticipate the reaction of S&Ls to these new funding vehicles.

The composite index of leading indicators is frequently followed as an indicator of the future pattern of credit demands. However, the index, despite its relatively good track record in tracing cyclical patterns, cannot be said to provide more than a rough gauge to interest-rate movements. Interest-rate turning points are more closely linked with the reference cycle, as reflected by the composite index of coincident indicators, particularly when adjusted for a lagging recognition that the economy had entered recession. Credit demands themselves, other expert opinion notwithstanding, do not give useful signals as to the peak in interest rates, save possibly over very short-run intervals. In part, this reflects the elasticity of balance sheets of financial intermediaries together with the fact that data to estimate supply and demand for funds are available on only a piecemeal basis for the financial system.

3. Interest rates themselves typically attempt to anticipate the peak in economic activity, resulting in a flattening and, in recent cycles, inversion in the yield curve. Inversion in prewar periods was generally linked to a liquidity crunch in the midst of monetary panic. More recently, the credit markets have exhibited sustained periods of substantial inversion. An inverted yield curve is a disequilibrium phenomenon that cannot persist in the absence of new information to alter expectations, since it projects future declines in rates. Persistent inversion requires that short-term rates continue to rise and, furthermore, is generally accompanied by more-than-proportional increases in long-term rates that will ultimately destroy the inversion. This process reflects the adjustments to:

> Disappointed expectations that rates will fall and produce capital appreciation (roughly) proportional to the duration of fixed income instruments.
>
> Larger risk premiums, since levels of interest rates have deviated more than expected and (generally) created a stretched financial fabric.
>
> Potential or actual political pressure for more (read: inflationary) expansionary monetary policies to relieve upward pressures on interest rates.

4. Postwar peak-to-trough declines in short-term interest rates have, on a percentage basis, been so similar as to enter the rule-of-thumb mythology. A similar stability in terms of percentage peak-to-trough decline in long-term interest rates during the postwar period can be seen in Exhibit 4. At the same time, however, the differential in call money and long-term Treasury yields at the trough has tended to shrink as shown in Exhibit 5. This may have reflected an implicit

Exhibit 4
Percent Decline in Interest Rates from Peak to Trough

	(1) Federal Funds	(2) Aaa Corporate Bonds	(3) Increases in Inflation Rate (CPI) in Prior Upturn	(4) (3) Divided by Trough Rate
1957–58...............	−82	−25	+5.7	1.57
1959–61...............	−71	−19	+2.6	0.59
1966–67...............	−34	−13	+4.1	0.77
1970–71...............	−59	−22	+5.3	0.70
1974–75...............	−64	−24	+9.1	1.15
1980..................	−49*	−21	+12.4	1.12

* Decline approximated 60 percent using weekly data.
Source: *Business Conditions Digest*, U.S. Department of Commerce.

Exhibit 5
Relative Behavior of Call Money and Long-Term Treasury Yields at Troughs

(1) Reference Cycle	(2) Federal Funds	(3) Long Treasury Bonds	(4) (3) − (2)
April 1958.............	0.63%	3.12%	2.49%
	(May 1958)	(April 1958)	
February 1961	1.16	3.73	2.57
	(July 1961)	(May 1961)	
November 1970	3.71	5.71	2.00
	(March 1971)	(March 1971)	
March 1975.............	5.22	6.66	1.44
	(May 1975)	(February 1975)	
July 1980..............	9.03	9.40	0.37
	(July 1980)	(June 1980)	

Note: Dates in parentheses are trough months on a month-average basis.
Source: *Business Conditions Digest*, U.S. Department of Commerce.

judgment on the part of the credit market at the trough that inflation would continue to decline—a judgment largely in error thus far in the postwar period. Another of the rules-of-thumb of the postwar period is that the cyclical decline in corporate bonds will typically retrace over half the preceeding trough-to-peak basis-point rise (see Exhibit 6).

Exhibit 6
High-Grade Corporate Bond Yields

	(1) Trough	(2) Succeeding Peak	(3) Basis Points Rise	(4) Basis Points Decline	(5) (4)/(3)
1953–54	2.74	4.81	207	120	58%
	(54:3)	(57:6)			
1957–58	3.61	5.37	176	100	57
	(58:6)	(59:10)			
1960–61	4.37	6.14	177	79	45
	(61:3)	(66:9)			
1966–67	5.35	9.70	435	216	50
	(62:2)	(70:6)			
1970–71	7.54*	10.44	290	254	88
	(71:2)	(74:9)			
1974–75	7.90	14.08	618	296	48
	(76:12)	(80:3)			
1980–81	11.12	16.97	585	—	—
	(80:6)	(81:9)			
6 Cycle Average					58%

Note: Dates in parentheses are dates of cyclical peaks and troughs in monthly average interest rates.)
* Trough in 1972 was disregarded due to price controls.
Source: *Business Conditions Digest*, U.S. Department of Commerce.

5.   Until recently, the Federal Reserve has tended to follow a policy of targeting interest rates. Use of an interest-rate target, however,
demands an accurate projection of the economic climate that will be
produced by that target in conjunction with other factors. Exhibit 7

Exhibit 7
Impact on Output of Real and Monetary Shocks under Alternative
Monetary Policies

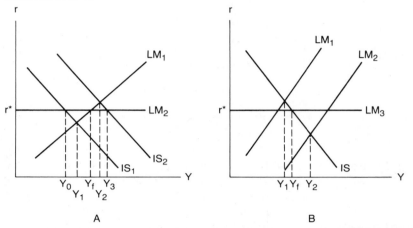

Notes: Definitions of variables are the same as for Exhibit 1. In Figure 7a, a real shock (IS_1
to IS_2) results in an income change of ($Y_3 - Y_0$) if monetary policy pegs interest rates (LM_2),
but $Y_2 - Y_1$ if policy constrains reserves. However, (Figure 7b), a monetary shock will change
income by $Y_2 - Y_1$. To justify a money stock (reserve) policy, one sufficient condition would be
that real shocks are larger than monetary shocks (i.e., that money demand is more stable than
net investment. See also [32]).
      Source: Adapted from Poole [57].

(from Poole, [56]) illustrates how an interest-rate target produces excessive shifts in monetary policy (as described by the LM function) in
response to real shocks in economic activity (a shift from IS_0 to IS_1 is
produced by a cyclical upswing). The interest-rate target, however,
cushions shocks produced by instability in money demand (shifts in
LM). Since the Federal Reserve has no special claim to prescience, its
interest-rate targets were frequently inappropriate for economic conditions. One test of the appropriateness of the Federal Reserve's various targets was the target's relationship to inflation expectations. (See
Exhibit 8.) Recall the Fisher equation (above). An attempt to maintain
an interest-rate target below inflation expectations (here proxied by
the average survey response to the Michigan Survey Research Center)
implies an opportunity to arbitrage goods against borrowing and pressures for accelerating monetary growth, *ultimately* forcing higher interest rates. The question of just when is "ultimately" is not an easy
one for which to find empirical regularities. The Federal Reserve has

Exhibit 8
Federal Funds Rate and Inflationary Expectations* (quarterly averages)

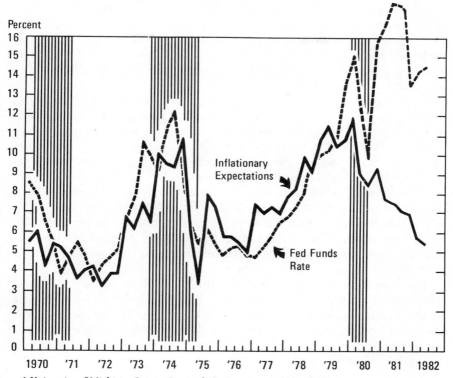

* University of Michigan Survey Research Center; mean expected price increase over next 12 months. Shaded areas indicate periods of contraction in business cycle activity.
Source: Federal Reserve Board; Survey Research Center, the University of Michigan.

chosen to alter its interest-rate targets more frequently in recent years, and target adjustments now tend to be tied to actual money supply growth relative to interim targets chosen by the Federal Reserve. Since these interim operating targets for money supply growth are not released until after the end of the interim period, however, they must be deduced by careful analysis of the operating factors within which monetary policy is conducted. These factors are particularly important for clues to the near-term (short-run) pressures on interest rates. They do not have good predictive power for longer-term trends in interest rates.

6. Cagan [32] found a "weak but significant association" between the lag in the upswing in interest rates and the duration of the following business expansion. A similar correlation was apparent for the depth of recession. The short recessions of 1960, 1970, and 1980 may reflect the nearly contemporaneous timing of reference-cycle and in-

terest-rate peaks. For this to continue to be true, however, given the increased attention to anticipating business cycles by credit market participants, is to make an improbable statement about the future duration of business cycles.

Major interest-rate turning points have tended to complement business-cycle turning points and, increasingly, to anticipate these reference-cycle turning points. What analytical tools are available for this purpose?

The most visible and easily available is the composite index of leading economic indicators. The index is composed of 12 indicators that tend to lead business activity and, moreover, were selected partly based on their ability to provide consistent leads with a minimum of false signals. Three consecutive one-month declines in the index do not necessarily signal impending recession; four are, however, rarely a false signal. The actual decline in the indicators prior to the peak in economic activity is not an indicator of the ultimate severity of the recession, but the author has found a good relationship between the peak-to-trough decline in the index and the depth of recession that has the intuitive appeal of rough correspondence to the cyclical component of overall economic activity.

Leading indicators have had a highly variable lead time (see Exhibit 9) and, during the ensuing period till recession, a substantial part of the cyclical upswing in interest rates is usually found, as credit demands become increasingly less easily postponed while credit supply is under pressure.

Exhibit 9
Leading Indicators and Cyclical Increases in Interest Rates

(1) *Cyclical Peak*	*(2)* *Lead in Months by Composite Index of Leading Economic Indicators*	*(3)* *Proportion of Total Cyclical Upswing Following Peak in Leading Economic Indicator Index in:*	
(1)	*(2)*	*(3)* *Yield on New Issues on Long-Term High-Grade Corporate Bonds*	*(4)* *Three- Month Treasury Bills*
June 1957....................	21 months	74%	51%
March 1960	10	26	45
September 1966	6	46	24
June 1970....................	17	55	39
September 1974	19	96	59
March 1980	17	94	40
Average, six cycles...........	15 months	65%	43%

Source: *Business Conditions Digest,* U.S. Department of Commerce.

An important reason for this variation lies not in the variation in cyclical experience so much as in the discrepancy between cycle and chronological time. The stages identified by Arthur Burns and Wesley Mitchell [7] in pioneering work at the National Bureau are always found in each business cycle, but as circumstances vary, the *time* necessary to complete each stage can show wide variations. Consequently, the student of business cycles seeks evidence to support an argument that the economy has passed from one stage to the next, using these points as roadposts to the potential for major sustainable turning points in interest rates, including the flattening of the yield curve and sharp run-up in interest rates that typically accompanies the final stages of the economic expansion. That evidence has become easier to gather with the widening range of easily available information. However, inflation, by increasing the dispersion and volatility of relative prices, has offset this advantage by making it more difficult to measure reference-cycle phases.

As laid out by Burns and Mitchell, the analytical study of business cycles encompasses nine stages: trough, peak, and subsequent trough, three intermediate periods of expansion and three of contraction. For statistical purposes, their approach was to measure peaks and troughs on a centered three-month average, then divide expansions and contractions into three stages of (arbitrarily) equal length.

Much of these studies predated large-scale computers. Computers permit easy computation of inflection points, producing nine stages as before but with the initial, intermediate (inflexion), and terminal stages of unequal length. The final, more judgemental process is then to correlate various indicators as an aid to deciding the economy's current position in the cycle.

At times, cyclical indicators frequently used as indicators of interest-rate movements may have only a casual correlation to rates. Even business-cycle phases lack a perfect correlation: From 1910 to 1948 there were six cycle phases (expansions and contractions) in which there were no identifiable corresponding swings in interest rates.[14] An additional dramatic example has been provided by the behavior of spot commodity prices and long-term Treasury bond yields in 1979–81. (See Exhibit 10.) Casual empiricism would suggest that the weakening in commodity prices suggests an impending decline in interest rates, since either demand is weakening (lowering inflationary expectations) or supply is unexpectedly high (again with presumably beneficial effects on inflation). In 1979 and 1980 major shifts in commodity prices were nearly contemporaneous with interest-rate movements, but no such pattern was evident in 1981. The negative correlation observed in 1981 can be rationalized; high interest rates,

---

[14] Phillip Cagan, "The Influence of Interest Rates on the Duration of Business Cycles," Tables 1–2, p. 15 in [32].

Exhibit 10
Long-Term Treasury Bonds and Spot Commodity Prices

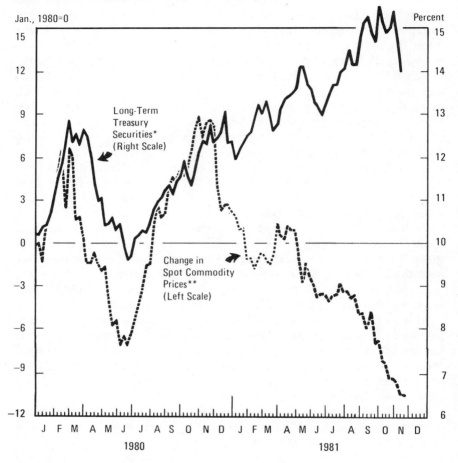

*   20 year constant maturity.
**   Journal of Commerce, 1947-49=100, change since 1/1/80. Index includes grains, food-
     stuffs, textiles and metals, but does not directly measure petroleum or precious metals.

by increasing the cost of carry, must either reduce cash prices, or be
matched by a rise in prices for forward (future) delivery, or both.[15] The
example illustrates the undesirability of using either forward or spot
prices independently in analyzing interest rates. The relationship between spot and forward prices reflects the following:

• Carrying costs including storage.

• Normal backwardation (a risk premium offered cash holders).

---

[15] Foreign exchange interest parity relationships spring from the same root.

- The risk premium for noncompliance with the forward contract specifications.
- The expected price change for the specific commodity.

Therefore the spot-futures arbitrage relationship will contain no new information about the *future* direction of interest rates. This also implies that analyses of the statistical relationships of spot and futures prices to forecast interest rates through inflation premia in commodity markets contain no new information. The residual information being offered by these markets as forecasts of interest rates is essentially "white noise"—a random walk that offers only the potential for arbitrage profits between markets.

Gauging a cyclical peak in economic activity has produced a relatively wide error bound on the basis of cyclical indices. Troughs can usually be gauged much more closely—largely because postwar recessions have tended to be of relatively short duration. The following compendium, by Roy Moor and Evelina Tainer of The First National Bank of Chicago, notes 12 signals of economic recovery found in the six postwar recessions to 1979.

	Signal of Recovery	Average Lead Time (months)
1.	Upturn in composite index of leading indicators.	3+ months
2.	Downturn in composite index of lagging indicators.	8 months
3.	Slowdown in repayments of consumer installment credit.	8+ months
4.	Consumer savings rate reverses the initial recession decline.	5 months
5.	Employment declines.	4 months
6.	Treasury bill rates decline.	8 months
7.	Long-term corporate bond yields decline.	7 months
8.	Net borrowed (free) reserves rise.	7+ months
9.	Deceleration in production decline (three-month average).	3 months
10.	Housing starts rise (year-to-year).	7+ months
11.	Crude material prices ease (year-to-year).	11 months
12.	Adjusted-for-inflation M2 declines.	2 months

Spread Relationships

On the basis of published indices, business-cycle turning points are rarely identical for all types of fixed income instruments. Some frequently heard shibboleths:

Municipal markets lag taxable securities. This is a special case of the preferred habitat thesis. Banks, casualty companies, and individuals are the primary buyers of tax-exempt issues. For this statement to be correct, spreads between taxable and tax-exempt securities can tighten at and after interest rate peaks to the extent that buyers have a reduced need for tax-exempt income. Similarly, spreads could widen prior to the peak as demands for tax-exempt income mount, reflecting the heated pace of business activity and bracket creep. The key to arbitraging these relationships is estimating the extent to which bracket creep and tax losses will exist in upturns and downturns, respectively, and estimating the extent to which alternative vehicles, such as leasing credits, will be used to defer and manage taxes.

Current-coupon corporate bonds will lag Treasury securities with comparable maturities in declining interest-rate environments. Potential price appreciation in a declining rate environment will be smaller for current-coupon corporate issues than for Treasury issues because of differences in call features. Whenever interest rates are viewed to be high relative to their sustainable long-run level, the lesser call protection offered by corporate issues will cause spreads to current-coupon Treasuries to widen. To be true in a declining-rate environment for noncallable securities, however, credit quality concerns must force risk premiums to rise. This frequently happens in the initial stages of recession then reverses as rates drop, leverage ratios improve, and balance sheets are restructured. Call option values also play a role here. At lower rate (more normal) levels, current coupon call options have less value, and spreads can tighten, even though quality premiums remain high.

Seasonal factors tend to lead to interest-rate peaks near midyear and interest-rate troughs at the first of the new year. In relatively efficient markets, predictable seasonal fluctuations will be anticipated. What remains will be either so variable or so damped that there is little or no profitable information from estimating the seasonal. Diller's analysis of seasonals (in [31], Chapter 2) for the early postwar period (1948–1965) found repetitive seasonality in the 1955–60 period, but seasonal movements were either damped or irregular in earlier and later periods. In the 1955–60 period seasonals tended to peak near year-end, trough in June, and peak again in September. The evidence was consistent with seasonal characteristics in the money demand function. Lawler's [43] recent study found that the spread between negotiable certificate of deposit and bill yields displayed a seasonal peak in February, with a June trough. Though Lawler did not draw this conclusion, the seasonality again appears related as much to Federal Reserve activity as to private sector activity, reflected in management of commercial bank balance sheets.

Longer Run Influences: Kondratieff and Kuznets Waves

War, natural calamities, sweeping technological advances, and other shocks can result in cycles overlaid on the more seasonal and cyclical swings in interest rates. The theme of very long cycles in prices and economic activity is identified with Nicolai Kondratieff, who postulated that economies followed regular cycles of roughly 50 years' duration (Phelps Brown and Hopkins [6] presented evidence of

50-year cycles for prices in the United Kingdom over the past eight centuries.) According to Kondratieff (see Exhibit 11) the first part of the 50-year cycle is typically composed of an upcycle lasting 20 years. In this up phase, inflation gradually accelerates as entrepreneurial confidence increases, economic policies are expansive, and capacity utilization—initially very low—increases, first to levels that encourage productivity improvements and new investment, but then to unsustainable levels. Economic volatility increases sharply, and the up phase usually terminates in heightened social tensions and even war. The termination of the up phase is generally followed by a 7- to 10-year interval of relative price stability, although bond prices remain close to their lows reached in the high inflation ending the up phase. The transition from recent excesses is typically accompanied by a swing to libertarian, laissez-faire, philosophies, and sustained attempts to cut government spending and deficits. The deflationary impact of these policies, on a financial system already strained by the prior inflation, sets off a self-feeding deflationary cycle that encompasses several business cycles with steep, lengthy counteractions, short recoveries, and sharply higher levels of bankruptcy.

To be sustainable, Kondratieff cycles must somehow involve systematic underprediction of inflation in the early up phase, and equally systematic errors in the deflation period. The improvement in the measurement and frequency of economic data and the safeguards built into the financial system in recent years have reduced the likelihood that we are entering the plateau phase of a Kondratieff-like cycle.

Kuznets' swings or "waves" occupy an intermediate position. In examining data over longer periods of time, Kuznets (for example [42]) found "long swings" in growth rates of real output and population spanning roughly 20 years. In the case of population, these swings have been linked to migration (which, given the selective character of international migration, has its own implications for growth rates) and technological change. Like Kondratieff cycles, moreover, Kuznets waves are associated with changes in capacity utilization. Immigration will lead to an accelerated demand for capital stock, rising real interest rates, and pressures for expansionary fiscal and monetary policies; outmigration can have the reverse effect. So long as international capital markets clear relatively efficiently, this need not have any long-term significance for interest rates, since international capital flows will shift capital from surplus to deficit countries (or asset prices will adjust). Neither labor nor capital market efficiency is perfect, however, and over/under building will produce cycles—long swings—that tend to produce unexpected pressures on credit markets over sustained periods of time.

Although an emphasis on long swing may seem at odds with the goal of predicting interest-rate movements over relatively short inter-

Exhibit 11
U.S. Wholesale Prices and the Idealized Kondratieff Wave

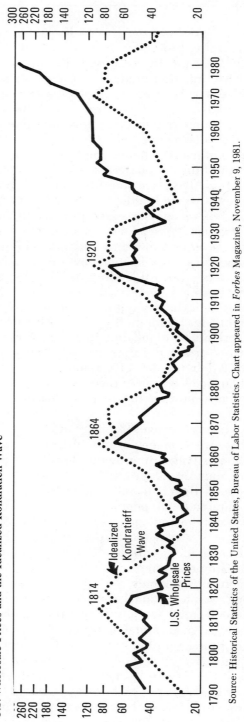

Source: Historical Statistics of the United States, Bureau of Labor Statistics. Chart appeared in *Forbes* Magazine, November 9, 1981.

vals, recall the discussion of market efficiency above. Success in forecasting the set of really *valuable* information (S) usually implies using information not generally variable or not generally used, or making use of new techniques to better understand existing information. To the extent that long waves have validity and are currently not being incorporated in existing models, they offer a relatively "cheap" source of new information, particularly since we might expect to find with efficient markets that *ex ante* changes in long-term rates increase with the forecast horizon.

FLOW-OF-FUNDS ANALYSIS

In contrast to those who forecast future interest rates on the basis of inflation and/or monetary policies, the flow-of-funds school projects supply and demand for credit by various participants.

Flow-of-funds methods do not forecast interest rates in a reduced-form relation. The goal instead is a more modest one, to anticipate directions in movements in interest rates as a result of an examination of the *sectoral* consistency of national income projections with the implication for financing. Underlying this approach is the implicit assumption that economic plans are being based on these national income projections and will be reflected in credit demands and supplies. Also implicit, however, is the assumption that sectoral financial flows change predictably and are only moderately sensitive to interest rates in other markets (preferred habitat). Otherwise, flow-of-funds models reverse the causality above, determining sector flows from wealth, NIA components, and interest rates, subject to aggregate constraints. Dependent and independent variables are reversed.

Emphasis on the various sources of and demands for loanable funds is in no way inconsistent with the emphasis on monetary variables by monetarists. Nobel laureate Sir John Hicks [37, p. 135], writing in 1938, made perhaps the most direct statement on this point:

> Is the rate of interest determined by the supply and demand for loanable funds (that is to say, by borrowing and lending); or is it determined by the supply and demand for money itself? This last view is put forward by Mr. Keynes in his *General Theory*. I shall hope to show that it makes no difference whether we follow his way of putting it, or whether we follow those writers who adopt what appears at present to be a rival view. Properly followed up, the two approaches lead to exactly the same results.

Hick's reconciliation noted that equilibrium was inconsistent with more than one set of spot rates.[16] Walras' Law could then be invoked

---

[16] If, in our n-commodity system, demands for n−1 products equal the supplies of n−1 products, then the nth demand must equal its supply. The proof uses the fact that only n−1 relative prices need to be determined and that income to be spent on the products, at any point in time, is given.

to show that in an economy with commodities (n−1 relative prices), a loan or credit market, and money and with equilibrium in the n−1 relative prices, if the loan/credit market were in equilibrium, then the supply of money must equal the demand for money. Put another way, the n commodity markets and the supply and demand for money will determine the n−1 relative prices and the price level that are consistent with only one interest rate; and that is the interest rate that clears the loan market, since only one spot rate can exist for a given maturity.

The differences between those who would forecast interest rates on the basis of the supply of and demand for money and those who would use the supply of and demand for credit are only superficial at this level of analysis. The *real* argument relates to how best to determine the interest rate that is also consistent with simultaneously clearing the n goods markets. Monetarists implicitly view expectations of inflation as the primary determinant of the level and direction of interest rates and focus on this component of the Fisher equation. This view carries over to policy recommendations, which emphasize that commodity (real or goods) markets will clear quickly and efficiently in the absence of government intervention. By implication, the real rate of interest, or marginal efficiency of capital, is relatively stable. Analysts preferring flow of funds do so because they view money demand as unstable (or money supply as undefineable, or both) and see the real rate of interest as both unstable and capable of being heavily influenced by activities in certain key markets.

Viewed objectively, these differences are often a matter of the time frame of analysis. Short term, there is a limited correlation of interest rates with inflation, and at least the appearance of instability in money demand relationships. Flow of funds, as a forecasting tool, has the apparent advantage of focusing on markets closely connected with credit demands and supply, and on particular regulatory barriers. Longer run, money demand appears stable, and inflation expectations become the proximate determinant of interest rates. One is tempted to say that which forecasting procedure to use depends primarily on the time reference.

However, it is important not to overemphasize this distinction. Monetarists refer to the impact of money on interest rates as having three stages: liquidity, income, and price expectations effects that partition the time path into short-term and long-run influences.[17]

---

[17] Studies of money demand generally support the contention that the demand for money is a stable function of a small number of variables—specifically, wealth or permanent income and an opportunity cost given by the real rate of return on alternative assets. A shift to a more expansionary monetary policy generates an initial drop in interest rates as economic actors attempt to shed excess balances through purchase of other assets. These purchases bid up the price of other assets (bid down the opportunity cost of money) to enable the initial increase to be held. However, it also encourages increased production of these assets (the income effect), which bids up the

Beyond the forecasting horizon, it is often difficult to categorize flow-of-funds approaches to interest rates because different forecasters identify different pressure points at different points in the business cycle as the predominant determinant of the direction and level of interest rates.

Comments, below, are generally offered as a guide:

1.   Flow-of-funds data are prepared by staff of the Board of Governors of the Federal Reserve from data produced by a large number of different sources. Data frequently must be massaged in one way or another to produce comparability.[18] The Board's personnel do an excellent job with this difficult task. Nevertheless, estimates are subject to wider error bounds than many financial data. For this reason, flow-of-funds forecasts tends to focus on Treasury financing, bank, bond, and mortgage borrowing, and consumer credit. One way to assess the potential for error is to study the statistical discrepancy between asset and liability statistics in the various sectors (see Exhibit 12).

Exhibit 12
Average Statistical Discrepancy for Selected Sectors (1978–80 averages)

Sector	$billions	Discrepancy As a Percent of Sector Net Increase in Liabilities
Households, personal trusts, and nonprofit organizations	−59	39%
Nonfinancial corporate business (excluding farms)	35	23
U.S. government................................	4	6
Commercial banking	−10	8

Source: Board of Governors of the Federal Reserve.

2.   The concept of "crowding out" plays an important role in many flow-of-funds analyses. In Exhibit 13 higher Treasury borrowing raises interest rates from i_0 to i_1, reducing business external borrowing for (e.g.) fixed investment by $B_0 - B_1$ and lowering consumer borrow-

demand for money and lowers prices of the competing assets whose production has been increased (raising the real interest rate). Finally, by increasing capacity utilization and raising asset prices, this process produces an upward adjustment in price expectations and money interest rates. Empirical studies find the liquidity effect of an unanticipated monetary expansion to be at most six months and the income effect to be somewhat longer and more variable. For an anticipated expansion, however, liquidity and income effects have already been largely if not totally discounted. For an elaboration, see, for example, Friedman [24], Gibson and Kaufman [27], Barro [2], and Miskin [49]. However, the variability of liquidity and income effects (depending on the validity of expectations, initial economic conditions, etc.) and the evidence of market efficiency referred to earlier in this chapter are used to justify the monetarist focus on price expectations for interest-rate forecasts and a longer run perspective.

[18] For example, bond issuance volume in the public and private new-issue markets must be gathered; retired and maturing issues must then be netted from this gross total.

Exhibit 13
Crowding Out

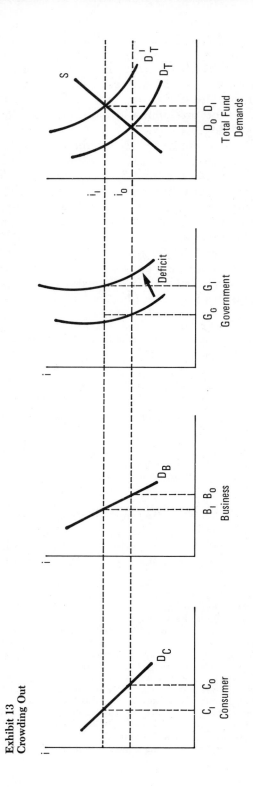

ing by $C_0 - C_1$. This neglects the cause of the initial deficit, which might have been lower tax receipts because reduced activity cut underlying consumer and business activity to levels consistent with C_1 and B_1, respectively. Furthermore, the analysis neglects the impact of a deficit created by expansionary fiscal policy on private output through operating on perceived wealth and asset values for underlying (more utilized) capital stock. The impact, for example, *might* be to produce additional internal funds, short term to fund the deficit. Longer run, of course, expansionary policies will increase external cash needs to increment capacity. It also helps to assume only a limited elasticity of supply of savings—an assumption that has considerable support empirically. Otherwise, "crowding out" must be relatively minor, and interest-rate forecasts based on flow of funds would show little variation.[19] On balance, Exhibit 13 contains a dangerous simplicity; the actual support for crowding out, short term, must be empirical.

3. Structural or regulatory constraints that prevent markets from arbitraging play a key role in many flow-of-funds forecasts. Regulation Q, which limited the monetary interest rates that banks and savings associations could pay on certain types of deposits, has been an effective throttle on home mortgage lending whenever market interest rates rose above these ceilings. This effectively increased credit supplies to other participants and subsidized their cost of credit in high interest-rate environments. In recent years several deposit forms not subject to Regulation Q have developed, and the regulation itself is scheduled to be totally phased out in stages to 1986. Another less documented "structural" constraint sometimes seen in flow-of-funds analyses conforms with preferred habitat by arguing that significant new Treasury debt can only be sold at a sharp concession to current debt holdings—in other words, a very inelastic demand function exists for additions to current holdings.

4. Within the flow-of-funds school are at least two disparate groups. One group emphasizes aggregate financial ratios. Current or prospective financial conditions, in this view, will result in financial ratios that are so extreme as to lead to extremely inelastic credit supplies thereby widening quality differentials and increasing the probability of a credit crunch as these stretched ratios strain the normal intermediary function. We might call this the intermediary school. The second group also uses ratios but emphasizes ratios dealing with wealth, maturity mismatch, and debt service capacity—the "real balance" school. This second group emphasizes (explicitly or implicitly) that interest rates are the "terms of trade" between consuming in the present and postponing current consumption. The major difference

---

[19] As a general rule, this is the typical result for model-based forecasts because of the need to damp the large statistical noise in the data.

between the groups, then, is that the intermediary school focuses on the potential for a given supply of savings to be channeled to various borrowers and the potential for key borrowers or intermediaries to be shut out of the credit market as a result of an actual or perceived deterioration in their risk-bearing ability. By contrast, the "real balance" group's focus is on how elastic this initial supply of savings will be to changes in economic conditions (both income and price effects), implicitly assuming the efficiency of the intermediation process.

5. In some ways the term *flow of funds* is a misnomer that tends to concentrate attention on sources of new funds and incremental demands at the expense of changes in asset allocation among existing assets. Such shifts have the potential to dwarf incremental flows. For example, money market funds total more than $150 billion, and a further $600 billion is in six-month to 2½-year thrift and bank certificates. A 10 percent shift out of these funds is on the scale of 75 percent of personal savings flows. Furthermore, recent work on asset models has stressed that markets often clear by changes in price, with modest flows. Arbitrage of international and domestic short-term money markets is a frequent example; so are the equity markets, in which net flows of funds are a miniscule part of outstanding market values.

PRODUCING A FORECAST

What might seem like the most difficult is actually the easiest part of this exercise, which is why it has been delayed until the end. Following are five ways of producing a forecast.

1. Forecasts can be read directly from the forward rate structure. In the absence of additional information or confidence in one's expertise, this is the rational choice. Exhibit 14 is an example of forward rates calculated by one analytical service near year-end 1981. To these

Exhibit 14
Estimated U.S. Treasury Term Structure, December 29, 1981

Maturity	Spot Rates	Current Yield on Par Bond	Discount Function	Forward Rates
1 mo...............	10.14%	10.51%	0.992%	10.14%
2 mo...............	11.24	11.64	0.982	12.93
3 mo...............	12.12	12.55	0.971	14.47
6 mo...............	13.52	14.00	0.937	15.32
12 mo..............	13.46	13.94	0.878	13.89
2 yr...............	13.52	14.01	0.770	14.03
3 yr...............	13.64	14.11	0.673	14.41
5 yr...............	13.74	14.20	0.515	14.32
7 yr...............	13.74	14.20	0.395	14.18
10 yr..............	13.66	14.17	0.267	13.95
15 yr..............	13.45	14.06	0.142	13.46
20 yr..............	13.35	14.02	0.075	13.62
30 yr..............	13.33	14.01	0.021	13.58

Source: Gifford Fong and Associates, used by permission.

forward rates must be added any liquidity or term premiums. Further-more, the geometric mean of a series of forward rates is the spot rate, and coupon premium, default, and call options must be added to produce a forecast of a particular interest rate. The latter are generally estimated from historical data of actual rates regressed on spot rates and proxy variables—sector and rating dummies for default risk and coupon scales, the theoretical value of the call option, and so on. (One approach to measuring the call option is found in Yawitz and Marshall [73].) For short-term rates, however, evidence to date supports using one or more of the techniques below or a survey of forecasters.

2. Use a large-scale econometric model. The evidence to date is ambiguous on this point. If experts have provided their judgemental review, there may be some gain in using this as a tool for forecasting short-term rates [e.g., Throop, [66] and Pesando [55]].

3. Produce a "monetarist" forecast. These come in several vari-ants. Perhaps the simplest solves for the interest-rate path consistent with a projected growth of the money stock, given the assumption of a stable money demand function. This involves projection of the price and income components for the money demand function and finding interest rates consistent with these projections. A variant on this method would assume some portion of the differential between money supply and money demand is made up each period that money supply growth is different than "expectations" (based either on pub-licly announced targets or distributed lags, for example, Barro [2]). Naturally, the success of this procedure is dependent on the ability to correctly predict income, price, and adjustment components—a fur-ther reason monetarists tend to focus their horizon for interest-rate forecasts on the two- to five-year period where price expectations become the most important determinant. For these longer-run fore-casts, longer-run growth of the money stock, and its first and second derivatives, become the prime components of a forecast.[20]

A simple example of a short-term, monetarist forecast is given be-low. There is general agreement that a good specification of the de-mand for money in terms of a small number of variables, is:

$$\frac{M}{NP} = a + b \left(\frac{Y}{PN}\right) + c(R_0) + d(R_B) + e \left(\frac{M_{-1}}{P_{-1}N_{-1}}\right) \qquad (4)$$

where all variables are expressed in logarithmic form, and are de-fined as follows:

M = any variant of M_1 or M_2, depending on one's preference
Y = real (preferably permanent) income (often proxied by real GNP)

---

[20] The fact that the second derivative of monetary growth is damped about zero has not, apparently, prevented its being an important part of the judgment on the direction of interest rates two to three years out!

N = population

P = a broad-based price index, usually proxied by the GNP defla-
tor because of the absence of a broad-based price index for
assets.

R_0 = an interest-rate proxying for the opportunity cost of money.
Both short-term and long-term rates have been used without
real discrimination, though a "transactions" view of money
demand would favor the short-term rate.

R_B = the "own" rate—passbook savings or (more recently), NOW
accounts, preferably adjusted upward for nonpecuniary returns.

The subscript "−1" indicates a one period lag, to allow for partial
adjustment in observed data.

Assuming one determined a desired specification, (4) could be estimated over some prior period using R_0 as an independent variable,
and incorporating any desired shift variables (for price controls,
changing commitment pricing terms on bank lines, etc.) The use of a
lagged term to capture serial correlation is a serious statistical weakness from a forecasting standpoint. Forecasts would use these estimated coefficients to solve for R_0:

$$R_0 = \frac{1}{c}\frac{M}{NP} - \frac{b}{c}\left(\frac{Y}{PN}\right) - \frac{d}{c}(R_B) + \frac{e}{c}\left(\frac{M_{-1}}{P_{-1}N_{-1}}\right) - \frac{a}{c} \tag{5}$$

using forecasts of M/NP and Y/PN; R_B is (generally) slowly changing
or predictable on the basis of legislation, and $M_{-1}/(P_{-1}N_{-1})$ is known.
M can be forecast using Federal Reserve targets, if desired. N is predictable; forecasts of Y and P can be naive (last period's growth rate),
sourced from consensus forecasts, or even based on recent and projected money stock growth. (A close correlation exists between nominal income growth over six-month spans and money supply growth
over prior six-month spans.)

There is less agreement on stability of this relationship.[21] More
important, unless consistent forecasts of M, Y, and P have been created, the solution for R_0 lacks validity, since the coefficients were
calculated based on a certain consistency. (This is a variant of the
previous descriptions of rational expectations.)

4.   Forecasts using business cycle turning points, of course, rely on
an ability to outperform the composite index of leading economic
indicators or one of its variants (such as the ratio of composite coincident to composite lagging indicators). There have been a number of
books on business cycles, but the Mitchell/Burns anthology and its
offspring remains required reading for serious students. Also recommended is the critique of recent research by Lucas [44].

---

[21] Two solutions for the above equation are given in Hafer and Hein [32, pp. 13–14]
and [71].

5. Different emphasis, as noted, make it more difficult to precisely describe the creation of a forecast using flow of funds. Instead, major areas are detailed below.[22]

a. The basic flow-of-funds forecast typically contains key trigger points:
   (1) The differential, *ex ante*, between investment demand and the flow of savings. To close this differential, prices and quantities must adjust (markets clear) and ensure *ex post* equality.
   (2) The size and timing of the federal government's financing needs, as a key component of *ex ante* savings flows.
   (3) The outlook for inventories and corporate cash flows as a guide to external cash needs.
   (4) In recent years, sources of funds from abroad.
   (5) Asset allocation by banks and insurance companies ("preferred habitat").

b. Start with national income (NIA) projections as a guide to flow of funds and as a check on the internal consistency of the national income projections. (Refer to Exhibit 15 for NIA components to gross saving and investment.).

Exhibit 15

	1980 ($billions)
Gross Savings:	
Personal savings	$101.3
Undistributed corporate profits	107.2
Corporate inventory valuation adjustment	−45.7
Capital consumption adjustment	−17.2
Corporate capital consumption allowance	175.4
Noncorporate corporate capital consumption allowance	111.9
Total gross private savings NIA	432.9
Plus	
Federal government surplus	−61.2
State and local surplus	29.1
Consumer durables	211.9
Equals: gross savings, flow of funds	612.7
Gross Investment:	
Consumer durables	211.9
Residential	105.3
Plant and equipment	296.0
Inventory change	−5.9
Oil leases/mineral rights (U.S. government sales)	6.5
Total gross investment	613.8
Statistical Discrepancy	1.1

Source: Federal Reserve.

---

[22] This discussion relies heavily on von Furstenberg [26].

Sources of savings include:

(1)   Household and personal savings. To personal savings from income from current production (NIA), add:

- The surplus of railroad retirement and state and local retirement funds because these funds are also available for investment.
- Capital gains distributions of investment companies.
- Consumer durables (NIA, and thus gross of depreciation).
- Depreciation on other household assets.

(2)   Nonfinancial business savings. To undistributed corporate profits, add capital consumption allowances, but subtract a minor item, capital gains dividends of investment companies, and the undistributed profits of the financial sector (including retained earnings of government entities).

(3)   Foreign sector saving. This is the negative of net foreign investment.

(1), (2), and (3) constitute private sources; to this, to determine gross savings, (4) must be added.

(4)   Government savings—both the federal government's overall cash surplus or deficit and the surplus or deficit of state and local governments.

Since gross savings must equal gross investment, the forecast of the sum of (1)–(4) is compared with uses for these funds:

- Residential construction.
- Nonresidential outlays for structures and equipment.
- Inventories
- Consumer durables.

To this point, the forecast is basically equivalent to describing the IS relationship. This means that it is consistent with *any* level of interest rates, although a particular interest rate would be specified were a level of economic activity known. In fact, the IS relationship specifies jointly attainable combinations of output, y and interest rates, r. Since y and r are jointly determined, however, it is not sufficient to form an interest-rate forecast. Even at this level of generality, however, two features might be noted:

- Personal savings are only a part of the economy's gross savings pool. International comparisons of savings that focus only on this subcomponent may seriously distort the overall relationship. Japan's substantially higher personal savings rate, for example, is partly offset by a much higher government deficit and more leveraged business sector.
- At this level of aggregation, savings and investment "appear" to be independent of financial markets. The role of financial markets is to channel or gather an excess or deficiency of funds from various sectors to ration across various

sectors requiring net financial investment. Their success determines the ultimate combination of output and interest rates (y_0, r_0).

Exhibit 16 shows the derivation for 1980 of net financial investment. (Statistical discrepancies have been subsumed in net financial investment for each sector.)

c. From this point, the flow-of-funds forecast, whether econometric or intuitive, is successively disaggregative. That is partly because there is only a *weak* relationship between actual credit/GNP in aggregate and the trend in interest rates. (See Exhibit 17.)

Forecasts for NIA components, by sector, determine net financial investment for each sector (Exhibit 16).

Net financial investment, in turn, equals net acquisition of financial assets less debt issuance for each sector. In terms of Exhibit 16, this obviously places the onus on the household and financial sectors to finance business and government activities under most economic environments.

Also shown in Exhibit 16 are gross flows underlying net activity. These should also be carefully examined. Too small a proportion of gross to net flows *suggests* an unexpectedly greater degree of monetary stringency with consequent upward pressure on interest rates.

Once a sector-by-sector description of net financial investment has been created using NIA data, it is necessary to determine what funds will be available to or demanded from the credit markets. This involves projecting reasonable values for items in lines 11 through 17 of Exhibit 16, and comparing these items with net financial investment to arrive at net investment in credit markets and related instruments (line 19). Several of the line items in line 11 to 17 are linked to other forecasts. Demand deposit and currency growth, for example, must be consistent with one's view of the policy measures followed by the Federal Reserve. Insurance and pension reserves tend to follow a relatively predictable trend. The relatively unpredictable items are the distribution of household assets between money market funds and time deposits, and business demands for time deposits, particularly since distinguishing these demands from security R/P and other liquid assets is a very artificial one.

Line 19 of Exhibit 16 is the penultimate goal in creating a forecast. This is the forecast, by sector, of funds that will be provided to the credit markets and related instruments. Note the implication, for example, of a relatively large figure for the household sector in line 10 coupled with a decline in line 18. The implication is that much more of the household's credit acquisition will be direct or through nontraditional intermediaries.

Data in Exhibit 18 show that in 1980, household borrowing for

Exhibit 16

Derivation of Net Financial Investment, 1980 ($ billions)

Sector

Case Number	Transactions Category	Households u	Households s	Business u	Business s	Net Foreign Sector u	Net Foreign Sector s	State and Local Governments u	State and Local Governments s	U.S. Government u	U.S. Government s	Federally Sponsored Credit Agencies u	Federally Sponsored Credit Agencies s	Monetary Authority u	Monetary Authority s	Commercial Banking u	Commercial Banking s	Private Nonbank Finance u	Private Nonbank Finance s	Total, All Sectors u	Total, All Sectors s
1	Gross saving	402.9			257.6	0.0			2.7		−70.0		0.9		0.4		8.2				612.7
2	Capital consumption		230.8		225.0												5.0				465.4
3	Net savings (1 − 2)	172.0			32.6				2.7		−70.0		0.9		0.4		3.2				147.3
4	Gross investment (5 + 10)	402.9		257.7		0.0		2.7		−70.0		0.9		0.4		8.2				612.7	612.7
5	Private capital expenditures (6 to 9)	313.1		285.4				0.0				0.0		0.0		11.3				612.7	
6	Consumer durables	211.9																		211.9	
7	Residential construction	93.8		11.4																105.3	
8	Plant and Equipment	7.4		273.6												11.3		2.9		295.0	
9	Inventory change/mineral rights			0.6																0.6	
10	Net financial investment (1 − 5) = (18 − 19)	89.8		−27.8		0.0		2.7		−70.0		0.9		0.4		−3.2		7.1			
11	Demand deposits and currency	10.9		2.4		0.7		−1.1		−3.6		0.1		2.3	9.0	0.7	4.9	3.7	2.1	16.0	16.0
12	Time/savings deposits	131.2		1.7		1.2		−1.7		−0.2							91.7	128	53.4	145.1	145.1
13	Money funds	29.2																	29.2	29.2	29.2
14	Gold/foreign exchange/SDRs						5.5				4.3			3.9	2.6					8.1	8.1
15	Life insurance reserves	11.5																	11.5	11.5	11.5
16	Pension fund reserves	77.5																	42.3	77.5	77.5
17	Interbank items					−24.5		*	26.5	*	8.8			−1.9	−1.0	−4.5	−29.8			−30.8	−30.8
18	Net investment in liquid or insurance claims (11 to 17)	260.3		4.1		−28.1		−29.3		−8.3		0.8		−6.3		−70.6		−122.0		0	
19	Net investment in credit markets and related investments (10 − 18)	−170.5		−31.9		28.1		32.1		−61.7		0.1		+6.3		67.4		129.1		0	
20	Statistical discrepancy Incl. in (10)	−79.6		44.5		28.5		9.8		−0.8		0.6				−10.6		−0.9		−8.6	
21	= 19 − 20	90.9		−76.4		−0.4		22.3		−60.5		−1.5		−6.3		56.8		128.2		8.6	

Note: u = use; s = source. Details may not add to totals due to rounding.
* Included in household sector.
Source: November, 1981 Flow of Funds Accounts, Board of Governors of the Federal Reserve System.

Exhibit 17
Credit Demand and Long-Term Interest Rates

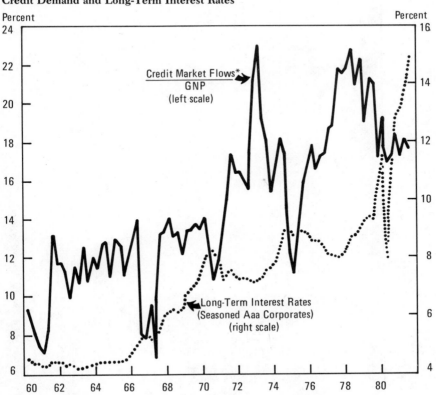

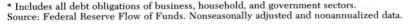

* Includes all debt obligations of business, household, and government sectors.
Source: Federal Reserve Flow of Funds. Nonseasonally adjusted and nonannualized data.

consumer credit and home mortgage debt accounted for 46 percent of household net investment in credit markets and related instruments, a comparatively small proportion because of the negligible rise in consumer credit. Similarly, a growing projection of funds by commercial banks relative to nonbank finance (comparing 1980 to prior years, not shown here) would tend to suggest business would be "forced" to use more bank financing, or go directly to investors, bypassing intermediaries. To go from this statement to the implication that long-term interest rates would be under upward pressure, however, requires an additional assumption. This is that businesses will pay a premium to have the somewhat longer maturity offered by public debt markets, or that banks will refuse to offer longer term fixed-rate claims, or some combination of these factors. (One reason often given in recent years to expect such a premium has been the deterioration in business balance sheet flexibility.)

Exhibit 18

Sector

Case Number	Transactions Category	Households		Business		Net Foreign Sector		State and Local Government		U.S. Government		Federally Sponsored Credit Agencies		Monetary Authority		Commercial Banking		Private Nonbank Finance		Total, All Sectors	
		u	s	u	s	u	s	u	s	u	s	u	s	u	s	u	s	u	s	u	s
17	Net investment in credit market and related investments (from table 8)	-17.5		-31.9		28.1		32.1		-61.7		0.8		6.3		67.4		129.1			0.0
22	Credit market investments (lines 22 to 31)	-27.6	101.7	3.7	123.7	15.6	27.1	44.5	25.3	23.7	79.2	42.1	43.0[c,d]	4.5	0.0	99.7	7.1	155.6	10.4	412.4	417.4
23	U.S. government securities	20.5		-2.1		10.5		23.6			79.3			4.5		25.6		39.7		122.3	122.3
24	State and local obligation	3.0		-0.2				0.3	24.4							13.6		10.1		26.9	26.9
25	Corporate/foreign bonds	3.6			30.4	5.1	0.8	9.7				25.6[c]				0.6	1.5	20.1	5.6	38.4	38.4
26	Home mortgages	6.3	83.4		-1.6			8.0		2.7						11.3		27.1	-0.8	81.0	81.0
27	Other mortgages	1.8	1.5		38.9			2.8		4.8	-0.1	7.1[d]				8.1		15.5	-0.1	40.1	40.1
28	Consumer credit	2.3			2.1											-9.7		9.9		2.3	2.3
29	Bank loans, not elsewhere classified	5.6			31.7	11.5										48.4		10.0	-0.5	48.4	48.4
30	Other loans[b]	8.9	—		15.2	4.7		0.9		16.2		10.4						10.0	7.1	36.6	36.6
31	Commercial paper/banker's acceptances	-3.6	—	3.9	6.6	10.1										1.8	5.6	23.2	-0.9	21.4	21.4
32	Related instruments (lines 33 to 37)	-89.2	7.1	10.4	12.9	3.0	2.1	2.8	5.3	-2.5	3.7	0.8		0.5	-1.3	-4.3	20.8	7.6	23.7	67.0	67.0
33	Corporate equity issuance (net)	-1.9				5.4											0.4	12.3	5.7	21.1	21.1
34	Security credit	4.1	5.0							-2.8								5.1	4.9	10.0	10.0
35	Taxes payable				-6.7					1.4	3.7					0.8			3.1	-3.9	-3.9
36	Trade credit (net)	2.2	2.1	33.2		1.8	1.0	-1.1	1.8								0.5			40.0	40.0
37	Equity in noncorp enterprises	-18.3			-18.3															-18.3	-18.3
38	Other	-75.3	66.1	-10.3		6.8				-1.1		0.8		0.5		-5.2	20.0	-9.9	10.0	18.1	18.1
20	Statistical discrepancy incl. in lines 22, 32	-79.6		44.5		28.5		9.8		-0.8		0.6		-1.3		-10.6		-0.9		-8.6	

[a] Line 19 also equals the negative of net sources in Lines 21 and 32.
[b] Includes: Finance company loans to business, U.S. government loans, sponsored credit agency loans, and policy loans.
[c] Includes: $18.0 billion of mortgage pools.
[d] Includes: $16.0 billion of mortgage pools.
[e] Includes: $7.1 billion of advances from FHLB.

Source: November, 1981 Flow of Funds Accounts, Board of Governors of the Federal Reserve System.

Comparing entries in Exhibit 18 over time also helps to pinpoint how Treasury and off-budget financing might be met. Again, some forecasters choose to draw implications, based strongly or weakly on preferred habitat, of the pressures on interest rates necessary to permit the Treasury to fund a greater-than-normal (let alone greater-than-expected) deficit, particularly if the distribution of funds for the credit markets deviates from normal and/or large inelastic entries can already be identified. (An example of the latter would be heavy business trade credit needs).

Typical practice is to complete as many items of the array in Exhibit 18 from trend extrapolation or compatible figures to NIA extrapolations. Upward pressures on interest rates—and revisions to NIA estimates—are indicated by a failure of expected financial demands, whether from Treasury or private users, to meet sources. Usually, a first pass is made using only private sector uses cued to NIA projections. (For example, projections for housing sales and starts cue mortgage activity, consumer durables and employment gains can be related to consumer credit, and inventory activity will be reflected in business short-term credit needs.) These demands then leave remaining sources to meet the Treasury's deficit (or can be incremented by a surplus). This gap indicates whether pressures on interest rates, given the NIA projections, would be significant (and in some circumstances, the potential for declines in rates). A judgement on what sectors will prove most interest-elastic to meet Treasury funding requirements is then made, and NIA activity recalculated to arrive at new sources and uses. Computer simulation permits a simultaneous solution.

The problems that face all large models, described earlier, face modeling flow of funds. As noted previously, too, the size of the statistical discrepancy means that the standard errors attaching to projections of microelements of individual accounts must be considered to be very large. Successful flow-of-funds forecasters generally weld experience, subjective beliefs, and a substantial element of luck to detailed economic analysis.

Although this may appear to be more art than science and, as described, is a process of successive iteration, with each new entry requiring a cross-check of other projections, it must be emphasized again that flow-of-funds methods do not forecast interest rates in a reduced-form-equation fashion. The goal is a more modest one—to anticipate directions in the movement of interest rates as a result of the examination of the *sectoral* consistency of NIA projections with the implications, given institutional limitations, for financing sectoral demands. Underlying this approach is the implicit assumption that economic plans are being based on these NIA projections and will be reflected in credit demands and supplies. This need not be true. For example, Wojnilower's summation of his techniques (in [72, p. 232]) explicitly recognized that professional projections may dovetail poorly with results:

> The most interesting case of schizoid expectations comes from the financial community, although here my evidence is unfortunately entirely anecdotal. That financial managers in their professional capacities have had a more optimistic outlook than the public on security prices is surely attested by the fact that institutions have continued to acquire massive amounts of bonds in the face of virtually continual declines in real and all too often also nominal values. Meanwhile the public has clearly shifted its investment mix toward increasing its borrowings and its real estate assets, producing palpably superior investment performance.

Flow-of-funds models have a further advantage that also helps to account for their popularity. Like the "stories" that color perceptions of individual equity issues (despite the weight of evidence that on average these stories are fully discounted by current stock prices), flow of funds can be used to emphasize a particular component that the analyst views as the *current* crucial factor in interest-rate movements. The fallacy of composition, that what is true of the individual need not be true of the whole, is equally applicable for flow-of-funds analysis (personal versus gross savings for example), but flow of funds can add the emperor's new clothes to what is otherwise the naked and relatively efficient operation of Adam Smith's "invisible hand." By giving color to a view of the operation of the economy, flow-of-funds analysis can provide a service that is as much a marketing technique as an analytical underpinning. It is a technique that many special-interest groups have honed to near perfection in interaction with government to justify federal guarantees or other subsidies that have ballooned total funding in recent years.

CONCLUSIONS

Serious studies generally indicate that short-term forecasts of long-term interest rates contain little or no value added. Forecasts of short-term interest rates, however, have been made successfully, by comparison with naive extrapolations, both because there is no theoretical necessity for short-term rates, short term, to follow a random walk and because the Federal Reserve has frequently chosen to act in a predictable fashion.

The evidence that short-term, long-term interest rates follow a random walk has been used to:

1. Support option strategies directed toward fixed income investments, such as immunization, that shift the forecast horizon to a longer term perspective (but may offset this advantage by concentrating reinvestment risk).

2. Relate interest rates and inflation over longer periods of time.
    Deregulation, in this writer's opinion, has only temporarily dis-
    turbed this relationship, and presumably shifted it to a different
    plateau.
3. Justify an approach that views flow of funds as primarily a consis-
    tency check and marketing guide, rather than an efficient tool for
    forecasting rates.

    As in all other markets, however, the maxim in forecasts is *caveat
    emptor.*

BIBLIOGRAPHY

1. Barro, Robert J. "Rational Expectations and the Role of Monetary Pol-
    icy." *The Journal of Monetary Economics*, January, 1976, pp. 1–32.
2. _____. "Unanticipated Money, Output, and the Price Level in the
    United States." *The Journal of Political Economy*, August 1978, pp.
    549–80.
3. Black, Fischer. "The ABC's of Business Cycles." *Financial Analysts
    Journal*, November/December 1981, pp. 75–80.
4. Blinder, Alan, and Stanley Fischer. "Inventories, Rational Expectations
    and the Business Cycle." National Bureau of Economic Research Work-
    ing Paper, No. 381, August 1979.
5. Bomberger, William A., and W. J. Frazer. "Interest Rates, Uncertainty,
    and the Livingston Data." *The Journal of Finance*, June 1981, pp.
    661–75.
6. Brown, Earnest Phelps, and Shiela Hopkins. "Seven Centuries of the
    Price of Consumables, Compared with Builders' Wage Rates."
    Economica, November 1956, pp. 296–314.
7. Burns, Arthur C., and Wesley C. Mitchell. *Measuring Business Cycles.*
    New York: National Bureau of Economic Research, 1947.
8. Cagan, Phillip. *Determinants and Effects of Changes in the Stock of
    Money 1875–1960.* New York: National Bureau of Economic Research,
    Columbia University Press, 1965.
9. Chow, G. C. "Multiplier, Accelerator, and Liquidity Preference." *Re-
    view of Economics and Statistics*, January 1967, pp. 1–15.
10. Cox, John C.; Jonathan E. Ingersoll, Jr.; and Steven A. Ross. "Duration
    and the Measurement of Basis Risk." *The Journal of Business*, January
    1979, pp. 51–61.
11. _____. "A Reexamination of Traditional Hypotheses About the Term
    Structure of Interest Rates." *Journal of Finance*, September 1981, pp.
    769–93.
12. Culbertson, John M. *Macroeconomic Theory and Stabilization Policy.*
    New York: McGraw-Hill, 1968.
13. Dobson, Steven W.; Robert C. Sutch; and David E. Vanderford. "An
    Evaluation of Alternative Empirical Models of the Term Structure of
    Interest Rates." *Journal of Finance*, September 1976, pp. 1035–65.
14. Dwyer, Gerald P. "Are Expectations of Inflational Rational?" *Journal of
    Monetary Economics*, February 1981, pp. 59–84.

15. Echols, Michael E., and Jan W. Elliot. "Rational Expectations in a Disequilibrium Model of the Term Structure." *American Economic Review*, March 1976, pp. 28–44.

16. Evans, Paul. "Why Have Interest Rates Been So Volatile?" Federal Reserve Bank of San Francisco, *Economic Review*, Summer 1981, pp. 7–20.

17. Fama, Eugene. "Short-Term Interest Rates as Predictors of Inflation." *American Economic Review*, June 1975, pp. 427–48.

18. Fama, Eugene, and G. William Schwert. "Inflation, Interest and Relative Prices." *Journal of Business*, April 1979, pp. 183–210.

19. Feldstein, Martin. "Inflation, Income Taxes and the Rate of Interest: A Theoretical Analysis." *American Economic Review*, December 1976, pp. 809–20.

20. Feldstein, Martin, and Otto Eckstein. "The Fundamental Determinants of the Interest Rate." *Review of Economics and Statistics*, August 1970, pp. 363–75.

21. Fildes, Robert A., and M. D. Fitzgerald. "Efficiency and Premiums in the Short-Term Money Market." *Journal of Money, Credit and Banking*, November 1980, Part I, pp. 615–29.

22. Fisher, Irving. *The Theory of Interest*. New York: MacMillan, 1930.

23. Friedman, Benjamin, and William G. Dewald. *Financial Market Behavior Capital Formation and Economic Performance*. Conference papers published by the *Journal of Money, Credit and Banking*, vol. 12, part 2 (May 1980).

24. Friedman, Milton. *The Optimum Quantity of Money and Other Essays*. New York: Aldine Publishers, 1969. (See especially essays 5, 6, 10.)

25. Friedman, Milton, and Anna J. Schwartz. *Monetary Trends in the United States and the United Kingdom*. Chicago: National Bureau of Economic Research, University of Chicago Press, forthcoming, 1982.

26. von Fustenberg, George M. "Flow of Funds Analysis and the Economic Outlook." *Annals of Economic and Social Measurement*, February 1977, pp. 1–25.

27. Gibson, William E., and George Kaufman. "The Sensitivity of Interest Rates to Changes in Money and Income." *The Journal of Political Economy*, May/June 1968, pp. 472–78.

28. Gordon, R. A., and L. Klein, eds. *Readings in Business Cycles*. Homewood, Ill.: Richard D. Irwin, 1965.

29. Gordon, Robert J. "Large-Scale Econometric Models." Mimeographed. Washington, D.C.: U.S. Department of the Treasury, 1970.

30. Grossman, Jacob. "The Rationality of Money Supply Expectations and the Short-Run Response of Interest Rates to Monetary Surprises." *Journal of Money, Credit and Banking*, November 1981, pp. 409–24.

31. Guttentag, Jack M., ed. *Essays on Interest Rates*. Vol. 2. New York: National Bureau of Economic Research, Columbia University Press, 1971. (Especially essays 1, 2.)

32. Guttentag, Jack M., and Phillip Cagan, eds. *Essays on Interest Rates*. Vol. 1. New York: National Bureau of Economic Research, Columbia University Press, 1969.

33. Hafer, R. W., and Scott Hein. "The Dynamics and Estimation of Short-Run Money Demand." Federal Reserve Bank of St. Louis *Review*, March 1980, pp. 26–35.

34. Hartman, David G. "The International Financial Market and U.S. Interest Rates." Working Paper No. 598, National Bureau of Economic Research, New York, 1981.

35. Hein, Scott. "Dynamic Forecasting and the Demand for Money." Federal Reserve Bank of St. Louis *Review,* June-July 1980, pp. 13–23.

36. Hicks, Sir John R. "Mr. Keynes and the Classics." *Econometrica,* April 1937, pp. 147–59.

37. _____. *Value and Capital.* 2d ed. London: Oxford at the Clarendon Press, 1946.

38. Houglet, Michel X. *Estimating the Term Structure of Interest Rates for Nonhomogeneous Bonds.* Ph.D. dissertation, University of California, Berkeley, 1980.

39. Ibbotson, Roger G., and Rex A. Sinquefield. *Stocks, Bonds, Bills, and Inflation: Historical Returns (1926–1978).* 2d ed. Charlottesville, Va.: The Financial Analysts Research Foundation, 1979.

40. Kane, E. J. "Arbitrage Pressure and Divergences between Forward and Futures Interest Rates." Working Paper No. CSFM–21 Center for the Study of Futures Markets, Columbia Business School, New York, May 1980.

41. Kessel, Reuben A. *The Cyclical Behavior of The Term Structure of Interest Rates.* New York: National Bureau of Economic Research, Columbia University Press, 1965.

42. Kuznets, Simon. *Economic Growth of Nations.* Cambridge, Mass.: Harvard University Press, 1971.

43. Lawler, T. A. "Seasonal Movements in Short-Term Yield Spreads." Federal Reserve Bank of Richmond *Economic Review,* July/August 1978.

44. Lucas, Robert. "Methods and Problems of Business Cycle Theory." *The Journal of Money, Credit and Banking,* November 1980, Part II, pp. 696–715.

45. Lutz, F. A. *The Theory of Interest.* 2d ed. New York: Aldine Publishers, 1967.

46. McCulloch, J. Huston. "The Tax-Adjusted Yield Curve." *Journal of Finance,* June 1975, pp. 811–30.

47. McNees, Stephen K. "The Recent Record of Thirteen Forecasters." *New England Economic Review,* Federal Reserve Bank of Boston, September/October 1981.

48. Meltzer, Allan H. "Keynes' General Theory: A Different Perspective." *Journal of Economic Literature,* March 1981, pp. 34–64.

49. Miskin, Frederic. "Monetary Policy and Long-Term Interest Rates." *Journal of Monetary Economics,* February 1981, pp. 29–55.

50. Modigliani, Franco, and R. J. Shiller. "Inflation, Rational Expectations and the Term Structure of Interest Rates." *Economica,* February 1973, pp. 12–43.

51. Modigliani, Franco, and Richard Sutch, "Innovations in Interest Rate Policy." *American Economic Review, Papers and Proceedings,* May 1966, pp. 178–97.

52. Mundell, R. A. *Monetary Theory.* Pacific Palisades, Calif.: Goodyear Publishing, 1971.

53. Nelson, Charles R. *The Term Structure of Interest Rates,* New York: Basic Books, 1972.

54. Nelson, Charles R., and G. William Schwert. "Short-Term Interest Rates as Predictors of Inflation: On Testing the Hypothesis that the Real Rate is Constant." *American Economic Review*, June 1977, pp. 478–86.

55. Pesando, James E. "On Forecasting Long-Term Interest Rates: Is the Success of the No-Change Prediction Surprising?" *Journal of Finance*, September 1980, pp. 1045–47.

56. Poole, William R. "Optimal Choice of Monetary Policy Instruments in a Simple Stochastic Macro Model." *Quarterly Journal in Economics*, May 1970, pp. 197–216.

57. _____. The Relationship of Monetary Decelerations to Business Cycle Peaks: Another Look at the Evidence." *Journal of Finance*, June 1975, pp. 697–712.

58. Reinganum, Marc. "The Arbitrage Pricing Theory: Some Empirical Results." *Journal of Finance*, May 1981, pp. 313–21.

59. Roll, Richard. *The Behavior of Interest Rates*. Amsterdam: North Holland, 1970.

60. Ross, Stephen A. "The Arbitrage Theory of Capital Asset Pricing." *Journal of Economic Theory*, December 1976, pp. 341–60.

61. Salomon Brothers, *Prospects for Financial Markets*. Annual. New York: Salomon Brothers Bond Market Research.

62. Santoni, G. J., and Courtenay C. Stone. "What Really Happened to Interest Rates: A Longer-Run Analysis." Federal Reserve Bank of St. Louis *Review*, November 1981, pp. 3–14.

63. Singleton, Kenneth J. "Maturity-Specific Disturbances and the Term Structure of Interest Rates." *Journal of Money, Credit and Banking*, November 1980, part 1, pp. 603–14.

64. Stokes, Houston H., and H. Neuberger. "The Effect of Monetary Changes on Interest Rates: A Box-Jenkins Approach." *Review of Economics and Statistics*, November 1979, pp. 534–48.

65. Telser, Lester G. "A Critique of Some Recent Empirical Research on the Explanation of the Term Structure of Interest Rates." *Journal of Political Economy*, August 1967, pp. 546–61.

66. Throop, Adrian W. "Interest-Rate Forecasts and Market Efficiency." Federal Reserve Bank of San Francisco, *Economic Review*, Spring 1981, pp. 29–43.

67. Tobin, James, and William Brainard. "Pitfalls in Financial Model Building." *American Economic Review, Papers and Proceedings*, May 1968, pp. 99–122.

68. Turnbull, Stuart M. "Measurement of the Real Rate of Interest and Related Problems in a World of Uncertainty." *Journal of Money, Credit and Banking*, May 1981, pp. 177–91.

69. Wecker, William. "Predicting the Turning Points of a Time Series." *The Journal of Business*, January 1979, pp. 35–50.

70. Wendel, Helmut F. "Interest-Rate Expectations." Washington, D.C.: Board of Governors of the Federal Reserve System, 1968.

71. Wenninger, John; Lawrence Radecki; and Elizabeth Hammond. "Recent Instability in the Demand for Money." Federal Reserve Bank of New York, *Quarterly Review*, Summer 1981, pp. 1–9.

72. Wojnilower, Albert R. "The Central Role of Credit Crunches in Recent Financial History." *Brookings Papers on Economic Activity,* vol. 2 (1980), 30th Conference, pp. 277–326.

73. Yawitz, Jess B., and W. J. Marshall. "Measuring the Effect of Callability on Bond Yields." *Journal of Money, Credit and Banking,* February 1981, pp. 60–71.

Appendixes

Tax Consequences of Exchange Offers

A

NICHOLAS J. LETIZIA, J.D., C.P.A.
Donaldson, Lufkin & Jenrette

ANTHONY J. TARANTO
Thomas J. Lipton, Inc.

Security swaps between an issuing corporation and a security holder can result in tax consequences far beyond recognition of taxable gain or loss. The form of exchange can impact the carry-over of tax attributes, basis, holding period and characterization of income as capital gain or ordinary. The tax effects of proposed exchanges must be reviewed with great scrutiny to ensure that the mode of the transaction will not result in a deleterious tax impact to the corporation or investor. The myriad complex rules containing rudimentary mechanical features as well as highly subjective areas provide sufficient latitude to mandate adequate transactional tax planning. The flexibility of the tax rules often permits desired business objectives to be realized through selection of the proper form of a proposed transaction.

Fundamentally, a recognized tax event does not result, notwithstanding the presence of an economic or accounting gain or loss, if in substance the position of an investor remains unchanged. This is true irrespective of whether there has been an alteration in the legal entity in which the investment is made.

Specific rules define the types of exchanges that qualify as tax-free reorganizations. The transaction at the corporate level must qualify as a tax-free reorganization in order for an exchange of securities to be tax

1053

free to the exchanging shareholders. If two individuals swapped their respective 100 shares in different public corporations on a strictly private basis, each individual would recognize gain or loss equal to the difference between the fair market value of the stock received and the basis in the stock surrendered.

There are four basic types of tax-free reorganizations: (1) acquisitive, (2) divisive, (3) refinancing, and (4) bankruptcy arrangements. *Acquisitive exchanges* involve the acquisition of another corporation. The acquisition can be in the form of an asset or stock transaction; it can result in a direct investment in a newly acquired subsidiary or in a combination of business enterprises by way of merger or consolidation. *Divisive exchanges* involve the separation of a subsidiary from an affiliated group or a division from a single corporation. *Refinancing exchanges* involve alterations of a corporation's capital structure or attempts to minimize debt-carrying expenses due to a decline in interest rates. *Bankruptcy arrangements* involve the judicially supervised reorganization of a corporation in order that such enterprise may continue to operate as a going concern.

The potential transactions that can be characterized as any of the four basic types of exchanges are legion. This chapter will focus only on the general tax impact on an investor who exchanges securities pursuant to transactions that qualify as tax-free reorganizations. Investors should be cautioned that prior to assenting to an exchange, competent tax counsel should be procured.

GENERAL CONCEPTS

Generally, absent specific statutory authority, all realized gains and losses are subject to tax. Certain nonrecognition rules permit the postponement of tax irrespective of economic realization, since Congress has decided that a mere change in the form of an investment, in some instances, should not be taxed. This deferral is grounded on the public policy that a mere alteration of the form of an investment should not be recognized if the economic substance of such investment remains unchanged.

This principle underscores sections 351, 355, and 368 of the Internal Revenue Code of 1954. These provisions constitute the primary definitional infrastructure that regulate the four basic types of exchanges. They are not elective; rather, if a transaction satisfies the requirements of any of these sections, a reorganization will be deemed to be tax free. However, certain operative rules could result in partial or full taxability. Although a transaction may satisfy the definitional rules, the operative rules must be applied at the exchanging-investor level.

These deferral provisions generally permit the tax-free swap of stock or securities, provided the transaction is tax free at the corporate level. "Securities" are limited to debt obligations. The security holder's basis and holding period for long-term capital gain or loss treatment remain unchanged.

A problem exists as to what type of debt instrument constitutes a security. The Internal Revenue Service and the courts hold that only long-term debt obligations can qualify as securities. For certain purposes, the Internal Revenue Service has ruled that debt instruments having a maturity of less than five years are not securities. Notwithstanding this ruling, the ultimate determination of whether an instrument is a security depends on the facts and circumstances of a particular case. This ruling as well as judicial decisions obviously indicate that term is a principal factor in determining whether or not an instrument is a security.

Problems may be present if (1) debt instruments having different face values are swapped, (2) shares of stock are swapped for securities, (3) securities are swapped for shares of stock, (4) other property (including liabilities assumed or taken subject to) is received in addition to stock or securities, or (5) original-issue discount or amortizable bond premium exists.

Generally, the receipt of property other than stock or securities in an exchange for stock or securities is a taxable event. Such nonqualified property is called *boot*. The character of boot as capital gain or ordinary income depends on the particular facts and circumstances. The maximum gain that could be recognized is the amount of boot received. Typically, an investor realizes capital gain, since the underlying debt instrument is a capital asset. Similarly, assumed liabilities and liabilities to which property is taken subject are treated as boot; however, no taxable event occurs unless the sum of any such liabilities exceeds the basis of the stock or securities tendered in an exchange. The basis of the stock or securities received is increased by any boot recognized. Finally, the excess face value of securities received over securities surrendered is treated as boot.

Stock for debt exchanges (vertical or upstream exchanges) involve upgrading an investment to a senior position in terms of legal rights appurtenant thereto. Debt for stock exchanges (vertical or downstream exchanges) involve a dimunition of legal rights. Vertical exchanges do not change the otherwise tax-free status of a transaction unless stock is exchanged solely for debt. If stock is exchanged for stock and securities a portion of the gain may be taxable as boot.

Horizontal debt exchanges (i.e., debt for debt), also do not frustrate an otherwise tax-free exchange.

Original issue discount is the discount equal to the difference between the issue price of a debt obligation and such obligation's face value. Section 1232 requires that such discount be recognized as interest income during the life of the bond.[1] The investor's basis in a debt obligation is increased by the amount of original-issue discount recognized. Accordingly, at the time of maturity, the investor's basis in a debt obligation would equal the face value of such obligation so no gain or loss is realized. Market discount, on the other hand, is not amortized.

Amortizable bond premium is the excess of the price paid for a bond over its face value. At the election of the taxpayer, such differences may be amortized over the unexpired life of the instrument.[2] This amortization results in a current ordinary deduction and a corresponding basis reduction so that no gain or loss is realized at maturity. Market premium as well as bond premium at the time of the original issuance may be amortized pursuant to this election.

The following sections of this chapter will consider certain specific types of exchanges.

DEBT INSTRUMENTS HAVING DIFFERENT FACE VALUES ARE SWAPPED

If the face value of the securities received exceeds the face value of the securities surrendered, the fair market value of the excess "face value" is treated as boot. The taxpayer's gain on the security swap is recognized to the extent of the boot.

If more than one security is received, the amount of boot recognized is determined by allocating the excess face value among the securities received. This allocation is made by multiplying the fair market value of each security received by a fraction, the numerator of which is the face value of all securities received over securities surrendered and the denominator is the total face value of the securities received.

For example, suppose an individual exchanged a security with a face value of $2,000 for two different securities, each with a face value of $1,500. One of the securities, X, received has a fair market value (FMV) of $1,500; the other, Y, has a fair market value of $1,200. The boot or other property is calculated as follows:

$$\frac{\text{Total excess face value}}{\text{Total face value of securities received}} = \frac{\$1,000}{\$3,000} = \frac{1}{3}$$

Accordingly, one-third of the fair market value of each security received constitutes boot. Therefore, boot is calculated as follows:

---

[1] See Chapter 3.

[2] See Chapter 3. The taxpayer *must* amortize the premium of a tax-exempt obligation.

$$\text{For security X FMV:} \quad \$1,500 \times \tfrac{1}{3} = \$500$$
$$\text{For security Y FMV:} \quad \$1,200 \times \tfrac{1}{3} = \underline{\quad 400}$$
$$\text{Total Boot} \qquad\qquad\qquad\qquad\quad \$900$$

SHARES OF STOCK FOR SECURITIES— UPSTREAM EXCHANGE

An investor must beware of the consequences of an upstream exchange (stock received in exchange for debt securities). This type of swap is a taxable event. In a situation in which an investor has upgraded his status from shareholder to creditor, the investor will have to recognize gain as though he had received money in the swap. In effect, the investor is deemed to have sold his equity interest at a price equal to the fair market value of the securities received.

This transaction is not within the ambit of the nonrecognition rules, since the investor does not maintain a continuing equity interest in the corporation. Gain is equal to the difference between the fair market value of the securities received and the basis in the stock surrendered. This rule is illustrated below.

Suppose X, an individual, owns stock in Z Corporation, having a basis of $200 and a fair market value of $400. X exchanges her stock for Z Corporation securities having a face value of $1,000 and a fair market value of $400. X must recognize the difference between her basis of $200 in Z Corporation's stock and the fair market value, $400, of the securities received. X's basis in the Z Corporation's securities is $400.

If a shareholder receives both stock and securities in exchange for stock, the transaction is partially taxable, since no securities were surrendered. The face value of the securities received is treated as boot. If securities were surrendered, the rules discussed above would limit the amount of boot to the excess face value of the securities received over the securities surrendered.

SECURITIES FOR STOCK—DOWNSTREAM EXCHANGE

If securities are exchanged solely for stock, the transaction is wholly tax free. Similarly, if stock and securities are exchanged solely for stock, no gain or loss is recognized. This transaction is not partially taxable as in the case of an exchange of stock and securities solely for securities, since stock never constitutes boot.

BOOT

Securities that are not to be treated as "nonrecognition property" must be treated as boot. The term *boot* also applies to other property (including the relief of liabilities) and money, which is not considered nonrecognition property under the tax rules. Gain in this type of transaction is recognized, but only to the extent of the boot received. A few examples will illustrate this point:

1. In a transaction, which qualifies under a plan of reorganization, the investor swaps stock with a basis of $800 for:

Stock (FMV)...	$1,000
Cash...	500
Securities (FMV)...	500
Total market value of property received.....................	2,000
Less: Basis of stock surrendered............................	800
Gain realized...	$1,200

Gain to be recognized by the taxpayer is limited to the lesser of the realized gain of $1,200 or $1,000 the value of the boot received $1,000

2. Assume the same facts as in Example 1 except the basis of the stock surrendered by the investor was $3,000 and not $1,200. The investor would have a realized loss on the swap of $1,000; however, the investor would not be permitted to recognize any loss on the transaction.

3. Assume the same facts as Example 1, except the basis of the stock surrendered is $1,200. The realized gain on this exchange would be $800, which also would be recognized gain. The recognized gain is $800 and not $1,000 because the recognized gain to the taxpayer is limited to the lesser of the amount of boot received or the realized gain.

The nature of the gain recognized is beyond the scope of this chapter. Simply stated, if boot has the effect of a dividend, the gain will be taxed as a dividend at ordinary rates. In many instances, however, distributions of boot will be taxed as capital gains.

BASIS AND HOLDING PERIOD

The basis of stock and/or securities received as nonrecognition property has the same basis as the stock and/or securities surrendered. If the exchange is partially taxable, the basis of the nonrecognition property is decreased by the fair market value of such nonrecognition property and increased by any gain recognized. The basis of any boot received is its fair market value. Specific rules are provided for allocating basis on relative fair market value if different classes of stock or securities are received as nonrecognition property.

The holding period for determining whether a subsequent disposition of nonrecognition property results in a long-term or short-term capital gain includes the holding period of the stock and/or securities surrendered. The holding period of nonrecognition property received as boot begins on the day following the exchange.

CONCLUSION

Except in rare cases, realized gains are subject to recognition for federal income tax purposes. Certain exchanges of stock and securities pursuant to a tax-free reorganization are examples of such rare cases. As illustrated above, these transactions may result in partial recognition of gain but never in a recognition of loss. Losses are deferred by virtue of the carryover basis rules until investors dispose of their interest in taxable transactions.

To the layperson these rules may appear overly complex and somewhat illogical. Complexity is required because of the multitude of various transactions that in substance constitute a mere change in form of investment and not economic interest. Such changes in form are ignored. Partial recognition only occurs if a transaction alters the economic interest of an investor through the receipt of boot. The limitation on deductibility of losses is completely consistent with the underlying rationale of the tax law that transactions designed with the sole purpose of avoiding tax will be ignored. Despite their complexity, these rules render equitable results in most instances.

Individual Retirement, Simplified Employee Pension, and Keogh Plans

B CHRISTOPHER J. RYAN, J.D.
Attorney
Ruskin, Schlissel, Moscou & Evans

INTRODUCTION

All three of the plans heading the title of this chapter have one central characteristic in common. All provide an avenue by which individuals can accumulate retirement funds on a tax-favored basis. Each plan will be treated separately in the following pages.

INDIVIDUAL RETIREMENT PLANS (IRAs)

An individual retirement plan is a personal retirement savings program to which eligible individuals may contribute tax-deductible payments with the benefit of tax-deferred buildup of income. In tax years beginning in 1977 and later, some individuals may also contribute to plans for their spouses. There are three types of individual retirement plans:

Individual Retirement Account. An individual retirement account is a trust or custodial account established for the exclusive benefit of an individual or the individual's beneficiaries. The trustee or custodian must be a bank, a federally insured credit union, building and loan association, insurance company, brokerage firm, or other "person" who is eligible to act as a trustee or custodian under rules promulgated by the IRS.

No part of the trust funds can be invested in life insurance contracts. Assets of the trust cannot be commingled with other property except where there is a common trust fund or common investment fund. The individual's interest in the IRA must be nonforfeitable. The trust instrument must provide that distributions will begin no later than the close of the taxable year in which the individual reaches age 70½.[1]

Individual Retirement Annuity. An individual retirement annuity is either an annuity or endowment contract purchased from an insurance company. The contract must be nontransferable and nonforfeitable. A contract will be considered transferable if it can be used as security for a loan other than a loan from the issuer in an amount not greater than the cash value of the contract. Even so, a policy loan would cause the contract to cease to be an individual retirement annuity or endowment contract as of the first day of the owner's tax year in which the loan was made. Premiums may not be fixed, nor may they exceed $2,000 a year. Distributions must begin no later than the close of the taxable year in which the individual reaches the age of 70½, and the period in which distribution may be made is limited.[2]

Individual Retirement Bonds. Individual retirement bonds are retirement bonds issued by the federal government. These bonds currently earn 8 percent interest, compounded twice a year. Interest will be paid only upon redemption and not at all if the bond is redeemed within 12 months after issuance. It will cease to bear interest at the buyer's age of 70½ or, if earlier, five years after the death of the registered buyer. Except in the case of a rollover contribution, the buyer may not purchase more than $2,000 in a tax year on the behalf of any one individual, and the bond must be non-transferable.[3]

Retirement bonds are available at any Federal Reserve Bank or directly from the U.S. Treasury. They are issued in denominations of $50, $75, $100, and $500.

Eligible Persons

Everybody is eligible to participate in an IRA despite the fact that they may already be participants in a qualified pension plan (including a Keogh plan).[4] Also a person already receiving benefits from social security or some other government or private retirement plan can participate in an IRA plan.

If a husband and wife are eligible, each may make deductible contributions to a separate plan, whether they file joint or separate re-

---

[1] Internal Revenue Code, Section 408(a).
[2] Internal Revenue Code, Section 408(b).
[3] Internal Revenue Code, Section 409.
[4] Internal Revenue Code, Section 219(b)(2).

turns. The deduction is figured individually and without regard to community property laws.[5]

Contributions and Distributions

The limit on the contributions a qualified individual may make to his or her IRA account is 100 percent of annual income up to a maximum of $2,000, and the maximum is $2,250 for a spousal IRA.[6] For this reason and the additional reason that IRAs were never very popular with the persons eligible for them, financial institutions were not enamoured of the plans when they measured the burdensome filings required by the IRS of them as custodians and trustees.

However, IRAs are enjoying increasing popularity as the result of skyrocketing interest rates and the public's growing awareness of investment plans illustrated by the success of the money market funds, many of which offer separate IRA accounts within the fund itself. This results in a person being able to earn, at the time of this writing, 17 percent tax free on the corpus of an account, and contributions to the account are tax deductible whether or not the individual itemizes deductions. Excess contributions are subject to a 6 percent nondeductible excise tax, which recurs annually until the excess contribution is eliminated.[7]

The earliest age at which a person can begin receiving IRA payments without tax penalty is age 59½, unless he or she becomes disabled. In contrast, the person must begin receiving payments no later than age 70½. Funds distributed prematurely are taxed at ordinary income in the year of distribution and are subject to a nondeductible 10 percent excise tax on the amount of the distribution.[8]

Once reaching age 59½ and beginning to receive distributions, the individual pays federal income tax on the proceeds in each year payments are received. If the IRA is paid out in one lump sum, the individual pays income tax on the entire amount in one year. For those people receiving the distribution as an annuity or over a period of years, tax payments are spread over several years. Naturally, a lump-sum distribution leads to bunching of taxable income, but the individual can take advantage of the regular five-year income-averaging rules. However, he or she would not be eligible for special 10-year averaging that applies to lump-sum payments from other retirement plans.

---

[5] Regulation under Internal Revenue Code 1954 Section 408(g). If a nonworking spouse is the beneficiary of the IRA, the amount goes to $2,250 provided the couple files a joint return. If the contributions are not equal for both spouses, the ceiling is $2,000.

[6] Regulation under Internal Revenue Code 1954 Section 219(b).

[7] Regulation under Internal Revenue Code 1954 Section 408(d) (4).

[8] Regulation under Internal Revenue Code 1954 Section 408.

If a person dies before beginning to receive retirement benefits, the funds accumulated in the account must be distributed to the beneficiary in a lump sum within five years of the person's death or be applied to the purchase of an annuity for the beneficiary. If the contributor dies during retirement, the beneficiary will receive any remaining payments to which the contributor was entitled.

Employer-Sponsored IRAs

An employer can establish IRAs for its employees and for nonworking spouses of these employees. The employer can deduct its contributions to the IRAs. And, although the contribution is included in the employee's compensation and is subject to social security and unemployment taxes, the employee can also deduct the contribution.

A trust that will be treated as an individual retirement account may be set up by an employer or association of employees if the trust meets all the requirements of an individual retirement account and there is a separate accounting maintained for each employee. The assets of an employer or association trust may be held in a common fund for the account of all individuals who have an interest in the trust. Such trusts may be composed of significant sums of money depending on the number of employees involved, particularly if the trust was created from the termination and rollover of a prior qualified pension plan.

Many small and medium-sized employers may view such a rollover as both favorable to the employer and employee for the following reasons. For the employer there is no requirement that an employer-sponsored IRA cover a certain number or group of employees. In fact the employer may discriminate in favor of employees who are either officers, stockholders, or highly paid. As to the employees, they can participate in the higher yields currently available in money market type IRAs if they act as the corporate trustee; and they have the flexibility to roll over their own IRAs to a brokerage firm or other qualified trustee should they leave the corporation, without running afoul of vesting requirements common to many qualified pension plans. Last, employees are also allowed a similar deduction for contributions up to the $2,000 limit to separate IRA plans or for voluntary contributions to employer plans.

Evolving IRAs

Because of the public's increasing awareness of the high interest rates available on money market instruments and bonds, many banks, brokerage firms, and mutual funds have established IRA plans. In the case of the brokerage firms, many offer self-directed accounts, whereby a person can invest part of the account in stocks, part in that firm's money market fund (provided he or she meets the firm's minimum investment requirements), and part in stock or commodity options or other financial services offered by the firm.

These self-directed accounts have proven very popular with the public because they allow the individual investor to purchase short-term or long-term interest-bearing securities offering unprecedented yields, rather than accepting the relatively uncompetitive rates that most banks and savings and loan associations offered in the past.

Finally, the popularity of IRAs and their counterpart Keoghs may receive a substantial boost from the Economic Recovery Tax Act of 1981, which raised the maximum IRA deductible contribution to $2,000 and the Keogh to $15,000 per year from the previous ceilings of $1,500 and $7,500 respectively.

SIMPLIFIED EMPLOYEE PENSION PLAN

A simplified employee pension (SEP) is an individual retirement account or individual retirement annuity, but not a retirement bond, which may accept employer contributions up to $15,000 or 15 percent of the employee's compensation not in excess of $200,000. It is owned by the employee, who may be self-employed or even an active participant in a qualified pension or profit sharing plan or a government plan, or for whom contributions were made to a 403(b) tax-sheltered annuity.[9] However, for an individual retirement plan or annuity to be a simplified employee pension, certain eligibility and contribution requirements must be met.

The employer must make contributions to any employee age 25 or older who has performed *services* for the employer in at least three of the immediately preceding five calendar years, and such employee must participate in the SEP. Services are defined as any interval of time in which an employee performs work for an employer. All eligible employees must participate (except employees whose compensation for the year was less then $200). Employees covered by a collective bargaining agreement in which retirement benefits were the subject of good-faith bargaining may be excluded from participation.[10]

If the employer's contribution to the SEP–IRA is less than the amount the employee could deduct for a contribution under the usual IRA rules (the lesser of $2,000 or 100 percent of compensation), the employee may make up the difference.[11]

---

[9] A 403(b) annuity is an annuity contract purchased for an employee by an employer that is exempt from tax under I.R.C. 501(a), and such an annuity is nonforfeitable except for failure to pay premiums.

[10] Internal Revenue Code, Section 408(k).

[11] Internal Revenue Code, Section 219(b).

Employer contributions must not discriminate in favor of an officer, a shareholder who owns more than 10 percent of the value of employer stock, a self-employed person, or a highly compensated employee. Employees who are excluded from participation as nonresident aliens or because they are covered by a collective bargaining agreement are not considered for purposes of determining whether or not there is discrimination.[12] Unless employer contributions bear a uniform relationship to total compensation, or earned income in the case of self-employed individuals, they will be considered discriminatory. Presumably, a uniform percentage of compensation would meet this requirement. Only limited integration with social security is permitted: The employer's share of social security taxes on employees may be taken into account as a contribution to the plan; however, if it is, the self-employment tax paid by any owner-employee in the plan must also be taken into account as a contribution made on his or her behalf. Integration of a simplified employee pension is not permitted in any year in which the employer also maintains an integrated pension, profit sharing, stock bonus, qualified bond purchase, or 403(b) tax-sheltered annuity plan.

Employer and Employee Deductions

Employer contributions are not subject to income tax withholding, FICA (social security tax), or FUTA (federal unemployment tax) if it is reasonable to believe that the employee will be entitled to deduct the amount on his or her income tax return.[13] However, in the case of an integrated plan, an employee who is an officer, more than 10 percent shareholder, or owner-employee must reduce the $15,000 (or $2,000 if making up a difference) element of the deduction limit by the amount of social security tax that was treated as an employee contribution.

Contributions to a SEP are made on a calendar-year basis. If the employer is a calendar-year taxpayer, it can make the contribution anytime during its tax year and claim a deduction for that year. Further, the employer may treat contributions made within the first 3½ months of the following year (that is, by April 15) as though made in the previous year. The maximum employer deduction is 15 percent of covered compensation for the calendar year. Any excess may be carried over and deducted in succeeding years up to a maximum of 15 percent of covered compensation. If the employer also contributes to a qualified profit sharing or stock bonus plan, the 15 percent deductible limit for that plan is reduced by the amount of the allowable deduc-

---

[12] Internal Revenue Code, Section 408(k) (3).
[13] Internal Revenue Code, Sections 3401(a) and 3306(6)(5).

tion for contributions to the simplified employee pensions with respect to participants in the stock bonus or profit sharing plan.[14]

An employee should include the employer's contribution to a SEP in gross income; however, this is effectively cancelled by an offsetting adjustment, provided the deduction does not exceed the $15,000 or 15 percent of compensation, whichever is less.

Advantages

The most significant advantage a SEP offers over traditional retirement plans (i.e., pension or profit sharing plans) is the minimum amount of paperwork and bookkeeping necessary to start and maintain the plan. Costs for consultants (lawyers, accountants, etc.) are generally much lower. Second, a SEP offers greater flexibility with respect to contributions. A corporation can contribute any amount it wants up to the maximum set by law, or it can choose not to make any contribution at all. Although this is generally true for profit sharing plans also, defined benefit plans are quite different. Employers maintaining defined benefit plans must satisfy stiff minimum funding standards every year, regardless of profits, or face penalty taxes.

SEP–IRAs also offer financial institutions who qualify as trustees or custodians under IRS regulations significant new business opportunities, since such corporate plans usually involve amounts in excess of $100,000 and therefore facilitate investment in certificates of deposit, Treasury bills, commercial paper, and (for the innovative) Eurodollars.

KEOGH PLANS

Self-employed retirement accounts are often referred to as KEOGH or HR–10 accounts. There are two basic income tax advantages for the self-employed person who adopts a Keogh plan:

1. To the extent that the contribution the self-employed person makes on his or her own behalf to a qualified plan is tax deductible, the person is deferring the tax on this income. (It will be taxable when ultimately received from the plan.)

2. Income earned on contributions to the plan (whether or not tax deductible when made) will escape tax while in the plan, thereby permitting a greater total compounding of earnings than would otherwise be possible.

Three basic terms should be defined before we attempt a description of a Keogh plan's requirements and benefits.

> *An employee* is any person who works for another person or a business firm for pay. Employees are also called common-law employees. It is

---

[14] Internal Revenue Code, Section 404.

possible to be an employee and be self-employed at the same time. A good example is a lawyer who is an employee of a corporation during regular working hours. The lawyer also has an office and practices law in the evening as a self-employed person.[15]

Self-employed person.   A person who has earned income from operating an unincorporated business (a sole proprietorship) or who performs personal services as a partner for a partnership is considered a self-employed person, even if there are no profits in a particular year.[16]

An *owner-employee* is a sole proprietor. In a partnership, a partner who owns either more than 10 percent interest in the profits or more than 10 percent interest in the capital of a partnership is also an owner-employee. A partner who owns 10 percent or less interest in the partnership is self-employed but is not an owner-employee.[17]

Requirements and Contributions

All employees with at least three years of service who are *not* (1) covered by a collective bargaining agreement under which retirement benefits were the subject of good-faith bargaining with the employer or (2) nonresident aliens must be covered under the *self-employed plan.* Eligible employees are prohibited from waiving participation in the plan, notwithstanding that such intended waiver would be purely voluntary on the employee's part.

Unlike corporate plans, no mimimum age requirement may be established in a plan covering self-employed individuals. Length of service is generally the sole factor in determining eligibility to participate. Employees who work 1,000 hours a year or more are regarded as full-time employees and must be covered, but those who work less than 1,000 hours a year do not have to be covered.

The above rules apply to the Keogh plans covering an owner-employee. A plan that does not cover an owner-employee need not cover all employees with three or more years of service. Instead the plan must meet the coverage requirements that apply to qualified pension plans. Plans covering owner-employees have additional limitations over and above those covering self-employed individuals none of whom are owner-employees (i.e., where no partner owns more than 10 percent of the partnership.) This is a critical distinction when figuring which requirements and limitations apply to persons covered by a Keogh plan.

The other critical distinction that must be made when analyzing a Keogh is how the rules are applied to "defined *benefit* plans" and "defined *contribution* plans." For clarity's sake a definition of these

---

[15] Department of Treasury Publication 560.
[16] Department of Treasury Publication 560.
[17] Department of Treasury Publication 560.

concepts will help the reader visualize dichotomies inherent in the complex IRS regulations covering Keogh plans.

A defined *contribution* plan provides an individual account for each person in the plan. Benefits are based on the amount contributed to each account and any income, expenses, gains, and losses, and any forfeiture of other accounts that may be allocated to the account. Forfeitures of accounts may not be allocated to self-employed persons or to owner-employees.[18]

A defined *benefit* plan sets retirement benefits. Contributions to the plan must be enough to produce those benefits. A defined benefit plan is a pension plan and can be in the form of an annuity, or bond purchase plan. Plans are for the benefit of employees or their beneficiaries. A sole proprietor is considered to be both an employee and employer. A partnership is considered to be the employer of each of the partners. A plan that includes self-employed persons must provide benefits for employees without discrimination.[19]

Whether a self-employed individual chooses either of the above plans will ordinarily be determined by that person's age and income.

Contributions to Defined Contributions Plans

Most Keogh accounts are defined contribution plans that require contributions based solely on the amount of earned income of a plan participant. Under defined contributions plans, the maximum annual contribution by the employer on behalf of any such self-employed individual is the lesser of $15,000 or 15 percent of his or her earned income. Unlike corporate plans, for which the $25,000 limitation that was effective in 1975 has been increased annually to $41,500 in 1981, the old $7,500 limitation for Keoghs has been in effect since the enactment of the Employee Retirement Income Security Act of 1974, and the new ceiling of $15,000 enacted by Congress in August 1981 was long overdue when compared to the corporate plans.

For purposes of the tax-deductible contribution limitation, only the first $200,000 of earned income of a self-employed person may be taken into account. This eliminates the possibility of a plan providing a maximum contribution for an owner-employee while providing less for other employees. Thus the plan must use at least a 7½ percent of a compensation contribution formula for all of the covered employees if a maximum contribution ($15,000) is to be made on behalf of an owner-employee whose earned income equals or exceeds $100,000. One benefit to the employer of covered employees is that if the employer covers at least one employee who is permitted to make voluntary contributions to a pension fund, the employer is permitted to

---

[18] Department of Treasury Publication 560.

[19] Department of Treasury Publication 560.

make an additional voluntary contribution equal to the lesser of 10 percent of the employee's income or $2,500 each year. Although voluntary contributions are not deductible, the income earned on the contributions is not taxed until distribution.

Further, self-employed persons are able to establish their own IRAs, even though they participate in a Keogh Plan or they make additional tax-deductible voluntary contributions to their Keogh plan.

Contributions to Defined Benefit Plans

In a defined benefit plan an actuary determines how much of a lump sum will be necessary to attain a certain monthly retirement income. Such plans must satisfy the requirements set forth in subsection (j) of Section 401 of the IRC. That section sets limits on the extent to which defined benefit plans can accrue benefits for self-employed individuals and shareholders employees. In general, a plan satisfies the requirements of this section only if the "basic benefit" accruing under the plan for each year of participation by the covered individual does not exceed the amount of his or her compensation that is covered under the plan (up to a maximum of $100,000). The Internal Revenue Code supplies the percentages in five-year intervals, and the regulations break them down by single years.

Annual contributions will vary widely from person to person, depending upon the age of the contributor and the contributor's income at the time the plan begins.

When May Distribution Be Made from a Keogh Plan?

A self-employed individual other than an owner-employee may receive a distribution of his or her account upon separation from service, regardless of age at the time of distribution.

Owner-employees, on the other hand, are subject to certain restrictions on distributions. Even if an owner-employee discontinued a business, no distribution could be made without penalty until he or she reached age 59½. An exception is provided if the owner-employee is disabled. However, the Economic Recovery Tax Act of 1981 adopted an amendment that permits early withdrawals from a terminated Keogh plan by an owner-employer without regard to the five-year ban on Keogh contributions for the owner-employee.

If a plan covers an owner-employee, the law requires that the owner-employee's entire account be distributed no later than age 70½ or that distributions begin no later than age 70½ and be payable as a single-life or joint surivor annuity for the life of the owner-employee and spouse. Otherwise distribution must be made in installments over a period that does not exceed the contributor's life expectancy and that of the spouse. The plan must also require that payments to a nonowner-employee or a common-law employee be distributed no later than the end of the year in which he or she reaches age 70½ or retires.

Investing Keogh Funds

A plan must be funded, and there are several ways to do it. A trust may be established to invest the funds of a plan. An annuity plan may purchase an annuity contract with incidental life insurance on the participants. Face-amounts certificates, which are treated as annuity contracts, may be bought by the employee, trust, or custodial account directly from an insurance company. A plan also may be funded with U.S. Retirement Plan Bonds. Finally, a custodial account may be established to invest the funds. Like IRAs discussed earlier in this chapter, there are several ways in which Keogh funds can be invested, some of which will be discussed below.

U.S. Government Retirement Bonds

The investment with the least expense and bother are U.S. government retirement bonds. Although the government bonds are easy to purchase, they currently pay only 8 percent, which is well below what one could obtain by investing in bank certificates of deposit or savings and loan time deposits. Therfore, it is difficult to see why anyone would choose this option.

If you invest retirement funds solely in time deposits, mutual fund shares, or life insurance, *only* a custodial account is necessary. Banks, savings and loans, and federally insured credit unions can all provide such accounts. If the plan is required to be funded by a trust, the trustee must be a bank or other "person" approved by the IRS as satisfying certain regulations.[20]

It is also possible to invest directly in money market instruments, notes, or bonds via a brokerage firm. With bond yields as high as they currently are, this may be an attractive way to lock in high returns for the major part of, if not all, of a persons accumulation period.

Many Keogh plans maintained by banks and brokerage houses allow participants to direct investments by the trustees or custodians. This enables owner-employees to have some of the degree of flexibility they might have in a corporate-type plan.

Transferring Funds

Transferring funds from a Keogh plan at one institution to a Keogh plan at another is very easy to do, and no tax penalties are incurred.

---

[20] Regulations under Internal Revenue Code 1954 Sec. 1.401–12.

This gives an investor important flexibility. For instance, an investor could take advantage of the high interest rates offered by notes, bonds, and money market instruments presently and switch later contributions into high dividend yielding stocks should those rates decline or into diamonds and bullion if inflation is the major worry. It should also be noted that Keogh plans can be rolled over into IRA plans, which in the right circumstances achieves substantial tax savings for the person making the rollover. And, in theory, a Keogh could be rolled over into an IRA, which could in turn be rolled over into a new employer's qualified plan, although IRS regulation apparently have not contemplated such an eventuality.

Keogh Plans and Tax Equity and Fiscal Responsibility Bill of 1982

As this chapter went to press the Tax Equity and Fiscal Responsibility Bill of 1982 was passed which made wide ranging changes in Keogh Plans to take effect December 31, 1983. For 1982 and 1983 Keogh contributions will still be limited to $15,000; however, in 1984, under the new act, that limit will be increased to $30,000. The act will generally eliminate the distinction in the tax law between corporate qualified retirement plans and Keogh Plans for the self-employed. A single set of provisions has been substituted for the two separate systems (corporate and Keogh) that used to apply.

Generally, maximums under corporate plans will be reduced in 1983 to a $90,000 benefit for pension plans and $30,000 of annual contributions for profit-sharing plans with no adjustment for inflation until 1986. The maximums for unincorporated professionals will be increased in 1984 to the corporate levels. Older individuals may be able to contribute as much as $100,000 or more annually to fund a $90,000 pension, a dramatic increase from the approximately $15,000 currently allowed for Keogh plans. Many of the special tax qualification rules relating to Keogh plans will be either eliminated or extended to corporate plans, with the net result that the technical distinction between corporate and Keogh plans will generally no longer exist after December 31, 1983.

Name Index

Subject Index